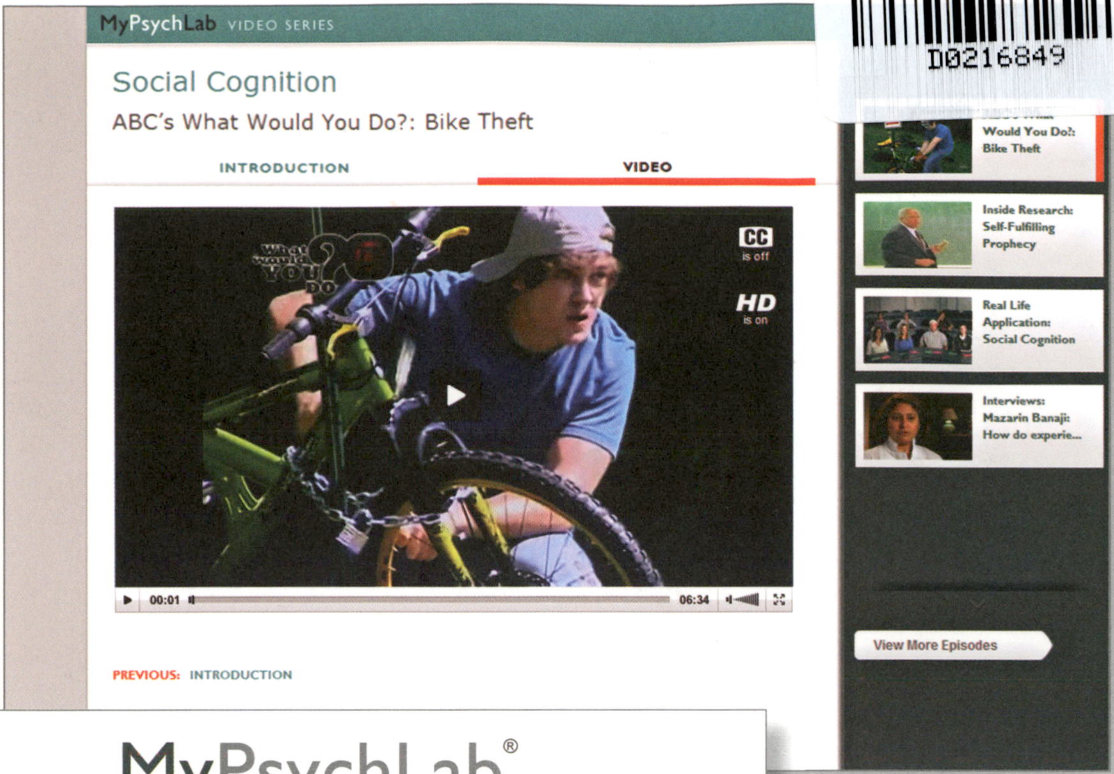

MyPsychLab®

Video Series *for* Social Psychology

Featuring ABC's *What Would You Do?*

CONTENTS

Why Do You Need This New Edition?

If you're wondering why you should buy this new edition of *Social Psychology*, here are 5 good reasons!

1. This edition includes new focus questions that are designed to help students preview and organize the material as they are reading. These focus questions appear at the beginning of each chapter and are repeated in the summary at the end of each chapter.
2. Each chapter has been substantially updated to contain the most current references and examples. Our goal is to tell the story of social psychology in a way that is engaging and compelling for students, and we have worked hard to ensure that this edition resonates strongly with our readers. Chapter Three, for example, contains 40 new references to research in social cognition. Chapter Five contains a major new section on self-esteem as well as several new examples, including a new figure on the prevalence of first-person pronouns in song lyrics over the past 30 years and a discussion of a recent episode of the popular TV show *30 Rock*.
3. This edition is integrated with the new **MyPsychLab** for Social Psychology. MyPsychLab offers students useful and engaging self-assessment tools, and it provides instructors with flexibility in assessing and tracking student progress. For instructors, MyPsychLab is a powerful tool for assessing student performance and adapting course content to students' changing needs, without requiring instructors to invest additional time or resources to do so. For this edition, students have access to a personalized study plan, based on Bloom's taxonomy, that helps them progress from less complex thinking (like remembering and understanding) to more complex thinking (like applying and analyzing).
4. Students and instructors will have access to the new **MyPsychLab Video Series for Social Psychology**. Current and cutting edge, this series features videos for social psychology covering the most recent research, science, and applications. Watch clips from ABC's wildly popular *What Would You Do*? series and discover how real people in real-world scenarios bring to life classic concepts in social psychology. The video series is also available to adopters on a DVD.
5. Adopters receive access to the **new Social Psychology PowerPoint Collection**. These PowerPoints provide an active format for presenting concepts from each chapter and incorporating relevant figures and tables. Instructors can choose from three PowerPoint presentations: a lecture presentation set that highlights major topics from the chapters, a highly visual lecture presentation set with embedded videos, or a PowerPoint collection of art files from the text.

PEARSON

Social Psychology

Eighth Edition

Elliot Aronson

Timothy D. Wilson

Robin M. Akert

PEARSON

Boston Columbus Indianapolis New York San Francisco Upper Saddle River
Amsterdam Cape Town Dubai London Madrid Milan Munich Paris Montréal Toronto
Delhi Mexico City São Paulo Sydney Hong Kong Seoul Singapore Taipei Tokyo

Editorial Director: Craig Campanella
Editor in Chief: Jessica Mosher
Executive Editor: Jeff Marshall
Acquisitions Editor: Amber Chow
Editorial Assistant: Diane Szulecki
VP, Director of Marketing: Brandy Dawson
Senior Marketing Manager: Nicole Kunzmann
Director of Production: Lisa Iarkowski
Managing Editor: Denise Forlow
Project Manager, Production: Shelly Kupperman
Senior Manufacturing and Operations Manager for Arts & Sciences: Mary Fischer
Operations Specialist: Diane Peirano
Creative Design Director: Leslie Osher
Interior/Cover Design: Jill Lehan
Digital Media Editor: Peter Sabatini
Digital Media Project Manager: Pam Weldin
Director of Development: Sharon Geary
Full-Service Project Management and Composition: Element LLC
Printer/Binder: Courier/Kendallville
Cover Printer: Lehigh-Phoenix Color/Hagerstown
Cover Image: Newscom
Text Font: Janson Text

Credits and acknowledgments borrowed from other sources and reproduced, with permission, in this textbook appear on the appropriate page of appearance.

Library of Congress Cataloging-in-Publication Data
Aronson, Elliot.
Social psychology / Elliot Aronson, Timothy D. Wilson, Robin M. Akert. —8th ed.
p. cm.
ISBN 978-0-205-79662-5 (alk. paper)
1. Social psychology. I. Wilson, Timothy D. II. Akert, Robin M. III. Title.
HM1033.A78 2013
302—dc23
2012024199

10 9 8 7 6 5 4 3 2 1

Student Edition
ISBN-10: 0-205-79662-1
ISBN-13: 978-0-205-79662-5

Instructor's Review Copy
ISBN-10: 0-205-79714-8
ISBN-13: 978-0-205-79714-1

Books à la Carte
ISBN-10: 0-205-24929-9
ISBN-13: 978-0-205-24929-9

PEARSON

To my grandchildren: Jacob, Jason, Ruth, Eliana, Natalie, Rachel and Leo Aronson. My hope is that your wonderful capacity for empathy and compassion will help make the world a better place.

—E.A.

To my family, Deirdre Smith, Christopher Wilson, and Leigh Wilson

—T.D.W.

To my mentor, colleague, and friend, Dane Archer

—R.M.A.

Brief Contents

Contents

Preface

When we began writing this book, our overriding goal was to capture the excitement of social psychology. We have been pleased to hear, in many kind letters and e-mail messages from professors and students, that we succeeded. One of our favorite responses was from a student who said that the book was so interesting that she always saved it for last, to reward herself for finishing her other work. With that one student, at least, we succeeded in making our book an enjoyable, fascinating story, not a dry report of facts and figures.

There is always room for improvement, however, and our goal in this, the eighth edition, is to make the field of social psychology an even better read. When we teach the course, there is nothing more gratifying than seeing the sleepy students in the back row sit up with interest and say, "Wow, I didn't know that! Now *that's* interesting." We hope that students who read our book will have that same reaction.

What's New in This Edition?

We are pleased to add a new feature to the eighth edition that we believe will appeal to students: focus questions designed to help them organize the material. These focus questions are located at the beginning of each chapter and repeated in the summary at the end of the chapter. In addition, we have retained and refined features that proved to be popular in the previous edition. For example, many of the sample test questions at the end of each chapter have been revised, mostly based on tests we have given to our students. Each chapter also has Try It! exercises that invite students to apply specific concepts to their everyday behavior, and one or more Connections features, which highlight a social psychology concept and connect it with an application in contemporary life. Each chapter ends with Use It!, designed to integrate the lessons of the chapter more generally. Each Use It! poses interesting and intriguing critical thinking questions and asks students to address the questions using one or more of the major concepts from the chapter. In all of these features, the goal is to challenge students to think critically about the material and apply it to their own lives.

We have updated the eighth edition substantially, with numerous references to new research. Here is a sampling of the new research that is covered:

- A signature of our book continues to be Chapter 2, "Methodology: How Social Psychologists Do Research," a readable, student-friendly chapter on social psychology research methods. This chapter has been updated for the eighth edition with new references and examples; its organization has also been improved in response to reviewer suggestions.
- In addition to having a new opening example, Chapter 3, "Social Cognition: How We Think About the Social World," has been updated with more than 40 references reflecting recent research. We added new sections on the importance of consciousness and perceptions of free will, as well as on embodiment and the priming of mind/body metaphors. The chapter also has a new Try It! exercise asking students to predict their own future versus a friend's future. This illustrates Pronin and Kugler's (2011) finding that people tend to believe that they have more free will than do other people.
- Chapter 4, "Social Perception: How We Come to Understand Other People," now combines the discussion of the fundamental attribution error and the correspondence bias, referring to it as one phenomenon. In addition to being updated with many new references, the chapter has also been streamlined and shortened.
- In Chapter 5,"The Self: Understanding Ourselves in a Social Context," we have added a major new section entitled "Self-Esteem: How We Feel About Ourselves," in which we discuss research on self-esteem, terror management theory, and narcissism. The section on self-awareness theory has been updated to reflect recent research on how often people think about themselves, including a new figure on the prevalence of first-person pronouns in song lyrics over the past 30 years. The examples have also been updated, including a discussion of a recent episode of the television show *30 Rock*.
- Chapter 6, "The Need to Justify Our Actions," has been extensively reorganized; the major headings are now "The Theory of Cognitive Dissonance," "Self-Justification in Everyday Life," and "Learning from Our Mistakes." "Dissonance Across Cultures" is now a subsection at the end of the first main section, under "Dissonance, Culture, and the Brain." Here we have added recent references to fMRI studies of brains in states of dissonance and the new replication of the Santos study of monkeys and dissonance. Combining these topics lets us say what seems hardwired about cognitive dissonance as a survival strategy and also how the expression of cognitive dissonance varies across cultures. Among the many new studies we have added to this chapter is a decade-long project on the use of counterattitudinal advocacy to reduce body-image dissatisfaction and eating disorders in women.
- Chapter 7, "Attitudes and Attitude Change: Influencing Thoughts and Feelings," includes nearly 50 references to recent research. The examples from contemporary culture have been updated, including recent examples of product placement in television shows and polling numbers of President Obama.

- Chapter 8, "Conformity: Influencing Behavior," includes many new references to recent research and a discussion of recent examples, such as an outbreak of what appears to be mass psychogenic illness in upstate New York in 2012.
- Chapter 9, "Group Processes: Influence in Social Groups," includes more than 40 references to recent research. We have replaced a previous Connections feature with a new one discussing the role of groupthink in the financial crisis of 2007. The sections on gender and leadership and culture and leadership are among those that have been updated.
- Chapter 10, "Interpersonal Attraction: From First Impressions to Close Relationships," has a new opening vignette and has some reorganization in response to reviewer suggestions. It is updated with references to dozens of new studies, including recent research on online dating and speed dating.
- Chapter 11, "Prosocial Behavior: Why Do People Help?" includes more than 30 references to recent research. We have added a new section on the effects of the media on prosocial behavior, including research on the effects of prosocial video games and song lyrics on helping behavior. The section on cultural differences in prosocial behavior has been substantially revised.
- Chapter 12, "Aggression: Why Do We Hurt Other People? Can We Prevent It?," has been reorganized and substantially updated. We examine the evidence that males around the world are more physically aggressive than females, and compare evolutionary and cultural explanations for why this is so. We discuss relational aggression, which is more characteristic of women, suggesting that both sexes can be equally aggressive. We have significantly revised and updated the material on "Violence in the Media," adding the results of the literature review in *Psychological Science in the Public Interest* and the meta-analyses of Ferguson and Sherry. We added sections on the cause-and-effect problem, data on how predisposing factors determine a child's or adult's response to media violence, and a discussion of other factors in a youth's environment that have stronger influences on aggression. In the concluding section, we added research showing that social rejection is the most significant risk factor for teenage suicide, despair, and violence.
- In Chapter 13, "Prejudice: Causes, Consequences, and Cures," we have replaced many old studies of prejudice in the 1960s to 1980s with more-contemporary studies and examples: anti-Muslim prejudice, the rise in anti-Mexican prejudice in the United States due to economic competition, prejudice against fat people (a term preferred by the National Association to Advance Fat Acceptance), prejudice against disabled people, the status of gay men and lesbians, and so on. The chapter now begins with four illustrations of prejudice in the news, to show the ubiquity and variety of prejudice. The section on discrimination now consists of two major examples: (1) the police and legal system's focus on arresting and incarcerating blacks rather than whites for drug offenses, although whites commit far more serious drug offenses and in greater numbers; and (2) examples of microaggressions, insults, and subtle discrimination in daily life.
- The three Social Psychology in Action chapters—"Making a Difference with Social Psychology: Attaining a Sustainable Future," "Social Psychology and Health," and "Social Psychology and the Law"—have been updated with many references to new research, but have also been shortened. When we teach the course, we find that students are excited to learn about these applied areas. At the same time, we recognize that some instructors have difficulty fitting the chapters into their courses. In this edition, our approach was to reduce the length of the applied chapters and to make it easy to integrate these chapters into different parts of the course. Whereas some teachers prefer to assign the chapters at the end of the course, others like to assign them in combination with earlier chapters. We believe that the way these chapters are revised for the eighth edition will make them compatible with either approach.

Teaching and Learning Resources

A really good textbook should become part of the classroom experience, supporting and augmenting the professor's vision for the class. ***Social Psychology*** offers a number of supplements that enrich both the professor's presentation of social psychology and the students' understanding of it.

Instructor Supplements

MyPsychLab®

- **MyPsychLab** The new MyPsychLab delivers proven results in helping individual students succeed. It provides engaging experiences that personalize, stimulate, and measure learning for each student. And it comes from a trusted partner with educational expertise and a deep commitment to helping students, instructors, and departments achieve their goals. For the 8th edition of Aronson, the new MyPsychLab contains a personalized study plan for each chapter that is organized according to Bloom's taxonomy, in order to help students move from remembering and understanding the concepts to apply and analyzing what they've learned. It also contains the new MyPsychLab Video Series for Social Psychology. MyPsychLab can be used by itself or linked to any learning management system. To learn more about how the new MyPsychLab combines proven learning applications with powerful assessment, visit www.mypsychlab.com.
- **MyPsychLab Video Series for Social Psychology** (0205847021) Current and cutting edge, the new *MyPsychLab Video Series* for social psychology features videos covering the most recent research, science, and applications. Watch clips from ABC's wildly popular *What Would You Do?* series and discover how real people in real-world scenarios bring to life classic concepts in social psychology. The video series is also available

to adopters on a DVD. Contact your Pearson representative for more information.

- **Class Preparation Tool** Finding, sorting, organizing and presenting your instructor resources is faster and easier than ever before with ClassPrep. This fully searchable database contains hundreds and hundreds of our best teacher resources, including lecture launchers and discussion topics, in-class and out-of-class activities and assignments, handouts, video clips, photos, illustrations, charts, graphs, and animations. Instructors can browse by topic, search by keyword, and filter results by asset type (photo, document, video, animation). Instructors can sort the resources into their own filing system; tag, rate, and comment on individual resources; and even download most of the resources. ClassPrep also offers instructors the option to upload their own resources and present directly from ClassPrep. ClassPrep is available for instructors through MyPsychLab. Please contact your Pearson representative for access.
- **Social Psychology PowerPoint Collection** (0205853595) The PowerPoints provide an active format for presenting concepts from each chapter and incorporating relevant figures and tables. Instructors can choose from three PowerPoint presentations: a lecture presentation set that highlights major topics from the chapters, a highly visual lecture presentation set with **embedded videos,** or a PowerPoint collection of the complete art files from the text. The PowerPoint files can be downloaded from www.pearsonhighered.com.
- **Classroom Response System** (0205853609) The Classroom Response System (CRS) facilitates class participation in lectures as well as a method of measurement of student comprehension. CRS also enables student polling and in-class quizzes. CRS is highly effective in engaging students with class lectures, in addition to adding an element of excitement to the classroom. Simply, CRS is a technology that allows professors to ask questions to their students through text-specific PowerPoint slides provided by Pearson. Students reply using handheld transmitters called "clickers," which capture and immediately display student responses. These responses are saved in the system gradebook and/or can later be downloaded to either a Blackboard or WebCT gradebook for assessment purposes.
- **Instructor's Resource Manual** (0205797121) The Instructor's Manual includes key terms, lecture ideas, teaching tips, suggested readings, chapter outlines, student projects and research assignments, Try It! exercises, critical thinking topics and discussion questions, and a media resource guide. It has been updated for the eighth edition with hyperlinks to ease facilitation of navigation within the IM.
- **Test Bank** (0205929273) Each of the more than 2,000 questions in this test bank is page-referenced to the text and categorized by topic and skill level. Each question in the test bank was reviewed by several instructors to ensure that we are providing you with the best and most accurate content in the industry.
- **MyTest Testing Software** (0205846939) This Web-based test-generating software provides instructors "best in class" features in an easy-to-use program. Create tests and easily select questions with drag-and-drop or point-and-click functionality. Add or modify test questions using the built-in Question Editor, and print tests in a variety of formats. The program comes with full technical support.

Student Supplements

MyPsychLab®

- **MyPsychLab** The new MyPsychLab delivers proven results in helping individual students succeed. It provides engaging experiences that personalize, stimulate, and measure learning for each student. And it comes from a trusted partner with educational expertise and a deep commitment to helping students, instructors, and departments achieve their goals. For the 8th edition of Aronson, the new MyPsychLab contains a personalized study plan for each chapter that is organized according to Bloom's taxonomy, in order to help students move from remembering and understanding the concepts to apply and analyzing what they've learned. It also contains the new MyPsychLab Video Series for Social Psychology. MyPsychLab can be used by itself or linked to any learning management system. To learn more about how the new MyPsychLab combines proven learning applications with powerful assessment, visit www.mypsychlab.com.
- **Student Study Guide** The Student Study Guide contains chapter overviews, learning objectives and outlines, a guided review section, study activities, key terms, and practice tests. It is available online. If you would like to include a printed study guide with your text, please contact your Pearson representative or visit the Pearson Custom Library at www.pearsoncustomlibrary.com.

Acknowledgments

Elliot Aronson is delighted to acknowledge the collaboration of Carol Tavris in helping him update this edition. He would also like to acknowledge the contributions of his best friend (who also happens to be his wife of 55 years), Vera Aronson. Vera, as usual, provided inspiration for his ideas and acted as the sounding board for and supportive critic of many of his semiformed notions, helping to mold them into more-sensible analyses.

Tim Wilson would like to thank his graduate mentor, Richard E. Nisbett, who nurtured his interest in the field and showed him the continuity between social psychological research and everyday life. He thanks his parents, Elizabeth and Geoffrey Wilson, for their overall support. Most of all, he thanks his wife, Deirdre Smith, and his children, Christopher and Leigh, for their love, patience, and understanding, even when the hour was late and the computer was still on.

Robin Akert is beholden to Jonathan Cheek, Julie Donnelly, Nan Vaida, Melody Tortosa, and Lila McCain for their feedback and advice, and to her family, Michaela and Wayne Akert, and Linda and Jerry Wuichet; their enthusiasm and boundless support have sustained her on this project as on all the ones before it. Finally, she wishes to express her gratitude to Dane Archer—mentor, colleague, and friend—who opened the world of social psychology to her and who has been her guide ever since.

We also thank Carol Tavris and Samuel Sommers for their tremendous help in revising some of the chapters for the eighth edition. Their vast knowledge of social psychology and adept way with words contributed greatly to this edition.

No book can be written and published without the help of many people working with the authors behind the scenes, and our book is no exception. We would like to thank the many colleagues who read one or more chapters of this edition and of previous editions of the book.

Reviewers of the Seventh Edition

Nathan Arbuckle, *Ohio State University*
Arthur Beaman, *University of Kentucky*
Anila Bhagavatula, *California State University–Long Beach*
Kosha Bramesfeld, *Pennsylvania State University*
Melissa Burkley, *Oklahoma State University*
Amber Bush Amspoker, *University of Houston*
Florette Cohen, *Rutgers University*
Traci Craig, *University of Idaho*
Megan Clegg-Kraynok, *West Virginia University*
Michael G. Dudley, *Southern Illinois University Edwardsville*
Kadimah Elson, *University of California, San Diego/Grossmont College*
Allen Gorman, *Radford University*
Jerry Green, *Tarrant County College*
H. Anna Han, *Ohio State University*
Lisa Harrison, *California State University, Sacramento*
Gina Hoover, *Ohio State University*
Jeffrey Huntsinger, *Loyola University Chicago*
Harold Hunziker Jr., *Corning Community College*
Alisha Janowsky, *University of Central Florida*
Bethany Johnson, *University of Nebraska–Omaha*
Stephen Kilianski, *Rutgers University*
Jessica Gonzalez, *Ohio State University*
Sara Gorchoff, *University of California, Berkeley*
John Lu, *Concordia University*
Robyn Mallett, *Loyola University Chicago*
Adam Meade, *North Carolina State University*
Dave Nalbone, *Purdue University–Calumet*
Matylda Osika, *University of Houston*
Paul Rose, *Southern Illinois University Edwardsville*
Fred Sanborn, *North Carolina Wesleyan College*
JoNell Strough, *West Virginia University*
David M. Tom, *Columbus State Community College*
Ruth Warner, *St. Louis University*
Jackie White, *University of North Carolina at Greensboro*
Tamara Williams, *Hampton University*
Garry Zaslow, *Nassau Community College*
Jie Zhang, *University at Buffalo*

Reviewers of Past Editions

Jeffrey B. Adams, *Saint Michael's College*
Bill Adler, *Collin County Community College*
John R. Aiello, *Rutgers University*
Charles A. Alexander, *Rock Valley College*
Sowmya Anand, *Ohio State University*
Art Aron, *State University of New York, Stony Brook*
Danny Axsom, *Virginia Polytechnic Institute and State University*
Joan W. Baily, *Jersey City State College*
Norma Baker, *Belmont University*
Austin Baldwin, *University of Iowa*
John Bargh, *New York University*
William A. Barnard, *University of Northern Colorado*
Doris G. Bazzini, *Appalachian State University*
Gordon Bear, *Ramapo College*
Susan E. Beers, *Sweet Briar College*
Kathy L. Bell, *University of North Carolina at Greensboro*
Leonard Berkowitz, *University of Wisconsin–Madison*
Ellen S. Berscheid, *University of Minnesota*
John Bickford, *University of Massachusetts, Amherst*
Thomas Blass, *University of Maryland*
C. George Boeree, *Shippensburg University*
Lisa M. Bohon, *California State University, Sacramento*
Jennifer Bosson, *The University of Oklahoma*
Chante C. Boyd, *Carnegie Mellon University*
Peter J. Brady, *Clark State Community College*
Kelly A. Brennan, *University of Texas, Austin*
Richard W. Brislin, *East-West Center of the University of Hawaii*
Jeff Bryson, *San Diego State University*
Amy Bush, *University of Houston*
Brad Bushman, *Iowa State University*
Thomas P. Cafferty, *University of South Carolina, Columbia*
Melissa A. Cahoon, *Wright State University*
Frank Calabrese, *Community College of Philadelphia*
Michael Caruso, *University of Toledo*
Nicholas Christenfeld, *University of California, San Diego*
Margaret S. Clark, *Carnegie Mellon University*
Russell D. Clark, III, *University of North Texas*
Susan D. Clayton, *Allegheny College*
Brian M. Cohen, *University of Texas, San Antonio*
Jack Cohen, *Camden County College*
Steven G. Cole, *Texas Christian University*
Eric J. Cooley, *Western Oregon State University*
Diana Cordova, *Yale University*
Jack Croxton, *State University of New York, Fredonia*
Keith E. Davis, *University of South Carolina, Columbia*
Mary Ellen Dello Stritto, *Ball State University*
Dorothee Dietrich, *Hamline University*
Kate Dockery, *University of Florida*
Susann Doyle, *Gainesville College*
Steve Duck, *University of Iowa*
Karen G. Duffy, *State University of New York, Geneseo*
Valerie Eastman, *Drury College*
Tami Eggleston, *McKendree College*

Timothy Elliot, *University of Alabama–Birmingham*
Steve L. Ellyson, *Youngstown State University*
Cindy Elrod, *Georgia State University*
Rebecca S. Fahrlander, *University of Nebraska at Omaha*
Alan Feingold, *Yale University*
Edward Fernandes, *East Carolina University*
Phil Finney, *Southeast Missouri State University*
Susan Fiske, *University of Massachusetts*
Robin Franck, *Southwestern College*
Denise Frank, *Ramapo College of New Jersey*
Timothy M. Franz, *St. John Fisher College*
William Rick Fry, *Youngstown State University*
Russell Geen, *University of Missouri*
Glenn Geher, *State University of New York at New Paltz*
David Gersh, *Houston Community College*
Frederick X. Gibbons, *Iowa State University*
Cynthia Gilliland, *Louisiana State University*
Genaro Gonzalez, *University of Texas*
Beverly Gray, *Youngstown State University*
Gordon Hammerle, *Adrian College*
Judith Harackiewicz, *University of Wisconsin–Madison*
Elaine Hatfield, *University of Hawaii, Manoa*
Vicki S. Helgeson, *Carnegie Mellon University*
Joyce Hemphill, *Cazenovia College*
Tracy B. Henley, *Mississippi State University*
Ed Hirt, *Indiana University*
David E. Hyatt, *University of Wisconsin–Oshkosh*
Marita Inglehart, *University of Michigan*
Carl Kallgren, *Behrend College, Pennsylvania State University, Erie*
Suzanne Kieffer, *University of Houston*
Stephen Kilianski, *Rutgers University*
Bill Klein, *Colby College*
James D. Johnson, *University of North Carolina, Wilmington*
Lee Jussim, *Rutgers University*
Fredrick Koenig, *Tulane University*
Alan Lambert, *Washington University, St. Louis*
Emmett Lampkin, *Kirkwook Community College*
Elizabeth C. Lanthier, *Northern Virginia Community College*
Patricia Laser, *Bucks County Community College*
G. Daniel Lassiter, *Ohio University*
Dianne Leader, *Georgia Institute of Technology*
Stephanie Madon, *Iowa State University*
John Malarkey, *Wilmington College*
Andrew Manion, *St. Mary's University of Minnesota*
Allen R. McConnell, *Michigan State University*
Joann M. Montepare, *Tufts University*
Richard Moreland, *University of Pittsburgh*
Carrie Nance, *Stetson University*
Todd D. Nelson, *Michigan State University*
Elaine Nocks, *Furman University*
Cheri Parks, *Colorado Christian University*
W. Gerrod Parrott, *Georgetown University*
David Peterson, *Mount Senario College*
Mary Pritchard, *Boise State University*
Cynthia K. S. Reed, *Tarrant County College*
Dan Richard, *University of North Florida*
Neal Roese, *University of Illinios*
Darrin L. Rogers, *Ohio State University*
Joan Rollins, *Rhode Island College*
Lee D. Ross, *Stanford University*
Alex Rothman, *University of Minnesota*
M. Susan Rowley, *Champlain College*
Delia Saenz, *Arizona State University*
Brad Sagarin, *Northern Illinois University*
Connie Schick, *Bloomsburg University*
Norbert Schwartz, *University of Michigan*
Gretchen Sechrist, *University at Buffalo*
Richard C. Sherman, *Miami University of Ohio*
Paul Silvia, *University of North Carolina at Greensboro*
Randolph A. Smith, *Ouachita Baptist University*
Linda Solomon, *Marymount Manhattan College*
Janice Steil, *Adelphi University*
Jakob Steinberg, *Fairleigh Dickinson University*
Mark Stewart, *American River College*
Lori Stone, *The University of Texas at Austin*
JoNell Strough, *West Virginia University*
T. Gale Thompson, *Bethany College*
Scott Tindale, *Loyola University of Chicago*
David Trafimow, *New Mexico State University*
Anne Weiher, *Metropolitan State College of Denver*
Gary L. Wells, *Iowa State University*
Paul L. Wienir, *Western Michigan University*
Kipling D. Williams, *University of Toledo*
Paul Windschitl, *University of Iowa*
Mike Witmer, *Skagit Valley College*
Gwen Wittenbaum, *Michigan State University*
William Douglas Woody, *University of Northern Colorado*
Clare Zaborowski, *San Jacinto College*
William H. Zachry, *University of Tennessee, Martin*
Leah Zinner, *University of Wisconsin–Madison*

We also thank the wonderful editorial staff of Pearson for their expertise and professionalism, including Craig Campanella (Editorial Director), Nicole Kunzmann (Marketing Manager), Michael Rosen (Editorial Assistant), Michael Halas (Media Editor), and Shelly Kupperman (Production Editor). Most of all, we thank Jeff Marshall (Executive Editor), whose tireless belief in our book, and vision for it, have truly made a difference. Finally, we thank Mary Falcon, but for whom we never would have begun this project.

Thank you for inviting us into your classroom. We welcome your suggestions, and we would be delighted to hear your comments about this book.

Elliot Aronson
elliot@cats.ucsc.edu

Tim Wilson
tdw@virginia.edu

Robin Akert
rakert@wellesley.edu

About the Authors

Elliot Aronson

When I was a kid, we were the only Jewish family in a virulently anti-Semitic neighborhood. I had to go to Hebrew school every day, late in the afternoon. Being the only youngster in my neighborhood going to Hebrew school made me an easy target for some of the older neighborhood toughs. On my way home from Hebrew school, after dark, I was frequently waylaid and roughed up by roving gangs shouting anti-Semitic epithets.

I have a vivid memory of sitting on a curb after one of these beatings, nursing a bloody nose or a split lip, feeling very sorry for myself and wondering how these kids could hate me so much when they didn't even know me. I thought about whether those kids were taught to hate Jews or whether, somehow, they were born that way. I wondered if their hatred could be changed—if they got to know me better, would they hate me less? I speculated about my own character. What would I have done if the shoe were on the other foot—that is, if I were bigger and stronger than they, would I be capable of beating them up for no good reason?

I didn't realize it at the time, of course, but eventually I discovered that these were profound questions. And some 30 years later, as an experimental social psychologist, I had the great good fortune to be in a position to answer some of those questions and to invent techniques to reduce the kind of prejudice that had claimed me as a victim.

Elliot Aronson is Professor Emeritus at the University of California at Santa Cruz and one of the most renowned social psychologists in the world. In 2002, he was chosen as one of the 100 most eminent psychologists of the twentieth century. Dr. Aronson is the only person in the 120-year history of the American Psychological Association to have received all three of its major awards: for distinguished writing, distinguished teaching, and distinguished research. Many other professional societies have honored his research and teaching as well. These include the American Association for the Advancement of Science, which gave him its highest honor, the Distinguished Scientific Research award; the American Council for the Advancement and Support of Education, which named him Professor of the Year of 1989; the Society for the Psychological Study of Social Issues, which awarded him the Gordon Allport prize for his contributions to the reduction of prejudice among racial and ethnic groups; and the William James Award from the Association for Psychological Science. In 1992, he was named a Fellow of the American Academy of Arts and Sciences. A collection of papers and tributes by his former students and colleagues, The Scientist and the Humanist, *celebrates his contributions to social psychological theory and its application to real-world problems. Dr. Aronson's own recent books for general audiences include* Mistakes Were Made (but not by ME), *with Carol Tavris, and a memoir,* Not by Chance Alone: My Life as a Social Psychologist.

Tim Wilson

One day when I was 8, a couple of older kids rode up on their bikes to share some big news: They had discovered an abandoned house down a country road. "It's really neat," they said. "We broke a window and nobody cared!" My friend and I hopped onto our bikes to investigate. We had no trouble finding the house—there it was, sitting off by itself, with a big, jagged hole in a first-floor window. We got off of our bikes and looked around. My friend found a baseball-sized rock lying on the ground and threw a perfect strike through another first-floor window. There was something exhilarating about the smash-and-tingle of shattering glass, especially when we knew there was nothing wrong with what we were doing. After all, the house was abandoned, wasn't it? We broke nearly every window in the house and then climbed through one of the first-floor windows to look around.

It was then that we realized something was terribly wrong. The house certainly did not look abandoned. There were pictures on the wall, nice furniture, books in shelves. We went home feeling frightened and confused. We soon learned that the house was the home of an elderly couple who were away on vacation. Eventually, my parents discovered what we had done and paid a substantial sum to repair the windows. For years, I pondered this incident: Why did I do such a terrible thing? Was I a bad kid? I didn't think so, and neither did my parents. How, then, could a good kid do such a bad thing? Even though the neighborhood kids said the house was abandoned, why couldn't my friend and I see the clear signs that someone lived there? How crucial was it that my friend was there and threw the first rock? Although I didn't know it at the time, these reflections touched on several classic social psychological issues, such as whether only bad people do bad things, whether the social situation can be powerful enough to make good people do bad things, and the way in which our expectations about an event can make it difficult to see it as it really is. Fortunately, my career as a vandal ended with this one incident. It did, however, mark the beginning of my fascination with basic questions about how people understand themselves and the social world—questions I continue to investigate to this day.

Tim Wilson did his undergraduate work at Williams College and Hampshire College and received his PhD from the University of Michigan. Currently Sherrell J. Aston Professor of Psychology at the University of Virginia, he has published numerous articles in the areas of introspection, attitude change, self-knowledge, and affective forecasting, as well as a recent book, Redirect: The Surprising New Science of Psychological Change. *His research has received the support of the National Science Foundation and the National Institute for Mental Health. He has been elected twice to the Executive Board of the Society for Experimental Social Psychology and is a Fellow in the American Psychological Society and the Society for Personality and Social Psychology. In 2009, he was named a Fellow of the American Academy of Arts and Sciences. Wilson has taught the Introduction to Social Psychology course at the University of Virginia for more than 30 years. In 2001 he was awarded the University of Virginia All-University Outstanding Teaching Award, and in 2010 was awarded the University of Virginia Distinguished Scientist Award.*

Robin Akert

One fall day when I was about 16, I was walking with a friend along the shore of the San Francisco Bay. Deep in conversation, I glanced over my shoulder and saw a sailboat capsize. I pointed it out to my friend, who took only a perfunctory interest and went on talking. However, I kept watching as we walked, and I realized that the two sailors were in the water, clinging to the capsized boat. Again I said something to my friend, who replied, "Oh, they'll get it upright—don't worry."

But I *was* worried. Was this an emergency? My friend didn't think so. And I was no sailor; I knew nothing about boats. But I kept thinking, "That water is really cold. They can't stay in that water too long." I remember feeling very confused and unsure. What should I do? Should I do anything? Did they really need help?

We were near a restaurant with a big window overlooking the bay, and I decided to go in and see if anyone had done anything about the boat. Lots of people were watching but not doing anything. This confused me too. Meekly, I asked the bartender to call for some kind of help. He just shrugged. I went back to the window and watched the two small figures in the water. Why was everyone so unconcerned? Was I crazy?

Years later, I reflected on how hard it was for me to do what I did next: I demanded that the bartender let me use his phone. In those days before "911," it was lucky that I knew there was a Coast Guard station on the bay, and I asked the operator for the number. I was relieved to hear the Guardsman take my message very seriously.

It had been an emergency. I watched as the Coast Guard cutter sped across the bay and pulled the two sailors out of the water. Maybe I saved their lives that day. What really stuck with me over the years was how other people behaved and how it made me feel. The other bystanders seemed unconcerned and did nothing to help. Their reactions made me doubt myself and made it harder for me to decide to take action. When I later studied social psychology in college, I realized that on the shore of the San Francisco Bay that day, I had experienced the "bystander effect" fully: The presence of other, apparently unconcerned bystanders had made it difficult for me to decide if the situation was an emergency and whether it was my responsibility to help.

Robin Akert graduated summa cum laude from the University of California at Santa Cruz, where she majored in psychology and sociology. She received her PhD in experimental social psychology from Princeton University. She is currently a Professor of Psychology at Wellesley College, where she was awarded the Pinanski Prize for Excellence in Teaching early in her career. She publishes primarily in the area of nonverbal communication, and recently received the AAUW American Fellowship in support of her research. She has taught the social psychology course at Wellesley College for nearly 30 years.

Special Tips for Students

"There is then creative reading as well as creative writing," said Ralph Waldo Emerson in 1837, and that aptly sums up what you need to know to be a proficient student: Be an active, creative consumer of information. How do you accomplish that feat? Actually, it's not difficult. Like everything else in life, it just takes some work—some clever, well-planned, purposeful work. Here are some suggestions about how to do it.

Get to Know the Textbook

Believe it or not, in writing this book, we thought carefully about the organization and structure of each chapter. Things are presented as they are for a reason, and that reason is to help you learn the material in the best way possible. Here are some tips on what to look for in each chapter.

Key terms are in boldface type in the text so that you'll notice them. We define the terms in the text, and that definition appears again in the margin. These marginal definitions are there to help you out if later in the chapter you forget what something means. The marginal definitions are quick and easy to find. You can also look up key terms in the alphabetical Glossary at the end of this textbook.

Make sure you notice the headings and subheadings. The headings are the skeleton that holds a chapter together. They link together like vertebrae. If you ever feel lost, look back to the previous heading and the headings before it—this will give you the "big picture" of where the chapter is going. It should also help you see the connections between sections.

The summary at the end of each chapter is a succinct shorthand presentation of the chapter information. You should read it and make sure there are no surprises when you do so. If anything in the summary doesn't ring a bell, go back to the chapter and reread that section. Most important, remember that the summary is intentionally brief, whereas your understanding of the material should be full and complete. Use the summary as a study aid before your exams. When you read it over, everything should be familiar. When you have that wonderful feeling of knowing more than is in the summary, you'll know that you are ready to take the exam.

Be sure to do the Try It! exercises. They will make concepts from social psychology concrete and help you see how they can be applied to your own life. Some of the *Try It!* exercises replicate social psychology experiments. Others reproduce self-report scales so you can see where you stand in relation to other people. Still others are short quizzes that illustrate social psychological concepts.

Visit our Web site at www.prenhall.com/aronson. You will be able to do more *Try It!* exercises, take interactive practice tests, and link to other sites.

Just Say No to the Couch Potato Within

Because social psychology is about everyday life, you might lull yourself into believing that the material is all common sense. Don't be fooled. The material presented in this book is more complicated than it might seem. Therefore, we want to emphasize that the best way to learn it is to work with it in an active, not passive, fashion. You can't just read a chapter once and expect it to stick with you. You have to go over the material, wrestle with it, make your own connections to it, question it, think about it, interact with it. Actively working with material makes it memorable and makes it your own. Because it's a safe bet that someone is going to ask you about this material later and you're going to have to pull it out of memory, do what you can to get it into memory now. Here are some techniques to use:

- Go ahead and be bold—use a highlighter! Go crazy—write in the margins! If you underline, highlight, circle, or draw little hieroglyphics next to important points, you will remember them better. We recall taking exams in college where we not only remembered the material, but could actually see in our minds the textbook page it was written on and the little squiggles and stars we'd drawn in the margin.
- Read the textbook chapter before the applicable class lecture, not afterward. This way, you'll get more out of the lecture, which will likely introduce new material in addition to what is in the chapter. The chapter will give you the big picture, as well as a lot of detail. The lecture will enhance that information and help you put it all together. If you haven't read the chapter first, you may not understand some of the points made in the lecture or realize which points are most important.
- Here's a good way to study material: Write out a key concept or a study in your own words, without looking at the book or your notes. Or say it out loud to yourself—again in your own words, with your eyes closed. Can you do it? How good was your version? Did you omit anything important? Did you get stuck at some point, unable to remember what comes next? If so, you now know that you need to go over that information in more detail. You can also study with someone else, describing theories and studies to each other and seeing if you're making sense.
- If you have trouble remembering the results of an important study, try drawing your own version of a graph of the findings (you can use our data graphs for an idea of how to proceed). If all the various points in a theory are confusing you, try drawing your own flowchart of how it works. You will probably find that you remember the research results much better in pictorial form than in words, and that the theory isn't so confusing (or missing a critical part) if you've outlined it. Draw the information a few times and it will stay with you.
- Remember, the more you work with the material, the better you will learn and remember it. Write it in your own words, talk about it, explain it to others, or draw visual representations of it.
- Last but not least, remember that this material is a lot of fun. You haven't even started reading the book yet, but we think you're going to like it. In particular, you'll see how much social psychology has to tell you about your real, everyday life. As this course progresses, you might want to remind yourself to observe the events of your daily life with new eyes—the eyes of a social psychologist—and try to apply what you are learning to the behavior of friends, acquaintances, strangers, and, yes, even yourself. Make sure you use the *Try It!* exercises and visit the Web site. You will find out how much social psychology can help us understand our lives. When you read the news, think about what social psychology has to say about current events and behaviors; we believe you will find that your understanding of daily life is richer. If you notice a news article that you think is an especially good example of "social psychology in action," please send it to us, with a full reference to where you found it and on what page. If we decide to use it in the next edition of this book, we'll list your name in the Acknowledgments.

We realize that ten years from now you may not remember all the facts, theories, and names you learn now. Although we hope you will remember some of them, our main goal is for you to take with you into your future a great many of the broad social psychological concepts presented herein—and, perhaps more important, a critical and scientific way of thinking. If you open yourself to social psychology's magic, we believe it will enrich the way you look at the world and the way you live in it.

1 Introducing Social Psychology

THE TASK OF THE PSYCHOLOGIST IS TO TRY TO UNDERSTAND AND PREDICT HUMAN BEHAVIOR. Different kinds of psychologists go about this task in different ways, and in this book we attempt to show you how social psychologists do it. Let's begin with a few examples of human behavior. Some of these might seem important; others might seem trivial; one or two might seem frightening. To a social psychologist, all of them are interesting. Our hope is that by the time you finish reading this book, you will find these examples as fascinating as we do.

- Abraham Biggs Jr., age 19, had been posting to an online discussion board for 2 years. Unhappy about his future and that a relationship had ended, Biggs announced on camera that he was going to commit suicide. He took an overdose of drugs and linked to a live video feed from his bedroom. None of his hundreds of observers called the police for more than 10 hours; some egged him on. Paramedics reached him too late, and Biggs died.
- Oscar is a middle-aged executive with a computer software company. As a student, Oscar had attended a large state university in the Midwest, where he was a member of Alpha Beta. He remembers having gone through a severe and scary hazing ritual to join, but believes it was worthwhile, since Alpha Beta was easily the best of all fraternities. A few years ago when his son, Sam, enrolled in the same university, Oscar urged him to pledge Alpha Beta. Sam did and was accepted. Oscar was relieved to learn that Sam was not required to undergo a severe initiation in order to become a member; times had changed, and hazing was now forbidden. When Sam went home for Christmas, Oscar asked him how he liked the fraternity. "It's all right, I guess," he said, "but most of my friends are outside the fraternity." Oscar was astonished. Why had he been so enamored of his fraternity brothers and his son wasn't? Was Alpha Beta now admitting a less desirable group of young men than in Oscar's day?
- In the mid-1970s, several hundred members of the Peoples Temple, a California-based religious cult, immigrated to Guyana under the guidance of their leader, the Reverend Jim Jones. Their aim was to found a model interracial community, called Jonestown, based on "love, hard work, and spiritual enlightenment." But within a few years some members wanted out, and they wrote to their congressman, claiming they were being held against their will. The congressman flew to Jonestown to investigate, but he and several other members of his party were shot and killed by a member of the Peoples Temple on Jones's orders. Jones grew despondent and began to speak over the public address system about the beauty of dying and the certainty that everyone would meet again in another place. The residents lined up in a pavilion, in front of a vat containing a mixture of Kool-Aid and cyanide. According to a survivor, almost all the residents drank willingly of the deadly solution. A total of 914 people died, including 80 babies and the Reverend Jones.

These stories pose fascinating questions about human social behavior: Why would people watch a troubled young man commit suicide in front of their eyes, when, by simply flagging the video to alert the Web site, they might

FOCUS QUESTIONS

- What is social psychology, and how is it different from other disciplines?
- What's more important: personality or situation?
- How did behaviorism and Gestalt psychology contribute to the development of social psychological thought?
- What are the differences between the self-esteem approach and the social cognition approach?
- How can social psychology help solve social problems?

have averted a tragedy? Why did Sam feel so much less attached to his fraternity than his father did? And how could large numbers of people be induced to kill their own children and then commit suicide? In this chapter, we will consider what these examples have in common and how social psychologists go about explaining them.

Social Psychology
The scientific study of the way in which people's thoughts, feelings, and behaviors are influenced by the real or imagined presence of other people

Social Influence
The effect that the words, actions, or mere presence of other people have on our thoughts, feelings, attitudes, or behavior

What Is Social Psychology?

Social psychology is the scientific study of the way in which people's thoughts, feelings, and behaviors are influenced by the real or imagined presence of other people: parents, friends, employers, teachers, strangers—indeed, by the entire social situation (Allport, 1985). When we think of social influence, the kinds of examples that readily come to mind are direct attempts at persuasion, whereby one person deliberately tries to change another person's behavior. This is what happens when advertisers use sophisticated techniques to persuade us to buy a particular brand of toothpaste, or when our friends try to get us to do something we don't really want to do ("Come on, have another beer—everyone is doing it"), or when the schoolyard bully uses force or threats to get smaller kids to part with their lunch money.

These direct attempts at **social influence** form a major part of social psychology and will be discussed in our chapters on conformity, attitudes, and group processes. To the social psychologist, however, social influence is broader than attempts by one person to change another person's behavior. It includes our thoughts and feelings as well as our overt acts. And it takes many forms other than deliberate attempts at persuasion. We are often influenced merely by the *presence* of other people, including perfect strangers who are not interacting with us. Other people don't even have to be present in order to influence us: We are governed by the imaginary approval or disapproval of our parents, friends, and teachers and by how we expect others to react to us. Sometimes these influences conflict with one another, and social psychologists are especially interested in what happens in the mind of an individual when they do. For example, conflicts frequently occur when young people go off to college and find themselves torn between the beliefs and values they learned at home and the beliefs and values of their professors or peers. (See the Try It!)

We will spend the rest of this introductory chapter expanding on these issues, so that you will get an idea of what social psychology is, what it isn't, and how it differs from other, related disciplines.

Our thoughts, feelings, and behaviors are influenced by our immediate surroundings as well as by our cultural and family background. These students share a college identity but differ in ethnicity and religion.

TRY IT! How Do Values Change?

Think of the major values that govern people's lives: love, money, sex, wealth, religion, freedom, compassion for others, security, children, duty, loyalty, and so on. Make three lists of the 10 values that are most important to (1) you, (2) your parents, and (3) your closest friends in college. Note the similarities and differences in your lists. How do these differences affect you? Do you find yourself rejecting one set of values in favor of the other? Are you trying to make a compromise between the two? Are you attempting to form a new set of values that are your own?

Social Psychology, Science, and Common Sense

Throughout history, philosophy has been a major source of insight about human nature. Indeed, the work of philosophers is part of the foundation of contemporary psychology. This has more than mere historical significance: Psychologists have looked to philosophers for insights into the nature of consciousness (e.g., Dennett, 1991) and how people form beliefs about the social world (e.g., Gilbert, 1991). Sometimes, however, even great thinkers find themselves in disagreement with one another. When this occurs, how are you supposed to know who is right? Are there some situations where Philosopher A might be right, and other conditions where Philosopher B might be right? How would you determine this?

We social psychologists address many of the same questions that philosophers do, but we attempt to look at these questions scientifically—even questions concerning that great human mystery, love. In 1663, the Dutch philosopher Benedict Spinoza offered a highly original insight. He proposed that if we love someone whom we formerly hated, that love will be stronger than if hatred had not preceded it. Spinoza's proposition is beautifully worked out. His logic is impeccable. But how can we be sure that it holds up? Does it always hold up? What are the conditions under which it does or doesn't? These are *empirical* questions, meaning that their answers can be derived from experimentation or measurement rather than by personal opinion (Aronson, 1999; Aronson & Linder, 1965).

Now let's take another look at the examples at the beginning of this chapter. Why did these people behave the way they did? One way to answer this question would simply be to ask them. We could ask the people who observed Abraham Biggs's suicide why they didn't call the police; we could ask Sam why he wasn't especially excited about his fraternity brothers. The problem with this approach is that people are not always aware of the origins of their own responses and feelings (Gilbert, 2008; Nisbett & Wilson, 1977; Wilson, 2002). People might come up with plenty of excuses for not calling the police to rescue Biggs, but those excuses might not be the *reason* they did nothing. It is unlikely that Sam could pinpoint why he liked his fraternity brothers less than his father had liked his.

After the mass suicide at Jonestown, everyone had an explanation. Some people claimed (mistakenly) that the Reverend Jones used hypnotism and drugs to weaken the resistance of his followers. Others claimed (also mistakenly) that the people who were attracted to his cult were emotionally disturbed in the first place. As you will learn throughout this book, such speculations are almost always wrong, or at the very least oversimplified, because they underestimate the power of the situation. It is difficult for most people to grasp just how powerful a cult can be in affecting the hearts and minds of otherwise healthy and well-educated people.

If we rely on commonsense explanations of one particular tragic event, moreover, we don't learn very much that helps us understand other, similar ones. The attacks on the World Trade Center and the Pentagon on September 11, 2001, made Americans wonder what kind of "crazy, deranged" people become suicide bombers. Yet the evidence repeatedly finds that the people in suicide cults, like most suicide bombers today, were mentally healthy and, for the most part, bright and well educated. Name-calling may make some people feel better, but it is no substitute for understanding the

British soldiers stand near burning vehicles in Kabul, Afghanistan, after a suicide car bomber killed soldiers on a NATO-led peacekeeping mission. What causes a person to become a suicide bomber? Popular theories say such people must be mentally ill, alienated loners, or psychopaths. But social psychologists would try to understand the circumstances and situations that drive otherwise healthy, well-educated, bright people to commit murder and suicide for the sake of a religious or political goal.

complexities of the situations that caused these people to kill themselves for their leaders or for a political or religious conviction.

Social psychologists are not opposed to folk wisdom—far from it. You will find plenty of wise observations from journalists, social critics, and novelists in the margins of this book. The primary problem with relying entirely on such sources is that, more often than not, they disagree with one another, and there is no easy way of determining which of them is correct. Consider what folk wisdom has to say about the factors that influence how much we like other people. We know that "birds of a feather flock together." With a little effort, each of us could come up with lots of examples where indeed we liked to hang around with people who shared our backgrounds and interests. But folk wisdom also tells us that "opposites attract." If we tried, we could also come up with examples where we were attracted to people with different backgrounds and interests. Well, which is it? Similarly, are we to believe that "out of sight is out of mind" or that "absence makes the heart grow fonder," that "haste makes waste" or that "he who hesitates is lost"?

And which answer best explains why the Jonestown massacre occurred?

- The Reverend Jones attracted people who were already psychologically depressed.
- Only mentally ill people join cults.
- Jones was such a powerful, charismatic figure that virtually anyone—even strong, nondepressed individuals like you or us—would have succumbed to his influence.
- People cut off from society are particularly vulnerable to social influence.
- All of the above.
- None of the above.

Social psychologists would want to know which of these explanations—or another one entirely—is the most likely. To do this, we have devised an array of scientific methods to test our assumptions, guesses, and ideas about human social behavior, empirically and systematically rather than by relying on folk wisdom, common sense, or the opinions and insights of philosophers, novelists, political pundits, and our grandmothers. Doing experiments in social psychology presents many challenges, primarily because we are attempting to predict the behavior of highly sophisticated organisms in a variety of complex situations. As scientists, our goal is to find objective answers to a wide array of important questions: What are the factors that cause aggression? How might we reduce prejudice? What variables cause two people to like or love each other? Why do certain kinds of political advertisements work better than others?

To answer questions like these, the first task of the social psychologist is to make an educated guess, called a *hypothesis*, about the specific situations under which one outcome or the other would occur. Just as a physicist performs experiments to test hypotheses about the nature of the physical world, the social psychologist performs experiments to test hypotheses about the nature of the social world. The next task is to design well-controlled experiments sophisticated enough to tease out the situations that would result in one or another outcome. This enriches our understanding of human nature and allows us to make accurate predictions once we know the key aspects of the prevailing situation. (In Chapter 2 we will discuss the scientific methods that social psychologists use.)

To elaborate, let's return to our discussion about the kinds of people we like and the relationship between absence and liking. Social psychologists would suggest that there are some conditions under which birds of a feather do flock together, and other conditions under which opposites do attract. Similarly, there are some conditions under which absence does make the heart grow fonder, and others under which out of sight does mean out of mind. So each proverb can be true. That statement helps, but is it good enough? Not really, because if you want to understand human behavior, knowing that each can be true is not sufficient. Part of the job of the social psychologist is to do the research that specifies the conditions under which one or another is most likely to take place.

Watch on **MyPsychLab**
To learn more about how psychology helps us understand ourselves, watch the MyPsychLab video ***The Complexity of Humans: Phil Zimbardo.***

How Social Psychology Differs from Its Closest Cousins

If you are like most people, when you read the examples that opened this chapter and started thinking about how those events might have come about, you assumed that the individuals involved had some weaknesses, flaws, and personality traits that led them to respond as they did. What character traits might these be? Some people are leaders and others are followers; some people are public-spirited and others are selfish. Perhaps the people who failed to get help for Abraham Biggs were lazy, timid, selfish, or heartless. Given what you know about their behavior, would you want any of them as a friend?

Personality psychologists study qualities of the individual that might make a person shy, conventional, rebellious, and willing to wear a turquoise wig in public or a yellow shirt in a sea of blue. Social psychologists study the powerful role of social influence on how all of us behave.

Individual Differences
The aspects of people's personalities that make them different from other people

Would you loan them your car or trust them to take care of your new puppy? As for Sam, perhaps he is not as much of an extrovert or joiner as his dad was. And, most seriously, perhaps the people at Jonestown ended their own lives and their children's because they were all conformists or weak-willed or suffered from mental disorders.

Asking and trying to answer questions about people's behavior in terms of their traits is the work of personality psychologists, who generally focus on **individual differences**, the aspects of people's personalities that make them different from others. Research on personality increases our understanding of human behavior, but social psychologists believe that explaining behavior primarily through personality factors ignores a critical part of the story: the powerful role played by social influence. Remember that it was not just a handful of people who committed suicide at Jonestown, but almost 100% of the people in the village. Although it is conceivable that they were all mentally ill or had the same constellation of personality traits, this is highly improbable. If we want a richer, more thorough explanation of this tragic event, we need to understand what kind of power and influence a charismatic figure like Jim Jones possessed, the nature of the impact of living in a closed society cut off from other points of view, and other factors that could cause mentally healthy people to obey him.

Here is a more mundane example. Suppose you go to a party and see a great-looking fellow student you have been hoping to get to know better. The student is looking pretty uncomfortable, however—standing alone, not making eye contact, not talking to anyone who comes over. You decide you're not so interested; this person seems pretty aloof, standoffish, even arrogant. But a few weeks later you see the student again, now being outgoing, funny, and appealing. So which is it? What is this person "really" like? Shy or arrogant, charming and welcoming? It's the wrong question; the answer is both and neither. All of us are capable of being shy in some situations and outgoing in others. A much more interesting question is this: What factors are different in these two situations that have such a profound effect on behavior? That is a social psychological question. (See the following Try It!)

Social psychology is related to other disciplines in the social sciences, including sociology, economics, and political science. Each of these examines the influence of social factors on human behavior, but important differences set social psychology apart—most notably in their level of analysis. For biologists, the level of analysis might be the gene or neurotransmitter. For personality and clinical psychologists, the level of the analysis is the individual. *For the social psychologist, the level of analysis is the individual in the context of a social situation.* For example, to understand why people intentionally hurt one another, the social psychologist focuses on the psychological processes that trigger aggression in specific situations. To what extent is aggression preceded by frustration? Does frustration always precede aggression? If people are feeling frustrated, under what conditions will they vent their frustration with an overt, aggressive act? What factors might preclude an aggressive response by a frustrated individual? Besides frustration, what other factors might cause aggression? We will address these questions in Chapter 12.

TRY IT! Social Situations and Behavior

1. Think about one of your friends or acquaintances whom you regard as a shy person. (You may use yourself!) For a moment, try not to think about him or her as "a shy person," but rather as someone who has difficulty relating to people in some situations but not in others.
2. Make a list of the social situations you think are most likely to bring out your friend's shy behavior.
3. Make a list of the social situations that might bring forth more-outgoing behaviors on your friend's part. Being with a small group of friends he or she is at ease with? Being with a new person, but one who shares your friend's interests?
4. Set up a social environment that you think would make your friend comfortable and relaxed. Pay close attention to the effect that it has on your friend's behavior.

Other social sciences are more concerned with broad social, economic, political, and historical factors that influence events in a given society. Sociology is concerned with such topics as social class, social structure, and social institutions. Of course, because society is made up of collections of people, some overlap is bound to exist between the domains of sociology and those of social psychology. The major difference is that sociology, rather than focusing on the individual, looks toward society at large. *The level of analysis is the group or institution.* So while sociologists, like social psychologists, are interested in aggression, sociologists are more likely to be concerned with why a particular society (or group within a society) produces different levels of aggression in its members. Why is the murder rate in the United States so much higher than in Canada or Europe? Within the United States, why is the murder rate higher in some social classes and geographic regions than in others? How do changes in society relate to changes in aggressive behavior?

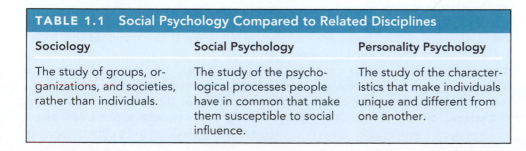

The people in this photo can be studied from a variety of perspectives: as individuals or as members of a family, a social class, an occupation, a culture, or a region. Sociologists study the group or institution; social psychologists study the influence of those groups and institutions on individual behavior.

The difference between social psychology and other social sciences in the level of analysis they examine reflects another difference between the disciplines: what they are trying to explain. *The goal of social psychology is to identify universal properties of human nature that make everyone susceptible to social influence, regardless of social class or culture.* The laws governing the relationship between frustration and aggression, for example, are hypothesized to be true of most people in most places, not just members of one social class, age group, or race.

However, because social psychology is a young science that developed mostly in the United States, many of its findings have not yet been tested in other cultures to see if they are universal. Nonetheless, our goal as social psychologists is to discover such laws. And increasingly, as methods and theories developed by American social psychologists are adopted by European, Asian, African, Middle Eastern, and South American social psychologists, we are learning more about the extent to which these laws are universal, as well as cultural differences in the way these laws are expressed (see Chapter 2). *Cross-cultural research* is therefore extremely valuable, because it sharpens theories, either by demonstrating their universality or by leading us to discover additional variables whose incorporation helps us make more-accurate predictions of human behavior. We will encounter many examples of cross-cultural research in subsequent chapters.

In sum, social psychology is located between its closest cousins, sociology and personality psychology (see Table 1.1). Social psychology and sociology share an interest in the way the situation and the larger society influence behavior. But social psychologists focus more on the psychological makeup of individuals *that renders people susceptible* to social influence. And although social psychology and personality psychology both emphasize the psychology of the individual rather than focusing on what makes people different from one another, social psychology emphasizes the *psychological processes* shared by most people around the world that make them susceptible to social influence.

Watch on **MyPsychLab**
Consider social psychology and related fields as you watch the MyPsychLab video ***Alan Kazdin: Would you suggest psychology students keep their eyes open to other disciplines?***

TABLE 1.1 Social Psychology Compared to Related Disciplines

Sociology	Social Psychology	Personality Psychology
The study of groups, organizations, and societies, rather than individuals.	The study of the psychological processes people have in common that make them susceptible to social influence.	The study of the characteristics that make individuals unique and different from one another.

The Power of the Situation

Suppose you stop at a roadside restaurant for a cup of coffee and a piece of pie. The server comes over to take your order, but you are having a hard time deciding which pie you want. While you are hesitating, she impatiently taps her pen against her notepad, rolls her eyes toward the ceiling, scowls at you, and finally snaps, "Hey, I haven't got all day, you know!" Like most people, you would probably think that she is a nasty or unpleasant person.

But suppose, while you are deciding whether to complain about her to the manager, a regular customer tells you that your "crabby" server is a single parent who was kept awake all night by the moaning of her youngest child, who was terribly sick; that her car broke down on her way to work and she has no idea where she will find the money to have it repaired; that when she finally arrived at the restaurant, she learned that her coworker was too drunk to work, requiring her to cover twice the usual number of tables; and that the short-order cook keeps screaming at her because she is not picking up the orders fast enough to please him. Given all that information, you might conclude that she is not necessarily a nasty person, just an ordinary human being under enormous stress.

The key fact, therefore, is that, without important information about a situation, most people will try to explain someone's behavior in terms of the personality of the individual; they focus on the fish, and not the water the fish swims in. But if the water is murky, contaminated, or full of predators, the fish is not going to be very happy. The fact that many people often fail to take the situation into account is important to social psychologists, because it has a profound impact on how human beings relate to one another—such as, in the case of the server, whether they feel sympathy toward another person or impatience and anger.

Thus, the social psychologist is up against a formidable barrier known as the **fundamental attribution error**: the tendency to explain our own and other people's behavior entirely in terms of personality traits and to underestimate the power of social influence. Explaining behavior this way often gives us a feeling of false security. For example, when trying to explain repugnant or bizarre behavior, such as suicide bombers or the people of Jonestown taking their own lives and killing their own children, it is tempting and, in a strange way, comforting to write off the victims as flawed human beings. Doing so gives the rest of us the feeling that it could never happen to us. Ironically, this in turn increases our personal vulnerability to possibly destructive social influences by making us less aware of our own susceptibility to social psychological processes. Moreover, by failing to fully appreciate the power of the situation, we tend to oversimplify the problem, which then decreases our understanding of the causes of many human actions. Among other things, this oversimplification can lead us to blame the victim in situations where the individual was overpowered by social forces too difficult for most of us to resist, as in the Jonestown tragedy.

To take a more everyday example, imagine a situation in which people are playing a two-person game wherein each player must choose one of two strategies: They can play competitively and try to win as much money as possible and make sure their partner loses as much as possible, or they can play cooperatively and try to make sure both they and their partner win some money. We will discuss the details of this game in Chapter 9. For now, just consider that there are only two basic strategies to use when playing the game: competition or cooperation. How do you think each of your friends would play this game?

Few people find this question hard to answer; we all have a feeling for the relative competitiveness of our friends. Accordingly, you might say, "I am certain that my friend Jennifer, who is a hard-nosed business major, would play this game more competitively than my friend Anna, who is a really caring, loving person." But how accurate are you likely to be? Should you be thinking about the game itself rather than who is playing it?

Fundamental Attribution Error

The tendency to overestimate the extent to which people's behavior is due to internal, dispositional factors and to underestimate the role of situational factors

To find out, Lee Ross and his students conducted the following experiment (Liberman, Samuels, & Ross, 2004). They chose a group of students at Stanford University who were considered by the resident assistants in their dorm to be either especially cooperative or especially competitive. The researchers did this by describing the game to the RAs and asking them to think of students in their dormitories who would be most likely to adopt the competitive or cooperative strategy. As expected, the RAs easily identified students who fit each category.

Next, Ross invited these students to play the game in a psychology experiment. There was one added twist: The researchers varied a seemingly minor aspect of the social situation—what the game was called. They told half the participants that the name was the Wall Street Game and half that it was the Community Game. Everything else about the game was identical. Thus, people who were judged as either competitive or cooperative played a game that was called either the Wall Street Game or the Community Game, resulting in four conditions.

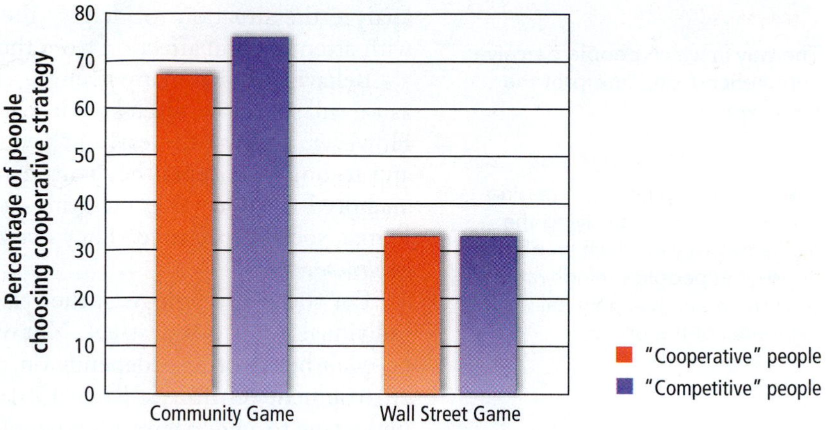

FIGURE 1.1

Why the Name of the Game Matters

In this experiment, when the name of the game was the "Community Game," players were far more likely to behave cooperatively than when it was called the "Wall Street Game"—regardless of their own cooperative or competitive personality traits. The game's title conveyed social norms that trumped personality and shaped the players' behavior.

(Adapted from Liberman, Samuels, & Ross, 2004)

Again, most of us go through life assuming that what really counts is an individual's personality, not something about the individual's immediate situation and certainly not something as trivial as what a game is called, right? Not so fast! As seen in Figure 1.1, the name of the game made a tremendous difference in how people behaved. When it was called the Wall Street Game, approximately two thirds of the students responded competitively, whereas when it was called the Community Game, only a third responded competitively. The name of the game sent a powerful message about how the players should behave. It alone conveyed a social norm about what kind of behavior was appropriate in this situation. In Chapter 7, we will see that social norms can shape people's behaviors in all kinds of remarkable ways.

In this situation, a student's personality made no measurable difference in the student's behavior. The students labeled *competitive* were no more likely to adopt the competitive strategy than those who were labeled *cooperative*. This pattern of results is one we will see throughout this book: Aspects of the social situation that may seem minor can overwhelm the differences in people's personalities (Ross & Ward, 1996). This is not to say that personality differences do not exist or are unimportant; they do exist and frequently are of great importance. But social and environmental situations are so powerful that they have dramatic effects on almost everyone. This is the domain of the social psychologist.

The Power of Social Interpretation

It is one thing to say that the social situation has profound effects on human behavior, but what exactly do we mean by the social situation? One strategy for defining it would be to specify the objective properties of the situation, such as how rewarding it is to people, and then document the behaviors that follow from these objective properties.

This is the approach taken by **behaviorism**, a school of psychology maintaining that to understand human behavior, one need only consider the reinforcing properties of the environment: When behavior is followed by a reward (such as money, attention, praise, or other benefits), it is likely to continue; when behavior is followed by a punishment (such as pain, loss, or angry shouts), it is likely to become extinguished. Dogs come when they are called because they have learned that compliance is followed by positive reinforcement (e.g., food or petting); children memorize their multiplication tables more quickly if you praise them, smile at them, and paste a gold star on their foreheads following correct answers. Psychologists in this tradition, notably the pioneering behaviorist B. F. Skinner (1938), believed that all behavior could be understood by examining the rewards and punishments in the organism's environment. Thus, to understand Sam's lukewarm feelings about his fraternity, Alpha Beta, a behaviorist might

Behaviorism

A school of psychology maintaining that to understand human behavior, one need only consider the reinforcing properties of the environment.

Construal

The way in which people perceive, comprehend, and interpret the social world

Gestalt Psychology

A school of psychology stressing the importance of studying the subjective way in which an object appears in people's minds rather than the objective, physical attributes of the object

analyze the situation to identify the consequences of his actions: Are they rewarded with attention and affection from the other guys or punished by anger and rejection?

Behaviorism has many strengths, and its principles explain some behavior very well, as we will see in our discussion in Chapter 10 of the research on social exchange theory. However, because the early behaviorists chose not to deal with cognition, thinking, and feeling—concepts they considered too vague and mentalistic and not sufficiently anchored to observable behavior—they overlooked phenomena that are vital to the human social experience. They overlooked the importance of *how people interpret their environments*.

For social psychologists, the relationship between the social environment and the individual is a two-way street. Not only does the situation influence people's behavior; people's behavior also depends on their interpretation, or **construal**, of their social environment (Griffin & Ross, 1991; Ross & Nisbett, 1991). In fact, it is often more important to understand how people perceive, comprehend, and interpret the social world than it is to understand its objective properties (Lewin, 1943).

For example, if a person approaches you, slaps you on the back, and asks you how you are feeling, your response will depend not on what that person has done, but how you *interpret* that behavior. You might construe these actions differently depending on whether they come from a close friend who is concerned about your health, a casual acquaintance who is just passing the time of day, or an automobile salesperson attempting to be ingratiating for the purpose of selling you a used car. And your answer will vary also, even if the question about your health were worded the same and asked in the same tone of voice. You would be unlikely to say, "Actually, I'm feeling pretty worried about this kidney pain" to a salesperson, but you might tell your close friend.

This emphasis on construal has its roots in an approach called **Gestalt psychology**. First proposed as a theory of how people perceive the physical world, Gestalt psychology holds that we should study the subjective way in which an object appears in people's minds (the *gestalt*, or whole) rather than the way in which the objective, physical attributes of the object combine. For example, one way to understand how people perceive a painting would be to break it down into its individual elements, such as the exact amounts of primary colors applied to the different parts of the canvas, the types of brushstrokes used to apply the colors, and the different geometric shapes they form. We might then attempt to determine how these elements are combined by the perceiver to form an overall image of the painting. According to Gestalt psychologists, however, it is impossible to understand the way an object is perceived only by studying these building blocks of perception. The whole is different from the sum of its parts. One must focus on the phenomenology of the perceiver—on how an object appears to people—instead of on the individual objective elements of the stimulus.

Simulate on MyPsychLab

Learn more about Gestalt principles in the MyPsychLab simulation ***Gestalt Laws of Perception.***

The Gestalt approach was formulated in Germany in the first part of the twentieth century by Kurt Koffka, Wolfgang Köhler, Max Wertheimer, and their students and colleagues. In the late 1930s, several of these psychologists fled to the United States to escape the Nazi regime (Cartwright, 1979). Among the émigrés was Kurt Lewin, generally considered the founding father of modern experimental social psychology. As a young German Jewish professor in the 1930s, Lewin experienced the anti-Semitism rampant in Nazi Germany. The experience profoundly affected his thinking, and, once he moved to the United States, Lewin helped shape American social psychology, directing it toward a deep interest in exploring the causes and cures of prejudice and ethnic stereotyping.

Kurt Lewin: "If an individual sits in a room trusting that the ceiling will not come down, should only his 'subjective probability' be taken into account for predicting behavior or should we also consider the 'objective probability' of the ceiling's coming down as determined by engineers? To my mind, only the first has to be taken into account."

As a theorist, Lewin took the bold step of applying Gestalt principles beyond the perception of objects to social perception: how people perceive other people and their motives, intentions, and behaviors. Lewin was the first scientist to fully realize the importance of taking the perspective of the people in a situation. Social psychologists soon began to focus on the importance of how people construe their environments.

Construal has important implications. In a murder trial, when the prosecution presents compelling evidence it believes will prove the defendant guilty, the verdict always hinges on precisely how each jury member construes that evidence. These construals rest on a variety of events and perceptions that often bear no objective relevance to the case. During cross-examination, did a key witness come across as being too remote or too arrogant? Did the prosecutor appear to be smug, obnoxious, or uncertain?

A special kind of construal is what social psychologist Lee Ross calls "naïve realism," the conviction that all of us share that we perceive things "as they really are." If other people see the same things differently, therefore, it must be because *they* are biased (Ross, 2004, 2010; Ehrlinger, Gilovich, & Ross, 2005). Ross has been working closely with Israeli and Palestinian negotiators. These negotiations frequently run aground because of naïve realism; each side assumes that other reasonable people see things the same way they do. "[E]ven when each side recognizes that the other side perceives the issues differently," says Ross, "each thinks that the other side is biased while they themselves are objective and that their own perceptions of reality should provide the basis for settlement." So both sides resist compromise, fearing that their "biased" opponent will benefit more than they.

Fritz Heider, one of the early founders of social psychology, once observed, "Generally, a person reacts to what he thinks the other person is perceiving, feeling, and thinking, in addition to what the other person may be doing."

In a simple experiment, Ross took peace proposals created by Israeli negotiators, labeled them as Palestinian proposals, and asked Israeli citizens to judge them. The Israelis liked the Palestinian proposal attributed to Israel more than they liked the Israeli proposal attributed to the Palestinians. Ross concludes, "If your own proposal isn't going to be attractive to you when it comes from the other side, what chance is there that the *other* side's proposal is going to be attractive when it comes from the other side?" The hope is that once negotiators on both sides become fully aware of this phenomenon and how it impedes conflict resolution, a reasonable compromise will be more likely.

You can see that construals range from the simple (as in the example of the question "How are you feeling?") to the remarkably complex (international negotiations). And they affect all of us in our everyday lives. Imagine that Jason is a shy high school student who admires Maria from afar. As a budding social psychologist, you have the job of predicting whether or not Jason will ask Maria to the senior prom. To do this, you need to begin by viewing Maria's behavior through Jason's eyes—that is, by seeing how Jason interprets her behavior. If she smiles at him, does Jason construe her behavior as mere politeness, the kind of politeness she would extend to any of the dozens of nerds and losers in the senior class? Or does he view her smile as an encouraging sign, one that inspires him to gather the courage to ask her out? If she ignores him, does Jason figure that she's playing hard to get, or does he take it as a sign that she's not interested in him? To predict Jason's behavior, it is not enough to know the details of Maria's behavior; it is imperative to know how Jason interprets her behavior.

Research by social psychologists on construal shows why negotiation between nations can be so difficult: Each side thinks that it sees the issues clearly but that the other side is "biased."

Now suppose that after class one day, Maria kisses Jason on the cheek. Again, how he responds will depend on how he construes the situation: Does he interpret that kiss as a first step, a sign of romantic interest on Maria's part? Does he see it as an aloof, sisterly signal that Maria wants to be friends but nothing more? Or does he see it as a sign that Maria is interested in him but wants to proceed slowly? Were Jason to misinterpret the situation, he might commit a serious blunder: He might turn his back on what could have been the love of his life, or he might express his own passionate feelings inappropriately. In either case, social psychologists would say that the best strategy for understanding Jason's reaction would be to find a way to determine his construal of Maria's behavior rather than to dissect the objective nature of the kiss itself (its length, degree of pressure, etc.). But how are these construals formed? Stay tuned.

Where Construals Come From: Basic Human Motives

How will Jason determine why Maria kissed him? If it is true that subjective and not objective situations influence people, we need to understand how people arrive at their subjective impressions of the world. What are people trying to accomplish when they interpret the social world? When construing their environments, are most people concerned with making an interpretation that places them in the most positive light (e.g., Jason's believing "Maria is going to the prom with Eric because she is just trying to make me jealous") or with making the most accurate interpretation, even if it is unflattering (e.g., "Painful as it may be, I must admit that she would rather go to the prom with a sea slug than with me")? Social psychologists seek to understand the fundamental laws of human nature, common to all, that explain why we construe the social world the way we do.

We human beings are complex organisms. At any given moment, various intersecting motives underlie our thoughts and behaviors, including hunger, thirst, fear, a desire for control, and the promise of love, favors, and other rewards. (Some of these psychological motives are discussed in Chapters 10 and 11.) Two motives that concern us here are of primary importance: *the need to feel good about ourselves* and *the need to be accurate*. Sometimes, each of these motives pulls us in the same direction. Often, though, these motives tug us in opposite directions, where to perceive the world accurately requires us to face up to the fact that we have behaved foolishly or immorally.

Some people would construe this demonstration as an act of moral protest against same-sex marriage; others would construe it as an act of homophobia and prejudice. Each side is sure that they are right. Where do construals come from, and what are their consequences?

Leon Festinger, one of social psychology's most innovative theorists, was quick to realize that it is precisely when these two motives pull in opposite directions that we can gain our most valuable insights into the workings of the human mind. Imagine that you are the president of the United States and your country is engaged in a difficult and costly war overseas. You have poured hundreds of billions of dollars into that war, and it has consumed tens of thousands of American lives as well as thousands more lives of innocent civilians. The war seems to be at a stalemate; no end is in sight. You frequently wake up in the middle of the night, bathed in the cold sweat of conflict: On the one hand, you deplore all the carnage that is going on; on the other hand, you don't want to go down in history as the first American president to lose a war.

Some of your advisers tell you that they can see the light at the end of the tunnel, and that if you intensify the bombing or add thousands more troops, the enemy will soon capitulate and the war will be over. This would be a great outcome for you: Not only will you have succeeded in achieving your military and political aims, but history will consider you to have been a great leader as well. Other advisers, however, believe that intensifying the bombing will only strengthen the enemy's resolve; they advise you to sue for peace.

Which advisers are you likely to believe? As we shall see in Chapter 6, President Lyndon Johnson faced this exact dilemma in the mid-1970s, with the war in Vietnam; so did George W. Bush in the mid-2000s, when the war in Iraq did not end in 6 weeks as he had predicted when it began in 2003; so did Barack Obama, in deciding in 2009 whether to invest more troops in the war in Afghanistan. Most presidents have chosen to believe their advisers who suggest escalating the war, because if they succeed in winning, the victory justifies the human and financial cost; but withdrawing not only means going down in history as a president who lost a war, but also having to justify the fact that all those lives and all that money have been spent in vain. As you can see, the need to feel good about our decisions can fly in the face of the need to be accurate, and can have catastrophic consequences (Draper, 2008; McClellan, 2008; McNamara, 1995; Woodward, 2008). In Johnson's case, the decision to increase the bombing *did* strengthen the enemy's resolve, thereby prolonging the war in Vietnam.

The Self-Esteem Approach: The Need to Feel Good About Ourselves

Most people have a strong need to maintain reasonably high **self-esteem**—that is, to see themselves as good, competent, and decent (Aronson, 1998, 2007; Baumeister, 1993; Tavris & Aronson, 2007). Given the choice between distorting the world to feel good about themselves and representing the world accurately, people often take the first option.

Justifying Past Behavior Suppose a couple gets divorced after 10 years of a marriage made difficult by the husband's irrational jealousy. Rather than admitting the truth—that his jealousy and possessiveness drove her away—the husband blames the breakup of his marriage on the fact that his ex-wife was not responsive enough to his needs. His interpretation serves a purpose: It makes him feel better about himself (Simpson, 2010). Acknowledging major deficiencies in ourselves is very difficult, even when the cost is seeing the world inaccurately. The consequence of this distortion, of course, is that learning from experience becomes very unlikely. In his next marriage, the husband is likely to recreate the same problems.

We do not mean that people totally distort reality, denying the existence of all information that reflects badly on them; such extreme behavior is rare. Yet it is often possible for people to put a slightly different spin on the existing facts—one that puts them in the best possible light. Consider Roger. He's the guy whose shoes are almost always untied and who frequently has coffee stains on the front of his shirt. Most observers consider Roger a slob, but Roger probably describes himself as casual and noncompulsive. The fact that people distort their interpretation of reality so that they feel better about themselves is not surprising, but the ways in which this motive operates are often startling.

Watch on **MyPsychLab**
To learn more about how we justify our actions, watch the MyPsychLab video ***Carol Tavris: How does cognitive dissonance typically play out in society?***

Suffering and Self-Justification Let's go back to one of our early scenarios: the case of Oscar and his son, Sam. Why was Sam less enamored of his fraternity brothers than Oscar had been when he was in college? Recall that Oscar quickly formed the hypothesis that perhaps his fraternity was not attracting the kinds of wonderful people who were there when he was in college, and that personality psychologists might suggest that father and son differ in their degree of extroversion or other traits. This might be true. But social psychologists would suspect that a far more compelling explanation involves the hazing itself. Specifically, we would contend that a major factor that increased Oscar's liking for his fraternity brothers was the degrading hazing ritual he underwent, a ritual Sam was able to avoid. Why would something so negative cause Oscar to like his fraternity? Don't principles of behaviorism show that rewards, not punishments, make us like things associated with them? Quite so. But as we indicated earlier, social psychologists have discovered that this formulation is too simple to account for human thinking and motivation. Human beings have a need to justify their past behavior, and this need leads them to do many things a behaviorist could not explain.

Self-Esteem
People's evaluations of their own self-worth—that is, the extent to which they view themselves as good, competent, and decent

These first-year students are being "welcomed" to their university by seniors who subject them to hazing. Doing silly or dangerous things as part of a hazing ritual may be, well, silly or dangerous. At the same time, it does build cohesiveness.

Here's how it works. If Oscar goes through a severe hazing to become a member of the fraternity but later discovers unpleasant things about his fraternity brothers, he will feel like a fool: "Why did I go through all that pain and embarrassment to live in a house with a bunch of jerks? Only a moron would do a thing like that." To avoid feeling like a fool, he will try to justify his decision to undergo the hazing by distorting his interpretation of his fraternity experience. In other words, he will try to put a positive spin on his experiences.

Suppose that, having gone through all that hazing, Oscar moves into the fraternity house and begins to experience things that to an outside observer would not be very positive: The fraternity dues make a significant dent in Oscar's budget, the frequent parties take a toll on the amount of studying he can do, and consequently his grades suffer. Whereas an unmotivated observer—someone who didn't go through the hazing—might consider these aspects of fraternity life as definite negatives, Oscar is motivated to see them differently; indeed, he considers them a small price to pay for the sense of brotherhood he feels. He focuses on the good parts of living in the fraternity, and he distorts or dismisses the bad parts as inconsequential. The result of all this self-justification is to make Oscar more kindly disposed toward the fraternity and its members than Sam was, because Sam, not having gone through the hazing, had no need to justify his behavior and thus no need to see his fraternity experiences in a positive light. The end result? Oscar loved his fraternity and Sam did not.

Does this explanation sound far-fetched? How do we know that the people in the fraternity were not objectively nicer when Oscar was a member than when Sam was a member? In a series of well-controlled classic laboratory experiments, social psychologists investigated the phenomenon of hazing: The experimenters held constant everything in the situation, including the precise behavior of the fraternity members; the only thing they varied was the severity of the hazing that the students underwent in order to become members. The results demonstrated conclusively that the more unpleasant the procedure the participants underwent to get into a group, the better they liked the group—even though, objectively, the group members were the same people behaving the same way for everyone (Aronson & Mills, 1959; Gerard & Mathewson, 1966). We discuss this phenomenon more thoroughly in Chapter 6. The important points to remember here are that human beings are motivated to maintain a positive picture of themselves, in part by justifying their past behavior, and that under certain specifiable conditions, this leads them to do things that at first glance might seem surprising or paradoxical. They might prefer people and things for whom they have suffered to people and things they associate with ease and pleasure.

The Social Cognition Approach: The Need to Be Accurate

Even when people are bending the facts to see themselves in as favorable a way as they can, they do not completely distort reality. They know the difference between fantasizing about some hot rock star and believing in the fantasy that the rock star is in love with them. Human beings are quite skilled at thinking, contemplating, and deducing, and these astonishing talents begin early in life. It is impossible to observe the cognitive development of a child without being awestruck. Just think of the vast gains in knowledge and reasoning that occur in the first few years of life, as a child grows from a squirming, helpless newborn who can do little but eat, cry, poop, and sleep into a talkative 4-year-old who can utter complex sentences, hatch diabolical plots to frustrate a younger sibling, and create elaborate imaginary universes.

Social Cognition Given the amazing cognitive abilities of our species, it makes sense that social psychologists, when formulating theories of social behavior, would take into consideration the way in which human beings think about the world. We call this the cognitive approach to social psychology, or **social cognition** (Fiske & Taylor, 1991; Markus & Zajonc, 1985; Nisbett & Ross, 1980). Researchers who attempt to understand social behavior from the perspective of social cognition begin with the assumption that all people try to view the world as accurately as possible. They regard human beings as amateur sleuths who are doing their best to understand and predict their social world.

Unfortunately, we often make mistakes in that effort to understand and predict, because we almost never know all the facts we need to judge a given situation accurately. Whether it is a relatively simple decision, such as which breakfast cereal offers the best combination of healthfulness and tastiness, or a slightly more complex decision, such as our desire to buy the best car we can for under $18,000, or a much more complex decision, such as choosing a partner who will make us deliriously happy for the rest of our lives, it is usually impossible to gather all the relevant facts in advance. Moreover, we make countless decisions every day. Even if there were a way to gather all the facts for each decision, we lack the time or the stamina to do so.

Does this sound overblown? Aren't most decisions fairly easy? Let's take a closer look. We will begin by asking you an easy question: Which breakfast cereal is better for you, Lucky Charms or Quaker 100% Natural granola with oats, honey, and raisins? If you are like most of our students, you answered, "100% Natural." After all, everybody knows that Lucky Charms is a kids' cereal, full of sugar and cute little marshmallows, with a picture of a leprechaun on the box. Quaker's 100% Natural has a picture of all that healthy granola, the box is the color of natural wheat (light tan), and doesn't *natural* mean "good for you"? If that's the way you reasoned, you have fallen into a common cognitive trap: You have generalized from the cover to the product. A careful reading of the ingredients in small print will reveal that, per one cup serving, 100% Natural has 420 calories, 30 grams of sugar, and 12 grams of fat; no wonder *Men's Health* magazine rated it the worst packaged cereal in America. In contrast, a cup of Lucky Charms has 142 calories, 14 grams of sugar, and 1 gram of fat. Even in the simple world of cereals, things are not always what they seem.

Expectations About the Social World To add to the difficulty, sometimes our expectations about the social world interfere with perceiving it accurately. Our expectations can even change the *nature* of the social world. Imagine that you are an elementary school teacher dedicated to improving the lives of your students. At the beginning of the academic year, you review each student's standardized intelligence test scores. Early in your career, you were pretty sure that these tests could gauge each child's true potential. But after several years of teaching, you have become certain that these tests are accurate. You have come to see that, almost invariably, the kids who got high scores on these tests are the ones who did the best in your classroom, and the kids who got low scores performed poorly in class.

This scenario doesn't sound all that surprising, except for one fact: You might be wrong about the validity of the intelligence tests. It might be that the tests were not very accurate but that you unintentionally treated the kids with high scores and the kids with low scores differently. This is exactly what Robert Rosenthal and Lenore Jacobson (1968) found in their investigation of a phenomenon called the *self-fulfilling prophecy*: You expect that you or another person will behave in some way, so you act in ways to make your prediction come true (see Chapter 3). The researchers entered elementary school classrooms and administered a test. They then informed each teacher that, according to the test, a few specific students were "bloomers" who were about to take off and perform extremely well. In actuality, the test showed no such thing. The children labeled as bloomers were chosen at random by drawing names out of a hat and thus were no different, on average, from any of the other kids. Lo and behold, on returning to the classroom at the end of the school year, Rosenthal and Jacobson found that the bloomers were performing extremely well. The mere fact that the teachers were led to expect these students to do well caused an improvement in their performance. This striking phenomenon is no fluke; it has been replicated a number of times in many different schools (Rosenthal, 1995).

Social Cognition

How people think about themselves and the social world; more specifically, how people select, interpret, remember, and use social information to make judgments and decisions

How did it come about? Although this outcome seems almost magical, it is embedded in an important aspect of human nature. If you were one of those teachers and were led to expect two or three specific students to perform well, you would be more likely to treat those students in special ways: paying more attention to them, listening to them with more respect, calling on them more frequently, encouraging them, and trying to teach them more-challenging material. This, in turn, would almost certainly make these students feel happier, more respected, more motivated, and smarter—and, *voilà*, the prophecy is fulfilled. Thus, even when we are trying to perceive the social world as accurately as we can, there are many ways in which we can go wrong, ending up with the wrong impressions. We will see why in Chapters 3 and 4.

Social Psychology and Social Problems

To reiterate, social psychology can be defined as the scientific study of social influence. But perhaps you are wondering why we want to understand social influence in the first place. Who ca-res? And what difference does it make whether our behavior has its roots in the desire to be accurate or to bolster our self-esteem?

The most basic answer is simple: We are curious. Social psychologists are fascinated by human social behavior and want to understand it on the deepest possible level. In a sense, all of us are social psychologists. We all live in a social environment, and we are all more than mildly curious about such issues as how we become influenced, how we influence others, and why we fall in love with some people, dislike others, and are indifferent to still others. You don't have to be with people literally in order to be in a social environment. Facebook is a social psychologist's dream laboratory because it's all there: love, anger, bullying, bragging, affection, flirting, wounds, quarrels, friending and unfriending, pride and prejudice.

Watch on **MyPsychLab**

To learn more about cognitive dissonance, watch the MyPsychLab video ***Cognitive Dissonance: Need to Justify Our Actions.***

Leon Festinger: "The way I have always thought about it is that if the empirical world looks complicated, if people seem to react in bewilderingly different ways to similar forces, and if I cannot see the operation of universal underlying dynamics, then that is my fault. I have asked the wrong questions; I have, at a theoretical level, sliced up the world incorrectly. The underlying dynamics are there, and I have to find the theoretical apparatus that will enable me to reveal these uniformities."

Many social psychologists have another reason for studying the causes of social behavior: to contribute to the solution of social problems. From the very beginning of our young science, social psychologists have been keenly interested in such social challenges as reducing violence and prejudice and increasing altruism and tolerance. Contemporary social psychologists have continued this tradition and have broadened the issues of concern to include such endeavors as inducing people to conserve natural resources like water and energy (Dickerson et al., 1992), educating people to practice safer sex to reduce the spread of HIV and other sexually transmitted diseases (Aronson, 1997, 1998; Stone, 1994), understanding the relationship between viewing violence on television and the violent behavior of television watchers (Eron, 1996), developing effective negotiation strategies to resolve international conflict (Kelman, 1997; Ross, 2004, 2010), finding ways to reduce ethnic prejudice and violence in classrooms (Aronson & Patnoe, 1997), raising children's intelligence through environmental interventions and better school programs (Nisbett, 2009), and reducing the high school dropout rate of minority students (J. Aronson, 2010).

The ability to understand and explain complex and harmful social behavior brings with it the challenge to change it. For example, when the American government began to take the AIDS epidemic seriously, it mounted an advertising campaign that seemed intent on frightening people into practicing safer sex. This seems consistent with common sense: If you want people to do something they wouldn't ordinarily do, why not scare the daylights out of them?

This is not a stupid idea. There are many dysfunctional acts (e.g., cigarette smoking, drunk driving) for which the induction of fear can and does motivate people to take rational, appropriate action to preserve their health (Aronson, 2010a; Levy-Leboyer, 1988; Wilson, Purdon, & Wallston, 1988). But, based on years of systematic research on persuasion, social psychologists were quick to realize that in the specific situation of AIDS, arousing fear would almost certainly not produce the desired effect for most people, because most people do not want to think about dying or contracting a horrible illness while they are getting ready to have sex. Moreover, most people do not enjoy using condoms, because they feel that interrupting the sexual act to put on a condom tends to diminish the mood. Given these considerations, when people have been exposed to frightening messages about STDs and AIDS, instead of engaging in rational problem-solving behavior ("How can I protect myself and my partner?"), most tend to reduce that fear by engaging in denial ("It can't happen to me," "Surely no one I'd sleep with is HIV positive").

In this case, as you may have figured out, denial stems not from the desire to be accurate, but from the need to maintain self-esteem. If people can convince themselves that their sexual partners do not carry the HIV virus, they can continue to enjoy unprotected sex while maintaining a reasonably favorable picture of themselves as rational beings. By understanding how this process works, social psychologists have been able to create more effective programs for AIDS education and prevention, as we shall see (Aronson, 1997; Aronson, Fried, & Stone, 1991; Stone et al., 1994).

Social psychology can help us study social problems and find ways to solve them. Social psychologists might study whether children who watch violence on television become more aggressive themselves—and, if so, what kind of intervention might be beneficial.

Throughout this book, we will examine many other examples of the application of social psychology to real-world problems, including the effects of the mass media on attitudes and behavior (Chapter 7), violence and aggression (Chapter 12), and prejudice (Chapter 13). Beginning in the next chapter, you will find an occasional feature called Connections, in which we show how social psychology can be used to understand and solve problems in everyday life. For interested readers, we have also included four final chapters on the application of social psychology to contemporary issues involving health, the environment, law, and education. Finally, we hope that by understanding the fundamental causes of behavior as social psychologists study them, you will also be in a better position to change your own self-defeating or misguided behavior, improve your relationships, and make better decisions.

USE IT! Thinking Like a Social Psychologist

Lately, your once-easygoing, considerate roommate seems to have had a personality transplant, becoming grouchy, thoughtless, and rude. This has been going on for a couple of weeks, long enough to make you think about requesting a shift to a private room or asking for a different roommate. Before you do, what mistake might you be making? Hint: Think of the fundamental attribution error. How likely is it that your roommate's personality has undergone such a drastic change? What might be happening in your roommate's environment or stress levels to cause this change of behavior?

Summary

What is social psychology, and how is it different from other disciplines?

- **What Is Social Psychology?** Social psychology is defined as the scientific study of the way in which people's thoughts, feelings, and behaviors are influenced by the real or imagined presence of other people. Social psychologists are interested in understanding how and why the social environment shapes the thoughts, feelings, and behaviors of the individual.
  - **Social Psychology, Science, and Common Sense** Social psychologists approach the understanding of **social influence** differently from philosophers, journalists, or the layperson. Social psychologists develop explanations of social influence through *empirical methods*, such as experiments in which the variables being studied are carefully controlled. The goal of the science of social psychology is to discover universal laws of human behavior, which is why *cross-cultural research* is often essential.
  - **How Social Psychology Differs from Its Closest Cousins** When trying to explain social behavior, personality psychologists explain the behavior in terms of the person's individual character traits. Although social psychologists would agree that personalities vary, they explain social behavior in terms of the *power of the social situation* to shape how one acts. While social psychology is rooted in the study of the individual's internal

psychological processes, *the level of analysis for social psychology is the individual in the context of a social situation.* In contrast, sociologists focus their analysis on groupings of people organized in social categories such as family, race, religion, and economic class. Social psychologists seek to identify universal *properties of human nature* that make everyone susceptible to social influence regardless of social class or culture. Sociologists seek to explain *properties of societies.*

What's more important: personality or situation?

- **The Power of the Situation** Individual behavior is powerfully influenced by the social environment, but many people don't want to believe this. Social psychologists must contend with the **fundamental attribution error**, the tendency to explain our own and other people's behavior entirely in terms of personality traits and to underestimate the power of social influence. But social psychologists have shown time and again that social and environmental situations are usually more powerful than personality differences in determining an individual's behavior.

How did behaviorism and Gestalt psychology contribute to the development of social psychological thought?

- **The Power of Social Interpretation** Social psychologists have shown that the relationship between individuals and situations is a two-way street, so it is important to understand not only how situations influence individuals, but how people *perceive and interpret* the social world and the behavior of others. These perceptions are more influential than objective aspects of the situation itself. The term **construal** refers to the world as it is interpreted by the individual.

What are the differences between the self-esteem approach and the social cognition approach?

- **Where Construals Come From: Basic Human Motives** The way in which an individual construes (perceives, comprehends, and interprets) a situation is largely shaped by two basic human motives: *the need to be accurate* and *the need to feel good about ourselves.* At times these two motives tug in opposite directions; for example, when an accurate view of how we acted in a situation would reveal that we behaved selfishly.
  - **The Self-Esteem Approach: The Need to Feel Good About Ourselves** Most people have a strong need to see themselves as good, competent, and decent. People often distort their perception of the world to preserve their self-esteem.
  - **The Social Cognition Approach: The Need to Be Accurate** The social cognition perspective is an approach to social psychology that takes into account the way in which human beings think about the world. Individuals are viewed as trying to gain accurate understandings so that they can make effective judgments and decisions that range from which cereal to eat to whom they will marry. In actuality, individuals typically act on the basis of incomplete and inaccurately interpreted information.

How can social psychology help solve social problems?

- **Social Psychology and Social Problems** Social psychological theories about human behavior have been applied effectively to deal with a range of contemporary problems that include prejudice, energy shortages, the spread of AIDS, unhealthy habits, and violence in the schools. The best interventions for serious social problems are those based on scientifically grounded theories about human construal and behavior.

Chapter 1 Test

Study and Review on MyPsychLab

1. The topic that would most interest a social psychologist is
   - **a.** whether people who commit crimes tend to have more aggressive personalities than people who do not.
   - **b.** whether people who commit crimes have different genes from people who do not.
   - **c.** how the level of extroversion of different presidents affected their political decisions.
   - **d.** whether people's decision about whether to cheat on a test is influenced by how they imagine their friends would react if they found out.
   - **e.** the extent to which people's social class predicts their income.

2. How does social psychology differ from personality psychology?
   - **a.** Social psychology focuses on individual differences, whereas personality psychology focuses on how people behave in different situations.
   - **b.** Social psychology focuses on the processes that people have in common with one another that make them susceptible to social influence, whereas personality psychology focuses on individual differences.
   - **c.** Social psychology provides general laws and theories about societies, not individuals, whereas personality psychology studies the characteristics that make people unique and different from each other.
   - **d.** Social psychology focuses on individual differences, whereas personality psychology provides general laws and theories about societies, not individuals.

3. A stranger approaches Emily on campus and says he is a professional photographer. He asks if she will spend 15 minutes posing for pictures next to the student union. According to a social psychologist, Emily's decision will depend on which of the following?
   - **a.** How well dressed the man is.
   - **b.** Whether the man offers to pay her.
   - **c.** How Emily construes the situation.
   - **d.** Whether the man has a criminal record.

4. Researchers who try to understand human behavior from the perspective of *social cognition* assume that
   a. people try to view the world as accurately as possible.
   b. people almost always view the world accurately.
   c. people almost always make mistakes in how they view the world.
   d. people distort reality in order to view themselves favorably.
   e. the need for control is the most important motive behind a person's behavior.

5. The *fundamental attribution error* is best defined as the tendency to
   a. explain our own and other people's behavior entirely in terms of personality traits, thereby underestimating the power of social influence.
   b. explain our own and other people's behavior in terms of the social situation, thereby underestimating the power of personality factors.
   c. believe that people's group memberships influence their behavior more than their personalities.
   d. believe that people's personalities influence their behavior more than their group memberships.

6. Which of the following is least consistent with the *self-esteem approach* to how people view themselves and the social world?
   a. After Sarah leaves Bob for someone else, Bob decides that he never really liked her very much and that she had several annoying habits.
   b. Students who want to take Professor Lopez's seminar have to apply by writing a 10-page essay. Everyone who is selected ends up loving the class.
   c. Janetta did poorly on the first test in her psychology class. She admits to herself that she didn't study very much and vows to study harder for the next test.
   d. Sam has been involved in several minor traffic accidents since getting his driver's license. "There sure are a lot of terrible drivers out there," he says to himself. "People should learn to be good drivers like me."

Answer Key

1-d, 2-b, 3-c, 4-a, 5-a, 6-c

2 Methodology

How Social Psychologists Do Research

IN THIS INFORMATION AGE, WHEN PRETTY MUCH ANYTHING CAN BE FOUND ON THE INTERNET, PORNOGRAPHY IS MORE AVAILABLE THAN EVER BEFORE. One poll found that a quarter of all employees who have access to the Internet visit porn sites during their workdays ("The Tangled Web of Porn," 2008). It is thus important to ask whether exposure to pornography has harmful effects. Is it possible, for example, that looking at graphic sex increases the likelihood that men will become sexually violent?

There has been plenty of debate on both sides of this question. Legal scholar Catharine MacKinnon (1993) argued that "Pornography is the perfect preparation—motivator and instruction manual in one—for . . . sexual atrocities" (p. 28). In 1985, a group of experts, appointed by the attorney general of the United States, voiced a similar opinion, concluding that pornography is a cause of rape and other violent crimes. But in 1970, another commission reviewed much of the same evidence and concluded that pornography does *not* contribute significantly to sexual violence. Whom are we to believe? Is there a scientific way to determine the answer? We believe there is, and in this chapter we will discuss the kinds of research methods social psychologists employ, using research on pornography as an example.

We will also discuss another example, this one having to do not with the causes of violence, but how people react to it when they see it. If you happen to witness someone being attacked by another person, you might not intervene directly out of fear for your own safety. Most of us assume that we would help in some way, though, such as by calling the police. But there are so many examples of witnesses failing to help that it has acquired a name: the *bystander effect*. On March 11, 2011, in Bethesda, Maryland, Jayna Murray was brutally murdered by a coworker inside the clothing store where they worked. Two employees in an Apple store next door heard the murder through the walls, including cries for help from Murray, but did nothing to help (Johnson, 2011). In October of 2011 in Southern China, a 2-year-old girl was run over by two vans, minutes apart, and lay in the street dying. Neither car stopped, and a dozen people walked or rode past the girl without stopping to help (Branigan, 2011).

Perhaps the most famous case was the murder of Kitty Genovese, who was assaulted in the alley of an apartment complex in Queens, New York, in 1964. The attack lasted 45 minutes, and at the time the media reported that as many as 38 of the apartment residents either saw the attack from their windows or heard Genovese's screams, and yet no one attempted to help her, not even by calling the police. Although the details of this account have been called into question (Manning, Levine, & Collins, 2007), there is no doubt that bystanders often fail to help in emergencies, and the Genovese murder triggered a great deal of soul searching as to why. Some concluded that living in a metropolis dehumanizes us and leads inevitably to apathy, indifference to human suffering, and lack of caring. Is this true? Did big-city life cause the bystanders to ignore Kitty Genovese's screams for help, or was there some other explanation? How can we find out?

FOCUS QUESTIONS

- How do researchers develop hypotheses and theories?
- What are the strengths and weaknesses of the various research designs used by social psychologists?
- What impact do cross-cultural studies, the evolutionary approach, and research in social neuroscience have on the way in which scientists investigate social behavior?
- What is the basic dilemma of the social psychologist, and how do social psychologists solve this dilemma?

In October of 2011, a 2-year-old girl was struck by two vans in a row. A dozen people walked or rode past her. Why didn't they stop to help?

Social Psychology: An Empirical Science

A fundamental principle of social psychology is that many social problems, such as the causes of and reactions to violence, can be studied scientifically (Reis & Gosling, 2010; Wilson, Aronson, & Carlsmith, 2010; Reis & Judd, 2000). Before we discuss how social psychological research is done, we begin with a warning: The results of some of the experiments you encounter will seem obvious because social psychology concerns topics with which we are all intimately familiar—social behavior and social influence (Richard, Bond, & Stokes-Zoota, 2001). This familiarity sets social psychology apart from other sciences. When you read about an experiment in particle physics, it is unlikely that the results will connect with your personal experiences. We don't know about you, but we have never thought, "Wow! That experiment on quarks was just like what happened to me while I was waiting for the bus yesterday," or "My grandmother always told me to watch out for positrons and antimatter." When reading about the results of a study on helping behavior or aggression, however, it is quite common to think, "Come on. I could have predicted that. That's the same thing that happened to me last Friday."

The thing to remember is that, when we study human behavior, the results may appear to have been predictable—in retrospect. Indeed, there is a well-known human tendency called the **hindsight bias**, whereby people exaggerate how much they could have predicted an outcome *after* knowing that it occurred (Fischhoff, 2007; Nestler, Blank, & Egloff, 2010; Sanna & Schwarz, 2007). After we know the winner of a political election, for example, we begin to look for reasons why that candidate won. After the fact, the outcome seems inevitable and easily predictable, even if we were quite unsure who would win before the election. The same is true of findings in psychology experiments; it seems like we could have easily predicted the outcomes—after we know them. The trick is to predict what will happen in an experiment before you know how it turned out. To illustrate that not all obvious findings are easy to predict, take the Try It! quiz on the next page.

I love games. I think I could be very happy being a chess player or dealing with some other kinds of games. But I grew up in the Depression. It didn't seem one could survive on chess, and science is also a game. You have very strict ground rules in science, and your ideas have to check out with the empirical world. That's very tough and also very fascinating.

—Leon Festinger, 1977

Formulating Hypotheses and Theories

Research begins with a hunch, or hypothesis, that the researcher wants to test. There is lore in science that holds that brilliant insights come all of a sudden, as when Archimedes shouted, "Eureka! I have found it!" when the solution to a problem flashed into his mind. Although such insights do sometimes occur suddenly, science is a cumulative process, and people often generate hypotheses from previous theories and research.

Inspiration from Earlier Theories and Research Many studies stem from a researcher's dissatisfaction with existing theories and explanations. After reading other people's work, a researcher might believe that he or she has a better way of explaining people's behavior (e.g., why they fail to help in an emergency). In the 1950s, for example, Leon Festinger was dissatisfied with the ability of a major theory of the day, behaviorism, to explain why people change their attitudes. He formulated a new approach—dissonance theory—that made specific predictions about when and how people would change their attitudes. As we will see in Chapter 6, other researchers were dissatisfied with Festinger's explanation of the results he obtained, so they conducted further research to test other possible explanations. Social psychologists, like scientists

Hindsight Bias

The tendency for people to exaggerate how much they could have predicted an outcome after knowing that it occurred

TRY IT! Social Psychology Quiz: What's Your Prediction?

Answer the following questions, each of which is based on social psychological research.

1. Suppose an authority figure asks college students to administer near-lethal electric shocks to another student who has not harmed them in any way. What percentage of these students will agree to do it?
2. If you give children a reward for doing something they already enjoy doing, they will subsequently like that activity (a) more, (b) the same, or (c) less.
3. Who do you think would be happiest with their choice of a consumer product such as an art poster: (a) people who spend several minutes thinking about why they like or dislike each poster or (b) people who choose a poster without analyzing the reasons for their feelings?
4. Repeated exposure to a stimulus—such as a person, a song, or a painting—will make you like it (a) more, (b) the same, or (c) less.
5. You ask an acquaintance to do you a favor—for example, to lend you $10—and he or she agrees. As a result of doing you this favor, the person will probably like you (a) more, (b) the same, or (c) less.
6. When making a complex decision, is it best to (a) decide right away without any further thought, (b) think carefully about the different options, or (c) find something unrelated to distract you for a while and then make up your mind?
7. In the United States, female college students tend not to do as well on math tests as males do. Under which of the following circumstances will women do as well as men: (a) when they are told that there are no gender differences on the test, (b) when they are told that women tend to do better on a difficult math test (because under these circumstances they rise to the challenge), or (c) when they are told that men outperform women under almost all circumstances?
8. Which statement about the effects of advertising is most true? (a) Subliminal messages implanted in advertisements are more effective than normal, everyday advertising; (b) normal TV ads for painkillers or laundry detergents are more effective than subliminal messages implanted in ads; (c) both types of advertising are equally effective; or (d) neither type of advertising is effective.
9. In public settings in the United States, (a) women touch men more, (b) men touch women more, or (c) there is no difference—men and women touch each other equally.
10. Students walking across campus are asked to fill out a questionnaire on which they rate the degree to which student opinion should be considered on a local campus issue. Which group do you think believed that students should be listened to the most? (a) Those given a light clipboard with the questionnaire attached; (b) those given a heavy clipboard with the questionnaire attached; (c) the weight of the clipboard made no difference in people's ratings.

See page 45 for the answers.

in other disciplines, engage in a continual process of theory refinement: A theory is developed; specific hypotheses derived from that theory are tested; based on the results obtained, the theory is revised and new hypotheses are formulated.

Hypotheses Based on Personal Observations Social psychology deals with phenomena we encounter in everyday life. Researchers often observe something in their lives or the lives of others that they find curious and interesting, stimulating them to construct a theory about why this phenomenon occurred—and to design a study to see if they are right.

Consider the murder of Kitty Genovese that we described earlier. At the time, most people blamed her neighbors' failure to intervene on the apathy, indifference, and callousness that big-city life breeds. Two social psychologists who taught at universities in New York, however, had a different idea. Bibb Latané and John Darley were talking one day about the Genovese murder. Here is how Latané remembers their conversation: "One evening after [a] downtown cocktail party, John Darley … came back with me to my 12th Street apartment for a drink. Our common complaint was the distressing tendency of acquaintances, on finding that we called ourselves social psychologists, to ask why New Yorkers were so apathetic" (Latané, 1987, p. 78). Instead of focusing on "what was wrong with New Yorkers," Latané and Darley thought it would be more interesting and important to examine the social situation in which Genovese's neighbors found themselves. Maybe, they thought, the more people who witness an emergency, the less likely it is that any given individual will intervene. Genovese's neighbors might have assumed that someone else had called the police, a phenomenon Latané and Darley (1968) referred to as the *diffusion of responsibility.* Perhaps the bystanders would have been more likely to help had each thought he or she alone was witnessing the murder.

Simulate on **MyPsychLab**
To learn more about observational research, try the MyPsychLab simulation ***Observational Research: Laboratory vs. Naturalistic.***

After a researcher has a hypothesis, whether it comes from a theory, previous research, or an observation of everyday life, how can he or she tell if it is true? In science, idle speculation will not do; the researcher must collect data to test a hypothesis. Let's look at how the observational method, the correlational method, and the experimental method are used to explore research hypotheses such as Latané and Darley's (see Table 2.1).

TABLE 2.1 A Summary of Research Methods

Method	Focus	Question Answered
Observational	Description	What is the nature of the phenomenon?
Correlational	Prediction	From knowing X, can we predict Y?
Experimental	Causality	Is variable X a cause of variable Y?

Research Designs

Social psychology is a scientific discipline with a well-developed set of methods for answering questions about social behavior, such as the ones about violence with which we began this chapter. These methods are of three types: the *observational method*, the *correlational method*, and the *experimental method.* Any of these methods could be used to explore a specific research question; each is a powerful tool in some ways and a weak tool in others. Part of the creativity in conducting social psychological research involves choosing the right method, maximizing its strengths, and minimizing its weaknesses.

In this chapter, we will discuss these methods in detail. We, the authors of this book, are social psychologists who have done a great deal of research. We will therefore try to provide you with a firsthand look at both the joy and the difficulty of conducting social psychological studies. The joy comes in unraveling the clues about the causes of interesting and important social behaviors, just as a sleuth gradually unmasks the culprit in a murder mystery. Each of us finds it exhilarating that we have the tools to provide definitive answers to questions philosophers have debated for centuries. At the same time, as seasoned researchers, we have learned to temper this exhilaration with a heavy dose of humility, because there are formidable practical and ethical constraints involved in conducting social psychological research.

Observational Method
The technique whereby a researcher observes people and systematically records measurements or impressions of their behavior

Ethnography
The method by which researchers attempt to understand a group or culture by observing it from the inside, without imposing any preconceived notions they might have

The Observational Method: Describing Social Behavior

There is a lot to be learned by being an astute observer of human behavior. If the goal is to describe what a particular group of people or type of behavior is like, the **observational method** is very helpful. This is the technique whereby a researcher observes people and records measurements or impressions of their behavior. The observational method may take many forms, depending on what the researchers are looking for, how involved or detached they are from the people they are observing, and how much they want to quantify what they observe.

Ethnography One example is **ethnography**, the method by which researchers attempt to understand a group or culture by observing it from the inside, without imposing any preconceived notions they might have. The goal is to understand the richness and complexity of the group by observing it in action. Ethnography is the chief method of cultural anthropology, the study of human cultures and societies. As social psychology broadens its focus by studying social behavior in different cultures, ethnography is increasingly being used to describe different cultures and generate hypotheses about psychological principles (Fine & Elsbach, 2000; Hodson, 2004; Uzzel, 2000).

Consider this example from the early years of social psychological research. In the early 1950s, a group of people in the Midwest predicted that the world would come to an end in a violent cataclysm on a specific date. They also announced that they would be rescued in time by a spaceship that would land in their leader's backyard. Assuming that the end of the world was not imminent, Leon Festinger and his colleagues thought it would be interesting to observe this group closely and chronicle how they reacted when their beliefs and prophecy were disconfirmed (Festinger, Riecken, & Schachter, 1956). To monitor the hour-to-hour conversations of this group, the social psychologists found it necessary to become members and pretend that they too believed the world was about to end.

The key to ethnography is to avoid imposing one's preconceived notions on the group and to try to understand the point of view of the people being studied. Sometimes, however, researchers have a specific hypothesis that they want to test using the observational method. An investigator might be interested, for example, in how much aggression children exhibit during school recesses. In this case, the observer would be systematically looking for particular behaviors that are concretely defined before the observation begins. For example, aggression might be defined as hitting or shoving another child, taking a toy from another child without asking, and so on. The observer might stand at the edge of the playground and systematically record how often these behaviors occur. If the researcher were interested in exploring possible sex and age differences in social behavior, he or she would also note the child's gender and age. How do we know how accurate the observer is? In such studies, it is important to establish **interjudge reliability**, which is the level of agreement between two or more people who independently observe and code a set of data. By showing that two or more judges independently come up with the same observations, researchers ensure that the observations are not the subjective, distorted impressions of one individual.

Watch on **MyPsychLab**
Watch an interview with a researcher who uses quantitative, qualitative, and ethnographic methods in the MyPsychLab activity ***Academic Achievement and Academic Engagement among Early Adolescents: Diane Hughes.***

Archival Analysis The observational method is not limited to observations of real-life behavior. The researcher can also examine the accumulated documents, or archives, of a culture, a technique known as an **archival analysis** (Mullen, Rozell, & Johnson, 2001). For example, diaries, novels, suicide notes, popular music lyrics, television shows, movies, magazine and newspaper articles, and advertising all tell us a great deal about how a society views itself. Much like our example of aggression, specific, well-defined categories are created and then applied to the archival source. (See the following Try It! exercise.) Think back to the question of the relationship between pornography and violence. One problem with addressing this question is in defining what pornography is. As Supreme Court Justice Potter Stewart put it, "I know it when I see it," but describing its exact content is not easy.

Archival analysis is a good tool for answering this question, because it enables researchers to describe the content of documents present in the culture—in this case, the photographs and fictional stories that represent currently available pornography in the marketplace. One researcher, for example, studied the content of pornography in adults-only fiction paperback books sold at newsstands and regular bookstores (Smith, 1976). Another analyzed photographs posted on Internet Web sites (Mehta, 2001). One disturbing finding was that a lot of pornography involves the use of force (physical, mental, or blackmail) by a male to make a female engage in unwanted sex. Aggression against women is a major theme in some (though not all) pornography.

Observational research, in the form of archival analysis, can tell us a great deal about society's values and beliefs. The fact that sexual violence against women is common in pornography suggests that these images and stories appeal to many readers (Dietz & Evans, 1982; Gossett & Byrne, 2002) and leads to some troubling questions: Is pornography associated with sexually violent crimes against women that occur in our society? Do reading and looking at pornography cause some men to commit violent sexual acts?

Interjudge Reliability
The level of agreement between two or more people who independently observe and code a set of data; by showing that two or more judges independently come up with the same observations, researchers ensure that the observations are not the subjective, distorted impressions of one individual

Archival Analysis
A form of the observational method in which the researcher examines the accumulated documents, or archives, of a culture (e.g., diaries, novels, magazines, and newspapers)

TRY IT! Archival Analysis: Women, Men, and the Media

Try doing your own archival analysis to see how women and men are portrayed in the media. Choose three or four magazines that focus on different topics and audiences, for example, a newsmagazine, a "women's" magazine such as *Cosmopolitan*, a "men's" magazine such as *GQ*, and a literary magazine such as the *New Yorker*. In each magazine, open the pages randomly until you find an advertisement that has at least one picture of a person in it. Repeat so that you look at two or three such ads in each magazine.

Make a note of how much of the image is devoted to the person's face and whether the person in the ad is a woman or a man. Specifically, place the picture of each person into one of these categories, depending on what part of the person you can see: (a) the entire body, (b) from the waist up, or (c) primarily the head and face. Are there differences in the way women and men are portrayed? If so, why do you think this is? Now turn to page 45 to see how actual research of this sort turned out.

To answer these questions, research methods other than archival analysis must be used. Later in this chapter, we will see how researchers have used the correlational method and the experimental method to address important questions about sexual violence against women.

Limits of the Observational Method There are limits to the observational method. Certain kinds of behavior are difficult to observe because they occur only rarely or only in private. For example, had Latané and Darley chosen the observational method to study the effects of the number of bystanders on people's willingness to help a victim, we might still be waiting for an answer, given the infrequency of emergencies and the difficulty of predicting when they will occur.

Instead, Latané and Darley might have used an archival analysis—for example, by examining newspaper accounts of violent crimes and noting the number of bystanders and how many offered assistance to the victim. Yet here too the researchers would have quickly run into problems: Did each journalist mention how many bystanders were present? Was the number accurate? Were all forms of assistance noted in the newspaper article? Clearly, these are messy data. As is always the case with archival analysis, the researcher is at the mercy of the original compiler of the material; the journalists had different aims when they wrote their articles and may not have included all the information researchers would later need.

Perhaps most importantly, social psychologists want to do more than just describe behavior; they want to predict and explain it. To do so, other methods are more appropriate.

The Correlational Method: Predicting Social Behavior

A goal of social science is to understand relationships between variables and to be able to predict when different kinds of social behavior will occur. What is the relationship between the amount of pornography people see and their likelihood of engaging in sexually violent acts? Is there a relationship between the amount of violence children see on television and their aggressiveness? To answer such questions, researchers frequently use still another approach: the correlational method.

With the **correlational method**, two variables are systematically measured, and the relationship between them—how much you can predict one from the other—is assessed. People's behavior and attitudes can be measured in a variety of ways. Just as with the observational method, researchers sometimes make direct observations of people's behavior. For example, researchers might be interested in testing the relationship between children's aggressive behavior and how much violent television they watch. They too might observe children on the playground, but here the goal is to assess the relationship, or correlation, between the children's aggressiveness and other factors, such as TV viewing habits, which the researchers also measure.

Researchers look at such relationships by calculating the **correlation coefficient**, a statistic that assesses how well you can predict one variable from another—for example, how well you can predict people's weight from their height. A positive correlation means that increases in the value of one variable are associated with increases in the value of the other variable. Height and weight are positively correlated; the taller people are, the more they tend to weigh. A negative correlation means that increases in the value of one variable are associated with decreases in the value of the other. If height and weight were negatively correlated in human beings, we would look very peculiar; short people, such as children, would look like penguins, whereas tall people, such as NBA basketball players, would be all skin and bones! It is also possible, of course, for two variables to be completely unrelated, so that a researcher cannot predict one variable from the other (see Figure 2.1).

Surveys The correlational method is often used in **surveys**, research in which a representative sample of people are asked questions about their attitudes or behavior. Surveys are a convenient way to measure people's attitudes; for example, people can be telephoned and asked which candidate they will support in an upcoming election or how they feel about a variety of social issues. Researchers often apply the correlational method to survey results to predict how people's responses to one question predict their other responses. Psychologists often use surveys to help understand social behavior and

Correlational Method

The technique whereby two or more variables are systematically measured and the relationship between them (i.e., how much one can be predicted from the other) is assessed

Correlation Coefficient

A statistical technique that assesses how well you can predict one variable from another—for example, how well you can predict people's weight from their height

Surveys

Research in which a representative sample of people are asked (often anonymously) questions about their attitudes or behavior

FIGURE 2.1

The Correlation Coefficient

The diagrams below show three possible correlations in a hypothetical study of watching violence on television and aggressive behavior in children. The diagram at the left shows a strong positive correlation: The more television children watched, the more aggressive they were. The diagram in the middle shows no correlation: The amount of television children watched is not related to how aggressive they were. The diagram at the right shows a strong negative correlation: The more television children watched, the less aggressive they were.

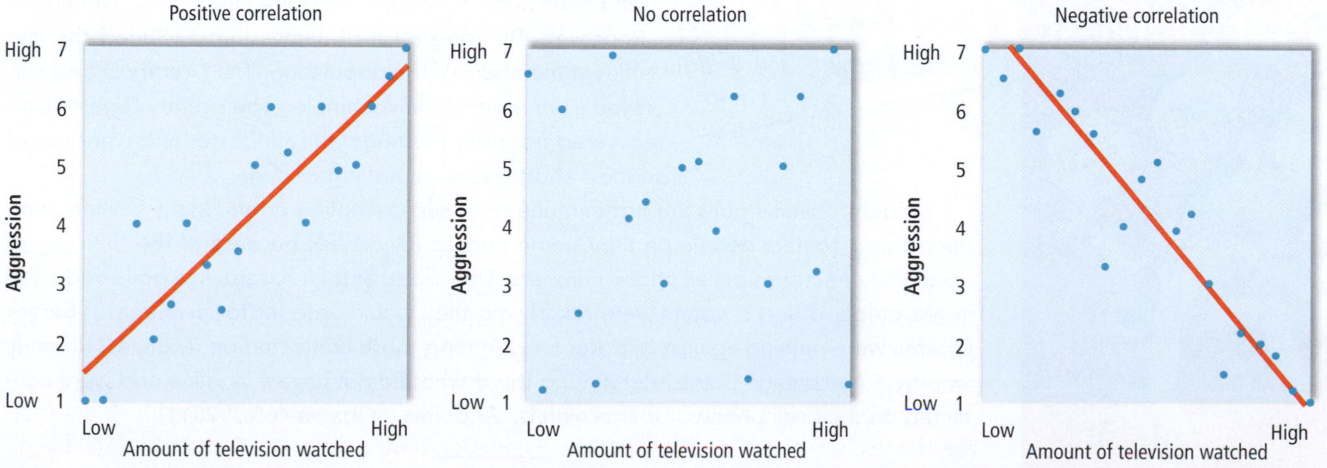

Random Selection

A way of ensuring that a sample of people is representative of a population by giving everyone in the population an equal chance of being selected for the sample

attitudes—for example, by seeing whether the amount of pornography men say they read is correlated with their attitudes toward women.

Surveys have a number of advantages, one of which is allowing researchers to judge the relationship between variables that are difficult to observe, such as how often people engage in safer sex. The researcher looks at the relationship between the questions asked on the survey, such as whether people who know a lot about how HIV is transmitted are more likely than other people to engage in safer sex.

Another advantage of surveys is the capability of sampling representative segments of the population. Answers to a survey are useful only if they reflect the responses of people in general—not just the people actually tested (called the *sample*). Survey researchers go to great lengths to ensure that the people they test are typical. They select samples that are representative of the population on a number of characteristics important to a given research question (e.g., age, educational background, religion, gender, income level). They also make sure to use a **random selection** of people from the population at large, which is a way of ensuring that a sample of people is representative of a population by giving everyone in the population an equal chance of being selected for the sample. As long as the sample is selected randomly, we can assume that the responses are a reasonable match to those of the population as a whole.

CONNECTIONS

Random Selection in Political Polls

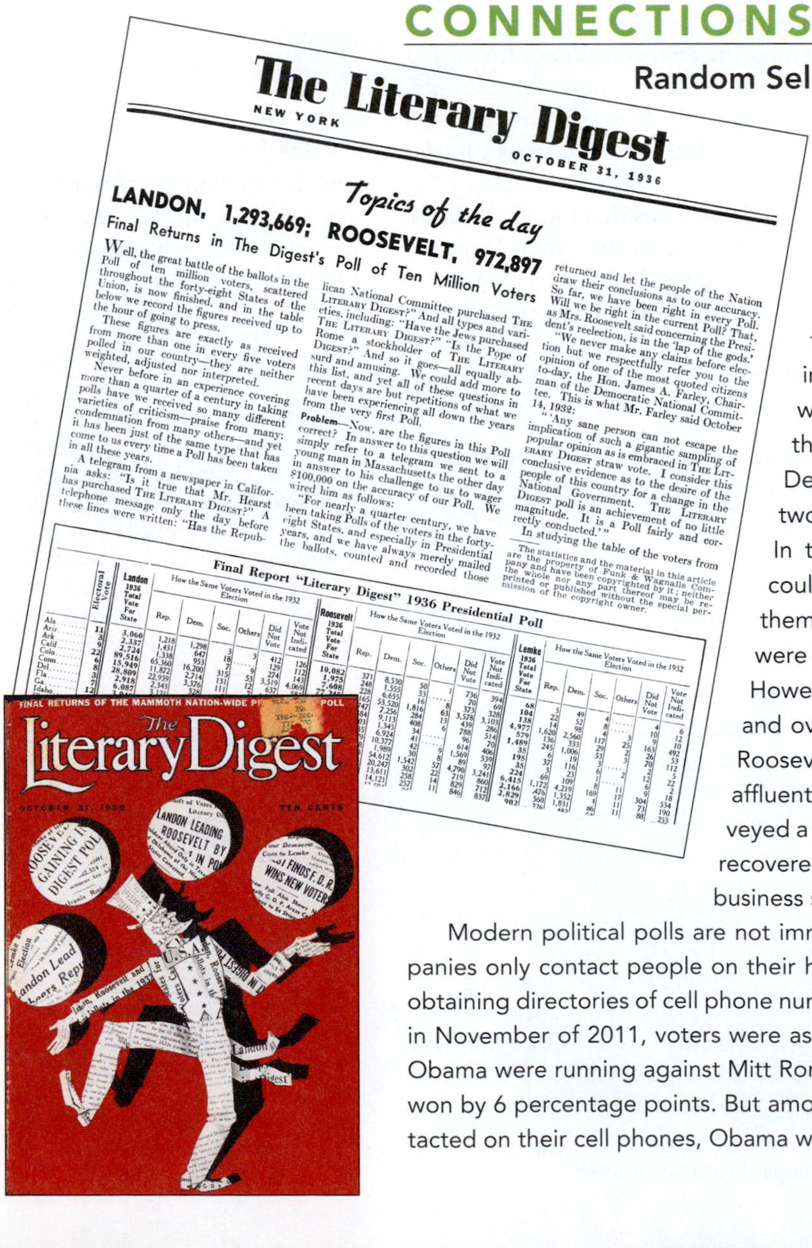
The Literary Digest
NEW YORK
OCTOBER 31, 1936

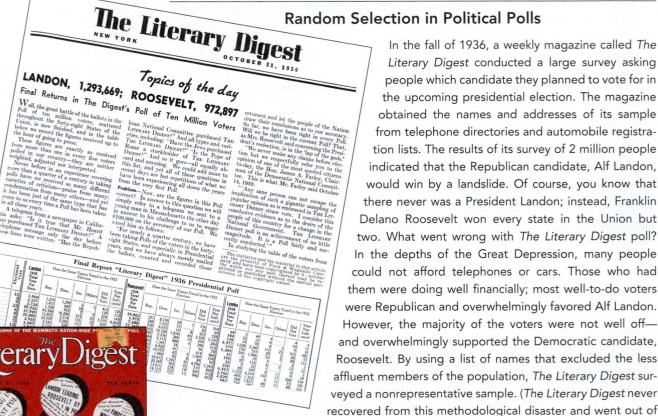

Topics of the day

LANDON, 1,293,669; ROOSEVELT, 972,897

Final Returns in The Digest's Poll of Ten Million Voters

Well, the great battle of the ballots in the Poll of ten million voters, scattered throughout the forty-eight States of the Union, is now finished, and in the table below we record the figures received up to the hour of going to press.

These figures are exactly as received from more than one in every five voters polled in our country—they are neither weighted, adjusted nor interpreted.

Never before in an experience covering more than a quarter of a century in taking polls have we received so many different varieties of criticism—praise from many; condemnation from many others—and yet it has been just of the same type that has come to us every time a Poll has been taken in all these years.

A telegram from a newspaper in California asks: "Is it true that Mr. Hearst has purchased The Literary Digest?" A telephone message only the day before these lines were written: "Has the Republican National Committee purchased The Literary Digest?" And all types and varieties, including: "Have the Jews purchased The Literary Digest?" "Is the Pope of Rome a stockholder of The Literary Digest?" And so it goes—all equally absurd and amusing. We could add more to this list, and yet all of these questions in recent days are but repetitions of what we have been experiencing all down the years from the very first Poll.

Problem—Now, are the figures in this Poll correct? In answer to this question we will simply refer to a telegram we sent to a young man in Massachusetts the other day in answer to his challenge to us to wager $100,000 on the accuracy of our Poll. We wired him as follows:

"For nearly a quarter century, we have been taking Polls of the voters in the forty-eight States, and especially in Presidential years, and we have always merely mailed the ballots, counted and recorded those returned and let the people of the Nation draw their conclusions as to our accuracy. So far, we have been right in every Poll. Will we be right in the current Poll? That, as Mrs. Roosevelt said concerning the President's reelection, is in the 'lap of the gods.'

"We never make any claims before election but we respectfully refer you to the opinion of one of the most quoted citizens to-day, the Hon. James A. Farley, Chairman of the Democratic National Committee. This is what Mr. Farley said October 14, 1932:

"'Any sane person can not escape the implication of such a gigantic sampling of popular opinion as is embraced in The Literary Digest straw vote. I consider this conclusive evidence as to the desire of the people of this country for a change in the National Government. The Literary Digest poll is an achievement of no little magnitude. It is a Poll fairly and correctly conducted.'"

In studying the table of the voters from

The statistics and the material in this article are the property of Funk & Wagnalls Company and have been copyrighted by it; neither the whole nor any part thereof may be reprinted or published without the special permission of the copyright owner.

Final Report "Literary Digest" 1936 Presidential Poll

Electoral Vote | Landon 1936 Total Vote For State | How the Same Voters Voted in the 1932 Election: Rep. Dem. Soc. Others Did Not Vote Vote Not Indicated | Roosevelt 1936 Total Vote For State | How the Same Voters Voted in the 1932 Election: Rep. Dem. Soc. Others Did Not Vote Vote Not Indicated | Lemke 1936 Total Vote For State | How the Same Voters Voted in the 1932 Election: Rep. Dem. Soc. Others Did Not Vote Vote Not Indicated

In the fall of 1936, a weekly magazine called *The Literary Digest* conducted a large survey asking people which candidate they planned to vote for in the upcoming presidential election. The magazine obtained the names and addresses of its sample from telephone directories and automobile registration lists. The results of its survey of 2 million people indicated that the Republican candidate, Alf Landon, would win by a landslide. Of course, you know that there never was a President Landon; instead, Franklin Delano Roosevelt won every state in the Union but two. What went wrong with *The Literary Digest* poll? In the depths of the Great Depression, many people could not afford telephones or cars. Those who had them were doing well financially; most well-to-do voters were Republican and overwhelmingly favored Alf Landon. However, the majority of the voters were not well off—and overwhelmingly supported the Democratic candidate, Roosevelt. By using a list of names that excluded the less affluent members of the population, *The Literary Digest* surveyed a nonrepresentative sample. (*The Literary Digest* never recovered from this methodological disaster and went out of business shortly after publishing its poll.)

Modern political polls are not immune from such sampling errors. Many polling companies only contact people on their home phones (landlines), because of the difficulty of obtaining directories of cell phone numbers. They do so at their hazard: In a poll conducted in November of 2011, voters were asked who they would vote for for president if Barack Obama were running against Mitt Romney. Among those contacted on landlines, Romney won by 6 percentage points. But among those who did not have a landline and were contacted on their cell phones, Obama won by 22 points ("Obama 46%," 2011).

A potential problem with survey data is the accuracy of the responses. Straightforward questions, regarding what people think about an issue or what they typically do, are relatively easy to answer. But asking survey participants to predict how they might behave in some hypothetical situation or to explain why they behaved as they did in the past is an invitation to inaccuracy (Schuman & Kalton, 1985; Schwarz, Groves, & Schuman, 1998). Often people simply don't know the answer—but they think they do. Richard Nisbett and Tim Wilson (1977) demonstrated this "telling more than you can know" phenomenon in a number of studies in which people often made inaccurate reports about why they responded the way they did. Their reports about the causes of their responses pertained more to their theories and beliefs about what should have influenced them than to what actually influenced them. (We discuss these studies at greater length in Chapter 5.)

Limits of the Correlational Method: Correlation Does Not Equal Causation The major shortcoming of the correlational method is that it tells us only that two variables are related, whereas the goal of the social psychologist is to identify the *causes* of social behavior. We want to be able to say that A causes B, not just that A is correlated with B.

If a researcher finds that there is a correlation between two variables, it means that there are three possible causal relationships between these variables. For example, researchers have found a correlation between the amount of violent television children watch and how aggressive they are (similar to the pattern shown in the graph on the left side in Figure 2.1, though not quite as strong; see Eron, 1982). One explanation of this correlation is that watching TV violence causes kids to become more violent themselves. It is equally probable, however, that the reverse is true: that kids who are violent to begin with are more likely to watch violent TV. Or there might be no causal relationship between these two variables; instead, both TV watching and violent behavior could be caused by a third variable, such as having neglectful parents who do not pay much attention to their kids. (Experimental evidence supports one of these causal relationships; we will discuss which one in Chapter 12.) When using the correlational method, it is wrong to jump to the conclusion that one variable is causing the other to occur. *Correlation does not prove causation.*

Unfortunately, forgetting this adage is one of the most common methodological errors in the social sciences. Consider a study of birth control methods and sexually transmitted diseases (STDs) in women (Rosenberg, Davidson, Chen, Judson, & Douglas, 1992). The researchers examined the records of women who had visited a clinic, noting which method of birth control they used and whether they had an STD. Surprisingly, the researchers found that women who relied on condoms had significantly more STDs than women who used diaphragms or contraceptive sponges. This result was widely reported in the popular press, with the conclusion that the use of diaphragms and sponges caused a lower incidence of disease. Some reporters urged women whose partners used condoms to switch to other methods.

A study conducted in the early 1990s found a correlation between the type of birth control women used and their likelihood of getting a sexually transmitted disease (STD). Those whose partners used condoms were more likely to have an STD than were women who used other forms of birth control. Does this mean that the use of condoms caused the increase in STDs? Not necessarily—see the text for alternative explanations of this research finding.

Can you see the problem with this conclusion? The fact that the incidence of disease was correlated with the type of contraception women used is open to a number of causal interpretations. Perhaps the women who used sponges and diaphragms had sex with fewer partners. (In fact, condom users were more likely to have had sex with multiple partners in the previous month.) Perhaps the partners of women who relied on condoms were more likely to have STDs than were the partners of women who used sponges and diaphragms. There is simply no way of knowing. Thus, the conclusion that the birth control methods protected against STDs cannot be drawn from this correlational study.

Experimental Method
The method in which the researcher randomly assigns participants to different conditions and ensures that these conditions are identical except for the independent variable (the one thought to have a causal effect on people's responses)

As another example of the difficulty of inferring causality from correlational designs, let's return to the question of whether pornography causes aggressive sexual acts against women, such as rape. In one study, male college students at a large midwestern university completed an anonymous survey on which they indicated whether they had ever engaged in sexually coercive behavior as well as the frequency with which they viewed various forms of pornography (Carr & VanDeusen, 2004). The researchers found a small but statistically significant correlation, such that the more pornography the students reported using, the greater the likelihood that they had committed sexual violence.

As suggestive as this finding is, it does not establish that using pornography made the student more likely to commit sexual violence. Can you think of alternative explanations for the correlation? It is possible that men who are aggressive toward women are more interested in pornography; that is, it is their aggression causing their attraction to pornography, and not the pornography causing their aggression (Malamuth et al., 2000). Alternatively, there could be some third variable, such as something in a man's upbringing or subculture, that makes him more likely to commit sexual violence and look at pornography. Other examples of the difficulty of inferring causality from correlational studies are shown in the following Try It!

The Experimental Method: Answering Causal Questions

The only way to determine causal relationships is with the **experimental method**. Here, the researcher systematically orchestrates the event so that people experience it in one way (e.g., they witness an emergency along with other bystanders) or another way

TRY IT! Correlation and Causation: Knowing the Difference

It can be difficult to remember that, when two variables are correlated, it doesn't necessarily mean that one caused the other; correlation does *not* allow us to make causal inferences. For each of the following examples, think about why the correlation was found. Even if it seems obvious which variable was causing the other, are there alternative explanations?

1. A politician extols the virtues of the Boy Scouts and Girl Scouts. In his salute to the Scouts, the politician mentions that few teenagers convicted of street crimes have been members of the Scouts. In other words, he is positing a negative correlation between activity in Scouting and frequency of criminal behavior. Why might this be?
2. A recent study found that college students who have "helicopter parents"—moms and dads who keep close track of their kids' academic life and intervene often—actually get lower grades than college students whose parents do not hover over them so closely. Does it follow that college students would do better in school if their parents backed off a little bit?
3. A study of soldiers stationed on army bases found that the number of tattoos a soldier had was correlated positively with becoming involved in a motorcycle accident. Why?
4. A study found that adolescents who are religious are less likely to commit crimes and more likely to wear seat belts than are adolescents who are not religious. Does religion make people more likely to obey the law?
5. A correlation exists between people's tendency to eat breakfast and how long they live, such that people who skip breakfast die younger. Does eating Wheaties lead to a long life?
6. A study reported that the more milk children drank, the more weight they gained. One researcher concluded that children who need to control their weight should cut down on their milk consumption. Is this a valid conclusion?
7. A recent survey found that people who watch public television have more sex than people who do not. "Who would have thought," the researchers reported, "that National Geographic Specials or Ken Burns' history of baseball could get people in the mood?" How would you explain this correlation?
8. A recent study in Britain found that kids who ate sweets daily at age 10 were much more likely to be arrested for a violent crime later in life than were kids who did not eat sweets daily at T0. Should we limit the number of candy bars that kids eat, so that they don't turn into violent criminals?

See page 45 for the answers.

(e.g., they witness the same emergency but are the sole bystander). The experimental method is the method of choice in most social psychological research, because it allows the experimenter to make causal inferences.

Theory is a good thing, but a good experiment lasts forever.

—Peter Leonidovich Kapista

The experimental method always involves a direct intervention on the part of the researcher. By carefully changing only one aspect of the situation (e.g., group size), the researcher can see whether this aspect is the cause of the behavior in question (e.g., whether people help in an emergency). Sound simple? Actually, it isn't. Staging an experiment to test Latané and Darley's hypothesis about the effects of group size involves severe practical and ethical difficulties. What kind of emergency should be used? Ideally (from a scientific perspective), it should be as true to the Genovese case as possible. Accordingly, you would want to stage a murder that passersby could witness. In one condition, you could stage the murder so that only a few onlookers were present; in another condition, you could stage it so that a great many onlookers were present.

Obviously, no scientist in his or her right mind would stage a murder for unsuspecting bystanders. But how can we arrange a realistic situation that is upsetting enough to be similar to the Genovese case without it being too upsetting? In addition, how can we ensure that each bystander experiences the same emergency except for the variable whose effect we want to test—in this case, the number of bystanders?

Let's see how Latané and Darley (1968) dealt with these problems. Imagine that you are a participant in their experiment. You arrive at the scheduled time and find yourself in a long corridor with doors to several small cubicles. An experimenter greets you and takes you into one of the cubicles, mentioning that five other students, seated in the other cubicles, will be participating with you. The experimenter leaves after giving you a pair of headphones with an attached microphone. You put on the headphones, and soon you hear the experimenter explaining to everyone that he is interested in learning about the kinds of personal problems college students experience.

To ensure that people will discuss their problems openly, he explains, each participant will remain anonymous; each will stay in his or her separate room and communicate with the others only via the intercom system. Further, the experimenter says, he will not be listening to the discussion, so that people will feel freer to be open and honest. Finally, the experimenter asks that participants take turns presenting their problems, each speaking for 2 minutes, after which each person will comment on what the others have said. To make sure this procedure is followed, he says, only one person's microphone will be turned on at a time.

The group discussion begins. You listen as the first participant admits that he has found it difficult to adjust to college. With some embarrassment, he mentions that he sometimes has seizures, especially when under stress. When his 2 minutes are up, you hear the other four participants discuss their problems; then it is your turn. When you have finished, the first person speaks again. To your astonishment, he soon begins to experience one of the seizures he mentioned earlier:

> I—er—um—I think I—I need—er—if—if could—er—er—somebody er—er—er—er—er—er—er—give me a little—er—give me a little help here because—er—I—er—I'm—er—er—h—h—having a—a—a real problem—er—right now and I—er—if somebody could help me out it would—it would—er—er s—s—sure be—sure be good . . . because—er—there—er—er—a cause I—er—I—uh—I've got a—a one of the—er—sei—er—er—things coming on and—and—and I could really—er—use some help so if somebody would—er—give me a little h—help—uh—er—er—er—er c—could somebody—er—er—help—er—uh—uh—uh (choking sounds) . . . I'm gonna die—er—er—I'm . . . gonna die—er—help—er—er—seizure—er (chokes, then quiet). (Darley & Latané, 1968, p. 379)

What would you have done in this situation? If you were like most of the participants in the actual study, you would have remained in your cubicle, listening to your fellow student having a seizure, and done nothing about it. Does this surprise you? Latané and Darley kept track of the number of people who left their cubicle to find the victim or the experimenter before the end of the victim's seizure. Only 31% of the participants sought help in this way. Fully 69% of the students remained in their cubicles and did nothing—just as Kitty Genovese's neighbors failed to offer assistance in any way.

Does this finding prove that the failure to help was due to the number of people who witnessed the seizure? How do we know that it wasn't due to some other factor? We know because Latané and Darley included two other conditions in their experiment. In these conditions, the procedure was identical to the one we described, with one crucial difference: The size of the discussion group was smaller, meaning that fewer people witnessed the seizure. In one condition, the participants were told that there were three other people in the discussion group besides themselves (the victim plus two others). In another condition, participants were told that there was only one other person in their discussion group (the victim). In this latter condition, each participant believed he or she was the only one who could hear the seizure.

Simulate on **MyPsychLab**

Learn more about the "seizure" experiment in the MyPsychLab simulation ***Bystander Intervention.***

Independent and Dependent Variables The number of people witnessing the emergency was the **independent variable** in the Latané and Darley (1968) study, which is the variable a researcher changes or varies to see if it has an effect on some other variable. The **dependent variable** is the variable a researcher measures to see if it is influenced by the independent variable; the researcher hypothesizes that the dependent variable will be influenced by the level of the independent variable. That is, the dependent variable is hypothesized to depend on the independent variable (see Figure 2.2). Latané and Darley found that their independent variable (the number of bystanders) did have an effect on the dependent variable (whether they tried to help). When the participants believed that four other people were witnesses to the seizure, only 31% offered assistance. When the participants believed that only two other people were aware of the seizure, helping behavior increased to 62%. When the participants believed that they were the only person listening to the seizure, nearly everyone helped (85%).

Independent Variable

The variable a researcher changes or varies to see if it has an effect on some other variable

Dependent Variable

The variable a researcher measures to see if it is influenced by the independent variable; the researcher hypothesizes that the dependent variable will depend on the level of the independent variable

These results indicate that the number of bystanders strongly influences the rate of helping, but it does not mean that the size of the group is the only cause of people's decision to help. After all, when there were four bystanders, a third of the participants still helped; conversely, when participants thought they were the only witness, some of them failed to help. Obviously, other factors influence helping behavior—the bystanders' personalities, their prior experience with emergencies, and so on. Nonetheless, Latané and Darley succeeded in identifying one important determinant of whether people help: the number of bystanders that people think are present.

Internal Validity in Experiments How can we be sure that the differences in help across conditions in the Latané and Darley seizure study were due to the different

Independent Variable	Dependent Variable
The variable that is hypothesized to influence the dependent variable. Participants are treated identically except for this variable.	The response that is hypothesized to depend on the independent variable. All participants are measured on this variable.
Example: Latané and Darley (1968)	
The number of bystanders	**How many participants helped?**
Participant + Victim	85%
Participant + Victim + Two others	62%
Participant + Victim + Four others	31%

FIGURE 2.2

Independent and Dependent Variables in Experimental Research

Researchers vary the independent variable (e.g., the number of bystanders people think are present) and observe what effect that has on the dependent variable (e.g., whether people help).

numbers of bystanders who witnessed the emergency? Could this effect have been caused by some other aspect of the situation? This is the beauty of the experimental method: We can be sure of the causal connection between the number of bystanders and helping, because Latané and Darley made sure that everything about the situation was the same in the different conditions except for the independent variable—the number of bystanders. Keeping everything but the independent variable the same in an experiment is referred to as *internal validity*. Latané and Darley were careful to maintain high internal validity by making sure that everyone witnessed the same emergency. They prerecorded the supposed other participants and the victim and played their voices over the intercom system.

You may have noticed, however, that there was a key difference between the conditions of the Latané and Darley experiment other than the number of bystanders: Different people participated in the different conditions. Maybe the observed differences in helping were due to characteristics of the participants instead of the independent variable. The people in the sole-witness condition might have differed in any number of ways from their counterparts in the other conditions, making them more likely to help. Maybe they were more likely to know something about epilepsy or to have experience helping in emergencies. If either of these possibilities is true, it would be difficult to conclude that it was the number of bystanders, rather than something about the participants' backgrounds, that led to differences in helping.

Fortunately, there is a technique that allows experimenters to minimize differences among participants as the cause of the results: **random assignment to condition**. This is the process whereby all participants have an equal chance of taking part in any condition of an experiment; through random assignment, researchers can be relatively certain that differences in the participants' personalities or backgrounds are distributed evenly across conditions. Because Latané and Darley's participants were randomly assigned to the conditions of their experiment, it is very unlikely that the ones who knew the most about epilepsy all ended up in one condition. Knowledge about epilepsy should be randomly (i.e., roughly evenly) dispersed across the three experimental conditions. This powerful technique is the most important part of the experimental method.

Even with random assignment, however, there is the (very small) possibility that different characteristics of people did not distribute themselves evenly across conditions. For example, if we randomly divide a group of 40 people into two groups, it is possible that those who know the most about epilepsy will by chance end up more in one group than in the other—just as it is possible to get more heads than tails when you flip a coin 40 times. This is a possibility we take seriously in experimental science. The analyses of our data come with a **probability level (*p*-value)**, which is a number, calculated with statistical techniques, that tells researchers how likely it is that the results of their experiment occurred by chance and not because of the independent variable. The convention in science, including social psychology, is to consider results *significant* (trustworthy) if the probability level is less than 5 in 100 that the results might be due to chance factors rather than the independent variables studied. For example, if we flipped a coin 40 times and got 40 heads, we would probably assume that this was very unlikely to have occurred by chance and that there was something wrong with the coin (we might check the other side to make sure it wasn't one of those trick coins with heads on both sides!). Similarly, if the results in two conditions of an experiment differ significantly from what we would expect by chance, we assume that the difference was caused by the independent variable (e.g., the number of bystanders present during the emergency). The *p*-value tells us how confident we can be that the difference was due to chance rather than the independent variable.

To summarize, the key to a good experiment is to maintain high **internal validity**, which we can now define as making sure that the independent variable, and *only* the independent variable, influences the dependent variable. This is accomplished by controlling all extraneous variables and by randomly assigning people to different experimental conditions (Campbell & Stanley, 1967). When internal validity is high, the experimenter is in a position to judge whether the independent variable causes

Random Assignment to Condition

A process ensuring that all participants have an equal chance of taking part in any condition of an experiment; through random assignment, researchers can be relatively certain that differences in the participants' personalities or backgrounds are distributed evenly across conditions

Probability Level (*p*-value)

A number calculated with statistical techniques that tells researchers how likely it is that the results of their experiment occurred by chance and not because of the independent variable or variables; the convention in science, including social psychology, is to consider results *significant* (trustworthy) if the probability level is less than 5 in 100 that the results might be due to chance factors and not the independent variables studied

Internal Validity

Making sure that nothing besides the independent variable can affect the dependent variable; this is accomplished by controlling all extraneous variables and by randomly assigning people to different experimental conditions

A good deal of social psychological research takes place in laboratory settings. How do social psychologists generalize from the findings of these studies to life outside the laboratory?

the dependent variable. This is the hallmark of the experimental method that sets it apart from the observational and correlational methods: Only the experimental method can answer causal questions, such as whether exposure to pornography causes men to commit violent acts.

For example, researchers have tested whether pornography causes aggression, by randomly assigning consenting participants to watch pornographic or nonpornographic films (the independent variable) and measuring the extent to which people acted aggressively toward women (the dependent variable). In a study by Donnerstein and Berkowitz (1981), males were angered by a female accomplice and then were randomly assigned to see one of three films: violent pornography (a rape scene), nonviolent pornography (sex without any violence), or a neutral film with no violence or sex (a talk show interview). The men were then given an opportunity to act aggressively toward the woman who had angered them, by choosing the level of electric shock she would receive in an ostensibly unrelated learning experiment (the accomplice did not really receive shocks, but participants believed that she would). The men who had seen the violent pornography administered significantly more-intense shocks to the woman than did the men who had seen the nonviolent pornography or the neutral film, suggesting that it is not pornography per se that leads to aggressive behavior, but the violence depicted in some pornography (Mussweiler & Förster, 2000). We review this area of research in more detail in Chapter 12.

External Validity in Experiments For all the advantages of the experimental method, there are some drawbacks. By virtue of gaining enough control over the situation so as to randomly assign people to conditions and rule out the effects of extraneous variables, the situation can become somewhat artificial and distant from real life. For example, one could argue that Latané and Darley strayed far from the original inspiration for their study, the Kitty Genovese murder. What does witnessing a seizure while participating in a laboratory experiment in a college building have to do with a brutal murder in a densely populated urban neighborhood? How often in everyday life do we have discussions with other people through an intercom system? Did the fact that the participants knew they were in a psychology experiment influence their behavior?

These are important questions that concern **external validity**, which is the extent to which the results of a study can be generalized to other situations and other people. Note that two kinds of generalizability are at issue: the extent to which we can generalize from the situation constructed by an experimenter to real-life situations (generalizability across *situations*) and the extent to which we can generalize from the people who participated in the experiment to people in general (generalizability across *people*).

When it comes to generalizability across situations, research in social psychology is sometimes criticized for being conducted in artificial settings that cannot be generalized to real life—for example, psychological experiments at a university. To address this problem, social psychologists attempt to increase the generalizability of their results by making their studies as realistic as possible. But this is hard to do in a laboratory setting in which people are placed in situations they would rarely, if ever, encounter in everyday life, such as occurred in Latané and Darley's group discussion of personal problems over an intercom system. Instead, psychologists attempt to maximize the study's **psychological realism**, which is the extent to which the psychological processes triggered in an experiment are similar to psychological processes that occur in everyday life (Aronson, Wilson, & Brewer, 1998). Even though Latané and Darley staged an emergency that in significant ways was unlike those encountered in everyday life, was it psychologically similar to real-life emergencies? Were the same psychological processes triggered? Did the participants

External Validity

The extent to which the results of a study can be generalized to other situations and to other people

Psychological Realism

The extent to which the psychological processes triggered in an experiment are similar to psychological processes that occur in everyday life have the same types of perceptions and thoughts, make the same types of decisions, and choose the same types of behaviors that they would in a real-life situation? If so, the study is high in psychological realism and we can generalize the results to everyday life.

Psychological realism is heightened if people feel involved in a real event. To accomplish this, experimenters often tell participants a **cover story**—a disguised version of the study's true purpose. Recall, for example, that Latané and Darley told people that they were studying the personal problems of college students and then staged an emergency. It would have been a lot easier to say to people, "Look, we are interested in how people react to emergencies, so at some point during this study we are going to stage an accident, and then we'll see how you respond." We think you'll agree that such a procedure would be very low in psychological realism. In real life, we never know when emergencies are going to occur, and we do not have time to plan our responses to them. If participants knew that an emergency was about to happen, the kinds of psychological processes triggered would have been quite different from those of a real emergency, reducing the psychological realism of the study.

Social psychologists are also concerned with generalizability across people. Latané and Darley's experiment, for example, documented an interesting, unexpected example of social influence whereby the mere knowledge that others were present reduced the likelihood that people helped. But what have we learned about people in general? The participants in their study were 52 male and female students at New York University who received course credit for participating in the experiment. Would the study have turned out the same way if a different population had been used? Would the number of bystanders have influenced helping behavior had the participants been middle-aged blue-collar workers instead of college students? Midwesterners instead of New Yorkers? Japanese instead of American?

The only way to be certain that the results of an experiment represent the behavior of a particular population is to ensure that the participants are randomly selected from that population. Ideally, samples in experiments should be randomly selected, just as they are in surveys. Increasingly, social psychologists are conducting research with diverse populations and cultures, some of it over the Internet (e.g., Lane, Banaji, & Nosek, 2007). But, unfortunately, it is impractical and expensive to select random samples for most social psychology experiments. It is difficult enough to convince a random sample of Americans to agree to answer a few questions over the telephone as part of a political poll, and such polls can cost thousands of dollars to conduct. Imagine the difficulty Latané and Darley would have had convincing a random sample of Americans to board a plane to New York to take part in their study, not to mention the cost of such an endeavor. Even trying to gather a random sample of students at New York University would not have been easy; each person contacted would have had to agree to spend an hour in Latané and Darley's laboratory.

Of course, concerns about practicality and expense are not good excuses for doing poor science. Many researchers address this problem by studying basic psychological processes that make people susceptible to social influence, assuming that these processes are so fundamental that they are universally shared. In that case, participants for social psychology experiments don't really have to come from many different cultures. Of course, some social psychological processes are likely to be quite dependent on cultural factors, and in those cases, we'd need diverse samples of people. The question then is, how can researchers tell whether the processes they are studying are universal?

Field Research One of the best ways to increase external validity is by conducting **field experiments**. In a field experiment, researchers study behavior outside the laboratory, in its natural setting. As in a laboratory experiment, the researcher controls the occurrence of an independent variable (e.g., group size) to see what effect it has on a dependent variable (e.g., helping behavior) and randomly assigns people to the different conditions. Thus, a field experiment has the same design as a laboratory experiment, except that it is conducted in a real-life setting rather than in the relatively artificial setting of the laboratory. The participants in a field experiment are unaware

Cover Story

A description of the purpose of a study, given to participants, that is different from its true purpose and is used to maintain psychological realism

Field Experiments

Experiments conducted in natural settings rather than in the laboratory

Social psychologists are interested in how generalizable their findings are to different kinds of people. What are the challenges in doing so? What approaches do social psychologists take?

that the events they experience are in fact an experiment. The external validity of such an experiment is high, because, after all, it is taking place in the real world, with real people who are more diverse than a typical college student sample.

Many such field studies have been conducted in social psychology. For example, Latané and Darley (1970) tested their hypothesis about group size and bystander intervention in a convenience store outside New York City. Two "robbers" (with full knowledge and permission of the cashier and manager of the store) waited until there were either one or two other customers at the checkout counter. They then asked the cashier to name the most expensive beer the store carried. The cashier answered the question and then said he would have to check in the back to see how much of that brand was in stock. While the cashier was gone, the robbers picked up a case of beer in the front of the store, declared, "They'll never miss this," put the beer in their car, and drove off.

Because the robbers were rather burly fellows, no one attempted to intervene directly to stop the theft. The question was, when the cashier returned, how many people would help by telling him that a theft had just occurred? As it turned out, the number of bystanders had the same inhibiting effect on helping behavior as in the laboratory seizure study: Significantly fewer people reported the theft when there was another customer-witness in the store than when they were alone.

It might have occurred to you to ask why researchers conduct laboratory studies at all, given that external validity is so much better with field experiments. Indeed, it seems to us that the perfect experiment in social psychology would be one that was conducted in a field setting with a sample randomly selected from a population of interest and with extremely high internal validity (all extraneous variables controlled, people randomly assigned to the conditions). Sounds good, doesn't it? The only problem is that it is very difficult to satisfy all these conditions in one study, making such studies virtually impossible to conduct.

There is almost always a trade-off between internal and external validity—that is, between being able to randomly assign people to conditions and having enough control over the situation to ensure that no extraneous variables are influencing the results, and making sure that the results can be generalized to everyday life. We have the most control in a laboratory setting, but the laboratory may be unlike real life. Real life can best be captured by doing a field experiment, but it is very difficult to control all extraneous variables in such studies. For example, the astute reader will have noticed that Latané and Darley's (1970) beer theft study differed from laboratory experiments in an important way: People could not be randomly assigned to the alone or in-pairs conditions. Were this the only study Latané and Darley had performed, we could not be sure whether the kinds of people who prefer to shop alone, as compared to the kinds of people who prefer to shop with a friend, differ in ways that might influence helping behavior. By randomly assigning people to conditions in their laboratory studies, Latané and Darley were able to rule out such alternative explanations.

The trade-off between internal and external validity has been referred to as the *basic dilemma of the social psychologist* (Aronson & Carlsmith, 1968). The way to resolve this dilemma is not to try to do it all in a single experiment. Most social psychologists opt first for internal validity, conducting laboratory experiments in which people are randomly assigned to different conditions and all extraneous variables are controlled; here there is little ambiguity about what is causing what. Other social psychologists prefer to maximize external validity by conducting field studies. And many social psychologists do both. Taken together, both types of studies meet the requirements of our perfect experiment.

Replications

Repeating a study, often with different subject populations or in different settings

Replications and Meta-Analysis **Replications** are the ultimate test of an experiment's external validity. Only by conducting studies in different settings, with different populations, can we determine how generalizable the results are. Often, though, when many studies on one problem are conducted, the results are somewhat variable. Several studies might find an effect of the number of bystanders on helping behavior, for example, while a few do not. How can we make sense of this? Does the number of bystanders make a difference or not? Fortunately, there is a statistical technique called **meta-analysis** that averages the results of two or more studies to see if the effect of an independent variable is reliable. Earlier we discussed *p*-values, which tell us the probability that the findings of one study are due to chance or to the independent variable. A meta-analysis essentially does the same thing, except that it averages the results of many different studies. If, say, an independent variable is found to have an effect in only 1 of 20 studies, the meta-analysis will tell us that that one study was probably an exception and that, on average, the independent variable is not influencing the dependent variable. If an independent variable is having an effect in most of the studies, the meta-analysis is likely to tell us that, on average, it does influence the dependent variable.

Meta-Analysis
A statistical technique that averages the results of two or more studies to see if the effect of an independent variable is reliable

Basic Research
Studies that are designed to find the best answer to the question of why people behave as they do and that are conducted purely for reasons of intellectual curiosity

Applied Research
Studies designed to solve a particular social problem

Most of the findings you will read about in this book have been replicated in several different settings, with different populations; we know, then, that they are reliable phenomena, not limited to the laboratory or to college sophomores. For example, Anderson and Bushman (1997) compared laboratory studies on the causes of aggression with studies conducted in the real world. In both types of studies, violence in the media caused aggressive behavior. Similarly, Latané and Darley's original findings have been replicated in numerous studies. Increasing the number of bystanders inhibited helping behavior with many kinds of people, including children, college students, and future ministers (Darley & Batson, 1973; Latané & Nida, 1981); in both small towns and large cities (Latané & Dabbs, 1975); in a variety of settings, such as psychology laboratories, city streets, and subway trains (Harrison & Wells, 1991; Latané & Darley, 1970; Piliavin, 1981; Piliavin & Piliavin, 1972); and with different kinds of emergencies, such as seizures, potential fires, fights, and accidents (Latané & Darley, 1968; Shotland & Straw, 1976; Staub, 1974), as well as with less-serious events, such as having a flat tire (Hurley & Allen, 1974). Many of these replications took place in real-life settings (e.g., on a subway train) where people could not possibly have known that an experiment was being conducted. We will frequently point out similar replications of the major findings we discuss in this book (Wilson, 2011).

Watch on **MyPsychLab**
To learn more about how psychological research progresses, watch the MyPsychLab video ***Alan Kazdin: What is the coolest thing you have ever discovered?***

Basic Versus Applied Research You may have wondered how people decide which specific topic to study. Why would a social psychologist decide to study helping behavior, cognitive dissonance theory, or the effects of pornography on aggression? Is he or she simply curious? Or does the social psychologist have a specific purpose in mind, such as trying to reduce sexual violence?

The goal in **basic research** is to find the best answer to the question of why people behave as they do, purely for reasons of intellectual curiosity. The researchers aren't trying to solve a specific social or psychological problem. In contrast, **applied research** is geared toward solving a particular social problem. Here, building a theory of behavior is usually secondary to solving the specific problem, such as alleviating racism, reducing sexual violence, or stemming the spread of AIDS.

In social psychology, the distinction between basic and applied research is fuzzy. Even though many researchers label themselves as either basic or applied scientists, the endeavors of one group are not independent of those of the other group. There are countless examples of advances in basic science that at the time had no known applied value but later proved to be the key to solving a significant applied problem. As we will see later in this book, for example, basic research with dogs, rats, and fish on the effects of feeling in control of one's environment has led to the development of techniques to improve the health of elderly nursing home residents (Langer & Rodin, 1976; Richter, 1957; Schulz, 1976; Seligman, 1975).

Most social psychologists would agree that, in order to solve a specific social problem, we must understand the psychological processes responsible for it. Indeed, Kurt Lewin (1951), one of the founders of social psychology, coined a phrase that has become a motto for the field: "There is nothing so practical as a good theory." He meant that to solve such difficult social problems as urban violence or racial prejudice, one must first understand the underlying

There is nothing so practical as a good theory.
—Kurt Lewin, 1951

psychological dynamics of human nature and social interaction. Even when the goal is to discover the psychological processes underlying social behavior, the findings often have clear applied implications, as you'll see throughout this book.

Watch on **MyPsychLab**
To learn more about the relevance of social psychology research, watch the MyPsychLab video ***Carol Tavris: Why did you hate your intro to psychology course?***

New Frontiers in Social Psychological Research

Social psychologists are always looking for new ways of investigating social behavior, and in recent years some exciting new methods have been developed. These methodological advances have been spurred on by new questions about the origins of social behavior, because new questions and new methods often develop hand in hand.

Culture and Social Psychology

Cross-Cultural Research
Research conducted with members of different cultures, to see whether the psychological processes of interest are present in both cultures or whether they are specific to the culture in which people were raised

Social psychology largely began as a Western science, conducted by Western social psychologists with Western participants. This raises the question of how universal the findings are. To study the effects of culture on social psychological process, social psychologists conduct **cross-cultural research** (Heine, 2010; Kitayama & Cohen, 2007; Nisbett, 2003; Smith & Bond, 1999). Some findings in social psychology are culture-dependent, as we will see throughout this book. In Chapter 3, for example, we will see that Westerners and East Asians rely on fundamentally different kinds of thought to perceive and understand the social world. In Chapter 5, we'll discuss cultural differences in the very way people define themselves. Whether we emphasize personal independence or social interdependence reflects our cultural values (Henrich, Heine, & Norenzayan, 2010).

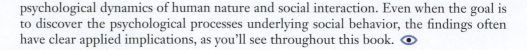

Some basic psychological processes are universal, whereas others are shaped by the culture in which we live. For example, are people's self-concepts shaped by cultural rules of how people must present themselves, such as the requirement by the Taliban regime in Afghanistan that women cover themselves from head to toe? Cross-cultural research is challenging but necessary for exploring how culture influences the basic ways in which people think about and interact with others.

Conducting cross-cultural research is not simply a matter of traveling to another culture, translating materials into the local language, and replicating a study there (Heine et al., 2002; van de Vijver & Leung, 1997). Researchers have to guard against imposing their own viewpoints and definitions, learned from their culture, onto another culture with which they are unfamiliar. They must also be sure that their independent and dependent variables are understood in the same way in different cultures (Bond, 1988; Lonner & Berry, 1986).

Suppose, for example, that you wanted to replicate the Latané and Darley (1968) seizure experiment in another culture. Clearly, you could not conduct the identical experiment somewhere else. The tape-recorded discussion of college life used by Latané and Darley was specific to the lives of New York University students in the 1960s and could not be used meaningfully elsewhere. What about more subtle aspects of the study, such as the way people viewed the person who had the seizure? Cultures vary considerably in how they define whether or not another person belongs to their social group; this factor figures significantly in how they behave toward that person (Gudykunst, 1988; Triandis, 1989). If people in one culture view the victim as a member of their social group but people in another culture perceive the victim as a member of a rival social group, you might find very different results in the two cultures—not because the psychological processes of helping behavior are different, but because people interpreted the situation differently. It can be quite daunting to conduct a study that is interpreted and perceived similarly in dissimilar cultures. Cross-cultural researchers are sensitive to these issues, and as more and more cross-cultural research is conducted carefully, we will be able to determine which social psychological processes are universal and which are culture-bound (Heine, 2010). For example, there is substantial evidence that playing violent video games makes people act in more aggressive ways and makes them less likely to help others. But is this true just in Western countries? A recent review of the literature compared studies of video games in the United States and Japan. As it happened, the deleterious effects of violent video games were the same in both countries (Anderson et al., 2010).

The Evolutionary Approach

Evolutionary theory was developed by Charles Darwin (1859) to explain the ways in which animals adapt to their environments. Central to the theory is **natural selection**, the process by which heritable traits that promote survival in a particular environment are passed along to future generations, because organisms with those traits are more likely to produce offspring. A common example is how giraffes came to have long necks. In an environment where food is scarce, giraffes that happened to have long necks could feed on foliage that other animals couldn't reach. These giraffes were more likely to survive and produce offspring than were other giraffes, the story goes, and the "long neck" gene thus became common in subsequent generations.

In biology, evolutionary theory is used to explain how different species acquired physical traits such as long necks. But what about social behaviors, such as the tendency to be aggressive toward a member of one's own species or the tendency to be helpful to others? Is it possible that social behaviors have genetic determinants that evolve through the process of natural selection, and, if so, is this true in human beings as well as animals? These are the questions posed by **evolutionary psychology**, which attempts to explain social behavior in terms of genetic factors that have evolved over time according to the principles of natural selection. The core idea is that evolution occurs very slowly, such that social behaviors that are prevalent today are due at least in part to adaptations to environments in our distant past (Buss, 2005; Neuberg, Kenrick, & Schaller, 2010). We will discuss in upcoming chapters how evolutionary theory explains social behavior (e.g., Chapter 10 on interpersonal attraction, Chapter 11 on prosocial behavior, and Chapter 12 on aggression). Here, in our chapter on research methods, it is important to note that a lively debate has arisen over the testability of evolutionary hypotheses. Because current behaviors are thought to be adaptations to environmental conditions that existed thousands of years ago, psychologists make their best guesses about what those conditions were and how specific kinds of behaviors gave people a reproductive advantage. But these hypotheses are obviously impossible to test with the experimental method. And just because hypotheses sound plausible does not mean they are true. For example, some scientists now believe that giraffes did not acquire a long neck in order to eat leaves in tall trees. Instead, they suggest, long necks first evolved in male giraffes to gain an advantage in fights with other males over access to females (Simmons & Scheepers, 1996). Which of these explanations is true? It's hard to tell. On the other hand, evolutionary approaches can generate novel hypotheses about social behavior that can be tested with the other methods described in this chapter.

Evolutionary Theory

A concept developed by Charles Darwin to explain the ways in which animals adapt to their environments

Natural Selection

The process by which heritable traits that promote survival in a particular environment are passed along to future generations; organisms with those traits are more likely to produce offspring

Evolutionary Psychology

The attempt to explain social behavior in terms of genetic factors that have evolved over time according to the principles of natural selection

Social Neuroscience

As we have seen, social psychology is concerned with how people's thoughts, feelings, and behaviors are influenced by the real or imagined presence of other people. Most research studies in social psychology, then, study just that—thoughts, feelings, and behaviors. Human beings are biological organisms, however, and social psychologists have become increasingly interested in the connection between biological processes and social behavior. These interests include the study of hormones and behavior, the human immune system, and neurological processes in the human brain. To study the brain and its relation to behavior, psychologists use sophisticated technologies, including electroencephalography (EEG), in which electrodes are placed on the scalp to measure electrical activity in the brain, and functional magnetic resonance imaging (fMRI), in which people are placed in scanners that measure changes in blood flow in their brains. Social psychologists take these measurements while participants think about and process social information, allowing them to correlate different kinds of brain activity with social information processing. This kind of research

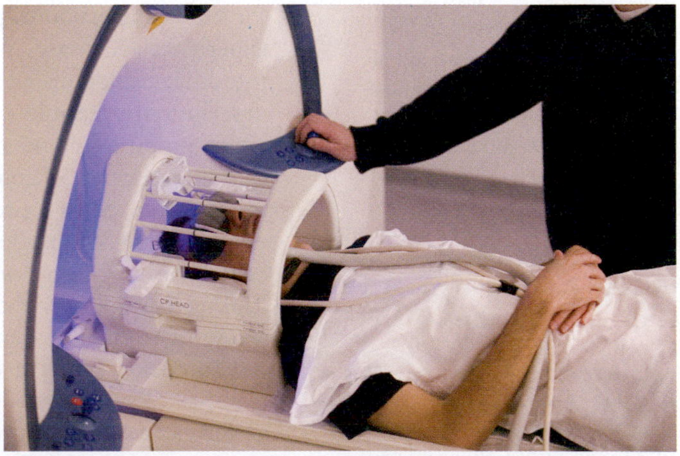

Social psychologists are studying the brain and its relation to behavior. They use technologies such as electroencephalography (EEG) and functional magnetic resonance imaging (fMRI).

Watch on MyPsychLab
To learn more about social neuroscience, watch the MyPsychLab video ***John Cacioppo: Can you tell us about your field?***

promises to open up a whole new area of inquiry into the relationship of the brain to behavior (Chiao et al., 2010; Harmon-Jones & Winkielman, 2007; Lieberman, 2010; Ochsner, 2007).

"DON'T TELL ME THIS NONSENSE DOESN'T VIOLATE THE CODE OF BIOETHICS."

Ethical Issues in Social Psychology

As you read this chapter, did it bother you to learn that researchers sometimes mislead people about the true purpose of their study or that, in Latané and Darley's seizure study, people were put in a situation that might have been upsetting? In their quest to create realistic, engaging situations, social psychologists frequently face ethical dilemmas. For scientific reasons, we want our experiments to resemble the real world as much as possible and to be as sound and well controlled as we can make them. But we also want to avoid causing our participants stress, discomfort, or unpleasantness. These two goals often conflict as the researcher goes about the business of creating and conducting experiments.

Researchers are concerned about the health and welfare of the individuals participating in their experiments. Researchers are also in the process of discovering important information about human social behavior, such as bystander intervention, prejudice, conformity, aggression, and obedience to authority. Many of these discoveries are bound to benefit society. Indeed, given the fact that social psychologists have developed powerful tools to investigate such issues scientifically, many scholars feel it would be immoral not to conduct experiments to explore them. To gain insight into such critical issues, however, researchers must create vivid events that are involving for the participants. Some of these events might make the participants uncomfortable, such as witnessing someone having a seizure. We can't resolve the dilemma by making pious claims that participants never experience discomfort in an experiment or by insisting that all is fair in science and then forging blindly ahead. Clearly, some middle ground is called for.

Informed Consent
Agreement to participate in an experiment, granted in full awareness of the nature of the experiment, which has been explained in advance

Deception
Misleading participants about the true purpose of a study or the events that will actually transpire

Institutional Review Board (IRB)
A group made up of at least one scientist, one nonscientist, and one member not affiliated with the institution that reviews all psychological research at that institution and decides whether it meets ethical guidelines; all research must be approved by the IRB before it is conducted

The dilemma is less problematic if researchers can obtain **informed consent** from their participants prior to their participation. To obtain informed consent, the researcher explains the nature of the experiment to participants before it begins and asks for their permission to participate. If participants are made fully aware of the kinds of experiences they are about to undergo and state that they are willing to participate, the ethical dilemma is resolved. In many social psychology experiments, this sort of description is feasible—and where it is feasible, it is done. But sometimes it is impossible. Suppose Latané and Darley had told their participants that a seizure was about to be staged, that it wouldn't be a real emergency, and that the point was to see if they offered help. Such a procedure would be bad science. In this kind of experiment, it's essential that the participant experience contrived events as if they were real; this is called a *deception experiment*. **Deception** in social psychological research involves misleading participants about the true purpose of a study or the events that transpire. (Note that not all research in social psychology involves deception.)

To ensure that the dignity and safety of research participants are protected, the American Psychological Association (2010) has published a list of ethical principles that govern all research in psychology (see Figure 2.3). In addition, any institution (such as a university) that seeks federal funding for psychological research is required to have an **institutional review board (IRB)** that reviews research before it is conducted. The board, which must include at least one scientist, one nonscientist, and one person who is not affiliated with the institution, reviews all research proposals and decides whether the procedures meet ethical guidelines. Any aspect of the experimental procedure that this committee judges to be overly stressful or upsetting must be changed or deleted

Selected Ethical Principles of Psychologists in the Conduct of Research

1. Psychologists seek to promote accuracy, honesty, and truthfulness in the science, teaching, and practice of psychology.
2. Psychologists respect the dignity and worth of all people, and the rights of individuals to privacy, confidentiality, and self-determination.
3. When psychologists conduct research in person or via electronic transmission or other forms of communication, they obtain the informed consent of the individual.
4. When obtaining informed consent psychologists inform participants about (1) the purpose of the research, expected duration, and procedures; (2) their right to decline to participate and to withdraw from the research once participation has begun; (3) the foreseeable consequences of declining or withdrawing; (4) reasonably foreseeable factors that may be expected to influence their willingness to participate such as potential risks, discomfort, or adverse effects; (5) any prospective research benefits; (6) limits of confidentiality; (7) incentives for participation; and (8) whom to contact for questions about the research and research participants rights.
5. Psychologists have a primary obligation and take reasonable precautions to protect confidential information obtained through or stored in any medium.
6. Psychologists do not conduct a study involving deception unless they have determined that the use of deceptive techniques is justified by the studys significant prospective scientific, educational, or applied value and that effective nondeceptive alternative procedures are not feasible.
7. Psychologists explain any deception that is an integral feature of the design and conduct of an experiment to participants as early as is feasible.
8. Psychologists provide a prompt opportunity for participants to obtain appropriate information about the nature, results, and conclusions of the research, and they take reasonable steps to correct any misconceptions that participants may have of which the psychologists are aware.

FIGURE 2.3

Procedures for the Protection of Participants in Psychological Research

The American Psychological Association, a professional organization that represents psychology in the United States, has established ethical guidelines that psychological researchers are expected to follow. Some of them are listed here.

(Adapted from APA Ethical Principles of Psychologists and Code of Conduct, 2010)

before the study can be conducted. (Note that some of the research described in later chapters was conducted before IRBs were required in the early 1970s. You will need to decide whether you would have approved these studies if you were on an IRB that judged them.)

When deception is used in a study, the postexperimental interview, called the debriefing session, is crucial. **Debriefing** is the process of explaining to the participants, at the end of an experiment, the true purpose of the study and exactly what transpired. If any participants have experienced discomfort, the researchers attempt to undo and alleviate it. During debriefing too the participants learn about the goals and purpose of the research. The best researchers question their participants carefully and listen to what they say, regardless of whether or not deception was used in the experiment. (For a detailed description of how debriefing interviews should be conducted, see Aronson et al., 1990.)

In our experience, virtually all participants understand and appreciate the need for deception, as long as the time is taken in the postexperimental debriefing session to review the purpose of the research and to explain why alternative procedures could not be used. Several investigators have gone a step further and assessed the impact on people of participating in deception studies (e.g., Christensen, 1988; Epley & Huff, 1998; Finney, 1987; Gerdes, 1979; Sharpe, Adair, & Roese, 1992). These studies have consistently found that people do not object to the kinds of mild discomfort and deceptions typically used in social psychological research. In fact, some studies have found that most people who participated in deception experiments reported learning more and enjoying the experiments more than did those who participated in nondeception experiments (Smith & Richardson, 1983). For example, Latané and Darley (1970) reported that, during their debriefing, the participants said that the deception was necessary and that they were willing to participate in similar studies in the future—even though they had experienced some stress and conflict during the study.

Debriefing

Explaining to participants, at the end of an experiment, the true purpose of the study and exactly what transpired

USE IT!

As we have seen in this chapter, social psychologists use empirical methods to test hypotheses about social behavior. Now that you know something about these methods, you are in a good position to judge the quality of research findings you read about in newspapers and magazines. As we saw, for example, one of the most common mistakes is for people to assume that because two variables are correlated with each other, one caused the other. We hope that when you hear about correlational findings in the media, a little light will go off in your head that causes you to challenge any causal conclusions that are drawn. Suppose, for example, that you are browsing through a promotional brochure for the *Consumers Reports on Health* newsletter, as one of us recently was, and you came across this tidbit: "Need more motivation to exercise? Exercise leads to better sex. In one study, men who exercised were five times as likely to achieve normal sexual function as a less-active group." Did the little light go off? This is a correlational finding—men who exercised more functioned better sexually—and we cannot draw the conclusion that it is the exercise that "leads to" (e.g., causes) better sex. Can you think of alternative explanations of this finding? Better yet, can you design an experiment that would test the hypothesis that exercise helps people's sex lives?

Summary

How do researchers develop hypotheses and theories?

- **Social Psychology: An Empirical Science** A fundamental principle of social psychology is that social influence can be studied scientifically.
  - **Formulating Hypotheses and Theories** Social psychological research begins with a hypothesis about the effects of social influence. Hypotheses often come from previous research findings; researchers conduct studies to test an alternative explanation of previous experiments. Many other hypotheses come from observations of everyday life, such as Latané and Darley's hunches about why people failed to help Kitty Genovese.

What are the strengths and weaknesses of the various research designs used by social psychologists?

- **Research Designs** Social psychologists use three research designs: the observational method, the correlational method, and the experimental method.
  - **The Observational Method: Describing Social Behavior** The **observational method**, whereby researchers observe people and systematically record their behavior, is useful for describing the nature of a phenomenon and generating hypotheses. It includes **ethnography**, the method by which researchers attempt to understand a group or culture by observing it from the inside, without imposing any preconceived notions they might have. Another method is **archival analysis**, whereby researchers examine documents or archives, such as looking at photographs in magazines to see how men and women are portrayed.
  - **The Correlational Method: Predicting Social Behavior** The **correlational method**, whereby two or more variables are systematically measured and the relationship between them assessed, is very useful when the goal is to predict one variable from another. For example, researchers might be interested in whether there is a correlation between the amount of violent television children watch and how aggressive they are. The correlational method is often applied to the results of surveys in which a representative group of people are asked questions about their attitudes and behaviors. To make sure that the results are generalizable, researchers randomly select survey respondents from the population at large. A limit of the correlational method is that *correlation does not equal causation.*
  - **The Experimental Method: Answering Causal Questions** The only way to determine causality is to use the **experimental method**, in which the researcher randomly assigns participants to different conditions and ensures that these conditions are identical except for the independent variable. The **independent variable** is the one researchers vary to see if it has a causal effect (e.g., how much TV children watch); the **dependent variable** is what researchers measure to see if it is affected (e.g., how aggressive children are). Experiments should be high in **internal validity**, which means that people in all conditions are treated identically, except for the independent variable (e.g., how much TV children watch). **External validity**—the extent to which researchers can generalize their results to other situations and people—is accomplished by increasing the realism of the experiment, particularly its psychological realism (the extent to which the psychological processes triggered in the

experiment are similar to those triggered in everyday life). It is also accomplished by **replicating** the study with different populations of participants. As in any other science, some social psychology studies are basic research experiments (designed to answer basic questions about why people do what they do), whereas others are applied studies (designed to find ways to solve specific social problems).

What impact do cross-cultural studies, the evolutionary approach, and research in social neuroscience have on the way in which scientists investigate social behavior?

- **New Frontiers in Social Psychological Research** In recent years, social psychologists have developed new ways of investigating social behavior.
  - **Culture and Social Psychology** To study the ways in which culture shapes people's thoughts, feelings, and behavior, social psychologists conduct cross-cultural research. This is not simply a matter of replicating the same study in different cultures; researchers have to guard against imposing their own viewpoints and definitions, learned from their culture, onto another culture with which they are unfamiliar.
  - **The Evolutionary Approach** Some social psychologists attempt to explain social behavior in terms of genetic factors that have evolved over time according to the principles of natural selection. Such ideas are hard to test experimentally but can generate novel hypotheses about social behavior that can be tested with the experimental method.
  - **Social Neuroscience** Social psychologists have become increasingly interested in the connection between biological processes and social behavior. These interests include the study of hormones and behavior, the human immune system, and neurological processes in the human brain.

What is the basic dilemma of the social psychologist, and how do social psychologists solve this dilemma?

- **Ethical Issues in Social Psychology** Social psychologists follow federal, state, and professional guidelines to ensure the welfare of their research participants. These include having an **institutional review board** approve their studies in advance, asking participants to sign **informed consent** forms, and **debriefing** participants afterwards about the purpose of the study and what transpired, especially if there was any deception involved.

Chapter 2 Test

Study and Review on MyPsychLab

1. The basic dilemma of the social psychologist is that
   a. it is hard to teach social psychology to students because most people believe strongly in personality.
   b. there is a trade-off between internal and external validity in most experiments.
   c. it is nearly impossible to use a random selection of the population in laboratory experiments.
   d. almost all social behavior is influenced by the culture in which people grew up.
   e. it is difficult to teach social psychology at 3:30 in the afternoon when people are sleepy.

2. Suppose a researcher found a strong negative correlation between college students' grade point average (GPA) and the amount of alcohol they drink. Which of the following is the best conclusion from this study?
   a. Students with a high GPA study more and thus have less time to drink.
   b. Drinking a lot interferes with studying.
   c. If you know how much alcohol a student drinks, you can predict his or her GPA fairly well.
   d. The higher a student's GPA, the more he or she drinks.
   e. People who are intelligent get higher grades and drink less.

3. A team of researchers wants to test the hypothesis that drinking wine makes people like jazz more. They randomly assign college students who are 21 or over to one room in which they will drink wine and listen to jazz or to another room in which they will drink water and listen to jazz. It happens that the "wine room" has a big window with nice scenery outside, while the "water room" is windowless, dark, and dingy. The most serious flaw in this experiment is that it
   a. is low in external validity.
   b. is low in internal validity.
   c. did not randomly select the participants from all college students in the country.
   d. is low in psychological realism.
   e. is low in mundane realism.

4. Mary wants to find out whether eating sugary snacks before an exam leads to better performance on the exam. Which of the following strategies would answer her question most conclusively?
   a. Identify a large number of students who perform exceptionally low and exceptionally high in exams, ask them whether they eat sugary snacks before exams, and see whether high performers eat more sugary snacks before exams than do low performers.
   b. Wait for exam time in a big class, ask everyone whether they ate sugary snacks before the exam, and see whether those who ate sugary snacks before the exam do better compared to those who didn't.
   c. Wait for exam time in a big class, give a random half of the students M&Ms before the exam, and see whether the students who ate M&Ms perform better.
   d. Pick a big class, give all students sugary snacks before one exam and salty snacks before the next exam; then see whether students score lower on average in the second exam.

5. A researcher conducts a study with participants who are college students. The researcher then repeats the study using the same procedures but with members of the general population (i.e., adults) as participants. The results are similar for both samples. The research has established ____________ through ____________.
   a. external validity, replication
   b. internal validity, replication
   c. external validity, psychological realism
   d. internal validity, psychological realism
   e. psychological realism, internal validity

6. In the Latané and Darley study, people sat in cubicles and heard over an intercom system someone having a seizure, to test psychological processes thought to be present in the Kitty Genovese murder. All of the following reasons *except one* explain why social psychologists do laboratory studies that differ so much from the real-life events that inspired them. Which one?
   a. It is usually easier to randomly assign people to conditions in controlled laboratory studies.
   b. The participants in lab studies are often more representative of the general population than are the people in the real-life examples.
   c. A great advantage to laboratory studies is the ability to maintain high internal validity and know for sure what is causing what.
   d. To see how much you can generalize from a lab study, you can replicate the study with different populations and in different situations.
   e. It is often possible to capture the same psychological processes in the laboratory as those that occur in real-life settings, if psychological realism is high.

7. Professor X wants to make sure his study of gifted youngsters will get published, but he's worried that his findings could have been caused by something other than the independent variable of who their first-grade teacher was. He is concerned with the ____________ of his experiment.
   a. probability level
   b. external validity
   c. replication
   d. internal validity

8. Suppose a psychologist decides to join a local commune to understand and observe its members' social relationships. This is
   a. cross-cultural research.
   b. meta-analysis.
   c. applied research.
   d. an experiment.
   e. ethnography.

9. Mary and Juan want to establish interjudge reliability in their study on child bullying and the amount of time spent playing video games. To ensure interjudge reliability, they should
   a. observe and code the violent behavior together so they can obtain a reliable coding system.
   b. independently observe and code the data to see if they come up with the same observations.
   c. have one of them observe and code the data and then explain his or her system to the other.
   d. have one observe and code child bullying, while the other should observe and code the amount of time the kids play video games.

10. All of the following except one are part of the guidelines for ethical research. Which is not?
   a. All research is reviewed by an IRB (institutional review board) that consists of at least one scientist, one nonscientist, and one person unaffiliated with the institution.
   b. A researcher receives informed consent from a participant unless deception is deemed necessary and the experiment meets ethical guidelines.
   c. When deception is used in a study, participants must be fully debriefed.
   d. There must be a cover story for every study, because all studies involve some type of deception.

Answer Key

1-b, 2-c, 3-b, 4-c, 5-a,
6-b, 7-d, 8-e, 9-b, 10-d

Scoring the TRY IT! exercises

Page 23

1. In studies conducted by Stanley Milgram (1974), up to 65% of participants administered what they thought were near-lethal shocks to another subject. (In fact, no real shocks were administered.)
2. (c) Rewarding people for doing something they enjoy will typically make them like that activity less in the future (e.g., Lepper, 1995, 1996; Lepper, Greene, & Nisbett, 1973).
3. (b) Wilson and colleagues (1993) found that people who did not analyze their feelings were the most satisfied with their choice of posters when contacted a few weeks later.
4. (a) Under most circumstances, repeated exposure increases liking for a stimulus (Zajonc, 1968).
5. (a) More (Jecker & Landy, 1969).
6. (c) Research by Dijksterhuis and Nordgren (2006) found that people who were distracted made the best choices, possibly because distraction allowed them to consider the problem unconsciously but not consciously.
7. (a) Research by Spencer, Steele, and Quinn (1999) and Steele (1997) found that when women think there are sex differences on a test, they do worse. When women were told that there were no gender differences in performance on the test, they did as well as men.
8. (b) There is no evidence that subliminal messages in advertising have any effect; considerable evidence shows that normal advertising is quite effective (Abraham & Lodish, 1990; Chaiken, Wood, & Eagly, 1996; Liebert & Sprafkin, 1988; Moore, 1982; Weir, 1984; Wilson, Houston, & Meyers, 1998).
9. (b) Men touch women more than vice versa (Henley, 1977).
10. (b) People given the heavy clipboard thought that student opinion should be weighed the most (Jostmann, Lakens, & Schubert, 2009).

Page 26

Two teams of researchers (Archer, 1983, and Akert, Chen, & Panter, 1991) performed an archival analysis of portrait art and news and advertising photographs in print and television media. They coded the photographs according to the number of images that were devoted to the person's face. Their results? Over 5 centuries, across cultures, and in different forms of media, men are visually presented in a more close-up style (focusing on the head and face), while women are shown in a more long-shot style (focusing on the body). These researchers interpret their findings as indicating a subtle form of sex-role stereotyping: Men are being portrayed in a stronger style that emphasizes their intellectual achievements, whereas women are being portrayed in a weaker style that emphasizes their total physical appearance.

Page 30

1. The politician ignored possible third variables that could cause both Scout membership and crime, such as socioeconomic class. Traditionally, Scouting has been most popular in small towns and suburbs among middle-class youngsters; it has never been very attractive or even available to youths growing up in densely populated, urban, high-crime areas.
2. Not necessarily. It might be the other way around—namely, that moms and dads are more likely to become helicopter parents if their kids are having academic problems. Or there could be a third variable that causes parents to hover and their kids to have academic problems.
3. Did tattoos cause motorcycle accidents? Or, for that matter, did motorcycle accidents cause tattoos? The researchers suggested that a third (unmeasured) variable was in fact the cause of both: A tendency to take risks and to be involved in flamboyant personal displays led to tattooing one's body and to driving a motorcycle recklessly.
4. It is possible that religion makes people more likely to obey the law. It is equally possible, however, that some other variable increases the likelihood that people will be religious and follow the rules—such as having parents who are religious.
5. Not necessarily. People who do not eat breakfast might differ from people who do in any number of ways that influence longevity—for example, in how obese they are, how hard-driving and high-strung they are, or even how late they sleep in the morning.
6. Not necessarily, because milk drinking may have little to do with weight gain. Children who drink a lot of milk might be more likely to eat cookies or other high-calorie foods.
7. It is possible that watching public television makes people want to have more sex. It is equally possible, however, that some third variable, such as health or education, influences both television preferences and sexual behavior. It is even possible that having sex makes people want to watch more public television. Based on the correlation the researchers reported, there is no way of telling which of these explanations is true.
8. Not necessarily. There could be a third variable that is causing kids to eat a lot of candy and to become violent later in life.

Note: For more examples on correlation and causation, see http://jfmueller.faculty.noctrl.edu/100/correlation_or_causation.htm

3 Social Cognition

How We Think About the Social World

IT WAS AN EPIC MATCH ON *JEOPARDY!*, THE TELEVISION QUIZ SHOW ON WHICH CONTESTANTS ARE GIVEN AN ANSWER AND HAVE TO PROVIDE THE CORRECT QUESTION. Two of the three contestants were among the best players of all time. Ken Jennings held the record for the longest winning streak on the show (he won 74 consecutive games), and Brad Rutter was the all-time money winner in the history of the show. What about the third contestant? Who would dare match his or her wits against these formidable opponents? Actually, it wasn't a "he" or "she," but an "it": a supercomputer named Watson, developed by IBM and named after that company's founder, Thomas J. Watson.

The match was nip and tuck at first, but by the third and last day Watson had built an insurmountable lead. Time after time, the supercomputer gave correct responses to esoteric clues. In the category, Legal 'Es', for example, Watson listened to the clue, "This clause in a union contract says that wages will rise or fall depending on a standard such as cost of living" and correctly responded, "What is escalator?" Ken Jennings, who described himself as "the Great Carbon-Based Hope against a new generation of thinking machines," conceded defeat by writing on his video screen, "I, for one, welcome our new computer overlords," paraphrasing a line from an episode of *The Simpsons* (Jennings, 2011; Markoff, 2011).

This was not the first time an IBM computer had outwitted human beings. In 1997, Gary Kasparov, the reigning chess champion of the world, conceded defeat in the sixth and decisive game against an IBM computer named Big Blue. But what was especially impressive about Watson's victory was that the supercomputer did not simply look up answers in a vast memory bank. The IBM researchers deliberately chose to compete in the game *Jeopardy!* because, in order to win, you have to understand natural language, with all its subtleties and double meanings. Watson had to figure out, for example, that the term "Legal 'Es'" was a pun on the word *legalese*, meaning that the answers would involve legal terms but that they would all begin with the letter *e*. The fact that it could do so, faster and more accurately than the best human beings ever to play the game, was impressive indeed.

Should we all feel a little less smart, like the commentator who remarked, after Big Blue defeated Gary Kasparov that he felt "a twinge of IQ loss and an increase in hairiness" (Dunn, 1997)? Well, computers are getting smarter and smarter, but they have a long way to go before they can match the human brain. When the field of artificial intelligence began in the 1950s, computer scientists believed that in a short amount of time they would produce computers that could outthink human beings in every way. But as powerful as computers are, and as good as they are at games like chess and *Jeopardy!*, there are key areas in which they don't come close to matching humans. For example, human beings are much better than computers at understanding the nuances of people's behavior and decoding their intentions, wishes, and desires. Because of this, computers fail miserably at games in which it is crucial to figure out what is going on inside people's heads and understand things from their point of view, such as poker (C. Wilson, 2011). Watson might know what *escalator* means in a legal context, but it would be hopeless at a game of Texas hold'em in which it had to figure out not only what cards its opponents had, but also what it means when they raise the pot by $50,000 with a nervous laugh. Are they bluffing? What do they think my hole cards are? What do they think I think their hole cards are?

FOCUS QUESTIONS

- What are the two major types of social cognition?
- What are the roles and functions of schemas and heuristics in automatic thinking?
- How does culture influence social thinking?
- What are some of the drawbacks of controlled thinking, and how can we improve its effectiveness?

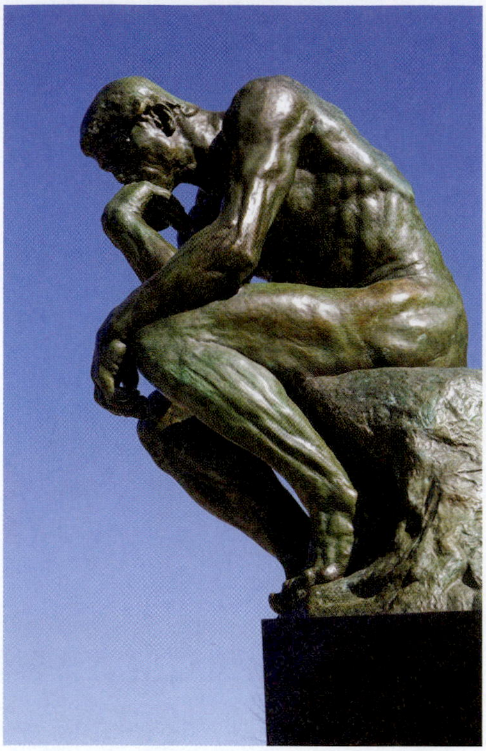

Rodin's famous sculpture, *The Thinker*, mimics controlled thinking, where people sit down and consider something slowly and deliberately. Even when we do not know it, however, we are engaging in automatic thinking, which is nonconscious, unintentional, involuntary, and effortless.

The Social Thinker

The human brain has evolved to be a powerful, finely tuned instrument for understanding other people, which is an important skill in playing poker. More generally, people are extremely good at **social cognition**, which, as we saw in Chapter 1, refers to the ways in which people think about themselves and the social world, including how they select, interpret, remember, and use social information. No computer can match us in this kind of thinking. That's not to say people are perfect social thinkers. Social psychologists have uncovered some fascinating mistakes to which we are prone, despite our uncanny cognitive abilities. In this chapter, we will see both the power and limits of social cognition.

To understand how people think about their social worlds and how accurate their impressions are likely to be, we need to distinguish between two different kinds of social cognition. One kind of thought is quick and automatic. When we meet someone for the first time, we often form lightning-quick impressions of him or her, without consciously deliberating about it. Similarly, we often make decisions "without thinking," such as jamming on the brakes of our car when we see a child step into the road (Bargh & Morsella, 2008; Dijksterhuis, 2010; Payne & Gawronski, 2010; Wilson, 2002). This is called *automatic thinking*. Other times, of course, people pause and think carefully about the right course of action. You may have spent hours deliberating over important decisions in your life, such as where to go to college, or whether to break up with your boyfriend or girlfriend. This is the second kind of social cognition—*controlled thinking*—which is more effortful and deliberate. Quite often the automatic and controlled modes of social cognition work well together. Think of the automatic pilot that flies modern airplanes, monitoring hundreds of complex systems and adjusting instantly to changes in atmospheric conditions. The autopilot does just fine most of the time, although occasionally it is important for the human pilot to take over and fly the plane manually. Humans too have "automatic pilots" that monitor their environments, draw conclusions, and direct their behaviors. But we can also "override" this automatic type of thinking and analyze a situation slowly and deliberately. We will begin by examining the nature of automatic thinking.

It is the mind which creates the world about us, and even though we stand side by side in the same meadow, my eyes will never see what is beheld by yours.

—George Gissing, *The Private Papers of Henry Ryecroft*, 1903

On Automatic Pilot: Low-Effort Thinking

People are very good at sizing up a new situation quickly and accurately. They figure out who is there, what is happening, and what might happen next. When you attended your first college class, for example, you probably made quick assumptions about who people were (the person standing at the lectern was the professor) and how to behave. We doubt that you confused the class with a fraternity party. And you probably reached these conclusions without even being aware that you were doing so.

Imagine a different approach: Every time you encounter a new situation, you stop and think about it slowly and deliberately, like Rodin's statue *The Thinker*. When you are introduced to someone new, you have to excuse yourself for 15 minutes while you analyze what you have learned and how much you like the person. Sounds exhausting, doesn't it? Fortunately, we form impressions of people quickly and effortlessly, without much conscious analysis of what we are doing. We do these things by engaging in an automatic analysis of our environments, based on our past experiences and knowledge of the world. **Automatic thinking** is thought that is nonconscious, unintentional, involuntary, and effortless. Although different kinds of automatic thinking meet these criteria to varying degrees (Bargh & Ferguson, 2000; Evans, 2008; Moors & De Houwer, 2006; Uleman, Saribay, & Gonzalez, 2008), for our purposes we can define automaticity as thinking that satisfies all or most of them.

Social Cognition

How people think about themselves and the social world; more specifically, how people select, interpret, remember, and use social information to make judgments and decisions

Automatic Thinking

Thinking that is nonconscious, unintentional, involuntary, and effortless

People as Everyday Theorists: Automatic Thinking with Schemas

Automatic thinking helps us understand new situations by relating them to our prior experiences. When we meet someone new, we don't start from scratch to figure out what he or she is like; we categorize the person as "an engineering student" or "like my cousin Helen." The same goes for places, objects, and situations. When we walk into a fast-food restaurant we've never visited, we know, without thinking, not to wait at a table for a waiter and a menu. We know that we have to go to the counter and order, because our past experience automatically tells us that this is what we do in fast-food restaurants.

More formally, people use **schemas**, which are mental structures that organize our knowledge about the social world. These mental structures influence the information we notice, think about, and remember (Bartlett, 1932; Heine, Proulx, & Vohs, 2006; Markus, 1977). The term *schema* is very general; it encompasses our knowledge about many things—other people, ourselves, social roles (e.g., what a librarian or an engineer is like), and specific events (e.g., what usually happens when people eat a meal in a restaurant). In each case, our schemas contain our basic knowledge and impressions that we use to organize what we know about the social world and interpret new situations. For example, our schema about the members of the Animal House fraternity might be that they're loud, obnoxious partygoers with a propensity for projectile vomiting.

The Function of Schemas: Why Do We Have Them? Schemas are very useful for helping us organize and make sense of the world and to fill in the gaps of our knowledge. Think for a moment what it would be like to have no schemas at all. What if everything you encountered was inexplicable, confusing, and unlike anything else you've ever known? Tragically, this is what happens to people who suffer from a neurological disorder called Korsakov's syndrome. People with this disorder lose the ability to form new memories and must approach every situation as if they were encountering it for the first time, even if they have actually experienced it many times before. This can be so unsettling—even terrifying—that some people with Korsakov's syndrome go to great lengths to try to impose meaning on their experiences. Neurologist Oliver Sacks (1987) gives the following description of a Korsakov patient named Thompson:

> He remembered nothing for more than a few seconds. He was continually disoriented. Abysses of amnesia continually opened beneath him, but he would bridge them, nimbly, by fluent confabulations and fictions of all kinds. For him they were not fictions, but how he suddenly saw, or interpreted, the world. Its radical flux and incoherence could not be tolerated, acknowledged, for an instant—there was, instead, this strange, delirious, quasi-coherence, as Mr. Thompson, with his ceaseless, unconscious, quick-fire inventions, continually improvised a world around him . . . *for such a patient must literally make himself (and his world) up every moment.* (pp. 109–110; emphasis in original)

In short, having continuity, being able to relate new experiences to our past schemas, is so important that people who lose this ability invent schemas where none exist.

> *Theory helps us to bear our ignorance of facts.*
> —George Santayana, *The Sense of Beauty*, 1896

Schemas are particularly useful when we are in confusing situations, because they help us figure out what is going on. Consider a classic study by Harold Kelley (1950) in which students in different sections of a college economics class were told that a guest lecturer would be filling in that day. To create a schema about what the guest lecturer would be like, Kelley told the students that the economics department was interested in how different classes reacted to different instructors and that the students would thus receive a brief biographical note about the instructor before he arrived. The note contained information about the instructor's age, background, teaching experience, and personality. One version said, "People who know him consider him to be a very warm person, industrious, critical, practical, and determined." The other version was identical except that the phrase "a very warm person" was replaced with "a rather cold person." The students received one of these personality descriptions at random.

Schemas

Mental structures people use to organize their knowledge about the social world around themes or subjects and that influence the information people notice, think about, and remember

People who know him consider him a rather cold person, industrious, critical, practical, and determined.

People who know him consider him a very warm person, industrious, critical, practical, and determined.

The guest lecturer then conducted a class discussion for 20 minutes, after which the students rated their impressions of him. Given that there was some ambiguity in this situation—after all, the students had seen the instructor for only a brief time—Kelley hypothesized that they would use the schema provided by the biographical note to fill in the blanks. This is exactly what happened. The students who expected the instructor to be warm gave him significantly higher ratings than the students who expected him to be cold, even though all the students had observed the exact same teacher behaving in the same way. The students who expected the instructor to be warm were also more likely to ask him questions and to participate in the class discussion. Has this happened to you? Have your expectations about a professor influenced your impressions of him or her? Did you find, oddly enough, that the professor acted just as you'd expected? Ask a classmate who had a different expectation about the professor what he or she thought. Do the two of you have different perceptions of the instructor based on the different schemas you were using?

Is this man an alcoholic or just down on his luck? Our judgments about other people can be influenced by schemas that are accessible in our memories. If you had just been talking to a friend about a relative who had an alcohol problem, you might be more likely to think that this man has an alcohol problem as well, because alcoholism is accessible in your memory.

Of course, people are not totally blind to what is actually out there in the world. Sometimes what we see is relatively unambiguous and we do not need to use our schemas to help us interpret it. For example, in one of the classes in which Kelley conducted his study, the guest instructor was quite self-confident, even a little arrogant. Given that arrogance is a relatively unambiguous trait, the students did not need to rely on their expectations to fill in the blanks. They rated the instructor as arrogant in both the warm and cold conditions. However, when they rated this instructor's sense of humor, which was less clear-cut, the students relied on their schemas: The students in the warm condition thought he was funnier than the students in the cold condition did. The more ambiguous our information is, then, the more we use schemas to fill in the blanks.

It is important to note that there is nothing wrong with what the students in Kelley's study did. As long as people have reason to believe their schemas are accurate, it is perfectly reasonable to use them to resolve ambiguity. If a stranger comes up to you in a dark alley and says, "Take out your wallet," your schema about such encounters tells you that the person wants to steal your money, not admire pictures of your family. This schema helps you avert a serious and perhaps deadly misunderstanding.

Which Schemas Are Applied? Accessibility and Priming The social world is full of ambiguous information that is open to interpretation. Imagine, for example, that you are riding on a city bus and a man gets on and sits beside you. He mutters incoherently to himself and rocks back and forth in his seat. At one point, he starts singing an old Beatles tune. How would you make sense of his behavior? You have several schemas you could use. Should you interpret his behavior with your "alcoholic" or "mentally ill person" schema? How will you decide?

The schema that comes to mind and guides your impressions of the man can be affected by **accessibility**, the extent to which schemas and concepts are at the forefront of the mind and are therefore likely to be used when making judgments about the social world (Higgins, 1996a; Sanna & Schwarz, 2004; Wheeler & DeMarree, 2009; Wyer & Srull, 1989). Something can become accessible for three reasons. First, some schemas are chronically accessible due to past experience (Chen & Andersen, 1999; Coane & Balota, 2009; Schlegel et al., 2009). This means that these schemas are constantly active and ready to use to interpret ambiguous situations. For example, if there is a history of alcoholism in your family, traits describing a person with alcoholism are likely to be chronically accessible to you, increasing the likelihood that you will assume that the man on the bus has had too much to drink. If someone you know has a mental illness, however, thoughts about how people with mental illnesses behave are likely to be more accessible than thoughts about someone with alcoholism, leading you to interpret the man's behavior very differently.

Second, something can become accessible because it is related to a current goal. The concept of mental illness might not be chronically accessible to you, but if you are studying for a test in your abnormal psychology class and need to learn about different kinds of mental disorders, this concept might be temporarily accessible. As a consequence, you might be more likely to notice the man on the bus and interpret his behavior as a sign of a mental disorder—at least until your test is over and you no longer have the goal of learning about mental illnesses (Eitam & Higgins, 2010; Kuhl, 1983; Martin & Tesser, 1996).

FIGURE 3.1

How We Interpret an Ambiguous Situation

The role of accessibility and priming.

Finally, schemas can become temporarily accessible because of our recent experiences (Bargh, 1996; Higgins & Bargh, 1987; Oishi, Schimmack, & Colcombe, 2003). This means that a particular schema or trait happens to be primed by something people have been thinking or doing before encountering an event. Suppose that right before the man on the bus sat down, you were reading *One Flew over the Cuckoo's Nest*, Ken Kesey's novel about patients in a mental hospital. Given that thoughts about mental patients were accessible in your mind, you would probably assume that the man had a mental illness. If, however, you had just looked out the window and seen a man leaning against a building drinking from a paper bag, you would probably assume that the man on the bus was drunk (see Figure 3.1). These are examples of **priming**, the process by which recent experiences increase the accessibility of a schema, trait, or concept. Reading Kesey's novel primes certain traits, such as those describing people with mental illnesses, making it more likely that these traits will be used to interpret a new event, such as the behavior of the man on the bus, even though this new event is completely unrelated to the one that originally primed the traits.

I know that often I would not see a thing unless I thought of it first.

—Norman Maclean, *A River Runs Through It*

The following classic experiment illustrates the priming effect (Higgins, Rholes, & Jones, 1977). Research participants were told that they would take part in two unrelated studies. In the first, a perception study, they would be asked to identify different colors

Accessibility

The extent to which schemas and concepts are at the forefront of people's minds and are therefore likely to be used when making judgments about the social world

Priming

The process by which recent experiences increase the accessibility of a schema, trait, or concept

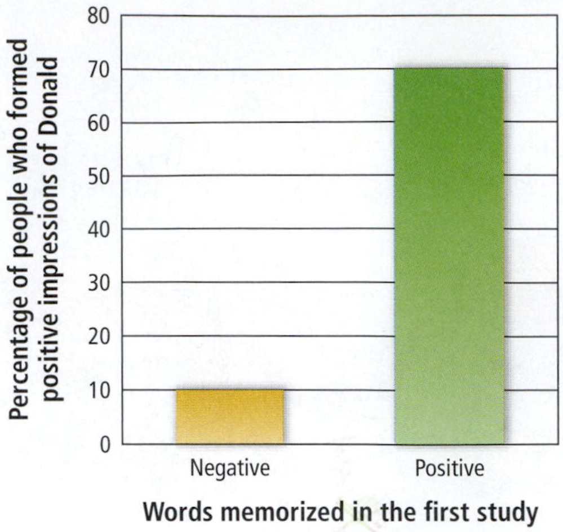

Description of Donald

Donald spent a great deal of time in his search of what he liked to call excitement. He had already climbed Mt. McKinley, shot the Colorado rapids in a kayak, driven in a demolition derby, and piloted a jet-powered boat—without knowing very much about boats. He had risked injury, and even death, a number of times. Now he was in search of new excitement. He was thinking perhaps he would do some skydiving or maybe cross the Atlantic in a sailboat. By the way he acted one could readily guess that Donald was well aware of his ability to do many things well. Other than business engagements, Donald's contacts with people were rather limited. He felt he didn't really need to rely on anyone. Once Donald made up his mind to do something it was as good as done no matter how long it might take or how difficult the going might be. Only rarely did he change his mind even when it might well have been better if he had.

FIGURE 3.2

Priming and Accessibility

In the second of a pair of studies, people were asked to read this paragraph about Donald and form an impression of him. In the first study, some of the participants had memorized words that could be used to interpret Donald in a negative way (e.g., reckless, conceited), while others had memorized words that could be used to interpret Donald in a positive way (e.g., adventurous, self-confident). As the graph shows, those who had memorized the negative words formed a much more negative impression of Donald than did those who had memorized the positive words.

(Based on data in Higgins, Rholes, & Jones, 1977.)

while at the same time memorizing a list of words. The second was a reading comprehension study in which they would read a paragraph about someone named Donald and then give their impressions of him. This paragraph is shown in Figure 3.2. Take a moment to read it. What do you think of Donald?

You might have noticed that many of Donald's actions are ambiguous—interpretable in either a positive or a negative manner—such as the fact that he piloted a boat without knowing much about it and that he wants to sail across the Atlantic. You might put a positive spin on these acts, deciding that Donald has an admirable sense of adventure. Or you could give the same behavior a negative spin, assuming that Donald is quite reckless.

How did the participants interpret Donald's behavior? As expected, it depended on whether positive or negative traits were primed and accessible. In the first study, the researchers divided people into two groups and gave them different words to memorize. People who had first memorized the words *adventurous*, *self-confident*, *independent*, and *persistent* later formed positive impressions of Donald, viewing him as a likable man who enjoyed new challenges. People who had first memorized *reckless*, *conceited*, *aloof*, and *stubborn* later formed negative impressions of Donald, viewing him as a stuck-up person who took needlessly dangerous chances.

But it was not just memorizing any positive or negative words that influenced people's impressions of Donald. In other conditions, research participants memorized words that were also positive or negative, such as *neat* or *disrespectful*. However, these traits didn't influence their impressions of Donald because the words did not apply to Donald's behavior. Thoughts, then, have to be both *accessible* and *applicable* before they will act as primes, exerting an influence on our impressions of the social world. Priming is a good example of automatic thinking, because it occurs quickly, unintentionally, and unconsciously. When judging others, people are usually not aware that they are applying concepts or schemas that they happened to be thinking about earlier.

Making Our Schemas Come True: The Self-Fulfilling Prophecy

Prophecy is the most gratuitous form of error.
—George Eliot (Mary Ann Evans Cross), 1871

People are not just passive recipients of information—they often act on their schemas in ways that change the extent to which these schemas are supported or contradicted. In fact, people can inadvertently

FIGURE 3.3

The Self-Fulfilling Prophecy

A sad cycle in four acts.

make their schemas come true by the way they treat other people (Jussim, Eccles, & Madon, 1996; Madon et al., 2011; Madon et al., 2006; Rosenthal & Jacobson, 1968; Scherr et al., 2011; Stinson et al., 2011). This **self-fulfilling prophecy** operates as follows: People have an expectation about what another person is like, which influences how they act toward that person, which causes that person to behave consistently with people's original expectations, making the expectations come true. Figure 3.3 illustrates the sad self-perpetuating cycle of a self-fulfilling prophecy.

Watch on **MyPsychLab**

To learn more about the self-fulfilling prophecy, watch the MyPsychLab video ***Self-Fulfilling Prophecy.***

In what has become one of the most famous studies in social psychology, Robert Rosenthal and Lenore Jacobson (1968) demonstrated the self-fulfilling prophecy in an elementary school. They administered a test to all the students in the school and told the teachers that some of the students had scored so well that they were sure to "bloom" academically in the upcoming year. In fact, this was not necessarily true: The students identified as "bloomers" were chosen at random by the researchers. As we discussed in Chapter 2, the use of random assignment means that, on average, the students designated as bloomers were no smarter or more likely to bloom than any of the other kids. The only way in which these students differed from their peers was in the minds of the teachers (neither the students nor their parents were told anything about the results of the test).

After creating the expectation in the teachers that certain students would do especially well, Rosenthal and Jacobson waited to see what would happen. They observed the classroom dynamics periodically, and, at the end of the school year, they gave all of the children an IQ test. Did the prophecy come true? Indeed it did. The students in each class who had been labeled as bloomers showed significantly greater gains in their IQ scores than the other students did (see Figure 3.4). The teachers' expectations had become reality. Rosenthal and Jacobson's findings have since been replicated in a number of both experimental and correlational studies (Jussim, Robustelli, & Cain, 2009; Madon et al., 2008; Madon et al., 2003; Madon et al., 2011; Natanovich & Eden, 2008).

Self-Fulfilling Prophecy

The case wherein people have an expectation about what another person is like, which influences how they act toward that person, which causes that person to behave consistently with people's original expectations, making the expectations come true

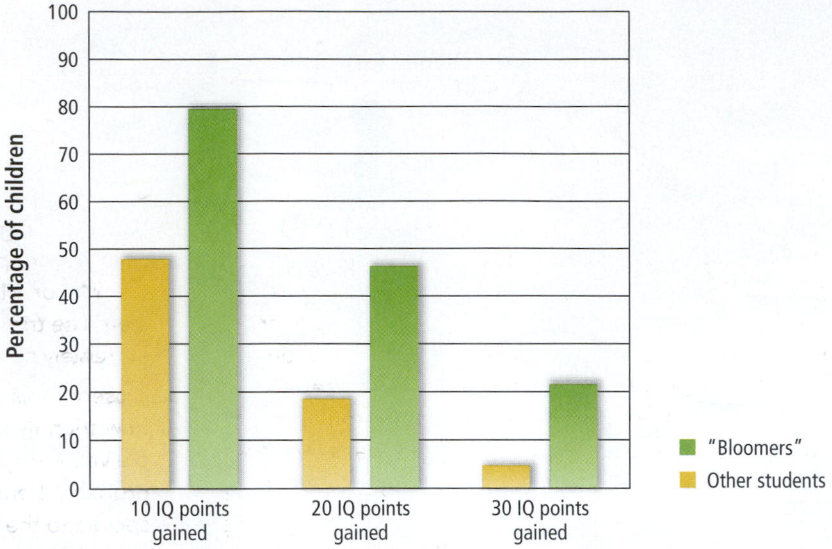

FIGURE 3.4

The Self-Fulfilling Prophecy: Percentage of First and Second Graders Who Improved on an IQ Test Over the Course of the School Year

Those whom the teachers expected to do well actually improved more than the other students.

(Adapted from Rosenthal & Jacobson, 1968)

What happened in the classrooms studied by Rosenthal and Jacobson (1968)? Did the teachers callously decide to give more attention and encouragement to the bloomers? Not at all. Most teachers are very dedicated and would be upset to learn that they favored some students over others. Far from being a conscious, deliberate act, the self-fulfilling prophecy is instead an example of automatic thinking (Chen & Bargh, 1997). Interestingly, the teachers in the Rosenthal and Jacobson study reported that they spent slightly less time with the students who were labeled as bloomers. In subsequent studies, however, teachers have been found to treat bloomers (the students they expect to do better) differently in four general ways: They create a warmer emotional climate for bloomers, giving them more personal attention, encouragement, and support; they give bloomers more material to learn and material that is more difficult; they give bloomers more and better feedback on their work; and they give bloomers more opportunities to respond in class and give them longer to respond (Brophy, 1983; Rosenthal, 1994; Snyder, 1984).

A distressing implication of the fact that the self-fulfilling prophecy occurs automatically is that our schemas may be quite resistant to change. Suppose a teacher has the schema that boys are innately better at math than girls and has inadvertently made this come true in his classroom, due to a self-fulfilling prophecy. "But Mr. Jones," we might reply, "how can you hold such a belief? There are plenty of girls who do very well in math." Mr. Jones would probably be unconvinced, because he would have data to support his schema. "In my classes over the years," he might note, "many more boys than girls have excelled at math." His error lies not with his characterization of the evidence but in his failure to realize his role in producing it. Robert Merton, an eminent sociologist, referred to this process as a "reign of error," whereby people can "cite the actual course of events as proof that [they were] right from the very beginning" (1948, p. 195).

Teachers can unintentionally make their expectations about their students come true by treating some students differently from others.

In real life, of course, psychologists do not give teachers false expectations about how well their students will do. But as the example of Mr. Jones indicates, teachers are only human, and they may acquire faulty expectations about their students based on the students' gender, race, social class, or family history. Any one of these factors could instill expectations in the minds of the teachers and lead to self-fulfilling prophecies, just as in the Rosenthal and Jacobson

TRY IT! Avoiding Self-Fulfilling Prophecies

1. Examine some of your own schemas and expectations about social groups, especially groups you don't particularly like. These might be members of a particular race or ethnic group, rival fraternity, or political party, or they could be people with a particular sexual orientation. Why don't you like members of this group? "Well," you might think, "one reason is that whenever I interact with these people, they seem cold and unfriendly." And you might be right. Perhaps they do respond to you in a cold and unfriendly fashion—not, however, because they are this way by nature but because they are responding to the way you have treated them.
2. Try this exercise to counteract the self-fulfilling prophecy: Find someone who is a member of a group you dislike and strike up a conversation with the person. For example, sit next to this person in one of your classes, or strike up a conversation at a party or gathering. Try to imagine that this individual is the friendliest, kindest, sweetest person you have ever met. Be as warm and charming as you can be. Don't go overboard; if, after never speaking to this person, you suddenly act like Mr. or Ms. Congeniality, you might arouse suspicion. The trick is to act as if you expect the person to be extremely pleasant and friendly.
3. Observe this person's reactions. Are you surprised by how friendly he or she was in responding to you? People you thought were inherently cold and unfriendly will probably behave in a warm and friendly manner in response to the friendly way you have treated them. If this doesn't work on your first encounter with the person, try it again on one or two later occasions. In all likelihood, you will find that friendliness really does breed friendliness (see Chapter 10).

study (Jussim & Harber, 2005). The same thing could happen outside the classroom, such as in the workplace, where bosses might influence their employees' behavior via self-fulfilling prophecies.

> *It is a capital mistake to theorize before you have all the evidence. It biases the judgment.*
>
> —Sherlock Holmes (Sir Arthur Conan Doyle), 1898

Limits of Self-Fulfilling Prophecies Does all of this mean that we are like putty in the hands of powerful people who have incorrect expectations about us? Suppose that Sarah is about to be interviewed for a job at a law firm by someone who has negative expectations about her qualifications, based, perhaps, on her gender, race, previous place of employment, or college. Will she be able to overcome these expectations and show the interviewer that she really is highly qualified for the job? Or, consistent with research on the self-fulfilling prophecy, will the interviewer mold Sarah's behavior in such a way that Sarah finds herself giving halting, inadequate answers to the questions?

Recent research confirms that self-fulfilling prophecies often occur but also demonstrates some of the conditions under which people's true nature will win out in social situations (Jussim & Harber, 2005; Madon et al., 2001; Madon et al., 2011). For example, self-fulfilling prophecies are most likely to occur when interviewers are not paying careful attention to the person they are interviewing (Biesanz, 2001; Harris & Perkins, 1995). When interviewers are motivated to form an accurate impression and are paying attention, they are often able to put their expectations aside and see what the person is really like. Thus, Sarah should hope that the lawyer interviewing her is not too busy or pressed for time. Otherwise, she might well fall prey to the interviewer's self-fulfilling prophecies. See the preceding Try It! for a way to overcome your own self-fulfilling prophecies.

To summarize, we have seen that the amount of information we face every day is so vast that we have to reduce it to a manageable size. In addition, much of this information is ambiguous or difficult to decipher. One way we deal with this "blooming, buzzing confusion"—in William James's words—is to rely on schemas, which help us reduce the amount of information we need to take in and help us interpret ambiguous information. These schemas are applied quickly, effortlessly, and unintentionally; in short, they are one form of automatic thinking. But are they the only way that people reduce ambiguity about the world? As we will see, people also reduce ambiguity with the use of metaphors about the mind and body.

It's Not Just in Our Head: Priming Metaphors About the Body and the Mind

Suppose that, as you are leaving a store one day, a stranger approaches you and says that her purse was just stolen and asks if you could spare a couple of dollars so that she could take the bus home. On the one hand, the woman could be telling the truth and really need someone to help her out, but on the other, she could be making the whole thing up in order to get money to buy drugs or alcohol. Will you decide to help her? As we have just seen, when faced with ambiguous situations such as this one, people rely on schemas and that are accessible in their minds. If the schema of helpfulness was just primed—maybe you just saw a clerk in the store go out of her way to help someone—you will be more likely to help the stranger.

But what if we told you that your decision will also depend on whether you just smelled something fresh and clean? Suppose, for example, that some window washers were cleaning the glass outside the store and that you could smell the citrusy aroma of the cleaning solution they were using. As preposterous as it may sound, research shows that that the scent of cleanliness increases the degree to which people trust strangers and their willingness to help others (Helzer & Pizarro, 2011; Schnall, Benton, & Harvey, 2008).

It turns out that it is not just schemas that can be primed and influence people's judgments and decisions. The mind is connected to the body, and when we think about something or someone, we do so with reference to how our bodies are reacting. Sometimes this is pretty straightforward; if we are tired, for example, we might interpret the world more negatively than if we are feeling peppy and full of energy. What is less obvious is that metaphors about the body and social judgments also influence our judgments and decisions (Lakoff & Johnson, 1999; Zhong & Liljenquist, 2006). For example, cleanliness is usually associated with morality, and dirtiness with immorality, as seen by such phrases as "washing away our sins" and "dirty thoughts." These are just metaphors, of course—thoughts aren't literally dirty. But priming metaphors about the relationship between the mind and the body influence what we do and think (Landau, Meier, & Keefer, 2010).

In one study, for example, participants sat down in a room that had just been sprayed with citrus-scented Windex or in a room with no odor. As the researchers predicted, those who were in the room that smelled clean were more trusting of a stranger and more likely to donate time and money to a charity (Liljenquist, Zhong, & Galinsky, 2009). In another study, participants who held a cup of hot coffee thought that a stranger was friendlier than did participants who held a cup of iced coffee. Holding the hot or cold beverage seems to have activated the metaphor that friendly people are "warm" and unfriendly people are "cold," thereby influencing people's impression of the stranger (Williams & Bargh, 2008). In yet another study, college students who filled out a survey attached to a heavy clipboard thought that student opinion should be given more consideration on a local campus issue than did students who filled out the survey attached to a light clipboard. Why? There is a metaphor that associates weight with importance, as indicated by the phrases, "carries weight" and "adding weight to the argument." Apparently, feeling the weight of the heavy clipboard primed this metaphor, causing participants to believe that student opinion should be given more weight (Jostmann, Lakens, & Schubert, 2009).

In each of these studies, a physical sensation (smelling something clean, feeling a hot beverage, holding something heavy) activated a metaphor that influenced judgments about a completely unrelated topic or person. This research shows that it is not just schemas that can be primed in ways that influence our judgments and behavior; priming metaphors about the relationship between the mind and the body can too.

Will this person's answers to the questionnaire be influenced by how heavy the clipboard is? Why or why not?

Another form of automatic thinking is to apply specific rules and shortcuts when thinking about the social world. These shortcuts are, for the most part, extremely useful, but as we will see, they can sometimes lead to erroneous inferences about the world.

Mental Strategies and Shortcuts

Think back to your decision of where to apply to college. One strategy you might have taken was to investigate thoroughly every one of the more than 3,000 colleges and universities in the United States. You could have read every catalog from cover to cover, visited every campus, and interviewed as many faculty members, deans, and students as you could find. Getting tired yet? Such a strategy would, of course, be prohibitively time-consuming and costly. Instead of considering every college and university, most high school students narrow down their choices to a small number of options and find out what they can about these schools.

This example is like many other decisions and judgments we make in everyday life. When deciding which job to accept, what car to buy, or whom to marry, we usually do not conduct a thorough search of every option ("OK, it's time for me to get married; I think I'll consult the Census Bureau's lists of unmarried adults in my town and begin my interviews tomorrow"). Instead, we use mental strategies and shortcuts that make the decisions easier, allowing us to get on with our lives without turning every decision into a major research project. These shortcuts do not always lead to the best decision. For example, if you had exhaustively studied every college and university in the United States, maybe you would have found one that you liked better than the one where you are now. Mental shortcuts are efficient, however, and usually lead to good decisions in a reasonable amount of time (Gigerenzer, 2008; Griffin & Kahneman, 2003; Gilovich & Griffin, 2002; Kahneman, 2011; Nisbett & Ross, 1980).

What shortcuts do people use? One, as we have already seen, is to use schemas to understand new situations. Rather than starting from scratch when examining our options, we often apply our previous knowledge and schemas. We have many such schemas, about everything from colleges and universities (e.g., what Ivy League colleges and big Midwestern universities are like) to other people (e.g., teachers' beliefs about the abilities of boys versus girls). When making specific kinds of judgments and decisions, however, we do not always have a ready-made schema to apply. At other times, there are too many schemas that could apply, and it is not clear which one to use. What do we do?

At times like these, people often use mental shortcuts called **judgmental heuristics** (Gigerenzer, 2008; Shah & Oppenheimer, 2008; Tversky & Kahneman, 1974). The word *heuristic* comes from the Greek word meaning "discover"; in the field of social cognition, heuristics are the mental shortcuts people use to make judgments quickly and efficiently. Before discussing these heuristics, we should note that they do not guarantee that people will make accurate inferences about the world. Sometimes heuristics are inadequate for the job at hand or are misapplied, leading to faulty judgments. In fact, a good deal of research in social cognition has focused on just such mistakes in reasoning; we will document many such mental errors in this chapter, such as the case of teachers who mistakenly believed that boys were smarter than girls. As we discuss the mental strategies that sometimes lead to errors, however, keep in mind that people use heuristics for a reason: Most of the time, they are highly functional and serve us well.

How Easily Does It Come to Mind? The Availability Heuristic Suppose you are sitting in a restaurant with several friends one night when it becomes clear that the waiter has made a mistake with one of the orders. Your friend Alphonse ordered the veggie burger with onion rings but instead got the veggie burger with fries. "Oh, well," he says, "I'll just eat the fries." This starts a discussion of whether he should have sent back his order, and some of the gang accuse Alphonse of not being assertive enough. Suppose he turns to you and asks, "Do you think I'm an unassertive person?" How would you answer?

Judgmental Heuristics
Mental shortcuts people use to make judgments quickly and efficiently

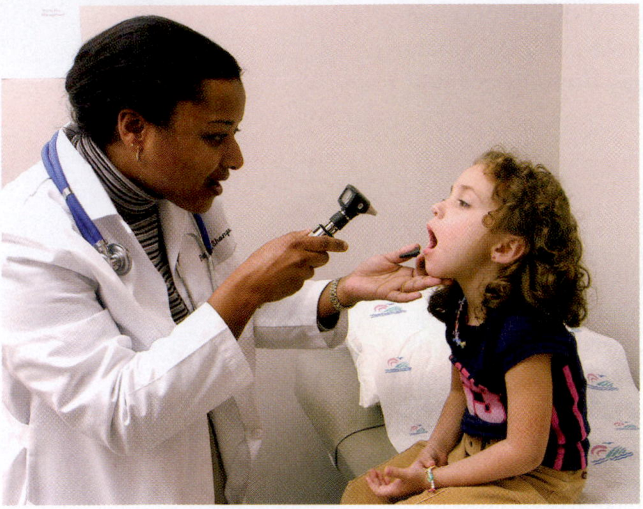

Physicians have been found to use the availability heuristic when making diagnoses. Their diagnoses are influenced by how easily they can bring different diseases to mind.

One way, as we have seen, would be to call on a ready-made schema that provides the answer. If you know Alphonse well and have already formed a picture of how assertive he is, you can recite your answer easily and quickly: "Don't worry, Alphonse, if I had to deal with a used-car salesman, you'd be the first person I'd call." Suppose, though, that you've never really thought about how assertive Alphonse is and have to think about your answer. In these situations, we often rely on how easily different examples come to mind. If it is easy to think of times Alphonse acted assertively (e.g., the time he stopped someone from butting in line in front of him at the movies), you will conclude that Alphonse is a pretty assertive guy. If it is easier to think of times Alphonse acted unassertively (e.g., the time he let a salesperson talk him into an expensive cell phone plan), you will conclude that he is pretty unassertive.

This mental rule of thumb is called the **availability heuristic**, which is basing a judgment on the ease with which you can bring something to mind (Caruso, 2008; Oppenheimer, 2004; Schwarz & Vaughn, 2002; Tversky & Kahneman, 1973). There are many situations in which the availability heuristic is a good strategy to use. If you can easily recall several instances when Alphonse stood up for himself, he probably is an assertive person; if you can easily recall several times when he was timid or meek, he probably is not. The trouble with the availability heuristic is that sometimes what is easiest to remember is not typical of the overall picture, leading to faulty conclusions.

When physicians are diagnosing diseases, for example, it might seem relatively straightforward for them to observe people's symptoms and figure out what disease, if any, they have. Sometimes, though, symptoms might be a sign of several different disorders. Do doctors use the availability heuristic, whereby they are more likely to consider diagnoses that come to mind easily? Several studies of medical diagnoses suggest that the answer is yes (Weber, 1993).

Consider Dr. Robert Marion's diagnosis of Nicole, a 9-year-old girl who came to his office one day. Nicole was normal in every way except that once or twice a year she had strange neurological attacks characterized by disorientation, insomnia, slurred words, and strange mewing sounds. Nicole had been hospitalized three times, had seen over a dozen specialists, and had undergone many diagnostic tests, including CT scans, brain-wave tests, and virtually every blood test there is. Still, the doctors were stumped. Within minutes of seeing her, however, Dr. Marion correctly diagnosed her problem as a rare inherited blood disorder called acute intermittent porphyria (AIP). The blood chemistry of people with this disorder often gets out of sync, causing a variety of neurological symptoms. It can be controlled with a careful diet and by avoiding certain medications.

How did Dr. Marion diagnose Nicole's disorder so quickly when so many other doctors failed to do so? He had just finished writing a book on the genetic diseases of historical figures, including a chapter on King George III of England, who—you guessed it—suffered from AIP. "I didn't make the diagnosis because I'm a brilliant diagnostician or because I'm a sensitive listener," Dr. Marion admitted. "I succeeded where others failed because [Nicole] and I happened to run into each other in exactly the right place, at exactly the right time" (Marion, 1995, p. 40).

In other words, Dr. Marion used the availability heuristic. AIP happened to come to mind quickly because Dr. Marion had just read about it, making the diagnosis easy. Although this was a happy outcome of the use of the availability heuristic, it is easy to see how it can go wrong. As Dr. Marion says, "Doctors are just like everyone else. We go to the movies, watch TV, read newspapers and novels. If we happen to see a patient who has symptoms of a rare disease that was featured on the previous night's 'Movie of the Week,' we're more likely to consider that condition when making a diagnosis" (Marion, 1995, p. 40). That's fine if your disease happens to be the topic of last night's movie. It's not so good if your illness isn't available in your doctor's memory, as was the case with the 12 doctors Nicole had seen previously.

Availability Heuristic

A mental rule of thumb whereby people base a judgment on the ease with which they can bring something to mind

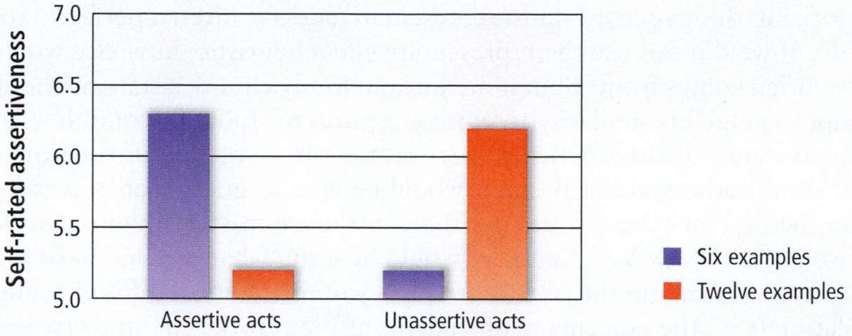

FIGURE 3.5

Availability and Assertiveness

People asked to think of 6 times they had behaved assertively found it easy to do so and concluded that they were pretty assertive people. People asked to think of 12 times they had behaved assertively found it difficult to think of so many examples and concluded that they were not very assertive people (see the left-hand side of the graph). Similar results were found among people asked to think of 6 or 12 times they had behaved unassertively (see the right-hand side of the graph). These results show that people often base their judgments on availability, or how easily they can bring information to mind.

(Adapted from Schwartz et al., 1991)

Do people use the availability heuristic to make judgments about themselves? It might seem as if we have well-developed ideas about our own personalities, such as how assertive we are, but we often lack firm schemas about our own traits (Markus, 1977). We thus might make judgments about ourselves based on how easily we can recall examples of our own behavior. To see if this is true, researchers performed a clever experiment in which they altered how easy it was for people to remember examples of their own past behaviors (Schwarz et al., 1991). In one condition, they asked people to think of 6 times they had acted assertively. Most people readily thought of times they turned down persistent salespeople and stood up for themselves. In another condition, the researchers asked people to think of 12 times they had acted assertively. This group had to try very hard to think of this many examples. All participants were then asked to rate how assertive they thought they really were.

The question was, did people use the availability heuristic (the ease with which they could bring examples to mind) to infer how assertive they were? As seen on the left side of Figure 3.5, they did. People asked to think of six examples rated themselves as relatively assertive because it was easy to think of this many examples. People asked to think of 12 examples rated themselves as relatively unassertive because it was difficult to think of that many. Other people were asked to think of 6 or 12 times they had acted unassertively, and similar results were found; those asked to think of six examples rated themselves as relatively unassertive (see the right side of Figure 3.5). In short, people use the availability heuristic when making judgments about themselves and other people (Caruso, 2008). Recently, a devious college professor used this technique to improve his course evaluations. He asked his students to list either 2 or 10 ways that the course could be improved and then to rate their overall impression of the course. Who gave the course the highest ratings? Those asked to list 10 ways it could be improved, because they found it hard to think of that many ways in which the course was lacking and thought, "If I can't come up with that many criticisms, it must be a great course!" (Fox, 2006).

How Similar Is A to B? The Representativeness Heuristic Suppose you attend a state university in New York. At the student union one day, you meet a student named Brian. Brian has blond hair and a deep tan, seems to be very mellow, and likes to go to the beach. What state do you think Brian is from? Because Brian matches a common stereotype for Californians, you might guess that he is from there. If so, you would be using the **representativeness heuristic**, which is a mental shortcut we use to classify something according to how similar it is to a typical case—such as how similar Brian is to your conception of Californians (Gilovich & Savitsky, 2002; Kahneman & Tversky, 1973; Kahneman & Frederick, 2002; Spina et al., 2010).

Representativeness Heuristic

A mental shortcut whereby people classify something according to how similar it is to a typical case

Categorizing things according to representativeness is often a perfectly reasonable thing to do. If we did not use the representativeness heuristic, how else would we decide where Brian comes from? Should we just randomly choose a state, without making any attempt to judge his similarity to our conception of students from New York State versus out-of-state students? Actually, there is another source of information we might use. If we knew nothing about Brian, it would be wise to guess that he was from New York State, because at state universities there are more in-state than out-of-state students. If we guessed New York State, we would be using what is called **base rate information**, information about the relative frequency of members of different categories in the population (e.g., the percentage of students at New York state universities who are from New York).

What do people do when they have both base rate information (e.g., knowing that there are more New Yorkers than Californians at a university) and contradictory information about the person in question (e.g., knowing that Brian is blond and mellow and likes to hang out at the beach)? Kahneman and Tversky (1973) found that people do not use base rate information sufficiently, paying most attention to how representative the information about the specific person is of the general category (e.g., Californians). Although this is not a bad strategy if the information about the person is very reliable, it can get us into trouble when the information is flimsy. Given that the base rate of Californians attending state universities in New York is low, you would need to have very good evidence that this person is a Californian before ignoring the base rate and guessing that he is one of the few exceptions. And given that it is not that unusual to find people from eastern states who have blond hair, are laid-back, and like to go to the beach, you would be wise to use the base rate in this instance.

We don't mean to imply that people totally ignore base rate information (Koehler, 1993, 1996). Baseball managers consider the overall likelihood of left-handed batters getting a hit off of left-handed pitchers when deciding whom to send up as a pinch hitter, and birdwatchers consider the prevalence of different species of birds in their area when identifying individual birds ("That probably wasn't a bay-breasted warbler, because they've never been seen in this area"). The point is that people often focus too much on individual characteristics of what they observe ("But it did seem to have a chestnut-colored throat; hmm, maybe it was a bay-breasted warbler") and too little on the base rates.

Simulate on **MyPsychLab**

To learn more about heuristics, try the MyPsychLab simulation ***Anchoring and Adjustment.***

Throughout history, for example, people have assumed that the cure for a disease must resemble—be representative of—the symptoms of the disease, even when this wasn't the case. At one time, eating the lungs of a fox was thought to be a cure for asthma, because foxes have a strong respiratory system (Mill, 1843). Such a reliance on representativeness may even impede the discovery of the actual cause of a disease. Around the turn of the twentieth century, an editorial in a Washington newspaper denounced the foolhardy use of federal funds to research far-fetched ideas about the causes of yellow fever, such as the absurd contention of one Walter Reed that yellow fever was caused by, of all things, a mosquito (Nisbett & Ross, 1980). How do heuristics influence your thinking? Take the quiz in the following Try It! to find out.

The Power of Unconscious Thinking

Part of the definition of automatic thinking is that it occurs unconsciously. Although it might seem magical that we can think without being aware that we are thinking, social psychologists are increasingly reaching the conclusion that we can do just that (Bargh & Morsella, 2008; Bos & Dijksterhuis, 2012; Dijksterhuis & Nordgren, 2006; Hassin, Uleman, & Bargh, 2005; Wilson, 2002). If we had to rely on slow, conscious thinking alone, we would be in a pickle, because we often need to make very fast decisions about what is happening around us, what to pay attention to, and which of our goals to pursue. We would be left scratching our heads while the world whizzed by. True enough, these fast, unconscious processes can sometimes lead to errors. Most of the time, however, unconscious thinking is critical to navigating our way through the world.

Base Rate Information

Information about the frequency of members of different categories in the population

CONNECTIONS

Personality Tests and the Representativeness Heuristic

Suppose you took a personality test, such as one of the many that are available online, and received the following feedback:

> You have a need for other people to like and admire you, and yet you tend to be critical of yourself. While you have some personality weaknesses, you are generally able to compensate for them. You have considerable unused capacity that you have not turned to your advantage. Disciplined and self-controlled on the outside, you tend to be worrisome and insecure on the inside. At times you have serious doubts as to whether you have made the right decision or done the right thing. You prefer a certain amount of change and variety and become dissatisfied when hemmed in by restrictions and limitations. You also pride yourself as an independent thinker and do not accept others' statements without satisfactory proof. But you have found it unwise to be too frank in revealing yourself to others. At times you are extroverted, affable, and sociable, while at other times you are introverted, wary, and reserved. Some of your aspirations tend to be rather unrealistic.

"Wow," you might think. "This test is amazing; it is uncanny how well it captured who I am." If so, you are not alone. Bertram Forer (1949) gave this feedback to a group of students and asked them to rate how well it described them, on a scale from 0 = very poor to 5 = excellent. The average rating was 4.26—a phenomenon that has come to be known as the "Barnum effect" after the circus owner and showman P. T. Barnum.

Why do most people believe that this personality description describes them so well? One culprit is the representativeness heuristic: The statements are vague enough that virtually everyone can find a past behavior that is similar to (representative of) the feedback. Consider the statement, "At times you have serious doubts as to whether you have made the right decision or done the right thing." All of us can think of times this was true of us—that is, of examples that are representative of this statement. Who hasn't second-guessed themselves about an important decision, such as where to go to college or what major to choose? Similarly, all of us can think of times when we were independent thinkers and times when we revealed too much about ourselves. The reason the feedback seems to describe us so well is that we do not go beyond the representative examples that come to mind and think, "Actually, there are just as many times when I didn't feel or act this way."

TRY IT! Reasoning Quiz

Answer each of the following questions.

1. Consider the letter *r* in the English language. Do you think this letter occurs more often as the first letter of words (e.g., *rope*) or more often as the third letter of words (e.g., *park*)?
   - **a.** more often as the first letter
   - **b.** more often as the third letter
   - **c.** about equally often as the first and as the third letter
2. Which of these do you think cause more fatalities in the United States?
   - **a.** accidents
   - **b.** strokes
   - **c.** accidents and strokes in approximately equal numbers
3. Suppose you flipped a fair coin 6 times. Which sequence is more likely to occur: HTTHTH or HHHTTT? (H = heads, T = tails)?
   - **a.** HTTHTH is more likely.
   - **b.** HHHTTT is more likely.
   - **c.** Both sequences are equally likely.
4. After flipping a coin and observing the sequence TTTTT, what is the probability that the next flip will be heads?
   - **a.** less than .5
   - **b.** .5
   - **c.** greater than .5

See page 73 for the answers.

Research has found that people's goals can be activated unconsciously by their recent experiences. For example, someone who walks by a church might have the "Golden Rule" activated without knowing it, making him or her more likely to give money to a homeless person.

Have you ever been chatting with someone at a party and suddenly realized that someone across the room has mentioned your name? The only way this could happen is if, while you were engrossed in conversation, you were unconsciously monitoring other conversations to see if something important came up (such as your name). This so-called "cocktail party" effect has been demonstrated under controlled experimental conditions (Harris & Pashler, 2004; Koch et al., 2011; Moray, 1959).

Another example of unconscious thinking is when we have competing goals and are not sure which one to act on. Suppose, for example, that you are taking a difficult math course in which the professor grades on a curve, guaranteeing that only a few people will get As. A classmate you don't know very well tells you he is having difficulty with some of the material and asks whether you can have coffee and go over your class notes with him. On the one hand, you want to be helpful, satisfying your goal to be a caring, compassionate person. On the other hand, you want to satisfy your goal of doing well in the class and are hesitant to hurt your chances by raising someone else's grade. Which goal do you act on? You could mull this over for a while, consciously weighing your options. Often, however, it is our nonconscious minds that choose the goal for us, basing the decision in part on which goal has been recently activated or primed (Aarts, Custers, & Holland, 2007; Bargh et al., 2001; Förster, Liberman, & Friedman, 2007; Hassin, in press).

Social psychologists have tested this hypothesis by priming people's goals in a subtle way and then seeing if it influences their behavior. In a study by Azim Shariff and Ara Norenzayan (2007), for example, participants were asked to make sentences out of sets of provided words—such as *felt*, *she*, *eradicate*, *spirit*, and *the*—from which they could make a sentence like "She felt the spirit." Next, as part of what was supposedly a different study, participants played an economics game in which they were given ten $1 coins and asked to divide them up between themselves and the next participant. Only the next participant would know what they decided, and that participant wouldn't know who they were. Think for a moment what you would do in this situation. Here's an opportunity to make a quick 10 bucks, and there is a definite temptation to pocket all the coins. But you might feel a little guilty hoarding all the money and leaving nothing for the next person. This is one of those situations in which there is a devil on one of our shoulders ("Don't be a fool—take it all!") and an angel on the other ("Do unto others as you would have them do unto you"). In short, people want the money, but this conflicts with their goal to be nice to others. Which goal wins out?

> *Outside consciousness there rolls a vast tide of life which is perhaps more important to us than the little isle of our thoughts which lies within our ken.*
>
> —E. S. Dallas (1866)

It depends in part on which goal has been recently primed. Remember the sentence-unscrambling task people did first? For some participants, the words people were given had to do with God (spirit, divine, God, sacred, and prophet), which were designed to prime the goal of acting kindly to one's neighbor. In the control condition, people got neutral words. An important detail is that participants did not make a connection between the sentence-making task and the economics game—they thought the two tasks were completely unrelated. Even so, the people who made sentences out of the words having to do with God left significantly more money for the next participant ($4.56 on average) than did people who got the neutral words ($2.56 on average). And it turned out that it was not just words about God that primed the goal of being more altruistic. In a third condition, the sentence task contained nonreligious words that had to do with fairness to others, such as *civic* and *contract*. People in this condition left nearly as much money for the next person as did people primed with God words ($4.44 on average). Studies such as this one show that goals can be activated and influence people's behavior without their knowing it, because people didn't realize that the words they got in the first task had anything to do with their decision about how to divide the money in the second task. The moral? Your decision about whether to help your classmate in your math class might depend on which goals have recently been primed. If you had just walked by your place of worship, for example, or read a book in which people were kind to others, you might be especially likely to help your classmate.

Cultural Differences in Social Cognition

It may have occurred to you to wonder whether the kinds of automatic thinking we have been discussing are present in all people throughout the world, or whether they are more common in some cultures than in others. If so, you are in good company; social psychologists have become increasingly interested in the influence of culture on social cognition.

Cultural Determinants of Schemas Although everyone uses schemas to understand the world, the *content* of our schemas is influenced by the culture in which we live. One researcher, for example, interviewed a Scottish settler and a local Bantu herdsman in Swaziland, a small country in southeastern Africa (Bartlett, 1932). Both men had been present at a complicated cattle transaction that had occurred a year earlier. The Scottish man needed to consult his records to recall how many cattle were bought and sold and for how much. The Bantu man promptly recited from memory every detail of the transaction, including from whom each ox and cow had been bought, the color of each animal, and the price of each transaction. The Bantu people's memory for cattle is so good that they do not bother to brand them; if a cow happens to wander away and get mixed up with a neighbor's herd, the owner simply goes over and takes it back, having no trouble distinguishing his animal from the dozens of others.

Clearly, an important source of our schemas is the culture in which we grow up. Cattle are a central part of the Bantu economy and culture, and therefore the Bantu have well-developed schemas about cattle. To an American, one cow might look like any other, though this person might have well-developed schemas, and hence an excellent memory, for transactions on the New York Stock Exchange or the latest contestants on *American Idol*. Schemas are a very important way by which cultures exert their influence—namely, by instilling mental structures that influence the very way we understand and interpret the world. In Chapter 5, we will see that people in different cultures have fundamentally different schemas about themselves and the social world, with some interesting consequences (Wang & Ross, 2007). For now, we point out that the schemas our culture teaches us strongly influence what we notice and remember about the world.

Take a quick look at these two photos and see if you notice any differences between them. As discussed in the text, the differences you notice may have to do with the culture in which you grew up.

Holistic Versus Analytic Thinking Culture influences social cognition in other fundamental ways. An analogy that is often used is that the human mind is like a toolbox filled with specific tools to help people think about and act in the social world. All humans have access to the same tools, but the culture in which they grow up can influence the ones they use the most (Norenzayan & Heine, 2005). If you live in a house that has screws instead of nails, you will use your screwdriver more than a hammer, but if your house contains nails and not screws, the screwdriver won't get much use.

By the same token, culture can influence the kinds of thinking people automatically use to understand their worlds. Not *all* kinds of thinking, mind you. The kinds of automatic thinking we have discussed so far, such as unconscious thinking and the use of schemas, appear to be used by all humans. But some basic ways in which people typically perceive and think about the world *are* shaped by culture. To illustrate these differences, take a quick look at the top picture on this page. Okay, now take a quick look at the picture right beneath it: Did you notice any differences between the two pictures? Your answer might depend on the culture in which you grew up. Richard Nisbett and his colleagues have found that people who grow up in Western cultures tend to have an **analytic thinking style**, a type of thinking in which people focus on the properties of objects without considering their surrounding context. For example, Westerners are most likely to focus on the planes because they are the main objects in the pictures. They are thus more likely to notice differences in these objects, such as the fact that the passenger plane has more windows in the second picture than in the first (Masuda & Nisbett, 2006). People who grow up in East Asian cultures (e.g., China, Japan, or Korea) tend to have a **holistic thinking style**, a type of thinking in which people focus on the overall context, particularly the ways in which objects relate to each other (Nisbett, 2003; Nisbett, 2001; Norenzayan & Nisbett, 2000).

For example, East Asians are more likely to notice differences in the backgrounds of the pictures, such as the fact that the shape of the control tower changes from one to the other. (Note that in the actual study, people saw 20-second videos of these scenes and tried to find all the differences between them. The pictures on the previous page are the last scenes from these two videos.) In Chapter 4, we will see that these differences in thinking styles also influence how we perceive emotions in other people. Suppose, for example, that you ran into a classmate who was surrounded by a group of friends. If you grew up in the West, you would likely focus only on your classmate's face (the object of your attention) to judge how he or she is feeling. If you grew up in East Asia, you would likely scan everyone's faces in the group (the overall context) and use this information to judge how your classmate is feeling (Masuda, Ellsworth, & Mesquita, 2008).

Where do these differences in holistic versus analytic thinking come from? Richard Nisbett (2003) suggests that they are rooted in the different philosophical traditions of the East versus West. Eastern thought has been shaped by the ideas of Confucianism, Taoism, and Buddhism, which emphasize the connectedness and relativity of all things. Western thought is rooted in the Greek philosophical tradition of Aristotle and Plato, which focuses on the laws governing objects, independent of their context. Recent research suggests, however, that the different thinking styles might also stem from actual differences in the environments in the different cultures. Yuri Miyamoto, Richard Nisbett, and Takahiko Masuda took photographs in randomly chosen city scenes in Japan and the United States. They matched the scenes as best they could; for example, the sizes of the cities were equivalent, as were the buildings that were photographed in each city (e.g., hotels and public elementary schools). The researchers hypothesized that the scenes in the Japanese cities would be "busier"—that is, they would contain more objects that competed for people's attention—than the scenes in the American cities. They were right. The Japanese scenes contained significantly more information and objects than the American scenes.

Could this be one reason why Americans focus more on a foreground object, whereas East Asians focus more on the overall context? To find out, Miyamoto and his colleagues did a second study in which they showed the pictures of American or Japanese cities to a sample of American and Japanese college students. The students were asked to imagine that they were in the scene depicted in the each picture, with the idea that the Japanese pictures would prime holistic thinking, whereas the American pictures would prime analytic thinking. Then the students completed the same airplane picture task described above, in which they tried to detect the differences between two similar pictures. As predicted, the people who saw the photos of Japanese cities were more likely to detect changes in the *background* of the test pictures, whereas people who saw the pictures of the American cities were more likely to detect changes in the *main object* of the pictures. This finding suggests that people in all cultures are capable of thinking holistically or analytically (they have the same tools in their mental toolbox), but that the environment in which people live, or even which environment has been recently primed, triggers a reliance on one of the styles (Boduroglu, Shah, & Nisbett, 2009; Cheung, Chudek, & Heine, 2011; Norenzayan, Choi, & Peng, 2007; Varnum et al., 2010). ◉

Analytic Thinking Style

A type of thinking in which people focus on the properties of objects without considering their surrounding context; this type of thinking is common in Western cultures

Holistic Thinking Style

A type of thinking in which people focus on the overall context, particularly the ways in which objects relate to each other; this type of thinking is common in East Asian cultures (e.g., China, Japan, and Korea)

◉ **Watch** on **MyPsychLab**

To learn more about cultural influences on social cognition, watch the MyPsychLab video *Cultural Psychology: Kaiping Peng.*

Controlled Social Cognition: High-Effort Thinking

It may have struck you as odd that we have spent so much of this chapter on automatic thinking, when controlled thinking is one of the hallmarks of what it is to be human. We are the only species (as far as we know) that has the ability to engage in conscious reflection about ourselves and the outside world, and we often use that ability to great purpose, solving difficult problems and planning for the future. After all, we are the species that has discovered the cures for fatal diseases, built architectural wonders, and put people on the moon. And we did so at least in part with **controlled thinking**, which is defined as thinking that is conscious, intentional, voluntary, and effortful. People can usually turn this on or turn off at will and are fully aware of what they are thinking. Further, this kind of thought is effortful in the sense that it requires mental energy. People have the capacity to think in a conscious, controlled way about only one thing at a time; they cannot be thinking about what they will eat for lunch today at the same time they are thinking through a complex math problem (Weber & Johnson, 2009).

So why so much emphasis on automatic thinking? The reason is that in the past few decades, social psychologists have discovered that this kind of thinking is much more powerful and prevalent than previously believed. As we saw earlier in this chapter, people's ability to think quickly and nonconsciously is quite impressive and is critical to our survival. Nonetheless, some social psychologists believe that the pendulum has swung too far in favor of automatic thinking and that we have underestimated the value and power of controlled thinking (Baumeister & Masicampo, 2010; Baumeister, Masicampo, & Vohs, 2011). A lively debate has ensued over the relative importance of each type of thought.

Controlled Thinking and Free Will

My first act of free will shall be to believe in free will.
—William James

One focus of this debate is on the age-old question of free will. Do we really have control over our actions, such that we can freely choose what to do at any given point in time? Maybe not as much as we think, if our behavior is under the control of automatic thought processes of which we are unaware.

"Well," you might reply, "I know that I have free will because I can decide right now whether to scratch my head, close this book, or stand up and dance like a chicken." Are you done with your chicken dance now? If so, consider this: Although it certainly seems like our ability to choose what we do demonstrates the existence of free will, it turns out that it is not that simple. Daniel Wegner (2002, 2004; Preston & Wegner, 2007) demonstrated that there can be an *illusion* of free will that is very much like the "correlation does not equal causation" problem we discussed in Chapter 2. Your thought "I think I'll do the chicken dance now" and your subsequent behavior (flapping your arms and hopping around the room) are correlated, making it seem like the thought caused the action. But they might actually have been produced by a third variable—namely an unconscious intention that caused both the conscious thought and the behavior.

Perhaps an example other than chicken dancing will make this clearer. Suppose you are sitting on the couch watching television and have the thought, "A bowl of ice cream sure would taste good right now." So you get up and go to the freezer and scoop out a serving of your favorite flavor. But maybe, as you were watching television, the desire for ice cream arose unconsciously first (perhaps primed by something you saw in a commercial). This unconscious desire led both to the conscious thought that you wanted ice cream and to your decision to get up and go to the freezer. In other words, the conscious thought "I want ice cream" was a consequence of an unconscious process, and was not the cause of your decision to go to the freezer. After all, sometimes people find themselves on the way to the refrigerator *without* having had the conscious thought that it was time for a snack. Their unconscious desire triggered the action without any intervening conscious thought.

Controlled Thinking
Thinking that is conscious, intentional, voluntary, and effortful

Facilitated communication was developed to allow communication-impaired people to express themselves. Unfortunately, it appears to be the case that the facilitators were unwittingly controlling the communications.

As another example, have you ever seen children in a video arcade furiously working the controls, believing that they are playing the game, when in fact they never put money in the machine and are watching the demonstration program? Occasionally, when the children pushed the controls in one direction, the game did appear to respond to the commands, making it hard for the children to realize that in fact they had no control over what was happening (Wegner, 2002). Adults are not immune from such illusions of control. People who are able to choose their lottery numbers, for example, are more confident that they will win than people who are assigned numbers (Langer, 1975). And what sports fans haven't felt that they have helped their favorite team by crossing their fingers or donning their lucky hat at a key moment in the game?

As these examples show, people sometimes believe that they are exerting more control over events than they really are. But it can also work the other way: People can actually be controlling things more than they realize. A number of years ago, a new technique called facilitated communication was developed to allow communication-impaired people, such as those with autism and cerebral palsy, to express themselves. A trained facilitator held the fingers and arm of a communication-impaired client at a computer keyboard to make it easier for the client to type answers to questions. This technique caused great excitement. People who had been unable to communicate with the outside world suddenly became quite verbose, voicing all sorts of thoughts and feelings with the aid of the facilitator—or so it seemed. Parents were thrilled by the sudden opportunity to communicate with their previously silent children.

Facilitated communication was soon discredited when it became clear that it was not the communication-impaired person who was doing the typing but, unwittingly, the facilitator. In one well-designed study, researchers asked separate questions over headphones of the facilitator and the communication-impaired person. The facilitator might have heard, "How do you feel about today's weather?" while the communication-impaired person heard, "How did you like your lunch today?" The answers that were typed matched the questions the facilitator heard (e.g., "I wish it were sunnier"), not the ones posed to the communication-impaired client (Mostert, 2010; Wegner, Fuller, & Sparrow, 2003; Wegner, Sparrow, & Winerman, 2004; Wheeler et al., 1993). The facilitators were not deliberately faking it; they genuinely believed that it was the communication-impaired person who was choosing what to type and that they were simply helping them move their fingers on the keyboard.

These examples illustrate that there can be a disconnect between our conscious sense of how much we are causing our own actions and how much we really are causing them. Sometimes we overestimate the amount of control we have, as when we believe that wearing our lucky hat will help our favorite sports team score a goal. Sometimes we underestimate the amount of control we have, as was the case with the facilitators who thought it was the client choosing what to type when they were unconsciously doing it themselves (Wegner, 2002).

Why does it matter what people believe? It turns out that the extent to which people believe they have free will has important consequences (Baumeister, Mele, & Vohs, 2010; Nichols, 2011). The more people believe in free will, for example, the more willing they are to help others in need and the less likely they are to engage in immoral actions such as cheating (Baumeister, Masicampo, & Dewall, 2009). In one study, college students either read a series of statements that implied the existence of free will, such as "I am able to overcome the genetic and environmental factors that sometimes influence my behavior," or a series of statements that implied the absence of free will, such as "Ultimately, we are biological computers—designed by evolution, built through genetics, and programmed by the environment" (Vohs & Schooler, 2008, p. 51). Next, all participants took a test composed of items from the Graduate Record Exam (GRE), scored their own tests, and paid themselves $1 for every correct answer. At least that is what participants were supposed to do. The question was, did some participants cheat and take extra money, beyond what they had actually earned? It turned out that people cheated significantly more when they read the statements implying that there is no free will than when they read the statements implying that there is free will. Why? When experiencing temptation, people who believe that they can control their actions probably exert more effort to do so, thinking, "I could easily steal some money, but I can control what I do, so it's up to me to be strong and do the right thing." In contrast, people who believe that there is no free will think, "I want the money, and I'm not really in control of my actions, so I might as well just go with that impulse." Thus, regardless of how much free will human beings *really* have, it is in society's best interest for us all to *believe* that we have it. (See the Try It! below for a demonstration of how much free will people think they have compared to other people.)

Counterfactual Thinking

Mentally changing some aspect of the past as a way of imagining what might have been

Mentally Undoing the Past: Counterfactual Reasoning

Another important question about controlled thinking is when people do it. When do we go off automatic pilot and think about things more slowly and consciously? One circumstance is when we experience a negative event that was a "close call," such as failing a test by just a point or two. Under these conditions, we engage in **counterfactual thinking**, which is mentally changing some aspect of the past as a way of imagining

TRY IT! Can You Predict Your (or Your Friend's) Future?

A. Please answer the following questions about *yourself*. In each row, circle *one* of the three possible options, according to which one best captures the genuine possibilities for what might happen during the year after you graduate from college.

1. have an exciting job or be in an exciting graduate program	have a boring job or be in a boring graduate program	both are possible
2. live in a really nice apartment or house	live in a really crappy apartment or house	both are possible
3. be in a long-term relationship	be single	both are possible
4. travel to Europe	not travel to Europe	both are possible
5. do something useful	waste time	both are possible
6. keep in close contact with my college friends	not keep in close contact with my college friends	both are possible

B. Please answer the following questions about *a college friend of your choosing*. In each row, circle *one* of the three possible options, according to which one best captures the genuine possibilities for what might happen during the year after he/she graduates from college.

1. have an exciting job or be in an exciting graduate program	have a boring job or be in a boring graduate program	both are possible
2. live in a really nice apartment or house	live in a really crappy apartment or house	both are possible
3. be in a long-term relationship	be single	both are possible
4. travel to Europe	not travel to Europe	both are possible
5. do something useful	waste time	both are possible
6. keep in close contact with his/her college friends	not keep in close contact with his/her college friends	both are possible

See page 73 for an explanation of how to interpret your answers.

Who do you think would be happier: someone who won a silver medal at the Olympics or someone who won a bronze? Surprisingly, research shows that silver medalists are often less happy, because they can more easily imagine how they might have come in first and won a gold.

what might have been (Kahneman & Miller, 1986; Markman et al., 2009; Roese, 1997; Tetlock, 2002; Wong, Galinsky, & Kray, 2009). "If only I had answered that one question differently," you might think, "I would have passed the test."

Counterfactual thoughts can have a big influence on our emotional reactions to events. The easier it is to mentally undo an outcome, the stronger the emotional reaction to it (Camille et al., 2004; Miller & Taylor, 2002; Niedenthal, Tangney, & Gavanski, 1994). One group of researchers, for example, interviewed people who had suffered the loss of a spouse or child. As expected, the more people imagined ways in which the tragedy could have been averted, by mentally undoing the circumstances preceding it, the more distress they reported (Davis et al., 1995; Branscombe et al., 1996).

Sometimes the emotional consequences of counterfactual reasoning are paradoxical. For example, who do you think would be happier: an Olympic athlete who won a silver medal (came in second) or an Olympic athlete who won a bronze medal (came in third)? Surely the one who got the silver, because they did better! Actually it is the reverse, because the silver medal winner can more easily imagine having won the event and therefore engages in more counterfactual reasoning—especially if the silver medalist expected to do better than the bronze medalist (McGraw, Mellers, & Tetlock, 2005). To test these hypotheses, Medvec, Madey, and Gilovich (1995) analyzed videotapes of the 1992 Olympics. Both immediately after their event and while they received their medals, silver medal winners appeared less happy than bronze medal winners. And during interviews with reporters, silver medal winners engaged in more counterfactual reasoning by saying things like, "I almost pulled it off; it's too bad." The moral seems to be that if you are going to lose, it is best not to lose by a slim margin.

Earlier we described controlled thinking as conscious, intentional, voluntary, and effortful. But like automatic thinking, different kinds of controlled thought meet these requirements to different degrees. Counterfactual reasoning is clearly conscious and effortful; we know we are obsessing about the past, and this kind of thinking often takes up so much mental energy that we cannot think about anything else. It is not, however, always intentional or voluntary. Even when we want to stop dwelling on the past and move on to something else, it can be difficult to turn off the kind of "if only" thinking that characterizes counterfactual reasoning (Andrade & Van Boven, 2010; Goldionger, 2003).

This is not so good if counterfactual thinking results in rumination, whereby people repetitively focus on negative things in their lives. Rumination has been found to be a contributor to depression (Lyubomirsky, Caldwell, & Nolen-Hoeksema, 1993; Watkins, 2008). Thus, it is not advisable to ruminate constantly about a bad test grade to the point where you can't think about anything else. Counterfactual thinking can be useful, however, if it focuses people's attention on ways they can cope better in the future. Thinking such thoughts as "If only I had studied a little harder, I would have passed the test" can be beneficial, to the extent that it gives people a heightened sense of control over their fate and motivates them to study harder for the next test (Nasco & Marsh, 1999; Roese & Olson, 1997).

Improving Human Thinking

The greatest of all faults, I should say, is to become conscious of none.

—Thomas Carlyle

One purpose of controlled thinking is to provide checks and balances for automatic thinking. Just as an airline captain can turn off the automatic pilot and take control of the plane when trouble occurs, controlled thinking takes over when unusual events occur. How successful are people at correcting their mistakes? How can they be taught to do better?

One approach is to make people a little more humble about their reasoning abilities. Often we have greater confidence in our judgments than we should (Buehler, Griffin, & Ross, 2002; Juslin, Winman, & Hansson, 2007; Merkle & Weber, 2011; Vallone et al., 1990). Teachers, for example, sometimes have greater confidence than is warranted in their beliefs about the abilities of boys versus girls. Anyone trying to improve human inference is thus up against an **overconfidence barrier** (Metcalfe, 1998). One approach, then, might be to address this overconfidence directly, getting people to consider the possibility that they might be wrong. This tack was taken by one team of researchers (Lord, Lepper, & Preston, 1984). They found that when asked to consider the opposite point of view to their own, people realized there were other ways to construe the world than their own way; consequently, they made fewer errors in judgment (Anderson, Lepper, & Ross, 1980; Hirt, Kardes, & Markman, 2004; Mussweiler, Strack, & Pfeiffer, 2000).

Overconfidence Barrier
The fact that people usually have too much confidence in the accuracy of their judgments

The sign of a first-rate intelligence is the ability to hold two opposed ideas at the same time.
—F. Scott Fitzgerald

Another approach is to directly teach people some basic statistical and methodological principles about how to reason correctly, with the hope that they will apply these principles in their everyday lives. Many of these principles are already taught in courses in statistics and research design, such as the idea that if you want to generalize from a sample of information (e.g., a group of welfare mothers) to a population (e.g., all welfare mothers), you must have a large, unbiased sample. Do people who take such courses apply these principles in their everyday lives? Are they less likely to make the kinds of mistakes we have discussed in this chapter? A number of studies have provided encouraging answers to these questions, showing that people's reasoning processes can be improved by college statistics courses, graduate training in research design, and even brief onetime lessons (Crandall & Greenfield, 1986; Malloy, 2001; Nisbett et al., 1987; Schaller, 1996).

TRY IT! How Well Do You Reason?

1. The city of Middleopolis has had an unpopular police chief for a year and a half. He is a political appointee who is a crony of the mayor, and he had little previous experience in police administration when he was appointed. The mayor has recently defended the chief in public, announcing that in the time since he took office, crime rates have decreased by 12%. Which of the following pieces of evidence would most deflate the mayor's claim that his chief is competent?
   a. The crime rates of the two cities closest to Middleopolis in location and size have decreased by 18% in the same period.
   b. An independent survey of the citizens of Middleopolis shows that 40% more crime is reported by respondents in the survey than is reported in police records.
   c. Common sense indicates that there is little a police chief can do to lower crime rates. These are for the most part due to social and economic conditions beyond the control of officials.
   d. The police chief has been discovered to have business contacts with people who are known to be involved in organized crime.
2. After the first 2 weeks of the major league baseball season, newspapers begin to print the top 10 batting averages. Typically, after 2 weeks, the leading batter has an average of about .450. Yet no batter in major league history has ever averaged .450 at the end of a season. Why do you think this is?
   a. A player's high average at the beginning of the season may be just a lucky fluke.
   b. A batter who has such a hot streak at the beginning of the season is under a lot of stress to maintain his performance record. Such stress adversely affects his playing.
   c. Pitchers tend to get better over the course of the season as they get more in shape. As pitchers improve, they are more likely to strike out batters, so batters' averages go down.
   d. When a batter is known to be hitting for a high average, pitchers bear down more when they pitch to him.
   e. When a batter is known to be hitting for a high average, he stops getting good pitches to hit. Instead, pitchers "play the corners" of the plate because they don't mind walking him.

See page 73 for the answers.

(Questions from Lehman, Lempert, & Nisbett, 1988, p. 442)

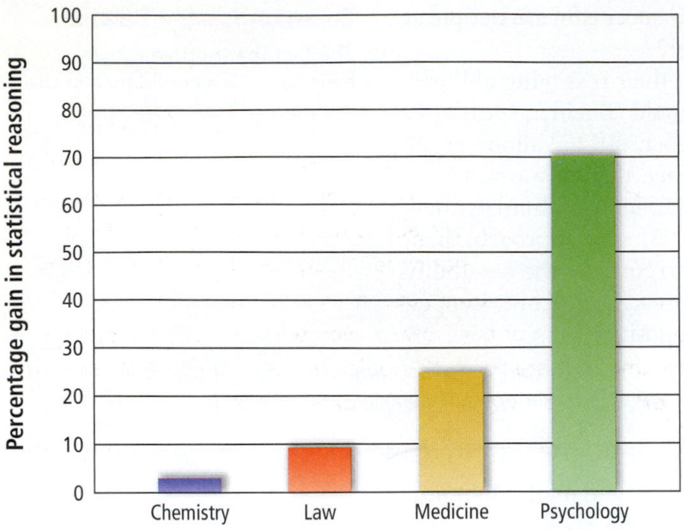

FIGURE 3.6

Performance on a Test of Statistical Reasoning Abilities by Graduate Students in Different Disciplines

After 2 years of graduate study, students in psychology and medicine showed more improvement on statistical reasoning problems than students in law and chemistry did.

(Adapted from Nisbett, Fong, Lehman, & Cheng, 1987)

Richard Nisbett and his colleagues (1987), for example, examined how different kinds of graduate training influenced people's reasoning on everyday problems involving statistical and methodological reasoning—precisely the kind of reasoning we have considered in this chapter, such as people's understanding of how to generalize from small samples of information (see the Try It! on the previous page for sample questions). The researchers predicted that students in psychology and medicine would do better on the statistical reasoning problems than students in law and chemistry would, because graduate programs in psychology and medicine include more training in statistics than programs in the other two disciplines do.

As Figure 3.6 shows, after 2 years of graduate work, students in psychology and medicine improved on the statistical reasoning problems more than students in law and chemistry did. The improvement among the psychology graduate students was particularly impressive. Interestingly, the students in the different disciplines performed equally well on sample items from the Graduate Record Exam, suggesting that they did not differ in overall intelligence. Instead, the different kinds of training they had received appeared to influence how accurately and logically they reasoned on everyday problems (Nisbett et al., 1987). Thus, there are grounds for being optimistic about people's ability to overcome the kinds of mistakes we have documented in this chapter. And you don't have to go to graduate school to do it. Sometimes it helps simply to consider the opposite, as participants in the Lord and colleagues' (1984) study did. Beyond this, formal training in statistics helps, at both the graduate and undergraduate levels. So if you were dreading taking a college statistics course, take heart: It might not only satisfy a requirement for your major, but improve your reasoning as well!

Watson Revisited

By now we have seen two very different modes of social cognition: one that is effortless, involuntary, unintentional, and unconscious (automatic thinking) and another that is more effortful, voluntary, intentional, and conscious (controlled thinking). As we mentioned at the beginning of the chapter, these two kinds of thought, in combination, are extremely powerful, particularly when it comes to understanding the social world. The IBM computer Watson may have succeeded on the TV show *Jeopardy!*, but we wouldn't recommend that you ask Watson to find you a romantic partner, raise your children, or help you negotiate a difficult business deal.

But as we've seen in this chapter, social cognition is by no means perfect. People make mistakes in reasoning, even to the point of unintentionally acting in ways to make their faulty theories come true (the self-fulfilling prophecy). How can we reconcile the fact that human beings have amazing cognitive abilities that have resulted in dazzling cultural and intellectual achievements but at the same time are prone to making consequential mental errors like the ones documented in this chapter?

Watch on **MyPsychLab**
To learn how children develop social cognition, watch the MyPsychLab video ***Development of Social Cognition.***

The best portrait of the social thinker is this: Whereas people are very sophisticated social thinkers who have amazing cognitive abilities, there is also plenty of room for improvement. The shortcomings of social thinking can be quite significant, as demonstrated by examples in this chapter and in later ones (e.g., racial prejudice—see Chapter 13). An apt metaphor for human thinking is that people are like "flawed scientists," brilliant thinkers who are attempting to discover the nature of the social world in a logical manner but who do so imperfectly. People are often blind to truths that don't fit their schemas and sometimes treat others in ways that make their schemas come true—something good scientists would never do.

USE IT!

By definition it is hard to recognize our own automatic thinking, because it is nonconscious, unintentional, involuntary, and effortless. We don't have a special window through which we can watch our automatic minds at work, which makes it difficult to know the extent to which we are making quick assumptions about other people and the extent to which these assumptions are correct. Can you think of any indirect clues that people get suggesting that they have made automatic assumptions about other people that are incorrect? For example, think back to the section of the chapter on self-fulfilling prophecies. Is there some way a middle school teacher could tell whether he or she is making false assumptions about the math abilities of the boys and girls in his or her class? What about you in your everyday life? When you meet someone for the first time and get to know him or her, how can you tell whether your initial assumptions are correct? Would it help to compare notes with other people who know this person?

Summary

What are the two major types of social cognition?

- **The Social Thinker** People are extremely good at **social cognition**, which refers to the ways in which people think about themselves and the social world. Although no computer can match us in this kind of thinking, we not are perfect social thinkers. Social psychologists have uncovered some fascinating mistakes to which we are prone, despite our uncanny cognitive abilities. Social thinking can be automatic or controlled.

What are the roles and functions of schemas and heuristics in automatic thinking?

- **On Automatic Pilot: Low-Effort Thinking** A great deal of social cognition—how people think about themselves and the social world—involves **automatic thinking**, which is nonconscious, unintentional, involuntary, and effortless.
  - **People as Everyday Theorists: Automatic Thinking with Schemas** An important part of automatic thinking is using our past knowledge to organize and interpret new information. More specifically, people use **schemas**, mental structures for organizing their knowledge about the social world around themes or subjects and for influencing what they notice, think about, and remember. Schemas are extremely useful tools for reducing ambiguity about the social world. They can cause problems, however, such as self-fulfilling prophecies, whereby a schema or expectation about another person influences how we act toward that person, which causes that person to behave consistently with our expectation.
  - **It's Not Just in Our Head: Priming Metaphors About the Body and the Mind** In addition to using schemas to reduce ambiguity about the world, people use metaphors about the mind and the body. Physical sensations (e.g., holding a heavy clipboard) can **prime** a metaphor (e.g., that important thoughts "have weight"), which then influences people's judgments (e.g., that student opinion should be given more weight on a campus issue).
  - **Mental Strategies and Shortcuts** Another form of automatic thinking is the use of **judgmental heuristics**, which are mental shortcuts people use to make judgments quickly and efficiently. Examples are the **availability heuristic**, whereby people base a judgment on the ease with which they can bring something to mind, and the **representativeness heuristic**, whereby people classify something according to how similar it is to a typical case. Heuristics are extremely useful and often produce accurate judgments, but can be misused, producing faulty judgments.
  - **The Power of Unconscious Thinking** Recent research suggests that a great deal of human thought occurs outside conscious awareness. People unconsciously monitor what is going on around them, in case something important occurs that requires their conscious attention. Even people's goals can be unconsciously activated.

How does culture influence social thinking?

- **Cultural Differences in Social Cognition** The human mind is like a toolbox filled with specific tools to help people think about and act in the social world. All humans have access to the same tools, but the culture in which they grow up can influence the ones they use the most. Western cultures tend to emphasize an **analytic thinking style**, a type of thinking in which people focus on the properties of objects without considering their surrounding context. People who grow up in East Asian cultures tend to have a **holistic thinking style**, a type of thinking in which people focus on the overall context, particularly the ways in which objects relate to each other.

What are some of the drawbacks of controlled thinking, and how can we improve its effectiveness?

- **Controlled Social Cognition: High-Effort Thinking** Not all social cognition is automatic; we also engage in **controlled thinking**, which is conscious, intentional, voluntary, and effortful.
  - **Controlled Thinking and Free Will** There can be a disconnect between our conscious sense of how much we are causing our own actions and how much we really are causing them. Sometimes we overestimate the amount of control we have, and sometimes we underestimate the amount of control we have. But the more people believe in free will, the more willing they are to help others in

need and the less likely they are to engage in immoral actions such as cheating.

- **Mentally Undoing the Past: Counterfactual Reasoning** One form of controlled thinking is **counterfactual reasoning**, whereby people mentally change some aspect of the past as a way of imagining what might have been.
- **Improving Human Thinking** In this chapter, we documented several ways in which social cognition can go wrong, producing faulty judgments. Research shows that some kinds of thinking, such as statistical reasoning, can be improved dramatically with training—such as by taking a course in statistics.

■ **Watson Revisited** Human beings are very sophisticated social thinkers who have amazing cognitive abilities. But we are also capable of consequential mistakes, such as self-fulfilling prophecies. People are like "flawed scientists"—brilliant thinkers who are attempting to discover the nature of the social world in a logical manner but do so imperfectly.

Chapter 3 Test

Study and Review on MyPsychLab

1. Over Thanksgiving break, your parents ask you if you can think of 12 reasons why your college is better than its archrival. You find it hard to come up with so many reasons and so end up thinking, "Hmm, maybe the schools aren't all that different." Which of the following mental strategies did you probably use to reach this conclusion?
   a. the representativeness heuristic
   b. base rate information
   c. the anchoring and adjustment heuristic
   d. the availability heuristic
   e. counterfactual thinking

2. Sam plays a carnival game in which he would have won a stuffed donkey if he had guessed the correct cup under which a ball was hidden. Unfortunately, from the line of 20 cups, he picked the cup directly to the left of the winning cup. According to social psychological research, he is *most likely* to
   a. experience cognitive dissonance.
   b. engage in counterfactual thinking.
   c. blame his mistake on the noise of the crowd.
   d. subsequently avoid similar games.

3. Which of the following is FALSE about research on free will?
   a. Sometimes people overestimate the amount of control they have over their behavior.
   b. Sometimes people underestimate the amount of control they have over their behavior.
   c. Studies have shown that people have free will over almost everything they do.
   d. The more people believe in free will, the more willing they are to help others in need.
   e. The more people believe in free will, the less likely they are to engage in immoral actions such as cheating.

4. Suppose you're driving home from watching a scary movie about a hitchhiker who was a murderer when you see someone talking loudly with a friend. Because you saw the movie, you assume that you are witnessing an argument that will probably end in a fight. This is an example of
   a. priming.
   b. base rate information.
   c. belief perseverance.
   d. controlled thinking.

5. Which of the following is LEAST true of the holistic thinking style discussed in this chapter?
   a. It is more common in East Asia than in the United States.
   b. It involves a focus on the context and ways in which objects relate to each other.
   c. People living in the West can think holistically if they are primed with pictures taken in Japan.
   d. The holistic style of thinking probably has a genetic basis.
   e. It may have its roots in the philosophic traditions of Confucianism, Taoism, and Buddhism.

6. Rob is definitely not the most attractive guy in the dorms, but he is extremely confident about who he is and how he looks. He is convinced that most women find him to be very attractive, and he in fact usually gets dates with women who are much more attractive than he is. What is the best explanation of Rob's success?
   a. self-affirmation theory
   b. the representativeness heuristic
   c. self-fulfilling prophecy
   d. self-esteem maintenance theory

7. All of the following are good examples of the self-fulfilling prophecy except one. Which one?
   a. A teacher believes that boys are better at math than girls, and boys in his class do better than girls in math.
   b. Bob thinks that members of the Alpha Beta Psi sorority are unfriendly and snobby. Whenever he meets members of this sorority, they are unfriendly toward him.
   c. Jill thinks her dog isn't very good at learning tricks. Her dog knows fewer tricks than most dogs.
   d. Sarah is worried that her son is not gifted in music, but he does better at his piano lessons than she expected.

8. According to this chapter, which is the best analogy to describe people's thinking abilities?
   a. People are cognitive misers.
   b. People are motivated tacticians.
   c. People are flawed scientists.
   d. People are skilled detectives.

9. Which of the following is MOST TRUE about the use of schemas?
   a. schemas are an example of controlled thinking
   b. when people have an incorrect schema, rarely do they act in a way to make it come true
   c. although schemas can lead to errors, they are a very useful way of organizing information about the world and filling in gaps in our knowledge
   d. the schema we use is influenced only by what information is chronically accessible and not by our goals or by what has been primed recently

10. Which of the following is the best summary of research on automatic thinking?

a. Automatic thinking is a problem because it usually produces mistaken judgments.

b. Automatic thinking is amazingly accurate and rarely produces errors of any consequence.

c. Automatic thinking is vital to human survival, but it is not perfect and can produce mistaken judgments that have important consequences.

d. Automatic thinking works best when it occurs consciously.

Answer Key

1-d, 2-b, 3-c, 4-a, 5-d,
6-c, 7-d, 8-c, 9-c, 10-c

Scoring the TRY IT! exercises

Page 61

1. The correct answer is (b), the third letter. Tversky and Kahneman (1974) found that most people thought that the answer was (a), the first letter. Why do people make this mistake? Because, say Tversky and Kahneman, they find it easier to think of examples of words that begin with *r*. By using the availability heuristic, they assume that the ease with which they can bring examples to mind means that such words are more common.
2. The correct answer is (b). Slovic, Fischhoff, and Lichtenstein (1976) found that most people think that (a) is correct (accidents). Why do people make this error? Again, it's the availability heuristic: Accidental deaths are more likely to be reported by the media, so people find it easier to bring to mind examples of such deaths than deaths from strokes.
3. The correct answer is (c). Both outcomes are equally likely, given that the outcomes of coin flips are random events. Tversky and Kahneman (1974) argue that, due to the representativeness heuristic, people expect a sequence of random events to "look" random. That is, they expect events to be representative of their conception of randomness. Many people, therefore, choose HTTHTH because this sequence is more representative of people's idea of randomness than HHHTTT. In fact, the chance that either sequence will occur is 1 out of 2^6 times, or 1 in 64. As another illustration of this point, if you were to buy a lottery ticket with four numbers, would you rather have the number 6957 or 1111? Many people prefer the former number because it seems more "random" and thus more likely to be picked. In fact, both numbers have a 1 in 1,000 chance of being picked.
4. The correct answer is (b). Many people choose (c) because they think that after five tails in a row, heads is more likely "to even things out." This is called the gambler's fallacy, which is the belief that prior random events (e.g., five tails in a row) have an influence on subsequent random events. Assuming that the coin is fair, prior tosses have no influence on future ones. Tversky and Kahneman (1974) suggest that the gambler's fallacy is due in part to the representativeness heuristic: Five tails and one head seems more representative of a chance outcome than six tails in a row.

Page 67

These questions are based on ones used by Pronin and Kugler (2010), who found that people tend to believe that they have more free will than do other people. In their study, they asked Princeton undergraduates to predict what would happen in the year after graduation, either to them or to a friend of their choosing. When the students answered the questions about themselves, they circled "both are possible" 52% of the time, whereas when they answered the questions about a friend, they circled "both are possible" only 36% of the time. In other words, the students seemed to think their friends' actions were more predetermined than were their own.

Page 69

1. (a) This question assesses methodological reasoning, the recognition that there are several reasons why crime has gone down other than actions taken by the police chief and that a better test of the mayor's claim is to compare the crime rate in Middleopolis with other, similar cities.
2. (a) This question assesses statistical reasoning, the recognition that large samples of information are more likely to reflect true scores and abilities than small samples of information. For example, if you flip a fair coin four times, it is not unusual to get all heads or all tails, but if you flip the coin a thousand times, it is extremely unlikely that you will get all heads or all tails. Applied to this example, this statistical principle says that when baseball players have a small number of at-bats, it is not unusual to see very high (or very low) averages just by chance. By the end of the season, however, when baseball players have hundreds of at-bats, it is highly unlikely that they will have a very high average just by luck.

4 Social Perception

How We Come to Understand Other People

OTHER PEOPLE ARE NOT EASY TO FIGURE OUT. Why are they the way they are? Why do they do what they do? The frequency and urgency with which we pose these questions are clear in a touching story, sent in by a reader to the *New York Times*. The reader explains that a female friend who had recently ended a relationship had decided to throw away a bag containing her ex's love letters, cards, and poems. She was stunned when her former boyfriend called the next day to ask why she had done this. How had he found out? It turns out that a homeless man found the letters when he was going through the garbage, read the correspondence, and became curious about how the two lovers' relationship had come to such an end. He went to a pay phone and called the boyfriend to find out, after finding his number in one of the letters. "I would have called you sooner," he told the former boyfriend, "but this was the first quarter I was given today" (De Marco, 1994).

FOCUS QUESTIONS

- How do people use nonverbal cues to understand others?
- What are implicit personality theories and where do they come from?
- How do we determine why people do what they do?
- What role does culture play in the formation of attributions?

The homeless man was down on his luck—no home, no money, reduced to rifling through garbage cans—and yet that endless fascination with the human condition still asserted itself. He needed to know why the couple broke up. He even spent his only quarter to find out.

We all have a fundamental fascination with explaining other people's behavior. But the reasons why people behave as they do are usually hidden from us. Unfortunately, we can't read other people's minds. All we have to go on is observable behavior: what people do, what they say, their facial expressions, gestures, tone of voice. We rely on our impressions and personal theories, putting them together as well as we can, hoping they will lead to reasonably accurate and useful conclusions.

Our desire to understand other people is so fundamental that it carries over into our hobbies and recreational lives. We go to movies, read novels, eavesdrop on conversations, and watch people flirt at bars, because thinking about the behavior even of strangers and fictional characters fascinates us (Weiner, 1985). This basic aspect of human cognition has been exploited brilliantly by reality TV programmers, who cast television shows with real people, not actors, and film them as they go about their lives. You can watch *Teen Mom* or *Hoarders*, *Keeping Up with the Kardashians* or *The Bachelor*. Why are these shows so popular with the American public? Because we enjoy figuring people out.

Consider the reality show *Jersey Shore*, which chronicles the daily life of half a dozen young adults sharing an apartment in a New Jersey beach town. They party, they hook up, they fight, they talk, they cry. They may be a lot like you and your friends, or they may be the complete opposite—either way, the choices they make in any given situation are fascinating. As we watch shows such as this one, we form impressions of the characters. We make attributions about them; that is, we reach conclusions about who we think they are and why they do what they do. These attributions help us understand their motivations, choices, and behavior—all of which are the topics of this chapter.

For example, season three of *Jersey Shore* focused heavily on the on-again, off-again romantic relationship between Sammi and Ronnie. To describe their relationship as an emotional train wreck seems charitable. As one television critic put it, "Here were two people who were desperately wrong for each other. But they were also desperately in love" (Franich, 2011a). How would they resolve the incredible number of problems they had? Would they stay together? *Should* they stay together? How did you "sum them up" as individuals? Here's how one television critic saw Sammi: "Everyone I know hates Sammi. When women look at her, they see a popular girl, a priss, a spoiled-rotten Queen Bee. She's the kind of girl other girls hope will get married to a benchwarming NFL player who will divorce her for a Victoria's Secret model, leaving her to a dwindling existence in some lesser corner of the *Real Housewives* universe. Men, on the other hand, look at Sammi and see every soul-seeking, high-maintenance girlfriend they've ever had" (Franich, 2011b). Don't think this critic is taking sides; here's his impression of Ronnie: "A guy who drinks like a sailor and fights like a frat dude and cries like a drunken fratboy sailor-baby and is secretly a shaved gorilla raised in human society as a social experiment" (Franich, 2011a). Ouch!

So, why do we enjoy shows such as these? Because thinking about other people and their behavior help us understand and predict our social world (Heider, 1958; Kelley 1967). In this chapter, we will discuss **social perception**—the study of how we form impressions of other people and how we make inferences about them. One important source of information that we use is people's nonverbal communication, such as their facial expressions, body movements, and tone of voice.

Watch on **MyPsychLab**
To learn more about nonverbal communication, watch the MyPsychLab video ***Flirting.***

Nonverbal Communication

What do we know about people when we first meet them? We know what we can see and hear, and even though we know we should not "judge a book by its cover," we do form impressions of others based on the slightest of cues. For example, Sam Gosling has conducted research on "what your stuff says about you," as presented in his book *Snoop* (2008). What's your room like? Messy, or orderly? What posters are on your wall? What objects are on your desk and shelves? All of these possessions can be used by observers (potential snoopers) as clues to what you are like. Recent research has also indicated that we form initial impressions of others based solely on their facial appearance, and we do this very quickly—in less than 100 milliseconds (Bar, Neta, & Linz, 2006; Willis & Todorov, 2006). We form these impressions even when the face reveals a neutral expression, not one showing emotion.

For example, people who have "baby faces"—features that are reminiscent of those of small children, with big eyes, a small chin and nose, and a high forehead—tend to be perceived as having childlike traits too: naïve, warm, and submissive (Zebrowitz & Montepare, 2008). Although such impressions will frequently be wrong, there is some evidence that we can make accurate judgments about others simply based on their facial appearance. For example, after brief glances at photographs of men's and women's faces, research participants were able to judge their sexual orientation at above chance levels of accuracy (Rule et al., 2008; Rule, Ambady, & Hallett, 2009). American participants rated the faces of Canadian political candidates (with whom they were totally unfamiliar) on the dimensions of powerfulness and warmth. Their first-impression ratings correlated with the actual election results: The more powerful the candidates looked, the more likely they were to win their election; the warmer they looked, the less likely they were to win (Rule & Ambady, 2010; Todorov et al., 2008).

When the eyes say one thing, and the tongue another, a practiced man relies on the language of the first.
—Ralph Waldo Emerson, *The Conduct of Life*

Besides revealing clues about ourselves through our possessions and basic facial appearance, our nonverbal expressions provide others with information about us (Ambady & Rosenthal, 1992, 1993; DePaulo, DePaulo, & Friedman, 1998; Gifford, 1991, 1994). **Nonverbal communication** refers to how people communicate, intentionally or unintentionally, without words. Facial expressions, tone of voice, gestures, body positions and movement, the use of touch, and eye gaze are the most frequently used and most revealing channels of nonverbal communication (Henley, 1977; Knapp & Hall, 2006).

Social Perception
The study of how we form impressions of and make inferences about other people

Nonverbal Communication
The way in which people communicate, intentionally or unintentionally, without words; nonverbal cues include facial expressions, tone of voice, gestures, body position and movement, the use of touch, and gaze

Nonverbal cues serve many functions in communication. They help us express our emotions, our attitudes, and our personality. For example, you express "I'm angry" by narrowing your eyes, lowering your eyebrows, and setting your mouth in a thin, straight line. You communicate your personality traits, such as being an extrovert, with broad gestures and frequent changes in voice pitch and inflection (Knapp & Hall, 2006). You can explore how you use one aspect of nonverbal communication—your voice—in the following Try It!

TRY IT! Using Your Voice as a Nonverbal Cue

Even though the words you say are full of information, the way you say them gives your listener even more of an idea of what you mean. You can take a perfectly straightforward sentence like "I don't know her" and give it many different meanings, depending on how you say it. Try saying that sentence out loud so that it communicates each of the emotions listed below. Experiment with the pitch of your voice (high or low), the speed with which you speak, the loudness or softness of your voice, and whether you stress some words and not others.

"I don't know her."

- You're angry.
- You're being sarcastic.
- You're scared.
- You're surprised.
- You're disgusted.
- You're very happy.

Now try this exercise with a friend. Turn your back to your friend as you repeat the sentence; you want your friend to have to rely on your voice as the only cue, without help from any facial expressions you might make. How well does he or she guess the emotions you are expressing? Have your friend try the exercise too. Can you understand his or her nonverbal vocal cues? If you don't always correctly identify the emotions in each other's voices, discuss what was missing or confusing in the voice. In this way, you'll be able to figure out, for example, what a "disgusted" voice sounds like as compared to an "angry" or "scared" voice.

Nonverbal forms of communication have typically been studied individually, in their separate "channels" (e.g., eye gaze or gestures), even though in everyday life nonverbal cues of many kinds occur all at the same time in a quite dazzling orchestration of information (Archer & Akert, 1980, 1984; Akert et al., 2010). Let's focus on a few of these channels and then turn to how we interpret the full symphony of nonverbal information as it occurs naturally.

An eye can threaten like a loaded and leveled gun, or can insult like hissing or kicking; or, in its altered mood, by beams of kindness, it can make the heart dance with joy.

—Ralph Waldo Emerson, *The Conduct of Life*

Facial Expressions of Emotion

The crown jewel of nonverbal communication is the facial-expressions channel. This aspect of communication has a long history of research, beginning with Charles Darwin's book *The Expression of the Emotions in Man and Animals* (1872). Its primacy is due to the exquisite communicativeness of the human face (Kappas, 1997; McHugo & Smith, 1996; Wehrle et al., 2000). Look at the photographs on page 78. We bet you can figure out the meaning of these expressions with very little effort.

Evolution and Facial Expressions Darwin's research on facial expressions has had a major impact on the field in many areas. We will focus on his belief that the primary emotions conveyed by the face are universal: All humans **encode,** or express, these emotions in the same way, and all humans can **decode,** or interpret them, with equal accuracy. Darwin's interest in evolution led him to believe that nonverbal forms of communication were species specific and not culture specific. He proposed that facial expressions were vestiges of once-useful physiological reactions. For example, if early hominids ate something that tasted terrible, they would have wrinkled their noses in displeasure and expelled the food from their mouths. Research by Joshua Susskind and his colleagues (2008) offers support for Darwin's view. They studied the facial expressions of disgust and fear and found, first, that the muscle movements of each emotion were completely the opposite of the other. Second, they found that the "fear face" enhances perception, while the "disgust face" decreases it. For fear, the facial and eye muscle movements increase sensory input, such as widening the visual field, increasing the volume of air in the nose, and speeding up eye movements—all of which are useful responses to something that is frightening. In contrast, for disgust, the muscle movements decrease input from these senses: Eyes narrow, less air is breathed in, and eye movements slow down, all of which are useful reactions to something that smells or tastes disgusting (Susskind et al., 2008).

Encode

To express or emit nonverbal behavior, such as smiling or patting someone on the back

Decode

To interpret the meaning of the nonverbal behavior other people express, such as deciding that a pat on the back was an expression of condescension and not kindness

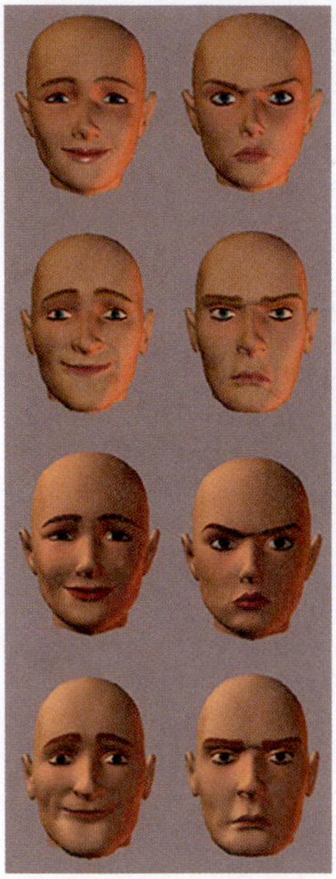

What emotion do you think is being displayed on each of these faces? Research by Becker et al. (2007) suggests that you might have found it easier to detect anger on the male faces and happiness on the female faces.

Darwin (1872) further proposed that facial expressions such as disgust and fear acquire evolutionary significance over time. Being able to communicate emotional states (e.g., the feeling of disgust, not for food but for another person or a situation) had survival value for the developing species (Hansen & Hansen, 1988; Izard, 1994; McArthur & Baron, 1983). For example, being able to perceive that another person is angry (and therefore potentially dangerous) would have great evolutionary significance for early humans—it might have meant the difference between life and death. D. Vaughn Becker and his colleagues (2007) have intriguing results in this area. They found that research participants were faster and more accurate at decoding angry expressions on male faces and at detecting happy expressions on female faces. Furthermore, when they subtly manipulated (via computer-generated faces) how male or female the face looked and the strength of the emotion shown, they again found a strong connection between anger and men's faces, and happiness and women's faces. The researchers suggest that from an evolutionary perspective, the costs and benefits of perceiving anger and happiness would vary depending on whether the encoder was male or female (Becker et al., 2007).

Was Darwin right when he stated that facial expressions of emotion are universal? The answer is yes, for the six major emotional expressions: anger, happiness, surprise, fear, disgust, and sadness. For example, in a particularly well-designed study, Paul Ekman and Walter Friesen (1971) traveled to New Guinea, where they studied the decoding ability of the South Fore, a preliterate tribe that, until that time, had had no contact with Western civilization. They told the Fore people brief stories with emotional content and then showed them photographs of American men and women expressing the six emotions; the Fores' job was to match the facial expressions of emotion to the stories. The Fores were as accurate as Western subjects had been. The researchers then asked the Fore people to demonstrate, while being photographed,

These photographs depict facial expressions of the six major emotions. Can you guess the emotion expressed on each face?

Answers (beginning in the upper left): Anger, fear, disgust, happiness, surprise, and sadness.

facial expressions that would match the stories they were told. These photographs, when later shown to American research participants, were also decoded accurately. This research yielded considerable evidence that the ability to interpret at least the six major emotions is cross-cultural—part of being human and not a product of people's cultural experience (Biehl et al., 1997; Ekman, 1993, 1994; Ekman et al., 1987; Elfenbein & Ambady, 2002; Haidt & Keltner, 1999; Izard, 1994; Matsumoto & Wilingham, 2006).

These six major emotions are also the first to appear in human development. Children as young as 6 months to a year express these emotions with the facial expressions we associate with adults. This is true as well for young children who have been blind from birth; they are able to display the basic emotions on their faces even though they have never seen them on other people's faces (Eibl-Eibesfeldt, 1975; Galati, Miceli, & Sini, 2001).

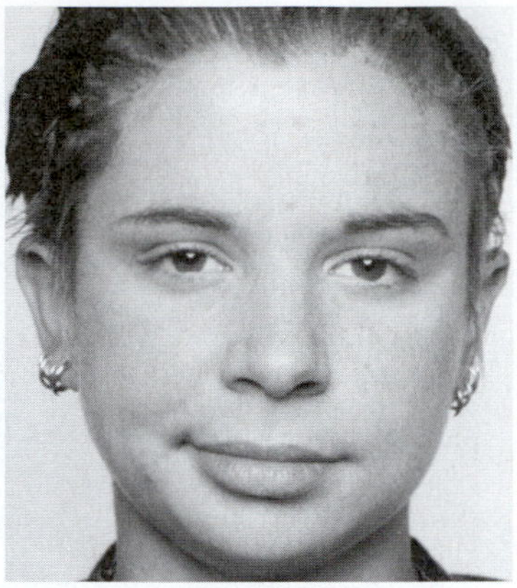

Recent research suggests that "contempt" may be a universally recognized expression.

Beyond the six major emotions, are there other emotional states that are communicated with distinctive and readily identifiable facial expressions across cultures? Researchers are exploring just this question for emotions such as contempt, anxiety, shame, pride, and embarrassment (Ekman, O'Sullivan, & Matsumoto, 1991; Harrigan & O'Connell, 1996; Keltner & Shiota, 2003). For example, research on the facial expression of *contempt* suggests that it is recognized cross-culturally like the six major emotions discussed earlier. Research participants from countries as culturally disparate as Estonia, Japan, the United States, Indonesia, Italy, India, and Vietnam recognized the contempt expression: a tightening and raising of the lip on only one side of the face, as shown in the photograph on the left (e.g., Haidt & Keltner, 1999; Matsumoto & Ekman, 2004).

Similarly, research has indicated that the emotion of *pride* exists cross-culturally. Pride is a particularly interesting emotional display, because it involves a facial expression as well as body posture and gesture cues. Specifically, the prototypical pride expression includes a small smile, the head tilted back slightly, a visibly expanded chest and posture, and the arms raised above the head or hands on hips (Tracy & Robins, 2004). Photographs of pride expressions were accurately decoded by research participants in the United States and Italy, and also by individuals from a preliterate, isolated tribe in Burkina Faso, West Africa (Tracy & Robins, 2008). Jessica Tracy and David Matsumoto (2008) explored pride and its opposite, *shame*, by coding the spontaneous expressions of winning and losing athletes in judo matches at the 2004 Olympic and Paralympic Games. Sighted and blind athletes from 37 countries were coded on their nonverbal behavior just after they had won or lost their judo match. The pride expression was associated to a significant extent with winning for both sighted and blind athletes around the world. Shame, expressed by slumped shoulders and a sunken chest, was significantly associated with losing for all the athletes except one group—sighted athletes from highly individualistic cultures such as those of the United States and Western Europe. In individualistic cultures, shame is a negative, stigmatized emotion that one hides rather than displays (Robins & Schriber, 2009).

Affect Blend

A facial expression in which one part of the face registers one emotion while another part of the face registers a different emotion

Why is Decoding Sometimes Inaccurate? Decoding facial expressions accurately is more complicated than we have indicated, for two reasons. People frequently display **affect blends** (Ekman & Friesen, 1975): One part of their face registers one emotion while another part registers a different emotion. Take a look at the accompanying photographs and see if you can tell which two emotions are being expressed in each face. An affect blend is the sort of expression you might display if a person told you something that was both horrible and inappropriate—you'd be disgusted with the content and angry that the person told you. A second reason why decoding facial expressions can be inaccurate has to do with culture.

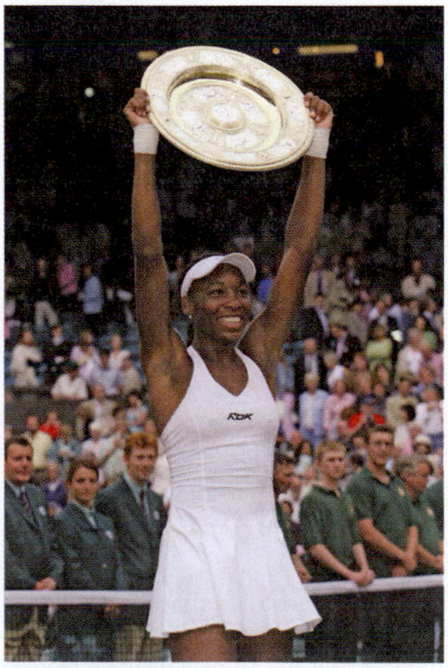

The nonverbal expression of pride, involving facial expression, posture, and gesture, is encoded and decoded cross-culturally.

Culture and the Channels of Nonverbal Communication

For decades, Paul Ekman and his colleagues have studied the influence of culture on the facial display of emotions (Ekman & Davidson, 1994; Ekman & Friesen, 1969;

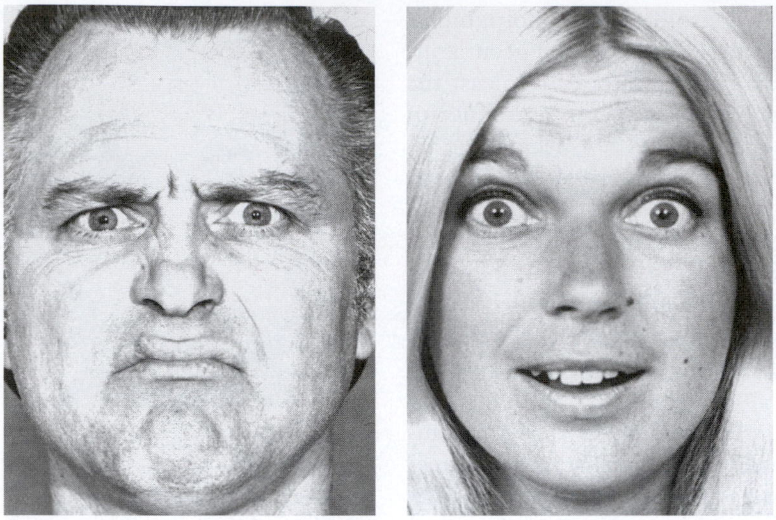

Often, people express more than one emotion at the same time. Can you tell which emotions these people are expressing? The answers are printed below.

(Adapted from Ekman & Friesen, 1975)

Answers: The man is expressing a blend of anger (the eye and eyebrow region) and disgust (the nose and mouth region). The woman is expressing a blend of surprise (eyes and eyebrows) and happiness (mouth). (It may help to cover half of the photograph with your hand to see each emotional expression clearly.)

Matsumoto & Ekman, 1989; Matsumoto & Hwang, 2010). They have concluded that **display rules** are particular to each culture and dictate what kinds of emotional expressions people are supposed to show. As we saw in our discussion of athletes' spontaneous expressions at the Olympics and Paralympics (Tracy & Matsumoto, 2008), the display rules of individualistic cultures discourage the expression of shame in front of others, while the display rules of collectivistic cultures allow (or even encourage) it.

Here is another example: American cultural norms discourage emotional displays in men, such as grief or crying, but allow the facial display of such emotions in women. In comparison, in Japan, traditional cultural rules dictate that women should not exhibit a wide, uninhibited smile (Ramsey, 1981). Japanese women will often hide a wide smile behind their hands, whereas Western women are allowed—indeed, encouraged—to smile broadly and often (Henley, 1977; La France, Hecht, & Paluck, 2003). Japanese norms lead people to cover up negative facial expressions with smiles and laughter and, in general, to display fewer facial expressions than are displayed in the West (Argyle, 1986; Aune & Aune, 1996; Gudykunst, Ting-Toomey, & Nishida, 1996; Richmond & McCroskey, 1995).

Simulate on MyPsychLab

To learn more about Paul Ekman's research, try the MyPsychLab simulation ***Recognizing Facial Expression of Emotions.***

There are, of course, other channels of nonverbal communication besides facial expressions. These nonverbal cues are strongly shaped by culture. Eye contact and gaze are particularly powerful nonverbal cues. In mainstream American culture, people typically become suspicious when a person doesn't "look them in the eye" while speaking, and they find it quite disconcerting to speak to someone who is wearing dark sunglasses. However, as you can see in Figure 4.1, in other parts of the world, direct eye gaze is considered invasive or disrespectful.

Another form of nonverbal communication is how people use personal space. Imagine that you are talking to a person who stands too close to you or too far away; these deviations from "normal" spacing will affect your impressions of that person. Cultures vary greatly in what is considered normative use of personal space (Hall, 1969; Hogh-Olesen, 2008). For example, most Americans like to have a bubble of open space, a few feet in radius, surrounding them. In comparison, in some other cultures it is normal for strangers to stand right next to each other, to the point of touching; someone who stands apart may be considered odd or suspicious.

Display Rules

Culturally determined rules about which nonverbal behaviors are appropriate to display

Emblems

Nonverbal gestures that have well-understood definitions within a given culture; they usually have direct verbal translations—such as the OK sign

Gestures of the hands and arms are also a fascinating means of communication. Americans are very adept at understanding certain gestures, such as the OK sign, in which one forms a circle with the thumb and forefinger and curves the rest of the fingers above the circle, and "flipping the bird," in which one bends all the fingers down at the first knuckle except the longest, middle finger. Gestures such as these, which have clear, well-understood definitions, are called **emblems** (Ekman & Friesen, 1975; Archer, 1997a). The important thing to keep in mind about emblems is that they are not universal; each culture has devised its own emblems, and these are not necessarily understandable to people from other cultures (see Figure 4.1). Thus, "flipping the bird" will be a clear communicative sign in American society, whereas in some parts of Europe you'd need to make a quick gesture with a cupped hand under your chin to convey the same message. On one occasion when President George H. W. Bush used the "V for victory" sign (forming a V shape), he did it backwards—with the palm of his hand facing him instead of the audience. Unfortunately, he flashed this gesture to a

Cultural Differences in Nonverbal Communication

Many forms of nonverbal behavior are specific to a given culture. Not only do some of the nonverbal behaviors of one culture mean nothing in another, but the same nonverbal behavior can exist in two cultures but have very different meanings in each. Such nonverbal differences can lead to misunderstanding when people from different societies interact. Some of these cultural differences are noted here.

Eye contact and gaze

In American culture, direct eye contact is valued; a person who won't "look you in the eye" is perceived as being evasive or even lying. However, in many parts of the world, direct eye contact is considered disrespectful, especially with superiors. For example, in Nigeria, Puerto Rico, and Thailand, children are taught not to make direct eye contact with their teachers and other adults. Cherokee, Navajo, and Hopi Native Americans use minimal eye contact as well. Japanese use far less direct eye contact than Americans do. In contrast, Arabs use a great deal of eye contact, with a gaze that would be considered piercing by people from some other cultures.

Personal space and touching

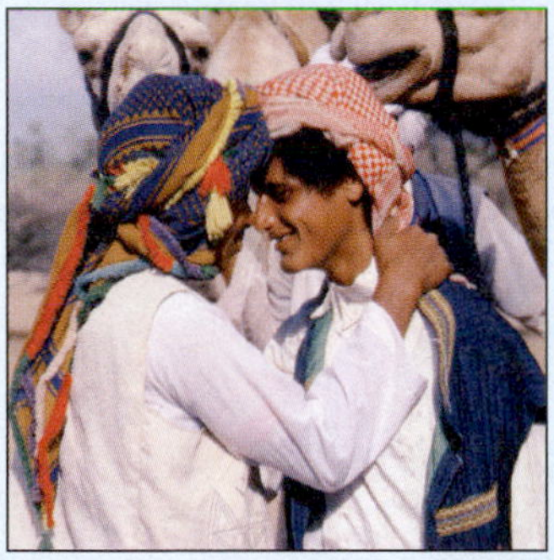

Societies vary in whether they are high-contact cultures, where people stand close to each other and touch frequently, or low-contact cultures, where people maintain more interpersonal space and touch less often. High-contact cultures include Middle Eastern, South American, and southern European countries. Low-contact cultures include North American, northern European, Asian, Pakistani, and Native American peoples. Cultures also differ in how appropriate they consider same-sex touching among friends. For example, in Korea and Egypt, men and women hold hands, link arms, or walk hip to hip with their same-sex friends, and these nonverbal behaviors carry no sexual connotation. In the United States, such behavior is much less common, particularly between male friends.

Hand and head gestures

The "OK" sign: The OK sign is formed by making a circle with your thumb and index finger, with your three other fingers extended upward. In the United States, this means "okay." However, in Japan, this hand gesture means "money." In France, it means "zero"; in Mexico, it means "sex." In Ethiopia, it means "homosexuality." Finally, in some South American countries, such as Brazil, it is an obscene gesture, carrying the same meaning as the American "flipping the bird" sign, where the middle finger is the only one extended.

The thumbs-up gesture: In the United States, raising one thumb upward with the rest of the fingers in the fist means "OK." Several European countries have a similar meaning for this gesture; for example, in France it means "excellent!" However, in Japan, the same gesture means "boyfriend," while in Iran and Sardinia, it is obscene.

The "hand-purse" gesture: This gesture is formed by straightening the fingers and thumb of one hand and bringing them together so the tips touch, pointing upwards. This gesture has no clear meaning in American culture. However, in Italy, it means "What are you trying to say?"; in Spain, it means "good"; in Tunisia, it means "slow down"; and in Malta, it means "you may seem good, but you are really bad."

Nodding the head: In the United States, nodding one's head up and down means "yes" and shaking it from side to side means "no." However, in some parts of Africa and India, the opposite is true: nodding up and down means "no," and shaking from side to side means "yes." To complicate this situation even more, in Korea, shaking one's head from side to side means "I don't know" (which in the United States is communicated by a shrug of the shoulders). Finally, Bulgarians indicate disagreement by throwing their heads back and then returning them to an upright position—which is frequently mistaken by Americans as meaning agreement.

FIGURE 4.1

Cultural Differences in Nonverbal Communication

According to covariation theory, we use the consistency, distinctiveness, and level of consensus to explain a person's behavior as mainly caused either by the person's situation or by the person's own characteristics or dispositions.

large crowd in Australia, and in Australia this emblem is the equivalent of "flipping the bird" (Archer, 1997a)!

To summarize, people's nonverbal communication can tell us a lot about people's attitudes, emotions, and personality traits. Nonverbal behavior gives us many bits of information—"data" that we then use to construct our overall impressions or theories about people. But nonverbal cues are just the beginning of social perception. We turn now to the cognitive processes people use when forming impressions of others.

Implicit Personality Theories: Filling in the Blanks

As we saw in Chapter 3, when people are unsure about the nature of the social world, they use their schemas to fill in the gaps. A schema is a mental shortcut: When all we have is a small amount of information, our schemas provide additional information to fill in the gaps (Fiske & Taylor, 1991; Markus & Zajonc, 1985). Thus, when we are trying to understand other people, we can use just a few observations of a person as a starting point and then, using our schemas, create a much fuller understanding. Schemas allow us to form impressions quickly, without having to spend weeks with people to figure out what they are like.

This kind of schema is called an **implicit personality theory**; it consists of our ideas about what kinds of personality traits go together (Asch, 1946; Schneider, 1973; Sedikides & Anderson, 1994; Werth & Foerster, 2002). We use a few known traits to determine what other characteristics a person has. When we form quick impressions of people, we often use two general schemas. One involves judgments of "warmth": A kind, warm person is also perceived as generous, trustworthy and helpful, whereas a cold person is seen as the opposite. The second schema, or implicit personality theory, involves "competence": A capable, can-do person is also seen as powerful and dominant, whereas an incompetent person is seen as the opposite (Fiske, Cuddy & Glick, 2006; Todorov, et al., 2008; Wojciszke, 2005). Researchers have discussed these two schemas as universal aspects of social cognition, with evolutionary significance. From an evolutionary perspective, perceptions of warmth and competence provide important information for survival (Fiske, et al., 2006). Who is it that you can trust and depend on, and who is it that you cannot? Note that relying on schemas can lead us astray. We might make the wrong assumptions about an individual; we might even resort to stereotypical thinking, where our schema, or stereotype, leads us to believe that the individual is like all the other members of his or her group. (We will discuss these issues in more depth in Chapter 13.)

Culture and Implicit Personality Theories

Implicit personality theories are developed over time and with experience. Although each of us may have a few idiosyncratic theories about which personality traits go together, we also share many similar theories with one another (Gervey et al., 1999). This occurs because implicit personality theories are strongly tied to culture. Like other beliefs, they are passed from generation to generation in a society, and one culture's implicit personality theory may be very different from another's (Anderson, 1995; Chiu et al., 2000; Vonk, 1995).

For example, when Americans perceive someone as "helpful," they also perceive them as "sincere"; a "practical" person is also "cautious" (Rosenberg, Nelson, & Vivekananthan, 1968). Another strong implicit personality theory in this culture involves physical attractiveness. We presume that "what is beautiful is good"—that people with physical beauty will also have a whole host of other wonderful qualities (Dion, Berscheid, & Walster, 1972; Eagly et al., 1991; Jackson, Hunter, & Hodge, 1995). In China, an implicit personality theory describes a person who embodies traditional

Implicit Personality Theory

A type of schema people use to group various kinds of personality traits together; for example, many people believe that someone who is kind is generous as well

Chinese values: creating and maintaining interpersonal harmony, inner harmony, and *ren qin*—a focus on relationships (Cheung et al., 1996).

Cultural variation in implicit personality theories was demonstrated in an intriguing study by Hoffman, Lau, and Johnson (1986). The researchers noted that different cultures have different ideas about personality types—the kinds of people for whom there are simple, agreed-on verbal labels. For example, in Western cultures, saying someone has an "artistic personality" implies that the person is creative, intense, temperamental, and has an unconventional lifestyle. The Chinese, however, do not have a schema or implicit personality theory for an artistic type. Granted, there are Chinese words to describe the individual characteristics of such people, such as *creative*, but there are no labels like "artistic" or "bohemian" that convey the whole constellation of traits implied by the English term. Conversely, in China there are categories of personality that do not exist in Western cultures. For example, a *shi gú* person is someone who is worldly, devoted to his or her family, socially skillful, and somewhat reserved.

Hoffman and his colleagues (1986) hypothesized that these cultural implicit personality theories influence the way people form impressions of others. To test this hypothesis, they wrote stories in English and Chinese, describing someone behaving like an artistic type or a shi gú type, without using those labels. They gave the English versions to a group of native English speakers who spoke no other languages and to a group of bilingual Chinese and English speakers. Another group of Chinese-English bilinguals received the versions written in Chinese.

If people were using their cultural theories to understand the stories they read, what would you expect to happen? One measure of the use of theories (or schemas) is the tendency to fill in the blanks—to believe that information fitting the schema was observed when in fact it was not. The researchers asked the participants to write down their impressions of the characters in the stories; they then looked to see whether the participants listed traits that were not in the stories but did fit the artistic or shi gú personality types. For example, the term *unreliable* was not used in the "artistic personality type" story but is consistent with that implicit personality theory.

When the native English speakers read about the characters in English, they were much more likely to form an impression that was consistent with the artistic type than with the shi gú type (see Figure 4.2). Similarly, when the Chinese-English bilinguals read the descriptions of the characters in English, they too formed an impression that was consistent with the artistic type but not with the shi gú type, because English provides a convenient label for the artistic type. In comparison, the Chinese-English bilinguals who read the descriptions in Chinese showed the opposite pattern of results. Their impression of the shi gú character was more consistent with that schema than their impression of the artist was, because the Chinese language provides a convenient label or implicit personality theory for this kind of person.

Decoding nonverbal behaviors and relying on implicit personality theories tends to occur automatically—we are not always consciously aware of using this information (Willis & Todorov, 2008). What about those times when we must work consciously to explain another person's behavior?

Implicit personality theories differ from culture to culture. Westerners assume that there is an artistic type of person—someone who is creative, intense, temperamental, and unconventional (for example, the artist Andy Warhol, above). The Chinese have a category of a *shi gú* person—someone who is worldly, devoted to his or her family, socially skillful, and somewhat reserved (below).

Causal Attribution: Answering the "Why" Question

We have seen that when we observe other people, we have a rich source of information—their nonverbal behavior—on which to base our impressions. From their nonverbal behavior, we can also make guesses about people's personalities, such as how friendly or outgoing they are. And once we get this

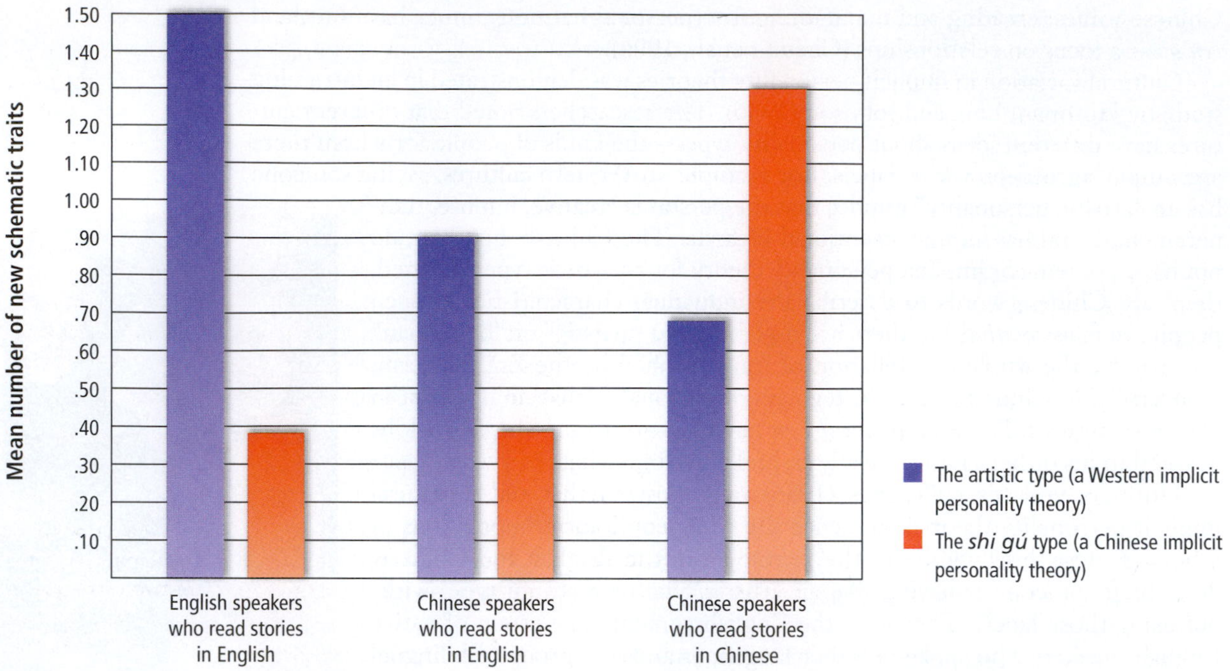

FIGURE 4.2

Implicit Personality Theories: How Our Culture and Language Shape Our Impressions of Others

People formed an impression of other people that was consistent with the implicit personality theory contained in their language. For example, when Chinese-English bilinguals read stories about people in English, they were likely to form impressions consistent with a Western implicit theory, the artistic personality. When Chinese-English bilinguals read the same stories in Chinese, they were likely to form impressions consistent with a Chinese implicit theory, the *shi gú* personality.

(Adapted from Hoffman, Lau, & Johnson, 1986)

far, we use our implicit personality theories to fill in the blanks: If a person is friendly, we generally infer that he or she must be sincere as well.

In the beginning was not the word, not the deed, not the silly serpent. In the beginning was why? Why did she pluck the apple? Was she bored? Was she inquisitive? Was she paid? Did Adam put her up to it? If not, who did?

—John le Carré, *The Russia House*, 1989

However, nonverbal behavior and implicit personality theories are not fail-safe indicators of what a person is really thinking or feeling. If you meet an acquaintance and she says, "It's great to see you!" does she really mean it? Perhaps she is acting more thrilled than she really feels, out of politeness. Perhaps she is outright lying and really can't stand you. The point is that even though nonverbal communication is sometimes easy to decode and our implicit personality theories can streamline the way we form impressions, there is still substantial ambiguity as to what a person's behavior really means (DePaulo, 1992; DePaulo, Stone, & Lassiter, 1985; Schneider, Hastorf, & Ellsworth, 1979).

Why did that acquaintance behave as she did? To answer this "why" question, we will use our immediate observations to form more-elegant and complex inferences about what people are really like and what motivates them to act as they do. How we go about answering these questions is the focus of **attribution theory**, the study of how we infer the causes of other people's behavior.

The Nature of the Attribution Process

Attribution Theory

A description of the way in which people explain the causes of their own and other people's behavior

Fritz Heider (1958) is frequently referred to as the father of attribution theory. His influential book defined the field of social perception, and his legacy is still very much evident in current research (Singer & Frith, 2006; Crandall et al., 2007). Heider discussed what he called "naive" or "commonsense" psychology. In his view, people were like amateur scientists, trying to understand other people's behavior by piecing together information until they arrived at a reasonable explanation or cause (Surian, Caldi, & Sperber, 2007; Weiner, 2008). Heider was intrigued by what seemed reasonable to people and by how they arrived at their conclusions.

One of Heider's most valuable contributions is a simple dichotomy: When trying to decide why people behave as they do—for example, why a father has just yelled at his young daughter—we can make one of two attributions. One option is to make an **internal attribution**, deciding that the cause of the father's behavior was something about him—his disposition, personality, attitudes, or character—an explanation that assigns the causes of his behavior internally. For example, we might decide that the father has poor parenting skills and disciplines his child in inappropriate ways. Alternatively, we might make an **external attribution**, deciding that something in the situation, not in the father's personality or attitudes, caused his behavior. If we conclude that he yelled because his daughter had just stepped into the street without looking, we would be making an external attribution for his behavior.

Notice that our impression of the father will be very different depending on the type of attribution we make. If we make an internal attribution, we'll have a negative impression of him. If we make an external attribution, we won't learn much about him—after all, most parents would have done the same thing if they were in that situation and their child had just disobeyed them by stepping into the street. Quite a difference!

This internal/external attribution dichotomy plays an extraordinarily important role in even the most intimate parts of our lives. Indeed, spouses in happy, satisfied marriages make very different attributions about their partners than spouses in troubled, distressed marriages. Satisfied spouses tend to make internal attributions for their partners' positive behaviors (e.g., "She helped me because she's such a generous person") and external attributions for their partners' negative behaviors (e.g., "He said something mean because he's so stressed at work this week"). In contrast, spouses in distressed marriages tend to display the opposite pattern: Their partners' positive behaviors are chalked up to external causes (e.g., "She helped me because she wanted to impress our friends"), while negative behaviors are attributed to internal causes (e.g., "He said something mean because he's a totally self-centered jerk"). When an intimate relationship becomes troubled, this second pattern of attributions about one's partner only makes the situation worse and can have dire consequences for the health and future of the relationship (Bradbury & Fincham, 1991; Fincham et al., 1997; McNulty, O'Mara, & Karney, 2008).

Internal Attribution

The inference that a person is behaving in a certain way because of something about the person, such as attitude, character, or personality

External Attribution

The inference that a person is behaving a certain way because of something about the situation he or she is in; the assumption is that most people would respond the same way in that situation

Covariation Model

A theory that states that to form an attribution about what caused a person's behavior, we systematically note the pattern between the presence or absence of possible causal factors and whether or not the behavior occurs

Explore on **MyPsychLab**

To learn more, explore ***Internal and External Attributions*** in MyPsychLab.

The Covariation Model: Internal Versus External Attributions

The first, essential step in the process of social perception is determining how people decide whether to make an internal or an external attribution. Harold Kelley's major contribution to attribution theory was the idea that we notice and think about more than one piece of information when we form an impression of another person (Kelley, 1967, 1973). For example, let's say you ask your friend to lend you her car, and she says no. Naturally, you wonder why. What explains her behavior? Kelley's theory, called the **covariation model**, says that you will examine multiple instances of behavior, occurring at different times and in different situations, to answer this question. Has your friend refused to lend you her car in the past? Does she lend it to other people? Does she normally lend you other possessions?

According to Fritz Heider, we tend to see the causes of a person's behavior as internal. For example, when a person on the street asks for money, we are likely to assume that he is at fault for being poor—perhaps lazy or drug-addicted. If we knew the person's situation—perhaps he has lost his job due to a factory closing or has a spouse whose medical bills have bankrupted them—we might come up with a different, external attribution.

TRY IT! Listen as People Make Attributions

Forming attributions is a major part of daily life, and you can watch the attribution process in action! All it takes is a group of friends and an interesting topic to discuss. Perhaps one of your friends is telling you about something that happened to her that day, or perhaps your group is discussing another person whom everybody knows. As they talk, pay very close attention to what they say. They will be trying to figure out why the person being discussed did what she did or said what he said. In other words, they will be making attributions. Your job is to try to keep track of their comments and label the attributional strategies they are using.

In particular, do they make internal attributions (about a person's character or personality), or do they make situational attributions (about all the other events and variables that make up a person's life)? Do your friends seem to prefer one type of attribution to the other? If their interpretation is dispositional, what happens when you suggest another possible interpretation, one that is situational? Do they agree or disagree with you? What kinds of information do they offer as "proof" that their attribution is right? Observing people when they are making attributions in real conversations will show you just how common and powerful this type of thinking is when people are trying to understand each other.

Kelley, like Heider before him, assumes that when we are in the process of forming an attribution, we gather information, or data. The data we use, according to Kelley, are about how a person's behavior "covaries" or changes across time, place, different actors, and different targets of the behavior. By discovering covariation in people's behavior (e.g., your friend refuses to lend you her car; she agrees to lend it to others), you are able to reach a judgment about what caused their behavior.

When we are forming an attribution, what kinds of information do we examine for covariation? Kelley (1967) identified three key types of information: *consensus*, *distinctiveness*, and *consistency*. Suppose that you are working at your part-time job at the Gap and you observe your boss yelling at another employee, Hannah, telling her that she's an idiot. Automatically, you ask that attributional question: "Why is the boss yelling at Hannah and being so critical? Is it something about the boss, something about Hannah, or something about the situation that surrounds and affects him?"

How would Kelley's (1967, 1972, 1973) model of covariation assessment answer this question? **Consensus information** refers to how other people behave toward the same stimulus—in this case, Hannah. Do other people at work also yell at Hannah and criticize her? **Distinctiveness information** refers to how the actor (the person whose behavior we are trying to explain) responds to other stimuli. Does the boss yell at and demean other employees in the store? **Consistency information** refers to the frequency with which the observed behavior between the same actor and the same stimulus occurs across time and circumstances. Does the boss yell at and criticize Hannah regularly and frequently, whether the store is filled with customers or empty?

Consensus Information
Information about the extent to which other people behave the same way toward the same stimulus as the actor does

Distinctiveness Information
Information about the extent to which one particular actor behaves in the same way to different stimuli

Consistency Information
Information about the extent to which the behavior between one actor and one stimulus is the same across time and circumstances

According to Kelley's theory, when these three sources of information combine into one of two distinct patterns, a clear attribution can be made. People are most likely to make an internal attribution (deciding that the behavior was due to something about the boss) when the consensus and distinctiveness of the act are low but its consistency is high (see Figure 4.3). We would be pretty confident that the boss yelled at Hannah because he is a mean and vindictive person if we knew that no one else yells at Hannah, that the boss yells at other employees, and that the boss yells at Hannah every chance he gets. People are likely to make an external attribution (in this case, about Hannah) if consensus, distinctiveness, and consistency are all high. Finally, when consistency is low, we cannot make a clear internal or external attribution, so we resort to a special kind of external or situational attribution, one that assumes something unusual or peculiar is going on in these circumstances—for example, that the boss just received very upsetting news and lost his temper with the first person he saw.

The covariation model assumes that people make causal attributions in a rational, logical way. People observe the clues, such as the distinctiveness of the act, and then

Why did the boss yell at his employee Hannah?			
People are likely to make an ***internal attribution***—it was something about the boss—if they see this behavior as	***low*** in consensus: The boss is the only person working in the store who yells at Hannah	***low*** in distinctiveness: The boss yells at all the employees	***high*** in consistency: The boss yells at Hannah almost every time he sees her
People are likely to make an ***external attribution***—it was something about Hannah—if they see this behavior as	***high*** in consensus: All of the employees yell at Hannah too	***high*** in distinctiveness: The boss doesn't yell at any of the other employees	***high*** in consistency: The boss yells at Hannah almost every time he sees her
People are likely to think it was something peculiar about the particular circumstances in which the boss yelled at Hannah if they see this behavior as	***low or high*** in consensus	***low or high*** in distinctiveness	***low*** in consistency: This is the first time that the boss has yelled at Hannah

FIGURE 4.3

The Covariation Model

Why did the boss yell at his employee Hannah? To decide whether a behavior was caused by internal (dispositional) factors or by external (situational) factors, people use consensus, distinctiveness, and consistency information.

draw a logical inference about why the person did what he or she did. Research has confirmed that people often do make attributions the way that Kelley's model says they should (Forsterling, 1989; Gilbert, 1998a; Hewstone & Jaspars, 1987; Hilton, Smith, & Kim, 1995; Orvis, Cunningham, & Kelley, 1975; White, 2002)—with two exceptions. Studies have shown that people don't use consensus information as much as Kelley's theory predicted; they rely more on consistency and distinctiveness information when forming attributions (McArthur, 1972; Wright, Luus, & Christie, 1990). Also, people don't always have the relevant information they need on all three of Kelley's dimensions. For example, you may not have consistency information because this is the first time you have ever asked your friend to borrow her car. In these situations, research has shown that people proceed with the attribution process using the information they do have and, if necessary, making inferences about the missing data (Fiedler, Walther, & Nickel, 1999; Kelley, 1973).

To summarize, the covariation model portrays people as master detectives, deducing the causes of behavior as systematically and logically as Sherlock Holmes would. However, as noted in Chapters 3 and 6, people aren't always logical or rational when forming judgments about others. Sometimes they distort information to satisfy their need for high self-esteem (see Chapter 6). At other times they use mental shortcuts that, although often helpful, can lead to inaccurate judgments (see Chapter 3). Unfortunately, the attributions we make are sometimes just plain wrong. In the next section, we will discuss some specific errors or biases that plague the attribution process. One shortcut is very common: the idea that people do what they do because of the kind of people they are, not because of the situation they are in.

Simulate on **MyPsychLab**

To learn more, try the MyPsychLab simulation ***Impression Formation and Attribution.***

The Fundamental Attribution Error: People as Personality Psychologists

One day in December 1955, a black seamstress in Montgomery, Alabama, refused to give up her seat on the city bus to a white man. At the time, segregationist "Jim Crow" laws in the South relegated African Americans to second-class status in all aspects of everyday life. For example, they had to sit in the back 10 rows of the bus; they could sit in the middle section if it was empty, but they had to give up their seats to white people when the bus got full. The front 10 rows were always reserved for white people only (Feeney, 2005). That day in 1955, Rosa Parks broke the law and refused to give up her seat. Later, she said, "People always say I didn't give up my seat because I was tired, but that wasn't true. I was not tired physically ... No, the only tired I was, was tired of giving in" (Feeney, 2005, p. A1, B8). Ms. Parks was convicted of violating the segregation laws and fined. In response, African Americans boycotted the Montgomery buses for over a year and mounted a legal challenge, which led to a successful Supreme Court decision in 1956 outlawing segregation on buses. Rosa Parks's brave act was the precipitating event of the American civil rights movement (Shipp, 2005).

On October 24, 2005, Rosa Parks died at the age of 92. To commemorate her, the American Public Transportation Association called for December 1 to be the "Tribute to Rosa Parks Day." Buses in major cities across the country designated one seat, behind the driver, to be kept empty for the day in her honor. Signs were posted on the windows adjacent to the seat, with Rosa Parks's photograph and the small caption "It all started on a bus," to alert riders (Ramirez, 2005).

A New York City journalist rode the buses that day to see if people would honor the request—after all, an empty seat on a big city bus is a coveted item. He found that the vast majority of riders did so, even during rush hour when just finding a place to stand is difficult. However, some people did sit in the special seat (Ramirez, 2005). Now this was an interesting development, both to the journalist and his fellow travelers. What were these people thinking? Why did they do it? It seemed to be a flagrant act of disrespect. How could one not honor Rosa Parks? Were these "sitters" prejudiced, even racist? Were they selfish or arrogant, believing that their personal needs were more important than anything else? In short, dispositional attributions were being made about these sitters, and they were negative attributions about the people's character and attitudes.

Rosa Parks, sitting at the front of the bus, after the Supreme Court ruled that bus segregation is illegal.

Being a good reporter, the journalist began asking the sitters why they chose to sit in this special seat. Lo and behold, a situational explanation emerged. They hadn't seen the sign. In fact, the small signs were badly placed and easy to miss in the midst of scheduling announcements (Ramirez, 2005). After the sign was pointed out to sitters, they reacted swiftly. One man "read it quickly, shuddered, then uttered a loud profanity in dismay. He scooted out of the seat. 'I didn't realize it was there ... It's history ... It means freedom'" (Ramirez, 2005, p. B1). Another rider, a black man, began to sit down but stopped halfway when he saw the sign. He said to another rider, a black woman, "'But people were sitting here.' The woman said gently, 'They couldn't see the sign.' 'Well,' the man said, peeling away the sign and moving it to the edge of the seat, 'they will now'" (Ramirez, 2005, p. B1). Thus, people on the bus were making the wrong attribution about the sitters. The other riders believed that their behavior was due to the kind of people they were (bad ones), instead of being due to the situation—in this case, a too small, badly written, and badly located sign.

The pervasive, fundamental theory or schema most of us have about human behavior is that people do what they do because of the kind of people they are, not because of the situation they are in. When thinking this way, we are more like personality psychologists, who see behavior as stemming from internal dispositions and traits, than like social psychologists, who focus on the impact of social situations on behavior. As we saw in Chapter 1, this tendency to overestimate the extent to which people's behavior is due to internal, dispositional factors, and to underestimate the role of situational factors, is called the **fundamental attribution error** (Heider, 1958; Jones, 1990; Ross, 1977; Ross & Nisbett, 1991). The fundamental attribution error has also been called the *correspondence bias* (Gilbert, 1998b; Gilbert & Jones, 1986; Gilbert & Malone, 1995; Jones, 1979, 1990).

Buses across the United States posted a sign like this one, asking riders to keep one seat empty to honor Rosa Parks.

(Richard Perry/*The New York Times*)

There have been many empirical demonstrations of the tendency to see people's behavior as a reflection of their dispositions and beliefs rather than as influenced by the situation (Gawronski, 2003; Jones, 1979, 1990; Miller, Ashton, & Mishal, 1990; Miller, Jones, & Hinkle, 1981; Vonk, 1999). For example, in a classic study, Edward Jones and Victor Harris (1967) asked college students to read an essay written by a fellow student that either supported or opposed Fidel Castro's rule in Cuba and then to guess how the author of the essay really felt about Castro (see Figure 4.4). In one condition, the researchers told the students that the author freely chose which position to take in the essay, thereby making it easy to guess how he really felt. If he chose to write in favor of Castro, clearly he must be sympathetic to Castro. In another condition, however, the students learned that the author had been assigned the position as a participant in a debate. One should not assume, then, that the writer believed what he or she wrote. Yet the participants in this study, and in dozens of others like it, assumed that the author really believed what he wrote, even when they knew he could not choose which position to take. As you can see in Figure 4.4, people moderated their guesses a little bit—there was not as much difference in their estimates of the author's attitude in the pro-Castro and anti-Castro conditions as there was in the choice condition—but they still assumed that the content of the essay reflected the author's true feelings.

> *Be not swept off your feet by the vividness of the impression, but say, "Impression, wait for me a little. Let me see what you are and what you represent."*
>
> —Epictetus, *Discourses*

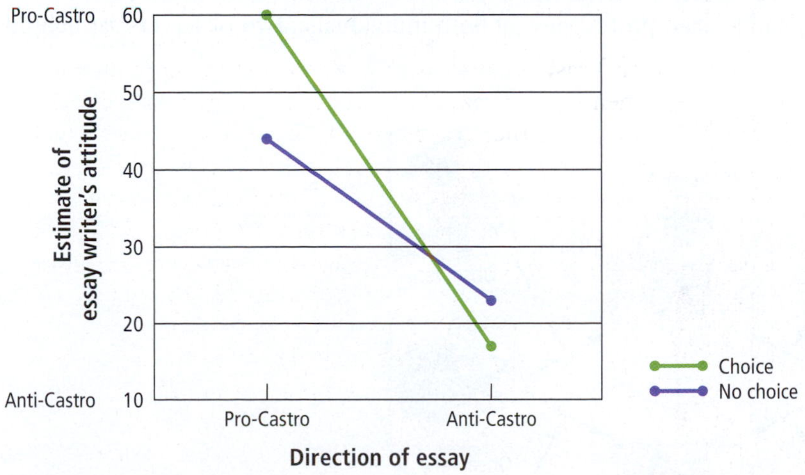

FIGURE 4.4

The Fundamental Attribution Error

Even when people knew that the author's choice of an essay topic was externally caused (i.e., in the no-choice condition), they assumed that what he wrote reflected how he really felt about Castro. That is, they made an internal attribution from his behavior.

(Adapted from Jones & Harris, 1967)

Fundamental Attribution Error

The tendency to overestimate the extent to which people's behavior is due to internal, dispositional factors and to underestimate the role of situational factors

Perceptual Salience
The seeming importance of information that is the focus of people's attention

Explore on MyPsychLab
To learn more, explore *Fundamental Attribution Error* in MyPsychLab.

Why is the fundamental attribution error so fundamental? It is not always wrong to make an internal attribution; clearly, people often do what they do because of the kind of people they are. However, considerable evidence indicates that social situations can strongly affect behavior; indeed, the major lesson of social psychology is that these influences can be extremely powerful. The point of the fundamental attribution error is that people often tend to underestimate external influences when explaining other people's behavior. Even when the influence of the situation on behavior is obvious, as in the Jones and Harris (1967) experiment, people persist in making internal attributions (Lord et al., 1997; Newman, 1996; Ross, 1977; Ross, Amabile, & Steinmetz, 1977; Ross & Nisbett, 1991).

The Role of Perceptual Salience in the Fundamental Attribution Error Why do people fall prey to the fundamental attribution error? One reason is that when we try to explain someone's behavior, our focus of attention is usually on the person, not on the surrounding situation (Baron & Misovich, 1993; Heider, 1944, 1958; Jones & Nisbett, 1972). In fact, the situational causes of another person's behavior are practically invisible to us (Gilbert & Malone, 1995). If we don't know what happened to someone earlier in the day (e.g., she received an F on her midterm), we can't use that situational information to help us understand her current behavior. And even when we know her situation, we still don't know how she interprets it; for example, the F may not have upset her because she's planning to drop the course anyway. If we don't know the meaning of the situation for her, we can't accurately judge its effects on her behavior. Much of the time, in fact, information about the situational causes of behavior is unavailable or difficult to interpret accurately (Gilbert, 1998b; Gilbert & Malone, 1995).

What information does that leave us? Although the situation may be close to invisible, the individual is extremely "perceptually prominent"—people are what our eyes and ears notice. And what we notice seems to be the reasonable and logical cause of the observed behavior (Heider, 1958). We can't see the situation, so we ignore its importance. People, not the situation, have **perceptual salience** for us; we pay attention to them, and we tend to think that they alone cause their behavior (Heider, 1958; Lassiter et al., 2002).

Several studies have confirmed the importance of perceptual salience—especially an elegant one by Shelley Taylor and Susan Fiske (1975). In this study, two male students engaged in a "get acquainted" conversation. (They were actually both accomplices of the experimenters and were following a script during their conversation.) At each session, six actual research participants also took part. They sat in assigned seats, surrounding the two conversationalists (see Figure 4.5). Two of them sat on each side of the actors; they had a clear, profile view of both individuals. Two observers sat behind

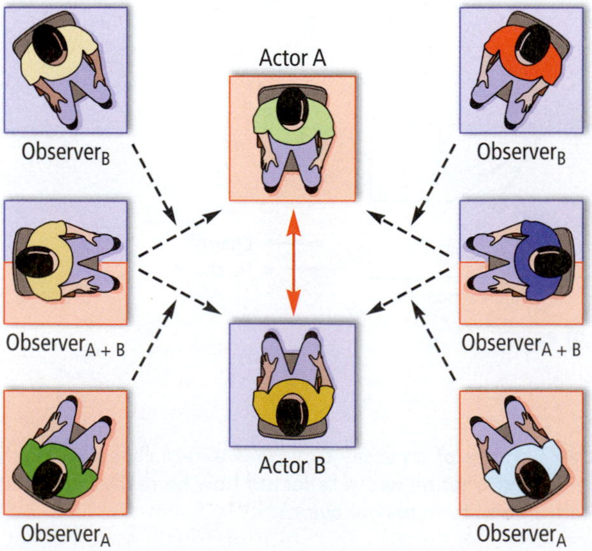

FIGURE 4.5
Manipulating Perceptual Salience
This is the seating arrangement for two actors and the six research participants in the Taylor and Fiske study. Participants rated each actor's impact on the conversation. Researchers found that people rated the actor they could see more clearly as having the larger role in the conversation.
(Adapted from Taylor & Fiske, 1975)

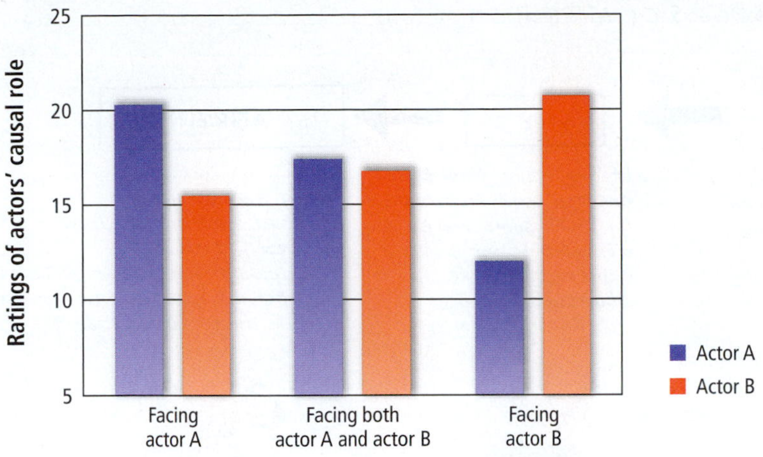

FIGURE 4.6

The Effects of Perceptual Salience

These are the ratings of each actor's causal role in the conversation. People thought that the actor they could see better had more impact on the conversation.

(Adapted from Taylor & Fiske, 1975)

each actor; they could see the back of one actor's head but the face of the other. Thus, the one who was visually salient—that is, the individual the participants could see better—was cleverly manipulated in this study.

After the conversation, the research participants were asked questions about the two men—for example, who had taken the lead in the conversation, and who had chosen the topics to be discussed? What happened? The person they could see better was the person they thought had more impact on the conversation (see Figure 4.6). Even though all the observers heard the same conversation, those who were facing student A thought he had taken the lead and chosen the topics, whereas those who were facing student B thought he had taken the lead and chosen the topics. In comparison, those who could see both students equally well thought both were equally influential.

Perceptual salience, or our visual point of view, helps explain why the fundamental attribution error is so widespread. We focus our attention more on people than on the surrounding situation because the situation is so hard to see or know; we underestimate or even forget about the influence of the situation when we are explaining human behavior. For example, when we hear someone argue strongly in favor of Castro's regime in Cuba, our first inclination is to explain this in dispositional terms: "This person must hold radical political views." We realize that this explanation might not be the whole story, however. We might think, "On the other hand, I know he was assigned this position as part of a debate" and adjust our attributions more toward a situational explanation. However, the problem is that people often don't adjust their judgments enough. In the Jones and Harris (1967) experiment, participants who knew that the essay writer did not have a choice of topics nevertheless thought he believed what he had written, at least to some extent. They adjusted insufficiently from the most salient information—the position advocated in the essay (Quattrone, 1982).

The Two-Step Process of Making Attributions In sum, we go through a **two-step process** when we make attributions (Gilbert, 1989, 1991, 1993; Krull, 1993). We make an internal attribution, assuming that a person's behavior was due to something about that person. We then attempt to adjust this attribution by considering the situation the person was in. But we often don't make enough of an adjustment in this second step. Indeed, when we are distracted or preoccupied, we often skip the second step, making an extreme internal attribution (Gilbert & Hixon, 1991; Gilbert & Osborne, 1989; Gilbert, Pelham, & Krull, 1988). Why? Because the first step (making the internal attribution) occurs quickly and spontaneously, whereas the

Two-Step Process of Attribution

Analyzing another person's behavior first by making an automatic internal attribution and only then thinking about possible situational reasons for the behavior, after which one may adjust the original internal attribution

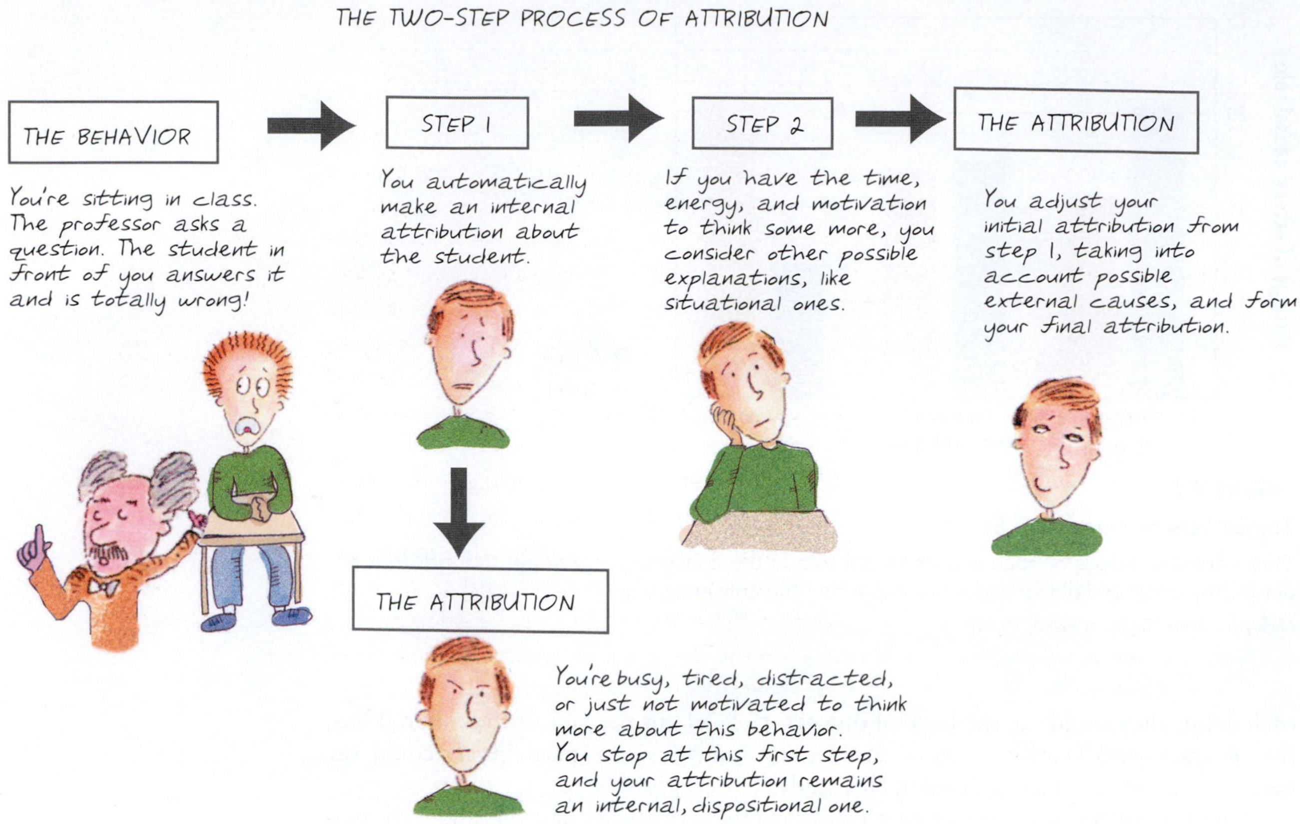

FIGURE 4.7

The Two-Step Process of Attribution

second step (adjusting for the situation) requires more effort and conscious attention (see Figure 4.7).

We will engage in this second step of attributional processing if we consciously slow down and think carefully before reaching a judgment, if we are motivated to reach as accurate a judgment as possible, or if we are suspicious about the behavior of the target person—for example, believing that he or she is lying or has ulterior motives (Hilton, Fein, & Miller, 1993; Risen & Gilovich, 2007; Webster, 1993).

Cultural Differences in Social Perception

Social psychologists are focusing more and more on the role of culture in many aspects of social perception. Does the culture in which we grow up influence how we perceive other people? Let's look at the evidence.

North American and some other Western cultures stress individual autonomy. A person is perceived as independent and self-contained; his or her behavior reflects internal traits, motives, and values (Markus & Kitayama, 1991). The intellectual history of this cultural value can be traced from the Judeo-Christian belief in the individual soul and the English legal tradition of individual rights (Menon et al., 1999; Kitayama et al., 2006). In contrast, East Asian cultures such as those in China, Japan, and Korea stress group autonomy. The individual derives his or her sense of self from the social group to which he or she belongs. The intellectual history of this belief derives from the Confucian tradition—for example, the "community man" (*qunti de fenzi*) or "social being" (*shehui de renge*), as well as from Taoism and Buddhism (Menon et al., 1999, p. 703; Zhu & Han, 2008).

Holistic versus Analytic Thinking Research has indicated that these differing cultural values affect the kind of information that people notice and pay attention to. As

CONNECTIONS

Police Interrogations and the Fundamental Attribution Error

Let's say you have been picked up by the police as a potential suspect in a crime (though, of course, you are innocent). Back at the police station, you reach the point in the process where a detective says you will now be "interviewed." You've watched enough episodes of *Law and Order* to know that this is the "interrogation" part. The detective tells you that you will be videotaped while answering questions, for possible later use in a court of law. As a student of social psychology, you should immediately ask, "Will the camera be focused only on me, or will it show me and the detective who's asking questions?" Why, you ask? Because recent research on videotaped police interrogations has shown that perceptual salience can trigger the fundamental attribution error, affecting how guilty the suspect is judged to be (Lassiter et al., 2002, 2010).

G. Daniel Lassiter and his colleagues (2007; Lassiter, 2010) presented 21 courtroom judges (who also had previous experience as both prosecutors and criminal defense attorneys) and 24 police officers (who had extensive experience conducting interrogations) with a videotaped suspect (actually a confederate) who confessed to a crime. These research participants were shown one of three videotaped camera-perspective versions: The focus was on the suspect only, on the detective only, or there was equal focus on the suspect and the detective. They were then asked to rate how "voluntary" the confession was, as opposed to "coerced." For both the judges and police officers, the videotape that focused only on the suspect produced significantly higher ratings of "voluntariness" than the other two videotape versions (Lassiter et al., 2007). The perceptual salience of the suspect, when shown all alone, triggered a fundamental attribution error, making him appear guiltier than when he was not as perceptually salient. These results are worrisome because videotaping only the suspect is standard operating procedure in real criminal investigations. In fact, only one country in the world thus far, New Zealand, has adopted an "equal focus" camera perspective (suspect + detective) for videotaped interrogations, and they have done so in response to concerns about attributional bias (Lassiter et al., 2006).

---

we discussed in Chapter 3, the values inherent in individualistic Western cultures cause people, as they grow up, to develop an *analytic thinking style*. This style involves focusing on the properties of objects (or people) while paying much less attention, if any, to the context or situation that surrounds that object. In contrast, the values of collectivistic cultures, such as those of East Asia (e.g., China, Korea, and Japan) cause people to develop a *holistic thinking style*. Here, people focus on the "whole picture"—that is the object (or person) and the context that surrounds that object, as well as the relationships that exist between them (Nisbett, 2003; Nisbett & Masuda, 2003). These differences in thinking styles influence how we perceive other people—for example, how we decode their facial expressions of emotion.

Imagine that you are talking to a group of friends. The expression on one friend's face catches your attention. She's frowning and her mouth is set in a tight line. What is she feeling? The analytic thinking style suggests that you would focus on her face alone and reach a decision. The holistic thinking style suggests that you would scan the faces of the others in the group, compare them to hers, and then reach a decision.

Takahiko Masuda and colleagues (2008) conducted a study much like this example on decoding facial expressions. They presented research participants in the United States and Japan with cartoon drawings of people in groups. One person in each cartoon was the central figure, shown in the foreground. This person had a facial expression that was happy, sad, angry, or neutral. The other people in the group had facial expressions that either matched the central figure or were different. The participants' task was to judge the central person's emotion on a 10-point scale. The researchers found that the facial

What emotion do you think the central person (the one in the middle) is experiencing in each of these cartoons? Your answer might depend on whether you live in a Western or East Asian culture (see the text as to why).

expressions on the group members' faces had little effect on Americans' ratings of the central figure. If that figure was smiling broadly, he received a high rating for "happy." It didn't matter what the rest of the group was expressing. In comparison, the facial expressions of the group members had a significant effect on the Japanese participants' ratings of the central figure. A broad smile was interpreted as very happy if the group members were also smiling; the same broad smile was interpreted as significantly less happy if the other group members were looking sad or angry. In short, the meaning of the cartoon character's facial expression depended upon his "context"—what the other cartoon characters standing next to him were feeling (Masuda et al., 2008). In addition, the researchers measured the eye-tracking movements of the participants as they looked at the cartoons. The Japanese spent more time looking at the cartoon characters in the background than did the Americans. Both groups began by looking at the central character, but after 1 second, the Japanese started to scan their eyes over the other characters significantly more than did the Americans (Masuda et al., 2008).

Social Neuroscience Evidence The eye-tracking results in the study by Masuda and colleagues (2008) suggest that something very interesting is going on, at a physiological level, in people who engage in analytic versus holistic thinking. Two groups of researchers have investigated this question, using different techniques. Trey Hedden and colleagues (2008) used functional magnetic resonance imaging (fMRI) to examine where in the brain cultural experience affects perceptual processing. Their participants, East Asians and European Americans, underwent fMRI while making judgments about the length of lines inside boxes. Some of the participants were told to ignore the box around each line ("ignore context") and some were told to pay attention to the box around each line ("attend to context"). Although participants were equally accurate at judging the lengths of the lines, they showed significantly more brain activity when they had to follow the instructions that were the opposite of their cultural thinking style. That is, American participants showed greater activation in higher-order cortical regions (frontal and parietal areas) when told to pay attention to the context, while East Asian participants showed greater activity in the same brain regions when told to ignore the context. Greater cortical activation means that the participant had to exert more attention (in a sense, had to work harder cognitively) when asked to perceive objects in a way that was not typical for him or her (Hedden et al., 2008).

The second group of researchers used event-related potentials (ERPs) to measure brain activity (Lewis, Goto, & Kong, 2008). While fMRI indicates which brain regions are active, ERPs provide a more fine-grained analysis of the onset and offset of neural firing. These researchers also presented participants with a series of simple perceptual tasks that involved visual information about "targets" and context. In an interesting twist, their participants were all Americans who had grown up in American culture but were of two different ethnic backgrounds: European American or East Asian American. The pattern of ERPs indicated that the European American participants paid more attention to the targets, while the East Asian American participants paid more attention to the context surrounding the targets.

Cultural Differences in the Fundamental Attribution Error Earlier we saw that people often commit the fundamental attribution error, overestimating the extent to which people's behavior is due to internal, dispositional factors and underestimating the role of situational factors. Is the fundamental attribution error stronger in Western than Eastern cultures?

As it turns out, people in individualist cultures do prefer dispositional attributions about others, relative to people in collectivist cultures, who prefer situational attributions. For example, Joan Miller (1984) asked people of two cultures—Hindus living in India and Americans living in the United States—to think of various examples of behaviors performed by their friends and to explain why those behaviors occurred. The American participants preferred dispositional explanations for the behaviors. In contrast, Indian participants preferred situational explanations for their friends' behaviors.

But, you might be thinking, perhaps the Americans and Indians generated different kinds of examples. Perhaps the Indians thought of behaviors that were really more situationally caused, whereas the Americans thought of behaviors that were really more dispositionally caused. To test this alternative hypothesis, Miller (1984) took some of the behaviors generated by the Indian participants and gave them to Americans to explain. The difference in internal and external attributions appeared again: Americans still found internal, dispositional causes for the behaviors that the Indians had thought were caused by the situation.

Another study compared newspaper articles in Chinese- and English-language newspapers. The researchers targeted two mass murders, one committed by a Chinese graduate student in Iowa and one committed by a Caucasian postal worker in Michigan (Morris & Peng, 1994). They coded all the news articles about the two crimes that appeared in the *New York Times* and the *World Journal*, a Chinese-language U.S. newspaper. The results showed that journalists writing in English made significantly more dispositional attributions about both mass murderers than journalists writing in Chinese did. For example, American reporters described one murderer as a "darkly disturbed man" with a "sinister edge" to his personality. Chinese reporters, when describing the same murderer, emphasized more situational causes, such as "not getting along with his adviser" and his "isolation from the Chinese community."

Finally, Ying-Yi Hong and colleagues (2003) investigated the fundamental attribution error with research participants who were Hong Kong Chinese college students. They described these students as bicultural—deriving their identity not only from their Hong Kong Chinese culture, but also from Western culture, to which they had had a great deal of exposure. The participants were first shown a series of photographs and answered brief questions about them. The purpose of the photographs was to "prime" one aspect of their bicultural identity. Half the participants saw photographs representing American culture, such as the American flag and the U.S. Capitol building. The other half saw photographs representing Chinese culture, such as a Chinese dragon and the Great Wall. Participants in the control condition saw photographs of geometric figures, which did not prime either culture. Next, in a supposedly unrelated task, participants were shown a photograph of a fish swimming in front of a school of other fish. They were asked to make an attribution: Why was this fish swimming in front of the other fish? Their responses were coded for dispositional reasons (e.g., "The fish is leading the other fish") or for situational reasons (e.g., "The fish is being chased by the other fish"). The researchers found that about 30% of the control group made situational attributions about the fish. However, participants primed with thoughts of one culture or the other showed significantly different patterns. Those primed with Chinese

Research has shown that when forming attributions, people in collectivistic cultures such as Japan are more likely to take situational information into account than are people in individualistic cultures.

Bicultural research participants were first "primed" with images from one of their cultural heritages: either images evoking Chinese culture or images evoking American culture, like these.

cultural images were even more likely to make situational attributions about the fish (nearly 50% of the participants), while those primed with American cultural images were even less likely to make situational attributions (about 15% of the participants), instead making dispositional attributions about the fish (Hong, Chiu, & Kung, 1997; Hong et al., 2000).

Thus, it appears that Western cultures cause people to think more like personality psychologists, viewing behavior in dispositional terms. In contrast, Eastern cultures seem to cause people to think more like social psychologists, considering the situational causes of behavior.

However, it would be a mistake to think that members of collectivist cultures don't *ever* make dispositional attributions. Of course they do—it's just a matter of degree. Recent research indicates that a tendency to think dispositionally about others is prevalent in many cultures. However, members of collectivistic cultures are more aware of how the situation affects behavior and more likely to take situational effects into account (Choi et al., 2003; Choi & Nisbett, 1998; Choi, Nisbett, & Norenzayan, 1999; Krull et al., 1999; Miyamoto & Kitayama, 2002). Thus, the difference is that people in collectivist cultures are more likely to go beyond dispositional explanations and consider information about the situation as well.

Resemblances are the shadows of differences. Different people see different similarities and similar differences.
—Vladimir Nabokov, *Pale Fire*

In conclusion, how can we summarize cultural differences in the attribution in terms of the two-step process we discussed earlier (see Figure 4.7)? What are people in collectivist cultures doing differently from people in individualist cultures? At what stage in this process do the two cultures diverge? Everyone appears to start off at the same point, making dispositional attributions about other people. What happens next is that people in collectivistic cultures look to the situation; they revise and correct their first impressions, taking the situation into account. Westerners tend to avoid this second step. Their first impression, the dispositional attribution, sticks (Choi et al., 2003; Hedden et al., 2008; Knowles et al., 2001; Lewis et al., 2008; Mason & Morris, 2010).

Self-Serving Attributions
Explanations for one's successes that credit internal, dispositional factors and explanations for one's failures that blame external, situational factors

Next, these research participants were asked to make an attribution about the behavior of the fish in the front of the pack. Would they make dispositional or situational attributions about the fish's behavior, given the cultural priming they had experienced earlier?

Self-Serving Attributions

Imagine that Alison goes to her chemistry class one day feeling anxious because she's getting her midterm grade that day. The professor returns her exam. Alison turns it over and sees that she has received an A. What will Alison think explains her grade? As you might guess, people tend to take personal credit for their successes but to blame their failures on external events beyond their control. Alison is likely to think that her success was due to the fact that she's good at chemistry and just plain smart. But what if Alison got a bad grade? Here, she is more likely to blame the professor for giving an unfair test. When people's self-esteem is threatened, they often make **self-serving attributions**. Simply put, these attributions refer to our tendency to take credit for our successes by making internal attributions but to blame others or the situation for our failures by making external attributions (Carver, De Gregorio, & Gillis, 1980; McAllister, 1996; Miller & Ross, 1975; Pronin, Lin, & Ross, 2002; Robins & Beer, 2001).

A particularly interesting arena for studying self-serving attributions is professional sports. When explaining their victories, athletes and coaches both point overwhelmingly to aspects of their own teams or players. In fact, an analysis of professional athletes' and coaches' explanations for their team's wins and losses found that 80% of the attributions for wins were to such internal factors. Losses were more likely to be attributed to external causes, outside of the team's control, such as bad luck or the superior play of the other team (Lau & Russell, 1980).

Who is more likely to make self-serving attributions? Roesch and Amirkhan (1997) wondered if in the realm of sports a player's skill, experience, and type of sport (team sports versus solo sports such as tennis) affected the type of attribution the player made about a sports outcome. They found that less-experienced athletes were more likely to make self-serving attributions than experienced ones. Experienced athletes realize that losses are sometimes their fault and that they can't always take credit for wins. Highly skilled athletes made more self-serving attributions than those with lower ability. The highly talented athlete believes that success is due to his or her prowess, while failure, an unusual and upsetting outcome, is due to teammates or other circumstances of the game. Finally, athletes in solo sports made more self-serving attributions than those in team sports. Solo athletes know that winning and losing rests on their shoulders. You can explore self-serving attributions by sports figures in the following Try It!

Why do we make self-serving attributions? Most people try to maintain their self-esteem whenever possible, even if that means distorting reality by changing a thought or belief. (We will discuss this concept at length in Chapter 6.) Here we see a specific attributional strategy that can be used to maintain or raise self-esteem: Just locate "causality"—the reason something happened—where it does you the most good (Greenberg, Pyszczynski, & Solomon, 1982; Snyder & Higgins, 1988; Shepard, Malone, & Sweeny, 2008). We are particularly likely to engage in self-serving attributions when we fail at something and we feel we can't improve at it. The external attribution truly protects our self-esteem, as there is little hope we can do better in the future. But if we believe we can improve, we're more likely to attribute our current failure to internal causes and then work on improving (Duval & Silvia, 2002).

A second reason has to do with how we present ourselves to others, a topic we'll explore in Chapter 5 (Goffman, 1959). We want people to think well of us and to admire

TRY IT! Self-Serving Attributions in the Sports News

Do athletes and coaches tend to take credit for their wins but make excuses for their losses? Find out for yourself the next time you look at the sports news after an important game. Analyze the athletes' comments to see what kinds of attributions they make about their performance. Is the pattern a self-serving one?

For example, after a win, does an athlete make internal attributions like "We won because of excellent teamwork; our defensive line really did their job today" or "My serve was totally on"? After a loss, does the athlete make external attributions like "All the injuries we've had this season have really hurt us" or "That line judge made every call against me"? According to the research, these self-serving attributions should occur more often than the opposite pattern—for example, where a winner says, "We won because the other team played so badly it was like they were dead" (external) or where a loser says, "I played terribly today. I stank" (internal).

Next, see if you can find examples that fit Roesch and Amirkhan's (1997) research. Are self-serving attributions more common among solo-sport athletes than team-sport athletes? Do the athlete "stars" make more self-serving attributions than their less talented colleagues? Finally, think about the three reasons we identify for why people make self-serving attributions (maintaining self-esteem, presenting yourself positively to others, and personal knowledge about your past performances). When a sports figure makes a self-serving attribution, which one of these three motives do you think is at work? For example, if New England Patriots quarterback Tom Brady or tennis champion Serena Williams attributed a loss to factors outside of themselves, do you think they would be protecting their self-esteem, trying to look good in front of others? Or would they be making the most logical attribution they could, given their experience (i.e., because they are so talented, most losses aren't their fault)?

us. Telling others that our poor performance was due to some external cause puts a "good face" on failure; many people call this strategy "making excuses" (Greenberg et al., 1982; Tetlock, 1981; Weary & Arkin, 1981).

A third reason people make self-serving attributions has to do with our earlier discussion about the kind of information that is available to people. Let's imagine the attributional process of another student in the chemistry class, Ron, who did poorly on the midterm. Ron knows that he studied very hard for the midterm, that he typically does well on chemistry tests, and that in general he is a very good student. The D on the chemistry midterm comes as a surprise. The most logical attribution Ron can make is that the test was unfair—the D grade wasn't due to a lack of ability or effort. The professor, however, knows that some students did well on the test; given the information that is available to the professor, it is logical for him to conclude that Ron, and not the fact that it was a difficult test, was responsible for the poor grade (Miller & Ross, 1975; Nisbett & Ross, 1980).

People also alter their attributions to deal with other kinds of threats to their self-esteem. One of the hardest things to understand in life is the occurrence of tragic events such as rapes, terminal diseases, and fatal accidents. Even when they happen to strangers we have never met, they can be upsetting. They remind us that if such tragedies can happen to someone else, they can happen to us. So we take steps to deny this fact. One way we do this is by making **defensive attributions**, which are explanations for behavior that defend us from feelings of vulnerability and mortality.

CONNECTIONS

The "Bias Blind Spot"

By now, we've discussed a number of attributional biases. Can you recall times when your thinking has reflected the fundamental attribution error or a self-serving attribution? What about other people? Do you think they fall prey to such biases more often than you do? Emily Pronin and colleagues have studied just this question and found evidence for a **bias blind spot**: We tend to think that others are more susceptible to attributional biases than we are, indicating a "blind spot" when reflecting on our own thought processes (Pronin, Lin, & Ross, 2002; Pronin, Gilovich, & Ross, 2004).

In order to study the bias blind spot, these researchers presented research participants with descriptions of a number of biases. We will focus on two here: self-serving attributions for success and failure, and "blaming the victim," or making a dispositional attribution about a victim's plight. The descriptions the participants read never used the word "bias" (which makes it sound like a "bad" thing); instead, they were described as "tendencies" to think a certain way, which were then explained. Participants were asked to rate how susceptible they thought they were to each of these tendencies in thinking, using a scale ranging from "not at all" to "strongly." Next, participants made the same ratings for how susceptible they thought the average American was to these tendencies in thinking.

The results indicated a striking difference between the two positions. Participants felt they were only "somewhat" susceptible to self-serving attributions, while the average American was rated as much more susceptible (see Figure 4.8). Similarly, participants felt they were barely susceptible to committing the "blaming the victim" attribution; but again, the average American was judged as much more likely to do so (see Figure 4.8).The same pattern of results was found when other participants were asked to rate themselves and their "average fellow classmate" (Pronin et al., 2002).

Thus, it appears that we realize that attributionally biased thinking can occur—in other people—but we're not so good at spotting it in ourselves. Our thoughts seem rational and sensible. We feel we have good reasons to support our conclusions, but other people, hey, they're susceptible to biases! Instead, we need to reflect on our judgment processes, check our conclusions, and remind ourselves that a bias blind spot may be lurking.

Defensive Attributions

Explanations for behavior that avoid feelings of vulnerability and mortality

Bias Blind Spot

The tendency to think that other people are more susceptible to attributional biases in their thinking than we are

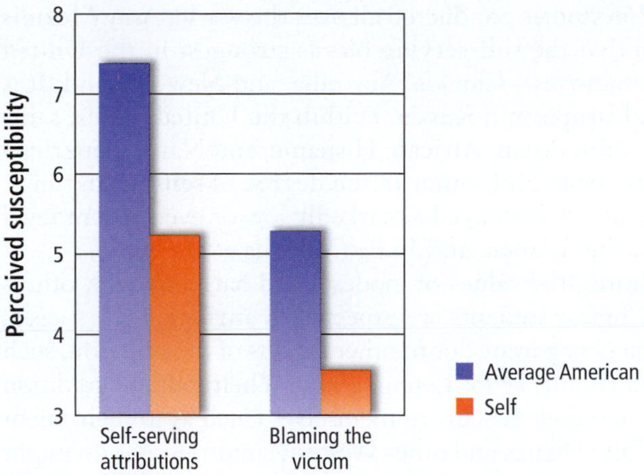

FIGURE 4.8

Perceived Susceptibility to Attributional Biases for Self and the Average American

Research participants rated their own susceptibility to two attributional biases and that of the "average American." They believed that others were significantly more likely to engage in biased thinking than they themselves were.

(Adapted from Pronin, Lin, & Ross, 2002)

One form of defensive attribution is to believe that bad things happen only to bad people—or at least, only to people who make stupid mistakes or poor choices. Therefore, bad things won't happen to us because we won't be that stupid or careless. Melvin Lerner (1980, 1998) has called this the **belief in a just world** —the assumption that people get what they deserve and deserve what they get (Hafer, 2000; Hafer & Begue, 2005; Aguiar et al., 2008).

The just-world belief has some sad and even tragic consequences. For example, suppose a female student on your campus was the victim of a date rape by a male fellow student. How do you think you and your friends would react? Would you wonder if she'd done something to trigger the rape? Was she acting suggestively earlier in the evening? Had she invited the man into her room?

Research by Elaine Walster (1966) and others has focused on such attributions, which these investigators call "blaming the victim" (e.g., Burger, 1981; Lerner & Miller, 1978; Stormo, Lang, & Stritzke, 1997). In several experiments, they have found that the victims of crimes or accidents are often seen as causing their fate. For example, not only do people tend to believe that rape victims are to blame for the rape (Abrams et al., 2003; Bell, Kuriloff, & Lottes, 1994), but also battered wives are often seen as responsible for their abusive husbands' behavior (Summers & Feldman, 1984). By using this attributional bias, the perceiver does not have to acknowledge that there is a certain randomness in life, that an accident or criminal may be waiting just around the corner for an innocent person like oneself. The belief in a just world keeps anxiety-provoking thoughts about one's own safety at bay.

Culture and Other Attributional Biases

Continuing to explore the link between culture and attributional biases, social psychologists have examined the self-serving bias and found a strong cultural component to it as well. For example, researchers asked industrial workers and their supervisors in Ghana, Africa, to assign causality for on-the-job accidents. Both groups made very self-serving attributions. Workers blamed factors in the situation, which absolved them of responsibility and blame; for example, they cited work overload, management pressure, and inadequate training. Supervisors blamed the workers—it was their carelessness, lack of skill, and ignorance that led to accidents (Gyekye & Salminen, 2004).

Belief in a Just World

A form of defensive attribution wherein people assume that bad things happen to bad people and that good things happen to good people

In a recent meta-analysis of 266 studies conducted all over the world, Amy Mezulis and her colleagues (2004) found that the self-serving bias is strongest in the United States and some other Western countries—Canada, Australia, and New Zealand. It is also prevalent in Africa, Eastern Europe, and Russia. Within the United States, samples of participants who were of white, Asian, African, Hispanic, and Native American descent did not differ significantly from each other in the degree of self-serving bias. On the other hand, some Asian cultures displayed a markedly low or even absent level of self-serving bias: Japan, the Pacific Islands, and India (Mezulis et al., 2004).

In many traditional Asian cultures, the values of modesty and harmony with others are highly valued. For example, Chinese students are expected to attribute their success to other people, such as their teachers or parents, or to other aspects of the situation, such as the high quality of their school (Bond, 1996; Leung, 1996). Their cultural tradition does not encourage them to attribute their success to themselves (such as to their talent or intelligence), as it does in the United States and other Western countries. As you might expect, Chinese research participants took less credit for their successes than U.S. participants did (Anderson, 1999; Lee & Seligman, 1997). Instead, Chinese students attributed their success to aspects of their situation, reflecting the values of their culture.

Do individualistic and collectivistic cultures differ in how they explain Olympic gold-medal success? Prior meta-analytic research has indicated that "cultural products" such as advertising, song lyrics, television shows, and art have content that reflects their culture's values: more individualistic content in Western cultures and more collectivistic content in countries such as Japan, Korea, China, and Mexico (Morling & Lamoreaux, 2008). Hazel Markus and her colleagues (2006) found that this applies to television and newspaper sports commentary as well. They coded Japanese and American media accounts of their countries' gold medal–winning athletes in the 2000 and 2002 Olympics. They found that U.S. media described the performance of American gold medalists in terms of their unique abilities and talents; in short, the athletes had demonstrated that they had "the right stuff" (Markus et al., 2006, p. 110). In comparison, Japanese media described the performance of Japanese gold medalists in much broader terms, including the individual's ability but also encompassing his or her past experiences of success and failure, and the role of other people such as coaches, teammates, and family in his or her success. Finally, American coverage focused more on positive aspects than negative ones (e.g., "[his] strength keeps him in the running"), consistent with a self-serving attributional style, while Japanese coverage focused more equally on positive and negative aspects (e.g., "Her second Olympics is a regrettable one. She was almost at the top, but she didn't have a perfect performance"; Markus et al., 2006, pp. 106–107). The following two quotes from gold medalists summarize the different ways in which culture influences how one defines and explains one's own behavior:

> *I think I just stayed focused. It was time to show the world what I could do ... I knew I could beat [her], deep down in my heart I believed it ... the doubts kept creeping in ... but I just said, "No, this is my night." (Misty Hyman, American gold medalist in the women's 200-m butterfly).* (Markus et al., 2006, p. 103)

> *Here is the best coach in the world, the best manager in the world, and all of the people who support me—all these things were getting together and became a gold medal. So I think I didn't get it alone, not only by myself (Naoko Takahashi, Japanese gold medalist in the women's marathon).* (Markus et al., 2006, p. 103)

Sports winners and losers often make very different, self-serving attributions to explain the outcome of the competition.

What about failure? Recall that in individualistic cultures such as the United States, people tend toward the self-serving bias, looking outside of themselves—to the situation—to explain failure. In collectivist cultures such as China, the reverse is true: People attribute failure to internal causes, not to external ones (Anderson, 1999; Oishi, Wyer, & Colcombe, 2000). In fact, in some Asian cultures such as Japan and Korea, self-critical attributions are extremely common and an important "glue" that holds groups together. When one criticizes one's self (the opposite of a self-serving attribution), others offer sympathy and compassion, which strengthens the interdependence of the group members (Kitayama & Uchida, 2003; Kitayama et al., 1995).

Recall that the belief in a just world is a defensive attribution that helps people maintain their vision of life as safe, orderly, and predictable. Is there a cultural component to it as well? Adrian Furnham (1993) argues that in a society where most people tend to believe the world is a just place, economic and social inequities are considered "fair." In such societies, people believe that the poor and disadvantaged have less because they deserve less. Thus, the just-world attribution can be used to explain and justify injustice. Preliminary research suggests that this is the case: In cultures with extremes of wealth and poverty, just-world attributions are more common than in cultures where wealth is more evenly distributed (Dalbert & Yamauchi, 1994; Furnham, 1993; Furnham & Procter, 1989). For example, research participants in India and South Africa received higher scores on the just-world belief scale than participants in the United States, Australia, Hong Kong, and Zimbabwe, who had scores in the middle of the scale. The lowest-scoring groups in the sample—those who believed the least in a just world—were the British and the Israelis (Furnham, 1993).

Watch on MyPsychLab
To learn more, watch the MyPsychLab video ***Explain "attribution" and the ways we look at people of different cultures.***

USE IT!

You're going to spend your whole life making attributions about other people. You'll need to make decisions about what kind of people they "really" are. Someone you can love? Someone you can't trust? How to do that accurately? That is the question. So much rides on "accuracy" in this area of life, and yet we often have, at best, imperfect knowledge upon which to base our judgments. Here's what you can do: First, remember that attributions come in two "flavors": *internal* and *external*. Remind yourself, often, to think about both as potential causes for another's behavior. Second, remember the bias blind spot. If you find yourself overrelying on one type information (perhaps falling prey to an attributional bias), force yourself to consider the other possibility. Play fair, in other words, when you make attributions. Human behavior is remarkably complex and is often a product of both the individual and the situation. Third, when you're forming an attribution about another, think of it as a hypothesis, one that you're working on but are willing to change when new information comes in. Fourth, acknowledge when you've been right, but also acknowledge when you've been wrong. Incorrect attributions can be an immense learning experience. In fact, we call that "gaining wisdom." So go out there, and be wise!

Summary

How do people use nonverbal cues to understand others?

- **Nonverbal communication** Nonverbal communication is used to express emotion, convey attitudes, and communicate personality traits. People can accurately decode subtle nonverbal cues.
  - **Facial Expressions of Emotion** The six major emotions are universal, encoded and decoded similarly by people around the world; they have evolutionary significance. **Affect blends** occur when one part of the face registers one emotion and another part, a different emotion. Mirror neurons are involved in emotional encoding and decoding, and help us experience empathy.
  - **Culture and the Channels of Nonverbal Communication** Other channels of nonverbal communication include eye gaze, touch, personal space, gesture, and tone of voice. **Display rules** are particular to each culture and dictate what kinds of emotional expressions people are supposed to show. **Emblems** are gestures with well-defined meanings and are culturally determined.

What are implicit personality theories and where do they come from?

- **Implicit Personality Theories: Filling in the Blanks** To understand other people, we observe their behavior but we also infer their feelings, traits, and motives. To do so, we use general notions or schemas about which personality traits go together in one person.
  - **Culture and Implicit Personality Theories** These general notions, or schemas, are shared by people in a culture and are passed from one generation to another.

How do we determine why people do what they do?

- **Causal Attribution: Answering the "Why" Question** According to **attribution theory**, we try to determine why people do what they do in order to uncover the feelings and traits that are behind their actions. This helps us understand and predict our social world.
  - **The Nature of the Attribution Process** When trying to decide what causes people's behavior, we can make one of two attributions: an **internal**, or dispositional, attribution or an **external**, situational, attribution.
  - **The Covariation Model: Internal Versus External Attributions** The **covariation model** focuses on observations of behavior across time, place, actors, and targets of the behavior. It examines how the perceiver chooses either an internal or an external attribution. We make such choices by using **consensus**, **distinctiveness**, and **consistency** information.
  - **The Fundamental Attribution Error: People as Personality Psychologists** In making attributions, people also use various mental shortcuts, including schemas and theories. One common shortcut is the **fundamental attribution error**, the tendency to believe that people's behavior corresponds to (matches) their dispositions. A reason for this bias is that a person's behavior has greater **perceptual salience** than does the surrounding situation. The **two-step process of attribution** states that the initial and automatic attribution tends to be dispositional, but it can be altered by situational information at the second step.
  - **Cultural Differences in Social Perception** Although people from individualistic and collectivistic cultures both demonstrate the fundamental attribution error, members of collectivist cultures are more sensitive to situational causes of behavior and more likely to rely on situational explanations, as long as situational variables are salient. A reliance on holistic versus analytic styles of thinking underlies this effect.
  - **Self-Serving Attributions** People's attributions are also influenced by their personal needs. **Self-serving attributions** occur when people make internal attributions for their successes and external attributions for their failures. **Defensive attributions** help people avoid feelings of mortality. One type of defensive attribution is the **belief in a just world**, where we believe that bad things happen to bad people and good things happen to good people. The **bias blind spot** indicates that we think other people are more susceptible to attributional biases in their thinking than we are.

What role does culture play in the formation of attributions?

- **Culture and Other Attributional Biases** There is evidence for cross-cultural differences in **self-serving** and **defensive attributions**. Typically, the difference occurs between Western, individualistic cultures and Eastern, collectivistic cultures.

Chapter 4 Test

Study and **Review** on **MyPsychLab**

1. Paul Ekman and Walter Friesen traveled to New Guinea to study the meaning of various facial expressions in the primitive South Fore tribe. What major conclusion did they reach?
   a. Facial expressions are not universal because they have different meanings in different cultures.
   b. The six major emotional expressions are universal.
   c. The six major emotional expressions are not universal.
   d. The members of the South Fore used different facial expressions than Westerners to express the same emotion.

2. What is a major assumption of Kelley's covariation model of attribution?
   a. We make quick attributions after observing one instance of someone's behavior.
   b. People make causal attributions using cultural schemas.
   c. People infer the cause of others' behaviors through introspection.
   d. People gather information to make causal attributions rationally and logically.

3. Which of the following psychological phenomena shows the least cultural variation?
   a. Self-serving attributions
   b. Implicit personality theories
   c. Anger and fear facial expressions
   d. Fundamental attribution error

4. Suppose that Mischa has found that when she sits in the first row of discussion classes she gets a better participation grade, regardless of how much she actually participates. Her positioning in front of the teacher could have an effect on how large of a role the teacher thinks Mischa has in discussion, due to
   a. the teacher's use of schemas.
   b. perceptual salience.
   c. the teacher's implicit personality theories.
   d. the two-step process of attribution.

5. Mr. Rowe and Ms. Dabney meet on a blind date. They get along well until they get into his black convertible to go to a movie. Ms. Dabney is quiet and reserved for the rest of the evening. It turns out that her brother had recently been in a serious accident in that same type of car and seeing it brought up those unwanted emotions. Mr. Rowe assumes that Ms. Dabney has a cold and reserved personality, thereby demonstrating
   a. a belief in a just world.
   b. the fundamental attribution error.
   c. perceptual salience.
   d. insufficient justification.

6. Suppose a certain student, Jake, falls asleep during every chemistry class. Further suppose that Jake is the only one who falls asleep in this class and he falls asleep in all of his other classes. According to Kelley's covariation theory of attribution, how will people explain his behavior?
   a. It is due to something unusual about Jake, because his behavior is low in consensus, high in distinctiveness, and high in consistency.
   b. Chemistry is really a boring class, because Jake's behavior is high in consensus, high in distinctiveness, and high in consistency.
   c. It is due to something unusual about Jake, because his behavior is low in consensus, low in distinctiveness, and high in consistency.
   d. It is due to something peculiar about the circumstances on a particular day, because his behavior is high in consensus.

7. Imagine that you are in Hong Kong reading the morning news and you notice a headline about a double murder that took place overnight. A suspect is in custody. Which of the following headlines is most likely to accompany the story?
   a. Dispute over Gambling Debt Ends in Murder
   b. Crazed Murdered Slays Two
   c. Homicidal Maniac Stalks Innocents
   d. Bloodthirsty Mobster Takes Revenge

8. Ming is from China; Jason is from the United States. Both participate in an experiment in which they take a test, are given feedback, and are told that they did very well. They are then asked to make attributions for their performance. Based on cross-cultural research on the self-serving bias, you would expect that
   a. Jason, but not Ming, will say that he succeeded due to his high ability.
   b. neither Ming nor Jason will say that they succeeded due to their high ability.
   c. both Ming and Jason will say that they succeeded due to their high ability.
   d. Ming, but not Jason, will say that he succeeded due to his high ability.

9. Which of the following statements best describes cultural differences in the fundamental attribution error?
   a. Members of collectivist cultures rarely make dispositional attributions.
   b. Members of Western cultures rarely make dispositional attributions.
   c. Members of collectivist cultures are more likely to go beyond dispositional explanations, considering information about the situation as well.
   d. Members of Western cultures are more likely to go beyond dispositional explanations, considering information about the situation as well.

10. It is 10 A.M. and Jamie is dragging himself to his next class to turn in a paper for which he pulled an all-nighter. Through a haze of exhaustion, on the way to class he sees a student slip and fall down. How would Jamie be most likely to interpret the cause of the student's behavior?
   a. Jamie's attribution will most heavily be influenced by his own personality.
   b. Given what we know about Jamie's current cognitive capacity, he will likely assume that the student fell because he or she was clumsy.
   c. Jamie would probably attribute the cause to the situation, such as the fact that it was raining and the sidewalks were slippery.
   d. Jamie would be so tired that he would not make any causal attributions.

Answer Key

1-b, 2-d, 3-c, 4-b, 5-b,
6-c, 7-a, 8-a, 9-c, 10-b

5 The Self

Understanding Ourselves in a Social Context

GREAT ATHLETES ARE BORN AND NOT MADE—OR SO IT SEEMS. "She's a natural," we hear, or "he's one in a million." Talent is important to athletic success, of course, which is why one of your authors became a psychologist instead of a professional baseball player. But is talent everything? Consider Michael Jordan, thought to be the most gifted basketball player who ever lived. Did you know he was cut from his high school team? (Yes, *that* Michael Jordan.) Rather than giving up, he redoubled his efforts, leaving home at 6:00 in the morning to practice before school. He eventually made it to the University of North Carolina, which has one of the top basketball programs in the country. But instead of resting on his laurels, Jordan constantly worked on his game. One year, after a disappointing loss that ended North Carolina's season, Jordan went right to the gym and spent hours working on his jump shot. Mia Hamm, who in her prime was the best women's soccer player in the world, had the same attitude. When she was 10, she talked herself onto an 11-year-old boys' team and eventually led them in scoring. In college she didn't think she was that good, but as she played against the top players in the country, she found herself "improving faster than I had ever dreamed possible" (Hamm, 1999, p. 4). After playing on teams that won the World Cup and an Olympic gold medal, here is what Hamm said about people who called her the best player in the world: "They're wrong. I have the potential, maybe, but I'm still not there" (Hamm, 1999, p. 15).

The point of these stories is not just that "practice makes perfect"; it's about the importance of how we see ourselves and our abilities. Some people view athletic talent as a gift you either have or you don't—the "one in a million" theory. The problem is that when such people do poorly, as every athlete does on occasion, it is a devastating sign that they don't have it. "I'm *not* one in a million and nothing can change that," they think. "So why bother practicing? Maybe I should take a psychology class instead." Others, such as Michael Jordan and Mia Hamm, view athletic performance as a skill that can be improved. Failure is a sign that they need to work harder, not that they should give up. As we will see in this chapter, how people view their own abilities and interpret the reasons for their behavior can be crucial determinants of their success. But how do people come to know themselves? More generally, what is the nature of the self, and how do people discover it? These are the questions to which we turn.

FOCUS QUESTIONS

- What is the self-concept, and how does it develop?
- How do we come to understand ourselves and define who we are?
- When are we likely to succeed at self-control, and when are we likely to fail?
- How do we portray ourselves so that others will see us as we want to be seen?
- What are the pros and cons of having high self-esteem?

The Origins of the Self

Who are you? How did you come to be this person you call "myself"? A good place to begin is with the question of whether we are the only species that has a "self." Although it is doubtful that other species can think of themselves as unique beings in the same way that we do, some fascinating

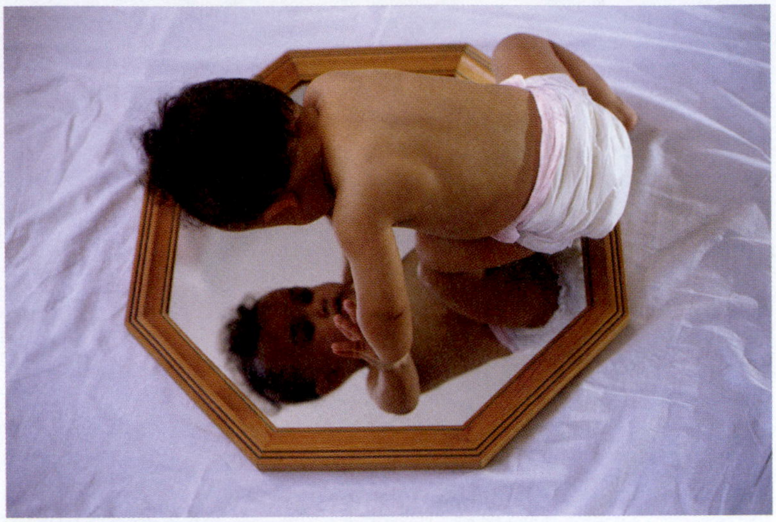

Researchers have examined whether other species have a self-concept, by seeing whether individuals recognize that an image in a mirror is them and not another member of their species. The same procedure has been used with human infants.

studies suggest that other species have at least a rudimentary sense of self (Gallup, 1997). To study whether animals have a self-concept, researchers place a mirror in an animal's cage until the mirror becomes a familiar object. The animal is then briefly anesthetized, and an odorless red dye is painted on its brow or ear. What happens when the animal wakes up and looks in the mirror? Members of the great ape family, such as chimpanzees and orangutans, immediately touch the area of their heads marked with the red spot, whereas lesser apes, such as gibbons, do not (Suddendorf & Collier-Baker, 2009).

These studies suggest that chimps and orangutans have a rudimentary self-concept. They realize that the image in the mirror is themselves and not another animal, and they recognize that they look different from how they looked before (Gallup, Anderson, & Shillito, 2002; Heschl & Burkart, 2006; Posada & Colell, 2007). What about other animals? As mentioned, lesser apes do not pass the mirror test, but there are cases in which individual members of other species have, including dolphins, an Asian elephant, and two magpies (Emery & Clayton, 2005; Plotnik & de Waal, 2006; Prior, Schwarz, & Gunturkun, 2008; Reiss & Marino, 2001). This raises the intriguing possibility that some species other than the great apes also have a rudimentary self-concept.

Wondering when a sense of self develops in humans, researchers used a variation of the red-dye test with toddlers and found that self-recognition develops at around 18 to 24 months of age (Hart & Matsuba, in press; Lewis & Ramsay, 2004). As we grow older, this rudimentary self-concept becomes more complex. One way psychologists have studied how people's self-concept changes from childhood to adulthood is by asking people of different ages to answer the simple question "Who am I?" Typically, a child's self-concept is concrete, with references to clear-cut, easily observable characteristics like age, sex, neighborhood, and hobbies. A 9-year-old answered the question this way: "I have brown eyes. I have brown hair. I have brown eyebrows. . . . I'm a boy. I have an uncle that is almost 7 feet tall" (Montemayor & Eisen, 1977, p. 317).

Watch on MyPsychLab
To learn more about the "mark" test, watch the MyPsychLab video ***Self Awareness in Toddlers.***

As we mature, we place less emphasis on physical characteristics and more on psychological states (our thoughts and feelings) and on considerations of how other people judge us (Hart & Damon, 1986; Livesley & Bromley, 1973; Montemayor & Eisen, 1977). Consider this 12th-grade high school student's answer to the "Who am I?" question:

> I am a human being. . . . I am a moody person. I am an indecisive person. I am an ambitious person. I am a very curious person. I am not an individual. I am a loner. I am an American (God help me). I am a Democrat. I am a liberal person. I am a radical. I am a conservative. I am a pseudoliberal. I am an atheist. I am not a classifiable person (i.e., I don't want to be). (Montemayor & Eisen, 1977, p. 318)

Clearly, this teenager has moved well beyond descriptions of her hobbies and appearance (Harter, 2003). But what exactly does the self do? In this chapter we will discuss four components of the self: *self-knowledge*, our beliefs about who we are and the way in which we formulate and organize this information; *self-control*, the way in which people make plans and execute decisions, such as your decision to read this book right now instead of going out for ice cream; *impression management*, the way in which we present ourselves to other people, trying to get them to see us the way we want to be seen; and *self-esteem*, the way we feel about ourselves—e.g., whether we view ourselves positively or negatively.

Self-Knowledge

How do you define who you are? As straightforward as this question might seem, the way in which you answer it likely reveals some fascinating cultural and social processes.

When Harvard-educated Masako Owada abandoned her promising career to marry Crown Prince Naruhito of Japan and assumed the traditional roles required of her, many Western women questioned her decision. At issue for many was cultural interdependence versus independence of the self.

Cultural Differences in Defining the Self

In June 1993, Masako Owada, a 29-year-old Japanese woman, married Crown Prince Naruhito of Japan. Masako was a brilliant career diplomat in the foreign ministry, educated at Harvard and Oxford. She spoke five languages and was on the fast track to a prestigious job as a diplomat. Her decision to marry the prince surprised many observers, because it meant she would have to give up her career. Indeed, she gave up any semblance of an independent life, becoming subservient to the prince and the rest of the royal family and spending much of her time participating in rigid royal ceremonies. Although some people hoped that she would modernize the monarchy, "so far the princess has not changed the imperial family as much as it has changed her" ("Girl Born to Japan's Princess," 2001).

How do you feel about Masako's decision to marry the prince? Your answer may say something about the nature of your self-concept and the culture in which you grew up. In many Western cultures, people have an **independent view of the self**, which is a way of defining oneself in terms of one's own internal thoughts, feelings, and actions and not in terms of the thoughts, feelings, and actions of others (Kitayama & Uchida, 2005; Markus & Kitayama, 1991, 2001; Nisbett, 2003; Oyserman & Lee, 2008; Triandis, 1995). Consequently, many Western observers were mystified by Masako's decision to marry the crown prince. They assumed that she was coerced into the marriage by a backward, sexist society that did not properly value her worth as an individual with an independent life of her own.

In contrast, many Asian and other non-Western cultures have an **interdependent view of the self**, which is a way of defining oneself in terms of one's relationships to other people and recognizing that one's behavior is often determined by the thoughts, feelings, and actions of others. Here, connectedness and interdependence between people are valued, whereas independence and uniqueness are frowned on. For example, when asked to complete sentences beginning with "I am," people from Asian cultures are more likely to refer to social groups, such as their family or religious group, than people from Western cultures are (Bochner, 1994; Triandis, 1989). To many Japanese and other Asians, Masako's decision to give up her career was not at all surprising and was a natural consequence of her view of herself as connected and obligated to others, such as her parents and the royal family. What is viewed as positive and normal behavior by one culture may be viewed very differently by another.

> *The squeaky wheel gets the grease.*
>
> —AMERICAN PROVERB
>
> *The nail that stands out gets pounded down.*
>
> —JAPANESE PROVERB

Ted Singelis (1994) developed a questionnaire that measures the extent to which people view themselves as interdependent or independent. Sample items from this scale are given in the Try It! on page 108. Singelis administered the questionnaire to students at the University of Hawaii at Manoa and found that Asian Americans agreed more with the interdependence than the independence items, whereas Caucasian Americans agreed more with the independence than the interdependence items.

We do not mean to imply that every member of a Western culture has an independent view of the self and that every member of an Asian culture has an interdependent view of the self. Within cultures, there are differences in the self-concept, and as contact between cultures increases, differences between cultures may decrease. It is interesting to note, for example, that Masako's decision to marry the prince was unpopular among at least some young Japanese women, who felt that her choice was not a positive sign of interdependence, but rather a betrayal of the feminist cause in Japan (Sanger, 1993). And the restricted life in the Imperial Household seems to have taken its toll on Princess Masako. In 2004 she stopped making public appearances, and the press office for the royal family announced that she was receiving therapy for an "adjustment disorder" (Kato, 2009).

Independent View of the Self

A way of defining oneself in terms of one's own internal thoughts, feelings, and actions and not in terms of the thoughts, feelings, and actions of other people

Interdependent View of the Self

A way of defining oneself in terms of one's relationships to other people, recognizing that one's behavior is often determined by the thoughts, feelings, and actions of others

TRY IT! A Measure of Independence and Interdependence

Instructions: Indicate the extent to which you agree or disagree with each of these statements.

	Strongly Disagree						Strongly Agree
1. My happiness depends on the happiness of those around me.	1	2	3	4	5	6	7
2. I will sacrifice my self-interest for the benefit of the group I am in.	1	2	3	4	5	6	7
3. It is important to me to respect decisions made by the group.	1	2	3	4	5	6	7
4. If my brother or sister fails, I feel responsible.	1	2	3	4	5	6	7
5. Even when I strongly disagree with group members, I avoid an argument.	1	2	3	4	5	6	7
6. I am comfortable with being singled out for praise or rewards.	1	2	3	4	5	6	7
7. Being able to take care of myself is a primary concern for me.	1	2	3	4	5	6	7
8. I prefer to be direct and forthright when dealing with people I've just met.	1	2	3	4	5	6	7
9. I enjoy being unique and different from others in many respects.	1	2	3	4	5	6	7
10. My personal identity, independent of others, is very important to me.	1	2	3	4	5	6	7

Note: These questions are taken from a scale developed by Singelis (1994) to measure the strength of people's interdependent and independent views of themselves. The actual scale consists of 12 items that measure interdependence and 12 items that measure independence. We have reproduced 5 of each type of item here: The first 5 are designed to measure interdependence, and the last 5 are designed to measure independence. For scoring instructions, turn to page 135.

(Adapted from Singelis, 1994)

Nonetheless, the difference between the Western and Eastern sense of self is real and has interesting consequences for communication between the cultures. Indeed, the differences in the sense of self are so fundamental that it is very difficult for people with independent selves to appreciate what it is like to have an interdependent self, and vice versa. After giving a lecture on the Western view of the self to a group of Japanese students, one psychologist reported that the students "sighed deeply and said at the end, 'Could this really be true?'" (Kitayama & Markus, 1994, p. 18). To paraphrase William Shakespeare, in Western society the self is the measure of all things. But however natural we consider this conception of the self to be, it is important to remember that it is socially constructed and therefore may differ from culture to culture.

Gender Differences in Defining the Self

Is there any truth to the stereotype that when women get together they talk about interpersonal problems and relationships, whereas men talk about anything but their feelings (usually sports)? Although this stereotype is clearly an exaggeration, it does have a grain of truth and reflects a difference in women's and men's self-concept (Baumeister & Sommer, 1997; Cross, Bacon, & Morris, 2000; Cross, Hardin, & Gercek-Swing, 2010; Gabriel & Gardner, 1999, 2004).

Women have more *relational interdependence*, meaning that they focus more on their close relationships, such as how they feel about their spouse or their child. Men have more *collective interdependence*, meaning that they focus on their memberships in larger groups, such as the fact that they are Americans or that they belong to a fraternity (Brewer & Gardner, 1996; Gabriel & Gardner, 1999). Starting in early childhood,

American girls are more likely to develop intimate friendships, cooperate with others, and focus their attention on social relationships, whereas boys are more likely to focus on their group memberships (Cross & Madson, 1997).

These differences persist into adulthood, such that women focus more on intimacy and cooperation with a small number of close others and are in fact more likely to discuss personal topics and disclose their emotions than men are (Caldwell & Peplau, 1982; Davidson & Duberman, 1982). Men focus more on their social groups, such as sports teams. For example, when women and men were asked to describe either a positive or negative emotional event in their lives, women tended to mention personal relationships, such as becoming engaged or the death of a family member (Gabriel & Gardner, 1999). Men talked about events involving larger groups, such as the time they joined a fraternity or their sports team lost an important game (see Figure 5.1). To see how much your self-concept is based on a sense of relational interdependence, answer the questions in the Try It! on page 110.

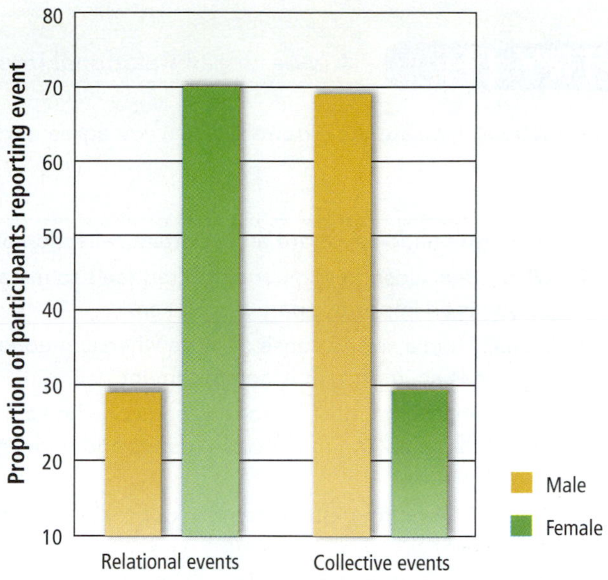

FIGURE 5.1

Gender Differences in Types of Interdependence

Male and female college students were asked to describe an important emotional event in their lives. Women reported more relational events, ones that had to do with close personal relationships. Men reported more collective events, ones that had to do with their membership in larger groups.

(From Gabriel & Gardner, 1999, p. 648)

When considering gender differences such as these, we need to be cautious: The psychological differences between men and women are far fewer than the ways in which they are the same (Deaux & LaFrance, 1998; Hyde, 2005). Nevertheless, there do appear to be differences in the way women and men define themselves in the United States, with women having a greater sense of relational interdependence than men.

Knowing Ourselves Through Introspection

We've seen that the cultures in which people grow up, and their gender, help shape their self-concept. But how do people come to know the selves that are shaped by culture and gender?

This might seem like a strange question. "Good grief," you might be thinking, "I don't need a social psychology textbook to tell me that! It's not exactly a mystery. I just think about myself—no big deal." In other words, you rely on **introspection**, looking inward to examine the "inside information" that you, and you alone, have about your thoughts, feelings, and motives. And, indeed, you do find some answers when you introspect. But there are two interesting things about introspection: People do not rely on this source of information as often as you might think (actually, people spend very little time thinking about themselves); and even when people do introspect, the reasons for their feelings and behavior can be hidden from conscious awareness (Wilson, 2002; Wilson & Dunn, 2004). In short, self-scrutiny isn't all it's cracked up to be, and if this were our only source of knowledge about ourselves, we would be in trouble.

> *Introspection is difficult and fallible ... the difficulty is simply that of all observation of whatever kind.*
>
> —William James, 1890

Focusing on the Self: Self-Awareness Theory How often do people think about themselves? To find out, researchers asked 365 high school juniors (in two American cities) what they were thinking about at several points in their day: when they woke up, 45 minutes later, at three random points in their day, and when they went to bed (Mor et al., 2010). The female students reported that they were thinking about themselves on 42% of these occasions, whereas the males reported that they were thinking about themselves on 32% of the occasions. Adolescence, of course, is a time of self-scrutiny, so these figures might not reflect how often adults focus on themselves. There is evidence, however, that the amount of time we spend thinking about ourselves is increasing, at least in the United States (Twenge & Foster, 2010). One recent study charted this in an interested way: Researchers coded the lyrics of the 10 most popular songs of the year, every year from 1980 to 2007. As a measure of self-focus in American culture, they counted the number of first-person singular pronouns in the lyrics (e.g., I, me), and found a

Introspection

The process whereby people look inward and examine their own thoughts, feelings, and motives

TRY IT! A Measure of Relational Interdependence

Instructions: Indicate the extent to which you agree or disagree with each of these statements.

	Strongly Disagree						Strongly Agree
1. My close relationships are an important reflection of who I am.	1	2	3	4	5	6	7
2. When I feel close to someone, it often feels to me as if that person is an important part of who I am.	1	2	3	4	5	6	7
3. I usually feel a strong sense of pride when someone close to me has an important accomplishment.	1	2	3	4	5	6	7
4. I think one of the most important parts of who I am can be captured by looking at my close friends and understanding who they are.	1	2	3	4	5	6	7
5. When I think of myself, I often think of my close friends or family also.	1	2	3	4	5	6	7
6. If a person hurts someone close to me, I feel personally hurt as well.	1	2	3	4	5	6	7
7. In general, my close relationships are an important part of my self-image.	1	2	3	4	5	6	7
8. Overall, my close relationships have very little to do with how I feel about myself.	1	2	3	4	5	6	7
9. My close relationships are unimportant to my sense of what kind of person I am.	1	2	3	4	5	6	7
10. My sense of pride comes from knowing who I have as close friends.	1	2	3	4	5	6	7
11. When I establish a close friendship with someone, I usually develop a strong sense of identification with that person.	1	2	3	4	5	6	7

For scoring instructions, turn to page 135.

(Adapted from Cross, Bacon, & Morris, 2000)

But as I looked into the mirror, I screamed, and my heart shuddered: for I saw not myself but the mocking, leering, face of a devil.

—Friedrich Nietzsche, *Thus Spake Zarathustra*

I swear to you … that to be overly conscious is a sickness, a real, thorough sickness.

—Fyodor Dostoevsky, *Notes from Underground*, 1864

steady increase over time (see Figure 5.2; DeWall et al., 2011). True, the Beatles released a song called "I, Me, Mine" in 1970, but such self-references have become even more common, such as Jennifer Hudson's "I Remember Me" or Ashlee Simpson's "I Am Me."

Sometimes it is external circumstances that turn the spotlight of consciousness on ourselves, such as seeing ourselves on a video or staring at ourselves in a mirror. For example, if you are watching a video taken by a friend with her new smartphone and you are the featured attraction, you will be in a state of self-awareness; you become the focus of your attention. According to **self-awareness theory**, when this happens we evaluate and compare our current behavior to our internal standards and values (Carver, 2003; Duval & Silvia, 2002; Duval & Wicklund, 1972; Phillips & Silva, 2005). In short, we become self-conscious, in the sense that we become objective, judgmental observers of ourselves, seeing ourselves as an outside observer would. Let's say that you feel you should quit smoking, and one day you catch an image of yourself in a store window smoking a cigarette. How do you think you will feel?

Self-Awareness Theory

The idea that when people focus their attention on themselves, they evaluate and compare their behavior to their internal standards and values

Seeing your reflection will make you aware of the disparity between your behavior and your internal standards. If you can change your behavior to match your internal guidelines (e.g., quit smoking), you will do so. If you feel you can't change your behavior, being in a state of self-awareness will be uncomfortable because you will be confronted with disagreeable feedback about yourself (Duval & Silvia, 2002). Apparently this happens pretty frequently. In studies in which researchers sample people at random points in their day—such as the one with high school juniors mentioned earlier (Mor et al., 2010)—the more often people say they were thinking about themselves, the more likely they are to be in a bad mood. Figure 5.3 illustrates how self-awareness makes us conscious of our internal standards and directs our subsequent behavior.

Sometimes people go even further in their attempt to escape the self. Such diverse activities as alcohol abuse, binge eating, and sexual masochism have one thing in common: All are effective ways of turning off the internal spotlight on oneself (Baumeister, 1991). Getting drunk, for example, is one way of avoiding negative thoughts about oneself, at least temporarily. The fact that people regularly engage in such dangerous behaviors, despite their risks, is an indication of how aversive self-focus can be (Hull, Young, & Jouriles, 1986; Leary & Tate, 2010).

Not all means of escaping the self, however, are so damaging. Many forms of religious expression and spirituality are also effective means of avoiding self-focus (Baumeister, 1991; Leary, 2004). Further, self-focus is not always aversive. If you have just experienced a major success, focusing on yourself can be pleasant indeed, because it highlights your positive accomplishments (Greenberg & Musham, 1981; Silvia & Abele, 2002). Self-focus can also be a way of keeping you out of trouble, by reminding you of your sense of right and wrong. For example, several studies have found that when people are self-aware (e.g., in front of a mirror), they are more likely to follow their moral standards, such as avoiding the temptation to cheat on a

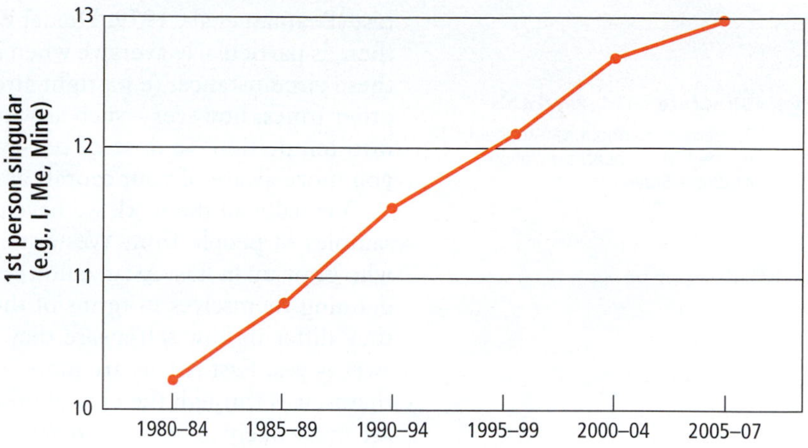

FIGURE 5.2

Use of First-Person Singular Pronouns in Popular Songs

As a measure of self-focus in American culture, researchers counted the number of first-person singular pronouns (e.g., I, me) in the lyrics of the 10 most popular songs of the year, every year from 1980 to 2007. As you can see, they found a steady increase over time.

Adapted from DeWall, Pond, Campbell, & Twenge (2011)

FIGURE 5.3

Self-Awareness Theory: The Consequences of Self-Focused Attention

When people focus on themselves, they compare their behavior to their internal standards.

(Adapted from Carver & Scheier, 1981)

test (Beaman et al., 1979; Diener & Wallbom, 1976; Gibbons, 1978). Self-awareness, then, is particularly aversive when it reminds people of their shortcomings, and under these circumstances (e.g., right after doing poorly on a test), people try to avoid it. At other times, however—such as when that little devil is on your shoulder pushing you into temptation—a dose of self-awareness is not such a bad thing because it makes you more aware of your morals and ideals.

Simulate on **MyPsychLab**
To learn more about self-concept, try the MyPsychLab simulation ***Multiple Selves.***

Virtually all the work we have described so far, however, has been conducted with samples of people from Western countries (primarily Americans). Given that people who grow up in East Asian cultures tend to have a more interdependent view of the self, defining themselves in terms of their relationships to other people, is it possible that they differ in how self-aware they tend to be? Recent research indicates that the answer is yes. East Asians are more likely to have an *outside perspective on the self*, viewing themselves through the eyes of other people. People who grow up in Western cultures are more likely to have an *insider perspective on the self*, focusing on their own private experiences without considering how other people see them (Cohen, Hoshino-Browne, & Leung, 2007; Heine et al., 2008). To be clear, people in both Eastern and Western cultures can adopt either perspective, but the "default" state people tend to adopt differs, with East Asians more likely to be in a state of self-awareness. How self-aware do you tend to be? Complete the Try It! on page 113 to find out.

I have often wished I had time to cultivate modesty ... But I am too busy thinking about myself.
—Dame Edith Sitwell

Judging Why We Feel the Way We Do: Telling More than We Can Know Even when we are self-aware and introspect to our heart's content, it can be difficult to know *why* we feel the way we do. Imagine trying to decide why you love someone. Being in love typically makes you feel giddy, euphoric, and preoccupied; in fact, the ancient Greeks thought love was a sickness. But why do you feel this way? Exactly what is it about your sweetheart that made you fall in love? We know it is something about our loved one's looks, personality, values, and background. But precisely what? How can we possibly describe the special chemistry that exists between two people? A friend of ours once told us he was in love with a woman because she played the saxophone. Was this really the reason? The heart works in such mysterious ways that it is difficult to tell.

Unfortunately, it's not just love that is difficult to explain. As we saw in Chapter 3, many of our basic mental processes occur outside of awareness (Wilson, 2002). This is not to say that we are thinkers without a clue—we are usually aware of the final result of our thought processes (e.g., that we are in love) but often unaware of the cognitive processing that led to the result. It's as if the magician pulled a rabbit out of a hat: You see the rabbit, but you don't know how it got there. How do we deal with this rabbit problem? Even though we often don't know why we feel a certain way, it seems we are always able to come up with an explanation. We are the proud owners of the most powerful brain to evolve on this planet, and we certainly put it to use. Unfortunately, it didn't come with an owner's manual. Introspection may not lead us to the true causes of our feelings and behavior, but we'll manage to convince ourselves that it did. Richard Nisbett and Tim Wilson referred to this phenomenon as "telling more than we can know," because people's explanations of their feelings and behavior often go beyond what they can reasonably know (Nisbett & Ross, 1980; Nisbett & Wilson, 1977; Wilson, 2002).

In one study, for example, college students recorded their daily moods every day for 5 weeks (Wilson, Laser, & Stone, 1982). The students also kept track of things that might predict their daily moods, such as the weather, their workload, and how much sleep they had gotten the night before. At the end of the 5 weeks, the students estimated how much their mood was related to these other variables. An analysis of the data showed that in many cases people were wrong about what predicted their mood. For example, most people believed that the amount of sleep they got predicted how good a mood they were in the next day, when in fact this wasn't true: The amount of sleep was unrelated to people's moods. The participants had introspected and found or generated some logical-sounding theories that weren't always right (Johansson et al., 2005; Wegner, 2002; Wilson, 2002).

We can never, even by the strictest examination, get completely behind the secret springs of action.
—Immanuel Kant

TRY IT! Measure Your Private Self-Consciousness

How much do you focus on yourself when you are alone? The following questions are taken from a scale developed by Fenigstein, Scheier, and Buss (1975) to measure private self-consciousness—the consistent tendency to be self-aware.

Instructions: Answer the following questions as honestly as possible on a scale from 1 to 5, where

1 = extremely uncharacteristic (not at all like me)
2 = somewhat uncharacteristic
3 = neither characteristic nor uncharacteristic
4 = somewhat characteristic
5 = extremely characteristic (very much like me)

1. I'm always trying to figure myself out.	1	2	3	4	5
2. Generally, I'm not very aware of myself.	1	2	3	4	5
3. I reflect about myself a lot.	1	2	3	4	5
4. I'm often the subject of my own fantasies.	1	2	3	4	5
5. I never scrutinize myself.	1	2	3	4	5
6. I'm generally attentive to my inner feelings.	1	2	3	4	5
7. I'm constantly examining my motives.	1	2	3	4	5
8. I sometimes have the feeling that I'm off somewhere watching myself.	1	2	3	4	5
9. I'm alert to changes in my mood.	1	2	3	4	5
10. I'm aware of the way my mind works when I work through a problem.	1	2	3	4	5

For scoring instructions, turn to page 135.

(Adapted from Fenigstein, Scheier, & Buss, 1975)

What these participants had relied on, at least in part, were their **causal theories**. People have many theories about what influences their feelings and behavior (e.g., "My mood should be affected by how much sleep I got last night") and often use these theories to help them explain why they feel the way they do (e.g., "I'm in a bad mood; I'll bet the fact that I got only 6 hours of sleep last night has a lot to do with it"). We learn many of these theories from the culture in which we grow up—ideas such as "absence makes the heart grow fonder," people are in bad moods on Mondays, or people who have been divorced are a poor choice for a successful second marriage. The only problem is that, as discussed in Chapter 3, our schemas and theories are not always correct and thus can lead to incorrect judgments about the causes of our actions.

The truth is, we never know for sure about ourselves… . Only after we've done a thing do we know what we'll do… . [That] is why we have spouses and children and parents and colleagues and friends, because someone has to know us better than we know ourselves.

—Richard Russo, *Straight Man*, 1997

We do not mean to imply that people rely solely on their causal theories when introspecting about the reasons for their feelings and behaviors. In addition to culturally learned causal theories, people have a great deal of information about themselves, such as how they have responded in the past and what they happen to have been thinking about before making a choice (Gavanski & Hoffman, 1987; Wilson, 2002). The fact remains, however, that introspecting about our past actions and current thoughts does not always yield the right answer about why we feel the way we do (Wilson & Bar-Anan, 2008).

The Consequences of Introspecting About Reasons In the first season of the TV show *30 Rock*, Liz Lemon, Tina Fey's character, has broken up with her boyfriend, Dennis, after he nailed multiple holes in her wall (in a failed attempt to install shelves) and brought home a Great Dane (knowing that she was allergic to dogs). But then Dennis came into the office and bared his soul in front of the whole gang, telling Liz that he would always love her. Should she get back together with him? Liz isn't sure, so

Causal Theories

Theories about the causes of one's own feelings and behaviors; often we learn such theories from our culture (e.g., "absence makes the heart grow fonder")

In an episode of the TV program *30 Rock*, Liz Lemon (played by Tina Fey) made a list of the reasons why she liked and disliked her boyfriend Dennis (played by Dean Winters). According to research on self-generated attitude change, the act of making this list might have changed her mind about how she felt, at least temporarily.

at her friend Jenna's suggestion, she makes a list of Dennis's pros and cons. She draws a line down the middle the paper and has no trouble filling up both sides. On the pro side, for example, she writes, "takes good care of his feet," "is funny when he goofs on his friends," and "has already seen me throw up two times." On the con side she writes, "dental hygiene," "wears acid wash denim," and "has already seen me throw up."

When Liz gets home that evening, she finds that Dennis has cleaned up her apartment, successfully built bookshelves, and mounted the television on the wall. So she takes out her list and adds to the pro side "fixed TV." The next day, her boss, Jack (Alec Baldwin's character), says something nice about Dennis, prompting Liz to add yet another entry to the pro side: "Jack likes Dennis." But things quickly fall apart when Dennis stops by again that evening. When she throws him out again, he slams the door, and the newly installed bookshelves and wall-mounted TV come crashing down. As Liz surveys the wreckage on her floor, she takes out her list, adds Dennis's latest behavior to the con list, and emphatically folds it up for the last time.

30 Rock is a fictional comedy, of course, and the episode just described is a spoof on a common activity, namely making a list of pros and cons about an important decision. But does putting reasons down on paper really clarify our thoughts, making it easier to decide what we really want? Actually, no. Tim Wilson and his colleagues found that analyzing the reasons for our feelings is not always the best strategy and in fact can make matters worse (Wilson, 2002; Wilson et al., 1989; Wilson, Hodges, & LaFleur, 1995).

As we saw in the previous section, it is hard to know exactly why we feel the way we do about something, especially in an area as complicated as romantic relationships. Some of the very same things Liz Lemon had on the pro side of her list, for example, also appeared on the con side. And some things are easier to put into words (e.g., "wears acid wash denim") than others (e.g., the special chemistry that can exist between two people). The problem is that we often convince ourselves that the reasons we generate reflect how we actually feel, even if they just happen to occur to us at the moment. One would think that Liz Lemon would know how she felt about Dennis; after all, she had been dating him for a while. But once she starting making her list of reasons, her feelings seemed to swing back and forth, depending on the latest entry on her list.

Research has confirmed this process of **reasons-generated attitude change**, which is attitude change resulting from thinking about the reasons for your attitudes. This happens because, when people analyze the reasons for their attitudes, they (a) bring to mind reasons that don't really reflect how they feel and (b) talk themselves into believing that this is how they feel. In a study by Wilson and Kraft (1993), for example, college students involved in relationships wrote down why things were going the way they were with their dating partner—much like Liz Lemon did. This caused them to change their minds about how their relationship was going; if they wrote down positive reasons, they became more positive, but if they wrote down negative reasons, they became more negative. Over time, though, the effects of analyzing reasons tends to wear off, and people's original "hard to explain" attitudes return. Thus, if people make important decisions right after analyzing reasons—such as deciding whether to break up with their boyfriend or girlfriend—they might make a decision they later regret. This is because right after analyzing reasons people tend to focus on the things that are easy to put into words (e.g., those acid-wash jeans) and ignore feelings that are hard to explain (e.g., that special chemistry). But it is the hard-to-explain feelings that often matter in the long run (Halberstadt & Levine, 1997; Reifman et al., 1996; Sengupta & Fitzsimons, 2004; Wilson, Lindsey, & Schooler, 2000).

Reasons-Generated Attitude Change

Attitude change resulting from thinking about the reasons for one's attitudes; people assume that their attitudes match the reasons that are plausible and easy to verbalize

In sum, it is often difficult for people to know exactly why they feel the way they do, and it can be dangerous to think too much about one's reasons. If introspection has its limits, how else might we find out what sort of person we are and what our attitudes are? We turn now to another source of self-knowledge: observations of our own behavior.

Knowing Ourselves by Observing Our Own Behavior

Suppose that a friend of yours asks you how much you like classical music. You hesitate because you never listened to classical music much when you were growing up, but lately you have found yourself listening to symphonies every now and then. "Well, I don't know," you reply. "I guess I like some kinds of classical music. Just yesterday I listened to a Beethoven symphony on the radio while I was driving to work." If so, you used an important source of self-knowledge: observations of one's own behavior (in this case, what you chose to listen to).

Self-Perception Theory

The theory that when our attitudes and feelings are uncertain or ambiguous, we infer these states by observing our behavior and the situation in which it occurs

I've always written poems ... I never know what I think until I read it in one of my poems.

—Virginia Hamilton Adair

Self-perception theory argues that when our attitudes and feelings are uncertain or ambiguous, we infer these states by observing our behavior and the situation in which it occurs (Bem, 1972). Let's consider each part of this theory. First, we infer our inner feelings from our behavior only when we are not sure how we feel. If you've always known that you love classical music, you do not need to observe your behavior to figure this out (Andersen, 1984; Andersen & Ross, 1984). Maybe, though, your feelings are murky; you've never really thought about how much you like it. If so, you are especially likely to use your behavior as a guide to how you feel (Chaiken & Baldwin, 1981; Wood, 1982).

Second, people judge whether their behavior really reflects how they feel or whether it was the situation that made them act that way. If you freely choose to listen to the classical music station—no one makes you do it—you are especially likely to conclude that you listen to that station because you like classical music. If it is your spouse and not you who turned to the station playing Beethoven, you are unlikely to conclude that you listen to classical music in your car because you like it.

Sound familiar? In Chapter 4, we discussed attribution theory—the way in which people infer someone else's attitudes and feelings by observing that person's behavior. According to self-perception theory, people use the same attributional principles to infer their own attitudes and feelings. For example, if you were trying to decide whether a friend likes classical music, you would observe her behavior and explain why she behaved that way. You might notice, for example, that she is always listening to classical music in the absence of any situational pressures or constraints—no one makes her play Mozart on her iPod. You would make an internal attribution for her behavior and conclude that she likes Mozart. Self-perception theory says that we infer our own feelings in the same way: We observe our behavior and explain it to ourselves; that is, we make an attribution about why we behaved that way (Critcher & Gilovich, 2010; Laird, 2007; Olson & Stone, 2005; Wilson, 2002). A large number of studies have supported self-perception theory, as we will now see.

Many programs try to get children to read more by rewarding them. But do these programs increase or decrease a child's love of reading?

Intrinsic Versus Extrinsic Motivation Imagine that you are an elementary school teacher who wants your students to develop a love of reading. Not only do you want your students to read more, but you also want them to develop a love of books. How might you go about accomplishing this? It is not going to be easy, because so many other things compete for your students' attention, such as television, video games, and text messaging.

If you are like many educators, you might decide that a good approach would be to reward the children for reading. Maybe that will get them to put down those cell phones and pick up a book—and develop a love of reading in the process. Teachers have always rewarded kids with a smile or a gold star on an assignment, of course, but recently they have turned to more-powerful incentives. A chain of pizza restaurants offers elementary school students in some school districts a certificate for a free pizza when they have read a certain number of books (see "Book It!" at www.bookitprogram.com). In others, teachers offer candy, brownies, and toys for academic achievement (Perlstein, 1999). One school district has taken this a step further by rewarding high school students with cash prizes if they do well on advanced placement exams (Hibbard, 2011).

Intrinsic Motivation

The desire to engage in an activity because we enjoy it or find it interesting, not because of external rewards or pressures

Extrinsic Motivation

The desire to engage in an activity because of external rewards or pressures, not because we enjoy the task or find it interesting

Overjustification Effect

The tendency for people to view their behavior as caused by compelling extrinsic reasons, making them underestimate the extent to which it was caused by intrinsic reasons

There is no doubt that rewards are powerful motivators and that pizzas and money will get kids to read more. One of the oldest and most fundamental psychological principles says that giving a reward each time a behavior occurs will increase the frequency of that behavior. Whether it be a food pellet delivered to a rat pressing a bar or a free pizza given to a child for reading, rewards can change behavior.

But people are not rats, and we have to consider the effects of rewards on what's inside—people's thoughts about themselves, their self-concept, and their motivation to read in the future. Does being paid to read, for example, change people's ideas about *why* they are reading? The danger of reward programs such as Book It! is that kids will begin to think they are reading to earn something, not because they find reading to be an enjoyable activity in its own right. When the reward programs end and pizzas are no longer forthcoming, children may actually read less than they did before.

This is especially likely to happen to children who already liked to read. Such children have high **intrinsic motivation**: the desire to engage in an activity because they enjoy it or find it interesting, not because of external rewards or pressures (Harackiewicz & Elliot, 1993, 1998; Harackiewicz & Hulleman, 2010; Hirt et al., 1996; Hulleman et al., 2010; Lepper, Corpus, & Iyengar, 2005; Ryan & Deci, 2000; Vansteenkiste et al., 2010). Their reasons for engaging in the activity have to do with themselves—the enjoyment and pleasure they feel when reading a book. In other words, reading is play, not work.

What happens when the children start getting rewards for reading? Their reading, originally stemming from intrinsic motivation, is now also spurred by **extrinsic motivation**, which is people's desire to engage in an activity because of external rewards or pressures, not because they enjoy the task or find it interesting. According to self-perception theory, rewards can hurt intrinsic motivation. Whereas before many children read because they enjoyed it, now they are reading so that they will get the reward. The unfortunate outcome is that replacing intrinsic motivation with extrinsic motivation makes people lose interest in the activity they initially enjoyed. This result is called the **overjustification effect**, which results when people view their behavior as caused by compelling extrinsic reasons (e.g., a reward), making them underestimate the extent to which their behavior was caused by intrinsic reasons (Deci, Koestner, & Ryan, 1999a, 1999b; Harackiewicz, 1979; Lepper, 1995; Lepper, Henderlong, & Gingras, 1999; Warneken & Tomasello, 2008).

In one study, for example, fourth- and fifth-grade teachers introduced four new math games to their students, and during a 13-day baseline period they noted how long each child played each math game. As seen in the leftmost line in Figure 5.4, the children initially had some intrinsic interest in the math games, in that they played them for several minutes during this baseline period. For the next several days, a reward program was introduced. Now the children could earn credits toward certificates and trophies by playing the math games. The more time they spent playing the games, the more credits they earned. As the middle line in Figure 5.4 shows, the reward program was effective in increasing the amount of time the children spent on the math games, showing that the rewards were an effective motivator.

The key question is what happened after the program ended and the kids could no longer earn rewards for playing the games. As predicted by the overjustification hypothesis, the children spent significantly less time on the math games than they had

initially, before the rewards were introduced (see the rightmost line in Figure 5.4). The researchers determined, by comparing these results to those of a control condition, that it was the rewards that made people like the games less and not the fact that everyone became bored with the games as time went by. In short, the rewards destroyed the children's intrinsic interest in the games; by the end of the study, they were hardly playing the games at all (Greene, Sternberg, & Lepper, 1976).

What can we do to protect intrinsic motivation from the dangers of society's reward system? Fortunately, there are conditions under which overjustification effects can be avoided. Rewards will undermine interest only if interest was initially high (Calder & Staw, 1975; Tang & Hall, 1995). If a child has no interest in reading, then getting him or her to read by offering rewards is not a bad idea, because there is no initial interest to undermine.

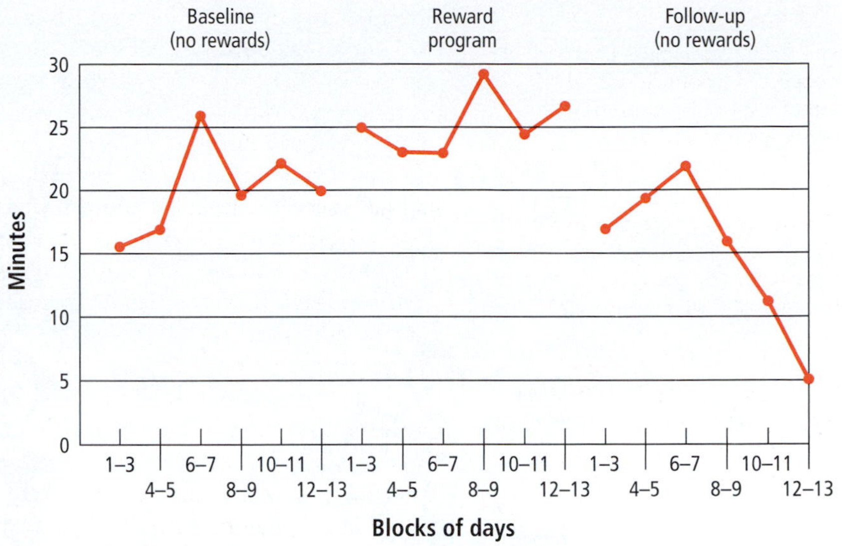

FIGURE 5.4

The Overjustification Effect

During the initial baseline phase, researchers measured how much time elementary school students played math games. During the reward program, they rewarded the children with prizes for playing with the games. When the rewards were no longer offered (during the follow-up phase), the children played with the games even less than they had during the baseline phase, indicating that the rewards had lowered their intrinsic interest in the games.

(Adapted from Greene, Sternberg, & Lepper, 1976)

Also, the type of reward makes a difference. So far, we have discussed **task-contingent rewards**, meaning that people get them simply for doing a task, regardless of how well they do it. Sometimes **performance-contingent rewards** are used, whereby the reward depends on how well people perform the task. For example, grades are performance-contingent because you get a high reward (an A) only if you do well. This type of reward is less likely to decrease interest in a task—and may even increase interest—as it conveys the message that you are good at the task (Deci & Ryan, 1985; Sansone & Harackiewicz, 1997). Thus, rather than giving kids a reward for playing math games regardless of how well they do (i.e., a task-contingent reward), it is better to reward them for doing well in math. Even performance-contingent rewards must be used with care; they too can backfire. Although people like the positive feedback these rewards convey, they do not like the apprehension caused by being evaluated (Harackiewicz, 1989; Harackiewicz, Manderlink, & Sansone, 1984). The trick is to convey positive feedback without making people feel nervous and apprehensive about being evaluated.

Understanding Our Emotions: The Two-Factor Theory of Emotion

How do you know which emotion you are experiencing at any given time? Is it fear or elation? This question probably sounds kind of silly: Don't we know how we feel without having to think about it? The way in which we experience emotions, however, has a lot in common with the kinds of self-perception processes we have been discussing.

> *I remember that the game [of basketball] lost some of its magical qualities for me once I thought seriously about playing for a living.*
>
> —Bill Russell, 1979

Stanley Schachter (1964) proposed a theory of emotion that says we infer what our emotions are in the same way we infer what kind of person we are or how interested we are in math games. In each case, we observe our behavior and then explain to ourselves why we are behaving that way. The only difference in these types of inferences is the kind of behavior we observe. Schachter says we observe our internal behaviors—how physiologically aroused we feel. If we feel aroused, we then try to figure out what is causing this arousal. For example, suppose you go for a 3-mile run one day and are walking back to your apartment. You go around a corner and nearly walk right into an extremely attractive person from your psychology class whom you are just getting to know. Your heart is pounding and you feel a little sweaty. Is it because love is blossoming between you and your new friend or simply because you just went for a run?

Schachter's theory is called the **two-factor theory of emotion**, because understanding our emotional states requires two steps: We must first experience physiological arousal, and then we must seek an appropriate explanation or label for it. Because our physical states are difficult to label on their own, we use information in the situation to help us make an attribution about why we feel aroused (see Figure 5.5 on next page).

Task-Contingent Rewards

Rewards that are given for performing a task, regardless of how well the task is done

Performance-Contingent Rewards

Rewards that are based on how well we perform a task

Two-Factor Theory of Emotion

The idea that emotional experience is the result of a two-step self-perception process in which people first experience physiological arousal and then seek an appropriate explanation for it

FIGURE 5.5

The Two-Factor Theory of Emotion

People first experience physiological arousal and then attach an explanation to it.

Imagine that you were a participant in a classic study by Stanley Schachter and Jerome Singer (1962) that tested this theory. When you arrive, the experimenter tells you he is studying the effects on people's vision of a vitamin compound called Suproxin. After a physician injects you with a small amount of Suproxin, the experimenter asks you to wait while the drug takes effect. He introduces you to another participant who, he says, has also been given some of the vitamin compound. The experimenter gives each of you a questionnaire to fill out, saying he will return in a little while to give you the vision tests.

You look at the questionnaire and notice that it contains some highly personal and insulting questions. For example, one question asks, "With how many men (other than your father) has your mother had extramarital relationships?" (Schachter & Singer, 1962, p. 385). The other participant reacts angrily to these offensive questions, becoming more and more furious, until he finally tears up his questionnaire, throws it on the floor, and stomps out of the room. How do you think you would feel? Would you feel angry as well?

As you've probably guessed, the real purpose of this experiment was not to test people's vision. The researchers set up a situation in which the two crucial variables—arousal and an emotional explanation for that arousal—would be present or absent, and then they observed which, if any, emotions people experienced. The participants did not really receive an injection of a vitamin compound. Instead, some participants received epinephrine, a hormone produced naturally by the human body that causes arousal (body temperature and heart and breathing rates increase), and the other half received a placebo that had no physiological effects.

Imagine how you would have felt had you received the epinephrine: As you read the insulting questionnaire, you begin to feel aroused. (Remember, the experimenter didn't tell you the shot contained epinephrine, so you don't realize that the injection is making you feel this way.) The other participant—who was actually an accomplice of the experimenter—reacts with rage. You are likely to infer that you are feeling flushed and aroused because you too are angry. You have met the conditions Schachter (1964) argues are necessary to experience an emotion: You are aroused, you have sought out and found a reasonable explanation for your arousal in the situation that surrounds you, and so you become furious. This is indeed what happened: The participants who had been given epinephrine reacted much more angrily than did participants who had been given the placebo.

A fascinating implication of Schachter's theory is that people's emotions are somewhat arbitrary, depending on what the most plausible explanation for their arousal happens to be. Schachter and Singer (1962) demonstrated this idea in two ways. First, they showed that they could prevent people from becoming angry by providing a nonemotional explanation for why they felt aroused. They did this by informing some of the people who received epinephrine that the injection would increase their heart rate, make their face feel warm and flushed, and cause their hands to shake slightly. When people actually began to feel this way, they inferred that it was not because they were angry but because the injection was taking effect. As a result, these participants did not react angrily to the questionnaire.

When people are aroused for one reason, such as occurs when they cross a scary bridge, they often attribute this arousal to the wrong source—such as attraction to the person they are with.

Second, Schachter and Singer showed that they could make participants experience a very different emotion by changing the most plausible explanation for their arousal. In another condition, participants did not receive the insulting questionnaire and the accomplice did not respond angrily. Instead, the accomplice acted in a euphoric, devil-may-care fashion, playing basketball with rolled-up pieces of paper, making paper airplanes, and playing with a hula hoop he found in the corner. How did the real participants respond? If they had received epinephrine but had not been told of its effects, they inferred that they must be feeling happy and euphoric and often joined in on the fun.

The Schachter and Singer experiment has become one of the most famous studies in social psychology because it shows that emotions can be the result of a self-perception process: People look for the most plausible explanation for their arousal. Sometimes the most plausible explanation is not the right one, and so people end up experiencing a mistaken emotion. The people who became angry or euphoric in the Schachter and Singer (1962) study did so because they felt aroused and thought this arousal was due to the obnoxious questionnaire or to the infectious, happy-go-lucky behavior of the accomplice. The real cause of their arousal, the epinephrine, was hidden from them, so they relied on situational cues to explain their behavior.

> *I could feel all the excitement of losing the big fish going through the transformer and coming out as anger at my brother-in-law.*
>
> —Norman Maclean, *A River Runs Through It*, 1976

Finding the Wrong Cause: Misattribution of Arousal To what extent do the results found by Schachter and Singer (1962) generalize to everyday life? (Recall from Chapter 2 that a test of a study's external validity is whether the results hold up outside the lab.) Do people form mistaken emotions in the same way as participants did in the study? In everyday life, one might argue, people usually know why they are aroused. If a mugger points a gun at us and says, "Give me your wallet!" we feel aroused and correctly identify this arousal as fear. If our heart is thumping while we walk on a deserted moonlit beach with the man or woman of our dreams, we correctly label this arousal as love or sexual attraction.

Many everyday situations, however, present more than one plausible cause for our arousal, and it is difficult to identify how much of the arousal is due to one source or another. Imagine that you go to see a scary movie with an extremely attractive date. As you are sitting there, you notice that your heart is thumping and you are a little short of breath. Is this because you are wildly attracted to your date or because the movie

Misattribution of Arousal
The process whereby people make mistaken inferences about what is causing them to feel the way they do

is terrifying you? It is unlikely that you could say, "Fifty-seven percent of my arousal is due to the fact that my date is gorgeous, 32 percent is due to the scary movie, and 11 percent is due to indigestion from all the popcorn I ate." Because of this difficulty in pinpointing the precise causes of our arousal, we sometimes misidentify our emotions. You might think that most of your arousal is a sign of attraction to your date when in fact a lot of it is due to the movie (or maybe even indigestion).

If so, you have experienced **misattribution of arousal**, whereby people make mistaken inferences about what is causing them to feel the way they do (Bar-Anan, Wilson, & Hassin, 2010; Ross & Olson, 1981; Oikawa, Aarts, & Oikawa, 2011; Zillmann, 1978). Consider how this worked in a field experiment by Donald Dutton and Arthur Aron (1974). An attractive young woman asked men visiting a park in British Columbia if they would fill out a questionnaire for her as part of a psychology project on the effects of scenic attractions on people's creativity. When they had finished, she said that she would be happy to explain her study in more detail when she had more time. She tore off a corner of the questionnaire, wrote down her name and phone number, and told the participant to give her a call if he wanted to talk with her some more. How attracted do you think the men were to this woman? Would they telephone her and ask for a date?

This is a hard question to answer. Undoubtedly, it depends on whether the men were involved with someone else, how busy they were, and so on. It might also depend, however, on how they interpreted any bodily symptoms they were experiencing. If they were aroused for some extraneous reason, they might mistakenly think that some of the arousal was the result of attraction to the young woman. To test this idea, Dutton and Aron (1974) had the woman approach males in the park under two very different circumstances.

In one condition, the men were walking across a 450-foot-long suspension bridge that spanned a deep canyon. The bridge was made of wooden planks attached to wire cables, and as they walked across, they had to stoop to hold on to the low handrail. A little way out over the canyon, the wind tended to catch the bridge and make it wobble from side to side. This is a scary experience, and most people who cross the bridge become more than a little aroused—their heart pounds against their chest, they breathe rapidly, and they begin to perspire. It was at this point that the attractive woman approached a man on the bridge and asked him to fill out her questionnaire. How attracted do you think he felt toward her?

In another condition, the woman waited until men had crossed the bridge and rested for a while on a bench in the park before approaching them. They had a chance to calm down—their hearts were no longer pounding, and their breathing rate had returned to normal. They were peacefully admiring the scenery when the woman asked them to fill out her questionnaire. How attracted were these men to the woman? The prediction from Schachter's two-factor theory is clear: The men approached on the bridge would be considerably more aroused and might mistakenly think that some of this arousal was the result of attraction to the beautiful woman. That is exactly what happened. A large proportion of the men approached on the bridge telephoned the woman later to ask her for a date, whereas relatively few of the men approached on the bench telephoned the woman (see Figure 5.6). This type of misattribution of arousal has been found in numerous subsequent studies, in both men and women (e.g., Meston & Frohlich, 2003; Zillmann, 1978). The moral is this: If you encounter an attractive person and your heart is going thump-thump, think carefully about why you are aroused—or you might fall in love for the wrong reasons!

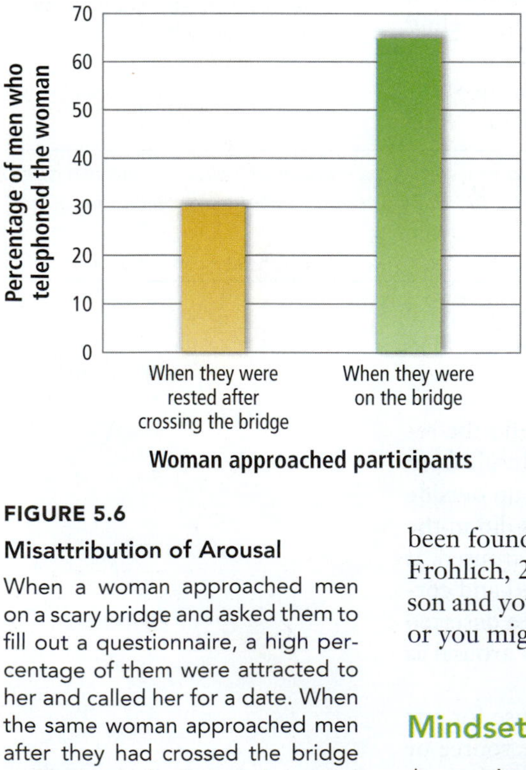

FIGURE 5.6
Misattribution of Arousal
When a woman approached men on a scary bridge and asked them to fill out a questionnaire, a high percentage of them were attracted to her and called her for a date. When the same woman approached men after they had crossed the bridge and had rested, relatively few called her for a date.
(Adapted from Dutton & Aron, 1974)

Mindsets: Understanding Our Own Abilities

As seen in our opening example about Michael Jordan and Mia Hamm, there is another important kind of self-knowledge: how we explain our own talents and abilities to ourselves. Some people believe that their abilities are set in stone; they either have them or

Sally is trying to give her daughter encouragement before she takes her final exams. But, according to research on fixed and growth mindsets, did she say the right thing? As discussed in this chapter, it is better for parents to convey to their children that their abilities are malleable qualities that can grow with hard work (the growth mindset) rather than communicate the idea that abilities are fixed quantities that you either have or do not have.

they do not. Psychologist Carol Dweck (2006) calls this a **fixed mindset**—the idea that we have a set amount of an ability that cannot change. According to this view, we have a fixed amount of intelligence, athletic ability, musical talent, and so on. Other people have what Dweck calls a **growth mindset**, which is the idea that their abilities are malleable qualities that they can cultivate and grow. Research shows that the mindset people have is crucial to their success: People with the fixed mindset are more likely to give up after setbacks and are less likely to work on and hone their skills; after all, if they fail it must be a sign that they simply don't have what it takes. People with the growth mindset, such as Michael Jordan and Mia Hamm, view setbacks as opportunities to improve through hard work (Cury et al., 2008).

Fixed Mindset
The idea that we have a set amount of an ability that cannot change

Growth Mindset
The idea that our abilities are malleable qualities that we can cultivate and grow

Mindsets are important not only to athletic performance, but also to how we view any ability, including how good we are at academics. Most students hit a bump in the road when they start college; for you, maybe it was a lower grade than you expected on a psychology or math test. How did you react to your disappointing grade? Dweck's research shows that students who have a fixed mindset about intelligence are more likely to give up and do poorly on subsequent tests, whereas those with growth mindsets are more likely to redouble their efforts and do better on subsequent tests. And she finds that the mindsets themselves can change; people with fixed views can learn to adopt the growth view. Thus, the next time you experience a setback—be it on the athletic field, in your classes, or in your personal relations—you might want to view it as an opportunity to work harder and improve, rather than as a sign that you "don't have what it takes."

Using Other People to Know Ourselves

The self-concept does not develop in a solitary context, but is shaped by the people around us. If we never interacted with other people, our own image would be a blur, because we would not see ourselves as having selves distinct from those of other people. Remember the mirror and red-dye test we discussed earlier, used to determine if animals have a self-concept? Variations of this test have been used to show that social contact is indeed crucial to the development of a self-concept. Gordon Gallup (1997) compared the behavior of chimpanzees raised in normal family groupings with that of chimps who were raised alone, in complete social isolation. The socially experienced chimps "passed" the mirror test; after red dye was put on their foreheads and they looked at themselves in a mirror, they immediately used their mirrored image to explore the red areas of their heads. However, the socially isolated chimps did not react to their reflections at all; they did not recognize themselves in the mirror, suggesting that they had not developed a sense of self.

There is little satisfaction in the contemplation of heaven for oneself if one cannot simultaneously contemplate the horrors of hell for others.
—P. D. JAMES, *THE CHILDREN OF MEN*, 1992

CONNECTIONS

How Should Parents Praise Their Children?

If you were to visit a home where parents are helping their children with their homework, you would find the parents doling out a lot of praise, at least in Western cultures. "Nice job on your geography project, Johnny. Your map of South America looks great!" "You got every math problem right, Susie—keep up the good work!" Many adults assume that it is beneficial to praise children because it makes them feel good about themselves and enhances their intrinsic motivation. As we saw earlier in this chapter, however, sometimes rewards can actually undermine intrinsic motivation. What should parents do?

The key is the message that the praise conveys (Bayat, 2011; Dweck, 2006; Henderlong & Lepper, 2002; Senko, Durik, & Harackiewicz, 2008; Zentall & Morris, 2010). We don't want children to develop a fixed mindset about their abilities, because if they do they won't react well to setbacks ("I guess this C on my spelling test means I'm a lousy speller"). It's better to focus on children's effort ("If you study harder for the next test, I bet you'll do better") to encourage a growth mindset—namely, the idea that hard work pays off when the going gets tough. When children do well, you shouldn't go overboard and praise them too much for their effort, however, because they might infer that this means they are low on ability, like the player on a basketball team who gets the Best Effort award instead of the Most Valuable Player award. Along with praise for effort, it is a good idea to make children feel that they have gained competence in the area (e.g., "You worked hard on your science project and really learned a lot; you've become quite an expert on plant pesticides"). Note that this praise avoids conveying the fixed mindset (that there is a set amount of ability in this area that people have or don't have). Instead, the praise should convey the message that they have gained competence through hard work. This is the mindset that Michael Jordan seemed to have, as seen at the beginning of the chapter. He practiced so hard that he went from a player cut from his high school team to the best player in the world. And by the way, what did his mother tell him when he didn't make his high school team? "I told him to go back and discipline himself," she said—in other words, to work harder, just the right message to foster a growth mindset (Williams, 2001, p. 92).

Watch on MyPsychLab
To learn more about the relationship between praise and self-esteem, watch the MyPsychLab video ***How can praising individuals in the "wrong way" limit their growth and their development of self-esteem?***

You may have noticed our comment that parents dole out a lot of praise "in Western cultures." There is some evidence that the situation is different in Eastern cultures, where people have a more interdependent sense of self. Praise is much less frequent in China and Japan because it is viewed as potentially harmful to children's character (Salili, 1996). Also, children in these countries appear to be more intrinsically motivated to begin with and more concerned with the desire to improve their performance (Heine et al., 1999; Lewis, 1995). Consequently, praise from adults may not be as necessary to motivate children in these cultures to engage in academic pursuits.

Knowing Ourselves by Comparing Ourselves to Others How do we use others to define ourselves? One way is to measure our own abilities and attitudes by seeing how we stack up against other people. Suppose you work in an office that subscribes to a charity fund. You can deduct from your monthly paycheck whatever you want and have it go to worthy organizations. You decide to donate $50 a month. How generous is this? Should you be feeling particularly proud of your philanthropic nature? One way to answer this question is to compare yourself to others. If you find out that your friend Sue donated only $10 per month, you are likely to feel that you are a very generous person who cares a lot about helping others. If you find out, however, that your friend Sue donated $100 per month, you probably will not view yourself as quite so generous.

Social Comparison Theory
The idea that we learn about our own abilities and attitudes by comparing ourselves to other people

This example illustrates **social comparison theory**, originally formulated by Leon Festinger (1954) and refined by many others (Buunk & Gibbons, 2007; Mussweiler, 2003; Suls & Wheeler, 2000). The theory holds that people learn about their own abilities and attitudes by comparing themselves to others. The theory revolves around two important questions: When do you engage in social comparison? And with whom do you choose to compare yourself? The answer to the first question is that people socially compare when there is no objective standard to measure themselves against and when they experience some uncertainty about themselves in a particular area (Suls & Fletcher, 1983; Suls & Miller, 1977). If the office donation program is new and you are not sure what amount would be generous, you are especially likely to compare yourself to others.

As to the second question—With whom do people compare themselves?—the answer depends on our goal. To illustrate this, suppose that it is the first day of your college Spanish class and you are wondering about your abilities and how well you will do in the class. With whom should you compare yourself: a student who mentions that she lived in Spain for 2 years, a student who says she took the course on a lark and has never studied Spanish before, or a student who has a similar background to yours? Not surprisingly, people find it most informative to compare themselves to others who have a similar background in the area in question (Goethals & Darley, 1977; Miller, 1982; Suls, Martin, & Wheeler, 2000). That is, comparing yourself to a student with a very similar background in Spanish—the one who, like you, took Spanish in high school but has never traveled to a Spanish-speaking country—will be most informative. If that student is doing well in the class, you probably will too (Thornton & Arrowood, 1966; Wheeler, Koestner, & Driver, 1982; Zanna, Goethals, & Hill, 1975).

Of course you're going to be depressed if you keep comparing yourself with successful people.

If we want to know what excellence is—the top level to which we can aspire—we engage in **upward social comparison**, which is comparing ourselves to people who are better than we are with regard to a particular trait or ability (Blanton et al., 1999). That is, if we want to know the "best of the best" so that we can dream of getting there some day, then clearly we should compare ourselves to the student who lived in Spain and see how well she is doing in the class. A problem with upward social comparison, however, is that it can be dispiriting, making us feel inferior. We'll never learn the language like that student who studied in Spain! (Boyce, Brown, & Moore, 2010; Muller & Fayant, 2010; Myers & Crowther, 2009.) If our goal is to feel good about ourselves and boost our egos, then we are better off engaging in **downward social comparison**—comparing ourselves to people who are worse than we are with regard to a particular trait or ability (Aspinwall & Taylor, 1993; Bauer & Wrosch, 2011; Chambers & Windschitl, 2009; Guenther & Alicke, 2010; Wehrens et al., 2010). That is, if you compare your performance in the class to that of the student who is taking Spanish for the first time, you will likely feel good about your own abilities, because you will surely have her beat. As another example, when interviewed by researchers, the vast majority of cancer patients spontaneously compared themselves to other patients who were more ill than they were, presumably as a way of making themselves feel more optimistic about the course of their own disease (Wood, Taylor, & Lichtman, 1985).

Another way we can feel better about ourselves is to compare our current performance with our own past performance. In a sense, people use downward social comparison here as well, though the point of comparison is a "past self," not someone else. In one study, people made themselves feel better by comparing their current self with a past self who was worse off. One student, for example, said that her "college self" was more outgoing and sociable than her "high school self," who had been shy and reserved (Ross & Wilson, 2003; Wilson & Ross, 2000).

Upward Social Comparison

Comparing ourselves to people who are better than we are with regard to a particular trait or ability

In short, the nature of our goals determines who we compare ourselves to. When we want an accurate assessment of our abilities and opinions, we compare ourselves to people who are similar to us. When we want information about what we can strive toward, we make upward social comparisons, though doing so can make us feel inferior. When our goal is to make ourselves feel better, we compare ourselves to those

Downward Social Comparison

Comparing ourselves to people who are worse than we are with regard to a particular trait or ability who are less fortunate (including our past selves); such downward comparisons make us look better.

Most people are other people. Their thoughts are someone else's opinions, their lives a mimicry, their passions a quotation.

—Oscar Wilde, 1905

Knowing Ourselves by Adopting Other People's Views As we just saw, sometimes we use other people as a measuring stick to assess our own abilities. When it comes to our views of the social world, however, often we adopt the views our friends hold. Have you ever noticed that people who hang out together tend to see the world in the same way? Maybe the roommates in the apartment across the hall were all supporters of Barack Obama for reelection in 2012 and all enjoy watching *American Idol* together, whereas the roommates in the apartment next door are Libertarians who supported Ron Paul and are big fans of *Glee*. One explanation for people holding common views, of course, is that "birds of a feather flock together"—that is, people who have similar views are attracted to each other and are more likely to become friends than are people who have dissimilar views. In Chapter 10 we will see evidence for this "birds of a feather" hypothesis (Newcomb, 1961).

But it is also true that people adopt the views of the people they hang out with, at least under certain conditions. Charles Cooley (1902) called this the "looking glass self," by which he meant that we see ourselves and the social world through the eyes of other people and often adopt those views. According to recent research, this is especially true when two people want to get along with each other (Hardin & Higgins, 1996; Huntsinger & Sinclair, 2010; Sinclair & Lun, 2010; Shteynberg, 2010). If a close friend thinks that *Glee* is the best TV show ever made, you will probably like it as well.

Perhaps it seems obvious that friends influence what each other thinks. What is surprising, however, is that such **social tuning**—the process whereby people adopt another person's attitudes—can happen even when we meet someone for the first time, if we want to get along with that person. And social tuning can happen unconsciously. Imagine, for example, that you were a participant in a study by Stacey Sinclair and her colleagues (Sinclair et al., 2005). When you arrive, the experimenter acts in either a likable or unlikable manner. In the likable condition she thanks you for participating and offers you some candy from a bowl, whereas in the unlikable condition she pushes the bowl of candy to the side and exclaims, "Just ignore this; some of the experimenters in my lab like to give subjects candy for their participation, but I think you are lucky just to get credit" (Sinclair et al., 2005, p. 588). You then sit at a computer and complete a simple task, in which you press one key every time the word *good* appears on the screen and another whenever the word *bad* appears.

Unbeknownst to you, the computer task is a measure of automatic prejudice. A photograph of a white or black face is flashed very rapidly right before the word *good* or *bad* appears. The faces are flashed so quickly that you do not consciously see them, and the computer measures how long it takes you to respond to the words. Previous research has shown that such subliminal flashes can influence people under controlled laboratory conditions (see Chapter 7 for a discussion of this research). In the present study, the assumption was that if people were prejudiced toward black people, then they should respond relatively quickly to "bad" when it was preceded by a black face and relatively slowly to "good" when it was preceded by a black face.

To see if people "tuned" their views to the experimenter, the researchers altered one other thing: In half of the sessions the experimenter wore a T-shirt that expressed antiracism views ("eracism"), and in half of the sessions she did not. The question was, did people unconsciously adopt the experimenter's antiracist views more when she was likable than when she was not? As seen in Figure 5.7, the answer is yes. When the experimenter was likable, participants showed less automatic prejudice when she was wearing the antiracism T-shirt than when she was not. Without even knowing it, they "tuned" their views toward hers. What about when she was unlikable? As seen in Figure 5.7, participants seemed to react against her views: They showed more automatic prejudice when she was wearing the antiracist T-shirt than when she was not. These results show that we tend to automatically adopt the views of people we like, but automatically reject the views of people we do not.

Social Tuning

The process whereby people adopt another person's attitudes

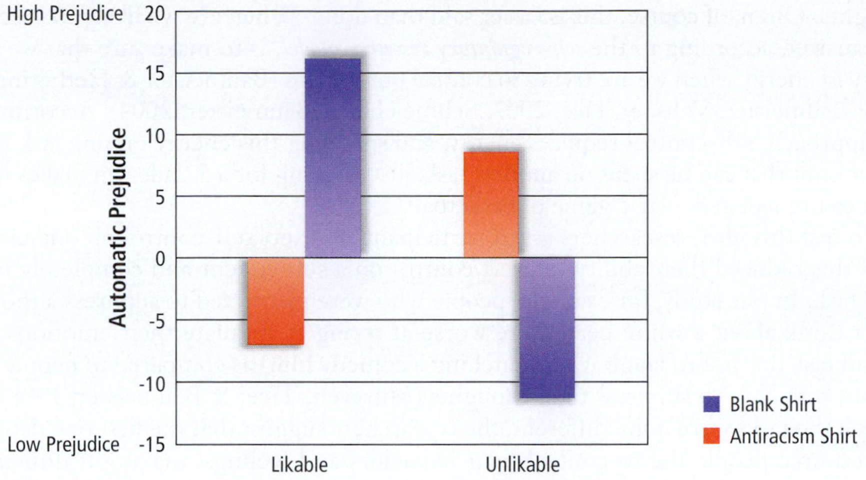

FIGURE 5.7

Social Tuning to a Likable Experimenter

Participants took a test of automatic prejudice toward black people, after interacting with an experimenter who was likable or unlikable and wore an antiracism T-shirt or a blank T-shirt. When the experimenter was likable, participants showed less automatic prejudice when she was wearing the antiracism T-shirt than when she was not (the higher the number on the scale, the more the anti-black prejudice). When the experimenter was unlikable, participants reacted against her views: They showed more automatic prejudice when she was wearing the antiracist T-shirt than when she was not. These results show that people tend to automatically adopt the views of people they like, but automatically reject the views of people they do not.

(Adapted from Sinclair, Lowery, Hardin, & Colangelo, 2005)

Self-Control: The Executive Function of the Self

Sarah has vowed to take the high road with her ex-boyfriend Jake, letting bygones be bygones and just forgetting about all the stupid things he did. "That's ancient history," she thinks. "Time to move on." One night she runs into Jake at a party and, wouldn't you know it, there he is with her friend Meghan, whom Jake swore he wasn't interested in. Sarah is sorely tempted to make a scene and tell them both off, but she grits her teeth, puts on her best smile, and acts as if she is the belle of the ball. She is proud of herself, but a little while later she finds herself devouring a bowl of potato chips, even though she had promised herself to eat a healthy diet and shed a few pounds. In this example Sarah is doing something familiar to us all—trying to exert self-control. She succeeds in one respect, by suppressing her desire to tell off her ex-boyfriend, but fails in another, by failing to keep to her healthy diet. What determines how successful we are at exerting self-control?

An important function of the self is to be the chief executive who makes choices about what to do in the present and plans for the future (Baumeister, Schmeichel, & Vohs, 2007; Carver & Scheier, 1998; Higgins, 1989, 2005; Vohs & Baumeister, 2011). We appear to be the only species, for example, that can imagine events that have not yet occurred and engage in long-term planning, and it is the self that does this planning and exerts control over our actions (Gilbert, 2006; Gilbert & Wilson, 2007). Regulating our behavior and choices in optimal ways, of course, can be easier said than done, as anyone who has been on a diet or tried to quit smoking knows.

One form of self-control that does not work very well (and often backfires) is *thought suppression*, whereby we try to push thoughts out of our minds. Often, the more we try not to think about something, such as an ex-boyfriend or the chips on the buffet table, the more those very thoughts keep coming to mind (Wegner, 1992, 1994; Wegner, Wenzlaff, & Kozak, 2004). A better strategy is to go ahead and think about the forbidden topic while trying to exert willpower when it comes to acting on those thoughts. Often, of course, this is easier said than done. When are we likely to succeed? The answer, according to the *self-regulatory resource model*, is to make sure that we have plenty of energy when we are trying to control our actions (Baumeister & Hetherington, 1996; Baumeister, Vohs, & Tice, 2007; Schmeichel & Baumeister, 2004). According to this approach, self-control requires energy, and spending this energy on one task limits the amount that can be spent on another task, just as going for a 5-mile run makes it difficult to immediately play a game of basketball.

To test this idea, researchers asked participants to exert self-control on one task, to see if this reduced their ability to exert control on a subsequent and completely unrelated task. In one study, for example, people who were instructed to suppress a thought (don't think about a white bear) were worse at trying to regulate their emotions on a second task (try not to laugh while watching a comedy film) as compared to people who did not first have to suppress their thoughts (Muraven, Tice, & Baumeister, 1998). Although the tasks were quite different, the researchers suggest that the first one depleted the resource people use to control their behaviors and feelings, making it difficult to engage in a subsequent act of self-control. This is why Sarah found it hard to avoid eating the potato chips—she had used up a lot of energy when checking her impulse to tell off her ex-boyfriend, making it difficult to exert self-control on something else.

Exactly what is this "energy" that we spend when exerting self-control? Recent research suggests that it is the level of glucose in the bloodstream at any given point (Gailliot & Baumeister, 2007). Glucose, a form of sugar, can be thought of as the fuel that supplies energy to the brain, and when people try hard to control their own actions, they need a lot of that fuel. Thus, if they use it up on one task (smiling sweetly at one's ex-boyfriend), there is less blood glucose available to fuel self-control on another task (avoiding the bowl of potato chips). The implications? Eat a healthy, regular diet without skipping meals, because we get blood glucose from food. One study found that people who drank lemonade sweetened with sugar were better able to exert self-control than people who drank lemonade with an artificial sweetener (Masicampo & Baumeister, 2008). Don't go overboard by loading up your diet with sugar, though, because that can have obvious negative effects (e.g., weight gain), and there is only so much your brain can use. But if you know that you are going to have to grit your teeth and try hard to control yourself in the near future—you know your ex-boyfriend or ex-girlfriend is going to be at the party—eating a little more sugar before you go might not be a bad idea.

What else can people do to increase their self-control? Research shows that practice makes perfect. That is, the more we try to exert self-control in one setting, the more successful we will be at it in the future (Bauer & Bauemeister, 2011). Another approach works when we find ourselves worn down from one attempt at self-control and are now faced with another temptation (e.g., that bowl of potato chips): It can help totake a break and relax for a few minutes to regain our energy (Tyler & Burns, 2008). Finally, research shows that it helps to form specific implementation intentions in advance of a situation in which you will need to exert self-control (Gollwitzer & Oettingen, 2011). That is, instead of saying to yourself, "I'm going to study a lot for the next test in my psychology class," make specific "if-then" plans that specify how and when you will study and how you will avoid temptations. For example, you might make these plans: "I'm going to the library right after class on Thursday, and if my roommate texts me and says I should join her at a party that night, I'll tell her that I'll meet up with her after I'm done studying."

Impression Management: All the World's a Stage

In 1991, David Duke decided to run for governor of Louisiana as a mainstream conservative Republican. He had some obstacles to overcome in convincing people to vote for him, because for most of his adult life he had been a white supremacist and an anti-Semite who in 1989 had sold Nazi literature from his office ("Duke," 1991). To

Impression management in action: In the 1970s, David Duke was a leader in the Ku Klux Klan; in 1991, he ran for governor of Louisiana as a mainstream conservative Republican. A remarkable change occurred in Duke's presentation of self during this time.

improve his appeal, he claimed that he no longer supported Nazi ideology or the Ku Klux Klan, of which he had been a leader (or "grand wizard") in the 1970s. He also tried to improve his appearance by undergoing facial cosmetic surgery. Duke's campaign rhetoric didn't fool too many Louisiana voters. They perceived the same racist message disguised in new clothes, and he was defeated by the Democratic candidate Edwin Edwards. In 2003, he was sentenced to 15 months in federal prison for allegedly using funds raised from supporters for personal investments and gambling (Murr & Smalley, 2003).

Though few politicians attempt as extreme a makeover as David Duke did, managing public opinion is hardly a new concept in politics. The public knew that President Franklin Roosevelt had suffered from polio, but the extent of his disability was kept secret. He used a wheelchair in private but never in public. Instead, he made speeches standing at a podium, supported by an aide to his side. Similarly, President John F. Kennedy presented himself as a healthy, vigorous man ready to face any challenge that came his way when in fact he suffered from degenerative bone disease and chronic back pain and was under heavy medication for much of his presidency (Dallek, 2002).

> *Keep up appearances whatever you do.*
>
> —Charles Dickens, 1843

These are extreme examples of **impression management**, which is the attempt by people to get others to see them the way they want to be seen (Gibson & Poposki, 2010; Goffman, 1959; Ham & Vonk, 2011; Schlenker, 2003; Uziel, 2010). Just as politicians try to put the best possible spin on their actions and manage the impressions others have of them, so do we in our everyday lives. As Erving Goffman (1959) pointed out, we are all like stage actors who are trying our best to convince the "audience" (the people around us) that we are a certain way, even if we really are not.

Impression Management
The attempt by people to get others to see them as they want to be seen

Ingratiation
The process whereby people flatter, praise, and generally try to make themselves likable to another person, often of higher status

Ingratiation and Self-Handicapping

People have many different impression management strategies (Jones & Pittman, 1982). One is **ingratiation**—using flattery or praise to make yourself likable to another, often a person of higher status (Jones & Wortman, 1973; Proost et al., 2010; Romero-Canyas et al., 2010). We can ingratiate through compliments, by agreeing with another's ideas, by commiserating and offering sympathy, and so on. If your boss drones on at a staff meeting, nearly putting the entire office to sleep, and you say, "Great job today, Sue. Loved your presentation," you are probably ingratiating. Ingratiation is a powerful

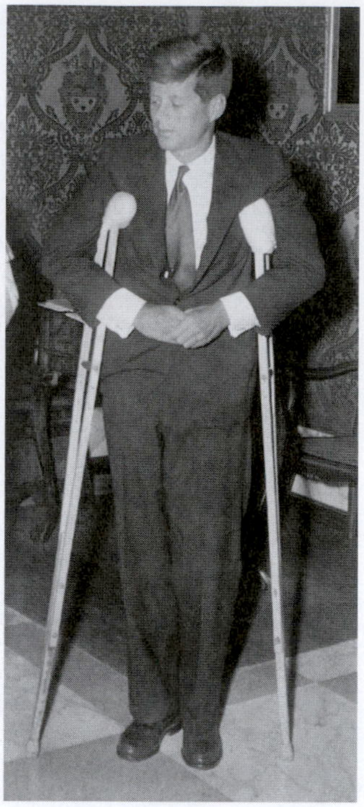

Virtually all politicians try to manage the impressions they convey to the public, sometimes distorting reality. President John F. Kennedy presented himself as a healthy, vigorous man, when in fact he suffered from degenerative bone disease and chronic back pain and was under heavy medication for much of his presidency.

technique, because we all enjoy having someone be nice to us—which is what the ingratiator is good at. However, such a ploy can backfire if the recipient of your ingratiation senses that you're being insincere (Jones, 1964; Kauffman & Steiner, 1968).

Another strategy, and the one that has attracted the most research attention, is **self-handicapping**. In this case, people create obstacles and excuses for themselves so that if they do poorly on a task, they can avoid blaming themselves. Doing poorly or failing at a task is damaging to your self-esteem. In fact, just doing less well than you expected or than you have in the past can be upsetting, even if it is a good performance. How can you prevent this disappointment? Self-handicapping is a rather surprising solution: You can set up excuses before the fact, just in case you do poorly (Arkin & Oleson, 1998; Jones & Berglas, 1978; McCrea, 2008; Rhodewalt & Vohs, 2005).

Let's say it's the night before the final exam in one of your courses. It's a difficult course, required for your major, and one in which you'd like to do well. A sensible strategy would be to eat a good dinner, study for a while, and then go to bed early and get a good night's sleep. The self-handicapping strategy would be to pull an all-nighter, do some heavy partying, and then wander into the exam the next morning bleary-eyed and muddle-headed. If you don't do well on the exam, you have an excuse to offer to others to explain your performance, one that deflects the potential negative internal attribution they might otherwise make (that you're not smart). If you ace the exam, well, so much the better—you did it under adverse conditions (no sleep), which suggests that you are especially bright and talented.

There are two major ways in which people self-handicap. In its more extreme form, called *behavioral self-handicapping*, people act in ways that reduce the likelihood that they will succeed on a task, so that if they fail they can blame it on the obstacles they created rather than on their lack of ability. The obstacles people have been found to use include drugs, alcohol, reduced effort on a task, and failure to prepare for an important event (Deppe & Harackiewicz, 1996; Lupien, Seery, & Almonte, 2010). Interestingly, research shows that men are more likely to engage in behavioral self-handicapping than are women (Hirt & McCrea, 2009; McCrea, Hirt, & Milner, 2008).

Self-Handicapping

The strategy whereby people create obstacles and excuses for themselves so that if they do poorly on a task, they can avoid blaming themselves

The second type, called *reported self-handicapping*, is less extreme. Rather than creating obstacles to success, people devise ready-made excuses in case they fail (Baumgardner, Lake, & Arkin, 1985; Hendrix & Hirt, 2009). We might not go so far as to pull an all-nighter before an important exam, but we might complain that we are not feeling well. People can arm themselves with all kinds of excuses: They blame their shyness, test anxiety, bad moods, physical symptoms, and adverse events from their past.

A problem with preparing ourselves with excuses in advance, however, is that we may come to believe these excuses and hence exert less effort on the task. Why work hard at something if you are going to do poorly anyway? Self-handicapping may prevent unflattering attributions for our failures, but it often has the perverse effect of causing the poor performance we feared to begin with. Further, even if self-handicappers avoid unflattering attributions about their performance (e.g., people thinking they aren't smart), they risk being disliked by their peers. People do not like others whom they perceive as engaging in self-handicapping strategies (Hirt, McCrea, & Boris, 2003; Rhodewalt et al., 1995). Women are particularly critical of other people who self-handicap. Thus, as we saw earlier, women are less likely to engage in the kind of self-handicapping in which they put obstacles in their own way, and they are more critical of others who do so (Hirt & McCrea, 2009; McCrea, Hirt, & Milner, et al., 2008). Why? Research shows that women place more value on trying hard to achieve something than men do and thus are more critical of people who seem not to try hard and then make up excuses for doing poorly.

To succeed in the world, we do everything we can to appear successful.

—François de La Rochefoucauld, 1678

Culture, Impression Management, and Self-Enhancement

People in all cultures are concerned with the impression they make on others, but the nature of this concern and the impression management strategies people use differ considerably from culture to culture (Lalwani & Shavitt, 2009). We have seen, for example, that people in Asian cultures tend to have a more interdependent view of themselves than people in Western cultures do. One consequence of this identity is that "saving face," or avoiding public embarrassment, is extremely important in Asian cultures. In Japan, people are very concerned that they have the "right" guests at their weddings and the appropriate number of mourners at the funerals of their loved ones—so concerned, in fact, that if guests or mourners are unavailable, they may go to a local "convenience agency" and rent some. These agencies (*benriya*) have employees who are willing to pretend—for a fee—that they are your closest friends. A woman named Hiroko, for example, worried that too few guests would attend her second wedding. No problem—she rented six, including a man to pose as her boss, at a cost of $1,500. Her "boss" even delivered a flattering speech about her at the wedding (Jordan & Sullivan, 1995). Although such impression management strategies might seem extreme to Western readers, the desire to manage public impressions is just as strong in the West (as exemplified by David Duke's attempts to change the way the public viewed him).

Self-Esteem: How We Feel About Ourselves

When Stuart Smalley, a fictional character played by Al Franken on Saturday Night Live, wants to make himself feel better, he looks at his image in the mirror and proudly proclaims how good, smart, and well liked he is. This routine is funny because Smalley's earnest words to the mirror clearly aren't working for him; he is actually a bumbling, insecure guy who doesn't have a clue about what is going on around him. Fortunately, when it comes to feeling good about ourselves, most of us have relatively high **self-esteem,** which is people's evaluation of their own self-worth—that is, the extent to which they view themselves as good, competent, and decent.

Self-Esteem

People's evaluations of their own self-worth—that is, the extent to which they view themselves as good, competent, and decent

Terror Management Theory
The theory that holds that self-esteem serves as a buffer, protecting people from terrifying thoughts about their own mortality

It might seem as though we should all strive to achieve as much self-esteem as possible; after all, why not shower ourselves with praise? Well, it is certainly true that we should try to avoid low self-esteem, which is a very unpleasant state that is associated with depression and the feelings that we are ineffective and not in control of our lives (Baumeister et al., 2003). What's more, high self-esteem protects us against thoughts about our own mortality. This is the basic tenet of **terror management theory**, which holds that self-esteem serves as a buffer, protecting people from terrifying thoughts about death (Greenberg, Solomon, & Pyszczynski, 1997; Pyszczynski et al., 2004). That is, in order to protect themselves from the anxiety caused by thoughts of their own deaths, people embrace cultural worldviews that make them feel like they are effective actors in a meaningful, purposeful world. People with high self-esteem are thus less troubled by thoughts about their own mortality than people with low self-esteem are (Schmeichel et al., 2009).

Another advantage of evaluating ourselves positively is that it motivates us to persevere when the going gets rough. In fact, it may even make us exaggerate how good we are at things and be overly optimistic about our futures, motivating us to try harder when we encounter obstacles in our path (Taylor & Brown, 1988). To illustrate this, consider two students who are thinking about their post-graduation job prospects. "I don't know," the first one thinks. "The economy isn't doing so well, and I don't think I have what it takes to compete with all those talented young people entering the job market. I'd say that there is only a 10% chance that I'll get my dream job right out of school." The second student thinks, "Yes, it's a tough market, but I think my prospects are great if I work hard and do well in school. I'm good enough to get my dream job." Now, for the sake of the argument, let's suppose that Student 1 is more correct than Student 2; it *is* a tough economy, after all, and few students land their first choice of job right away. But which student will work harder to achieve that goal? And which one is more likely to achieve it? Research shows that people who are optimistic—even unreasonably so—try harder, persevere more in the face of failure, and set higher goals than do people who are not (Nes & Segerstrom, 2006; Scheier, Carver, & Bridges, 2001). Obviously Student 2 shouldn't exaggerate his or her prospects too much; people who believe that they will be the next American Idol, when they can't carry a tune, are destined for failure and heartbreak. But a dose of optimism and confidence is a good thing, to the extent that it makes people work harder to achieve their goals.

Photo credit TK

In Greek mythology, Narcissus fell in love with his own reflection in a pool of water and was so fond of his own image that he couldn't leave and eventually died. Today, narcissism refers to the combination of excessive self-love and a lack of empathy toward others.

What happens when that dose is too large? There is a form of high self-esteem that is unhealthy, namely **narcissism**, which is the combination of excessive self-love and a lack of empathy toward others (Schriber & Robins, in press; Twenge & Campbell, 2009). Narcissists are extremely self-centered, concerned much more with themselves than with other people. On the Narcissistic Personality Inventory, a commonly used questionnaire measure, narcissists endorse such items as "I wish somebody would someday write my biography" and "I find it easy to manipulate people" (Raskin & Terry, 1988). That is, narcissists go far beyond optimists in their high opinions of themselves.

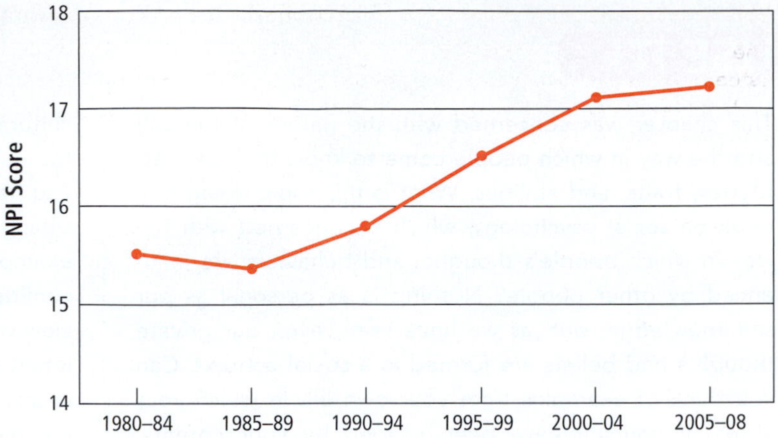

FIGURE 5.8

Are College Students Becoming More Narcissistic?

Scores on the Narcissistic Personality Inventory (NPI), a common measure of narcissism, have been going up among college students over the past several years.

(Adapted from Twenge & Foster, 2010)

If you were born after 1980, you might want not want to hear this, but narcissism has been increasing among college students in recent years. Jean Twenge and her colleagues (Twenge et al., 2008; Twenge & Foster, 2010) tracked down studies that administered the Narcissistic Personality Inventory to college students in the United States between the years 1982 and 2008. As seen in Figure 5.8, there has been a steady increase in scores on this test since the mid-1980s. And there is some evidence that narcissism is more prevalent in America than in other cultures (Campbell, Miller, & Buffardi, 2010; Foster, Campbell, & Twenge, 2003).

Why the increase in narcissism? Nobody knows, though Twenge and colleagues (2008) speculate that American culture has become increasingly self-focused. As we saw earlier, this is reflected in song lyrics, which have increasingly referred to "I" and "me," such as Uncle Kracker's song, "*Good to be me.*" There is so much self-focus among young people today, argues Jean Twenge, that she has dubbed them Generation Me (Twenge, 2006).

Well, you might ask, why is it a problem to be so self-focused? Won't that increase the chances of getting what we want in life? Actually, no. Narcissists do less well academically than others, are less successful in business, are more violent and aggressive, and are disliked by others, especially once people get to know them (Bushman & Baumeister, 2002; Twenge & Campbell, 2009).

Many young people are not so self-focused, of course, and devote countless hours to helping others through volunteer work. Ironically, in so doing they may have hit upon a way to become happier than with the narcissistic route. Imagine that you were in a study conducted by Dunn, Aknin, and Norton (2008). You are walking across campus one morning when a researcher approaches you and gives you an envelope with $20 in it. She asks you to spend it on yourself by 5:00 P.M. that day, such as by buying yourself a gift or paying off a bill. Sounds pretty nice, doesn't it? Now imagine that you were randomly assigned to another condition. Here you also get $20, but the researcher asks you to spend it on someone else by 5:00 P.M., such as by taking a friend out for lunch or donating it to a charity. How would that make you feel? It turns out that when the researchers contacted people that evening and asked how happy they were, those assigned to the "spend it on others" condition were happier than those asked to spend the money on themselves. A little less self-focus and a little more concern with others can actually make us happier.

Watch on **MyPsychLab**
To learn more about research on self-esteem, watch the MyPsychLab video ***Can you discuss your study of self-esteem and culture based on individuals' drawings of their social relationships?***

To recap, having high self-esteem is generally a good thing, to the extent that it makes people optimistic about their futures and work harder for what they want in life. There is a form of high self-esteem, however, that is quite problematic—namely narcissism—which, as we have seen, is extreme high self-regard combined with a lack of empathy toward others. The best combination is to feel good about ourselves but also to look out for and care about others.

Narcissism
The combination of excessive self-love and a lack of empathy toward others

USE IT!

This chapter was concerned with the nature of the self and the way in which people come to know their own attitudes, traits, and abilities. What is this topic doing in a book on social psychology, which is concerned with the way in which people's thoughts and behaviors are influenced by other people? Nothing is as personal as our self-knowledge, but, as we have seen, even our private thoughts and beliefs are formed in a social context. Can you think of examples from your own life in which your views of yourself have been shaped by your parents, friends, or teachers? Or, more broadly, by the community and culture in which you live? (See pages 108–109 on cultural and gender influences on the self.) Now let's turn the question around: Can you think of examples in which you have influenced someone else's self-views, such as a sibling, a close friend, or a romantic partner? Suppose, for example, that you have a friend who could use a bit of a confidence boost; he or she has an unrealistically negative view of his or her abilities (e.g., in academics, music, athletics, or driving ability). Based on what you have learned in this chapter, can you think of a couple of ways in which you might help this person gain confidence? (See, for example, pages 115–120 on intrinsic versus extrinsic motivation and pages 120–121 on mindsets.)

Summary

What is the self-concept, and how does it develop?

- **Origins of the Self** Studies show that great apes such as chimpanzees and orangutans pass the mirror self-recognition test, whereas lesser apes do not. In humans, self-recognition develops at around 18 to 24 months of age, and by adolescence the self-concept becomes much more complex. In adulthood, the self has four components: *self-knowledge*, our beliefs about who we are and the way in which we formulate and organize this information; *self-control*, the way in which we make plans and execute decisions; *impression management*, how we present ourselves to other people; and *self-esteem*, the way we feel about ourselves.

How do we come to understand ourselves and define who we are?

- **Self-Knowledge** We gain self-knowledge through a number of cultural and social influences.
  - **Cultural Differences in Defining the Self** People who grow up in Western cultures tend to have an independent view of the self, whereas people who grow up in Asian cultures tend to have an interdependent view of the self.
  - **Gender Differences in Defining the Self** Women tend to have relational interdependence, focusing more on close relationships, whereas men tend to have collective interdependence, focusing on their membership in larger groups.
  - **Knowing Ourselves Through Introspection** According to self-awareness theory, when people focus on themselves, they evaluate and compare their current behavior to their internal standards and values. According to research on "telling more than we can know," when people introspect about why they feel the way they do, they often use causal theories, many of which are learned from one's culture. When people think about the reasons for their attitudes, they assume that their attitudes match the reasons that are plausible and easy to verbalize, leading to reasons-generated attitude change.
  - **Knowing Ourselves by Observing Our Own Behavior** People also gain self-knowledge by observing their own behavior. **Self-perception theory** argues that when our attitudes and feelings are uncertain or ambiguous, we infer these states by observing our own behavior and the situation in which it occurs. An **overjustification effect** occurs when people focus on the extrinsic reasons for their behavior and underestimate their intrinsic reasons. According to the **two-factor theory of emotion,** emotional experience is the result of a two-step self-perception process in which people first experience arousal and then seek an appropriate explanation for it. Sometimes people make mistaken inferences about what is causing them to be aroused.
  - **Mindsets: Understanding Our Own Abilities** Some people have a **fixed mindset** about their abilities, which is the idea that they have a set amount of the ability that cannot change. Others have a **growth mindset**, the idea that their abilities are malleable qualities that they can cultivate and grow. People with a fixed mindset are more likely to give up after setbacks and are less likely to work on and hone their skills, whereas people with a growth mindset view setbacks as opportunities to improve through hard work.
  - **Using Other People to Know Ourselves** Our self-concepts are shaped by the people around us. According to **social comparison theory,** we learn about our own abilities and attitudes by comparing ourselves to other people. In addition, people tend to automatically

adopt the attitudes of those they like and want to interact with.

When are we likely to succeed at self-control, and when are we likely to fail?

- **Self-Control: The Executive Function of the Self** Self-control requires energy, and spending this energy on one task limits the amount that can be spent on another task. Recent research suggests that the level of glucose in the bloodstream is the mental "fuel" we spend on self-control.

How do we portray ourselves so that others will see us as we want to be seen?

- **Impression Management: All the World's a Stage** People try to get others to see them as they want to be seen.
  - **Ingratiation and Self-Handicapping** People have many different **impression management** strategies. One is **ingratiation**—using flattery or praise to make yourself likable to another, often a person of higher status. Another is **self-handicapping**, whereby people create obstacles and excuses for themselves so that if they do poorly on a task, they can avoid blaming themselves.
  - **Culture, Impression Management, and Self-Enhancement** The desire to manage the image we present to others is strong in all cultures, although the kinds of images we want to present depend on the culture in which we live.

What are the pros and cons of having high self-esteem?

- **Self-Esteem: How We Feel About Ourselves** Most of us have high self-esteem, which has the benefits of avoiding depression, allowing us to persevere in the face of failure, and, as shown by research on of **terror management theory**, protecting us from thoughts about our own mortality. There is a form of high self-esteem, however, that is quite problematic—namely **narcissism**—which is extreme high self-regard combined with a lack of empathy toward others. The best combination is to feel good about ourselves but also to look out for and care about others.

Chapter 5 Test

Study and Review on MyPsychLab

1. Which of the following statements is *least* true, according to research on self-knowledge?
   a. The best way to "know thyself" is to look inward, introspecting about ourselves.
   b. Sometimes the best way to know ourselves is to see what we do.
   c. We often try to figure out ourselves by comparing ourselves to others.
   d. One way we know ourselves is by using theories we learn from our culture.
   e. The way in which we know ourselves is often similar to the way in which we come to know other people.

2. Your friend Jane is interning at a law firm. When you ask her how it's going, she says, "Fine. I'm doing much better than the intern who started a month after me." What kind of social comparison is Jane making?
   a. upward social comparison
   b. downward social comparison
   c. impression comparison
   d. self-knowledge comparison

3. Suppose you meet Jessica, a student in your psychology class who is very friendly, and you like her immediately. She tells you about her recent trip to France and how much she loved it. Later on at a study-abroad session, you find yourself drawn to a program in Paris. This would be an example of
   a. reasons-generated attitude change.
   b. self-perception theory.
   c. social tuning.
   d. misattribution of arousal.
   e. upward social comparison.

4. Elise wants to increase her ability at self-control, such as by spending more time studying. Which of the following is *least* likely to work?
   a. When she is studying, she should try hard to suppress thoughts about the party she could have gone to.
   b. She should eat a small, sugary snack before studying.
   c. If she has just exerted self-control in one setting (e.g., dieting) and now needs to exert self-control in another setting (e.g., studying), she should take a break and relax for a few minutes.
   d. She should form specific implementation intentions, detailing when and where she will study in the upcoming days.

5. Your little sister enjoys taking time out of her day to make bead necklaces. A birthday party is coming up, and you decide you want to give a necklace to each person at the party. She offers to make a necklace for each of your friends, but for added motivation you give her a dollar for each one she makes. Which of the following is most likely to happen?
   a. After the party, your sister will enjoy making beads *more* than she did before, because you gave her a reward.
   b. After the party, your sister will enjoy making beads *less* than she did before, because you rewarded her for something she already liked to do.
   c. Because your sister already enjoys making beads, paying her for making them will have no effect on how much she enjoys the activity.
   d. Paying your sister for making the beads will increase her self-awareness.

6. According to research on sex differences in how people define themselves,
   a. women have higher collective interdependence in a family setting.
   b. men are low in relational interdependence only in situations that do not call for emotional sensitivity.
   c. women have lower relational independence.
   d. men have more collective interdependence than women.

7. On Halloween, you decide to do an experiment. When the trick-or-treaters arrive at your house, you have them stand in a line on your front porch. You stay outside with the group and let each child enter your house individually. You tell them they can take *one* piece of candy from the bowl that is sitting on a table. Half of the time you put the candy bowl in front of a big mirror. The other half of the time there is no mirror present. All of the children may be tempted to take more than one piece of candy. Which children will be *more* likely to give in to temptation?
   a. Those in the mirror condition.
   b. Those who are between 7 and 9 years old.
   c. Those in the no-mirror condition.
   d. Those who experience downward social comparison.

8. Catherine did very well on her math test. Which of the following statements should her mother tell her to increase the chances that Catherine will not give up on math if it later becomes more difficult for her?
   a. "You really worked hard for this test and your hard work paid off!"
   b. "You are such a smart kid, you excel in everything you do!"
   c. "You are so good in math, you obviously have a gift for this!"
   d. "I'm so glad to see you are doing better than all your classmates!"
   e. "Being good at math is in our family genes."

9. Which of the following is *true* about self-esteem and narcissism?
   a. The best way to be happy is to focus on ourselves and our own needs.
   b. Narcissists are disliked by others but do better academically and in business than other people.
   c. People who are optimistic (but not narcissistic) persevere more in the face of failure and set higher goals than do other people.
   d. Narcissism has been decreasing among college students in the United States over the past 30 years.

10. According to self-perception theory, which of the following audience members would enjoy the taping of *The Daily Show with Jon Stewart* the most?
   a. David, who sat right in front of the flashing applause sign and noticed that he clapped every time the sign said to.
   b. Stephen, who noticed that he was laughing more than other people.
   c. Zita, whose friends nudged her to get her to clap.
   d. Jimmy, who laughed a lot in order to make his friend Eleanor happy.

Answer Key

1-a, 2-b, 3-c, 4-a, 5-b,
6-d, 7-c, 8-a, 9-c, 10-b

Scoring the TRY IT! exercises

Page 108

To estimate your degree of interdependence, take the average of your answers to questions 1–5. To estimate your degree of independence, take the average of your answers to questions 6–10. On which measure did you come out higher? Singelis (1994) found that Asian Americans agreed more with the interdependence than the independence items, whereas Caucasian Americans agreed more with the independence than the interdependence items.

Page 110

To compute your score, first reverse the rating you gave to questions 8 and 9. That is, if you circled a 1, change it to a 7; if you circled a 2, change it to a 6; if you circled a 7, change it to a 1; and so on. Then add up your answers to the 11 questions. High scores reflect more of a tendency to define yourself in terms of relational interdependence. Cross, Bacon, and Morris (2000) found that women tend to score higher than men; in eight samples of college students, women averaged 57.2 and men averaged 53.4.

Page 113

Reverse your answers to questions 2 and 5. If you answered 1 to these questions, change it to a 5; if you answered 2, change it to a 4; and so on. Then add your ratings for all 10 questions. The higher your score, the more likely you are to focus your attention on yourself. Fenigstein, Scheier, and Buss (1975) found that the average score was 26 in a sample of college students.

6 The Need to Justify Our Actions

The Costs and Benefits of Dissonance Reduction

IT WAS SHOCKING NEWS: 39 PEOPLE WERE FOUND DEAD AT A LUXURY ESTATE IN RANCHO SANTA FE, CALIFORNIA, PARTICIPANTS IN A MASS SUICIDE. All were members of an obscure cult called Heaven's Gate. Each body was laid out neatly, feet clad in brand-new black Nikes, face covered with a purple shroud. The cult members died willingly and peacefully, leaving behind videotapes describing their reasons for suicide: They believed that the Hale-Bopp Comet, a recently discovered comet streaking across the night skies, was their ticket to a new life in paradise. They were convinced that in Hale-Bopp's wake was a gigantic spaceship whose mission was to carry them off to a new incarnation. To be picked up by the spaceship, they first needed to rid themselves of their current "containers." That is, they needed to leave their own bodies by ending their lives. Alas, no spaceship ever came.

Several weeks before the mass suicide, some members of the cult purchased an expensive, high-powered telescope. They wanted to get a clearer view of the comet and the spaceship that they believed was traveling behind it. A few days later, they returned the telescope and politely asked for their money back. When the store manager asked them if they had problems with the scope, they replied, "Well, gosh, we found the comet, but we can't find anything following it" (Ferris, 1997). Although the store manager tried to convince them that there was nothing wrong with the telescope and that nothing was following the comet, they remained unconvinced. Given their premise, their logic was impeccable: We know an alien spaceship is following behind the Hale-Bopp Comet. If an expensive telescope has failed to reveal that spaceship, then there is something wrong with the telescope.

Their thinking might strike you as strange, irrational, or stupid, but, generally speaking, the members of the Heaven's Gate cult were none of those things. Neighbors who knew them considered them pleasant, smart, and reasonable. What is the process by which intelligent, sane people can succumb to such fantastic thinking and self-destructive behavior? We will attempt to explain their actions at the end of this chapter. For now, we will simply state that their behavior is not unfathomable. It is simply an extreme example of a normal human tendency: the need to justify our actions and commitments.

FOCUS QUESTIONS

- What is the theory of cognitive dissonance, and how do people avoid dissonance to maintain a stable, positive self-image?
- How is the justification of effort a product of cognitive dissonance, and what are some practical applications for reducing dissonance?
- How can people avoid the traps of self-justification and other dissonance-reducing behavior?

The Theory of Cognitive Dissonance

During the past half-century, social psychologists have discovered that one of the most powerful determinants of human behavior stems from our need to preserve a stable, positive self-image (Aronson, 1969, 1998). Most people believe they are above average—more ethical and competent, better drivers, better leaders, better judges of character, and more attractive than the majority (Fine, 2008; Gilovich, 1991). But if most of us see ourselves as reasonable, moral, and smart, what happens when we are confronted with information implying that we have behaved in ways that are unreasonable, immoral, or stupid? That is the subject of this chapter.

Cognitive Dissonance

A drive or feeling of discomfort, originally defined as being caused by holding two or more inconsistent cognitions and subsequently defined as being caused by performing an action that is discrepant from one's customary, typically positive self-conception.

Maintaining a Positive Self-Image

The feeling of discomfort caused by performing an action that is discrepant from one's self-concept is called **cognitive dissonance**. Leon Festinger (1957) was the first to investigate the precise workings of this phenomenon and elaborated his findings in what is arguably social psychology's most important and most provocative theory.

Cognitive dissonance always produces discomfort, and in response we try to reduce it. The process is similar to the effects of hunger and thirst: Discomfort motivates us to eat or drink. But unlike satisfying hunger or thirst by eating or drinking, the path to reducing dissonance is not always simple or obvious. In fact, it can lead to fascinating changes in the way we think about the world and the way we behave. How can we reduce dissonance? There are three basic ways (see Figure 6.1):

- By changing our behavior to bring it in line with the dissonant cognition.
- By attempting to justify our behavior through changing one of the dissonant cognitions.
- By attempting to justify our behavior by adding new cognitions.

To illustrate each of these, let's look at something that millions of people do several times a day: smoke cigarettes. If you are a smoker, you are likely to experience dissonance because you know that this behavior significantly increases the risks of lung cancer, emphysema, and earlier death. How can you reduce this dissonance? The most direct way is to change your behavior and give up smoking. Your behavior would then be consistent with your knowledge of the link between smoking and cancer. Although many people have succeeded in quitting, it's not easy; many have tried and failed. What do these people do? It would be wrong to assume that they simply swallow hard, light up, and prepare to die. They don't. Researchers studied the behavior and attitudes of heavy smokers who attended a smoking cessation clinic but then relapsed into heavy smoking again. What do you suppose the researchers discovered? Heavy smokers who

FIGURE 6.1

How We Reduce Cognitive Dissonance

There are three basic ways of reducing dissonance: change your behavior, change your cognition, or add a new cognition.

tried to quit and failed managed to lower their perception of the dangers of smoking. In this way, they could continue to smoke without feeling terrible about it (Gibbons, Eggleston, & Benthin, 1997). A study of more than 360 adolescent smokers found the same thing: the greater their dependence on smoking and the greater the trouble they had quitting, the more justifications they came up with to keep smoking (Kleinjan, van den Eijnden, & Engels, 2009).

Smokers can come up with some pretty creative justifications. Some convince themselves that the data linking cigarette smoking to cancer are inconclusive. Or they say that smoking is worth the risk of cancer and emphysema because it is so enjoyable, and besides it relaxes them and reduces nervous tension and in this way actually improves their health. Some add a cognition that allows them to focus on the vivid exception: "Look at my grandfather. He's 87 years old, and he's been smoking a pack a day since he was 12. That proves it's not always bad for you." Another popular way of reducing dissonance through adding a new cognition is **self-affirmation**, in which a person focuses on one or more of his or her good qualities to lessen the dissonant sting caused by doing something foolish: "Yeah, I feel pretty stupid to still be smoking, but boy am I a good cook. In fact, let me tell you about this new recipe . . ." (Steele, 1988; McConnell & Brown, 2010).

Self-Affirmation

In the context of dissonance theory, a way of reducing dissonance by reminding oneself of one or more of one's positive attributes.

Impact Bias

The tendency to overestimate the intensity and duration of one's emotional reactions to future negative events.

These justifications may sound silly to the nonsmoker, but that is our point. As the smokers' rationales show, people experiencing dissonance will often deny or distort reality to reduce it. People who don't want to give up scientifically discredited ideas, refuse to practice safe sex, or receive bad news about their health can be equally "creative" in denying evidence and reducing their discomfort (Aronson, 1997; Croyle & Jemmott, 1990; Kassarjian & Cohen, 1965; Leishman, 1988).

Watch on MyPsychLab

To learn more, watch the MyPsychLab video ***Carol Tavris: What is cognitive dissonance?***

When you understand dissonance, you will see it in action all around you: in the politician who opposes prostitution but is caught with a high-priced call girl ("oh, a call girl isn't *really* a prostitute"), in the people who predict the end of the world but who, fortunately, turn out to be wrong ("our prediction was accurate; we just used numbers from the wrong chapter of the Bible"). In one study, researchers wondered how gay men who were strongly identified with their Christian church dealt with anti-gay pronouncements from their ministers. One way to resolve dissonance would be to change their behavior—that is, to change their church or even leave their religion. But those who decide to stay in the church resolve dissonance by focusing on the shortcomings of the minister; for example, they say, "It's not my religion that promotes this prejudice—it's the bigotry of this particular preacher" (Pitt, 2010).

Teenagers who smoke usually justify their actions with such cognitions as "Smoking is cool"; "I want to be like my friends"; "in movies, everyone smokes"; "I'm healthy; nothing is going to happen to *me*"; or "adults are always on my back about stuff I do"

Why We Overestimate the Pain of Disappointment

Imagine that you have just interviewed for the job of your dreams. You expect to be very disappointed if you don't get the job. Then, to your utter amazement, you *don't* get the job. How long do you think your disappointment will last? The answer is: It depends on how successfully you reduce the dissonance caused by not getting the job. When you first get the bad news, you will be disappointed; however, more than likely you will soon put a spin on it that makes you feel better. It was a dead-end job anyway. And that interviewer was a jerk.

Interestingly, people often do not anticipate how successfully they will reduce dissonance. When people think about how they will react to future negative events, they show an **impact bias**, whereby they overestimate the intensity and duration of their negative emotional reactions. For example, people overestimate how dreadful they will feel following a romantic breakup, loss of a job, or not getting into the dorm they wanted (Dunn, Wilson, & Gilbert, 2003; Gilbert et al., 1998; Mellers & McGraw, 2001; Wilson & Gilbert, 2005).

Given that people have successfully reduced dissonance in the past, why is it that they are not aware that they will do so in the future? The answer is that the process of *reducing dissonance is largely unconscious*. Indeed, dissonance reduction works better that way (Gilbert et al., 1998). It is not very effective to hear ourselves say, "I'll try to make myself feel better by *convincing myself* that the person who just rejected me is an idiot." It is more effective if we unconsciously transform our view of the interviewer; we feel better believing that anyone could see that he is an idiot (Bem & McConnell, 1970; Goethals & Reckman, 1973). Because the dissonance-reduction process is mostly unconscious, we do not anticipate that it will save us from future anguish.

Self-Esteem and Dissonance Who do you think feels the greatest dissonance after doing something cruel, foolish, or incompetent: a person with high self-esteem or low? The answer is the former; people with the highest self-esteem experience the most dissonance when they behave in ways that are contrary to their high opinion of themselves, and they will work harder to reduce it than will those with average levels of self-esteem. When people who have low self-esteem commit a stupid or immoral action, they do not feel as much dissonance, because the cognition "I have done an awful thing" is consonant with the cognition "I am a schlunk; I'm always doing awful things."

In a classic experiment, researchers predicted that individuals who had been given a boost to their self-esteem would be less likely to cheat, if given the opportunity to do so, than individuals who had a lower opinion of themselves (Aronson & Mettee, 1968). After all, if you think of yourself as a decent person, cheating would be dissonant with that self-concept. However, people who have had a temporary blow to their self-esteem, and thus are feeling low and worthless, might be more likely to cheat at cards, kick their dog, or do any number of things consistent with having a low opinion of themselves.

In this experiment, the self-esteem of college students was temporarily modified by giving the subjects false information about their personalities. After taking a personality test, one-third of the students were given positive feedback; they were told that the test indicated that they were mature, interesting, deep, and so forth. Another third of the students were given negative feedback; they were told that the test revealed that they were relatively immature, uninteresting, shallow, and the like. The remaining one-third of the students were not given any information about the results of the test. Immediately afterward, the students were scheduled to participate in an experiment conducted by a different psychologist who had no apparent relation to the personality inventory. As part of this second experiment, the participants played a game of cards against some of their fellow students. They were allowed to bet money and keep whatever they won. In the course of the game, they were given a few opportunities to cheat and thereby win a sizable sum of cash. The findings confirmed the prediction of dissonance theory: The students who had gotten the positive feedback were *least* likely to take the opportunity to cheat; the students who had gotten the negative feedback were *most* likely to cheat; and the control group fell in between.

If high self-esteem can serve as a buffer against dishonest or self-defeating behavior because people strive to keep their self-concepts consonant with their actions, this research has wide-ranging applications. For example, many African American children believe that they "don't have what it takes" to succeed academically, so they don't work hard, so they don't do as well as they might—all of this perfectly, if tragically, consonant. A team of social psychologists conducted a simple intervention, which they replicated three times with three different classrooms (Cohen et al., 2009). They bolstered African American children's self-esteem by having them do structured, self-affirming writing assignments. The children had to focus their attention on their good qualities in areas outside of academics and their most important values (e.g., religion, music, or love for their family). This self-affirmation raised their general self-esteem, which in turn reduced their academic anxiety, resulting in better performance. The lowest-achieving black students benefitted the most, and the benefits persisted in a follow-up study two years later. Thus, changing the students' negative self-perceptions had long-term benefits both on self-esteem and performance on objective exams.

Watch on **MyPsychLab**

To learn more about self-affirmation, watch the MyPsychLab video ***What is personality, and how does it relate to self-esteem?***

Do these results sound too good to be true? They are not. Still, we must be cautious in generalizing from them. Bolstering self-esteem can't be done in an artificial way. To be effective, this kind of intervention must be grounded in reality (Kernis, 2001). If a person were to look in the mirror and say, "Boy, I sure am terrific," it is unlikely to help much; the person has to focus on his or her actual strengths, positive values, and good qualities and then strive to make them consonant with his or her actions.

Rational Behavior versus Rationalizing Behavior

Most people think of themselves as rational beings, and generally they are right: We are certainly capable of rational thought. But as we've seen, the need to maintain our self-esteem leads to thinking that is not always rational; rather, it is *rationalizing*. People who are in the midst of reducing dissonance are so involved with convincing themselves that they are right that they frequently end up behaving irrationally and maladaptively.

During the late 1950s, when segregation was still widespread, two social psychologists did a simple experiment in a southern town (Jones & Kohler, 1959). They selected people who were deeply committed to a position on the issue of racial segregation: some strongly supported segregation; others opposed it just as strongly. Next, the researchers presented these individuals with a series of arguments on both sides of the issue. Some of the arguments were plausible, and others were rather silly. The question was: Which of the arguments would people remember best?

If the participants were behaving in a purely rational way, we would expect them to remember the plausible arguments best and the implausible arguments least, regardless of how they felt about segregation. But what does dissonance theory predict? A silly argument that supports your own position arouses some dissonance because it raises doubts about the wisdom of that position or the intelligence of people who agree with it. Likewise, a sensible argument on the other side of the issue also arouses some dissonance because it raises the possibility that the other side might be smarter or more accurate than you had thought. Because these arguments arouse dissonance, we try not to think about them.

This is exactly what the researchers found. The participants remembered the plausible arguments agreeing with their own position *and* the *implausible* arguments agreeing with the *opposing* position. Subsequent research has yielded similar results on many issues, from whether or not the death penalty deters people from committing murder to the risks of contracting HIV through heterosexual contact (e.g., Biek, Wood, & Chaiken, 1996; Edwards & Smith, 1996; Hart et al., 2009).

In sum, we humans do not always process information in an unbiased way. Sometimes, of course, we pursue new information because we want to be accurate in our views or make the wisest decisions. But once we are committed to our views and beliefs, most of us distort new information in a way that confirms them (Hart et al., 2009; Ross, 2010).

Once he is hooked on getting a truck, this young man will reason that "it certainly would be safer than a small car, and besides, the price of gasoline is bound to drop by the time I'm 40."

Decisions, Decisions, Decisions

Every time we make a decision, we experience dissonance. How come? Suppose you are about to buy a car, but you are torn between a van and a subcompact. You know that each has advantages and disadvantages: The van would be more convenient. You can sleep in it during long trips, and it has plenty of power, but it gets poor mileage and it's hard to park. The subcompact is a lot less roomy, and you wonder about its safety: but it is less expensive to buy, it's a lot zippier to drive, and it has a pretty good repair record. Before you decide, you will probably get as much information as you can. You go online and read what the experts say about each model's safety, gas consumption, and reliability. You'll talk with friends who own a van or a subcompact. You'll probably visit automobile dealers to test-drive the vehicles to see how each one feels. All this predecision behavior is perfectly rational.

Postdecision Dissonance
Dissonance aroused after making a decision, typically reduced by enhancing the attractiveness of the chosen alternative and devaluating the rejected alternatives

Let's assume you decide to buy the subcompact. We predict that your behavior will change in a specific way: You will begin to think more and more about the number of miles to the gallon as though it were the most important thing in the world. Simultaneously, you will almost certainly downplay the fact that you can't sleep in your subcompact. Who wants to sleep in their car on a long trip anyway? Similarly, you will barely remember that your new small car can put you at considerable risk of harm in a collision. How does this shift in thinking happen?

Distorting Our Likes and Dislikes In any decision, whether it is between two cars, two colleges, or two potential lovers, the chosen alternative is seldom entirely positive and the rejected alternative is seldom entirely negative. After the decision, your cognition that you are a smart person is dissonant with all the negative things about the car, college, or lover you chose; that cognition is also dissonant with all the *positive* aspects of the car, college, or lover you *rejected*. We call this **postdecision dissonance**. Cognitive dissonance theory predicts that to help yourself feel better about the decision, you will do some unconscious mental work to try to reduce the dissonance.

What kind of work? In a classic experiment, Jack Brehm (1956) posed as a representative of a consumer testing service and asked women to rate the attractiveness and desirability of several kinds of small appliances. Each woman was told that as a reward for having participated in the survey, she could have one of the appliances as a gift. She was given a choice between two of the products she had rated as being equally attractive. After she made her decision, each woman was asked to rerate all the products. After receiving the appliance of their choice, the women rated its attractiveness somewhat higher than they had the first time. Not only that, but they drastically lowered their rating of the appliance they might have chosen but decided to reject.

In other words, following a decision, to reduce dissonance we change the way we feel about the chosen and unchosen alternatives, cognitively spreading them apart in our own minds in order to make ourselves feel better about the choice we made.

The Permanence of the Decision The more important the decision, the greater the dissonance. Deciding which car to buy is clearly more important than deciding between a toaster and a coffeemaker; deciding which person to marry is clearly more important than deciding which car to buy. Decisions also vary in terms of how permanent they are—that is, how difficult they are to revoke. It is a lot easier to trade in your new car for another one than it is to get out of an unhappy marriage. The more permanent and less revocable the decision, the stronger is the need to reduce dissonance.

All sales are final. When will this customer be happier with her new flatscreen TV: ten minutes before the purchase? Ten minutes after the purchase?

In a simple but clever experiment, social psychologists intercepted people at a racetrack who were on their way to place $2 bets and asked them how certain they were that their horses would win (Knox & Inkster, 1968). The investigators also approached other bettors just as they were leaving the $2 window, after having placed their bets, and asked them the same question. Almost invariably, people who had already placed their bets gave their horses a much better chance of winning than did those who had not yet placed their bets. Because only a few minutes separated one group from another, nothing real had occurred to increase the probability of winning; the only thing that had changed was the finality of the decision—and hence the dissonance it produced.

Moving from the racetrack to the Harvard campus, other investigators tested the irrevocability hypothesis in a photography class (Gilbert & Ebert, 2002). In their study, participants were recruited through an advertisement for students interested in learning photography while taking part in a psychology experiment. Students were informed that they would shoot some photographs and print two of them. They would rate the two photographs and then get to choose one to keep. The other would be kept for administrative reasons. The students were randomly assigned to one of two conditions. In Condition One, students were informed that they had the option of exchanging photographs within a five-day period; in Condition Two, students were told that their choice was final. The researchers found that *prior* to making the choice between the two photographs, the students liked them equally. The experimenters then contacted the students two, four, and nine days after they had made their choice to find out if those who had a choice to exchange photographs liked the one they chose more or less than did those in the no-choice (irrevocable) condition. And, indeed, the students who had the option of exchanging photographs liked the one they finally ended up with less than did those who made the final choice on the first day.

Interestingly, when students were asked to predict whether keeping their options open would make them more or less happy with their decision, they predicted that keeping their options open would make them happier. They were wrong. Because they underestimated the discomfort of dissonance, they failed to realize that the finality of the decision would make them happier.

Lowballing
An unscrupulous strategy whereby a salesperson induces a customer to agree to purchase a product at a low cost, subsequently claims it was an error, and then raises the price; frequently, the customer will agree to make the purchase at the inflated price

Creating the Illusion of Irrevocability The irrevocability of a decision always increases dissonance and the motivation to reduce it. Because of this, unscrupulous salespeople have developed techniques for creating the illusion that irrevocability exists. One such technique is called **lowballing** (Cialdini, 2009; Cialdini et al., 1978; Weyant, 1996). Robert Cialdini, a distinguished social psychologist, temporarily joined the sales force of an automobile dealership to observe this technique closely. Here's how it works: You enter an automobile showroom intent on buying a particular car. Having already priced it at several dealerships, you know you can purchase it for about $18,000. You are approached by a personable middle-aged man who tells you he can sell you one for $17,679. Excited by the bargain, you agree to write out a check for the down payment so that he can take it to the manager as proof that you are a serious customer. Meanwhile, you imagine yourself driving home in your shiny new bargain. Ten minutes later the salesperson returns, looking forlorn. He tells you that in his zeal to give you a good deal, he miscalculated and the sales manager caught it. The price of the car comes to $18,178. You are disappointed. Moreover, you are pretty sure you can get it a bit cheaper elsewhere. The decision to buy is not irrevocable. And yet in this situation far more people will go ahead with the deal than if the original asking price had been $18,178, even though the reason for buying the car from this particular dealer—the bargain price—no longer exists (Cialdini, 2009; Cialdini et al., 1978).

Watch on **MyPsychLab**
To learn more about lowballing, watch the MyPsychLab video ***Becoming a detective of social influence: Robert Cialdini.***

There are at least three reasons why lowballing works. First, although the customer's decision to buy is reversible, a commitment of sorts does exist. Signing a check for a down payment creates the illusion of irrevocability, even though, if the car buyer thought about it, he or she would quickly realize that it is a nonbinding contract. In the world of high-pressure sales, however, even a temporary illusion can have real consequences. Second, the feeling of commitment triggered the anticipation of an exciting event: driving out with a new car. To have had the anticipated event thwarted (by not going ahead with the deal) would have been a big letdown. Third, although the final price is substantially higher than the customer thought it would be, it is probably only slightly higher than the price at another dealership. Under these circumstances, the

TRY IT! The Advantage of Finality

Ask five friends who are not in this psychology class the following question: Imagine you are shopping for a particular cell phone and you find it in two stores. The price for the phones is identical, but in Store A you have the option of exchanging the phone within 30 days, while in Store B all sales are final. One week after your purchase, which situation will make you happier with the cell phone: Store A (with the option to return the phone) or Store B (purchase not revocable)?

After he cheats, this student will try to convince himself that everybody would cheat if they had the chance.

customer in effect says, "Oh, what the heck. I'm here, I've already filled out the forms, I've written out the check—why wait?" Thus, by using dissonance reduction and the illusion of irrevocability, high-pressure salespeople increase the probability that you will decide to buy their product at their price.

The Decision to Behave Immorally Of course, decisions about cars, appliances, racehorses, and even presidential candidates are the easy ones. Often, however, our choices involve moral and ethical issues. When is it OK to lie to a friend, and when is it not? When is an act stealing, and when is it just "what everyone does"? How people reduce dissonance following a difficult moral decision has implications for their self-esteem and for whether they behave more *or less* ethically in the future.

Take the issue of cheating on an exam. Suppose you are a college sophomore taking the final exam in organic chemistry. Ever since you can remember, you have wanted to be a surgeon, and you think that your admission to medical school will depend heavily on how well you do in this course. A key question involves some material you know fairly well, but because so much is riding on this exam, you feel acute anxiety and draw a blank. You glance at your neighbor's paper and discover that she is just completing her answer to the crucial question. Your conscience tells you it's wrong to cheat, and yet, if you don't cheat, you are certain to get a poor grade. And if you get a poor grade, you are convinced that there goes medical school.

Regardless of whether you decide to cheat or not, the threat to your self-esteem arouses dissonance. If you cheat, your belief or cognition "I am a decent, moral person" is dissonant with your cognition "I have just committed an immoral act." If you decide to resist temptation, your cognition "I want to become a surgeon" is dissonant with your cognition "I could have nailed a good grade and admission to medical school, but I chose not to. Wow, was I stupid!"

Watch on **MyPsychLab**

To consider another type of cheating, watch the MyPsychLab video ***American Sex Lives 2004.***

Suppose that after a difficult struggle, you decide to cheat. According to dissonance theory, it is likely that you would try to justify the action by finding a way to minimize its negative aspects. In this case, an efficient path to reducing dissonance would involve changing your attitude about cheating. You would adopt a more lenient attitude toward cheating, convincing yourself that it is a victimless crime that doesn't hurt anybody, that everybody does it, and that, therefore it's not really so bad.

Suppose, by contrast, after a difficult struggle, you decide not to cheat. How would you reduce your dissonance? Again, you could change your attitude about the morality of the act, but this time in the opposite direction. That is, to justify giving up a good grade, you convince yourself that cheating is a heinous sin, that it's one of the lowest things a person can do, and that cheaters should be rooted out and severely punished.

How Dissonance Affects Personal Values What has happened is not merely a rationalization of your own behavior, but a change in your system of values. Thus, two people acting in two different ways could have started out with almost identical attitudes toward cheating. One came within an inch of cheating but decided to resist, while the other came within an inch of resisting but decided to cheat. After they had made their decisions, however, their attitudes toward cheating would diverge sharply as a consequence of their actions (see Figure 6.2 on next page).

These speculations were tested by Judson Mills (1958) in an experiment he performed in an elementary school. Mills first measured the attitudes of sixth graders toward cheating. He then had them participate in a competitive exam, with prizes awarded to the winners. The situation was arranged so that it was almost impossible to win without cheating. Mills made it easy for the children to cheat and created the illusion that they could not be detected. Under these conditions, as one might expect, some of the students cheated and others did not. The next day, the sixth graders were again asked to indicate how they felt about cheating. Sure enough, the children who had cheated became more lenient toward cheating, and those who had resisted the temptation to cheat adopted a harsher attitude.

Our prediction is that as you read this, you are thinking about your own beliefs about cheating and how they might relate to your own behavior. Not long ago, a scandal broke out at a Florida business school. In one course, a professor discovered, more than half the students had cribbed from an exam stolen in advance. When interviewed, those who cheated said things like, "Hey, no big deal. Everyone does it." Those who refrained from cheating said, "What the cheaters did was awful. They are lazy and unethical. And they are planning for careers in *business*?"

Take another look at Figure 6.2 and imagine yourself at the top of that pyramid, about to make any important decision, such as whether to stay with a current romantic partner or break up, use illegal drugs or not, choose this major or that one, get involved in politics or not. Keep in mind that once you make a decision, you are going to justify it to reduce dissonance, and that justification may later make it hard for you to change your mind . . . even when you should.

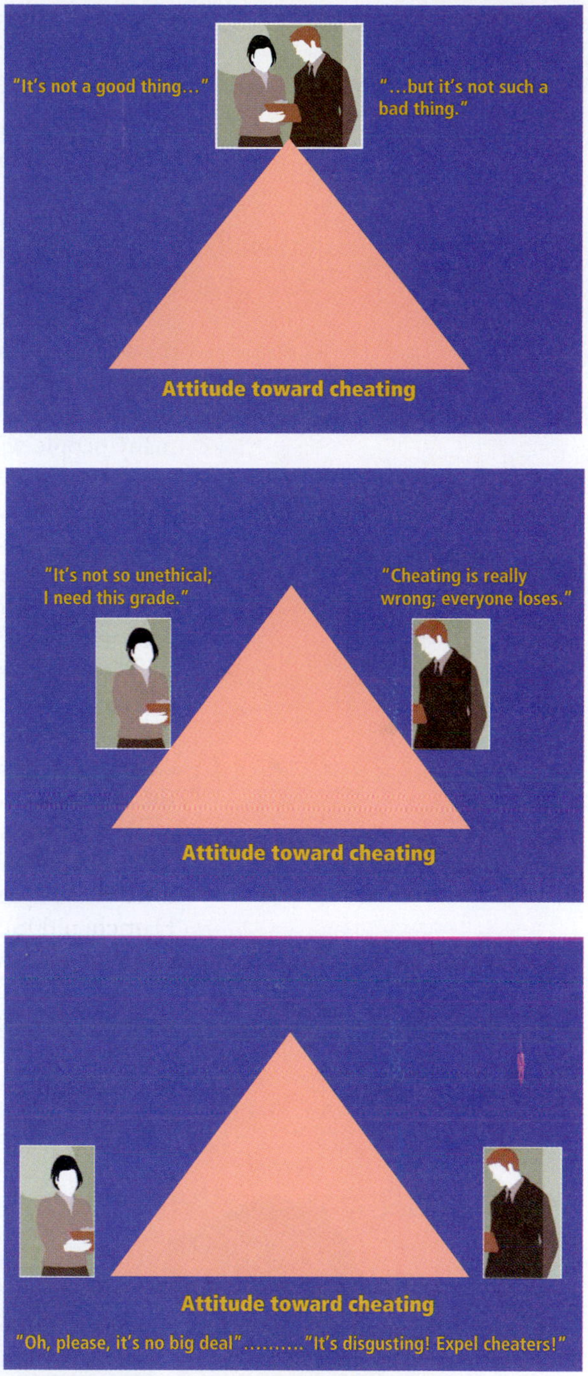

FIGURE 6.2

The Cheating Pyramid

Imagine two students taking an exam. Both are tempted to cheat. Initially, their attitudes toward cheating are almost identical, but then one impulsively cheats and the other does not. Their attitudes will then undergo predictable changes.

(Created by Carol Tavris. Used by permission.)

Dissonance, Culture, and the Brain

Cognitive dissonance theory has been supported by thousands of studies, some in related areas such as cognition (biases in how the brain processes information), memory (how we shape our current memories to be consonant with our self-concepts), and attitudes (see Chapter 7). Investigators are learning what aspects of cognitive dissonance seem to be universal, hardwired in the brain, and which vary across cultures.

Dissonance in the Brain Experiments with monkeys and chimps support the notion that cognitive dissonance has some built-in, adaptive functions. Remember the study in which homemakers ranked appliances and then, after getting to keep an appliance of their choice, lowered their ranking of the previously attractive appliance they did not choose? When monkeys and chimps are placed in a similar situation, having to choose between different-colored M&Ms instead of kitchen appliances, they later reduced their preference for the color of M&Ms they had not chosen (Egan, Santos, & Bloom, 2007; see also West et al., 2010). Among primates, this research suggests, it has been of evolutionary benefit to stick with a decision once made.

Neuroscientists have tracked brain activity to discover what parts of the brain are active when a person is in a state of dissonance and motivated to do something to reduce it (Harmon-Jones, 2010). Using fMRI technology, they can monitor neural activity in specific areas while people are experiencing various kinds of dissonance: for example, while they are rating their preferences for things they had chosen and those they had rejected, while they are arguing that the uncomfortable scanner experience was actually quite pleasant, or while they are confronted with unwelcome information. The areas of the brain that are activated during dissonance include the striatum and other highly specific areas within the prefrontal cortex, the site prominently involved in planning and decision making (Izuma et al., 2010; Qin et al., 2011; van Veen et al., 2009).

In a study of people who were trying to process dissonant or consonant information about their preferred presidential candidate, Drew Westen and his colleagues (2006) found that the reasoning areas of the brain virtually shut down when a person is confronted with dissonant information and the emotion circuits of the brain light up happily when consonance is restored. As Westen put it, people twirl the "cognitive kaleidoscope" until the pieces fall into the pattern they want to see, and then the brain

Justification of Effort
The tendency for individuals to increase their liking for something they have worked hard to attain

repays them by activating circuits involved in pleasure. It seems that the feeling of cognitive dissonance can literally make your brain hurt!

Dissonance Across Cultures We can find dissonance operating in almost every part of the world (e.g., Beauvois & Joule, 1996; Imada & Kitayama, 2010; Sakai, 1999), but it does not always take the same form, and the *content* of the cognitions that produce it may differ across cultures. In "collectivist" societies, where the needs of the group matter more than the needs of the individual, dissonance-reducing behavior might be less prevalent, at least on the surface (Triandis, 1995). In such cultures, we'd be more likely to find behavior aimed at maintaining group harmony and less likely to see people justifying their own personal misbehavior—but more likely to see people experiencing dissonance when their behavior shames or disappoints *others*.

Japanese social psychologist Haruki Sakai (1999), combining his interest in dissonance with his knowledge of Japanese community orientation, found that, in Japan, many people will vicariously experience dissonance on the part of someone they know and like. The observers' attitudes change to conform to those of their dissonance-reducing friends. In two other experiments, the Japanese justified their choices when they felt others were observing them while they were making their decision, but not later; this pattern was reversed for Americans (Imada & Kitayama, 2010). The perceived privacy or public visibility of the choice being made interacts with culture to determine whether dissonance is aroused and the choice needs to be justified.

Nonetheless, some causes of dissonance are apparently international and intergenerational. In multicultural America, immigrant parents and their young-adult children often clash over cultural values: the children want to be like their peers, but their elders want them to be like them. This conflict often creates enormous dissonance in the children because they love their parents but do not embrace all of their values. In a longitudinal study of Vietnamese and Cambodian adolescents in the United States, those who were experiencing the most cognitive dissonance were most likely to get into trouble, do less well in school, and fight more with their parents (Choi, He, & Harachi, 2008).

Self-Justification in Everyday Life

Suppose you put in a lot of effort to get into a particular club and it turns out to be a totally worthless organization, consisting of boring, pompous people doing trivial activities. You would feel pretty foolish, wouldn't you? A sensible person doesn't work hard to gain something worthless. Such a circumstance would produce significant dissonance; your cognition that you are a sensible, adept human being is dissonant with your cognition that you worked hard to get into a dismal group. How would you reduce this dissonance?

The harsh training required to become a marine will increase the recruits' feelings of cohesiveness and their pride in the corps.

The Justification of Effort

You might start by finding a way to convince yourself that the club and the people in it are nicer, more interesting, and more worthwhile than they appeared to be at first glance. How can one turn boring people into interesting people and a trivial club into a worthwhile one? Easy. Even the most boring people and trivial clubs have some redeeming qualities. Activities and behaviors are open to a variety of interpretations; if we are motivated to see the best in people and things, we will tend to interpret these ambiguities in a positive way. We call this the **justification of effort**, the tendency for individuals to increase their liking for something they have worked hard to attain.

TRY IT! Justifying Actions

Think about something that you have gone after in the past that required you to put in a lot of effort or that caused you considerable trouble. Perhaps you waited for several hours in a long line to get tickets to a concert; perhaps you sat in your car through an incredible traffic jam because it was the only way you could visit a close friend.

1. List the things you had to go through to attain your goal.
2. Do you think you tried to justify all that effort? Did you find yourself exaggerating the good things about the goal and minimizing any negative aspects of the goal? List some of the ways you might have exaggerated the value of the goal.
3. The next time you put in a lot of effort to reach a goal, you might want to monitor your actions and cognitions carefully to see if the goal was *really* worth it or whether there is any self-justification involved.

In a classic experiment, Elliot Aronson and Judson Mills (1959) explored the link between effort and dissonance reduction. In their experiment, college students volunteered to join a group that would be meeting regularly to discuss various aspects of the psychology of sex. To be admitted to the group, they volunteered to go through a screening procedure. For one-third of the participants, the procedure was demanding and unpleasant; for another third, it was only mildly unpleasant; and the final third was admitted to the group without any screening at all.

Each participant was then allowed to listen in on a discussion being conducted by the members of the group he or she would be joining. Although the participants were led to believe that the discussion was live, they were listening to a prerecorded tape. The taped discussion was designed to be as dull and bombastic as possible. After the discussion was over, each participant was asked to rate it in terms of how much he or she liked it, how interesting it was, how intelligent the participants were, and so forth.

As you can see in Figure 6.3, participants who expended little or no effort to get into the group did not enjoy the discussion much. They were able to see it for what it was—a dull and boring waste of time. Participants who went through a severe initiation, however, convinced themselves that the same discussion, though not as scintillating as they had hoped, was dotted with interesting and provocative tidbits and was therefore, in the main, a worthwhile experience. These findings have been replicated under a variety of circumstances: people justify the effort they have expended on everything from a worthless self-help program to a course of physical therapy (e.g., Coleman, 2010; Conway & Ross, 1984; Cooper, 1980; Gerard & Mathewson, 1966).

We are not suggesting that most people enjoy difficult, unpleasant experiences, nor that people enjoy things that are merely associated with unpleasant experiences. What we are asserting is that if a person agrees to go through a demanding or an unpleasant experience in order to attain some goal or object, that goal or object becomes more attractive. Thus, if you were walking to the discussion group and a passing car splashed mud all over you, you would not like that group any better. However, if you volunteered to jump into a mud puddle in order to be admitted to a group that turned out to be boring, you *would* like the group better. (See the Try It! above.)

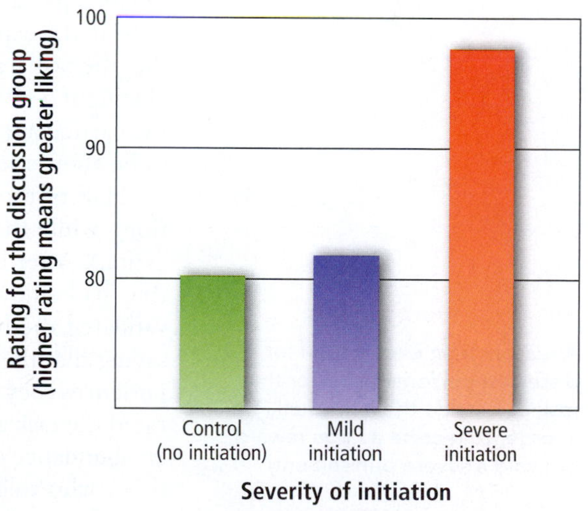

FIGURE 6.3

The Justification of Effort

The more effort we put into becoming members of a group, and the tougher the initiation, the more we will like the group we have just joined—even if it turns out to be a dud.

(Adapted from Aronson & Mills, 1959.)

External versus Internal Justification

Suppose your friend Jen shows you her expensive new dress and asks your opinion. You think it is atrocious and are about to say so, advising her to exchange it before another human being sees her in it, when she tells you that she has already had it altered, which means that she cannot return it. What do you say? Chances are you go through something like the following thought process: "Jen seems so happy and excited about her new dress. She spent a lot of money for it, and she can't take it back. If I say what I think, I'll upset her."

So you tell Jen that you like her dress. Do you experience much dissonance? We doubt it. Many thoughts are consonant with having told this lie, as outlined in your reasoning. In effect, your cognition that it is important not to embarrass or cause pain to people you like provides ample **external justification** for having told a harmless lie.

What happens, though, if you say something you don't believe when there *isn't* a good external justification for being insincere? What if your friend Jen is wealthy and can easily afford to absorb the cost of her ugly new dress? What if she sincerely wanted to know what you thought? Now the external justifications—the reasons for lying to Jen about the dress—are minimal. If you still withhold your true opinion, you will experience dissonance. When you can't find external justification for your behavior, you will attempt to find **internal justification**; you will try to reduce dissonance by changing something about yourself, such as your attitude or behavior.

Counterattitudinal Advocacy How can you do this? You might begin by looking harder for positive things about the dress that you hadn't noticed before. Within a short time, your attitude toward the dress will have moved in the direction of the statement you made. And that is how *saying becomes believing*. Its official term is **counterattitudinal advocacy**. It occurs when we claim to have an opinion or attitude that differs from our true beliefs. When we do this with little external justification—that is, without being motivated by something outside of ourselves—what we believe begins to conform more and more to the lie we told.

This proposition was first tested in a groundbreaking experiment by Leon Festinger and J. Merrill Carlsmith (1959). College students were induced to spend an hour performing a series of excruciatingly boring and repetitive tasks. The experimenter then told them that the purpose of the study was to determine whether or not people would perform better if they had been informed in advance that the tasks were interesting. They were each informed that they had been randomly assigned to the control condition—that is, they had not been told anything in advance. However, he explained, the next participant, a young woman who was just arriving in the anteroom, was going to be in the experimental condition. The researcher said that he needed to convince her that the task was going to be interesting and enjoyable. Because it was much more convincing if a fellow student rather than the experimenter delivered this message, would the participant do so? Thus, with his request, the experimenter induced the participants to lie about the task to another student.

Half of the students were offered \$20 for telling the lie (a large external justification), while the others were offered only \$1 for telling the lie (a small external justification). After the experiment was over, an interviewer asked the lie-tellers how much they had enjoyed the tasks they had performed earlier in the experiment. The results validated the hypothesis: The students who had been paid \$20 for lying—that is, for saying that the tasks had been enjoyable—rated the activities as the dull and boring experiences they were. But those who were paid only \$1 for saying the task was enjoyable rated the task as significantly more enjoyable. In other words, people who had received an abundance of external justification for lying told the lie but didn't believe it, whereas those who told the lie without much external justification convinced themselves that what they said was closer to the truth.

Can you induce a person to change an attitude about things that matter? Let's consider two issues that, for decades, have been of interest to students: the police and pot. Throughout American history, students have launched campus sit-ins and other demonstrations to protest segregation, sex discrimination, the Vietnam War, tuition increases, and, in 2011, Wall Street greed and lack of corporate accountability. Many of these protests were met with excessive force by the police, who used clubs, tear gas, and pepper spray on the students to disperse them. You can imagine how angry that action made the protesters and their supporters. Is it possible to change students'

External Justification

A reason or an explanation for dissonant personal behavior that resides outside the individual (e.g., in order to receive a large reward or avoid a severe punishment)

Internal Justification

The reduction of dissonance by changing something about oneself (e.g., one's attitude or behavior)

Counterattitudinal Advocacy

Stating an opinion or attitude that runs counter to one's private belief or attitude attitudes to make them more understanding and more supportive of the police? In a different domain, could you change the attitudes of those students who believe that marijuana is harmful and should be prohibited, persuading them to favor its use and legalization?

The answer, in both cases, is yes. And you can change these hot-button attitudes not by offering people large incentives to write a forceful essay supporting the police or the legalization of marijuana, but with small incentives. When Yale University students were offered a large cash reward for writing an essay supporting the excessive force used by the local police, they did not need to convince themselves that they believed what they had written; the external justification was enough. However, when they were induced to write a supportive essay for a small reward, they did, in fact, soften their attitudes toward the actions of the police (Cohen, 1962). Another study found the same pattern of results with students at the University of Texas who were opposed to the legalization of marijuana. When they were well paid for writing an essay favoring legalization, their real attitudes did not change. When they were given only a small fee, however, they needed to convince themselves that there was some truth in what they had written, and their attitudes became more prolegalization (Nel, Helmreich, & Aronson, 1969). In these studies, as in many others, the smaller the external incentive, the greater the attitude change.

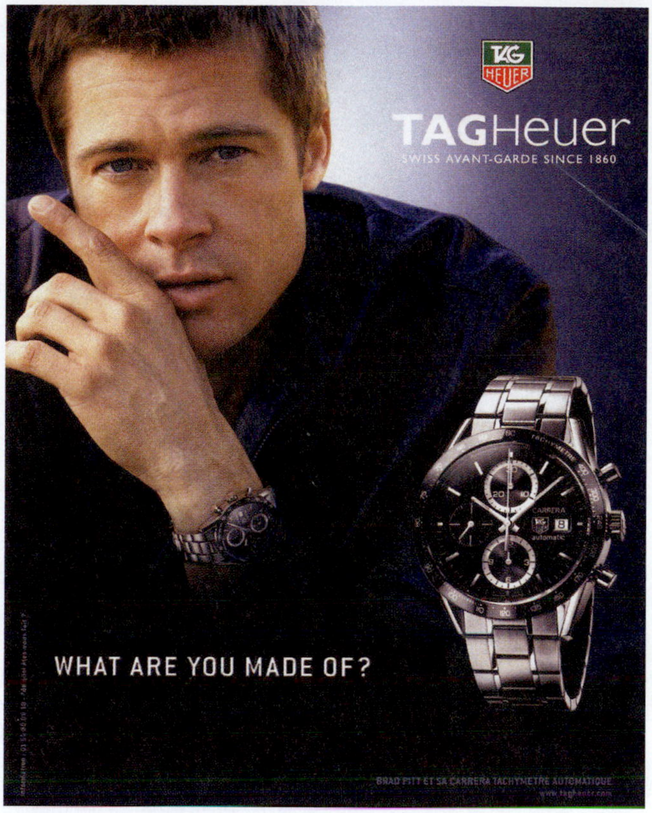

Celebrities are paid huge amounts of money to endorse products. Do you think that Brad Pitt believes the message he is delivering about this expensive watch? Is the justification for his endorsement internal or external?

Experiments on counterattitudinal advocacy have been applied to a wide range of real-world problems, from reducing prejudice to reducing the risk of eating disorders. In the former, white college students were asked to write a counterattitudinal essay publicly endorsing a controversial proposal at their university to double the amount of funds available for academic scholarships for African American students. Because the total amount of funds was limited, this meant cutting by half the amount of scholarship funds available to white students. As you might imagine, this was a highly dissonant situation. How might the students reduce dissonance? As they came up with more and more reasons in writing their essays, they ended up convincing themselves that they believed in that policy. And not only did they believe in it, but their general attitude toward African Americans became more favorable (Leippe & Eisenstadt, 1994, 1998). Later experiments with diverse groups have gotten the same results, including a decrease in white prejudice toward Asian students (Son Hing, Li, & Zanna, 2002) and, in Germany, German prejudice toward Turks (Heitland & Bohner, 2010).

Counterattitudinal advocacy has also been effective in dealing with a far different problem: eating disorders (such as bulimia) and dissatisfaction with one's body. In American society, where super-thin is considered beautiful, many women are dissatisfied with the size and shape of their own bodies, and the internalization of the media's "thin ideal" leads not only to unhappiness but also to constant dieting and eating disorders.

Explore on **MyPsychLab**
To learn more about Festinger and Carlsmith's research, try the MyPsychLab exploration ***Cognitive Dissonance and Attitude Change.***

For more than a decade, a team of researchers has been applying cognitive dissonance to counteract these self-destructive feelings and behaviors. In a series of experiments, high school and college women with body-image concerns were assigned to either dissonance or control conditions. Women in the dissonance condition had to compose their own arguments against the "thin is beautiful" image they had bought into, by writing an essay describing the emotional and physical costs of pursuing an unrealistic ideal body and by acting out that argument to discourage other women from pursuing the thin ideal. Participants in the dissonance condition showed significant increases in their satisfaction with their bodies, as well as a decrease in chronic dieting, and were happier and less anxious than women in the control conditions. Moreover, their risk of developing bulimia was greatly reduced (McMillan, Stice, & Rohde, 2011;

Parents can intervene to stop one sibling from tormenting another right at the moment of the incident, but what might they do to make it less likely to happen in the future?

Stice et al., 2006). Follow-up studies using variations of this method have found that its benefits are long lasting and that it is as effective for Latina and Asian/Hawaiian/Pacific Island women as for white and African American women (Rodriguez et al., 2008; Stice et al., 2008).

Punishment and Self-Persuasion

All societies run, in part, on punishment or the threat of punishment. You know, while cruising down the highway at 80 miles an hour, that if a cop spots you, you will pay a substantial fine, and if you get caught often, you will lose your license. So we learn to obey the speed limit when patrol cars are in the vicinity. By the same token, schoolchildren know that if they cheat on an exam and get caught, they could be humiliated by the teacher and punished. So they learn not to cheat while the teacher is in the room, watching them. But does harsh punishment teach adults to want to obey the speed limit? Does it teach children to value honest behavior? We don't think so. All it teaches is to try to avoid getting caught.

Let's look at bullying. It is extremely difficult to persuade children that it's not right or enjoyable to beat up other children (Olweus, 2002). But, theoretically, it is conceivable that under certain conditions they will persuade *themselves* that such behavior is unenjoyable. Imagine that you are the parent of a six-year-old boy who often beats up his four-year-old brother. You've tried to reason with your older son, to no avail. In an attempt to make him a nicer person (and to preserve the health and welfare of his little brother), you begin to punish him for his aggressiveness. As a parent, you can use a range of punishments, from the mild (a stern look) to the severe (spanking, forcing the child to stand in the corner for two hours, depriving him of TV privileges for a month). The more severe the threat, the higher the likelihood the youngster will cease and desist—while you are watching him. But he may hit his brother again as soon as you are out of sight. In short, just as most drivers learn to watch for the highway patrol while speeding, your six-year-old still enjoys bullying his little brother; he has merely learned not to do it while you are around to punish him.

Suppose that you threaten him with a mild punishment. In either case—under threat of severe punishment or of mild punishment—the child experiences dissonance. He is aware that he is not beating up his little brother, and he is also aware that he would like to beat him up. When he has the urge to hit his brother and doesn't, he implicitly asks himself, "How come I'm not beating up my little brother?" Under severe threat, he has a convincing answer in the form of a sufficient external justification: "I'm not beating him up because, if I do, my parents are going to punish me." This serves to reduce the dissonance.

The child in the mild threat situation experiences dissonance too. But when he asks himself, "How come I'm not beating up my little brother?" he doesn't have a convincing answer, because the threat is so mild that it does not provide a superabundance of justification. This is called **insufficient punishment**. The child is refraining from doing something he wants to do, and while he does have some justification for not doing it, he lacks complete justification. In this situation, he continues to experience dissonance; therefore, the child must find another way to justify the fact that he is not aggressing against his kid brother. The less severe you make the threat, the less external justification there is; the less external justification, the higher the need for internal justification. The child can reduce his dissonance by convincing himself that he doesn't want to beat up his brother. In time, he can go further in his quest for internal justification and decide that beating up little kids is not fun.

Insufficient Punishment

The dissonance aroused when individuals lack sufficient external justification for having resisted a desired activity or object, usually resulting in individuals devaluing the forbidden activity or object

To find out if this is in fact what happens, Elliot Aronson and J. Merrill Carlsmith (1963) devised an experiment with preschoolers. They couldn't very well have young children hitting each other for the sake of science, so they decided to change another behavior that was important to the children: their desire to play with some appealing toys. The experimenter first asked each child to rate the attractiveness of several toys. He then pointed to a toy that the child considered among the most attractive and told the child that he or she was not allowed to play with it. Half of the children were threatened with mild punishment if they disobeyed; the other half were threatened with severe punishment. The experimenter left the room for a few minutes, giving the children the time and opportunity to play with the other toys and to resist the temptation to play with the forbidden toy. None of the children played with the forbidden toy.

Next, the experimenter returned and asked each child to rate how much he or she liked each of the toys. Initially, everyone had wanted to play with the forbidden toy, but during the temptation period, when they had the chance, not one child played with it. Obviously, the children were experiencing dissonance. How did they respond to this uncomfortable feeling? The children who had received a severe threat had ample justification for their restraint. They knew why they hadn't played with the toy, and therefore they had no reason to change their attitude about it. These children continued to rate the forbidden toy as highly desirable; indeed, some even found it more desirable than they had before the threat.

But what about the others? Without much external justification for avoiding the toy—they had little to fear if they played with it—the children in the mild threat condition needed an *internal* justification to reduce their dissonance. Before long, they persuaded themselves that the reason they hadn't played with the toy was that they didn't like it. They rated the forbidden toy as less attractive than they had when the experiment began.

Self-Persuasion

A long-lasting form of attitude change that results from attempts at self-justification

The Lasting Effects of Self-Persuasion The forbidden-toy study was a good example of how self-justification leads to **self-persuasion** in the behavior of very young children. The children who were tempted to play with the forbidden toy but resisted came to believe that the toy wasn't so wonderful after all: they *persuaded themselves* of this belief to justify the fact that by obeying the adults, they had given up something they wanted. Self-persuasion is more permanent than direct attempts at persuasion precisely because, with self-persuasion, the persuasion takes place internally and not because of external coaxing, threats, or pressure.

Moreover, the effects of self-persuasion in young children can be lasting. In a replication of the forbidden-toy experiment, the overwhelming majority of the children who had been mildly threatened for playing with a terrific toy decided, on their own, not to play with it, even when given the chance several *weeks* later; the majority of the children who had been severely threatened played with the forbidden toy as soon as they could (Freedman, 1965). (See Figure 6.4.) Remember these findings when you become a parent! Parents who use punishment to encourage their children to adopt desirable values should keep the punishment mild—barely enough to produce a change in behavior—and the values will follow.

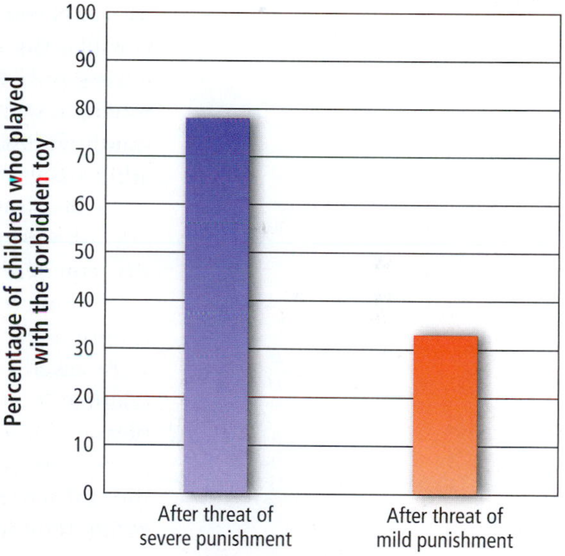

FIGURE 6.4

The Forbidden Toy Experiment

Children who had received a threat of mild punishment were far less likely to play with a forbidden toy (orange bar) than children who had received a threat of severe punishment (blue bar). Those given a mild threat had to provide their own justification by devaluing the attractiveness of the toy ("I didn't want to play with it anyhow"). The resulting self-persuasion lasted for weeks.

(Based on data in Freedman, 1965.)

Not Just Tangible Rewards or Punishments As we have seen, a sizable reward or a severe punishment provides strong external justification for an action. So if you want a person to do something or not to do something only once, the best strategy would be to promise a large reward or threaten a severe punishment. But if you want a person to become committed to an attitude or to a behavior, the *smaller* the reward or punishment that will lead to momentary compliance, the *greater* will be the eventual change in attitude and therefore the more permanent the effect. Large rewards and severe punishments, because they are strong external justifications, encourage compliance but prevent real attitude change (see Figure 6.5).

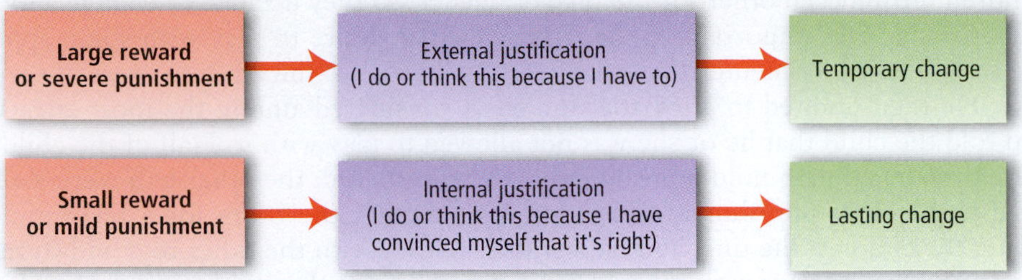

FIGURE 6.5

External versus Internal Justification

As this graphic summarizes, insufficient punishment or reward leads to self-justification, which in turn leads to self-persuasion and lasting change. Larger rewards or punishments may produce temporary compliance, which rarely lasts.

This phenomenon is not limited to tangible rewards and punishments; justifications can also come in more subtle packages. Take friendship. We like our friends, we trust our friends, we do favors for our friends. Suppose you are at a party at the home of a close friend. Your friend is passing around a strange-looking appetizer. "What is it?" you ask. "Oh, it's a fried grasshopper; I'd love you to try it." She's a good friend and you don't want to embarrass her in front of the others, so you pick one up and eat it. How much do you think you will like this new snack food?

Now suppose you are a guest at the home of a person you don't know well, and he hands you, as an appetizer, a fried grasshopper and tells you that he'd really like you to try it. You comply. Now the crucial question: In which of these two situations will you like the taste of the grasshopper better? Common sense might suggest that the grasshopper would taste better when recommended by a friend. But think about it for a moment; which condition involves less external justification? Common sense notwithstanding, dissonance theory makes the opposite prediction. In the first case, when you ask yourself, "How come I ate that disgusting insect?" you have ample justification: you ate it because your good friend asked you to. In the second case, you don't have this kind of outside justification, so you must create it. Namely, you must convince yourself that you *liked* the grasshopper.

Although this may seem a rather bizarre example of dissonance-reducing behavior, it's not as far-fetched as you might think. Indeed, in one experiment, army reservists were asked to eat fried grasshoppers as part of a research project on survival foods (Zimbardo et al., 1965). Reservists who ate grasshoppers at the request of a stern, unpleasant officer increased their liking for grasshoppers far more than those who ate grasshoppers at the request of a well-liked, pleasant officer. Those who complied with the unfriendly officer's request had little external justification for their actions. As a result, they adopted positive attitudes toward eating grasshoppers to justify their otherwise strange and dissonance-arousing behavior.

The Hypocrisy Paradigm

People often behave in ways that run counter to their own beliefs and their best interests. For example, although college students know that AIDS and other sexually transmitted diseases (STDs) are serious problems, only a small percentage use condoms. Not a surprise; condoms are inconvenient and unromantic, and they remind people of disease—the last thing they want to be thinking about in the heat of passion. No wonder that sexual behavior is often accompanied by denial: "Sure, STDs are a problem, but not for *me*."

How do you break through this wall of denial? In the 1990s, Elliot Aronson and his students set out to tackle this problem (Aronson, Fried, & Stone, 1991; Cooper, 2010; Stone et al., 1994). They asked two groups of college students to compose a speech

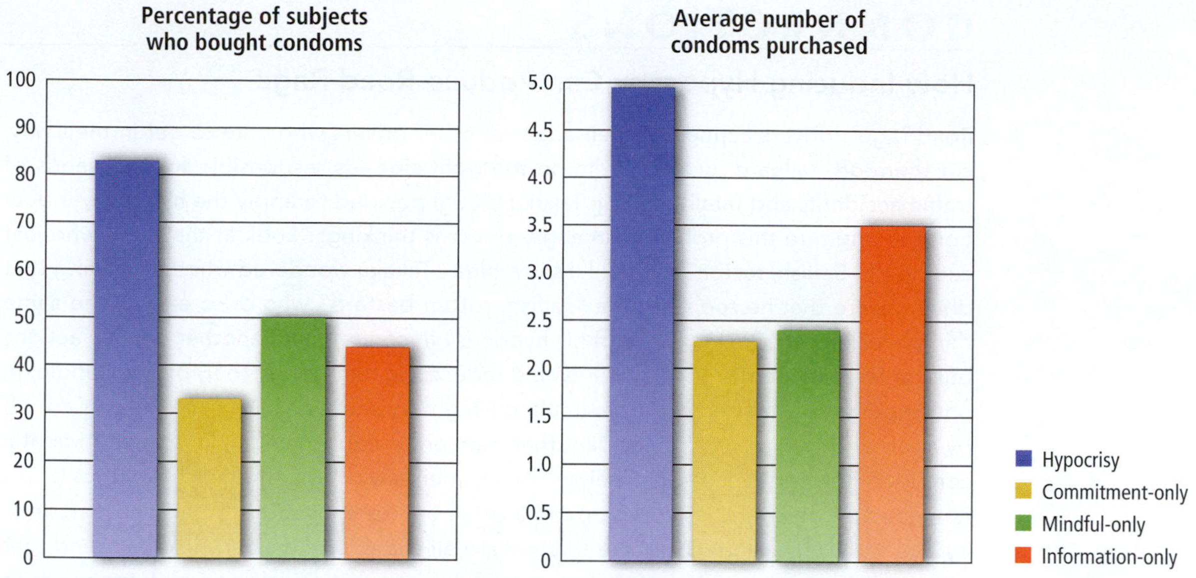

FIGURE 6.6

The Hypocrisy Paradigm

People who are made mindful of their hypocrisy (blue bars)—in this study, being made aware of the discrepancy between knowing that condoms prevent AIDS and other STDs but not using condoms themselves—begin to practice what they preach. Here, more of them bought condoms, buying more condoms than did students in other conditions—those who were simply given information about the dangers of AIDS, or who promised to buy them, or who were made aware that they weren't using them.

(Adapted from Stone, Aronson, Crain, Winslow, & Fried, 1994.)

describing the dangers of AIDS and advocating the use of condoms every time a person has sex. In one group, the students merely composed the arguments. In the second group, after composing their arguments, they were to recite them in front of a video camera and were told that an audience of high school students would watch the resulting tape. In addition, half of the students in each group were made mindful of their own failure to use condoms by making a list of the circumstances in which they had found it particularly difficult, awkward, or impossible to use them.

The participants in one group experienced the highest dissonance: those who made a video for high school students after the experimenter got them to think about their own failure to use condoms. Why? They were made aware of their own hypocrisy; they had to deal with the fact that they were preaching behavior that they themselves were not practicing. To remove the hypocrisy and maintain their self-esteem, they would need to start practicing what they were preaching. And that is exactly what the researchers found. When they gave each student the chance to buy condoms cheaply, the students in the hypocrisy condition were far more likely to buy condoms than students in any of the other conditions (see Figure 6.6). Moreover, when the researchers phoned the students several months after the experiment, they found that the effects held. People in the hypocrisy condition—the students who would have felt the most cognitive dissonance—reported far higher use of condoms than did those in the control conditions.

Using a similar research design of **hypocrisy induction**, researchers instructed undergraduate smokers to create an antismoking video that allegedly would be used to encourage high school students to quit smoking (Peterson, Haynes, & Olson, 2008). Again, the actors felt dissonance because their own behavior (smoking) contradicted the antismoking position they advocated on the video. This method of causing them to face their hypocrisy increased the participants' stated intention to quit smoking.

Hypocrisy Induction

The arousal of dissonance by having individuals make statements that run counter to their behaviors and then reminding them of the inconsistency between what they advocated and their behavior. The purpose is to lead individuals to more responsible behavior

CONNECTIONS

How Inducing Hypocrisy Can Reduce Road Rage

Road rage—drivers acting out their anger at other drivers who dare to get in their way, cut them off, tailgate, or pass them on the right side—is responsible for thousands of traffic accidents and fatalities. Seiji Takaku (2006) decided to apply the hypocrisy-induction paradigm to this problem. An angry driver is thinking: "Look at that SOB who just cut me off! Selfish, rotten bastard! I'll show him!" Takaku wondered whether making that driver aware that he too can be a "selfish, rotten bastard" who does exactly the same thing—making the driver aware of his hypocrisy in condemning another driver's actions but not his own identical behavior—would reduce the temptation to fly off the handle. In one experiment, he used video to simulate a highway situation in which a driver is cut off by another driver, a common incident that frequently leads to anger. In the experimental condition, the participants themselves first accidentally cut off another driver, thus being reminded of the fact that cutting people off is not an indication of a flawed personality, but rather the type of mistake that we are all capable of making. Takaku found that when people are reminded of their own fallibility, they are quicker to go from anger to forgiveness than if this reminder is not induced. The reminder reduces their perceived need to retaliate.

You might keep Takaku's method in mind the next time you find yourself fuming in traffic. And, by the way, that anger you feel at *other* cell phone users who drive while talking . . .?

Justifying Good Deeds and Harmful Acts

When we like people, we show it by treating them well. When we dislike people, we also often show it, perhaps by going out of our way to snub them. But it can also work the other way around: our own behavior toward a person affects whether we like or dislike that individual. Whenever we act either kindly or cruelly toward another person, self-justification sees to it that we never quite feel the same way about that person again. (See Try It!)

The Ben Franklin Effect: Justifying Acts of Kindness What happens when you do a favor for someone? In particular, what happens when you are subtly induced to do a favor for a person you don't much like; will you like the person more—or less? Dissonance theory predicts that you will like the person more after doing the favor. Can you say why?

> *We do not love people so much for the good they have done us as for the good we have done them.*
>
> —Leo Tolstoy, 1869

This phenomenon has been a part of folk wisdom for a long time. Benjamin Franklin confessed to having used it as a political

TRY IT! The Internal Consequences of Doing Good

When you walk down a city street and view people sitting on the sidewalk, panhandling, or pushing their possessions around in a shopping cart, how do you feel about them? Think about it for a few moments, and write down a list of your feelings. If you are like most college students, your list will reflect some mixed feelings. That is, you probably feel some compassion but also think these people are a nuisance, that if they tried harder, they could get their lives together. The next time you see a person panhandling or digging through the trash looking for food, take the initiative and give him or her a dollar. Say something friendly; wish them well. Note your feelings. Is there a change in how you perceive the person? Analyze any changes you notice in terms of cognitive dissonance theory.

strategy. While serving in the Pennsylvania state legislature, Franklin was disturbed by the political opposition and animosity of a fellow legislator. So he set out to win him over. He didn't do it by "paying any servile respect to him," Franklin wrote, but rather by inducing his opponent to do him a favor—namely, lending him a rare book he was eager to read. Franklin returned the book promptly with a warm thank-you letter. "When we next met in the House," Franklin said, "he spoke to me (which he had never done before), and with great civility; and he ever after manifested a readiness to serve me on all occasions, so that we became great friends and our friendship continued to his death. This is another instance of the truth of an old maxim I had learned, which says, 'He that has once done you a kindness will be more ready to do you another than he whom you yourself have obliged'" (Franklin, 1868/1900, pp. 216–217).

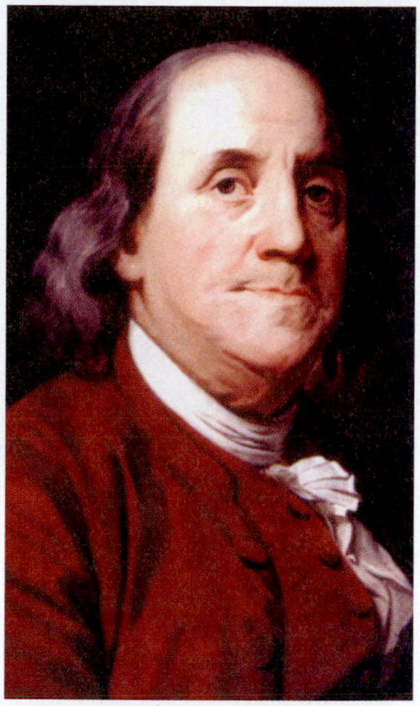

Without realizing it, Ben Franklin may have been the first dissonance theorist.

Benjamin Franklin was clearly pleased with the success of his blatantly manipulative strategy. But as scientists, we should not be convinced by his anecdote. We have no way to know whether Franklin's success was due to this particular gambit or to his all-around charm. That is why it is important to design and conduct an experiment that controls for such things as charm. Such an experiment was finally done—240 years later (Jecker & Landy, 1969). Students participated in an intellectual contest that enabled them to win a substantial sum of money. Afterwards, the experimenter approached one-third of them, explaining that he was using his own funds for the experiment and was running short, which meant he might be forced to close down the experiment prematurely. He asked, "As a special favor to me, would you mind returning the money you won?" The same request was made to a different group of subjects, not by the experimenter but by the departmental secretary, who asked them if they would return the money as a special favor to the (impersonal) psychology department's research fund, which was running low. The remaining participants were not asked to return their winnings at all. Finally, all of the participants were asked to fill out a questionnaire that included an opportunity to rate the experimenter. Participants who had been cajoled into doing a special favor for him found him the most attractive; they convinced themselves that he was a wonderful, deserving fellow. The others thought he was a pretty nice guy but not anywhere near as wonderful as did the people who had been asked to do him a favor (see Figure 6.7).

Think back to the experiment in which white students developed more favorable attitudes toward African Americans after having said publicly that they favored preferential treatment for black students. Can you see how the "Ben Franklin effect" might apply here, how this act of helping might have contributed to their change in attitudes?

Suppose you find yourself in a situation where you have an opportunity to lend a helping hand to an acquaintance, but because you are in a hurry or because it is inconvenient, you decline to help. How do you think this act of omission might affect your feelings for this person? As you might expect, in an experiment that investigated this precise situation, people justified their unwillingness to help by lowering their opinion of the acquaintance's qualities (Williamson et al., 1996). Not helping was simply an act of omission. But what if you harmed another person; what then might happen to your feelings?

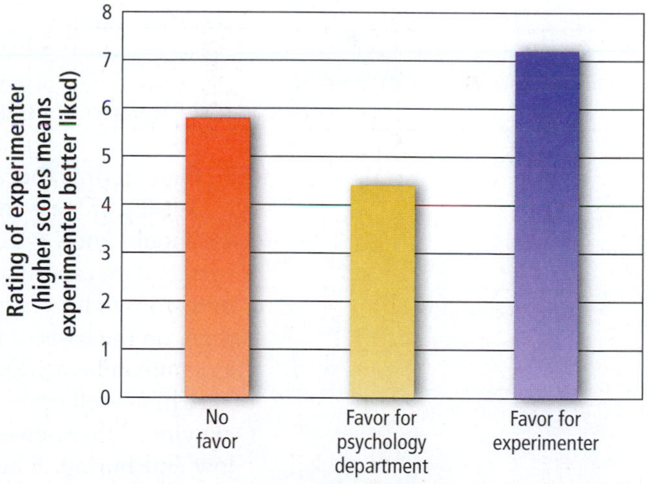

FIGURE 6.7

The Justification of Kindness

If we have done someone a personal favor (blue bar), we are likely to feel more positively toward that person than if we don't do the favor (orange bar) or do the favor because of an impersonal request (yellow bar).

(Based on data in Jecker & Landy, 1969.)

Dehumanizing the Enemy: Justifying Cruelty A sad, though universal, phenomenon is that all cultures are inclined to dehumanize their enemies by calling them cruel names and regarding them as "vermin," "animals," "brutes," and other nonhuman creatures. During World War II, Americans called the Germans and Japanese "krauts" and "Japs," respectively, and portrayed them in propaganda

The American guards at Iraq's Abu Ghraib prison treated their prisoners with a casual brutality that scandalized the world. What does dissonance theory predict about the consequences *for the guards* of dehumanizing the enemy?

posters as monsters; the Nazis portrayed the Jews as rats; during the Vietnam War, American soldiers referred to the Vietnamese as "gooks"; after the wars in Iraq and Afghanistan began, some Americans began referring to the enemy as "ragheads" because of the turbans or other headdresses that many Arabs and Muslims wear. The use of such language is a way of reducing dissonance: "I am a good person, but we are fighting and killing these other people; therefore, they must deserve whatever they get, because they aren't fully human like us."

Of course, many people have always held negative and prejudiced attitudes toward certain groups, and calling them names might make it easier for them to treat them brutally. To be certain that self-justification can *follow* acts of cruelty rather than only cause them, it is essential for the social psychologist to temporarily step back from the helter-skelter of the real world and test the proposition in the more controlled setting of the experimental laboratory.

A soldier who kills or injures fully armed enemy troops in the heat of battle is unlikely to experience much dissonance. When engaged in combat with an enemy soldier, it is a "you or me" situation; if the soldier had not killed the enemy, the enemy might have killed him. So even though wounding or killing another person is rarely taken lightly, it is not nearly so heavy a burden, and the dissonance not nearly as great, as it would be if the victim were an unarmed civilian, a child, or an old person.

These speculations are supported by the results of an experiment in which volunteers had to administer a supposedly painful electric shock to a fellow student (Berscheid, Boye, & Walster, 1968). As one might expect, these students disparaged their victim as a result of having administered the shock. But half of the students were told that there would be a turnabout: the other student would be given the opportunity to retaliate against them at a later time. Those who were led to believe that their victim would be able to retaliate later did not derogate the victim. Because the victim was going to be able to even the score, there was little dissonance, and therefore the harm-doers had no need to belittle their victim in order to convince themselves that he or she deserved it. The results of these laboratory experiments suggest that, during a war, military personnel are more likely to demean civilian victims (because these individuals can't retaliate) than military victims.

There's nothing people can't contrive to praise or condemn and find justification for doing so.

—Molière, *The Misanthrope*

Ideally, if we want to measure attitude change as a result of dissonant cognitions, we should know what the attitudes were before the dissonance-arousing behavior occurred. Two experimenters came up with a way to do this. They asked students, one at a time, to watch a young man (a confederate of the experimenters) being interviewed and then, on the basis of this observation, provide him with an analysis of his shortcomings as a human being (Davis & Jones, 1960). After saying things they knew were certain to hurt him—telling him they thought he was shallow, untrustworthy, and boring—they convinced themselves that he deserved to be insulted this way; why, he really *was* shallow and boring. Their opinion of him had become much more negative than it was prior to saying the hurtful things to him.

A more dramatic experiment on the justification-of-cruelty effect was done to examine the relationship between torture and blame. Suppose you read that a suspect in a particularly terrible crime has been tortured in an attempt to get him to reveal information. He insists he is innocent, but his interrogators simply increase the pain they are inflicting on him. Do you sympathize with the interrogator and blame the suspect for not confessing, or do you sympathize with the suffering suspect? Dissonance theory predicts that people who are *closest* to the situation—for example, being a prison staffer having to observe the torture—would reduce dissonance by seeing the victim as more likely to be guilty and therefore deserving of the pain inflicted on him. But those who are more distant from the situation—listening to the interrogation on the radio—would be more inclined to see the victim as innocent. And that is just what the experimenters found (Gray & Wegner, 2010). The closer people are to committing acts of cruelty, the greater their need to reduce the dissonance between "I am a good, kind person" and "I am causing another human being to suffer." The easiest route is to blame the victim: he is guilty, he started this, it's all his fault, he's not one of us anyway.

Think of the chilling implications of this research: namely, that people do not perform acts of cruelty and come out unscathed. Success at dehumanizing the victim virtually guarantees a continuation or even an escalation of the cruelty: it sets up an endless chain of violence, followed by self-justification (in the form of dehumanizing and blaming the victim), followed by still more violence and dehumanization. In this manner, unbelievable acts of human cruelty can escalate, such as the Nazi "Final Solution" that led to the murder of six million European Jews. Unfortunately, atrocities are not a thing of the past but are as recent as today's news.

Some Final Thoughts on Dissonance: Learning from Our Mistakes

At the beginning of this chapter, we raised a vital question regarding the followers of Heaven's Gate (as we did in Chapter 1 about the followers of the Reverend Jim Jones): How could intelligent people allow themselves to be led into what the overwhelming majority of us see as senseless behavior resulting in mass suicide? Of course, many factors were operating, including the charismatic power of each of the leaders, the existence of social support for the views of the group from other members, and the relative isolation of each group from dissenting views, producing a closed system—a little like living in a roomful of mirrors.

Yet, in addition to these factors, one of the single most powerful forces was the existence of a high degree of cognitive dissonance within the minds of the participants. After reading this chapter, you now realize that when individuals make an important decision and invest heavily in that decision (in terms of time, effort, sacrifice, and commitment), the result is a strong need to justify those actions and that investment. The more they give up and the harder they work, the greater will be the need to convince themselves that their views are correct. The members of the Heaven's Gate cult made monumental sacrifices for their beliefs: they abandoned their friends and families, left their professions, relinquished their money and possessions, moved to another part of the world, and worked hard and long for the particular cause they believed in—all increasing their commitment to the belief.

By understanding cognitive dissonance, therefore, you can understand why the Heaven's Gate people, having bought a telescope that failed to reveal a spaceship that wasn't there, concluded that the telescope was faulty. To have believed otherwise would have created too much dissonance to bear. That they went on to abandon their "containers," believing that they were moving on to a higher incarnation, is not unfathomable. It is simply an extreme manifestation of a process that we have seen in operation over and over again throughout this chapter.

Perhaps you are thinking, "Well, but they were a strange, isolated cult." But, as we have seen, dissonance reduction affects everyone. Much of the time, dissonance-reducing behavior can be useful because it allows us to maintain self-esteem. Yet if we were to spend all our time and energy defending our egos, we would never learn from our mistakes, bad decisions, and incorrect beliefs. Instead, we would ignore them, justify them, or, worse still, attempt to turn them into virtues. We would get stuck within the confines of our narrow minds and fail to grow or change. And, in extreme cases, we might end up justifying our own smaller Heaven's Gates—mistakes that can harm ourselves and others.

> *Both salvation and punishment for man lie in the fact that, if he lives wrongly, he can befog himself so as not to see the misery of his position.*
>
> —Leo Tolstoy

These athletes blew a big lead and lost the game. Will they make excuses, or will they learn from their mistakes?

It's bad enough when ordinary people get caught up in the self-justifying cycle, but when a political leader does so, the consequences can be devastating for the nation and the world (Tavris & Aronson, 2007). In 2003, President George W. Bush wanted to believe that Iraqi leader Saddam Hussein possessed weapons of mass destruction (WMD), nuclear and biochemical weapons that posed a threat to America and Europe. He needed this belief to be true to justify his decision to launch a preemptive war, although Iraq posed no immediate threat to the United States and none of its citizens had been involved in the attacks of 9/11. According to White House insider Scott McClellan (2009), this need led the president and his advisers to interpret CIA reports as definitive proof of Iraq's weapons of mass destruction, even though the reports were ambiguous and were contradicted by other evidence (Stewart, 2011; Wilson, 2005).

After the invasion of Iraq, administration officials, when asked "Where are the WMD?," said that Iraq is a big country and that Saddam Hussein had them well hidden, but they were sure they would be found. As the months dragged on and still no WMD were discovered, the administration officials had to admit that there were none. Now what? How did President Bush and his staff reduce dissonance between "We believed there were WMD that justified this war" and "We were wrong"? By adding new cognitions to justify the war: Now they said that the U.S. mission was to liberate the nation from a cruel dictator and give the Iraqi people the blessings of democratic institutions. Even if things are not going well now, they said, history will vindicate us in 10 or 20 or 50 years. To an observer, these justifications are inadequate; after all, there are many brutal dictators in the world, and no one can foresee the long-term results of any war begun for a short-term purpose. But to President Bush and his advisers, the justifications seemed reasonable (Bush, 2010).

Of course we cannot be certain what was going on in President Bush's mind, but some five decades of research on cognitive dissonance suggests that the president and his advisers may not have been intentionally deceiving the American people; it is more likely that, like the members of Heaven's Gate, they were deceiving themselves, blinding themselves to the possibility of being wrong. Needless to say, Mr. Bush was not the only leader to engage in this kind of self-justifying behavior. The memoirs of some of our most beleaguered former presidents, Democrat and Republican alike, are full of the kinds of self-serving, self-justifying statements that can best be summarized as "If I had it all to do over again, I would not change much. Actually, I wouldn't change anything except how my opponents treated me unfairly" (Johnson, 1991; Nixon, 1990).

Few of us will ever wield the power of a world leader or end our lives in a cult waiting for a spaceship to transport us to another planet. But, on a smaller scale, in our zeal to protect our self-concept, we often make foolish mistakes and compound that failure by blinding ourselves to the possibility of learning from them. Is there hope? We think so. Although the process of self-justification is unconscious, once we know that we are prone to justify our actions, we can begin to monitor our thinking and, in effect, "catch ourselves in the act." If we can learn to examine our behavior critically and dispassionately, we stand a chance of breaking out of the cycle of action followed by self-justification followed by more committed action.

Admittedly, acknowledging our mistakes and taking responsibility for them is easier said than done. Imagine that you are a prosecutor who has worked hard for many years to put "bad guys" in prison. You're the good guy. How will you respond to the dissonant information that DNA testing suggests that a few of those bad guys you put away might be innocent? Will you welcome this evidence with an open mind, because you would like justice to be done, or will you reject it, because it

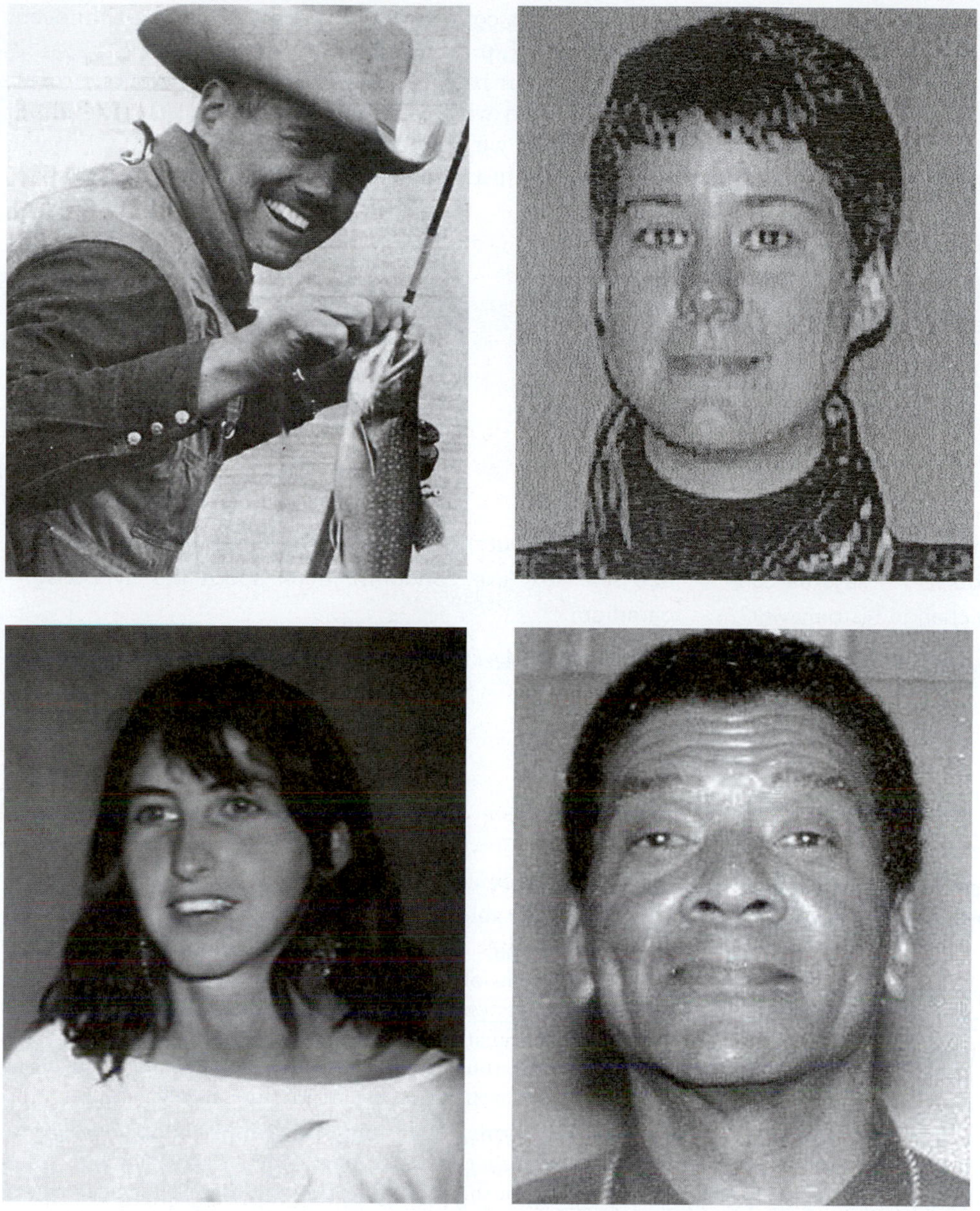

The members of the Heaven's Gate cult were just plain folks of all races, backgrounds, and walks of life. Yet almost all of them eventually committed suicide because of their commitment to the cult and its beliefs, an extreme result of the mechanism of cognitive dissonance that all of us experience.

might show that you were wrong? Unfortunately—but not surprisingly for those who understand dissonance theory—many prosecutors in America make the latter choice: they resist and block the efforts by convicted prisoners to reopen their cases and get DNA tests (Tavris & Aronson, 2007). Their dissonance-reducing reasoning is something like this: "Well, even if he wasn't guilty of *this* crime, he was surely guilty of something else; after all, he's a bad guy."

But at least one prosecutor chose to resolve that dissonance in a more courageous way. Thomas Vanes had routinely sought the death penalty or extreme prison sentences for defendants convicted of horrible crimes. One man, Larry Mayes, served more than 20 years for rape before DNA testing cleared him of the crime. "When [Mayes] requested a DNA retest on that rape kit," he wrote, "I assisted in tracking down the old evidence, convinced that the current tests would put to rest his long-standing claim of innocence. But he was right, and I was wrong. Hard facts trumped opinion and belief, as they should. It was a sobering lesson, and none of the easy-to-reach rationalizations (just doing my job, it was the jurors who convicted him, the appellate courts had upheld the conviction) completely lessen the sense of

Watch on MyPsychLab
As you watch the MyPsychLab video ***AP Exclusive: Abusive Priests Live Unmonitored,*** consider how cognitive dissonance and self-justification relate to the situation in question.

responsibility—moral, if not legal—that comes with the conviction of an innocent man" (quoted in Tavris & Aronson, 2007, p. 157).

Throughout our lives, all of us, in our roles as family members, workers, professionals, and citizens, will be confronted with evidence that we were wrong about something important to us—something we did or something we believed. Will you step off the pyramid in the direction of justifying that mistake . . . or will you strive to correct it?

USE IT!

You have a friend who drives after binge drinking. You keep telling him that it is dangerous to do it. He says he can handle it. How could you get him to change his behavior?

Hint: Think about the research on getting students to practice safe sex (use condoms); think about the hypocrisy paradigm.

Summary

What is theory of cognitive dissonance, and how do people avoid dissonance to maintain a stable, positive self-image?

- **The Theory of Cognitive Dissonance** Most people need to see themselves as intelligent, sensible, and decent folks who behave with integrity. This chapter is about the behavior changes and cognitive distortions that occur when we are faced with evidence that we have done something that is not intelligent, sensible, or decent—the mental effort we expend to maintain that positive self-image.
  - **Maintaining a positive self-image** According to **cognitive dissonance theory**, people experience discomfort (dissonance) when they behave in ways that are inconsistent with their conception of themselves (self-image). To reduce the dissonance, people either (1) change their behavior to bring it in line with their cognitions about themselves, (2) justify their behavior by changing one of their cognitions, or (3) attempt to justify their behavior by inventing new cognitions. One common kind of new cognition is *self-affirmation*, focusing on a positive quality to offset feelings of having acted foolishly. When people's self-esteem is temporarily enhanced, they are less likely to cheat or commit other unethical acts, and more likely to work hard to improve their grades, so as to keep their behavior consonant with their self-concept. But people are not good at anticipating how they will cope with future negative events; they show an **impact bias**, overestimating how bad they will feel, because they don't realize that they will be able to reduce dissonance.
  - **Rational behavior versus rationalizing behavior** Humans often process information in a biased way, one that fits our preconceived notions. The explanation for this is that information or ideas that disagree with our views arouse dissonance. And we humans avoid dissonance even at the expense of rational behavior.
  - **Decisions, decisions, decisions** Decisions arouse dissonance because they require choosing one thing and not the other. The thought that we may have made the wrong choice causes discomfort—**postdecision dissonance**—because it would threaten our self-image as one who makes good decisions. After the choice is final, the mind diminishes the discomfort through solidifying the case for the item chosen or the course of action taken. That is how dissonance reduction can change a person's values and morality: once an unethical act is committed, the person experiencing dissonance justifies it, thereby increasing the likelihood of committing it again.
  - **Dissonance, culture, and the brain** Dissonance seems to be hardwired in the brain; different parts of the brain are activated when people are in a state of mental conflict or have made a choice. Because postdecision dissonance has been observed in monkeys but not other species, many researchers believe it must have an evolutionarily adaptive purpose in primates. However, although

cognitive dissonance seems to be universal, occurring in non-Western cultures as well as Western ones, the content of what creates dissonant cognitions and the process and intensity of dissonance reduction do vary across cultures, reflecting the difference in cultural norms.

How is the justification of effort a product of cognitive dissonance, and what are some practical applications for reducing dissonance?

- **Self-Justification in Everyday Life** Researchers have studied the forms of dissonance reduction and their application in many spheres of life.
  - **The justification of effort** People tend to increase their liking for something they have worked hard to attain, even if the thing they have attained is not something they would otherwise like. This explains the intense loyalty that initiated recruits feel for their fraternities and military institutions after undergoing hazing.
  - **External versus internal justification** When we perform an action because of the ample external reward to do it, then the action has little or no effect on our attitudes or beliefs. However, if the reward is not big enough to justify the action, we find ourselves experiencing cognitive dissonance because there is little **external justification** for what we did. This activates an **internal justification** process to justify the action to ourselves. The internal process of self-justification has a much more powerful effect on an individual's long-term values and behaviors than does a situation where the external justifications are evident. When people publicly advocate something that is counter to what they believe or how they behave, called **counterattitudinal advocacy**, they will feel dissonance. Counterattitudinal advocacy has been used to change people's attitudes in many ways, from their prejudices to self-defeating beliefs and harmful practices such as bulimia.
  - **Punishment and self-persuasion** Another way of getting people to change is not by administering severe punishment, but **insufficient or mild punishment**, as the forbidden-toy experiment demonstrated. The less severe the threat or the smaller the reward, the less external justification the person has for compliance, and thus the greater the need for internal justification. The resulting **self-persuasion** becomes internalized and lasts longer than temporary obedience to avoid a punishment.
  - **The hypocrisy paradigm** Inducing **hypocrisy**—making people face the difference between what they say and what they do—is one way to use the human tendency to reduce dissonance to foster socially beneficial behaviors. In the case of an AIDS-prevention experiment, participants videotaped speeches about the importance of using condoms and they were made aware of their own failure to use them. To reduce dissonance, they changed their behavior—they purchased condoms.
  - **Justifying good deeds and harmful acts** A clever application of cognitive dissonance theory is to get someone to like you by having them do you a favor. The reason this works is that the person needs to internally justify the fact that they did something nice for you. The converse is true as well. If you harm another person, to reduce the threat to your self-image that could come from doing a bad deed, you will tend to justify what you did by denigrating your victim: the person deserved it, or he or she is not "one of us" anyway. In extreme cases such as conflict and war, many people will embrace the cognition that the victim or enemy deserved everything they got because they are less than human.

How can people avoid the traps of self-justification and other dissonance-reducing behavior?

- **Some Final Thoughts on Dissonance: Learning from Our Mistakes** Much of the behavior described in this chapter may seem startling: people coming to dislike others more after doing them harm, people liking others more after doing them a favor, people believing a lie they've told only if there is little or no reward for telling it. These behaviors would be difficult for us to understand if it weren't for the insights provided by the theory of cognitive dissonance. There are times when dissonance reduction is counterproductive because it solidifies negative values and behaviors, and this applies to everyone from members of small cults to national leaders. Although the process of reducing dissonance is unconscious, it is possible to intervene in the process. Knowing that humans are dissonance-reducing animals can make us more aware of the process. The next time we feel the discomfort of having acted counter to our values, we can consciously pause the self-justification process to reflect on our action.

Chapter 6 Test

Study and Review on MyPsychLab

1. Based on the "Ben Franklin effect," you are most likely to increase your liking for Tony when
   a. Tony lends you $10.
   b. you lend Tony $10.
   c. Tony returns the $10 you loaned him.
   d. Tony finds $10.

2. After spending two years fixing up an old house themselves, which involved many hours of tedious work, Abby and Brian are even more convinced that they made the right choice of house. According to the dissonance theory, this is an example of

a. counterattitudinal advocacy.
b. insufficient punishment.
c. the Ben Franklin effect.
d. justifying their effort.

3. Your friend Amy asks you what you think of the shoes she just bought. Privately, you think they are the ugliest shoes you have ever seen, but you tell her you love them. In the past, Amy has always valued your honest opinion and doesn't care that much about the shoes, which were inexpensive. Because the external justification for your fib was ________, you will probably ____________.
   a. high, decide you like the shoes
   b. high, maintain your view that the shoes are ugly
   c. low, decide you like the shoes
   d. low, maintain your view that the shoes are ugly

4. Meghan has been accepted to two top graduate schools. According to cognitive dissonance theory, under which of the following conditions will she experience the most dissonance?
   a. When she is thinking about the pros and cons of both programs before making up her mind.
   b. When she is pretty sure which program she wants to attend but has not yet notified the school of her decision.
   c. Right after she decides which program to attend and notifies the school of her decision.
   d. Meghan will experience an equal amount of dissonance in each of the above three circumstances.

5. You are required to sell $30 souvenir books for a club fund-raiser. How could you use the technique of lowballing to improve your sales?
   a. Start by offering the books at $70 each and pretend to bargain with customers, making $30 your "final offer."
   b. Start by selling the books at $25, but once the customer has retrieved his or her checkbook, tell him or her you made a mistake and the books are actually $5 more expensive than you thought.
   c. Offer the customers additional incentives to buy the book, such as free cookies with every purchase.
   d. Start by selling the books at $40, but tell the customer he or she will get $10 back in the mail in three weeks.

6. Suppose you are babysitting for two boys, brothers who are ages six and three. The older child often beats up his younger brother. What would be the most effective way to make him stop?
   a. Threaten the older child with mild punishment, like sitting in time-out for five minutes, and hope that he obeys.
   b. Threaten the older child with mild punishment, like sitting in time-out for five minutes, and don't worry about whether he obeys.
   c. Threaten the older child with harsh punishment, like spanking him.
   d. Talk to the younger child about ways he can defend himself.

7. Which of the following techniques relating to *post-decision dissonance* could a clothing store use to increase customer satisfaction?
   a. Cut all prices in half.
   b. Ask customers to make a radio ad saying how great the store is.
   c. Charge a membership fee to shop at the store.
   d. Make all sales final.

8. A school principal who wants to reduce vandalism has several students who are notorious for graffiti give a speech to the entire school about the negative aspects of damaging school property. Which of the following should the principal do to make it most likely that these students will stop vandalizing the school, according to research using the hypocrisy paradigm?
   a. He should have every student deliver a speech, not just those who have already committed vandalism.
   b. He should have them deliver speeches about the positive aspects of vandalism as well as the negative aspects.
   c. After they make the speech, he should ask them to remember times they have committed vandalism.
   d. Right after students deliver the speech, he should ask them to volunteer to help clean up the school parking lot.

9. Imagine that before a test, the professor told Jake that if he is caught cheating, he will be expelled. Imagine that the professor told Amanda that if caught cheating, her only punishment will be to write a short paper about why cheating is wrong. If both students don't cheat, what would dissonance theory predict?

- **a.** Amanda will feel more honest than Jake will.
- **b.** Jake will feel more honest than Amanda will.
- **c.** Amanda and Jake will feel equally honest.
- **d.** Neither Jake nor Amanda will feel honest, because they were both threatened.

10. Bess undergoes treatment for drug addiction. According to cognitive dissonance theory, after she leaves the clinic, Bess is most likely to stay off drugs if the treatment at the clinic was

- **a.** involuntary (she was ordered to undergo treatment) and a difficult ordeal.
- **b.** involuntary (she was ordered to undergo treatment) and an easy experience.
- **c.** voluntary (she chose to undergo treatment) and an easy experience.
- **d.** voluntary (she chose to undergo treatment) and a difficult ordeal.

Answer Key

1-b, 2-d, 3-c, 4-c, 5-b,
6-a, 7-d, 8-c, 9-a, 10-d

7 Attitudes and Attitude Change

Influencing Thoughts and Feelings

Independent Tobacco Experts Ag
LUCKY STRIKE FIRST C
over any other brand!
*An impartial Crossley poll covering all the Southern tobacco markets shows that more independent tobacco auctioneers, buyers and warehousemen smoke Lucky Strike than any other brand.
Certified by Crossley, Incorporated
Archibald M. Crossley, President

IT SEEMS AS IF ADVERTISING HAS MADE INROADS EVERYWHERE WE LOOK. Ads are rampant on the Internet, in public restrooms, on video screens at cash machines and gasoline pumps, and even on motion sickness bags on airplanes (Story, 2007). But Andrew Fischer, a 20-year-old from Omaha, Nebraska, wins the prize for advertising innovation. Fischer placed an ad on eBay, offering to wear someone's logo or message on his forehead for 30 days (in the form of a nonpermanent tattoo). The bidding was furious—especially after the national press wrote about Fischer—and was finally won by a company called SnoreStop that makes products to keep people from snoring. They paid Fischer a whopping $37,375, and he dutifully imprinted their logo on his forehead. "For 40 grand, I don't regret looking like an idiot for a month," reported Fischer (Newman, 2009, p. B3).

It is easy to laugh at the lengths to which advertisers will go, brushing them off as absurd but harmless attempts to influence us. We should keep in mind, though, that advertising can have powerful effects. Consider the history of cigarette ads. In the nineteenth century, most consumer goods, including tobacco products, were made and sold locally. But as the Industrial Revolution led to the mass production of many consumer products, manufacturers sought broader markets. Advertising was the natural result. In the 1880s, cigarettes were being mass-produced for the first time, and moguls such as James Buchanan Duke began to market their brands aggressively. Duke placed ads for his brands in newspapers, rented space on thousands of billboards, hired famous actresses to endorse his brands, and gave gifts to retailers who stocked his products. Other cigarette manufacturers soon followed suit (Kluger, 1996).

Although these efforts were phenomenally successful—sales of cigarettes skyrocketed in the United States—there was still a vast untapped market, namely, women. Until the early twentieth century, men bought 99% of cigarettes sold. It was socially unacceptable for women to smoke; those who did were considered to have questionable morals. This began to change with the burgeoning women's rights movement and the fight to achieve the right to vote. Ironically, smoking cigarettes became a symbol of women's emancipation (Kluger, 1996). Cigarette manufacturers were happy to encourage this view by targeting women in their advertisements. Because it was unacceptable for women to smoke in public, early cigarette ads never showed a woman actually smoking. Instead, they tried to associate smoking with sophistication and glamour or convey that cigarettes helped control weight ("Reach for a Lucky instead of a sweet"). By the 1960s, cigarette advertisements were making a direct link between women's liberation and smoking, and a new brand was started (Virginia Slims) specifically for this purpose ("You've come a long way, baby"). Women began to purchase cigarettes in droves. In 1955, 52% of men and 34% of women smoked in the United States (Centers for Disease Control and Prevention, n.d.). Fortunately, the smoking rate has decreased overall since then, but the gap between men and women has narrowed. In 2009, 23% of adult men smoked, compared to 18% of adult women (Centers for Disease Control and Prevention, 2010).

To make up for the shrinking market in the United States, tobacco companies have aggressively marketed cigarettes in other countries. The World

FOCUS QUESTIONS

- What are the different kinds of attitudes, and on what are they based?
- How can external factors such as social influence and internal factors such as emotions and confidence change attitudes?
- What are some strategies for resisting persuasive messages?
- Under what conditions do attitudes predict behavior?
- How does advertising change people's attitudes? What is the role of subliminal messages and cultural stereotypes in advertising?

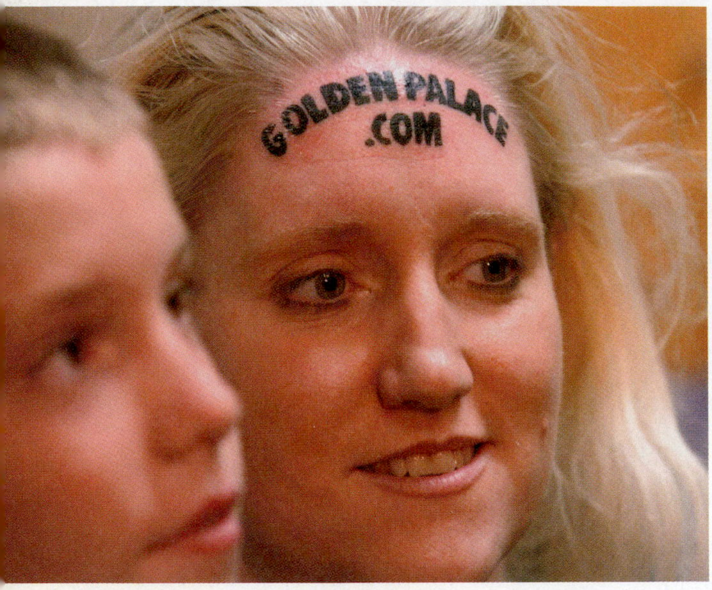

People have begun offering their bodies as venues for advertisers. A Utah woman, shown here, received $10,000 to advertise Golden Palace casino on her forehead. She plans to use the money to send her son to private school.

Health Organization estimates that 50,000 teenagers a day begin smoking in Asia alone and that smoking may eventually kill *one-quarter* of the young people currently living in Asia (Teves, 2002).

Is advertising responsible? To what extent can advertising shape people's attitudes and behavior? Exactly what is an attitude, anyway, and how is it changed? These questions, which are some of the oldest in social psychology, are the subject of this chapter.

The Nature and Origin of Attitudes

Each of us *evaluates* our worlds. We form likes and dislikes of virtually everything we encounter; indeed, it would be odd to hear someone say, "I feel completely neutral toward anchovies, chocolate, Radiohead, and Barack Obama." Simply put, **attitudes** are evaluations of people, objects, or ideas (Ajzen & Fishbein, 2005; Banaji & Heiphetz, 2010; Bohner & Dickel, 2011; Eagly & Chaiken, 2007; Petty et al., 2005). Attitudes are important because they often determine what we do—whether we eat anchovies and chocolate, attend Radiohead concerts, and vote for Barack Obama.

Where Do Attitudes Come From?

One provocative answer to the question of where attitudes come from is that at least some are linked to our genes (Dodds et al., 2011; Tesser, 1993). Evidence for this conclusion comes from the fact that identical twins share more attitudes than do fraternal twins, even when the identical twins were raised in different homes and never knew each other. One study, for example, found that identical twins had more similar attitudes toward such things as the death penalty and jazz than fraternal twins did (Martin et al., 1986). Now, we should be careful how to interpret this evidence. No one is arguing that there are specific genes that determine our attitudes; it is highly unlikely, for example, that there is a "jazz loving" gene that determines your music preferences. It appears, though, that some attitudes are an indirect function of our genetic makeup. They are related to things such as our temperament and personality, which are directly related to our genes (Olson et al., 2001). People may have inherited a temperament and personality from their parents that make them predisposed to like jazz more than rock and roll.

Even if there is a genetic component, our social experiences clearly play a major role in shaping our attitudes. Social psychologists have focused on these experiences and how they result in different kinds of attitudes. They have identified three components of attitudes: the *cognitive component*, or the thoughts and beliefs that people form about the attitude object, the *affective component*, or people's emotional reactions toward the attitude object, and the *behavioral component*, how people act toward the attitude object. Importantly, any given attitude can be based more on one type of experience than on another (Zanna & Rempel, 1988).

Attitudes
Evaluations of people, objects, and ideas

Cognitively Based Attitude
An attitude based primarily on people's beliefs about the properties of an attitude object

Affectively Based Attitude
An attitude based more on people's feelings and values than on their beliefs about the nature of an attitude object

Cognitively Based Attitudes Sometimes our attitudes are based primarily on the relevant facts, such as the objective merits of an automobile. How many miles to the gallon does it get? What are its safety features? To the extent that people's evaluation is based primarily on their beliefs about the properties of an attitude object, we say it is a **cognitively based attitude**. The purpose of this kind of attitude is to classify the pluses and minuses of an object so that we can quickly tell whether we want to have anything to do with it. Consider your attitude toward a utilitarian object like a vacuum cleaner. Your attitude is likely to be based on your beliefs about the objective merits of particular brands, such as how well they vacuum up dirt and how much they cost—not on how sexy they make you feel.

Affectively Based Attitudes An attitude rooted more in emotions and values than on an objective appraisal of pluses and minuses is called an **affectively based attitude**

Some attitudes are based more on emotions and values than on facts and figures. Attitudes toward gay marriage may be such a case.

(Breckler & Wiggins, 1989; Zanna & Rempel, 1988). Sometimes we simply like a car, regardless of how many miles to the gallon it gets. Occasionally we even feel strongly attracted to something—such as another person—in spite of having negative beliefs about him or her (e.g., knowing the person is a "bad influence").

As a guide to which attitudes are likely to be affectively based, consider the topics that etiquette manuals suggest should not be discussed at a dinner party: politics, sex, and religion. People seem to vote more with their hearts than their minds, for example, caring more about how they feel about a candidate than their beliefs about his or her specific policies (Abelson et al., 1982; Granberg & Brown, 1989; Westen, 2007). In fact, it has been estimated that one-third of the electorate knows virtually nothing about specific politicians but nonetheless has strong feelings about them (Redlawsk, 2002; Wattenberg, 1987).

If affectively based attitudes do not come from examining the facts, where do they come from? They have a variety of sources. They can stem from people's values, such as their basic religious and moral beliefs. People's feelings about such issues as abortion, the death penalty, and premarital sex are often based more on their values than on a cold examination of the facts. The function of such attitudes is not so much to paint an accurate picture of the world as to express and validate one's basic value system (Maio & Olson, 1995; Schwartz, 1992; Smith, Bruner, & White, 1956; Snyder & DeBono, 1989). Other affectively based attitudes can result from a sensory reaction, such as liking the taste of chocolate (despite its number of calories), or an aesthetic reaction, such as admiring a painting or the lines and color of a car. Still others can be the result of conditioning (Hofmann et al., 2010).

Classical conditioning works this way: A stimulus that elicits an emotional response is accompanied by a neutral, nonemotional stimulus until eventually the neutral stimulus elicits the emotional response by itself. For example, suppose that when you were a child you experienced feelings of warmth and love when you visited your grandmother. Suppose also that her house always smelled faintly of mothballs. Eventually, the smell of mothballs alone will trigger the emotions you experienced during your visits, through the process of classical conditioning (Dedonder et al., 2010; De Houwer, in press; Walther & Langer, 2010; Olson & Fazio, 2006).

In **operant conditioning**, behaviors we freely choose to perform become more or less frequent, depending on whether they are followed by a reward (positive reinforcement) or punishment. How does this apply to attitudes? Imagine that a 4-year-old white girl goes to the playground with her father and begins to play with an African American girl. Her father expresses strong disapproval, telling her, "We don't play with that kind of child." It won't take long before the child associates interacting with African Americans with disapproval, and therefore adopts her father's racist attitudes. Attitudes can take on a positive or negative affect through either classical or operant conditioning, as shown in Figure 7.1 (Cacioppo et al., 1992; Kuykendall & Keating, 1990).

Although affectively based attitudes come from many sources, we can group them into one family because they (1) do not result from a rational examination of the issues, (2) are not governed by logic (e.g., persuasive arguments about the issues seldom change an affectively based attitude), and (3) are often linked to people's values, so that trying to change them challenges those values (Katz, 1960; Smith; Bruner, & White, 1956). How can we tell if an attitude is more affectively or cognitively based? See the following Try It! for one way to measure the bases of people's attitudes.

We never desire passionately what we desire through reason alone.

—François de La Rochefoucauld, *Maxims*, 1665

That is the way we are made; we don't reason; where we feel, we just feel.

—Mark Twain, *A Connecticut Yankee in King Arthur's Court*, 1885

Classical Conditioning

The phenomenon whereby a stimulus that elicits an emotional response (e.g., your grandmother) is repeatedly paired with a neutral stimulus that does not (e.g., the smell of mothballs), until the neutral stimulus takes on the emotional properties of the first stimulus

Operant Conditioning

The phenomenon whereby behaviors we freely choose to perform become more or less frequent, depending on whether they are followed by a reward (positive reinforcement) or punishment

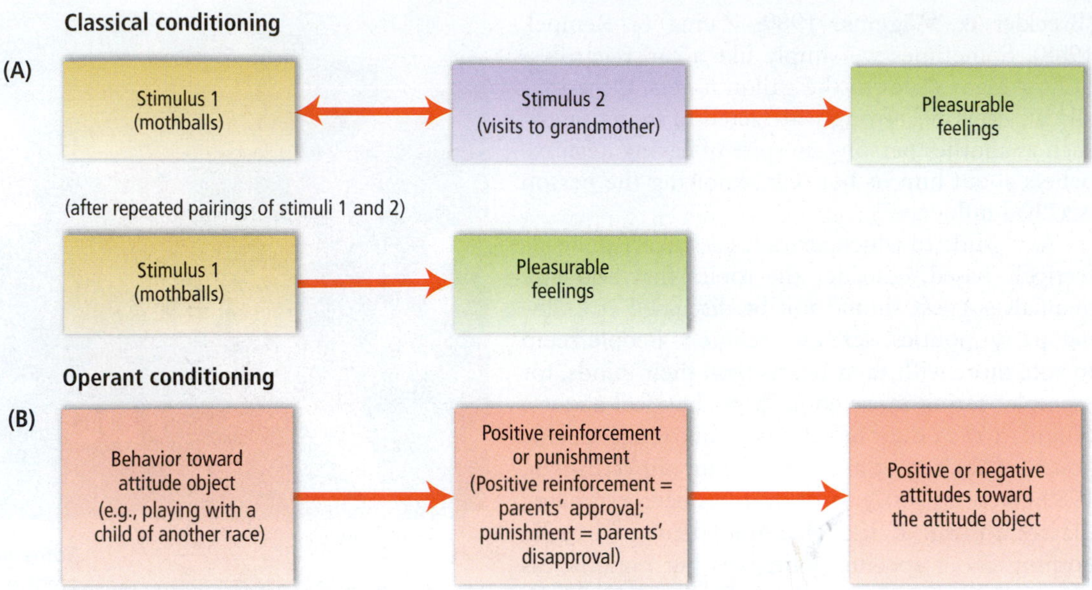

FIGURE 7.1

Classical and Operant Conditioning of Attitudes

Affectively based attitudes can result from either classical or instrumental conditioning.

TRY IT! Affective and Cognitive Bases of Attitudes

Fill out this questionnaire to see how psychologists measure the affective and cognitive components of attitudes.

1. Circle the number on each scale that best describes your feelings toward snakes.

hateful	−3	−2	−1	0	1	2	3	love
sad	−3	−2	−1	0	1	2	3	delighted
annoyed	−3	−2	−1	0	1	2	3	happy
tense	−3	−2	−1	0	1	2	3	calm
bored	−3	−2	−1	0	1	2	3	excited
angry	−3	−2	−1	0	1	2	3	relaxed
disgusted	−3	−2	−1	0	1	2	3	acceptance
sorrowful	−3	−2	−1	0	1	2	3	joy

2. Circle the number on each scale that best describes the traits or characteristics of snakes.

useless	−3	−2	−1	0	1	2	3	useful
foolish	−3	−2	−1	0	1	2	3	wise
unsafe	−3	−2	−1	0	1	2	3	safe
harmful	−3	−2	−1	0	1	2	3	beneficial
worthless	−3	−2	−1	0	1	2	3	valuable
imperfect	−3	−2	−1	0	1	2	3	perfect
unhealthy	−3	−2	−1	0	1	2	3	wholesome

Add up your responses to Question 1 and, separately, your responses to Question 2.

Question 1 measures the affective component of your attitude toward snakes, whereas Question 2 measures the cognitive component of attitudes. Most people's attitudes toward snakes are more affectively than cognitively based. If this is true of you, your total score for Question 1 should depart more from zero (in a negative direction for most people) than your total score for Question 2.

Now go back and fill out the scales again, substituting *vacuum cleaners* for *snakes*. Most people's attitudes toward a utilitarian object such as a vacuum cleaner are more cognitively than affectively based. If this is true of you, your total score for Question 2 should depart more from zero than your total score for Question 1.

Behaviorally Based Attitudes A **behaviorally based attitude** stems from people's observations of how they behave toward an object. This may seem a little odd: How do we know how to behave if we don't already know how we feel? According to Daryl Bem's (1972) *self-perception theory*, under certain circumstances people don't know how they feel until they see how they behave. For example, suppose you asked a friend how much she likes to exercise. If she replies, "Well, I guess I like it, because I always seem to be going for a run or heading over to the gym to work out," we would say she has a behaviorally based attitude. Her attitude is based more on an observation of her behavior than on her cognitions or affect.

As noted in Chapter 5, people infer their attitudes from their behavior only under certain conditions. First, their initial attitude has to be weak or ambiguous. If your friend already has a strong attitude toward exercising, she does not have to observe her behavior to infer how she feels about it. Second, people infer their attitudes from their behavior only when there are no other plausible explanations for their behavior. If your friend believes she exercises to lose weight or because her doctor has ordered her to, she is unlikely to assume that she runs and works out because she enjoys it. (See Chapter 5 for a more detailed description of self-perception theory.)

Behaviorally Based Attitude
An attitude based on observations of how one behaves toward an object

Explicit Attitudes
Attitudes that we consciously endorse and can easily report

Implicit Attitudes
Attitudes that are involuntary, uncontrollable, and at times unconscious

How can I know what I think till I see what I say?
—Graham Wallas, *The Art of Thought*, 1926

Explicit Versus Implicit Attitudes

Once an attitude develops, it can exist at two levels. **Explicit attitudes** are ones we consciously endorse and can easily report; they are what we think of as our evaluations when someone asks us a question like "What is your opinion about affirmative action?" People can also have **implicit attitudes**, which are involuntary, uncontrollable, and at times unconscious evaluations (Gawronski & Bodenhausen, 2012; Gawronski & Payne, 2010; Greenwald & Banaji, 1995; Nosek, Hawkins, & Frazier, 2011; Wilson, Lindsey, & Schooler, 2000).

Consider Sam, a white, middle-class college student who genuinely believes that all races are equal and abhors any kind of racial bias. This is Sam's explicit attitude, in the sense that it is his conscious evaluation of members of other races that governs how he chooses to act. For example, consistent with his explicit attitude, Sam recently signed a petition in favor of affirmative action policies at his university. Sam has grown up in a culture in which there are many negative stereotypes about minority groups, however, and it is possible that some of these negative ideas have seeped into him in ways of which he is not fully aware (Devine, 1989). When he is around African Americans, for example, perhaps some negative feelings are triggered automatically and unintentionally. If so, he has a negative implicit attitude toward African Americans, which is likely to influence behaviors he is not monitoring or controlling, such as how nervous he acts around African Americans (Greenwald et al., 2009). People can have explicit and implicit attitudes toward virtually anything, not just other races. For example, students can believe explicitly that they hate math but have a more positive attitude at an implicit level (Galdi, Arcuri, & Gawronski, 2008; Kawakami et al., 2008; Ranganath & Nosek, 2008; Steele & Ambady, 2006). How do we know this? A variety of techniques have been developed to measure people's implicit attitudes. One of the most popular is the Implicit Association Test, or IAT, which we discuss in Chapter 13.

People can have both explicit and implicit attitudes toward the same topic. Social psychologists have been especially interested in people's explicit and implicit attitudes toward members of other races.

Research on implicit attitudes is in its infancy, and social psychologists are actively investigating the nature of these attitudes, how to measure them, and their relation to explicit attitudes (Briñol & Petty, 2012; Albarracin, Hart, & McCulloch, 2006; Fazio & Olson, 2003; Gawronski & Bodenhausen, 2012; Kruglanski & Dechesne, 2006). Progress is being made on a variety of fronts, including the question of where implicit attitudes come from. Laurie Rudman, Julie Phelan, and Jessica Heppen (2007), for example, found evidence that implicit attitudes are rooted more in people's childhood experiences, whereas explicit attitudes are rooted more in their recent experiences. In one study, the researchers measured college students' implicit and explicit attitudes toward overweight people. They also asked the students to report their current weight and their weight when they were growing up. Participants' implicit attitudes toward overweight people were predicted by their childhood weight but not their current weight, whereas their explicit attitudes were predicted by their current weight but not their childhood weight. Consider, for example, someone who was overweight as a child but is of normal weight as an adult. This person's implicit attitude toward overweight people would likely be positive, because it is rooted in his or her childhood experiences with obesity. The person's explicit attitude toward overweight people would likely be negative, because it is based on the fact he or she does not currently have a weight problem. An additional finding from this study was that people whose mother was overweight and were close to their mothers had positive implicit attitudes toward overweight people, even if they held negative explicit attitudes. In short, people can often have different attitudes toward the same thing, one rooted more in childhood experiences and the other based more on their adult experiences.

We will return in Chapter 13 to a discussion of implicit attitudes as they apply to stereotyping and prejudice. The focus in the remainder of this chapter will be on how explicit attitudes change and their relation to behavior.

How Do Attitudes Change?

Attitudes do sometimes change. In America, for example, the popularity of the president often rises and falls with surprising speed. Right after President Obama assumed office, in January of 2009, 67% of Americans said they approved of the job he was doing. By November of 2010, as the economic recovery in the United States sputtered, his approval rating had dropped to 47%. Then, right after Osama Bin Laden was killed in a raid by U.S. Navy Seals in May of 2011, his approval rating shot back up to 60%, only to fall back to 46% by October of 2011 (AP-GfK Poll, 2011).

The ability to kill or capture a man is a relatively simple task compared with changing his mind.

—Richard Cohen, 1991

When attitudes change, they often do so in response to social influence. Our attitudes toward everything from a presidential candidate to a brand of laundry detergent can be influenced by what other people do or say. This is why attitudes are of such interest to social psychologists; even something as personal and internal as an attitude is a highly social phenomenon, influenced by the imagined or actual behavior of other people. The entire premise of advertising, for example, is that your attitudes toward consumer products can be influenced by publicity. Remember Andrew Fischer? After he tattooed SnoreStop onto his forehead, Web sales of the product increased by 500%, aided by coverage of Fischer's stunt in the national press (Puente, 2005). Let's take a look at the conditions under which attitudes are most likely to change.

Sometimes attitudes change dramatically over short periods of time. For example, Americans' approval rating of President Obama has gone up and down since he assumed the presidency.

Changing Attitudes by Changing Behavior: Cognitive Dissonance Theory Revisited

We have already discussed one way that attitudes change: when people behave inconsistently with their attitudes and cannot find external justification for their behavior. We refer, of course, to cognitive dissonance theory. As we noted in Chapter 6, people experience dissonance when they do something that threatens their image of themselves as decent, kind, and honest—particularly if there is no way they can explain away this behavior as due to external circumstances.

If you wanted to change some friends' attitude toward smoking, you might succeed by getting them to give antismoking speeches. You would want to make it hard for your friends to find external reasons for giving the speech; for example, you would not want them to justify their actions by saying, "I'm doing it as a special favor for my friend" or "I'm getting paid handsomely for doing it." That is, as we saw in Chapter 6, the goal is to get your friends to find *internal justification* for giving the speech, whereby they reduce the dissonance of giving the speech by deciding that they believe what they are saying. But what if your goal is to change attitudes on a mass scale? Suppose you were hired by the American Cancer Society to come up with an antismoking campaign that could be used nationwide to counteract the kind of tobacco advertisements we discussed at the beginning of this chapter. Although dissonance techniques are powerful, they are very difficult to carry out on a mass scale (e.g., it would be hard to have all American smokers make antismoking speeches under just the right conditions of internal justification). To change as many people's attitudes as possible, you would have to resort to other techniques of attitude change. You would probably construct some sort of **persuasive communication**, which is a communication such as a speech or television advertisement that advocates a particular side of an issue. How should you construct your message so that it would change people's attitudes?

By persuading others, we convince ourselves.
—JUNIUS

Watch on **MyPsychLab**
What do you think of the antismoking message in the MyPsychLab video ***Smoking Damage?***

Persuasive Communications and Attitude Change

Suppose the American Cancer Society has given you a six-figure budget to develop your advertising campaign. Should you pack your public service announcement with facts and figures? Or should you take a more emotional approach, including in your message frightening visual images of diseased lungs? Should you hire a movie star to deliver your message or a Nobel Prize–winning medical researcher? Should you take a friendly tone and acknowledge that it is hard to quit smoking, or should you take a hard line and tell smokers to quit cold turkey? You can see the point: Constructing a truly persuasive communication is complicated.

Of the modes of persuasion furnished by the spoken word there are three kinds. The first kind depends on the personal character of the speaker; the second on putting the audience into a certain frame of mind; the third on the proof, or apparent proof, provided by the words of the speech itself.
—ARISTOTLE, *RHETORIC*

Luckily, social psychologists, beginning with Carl Hovland and his colleagues, have conducted many studies over the years on what makes a persuasive communication effective (Hovland, Janis, & Kelley, 1953). Drawing on their experiences during World War II, when they worked for the United States Army to increase the morale of soldiers (Stouffer et al., 1949), Hovland and his colleagues conducted many experiments on the conditions under which people are most likely to be influenced by persuasive communications. In essence, they studied "who says what to whom," looking at the source of the communication (e.g., how expert or attractive the speaker is), the communication itself (e.g., the quality of the arguments, whether the speaker presents both sides of the issue), and the nature of the audience (e.g., which kinds of appeals work with hostile or friendly audiences). Because these researchers were at Yale University, this approach to the study of persuasive communications is known as the **Yale Attitude Change approach**.

This approach yielded a great deal of useful information on how people change their attitudes in response to persuasive communications; some of this information is summarized in Figure 7.2. As the research mounted, however, a problem became apparent: Many aspects of persuasive communications turned out to be important, but it was not clear which were more important than others—that is, it was unclear when one factor should be emphasized over another.

For example, let's return to that job you have with the American Cancer Society. The marketing manager wants to see your ad next month. If you were to read the many Yale Attitude Change studies, you might find lots of useful information about who should say what to whom in order to construct a persuasive communication. However, you might also find yourself saying, "There's a lot of information here, and I'm not sure where I should place the most emphasis. Should I focus on who delivers the ads? Or should I worry more about the content of the message?"

Persuasive Communication
Communication (e.g., a speech or television ad) advocating a particular side of an issue

Yale Attitude Change Approach
The study of the conditions under which people are most likely to change their attitudes in response to persuasive messages, focusing on the source of the communication, the nature of the communication, and the nature of the audience

The Central and Peripheral Routes to Persuasion Some well-known attitude researchers have asked the same questions: When is it best to stress factors central to the communication, such as the strength of the arguments, and when is it best to stress factors peripheral to the logic of the arguments, such as the credibility or attractiveness

Figure 7.2
The Yale Attitude Change Approach

Researchers at Yale University initiated research on what makes a persuasive communication effective, focusing on "who said what to whom."

The Yale Attitude Change Approach

The effectiveness of persuasive communications depends on who says what to whom.

Who: The Source of the Communication

- Credible speakers (e.g., those with obvious expertise) persuade people more than speakers lacking in credibility (Hovland & Weiss, 1951; Jain & Posavac, 2000).
- Attractive speakers (whether due to physical or personality attributes) persuade people more than unattractive speakers do (Eagly & Chaiken, 1975; Petty, Wegener, & Fabrigar, 1997).

What: The Nature of the of the Communication

- People are more persuaded by messages that do not seem to be designed to influence them (Petty & Cacioppo, 1986; Walster & Festinger, 1962).
- Is it better to present a one-sided communication (one that presents only arguments favoring your position) or a two-sided communication (one that presents arguments for and against your position)? In general, two-sided messages work better, if you are sure to refute the arguments on the other side (Crowley & Hoyer, 1994; Igou & Bless, 2003; Lumsdaine & Janis, 1953).
- Is it better to give your speech before or after someone arguing for the other side? If the speeches are to be given back to back and there will be a delay before people have to make up their minds, it is better to go first. Under these conditions, there is likely to be a primacy effect, wherein people are more influenced by what they hear first. If there is a delay between the speeches and people will make up their minds right after hearing the second one, it is better to go last. Under these conditions, there is likely to be a recency effect, wherein people remember the second speech better than the first one (Haugtvedt & Wegener, 1994; Miller & Campbell, 1959).

To Whom: The Nature of the Audience

- An audience that is distracted during the persuasive communication will often be persuaded more than one that is not (Albarracin & Wyer, 2001; Festinger & Maccoby, 1964).
- People low in intelligence tend to be more influenceable than people high in intelligence, and people with moderate self-esteem tend to be more influenceable than people with low or high self-esteem (Rhodes & Wood, 1992).
- People are particularly susceptible to attitude change during the impressionable ages of 18 to 25. Beyond those ages, people's attitudes are more stable and resistant to change (Krosnick & Alwin, 1989; Sears, 1981).

of the person delivering the speech (Chaiken, 1987; Chaiken, Wood, & Eagly, 1996; Petty & Cacioppo, 1986; Petty et al., 2005; Petty & Briñol, 2008)? The **elaboration likelihood model** of persuasion (Petty & Cacioppo, 1986; Petty, Barden, & Wheeler, 2009), for example, specifies when people will be influenced by what the speech says (i.e., the logic of the arguments) and when they will be influenced by more-superficial characteristics (e.g., who gives the speech or how long it is).

Elaboration Likelihood Model

A model explaining two ways in which persuasive communications can cause attitude change: *centrally,* when people are motivated and have the ability to pay attention to the arguments in the communication, and *peripherally,* when people do not pay attention to the arguments but are instead swayed by surface characteristics (e.g., who gave the speech)

Central Route to Persuasion

The case in which people elaborate on a persuasive communication, listening carefully to and thinking about the arguments, which occurs when people have both the ability and the motivation to listen carefully to a communication

Peripheral Route to Persuasion

The case in which people do not elaborate on the arguments in a persuasive communication but are instead swayed by peripheral cues

The theory states that under certain conditions people are motivated to pay attention to the facts in a communication, so they will be most persuaded when these facts are logically compelling. That is, sometimes people elaborate on what they hear, carefully thinking about and processing the content of the communication. Petty and Cacioppo (1986) call this the **central route to persuasion**. Under other conditions, people are not motivated to pay attention to the facts; instead, they notice only the surface characteristics of the message, such as how long it is and who is delivering it. Here people will not be swayed by the logic of the arguments, because they are not paying close attention to what the communicator says. Instead, they are persuaded if the surface characteristics of the message—such as the fact that it is long or is delivered by an expert or attractive communicator—make it seem like a reasonable one. Petty and Cacioppo call this the **peripheral route to persuasion** because people are swayed by things peripheral to the message itself. If you happen to follow the reality TV star Khloe Kardashian on Twitter, for example, you may have received her tweet that a particular brand of jeans "makes your butt look scary good." Celebrities are reportedly being paid as much as $10,000 a post to tweet about the virtues of various products (Rexrode, 2011).

What determines whether people take the central versus the peripheral route to persuasion? The key is whether people have both the motivation and the ability to pay attention to the facts. If people are truly interested in the topic and thus motivated to pay close attention to the arguments, *and* if people have the ability to pay attention—for example, if nothing is distracting them—they are more likely to take the central route (see Figure 7.3).

The Motivation to Pay Attention to the Arguments One thing that determines whether people are motivated to pay attention to a communication is the personal relevance of the topic: How important is the topic to a person's well-being? For example, consider the issue of whether Social Security benefits should be reduced. How personally relevant is this to you? If you are a 72-year-old whose sole income is from Social Security, the issue is extremely relevant; if you are a 20-year-old from a well-to-do family, the issue has little personal relevance.

Sometimes attitude change occurs via a peripheral route, whereby people are persuaded by things other than arguments about the facts. For example, sometimes we are swayed more by who delivers a persuasive communication than by the strength of the message. An endorsement by Oprah Winfrey, for example, can turn a book into an instant best seller.

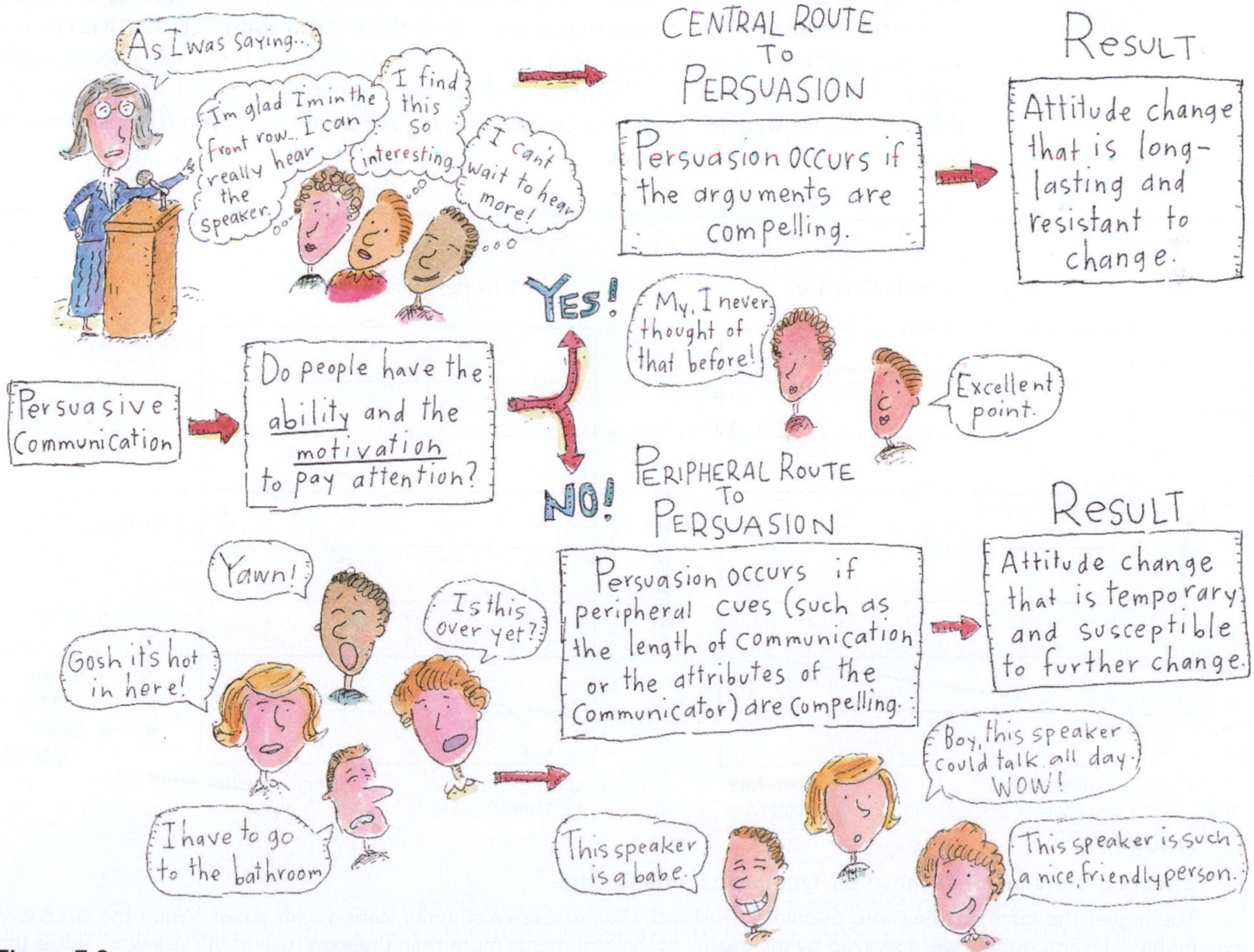

Figure 7.3

The Elaboration Likelihood Model

The elaboration likelihood model describes how people change their attitudes when they hear persuasive communications.

The more personally relevant an issue is, the more willing people are to pay attention to the arguments in a speech and therefore the more likely people are to take the central route to persuasion. In one study, for example, college students were asked to listen to a speech arguing that all college seniors should be required to pass a comprehensive exam in their major before they graduate (Petty, Cacioppo, & Goldman, 1981). Half of the participants were told that their university was seriously considering requiring comprehensive exams. For these students, the issue was personally relevant. For the other half, it was a "ho-hum" issue—they were told that their university might require such exams but would not implement them for 10 years.

The researchers then introduced two variables that might influence whether people would agree with the speech. The first was the strength of the arguments presented. Half of the participants heard arguments that were strong and persuasive (e.g., "The quality of undergraduate teaching has improved at schools with the exams"), whereas the others heard arguments that were weak and unpersuasive (e.g., "The risk of failing the exam is a challenge most students would welcome"). The second variable was a peripheral cue—the prestige of the speaker. Half of the participants were told that the author of the speech was an eminent professor at Princeton University, whereas the others were told that the author was a high school student.

When deciding how much to agree with the speaker's position, the participants could use one or both of these different kinds of information; they could listen carefully to the arguments and think about how convincing they were, or they could simply go by who said them (i.e., how prestigious the source was). As predicted by the elaboration likelihood model, the way in which people were persuaded depended on the personal relevance of the issue. The left panel of Figure 7.4 shows what happened when the issue was highly relevant to the listeners. These students were greatly influenced by the quality of the arguments (i.e., persuasion occurred via the central route). Those who heard strong arguments agreed much more with the speech than did those who heard weak arguments. It didn't matter who presented the arguments, the Princeton professor or the high school student. A good argument was a good argument, even if it was written by someone who lacked prestige.

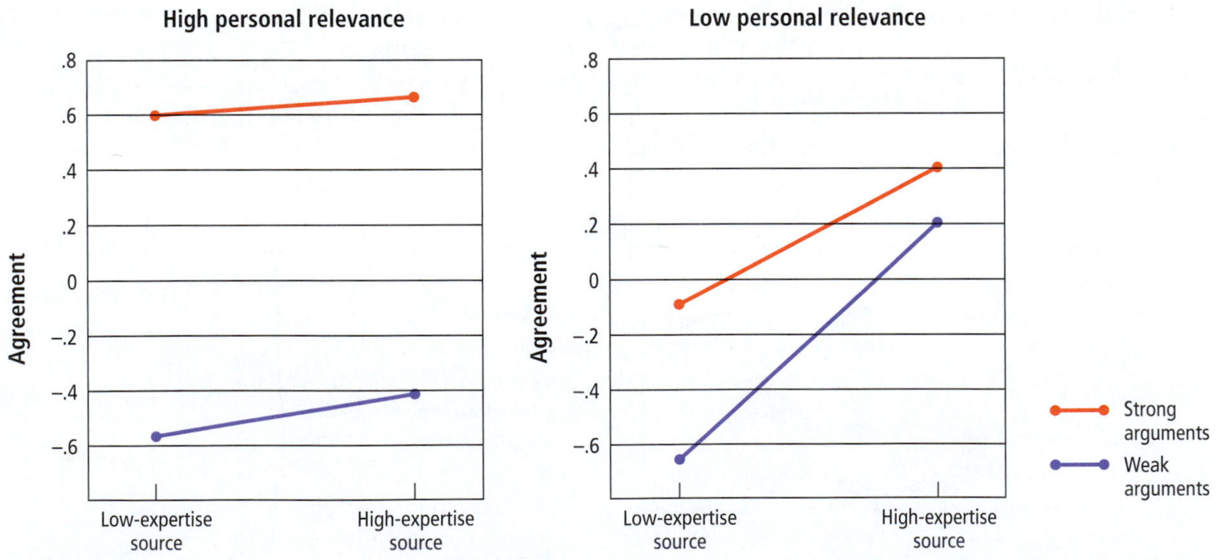

FIGURE 7.4

Effects of Personal Relevance on Type of Attitude Change

The higher the number, the more people agreed with the persuasive communication. Left panel: When the issue was highly relevant, people were swayed by the quality of the arguments more than the expertise of the speaker. This is the central route to persuasion. Right panel: When the issue was low in relevance, people were swayed by the expertise of the speaker more than the quality of the arguments. This is the peripheral route to persuasion.

(Based on data in Petty, Cacioppo, & Goldman, 1981)

What happens when a topic is of low relevance? As seen in the right panel of Figure 7.4, what mattered was not the strength of the arguments but who the speaker was. Those who heard the strong arguments agreed with the speech only slightly more than those who heard the weak arguments, whereas those who heard the Princeton professor were much more swayed than those who heard the high school student.

This finding illustrates a general rule: When an issue is personally relevant, people pay attention to the arguments in a speech—the "proof" of the speech, in Aristotle's words—and will be persuaded to the extent that the arguments are sound. When an issue is not personally relevant, people pay less attention to the arguments. Instead, they will take a mental shortcut, following such peripheral rules as "Prestigious speakers can be trusted" (Chen & Chaiken, 1999; Fabrigar et al., 1998).

In addition to the personal relevance of a topic, people's motivation to pay attention to a speech depends on their personality. Some people enjoy thinking things through more than others do; they are said to be high in the **need for cognition** (Cacioppo et al., 1996; Petty et al., 2009). This is a personality variable that reflects the extent to which people engage in and enjoy effortful cognitive activities. People high in the need for cognition are more likely to form their attitudes by paying close attention to relevant arguments (i.e., via the central route), whereas people low in the need for cognition are more likely to rely on peripheral cues such as how attractive or credible a speaker is. The Try It! exercise on the following page can show you how high you are in the need for cognition.

> *I'm not convinced by proofs but signs.*
> —Coventry Patmore

The Ability to Pay Attention to the Arguments Sometimes it is difficult to pay attention to a speech, even if we want to. Maybe we're tired, maybe we're distracted by construction noise outside the window, maybe the issue is too complex and hard to evaluate. When people are unable to pay close attention to the arguments, they are swayed more by peripheral cues (Petty & Brock, 1981; Petty et al., 2005). For example, a few years ago an exchange of letters appeared in an advice column about whether drugs such as cocaine and marijuana should be legalized. Readers wrote in with all sorts of compelling arguments on both sides of the issue, and it was difficult to figure out which arguments had the most merit. One reader resolved this dilemma by relying less on the content of the arguments than on the prestige and expertise of the source of the arguments. She noted that several eminent people have supported the legalization of drugs, including a Princeton professor who wrote in the prestigious publication *Science*; the eminent economist Milton Friedman; Kurt Schmoke, the former mayor of Baltimore; columnist William F. Buckley; and former secretary of state George Schultz. She decided to support legalization as well, not because of the strength of prolegalization arguments she had read, but because that's the way several people she trusted felt—a clear case of the peripheral route to persuasion.

How to Achieve Long-Lasting Attitude Change Now that you know a persuasive communication can change people's attitudes in either of two ways—via the central or the peripheral route—you may be wondering what difference it makes. Does it really matter whether it was the logic of the arguments or the expertise of the source that changed students' minds about comprehensive exams in the Petty and colleagues (1981) study? Given the bottom line—they changed their attitudes—why should any of us care how they got to that point?

If we are interested in creating long-lasting attitude change, we should care a lot. People who base their attitudes on a careful analysis of the arguments will be more likely to maintain this attitude over time, more likely to behave consistently with this attitude, and more resistant to counterpersuasion than people who base their attitudes on peripheral cues (Chaiken, 1980; Mackie, 1987; Petty, Haugtvedt, & Smith, 1995; Petty & Wegener, 1999). In one study, for example, people changed their attitudes either by analyzing the logic of the arguments or by using peripheral cues. When the participants were telephoned 10 days later, those who had analyzed the logic of the arguments were more likely to have maintained their new attitude—that is, attitudes that changed via the central route to persuasion lasted longer (Chaiken, 1980).

Need for Cognition

A personality variable reflecting the extent to which people engage in and enjoy effortful cognitive activities

TRY IT! The Need for Cognition

Indicate to what extent each statement is characteristic of you, using the following scale.

1 = extremely uncharacteristic of you (not at all like you)
2 = somewhat uncharacteristic
3 = uncertain
4 = somewhat characteristic
5 = extremely characteristic of you (very much like you)

1. I would prefer complex to simple problems. ________
2. I like to have the responsibility of handling a situation that requires a lot of thinking. ________
3. Thinking is not my idea of fun. ________
4. I would rather do something that requires little thought than something that is sure to challenge my thinking abilities. ________
5. I try to anticipate and avoid situations where there is a likely chance I will have to think in depth about something. ________
6. I find satisfaction in deliberating hard and for long hours. ________
7. I only think as hard as I have to. ________
8. I prefer to think about small, daily projects to long-term ones. ________
9. I like tasks that require little thought once I've learned them. ________
10. The idea of relying on thought to make my way to the top appeals to me. ________
11. I really enjoy a task that involves coming up with new solutions to problems. ________
12. Learning new ways to think doesn't excite me very much. ________
13. I prefer my life to be filled with puzzles that I must solve. ________
14. The notion of thinking abstractly is appealing to me. ________
15. I would prefer a task that is intellectual, difficult, and important to one that is somewhat important but does not require much thought. ________
16. I feel relief rather than satisfaction after completing a task that required a lot of mental effort. ________
17. It's enough for me that something gets the job done; I don't care how or why it works. ________
18. I usually end up deliberating about issues even when they do not affect me personally. ________

This scale measures the *need for cognition*, which is a personality variable reflecting the extent to which people engage in and enjoy effortful cognitive activities (Cacioppo et al., 1996). People high in the need for cognition are more likely to form their attitudes by paying close attention to relevant arguments (i.e., via the central route), whereas people low in the need for cognition are more likely to rely on peripheral cues, such as how attractive or credible a speaker is.

See page 195 for instructions on how to add up your score on this measure.

Emotion and Attitude Change

Now you know exactly how to construct your ad for the American Cancer Society, right? Well, not quite. Before people will consider your carefully constructed arguments, you have to get their attention. If you are going to show your antismoking ad on television, for example, how can you be sure people will watch the ad when it comes on, instead of changing the channel or heading for the refrigerator? One way is to grab people's attention by playing to their emotions.

Fear-Arousing Communications One way to get people's attention is to scare them—for example, by showing pictures of diseased lungs and presenting alarming data about the link between smoking and lung cancer. This kind of persuasive message (attempting to change people's attitudes by stirring up their fears) is called a **fear-arousing communication.** Public service ads often take this approach by trying to scare people into practicing safer sex, wearing seat belts, and staying away from drugs. For example, since January 2001 cigarette packs sold in Canada have been required to display graphic pictures of diseased gums and other body parts that cover at least 50% of the outside label. The U.S. Food and Drug Administration has ruled that all cigarette packs sold in the United States must contain similar images, but this ruling has been challenged in the courts by the tobacco industry (Pickler, 2011).

Fear-Arousing Communication
Persuasive message that attempts to change people's attitudes by arousing their fears

Do fear-arousing communications work? It depends on whether the fear influences people's ability to pay attention to and process the arguments in a message. If a moderate amount of fear is created and people believe that listening to the message will teach them how to reduce this fear, they will be motivated to analyze the message carefully and will likely change their attitudes via the central route (Petty, 1995; Rogers, 1983).

Consider a study in which a group of smokers watched a graphic film depicting lung cancer and then read pamphlets with specific instructions about how to quit smoking (Leventhal, Watts, & Pagano, 1967). As shown by the bottom line in Figure 7.5, people in this condition reduced their smoking significantly more than people who were shown only the film or only the pamphlet. Why? Watching the film scared people, and giving them the pamphlet reassured them that there was a way to reduce this fear—by following the instructions on how to quit. Seeing only the pamphlet didn't work very well, because there was little fear motivating people to read it carefully. Seeing only the film didn't work very well either, because people are likely to tune out a message that raises fear but does not give information about how to reduce it. This may explain why some attempts to frighten people into changing their attitudes and behaviors fail: They succeed in scaring people but do not provide specific recommendations to help them reduce their fear (Aronson, 2008; Hoog, Stroebe, & de Wit, 2005; Ruiter, Abraham, & Kok, 2001).

As of 2013, FDA rules call for all cigarette packs sold in the United States to display pictures that warn about the dangers of smoking, such as the one shown here. Do you think that this ad would scare people into quitting?

Fear-arousing appeals will also fail if they are so strong that they overwhelm people. If people are scared to death, they will become defensive, deny the importance of the threat, and be unable to think rationally about the issue (Janis & Feshbach, 1953; Liberman & Chaiken, 1992). So if you have decided to arouse people's fear in your ad for the American Cancer Society, keep these points in mind: Try to create enough fear to

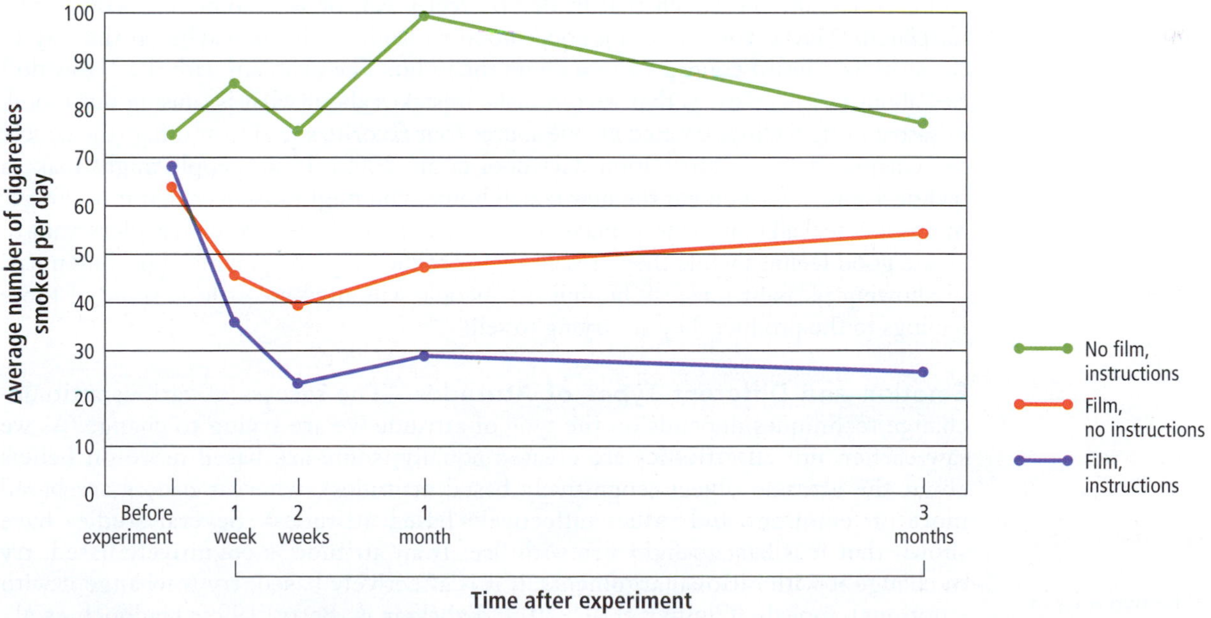

FIGURE 7.5

Effects of Fear Appeals on Attitude Change

People were shown a scary film about the effects of smoking, instructions about how to stop smoking, or both. Those who were shown both had the biggest reduction in the number of cigarettes they smoked.

(Adapted from Leventhal, Watts, & Pagano, 1967)

"While we're waiting for His Honor, may I offer the jury a selection of hand-dipped Swiss chocolates, compliments of my client?"

Henry Martin/The New Yorker Collection/www.cartoonbank.com

motivate people to pay attention to your arguments, but not so much fear that people will tune out or distort what you say, and include some specific recommendations about how to stop smoking so people will be reassured that paying close attention to your arguments will help them reduce their fear.

Emotions as a Heuristic Another way in which emotions can cause attitude change is by acting as a signal for how we feel about something. According to the **heuristic–systematic model of persuasion** (Chaiken, 1987), when people take the peripheral route to persuasion, they often use heuristics. Recall from Chapter 3 that heuristics are mental shortcuts people use to make judgments quickly and efficiently. In the present context, a heuristic is a simple rule people use to decide what their attitude is without having to spend a lot of time analyzing every detail about the topic at hand. Examples of such heuristics are "Experts are always right" and "Length equals strength" (i.e., long messages are more persuasive than short ones).

Interestingly, our emotions and moods can themselves act as heuristics to determine our attitudes. When trying to decide what our attitude is about something, we often rely on the "How do I feel about it?" heuristic (Clore & Huntsinger, 2007; Forgas, 2011; Kim, Park, & Schwarz, 2010; Schwarz & Clore, 1988; Storbeck & Clore, 2008). If we feel good, we must have a positive attitude; if we feel bad, it's thumbs down. Now this probably sounds like a pretty good rule to follow, and, like most heuristics, it is—most of the time. Suppose you need a new couch and go to a furniture store to look around. You see one in your price range and are trying to decide whether to buy it. If you use the "How do I feel about it?" heuristic, you do a quick check of your feelings and emotions. If you feel great while you're sitting on the couch in the store, you will probably buy it.

The only problem is that sometimes it is difficult to tell where our feelings come from. Is it really the couch that made you feel great, or is it something completely unrelated? Maybe you were in a good mood to begin with, or maybe on the way to the store you heard your favorite song on the radio. The problem with the "How do I feel about it?" heuristic is that we can make mistakes about what is causing our mood, misattributing feelings created by one source (our favorite song) to another (the couch; see Chapter 5 on misattribution; Claypool et al., 2008). If so, people might make a bad decision. After you get the new couch home, you might discover that it no longer makes you feel all that great. It makes sense, then, that advertisers and retailers want to create good feelings while they present their product (e.g., by playing appealing music or showing pleasant images), hoping that people will attribute at least some of those feelings to the product they are trying to sell.

Emotion and Different Types of Attitudes The success of various attitude-change techniques depends on the type of attitude we are trying to change. As we saw earlier, not all attitudes are created equally; some are based more on beliefs about the attitude object (cognitively based attitudes), whereas others are based more on emotions and values (affectively based attitudes). Several studies have shown that it is best to fight fire with fire: If an attitude is cognitively based, try to change it with rational arguments; if it is affectively based, try to change it with emotional appeals (Conner et al., 2011; Fabrigar & Petty, 1999; Haddock et al., 2008; Shavitt, 1989).

Heuristic–Systematic Model of Persuasion

An explanation of the two ways in which persuasive communications can cause attitude change: either systematically processing the merits of the arguments or using mental shortcuts (heuristics), such as "Experts are always right"

Consider a study of the effectiveness of different kinds of advertisements (Shavitt, 1990). Some ads stress the objective merits of a product, such as an ad for an air conditioner or a vacuum cleaner that discusses its price, efficiency, and reliability. Other ads stress emotions and values, such as ones for perfume or designer jeans that try to

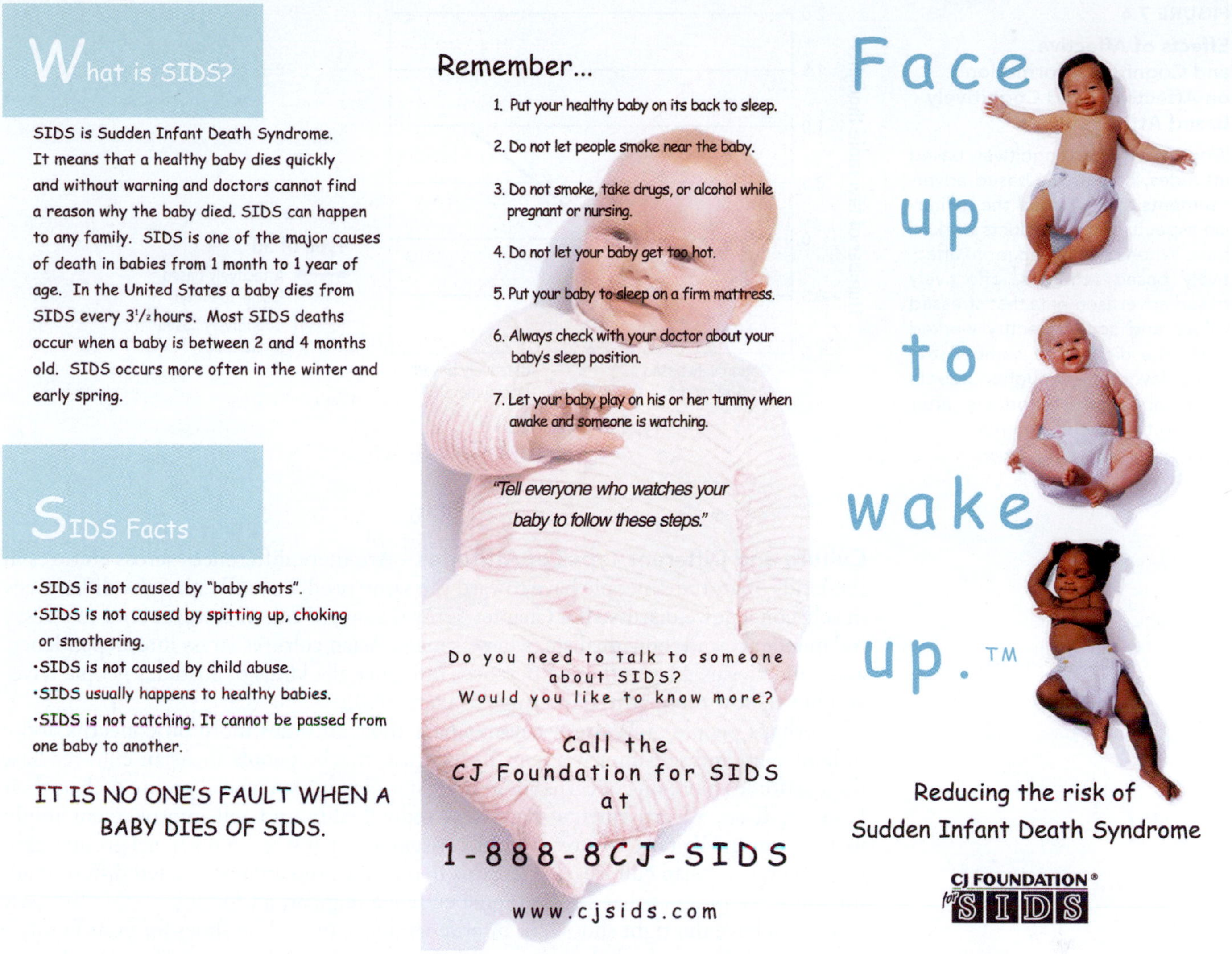

Many advertisements attempt to use emotions to persuade people. This ad uses a combination of cuteness (images of babies) and apprehension ("face up to wake up") to educate parents that it is safest for babies to sleep on their backs.

associate their brands with sex, beauty, and youthfulness rather than saying anything about the objective qualities of the product. Which kind of ad is most effective?

To find out, participants looked at different kinds of advertisements. Some were for "utilitarian products" such as air conditioners and coffee. People's attitudes toward such products tend to be formed after an appraisal of the utilitarian aspects of the products (e.g., how energy efficient an air conditioner is) and thus are cognitively based. The other items were "social identity products" such as perfume and greeting cards. People's attitudes toward these types of products tend to reflect a concern with how they appear to others and are therefore more affectively based.

It is useless to attempt to reason a man out of a thing he was never reasoned into.

—Jonathan Swift

As shown in Figure 7.6, people reacted most favorably to the ads that matched the type of attitude they had. If people's attitudes were cognitively based (e.g., toward air conditioners or coffees), the ads that focused on the utilitarian aspects of these products, such as the features of the air conditioner, were most successful. If people's attitudes were more affectively based (e.g., toward perfume or greeting cards), the ads that focused on values and social identity concerns were most successful. The graph displayed in Figure 7.6 shows the number of favorable thoughts people had in response to the different kinds of ads. Similar results were found on a measure of how much people intended to buy the products. Thus, if you ever get a job in advertising, the moral is to know what type of attitude most people have toward your product and then tailor your advertising accordingly.

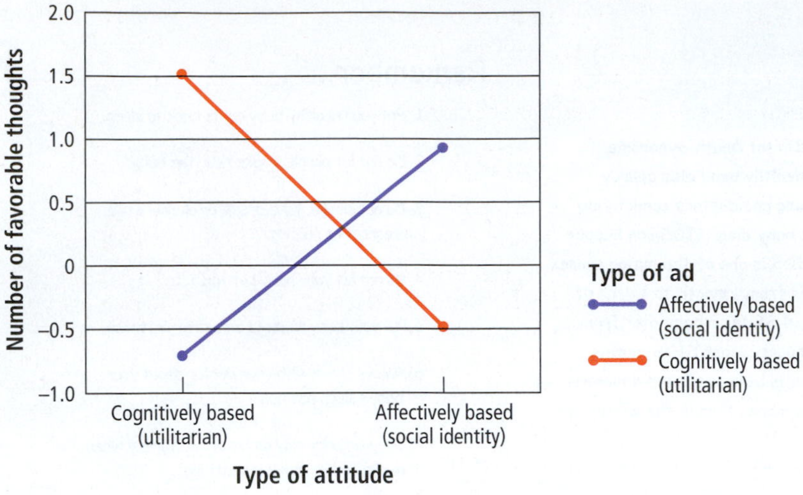

FIGURE 7.6

Effects of Affective and Cognitive Information on Affectively and Cognitively Based Attitudes

When people had cognitively based attitudes, cognitively based advertisements that stressed the utilitarian aspects of the products worked best. When people had more affectively based attitudes, affectively based advertisements that stressed values and social identity worked best. The higher the number, the more favorable thoughts people listed about the products after reading the advertisements.

(Based on data in Shavitt, 1990)

Culture and Different Types of Attitudes Are there differences across cultures in the kinds of attitudes people have toward the same products, reflecting the differences in self-concept we discussed in Chapter 5? As we saw, Western cultures tend to stress independence and individualism, whereas many Asian cultures stress interdependence and collectivism. Maybe these differences influence the kinds of attitudes people have and hence how those attitudes change (Aaker, 2000).

Perhaps people in Western cultures base their attitudes more on concerns about individuality and self-improvement. In contrast, maybe people in Asian cultures base their attitudes more on concerns about their standing in their social group, such as their families. If so, advertisements that stress individuality and self-improvement might work better in Western cultures, and advertisements that stress one's social group might work better in Asian cultures. To test this hypothesis, researchers created different ads for the same product that stressed independence (e.g., an ad for shoes said, "It's easy when you have the right shoes") or interdependence (e.g., "the shoes for your family") and showed them to both Americans and Koreans (Han & Shavitt, 1994). The Americans were persuaded most by the ads stressing independence, and the Koreans were persuaded by the ads stressing interdependence. The researchers also analyzed actual magazine advertisements in the United States and Korea and found that these ads were in fact different: American ads tended to emphasize individuality, self-improvement, and benefits of the product for the individual consumer, whereas Korean ads tended to emphasize the family, concerns about others, and benefits for one's social group. In general, then, advertisements work best if they are tailored to the kind of attitude they are trying to change.

Confidence in One's Thoughts and Attitude Change

Although you know a lot by now about how to craft your persuasive message for the American Cancer Society, there is one other thing you might want to take into account: how confident people are in the thoughts that your message triggers. Suppose your message succeeds in getting smokers to think, "Wow, there are a lot of dangers to smoking I didn't know about." That's all well and good, but you also want to make sure that people have a lot of *confidence* in those thoughts. If they roll their eyes and think, "I'm not so sure about any of that," your message isn't going to have much effect (Briñol & Petty, 2009, 2012). Although that probably seems straightforward enough, the *way* in which people gain confidence in their thoughts isn't always so obvious. Consider a study by Briñol and Petty (2003) in which participants were asked to test out the durability of some new headphones. Some were asked to shake their heads from side to side while wearing them, whereas others were asked to nod their heads up and down. While they were doing this, the participants listened to an editorial arguing that all students should be required to carry personal identification cards on campus. One final twist was that half of the participants heard strong, persuasive arguments (e.g., that ID cards would make the campus safer for students) whereas the other half heard weak, unconvincing arguments (e.g., that if students carried the cards, security guards would have more time for lunch).

As you have no doubt gathered, the point of the study was not to test the headphones but to see whether shaking or nodding one's head while listening to a persuasive communication influenced how persuaded people were by the message. The idea was that even though the head movements had nothing to do with the editorial, they might influence how confident people felt in the arguments they heard. Nodding one's head up and down, as people do when they say yes, might make them feel more confident than when they shake their head side to side, as they do when they say no. This is exactly what happened, which had some interesting consequences. When the arguments in the editorial were strong, people who nodded their heads agreed with them more than did people who shook their heads, because the head nodders had more confidence in the strong arguments that they heard (see the left side of Figure 7.7). But when the arguments were weak, head nodding had the opposite effect. It gave people more confidence that the arguments they heard were in fact weak and unconvincing, making them *less* convinced than people who shook their heads from side to side (see the right side of Figure 7.7). The moral? Anything you can do to increase people's confidence in their thoughts about your message will make it more effective, as long as your arguments are strong and convincing.

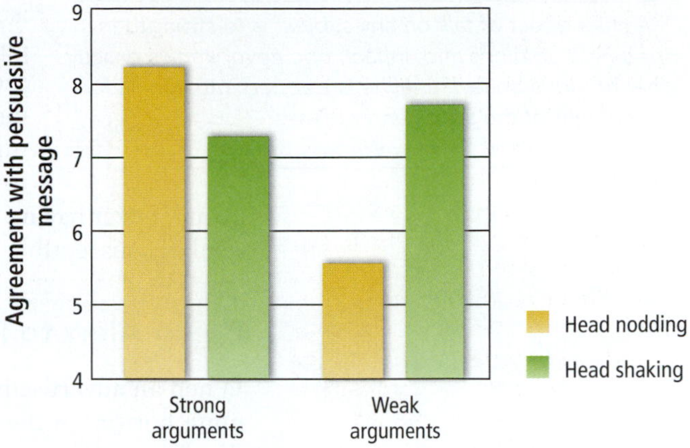

FIGURE 7.7

Effects of Confidence in One's Thoughts on Persuasion

People who nodded their heads up and down, compared to those who shook their heads from side to side, had greater confidence in their thoughts about the message (e.g., "Wow, this is really convincing" when the arguments were strong, and "Wow, this is really dumb" when the arguments were weak).

(Figure adapted from Briñol & Petty, 2003)

Resisting Persuasive Messages

By now you are no doubt getting nervous (and not just because the chapter hasn't ended yet). With all these clever methods to change your attitudes, are you ever safe from persuasive communications? Indeed you are, or at least you can be if you use some strategies of your own. Here's how to make sure all those persuasive messages that bombard you don't turn you into a quivering mass of constantly changing opinion.

Watch on **MyPsychLab**

To learn more about resisting mindless persuasion, watch the MyPsychLab video ***What's In It For Me? How am I being influenced?***

Attitude Inoculation

One thing you can do is consider the arguments against your attitude before someone attacks it. The more people have thought about pro and con arguments beforehand using the technique known as **attitude inoculation** (Ivanov, Pfau, & Parker, 2009; McGuire, 1964), the better they can ward off attempts to change their minds using logical arguments. By considering "small doses" of arguments against their position, people become immune to later, full-blown attempts to change their attitudes. Having considered the arguments beforehand, people are relatively immune to the effects of the later communication, just as exposing people to a small amount of a virus can inoculate them against exposure to the full-blown viral disease. In contrast, if people have not thought much about the issue—that is, if they formed their attitude via the peripheral route—they are particularly susceptible to an attack on that attitude using logical appeals.

Attitude Inoculation

Making people immune to attempts to change their attitudes by initially exposing them to small doses of the arguments against their position

In one study, for example, William McGuire (1964) "inoculated" people by giving them brief arguments against *cultural truisms*, beliefs that most members of a society accept uncritically, such as the idea that we should brush our teeth after every meal. Two days later, people came back and read a much stronger attack on the truism, one that contained a series of logical arguments about why brushing your teeth too frequently

The chief effect of talk on any subject is to strengthen one's own opinions and, in fact, one never knows exactly what he does believe until he is warmed into conviction by the heat of the attack and defense.

—Charles Dudley Warner, *Backlog Studies*, 1873

is a bad idea. The people who had been inoculated against these arguments were much less likely to change their attitudes than were those in a control group who had not been inoculated. Why? The individuals who were inoculated with weak arguments had time to think about why these arguments were false, making them more able to contradict the stronger attack they heard 2 days later. The control group, never having thought about how often people should brush their teeth, was particularly susceptible to the strong communication arguing against frequent brushing.

Being Alert to Product Placement

When an advertisement comes on during a TV show, people often decide to press the mute button on the remote control (or the fast-forward button if they have recorded the show). To counteract this tendency to avoid ads, advertisers look for ways of displaying their wares during the show itself. Many companies pay the makers of a TV show or movie to incorporate their product into the script (Kang, 2008). If you were a fan of the NBC television program *Chuck*, for example, you may have noticed that the characters ate a lot of Subway sandwiches. That is no coincidence, because Subway was a sponsor of the show. In fact, one reason that NBC executives decided to renew the program in 2009 was because the Subway restaurant chain paid to have their products featured in the plots of the show (Carter, 2009). If you have ever watched *American Idol*, you've probably noticed that ever-present Coca-Cola cup in front of each judge. Maybe the revolving groups of judges over the years have all loved Coke, but more likely the Coca-Cola company paid to have their product prominently displayed. They are not alone: In 2007, $2.7 billion was spent on similar product placement (Van Reijmersdal, Neijens, & Smit, 2009).

Watch on MyPsychLab
To learn more about product placement, watch the MyPsychLab video ***Different Forms of Advertising.***

One reason product placement can work is that people do not realize that someone is trying to influence their attitudes and behavior. Our defenses are down; when we see a character on a show such as *Chuck* eating a Subway sandwich, we don't think about the fact that someone is trying to influence our attitudes, and we don't generate counterarguments (Burkley, 2008; Levitan & Visser, 2008; Wheeler, Briñol, & Hermann, 2007). Children are especially vulnerable. One study, for example, found that the more children in grades 5 to 8 had seen movies in which adults smoked cigarettes, the more positive were their attitudes toward smoking (Heatherton & Sargent, 2009; Wakefield, Flay, & Nichter, 2003).

This leads to the question of whether forewarning people that someone is about to try to change their attitudes is an effective tool against product placement, or persuasion more generally. It turns out that it is. Several studies have found that warning people about an upcoming attempt to change their attitudes makes them less susceptible to that attempt. When people are forewarned, they analyze what they see and hear more carefully and as a result are likely to avoid attitude change. Without such warnings, people pay little attention to the persuasive attempts and tend to accept the messages at face value (Knowles & Linn, 2004; Sagarin & Wood, 2007; Wood & Quinn, 2003). So before letting kids watch TV or sending them off to the movies, it is good to remind them that they are likely to encounter several attempts to change their attitudes.

Product placement, in which a commercial product is incorporated into the script of a movie or television show, is becoming more common.

Resisting Peer Pressure

We've seen that many attacks on our attitudes consist of appeals to our emotions. Can we ward off this kind of opinion change technique just as we can ward off the effects of logical appeals? This is an important question, because many critical changes in attitudes and behaviors occur not in response to logic, but via more-emotional appeals. Consider the way in which many

> *A companion's words of persuasion are effective.*
> —HOMER

adolescents begin to smoke, drink, or take drugs. Often they do so in response to pressure from their peers, at an age when they are particularly susceptible to such pressure. Indeed, one study found that the best predictor of whether an adolescent smokes marijuana is whether he or she has a friend who does so (Allen, Donohue, & Griffin, 2003; Yamaguchi & Kandel, 1984).

Think about how this occurs. It is not as if peers present a set of logical arguments ("Hey, Jake, did you know that recent studies show that moderate drinking may have health benefits?"). Instead, peer pressure is linked more to people's values and emotions, playing on their fear of rejection and their desire for freedom and autonomy. In adolescence, peers become an important source of social approval—perhaps the most important—and can dispense powerful rewards for holding certain attitudes or behaving in certain ways, such as using drugs or engaging in unprotected sex. What is needed is a technique that will make young people more resistant to attitude change attempts via peer pressure so that they will be less likely to engage in dangerous behaviors.

One possibility is to extend the logic of McGuire's inoculation approach to more–affectively based persuasion techniques such as peer pressure. In addition to inoculating people with doses of logical arguments that they might hear, we could also inoculate them with samples of the kinds of emotional appeals they might encounter.

Consider Jake, a 13-year-old who is hanging out with some classmates, many of whom are smoking cigarettes. The classmates begin to tease Jake about not smoking, calling him a wimp. One of them even lights a cigarette and holds it in front of Jake, daring him to take a puff. Many 13-year-olds, facing such pressure, would cave in and smoke that cigarette. But suppose that we have immunized Jake from such social pressures by exposing him to mild versions of them and showing him ways to combat these pressures. We might have him role-play a situation where a friend calls him a chicken for not smoking a cigarette and teach him to respond by saying, "I'd be more of a chicken if I smoked it just to impress you." Would this help him resist the more powerful pressures exerted by his classmates?

Reactance Theory

The idea that when people feel their freedom to perform a certain behavior is threatened, an unpleasant state of reactance is aroused, which they can reduce by performing the threatened behavior

Several programs designed to prevent smoking in adolescents suggest that it would. In one, psychologists used a role-playing technique with seventh graders, very much like the one we just described (McAlister et al., 1980). The researchers found that these students were significantly less likely to smoke 3 years after the study, compared to a control group that had not participated in the program. This result is encouraging and has been replicated in similar programs designed to reduce smoking and drug abuse (Botvin & Griffin, 2004; Chou et al., 1998).

A number of interventions designed to prevent smoking in adolescents have had some success. Many celebrities have lent their names and pictures to the effort, such as actor Jackie Chan, who was the spokesperson for an anti-smoking campaign in Taiwan.

When Persuasion Attempts Boomerang: Reactance Theory

Suppose you want to make sure that your child never smokes. "Might as well err on the side of giving too strong a message," you might think, absolutely forbidding your child to even look at a pack of cigarettes. "What's the harm?" you figure. "At least this way my child will get the point about how serious a matter this is."

Actually, there is harm to administering strong prohibitions: The stronger they are, the more likely they will boomerang, causing an increase in interest in the prohibited activity. According to **reactance theory** (Brehm, 1966), people do not like to feel that their freedom to do or think whatever they want is being threatened. When they feel that their freedom is threatened, an unpleasant state of reactance is aroused, and people can reduce this reactance by performing the threatened behavior (e.g., smoking).

In one study, for example, researchers placed one of two signs in the bathrooms on a college campus, in an attempt to get people to stop writing graffiti on the restroom walls (Pennebaker & Sanders, 1976). One sign read, "Do not write on these walls under any circumstances." The other gave a milder prohibition: "Please don't write on these walls." The researchers returned 2 weeks later and observed how much graffiti had been written since they posted the signs. As they predicted, significantly more people wrote graffiti in the bathrooms with the "Do not write …" sign than with the "Please don't write …" sign. Similarly, people who receive strong admonitions against smoking, taking drugs, or getting their nose pierced become more likely to perform these behaviors to restore their sense of personal freedom and choice (Erceg, Hurn, & Steed, 2011; Miller et al., 2007).

When Do Attitudes Predict Behavior?

Remember the advertising campaign you were hired to develop for the American Cancer Society? The reason they and other groups are willing to spend so much money on ad campaigns is because of a simple assumption: When people change their attitudes (e.g., they don't like cigarettes as much), they change their behavior as well (e.g., they stop smoking).

Actually, the relationship between attitudes and behavior is not so simple, as shown in a classic study (LaPiere, 1934). In the early 1930s, Richard LaPiere embarked on a cross-country sightseeing trip with a young Chinese couple. Prejudice against Asians was common in the United States at this time, so at each hotel, campground, and restaurant they entered, LaPiere worried that his friends would be refused service. To his surprise, of the 251 establishments he and his friends visited, only one refused to serve them.

Struck by this apparent lack of prejudice, LaPiere decided to explore people's attitudes toward Asians in a different way. After his trip, he wrote a letter to each establishment he and his friends had visited, asking if it would serve a Chinese visitor. Of the many replies, only *one* said it would. More than 90% said they definitely would not; the rest were undecided. Why were the attitudes people expressed in writing the reverse of their actual behavior?

We give advice but we do not influence people's conduct.

—François de La Rochefoucauld, *Maxims*, 1665

LaPiere's study was not, of course, a controlled experiment. As he acknowledged, there are several reasons why his results may not show an inconsistency between people's attitudes and behavior. He had no way of knowing whether the proprietors who answered his letter were the same people who had served him and his friends, and even if they were, people's attitudes could have changed in the months between the time they served the Chinese couple and the time they received the letter. Nonetheless, the lack of correspondence between people's attitudes and what they actually did was so striking that we might question the earlier assumption that behavior routinely follows from attitudes. This is especially the case in light of research performed after LaPiere's study, which also found that people's attitudes can be poor predictors of their behavior (Wicker, 1969).

How can this be? Does a person's attitude toward Asians or political candidates really tell us nothing about how he or she will behave? How can we reconcile LaPiere's findings—and other studies like it—with the fact that many times behavior and attitudes *are* consistent? It turns out that attitudes do predict behavior, but only under certain specifiable conditions (DeBono & Snyder, 1995; Glasman & Albarracín, 2006). One key factor is knowing whether the behavior we are trying to predict is spontaneous or planned (Fazio, 1990).

Predicting Spontaneous Behaviors

Sometimes we act spontaneously, thinking little about what we are about to do. When LaPiere and his Chinese friends entered a restaurant, the manager did not have a lot of time to reflect on whether to serve them; he or she had to make a snap decision. Similarly, when someone stops us on the street and asks us to sign a petition in favor of a change in the local zoning laws, we usually don't stop and think about it for 5 minutes—we decide whether to sign the petition on the spot.

Attitudes will predict spontaneous behaviors only when they are highly accessible to people (Fazio, 1990, 2007; Kallgren & Wood, 1986). **Attitude accessibility** refers to the strength of the association between an object and an evaluation of it, which is typically measured by the speed with which people can report how they feel about the object or issue (Fazio, 2000). When accessibility is high, your attitude comes to mind whenever you see or think about the attitude object. When accessibility is low, your attitude comes to mind more slowly. It follows that highly accessible attitudes will be more likely to predict spontaneous behaviors, because people are more likely to be thinking about their attitude when they are called on to act. But what makes attitudes accessible in the first place? One important determinant is the degree of behavioral experience people have with the attitude object. Some attitudes are based on hands-on experience, such as a person's attitude toward the homeless after volunteering at a homeless shelter. Other attitudes are formed without much experience, such as a person's attitude toward the homeless that is based on reading about them in the newspaper. The more-direct experience people have with an attitude object, the more accessible their attitude is, and the more accessible it is, the more likely their spontaneous behaviors will be consistent with their attitudes (Glasman & Albarracin, 2006).

Attitude Accessibility

The strength of the association between an attitude object and a person's evaluation of that object, measured by the speed with which people can report how they feel about the object

Theory of Planned Behavior

The idea that people's intentions are the best predictors of their deliberate behaviors, which are determined by their attitudes toward specific behaviors, their subjective norms, and their perceived behavioral control

Predicting Deliberative Behaviors

Most of us take our time and deliberate about where to go to college, whether to accept a new job, or where to spend our vacation. Under these conditions, the accessibility of our attitude is less important. Given enough time to think about an issue, even people with inaccessible attitudes can bring to mind how they feel. It is only when we have to decide how to act on the spot, without time to think it over, that accessibility matters (Eagly & Chaiken, 1993; Fazio, 1990).

The best-known theory of how attitudes predict deliberative behaviors is the **theory of planned behavior** (Ajzen & Albarracin, 2007; Ajzen & Fishbein, 1980, 2005). According to this theory, when people have time to contemplate how they are going to behave, the best predictor of their behavior is their intention, which is determined by three things: their attitudes toward the specific behavior, their subjective norms, and their perceived behavioral control (see Figure 7.8). Let's consider each of these in turn.

Specific Attitudes The theory of planned behavior holds that only specific attitudes toward the behavior in question can be expected to predict that behavior. In one study, researchers asked a sample of married women for their attitudes toward birth control pills, ranging from the general (their attitude toward birth control) to the specific (their attitude toward using birth control pills during the next 2 years; see Table 7.1). Two years later, they asked the women whether they had used birth control pills at any

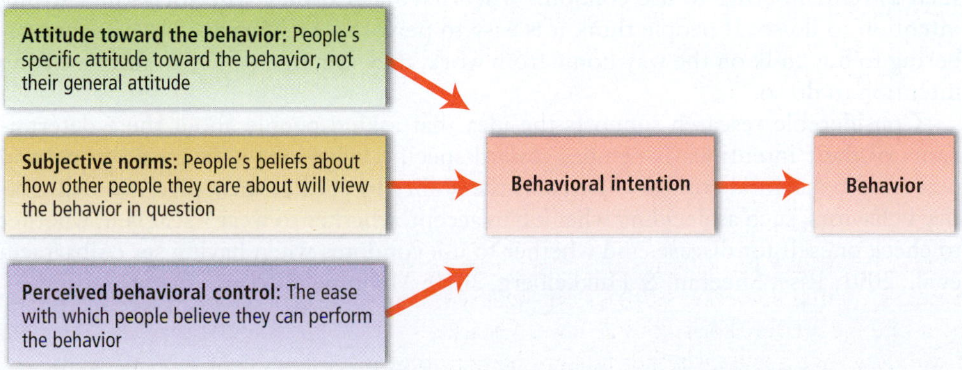
Attitude toward the behavior: People's specific attitude toward the behavior, not their general attitude
Subjective norms: People's beliefs about how other people they care about will view the behavior in question
Perceived behavioral control: The ease with which people believe they can perform the behavior
Behavioral intention
Behavior

FIGURE 7.8

The Theory of Planned Behavior

According to this theory, the best predictors of people's planned, deliberative behaviors are their behavioral intentions. The best predictors of their intentions are their attitudes toward the specific behavior, their subjective norms, and their perceived behavioral control of the behavior.

(Adapted from Ajzen, 1985)

TABLE 7.1 Specific Attitudes Are Better Predictors of Behavior

Different groups of women were asked about their attitudes toward birth control. The more specific the question, the better it predicted their actual use of birth control.

Note: If a correlation is close to 0, it means that there is no relationship between the two variables. The closer the correlation is to 1, the stronger the relationship between attitudes and behavior.

Attitude Measure	Attitude – Behavior Correlation
Attitude toward birth control	0.08
Attitude toward birth control pills	0.32
Attitude toward using birth control pills	0.53
Attitude toward using birth control pills during the next 2 years	0.57

(Adapted from Davidson & Jaccard, 1979)

time since the last interview. As Table 7.1 shows, the women's general attitude toward birth control did not predict their use of birth control at all. This general attitude did not take into account other factors that could have influenced their decision, such as concern about the long-term effects of the pill and their attitude toward other forms of birth control. The more specific the question was about the act of using birth control pills, the better this attitude predicted their actual behavior (Davidson & Jaccard, 1979).

This study helps explain why LaPiere (1934) found such inconsistency between people's attitudes and behaviors. His question to the proprietors—whether they would serve "members of the Chinese race"—was very general. Had he asked a much more specific question—such as whether they would serve an educated, well-dressed, well-to-do Chinese couple accompanied by a white American college professor—the proprietors might have given an answer that was more in line with their behavior.

If actions are to yield all the results they are capable of, there must be a certain consistency between them and one's intentions.

—François de La Rochefoucauld, *Maxims*, 1665

Subjective Norms In addition to measuring attitudes toward the behavior, we also need to measure people's subjective norms—their beliefs about how people they care about will view the behavior in question (see Figure 7.8). To predict someone's intentions, knowing these beliefs can be as important as knowing the person's attitudes. For example, suppose we want to predict whether Kristen intends to go to a hip-hop concert and we know that she doesn't like hip-hop music. We would probably say she won't go. But suppose we also know that Kristen's best friend, Tony, really wants her to go. Knowing this subjective norm—her belief about how a close friend views her behavior—we might make a different prediction.

Perceived Behavioral Control Finally, as seen in Figure 7.8, people's intentions are influenced by the ease with which they believe they can perform the behavior—perceived behavioral control. If people think it is difficult to perform the behavior, such as remembering to use condoms when having sex, they will not form a strong intention to do so. If people think it is easy to perform the behavior, such as remembering to buy milk on the way home from work, they are more likely to form a strong intention to do so.

Considerable research supports the idea that asking people about these determinants of their intentions—attitudes toward specific behaviors, subjective norms, and perceived behavioral control—increases the ability to predict their planned, deliberative behaviors, such as deciding what job to accept, whether to wear a seat belt, whether to check oneself for disease, and whether to use condoms when having sex (Albarracín et al., 2001; Rise, Sheeran, & Hukkelberg, 2010; Manning, 2009).

CONNECTIONS

Do Media Campaigns to Reduce Drug Use Work?

Smoking and drinking are common in movies, and sometimes public figures admired by many youth glamorize the use of drugs and alcohol. Advertising, product placement, and the behavior of admired figures can have powerful effects on people's behavior, including tobacco and alcohol use (Pechmann & Knight, 2002; Saffer, 2002). This raises an important question: Do public service ads designed to reduce people's use of drugs such as alcohol, tobacco, and marijuana work?

By now you know that changing people's attitudes and behavior can be difficult, particularly if people are not very motivated to pay attention to a persuasive message or are distracted while trying to pay attention. If persuasive messages are well crafted, they can have an effect, however, and in this chapter we have seen many successful attempts to change people's attitudes. What happens when researchers take these techniques out of the laboratory and try to change real-life attitudes and behavior, such as people's attraction to and use of illegal drugs?

A meta-analysis of studies that tested the effects of a media message (conveyed via television, radio, electronic, and print media) on substance abuse (including illegal drugs, alcohol, and tobacco) in youths was encouraging (Derzon & Lipsey, 2002). After a media campaign that targeted a specific substance, such as tobacco, kids were less likely to use that substance. Television and radio messages had bigger effects than messages in the print media (Ibrahim & Glantz, 2007).

In one particularly impressive study, researchers developed 30-second television spots in which teen actors conveyed the risks of smoking marijuana, such as its effects on people's relationships, level of motivation, and judgment (Palmgreen et al., 2001). The ads were shown for 4-month intervals at different times in two similar communities—Fayette County, Kentucky, and Knox County, Tennessee. The researchers interviewed randomly chosen teenagers in both communities and assessed their attitudes and use of marijuana during the previous 30 days.

The ads had no detectable effect among teenagers who were low in sensation seeking, which is a personality trait having to do with how much people are attracted to novel, emotionally exciting activities. These people did not use marijuana much to begin with, so we would not expect the public service ads to change their behavior. Among the teenagers who were high in sensation seeking, however, the ads had a definite impact. When the ads were shown in Fayette County but not Knox County, the percentage of Fayette teenagers who reported using marijuana in the preceding 30 days dropped from about 38% to 28%. The percentage of Knox County teenagers who said they used marijuana increased during this same time period. When the ads were shown in Knox County, reported marijuana use also dropped by about 10%. These drops were not huge; it is not as if every teenager who saw the ads decided against smoking marijuana. Undoubtedly, some teenagers never saw the ads, and many who did were unaffected. From a public health perspective, however, a 10% drop is impressive, providing some hope for the success of media campaigns that promote healthier behavior.

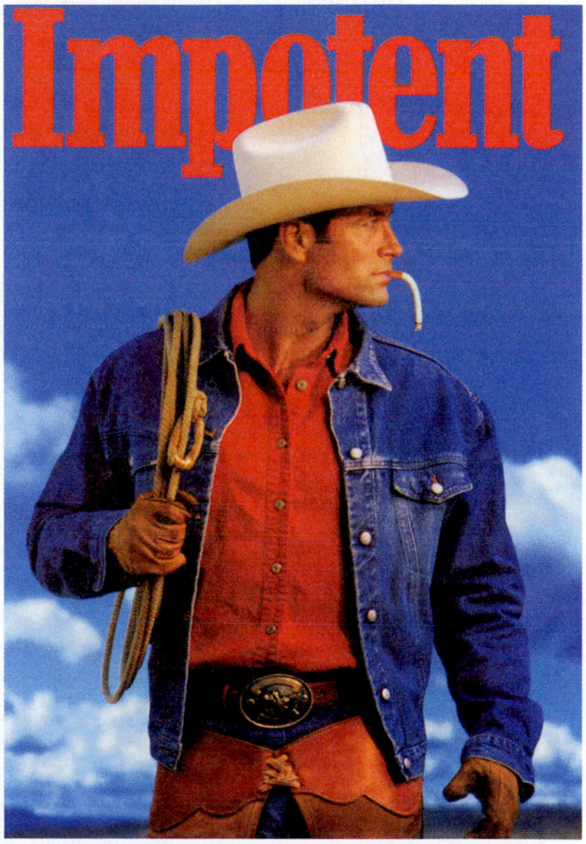

A recent meta-analysis showed that public campaigns to reduce drug use can work. Do you think this ad is effective, based on what you have read in this chapter?

The Power of Advertising

A curious thing about advertising is that most people think it works on everyone but themselves (Wilson & Brekke, 1994). People typically comment, "There is no harm in watching commercials. Some of them are fun, and they don't have much influence on me." Are they right? This is an important question for social psychology, because most of the research on attitudes and behavior we have discussed so far was conducted in the laboratory with college students. As we saw at the beginning of the chapter, each of us is confronted with hundreds of attempts to change our attitudes every day, in the form of advertisements. Do these ads really work, or are companies wasting the billions of dollars a year they are spending on advertising?

You can tell the ideals of a nation by its advertisements.
—George Norman Douglas, *South Wind*, 1917

It turns out that people are influenced by advertisements more than they think (Abraham & Lodish, 1990; Capella, Webster, & Kinard, 2011; Ryan, 1991; Wells, 1997; Wilson, Houston, & Meyers, 1998). The best evidence that advertising works comes from studies using what are called *split cable market tests.* Advertisers work in conjunction with cable television companies and grocery stores, showing a target commercial to a randomly selected group of people. They keep track of what people buy by giving potential consumers special ID cards that are scanned at checkout counters; thus, they can tell whether people who saw the commercial for ScrubaDub laundry detergent actually buy more ScrubaDub—the best measure of advertising effectiveness. The results of over 300 split cable market tests indicate that advertising does work, particularly for new products (Lodish et al., 1995).

How Advertising Works

How does advertising work, and what types of ads work best? The answers follow from our earlier discussion of attitude change. If advertisers are trying to change an affectively based attitude, then, as we have seen, it is best to fight emotions with emotions. Many advertisements take the emotional approach—for example, ads for different brands of soft drinks. Given that different brands of colas are not all that different, many people do not base their purchasing decisions on the objective qualities of the different brands. Consequently, soda advertisements do not stress facts and figures. As one advertising executive noted, "The thing about soda commercials is that they actually have nothing to say" ("Battle for Your Brain," 1991). Instead of presenting facts, soft drink ads play to people's emotions, trying to associate feelings of excitement, youth, energy, and sexual attractiveness with the brand.

Watch on MyPsychLab
To learn more about how psychologists study advertising, watch the MyPsychLab video ***Social Influence: Robert Cialdini.***

If people's attitudes are more cognitively based, we need to ask an additional question: How personally relevant is the issue? Consider, for example, the problem of heartburn. This is not a topic that evokes strong emotions and values in most people—it is more cognitively based. To people who suffer from frequent heartburn, however, the topic clearly has direct personal relevance. In this case, the best way to change people's attitudes is to use logical, fact-based arguments: Convince people that your product will reduce heartburn the best or the fastest and people will buy it (Chaiken, 1987; Petty & Cacioppo, 1986).

What if you are dealing with a cognitively based attitude that is not of direct personal relevance to people? For example, what if you are trying to sell a heartburn medicine to people who experience heartburn only every now and then and do not consider it a big deal? Here you have a problem, because people are unlikely to pay close attention to your advertisement. You might succeed in changing their attitudes via the peripheral route, such as by having attractive movie stars endorse your product. The problem with this, as we have seen, is that attitude change triggered by simple peripheral cues is not long lasting (Chaiken, 1987; Petty & Cacioppo, 1986). So if you have a product that does not trigger people's emotions and is not directly relevant to their everyday lives, you are in trouble.

But don't give up. The trick is to *make* your product personally relevant. Let's take a look at some actual ad campaigns to see how this is done. Consider the case of Gerald Lambert, who early in the twentieth century inherited a company that made a surgical antiseptic used to treat throat infections—Listerine. Seeking a wider market for his product, Lambert decided to promote it as a mouthwash. The only problem was that no one at the time used a mouthwash or even knew what one was. So having invented the cure, Lambert invented the disease. Look at the ad for Listerine, which appeared in countless magazines over the years. Even though today we find this ad incredibly sexist, at the time it successfully played on people's fears about social rejection and failure. The phrase "Often a bridesmaid, never a bride" became one of the most famous in the history of advertising. In a few cleverly chosen words, it succeeded in making a problem—halitosis—personally relevant to millions of people.

Often a bridesmaid...
never a bride!
Janice is a familiar type. She's popular with the girls . . . attractive to men *for a while*. Men seem serious—then just courteous—finally, oblivious. Halitosis (unpleasant breath) is a roadblock to romance. And the tragedy is, you're never aware that you're offending!
The most common cause of bad breath is germs . . . Listerine kills germs by millions
And why should anyone risk halitosis when Listerine Antiseptic ends it so quickly? Germs—which ferment the proteins always present in your mouth—are the most common cause of bad breath. The more you reduce these germs, the longer your breath stays sweeter. Listerine kills germs on contact . . . by millions.
Tooth paste can't kill germs the way Listerine does
Tooth paste can't kill germs the way Listerine does, because no tooth paste is antiseptic. Listerine IS antiseptic. That's why Listerine stops bad breath four times better than tooth paste. Gargle Listerine full-strength every morning, every night, before every date!
THE MOST WIDELY USED ANTISEPTIC IN THE WORLD!
LISTERINE ANTISEPTIC...STOPS BAD BREATH
4 times better than tooth paste

This ad is one of the most famous in the history of advertising. Although today it is easy to see how sexist and offensive it is, when it appeared in the 1930s it succeeded in making a problem (bad breath) personally relevant by playing on people's fears and insecurities about personal relationships. Can you think of contemporary ads that try to raise similar fears?

Subliminal Advertising: A Form of Mind Control?

In September 2000, during the heat of the U.S. presidential campaign between George W. Bush and Al Gore, a man in Seattle was watching a political advertisement on television. At first the ad looked like a run-of-the-mill political spot in which an announcer praised the benefits of George W. Bush's prescription drug plan and criticized Al Gore's plan. But the viewer thought that he noticed something odd. He videotaped the ad the next time it ran and played it back at a slow speed, and sure enough, he *had* noticed something unusual. As the announcer said, "The Gore prescription plan: Bureaucrats decide … ," the word RATS flashed on the screen very quickly—for one thirtieth of a second at normal viewing speed. The alert viewer notified officials in the Gore campaign, who quickly contacted the press. Soon the country was abuzz about a possible attempt by the Bush campaign to use subliminal messages to create a negative impression of Al Gore. The Bush campaign denied that anyone had deliberately inserted the word RATS, claiming that it was "purely accidental" (Berke, 2000).

The RATS incident was neither the first nor the last controversy over the use of **subliminal messages**, defined as words or pictures that are not consciously perceived but may influence people's judgments, attitudes, and behaviors. In the late 1950s, James Vicary supposedly flashed the messages "Drink Coca-Cola" and "Eat popcorn" during a commercial movie and claimed that sales at the concession counter skyrocketed (according to some reports, Vicary made up these claims; Weir, 1984). Wilson Bryan Key (1973, 1989) has written several best-selling books on hidden persuasion techniques, which claim that advertisers routinely implant sexual messages in print advertisements, such as the word *sex* in the ice cubes of an ad for gin, and male and female genitalia in everything from pats of butter to the icing in an ad for cake mix. Key (1973) argues that these images are not consciously perceived but put people in a good mood and make them pay more attention to the advertisement. More recently, gambling casinos in Canada removed a brand of slot machines after it was revealed that the machines flashed the winning symbols on every spin, at a speed too fast for the players to see consciously (Benedetti, 2007).

Subliminal Messages
Words or pictures that are not consciously perceived but may nevertheless influence people's judgments, attitudes, and behaviors

During the 2000 U.S. presidential race, George W. Bush aired a television ad about his prescription drug plan, during which the word RATS was flashed on the screen for a split second. Do subliminal messages like this one have any effect on people's attitudes?

Subliminal messages are not just visual; they can be auditory as well. There is a large market for audiotapes that contain subliminal messages to help people lose weight, stop smoking, improve their study habits, raise their self-esteem, and even shave a few strokes off their golf scores. But are subliminal messages effective? Do they really make us more likely to buy consumer products or help us lose weight and stop smoking? Most members of the public believe that subliminal messages can shape their attitudes and behaviors, even though they are not aware that the messages have entered their minds (Zanot, Pincus, & Lamp, 1983). Are they right?

Debunking the Claims About Subliminal Advertising Few of the proponents of subliminal advertising have conducted controlled studies to back up their claims. Fortunately, many studies of subliminal perception have been conducted, allowing us to evaluate the sometimes outlandish claims that are made. Simply stated, there is no evidence that the types of subliminal messages encountered in everyday life have any influence on people's behavior. Hidden commands do not cause us to line up and buy popcorn any more than we normally do, and the subliminal commands on self-help tapes do not (unfortunately!) help us quit smoking or lose weight (Brannon & Brock, 1994; Broyles, 2006; Nelson, 2008; Pratkanis, 1992; Theus, 1994; Trappey, 1996). For example, one study randomly assigned people to listen to a subliminal self-help tape designed to improve people's memory or to one designed to raise their self-esteem (Greenwald et al., 1991). Neither of the tapes had any effect on people's memory or self-esteem. Even so, participants were convinced that the tapes had worked, which explains why people spend millions of dollars on subliminal self-help tapes each year. It would be nice if we could all improve ourselves simply by listening to music with subliminal messages, but this study and others like it show that subliminal tapes are no better at solving our problems than patent medicines or visits to an astrologist.

PEOPLE HAVE BEEN TRYING TO FIND THE BREASTS IN THESE ICE CUBES SINCE 1957.
The advertising industry is sometimes charged with sneaking seductive little pictures into ads.
Supposedly, these pictures can get you to buy a product without your even seeing them.
Consider the photograph above. According to some people, there's a pair of female breasts hidden in the patterns of light refracted by the ice cubes.
Well, if you really searched you probably *could* see the breasts. For that matter, you could also see Millard Fillmore, a stuffed pork chop and a 1946 Dodge.
The point is that so-called "subliminal advertising" simply doesn't exist. Overactive imaginations, however, most certainly do.
So if anyone claims to see breasts in that drink up there, they aren't in the ice cubes.
They're in the eye of the beholder.
ADVERTISING
ANOTHER WORD FOR FREEDOM OF CHOICE.
American Association of Advertising Agencies

There is no scientific evidence that implanting sexual images in advertising boosts sales of a product. In fact, subliminal advertising is rarely used and is outlawed in many countries. The public is very aware of the subliminal technique, however—so much so that advertisers sometimes poke fun at subliminal messages in their ads.

Laboratory Evidence for Subliminal Influence You may have noticed that we said that subliminal messages don't work when "encountered in everyday life." There *is* evidence that people can be influenced by subliminal messages under carefully controlled laboratory conditions (Dijksterhuis, Aarts, & Smith, 2005; Verwijmeren et al., 2011). In one study, for example, Dutch college students saw subliminal flashes of the words "Lipton Ice" (a brand of ice tea) or a nonsense word made of the same letters (Karremans, Stroebe, & Claus, 2006). All the students were then asked whether they would prefer Lipton Ice or a brand of Dutch mineral water if they were offered a drink at that moment. If students were not thirsty at the time, the subliminal flashes had no effect on their drink preference. But if students were thirsty, those who had seen the subliminal flashes of "Lipton Ice" were significantly more likely to choose that drink than were students who had seen subliminal flashes of the nonsense word. Several other laboratory studies have found similar effects of pictures or words flashed at subliminal levels (e.g., Bargh & Pietromonaco, 1982; Bermeitinger et al., 2009; Dijksterhuis & Aarts, 2002; Strahan, Spencer, & Zanna, 2002).

Does this mean that advertisers will figure out how to use subliminal messages in everyday advertising? Maybe, but it hasn't happened yet. To get subliminal effects, researchers have to make sure that the illumination of the room is just right, that people are seated just the right distance from a viewing screen, and that nothing else is occurring to distract people as the subliminal stimuli are flashed. Further, even in the laboratory, there is no evidence that subliminal messages can get people to act counter to their wishes, values, or personalities (Neuberg, 1988). Thus, it is highly unlikely that the word *rats* in the Bush campaign ad converted people from Gore supporters to Bush supporters.

Advertising, Cultural Stereotypes, and Social Behavior

Ironically, the hoopla surrounding subliminal messages has obscured the fact that ads are more powerful when people consciously perceive them. We have seen plenty of evidence that the ads people perceive consciously every day can substantially influence their behavior even though the ads do not contain subliminal messages. It is interesting that people fear subliminal advertising more than regular advertising when it is regular advertising that is more powerful (Wilson, Gilbert, & Wheatley, 1998). The following Try It! will help you see whether this is true of people you know.

Further, advertising influences more than just our consumer attitudes. Advertisements transmit cultural stereotypes in their words and images, subtly linking products with desired images (e.g., beer ads linking beer consumption with sex). Advertisements can also reinforce and perpetuate stereotypical ways of thinking about social groups. Until recently, ads almost always showed groups of whites (token individuals of color are now mixed into the group), couples that are heterosexual, families that are traditional (with a mom, dad, son, and daughter), and so on. You would think that divorced families, the middle-aged and the elderly, people of color, lesbians and gay men, the physically disabled, and others just didn't exist.

TRY IT! Advertising and Mind Control

Here is an exercise on people's beliefs about the power of advertising that you can try on your friends. Ask about 10 friends the following questions—preferably friends who have not had a course in social psychology! See how accurate their beliefs are about the effects of different kinds of advertising.

1. Do you think that you are influenced by subliminal messages in advertising? (Define *subliminal messages* for your friends as words or pictures that are not consciously perceived but nevertheless supposedly influence people's judgments, attitudes, and behaviors.)
2. Do you think that you are influenced by everyday advertisements that you perceive consciously, such as television ads for laundry detergent and painkillers?
3. Suppose you had a choice to listen to one of two speeches that argued against a position you believe in, such as whether marijuana should be legalized. In Speech A, a person presents several arguments against your position. In Speech B, all of the arguments are presented subliminally—you will not perceive anything consciously. Which speech would you rather listen to: A or B?

Tally the results here.

Question 1	Question 2	Question 3
Yes:	Yes:	Yes:
No:	No:	No:

Turn to page XX to see if your results match those of actual studies. Show off your knowledge to your friends. Ask them why they are more wary of subliminal messages than everyday advertising when it is everyday ads and not subliminal messages that change people's minds. Why do *you* think that people are most afraid of the kinds of ads that are least effective? What does this say about people's awareness of their own thought processes?

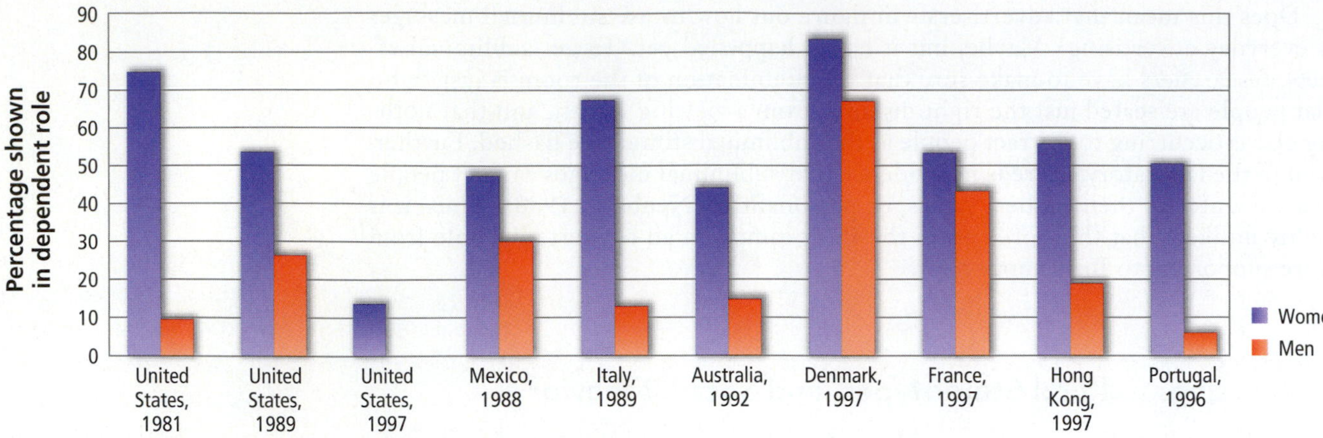

FIGURE 7.9

Portrayals of Women and Men in Television Advertising

The ways in which women and men are portrayed in television commercials have been examined throughout the world. In every country, women were more likely to be portrayed in powerless, dependent roles than men were.

(Based on data in Furnham & Mak, 1999)

Gender stereotypes are particularly pervasive in advertising imagery. Men are doers; women are observers. Several studies have examined television commercials throughout the world and coded how men and women are portrayed. As seen in Figure 7.9, one review found that women were more likely to be portrayed in dependent roles (that is, not in a position of power but dependent on someone else) than men in every country that was examined (Furnham & Mak, 1999). More recent studies have found that these stereotypical views of women persist in advertising (Conley & Ramsey, 2011; Eisend, 2010).

Well, you might think, television commercials reflect the stereotypes of a society but play little role in shaping those stereotypes or influencing people's attitudes and behavior. Actually, the images conveyed in advertisements are far from harmless. As we will see in Chapter 8, a thin body style for women is glamorized in the media. The women shown in magazines, movies, and television programs are getting thinner all the time, are thinner than women in the actual population, and are often so thin that they would qualify for a diagnosis of anorexia (Fouts & Burggraf, 1999, 2000; Wiseman et al., 1992). The message to women and young girls? To be beautiful you must be thin. This message is hittinng home: Girls and women in America are becoming increasingly dissatisfied with the way they look. In one survey, nearly half of college women said they were unhappy with their bodies (Bearman, Presnell, & Martinez, 2006; Monteath & McCabe, 1997), and this dissatisfaction was unrelated to the women's *actual* body size (Grabe & Hyde, 2006). What's worse, body dissatisfaction has been shown to be a risk factor for eating disorders, low self-esteem, and depression (Slevec & Tiggemann, 2011; Stice et al., 2011). But is there a causal connection between the way women are depicted in the media and women's feelings about their own bodies? It appears that there is. Experimental studies show that women who are randomly assigned to look at media decpictions of thin women show a dip in their body self-image (Grabe, Ward, & Hyde, 2008). In Chapter 8 we will see that the media has influenced men's images of their bodies as well. In this chapter we have seen that the media can have powerful effects on people's attitudes, both directly (e.g., advertisements that target our attitudes toward a particular product) and indirectly (e.g., the ways in which women and men are portrayed).

Watch on **MyPsychLab**

To learn more about media influence on attitudes about our bodies, watch the MyPsychLab video ***Body Image Part 1: Kianna, 12 Years Old.***

USE IT!

To what extent do you think your attitudes and behavior are shaped by advertising? Imagine that you are watching television and an ad comes on for a particular brand of pain relief medicine. Or suppose that instead of seeing an ad for this brand, you see it as part of a product placement in a TV show (maybe you see Randy Jackson, a judge on *American Idol*, take a sip from his Coca-Cola cup). It might seem far-fetched that seeing an ad or a product placed within a show can dramatically influence what you choose to buy the next time you are at the drug store, but after reading this chapter, can you be so sure? Assuming that you do not want to be at the mercy of the advertising industry, what steps might you take to resist the impact of advertising? Think back to the section on resisting persuasive messages (pages 19–22): Are there strategies you could adopt to avoid being influenced? Of course, you might not think it is worth the effort to muster your defenses against ads for pain relievers. But what about attempts to get you to vote for a particular political candidate or to develop positive attitudes toward cigarettes? None of us, of course, is an automaton that marches completely to the tune of Madison Avenue. It is worth thinking, however, about how much we want to be influenced by advertising and steps we can take to avoid that influence.

Summary

What are the different kinds of attitudes, and on what are they based?

- **The Nature and Origin of Attitudes** An **attitude** is a person's enduring evaluation of people, objects, and ideas.
  - **Where Do Attitudes Come From?** Although some attitudes may have a weak genetic basis, they are based mostly on our experiences. **Cognitively based attitudes** are based mostly on people's beliefs about the properties of the attitude object. **Affectively based attitudes** are based more on people's emotions and values; they can be created through **classical conditioning** or **operant conditioning**. **Behaviorally based attitudes** are based on people's actions toward the attitude object.
  - **Explicit Versus Implicit Attitudes** Once an attitude develops, it can exist at two levels. **Explicit attitudes** are ones we consciously endorse and can easily report. **Implicit attitudes** are involuntary, uncontrollable, and at times unconscious.

How can external factors such as social influence and internal factors such as emotions and confidence change attitudes?

- **How Do Attitudes Change?** Attitudes often change in response to social influence.
  - **Changing Attitudes by Changing Behavior: Cognitive Dissonance Theory Revisited** One way that attitudes change is when people engage in counterattitudinal advocacy for low external justification. When this occurs, people find internal justification for their behavior, bringing their attitudes in line with their behavior.
  - **Persuasive Communications and Attitude Change** Attitudes can also change in response to a **persuasive communication**. According to the **Yale Attitude Change approach**, the effectiveness of a persuasive communication depends on aspects of the communicator, or source of the message; aspects of the message itself (e.g., its content); and aspects of the audience. The **elaboration likelihood model** specifies when people are persuaded more by the strength of the arguments in the communication and when they are persuaded more by surface characteristics. When people have both the motivation and ability to pay attention to a message, they take the **central route to persuasion**, where they pay close attention to the strength of the arguments. When they have low motivation or ability, they take the **peripheral route to persuasion**, where they are swayed by surface characteristics, such as the attractiveness of the speaker.
  - **Emotion and Attitude Change** Emotions influence attitude change in a number of ways. **Fear-arousing communications** can cause lasting attitude change if a moderate amount of fear is aroused and people believe they will be reassured by the content of the message. Emotions can also be used as heuristics to gauge one's attitude; if people feel good in the presence of an object, they often infer that they like it, even if those good feelings were caused by something else. Finally, the effectiveness of persuasive communications also depends on the type of attitude people have. Appeals to emotion and social identity work best if the attitude is based on emotion and social identity.
  - **Confidence in One's Thoughts and Attitude Change** People's confidence in their thoughts about an attitude object affects how much they will influenced by a persuasive communication. People's confidence can be affected by such things as whether they are nodding or shaking their head while listening to a persuasive message.

What are some strategies for resisting persuasive messages?

- **Resisting Persuasive Messages** Researchers have studied a number of ways by which people can avoid being influenced by persuasive messages.

- **Attitude Inoculation** One way is to expose people to small doses of arguments against their position, which makes it easier for them to defend themselves against a persuasive message they hear later.
- **Being Alert to Product Placement** Increasingly, advertisers are paying to have their products shown prominently in TV shows and movies. Forewarning people about attempts to change their attitudes, such as product placement, makes them less susceptible to attitude change.
- **Resisting Peer Pressure** Teaching kids how to resist peer pressure can make them less vulnerable to it.
- **When Persuasion Attempts Boomerang: Reactance Theory** According to **reactance theory**, people experience an unpleasant state called reactance when their freedom of choice is threatened. Attempts to manage people's attitudes can backfire if they make people feel that their choices are limited.

Under what conditions do attitudes predict behavior?

- **When Do Attitudes Predict Behavior?** Under what conditions will people's attitudes dictate how they actually behave?
  - **Predicting Spontaneous Behaviors** Attitudes predict spontaneous behaviors only when they are relatively accessible. **Attitude accessibility** refers to the strength of the association between an object and an evaluation of it.
  - **Predicting Deliberative Behaviors** According to the **theory of planned behavior**, deliberative (nonspontaneous) behaviors are a function of people's attitude toward the specific act in question, subjective norms (people's beliefs about how others view the behavior in question), and how much people believe they can control the behavior.

How does advertising change people's attitudes? What is the role of subliminal messages and cultural stereotypes in advertising?

- **The Power of Advertising** Advertising has been found to be quite effective at changing people's attitudes, as indicated by split cable market tests, where advertisers show different advertisements to different samples of cable subscribers and then look at what they buy.
  - **How Advertising Works** Advertising works by targeting affectively based attitudes with emotions, by targeting cognitively based attitudes with facts, and by making a product seem personally relevant.
  - **Subliminal Advertising: A Form of Mind Control?** There is no evidence that subliminal messages in advertisements have any influence on people's behavior. Subliminal influences have been found, however, under controlled laboratory conditions.
  - **Advertising, Cultural Stereotypes, and Social Behavior** In addition to changing people's attitudes toward commercial products, advertisements often transmit cultural stereotypes.

Chapter 7 Test

Study and Review on MyPsychLab

1. All of the following are true about attitudes *except* one. Which one is false?
   a. Attitudes are evaluations of people, objects, and ideas.
   b. Attitudes are related to our temperament and personality.
   c. Attitudes rarely change over time.
   d. Attitudes can be changed with persuasive communications.
   e. Under the right conditions attitudes predict people's behavior.

2. Paige wants to buy a puppy. She does some research and decides to buy an English springer spaniel rather than a Great Dane because they are smaller, more active, and good with children. Which type of attitude influenced her decision?
   a. affectively based attitude
   b. behaviorally based attitude
   c. explicitly based attitude
   d. cognitively based attitude

3. People will be most likely to change their attitudes about smoking if an antismoking advertisement
   a. uses extremely graphic pictures of how smoke can harm the body and warns of the risks of smoking.
   b. gives people subliminal messages about the risks of smoking as well as recommendations of how to quit.
   c. uses graphic pictures of the damages of smoking on the body and then provides specific recommendations on how to quit smoking.
   d. uses success stories of how people quit smoking.

4. Emilia would be most likely to pay attention to facts about the danger of AIDS during a school assembly *and* remember the facts for a long time if
   a. the speaker emphasized statistical information about AIDS throughout the world.
   b. the speaker emphasized how the disease has spread in her community and there isn't anything distracting Emilia from listening.
   c. the speaker emphasized how the disease has spread in her community and at the same time Emilia's best friend is whispering to her about a big party that weekend.
   d. the speaker is a nationally known expert on AIDS.

5. According to reactance theory, what of the following public service messages would be *least* likely to get people to wear seatbelts?
   a. "Please wear your seatbelt every time you drive."
   b. "Wear your seatbelt to save lives."
   c. "It's the law—you must wear your seatbelt."
   d. "Buckle up your children—you might save their lives."

6. You are trying to sell a new electronic toothbrush at the airport to busy, distracted travelers. Which of the following strategies is *least* likely to be successful at getting people to buy a toothbrush?

a. Make up a flier that gives convincing reasons why the toothbrush is so good.
b. Make a large sign that says, "9 out of 10 dentists recommend this toothbrush!"
c. Put up a large banner featuring a picture of your friend who looks like Brad Pitt posing with the toothbrush.
d. Stop people and say, "Do you know that this is the toothbrush that is used the most by Hollywood stars?"

7. Under which of the following conditions would people be most likely to vote for a political candidate? They

a. like the candidate's policies but have negative feelings toward him or her.
b. know little about the candidate's policies but have positive feelings toward him or her.
c. see subliminal ads supporting the candidate on national television.
d. see television ads supporting the candidate while they are distracted by their children.

8. All of the following are examples of ways to resist persuasion *except*

a. making people immune to change of opinions by initially exposing them to small doses of arguments against their position.
b. warning people about advertising techniques such as product placement.
c. forbidding people to buy a product.
d. role-playing using milder versions of real-life social pressures.

9. On a survey, Milo reports that he agrees with wearing a seatbelt. According to the theory of planned behavior, what else will predict whether Milo will wear a seatbelt on a given day?

a. He generally agrees that safe driving is important.
b. His best friend, Trevor, was in the car and he also wore a seatbelt.
c. His attitude toward seatbelts was not very accessible.
d. Milo believes that it is hard to remember to wear his seatbelt.

10. Suppose that while you are watching a film at a movie theater the words "Drink Coke" are flashed on the screen at speeds too quick for you to see consciously. According to research on subliminal perception, which of the following is most true?

a. You will get up and buy a Coke, but only if you are thirsty.
b. You will get up and buy a Coke, but only if you prefer Coke to Pepsi.
c. You will be *less* likely to get up and buy a Coke.
d. You will be no more likely to buy a Coke than if the subliminal messages were not flashed.

Answer Key

1-c, 2-d, 3-c, 4-b, 5-c,
6-a, 7-b, 8-c, 9-b, 10-d

Scoring the TRY IT! exercises

Page 176

Scoring: First, reverse your responses to items 3, 4, 5, 7, 8, 9, 12, 16, and 17. Do so as follows: If you gave a 1 to these questions, change it to a 5; if you gave a 2, change it to a 4; if you gave a 3, leave it the same; if you gave a 4, change it to a 2; if you gave a 5, change it to a 1. Then add up your answers to all 18 questions.

People who are high in the need for cognition score slightly higher in verbal intelligence but no higher in abstract reasoning. And there are no gender differences in the need for cognition.

Page 191

Question 1: Wilson, Gilbert, and Wheatley (1998) found that 80% of college students preferred not to receive a subliminal message because it might influence them in an undesirable way.

Question 2: Wilson, Gilbert, and Wheatley (1998) found that only 28% of college students preferred not to receive a regular everyday TV ad because it might influence them in an undesirable way.

Question 3: When Wilson, Houston, and Meyers (1998) asked college students to choose to listen to the type of speech they thought would influence them the least, 69% chose the regular speech and 31% chose the subliminal speech. Ironically, it was the regular speech that changed people's minds the most.

8 Conformity

Influencing Behavior

On April 9, 2004, a man called a McDonald's restaurant in Mount Washington, Kentucky, and identified himself as a police detective to the assistant manager, Donna Jean Summers, 51. He told her she had a problem: One of her employees had stolen from the restaurant. He said he had talked to McDonald's corporate headquarters and to the store manager, whom he named correctly. The policeman gave Ms. Summers a rough description of the perpetrator, a teenage female, and she identified one of her employees (whom we will call Susan, to protect her identity). The police detective told the assistant manager that she needed to search Susan immediately for the stolen money, or else Susan would be arrested, taken to jail, and searched there (Wolfson, 2005).

You might be thinking that this all sounds a bit odd. Ms. Summers said later that she was initially confused, but the caller was very authoritative and presented his information in a convincing manner. And, after all, he was a policeman. We're supposed to obey the police. During the phone call, Ms. Summers thought she heard police radios in the background.

So she called Susan into a small room and locked the door. Susan was 18 and had been a perfect employee for several months. The policeman on the phone told Ms. Summers what to do and what to say. Following his instructions, she ordered Susan to take off her clothing, one item at a time, until she was standing naked. Ms. Summers put all the clothes in a bag and put the bag outside the room, as instructed by the caller. Susan was now crying, fearful of the allegations and humiliated by the strip search. It was 5:00 P.M. Unfortunately for Susan, the next 4 hours would involve even further degradation and sexual abuse, all because of orders given by the "policeman" on the phone (Barrouquere, 2006).

Susan was not the first fast-food employee to be victimized in this manner. Phone calls to restaurant managers, ordering them to abuse their employees, had been occurring around the country since 1999. It just took law enforcement some time to put the whole picture together, given that the perpetrator was using a calling card, which is difficult to trace. In all, managers of 70 restaurants, representing a dozen different chains in 32 states, received these phone calls and obeyed the caller's instructions (Barrouquere, 2006; Gray, 2004; Wolfson, 2005). The caller, as you have probably guessed, was not a policeman, but was perpetrating a horrible hoax.

Susan had been standing naked in the small, locked room for an hour. Ms. Summers needed to get back to supervising the cooking area, so the "policeman" told her to find someone else to guard Susan. She called her fiancé, Walter Nix, Jr., 42, who agreed to come to the restaurant. Mr. Nix locked himself into the room with the naked and increasingly terrified teenager. At this point, the events become even more bizarre and disturbing. Mr. Nix also believed the caller was who he said he was, and Mr. Nix proved even more obedient. In a series of escalating demands over 3 hours, the "detective" told Mr. Nix to force Susan to acquiesce to various sexual demands. The caller also talked directly to Susan, threatening her with what would happen if she didn't obey. "I was scared because they were a higher authority to me. I was scared for my safety because I thought I was in trouble with the law," she said (Wolfson, 2005, p. 3).

FOCUS QUESTIONS

- What is conformity and why does it occur?
- How does informational social influence motivate people to conform?
- How does normative social influence motivate people to conform?
- How can we use our knowledge of social influence for positive purposes?
- What have studies demonstrated about people's willingness to obey someone in a position of authority?

Hours later, the caller told Mr. Nix to replace himself with another man. Thomas Simms, a 58-year-old employee, was called into the room. As he put it later, he knew immediately "something is not right about this" (Wolfson, 2005, p. 7). He refused to obey the man on the phone. He called in Ms. Summers and convinced her something was wrong. "I knew then I had been had," she said. "I lost it. I begged [Susan] for forgiveness. I was almost hysterical" (Wolfson, 2005, p. 7). At this point, the "detective" hung up the phone. Susan's abuse was finally over.

After an investigation that involved police detectives in several states, a Florida man, David R. Stewart, 38, was arrested and charged as the telephone hoaxer. Married and the father of five, Stewart worked as a prison guard and was formerly a security guard and volunteer sheriff's deputy. At his trial in 2006, with only circumstantial evidence against him, the jury returned a verdict of not guilty. There have been no further fast-food hoax phone calls (ABC News, 2007). The assistant manager, Donna Summers, and her (no longer) fiancé, Walter Nix Jr., pleaded guilty to various charges. Ms. Summers was sentenced to probation, and Mr. Nix was sentenced to 5 years in prison. Susan, who now suffers from panic attacks, anxiety, and depression, sued the McDonald's corporation for failing to warn employees nationally after the first hoaxes occurred at their restaurants. She was awarded $6.1 million in damages by a Kentucky jury (Barrouquere, 2006; Neil, 2007; Wolfson, 2005).

In one of the saddest comments on this event, Susan's therapist said that Susan followed orders that night because her experience with adults "has been to do what she is told, because good girls do what they are told" (Wolfson, 2005). Indeed, every day people try to influence us to do what they want, sometimes through direct requests and sometimes through more-subtle processes. The most powerful form of social influence produces obedience and occurs when an authority figure gives an order. The fast-food restaurant hoax shows us how overly obedient people can be. A more subtle form of social influence involves conformity. Here, others indicate to us less directly what is appropriate, and we come to sense that it is in our best interest to go along with them. In this chapter, we will focus on the potentially positive and negative effects of these social influence processes.

Conformity: When and Why

Which one of the two quotations on the left do you find more appealing? Which one describes your immediate reaction to the word *conformity*? We wouldn't be surprised if you preferred the second quotation. American culture stresses the importance of not conforming (Hofstede, 1986; Kim & Markus, 1999; Kitayama et al., 2009; Markus, Kitayama, & Heiman, 1996). We picture ourselves as a nation of rugged individualists, people who think for themselves, stand up for the underdog, and go against the tide to fight for what we think is right. This cultural self-image has been shaped by the manner in which our nation was founded, by our system of government, and by our society's historical experience with western expansion—the "taming" of the Wild West (Kitayama et al., 2006; Turner, 1932).

Do as most do, and [people] will speak well of thee.

—Thomas Fuller

It were not best that we should all think alike; it is difference of opinion that makes horse races.

—Mark Twain

American mythology has celebrated the rugged individualist in many ways. For example, one of the longest-running and most successful advertising campaigns in American history featured the "Marlboro Man." As far back as 1955, the photograph of a cowboy alone on the range was an archetypal image. It also sold a lot of cigarettes. Clearly, it told us something about ourselves that we want and like to hear: that we make up our own minds; that we're not spineless, weak conformists (Cialdini, 2005; Pronin, Berger, & Molouki, 2007). More recently, consider the example of Apple Computer, currently the most valuable publicly traded company in the world (Rooney, 2012). For several years, Apple's advertising slogan captured a similar sentiment of simply stated nonconformity: "Think different."

But are we, in fact, nonconforming creatures? Are the decisions we make always based on what we think, or do we sometimes use other people's behavior to help us decide what to do? In spite of Apple's advertising telling customers to "think different," take a careful look around the lecture hall next time you're in class and count how many laptops in the room share the identical glowing Apple logo. The computer of the nonconformist is now everywhere.

On a far more sobering note, as we saw in Chapter 6, the mass suicide of the Heaven's Gate cult members suggests that people sometimes conform in extreme and astonishing ways—even when making such a crucial decision as whether or not to take their own lives. But, you might argue, surely this is an extremely unusual case. Perhaps the followers of Marshall Applewhite were disturbed people who were somehow predisposed to do what a charismatic leader told them to do. There is, however, another, more chilling possibility: Maybe most of us would have acted the same way had we been exposed to the same long-standing, powerful conformity pressures as were the members of Heaven's Gate. According to this view, almost anyone would have conformed in these same extreme circumstances.

Under strong social pressure, individuals will conform to the group, even when this means doing something immoral. In 2004, American soldiers' degrading abuse of Iraqis held at the Abu Ghraib prison sparked an international scandal and a great deal of soul-searching back home. In this now-infamous photograph, Specialist Charles Graner flashes a thumbs-up sign over the dead body of an Iraqi prisoner. Why did the soldiers humiliate their captives (and seem to enjoy themselves as they did it)? As you read this chapter, you will see how the social-influence pressures of conformity and obedience can cause decent people to commit indecent acts.

If this statement is true, we should be able to find other situations in which people, put under strong social pressures, conformed to a surprising degree. And, in fact, we can. For example, in 1961, activists in the American civil rights movement incorporated Mohandas Gandhi's principles of nonviolent protest into their demonstrations to end segregation. They trained their "Freedom Riders" (so named because they boarded buses and disobeyed "back of the bus" seating rules) in the passive acceptance of violent treatment. Thousands of southern African Americans, joined by a smaller number of northern whites, many from college campuses, demonstrated against the segregationist laws of the South. In confrontation after confrontation, the civil rights activists reacted nonviolently as they were beaten, clubbed, hosed, whipped, raped, and even killed by southern sheriffs and police (Powledge, 1991; Nelson, 2010). Their powerful show of conformity to the ideal of nonviolent protest helped usher in a new era in America's fight for racial equality.

But just a few years later, social pressure resulted in a tragic rather than heroic course of events. On the morning of March 16, 1968, American soldiers in Vietnam boarded helicopters that would take them to the village of My Lai. One pilot radioed that he saw Vietcong soldiers below, and so the soldiers jumped off the helicopters, rifles blazing. They soon realized that the pilot was wrong—there were no enemy soldiers, only women, children, and elderly men cooking breakfast over small fires. Inexplicably, the leader of the platoon ordered one of the soldiers to kill the villagers. Other soldiers began firing too, and the carnage spread, ultimately ending with the deaths of 450 to 500 Vietnamese civilians (Hersh, 1970). Similar processes of social influence have been implicated in more-recent military atrocities, including the humiliation of Iraqi captives at the Abu Ghraib prison starting in 2003 (Hersh, 2004), the killing of thousands of Iraqi civilians and destruction of tens of thousands of houses in Fallujah in 2004 (Marqusee, 2005), and American soldiers urinating on the corpses of Taliban fighters in Afghanistan in 2011 (Martinez, 2012).

In all these examples, people found themselves caught in a web of social influence. In response, they changed their behavior and conformed to the expectations of others (O'Gorman, Wilson, & Miller, 2008). For social psychologists, this is the essence of **conformity**: changing one's behavior due to the real or imagined influence of others (Kiesler & Kiesler, 1969; Aarts & Dijksterhuis, 2003). As these examples show, the consequences of conformity can span a wide range, from usefulness and bravery to hysteria and tragedy. But why did these people conform? Some probably conformed because they did not know what to do in a confusing or unusual situation. The behavior of the people around them served as a cue as to how to respond, and they decided to act in a similar manner. Other people probably conformed because they did not wish to be ridiculed or punished for being different from everybody else. They chose to act the way the group expected so that they wouldn't be rejected or thought less of by group members. Let's see how each of these reasons for conforming operates.

Conformity

A change in one's behavior due to the real or imagined influence of other people

Informational Social Influence: The Need to Know What's "Right"

How should you address your psychology professor—as Dr. Berman, Professor Berman, Ms. Berman, or Patricia? How should you vote in the upcoming ballot referendum that would raise your tuition to cover expanded student services? Do you cut a piece of sushi or eat it whole? Did the scream you just heard in the hallway come from a person joking with friends or from the victim of a mugging?

In these and many other situations, we feel uncertain about what to think or how to act. We simply don't know enough to make a good or accurate choice. Luckily, we have a powerful and useful source of knowledge available to us—the behavior of other people. Asking others what they think or watching what they do helps us reach a definition of the situation (Kelley, 1955; Thomas, 1928). When we subsequently act like everyone else, we are conforming, but this doesn't mean we are weak, spineless individuals with no self-reliance. Instead, the influence of other people leads us to conform because we see those people as a source of information to guide our behavior. We conform in such a way because we believe that others' interpretation of an ambiguous set of circumstances is more accurate than ours and will help us choose an appropriate course of action. This is called **informational social influence** (Cialdini, 2000; Cialdini & Goldstein, 2004; Deutsch & Gerard, 1955).

As an illustration of how other people can be a source of information, imagine that you are a participant in the following experiment by Muzafer Sherif (1936). In the first phase of the study, you are seated alone in a dark room and asked to focus your attention on a dot of light 15 feet away. The experimenter asks you to estimate in inches how far the light moves. You stare earnestly at the light and, yes, it moves a little. You say, "about 2 inches," though it is not easy to tell exactly. The light disappears and then comes back; you are asked to judge again. The light seems to move a little more this time, and you say, "4 inches." After several of these trials, the light seems to move about the same amount each time—about 2 to 4 inches.

> *"It's always best on these occasions to do what the mob do." "But suppose there are two mobs?" suggested Mr. Snodgrass. "Shout with the largest," replied Mr. Pickwick.*
>
> —Charles Dickens, *Pickwick Papers*

The interesting thing about this task is that the light was not actually moving at all. It looked as if it was moving because of a visual illusion called the autokinetic effect: If you stare at a bright light in a uniformly dark environment (e.g., a star on a dark night), the light will appear to waver back and forth. This occurs because you have no stable reference point with which to anchor the position of the light. The distance that the light appears to move varies from person to person but becomes consistent for each person over time. In Sherif's experiment, the subjects all arrived at their own stable estimate during the first phase of the study, but these estimates differed from person to person. Some people thought the light was moving only an inch or so; others thought it was moving as much as 10 inches.

Sherif chose the autokinetic effect because he wanted a situation that would be ambiguous—where the correct definition of the situation would be unclear to his participants. In the second phase of the experiment, a few days later, the participants were paired with two other people, each of whom had had the same prior experience alone with the light. Now the situation became a truly social one, as all three made their judgments out loud. Remember, the autokinetic effect is experienced differently by different people; some see a lot of movement and some see not much at all. After hearing their partners give judgments that were different from their own, what did people do?

Over the course of several trials, people reached a common estimate, and each member of the group conformed to that estimate. These results indicate that people were using each other as a source of information, coming to believe that the group estimate was the correct one (see Figure 8.1). An important feature of informational social influence is that it can lead to **private acceptance**, when people conform to the behavior of others because they genuinely believe that these other people are right.

Informational Social Influence

The influence of other people that leads us to conform because we see them as a source of information to guide our behavior; we conform because we believe that others' interpretation of an ambiguous situation is more correct than ours and will help us choose an appropriate course of action

Private Acceptance

Conforming to other people's behavior out of a genuine belief that what they are doing or saying is right

It might seem equally plausible that people publicly conformed to the group but privately maintained the belief that the light was moving only a small amount. For example, maybe someone privately believed that the light was moving 10 inches but

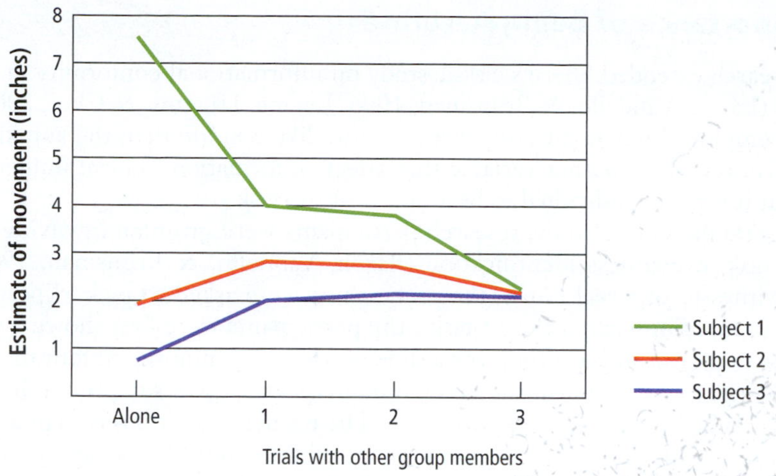

FIGURE 8.1

One Group's Judgments in Sherif's (1936) Autokinetic Studies

People estimated how far a point of light appeared to move in a dark room. When they saw the light by themselves, their estimates varied widely. When they were brought together in groups and heard other people announce their estimates, people conformed to the group's estimate of how much the light moved, adjusting their private beliefs based on the information other group members provided.

(Adapted from Sherif, 1936)

announced that it had moved 3 inches, the group estimate, to avoid standing out from the crowd or looking foolish. This would be a case of **public compliance**, conforming publicly without necessarily believing in what the group is saying or doing. Sherif cast doubt on this interpretation of his study, however, by asking people to judge the lights once more by themselves, after participating in groups. Even though they no longer had to worry about looking silly in front of other participants, they continued to give the answer the group had given earlier. One study even found that people still conformed to the group estimate when they participated individually a year later (Rohrer et al., 1954). These results suggest that people were relying on each other to define reality and came to privately accept the wisdom of the group estimate.

Public Compliance

Conforming to other people's behavior publicly without necessarily believing in what the other people are doing or saying.

The power of conformity to produce private acceptance has been demonstrated in several areas of life, including energy conservation. For example, Jessica Nolan and her colleagues (2008) gave a sample of California residents information urging them to conserve electricity in their homes. The household members received one of four messages. Three of these presented basic reasons to conserve: to protect the environment, to benefit society, or to save money. The fourth message contained information designed to promote conformity: The participants were told that the majority of their neighbors conserved electrical energy. The researchers then measured actual energy usage from the homes' electrical meters. They found that the fourth message, containing information about the behavior of one's neighbors, caused people to conserve significantly more energy than did the other three messages (Nolan et al., 2008). Similarly, Goldstein, Cialdini, and Griskevicius (2008) managed to increase hotel guests' compliance with the "reuse your bath towels and save energy" request, a widely used hotel management technique that hasn't always proved popular with guests. The researchers found that an informational sign in the bathroom, stating that the majority of guests in this room reuse their towels, was significantly more effective than the general appeal for help usually used by hotels ("Help save the environment"; Goldstein et al., p. 473).

Eight thousand pumpkins meet the Eiffel Tower. While the holiday is based on ancient British and Irish traditions surrounding All Hallows' Eve, Halloween as we know it is a completely American phenomenon—until October 1997, that is, when "Ah-lo-ween" was introduced to the French public by retailers in an effort to boost consumer spending to spark a sagging French economy (Cohen, 1997). Informational social influence is how the French literally learned what this holiday is about. As of Halloween 1997, they had no idea of what "treek au treeting" was. However, by Halloween 2000, French shops were decorated in black and orange, carved pumpkins were displayed, and nightclubs held costume competitions.

(Associated Press, 2002)

The Importance of Being Accurate

Later research extended Sherif's classic study on informational conformity in interesting ways (Baron, Vandello, & Brunsman, 1996; Levine, Higgins, & Choi, 2000). This research employed judgment tasks that are more like real life than the autokinetic effect. It also revealed another variable that affects informational social influence: how important it is to the individual to be accurate at the task.

For example, in one study, research participants were given an involving but ambiguous task: eyewitness identification (Baron, Vandello, & Brunsman, 1996). Just like eyewitnesses of a real crime, the participants were asked to pick a "perpetrator" out of a lineup. For each of the 13 tasks, the participants were first shown a slide of a man—the perpetrator. Next they saw a slide of a lineup composed of four men, one of whom was the perpetrator. In the lineup, the perpetrator was sometimes dressed differently than he had been in the prior slide. The participant's job was to pick him out. The task was made very difficult (to the point of ambiguity) by presenting the slides extremely quickly. Participants saw each slide for only half a second. The eyewitness task took place in a group consisting of the participant and three confederates. Each of the four said their answers out loud after viewing each pair of slides. On the critical seven trials, where informational social influence would be measured, the three confederates answered before the participant—and all the confederates gave the same wrong answer.

The researchers also manipulated how important it was to the research participants to be accurate at the task. In the high-importance condition, they were told that the upcoming task was a real test of eyewitness identification ability and that police departments and courts would soon be using it to differentiate good eyewitnesses from poor ones. Participants' scores would therefore establish standards against which future eyewitness performance would be judged. In addition, those who were most accurate at the task would receive a $20 bonus from the experimenters. In contrast, in the low-importance condition, the research participants were told that the study was a first attempt to study eyewitness identification and that the slide task was still being developed. Thus, as the participants began the task, they were in two very different states of mind. Half thought their performance was very important and would have ramifications for the legal community. They were motivated to do well (and earn their $20). The other half saw this as just a regular research study like any other. Their performance didn't seem that important to the experimenters.

Even for judgments of the utmost importance—such as when an eyewitness to a crime later tries to identify the culprit—informational social influence influences our perceptions.

The high-importance condition mirrors the concerns of many situations in everyday life—your judgments and decisions have consequences, and you're motivated to "get things right." Will that make you more or less susceptible to informational social influence? The researchers found that it makes you *more* susceptible. In the low-importance condition, participants conformed to the confederates' judgments and gave the same wrong answers on 35% of the critical trials. In the high-importance condition, participants conformed to the confederates' judgments on 51% of the critical trials.

But relying on other people as a source of information is a strategy that also comes with risks. In a different eyewitness study, pairs of eyewitnesses each watched separate videos of what they believed to be the exact same event (Gabbert, Memon, & Allan, 2003). Unbeknownst to participants, each member of the pair viewed a slightly different video. Among pairs that were allowed to discuss the video before each eyewitness took an individual memory test, 71% of witnesses went on to mistakenly recall having personally seen items that only their partner had actually seen. This experiment illustrates the major risk of using other people around you for information: What if those other people are wrong? Indeed, this is why most police procedures require that eyewitnesses be interviewed individually by investigators (and view lineups individually as well).

When Informational Conformity Backfires

A dramatic form of informational social influence occurs during crises, when an individual is confronted with a frightening, potentially dangerous situation to which he or she is ill-equipped to respond (Killian, 1964). The person may have no idea of what is really happening or what he or she should do. When one's personal safety is involved, the need for information is acute—and the behavior of others is very informative.

Consider what happened on Halloween Night in 1938. Orson Welles, the gifted actor and film director, and the Mercury Theater broadcast a radio play based loosely on H. G. Wells's science fiction fantasy *War of the Worlds*. Remember, this was the era before television; radio was a primary source of entertainment (with music, comedy, and drama programs) and it was the only source for fast-breaking news. That night, the drama that Welles and his fellow actors broadcast—portraying the invasion of Earth by hostile Martians—was so realistic that at least a million listeners became frightened and alerted the police; several thousand were so panic-stricken that they tried to flee the "invasion" in their cars (Cantril, 1940).

Why were so many Americans convinced that what they heard was a real news report of an actual invasion by aliens? Hadley Cantril (1940), who studied this real-life "crisis," suggested two reasons. One was that the play parodied existing radio news shows very well, and many listeners missed the beginning of the broadcast (when it was clearly identified as a play) because they had been listening to a popular show on another station. The other culprit, however, was informational social influence. Many people were listening with friends and family. As the *War of the Worlds* scenario became increasingly frightening, they naturally turned to each other, out of uncertainty, to see whether they should believe what they heard. Seeing looks of concern and worry on their loved ones' faces added to the panic people were beginning to feel. "We all kissed one another and felt we would all die," reported one listener (Cantril, 1940, p. 95).

Ninety-nine percent of the people in the world are fools, and the rest of us are in great danger of contagion.
—THORNTON WILDER, *THE MATCHMAKER*

A late-nineteenth-century social scientist Gustav Le Bon (1895) was the first researcher to document how emotions and behavior can spread rapidly through a crowd—an effect he called **contagion** (Fowler & Christakis, 2008; Hatfield, Cacioppo, & Rapson, 1993; Levy & Nail, 1993). As we have learned, in a truly ambiguous situation, people become more likely to rely on the interpretation of others. Unfortunately, in a truly ambiguous and confusing situation, other people may be no more knowledgeable or accurate than we are. If other people are misinformed, we will adopt their mistakes and misinterpretations. Depending on others to help us define the situation can therefore lead us into serious inaccuracies.

Yes, we must, indeed, all hang together or, most assuredly, we shall all hang separately.
—BENJAMIN FRANKLIN AT THE SIGNING OF THE DECLARATION OF INDEPENDENCE, 1776

An extreme example of misdirected informational social influence is **mass psychogenic illness** (Bartholomew & Wessely, 2002; Colligan, Pennebaker, & Murphy, 1982), the occurrence in a group of people of similar physical symptoms with no known physical cause. For example, in 1998, a high school teacher in Tennessee reported the smell of gasoline in her classroom; soon she experienced headache, nausea, shortness of breath, and dizziness. As her class was being evacuated, others in the school reported similar symptoms. The decision was made to evacuate the entire school. Everyone watched as emergency medical workers ushered the teacher and students into ambulances. Local experts investigated and could find nothing wrong with the school. Classes resumed—and more people reported feeling sick. Again the school was evacuated and closed. Experts from numerous government agencies were called in to conduct an environmental investigation. And again nothing was found to be wrong with the school. When it reopened this time, the epidemic of mysterious illness was over (Altman, 2000).

Contagion
The rapid spread of emotions or behaviors through a crowd

Mass Psychogenic Illness
The occurrence in a group of people of similar physical symptoms with no known physical cause

The *Southern Standard* headlined a frightening and mysterious event at a local Tennessee high school. An investigation found that the "poisonings" were a case of mass psychogenic illness.

Discussion regarding the possibility of mass psychogenic illness once again made headlines in early 2012, as more than a dozen students in an upstate New York high school developed a condition resembling Tourette's syndrome (a neurological condition characterized by involuntary tics, body movements, and vocalizations) that seemed to have no identifiable cause (Szalavitz, 2012). What is particularly interesting about incidents like these (as well as other peculiar forms of conformity) is the powerful role that the mass media play in their dissemination. These days, information is spread quickly and efficiently to all segments of the population through not only radio and television, but also texting and social media. Whereas in the Middle Ages it took 2 hundred years for the "dancing manias" (a kind of psychogenic illness) to crisscross Europe (Sirois, 1982), today it takes only minutes for millions of people around the world to learn about an unusual event via computers and smartphones. Luckily, the mass media also have the power to quickly squelch contagion by introducing more-logical explanations for ambiguous events.

When Will People Conform to Informational Social Influence?

Let's review the situations that are the most likely to produce conformity because of informational social influence.

When the Situation is Ambiguous Ambiguity is the most crucial variable for determining how much people use each other as a source of information. When you are unsure of the correct response, the appropriate behavior, or the right idea, you will be most open to influence from others. The more uncertain you are, the more you will rely on others (Allen, 1965; Renfrow & Gosling, 2006; Tesser, Campbell, & Mickler, 1983; Walther et al., 2002). Situations such as the military atrocities discussed above were ambiguous ones for the people involved—ideal circumstances for informational social influence to take hold. Most of the soldiers were young and inexperienced. When they saw a few other soldiers shooting at the villagers or humiliating prisoners, many of them thought this was what they were supposed to do too, and they joined in.

When the Situation is a Crisis Crisis often occurs simultaneously with ambiguity. In a crisis situation, we usually do not have time to stop and think about exactly which course of action we should take. We need to act—immediately. If we feel scared and panicky and are uncertain what to do, it is only natural for us to see how other people are responding and to do likewise. Unfortunately, the people we imitate may also feel scared and panicky and not be behaving rationally.

Soliders, for example, are undoubtedly scared and on edge during their tours of duty. Further, in many wars it is not easy to tell who the enemy is. In the Vietnam War, civilians who were sympathizers of the Vietcong were known to have laid mines in the path of U.S. soldiers, fired guns from hidden locations, and thrown or planted grenades. Similarly, in Iraq and Afghanistan it was difficult to tell if people were civilians or combatants, allies or enemies. It is perhaps not surprising, then, that these soldiers often turned to others around them to gauge the proper course of action. Had these individuals not been in the midst of a chronic crisis situation, and instead had more time to think about their actions, perhaps tragedy and scandal would have been avoided.

When Other People are Experts Typically, the more expertise or knowledge a person has, the more valuable he or she will be as a guide in an ambiguous situation (Allison, 1992; Cialdini & Trost, 1998). For example, a passenger who sees smoke coming out of an airplane engine will probably check the flight attendants' reaction rather than their seatmates'; however, experts are not always reliable sources of information.

Imagine the fear felt by the young man listening to the *War of the Worlds* broadcast who called his local police department for an explanation, only to learn that the police too thought the events described on the radio were actually happening (Cantril, 1940)!

The desire to be accepted and liked by others can lead to dangerous behavior. Here, Brazilian teenagers "surf" on top of trains because it has become the popular thing to do in their peer group.

Normative Social Influence: The Need to Be Accepted

In the 1990s in Rio de Janeiro, Brazil, teenage boys and girls engaged in a dangerous and reckless game: "surfing" on the tops of trains, standing with arms outstretched as the trains sped along. Despite the fact that an average of 150 teenagers died each year from this activity and 400 more were injured by falling off the trains or hitting the 3,000-volt electric cable, the surfing continued (Arnett, 1995). More recently, in the United States and Australia, teenagers surfing on speeding cars has become a growing problem. Severe injuries and deaths from car surfing have been reported in Massachusetts, Ohio, Arizona, Wisconsin, and New South Wales, Australia (Daniel & Nelson, 2004; Ma, 2009).

Why do some adolescents engage in such risky behavior? Why does anyone follow the group's lead when the resulting behavior is far from sensible and may even be dangerous? We doubt that the Brazilian, American, or Australian teenagers risked their lives due to informational conformity. It is difficult to argue that a boy or girl staring at a train would say, "Gee, I don't know what to do. I guess standing on top of a speeding train makes sense." This example suggests that there must be something else besides the need for information that can explain conformity. And there is: We also conform so that we will be liked and accepted by other people (Maxwell, 2002). We conform to the group's **social norms**—implicit (and sometimes explicit) rules for acceptable behaviors, values, and beliefs (Deutsch & Gerard, 1955; Kelley, 1955; Miller & Prentice, 1996). Groups have certain expectations about how the group members should behave, and members in good standing conform to these rules. Members who do not are perceived as different, difficult, and eventually deviant.

Deviant group members are often ridiculed, punished, or even rejected by other group members (James & Olson, 2000; Kruglanski & Webster, 1991; Levine, 1989; Miller & Anderson, 1979). For example, in Japan a whole class (or even the entire school) will sometimes turn against one student perceived as different, alternately harassing and shunning the individual. In a highly cohesive, group-oriented culture such as Japan, this kind of treatment has had tragic results: Twelve teenage victims of bullying killed themselves in one year (Jordan, 1996). Another social phenomenon in Japan is the *hikikomori*, teenagers (mostly male) who have withdrawn from all social interaction. They spend all their time alone, in their bedrooms in their parents' homes. Some hikikomori have remained sequestered for over a decade. Japanese psychologists state that many hikikomori were the victims of severe bullying before their withdrawal (Jones, 2006). Recently, researchers in the United States and Great Britain have begun to study cyberbullying in middle and secondary schools. This form of bullying, using cell phones and the Internet, is increasingly frequent, affecting as many as 11% of middle school children (Kowalski & Limber, 2007; Smith et al., 2008; Wilton & Campbell, 2011).

We human beings are by nature a social species. Few of us could live happily as hermits, never seeing or talking to another person. Through interactions with others, we receive emotional support, affection, and love, and we partake of enjoyable experiences. Other people are extraordinarily important to our sense of well-being. Research on individuals who have been isolated for long periods of time indicates that being deprived of human contact is stressful, traumatic, and psychologically painful (Baumeister & Leary, 1995; Schachter, 1959; Williams & Nida, 2011).

Social Norms

The implicit or explicit rules a group has for the acceptable behaviors, values, and beliefs of its members

Normative Social Influence

The influence of other people that leads us to conform in order to be liked and accepted by them; this type of conformity results in public compliance with the group's beliefs and behaviors but not necessarily in private acceptance of those beliefs and behaviors

Given this fundamental human need for social companionship, it is not surprising that we often conform to gain acceptance from others. Conformity for normative reasons occurs in situations where we do what other people are doing, not because we are using them as a source of information, but so that we won't attract attention, be made fun of, get into trouble, or be rejected. Thus, **normative social influence** occurs when the influence of other people leads us to conform to be liked and accepted by them. This type of conformity results in public compliance with the group's beliefs and behaviors, but not necessarily in private acceptance (Cialdini, Kallgren, & Reno, 1991; Deutsch & Gerard, 1955; Levine, 1999; Nail, McDonald, & Levy, 2000).

You probably don't find it too surprising that people sometimes conform to be liked and accepted by others. You might be thinking, where's the harm? If the group is important to us and wearing the right clothes or using the right slang will gain us acceptance, why not go along? But when it comes to more-important kinds of behaviors, such as hurting another person, surely we will resist such conformity pressures. And of course we won't conform when we are certain of the correct way of behaving and the pressures are coming from a group that we don't care all that much about. Or will we?

Explore on **MyPsychLab**
To explore social influence further, try the MyPsychLab activity ***Urban Legends***.

Conformity and Social Approval: The Asch Line-Judgment Studies

To find out, Solomon Asch (1951, 1956) conducted a series of now-classic studies exploring the power of normative social influence. Asch devised the studies assuming that there are limits to how much people will conform. Naturally, people conformed in the Sherif studies (see page 200), he reasoned, because the situation was highly ambiguous—trying to guess how much a light was moving. But when a situation was wholly unambiguous, Asch expected that people would act like rational, objective problem solvers. When the group said or did something that contradicted an obvious truth, surely people would resist social pressures and decide for themselves what was going on.

To test his hypothesis, Asch conducted the following study. Had you been a participant, you would have been told that this was an experiment on perceptual judgment and that you would be taking part with seven other students. Here's the scenario: The experimenter shows everyone two cards, one with a single line on it, the other with three lines labeled 1, 2, and 3. He asks each of you to judge and then announce out loud which of the three lines on the second card is closest in length to the line on the first card (see Figure 8.2).

It is crystal clear that the correct answer is the second line. Not surprisingly, each participant says, "Line 2." Your turn comes next to last, and of course you say, "Line 2" as well. The last participant concurs. The experimenter then presents a new set of cards and asks the participants again to make their judgments and announce them out loud.

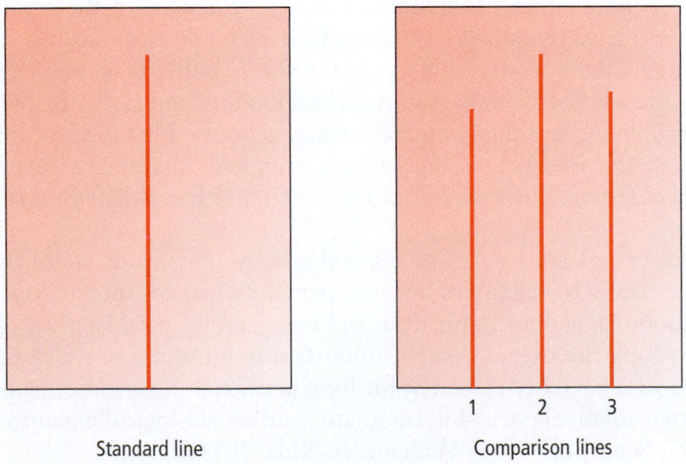

FIGURE 8.2

The Judgment Task in Asch's Line Studies

In a series of studies of normative social influence, participants judged which of the three comparison lines on the right was closest in length to the standard line on the left. The correct answer was always obvious (as it is here). However, members of the group (actually confederates) gave the wrong answer out loud. Now the participant faced a dilemma: Give the right answer and go against the whole group, or conform to their behavior and give an obviously wrong answer?

(Adapted from Asch, 1956)

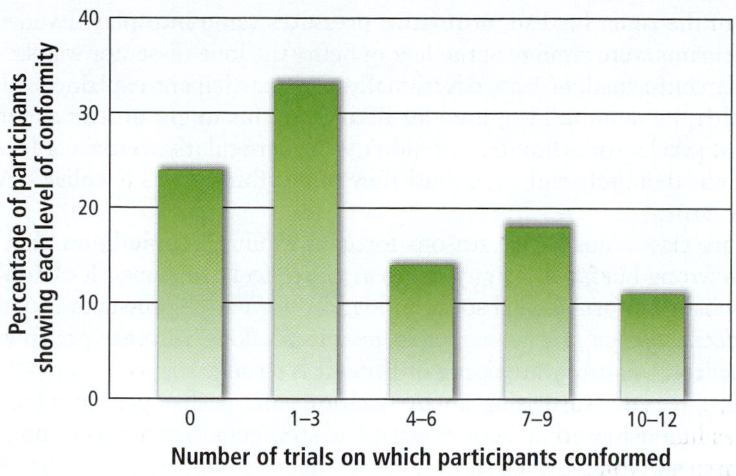

FIGURE 8.3

Results of the Asch Line-Judgment Study

Participants in the Asch line study showed a surprisingly high level of conformity, given how obvious it was that the group was wrong in its judgments. Seventy-six percent of the participants conformed on at least one trial; only 24% of participants never conformed at all (see bar labeled zero). Most participants conformed on one to three of the 12 trials in which the group gave the wrong answer. However, a sizable number of participants conformed to the group's incorrect response nearly every single time (see the two bars on the right).

(Adapted from Asch, 1957)

Again, the answer is obvious, and everyone gives the correct answer. At this point, you are probably thinking, "What a waste of time. I've got a paper due tomorrow. I need to get out of here."

As your mind starts to wander, though, something surprising happens. The experimenter presents a third set of lines, and again the answer is obvious—line 3 is clearly the closest in length to the target line. But the first participant announces that the correct answer is line 1! "This guy must be so bored that he fell asleep," you think. Then the second person announces that line 1 is the correct answer. The third, fourth, fifth, and sixth participants all agree; it's now your turn to judge. Startled at this point, you are probably looking at the lines very closely to see if you missed something. But no, line 3 is clearly the right answer. What will you do? Will you stand up for what you believe to be the truth, blurting out, "Line 3," or will you go along with the group and give the obviously wrong answer, "Line 1"?

As you can see, Asch set up a situation to discover if people would conform even when the right answer was absolutely obvious. In each group, all the individuals except for the actual participant were confederates of the research term who had been instructed to give the wrong answer on 12 of the 18 trials. What happened? Contrary to what Asch expected, a considerable amount of conformity occurred: Seventy-six percent of the participants conformed and gave an obviously incorrect response on at least one trial. On average, people conformed on about a third of the trials on which the accomplices gave the incorrect answer (see Figure 8.3).

It isn't difficult to keep alive, friends—just don't make trouble—or if you must make trouble, make the sort of trouble that's expected.

—Robert Bolt, *A Man for All Seasons*

Why did people conform so much of the time? Participants couldn't have needed information from others to help them decide, as they did in the Sherif study, because the situation was not ambiguous. The right answers were so obvious that when people in a control group made the judgments by themselves, they were accurate more

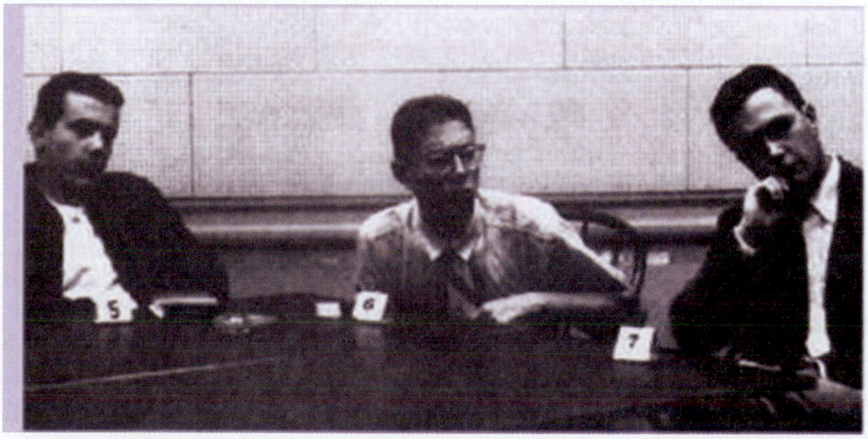

Participants in an Asch line study. The real participant is seated in the middle. He is surrounded by the experimenter's accomplices, who have just given the wrong answer on the line task.

than 98% of the time. Instead, normative pressures came into play. Even though the other participants were strangers, the fear of being the lone dissenter was so strong that most people conformed, at least occasionally. One participant explained: "Here was a group; they had a definite idea; my idea disagreed; this might arouse anger . . . I was standing out [like] a sore thumb . . . I didn't want particularly to make a fool of myself . . . I felt I was definitely right . . . [but] they might think I was peculiar" (Asch, 1956, Whole No. 416).

These are classic normative reasons for conforming: People know that what they are doing is wrong but go along anyway so as not to feel peculiar or look foolish. Notably, in contrast to informational social influence, normative pressures usually result in *public compliance without private acceptance*; people go along with the group even if they do not believe in what they are doing or think it is wrong.

What is especially surprising about Asch's results is that people were concerned about looking foolish even in front of complete strangers. It is not as if the participants were in danger of being ostracized by a group that was important to them. Yet decades of research since the original Asch study have indicated that conformity for normative reasons can occur simply because we do not want to risk social disapproval, even from complete strangers we will never see again (Bond & Smith, 1996; Cialdini & Goldstein, 2004; Tanford & Penrod, 1984).

In a variation of his study, Asch (1957) demonstrated just how powerful social disapproval can be in shaping a person's behavior. As before, the confederates gave the wrong answer 12 out of 18 times, but in this version participants wrote their answers on a piece of paper instead of saying them out loud. Now people did not have to worry about what the group thought of them, because the group would never find out what their answers were. Conformity dropped dramatically, occurring on an average of only 1.5 of the 12 trials (Insko et al., 1985; Nail, 1986). As Serge Moscovici (1985) observed, the Asch studies are "one of the most dramatic illustrations of conformity, of blindly going along with the group, even when the individual realizes that by doing so he turns his back on reality and truth" (p. 349).

Simulate on **MyPsychLab**

Put yourself in the Asch experiment by trying the MyPsychLab simulation ***Social Influence (1)***.

Research by Gregory Berns and his colleagues has provided biological evidence for just how unpleasant and uncomfortable it is to resist normative social influence (Berns et al., 2005). Berns and his research team used functional magnetic resonance imaging (fMRI) to examine the changes in brain activity of research participants as they either normatively conformed to a group's judgment or maintained their independence and disagreed with the group.

Instead of judgments of line length, the task in this study involved mental rotation. While in the fMRI scanner, participants were shown a three-dimensional figure and then asked if a second figure (rotated in a different direction) was the same as the first figure or different. They indicated their answers by pushing a button. The task was slightly more difficult than Asch's line-judgment task; the baseline error rate, when participants made judgments alone, was 13.8%, compared to Asch's (1951, 1956) baseline error rate of 2%.

Before being placed in the fMRI scanner, participants met and interacted with four other participants who were, as you've probably guessed, actually confederates. These four would be doing the same mental rotation task, but only the participant would have his or her brain activity monitored. During the task, the participant completed one-third of the trials with no knowledge of the answers of the other four people. On the remaining two-thirds of the trials, the participant saw the four group members' answers on a visual display. Half the time the group had all chosen the wrong answer, and the other half of the time they had all chosen the right answer.

Now, what did the participants do, and, most importantly, what areas of their brains were activated when they did it? First, as with the original Asch study, participants conformed to the group's wrong answers some of the time (41% of the trials, to be exact). On the baseline trials, where the participants answered alone, the fMRI results indicated increased activity in the posterior brain areas dedicated to vision and perception. When the participants conformed to the group's wrong

Customs do not concern themselves with right or wrong or reason. But they have to be obeyed; one reasons all around them until [one] is tired, but [one] must not transgress them, it is sternly forbidden.

—Mark Twain

answers, activation occurred in the same areas; however, when participants chose to give the right answer and thus disagree with the group's unanimous wrong answer, the visual/perceptual areas of the brain were not activated. Instead, different areas of the brain became active: the amygdala, an area devoted to negative emotions, and the right caudate nucleus, an area devoted to modulating social behavior (Berns et al., 2005). Thus, this brain-imaging research supports the idea that normative social influence occurs because people feel negative emotions, such as discomfort and tension, when they go against the group (Spitzer et al., 2007).

The Importance of Being Accurate, Revisited

Now, you may be thinking, "OK, so we conform to normative social influence, but hey, only when it's something little. Who cares whether you give the right answer on a line-judgment task? It doesn't matter, nothing is at stake—I'd never conform to the group's wrong answer if something important was involved!" And this would be a very good criticism. Recall our discussion of importance in connection with informational social influence; we found that in ambiguous situations, the more important the decision or choice a person has to make, the more the person conforms for informational reasons. What about in nonambiguous situations? Maybe the more important the decision or choice is, the less the person would conform? When it's important to you to be right, are you strong enough to withstand group pressure and disagree with the group?

Recall the first study of eyewitness identification that we discussed earlier, in which Baron and his colleagues (Baron, Vandello, & Brunsman, 1996) included experimental conditions that triggered social influence. In the study research, participants viewed pairs of slides, one of the perpetrator alone and one of the perpetrator in a lineup. Participants watched the slides in groups with two confederates. When studying informational conformity, the researchers made the task fiendishly difficult and therefore ambiguous—the slides were projected for only half a second. In order to study normative social influence, however, the researchers made the same task ridiculously easy: The participants viewed each slide for a full 5 seconds, and they were shown each pair of slides twice. Now the task becomes analogous to Asch's line-judging task; basically, if you're awake, you'll get the right answer. Baron and colleagues proved that the task was easy, by having individuals in a control group each view the slides alone. The controls answered correctly on 97% of the trials.

Baron and colleagues again manipulated the importance of the participants being accurate, in the same ways we discussed earlier. Half were led to believe that it was very important that they give the right answers, and half were told it really didn't matter how they did. Now how will participants respond when the confederates give the obviously wrong answer? Will they conform to the group on at least some of the trials, as the participants in the Asch study did? Or will the participants who believe accuracy is very important give the correct answers every time, standing up to the group and ignoring the normative pressure to agree with them?

The researchers found that participants in the low-importance condition conformed to the group on 33% of the critical trials—very close to the rate in Asch's line-judgment task. What happened to the participants in the high-importance condition? Instead of standing up to the group across the board, they caved in on at least some trials. They did conform less to the obviously wrong answers of the group; on only 16% of the critical trials did they echo the group's blatantly wrong answer. But they still conformed sometimes! These findings underscore the power of normative social influence: Even when the group is wrong, the right answer is obvious, and there are strong incentives to be accurate, some people still find it difficult to risk social disapproval, even from strangers (Baron et al., 1996; Hornsey et al., 2003). And as the examples of train- and car-surfing demonstrate, this desire to be accepted can have tragic consequences.

Normative social influence most closely reflects the negative stereotype of conformity we referred to earlier: the belief that those who conform are spineless and weak. Ironically, while this type of social pressure can be difficult to resist, people are often quick to deny that they've been influenced by normative considerations. Recall the energy conservation study by Nolan and colleagues (2008) described earlier. In this study, researchers assessed the effectiveness of different arguments for reducing electricity use among Californians. The most persuasive message was telling consumers that their neighbors were conserving energy. But participants *believed* that this message had little effect on them, especially compared to participants who received information regarding protecting the environment or saving money. As Nolan and her coauthors conclude, we often underestimate the power of normative social influence.

But your denial that normative pressures affect you doesn't stop others from trying to exert influence through such processes. How else to explain why some television producers hire professional laughers to sit in the studio audience to make their comedies seem funnier (Warner, 2011)? Or why some sports teams pay abnormally enthusiastic fans to rile up fellow spectators at their home games (Sommers, 2011)? Clearly, the desire to fit in and be accepted is part of human nature, whether or not we're willing to admit it.

The Consequences of Resisting Normative Social Influence

One way to observe the power of normative social pressure is to examine the consequences when people manage to resist it. If a person refuses to do as the group asks and thereby violates its norms, what happens? Think about the norms that operate in your group of friends. Some friends have an egalitarian norm for making group decisions. For example, when choosing a movie, everyone gets to state a preference; the choice is then discussed until agreement is reached. What would happen if, in a group with this kind of norm, you stated at the outset that you only wanted to see *Rebel Without a Cause* and would not agree to watch anything else? Your friends would be surprised by your behavior; they would also be annoyed with you or even angry. If you continued to disregard the friendship norms of the group by failing to conform, two things would most likely happen. First, the group would try to bring you "back into the fold," chiefly through increased communication. Teasing comments and long discussions would ensue as your friends tried to figure out why you were acting so strangely and tried to get you to conform to their expectations (Garfinkle, 1967). If these tactics didn't work, your friends would most likely say negative things to you and about you and start to withdraw from you (Festinger & Thibaut, 1951). Now, in effect, you've been rejected (Abrams et al., 2000; Hornsey et al., 2006; Levine, 1989; Marques et al., 2001; Milgram & Sabini, 1978).

Stanley Schachter (1951) demonstrated how the group responds to an individual who ignores the group's normative influence. He asked groups of college students to read and discuss a case history of "Johnny Rocco," a juvenile delinquent. Most of the students took a middle-of-the-road position about the case, believing that Rocco should receive a judicious mixture of love and discipline. Unbeknownst to the participants, however, Schachter had planted an accomplice in the group who was instructed to disagree with the group's recommendations. The accomplice consistently argued that Rocco should receive the harshest amount of punishment, regardless of what the other group members argued.

> *Success or failure lies in conformity to the times.*
> —Niccolò Machiavelli, *The Prince*

How was the deviant treated? He became the target of the most comments and questions from the real participants throughout most of the discussion, and then, near the end, communication with him dropped sharply. The other group members had tried to convince the deviant to agree with them; when it appeared that it wouldn't work, they started to ignore him. In addition, they punished him. After the discussion, they were asked to fill out questionnaires that supposedly pertained to future discussion meetings of their group. The participants were asked to nominate one group member who should be eliminated from further discussions if the group size had to be reduced. They nominated the deviant. They were also asked to assign group members to various tasks in future discussions. They assigned the unimportant or boring jobs, such as taking notes, to the deviant. Social groups are well versed in how to bring a nonconformist into line. No wonder we respond as often as we do to normative pressures! You can find out what it's like to resist normative social influence in the following Try It!

TRY IT! Unveiling Normative Social Influence by Breaking the Rules

Every day, you talk to a lot of people—friends, professors, coworkers, and strangers. When you have a conversation, whether long or short, you follow certain interaction "rules" that operate in American culture. These rules for conversation include nonverbal forms of behavior that Americans consider "normal" as well as "polite." You can find out how powerful these norms are by breaking them and noting how people respond to you; their responses demonstrate the power of normative social influence.

For example, in conversation, we stand a certain distance from each other—not too far and not too close. About 2 to 3 feet is typical in mainstream U.S. culture. In addition, we maintain a good amount of eye contact when we are listening to the other person; in comparison, when we're talking, we look away from the person more often.

What happens if you break these normative rules? Try having a conversation with a friend and stand either too close or too far away (e.g., 1 foot or 7 feet). Have a typical, normal conversation with your friend—only the spacing you use with this person should be different. Note how your friend responds. If you're too close, your friend will probably back away; if you continue to keep the distance small, he or she may act uncomfortable and even end your conversation sooner than usual. If you're too far away, your friend will probably come closer; if you back up, he or she may think you are in a strange mood. In either case, your friend's response will probably include looking at you a lot, having a puzzled look on his or her face, acting uncomfortable or confused, and talking less than normal or ending the conversation.

You have acted in a nonnormative way, and your conversational partner is, first, trying to figure out what is going on and, second, responding in a way to get you to stop acting oddly. From this one brief exercise, you will get the idea of what would happen if you behaved oddly all the time—people would try to get you to change, and then they would probably start avoiding or ignoring you.

When you're finished, "debrief" your friend, explaining the exercise, so that your behavior is understood. The relief you feel upon revealing why you were acting so peculiarly is yet one more demonstration of the strength of normative pressure and the challenge inherent to resisting it.

Normative Social Influence in Everyday Life

Normative social influence operates on many levels in our daily lives. For example, although few of us are slaves to fashion, we tend to wear what is considered appropriate and stylish at a given time. Men's wide neckties, popular in the 1970s, gave way to narrow ties in the 1980s before widening again in the 1990s and seeing a resurgence of skinny ties today; women's hemlines dropped from mini to maxi and then rose again. Normative social influence is at work whenever you notice a particular look shared by people in a certain group, and, no matter what it is, it will look outdated just a few years later until the fashion industry revives it in a new trend.

By 2007, the Crocs fad was in full force as kids (and parents) everywhere could be found out and about in these plastic clogs with Swiss-cheese holes. Five years later, reviews are decidedly more mixed: an anti-Croc page on Facebook currently has more than 1.6 million fans.

Fads are another fairly frivolous example of normative social influence. Certain activities or objects can suddenly become popular and sweep the country. For example, in the late 1950s, every child had to have a Hula Hoop or risk social ostracism, in the 1970s people actually paid for the right to own a Pet Rock, and in the 1990s Beanie Baby mania swept up children and adults alike. College students swallowed live goldfish in the 1930s, crammed as many people as possible into telephone booths in the 1950s, and "streaked" (ran naked) at official gatherings in the 1970s. These fads seem silly now, but ask yourself, could there be "fads" that you are following now?

Social Influence and Women's Body Image A more sinister form of normative social influence involves people's attempts to conform to cultural definitions of an attractive body—historically, a particularly problematic proposition for women. Although many, if not most, world societies throughout history have considered plumpness in females attractive, Western culture, and especially American culture, currently values unrealistic thinness in the female form (Grossbard et al., 2009; Jackson, 1992; Weeden & Sabini, 2005).

FIGURE 8.4

What Is the "Ideal" Female Body Across Cultures?

Researchers divided 54 cultures into groups, depending on the reliability of their food supply. They then determined what was considered the "ideal" female body in each culture. Heavy female bodies were considered the most beautiful in cultures with unreliable food supplies. As the reliability of the food supply increased, the preference for a moderate-to-heavy body type decreased. Only in cultures where food was very readily available was the slender body valued more.

(Adapted from Anderson, Crawford, Nadeau, & Lindberg, 1992)

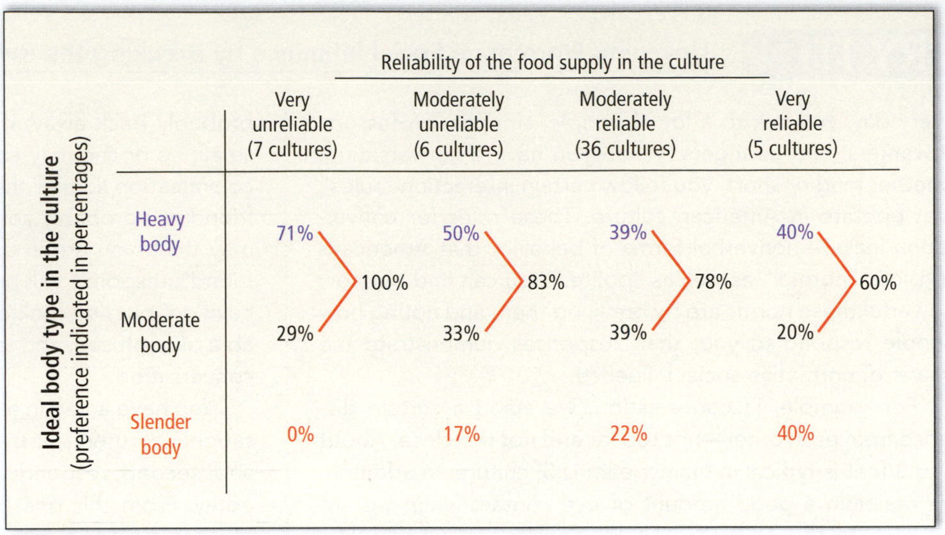

Why should preference for female body type vary by culture? To explore this question, Judith Anderson and her colleagues (Anderson et al., 1992) analyzed what people in 54 cultures considered the ideal female body: a heavy body, a body of moderate weight, or a slender body. The researchers also analyzed how reliable the food supply was in each culture. They hypothesized that in societies where food was frequently scarce, a heavy body would be considered the most beautiful. These would be women who had enough to eat and therefore were healthy and fertile. As you can see in Figure 8.4, their hypothesis was supported. Heavy body types in women were preferred over slender or moderate ones in cultures with unreliable food supplies. As the reliability of the food supply increases, the preference for heavy-to-moderate bodies decreases. Most dramatic is the increase in preference for the slender body across cultures. Only in cultures with very reliable food supplies (such as the United States) was the slender body type highly valued.

No woman can be too slim or too rich.
—Wallis Simpson, Duchess of Windsor

What is the American standard for the female body? Has it changed over time? In the 1980s, Brett Silverstein and her colleagues (Silverstein et al., 1986) analyzed photographs of women appearing in *Ladies' Home Journal* and *Vogue* magazines from 1901 to 1981. The researchers measured the women's busts and waists, creating a bust-to-waist ratio. A high score indicates a heavier, more voluptuous body, while a lower score indicates a thinner, lean body type. Their results show a startling series of changes in the cultural definition of female bodily attractiveness over the course of 80 years (see Figure 8.5).

At the turn of the twentieth century, an attractive woman was voluptuous and heavy; by the "flapper" period of the 1920s, the desired look for women was rail-thin and flat-chested. The normative body changed again in the 1940s, when World War II "pinup girls" such as Betty Grable exemplified a heavier standard. The curvaceous female body remained popular during the 1950s; witness, for example, Marilyn Monroe. However, the "swinging 1960s" fashion look, exemplified by the reed-thin British model Twiggy, introduced once again a very thin silhouette. The average bust-to-waist ratio has been low since 1963, marking the longest period of time in recent history that American women have been exposed to an extremely thin standard of physical attractiveness (Barber, 1998; Wiseman et al., 1992). In fact, a recent meta-analysis of research studies indicates that Americans have adopted the "thin is beautiful" standard for women even more strongly in the 2000s than in the 1990s (Grabe et al., 2008). Though, interestingly, this pattern seems to hold more so for whites; recent analysis of beauty ideals for African American women reveals greater acceptance of larger, more curvaceous body types (Dawson-Andoh et al., 2010).

Interestingly, the standards for physical attractiveness for women in other cultures have also undergone changes in recent decades. Since World War II, the preferred look in Japan has taken on a "Westernized" element—long-legged, thin bodies, or what is

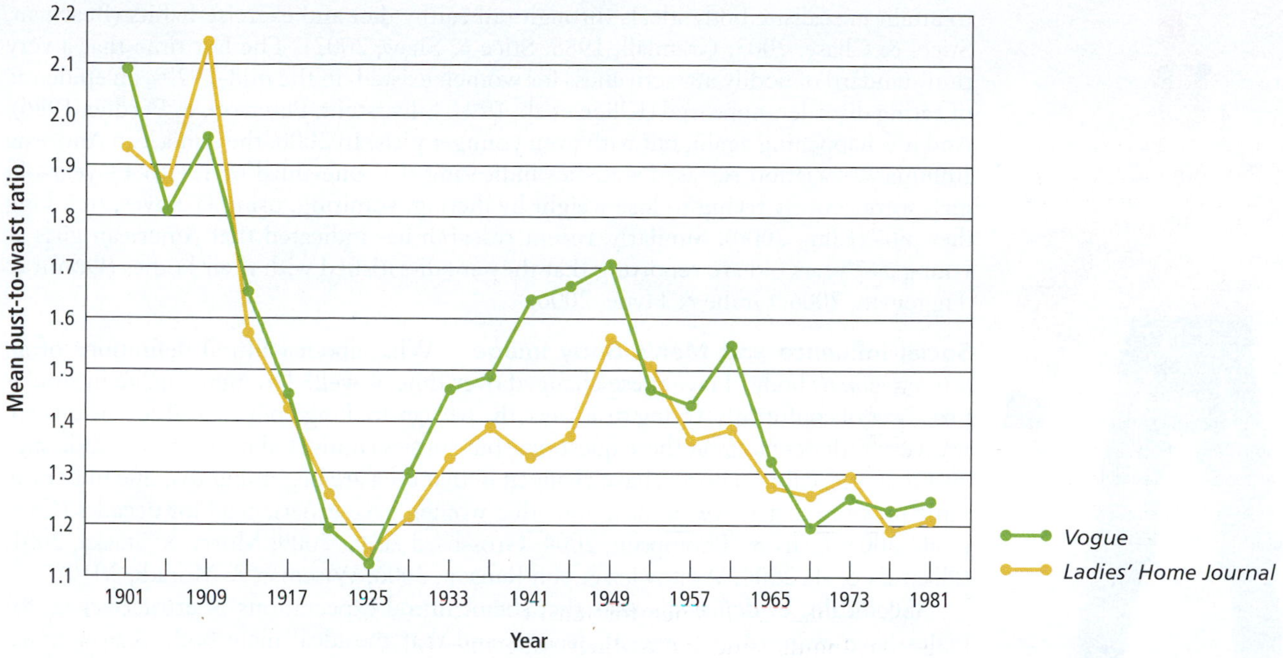

FIGURE 8.5

The Mean Bust-to-Waist Ratios of Models in *Vogue* and *Ladies' Home Journal*, 1901–1981

What is considered an attractive female body changed dramatically during the twentieth century, from heavy women at the beginning of the 1900s, to rail-thin women during the 1920s, to somewhat heavier and more-curvaceous women during the 1940s and 1950s, to a return to very thin women in the 1960s and thereafter.

(Adapted from Silverstein, Perdue, Peterson, & Kelly, 1986)

called the "*hattou shin* beauty" (Mukai, Kambara, & Sasaki, 1998). And this cultural shift has had an effect—Japanese women experience strong normative pressures to be thin (Mukai, 1996). Indeed, researchers have found that Japanese women are even more likely than American women to perceive themselves as being overweight. They also report greater dissatisfaction with their bodies than do American women. All this occurs despite the fact that the Japanese women in the sample were significantly thinner than the American women. In addition, these researchers found that participants' "need for social approval," as measured on a questionnaire, was a significant predictor of eating disorders for the Japanese women but not for the American women. Japanese culture places a greater emphasis on conformity than American culture does, and hence the normative pressure to be thin operates with even more serious consequences for Japanese women (Mukai et al., 1998).

Cultural standards for women's bodies are changeable. Whereas today's female models and movie stars tend to be lean and muscle-toned, the female icons of the 1940s and 1950s, such as Marilyn Monroe, were curvaceous, heavier, and less muscular.

How do women learn what kind of body is considered attractive at a given time in their culture (and how they compare to these standards)? From family and friends and the media. Various contemporary media, from magazine ads to TV sitcoms, have been implicated in sending a message that the ideal female body is thin (Barriga, Shapiro, & Jhaveri, 2009; Cusumano & Thompson, 1997; Fouts & Burggraf, 2000). Women tend to perceive themselves as overweight and as heavier than they actually are (Cohn & Adler, 1992), and this effect is heightened if they've just been exposed to media portrayals of thin women (Bessenoff, 2006; Diedrichs & Lee, 2011; Fredrickson et al., 1998; Grube, Ward, & Hyde, 2008; Strahan et al., 2008). Given that the average U.S. woman is 5'4" and 140 pounds, and the average advertising model in the United States is 5'11" and 117 pounds, this result is not surprising (Locken & Peck, 2005).

The sociocultural pressure for thinness that is currently operating on women has potentially serious consequences. It can even be fatal, as it leads some women to attempt to attain unrealistic body ideals through unhealthy diet and exercise habits (Bearman, Stice, & Chase, 2003; Crandall, 1988; Stice & Shaw, 2002). The last time that a very thin standard of bodily attractiveness for women existed, in the mid-1920s, an epidemic of eating disorders appeared (Killen et al., 1994; Silverstein, Peterson, & Perdue, 1986). And it is happening again, but with even younger girls: In 2000, the American Anorexia Bulimia Association released statistics indicating that one-third of 12- to 13-year-old girls were actively trying to lose weight by dieting, vomiting, using laxatives, or taking diet pills (Ellin, 2000). Similarly, recent research has indicated that American girls as young as 7 years old are reporting that they are dissatisfied with their bodies (Dohnt & Tiggeman, 2006; Grabe & Hyde, 2006).

Has the American cultural ideal of the male body changed over time? Harrison Pope and his colleagues (1999) measured the waist, chest, and biceps of the most popular action-figure toys of the last three decades. The researchers found that the toy figures had grown much more muscular over time, far exceeding the muscularity of even the largest human bodybuilders. The researchers suggest that such unrealistic images of the male body may contribute to body-image disorders in boys.

Social Influence and Men's Body Image What about cultural definitions of an attractive *male* body? Have these changed over time as well? Do men engage in similar processes of conformity, trying to achieve the perfect-looking body? Until recently, there was very little research on these questions, but studies conducted in the past decade suggest that, yes, cultural norms have changed in that men are beginning to come under the same pressure to achieve an ideal body that women have experienced for decades (Cafri et al., 2005; Cafri & Thompson, 2004; Grossbard et al., 2009; Morry & Staska, 2001; Olivardia et al., 2004; Wojtowicz & von Ranson, 2006; Wiseman & Moradi, 2010).

Specifically, evidence suggests that sociocultural expectations of attractiveness for males have changed over recent decades and that the ideal male body is now much more muscular. For example, Harrison Pope and his colleagues (Pope, Olivardia, Gruber, & Borowiecki, 1999) analyzed boys' toys such as G.I. Joe dolls by measuring their waists, chests, and biceps. The changes in G.I. Joe from 1964 to 1998 are startling, as you can see in the photographs from their research.

They also coded advertisements since 1950 in two women's magazines, *Glamour* and *Cosmopolitan*, for how often male and female models were pictured in a state of undress. For women, the percentage remained at about 20% over the decades, but for men a change was clear. In 1950, fewer than 5% of ads showed men in some state of undress; by 1995, that figure had risen to as much as 35% (Pope, Phillips, & Olivardia, 2000).

Do these presentations of (nearly) naked—and perfect—male bodies affect men's perceptions of themselves? Ida Jodette Hatoum and Deborah Belle (2004) investigated this question by focusing on the relationship between media consumption and bodily concerns in a sample of college men. They found that reading male-oriented magazines such as *Maxim*, *Details*, *Esquire*, *Men's Fitness*, and *Men's Health*—all of which present the "hypermuscular" male body—was significantly correlated with negative feelings about one's own body. In addition, these researchers found that the more men were exposed to these male-directed magazines (as well as to movies), the more they valued thinness in women.

Pope and colleagues (Pope, Gruber et al., 2000) asked men in the United States, France, and Austria to alter a computer image of a male body in terms of fat and muscle until it reflected, first, their own bodies; second, the body they'd like to have; and, finally, the body they thought women would find most attractive. The men were quite accurate in their depiction of their own bodies; however, men in all three countries chose an ideal body that had on average 28 more pounds of muscle than their own. This muscular ideal was also the body they chose for what they thought women would find attractive. (However, when women completed the task, they chose a very normal, average-looking male body as their ideal.)

Researchers have also found that adolescent and young men report feeling pressure from parents, peers, and the media to be more muscular; they respond to this pressure by developing strategies to achieve the ideal, "six-pack" body (Bergstrom & Neighbors, 2006; McCabe & Ricciardelli, 2003a, 2003b; Ricciardelli & McCabe, 2003). For example, results from a number of studies indicate that 21% to 42% of young men have altered their eating habits in order to gain muscle mass and/or weight, while 12% to 26% have dieted in order to reduce body fat/weight. An increasing number are also using risky substances such as steroids or ephedrine to achieve a more muscular physique (Cafri et al., 2005). All these data suggest that informational and normative social influence is now operating on men as well as women, affecting their perceptions of their own bodies' attractiveness.

When Will People Conform to Normative Social Influence?

Although conformity is commonplace, people don't always cave in to peer pressure. We certainly do not all agree on many major issues, such as abortion, affirmative action, or same-sex marriage. Exactly when are people most likely to conform to normative pressures? Some answers to this question are provided by Bibb Latané's (1981) **social impact theory**. According to this theory, the likelihood that you will respond to social influence depends on three variables regarding the group in question:

Social Impact Theory
The idea that conforming to social influence depends on the group's importance, its immediacy, and the number of people in the group

1. *Strength:* How important to you is the group?
2. *Immediacy:* How close is the group to you in space and time during the attempt to influence you?
3. *Number:* How many people are in the group?

Social impact theory predicts that conformity will increase as strength and immediacy increase. Clearly, the more important a group is to us and the closer group members are to us physically, the more likely we will be to conform to its normative pressures.

Social influence operates differently when it comes to group size. As the size of the group increases, each additional person has less of an influencing effect—going from three people to four makes more of a difference than going from 53 people to 54. If we feel pressure from a group to conform, adding another person to the majority makes much more of a difference if the group is small rather than large. Latané constructed a mathematical model that captures these hypothesized effects of strength, immediacy, and number and has applied this formula to the results of many conformity studies (Bourgeois & Bowen, 2001; Latané, 1981; Latané & Bourgeois, 2001; Latané & L'Herrou, 1996).

For example, gay men who lived in communities that were highly involved in AIDS awareness activities (where strength, immediacy, and number would all be high) reported feeling more social pressure to avoid risky sexual behavior and stronger intentions to do so than gay men who lived in less-involved communities (Fishbein et al., 1993). Similarly, a recent study of heterosexual dating couples (a relationship typically high in strength and immediacy) reveals that an individual's own tendency to engage in heavy drinking is significantly predicted by the norm set by his or her partner's drinking tendencies (Mushquash et al., 2011).

Watch on **MyPsychLab**
To learn more, watch the MyPsychLab video ***Conformity and Influence in Groups***.

Let's see in more detail what social impact theory says about the conditions under which people will conform to normative social pressures.

When the Group Grows Larger At what point does group size stop influencing conformity? Asch (1955) and later researchers found that conformity increased as the number of people in the group increased, but once the group reached four or five other people, conformity does not increase much (Bond, 2005; Campbell & Fairey, 1989; Gerard, Wilhelmy, & Conolley, 1968)—just as social impact theory suggests (see Figure 8.6). In short, it does not take an extremely large group to create normative social influence, but the larger the group, the stronger the social pressure.

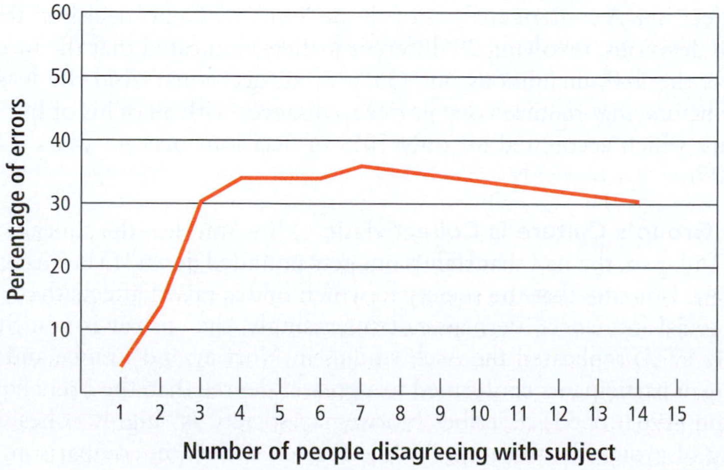

FIGURE 8.6
Effects of Group Size on Conformity
Asch varied the size of the unanimous majority in his study and found that once the majority numbered four, adding more people had little influence on conformity.
(Adapted from Asch, 1955)

When the Group is Important Another tenet of social impact theory is that the strength of the group—defined as how important the group is to us—makes a difference. Normative pressures are much stronger when they come from people whose friendship, love, and respect we cherish, because there is a large cost to losing this love and respect (Abrams et al., 1990; Guimond, 1999; Hogg, 1992; Nowak, Szamrej, & Latané, 1990; Wolf, 1985). One consequence of this conclusion is that it can be dangerous to have policy decisions made by highly cohesive groups, because they care more about pleasing each other and avoiding conflict than arriving at the best, most logical decision. We will see several examples of this phenomenon in Chapter 9.

We should note, however, that the very act of conforming normatively to important groups *most* of the time can earn you the right to deviate occasionally without serious consequences. This interesting observation was made by Edwin Hollander (1960, 1985), who stated that conforming to a group over time earns you **idiosyncrasy credits**, much like putting money in the bank to save for future use. It's as if your past conformity allows you, at some point in the future, to deviate from the group (to "make withdrawals") without getting into too much trouble. Let's say, for example, that your friends are all in agreement that they want to go out for Chinese food. You, however, feel like Mexican food tonight, and rather than simply going along with group consensus, you decide to stick to your guns and lobby for burritos. If you have typically followed their friendship norms in other areas in the past, your friends will be less likely to become upset with you for your current nonconformity, for you've earned the right to deviate from their normative rules in this area on this occasion.

When one has no Allies in the Group Normative social influence is most powerfully felt when everyone in the group says or believes the same thing—for example, when your group of friends all believe that *The Lord of the Rings* was the greatest movie trilogy ever made. Resisting such unanimous social influence is difficult or even impossible, unless you have an ally. If another person disagrees with the group—say, by nominating the original *Star Wars* movies as the best trilogy ever—this behavior will help you buck the tide as well.

To test the importance of having an ally, Asch (1955) conducted another version of his conformity experiment. He had six of the seven confederates give the wrong answer, while one confederate gave the right answer on every trial. Now the subject was not alone. Though still disagreeing with the majority of the group, having one ally helped the subject resist normative pressures. People conformed on an average of only 6% of the trials in this study, compared to 32% when all of the confederates gave the wrong answer. Several other studies have found that observing another person resist normative social influence emboldens the individual to do the same (Allen & Levine, 1969; Morris & Miller, 1975; Nemeth & Chiles, 1988).

The difficulty of being the lone dissenter is apparent even in the U.S. Supreme Court. After hearing a case, the nine justices first determine, informally, whether they are unanimous or split in their decision. Some justices then write drafts and others decide which draft they will sign. There are informal attempts at influence, and eventually all make a decision. A content analysis of all the Supreme Court decisions from 1953 to 2001 (4,178 decisions, involving 29 different justices) indicated that the most common decision was the 9–0, unanimous one (35% of all decisions). And the least common decision? The one that required one justice to disagree with all of his or her colleagues, the 8–1 split, which accounted for only 10% of decisions over 48 years (Granberg & Bartels, 2005).

When the Group's Culture is Collectivistic "In America, the squeaky wheel gets the grease. In Japan, the nail that stands out gets pounded down" (Markus & Kitayama, 1991, p. 224). Is it true that the society in which one is raised affects the frequency of normative social influence? Perhaps not surprisingly, the answer is yes. Stanley Milgram (1961, 1977) replicated the Asch studies in Norway and France and found that the Norwegian participants conformed to a greater degree than the French participants did. Milgram (1961, p. 51) describes Norwegian society as "highly cohesive," with "a deep feeling of group identification," while French society, in comparison, shows "far

Idiosyncrasy Credits

The tolerance a person earns, over time, by conforming to group norms; if enough idiosyncrasy credits are earned, the person can, on occasion, behave deviantly without retribution from the group

TRY IT! Fashion: Normative Social Influence in Action

You can observe social impact theory in action by focusing on fashion—specifically, the clothes and accessories that you and your group of friends wear, as well as the look of other groups on campus. You can also observe what happens when you break those normative rules for fashion.

When you are with a group of friends and acquaintances, note carefully how everyone is dressed. Pretend that you are from another culture and not acquainted with the norms of this group; this will help you notice details that you might otherwise overlook. For example, what kinds of pants, shoes, shirts, jewelry, and other items are worn by this group? Are there similarities in their haircuts? Can you discover their fashion "rules"?

Next, spend some time on campus "people-watching," specifically observing what other groups of people are wearing. Can you discern different subgroups on your campus, defined by their style of dress? If so, there are different types of normative conformity operating on your campus; groups of friends are dressing according to the rules of their subgroup and not according to the rules of the campus as a whole.

Finally, if you are brave enough, break some normative fashion rules and see what happens. You can do this subtly or you can be very obvious. (But do be sensible; don't get yourself arrested!) For example, try wearing a suit and tie or a formal dress to the dining hall one day. Wear pajamas to class or to your professor's office hours. Wear a garbage bag (with holes cut out for your head and arms) over regular clothing. In any of these cases, just walk around as usual, seeming unaware that you are doing or wearing anything strange at all. How do people react to you? What will your friends say? Strangers will stare at you, but will they also avoid you?

Your group of friends (as well as the students at your school in general) may well have the qualities that social impact theory discusses: The group is important to you, the group is large, and the group is unanimous (which would be the case if your group of friends or your college student body has definite fashion norms). If you stop conforming to this normative social influence, the other group members will likely feel uncomfortable and exert some kind of pressure on you, trying to get you to return to a state of conformity.

less consensus in both social and political life." In another cross-cultural study of normative social influence, people in Lebanon, Hong Kong, and Brazil conformed to a similar extent (both to each other and to the American sample), whereas participants from the Bantu tribe of Zimbabwe conformed to a much greater degree (Whittaker & Meade, 1967). As the researchers point out, conformity has a very high social value in Bantu culture.

The extent to which conformity is valued varies across cultures. In the Opening Ceremony of the 2008 Beijing Olympics, a worldwide television audience was mesmerized by the sight of 2,008 drummers performing in perfect synchronization.

Although Japanese culture is more highly conforming than our own in many areas, two Asch-type studies found that when the group unanimously gave the incorrect answer, Japanese students were less conformist in general than North Americans (Frager, 1970; Williams & Sogon, 1984). In Japan, cooperation and loyalty are directed to the groups to which one belongs and with which one identifies; there is little expectation that one should conform to the behavior of strangers, especially in such an artificial setting as a psychology experiment. Similarly, conformity was much higher in a British sample when the participants thought the other group members were psychology majors like themselves rather than art history majors (Abrams et al., 1990). Similarly, German research participants have shown less conformity in the Asch experiment than North Americans (Timaeus, 1968); in Germany, conformity to strangers is less valued than conformity to a few well-defined groups (Moghaddam, Taylor, & Wright, 1993).

A more systematic review of the role of culture in conformity is provided by a meta-analysis of 133 Asch line-judgment studies conducted in 17 countries: United States, Canada, Britain, France, the Netherlands, Belgium, Germany, Portugal, Japan, Hong Kong, Fiji, Zimbabwe, Congo, Ghana, Brazil, Kuwait, and Lebanon (Bond & Smith, 1996). Participants from collectivistic cultures showed higher rates of conformity on the line task than participants from individualistic cultures. In collectivistic cultures, conformity is seen as a valued trait, not as a somewhat negative one, as in the United States. Agreeing with others is not viewed as an act of submission or cowardice in collectivist cultures, but an act of tact and sensitivity (Hodges & Geyer, 2006; Smith & Bond, 1999). Because the emphasis is on the group and not the individual, people in collectivistic cultures value normative social influence because it promotes harmony and supportive relationships in the group (Guisinger & Blatt, 1994; Kim et al., 1994; Markus et al., 1996; Zhang et al., 2007).

J. W. Berry (1967; Kim & Berry, 1993) explored the issue of conformity as a cultural value by comparing two cultures that had very different strategies for accumulating food. He hypothesized that societies that relied on hunting or fishing would value independence, assertiveness, and adventurousness—traits that were needed to find and bring home food. He also postulated that societies that were primarily agricultural would value cooperativeness, conformity, and acquiescence—traits that made close living and interdependent farming more successful. Berry used an Asch-type conformity task to compare the Inuit people of Baffin Island in Canada, a hunting and fishing society, to the Temne of Sierra Leone in Africa, a farming society. Consistent with Berry's hypothesis, the Temne showed a significant tendency to accept the suggestions of fellow group members in the study, while the Inuit almost completely disregarded them. As one Temne put it, "When the Temne people choose a thing, we must all agree with the decision—this is what we call cooperation"; in contrast, the few times the Inuit did conform to the group's wrong answer, they did so with "a quiet, knowing smile" (Berry, 1967, p. 417).

Minority Influence: When the Few Influence the Many

We shouldn't leave our discussion of normative social influence with the impression that groups affect individuals but the individual never has an effect on the group. As Serge Moscovici (1985, 1994; Moscovici, Mucchi-Faina, & Maass, 1994) says, if groups always succeeded in silencing nonconformists, rejecting deviants, and persuading everyone to go along with the majority point of view, how could change ever be introduced into the system? We would all be like little robots, marching along with everyone else in monotonous synchrony, never able to adapt to changing reality. Clearly, this is not the case (Imhoff & Erb, 2009).

> *People create social conditions, and people can change them.*
>
> —Tess Onwueme

Instead, the individual, or the minority of group members, can influence the behavior or beliefs of the majority (Moscovici, 1985, 1994; Mucchi-Faina & Pagliaro, 2008; Sinaceur et al., 2010). This is called **minority influence**. The key is consistency: People with minority views must express the same view over time, and different members of the minority must agree with one another. If a person in the minority wavers

Minority Influence
The case where a minority of group members influences the behavior or beliefs of the majority

between two different viewpoints or if two individuals express different minority views, the majority will dismiss them as people who have peculiar and groundless opinions. If, however, the minority expresses a consistent, unwavering view, the majority is more likely to take notice and even adopt the minority view (Moscovici & Nemeth, 1974). For example, in the 1970s, a minority of scientists began to call attention to evidence of human-caused climate change. Today, the majority is paying attention, and political leaders from the industrialized nations have met to discuss possible worldwide solutions. As another example, in the 1960s, a minority of feminists began to address women as Ms. instead of Miss or Mrs. Today, Ms. is the standard form of address in the workplace and many other contexts (Zimmer, 2009).

In a meta-analysis of nearly 1 hundred studies, Wendy Wood and her colleagues describe how minority influence operates (Wood et al., 1994). People in the majority can cause other group members to conform through normative influence. As in the Asch experiments, the conformity that occurs may be a case of public compliance without private acceptance. People in the minority can rarely influence others through normative means. In fact, majority group members may be hesitant to agree publicly with the minority; they don't want anyone to think that they side with those unusual, strange views. Minorities therefore exert their influence on the group via the other principal method: informational social influence. The minority can introduce new and unexpected information to the group and cause the group to examine the issues more carefully. Such careful examination may cause the majority to realize that the minority view has merit, leading the group to adopt all or part of the minority's view. In short, majorities often obtain public compliance because of normative social influence, whereas minorities are more likely to achieve private acceptance because of informational social influence (De Dreu & De Vries, 2001; Levine, Moreland, & Choi, 2001; Wood et al., 1996.)

Never let anyone keep you contained, and never let anyone keep your voice silent.

—Adam Clayton Powell

CONNECTIONS

The Power of Propaganda

One extraordinary example of social influence is propaganda, especially as perfected by the Nazi regime in the 1930s. Propaganda is defined as "the deliberate, systematic attempt to shape perceptions, manipulate cognitions, and direct behavior to achieve a response that furthers the desired intent of the propagandist" (Jowett & O'Donnell, 1999, p. 6).

Adolf Hitler was well aware of the power of propaganda as a tool of the state. In *Mein Kampf* (1925), written before he came to power, Hitler stated, "Its task is not to make an objective study of the truth . . . and then set it out before the masses with academic fairness; its task is to serve our right, always and unflinchingly" (pp. 182–183). In 1933, Hitler appointed Joseph Goebbels as head of the newly created Nazi Ministry of Popular Enlightenment and Propaganda. It was a highly efficient agency that permeated every aspect of Germans' lives. Nazis controlled all forms of the media, including newspapers, films, and radio. They also disseminated Nazi ideology through the extensive use of posters and "spectacles"—lavish public rallies that aroused powerful emotions of loyalty and patriotism among massive crowds (Jowett & O'Donnell, 1999; Zeman, 1995). Nazi propaganda was taught in schools and further promoted in Hitler Youth groups. The propaganda always presented a consistent, dogmatic message: The German people must take action to protect their racial purity and to increase their *Lebensraum* (living space) through conquest (Staub, 1989).

The concerns with *Lebensraum* led to World War II; the concerns with racial purity led to the Holocaust. How could the German people have acquiesced to the destruction of European Jewry? A major factor was prejudice (which we will discuss further in Chapter 13). Anti-Semitism was not a new or a Nazi idea. It had existed in Germany and in many other parts of Europe for hundreds of years. Propaganda is most successful when it taps into an audience's

Nazi propaganda permeated all facets of German life in the 1930s and 1940s. Here, huge crowds attend the 1934 Nuremberg rally. Such large public gatherings were a technique frequently used by Goebbels and Hitler to promote loyalty and conformity to the Nazi party.

preexisting beliefs. Thus, the German people's anti-Semitism could be quite easily strengthened and expanded by Goebbels's ministry. Jews were described in the Nazi propaganda as destroyers of Aryan racial purity and thus a threat to German survival. They were "pests, parasites, bloodsuckers" (Staub, 1989, p. 103) and were compared to "a plague of rats that needed to be exterminated" (Jowett & O'Donnell, 1999, p. 242); however, anti-Semitism is not a sufficient cause in and of itself for the extermination of Jews. Germany was initially no more prejudiced against Jews than its neighboring countries (or even the United States) in the 1930s, but none of these other countries came up with the concept of a "final solution" as Germany did (Tindale et al., 2002).

Although prejudice was an important precursor, more is needed to explain the Holocaust. Clearly, the propaganda operated as persuasive messages leading to attitude change, as we discussed in Chapter 7. But the propaganda also initiated social influence processes. In a totalitarian, fascist regime, the state is the "expert"—always present, always right, and always to be obeyed. Propaganda would persuade many Germans through informational conformity. They learned new "facts" (which were really lies) about the Jews and learned new solutions to what the Nazis had defined as the "Jewish question." The propaganda did an excellent job of convincing Germans that the Jews were a threat. As we saw earlier, people experiencing a crisis—in this case, runaway inflation and economic collapse in Germany—are more likely to conform to information delivered by an expert.

But surely, you are thinking, there must have been Germans who did not agree with the Nazi propaganda. Yes, there were, but it certainly wasn't easy. Just think about the position they were in. The Nazi ideology so permeated daily life that children and teenagers in Hitler Youth groups were encouraged to spy on their own parents and report them to the Gestapo if they were not "good" Nazis (Staub, 1989). Neighbors, coworkers, salespeople in shops, or passersby on the street—they could all turn you in if you said or did something that indicated you were disloyal. This situation is ripe for normative conformity, where public compliance occurs without, necessarily, private acceptance. Rejection, ostracism, even torture or death were strong motivators for normative conformity, and many ordinary Germans conformed to Nazi propaganda. Whether they did so for informational or normative reasons, their conformity permitted the Holocaust to occur. In the early years of the Third Reich, Hitler was very concerned about public resistance to his ideas (Staub, 1989). Unfortunately, because of social influence processes, prejudice, and the totalitarian system, public resistance never arose with sufficient strength to challenge Hitler's regime.

To swallow and follow, whether old doctrine or new propaganda, is a weakness still dominating the human mind.

—Charlotte Perkins Gilman

Using Social Influence to Promote Beneficial Behavior

We have seen how informational and normative conformity occurs. Even in a highly individualistic culture such as the United States, conformity of both types is common. Is there a way that we can use this tendency to conform to change people's behavior for the common good? Robert Cialdini, Raymond Reno, and Carl Kallgren have developed a model of normative conduct in which social norms (the rules that a society has for acceptable behaviors, values, and beliefs) can be used to subtly induce people to conform to correct, socially approved behavior (Cialdini, Kallgren, & Reno, 1991; Jacobson, Mortensen, & Cialdini, 2011; Kallgren, Reno, & Cialdini, 2000; Schultz et al., 2007).

For example, we all know that littering is wrong. But when we've finished enjoying a snack at the beach or in a park, what determines whether we toss the wrapper on the ground or carry it with us until we come to a trash can? Let's say we wanted to decrease littering or increase voter participation or encourage people to donate blood. How would we go about doing it?

Cialdini and his colleagues (1991) suggest that first we need to focus on what kind of norm is operating in the situation. Only then can we invoke a form of social influence that will encourage people to conform in socially beneficial ways. A culture's social norms are of two types. **Injunctive norms** have to do with what we think other people approve or disapprove of. Injunctive norms motivate behavior by promising rewards (or punishments) for normative (or nonnormative) behavior. For example, an injunctive norm in our culture is that littering is wrong and that donating blood is a good thing to do. **Descriptive norms** concern our perceptions of the way people actually behave in a given situation, regardless of whether the behavior is approved or disapproved of by others. Descriptive norms motivate behavior by informing people about what is effective or adaptive behavior. For example, while we all know that littering is wrong (an injunctive norm), we also all know that there are times and situations when people are likely to do it (a descriptive norm)—for example, dropping peanut shells on the ground at a baseball game or leaving your trash behind at your seat in a movie theater. Descriptive norms also tell us that relatively few people donate blood and that only a small percentage of registered voters actually vote. In sum, an injunctive norm relates to what most people in a culture approve or disapprove of; a descriptive norm relates to what people actually do (Kallgren et al., 2000; White et al., 2009).

Injunctive Norms
People's perceptions of what behaviors are approved or disapproved of by others

Descriptive Norms
People's perceptions of how people actually behave in given situations, regardless of whether the behavior is approved or disapproved of by others

The Role of Injunctive and Descriptive Norms

In a series of studies, Cialdini and colleagues have explored how injunctive and descriptive norms affect people's likelihood to litter. For example, in one field experiment, patrons of a city library were returning to their cars in the parking lot when a confederate approached them (Reno, Cialdini, & Kallgren, 1993). In the control group, the confederate just walked by. In the *descriptive norm condition*, the confederate was carrying an empty bag from a fast-food restaurant and dropped the bag on the ground before passing the participant. By littering, the confederate was subtly communicating, "this is what people do in this situation." In the *injunctive norm condition*, the confederate was not carrying anything but instead picked up a littered fast-food bag from the ground before passing the participant. By picking up someone else's litter, the confederate was subtly communicating that "littering is wrong." These three conditions occurred in one of two environments: Either the parking lot was heavily littered (by the experimenters, using paper cups, candy wrappers, and so on), or the area was clean and unlittered (cleaned up by the experimenters).

At this point, research participants have been exposed to one of two types of norms about littering or to no norm at all (the control group). And all this has happened in a littered or a clean environment. How were participants' own littering tendencies affected in these environments? When they got back to their cars, they found a large handbill slipped under the driver's side of the windshield. The handbill appeared on all the other cars too (not surprising, since the experimenters put them there). The participant had two choices at this point: throw the handbill on the ground, littering, or bring the handbill inside their car to dispose of it later. What did they do? Who refrained from littering?

Invoking conformity to social norms can be used in the effort to address societal problems such as littering.

The control group tells us the baseline of what percentage of people typically litter in this situation. As you can see in Figure 8.7, the researchers found that slightly more than one-third of people threw the handbill on the ground; it didn't matter if the area was already littered or if it was clean. In the descriptive norm condition, the confederate's littering communicated two different messages, depending on the condition of the parking lot. In the littered parking lot, the confederate's behavior reminded participants that people often litter here—the confederate served as just one salient example of the type of behavior that had led to such a messy parking lot in the first place. In the clean parking lot, however, the confederate's behavior communicated a different message. Now, the behavior stood out as unusual—it reminded participants that most people don't litter in this area, which is why it looked so clean otherwise. Hence, we would expect the confederate's littering behavior to remind participants of a descriptive norm against littering more in the clean environment than in the littered one, and this is what the researchers found (see Figure 8.7). Finally, what about the injunctive norm condition? This kind of norm was less context-dependent: Seeing the confederate picking up someone else's litter invokes the injunctive norm that littering is wrong in both the clean and the littered environments, thereby leading to the lowest amount of littering in the study (see Figure 8.7; Reno et al., 1993).

In light of studies such as this one, researchers have concluded that injunctive norms are more powerful than descriptive norms in producing desirable behavior (Cialdini, 2003; Kallgren et al., 2000). This should not surprise you, because injunctive norms tap into normative conformity—we conform (for example, refraining from littering) because someone's behavior reminds us that our society disapproves of littering. We will look like selfish slobs if we litter, and we will feel embarrassed if other people see us litter. While norms are always present to some extent—we *know* that littering is bad—they are not always *salient* to us (Jonas et al., 2008; Kallgren et al., 2000). To promote socially beneficial behavior, something in the situation needs to draw our attention to the relevant norm. Thus, anything that highlights *injunctive norms*—what society approves and disapproves of—can be used to create positive behavioral change.

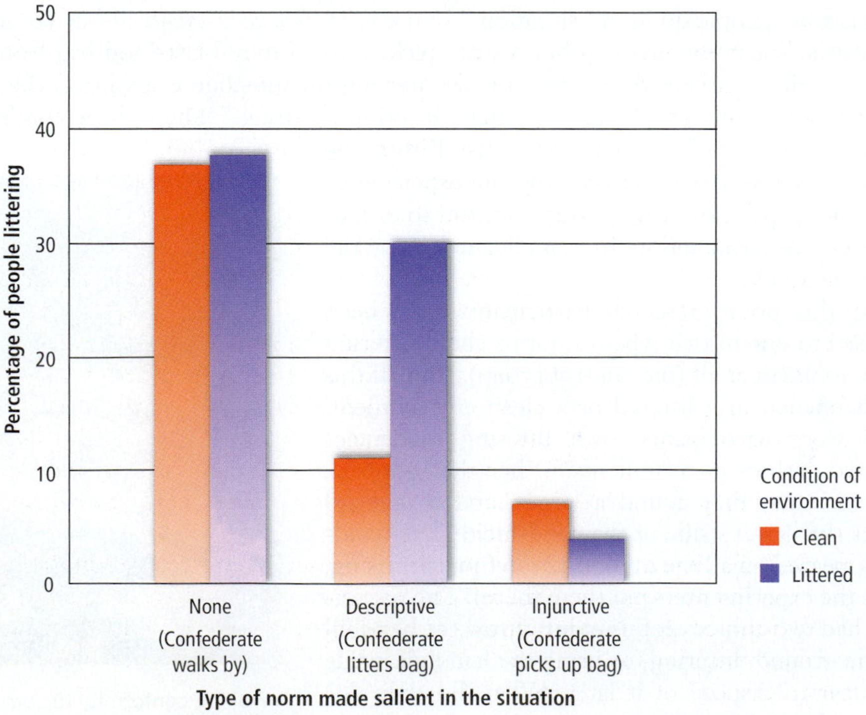

FIGURE 8.7

The Effect of Injunctive and Descriptive Norms on Littering

The data for the control group (left) indicate that 37% to 38% of people litter a handbill found on their car windshield whether the environment (a parking lot) is littered or clean. When a descriptive norm is made salient, littering decreases significantly only in the clean environment (middle). When an injunctive norm is made salient, littering decreases significantly in both types of environment, indicating that injunctive norms are more consistently effective at changing behavior.

(Adapted from Reno, Cialdini, & Kallgren, 1993)

Using Norms to Change Behavior: Beware the "Boomerang Effect"

In recent years, university administrators have tried a new technique for decreasing alcohol binge drinking on their campuses. The idea is that students typically overestimate how much their peers drink each week (Berkowitz, 2004; Lewis et al., 2007; Perkins, 2007). Thus, telling them, "Students at your school, on average, consume only X number of drinks a week" should lead them to decrease their own alcohol intake as they conform to this lower level. However, researchers have noted a major problem with this approach: Sometimes, it backfires, or "boomerangs." That is, for students who already drink very little (or not at all), finding out that the average student on campus drinks more than they do leads them to *increase* their own alcohol intake to be more like everyone else! In short, the public service message meant to decrease alcohol consumption can actually have the effect of increasing it (Perkins, Haines, & Rice, 2005; Wechsler et al., 2003). Accordingly, your efforts to change others' behavior through processes of conformity must consider that there are different types of people receiving your message: Those performing the undesirable behavior at an *above-average* level (whom you want to convince to decrease their behavior) and those who are performing the undesirable behavior at a *below-average* level (who you want to continue doing what they're already doing rather than to "boomerang" by increasing the undesirable behavior).

P. Wesley Shultz and colleagues tested this idea by focusing on a desirable behavior we've already discussed in this chapter: conserving electrical energy in the home (Shultz et al., 2007). Residents of a California neighborhood agreed to take part in the study. Their baseline energy usage was measured, and they were divided into two groups: those whose energy consumption was above the average for their neighborhood and those whose energy consumption was below the average. The households were then randomly assigned to receive one of two kinds of feedback about their energy usage over several weeks. In the *descriptive norm condition*, they were told how much energy they had used that week, told how much energy the average household in their neighborhood had used (the descriptive norm information), and given suggestions for how to conserve energy. In the *descriptive norm plus injunctive norm condition*, they received all of the above information plus one subtle, but important, addition: If they had consumed less energy than the average household, the researcher drew a smiley face next to the information. If they had consumed more energy than the average household, the researcher drew a sad face instead. The happy or sad face communicated the *injunctive* part of the message—the recipients were receiving either approval or disapproval for the amount of energy they had used.

Weeks later, researchers measured energy usage again. Did the messages help convince people to conserve energy? Did those who already used low amounts stray from the path of conservation righteousness and "boomerang," deciding that it would not be so bad for them to be a little less efficient just like their wasteful neighbors? First, the results indicated that the descriptive norm message had a positive effect on those who consumed more energy than average; they cut back and conserved. However, the descriptive norm message had a boomerang effect on those who consumed less energy than average. Once they learned what their neighbors were doing (using electricity like crazy), they felt liberated to increase their own usage!

On the other hand, the "descriptive norm plus injunctive norm" message was uniformly successful. Those whose consumption was more than average decreased their usage when they received this message. Most importantly, those whose consumption was below average to begin with did not boomerang when they received this message—they maintained their low level of energy use, the same level as before the study started. Thus, the smiley face reminded them that they were doing the right thing, and they kept on doing it (Schultz et al., 2007).

This study has had a major impact on energy conservation strategies in the United States. The use of smiley and sad faces to give injunctive norm feedback, combined with descriptive norm energy-usage information, is now being used by utility companies in various major metropolitan areas, including Boston, Chicago, Sacramento, and Seattle (Kaufman, 2009).

Obedience to Authority

We are socialized, beginning as children, to obey authority figures who we perceive as legitimate (Blass, 2000; Staub, 1989). We internalize the social norm of obedience such that we usually obey rules and laws even when the authority figure isn't present—you stop at red lights even if the cops aren't parked at the corner. However, obedience can have extremely serious and even tragic consequences as well. People will obey the orders of an authority figure to hurt or even kill other human beings.

As with many eras, the past century was marked by repeated atrocities and genocides—in Germany and the rest of Europe, Armenia, the Ukraine, Rwanda, Cambodia, Bosnia, Sudan, and elsewhere. One of the most important questions facing the world's inhabitants, therefore, becomes, where does obedience end and personal responsibility begin? The philosopher Hannah Arendt (1965) was particularly interested in understanding the causes of the Holocaust. How could Hitler's Nazi regime in Germany accomplish the murder of 6 million European Jews and millions of others, based on ethnicity, sexual orientation, or political beliefs? Arendt argued that most participants in the Holocaust were not sadists or psychopaths who enjoyed the mass murder of innocent people, but rather ordinary citizens subjected to complex and powerful social pressures. As a journalist, she covered the trial of Adolf Eichmann, the Nazi official responsible for the transportation of Jews to the death camps, and concluded that he was not the bloodthirsty monster that many people made him out to be, but a commonplace bureaucrat who did what he was told without questioning his orders (Miller, 1995).

Our point is not that Eichmann—or the soldiers at My Lai or the Khmer Rouge in Cambodia or the Serbs in Bosnia—should be excused for the crimes they committed. The point is that it is too easy to explain their behavior as the acts of madmen. It is more fruitful—and more frightening—to view their behavior as the acts of ordinary people exposed to extraordinary social influence. But how can we be sure that these atrocities were not caused solely by evil, psychopathic people, but rather by powerful social forces operating on people of all types? The way to find out is to study social pressure in the laboratory under controlled conditions. We could take a sample of ordinary citizens, subject them to various kinds of social influence, and see to what extent they will conform and obey. Can an experimenter influence ordinary people to commit immoral acts, such as inflicting severe pain on an innocent bystander? Stanley Milgram (1963, 1974, 1976) decided to find out, in what has become the most famous series of studies in social psychology.

Imagine that you were a participant in one of Milgram's studies. You answer an ad in the newspaper, asking for participants in a study on memory and learning. When you arrive at the laboratory, you meet another participant, a 47-year-old, somewhat overweight, pleasant-looking fellow. The experimenter, wearing a white lab coat, explains that one of you will play the role of a teacher and the other the role of a learner. You draw a slip of paper out of a hat and discover that you will be the teacher. It turns out that your job is to read to the other participant a list of word pairs (e.g., *blue–box*, *nice–day*) and then test him on the list. The experimenter instructs you to deliver an electric shock to the learner whenever he makes a mistake, because the purpose of the study is to examine the effects of punishment on learning.

Victims of the Holocaust from the Bergen-Belsen concentration camp, 1945.

You watch as the other participant—the learner—is strapped into a chair in an adjacent room and electrodes are attached to his arm. You are seated in front of a shock generator whose 30 switches deliver varying levels of shock in 15-volt increments, from 15 to 450 volts. There are labels accompanying these switches, from "Slight Shock" to "Danger: Severe Shock" to an ominous "XXX" next to the highest levels (see the photos on page 226). The experimenter tells you that the first time the learner makes a mistake, you should give him a shock of 15 volts—the smallest amount—and then increase the amount by

15 volts for each subsequent mistake he makes. So that you will know what the shocks are like, the experimenter gives you a sample shock of 45 volts, which is rather painful.

You read the list of word pairs to the learner and then begin the testing phase. After announcing the first word of each pair, you give four possible answers; the learner responds by pressing one of four switches, illuminating a light on the answer box in front of you. Everything begins smoothly as the learner gets the first few right. Then he gets some wrong, and as instructed, you deliver a shock each time. At this point, you are probably getting concerned about the number and severity of the shocks you will have to give. When you get to the 75-volt level, the learner, whom you can hear over an intercom, emits a painful "Ugh!" Perhaps you pause and ask the experimenter what you should do. "Please continue," he responds without hesitation. As the learner continues to make mistakes, you deliver a few more shocks. The learner protests, shouting, "Ugh! Experimenter! That's all! Get me out of here!" You look at the experimenter with concern. He tells you calmly, "It is absolutely essential that you continue." (See Figure 8.8.)

Learner's Protests

75 volts: Ugh!

90 volts: Ugh!

105 volts: Ugh! (louder)

120 volts: Ugh! Hey this really hurts.

135 volts: Ugh!!

150 volts: Ugh!!! Experimenter! That's all. Get me out of here. I told you I had heart trouble. My heart's starting to bother me now. Get me out of here, please. My heart's starting to bother me. I refuse to go on. Let me out.

165 volts: Ugh! Let me out! (shouting)

180 volts: Ugh! I can't stand the pain. Let me out of here! (shouting)

195 volts: Ugh! Let me out of here. Let me out of here. My heart's bothering me. Let me out of here! You have no right to keep me here! Let me out! Let me out of here! Let me out! Let me out of here! My heart's bothering me. Let me out! Let me out!

210 volts: Ugh! Experimenter! Get me out of here. I've had enough. I won't be in the experiment anymore.

225 volts: Ugh!

240 volts: Ugh!

255 volts: Ugh! Get me out of here.

270 volts: Ugh! (agonized scream) Let me out of here. Let me out of here. Let me out of here. Let me out. Do you hear? Let me out of here.

285 volts: Ugh! (agonized scream)

300 volts: Ugh! (agonized scream) I absolutely refuse to answer anymore. Get me out of here. You can't hold me here. Get me out. Get me out of here.

315 volts: Ugh! (intensely agonized scream) I told you I refuse to answer. I'm no longer part of this experiment.

330 volts: Ugh! (intense and prolonged agonized scream) Let me out of here. Let me out of here. My heart's bothering me. Let me out, I tell you. (hysterically) Let me out of here. Let me out of here. You have no right to hold me here. Let me out! Let me out! Let me out of here! Let me out!

Instructions Used by the Experimenter to Achieve Obedience

Prod 1: Please continue *or* Please go on.

Prod 2: The experiment requires that you continue.

Prod 3: It is absolutely essential that you continue.

Prod 4: You have no other choice; you must go on.

The prods were always made in sequence: Only if prod 1 had been unsuccessful could prod 2 be used. If the subject refused to obey the experimenter after prod 4, the experiment was terminated. The experimenter's tone of voice was at all times firm but not impolite. The sequence was begun anew on each occasion that the subject balked or showed reluctance to follow orders.

Special prods. If the subject asked whether the learner was likely to suffer permanent physical injury, the experimenter said:

Although the shocks may be painful, there is no permanent tissue damage, so please go on. [Followed by prods 2, 3, and 4 if necessary.]

If the subject said that the learner did not want to go on, the experimenter replied: Whether the learner likes it or not, you must go on until he has learned all the word pairs correctly. So please go on. [Followed by prods 2, 3, and 4 if necessary.]

FIGURE 8.8

Transcript of the learner's protests in Milgram's obedience study and of the prods used by the experimenter to compel people to continue giving shocks.

(Adapted from Milgram, 1963, 1974)

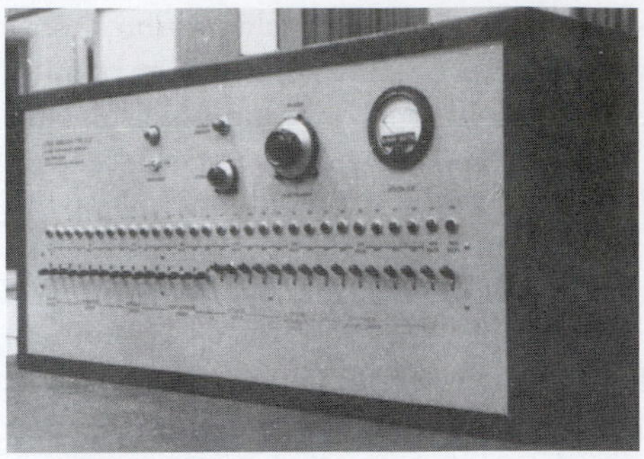

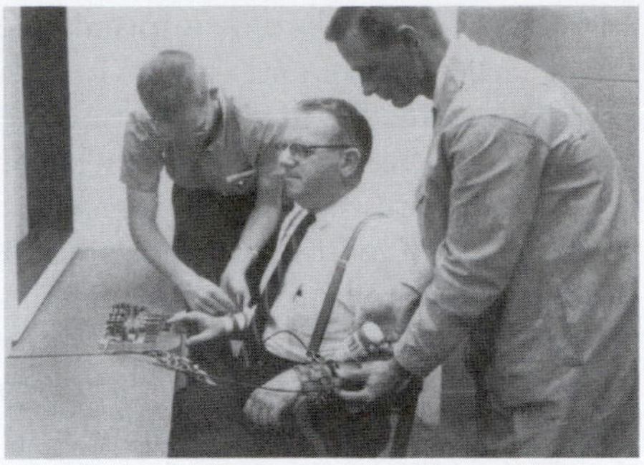

Left: The shock generator used in Milgram's research. *Right:* The learner (an accomplice of the experimenter) is strapped into the chair, and electrodes are attached to his arm.

(Adapted from Milgram, 1974)

What would you do? How many people do you think would continue to obey the experimenter, increasing the levels of shock all the way up the shock panel until they had delivered the maximum amount of 450 volts?

When this question was posed to psychology majors at Yale University, they estimated that only about 1% of the population would go to this extreme. A sample of middle-class adults and a panel of psychiatrists made similar predictions. Based on our discussion of conformity thus far, however, perhaps you are not so optimistic. Indeed, most of Milgram's participants succumbed to the pressure of an authority figure. The average maximum shock delivered was 360 volts, and 62.5% of the participants went all the way to the end of the panel, delivering the 450-volt shock. A full 80% of the participants continued giving the shocks even after the learner, who earlier had mentioned that he had a heart condition, screamed, "Let me out of here! Let me out of here! My heart's bothering me. Let me out of here! ... Get me out of here! I've had enough. I won't be in the experiment any more" (Milgram, 1974, p. 56).

It is important to note that the learner was actually an accomplice of the experimenter who was acting rather than suffering—he did not receive any actual shocks. It is equally important to note that the study was very convincingly done so that people believed they really were shocking the learner. Here is Milgram's description of one participant's response to the teacher role:

> I observed a mature and initially poised businessman enter the laboratory smiling and confident. Within 20 minutes he was reduced to a twitching, stuttering wreck, who was rapidly approaching a point of nervous collapse. He constantly pulled on his earlobe, and twisted his hands. At one point he pushed his fist into his forehead and muttered, "Oh God, let's stop it." And yet he continued to respond to every word of the experimenter, and obeyed to the end. (Milgram, 1963, p. 377)

Why did so many research participants (who ranged in age from the twenties to the fifties and included blue-collar, white-collar, and professional workers) conform to the wishes of the experimenter, to the point where they genuinely believed they were inflicting great pain on another human being? Why were the college students, middle-class adults, and psychiatrists so wrong in their predictions about what people would do? In a dangerous way, each of the reasons that explain why people conform combined to cause Milgram's participants to obey—just as many Germans did during the Holocaust and soldiers have done during recent atrocities in Iraq and Afghanistan. Let's take a close look at how this played out in Milgram's research.

Watch on **MyPsychLab**
To learn more, watch the MyPsychLab video ***Classic Footage of Milgram's Obedience Study***.

The Role of Normative Social Influence

First, it is clear that normative pressures made it difficult for people in Milgram's studies to refuse to continue. As we have seen, if someone really wants us to do something, it can be difficult to say no. This is particularly true when the person is in a position of authority over us. Milgram's participants probably believed that if they refused to continue, the experimenter would be disappointed, hurt, or maybe even angry—all of which put pressure on them to continue. It is important to note that this study, unlike the Asch study, was set up so that the experimenter actively attempted to get people to conform, giving commands such as "It is absolutely essential that you continue." When an authority figure is so insistent that we obey, it is difficult to say no (Blass, 1991, 2000, 2003; Hamilton, Sanders, & McKearney, 1995; Meeus & Raaijmakers, 1995; Miller, 1986).

The fact that normative pressures were present in the Milgram study is clear from a variation that he conducted. This time, there were three teachers, two of whom were confederates. One confederate was instructed to read the list of word pairs; the other, to tell the learner whether his response was correct. The (real) participant's job was to deliver the shocks, increasing their severity with each error, as in the original study. At 150 volts, when the learner gave his first vehement protest, the first confederate refused to continue, despite the experimenter's command that he do so. At 210 volts, the second confederate refused to continue. The result? Seeing their peers disobey made it much easier for the actual participants to disobey too. Only 10% of the participants gave the maximum level of shock in this version of the study (see Figure 8.9). This result is similar to Asch's finding that people did not conform nearly as much when one accomplice bucked the majority.

The Role of Informational Social Influence

Despite the power of the normative pressures in Milgram's original study, they are not the sole reason people complied. The experimenter was authoritative and insistent, but he was hardly pointing a gun at participants and telling them to "conform or else"; the participants were free to get up and leave anytime they wanted to. Why didn't they, especially when the experimenter was a stranger they had never met before and probably would never see again?

As we saw earlier, when people are in a confusing situation and unsure of what they should do, they use other people to help define the situation. Informational social influence is especially powerful when the situation is ambiguous, when it is a crisis, and when the other people in the situation have some expertise. All three of these characteristics describe the situation Milgram's participants faced. The scenario—a study of the effects of punishment on learning—seemed straightforward enough when the experimenter explained it, but then it turned into something else altogether. The learner cried out in pain, but the experimenter told the participant that the shocks did not cause any permanent damage. The participant didn't want to hurt anyone, but he or she had agreed to be in the study and to follow the directions. When in such a state of conflict, it was only natural for the participants to use an expert—the experimenter in the scientific-looking white lab coat—to help them decide what was the right thing to do (Hamilton et al., 1995; Krakow & Blass, 1995; Miller, 1986; Miller, Collins, & Brief, 1995).

Another version of Milgram's study supports the idea that informational influence was operative. This version was identical to the original one except for three critical changes: First, the experimenter never said which shock levels were to be given, leaving this decision up to the participant. Second, before the study began, the experimenter received a telephone call and had to leave the room, telling the participant to continue without him. Third, there was a confederate playing the role of an additional teacher, whose job was to record how long it took the learner to respond to each word pair. When the experimenter left, this other "teacher" said that he had just thought of a good system: How about if they increased the level of shock each time the learner made a mistake? He insisted that the real participant follow this procedure.

Note that in this situation the expertise of the person giving the commands is nonexistent: He was just a regular person, no more knowledgeable than the participants themselves. Because he lacked expertise, people were much less likely to use him as a source of information about how they should respond. As seen in Figure 8.9, in this version, full compliance dropped from 62.5%, to only 20%. (The fact that 20% still gave the maximum shock suggests that some people were so uncertain about what to do that they used even a nonexpert as a guide.)

An additional variation conducted by Milgram underscores the importance of authority figures as experts in eliciting such

When you think of the long and gloomy history of man, you will find more hideous crimes have been committed in the name of obedience than in the name of rebellion.
—C. P. SNOW

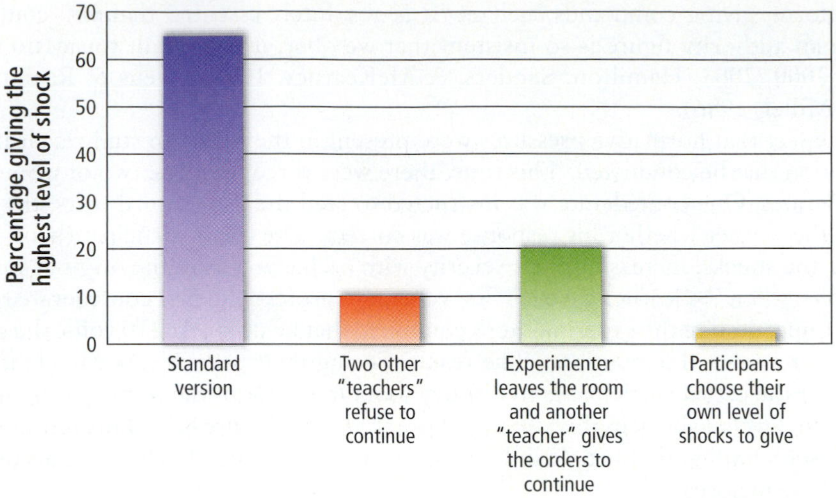

FIGURE 8.9

Results of Different Versions of the Milgram Study

Obedience is highest in the standard version, where the participant is ordered to deliver increasing levels of shock to another person (left panel). Obedience drops when other participants model disobedience or when the authority figure is not present (two middle panels). Finally, when no orders are given to increase the shocks, almost no participants do so (right panel). The contrast in behavior between the far-left and far-right panels indicates just how powerful a tendency obedience is.

(Adapted from Milgram, 1974)

obedience. In this variation, two experimenters gave the real participants their orders. At 150 volts, when the learner first cried out that he wanted to stop, the two experimenters began to disagree about whether they should continue the study. At this point, 100% of the participant-teachers stopped responding. Note that nothing the victim ever did caused all the participants to stop obeying; however, when the authorities' definition of the situation became unclear, the participants broke out of their conforming role.

Other Reasons Why We Obey

Both normative and informational social influences were very strong in Milgram's research; however, these reasons for complying still fall short of fully explaining why people acted in a manner that seems so inhumane. They seem to account for why people initially complied with the experimenter's instructions, but after it became increasingly obvious what was happening to the learner, why didn't participants realize that what they were doing was terribly wrong and stop? Just as the fast-food restaurant managers continued to abuse their employees long after the demands of the "policeman" on the phone shifted from bizarre to illegal, many of Milgram's participants pressed the shock levers time after time after time, despite the cries of anguish from a fellow human being.

Conforming to the Wrong Norm To understand this continued compliance, we need to consider additional aspects of the situation. We don't mean to imply that Milgram's participants were completely mindless or unaware of what they were doing. All were terribly concerned about the plight of the victim. The problem was that they were caught in a web of conflicting norms, and it was difficult to determine which ones to follow. At the beginning of the study, it was perfectly reasonable to heed the norm that says, "Obey expert, legitimate authority figures." The experimenter was confident and knowledgeable, and the study seemed as if it was a reasonable test of an interesting hypothesis. So why not cooperate and do as you are told?

But, gradually, the rules of the game changed, and this "obey authority" norm was no longer appropriate. The experimenter, who seemed so reasonable before, was now asking people to inflict great pain on their fellow participant. But once people are following one norm, it can be difficult to switch midstream or to realize that this norm is no longer appropriate and that another norm, "Do not inflict needless harm on a fellow human being," should be followed. For example, suppose the experimenter had explained, at the outset, that he would like people to deliver possibly fatal shocks to the other participant. How many people would have agreed? Very few, we suspect, because it would have been clear that this violated an important social and personal norm about inflicting harm on others. Instead, the experimenter pulled a kind of "bait and switch" routine, whereby he first made it look like an "obey authority" norm was appropriate and then gradually violated this norm (Collins & Brief, 1995).

It was particularly difficult for people to abandon the "obey authority" norm in the Milgram study because of three key aspects of the situation. First, the study was fast paced, preventing the participants from reflecting on what they were doing. They were busy recording the learner's responses, keeping track of the word pairs, and determining whether the learner's responses were right or wrong. Given that they had to attend carefully to these details and move along at a fast pace, it was difficult for them to realize that the norm that was guiding their behavior—cooperating with the authority figure—was, after a while, no longer appropriate (Conway & Schaller, 2005; Modigliani & Rochat, 1995). We suspect that if, halfway through the study, Milgram's participants had been told to take a break or had been left in the room by themselves for a period of time, many more would have successfully redefined the situation and refused to continue.

Self-justification A second important aspect of the situation in the Milgram study is that, as alluded to above, the experimenter asked people to increase the shocks in very small increments. The participants did not go from giving a small shock to giving a potentially lethal one. Instead, at any given point, they only faced a smaller decision about whether to increase by a meager 15 volts the amount of shock they had just given. As we saw in Chapter 6, every time a person makes an important or difficult decision, dissonance is produced, with resultant pressures to reduce it. An effective way of reducing dissonance produced by a difficult decision is to decide that the decision was fully justified. But because reducing dissonance provides a justification for the preceding action, in some situations it makes a person vulnerable to further escalating the previously chosen activity.

Thus, in the Milgram study, the participants' initial agreement to administer the first shock created internal pressure on them to continue to obey. As the participants administered each successive level of shock, they had to justify it in their own minds. After they had justified a particular shock level, it became very difficult for them to decide on a place where they should draw the line and stop. How could they say, in effect, "OK, I gave him 200 volts, but not 215—never 215!" Each succeeding shock and its justification laid the groundwork for the next shock and would have been dissonant with quitting; 215 volts is not *that* different from 200, and 230 is not *that* different from 215. Those who did break off the series did so against enormous internal pressure to continue (Darley, 1992; Gilbert, 1981; Miller et al., 1995).

The Loss of Personal Responsibility The third reason why it was difficult for participants to abandon the "obey authority" norm in the Milgram studies is a particularly troubling one. When you are the research participant (or the employee) and the other person is a legitimate authority figure (the experimenter, the boss, the military commander, the police officer), you are the "puppet" and they are pulling the strings. They define what it is you are supposed to do, and they are responsible for the end results—after all, it was their idea and you were "just following orders." Milgram (1974) stressed that the loss of a sense of personal responsibility for one's actions was a critical component explaining the results of the obedience studies.

A particularly disturbing job is that of prison guards who must carry out a capital punishment sentence. How do these guards respond to a job where they are told to kill another person? Clearly, they need to reduce their cognitive dissonance. Taking a life is a supremely problematic and disturbing act, so they very much need to engage in self-justification in order to do it. Michael Osofsky, Albert Bandura, and Philip Zimbardo (2005) studied guards on the execution teams of three southern state prisons and compared them to their fellow guards who did not conduct executions. All the guards responded anonymously to a questionnaire that asked them to rate their level of agreement with statements such as "Because of the nature of their crime, murderers have lost the right to live" and "Those who carry out state executions should not be criticized for following society's wishes."

The researchers found a highly significant difference in the attitudes of the two types of guards. The execution-team guards demonstrated much more "moral disengagement" from their work than did the other guards. The execution-team guards denied all personal responsibility for the executions. They felt they were just following orders—in this case, those of a judge and jury. They also engaged in high levels of justification in other areas. As compared to the regular prison guards, they dehumanized the prisoners more, seeing them as lacking important human qualities. They perceived the prisoners as more of a threat to society, such that it was necessary that they be killed. All these attitudes helped the execution guards reduce their qualms about the morality of what they did at work. As one guard put it, "I had a job to do, that's what we did. Our job was to execute this man and we were going to do it in a professional manner" (Osofsky, Bandura, & Zimbardo, 2005, p. 386).

The Obedience Studies, Then and Now

Stanley Milgram's study of obedience is widely considered to be one of the most important contributions to the field of psychology (Benjamin & Simpson, 2009). His work, conducted in the early 1960s, was replicated in the following years by researchers in 11 countries, involving approximately 3,000 research participants (Blass, 2009). However, Milgram's research paradigm also ignited a storm of protest (and soul-searching) in the research community over the ethical treatment of research participants.

Milgram's research was criticized by some as unethical for several reasons. First, the study involved *deception*. For example, participants were told it was a study on memory and learning, when of course it was not; participants were told the electric shocks were real, when of course they were not. Second, there was no true *informed consent* on the part of participants. When they agreed to be in the study, they were not informed as to its true nature, and thus they never really consented to take part in the scenario they eventually experienced. Third, their role as teacher caused them *psychological distress* during the course of the study; for many participants, this occurred at a high level. Fourth, it was not made clear to participants that they had the *right to withdraw* from the study at any time; in fact, the experimenter stated the exact opposite—for example, that they "had to continue." Fifth, the participants experienced *inflicted insight*. When the study ended, some of them had learned unpleasant things about themselves that they had not agreed to beforehand (Baumrind, 1964, 1985; Milgram, 1964; Miller, 2009).

Although the ethical issues surrounding Milgram's study were not, as is often suggested, the reason formal ethical guidelines for research participants were created in the United States in 1966 (they were primarily created to protect participants in medical research), these new guidelines made conducting obedience research such as Milgram's increasingly problematic (Benjamin & Simpson, 2009). Indeed, decades would pass without researchers conducting follow-up studies of obedience using Milgram's procedure (Blass, 2009), and many students learned in their psychology courses that such studies could never be run again. But that all changed in 2006.

That year, Jerry M. Burger (2009) conducted the first obedience study in the United States in 30 years. Much had changed in the country over these decades. Had the likelihood of being obedient, even to the point of inflicting harm, changed as well? In order to conduct this study under modern ethical guidelines, Burger (2009) had to make a number of changes to the procedure. First, he reduced the psychological distress experienced by participants by stopping the study after 150 volts, when the learner is first heard yelling that he wants out and refuses to go on. Analysis of data from eight of Milgram's study versions indicated that when disobedience occurred, it was most likely to happen at this point in the study; most previous participants who passed the 150-volt mark tended to go all the way to end of the shock panel (Packer, 2008). Thus, Burger could compare obedience versus disobedience up to this critical 150-volt juncture and then end the study without further subjecting participants to the many, many levels of shock (and stress) that remained. Second, participants were prescreened by a clinical psychologist, and those who were identified as even slightly likely to have a negative reaction to the experience were excluded from the study (38% were excluded). Finally, Burger (2009) explicitly and repeatedly told his participants that they could leave the study at any time, as could the learner.

In most respects, though, Burger's (2009) study was like the original. His experimenter used the same four "prods" that Milgram's used (e.g., "It is absolutely essential that you continue") to order participants to continue when they began to waver. Burger's participants, like Milgram's, were adult residents recruited through newspaper advertisements and flyers. Their age range of 20 to 81 years was broader than Milgram's, though their average age of about 43 years was similar. They were ethnically more diverse than Milgram's participants, and they were also more highly educated: Forty percent of Burger's sample had college degrees, and another 20% had master's degrees. Both men and women participated as teachers in Burger's study; Milgram had female participants in only one of his many study versions. Finally, because the Milgram obedience studies are quite well known, Burger excluded participants who had taken more than two college-level psychology courses.

What did Burger (2009) find? Are people more disobedient today than they were in Milgram's time 45 years ago? After all, during the intervening decades, as large numbers of Americans took part in the civil rights movement and various antiwar movements, they had accepted the injunctive norm that questioning authority was the right thing to do. Americans had also grown less complacent and accepting of their government at both the state and federal level (Cohen, 2008). Did these cultural experiences translate into a newly empowered, disobedient participant? Sadly, the answer is no; they did not. Burger (2009) found no significant difference in obedience rates between his participants and Milgram's. After the critical 150-volt shock had been delivered (and the learner cried out to be released), 70% of Burger's participants had obeyed and were ready to continue (at which point, Burger ended the study). At this same point in the comparable Milgram study, 82.5% were obedient and continued; the difference between 70% and 82.5% is not statistically significant. Similarly, Burger (2009) found no significant difference in obedience between his male and female participants, which was also the case in Milgram's research.

Note that Burger's ethically necessary changes in methodology also complicate a direct comparison to Milgram's results (Miller, 2009). Some of Burger's changes may have decreased the likelihood of obedience; others may have increased its likelihood. For example, perhaps repeated reminders beforehand that they could withdraw from the study at any time made it easier for participants to ultimately disobey. But the most profound change that Burger made was stopping the study after 150 volts. While this makes the procedure more ethical, it means we have no idea how many participants, today, would go all the way to the 450-volt shock (Twenge, 2009). Much of the extraordinary power of the Milgram obedience studies came from participants' choices after 150 volts, as they continued step by small step to the last switch on the shock generator. It is during this part of the study that participants felt the most conflicted and anxious. It is here that they revealed their response to a pressing moral conflict (Miller, 2009). This information is lost in the present replication. And as such, it reminds us that scientific inquiry has two, sometimes competing aims: to discover new knowledge, and to do no harm.

Simulate on **MyPsychLab**
To learn more, try the MyPsychLab ***Closer Look Simulation: Social Psychology.***

It's not About Aggression Before leaving our discussion of Milgram's research, we should mention one other possible interpretation of his results: Did the participants act so inhumanely because there is an inherently evil side to human nature, lurking just below the surface, ready to be expressed with the flimsiest excuse? To test this hypothesis, Milgram conducted another version of his study. Everything was the same except that the experimenter told the participants that they could choose any level of shock they wished to give the learner when he made a mistake. Milgram gave people permission to use the highest levels, telling them that there was a lot to be learned from all levels of shock. This instruction should have allowed any aggressive urges to be expressed unchecked. Instead, the participants chose to give very mild shocks (see Figure 8.9 on page 228). Only 2.5% of the participants gave the maximum shock. Thus, the Milgram studies do not show that all people have an evil streak that shines through when the surface is scratched (Reeder, Monroe, & Pryor, 2008). Instead, these studies demonstrate that social pressures can combine in insidious ways to make humane people act in an inhumane manner. Let us conclude this chapter with the words of Stanley Milgram:

> Even Eichmann was sickened when he toured the concentration camps, but in order to participate in mass murder he had only to sit at a desk and shuffle papers. At the same time the man in the camp who actually dropped [the poison] into the gas chambers is able to justify his behavior on the grounds that he is only following orders from above. Thus there is fragmentation of the total human act; no one man decides to carry out the evil act and is confronted with its consequences. The person who assumes full responsibility for the act has evaporated. Perhaps this is the most common characteristic of socially organized evil in modern society.
>
> (1976, pp. 183–184)

USE IT!

The topics of conformity and obedience bring to mind the great opening sentence in Charles Dickens's novel *A Tale of Two Cities*: "It was the best of times, it was the worst of times." These types of social influence are incredibly useful in maintaining social order. Without them, life would be chaotic, even dangerous. However, they have their "dark side" as well, even to the point of promoting and enabling genocide. What can you do to protect yourself from the potentially negative effects of social influence? Probably the most difficult is informational conformity; by definition, you conform to others because you don't know what's going on. Therefore, it is very difficult to know if they're wrong. Typically, it's best to rely on an expert instead of a nonexpert, but even this advice can be tricky. Resisting normative conformity is more straightforward. You'll know what the right thing to do is, but will you be able to withstand the disapproval of others? Remember that having an ally will help you to stand up to group pressure. Obedience also presents a fairly straightforward scenario. You'll know when you've been given an order that goes against your ethical or moral beliefs. As with normative conformity, it will be a matter of whether or not you are willing and able to withstand the repercussions of your disobedience. Luckily, learning about these types of social influence will make you more aware in the future of when it is appropriate to agree with the group and when it is not.

Summary

What is conformity and why does it occur?

- **Conformity: When and Why** Conformity occurs when people change their behavior due to the real (or imagined) influence of others. There are two main reasons people conform: informational and normative social influences.

How does informational social influence motivate people to conform?

- **Informational Social Influence: The Need to Know What's "Right"** Informational social influence occurs when people do not know what is the correct (or best) thing to do or say. They look to the behavior of others as an important and needed source of information, and they use it to choose appropriate courses of action for themselves. Informational social influence usually results in private acceptance, in which people genuinely believe in what other people are doing or saying.
  - **Importance of Being Accurate** In situations where it is important to be accurate, the tendency to conform to other people through informational social influence increases.
  - **When Informational Conformity Backfires** Using other people as a source of information can backfire when they are wrong about what's going on. Contagion occurs when emotions and behaviors spread rapidly throughout a group; one example is **mass psychogenic illness**.
  - **When Will People Conform to Informational Social Influence?** People are more likely to conform to informational social influence when the situation is ambiguous, when they are in a crisis, or if experts are present.

How does normative social influence motivate people to conform?

- **Normative Social Influence: The Need to Be Accepted** **Normative social influence** occurs when we change our behavior to match that of others because we want to remain a member of the group in good standing and continue to gain the advantages of group membership. We conform to the group's **social norms**, implicit or explicit rules for acceptable behaviors, values, and attitudes. Normative social influence usually results in **public compliance**, but not private acceptance of other people's ideas and behaviors.
  - **Conformity and Social Approval: The Asch Line-Judgment Studies** In a series of classic studies, Solomon Asch found that people would conform, at least some of the time, to the obviously wrong answer of the group.
  - **The Importance of Being Accurate, Revisited** When it is important to be accurate, people are more likely to resist normative social influence and go against the group, giving the right answer.
  - **The Consequences of Resisting Normative Social Influence** Resisting normative social influence can lead to ridicule, ostracism, and rejection by the group.
  - **Normative Social Influence in Everyday Life** Normative social influence operates on many levels in social life: It influences our eating habits, hobbies, fashion, body image, and so on, and it promotes polite behavior in society.
  - **When Will People Conform to Normative Social Influence?** **Social impact theory** specifies when normative social influence is most likely to occur by referring to the strength, immediacy, and size of the group. We are more likely to conform when the group is one we care about, when the group members are unanimous in their thoughts or behaviors, when the group has three or more members, and when we are members of collectivist cultures. Past conformity gives people **idiosyncrasy credits**, allowing them to deviate from the group without serious consequences.
  - **Minority Influence: When the Few Influence the Many** Under certain conditions, an individual (or small number of people) can influence the majority. The key is consistency in the presentation of the minority viewpoint.

How can we use our knowledge of social influence for positive purposes?

- **Using Social Influence to Promote Beneficial Behavior** Social influence techniques can be used to promote socially beneficial behavior in others. Communicating **injunctive norms** is a more powerful way to create change than communicating **descriptive norms**. In addition, one must be careful that descriptive norms do not create a "boomerang effect."
  - **The Role of Injunctive and Descriptive Norms**

What have studies demonstrated about people's willingness to obey someone in a position of authority?

- **Obedience to Authority** In the most famous series of studies in social psychology, Stanley Milgram examined obedience to authority figures. He found chilling levels of obedience, to the point where a majority of participants administered what they thought were potentially lethal shocks to a fellow human being.
  - **The Role of Normative Social Influence** Normative pressures make it difficult for people to stop obeying authority figures. They want to please the authority figure by doing a good job.
  - **The Role of Informational Social Influence** The obedience studies created a confusing situation for participants, with competing, ambiguous demands. Unclear about how to define what was going on, they followed the orders of the expert.
  - **Other Reasons We Obey** Participants conformed to the wrong norm: They continued to follow the "obey authority" norm when it was no longer appropriate. It was difficult for them to abandon this norm for three reasons: the fast-paced nature of the study, the fact that the shock levels increased in small increments, and their loss of a feeling of personal responsibility.
  - **The Obedience Studies, Then and Now** Milgram's research design was criticized on ethical grounds, involving deception, informed consent, psychological distress, the right to withdraw, and inflicted insight. A recent U.S. replication of the Milgram study found that the level of obedience in 2006 was not significantly different from that found in the classic study in the 1960s. Similarly, there was no difference in obedience between men and women participants in either time period.

Chapter 8 Test

Study and **Review** on **MyPsychLab**

1. All of the following are examples of informational social influence *except*
   a. you are running a race, but because you are unsure of the route, you wait to check which of two roads the other runners follow.
   b. you've just started work at a new job, and a fire alarm goes off; you watch your coworkers to see what to do.
   c. when you get to college you change the way you dress so that you "fit in" better—that is, so that people will like you more.
   d. you ask your adviser which classes you should take next semester.
   e. mass psychogenic illness.

2. Which of the following is true, according to social impact theory?
   a. People conform more to others who are physically close than to others who are physically distant.
   b. People conform more if the others are important to them.

c. People conform more to three or more people than to one or two people.
d. All of the above are true.
e. Only (a) and (b) are true.

3. In Asch's line studies, participants who were alone when asked to report the length of the lines gave the correct answer 98% of the time. When they were with the confederates, however (i.e., all of whom gave the wrong answer on some trials), 76% of participants gave the wrong answer at least once. This suggests that Asch's studies are an illustration of
   a. public compliance with private acceptance.
   b. the fundamental attribution error.
   c. public compliance without private acceptance.
   d. informational influence.
   e. private compliance.

4. Which of the following situations demonstrates mass psychogenic illness?
   a. You share the happiness a close friend experiences when she learns that she's won the state lottery.
   b. During the past week, complaints of dizziness and fainting spells spread throughout the dorm though no physical cause can be identified.
   c. After looking through a medical dictionary, you fear that you have three separate illnesses.
   d. Panic spreads throughout a crowd when someone yells, "Killer bees!"

5. Whereas ______________ may be the mechanism by which women learn what kind of body type is considered attractive, ______________ explains their attempts to obtain such a shape through dieting and other means.
   a. contagion influence, minority influence
   b. minority influence, contagion influence
   c. informational social influence, normative social influence
   d. normative social influence, informational social influence

6. Which of the following is most true about informational social influence?
   a. When deciding whether to conform, people should ask themselves whether the other people know more about what is going on than they do.
   b. People should always try to resist it.
   c. People are most likely to conform when other people have the same level of expertise as they do.
   d. Often, people publicly conform but do not privately accept this kind of influence.

7. Brandon knows that society considers underage drinking to be wrong; he also knows, however, that on a Saturday night at his university many of his friends will engage in this behavior. His belief that most of the public would disapprove of underage drinking is ______________, while his perception that many teenagers drink under certain circumstances is ______________.
   a. an injunctive norm, a descriptive norm
   b. a descriptive norm, an injunctive norm
   c. a descriptive norm, conformity
   d. an injunctive norm, conformity

8. Tom is a new student at his university. During the first week of classes, he notices a fellow student from one of his classes getting on a bus. Tom decides to follow the student and discovers that this bus takes him right to the building where his class meets. This best illustrates what kind of conformity?

- **a.** Obedience to authority
- **b.** Informational social influence
- **c.** Public compliance
- **d.** Normative social influence
- **e.** Mindless conformity

9. Which of the following best describes an example of normative social influence?

- **a.** Sarah is studying with a group of friends. When comparing answers on the practice test, she discovers that they all answered the question differently than she had. Instead of speaking up and telling them she thinks the answer is something else, she agrees with their answer, because she figures they must be right.
- **b.** Sarah is supposed to bring a bottle of wine to a dinner party she is attending. She doesn't drink wine herself but figures she can just ask the store clerk for advice on what kind to buy.
- **c.** Sarah is out to lunch with her boss and coworkers. Her boss tells a joke that makes fun of a certain ethnic group and everyone else laughs. Sarah doesn't think the joke is funny but laughs anyway.
- **d.** Sarah is flying on an airplane for the first time. She is worried when she hears the engine make a strange noise but feels better after she looks at the flight attendants and sees that they are not alarmed.

10. Which of the following had the least influence on participants' willingness to keep giving shocks in the Milgram studies?

- **a.** Normative social influence
- **b.** Activation of the "obey authority" norm
- **c.** Self-justification
- **d.** Informational social influence
- **e.** Participants' aggression

Answer Key

1-c, 2-d, 3-c, 4-b, 5-c,
6-a, 7-a, 8-b, 9-d, 10-e

9 Group Processes

Influence in Social Groups

On March 19, 2003, an unseasonably cool spring day in Washington, D.C., President George W. Bush convened a meeting with his top advisers in the Situation Room, the nerve center in the basement of the White House. Months of planning had come down to this moment—final approval of the invasion of Iraq. The president first asked whether any of his advisers had any last thoughts or recommendations. When none did, he asked the staff to establish a secure video link with General Tommy Franks, the commander of all U.S. armed forces in the Middle East. Franks and his senior field commanders, who were at Prince Sultan Air Force Base in Saudi Arabia, gave President Bush a final briefing, after which General Franks concluded, "The force is ready to go, Mr. President." President Bush then gave a prepared statement: "For the peace of the world and the benefit and freedom of the Iraqi people, I hereby give the order to execute Operation Iraqi Freedom. May God bless the troops" (Woodward, 2004, p. 379).

With these words, President Bush set in motion a controversial war that will undoubtedly be debated by historians for decades to come. For social psychologists, a fascinating question is how the decision to invade Iraq was made—indeed, how important decisions of any kind are made. Do groups of experts make better decisions, for example, than do individuals? The American government has at its disposal a huge number of talented people with expertise in world affairs, national security, human rights, and military intelligence, and it might seem that drawing upon and combining this expertise would lead to the best decisions. Groups don't always make good decisions, however—especially when they are blinded by the desire to maintain cohesiveness or to please a dominant leader. In this chapter, we will focus on questions about the nature of groups and how they influence people's behavior, which are some of the oldest topics in social psychology (Forsyth & Burnette, 2010; Hackman & Katz, 2010; Kerr & Tindale, 2004; Wittenbaum & Moreland, 2008).

FOCUS QUESTIONS

- What are groups and why do people join them?
- In what ways do people act differently when other people are around? What are the key variables that determine what the effects of others will be on individual performance?
- When people make decisions, are two (or more) heads better than one? Why or why not?
- When individuals or groups are in conflict, what determines the likelihood that this conflict will escalate or that it will be resolved?

What Is a Group?

Six students studying at a table in the library are not a group. But if they meet to study for their psychology final together, they are. A **group** consists of three or more people who interact and are interdependent in the sense that their needs and goals cause them to influence each other (Cartwright & Zander, 1968; Lewin, 1948). (Two people are generally considered to be a dyad rather than a group; Moreland, 2010). Like a president's advisers working together to reach a foreign policy decision, citizens meeting to solve a community problem, or people who have gathered to blow off steam at a party, groups consist of people who have assembled for some common purpose.

Group
Three or more people who interact and are interdependent in the sense that their needs and goals cause them to influence each other.

Think for a moment of the number of groups to which you belong. Don't forget to include your family, campus groups (such as clubs or political organizations), community groups (such as churches or synagogues), sports teams, and more-temporary groups (such as your classmates in a small seminar). All

Groups have a number of benefits. They are an important part of our identity, helping us define who we are, and are a source of social norms, the explicit or implicit rules defining what is acceptable behavior.

of these count as groups because you interact with the other members and you are interdependent: You influence them, and they influence you.

Why Do People Join Groups?

Forming relationships with other people fulfills a number of basic human needs—so basic, in fact, that there may be an innate need to belong to groups. Some researchers argue that in our evolutionary past there was a substantial survival advantage to establishing bonds with other people (Baumeister & Leary, 1995; DeWall & Richman, 2011). People who bonded together were better able to hunt for and grow food, find mates, and care for children. Consequently, they argue, the need to belong has become innate and is present in all societies. Consistent with this view, people in all cultures are motivated to form relationships with other people and to resist the dissolution of these relationships (Gardner, Pickett, & Brewer, 2000; Manstead, 1997). People monitor their status in groups and look for any sign that they might be rejected (Blackhart et al., 2009; Kerr & Levine, 2008; Leary & Baumeister, 2000; Pickett & Gardner, 2005). One study found that people who were asked to recall a time when they had been rejected by other people estimated that the temperature of the room was 5 degrees lower than did people who were asked to recall a time when they were accepted by other people (IJzerman & Semin, 2010; Zhong & Leonardelli, 2008). Social rejection is, literally, chilling.

Not only do people have a strong need to belong to social groups, but they also have a need to feel distinctive from those who do *not* belong to the same groups. If you go to a large state university, you might have a sense of belonging, but being a member of such a large collective is unlikely to make you feel distinctive from others. Groups that are relatively small can fulfill both functions, by giving us a sense of belonging with our fellow group members and also making us feel special and distinctive. This helps explain why people are attracted to smaller groups at their college universities, such as fraternities or sororities (Brewer, 1991, 2007; Tasdemir, 2011).

Watch on **MyPsychLab**

To learn more about the effects of belonging to a group, watch the MyPsychLab video ***Group Learning.***

Another important function of groups is that they help us define who we are. As we saw in Chapter 8, other people can be an important source of information, helping us resolve ambiguity about the nature of the social world (Darley, 2004). All groups make assumptions about the nature of the social world and thus provide a lens through which we can understand the world and our place in it (Hogg, Hohman, & Rivera, 2008). So groups become an important part of our identity—witness the number of times people wear shirts emblazoned with the name of one of their groups (e.g., a campus organization). Groups also help establish social norms, the explicit or implicit rules defining what is acceptable behavior.

The Composition and Functions of Groups

The groups to which you belong probably vary in size from a few members to several dozen members. Most groups, however, have three to six members (Desportes & Lemaine, 1988; Levine & Moreland, 1998; McPherson, 1983). If groups become too large, you cannot interact with all the members; for example, the college or university that you attend is not a group, because you are unlikely to meet and interact with every other student.

Another important feature of groups is that the members tend to be alike in age, sex, beliefs, and opinions (George, 1990; Levine & Moreland, 1998; Magaro & Ashbrook, 1985). There are two reasons for the homogeneity of groups. First, many groups tend to attract people who are already similar before they join (Alter & Darley, 2009; Feld, 1982). As we'll see in Chapter 10, people are attracted to others who share their attitudes and thus are likely to recruit fellow group members who are similar to them. Second, groups tend to operate in ways that encourage similarity in the members (Moreland, 1987). This can happen in a number of important ways, some of which we discussed in Chapter 8.

Social Norms As we saw in Chapter 8, *social norms* are a powerful determinant of our behavior (Hogg, 2010; Kameda, Takezawa, & Hastie, 2005). All societies have norms about which behaviors are acceptable, some of which all members are expected to obey (e.g., we should be quiet in libraries) and some of which vary from group to group (e.g., rules about what to wear to weddings and funerals). If you belong to a fraternity or sorority, you can probably think of social norms that govern behavior in your group, such as whether alcoholic beverages are consumed and how you are supposed to feel about rival fraternities or sororities. It is unlikely that other groups to which you belong share these norms. The power of norms to shape behavior becomes clear when we violate them too often: We are shunned by other group members and, in extreme cases, pressured to leave the group (Marques, Abrams, & Serodio, 2001; Schachter, 1951).

Social Roles Most groups have a number of well-defined **social roles**, which are shared expectations in a group about how particular people are supposed to behave (Hare, 2003). Whereas norms specify how all group members should act, roles specify how people who occupy certain positions in the group should behave. A boss and an employee in a business occupy different roles and are expected to act in different ways in that setting. Like social norms, roles can be very helpful, because people know what to expect from each other. When members of a group follow a set of clearly defined roles, they tend to be satisfied and perform well (Barley & Bechky, 1994; Bettencourt & Sheldon, 2001).

Social Roles
Shared expectations in a group about how particular people are supposed to behave.

There are, however, potential costs to social roles. People can get so far into a role that their personal identities and personalities get lost. Suppose that you agreed to take part in a 2-week psychology experiment in which you were randomly assigned to play the role of a prison guard or a prisoner in a simulated prison. You might think that the role you were assigned to play would not be very important; after all, everyone knows that it is only an experiment and that people are just pretending to be guards or prisoners. Philip Zimbardo and his colleagues, however, had a different hypothesis. They believed that social roles can be so powerful that they overwhelm our personal identities to the point that we become the role we are playing.

To see if this is true, Zimbardo and colleagues conducted an unusual study. They built a mock prison in the basement of the psychology department at Stanford University and paid students to play the role of guard or prisoner (Haney, Banks, & Zimbardo, 1973; Zimbardo, 2007). The role students played was determined by the flip of a coin. The guards were outfitted with a uniform of khaki shirts and pants, a whistle, a police nightstick, and reflecting sunglasses, and the prisoners with a loose-fitting smock with an identification number stamped on it, rubber sandals, a cap made from a nylon stocking, and a locked chain attached to one ankle.

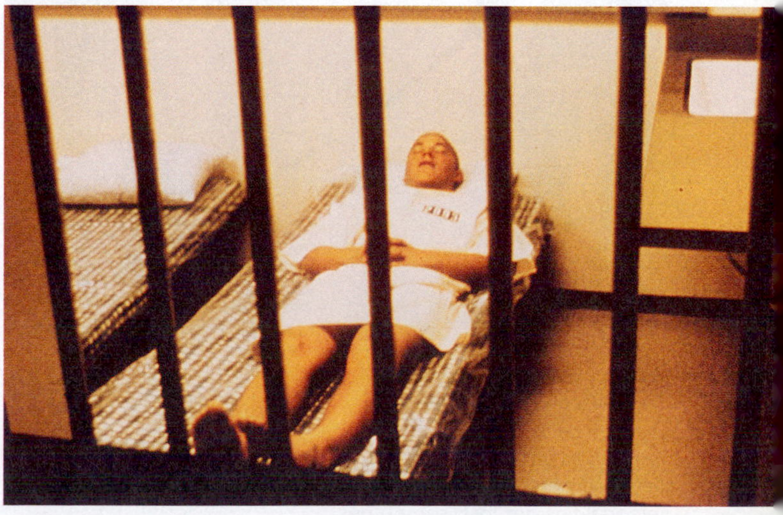

Philip Zimbardo and his colleagues randomly assigned students to play the role of prisoner or guard in a mock prison. The students assumed these roles all too well.

The researchers planned to observe the students for 2 weeks to see whether they began to act like real prison guards and prisoners. As it turned out, the students quickly assumed these roles—so much so that the researchers ended the experiment after only 6 days. Many of the guards became quite abusive, thinking of creative ways of verbally harassing and humiliating the prisoners. The prisoners became passive, helpless, and withdrawn. Some prisoners, in fact, became so anxious and depressed that they had to be released from the study earlier than the others. Remember, everyone knew that they were in a psychology experiment and that the prison was only make-believe. The roles of guard and prisoner were so compelling and powerful, however, that this simple truth was often overlooked. People got so far into their roles that their personal identities and sense of decency somehow got lost.

Prison Abuse at Abu Ghraib Does this sound familiar? In 2004, it came to light that American military guards had been abusing prisoners in Abu Ghraib, a prison in Iraq (Hersch, 2004). A report written by U.S. Major General Taguba, who investigated the claims of abuse, documented numerous cases of physical beatings, sexual abuse, and psychological humiliation. The American public was shocked by pictures of U.S. soldiers smiling as they stood in front of naked Iraqi prisoners, as if they were posing in front of local landmarks for the folks back home.

Did a few bad apples happen to end up in the unit guarding the prisoners? Not according to Phillip Zimbardo (2007), who has analyzed the similarities between the abuse at Abu Ghraib and the prison study he conducted 30 years earlier. "What's bad is the barrel," Zimbardo argued. "The barrel is the barrel I created by my prison—and we put good boys in, just as in this Iraqi prison. And the barrel corrupts. It's the barrel of the evil of prisons—with secrecy, with no accountability—which gives people permission to do things they ordinarily would not" (quoted in O'Brien, 2004). The military guards at Abu Ghraib were under tremendous stress, had received scant training, had little supervision, and were asked to set their own rules for interrogation. It was easy to dehumanize the prisoners, given that the guards didn't speak their language and that many of the prisoners were naked (due to a shortage of prison suits). "You start looking at these people as less than human," said one guard, "and you start doing things to 'em that you would never dream of" (Zimbardo, 2007, p. 352).

Watch on **MyPsychLab**
To learn more about the Stanford prison experiment, watch the MyPsychLab video ***The Power of the Situation: Phil Zimbardo.***

This is not to say that the soldiers should be excused for their actions. The abuse came to light when 24-year-old Joe Darby, an Army Reservist at Abu Ghraib, reported what was happening, and, as in Zimbardo's study, there were some guards who treated the prisoners well. Thus, not everyone was caught in the web of their social roles, unable to resist. But as much as we would like to think that we would be one of these heroes, the lesson from the Zimbardo prison study—and Milgram's studies of obedience, discussed in Chapter 8—is that most of us would not resist the social influences in these powerful situations and would perhaps perform acts we thought we were incapable of.

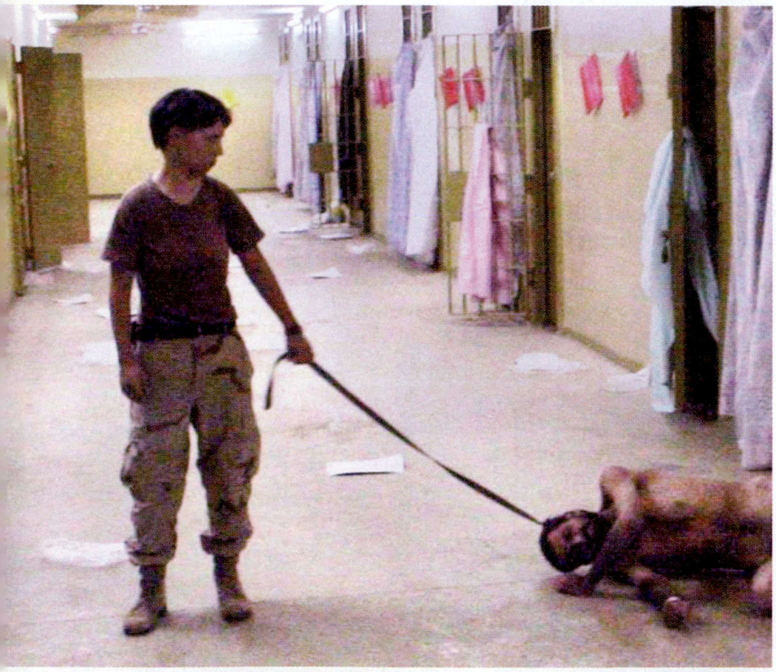

Social roles can be very helpful, because people know what to expect from each other. However, people can get too far into a role that their personal identities and personalities get lost, sometimes with tragic consequences. Some people think that the abuse at the Abu Ghraib prison in Iraq was due to soldiers getting too far into their roles as prison guards.

Gender Roles Of course, not all social roles involve such extreme behavior. But even in everyday life, roles can be problematic when they are arbitrary or unfair. All societies, for example, have expectations about how people who occupy the roles of women and men should behave. In many cultures, women are expected to assume the role of wife and mother and have limited opportunities to pursue other careers. In the United States and other countries, these expectations are changing, and women have more opportunities than ever before. Conflict can result, however, when expectations change for some roles but not for others assumed by the same person. In India, for example, women were traditionally permitted to take only the roles of wife, mother, agricultural laborer, and domestic worker. As their rights have improved, women are increasingly working at other professions. At home, though, many husbands still expect their wives to assume the traditional role of child rearer and household manager, even if their wives have other careers. Conflict results, because many women are expected to "do it all"—maintain a career, raise the children, clean the house, and attend to their husband's needs (Brislin, 1993; Wax, 2008). Such conflicts are not limited to India; many American readers will find this kind of role conflict all too familiar (Eagly & Diekman, 2003; Kite, Deaux, & Haines, 2008; Marks, Lam, & McHale, 2009; Rudman, 1998).

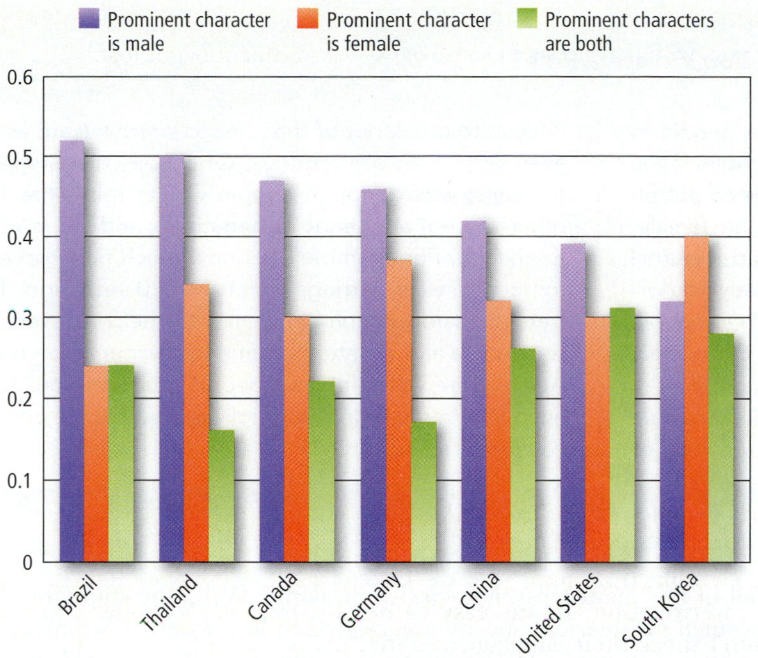

FIGURE 9.1

Percentage of Prominent Characters in Television Commercials Who Were Men, Women, or Both Men and Women

Researchers examined television commercials that were broadcast in seven countries and coded the gender of the prominent characters (the ones who were in the foreground demonstrating or commenting on the product being advertised). This figure shows, for each country, the percentage of the prominent characters who were men, women, or both men and women.

(Based on data in Paek, Nelson, & Vilela, 2011)

Gender roles vary from country to country and change over time within countries. To look at cultural differences in gender roles, researchers examined the content of over 2,600 television commercials that were broadcast in the year 2002 in seven countries: Brazil, Canada, China, Germany, South Korea, Thailand, and the United States (Paek, Nelson, & Vilela, 2011). They coded the gender of the prominent characters in the commercials, namely the people who were in the foreground demonstrating or commenting on the product being advertised. As seen in Figure 9.1, the gender of the main characters in commercials varied widely by country. In Brazil, the prominent characters were much more likely to be male than female, whereas in the United States and South Korea, there was much less of a gender difference. South Korea was the only country in which women were more likely than men to be the prominent character. The authors of the study point out that South Korean women have made substantial economic advances in recent years; however, they also note that even when women are shown prominently in South Korean television ads, they are much more likely than men to be shown in the role of homemaker.

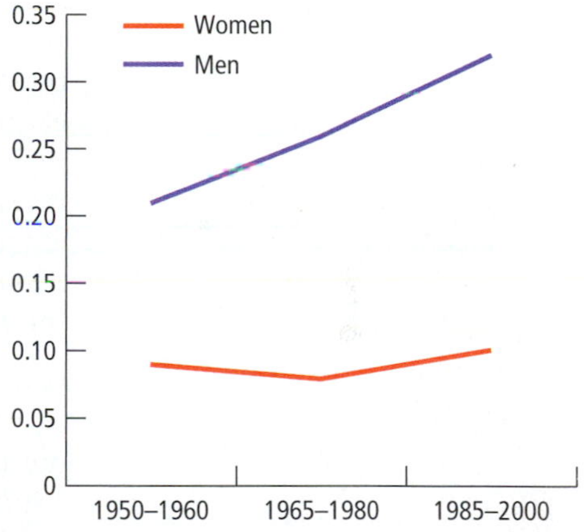

FIGURE 9.2

Percentage of Ads Showing Women Versus Men in a Subordinate Role, by Time Period

Researchers analyzed advertisements that appeared in U.S. magazines from 1950 to 2000 and coded the percentage of ads in each year that showed women in a subordinate role versus men in a subordinate role (such as showing deference to someone or receiving guidance from another person). This figure shows the percentage of ads in each category for three different time periods.

(Based on data in Mager & Helgeson, 2011)

In the United States, gender roles have changed a lot over the past several decades. Women did not achieve the right to vote until 1920. In 1950, about a third of women had a job outside the home; by 1998, 60% did. In 1965, the United States Supreme Court struck down the last state law that prohibited the use of contraceptives by married couples. In 1976, Nebraska was the first state to pass a law making it illegal for a man to rape his wife. In 2009, women held about half of the nation's jobs (Rampell, 2009). But an analysis of magazine advertisements that appeared in U.S. magazines from 1950 to 2000 suggests that we have a ways to go (Mager & Helgeson, 2011). These researchers coded the percentage of ads in each year that showed women in a subordinate role versus men in a subordinate role, such as showing deference to someone or receiving guidance from another person. As seen in Figure 9.2, women were far more likely than men to be shown in a subordinate role. Perhaps more surprisingly, the percentage of times that women were shown this way has actually increased over time. Advertisements are but one small peek into a culture, of course, and as we noted, there are many ways in which women have made advances in the United States. But the content analysis of advertisements does suggest that women continue to be portrayed in more-subordinate roles than are men.

TRY IT! What Happens When You Violate a Role?

Pick a behavior that is part of the role for your gender in your culture, and deliberately violate it. For example, if you are male in the United States, you might decide to put on makeup or carry a purse to your next class. If you are female, you might wear a jacket and tie to a party. Keep a journal describing how others react to you. More than likely, you will encounter a good deal of social disapproval, such as people staring at you or questioning your behavior. For this reason, you want to avoid role violations that are too extreme.

The social pressure that is brought to bear on people who do not conform to their roles explains why it can be so difficult to break out of the roles to which we are assigned, even when they are arbitrary. Of course, there is safety in numbers; when enough people violate role expectations, others do not act nearly as negatively, and the roles begin to change. For example, it is now much more acceptable for men to wear earrings than it was 20 years ago. To illustrate this safety in numbers, enlist the help of several same-sex friends and violate the same role expectation together. Again, note carefully how people react to you. Did you encounter more or less social disapproval in the group than you did as an individual?

Does all of this matter, psychologically speaking? Well, one study found that the status of women in American society was related to how assertive women considered themselves to be (Twenge, 2001). During the period of 1931 to 1945, women's status increased; they earned college degrees and worked outside the home in increasing numbers. During this same time period, women's ratings of their own assertiveness increased. Between the years 1946 and 1967, however, the stay-at-home mom became the norm. Women increasingly dropped out of the workforce and fewer women went to college. During this time period, women's ratings of their own assertiveness dropped. Between 1968 and 1993, women's status improved again as the feminist movement took hold in the United States; by the early 1990s, for example, women were again earning more college degrees than men. And wouldn't you know it, women's ratings of their own assertiveness reversed course during this time period, increasing again. This research suggests that the roles that people assume in groups, and in society at large, are powerful determinants of their feelings, behavior, and personality (Eagly & Steffen, 2000; Eagly, Diekman, Johannesen-Schmidt, & Koenig, 2004). The Try It! exercise on this page describes a way you can experience this for yourself.

Group Cohesiveness Another important aspect of group composition is how cohesive the group is. The qualities of a group that bind members together and promote mutual liking are known as **group cohesiveness** (Dion, 2000; Friedkin, 2004; Hogg, 1993; Holtz, 2004). If a group has formed primarily for social reasons, such as a group of friends who like to go to the movies together on weekends, then, the more cohesive the group is, the better. This is pretty obvious; would you rather spend your free time with a bunch of people who don't care much for each other or a tight-knit bunch of people who feel committed to you and the other members of the group? As might be expected, the more cohesive a group is, the more its members are likely to stay in the group, take part in group activities, and try to recruit new like-minded members (Levine & Moreland, 1998; Pickett, Silver, & Brewer, 2002; Sprink & Carron, 1994).

If the function of the group is to work together and solve problems, however—as it is for a military unit or sales team at a company—then the story is not quite so simple. Doing well on a task causes a group to become more cohesive (Mullen & Cooper, 1994), but is the reverse true? Does cohesiveness cause a group to perform well? It does if the task requires close cooperation between the group members, such as the case of a football team executing a difficult play or a military unit carrying out a complicated maneuver (Gully, Devine, & Whitney, 1995). Sometimes, however, cohesiveness can get in the way of optimal performance if maintaining good relations among group members becomes more important than finding good solutions to a problem. Is it possible, for example, that the cohesiveness felt by President Bush and his advisers got in the way of clear thinking about whether to invade Iraq? We will return to this question later in the chapter, when we discuss group decision making.

Group Cohesiveness

Qualities of a group that bind members together and promote liking between members.

Individual Behavior in a Group Setting

Do you act differently when other people are around? Simply being in the presence of other people can have a variety of interesting effects on our behavior. We will begin by looking at how a group affects your performance on something with which you are very familiar—taking a test in a class.

Social Facilitation: When the Presence of Others Energizes Us

> *Mere social contact begets . . . a stimulation of the animal spirit that heightens the efficiency of each individual workman.*
>
> —KARL MARX, *DAS KAPITAL*, 1867

It is time for the final exam in your psychology class. You have spent countless hours studying the material, and you feel ready. When you arrive, you see that the exam is scheduled in a tiny room already packed with students. You squeeze into an empty desk, elbow to elbow with your classmates. The professor arrives and says that if any students are bothered by the close quarters, they can take the test by themselves in one of several smaller rooms down the hall. What should you do?

The question is whether being with other people will affect your performance (Geen, 1989; Guerin, 1993; Zajonc, 1965). The presence of others can mean one of two things: (1) performing a task with coworkers who are doing the same thing you are or (2) performing a task in front of an audience that is not doing anything but observing you. Note that the question is a basic one about the mere presence of other people, even if they are not part of a group that is interacting. Does the simple fact that other people are around make a difference, even if you never speak or interact with them in any way?

To answer this question, we need to talk about insects—cockroaches, in fact. Believe it or not, a classic study using cockroaches as research participants suggests an answer to the question of how you should take your psychology test. Robert Zajonc and his colleagues (Zajonc, Heingartner, & Herman, 1969) built a contraption to see how a cockroach's behavior was influenced by the presence of its peers. The researchers placed a bright light (which cockroaches dislike) at the end of a runway and timed how long it took a roach to escape the light by running to the other end, where it could scurry into a darkened box (see the left side of Figure 9.3). The question was, did roaches perform this simple feat faster when they were by themselves or when they were in the presence of other cockroaches?

You might be wondering how the researchers managed to persuade other cockroaches to be spectators. They simply placed other roaches in clear plastic boxes next to the runway. These roaches were in the bleachers, so to speak, observing the solitary cockroach do its thing (see Figure 9.3). As predicted, the individual cockroaches performed the task faster when other roaches were there than when they were by themselves.

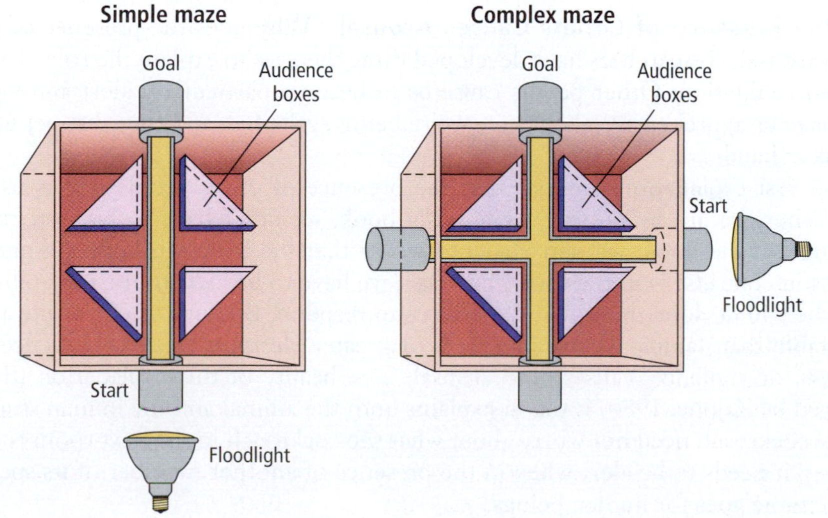

FIGURE 9.3

Cockroaches and Social Facilitation

In the maze on the left, cockroaches had a simple task: to go from the starting point down the runway to the darkened box. They performed this feat faster when other roaches were watching than when they were alone. In the maze on the right, the cockroaches had a more difficult task. It took them longer to solve this maze when other roaches were watching than when they were alone.

(Based on data in Zajonc, Heingartner, & Herman, 1969)

Research on social facilitation finds that people do better on a well-learned task when in the presence of others than when they are alone. If students have studied hard and know the material well, they might be better off taking an exam in a room with lots of other people.

We would not give advice on how you should take your psychology test based on one study that used cockroaches. But the story does not end here. Dozens of studies have been done on the effects of the mere presence of other people, involving human beings as well as other species such as ants and birds (e.g., Aiello & Douthitt, 2001; Rajecki, Kidd, & Ivins, 1976; Sharma et al., 2010). The findings of these studies are remarkably consistent: As long as the task is a relatively simple, well-learned one—as escaping a light is for cockroaches—the mere presence of others improves performance.

Simple Versus Difficult Tasks Before concluding that you should stay in the crowded classroom to take your exam, we need to consider a different set of findings. Remember that we said the presence of others enhances performance on *simple, well-learned* tasks, as escaping a light is for a cockroach. What happens when we give people a more difficult task to do and place them in the presence of others? To find out, Zajonc and his colleagues (1969) included another condition in the cockroach experiment. This time, the cockroaches had to solve a maze that had several runways, only one of which led to the darkened box (see the right side of Figure 9.3). When working on this more difficult task, the opposite pattern of results occurred: The roaches took *longer* to solve it when other roaches were present than when they were alone. Many other studies have also found that people and animals do worse in the presence of others when the task is difficult (e.g., Bond & Titus, 1983; Geen, 1989).

Arousal and the Dominant Response In an influential article, Robert Zajonc (1965) offered an elegant theoretical explanation for why the presence of others facilitates a well-learned response but inhibits a less practiced or new response. The presence of others increases physiological arousal (i.e., our bodies become more energized). When such arousal exists, it is easier to perform a dominant response (e.g., something we're good at) but harder to do something complex or learn something new. Consider, for example, a behavior that is second nature to you, such as riding a bicycle or writing your name. Arousal caused by the presence of other people watching you should make it even easier to perform these well-learned tasks. But let's say you have to do something more complex, such as learning a new sport or working on a difficult math problem. Now arousal will lead you to feel flustered and do less well than if you were alone (Schmitt et al., 1986). This phenomenon became known as **social facilitation**, which is the tendency for people to do better on simple tasks and worse on complex tasks when they are in the presence of others and their individual performance can be evaluated.

Social Facilitation
The tendency for people to do better on simple tasks and worse on complex tasks when they are in the presence of others and their individual performance can be evaluated.

Why the Presence of Others Causes Arousal Why does the presence of others lead to arousal? Researchers have developed three theories to explain the role of arousal in social facilitation: Other people cause us to become particularly alert and vigilant, they make us apprehensive about how we're being evaluated, and they distract us from the task at hand.

The first explanation suggests that the presence of other people makes us more alert. When we are by ourselves reading a book, we don't have to pay attention to anything but the book; we don't have to worry that the lamp will ask us a question. When someone else is in the room, however, we have to be alert to the possibility that he or she will do something that requires us to respond. Because other people are less predictable than lamps, we are in a state of greater alertness in their presence. This alertness, or vigilance, causes mild arousal. The beauty of this explanation (the one preferred by Zajonc, 1980) is that it explains both the animal and the human studies. A solitary cockroach need not worry about what the cockroach in the next room is doing; however, it needs to be alert when in the presence of another member of its species—and the same goes for human beings.

The second explanation focuses on the fact that people are not cockroaches and are often concerned about how other people are evaluating them. When other people can see how you are doing, the stakes are raised: You feel as if the other people are evaluating you and will feel embarrassed if you do poorly and pleased if you do well. This concern about being judged, called *evaluation apprehension*, can cause mild arousal. According to this view, then, it is not the mere presence of others but the presence of others who are evaluating us that causes arousal and subsequent social facilitation (Blascovich et al., 1999; Bond, Atoum, & Van Leeuwen, 1996; Muller & Butera, 2007; Seta & Seta, 1995).

The third explanation centers on how distracting other people can be (Baron, 1986; Muller, Atzeni, & Fabrizio, 2004). It is similar to Robert Zajonc's (1980) notion that we need to be alert when in the presence of others, except that it focuses on the idea that any source of distraction—be it the presence of other people or noise from the party going on in the apartment upstairs—will put us in a state of conflict because it is difficult to pay attention to two things at the same time. This divided attention produces arousal, as any parent knows who has ever tried to read the newspaper while his or her 2-year-old clamors for attention. Consistent with this interpretation, nonsocial sources of distraction, such as a flashing light, cause the same kinds of social facilitation effects as the presence of other people (Baron, 1986).

We have summarized research on social facilitation in the top half of Figure 9.4 (we will discuss the bottom half in a moment). This figure illustrates that there is more than one reason why the presence of other people is arousing. The consequences of this arousal, however, are the same: When people are around other people, they do better on tasks that are simple and well learned, but they do worse on tasks that are complex and require them to learn something new.

Where, then, should you take your psychology exam? We recommend that you stay with your classmates, assuming you know the material well, so that it is relatively simple for you to recall it. The arousal produced by being elbow to elbow with your classmates should improve your performance. But when you study for an exam—that is, when

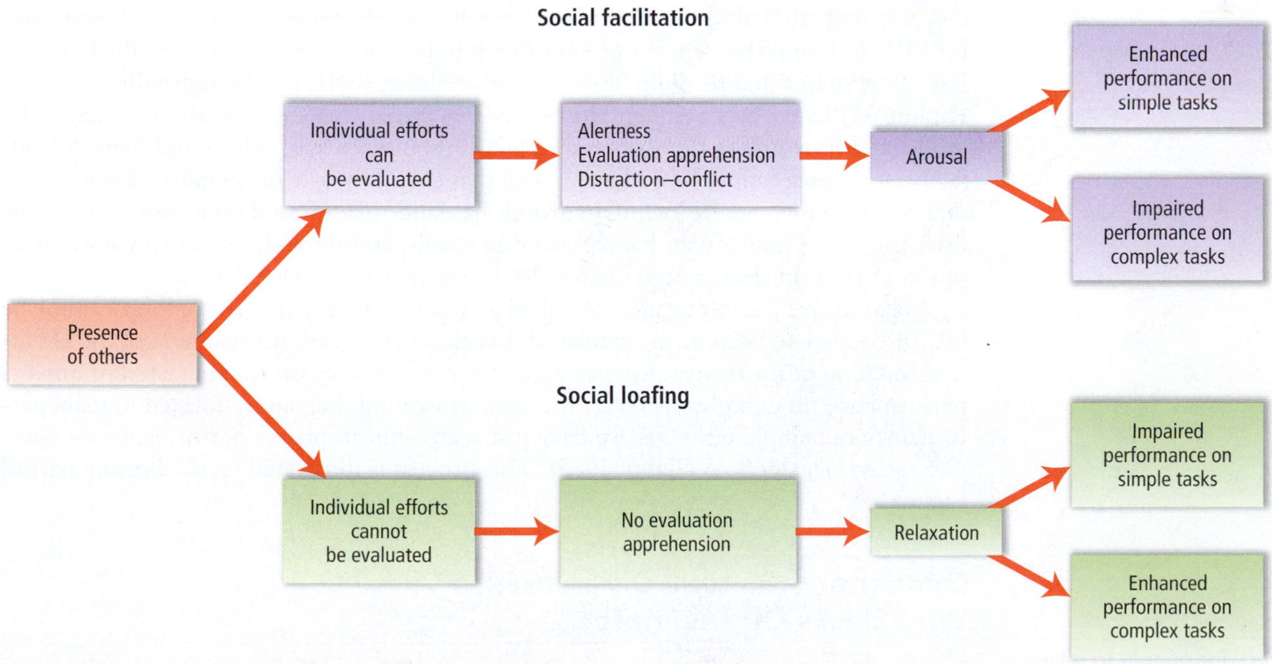

FIGURE 9.4

Social Facilitation and Social Loafing

The presence of others can lead to social facilitation or social loafing. The important variables that distinguish the two are evaluation, arousal, and the complexity of the tasks.

you learn new material—you should do so by yourself, away from other people. In this situation, the arousal caused by others will make it more difficult to concentrate. And, oh yes, it is not only the presence of real people who can influence our behavior—so can the presence of our favorite TV characters. In a recent study, college students performed a simple or complex task while a picture of their favorite TV character or some other TV character was displayed on a computer screen. When the TV character was people's favorite—such as George from *Grey's Anatomy*—it was as if a real person was in the room: People did better on the simple task but worse on the complex task. When the TV character wasn't people's favorite, their performance was unaffected (Gardner & Knowles, 2008).

Simulate on **MyPsychLab**
To learn more about how the presence of others affects performance, try the MyPsychLab simulation ***Social Facilitation.***

Social Loafing: When the Presence of Others Relaxes Us

When you take your psychology exam, your individual efforts will be evaluated (you will be graded on the test). This is typical of the condition for research on social facilitation we have reviewed: People are working on something (either alone or in the presence of others), and their individual efforts are easily observed and evaluated. Often when people are in the presence of others, however, their individual efforts cannot be distinguished from those of the people around them. Such is the case when you clap after a concert (no one can tell how loudly you are clapping) or when you play an instrument in a marching band (your instrument blends in with all the others).

Which of us . . . is to do the hard and dirty work for the rest—and for what pay?

—John Ruskin

These situations are the opposite of the kinds of social facilitation settings we have just considered. In social facilitation, the presence of others puts the spotlight on you, making you aroused. But if being with other people means we can merge into a group, becoming less noticeable than when we are alone, we should become relaxed. Because no one can tell how well we are doing, we should feel less evaluation apprehension and thus be less willing to try our hardest. What happens then? Will this relaxation produced by becoming lost in the crowd lead to better or worse performance? Again, the answer depends on whether we are working on a simple or a complex task.

Let's first consider simple tasks, such as trying to pull as hard as you can on a rope. The question of how working with others would influence performance on such a task was first studied in the 1880s by a French agricultural engineer, Max Ringelmann (1913). He found that when a group of men pulled on a rope, each individual exerted less effort than when he did it alone. A century later, social psychologists Bibb Latané, Kipling Williams, and Stephen Harkins (1979) called this **social loafing**, which is the tendency for people to relax when they are in the presence of others and their individual performance cannot be evaluated, such that they do worse on simple tasks but better on complex tasks. Social loafing in groups has since been found on a variety of simple tasks, such as clapping your hands, cheering loudly, and thinking of as many uses for an object as you can (Karau & Williams, 2001; Shepperd & Taylor, 1999).

What about complex tasks? Recall that when performance in a group cannot be identified, people become more relaxed. Recall also our earlier discussion of the effects of arousal on performance: Arousal enhances performance on simple tasks but impairs performance on complex tasks. By the same reasoning, becoming relaxed impairs performance on simple tasks—as we have just seen—but improves performance on complex tasks (Jackson & Williams, 1985). This process is illustrated on the bottom part of Figure 9.4.

Gender and Cultural Differences in Social Loafing: Who Slacks Off the Most?

Social Loafing
The tendency for people to relax when they are in the presence of others and their individual performance cannot be evaluated, such that they do worse on simple tasks but better on complex tasks.

Jane and John are working with several classmates on a class project, and no one can assess their individual contributions. Who is more likely to slack off and let the other do most of the work: John or Jane? If you said John, you are probably right. In a review of more than 150 studies of social loafing, the tendency to loaf was found to be stronger in men than in women (Karau & Williams, 1993). As discussed in Chapter 5, women tend to be higher than men in *relational interdependence*, which is the tendency to focus on and care about personal relationships with other individuals. Perhaps it is this focus that makes women less likely to engage in social loafing when in groups (Eagly, 1987; Wood, 1987).

Research has also found that the tendency to loaf is stronger in Western cultures than Asian cultures, which may be due to the different self-definitions prevalent in these cultures (Karau & Williams, 1993). Asians are more likely to have an *interdependent view of the self*, which is a way of defining oneself in terms of relationships to other people (see Chapter 5). This self-definition may reduce the tendency toward social loafing when in groups. We should not, however, exaggerate these gender and cultural differences. Women and members of Asian cultures do engage in social loafing when in groups; they are just less likely to do so than men or members of Western cultures (Chang & Chen, 1995; Hong, Wyer, & Fong, 2008).

The robes and hoods of the Ku Klux Klan cloak its members in anonymity; their violent behavior is consistent with research on deindividuation.

To summarize, you need to know two things to predict whether the presence of others will help or hinder your performance: whether your individual efforts can be evaluated and whether the task is simple or complex. If your performance can be evaluated, the presence of others will make you alert and aroused. This will lead to social facilitation effects, where people do better on simple tasks but worse on complex tasks (see the top of Figure 9.4). If your efforts cannot be evaluated (i.e., you are one cog in a machine), you are likely to become more relaxed. This leads to social loafing effects, where people do worse on simple tasks but better on complex ones (see the bottom of Figure 9.4).

These findings have numerous implications for the way in which groups should be organized. On the one hand, if you are a manager who wants your employees to work on a relatively simple problem, a little evaluation apprehension is not such a bad thing—it should improve performance. You shouldn't place your employees in groups where their individual performance cannot be observed, because social loafing (lowered performance on simple tasks) is likely to result. On the other hand, if you want your employees to work on a difficult, complex task, then lowering their evaluation apprehension—by placing them in groups in which their individual performance cannot be observed—is likely to result in better performance.

Deindividuation: Getting Lost in the Crowd

If you are going to make people more anonymous, you should be aware of other consequences of being a face in the crowd. So far, we have discussed the ways in which a group affects how hard people work and how successfully they learn new things. Being in a group can also cause **deindividuation**, which is the loosening of normal constraints on behavior when people can't be identified (such as when they are in a crowd; Lea, Spears, & de Groot, 2001). In other words, getting lost in a crowd can lead to an unleashing of behaviors that we would never dream of doing by ourselves. Throughout history, there have been many examples of groups of people committing horrendous acts that no individual would do on his or her own. The massacre at My Lai during the Vietnam War, when a group of American soldiers systematically murdered hundreds of defenseless women, children, and elderly men (see Chapter 8), was one such instance. In the summer of 2011, mobs of people throughout England committed acts of looting, arson, and violence. In the United States, hysterical fans at rock concerts have trampled each other to death. And the United States has a shameful history of whites—often cloaked in the anonymity of white robes—lynching African Americans.

Deindividuation

The loosening of normal constraints on behavior when people can't be identified (such as when they are in a crowd).

Brian Mullen (1986) content-analyzed newspaper accounts of 60 lynchings committed in the United States between 1899 and 1946 and discovered an interesting fact: The more people there were in the mob, the greater the savagery and viciousness with which they killed their victims. Similarly, Robert Watson (1973) studied 24 cultures and found that warriors who hid their identities before going into battle—for example, by using face and body paint—were significantly more likely to kill, torture, or mutilate captive prisoners than were warriors who did not hide their identities.

Deindividuation Makes People Feel Less Accountable Why does deindividuation lead to impulsive (and often violent) acts? One reason is that people feel less accountable for their actions because it reduces the likelihood that any individual will be singled out and blamed (Diener, 1980; Postmes & Spears, 1998; Zimbardo, 1970). In Harper Lee's novel *To Kill a Mockingbird*, for example, a mob of white Southerners assembled to lynch Tom Robinson, a black man falsely accused of rape. Here is a classic case of deindividuation: It was night, the men were dressed alike, and it was difficult to tell one from another. But then Scout, the 8-year-old daughter of Robinson's attorney, Atticus, recognized one of the farmers and greeted him by name. She unwittingly performed a brilliant social psychological intervention by increasing the extent to which the mob felt like individuals who were accountable for their actions. And, indeed, the mob disbanded and went home at that point.

Deindividuation Increases Obedience to Group Norms In a meta-analysis of more than 60 studies, researchers found that becoming deindividuated also increases the extent to which people obey the group's norms (Postmes & Spears, 1998). Sometimes the norms of a specific group of which we are a member conflict with the norms of other groups or of society at large. When group members are together and deindividuated, they are more likely to act according to the group norms than the other norms. In *To Kill a Mockingbird*, for example, the norms of the lynch mob were to take the law into their own hands, but clearly these norms conflicted with other rules and laws (e.g., "Thou shalt not kill"). Because of the conditions promoting deindividuation, they were about to act on the group's norms and ignore the others until Scout stepped in and reminded them that they were individuals. Thus, it is not just that deindividuation reduces the likelihood that one person will stand out and be blamed, but also that it increases adherence to the specific group's norms.

If you can keep your head when all about you are losing theirs . . .

—Rudyard Kipling, "If," 1909

Consequently, deindividuation does not always lead to aggressive or antisocial behavior—it depends on what the norm of the group is. Imagine that you are at a rowdy college party at which everyone is dancing wildly to very loud music. To the extent that you feel deindividuated—it is dark, and you are dressed similarly to other people—you are more likely to join the group and let loose on the dance floor. Thus, it is the specific norm of the group that determines whether deindividuation will lead to positive or negative behaviors (Gergen, Gergen, & Barton, 1973; Johnson & Downing, 1979). If the group is angry and the norm is to act violently, deindividuation will make people in the group act aggressively. If we are at a party and the norm is to eat a lot, being deindividuated will increase the likelihood that we will eat the entire bowl of guacamole.

Deindividuation in Cyberspace Have you ever participated in an Internet forum in which people post anonymous comments about some issue or event? If so, you have probably witnessed deindividuation at work, whereby people feel less inhibited about what they write because of their anonymity. In January 2006, the *Washington Post* had to temporarily shut down the blog on its Web site after the site was deluged with postings from angry readers, many of whom wrote obscene or insulting comments.

Before blogs and Internet forums became popular, angry readers could have written letters to the editor or vented their feelings to their coworkers at the watercooler. In both cases, their discourse would have likely been more civil, free of the profanities used by many of the people who posted comments on the *Post*'s blog—in no small part because people are not anonymous in these settings (most newspapers require people to sign letters to the editor). The Internet has provided new ways in which people can communicate with each other anonymously, and just as research on deindividuation predicts, in these settings people often feel free to say things they would never dream of saying if they could be identified (Lee, 2004). There are advantages, of course, to free and open discussion of difficult topics, but the cost seems to be a reduction in common civility, as the editors of the *Post*'s blog discovered.

Group Decisions: Are Two (or More) Heads Better Than One?

Nor is the people's judgement always true: The most may err as grossly as the few.
—John Dryden, *Absalom and Achitophel*, 1682

We have just seen that the presence of other people influences individual behavior in a number of interesting ways. We turn now to one of the major functions of groups: to make decisions. Most important decisions in the world today are made by groups, because it is assumed that groups make better decisions than individuals do. In the American judicial system, many verdicts are determined by groups of individuals (juries), not single individuals (for a discussion of jury decision making, see Social Psychology in Action 3, "Social Psychology and the Law"). The United States Supreme Court is made up of nine justices, not just one member of the judiciary. Similarly, governmental and corporate decisions are often made by groups of people who meet to discuss the issues, and U.S. presidents have a cabinet and the National Security Council to advise them.

Is it true that two (or more) heads are better than one? Most of us assume the answer is yes. A lone individual may be subject to all sorts of whims and biases, whereas several people together can exchange ideas, catch each other's errors, and reach better decisions. We have all taken part in group decisions in which we listened to someone else and thought to ourselves, "Hmm, that's a really good point—I never would have thought of that." In general, groups do better than individuals if they rely on the person with the most expertise and if people are motivated to search for the answer that is best for the entire group and not just for themselves (De Dreu, Nijstad, & van Knippenberg, 2008). Sometimes, though, two or more heads are not better than one—or at least no better than two heads working alone (Hackman & Katz, 2010; Kerr & Tindale, 2004). Several factors can cause groups to make worse decisions than would individuals.

Process Loss: When Group Interactions Inhibit Good Problem Solving

One problem is that a group will do well only if the most talented member can convince the others that he or she is right—which is not always easy, given that many of us bear a strong resemblance to mules when it comes to admitting we are wrong. You undoubtedly know what it's like to try to convince a group to follow your idea, be faced with opposition and disbelief, and then have to sit there and watch the group make the wrong decision. This is called **process loss**, which is any aspect of group interaction that inhibits good problem solving (Hurley & Allen, 2007; Steiner, 1972). Process loss can occur for a number of reasons. Groups might not try hard enough to find out who the most competent member is and instead rely on someone who really doesn't know what he or she is talking about. The most competent member might find it difficult to disagree with everyone else in the group (recall our discussion of normative social pressures in Chapter 8). Other causes of process loss involve communication problems within the group: In some groups, people don't listen to each other; in others, one person is allowed to dominate the discussion while the others tune out (Sorkin, Hays, & West, 2001; Watson et al., 1998).

Failure to Share Unique Information Suppose you are meeting with three other people to decide whether to support a particular candidate for Student Council president. You all know some of the same things about the candidate, such as the fact that she was president of her sophomore class and is an economics major. But each of you has unique information as well. Maybe you are the only one who knows that she was punished for underage drinking in her first-year dorm, whereas one of the other group members is the only one who knows that she volunteers every week at a local homeless shelter. Obviously, the four of you will make the best decision if you share with each other everything you know about the candidate.

But there is a funny thing about groups: They tend to focus on the information they share and ignore facts known to only some members of the group (Stasser & Titus,

Process Loss
Any aspect of group interaction that inhibits good problem solving.

1985; Toma & Butera, 2009; Wittenbaum & Park, 2001). One study, for example, used a situation similar to the one we have just described, in which students decided who among several candidates was most qualified to be Student Council president (Stasser & Titus, 1985). In the shared information condition, groups of four participants were given the same packet of information to read, which indicated that Candidate A was the best choice for office. Not surprisingly, when the groups met to discuss the candidates, almost all of the members chose Candidate A. In the unshared information condition, each participant in the group received a different packet of information. All participants learned that Candidate A had the same four negative qualities, but each learned that Candidate A also had two unique positive qualities—that is, positive qualities that were different from those listed in other participants' packets. Thus, if the four participants shared with each other the information that was in their packets, they would learn that Candidate A had a total of eight positive qualities and four negative qualities. Instead, most of the groups in the unshared information condition never realized that Candidate A had more good than bad qualities, because when they met they focused on the information they shared rather than on the information they did not. As a result, few of these groups chose Candidate A.

Subsequent research has focused on ways to get groups to focus more on unshared information (Campbell & Stasser, 2006; Scholten et al., 2007; Stasser & Birchmeier, 2003). Unshared information is more likely to be brought up later in the discussion, suggesting that group discussions should last long enough to get beyond what everyone already knows (Fraidin, 2004; Larson et al., 1998). It also helps to tell group members not to share what their initial preferences are at the outset of the discussion; if they do, they will focus less on unique, unshared information (Mojzisch & Schulz-Hardt, 2010). Another approach is to assign different group members to specific areas of expertise so that they know that they alone are responsible for certain types of information (Stasser, Stewart, & Wittenbaum, 1995; Stewart & Stasser, 1995).

The only sin which we never forgive in each other is difference of opinion.
—Ralph Waldo Emerson, *Society and Solitude*, 1870

This last lesson has been learned by many couples, who know to rely on each other's memories for different kinds of information. One member of a couple might be responsible for remembering the times of social engagements, whereas the other might be responsible for remembering when to pay the bills (Wegner, Erber, & Raymond, 1991). The combined memory of two people that is more efficient than the memory of either individual is called **transactive memory** (Peltokorpi, 2008; Rajaram & Pereira-Pasarin, 2010; Wegner, 1995). By learning to specialize their memories and knowing what their partner is responsible for, couples often do quite well in remembering important information. The same can be true of groups, if they develop a system whereby different people are responsible for remembering different parts of a task (Ellis, Porter, & Wolverton, 2008; Lewis et al., 2007; Moreland, 1999). In sum, the tendency for groups to fail to share important information known to only some of the members can be overcome if people learn who is responsible for what kinds of information and take the time to discuss these unshared data (Stasser, 2000).

Groupthink: Many Heads, One Mind Earlier we mentioned that group cohesiveness can get in the way of clear thinking and good decision making. Using real-world events, Irving Janis (1972, 1982) developed an influential theory of group decision making that he called **groupthink**, a kind of thinking in which maintaining group cohesiveness and solidarity is more important than considering the facts in a realistic manner. According to Janis's theory, groupthink is most likely to occur when certain preconditions are met, such as when the group is highly cohesive, isolated from contrary opinions, and ruled by a directive leader who makes his or her wishes known. One of his examples was the decision by President John F. Kennedy and his advisers to invade Cuba in 1961. This was during the Cold War, when there were many tensions between the Soviet Union and the United States, and the Communist revolution in Cuba (with the support of the Soviet Union) was seen as an enormous threat. The idea was to land a small force of CIA-trained Cuban exiles on the Cuban coast, who would then instigate and lead a mass uprising against Fidel Castro, the Cuban leader. What looked good on paper to Kennedy and his advisers turned out to be a fiasco. Soon after the invasion was

Transactive Memory

The combined memory of two people that is more efficient than the memory of either individual.

Groupthink

A kind of thinking in which maintaining group cohesiveness and solidarity is more important than considering the facts in a realistic manner.

launched, Castro's forces captured or killed nearly all the U.S.-backed forces. Friendly Latin American countries were outraged that the United States had invaded one of their neighbors, and Cuba became even more closely allied with the Soviet Union. Later, President Kennedy would ask, "How could we have been so stupid?" (Sorenson, 1966).

The reason, according to Janis (1982), was that the decision met many of the symptoms of groupthink. Kennedy and his team were riding high on their close victory in the 1960 election and were a tight-knit, homogeneous group. Because they had not yet made any major policy decisions, they lacked well-developed methods for discussing the issues. Moreover, Kennedy made it clear that he favored the invasion, and he asked the group to consider only details of how it should be executed instead of questioning whether it should proceed at all.

"All those in favor say 'Aye.'" *"Aye."* *"Aye."* *"Aye."* *"Aye."* *"Aye."*

Henry Martin/The New Yorker Collection/ www.cartoonbank.com

When these preconditions of groupthink are met, several symptoms appear (see Figure 9.5). The group begins to feel that it is invulnerable and can do no wrong. People do not voice contrary views (they exercise self-censorship), because they are afraid of ruining the group's high morale or because they fear being criticized by the others. For example, Arthur Schlesinger, one of Kennedy's advisers, reported that he had severe doubts about the Bay of Pigs invasion but did not express these concerns during the discussions, out of a fear that "others would regard it as presumptuous of him, a college professor, to take issue with august heads of major government institutions" (Janis, 1982, p. 32). If anyone does voice a contrary viewpoint, the rest of the group is quick to criticize, pressuring the person to conform to the majority view. This kind of behavior creates an

Antecedents of groupthink

The group is highly cohesive: The group is valued and attractive, and people very much want to be members.

Group isolation: The group is isolated, protected from hearing alternative viewpoints.

A directive leader: The leader controls the discussion and makes his or her wishes known.

High stress: The members perceive threats to the group.

Poor decision-making procedures: No standard methods to consider alternative viewpoints.

→

Symptoms of groupthink

Illusion of invulnerability: The group feels it is invincible and can do no wrong.

Belief in the moral correctness of the group: "God is on our side."

Stereotyped views of out-group: Opposing sides are viewed in a simplistic, stereotyped manner.

Self-censorship: People decide not to voice contrary opinions so as not to "rock the boat."

Direct pressure on dissenters to conform: If people do voice contrary opinions, they are pressured by others to conform to the majority.

Illusion of unanimity: An illusion is created that everyone agrees—for example, by not calling on people known to disagree.

Mindguards: Group members protect the leader from contrary viewpoints.

→

Defective decision making

Incomplete survey of alternatives

Failure to examine risks of the favored alternative

Poor information search

Failure to develop contingency plans

FIGURE 9.5

Groupthink: Antecedents, Symptoms, and Consequences

Under some conditions, maintaining group cohesiveness and solidarity is more important to a group than considering the facts in a realistic manner (see "Antecedents"). When this happens, certain symptoms of groupthink occur, such as the illusion of invulnerability (see "Symptoms"). These symptoms lead to defective decision making.

(Based on data in Janis & Mann, 1977.)

illusion of unanimity, where it looks as if everyone agrees. On the day the group voted on whether to invade, President Kennedy asked all those present for their opinion—except Arthur Schlesinger.

The perilous state of groupthink causes people to implement an inferior decision-making process. As seen at the far right in Figure 9.5, for example, the group does not consider the full range of alternatives, does not develop contingency plans, and does not adequately consider the risks of its preferred choice. Can you think of other governmental decisions that were plagued by groupthink? Some have suggested that President Bush's decision to invade Iraq in 2003 was such a case. President Bush's former press secretary, Scott McClelland, for example, wrote that once the president made his view known "it was rarely questioned," because "that is what Bush expected and made known to his top advisers" (McClelland, 2008, p. 128). On the other hand, President Bush was not known as a highly directive leader who dominated group discussions. We leave it to future historians to decide whether this important decision resulted from sound decision-making processes or from symptoms of groupthink.

A lot of water has gone over the dam since the theory of groupthink was first proposed, and a number of researchers have put it to the test (Packer, 2009; Tetlock et al., 1992; Turner et al., 2006; Turner, Pratkanis, & Struckman, 2007). The upshot of this research is that defective group decision making may be more common than the original theory assumed. The groupthink theory held that a specific set of conditions had to be met in order for groupthink to occur—namely the antecedents listed on the left side of Figure 9.5 (e.g., the group has to be highly cohesive). It now appears that groupthink can occur even when some of these antecedents are missing. It may be enough for people to identify strongly with the group, have clear norms about what the group is supposed to do, and have low confidence that the group can solve the problem (Baron, 2005; Henningsen et al., 2006). Research has also found, however, that some people are particularly likely to challenge a group decision that is wrong. One study, for example, examined the extent to which bicultural individuals—those who have two cultural backgrounds, as is the case with many first-generation Asian Americans—were willing to challenge a group decision that was incorrect. The study found that the bicultural individuals who identified strongly with one or the other of their cultures were the most likely to conform to the group, even when it was wrong. Interestingly, it was the bicultural individuals who felt the most torn about their identity—who had a foot in two different cultures—that were the *least* likely to conform (i.e., most likely to challenge the group when it was wrong). Having experience with two different cultures, and identifying with both, may make people more immune to group pressure (Mok & Morris, 2010).

Watch on **MyPsychLab**
To learn more about decision making and groupthink, watch the MyPsychLab video ***IT Video: Group Thinking.***

Avoiding the Groupthink Trap A wise leader can take several steps to ensure that his or her group is immune to the groupthink style of decision making (Flowers, 1977; McCauley, 1989; Zimbardo & Andersen, 1993).

- **Remain impartial.** The leader should not take a directive role, but should remain impartial.
- **Seek outside opinions.** The leader should invite outside opinions from people who are not members of the group and who are thus less concerned with maintaining group cohesiveness.
- **Create subgroups.** The leader should divide the group into subgroups that first meet separately and then meet together to discuss their different recommendations.
- **Seek anonymous opinions.** The leader might also take a secret ballot or ask group members to write down their opinions anonymously; doing so would ensure that people give their true opinions, uncensored by a fear of recrimination from the group.

Fortunately, President Kennedy learned from his mistakes with the Bay of Pigs decision, and when he encountered his next major foreign policy decision, the Cuban missile crisis, he took many of these steps to avoid groupthink. When his advisers met to decide what to do about the discovery that the Soviet Union had placed nuclear-tipped missiles in Cuba, pointed towards the United States, Kennedy often absented himself from the group so as not to inhibit discussion. He also brought in outside experts (e.g., Adlai Stevenson) who were not members of the in-group. That Kennedy successfully negotiated the removal of the Soviet missiles was almost certainly due to the improved methods of group decision making he adopted.

CONNECTIONS

Was the Financial Crisis of 2007 a Result of Groupthink?

The concept of groupthink has become widely known in the general culture, and writers and pundits alike have blamed it for many bad decisions. A *New York Times* article, for example, claimed that experts on the Federal Reserve Board should have predicted the financial crisis of 2007, but didn't because they exhibited symptoms of groupthink (Shiller, 2008).

By way of background, the financial crisis that began in 2007 in the United States was so severe that it has been called the Great Recession. Before that point, housing prices were skyrocketing; between 1996 and 2007, the average price of a house in the United States more than doubled. But then interest rates began to rise and home prices started to fall. More and more people couldn't afford to pay their mortgages, and banks foreclosed their properties. Banks themselves began to fail at an alarming rate. Between October of 2007 and March of 2009, the stock market lost over half of its value. Many people lost their jobs; in January of 2007, the unemployment rate was 4.6%, but by October of 2009, it was more than double that.

Why didn't financial experts see all of this coming? Well, according to the article in the *New York Times*, some did, but their voices weren't heeded: "Lots of people were worried about the housing boom and its potential for creating economic disaster. It's just that the Fed did not take them very seriously" (Shiller, 2008, p. BU5). The author suggests that some experts fell prey to groupthink, by buckling under the pressure of majority opinion and not voicing their concerns loudly enough due to self-censorship. He suggests that the chair of the Federal Reserve Board, Alan Greenspan, like other leaders before him, may have underestimated how much dissent there was among his experts because of groupthink processes. Does this claim hold up, based on what we know from research in social psychology?

Yes and no. To the extent that experts on the Federal Reserve Board failed to voice their concerns and that there was an illusion of unanimity on the Board, some of the symptoms of groupthink were present (see Figure 9.5). But the term *groupthink* is usually reserved for members of highly cohesive groups that exert direct pressure on each other to conform and believe in the moral correctness of the group. Furthermore, the Federal Reserve Board was not solely responsible for the financial crisis. In January of 2011, the Financial Crisis Inquiry Commission concluded that, yes, the Federal Reserve Board deserved some of the blame, but that the crisis was also caused by "dramatic breakdowns of corporate governance, profound lapses in regulatory oversight, and near fatal flaws in our financial system" (Financial Crisis Inquiry Report, 2011, pp. xxvii–xxviii). Thus, there may have been some elements of groupthink leading up to the crisis, but we can't blame it for the entire economic downturn.

Some have argued that the financial crisis of 2007 was triggered by groupthink among financial experts. Based on what you have read about groupthink, do you think this is true?

Group Polarization: Going to Extremes

Maybe you are willing to grant that groups sometimes make poor decisions. Surely, though, groups will usually make less-risky decisions than a lone individual will. One individual might be willing to bet the ranch on a risky proposition, but if others help make the decision, they will interject reason and moderation. Or will they? The question of whether groups or individuals make more-risky decisions has been examined in numerous studies. Participants are typically given the Choice Dilemmas Questionnaire (CDQ), a series of stories that presents a dilemma for the main character and asks the reader to choose how much probability of success there would have to be before the reader would recommend the risky alternative (Kogan & Wallach, 1964). An example of a CDQ item about a chess player appears in the following Try It! exercise. People choose their answers alone and then meet in a group to discuss the options, arriving at a unanimous group decision for each dilemma.

Many of the initial studies found, surprisingly, that groups make riskier decisions than individuals do. For example, when deciding alone, people said that the chess player should make the risky gambit only if there were at least a 30% chance of success. But after discussing the problem with others in a group, people said that the chess player should go for it even if there were only a 10% chance of success (Wallach, Kogan, & Bem, 1962). Findings such as these have become known as the *risky shift*. But further research has made clear that such shifts are not the full story. It turns out that groups tend to make decisions that are more extreme, in the same direction as the individual's initial predispositions, which happened to be risky in the case of the chess problem. What would happen if people were initially inclined to be conservative? In cases such as these, groups tend to make even more-conservative decisions than individuals do.

Consider this problem: Roger, a young married man with two children, has a secure but low-paying job and no savings. Someone gives him a tip about a stock that will triple in value if the company's new product is successful, but will plummet if the new product fails. Should Roger sell his life insurance policy and invest in the company? Most people recommend a safe course of action here: Roger should buy the stock only if the new product is very certain to succeed. When they talk it over in a group, they become even more conservative, deciding that the new product would have to have a nearly 100% chance of success before they would recommend that Roger buy stock in the company.

The tendency for groups to make decisions that are more extreme than the initial inclination of its members—toward greater risk if people's initial tendency is to be risky

TRY IT! Choice Dilemmas Questionnaire

You'll need four or five friends for this exercise. First, copy the following questionnaire and give it to each of your friends to complete individually, without talking to anyone else. Then bring them all together and ask them to discuss the dilemma and arrive at a unanimous decision. They should try to reach a consensus such that every member of the group agrees at least partly with the final decision. Finally, compare people's initial decisions (made alone) with the group decision. Who made the riskier decisions on average: people deciding by themselves or the group?

The Choice Dilemmas Questionnaire

A low-ranked participant in a national chess tournament, playing an early match against a highly favored opponent, has the choice of attempting or not attempting a deceptive but risky maneuver that might lead to quick victory if it is successful or almost certain defeat if it fails. Indicate the lowest probability of success that you would accept before recommending that the chess player employ the risky move.

_________ 1 chance in 10 of succeeding
_________ 3 chances in 10 of succeeding
_________ 5 chances in 10 of succeeding
_________ 7 chances in 10 of succeeding
_________ 9 chances in 10 of succeeding
_________ I would not recommend taking the chance.

Remember, groups tend to make riskier decisions than individuals on problems such as these. Did you find the same thing? Why or why not? If the group did make a riskier decision, was it due more to the persuasive arguments interpretation discussed in the text, the social comparison interpretation, or both?
(Adapted from Wallach, Kogan, & Bem, 1962)

and toward greater caution if people's initial tendency is to be cautious—is known as **group polarization** (Brown, 1965; Palmer & Loveland, 2008; Rodrigo & Ato, 2002; Teger & Pruitt, 1967).

Group Polarization
The tendency for groups to make decisions that are more extreme than the initial inclinations of its members.

Group polarization occurs for two main reasons. According to the persuasive arguments interpretation, all individuals bring to the group a set of arguments, some of which other individuals have not considered, supporting their initial recommendation. For example, one person might stress that cashing in the life insurance policy is an unfair risk to Roger's children should he die prematurely. Another person might not have considered this possibility; thus, he or she becomes more conservative as well. A series of studies supports this interpretation of group polarization, whereby each member presents arguments that other members have not considered (Burnstein & Sentis, 1981; Burnstein & Vinokur, 1977).

Great Person Theory
The idea that certain key personality traits make a person a good leader, regardless of the situation.

Transactional Leaders
Leaders who set clear, short-term goals and reward people who meet them.

Transformational Leaders
Leaders who inspire followers to focus on common, long-term goals.

According to the social comparison interpretation, when people discuss an issue in a group, they first check out how everyone else feels. What does the group value: being risky or being cautious? To be liked, many people then take a position that is similar to everyone else's but a little more extreme. In this way, the individual supports the group's values and also presents himself or herself in a positive light—a person in the vanguard, an impressive thinker. Both the persuasive arguments and the social comparison interpretations of group polarization have received research support (Blaskovich, Ginsburg, & Veach, 1975; Brown, 1986; Isenberg, 1986; Zuber, Crott, & Werner, 1992).

Leadership in Groups

There is properly no history, only biography.
—Ralph Waldo Emerson, *Essays, History*, 1841

A critical question we have not yet considered is the role of the leader in group decision making. The question of what makes a great leader has intrigued psychologists, historians, and political scientists for some time (Bass, 1990; Chemers, 2000; Fiedler, 1967; Hogg, 2010; Hollander, 1985; Klenke, 1996; Simonton, 1987). One of the best-known answers to this question is the **great person theory**, which maintains that certain key personality traits make a person a good leader, regardless of the nature of the situation the leader faces.

If the great person theory is true, we ought to be able to isolate the key aspects of personality that make someone a great leader. Is it a combination of intelligence, charisma, and courage? Is it better to be introverted or extroverted? Should we add a dollop of ruthlessness to the mix as well, as Niccolò Machiavelli suggested in 1513 in his famous treatise on leadership, *The Prince*? Or do highly moral people make the best leaders?

Leadership and Personality Numerous studies have found weak relationships between personality and leadership abilities. Compared to nonleaders, for example, leaders tend to be slightly more intelligent, extroverted, driven by the desire for power, charismatic, socially skilled, open to new experiences, confident in their leadership abilities, less neurotic, and have a moderate degree of assertiveness (Ames & Flynn, 2007; Chemers, Watson, & May, 2000; Judge et al., 2002; Van Vugt, 2006). What is most telling, however, is the absence of strong relationships. Surprisingly few personality characteristics correlate strongly with leadership effectiveness, and the relationships that have been found tend to be modest (Avolio, Walumbwa, & Weber, 2009; von Wittich & Antonakis, 2011). For example, Dean Simonton (1987, 2001) gathered information about one hundred personal attributes of all U.S. presidents, such as their family backgrounds, educational experiences, occupations, and personalities. Only three of these variables—height, family size, and the number of books a president published before taking office—correlated with how effective the presidents were in office. Tall presidents, those from small families, and those who have published books are most likely to become effective leaders, as rated by historians. The other 97 characteristics, including personality traits, were not related to leadership effectiveness at all.

What determines whether someone, such as Martin Luther King, Jr., is a great leader? Is it a certain constellation of personality traits, or is it necessary to have the right person in the right situation at the right time?

Leadership Styles Although great leaders may not have specific kinds of personalities, they do appear to adopt specific kinds of leadership styles. **Transactional leaders** set clear, short-term goals and reward people who meet them. **Transformational leaders**, on the other hand, inspire followers to focus on common, long-term goals (Bass, 1998; Burns, 1978). Transactional leaders do a good job of making sure the needs of the organization are met and that things run smoothly. It is transformational leaders, however, who think outside the box, identify important long-term goals, and inspire their followers to exert themselves to meet these goals.

Interestingly, these leadership styles are not closely linked with personality traits; it is not as if people are "born to be" one or the other type of leader (Judge, Colbert, & Ilies, 2004; Nielsen & Cleal, 2011). Further, these styles are not mutually exclusive; in fact, the most effective leader is one who adopts both styles (Judge & Piccolo, 2004). If no one was minding the day-to-day operation of an organization, and people were not being rewarded for meeting short-term objectives, the organization would suffer. At the same time, it is important as well to have a charismatic leader who inspires people to think about long-term objectives.

The Right Person in the Right Situation As you know by now, one of the most important tenets of social psychology is that, to understand social behavior, it is not enough to consider personality traits alone—we must take the social situation into account as well. The inadequacy of the great person theory does not mean that personal characteristics are irrelevant to good leadership. Instead, being good social psychologists, we should consider both the nature of the leader and the situation in which the leading takes place.

A business leader, for example, can be highly successful in some situations but not in others. Consider the late Steve Jobs, who, at age 21, founded the Apple Computer Company with Stephen Wozniak. Jobs was anything but an MBA type of corporate leader. A product of the 1960s' counterculture, he turned to computers only after experimenting with LSD, traveling to India, and living on a communal fruit farm. In the days when there were no personal computers, Jobs's offbeat style was well suited to starting a new industry. Within 5 years, he was the leader of a billion-dollar company. But Jobs's unorthodox style was ill suited to managing a large corporation in a competitive market. Apple's earnings began to suffer, and in 1985 Jobs was forced out. Undeterred, Jobs cofounded Pixar in 1986, the first major company to make computer-generated animation, and sold it to the Disney Company in 2006 for $7.4 billion. And in the 1990s, the Apple company faced some of the same technological challenges it did at its inception, having to revamp the operating system for its Macintosh computers and regain market share. Whom did Apple hire to lead this new challenge? Steve Jobs, of course.

A comprehensive theory of leadership thus needs to focus on the characteristics of the leader, the followers, and the situation. The best-known theory of this type is the **contingency theory of leadership**, which argues that leadership effectiveness depends both on how task-oriented or relationship-oriented the leader is and on the amount of control and influence the leader has over the group (Fiedler, 1967, 1978). There are basically two kinds of leaders, the theory argues: those who are **task-oriented**, concerned more with getting the job done than with workers' feelings and relationships, and those who are **relationship-oriented**, concerned more with workers' feelings and relationships. Task-oriented leaders do well in *high-control work situations*, when the leader has excellent interpersonal relationships with subordinates, his or her position in the company is clearly perceived as powerful, and the work needing to be done by the group is structured and well defined. They also do well in *low-control work situations*, when the leader has poor relationships with subordinates and the work needing to be done is not clearly defined. What about relationship-oriented leaders? They are most effective in *moderate-control work situations*. Under these conditions, the wheels are turning fairly smoothly, but some attention is needed to the squeakiness caused by poor relationships and hurt feelings. The leader who can soothe such feelings will be most successful (see Figure 9.6). The contingency theory of leadership has been supported in studies of numerous types of leaders, including business managers, college administrators, military commanders, and postmasters (Ayman, 2002; Chemers, 2000; Schriesheim, Tepper, & Tetrault, 1994; Van Vugt & DeCremer, 1999).

Contingency Theory of Leadership
The idea that leadership effectiveness depends both on how task-oriented or relationship-oriented the leader is and on the amount of control and influence the leader has over the group.

Task-Oriented Leader
A leader who is concerned more with getting the job done than with workers' feelings and relationships.

Relationship-Oriented Leader
A leader who is concerned more with workers' feelings and relationships.

Gender and Leadership If you've seen an episode of the television show *Mad Men*, which is about an advertising agency in the 1960s, you know that it was not that long ago that businessmen were exactly that: men. Since that time, women started working outside the home in increasing numbers, and, as we noted earlier, the workforce in the United States is now about half women. But are women as likely as men to become leaders in business, politics, and other organizations? Barriers to

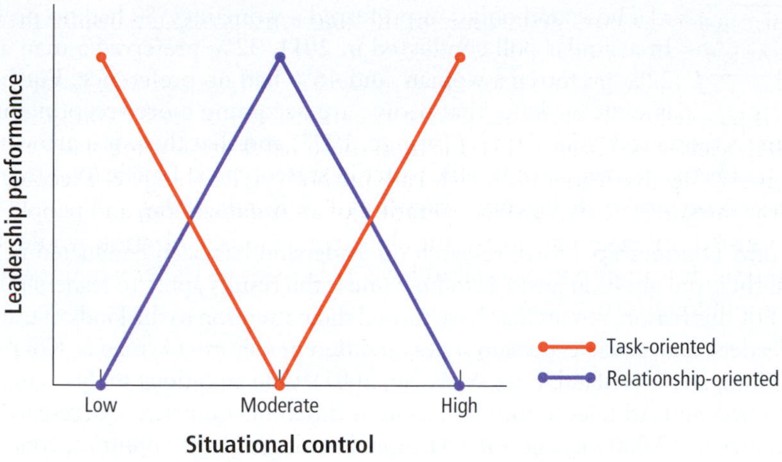

FIGURE 9.6

Fiedler's Contingency Theory of Leadership

According to Fiedler, task-oriented leaders perform best when situational control is high or low, whereas relationship-oriented leaders perform best when situational control is moderate.

advancement by women are breaking down; in 2008, for example, a woman (Hillary Clinton) came close to winning the Democratic nomination for president, and another woman (Sarah Palin) ran for vice president on the Republican ticket for the first time. In 2009, a woman (Nancy Pelosi) became the first female Speaker of the House of Representatives. Unfortunately, the barriers have not completely disappeared. In 2011, only 12 of the CEOs of Fortune 500 companies were women, and the boards of directors of U.S. companies included only 16% women (Catalyst, 2011). Things are not much different elsewhere. That 16% figure is actually among the highest in the world, except for Scandinavian countries (Norway has the highest percentage of women on boards of directors at 40%).

Leadership cannot really be taught. It can only be learned.

—HAROLD GENEEN, 1984

One reason that it is difficult for women to achieve leadership positions is because many people believe that good leaders have *agentic* traits (assertive, controlling, dominant, independent, self-confident), which are traditionally associated with men. In contrast, women are expected to be more *communal* (concerned with the welfare of others, warm, helpful, kind, affectionate). Thus, if women behave in the way they are "supposed" to behave, they are often viewed as having less leadership potential. But if women succeed in attaining a leadership position and act in ways that leaders are expected to act—namely, in agentic, forceful ways—they are criticized for not "acting like a woman should" (Brescoll, Dawson, & Uhlmann, 2010; Eagly, Johannesen-Schmidt, & van Engen, 2003; Eagly & Karau, 2002; Koenig et al., 2011).

Here's another danger that women leaders face: Because they are perceived as being more communal, they are often thought to be better at managing crises, particularly ones that involve interpersonal problems, such as a conflict between high-level managers. That might seem like a good thing—trusting women leaders to solve problems—but it has a downside in which women are more likely to be put in precarious, high-risk positions where it is difficult to succeed. Michelle Ryan and her colleagues have called this a "glass cliff" (Ryan et al. 2008, 2011). Even when women have broken through the "glass ceiling" into top leadership positions, they are more likely than men to be put in charge of units that are in crisis and in which the risk of failure is high. Ryan and her colleagues found this to be true in studies of hiring in real-world companies, as well as in controlled laboratory studies in which people read descriptions of companies and recommended people for leadership positions. Participants were more likely to recommend a woman when an organizational unit was in crisis and a man when the unit was running smoothly—which makes it more likely that women will fail in their leadership positions.

If women seeking leadership roles conform to society's expectations about how they ought to behave, by being warm and communal, they are often perceived as having low leadership potential. If they become leaders and act in ways that leaders are expected to act—namely, in agentic, forceful ways—they are often perceived negatively for not "acting like a woman should."

The better news is that prejudice toward women leaders appears to be lessening over time. In a Gallup poll conducted in 1953, 66% of people said that they preferred a man

I wonder men dare trust themselves with men.
—William Shakespeare, *The Life of Timon of Athens*

as a boss, and only 5% preferred a woman (25% had no preference). In a similar poll conducted in 2011, 32% preferred a man as a boss, 22% preferred a woman, and 46% had no preference. Further, there is some evidence that people are becoming more accepting of women who act in stereotypical "male" ways (Twenge, 1997) and that there is a growing recognition that effective leaders must be able to act in stereotypical female (communal) ways as well as stereotypical male (agentic) ways (Eagly & Karau, 2002).

Culture and Leadership Most research on leadership has been conducted in Western countries; thus, the question arises as to how much the results apply to leadership in other cultures. For this reason, researchers have turned their attention to the kinds of traits people value in leaders, and actual leadership styles, in different cultures (Ayman & Korabik, 2010; Eagly & Chin, 2010; Gelfand, Erez, & Aycan, 2007). One ambitious study examined leadership practices and attitudes toward leaders in 62 different countries. The researchers gave questionnaires to 17,000 managers in 951 organizations in those countries, conducted extensive interviews, convened group discussions, and analyzed the content of media in each country. Not surprisingly, different cultures valued different traits in leaders. For example, autonomous leadership, defined as being independent of one's superiors and keeping one's distance from subordinates and to spend a lot of time working alone, was valued more in most Eastern European countries than it was in most Latin American countries. But there was universal agreement about the value of two leadership qualities: charisma and being team-oriented (House et al., 2004). Questions about cultural differences in leadership are receiving increasing attention, because in a global economy work groups are becoming more diverse and managers from different cultures have increasingly frequent contact.

Conflict and Cooperation

We have already examined how people work together to make decisions; in these situations, group members have a common goal. Often, however, people have incompatible goals, placing them in conflict with each other. This can be true of two individuals, such as romantic partners who disagree about who should clean the kitchen, or two groups, such as a labor union and company management who disagree over wages and working conditions. It can also be true of nations, such as in the long-standing conflict between Israel and its Arab neighbors or between the Shiites, Sunnis, and Kurds in Iraq. The opportunity for interpersonal conflict exists whenever two or more people interact. Sigmund Freud (1930) went so far as to argue that conflict is an inevitable by-product of civilization because the goals and needs of individuals often clash with the goals and needs of their fellow human beings. The nature of conflict, and how it can be resolved, has been the topic of a great deal of social psychological research (Cohen & Insko, 2008; De Dreu, 2010; Deutsch, 1973; Thibaut & Kelley, 1959).

Sometimes people are able to resolve conflicts peacefully, such as a couple that has an amicable divorce. At other times conflicts escalate into rancor and violence. Social psychologists have performed experiments to test ways in which conflict resolution is most likely to occur.

Many conflicts are resolved peacefully, with little rancor. Couples can find a way to resolve their differences in a mutually acceptable manner, and labor disputes are sometimes settled with a handshake. All too often, however, conflict erupts into open hostilities. The divorce rate in the United States is distressingly high. People sometimes resort to violence to resolve their differences, as shown by the high rate of murders in the United States, which has been called "the murder capital of the civilized world." Warfare between nations remains an all-too-common solution to international disputes. Obviously, it is of great importance to find ways of resolving conflicts peacefully.

Social Dilemmas

What is best for an individual is not always best for the group as a whole. Consider a publishing venture by the novelist Stephen King. He wrote two installments of a novel called *The Plant* and posted them on the Internet, asking readers to pay $1 per installment. The deal he offered was simple: If at least 75% of the people who downloaded the installments paid the fee, he would keep writing and posting new installments. If fewer than 75% of the people paid, he would stop writing and people would never get the rest of the novel.

King had devised a classic **social dilemma**, a conflict in which the most beneficial action for an individual will, if chosen by most people, be harmful to everyone (Weber, Kopelman, & Messick, 2004). It was to any individual's financial advantage to download King's novel free of charge and let other people pay. However, if too many people took this approach, everyone would lose, because King said he would stop writing the novel. At first, people acted for the good of all; more than 75% paid for the first installment. As with many other social dilemmas, however, people eventually acted in their own self-interest, to the detriment of all. The number of people who paid for their later installments dropped below 75%, and King stopped posting new ones, saying on his Web site that the novel was "on hiatus."

The Panera restaurant chain has had more success with this approach. In 2010 they began opening Panera Cares restaurants, which look and operate like other Paneras except for one thing: People aren't required to pay anything if they don't want to. There are suggested prices for all menu items, but customers are allowed to pay whatever they want. The CEO and founder of the restaurant chain, Ronald Shaich, had a vision in which people in real need could come get a good meal and pay whatever they could afford; the costs would be offset, he hoped, by customers who could afford to pay more than the suggested prices. So far it's working. At the first three Panera Cares restaurants to open—in St. Louis, Detroit, and Portland—about three in five people pay the suggested prices, one in five pays less, and one in five pays more. Those who pay less are usually people who couldn't otherwise afford to eat out, such as a teacher who was laid off after 25 years and low-income families who come in to celebrate a birthday. True, some people take advantage of the system, such as three college students who paid \$3 for a \$40 meal. But enough people pay more than the suggested price to offset those who pay less, and the three stores are self-sustaining (Salter, 2011). What determines how people respond in social dilemmas such as these? Social psychologists have attempted to find out by studying these conflicts experimentally, testing both their causes and resolutions in the laboratory.

One of the most common ways of studying social dilemmas in the laboratory is with a game called "the prisoner's dilemma." In each trial, two players have to choose one of two options without knowing what the other player will choose. The number of points they win depends on the options chosen by both people. Suppose that you were playing the game with a friend. As shown in the following Try It! exercise, you have to choose Option X or Option Y without knowing which option your friend will choose. Your payoff—the amount of money you win or lose—depends on the choices of both you and your friend. For example, if both you and your friend choose Option X, you both win \$3. If, however, you choose Option Y and your friend chooses Option X, you win \$6 and your friend loses \$6. Which option would you choose?

Many people begin by choosing Option Y. At worst you will lose \$1, and at best you will win the highest possible amount, \$6. Choosing Option X raises the possibility that both sides will win some money, but this is also a risky choice. If your partner chooses Y while you choose X, you stand to lose a great deal. Because people often do not know how much they can trust their partners, Option Y frequently seems like the safest choice (Rapoport & Chammah, 1965). The rub is that both players will probably think this way, ensuring that both sides lose (see the lower right-hand corner of the table in the Try It! exercise).

People's actions in these games seem to mirror many conflicts in everyday life. To find a solution desirable to both parties, people must trust each other. Often they do not, and this lack of trust leads to an escalating series of competitive moves so that in the end no one wins (Insko & Schopler, 1998; Kelley & Thibaut, 1978; Lount et al., 2008). Two countries locked in an arms race, for example, may feel that they cannot afford to disarm, out of fear that the other side will take advantage of their weakened position. The result is that both sides add furiously to their stockpile of weapons, neither gaining superiority over the other and both spending money they could use to solve domestic problems (Deutsch, 1973). Such an escalation of conflict is also seen all too often among couples who are divorcing. Sometimes the goal seems more to hurt the other person than to further one's own needs (or the children's). In the end, both suffer because, metaphorically speaking, they both choose Option Y too often.

Social Dilemma

A conflict in which the most beneficial action for an individual will, if chosen by most people, have harmful effects on everyone.

TRY IT! The Prisoner's Dilemma

YOUR FRIEND'S OPTIONS	Your Options: OPTION X	Your Options: OPTION Y
Option X	You win $3 Your friend wins $3	You win $6 Your friend loses $6
Option Y	You lose $6 Your friend wins $6	You lose $1 Your friend loses $1

Play this version of the prisoner's dilemma game with a friend. First, show the table to the friend, and explain how the game works: On each trial of the game, you and your friend can choose Option X or Option Y, without knowing what the other will choose. You should each write your choice on folded pieces of paper that are opened at the same time. The numbers in the table represent imaginary money that you and your friend win or lose on each trial. For example, if you choose Option X on the first trial and your friend chooses Option Y, you lose an imaginary $6 and your friend wins an imaginary $6. If both of you choose Option Y, you both lose an imaginary $1. Play the game for 10 trials, and keep track of how much each of you wins or loses. Did you and your friend choose the cooperative option (Option X) or the competitive option (Option Y) more often? Why? Did a pattern of trust or mistrust develop over the course of the game?

Increasing Cooperation in the Prisoner's Dilemma Such escalating conflict, though common, is not inevitable. Many studies have found that when people play the prisoner's dilemma game, they will, under certain conditions, adopt the more cooperative response (Option X), ensuring that both sides end up with a positive outcome. Not surprisingly, if people are playing the game with a friend or if they expect to interact with their partner in the future, they are more likely to adopt a cooperative strategy that maximizes both their profits and their partner's (Cohen & Insko, 2008). Also, subtly changing the norms about what kind of behavior is expected can have large effects on how cooperative people are. One study found that simply changing the name of a game from the "Wall Street Game" to the "Community Game" increased the percentage of people who cooperated from 33% to 71% (Liberman, Samuels, & Ross, 2004). Another, conducted with Chinese college students in Hong Kong, found that showing people symbols of Chinese culture before the game (e.g., a Chinese dragon) made people more cooperative, whereas showing people symbols of American culture (e.g., an American flag) made them more competitive (Wong & Hong, 2005).

To increase cooperation, you can also try the **tit-for-tat strategy**, which is a way of encouraging cooperation by at first acting cooperatively but then always responding the way your opponent did (cooperatively or competitively) in the previous trial. This strategy communicates a willingness to cooperate and an unwillingness to sit back and be exploited if the partner does not cooperate. The tit-for-tat strategy is usually successful in getting the other person to respond with the cooperative, trusting response (Axelrod, 1984; Klapwijk & Van Lange, 2009; Leite, 2011; Messick & Liebrand, 1995; Wubben, De Cremer, & van Dijk, 2009). Using this tactic in the arms race would mean matching not only any military buildup made by an unfriendly nation, but also any conciliatory gesture, such as a ban on nuclear testing.

Another proven strategy is to allow individuals rather than opposing groups to resolve a conflict, because two individuals who play the prisoner's dilemma are more likely to cooperate than two groups who play the same game (Schopler & Insko, 1999). The reason for this is that people are more likely to assume that another individual is cooperative at heart and can be trusted, but that most groups of individuals will, given the opportunity, stab us in the back. Does this mean that world leaders would be more cooperative when negotiating one-on-one than when groups of advisers from the two nations meet? Possibly. In 1985, Ronald Reagan and Mikhail Gorbachev, then leaders of the United States and the Soviet Union, met for the first time, in Switzerland, to discuss arms reduction. After formal meetings between the leaders and their aides stalled, Reagan and Gorbachev took a walk to a boathouse, accompanied only by translators. According to some reports, the two men came close to agreeing to dismantle all of their nuclear missiles—until their aides got wind of this "preposterous" idea and squelched it (Korda, 1997).

Tit-for-Tat Strategy

A means of encouraging cooperation by at first acting cooperatively but then always responding the way your opponent did (cooperatively or competitively) on the previous trial.

Using Threats to Resolve Conflict

When involved in a conflict, many of us are tempted to use threats to get the other party to cave in to our wishes, believing that we should, in the words of Teddy Roosevelt, "speak softly and carry a big stick." Parents commonly use threats to get their children to behave, and teachers often threaten their students with demerits or a visit to the principal. More alarming is the increasing number of youths in the United States who carry weapons and use them to resolve conflicts that used to be settled with a playground scuffle. Threats are commonly used on an international scale as well, to further the interests of one nation over another (Turner & Horvitz, 2001).

A classic series of studies by Morton Deutsch and Robert Krauss (1960, 1962) indicates that threats are not an effective means of reducing conflict. These researchers developed a game in which two participants imagined that they were in charge of trucking companies named Acme and Bolt. The goal of each company was to transport merchandise as quickly as possible to a destination. The participants were paid 60 cents for each "trip" but had 1 cent subtracted for every second it took them to make the trip. The most direct route for each company was over a one-lane road on which only one truck could travel at a time. This placed the two companies in direct conflict, as seen in Figure 9.7. If Acme and Bolt both tried to take the one-lane road, neither truck could pass, and both would lose money. Each company could take an alternate route, but this was much longer, guaranteeing that they would lose at least 10 cents in each trial.

After a while, most participants worked out a solution that allowed both trucks to make a modest amount of money. They took turns waiting until the other party crossed the one-lane road; then they would take that route as well. In another version of the study, the researchers gave Acme a gate that could be lowered over the one-lane road, thereby blocking Bolt from using that route. You might think that using force—the gate—would increase Acme's profits, because all Acme had to do was to threaten Bolt to "stay off the one-lane road or else." In fact, quite the opposite happened. When one side had the gate, both participants lost more than when neither side had the gate—as seen in the left panel of Figure 9.8. This figure shows the total amount earned or lost by both sides. (Acme won slightly more than Bolt when it had the gate, but won substantially more when neither side had a gate.) Bolt did not like to be threatened and often retaliated by parking its truck on the one-lane road, blocking the other truck's progress. Meanwhile, the seconds ticked away and both sides lost money.

> *My own belief is that Russian and Chinese behavior is as much influenced by suspicion of our intentions as ours is by suspicion of theirs. This would mean that we have great influence over their behavior—that, by treating them as hostile, we assure their hostility.*
>
> —J. William Fulbright, April 4, 1971

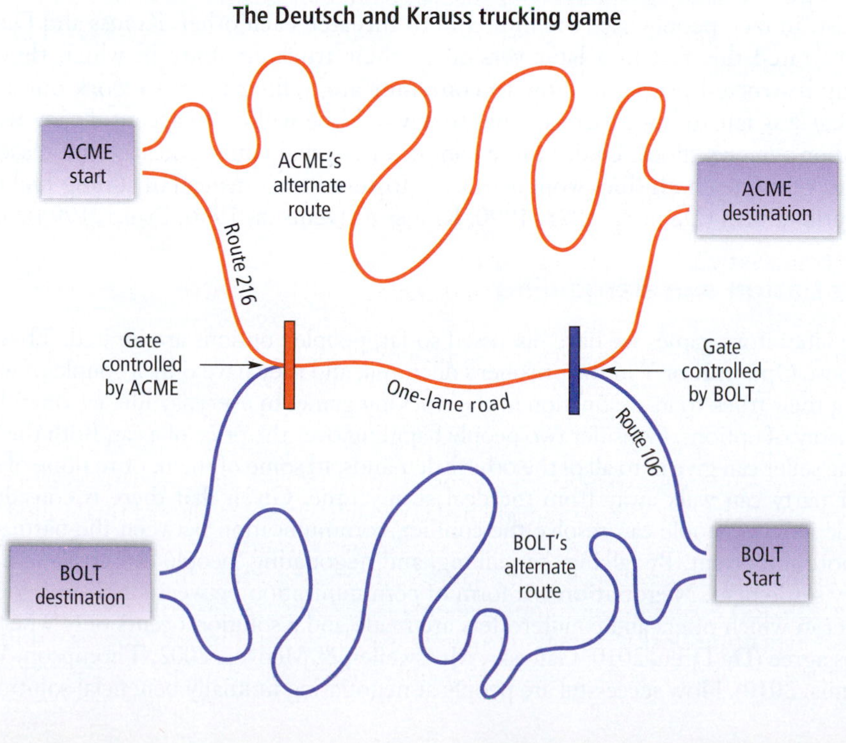

FIGURE 9.7

The Trucking Game

Participants play the role of the head of either Acme or Bolt Trucking Company. In order to earn money, they have to drive their truck from the starting point to their destination as quickly as possible. The quickest route is the one-lane road, but both trucks cannot travel on this road at the same time. In some versions of the studies, participants were given gates that they used to block the other's progress on the one-lane road.

(From Deutsch & Krauss, 1962.)

FIGURE 9.8

Results of the Trucking-Game Studies

The left-hand panel shows the amount of money the participants made (summed over Acme and Bolt) when they could not communicate. When threats were introduced by giving one ("unilateral threat") or both sides ("bilateral threat") a gate, both sides lost more money. The right-hand panel shows the amount of money the participants made when they were required to communicate in every trial. Once again, giving them gates reduced their winnings.

(Based on data in Deutsch & Krauss, 1962.)

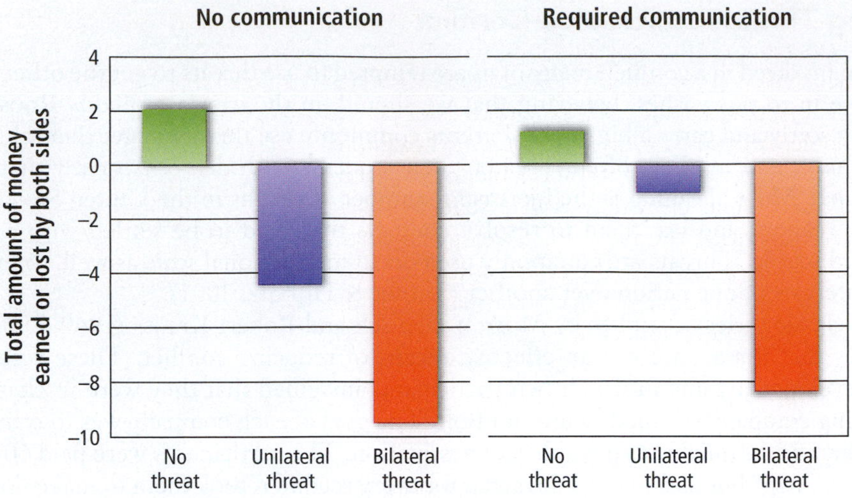

What would happen if the situation were more equitable, with both sides having gates? Surely they would learn to cooperate very quickly, recognizing the stalemate that would ensue if both of them used their gates—right? To the contrary (as you can see in the left panel of Figure 9.8), both sides lost more money in the bilateral threat condition than in any of the others. The owners of the trucking companies both threatened to use their gates and did so with great frequency.

Effects of Communication

There is a way in which the Deutsch and Krauss trucking game does not approximate real life: The two sides were not allowed to communicate with each other. Would the two adversaries work out their differences if they could talk them over? To find out, Deutsch and Krauss ran a version of their study in which the participants were required to communicate on every trial. Surely if people talked to each other, they would cooperate more. But as seen in the right panel of Figure 9.8, no dramatic increase in profits occurred. Making people communicate reduced losses somewhat when Acme alone had the gate (the unilateral threat condition) but failed to increase cooperation in either of the two other conditions (no threat, bilateral threat). Overall, requiring people to communicate did not raise profits dramatically. Why not?

The problem with the communication in the trucking studies is that it did not foster trust. In fact, people used the intercom to threaten each other. Krauss and Deutsch demonstrated this fact in a later version of their trucking study in which they specifically instructed people on how to communicate, telling them to work out a solution that was fair to both parties—that they would be willing to accept if they were in the other person's shoes. Under these conditions, verbal communication increased the amount of money both sides won, because it fostered trust instead of adding fuel to the competitive fires (Deutsch, 1973, 1990; Krauss & Deutsch, 1966; Pruitt, 1998).

Watch on **MyPsychLab**

To learn more about conflict resolution in groups, watch the MyPsychLab video ***In the Real World: Resolving Conflict.***

Negotiation and Bargaining

In the laboratory games we have discussed so far, people's options are limited. They have to choose Option X or Y in the prisoner's dilemma, and they have only a couple of ways of getting their truck to its destination in the trucking game. In everyday life, we often have a wide array of options. Consider two people haggling over the price of a car. Both the buyer and the seller can give in to all of the other's demands, to some of them, or to none of them. Either party can walk away from the deal at any time. Given that there is considerable latitude in how people can resolve the conflict, communication between the parties is all the more important. By talking, bargaining, and negotiating, people can arrive at a satisfactory settlement. **Negotiation** is a form of communication between opposing sides in a conflict in which offers and counteroffers are made and a solution occurs only when both parties agree (De Dreu, 2010; Galinsky, Mussweiler, & Medvec, 2002; Thompson, Wang, & Gunia, 2010). How successful are people at negotiating mutually beneficial solutions?

Negotiation

A form of communication between opposing sides in a conflict in which offers and counteroffers are made and a solution occurs only when both parties agree.

One limit to successful negotiation is that people often assume that they are locked in a conflict in which only one party can come out ahead. They don't realize that a solution favorable to both parties is available. A couple getting a divorce, for example, might lock horns and find it impossible to reach a financial settlement, until they realize that they have different priorities. Perhaps it is most important to one person to keep the furniture and the season tickets to the orchestra, whereas the other wants the china and the vintage collection of vinyl records. This type of compromise, called an **integrative solution**, is an outcome to a conflict whereby the parties make trade-offs on issues according to their different interests; each side concedes the most on issues that are unimportant to it but are important to the other side.

Neutral mediators often help solve labor disputes, legal battles, and divorce proceedings. Mediators can be in a better position to recognize that there are mutually agreeable solutions to a conflict.

It might seem that such integrative solutions would be relatively easy to achieve. After all, the two parties simply have to sit down and figure out which issues are the most important to each. However, people often find it difficult to identify integrative solutions (Moran & Ritov, 2007; Thompson, 1997). For example, the more people have at stake in a negotiation, the more biased their perceptions of their opponent. They will tend to distrust proposals made by the other side and to overlook interests they have in common (O'Connor & Carnevale, 1997; Ross & Ward, 1995, 1996). This is one reason why people often use neutral mediators to solve labor disputes, legal battles, and divorce proceedings: Mediators are often in a better position to recognize that there are mutually agreeable solutions to a conflict (Carnevale, 1986; Kressel & Pruitt, 1989; Ross & LaCroix, 1996).

Yet there remains another wall. This wall constitutes a psychological barrier between us, ... [a] barrier of distorted and eroded interpretation of every event and statement. . . . I ask, why don't we stretch our hands with faith and sincerity so that together we might destroy this barrier?

—Former Egyptian President Anwar al-Sadat, speaking before the Israeli Knesset, 1977

What about the role of communication in negotiation? As we saw earlier, communication is only helpful if it allows parties to develop trust. It appears that this is easier in old-fashioned face-to-face negotiations than in electronic communications such as e-mail, instant messaging, text messaging, and video conferencing. The modern techniques have many advantages, of course, but a disadvantage is that it is harder to get to know people and learn to trust them. A meta-analysis of several studies found that negotiations conducted over electronic media were more hostile, and resulted in lower profits, than face-to-face negotiations (Stuhlmacher & Citera, 2005).

The bottom line? When you are negotiating with someone, it is important to keep in mind that integrative solutions are often available. Try to gain the other side's trust, communicate your own interests in an open manner (ideally in person or with the help of a mediator), and try taking the other person's perspective (Trötschel et al., 2011). Remember that the way you construe the situation is not necessarily the same as the way the other party construes it. You may well discover that the other side communicates its interests more freely as a result, increasing the likelihood that you will find a solution beneficial to both parties.

Integrative Solution

A solution to a conflict whereby the parties make trade-offs on issues according to their different interests; each side concedes the most on issues that are unimportant to it but important to the other side.

USE IT!

Chances are you will soon find yourself in a group that needs to make a decision. Perhaps you are an officer in a student organization that is making budget decisions, part of a team of students deciding how to proceed on a class project, or a member of a fraternity or sorority deciding whom to admit. Based on what you have learned in this chapter, will you act any differently to make sure that your group makes the best decision? What kinds of *process loss* should you be alert to, for example, that might impede good decision making? (See page 249.) How can you make sure that people share information that others don't have? (See page 249.) Is it possible that you and your friends will be subject to *groupthink*, and, if so, how can you prevent it? (See page 250.) Lastly, can you predict who is likely to become the leader in your groups and how effective they will be? What should you do to increase the chances that you will be chosen as the leader? (See pages 255–258.) Good luck!

Summary

What are groups and why do people join them?

- **What Is a Group?** A **group** consists of three or more people who interact with each other and are interdependent.
  - **Why Do People Join Groups?** The *need to belong* to groups may be innate. Groups also serve as a source of information about the social world and are an important part of our social identities. People are very sensitive to rejection from groups and do what they can to avoid it. Groups also make people feel distinctive from members of other groups.
  - **The Composition and Functions of Groups** Groups tend to consist of homogeneous members, in part because groups have *social norms* that people are expected to obey. Groups also have well-defined social roles, shared expectations about how people are supposed to behave. People can get so far into a social role that their personal identities and personalities get lost. Social roles are shaped by our culture. Gender roles have changed a lot over the past several decades in the United States, although studies of advertisements indicate that women are still portrayed in subordinate roles more often than men are. Group cohesiveness, qualities of a group that bind members together and promote liking between members, is another important property of groups that influences the group's performance.

In what ways do people act differently when other people are around? What are the key variables that determine what the effects of others will be on individual performance?

- **Individual Behavior in a Group Setting** Research has compared the performance of people who are by themselves versus in groups.
  - **Social Facilitation: When the Presence of Others Energizes Us** When people's individual efforts on a task can be evaluated, the mere presence of others leads to social facilitation: Their performance is enhanced on simple tasks but impaired on complex tasks.
  - **Social Loafing: When the Presence of Others Relaxes Us** When people's individual efforts *cannot* be evaluated, the mere presence of others leads to relaxation and social loafing: Performance is impaired on simple tasks but enhanced on complex tasks.
  - **Gender and Cultural Differences in Social Loafing: Who Slacks Off the Most?** Social loafing is more prevalent among men than women, and more prevalent in Western than Asian cultures.
  - **Deindividuation: Getting Lost in the Crowd** The mere presence of others can also lead to deindividuation, which is the loosening of normal constraints on behavior when people are in crowds.

When people make decisions, are two (or more) heads better than one? Why or why not?

- **Group Decisions: Are Two (or More) Heads Better Than One?** Research has compared how people make decisions when they are by themselves versus in groups.
  - **Process Loss: When Group Interactions Inhibit Good Problem Solving** Groups make better decisions than individuals if they are good at pooling ideas and listening to the expert members of the group. Often, however, process loss occurs, which is any aspect of group interaction that inhibits good decision making. For example, groups often focus on the information they have in common and fail to share unique information. Tightly knit, cohesive groups are also prone to groupthink, which occurs when maintaining group cohesiveness and solidarity becomes more important than considering the facts in a realistic manner.
  - **Group Polarization: Going to Extremes** Group polarization causes groups to make more extreme decisions in the direction toward which its members were initially leaning; these group decisions can be more risky or more cautious, depending on which attitude is valued in the group.
  - **Leadership in Groups** There is little support for the great person theory, which argues that good leadership is a matter of having the right personality traits. Leaders do adopt specific kinds of leadership styles, such as transactional or transformational. Leadership effectiveness is a function of both the kind of person a leader is and the nature of the work situation. Although strides have been made, women are still underrepresented in leadership positions. Women who become leaders often face a "glass cliff" whereby they are put in charge of work units that are in crisis and in which the risk of failure is high. Further, there is a double bind for women leaders: If they conform to societal expectations about how they ought to behave, by being warm and communal, they are often perceived as having low leadership potential. If they succeed in attaining a leadership position and act in ways that leaders are expected to act—namely, in agentic, forceful ways—they are often perceived negatively for not "acting like a woman should."

When individuals or groups are in conflict, what determines the likelihood that this conflict will escalate or that it will be resolved?

- **Conflict and Cooperation** Research has examined how people resolve conflicts when they have incompatible goals.
  - **Social Dilemmas** These occur when the most beneficial action for an individual will, if chosen by most people, have harmful effects on everyone. A commonly studied social dilemma is the prisoner's dilemma, in which two people must decide whether to look out for only their own interests or for their partner's interests as well. Creating trust is crucial in solving this kind of conflict.
  - **Using Threats to Resolve Conflict** Research has found that using threats tends to escalate rather than resolve conflicts.
  - **Effects of Communication** Communication resolves conflict only when it promotes trust.
  - **Negotiation and Bargaining** When two sides are negotiating and bargaining it is important to look for an integrative solution, whereby each side concedes the most on issues that are unimportant to it but are very important to its adversary.

Chapter 9 Test

Study and Review on MyPsychLab

1. Why are groups homogeneous (alike in age, sex, beliefs, and opinions)?
   a. People who are already similar to each tend to join the same group.
   b. Evolutionary pressures caused people with similar genes to join groups.
   c. Groups encourage similarity in their members.
   d. (a) and (c)
   e. (a), (b), and (c)

2. Group cohesiveness is best defined as
   a. shared expectations in a group about how people are supposed to behave.
   b. qualities that bind members together and promote liking between members.
   c. expectations about the roles and behaviors of men and women.
   d. the tendency for people to do better on simple tasks and worse on complex tasks in the presence of others.

3. You are trying to decide whether to take a test in a lecture hall where you will be surrounded by lots of other people or in a room by yourself. Assuming that you have studied for the test and know the material, you should take the test in the ____________ because it will result in ____________ .
   a. hallway, social loafing
   b. hallway, social facilitation
   c. classroom, social loafing
   d. hallway, deindividuation
   e. classroom, social facilitation

4. The tendency to engage in social loafing is stronger in ____________ than ____________; it is also stronger in ____________ than ____________.
   a. men, women; Asian cultures, Western cultures
   b. women, men; Asian cultures, Western cultures
   c. men, women; Western cultures, Asian cultures
   d. women, men; Western cultures, Asian cultures

5. On his way back from class, Matt encounters an angry mob ready to storm the dining hall to demand better food. Matt likes the food as it is and wants to stop the mob. What would be the most effective solution?
   a. Increasing group cohesiveness by inviting the entire mob to his house for tea.
   b. Passing out blue shirts for everyone to wear.
   c. Reducing process loss in the group by making sure that its most expert members have the most influence.
   d. Finding a friend in the group, calling out her name, and talking to her loudly about an upcoming test.

6. Four psychology students working on a group project together are trying to figure out how they should avoid groupthink when making decisions about their project. Which of these ideas would be the *least* helpful?
   a. Bonding by going to see a movie together before starting the project.
   b. Assigning each group member to be responsible for a different chapter in their textbook so that they cover all the details.
   c. Having a student not in their group review the project.
   d. Designating a leader to oversee the project, one who is nondirective and encourages people to give honest feedback.

7. Bill and Pam, a married couple, are buying a house and have narrowed their choice down to two options. Bill remembers that one house had a beautiful kitchen; Pam, however, remembers that there were roaches in the broom closet. By sharing this information with each other, Pam and Bill are using ____________ to avoid ____________.
   a. mindguards, groupthink
   b. social roles, deindividuation
   c. transactive memory, process loss
   d. subgroups, group polarization

8. Which of the following is *least likely* to lead to process loss in a group?
   a. A group leader has high charisma but very little expertise.
   b. The group members have never met before.
   c. Group members do not share information that others lack.
   d. Some members in the group do not listen to each other.
   e. The most competent member doesn't feel free to speak up.

9. Which of the following is true about research on leadership?
   a. Female leaders are more likely than male leaders to be put in precarious, high-risk positions where it is difficult to succeed.
   b. The best leaders are born that way.
   c. People in all cultures value the same traits in leaders.
   d. If a woman succeeds in becoming a leader of an organization and acts in an agentic way, she is evaluated in the same way that male leaders are.

10. When is communication most effective for resolving conflict?
    a. When people communicate through electronic means (e.g., over e-mail).
    b. When it is required.
    c. When the stakes are high for people on both sides of a conflict.
    d. When a mediator is used.

Answer Key

1-d, 2-b, 3-e, 4-c, 5-d,
6-a, 7-c, 8-b, 9-a, 10-d

10 Interpersonal Attraction

From First Impressions to Close Relationships

Laura and Denny Allen have an awful lot in common. Born in the same hospital in Oregon nearly 70 years ago, they both grew up in the Portland area and attended Oregon State University. They both dedicated their careers to fields in which they could better the lives of those around them; for Laura it was educational consulting for gifted children, for Denny it was working as an environmental health professional and food inspector (Willis, 2012).

Laura and Denny, now retired, both enjoy traveling overseas. They have a passion for volunteering. They love dogs, wine making, and hunting for wild mushrooms. In terms of politics and religion? You guessed it—their beliefs line up almost perfectly.

There's something pleasantly reassuring about stories of compatible soul mates who meet as youngsters and contentedly spend their lives together, isn't there? Except this description doesn't apply to the Allens.

Yes, the Allens are a happily married couple who live together in Wilsonville, Oregon, with their two pugs (named Georgia and Olive, in case you were wondering). But Laura and Denny have only been married for 5 years. Despite living in neighboring parts of the state for decades, the Allens didn't meet until recently—when they both signed up for the same Internet dating site.

Interpersonal attraction, like much of human nature, can be studied scientifically. And it's a good thing too, because many of our assumptions about falling in love turn out to be mistaken, as we'll discuss throughout this chapter. One such case is the belief that opposites attract: Research offers the clear conclusion that similarity is a stronger predictor of who we're drawn to (Heine, Foster, & Spina, 2009). And as to the idea that women are pickier than men in selecting mates, they often are, but not for the biologically based reasons you might assume (Finkel & Eastwick, 2009).

And what about the expectation that Internet dating is only for young people? By 2009, 22% of heterosexual couples reported meeting online, a number that rises to a whopping 61% for same-sex couples (Finkel et al., 2012). These numbers—as well as Web sites with names like seniormatch.com, seniorpeoplemeet.com, and silversingles.com—demonstrate that no longer do we live in a society in which only small subsets of the population are looking for relationships online.

In fact, social psychologists even study dating Web sites themselves, as explored in the final section of this chapter. For example, in 2012, Eli Finkel and colleagues reviewed data regarding online dating and concluded that although the practice has never been more popular than it is today, many of the promises made by these sites go unfulfilled. Specifically, the idea of mathematical algorithms that can point users toward ideally compatible mates has little in the way of empirical support. Sure, more Americans than ever are pairing up online, but the success rate for dates facilitated by Web site is no higher than the success rate for dates engineered through more old-fashioned routes, like meeting at a bar or getting fixed up by friends (Finkel et al., 2012).

The compatibility analyses of dating Web sites don't live up to their promises for a variety of reasons, according to Finkel and his colleagues. First, as you read about in Chapter 5, sometimes we don't have a good sense of why we do what we do or what will make us happy. By the same token, we aren't always accurate when it comes to predicting the mate characteristics that will lead to a satisfying relationship. Second, most dating Web site algorithms focus on matching people by personality traits or other stable characteristics. But many of the best predictors of relationship satisfaction—like communication style and sexual compatibility—can't be assessed until people actually get to know each other (Finkel et al., 2012).

FOCUS QUESTIONS

- How do humans decide whom they like and want to get to know better?
- What is love, and how do we form close relationships?
- What does research tell us about romantic breakups?
- How do new technologies influence how we form close relationships?

Propinquity Effect
The finding that the more we see and interact with people, the more likely they are to become our friends

Thus, even processes as basic to the human condition as falling in love and choosing a life partner show the effects of social psychology: the limitations of self-knowledge and the influence of the situation. As mystically romantic a view as many of us hold of love, the experience of falling for someone can still be studied using psychological theories and methods. In this chapter, we will explore what makes us feel attracted to other people, whether as friends or lovers, and how relationships develop and progress.

What Causes Attraction?

When social psychologist Ellen Berscheid asked people of various ages what made them happy, at or near the top of their lists were making friends and having positive, warm relationships (Berscheid, 1985; Berscheid & Peplau, 1983; Berscheid & Reis, 1998). The absence of meaningful relationships with other people makes people feel lonely, worthless, hopeless, helpless, and powerless (Baumeister & Leary, 1995; Cacioppo & Patrick, 2008; Hartup & Stevens, 1997; Stroebe & Stroebe, 1996). In fact, social psychologist Arthur Aron states that a central human motivation is "self-expansion." This is the desire to overlap or blend with another person, so that you have access to that person's knowledge, insights, and experience and thus broaden and deepen your own experience of life (Aron, Aron, & Norman, 2004; Aron, Mashuk, & Aron, 2004). We will begin this chapter by discussing the antecedents of attraction, from the initial liking of people meeting for the first time to the love that develops in close relationships.

The Person Next Door: The Propinquity Effect

One of the simplest determinants of interpersonal attraction is proximity (sometimes called *propinquity*). The people who, by chance, are the ones you see and interact with the most often are the most likely to become your friends and lovers (Berscheid & Reis, 1998).

Now, this might seem obvious. But the striking thing about proximity and attraction, or the **propinquity effect**, is that it works in a very narrow sense. For example, consider a classic study conducted in a housing complex for married students at MIT. Leon Festinger, Stanley Schachter, and Kurt Back (1950) tracked friendship formation among the couples in the various apartment buildings. One section of the complex, Westgate West, was composed of 17 two-story buildings, each having 10 apartments. Residents had been assigned to apartments at random, and nearly all were strangers when they moved in. The researchers asked residents to name their three closest friends in the complex. Just as the propinquity effect would predict, 65% of the friends mentioned lived in their same building, even though the other buildings were not far away.

Even more striking was the pattern of friendships within a building. Each Westgate West building was designed like the drawing in Figure 10.1: Most of the front doors were only 19 feet apart, and the greatest distance between apartment doors was only 89 feet. The researchers found that 41% of the next-door neighbors indicated that they

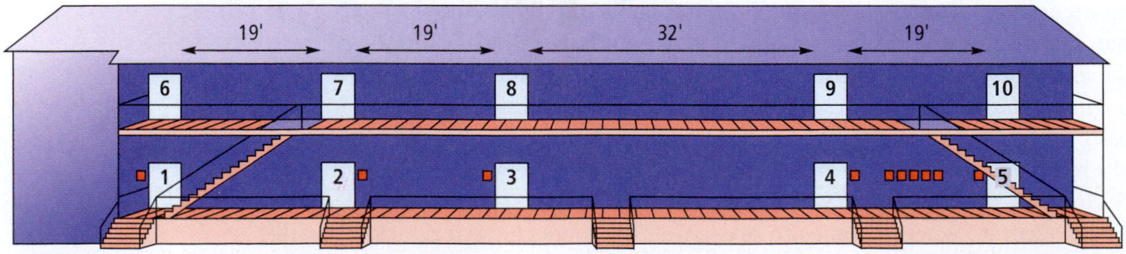

FIGURE 10.1
The Floor Plan of a Westgate West Building
All the buildings in the housing complex had the same floor plan.
(Adapted from Festinger, Schachter, & Back, 1950)

TRY IT! Mapping the Effect of Propinquity in Your Life

Try examining the relationship between your friends and acquaintances and the places where you spend time regularly. Does propinquity explain who your friends are?

First, pick a physical space to focus on. You could choose your dormitory, your apartment building, or the location where you work. (We'll use a dormitory for our example.) Draw a rough floor plan. Include the location of all the doors, stairs or elevators, bathrooms, common rooms, laundry rooms, and so on. Mark your room with a large X.

Second, think about your close friends on the floor or in the building. Mark their rooms with the number 1. Next, think about whom your not-as-close friends are; mark their rooms with a 2. Finally, think about your acquaintances—people you say hello to or chat with briefly now and then but aren't really close enough to be considered friends. Mark their rooms with a 3.

Now examine the pattern of friendships on your map. Are your friends clustered near your room in physical space? Are the rooms with the numbers 1 and 2 among the closest to your room in physical space? Are they physically closer to your room than the ones with number 3? And what about the dorm rooms that didn't get a number (meaning that you don't really know these people or interact with them)—are these rooms the farthest from yours, on average?

Finally, examine your propinquity map for the presence of functional distance. Do aspects of the architectural design of your dorm make you more likely to cross paths with some residents than others? For example, the location of the bathrooms, kitchen, living rooms, stairs, and mailboxes can play an important role in propinquity and friendship formation. These are all places where you go frequently; when walking there and back, you pass some people's rooms more than others'. Are you more likely to know the people who are located along your path? If so, propinquity has played an important role in determining your relationships!

were close friends, 22% of those who lived two doors apart said so, and only 10% of those who lived on opposite ends of the hall indicated that they were close friends.

Festinger and his colleagues (1950) demonstrated that attraction and propinquity rely not only on actual physical distance but also on "functional distance." Functional distance refers to aspects of architectural design that determine which people you cross paths with most often. For example, consider the friendship choices of the residents of apartments 1 and 5 in Figure 10.1. Living at the foot of the stairs or near the mailboxes meant that a couple saw a great deal of upstairs residents. Sure enough, apartment dwellers in apartments 1 and 5 throughout the complex had more friends upstairs than dwellers in the other first-floor apartments did. (You can map out propinquity effects in your own life with the preceding Try It! exercise.)

Propinquity works because of familiarity, or the **mere exposure effect**: The more exposure we have to a stimulus, the more apt we are to like it (Moreland & Topolinski, 2010; Zajonc, 1968). In reality, familiarity doesn't usually breed contempt; it breeds liking. We typically associate positive feelings with things that are familiar, like comfort food, songs we remember from childhood, certain corporate logos, and the sound of the local play-by-play announcer's voice. The same is true for the people we encounter. The more often we see certain people, and the more familiar they become, the more friendship blooms. However, there is one caveat: If the person in question is an obnoxious jerk, then, not surprisingly, the more exposure you have, the greater your dislike becomes (Norton, Frost, & Ariely, 2007). But in the absence of such negative qualities, familiarity breeds attraction and liking (Bornstein, 1989; Griffin & Sparks, 1990; Moreland & Beach, 1992; Lee, 2001).

> *Contrary to popular belief, I do not believe that friends are necessarily the people you like best; they are merely the people who got there first.*
>
> —Sir Peter Ustinov, *Dear Me*, 1977

A good example of the propinquity and mere exposure effects is your college classroom. All semester long, you see the same people. Does this increase your liking for them? Researchers tested this hypothesis with German students by randomly assigning them on the first day of class to permanent seats for the semester (Back, Schmukle, & Egloff, 2008). That first day, they had students rate each member of the class on likability and the extent to which they would like to get to know each other. These initial ratings indicated that students who sat in neighboring seats or in the same row had higher initial attraction scores than those seated far apart. A year later, they asked these students to rate the members of their original class again in terms of how much they liked them, how well

Mere Exposure Effect
The finding that the more exposure we have to a stimulus, the more apt we are to like it

Close friendships are often made in college, in part because of prolonged propinquity.

they knew them, and to what degree they were friends. Once again, those who had sat side by side or in the same row the prior semester were significantly more likely to be friends a year later than those who sat far apart. The propinquity effect means that some of our relationships develop simply because we were "at the right place, at the right time."

Similarity

As we saw, propinquity increases familiarity, which leads to liking, but something more is needed to fuel a growing friendship or a romantic relationship. (Otherwise, every pair of roommates would be best friends!) That "fuel" is often *similarity*—a match between our interests, attitudes, values, background, or personality and those of another person. As we discussed in Chapter 1, folk wisdom captures this idea in the expression "Birds of a feather flock together" (the concept of *similarity*). But folk wisdom also has another saying, "Opposites attract" (the concept of *complementarity*). Luckily, we don't have to remain forever confused by contradictory advice from old sayings; as mentioned in the opening to this chapter, research evidence demonstrates that it is overwhelmingly similarity and not complementarity that draws people together (AhYun, 2002; Berscheid & Reis, 1998; Byrne, 1997; Heine et al., 2009; McPherson, Smith-Lovin, & Cook, 2001).

Opinions and Personality A large body of research indicates that the more similar someone's opinions are to yours, the more you will like the person (e.g., Byrne & Nelson, 1965; Lutz-Zois et al., 2006). For example, in a classic study, Theodore Newcomb (1961) randomly assigned male students at the University of Michigan to be roommates in a particular dormitory at the start of the school year. Would similarity predict friendship formation? The answer was yes: Men became friends with those who were demographically similar (e.g., shared a rural background), as well as with those who were similar in attitudes and values (e.g., were also engineering majors or also held comparable political views). It's not just attitudes or demographics that are important. Similar personality characteristics also promote liking and attraction. For example, in a study of gay men's relationships, those who scored high on a test of stereotypical male traits desired a partner who was most of all logical—a stereotypical masculine trait. Gay men who scored high on a test of stereotypical female traits desired a partner who was most of all expressive—a stereotypical feminine trait (Boyden, Carroll, & Maier, 1984). Similar personality characteristics are important for heterosexual couples and for friends as well (Acitelli, Kenny, & Weiner, 2001; Caspi & Harbener, 1990; Gonzaga, Campos, & Bradbury, 2007; Klohnen & Luo, 2003; Weaver & Bosson, 2011).

Interests and Experiences The situations you choose to be in are usually populated by people who have chosen them for similar reasons. You're sitting in a social psychology class, surrounded by people who also chose to take social psychology this semester. You sign up for salsa dance lessons; the others in your class also want to learn Latin dancing. Thus, we choose to enter into certain social situations where we then find similar others. For example, in a study of the patterns of students' friendships that focused on the effects of "tracking" (grouping students by academic ability), researchers found that students were significantly more likely to choose friends from inside their track than from outside it (Kubitschek & Hallinan, 1998). Clearly, propinquity and initial similarity play a role in the formation of these friendships. However, the researchers add that similarity plays yet another role: Over time, students in the same academic track share many of the same experiences, which are different from the experiences of those in other tracks. Thus, new similarities are created and discovered, fueling the friendships. In short, shared experiences promote attraction (Pinel et al., 2006).

Appearance Finally, similarity also operates when it comes to more-superficial considerations. Sean Mackinnon, Christian Jordan, and Anne Wilson (2011) conducted a series of studies examining physical similarity and seating choice. In one study, they simply analyzed the seating arrangement of college students in a library computer lab, making observations multiple times over the course of several different days. Results indicated that students who wore glasses sat next to other students with glasses far more often than random chance alone would predict. A second study found the same pattern by hair color.

In a third study, participants arrived at a psychology lab and were introduced to a partner who was already sitting. Handed a chair, they were told to have a seat, after which point the research team secretly measured how close to the partner's chair they put down their own chair. A separate set of researchers later evaluated photos of both the participant and the partner. Pairs judged as more physically similar had, on average, sat closer to each other. Without even realizing it, you are often drawn to those who look like you, to the point where people are even more likely to ask out on dates others who are similar to them in terms of attractiveness level (Taylor et al., 2011; Walster et al., 1966).

"I don't care if she is a tape dispenser. I love her."

Sam Gross/The New Yorker Collection/ www.cartoonbank.com.

Some Final Comments about Similarity Here are two additional points about similarity. First, while similarity is very important in close relationships, it is important to make a distinction between "actual" (or real) similarity and "perceived" similarity (that is, the degree to which one *believes* oneself to be similar to another; Morry, 2007). In a recent meta-analysis, R. Matthew Montoya and his colleagues found that in long-term relationships, "perceived" similarity predicted liking and attraction better than "actual" similarity did. Thus, *feeling* similar to another is what's really important—so much so that we will create beliefs about the similarity between ourselves and intimate others even when they don't exist (Montoya, Horton, & Kirchner, 2008).

Second, a *lack* of similarity does appear to play an important role in one type of relationship. Sometimes when we begin a romantic relationship, we want a serious, committed relationship; but sometimes, we just want a "fling." David Amodio and Carolin Showers (2005) found that whether similarity or complementarity was important depended on the level of commitment that research participants felt toward their romantic partner. If participants wanted a committed relationship, they chose a similar partner; however, if they felt a low level of commitment to the relationship, they favored dissimilar partners. Thus, in low-commitment relationships, we may go out of our way to choose someone who is strikingly different from us. A relationship with this sort of person represents more of an adventure; however, as we'll see as we progress through this chapter, relationships based on differences, rather than similarities, can be difficult to maintain.

An administrator in the Housing Office of Barnard College sorts through roommate applications, placing them in piles according to their similar answers to questions about living habits and interests.

(Willie J. Allen Jr./*The New York Times*)

Reciprocal Liking

We like to be liked. In fact, just knowing that a person likes us fuels our attraction to that individual. Liking is so powerful that it can even make up for the absence of similarity. For example, in one experiment, when a young woman expressed interest in male research participants simply by maintaining eye contact, leaning toward them, and listening attentively, the men expressed great liking for her despite the fact that they knew she disagreed with them on important issues (Gold, Ryckman, & Mosley, 1984). Whether the clues are nonverbal or verbal, perhaps the most crucial determinant of whether we will like person A is the extent to which we believe person A likes us (Berscheid & Walster, 1978; Kenny, 1994b; Kenny & La Voie, 1982; Kubitschek & Hallinan, 1998; Montoya & Insko, 2008).

Life is to be fortified by many friendships. To love, and to be loved, is the greatest happiness of existence.
Love to faults is always blind, Always is to joy inclin'd.
—WILLIAM BLAKE, *LOVE TO FAULTS*

Just how powerful is reciprocal liking? According to recent research, it is powerful enough to neutralize our basic tendency to pay more attention to attractive faces. Nicolas Koranyi and Klaus Rothermund (2012) used a computer program to present a series of opposite-sex faces to German research participants. Each photo appeared for the same half-second duration, but its location in one of the four corners of the screen was determined at random. Immediately after each photo appeared, a geometrical shape was shown, once again randomly located in one of the four corners of the screen. Participants' task was to identify as quickly as possible whether the shape was a circle or a square. When the shape showed up in the same location as the previous photo, the task was easy: Participants were already looking in that vicinity and quickly identified the shape. When the shape appeared in a different area, however, the task was harder: With their eyesight still fixated on the spot where the face just was, participants had to shift their visual attention to find the shape. This shift proved particularly challenging when the previous photo was an attractive one, as we have a tendency to linger and look longer at good-looking faces.

But not all respondents showed this bias to stare a bit longer at attractive faces. Who was able to break the spell of the pretty face? It was the participants who had previously been asked to imagine that they had just learned that someone whom they had a crush on also had feelings for them. As the researchers suggest, it makes sense that this type of interest from someone else would disrupt our otherwise chronic focus on the attractive alternatives out there. Think about it: If our attention were repeatedly hijacked by *every* pretty face that passed by, we'd never get the chance to turn initial interactions into more-meaningful, sustained romantic relationships. Koranyi and Rothermund's (2012) results weren't limited to just imagining reciprocated liking, either. In a second study, the researchers created a heterosexual Internet dating site and asked participants to identify three opposite-sex students whom they'd be interested in dating. One week later, participants completed the same face/shape computer task; as expected, they were slower to identify shapes when preceded by attractive faces. But next they were told about one opposite-sex participant who had reciprocated their dating interest. When they then ran through the same face/shape task a second time, suddenly they showed no attentional bias for attractive faces. Basking in the glow of reciprocated liking is enough to stop a wandering eye and convince you, at least for a while, that the grass may not be greener on the other side.

Physical Attractiveness and Liking

Speaking of pretty faces, propinquity, similarity, and reciprocal liking are not the only determinants of whom we come to like. How important is physical appearance to our first impressions? In field experiments investigating actual behavior (rather than what they *say* they will do), people overwhelmingly go for physical attractiveness. For example, in a classic study, Elaine Walster Hatfield and her colleagues (Walster, et al., 1966) randomly matched 752 incoming students at the University of Minnesota for a blind date at a dance during freshman orientation week. Although the students had previously taken a battery of personality and aptitude tests, the researchers paired them up at random. On the night of the dance, the couples spent a few hours together dancing and chatting. They then evaluated their date and indicated the strength of their desire to see that person again. Of the many possible characteristics that could have determined whether they liked each other—such as their partner's intelligence, independence, sensitivity, or sincerity—the overriding determinant was physical attractiveness.

It is only shallow people who do not judge by appearances.
—OSCAR WILDE, *THE PICTURE OF DORIAN GRAY*, 1891

What's more, there was no great difference between men and women on this count. This is an interesting point, for several studies have found that men and women pay equal attention to the physical attractiveness of others (Duck, 1994a, 1994b; Lynn & Shurgot, 1984; Speed & Gangestad, 1997; Woll, 1986), but other studies have reported that men value attractiveness more than women do (Buss, 1989; Buss & Barnes, 1986; Howard, Blumstein, & Schwartz, 1987). A meta-analysis of many studies found that while both sexes value attractiveness, men value it a bit more (Feingold, 1990); however, this gender difference was greater when men's and women's attitudes were being measured than when their actual behavior was being measured. Thus, it may be that men are more likely than women to *say* that physical attractiveness is important to them but that when it comes to actual behavior, the sexes are fairly similar in how they respond to the physical attractiveness of others. Indeed, across multiple studies, both genders rated physical attractiveness as the single most important characteristic that triggers sexual desire (Graziano et al., 1993; Regan & Berscheid, 1995, 1997).

Simulate on **MyPsychLab**
To learn more, try the MyPsychLab simulation ***Perceptions of Attractiveness.***

This powerful role of physical appearance in attraction is not limited to heterosexual relationships. When gay men participated in a "blind date" study like the one described earlier, they responded just as the heterosexual men and women had: The physical attractiveness of their dates was the strongest predictor of liking (Sergios & Cody, 1985).

What is Attractive? Is physical attractiveness "in the eye of the beholder," or do we all share the same notions of what is beautiful and handsome? From early childhood, the media tell us what is beautiful, and they tell us that beauty is associated with goodness. For example, illustrators of most traditional children's books, as well as the people who draw characters in Disney movies, have taught us that the heroines—as well as the princes who woo and win them—look alike. For example, the heroines all have regular features; small, pert noses; big eyes; shapely lips; blemish-free complexions; and slim, athletic bodies—rather like Barbie dolls.

Oh, what vileness human beauty is, corroding, corrupting everything it touches.
—Orestes, 408 B.C.

Bombarded as we are with media depictions of attractiveness, it is not surprising to learn that we share criteria for defining beauty (Fink & Penton-Voak, 2002; Tseëlon, 1995). Michael Cunningham (1986) designed a creative study to determine these standards of beauty. He asked college men to rate the attractiveness of 50 photographs of women, taken from a college yearbook and from an international beauty-pageant program. Cunningham then carefully measured the relative size of the facial features in each photograph. He found that high attractiveness ratings for female faces were associated with large eyes, a small nose, a small chin, prominent cheekbones, narrow cheeks, high eyebrows, large pupils, and a big smile. Researchers then examined women's ratings of male beauty in the same way (Cunningham, Barbee, & Pike, 1990). They found that men's faces with large eyes, prominent cheekbones, a large chin, and a big smile received higher attractiveness ratings.

She's beautiful and therefore to be woo'd.
—William Shakespeare

There is some overlap in the men's and women's ratings. Both sexes admire large eyes in the opposite sex; as mentioned in Chapter 4, these are considered a "baby face" feature, for newborn mammals have very large eyes relative to the size of their faces. Baby-face features are thought to be attractive because they elicit feelings of warmth and nurturance in perceivers—think of our typical response to infants, kittens, and puppies (e.g., Berry, 1995; Livingston & Pearce, 2009; Zebrowitz, 1997; Zebrowitz & Montepare, 1992). Both sexes also admire prominent cheekbones, an adult feature that is found only in the faces of those who are sexually mature. Note that the female face that is considered beautiful has more baby-face features (small nose, small chin) than the handsome male face, suggesting that beauty in the female is associated more with childlike qualities than male beauty is.

Photography models represent facial standards of beauty for men and women.

Cultural Standards of Beauty Are people's perceptions of what is beautiful or handsome similar across cultures? The answer is a surprising yes (Cunningham et al., 1995; Jones & Hill, 1993; McArthur & Berry, 1987; Rhodes et al., 2001). Even though racial and ethnic groups do vary in their specific facial features, people from a wide range of cultures agree on what is physically attractive in the human face. Researchers asked participants from various countries, ethnicities, and racial groups to rate the physical attractiveness of photographed faces of people who also represented various countries, ethnicities, and racial groups. Their ratings agreed to a remarkable extent. For example, one review of this literature found that the correlations between participants' ratings ranged from 0.66 to 0.93 (Langlois & Roggman, 1990), which are very strong correlations (see Chapter 2). A meta-analysis of several studies by Judith Langlois and her colleagues (2000) also found evidence for cross-cultural agreement in what constitutes a beautiful or handsome face. In short, perceivers think some faces are just better looking than others, regardless of cultural background (Berscheid & Reis, 1998).

Beauty is a greater recommendation than any letter of introduction.

—Aristotle, fourth century b.c.

How can we explain these results? Researchers have suggested that humans came to find certain dimensions of faces attractive during the course of our evolution (Langlois & Roggman, 1990; Langlois, Roggman, & Musselman, 1994). We know, for example, that even infants prefer photographs of attractive faces to unattractive ones, and infants prefer the same photographs that adults prefer (Langlois et al., 1991; Langlois, Roggman, & Rieser-Danner, 1990). One aspect of beauty that is preferred in both men and women is symmetry, where the size, shape, and location of the features on one side of the face match those on the other (Little et al., 2008; Langlois et al., 2000; Rhodes, 2006). Evolutionary psychologists suggest that we're attracted to symmetrical features because they serve as markers of good health and reproductive fitness—that is, facial symmetry is an indicator of "good genes" (Grammer & Thornhill, 1994).

A series of studies explored this preference by creating composite photographs of faces. Faces were morphed (i.e., combined digitally) to create a composite that was the mathematical average of the features of multiple faces; ultimately, 32 faces were combined into a single composite. When shown to research participants, composite photographs were judged as more attractive than were all the separate faces that had created them, and this held true for both male and female photographs (Langlois & Roggman, 1990; Langlois et al., 1994). The "averaged" composite face was more attractive because it had lost some of the atypical or asymmetrical variation that was present in the individual faces.

Does this mean that we find "average" faces the most attractive? Clearly not, for we respond to the physical appearance of movie stars and models because their looks are "above average" compared to most humans. David Perret and his colleagues made this point clear in the following study (Perret, May, & Yoshikawa, 1994). They created composite faces of two types: One composite was based on 60 photographs that had each been rated as average in attractiveness. The other composite was based on 60 photographs that had each been rated as highly attractive. Composites of these two types were made using photographs of Caucasian women, Caucasian men, Japanese women, and Japanese men. Research participants in Great Britain and Japan then rated all the composite faces for attractiveness.

The researchers found, first, that the composites of highly attractive faces were rated as significantly more attractive than the composites of average attractive faces. Second, Japanese and British participants showed the same pattern when judging the faces, reinforcing the idea that similar perceptions of facial attractiveness exist cross-culturally. Finally, what did those composites of highly attractive faces look like? Their

Physical attractiveness of composite faces. Langlois and Roggman (1990) created composites of faces using a computer. Pictured here is the first step in the process: The first two women's photos are merged to create the "composite person" at the far right. This composite person has facial features that are the mathematical average of the facial features of the two original women.

(From Langlois, Roggman, & Musselman, 1994)

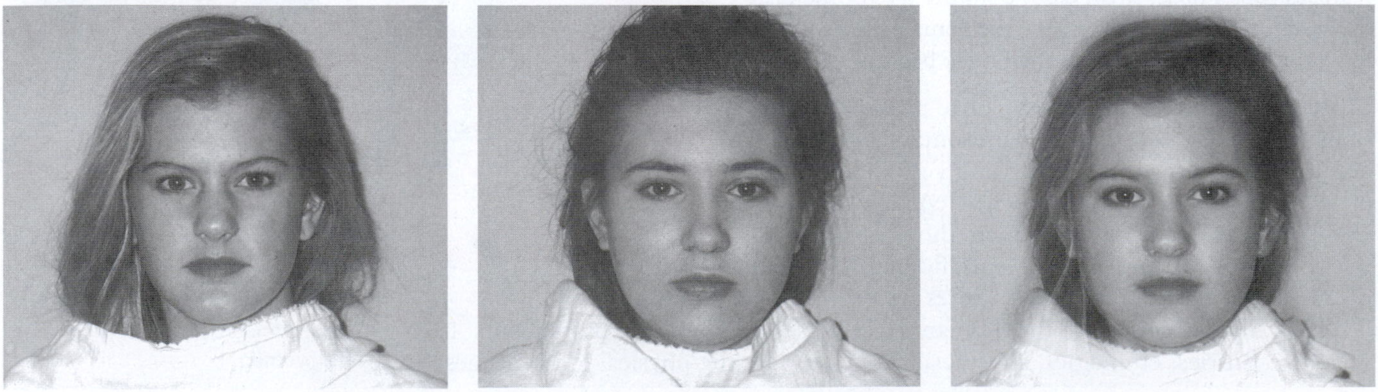

facial shapes, whether Japanese or Caucasian, matched the descriptions that Michael Cunningham and his colleagues (Cunningham, 1986; Cunningham, Barbee, & Pike, 1990) found in their research. For example, the Japanese and Caucasian "highly attractive" female composites had higher cheekbones, a thinner jaw, and larger eyes than the "average attractive" composites did (Perrett et al., 1994).

The Power of Familiarity In the end, the crucial variable that explains interpersonal attraction may actually be familiarity (Berscheid & Reis, 1998). We've seen that "averaging" faces together produces one face that looks typical, familiar, and physically attractive (see also Halberstadt & Rhodes, 2000). Recent research has found evidence for an even more startling familiarity effect: When research participants rated the attractiveness of faces, they preferred the faces that most resembled their own! The researchers morphed a picture of each participant's face (without the participant's knowledge) into that of a person of the opposite sex. When presented with this photo of their opposite-sex "clone," participants gave it high ratings of attractiveness (Little & Perrett, 2002). This preference for the familiar appears to be shared by people in close relationships. Research participants who were members of the same family or close friends agreed much more with each other when they rated photographs of faces for attractiveness than they did with strangers (Bronstad & Russell, 2007).

Familiarity also underlies the other concepts we've discussed thus far: propinquity (people we see frequently become familiar through mere exposure), similarity (people who are similar to us will also seem familiar to us), and reciprocal liking (people who like each other get to know and become familiar with each other). All these attraction variables may be expressions of our "underlying preference for the familiar and safe over the unfamiliar and potentially dangerous" (Berscheid & Reis, 1998, p. 210).

Assumptions about Attractive People It's important to realize that beauty "matters"—even when it shouldn't. We're attracted to that which is beautiful, and that can lead to inequity in everyday life. A particularly chilling example of the unfair benefit of beauty was discovered by Lina Badr and Bahia Abdallah (2001), who rated the facial physical attractiveness and health status of premature infants born in hospitals in Beirut, Lebanon. They found that physical attractiveness significantly predicted the health outcomes of these infants above and beyond factors such as their medical condition. The more attractive the infant, the more quickly he or she gained weight and the shorter his or her stay in the hospital. The reason? Neonatal nurses responded more to the "prettier" infants and gave them better care.

Physical attractiveness confers other benefits as well. People of above-average looks tend to earn 10% to 15% more than those of below-average appearance (French, 2002; Hammermesh & Biddle, 1994; Judge, Hurst, & Simon, 2009; Mobius & Rosenblat, 2006). Attractiveness even helps win elections. Panu Poutvaara and his colleagues (2006) presented photographs of Finnish political candidates to research participants in many other countries (who would have no prior knowledge of these candidates) and asked them to rate the politicians on a variety of attributes including attractiveness. They found that the ratings of attractiveness were the best predictors of the actual number of votes each candidate had gotten in the real elections. A higher beauty rating predicted an increase of between 2.5 and 2.8 percentage points in the vote total for female candidates and between 1.5 and 2.1 percentage points for male candidates, amounts that could tip the balance of a close election (Poutvaara, Berggren, & Jordahl, 2006).

Many studies have found that physical attractiveness affects the attributions people make about others. Specifically, we tend to attribute to beautiful people positive qualities that have nothing to do with their looks. This is called the "what is beautiful is good" stereotype (Ashmore & Longo, 1995; Calvert, 1988; Dion, Berscheid, & Walster, 1972; Lemay, Clark, & Greenberg, 2010). Meta-analyses have revealed that physical attractiveness has the largest effect on both men's and women's attributions when they are judging social competence: The beautiful are thought to be more sociable, extroverted, and popular than the less attractive (Eagly et al., 1991; Feingold, 1992b). They are also seen as more sexual, happier, and more assertive.

TABLE 10.1 How Culture Affects the "What Is Beautiful Is Good" Stereotype

The "what is beautiful is good" stereotype has been explored in both individualistic cultures (e.g., North America) and collectivistic cultures (e.g., Asia). Male and female participants in the United States and Canada and in South Korea rated photographs of people with varying degrees of physical attractiveness. Responses indicated that some of the traits that make up the stereotype are the same across cultures, while other traits associated with the stereotype are different in the two cultures. In both cultures, the physically attractive are seen as having more of the characteristics that are valued in that culture than do the less physically attractive.

Traits Shared in the Korean, American, and Canadian Stereotype

sociable	extraverted	likable
happy	popular	well-adjusted
friendly	mature	poised
sexually warm and responsive		

Additional Traits Present in the American and Canadian Stereotype

strong	assertive	dominant

Additional Traits Present in the Korean Stereotype

sensitive	empathic	generous
honest	trustworthy	

Sources: Eagly, Ashmore, Makhijani, & Longo (1991); Feingold (1992b); Wheeler & Kim (1997).

Do these stereotypes about the beautiful operate across cultures? The answer appears to be yes (Anderson, Adams, & Plaut, 2008; Chen, Shaffer, & Wu, 1997). For example, college students in South Korea were asked to rate a number of yearbook photographs (Wheeler & Kim, 1997). Both male and female participants thought the more physically attractive people would also be more socially skilled, friendly, and well adjusted—the same group of traits that North American participants thought went with physical attractiveness (see Table 10.1). But Korean and North American students differed in some of the other traits they assigned to the beautiful, highlighting differences in what is considered important in each culture (Markus et al., 1996; Triandis, 1995). For the American and Canadian students—who live in more-individualistic cultures that value independence, individuality, and self-reliance—the "beautiful" stereotype included traits of personal strength. These traits were not part of the Korean "beautiful" stereotype. Instead, for these students, who live in a more collectivistic culture that values harmonious group relations, the "beautiful" stereotype included integrity and concern for others (see Table 10.1).

Interestingly, the stereotype that the beautiful are particularly gifted in the area of social competence has some research support; highly attractive people *do* develop good social interaction skills and report having more-satisfying interactions with others than do less-attractive people (Feingold, 1992b; Langlois et al., 2000; Meier et al., 2010; Reis et al., 1982). Undoubtedly, this "kernel of truth" in the stereotype occurs because the beautiful, from a young age, receive a great deal of social attention that in turn helps them develop good social skills. You probably recognize the self-fulfilling prophecy at work here (see Chapter 3): The way we treat people affects how they behave and ultimately how they perceive themselves.

Can a "regular" person be made to act like a "beautiful" one through the self-fulfilling prophecy? To find out, researchers gave college men a photo and a packet of information about a woman with whom they were about to have a phone conversation (Snyder, Tanke, & Berscheid, 1977). But the photograph was rigged; at random, the men were either given a photo that a previous group of raters had judged to be attractive or one that a previous group had rated as unattractive. In both cases, this photo was *not* of the actual woman they were about to speak with. The experimental purpose of the photograph was to invoke the men's stereotype that "what is beautiful is good"—to test the possibility that the woman would be more likable, poised, and fun to talk to if her male conversation partner believed she was attractive than if he believed she was unattractive. Did the men's beliefs about appearance change the reality of how the women behaved?

In short, yes! The men who thought they were talking to an attractive woman responded to her in a warmer, more sociable manner than the men who thought they were talking to an unattractive woman. Not only that, but the men's behavior actually influenced how the women themselves behaved. When independent observers listened to a tape recording of only the woman's half of the conversation (without knowing anything about the photograph the men had seen), they rated the women whose male partners thought they were physically attractive as more confident, animated, and warm than they rated those women whose male partners thought they were unattractive. In other words, because the male partner thought he was talking to an attractive woman, he spoke to her in a way that brought out her best and most sparkling qualities. Subsequent studies have found similar results with the gender roles reversed (Andersen & Bem, 1981), reminding us that it is a myth that physical attractiveness only affects women's lives. Indeed, meta-analyses that have examined the effect of attractiveness across hundreds of studies have found that physical attractiveness is often as important a factor in men's lives as it is in women's (Eagly et al., 1991; Feingold, 1992b; Langlois et al., 2000).

Evolution and Mate Selection

The poet Robert Browning asked, "How do I love thee? Let me count the ways." For psychologists, the question is "*Why* do I love thee?" Some researchers believe that the answer lies in an **evolutionary approach to mate selection**. The basic tenet of evolutionary biology is that an animal's "fitness" is measured by its reproductive success (i.e, its capability to pass on its genes to the next generation). Reproductive success is not just part of the game; it *is* the game. This biological concept has been applied to social behavior by psychologists, who define **evolutionary psychology** as the attempt to explain social behavior in terms of genetic factors that have evolved over time according to the principles of natural selection. For example, as detailed above, one explanation for your tendency to find symmetrical faces more attractive is that symmetry indicates positive health and "good genes."

Evolution and Sex Differences Evolutionary psychology also makes some particularly interesting (and controversial) predictions regarding sex differences in mate preference. Specifically, evolutionary psychologists argue that men and women have very different agendas when it comes to mate selection, due to their differing roles in producing (and raising) offspring. For females, reproduction is costly in terms of time, energy, and effort: They must endure the discomforts and risks of pregnancy and birth, and, traditionally, theirs is the primary responsibility for caring for the infant until maturity. Reproducing, then, is serious business, so females, the theory goes, must consider carefully when and with whom to reproduce. In comparison, reproduction is a low-cost, short-term investment for males. The evolutionary approach to mate selection concludes that reproductive success for the two sexes translates into two very different behavior patterns: Throughout the animal world, males' reproductive success is measured by the *quantity* of their offspring. They pursue frequent pairings with many females in order to maximize their number of surviving progeny. In contrast, females' reproductive success lies in successfully raising each of their offspring to maturity. They pair less frequently and only with carefully chosen males, because the cost to them of raising and ensuring the survival of each offspring is so high (Berkow, 1989; Symons, 1979).

> *Men seek to propagate widely, whereas women seek to propagate wisely.*
>
> —Robert Hinde

Now, what does all of this have to do with how people fall in love? David Buss and his colleagues argue that the evolutionary approach explains the different strategies and tendencies of men and women in romantic relationships (Buss, 1985, 1988a, 1996a, 1996b; Buss & Schmitt, 1993). Buss (1988b) explains that finding (and keeping) a mate requires one to display one's resources—the aspects of oneself that will appear attractive to potential mates. This approach argues that, across millennia, human beings have been selected through evolution to respond to certain external cues in the opposite sex. Women, facing high reproductive costs, will look for a man who can supply

Evolutionary Approach to Mate Selection

A theory derived from evolutionary biology that holds that men and women are attracted to different characteristics in each other (men are attracted by women's appearance; women are attracted by men's resources) because this maximizes their chances of reproductive success

Evolutionary Psychology

The attempt to explain social behavior in terms of genetic factors that have evolved over time according to the principles of natural selection the resources and support she needs to raise a child. Men will look for a woman who appears capable of reproducing successfully. More precisely, men will respond to the physical appearance of women because age and health denote reproductive fitness, and women will respond to the economic and career achievements of men because these variables represent resources they and their offspring need (Buss, 1988b).

Many studies have provided support for these predictions. For example, Buss and colleagues (Buss, 1989; Buss et al., 1990) asked more than 9 thousand adults in 37 countries how desirable various characteristics were in a marriage partner. In general, women valued ambition, industriousness, and earning capacity in a potential mate more than the men did. The men valued physical attractiveness in a mate more than the women did. It should be noted, however, that the top characteristics on both men's and women's lists were the same—involving honesty, trustworthiness, and a pleasant personality (Buss & Barnes, 1986; Hatfield & Sprecher, 1995; Regan & Berscheid, 1997; Sprecher, Sullivan, & Hatfield, 1994). Other surveys have indicated that men prefer spouses who are younger than they are (youth indicating reproductive fitness), while women prefer spouses around their own age or older (Buss, 1989; Kenrick & Keefe, 1992).

Alternate Perspectives on Sex Differences The evolutionary approach to attraction and love has inspired its share of debate. For example, one could argue that evolutionary advantages to having multiple sexual partners should not be limited to men, but should also apply to women. With multiple partners, females would increase the odds of getting resources for their offspring, as well as benefit from genetic diversity. Females could choose an attractive male with "good genes" with whom to procreate and another male with whom to raise the offspring (Campbell, 2002; Gangestad & Simpson, 2000; Gangestad & Thornhill, 1998). It may also be the case that men value physical attractiveness in a partner, not because of evolved tendencies, but simply because they have been taught by society to value it—they have been conditioned by decades of advertising and media images to value beauty in women and to have a more recreational approach to sex than women do (Hatfield & Rapson, 1993). Similarly, research has found that in some situations, women value physical attractiveness just as much as men—specifically, when they are considering a potential sexual partner as opposed to a potential marriage partner (Regan & Berscheid, 1997; Simpson & Gangestad, 1992).

Other researchers offer additional arguments that the preference for different qualities in a mate can be explained without resorting to evolutionary principles: Around the world, women typically have less power, status, wealth, and other resources than men do. Therefore, in many societies women need to rely on men to achieve economic security, and they must consider this characteristic when choosing a husband (Rosenblatt, 1974). To test this hypothesis, Steven Gangestad (1993) correlated the extent to which women in several countries had access to financial resources and the extent to which women reported male physical attractiveness as an important variable in a mate. His results revealed that the more economic power women had in a given culture, the more highly women prioritized a man's physical attractiveness (Gangestad, 1993).

Watch on MyPsychLab
To learn more about evolutionary theories of mate selection, watch the MyPsychLab video ***Thinking Like a Psychologist: Evolutionary Psychology.***

As you can see, when discussing human mate preference, it is often difficult to disentangle "nature" (inborn preferences) from "nurture" (cultural norms and gender roles). When we hear about sex differences related to mate selection and attraction, our first instinct is often to turn to biological or evolutionary explanations (Conley et al., 2011). But a closer look often reveals that many of these differences are also attributable to situational factors. Take, for instance, the proposition that women are pickier than men when it comes to selecting a mate. Indeed, whether you look at online dating, speed-dating events, or old-fashioned face-to-face date requests, research indicates that women are significantly more discriminating in who they'll go out with than men are (Clark & Hatfield, 1989; Hitsch, Hortaçsu, & Ariely, 2010; Schützwohl et al., 2009; Penke, Fasolo, & Lenton, 2007). This makes sense from an evolutionary perspective. The argument would be that women *have* to be picky because they can't afford to make mistakes; unlike men, their fertility window is relatively narrow across the lifespan, and each decision to reproduce also requires more time and resources.

But consider the provocative results of a speed-dating study recently conducted by Eli Finkel and Paul Eastwick (2009). College students in this study had brief

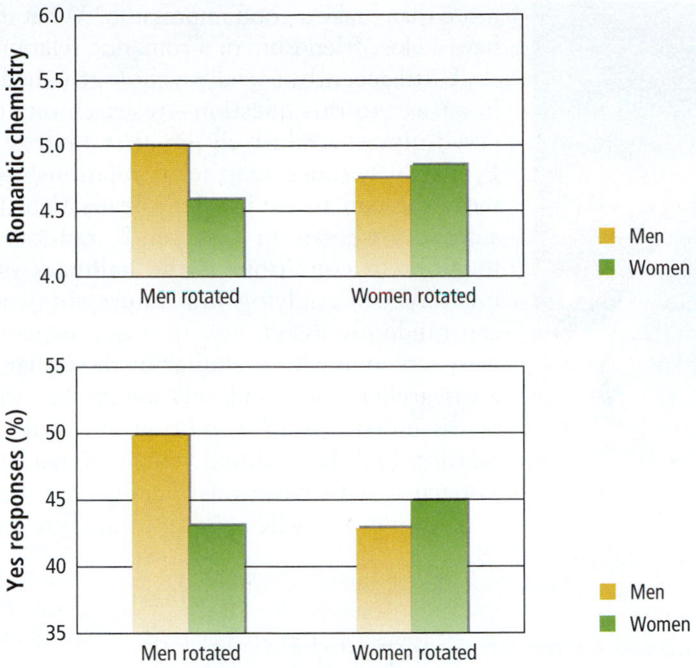

FIGURE 10.2

How Speed-Dating Rules Affect Attraction

In one version of Finkel and Eastwick's (2009) study, male college students rotated from one 4-minute speed date to the next as female students remained seated. As expected, the women were "pickier" than the men, perceiving less romantic chemistry and rating fewer of their speed-dating partners as people they'd like to get to know better. But changing the structure of the speed dates also changed these ratings: When the women rotated around and the men remained seated, women were no longer the pickier gender—if anything, now the *men* became slightly stingier when it came to perceptions of attraction.

(Adapted from Finkel & Eastwick, 2009)

conversations with a dozen different opposite-sex individuals. In these speed-dating sessions, the women remained seated while the men in attendance rotated in a circle, spending 4 minutes with each prospective dating partner before moving on to the next person. After each of the 12 women had been visited by each of the 12 men, all participants completed a questionnaire assessing their attraction to these potential mates (and later, from the comfort of their own homes, they recorded on the study Web site whether or not they'd be interested in seeing each person again). Once again, women were more selective than men, reporting lower levels of romantic desire and identifying fewer prospective mates that they'd like to get to know better (see Figure 10.2).

But an interesting thing happened when the researchers made a minor tweak to the speed-dating situation. In a second set of events, they had men and women swap roles. Now the men remained seated and the women rotated around—a simple modification, but one that stood regular dating protocol on its head. Instead of women sitting still while male suitors paraded in a circle, now the men remained stationary as women approached them. The "dates" themselves were still the same: 4-minute conversations after which both parties were asked for their impressions. But from a situational standpoint, this was traditional dating in reverse (Conley et al., 2011). And in this bizarro dating world where women did the approaching, women were no longer pickier than men. If anything, the female participants now reported more chemistry with their partners and identified more prospective mates that they wanted to see again.

Finkel and Eastwick's (2009) results suggest that the sex differences in mate selectivity do not simply reflect evolution or biology, but are also attributable to the established dating paradigm in most societies, in which men are the approachers and women the approachees. Being approached gives you control in the world of dating, regardless of sex or gender; being approached also means feeling in demand and having options. And so it is that, as with many aspects of human nature, we need both "nature" and "nurture" explanations to fully understand the psychology of attraction and mate selection.

Watch on **MyPsychLab**

To learn more about research on speed dating, watch the MyPsychLab video ***In The Real World: Speed Dating.***

Love and Close Relationships

By this point in the chapter, you have learned enough about attraction to make a favorable first impression the next time you meet someone. Suppose you want Claudia to like you. You should hang around her so that you become familiar, emphasize your similarity to her, and let her know you enjoy her company. But what if you want to do

This scene from the *Twilight* saga exemplifies the early stages of love.

more than make a good impression? What if you want to have a close friendship or a romantic relationship?

Until recently, social psychologists had little to say in answer to this question—research on attraction focused almost exclusively on first impressions. Why? Primarily because long-term relationships are much more difficult to study scientifically than first impressions. As we saw in Chapter 2, random assignment to different conditions is the hallmark of an experiment. When studying first impressions, a researcher can randomly assign you to a get-acquainted session with someone who is similar or dissimilar to you. But a researcher can't randomly assign you to the similar or dissimilar "lover" condition and make you have a relationship! In addition, the feelings and intimacy associated with close relationships can be difficult to measure. Psychologists face a daunting task when trying to analyze such complex feelings as love and passion.

Defining Love: Companionship and Passion

Despite the difficulties inherent to studying close relationships, social psychologists have made some interesting discoveries about the nature of love, how it develops, and how it flourishes. Let's begin with perhaps the most difficult question: What, exactly, is love? Early attempts to define love distinguished between liking and loving, showing that, as you might expect, love is something different from "lots of liking"—and not just in terms of sexual desire (Rubin, 1970).

> *Love is or it ain't. Thin love ain't love at all.*
>
> —Toni Morrison

For Shakespeare's Romeo and Juliet, love was passionate, turbulent, and full of longing; same goes for the Bella, Edward, and Jacob triangle of the *Twilight* series. Your grandparents, if they've remained married for a long time, probably exemplify a calmer, more tranquil (and probably less supernatural) kind of love. We use the word *love* to describe all of these relationships, though each one seems to be of a different kind (Berscheid & Meyers, 1996, 1997; Fehr, 1994; Fehr & Russell, 1991; Vohs & Baumeister, 2004).

> *Love is something so divine, Description would but make it less; 'Tis what I feel, but can't define, 'Tis what I know, but can't express.*
>
> —Beilby Porteus

Social psychologists have recognized that a good definition of love must include the passionate, giddy feelings of romantic love as well as the deep, long-term devotion of married couples, lifelong friends, or siblings. In defining love, then, we generally distinguish between *companionate love* and *passionate love* (Hatfield, 1988; Hatfield & Rapson, 1993; Hatfield & Walster, 1978). **Companionate love** consists of feelings of intimacy and affection we have for someone that are not accompanied by passion or physiological arousal. People can experience companionate love in nonsexual close friendships, or in sexual relationships in which they experience great feelings of intimacy but not as much of the heat and passion as they once felt.

Companionate Love

The feelings of intimacy and affection we have for someone that are not accompanied by passion or physiological arousal

Passionate Love

An intense longing we feel for a person, accompanied by physiological arousal; when our love is reciprocated, we feel great fulfillment and ecstasy, but when it is not, we feel sadness and despair

Passionate love involves an intense longing for another person, characterized by the experience of physiological arousal—the feeling of shortness of breath and a thumping heart in someone's presence (Fisher, 2004; Regan & Berscheid, 1999). When things are going well (the other person loves us too), we feel great fulfillment and ecstasy. When things are not going well (our love is unrequited), we feel great sadness and despair. Cross-cultural research comparing an individualistic culture (the United States) and a collectivistic culture (China) indicates that American couples tend to value passionate love more than Chinese couples do, and Chinese couples tend to value companionate love more than American couples do (Gao, 1993; Jankowiak, 1995; Ting-Toomey & Chung, 1996). In comparison, the Taita of Kenya, in East Africa, value both equally; they conceptualize romantic love as a combination

TABLE 10.2 Cross-Cultural Evidence for Passionate Love Based on Anthropological Research in 166 Societies

Cultural Area	Passionate Love Present	Passionate Love Absent
Mediterranean	22 (95.7%)	1 (4.3%)
Sub-Saharan Africa	20 (76.9%)	6 (23.1%)
Eurasia	32 (97.0%)	1 (3.0%)
Insular Pacific	27 (93.1%)	2 (6.9%)
North America	24 (82.8%)	5 (17.2%)
South and Central America	22 (84.6%)	4 (15.4%)

Source: Data from Jankowiak & Fischer (1992).

of companionate and passionate love. The Taita consider this the best kind of love, and achieving it is a primary goal in their society (Bell, 1995). Reviewing the anthropological research on 166 societies, William Jankowiak and Edward Fischer (1992) found evidence for passionate love in 147 of them, as you can see in Table 10.2.

Try to reason about love, and you will lose your reason.
—French Proverb

Elaine Hatfield and Susan Sprecher (1986) developed a questionnaire to measure passionate love. As measured by this scale, passionate love consists of strong, uncontrollable thoughts; intense feelings; and overt acts toward the target of one's affection. Find out if you are experiencing (or have experienced) passionate love by filling out the questionnaire in the following Try It! exercise.

TRY IT! Passionate Love Scale

These items ask you to describe how you feel when you are passionately in love. Think of the person whom you love most passionately right now. If you are not in love right now, think of the last person you loved passionately. If you have never been in love, think of the person you came closest to caring for in that way. Choose your answers as you remember how you felt when your feelings were the most intense.

For each of the 15 items, choose the number between 1 and 9 that most accurately describes your feelings. The answer scale ranges from 1 (not at all true) to 9 (definitely true). Write the number you choose next to each item.

1 2 3 4 5 6 7 8 9

1 ↑ Not at all true; 5 ↑ Moderately true; 9 ↑ Definitely true

1. I would feel deep despair if ________ left me.
2. Sometimes I feel I can't control my thoughts; they are obsessively on ________.
3. I feel happy when I am doing something to make ________ happy.
4. I would rather be with ________ than anyone else.
5. I'd get jealous if I thought ________ were falling in love with someone else.
6. I yearn to know all about ________.
7. I want ________—physically, emotionally, mentally.
8. I have an endless appetite for affection from ________.
9. For me, ________ is the perfect romantic partner.
10. I sense my body responding when ________ touches me.
11. ________ always seems to be on my mind.
12. I want ________ to know me—my thoughts, my fears, and my hopes.
13. I eagerly look for signs indicating ______'s desire for me.
14. I possess a powerful attraction for ________.
15. I get extremely depressed when things don't go right in my relationship with ________.

Scoring: Add up your scores for the 15 items. The total score can range from a minimum of 15 to a maximum of 135. The higher your score, the more your feelings for the person reflect passionate love; the items to which you gave a particularly high score reflect those components of passionate love that you experience most strongly.

(Adapted from Hatfield & Sprecher, 1986)

CONNECTIONS

This Is Your Brain . . . in Love

Falling in love is an extraordinary feeling—you are giddy, euphoric, full of energy, and more or less obsessed with your new beloved. These powerful emotions, experienced by people in many different cultures, suggest that romantic love may have evolved as a primary component of the human mating system. Is something special happening in our brains when we fall in love?

To find out, a team of researchers recruited college students in the greater New York area who described themselves as currently being "intensely in love" (Aron et al., 2005). They asked these research participants to bring two photographs to the experimental session: one of their beloved and one of an acquaintance of the same age and sex as their beloved. After filling out some questionnaires (including the Try It! Passionate Love Scale on page 281), the participants were ready for the main event. They slid into a functional MRI (fMRI) scanner, which records increases and decreases in blood flow in the brain, indicating which regions of the brain have neural activity at any given time. While the participant was in the scanner, the experimenters alternated projecting on a screen one photograph and then the other, interspersed with a mathematical distraction task.

The researchers found that two specific areas, deep within the brain, were activated when participants looked at the photograph of their romantic partner, but not when they looked at the photograph of their acquaintance (or engaged in the math task). Furthermore, those participants who self-reported higher levels of romantic love showed greater activation in these areas when looking at their beloved than those who reported lower levels (Aron et al., 2005). These two brain areas were the ventral tegmental area (VTA) and the caudate nucleus, which communicate with each other as part of a circuit. A great deal is already known about what causes these areas of the brain to fire and what kind of processing they do—and now, this knowledge can be applied to the experience of passionate love.

Falling in love activates a reward center in the brain that is also activated by eating chocolate.

Specifically, prior research has found that the VTA becomes active when people ingest cocaine—a drug that induces feelings of pleasure, euphoria, restlessness, sleeplessness, and loss of appetite (reactions that are also reminiscent of falling in love). The VTA, rich in the neurotransmitter dopamine, also fires when people eat chocolate. Thus, the VTA and the caudate nucleus constitute a major reward and motivation center of the brain. For example, fMRI studies of gamblers' brains as they gambled showed greatly increased activity in these dopamine-rich areas when they won—a rewarding and motivating event for them (Aron et al., 2005). Thus, when people say that falling in love is "addictive," "like a drug," or "like winning the lottery," they're right. All these experiences activate the same areas of the brain: dopamine-rich centers of pleasure, reward, and motivation (Bartels & Zeki, 2000, 2004; Fisher, 2004).

Culture and Love

As indicated above, the process of finding a romantic partner varies across the world. For example, in villages in Nepal, dating is forbidden, and even casual meetings between young men and women are considered inappropriate. Traditionally, one's future spouse is chosen by one's parents, who focus on the potential mate's social standing: family, caste, and economic resources. In these arranged marriages, the bride and groom often speak to each other for the first time on their wedding day. It is not unusual for the bride to cry during the ceremony and for the groom to look stunned and resigned (Goode, 1999). But despite what might seem an inauspicious beginning, many of these unions turn out to be very successful, especially when considered in light of the high divorce rate of unarranged marriages in the United States.

Beyond differences in custom and ceremony, cultures also differ with regard to how people think about, define, and experience love. As we have discussed throughout this book, Western and Eastern cultures vary with respect to how they conceptualize the needs of individuals and of the group or the society (Hofstede, 1984; Kim & Markus, 1999; Markus, Kitayama, & Heiman, 1996; Triandis, 1995). Social psychologists have noted that, while romantic love is an important, even crucial, basis for marriage in individualistic societies, it is less emphasized in collectivistic ones. In individualistic societies, romantic love is a heady, highly personal experience. One immerses oneself in the new partner, virtually ignoring friends and family for a while. The decision regarding whom to become involved with or marry is for the most part a personal one. In comparison, in collectivistic societies, the individual in love must consider the wishes of family and other group members, which sometimes includes agreeing to an arranged marriage (Dion & Dion, 1988, 1993; Fiske et al., 1998; Levine et al., 1995). Interestingly, though, in recent decades Western ways of finding a partner have begun to permeate collectivistic cultures through the media (Hatfield & Rapson, 2002). In Nepal, for example, prospective brides and grooms now write each other letters, getting to know each other a bit before the wedding (Goode, 1999).

Although people all over the world experience love, how love is defined varies across cultures.

How romantic love is defined varies across individualistic and collectivistic cultures. Researchers have found that Canadian college students have different attitudes about love, depending on their ethnocultural background: Asian (Chinese, Korean, Vietnamese, Indian, Pakistani), Anglo-Celtic (English, Irish, Scottish), or European (Scandinavian, Spanish, German, Polish). In comparison to their peers, Asian Canadian respondents are significantly more likely to identify with a companionable, friendship-based romantic love, a "style of love that would not disrupt a complex network of existing family relationships" (Dion & Dion, 1993, p. 465). Other researchers have found that in West African settings, relationships with one's parents, siblings, and other relatives are seen as more important and consequential than the more recent relationship one has formed with one's spouse. In many areas of West Africa, happily married couples do not live together in the same house, nor do they expect to sleep together every night. In stark contrast to the pattern of intimate relationships in individualistic cultures, their connection and obligation to their extended family members takes precedence over those to their spouse. In individualistic cultures, the opposite is typically true (Adams, Anderson, & Adonu, 2004). As another example of cross-cultural research, college students in 11 countries around the world were asked, "If a man (woman) had all the qualities you desired, would you marry this person if you were not in love with him (her)?" This study found that marrying for love was most important to participants in Westernized countries (e.g., the United States, Brazil, England, and Australia) and of least importance to participants in Asian countries (e.g., India, Pakistan, and Thailand; Levine et al., 1995).

The results of these studies indicate that the concept of romantic love is culturally specific (Dion & Dion, 1996; Gao & Gudykunst, 1995; Hatfield & Rapson, 2002; Hatfield & Sprecher, 1995; Sprecher, Aron et al., 1994). We all love, but we do not necessarily all love in the same way—or at least we don't describe it in the same way (Landis & O'Shea, 2000). For example, the Japanese use the word *amae* as an extremely positive emotional state in which one is a totally passive love object, indulged and taken care of by one's romantic partner, much like a mother-infant relationship. Amae has no equivalent word in English or in any other Western language; the closest is the word *dependency*, an emotional state that Western cultures consider unhealthy in adult relationships (Dion & Dion, 1993; Doi, 1988; Farrer, Tsuchiya, & Bagrowicz, 2008).

Similarly, the Chinese concept of *gan qing* differs from the Western view of romantic love. Gan qing is achieved by helping and working for another person; for example, a "romantic" act would be fixing someone's bicycle or helping someone learn new material (Gao, 1996). In Korea, a special kind of relationship is expressed by the concept of *jung*. Much more than "love," jung is what ties two people together. Couples in new relationships may feel strong love for each other, but they have not yet developed strong jung—that takes time and mutual experiences. Interestingly, jung can develop in negative relationships too—for example, between business rivals who dislike each other. Jung may unknowingly grow between them over time, with the result that they will feel that a strange connection exists between them (Lim & Choi, 1996; Kline, Horton, & Zhang, 2008).

Phillip Shaver and his colleagues (Shaver, Wu, & Schwartz, 1992) wondered if romantic or passionate love was associated with the same emotions in different cultures. They asked research participants in the United States, Italy, and China to sort emotional words into categories; their analysis indicated that love has similar and different meanings cross-culturally. The most striking difference was the presence of a "sad love" cluster in the Chinese sample. The Chinese had many love-related concepts that were sad, such as words for "sorrow-love," "tenderness-pity," and "sorrow-pity." Although this "sad love" cluster made a small appearance in the U.S. and Italian samples, it was not perceived as a major aspect of love in these Western societies.

Other researchers wondered what the lyrics of popular American and Chinese love songs would reveal about the experience of love in each culture (Rothbaum & Tsang, 1998). Finding that the Chinese love songs had significantly more references to suffering and to negative outcomes than the American love songs, the researchers looked to the Chinese concept of *yuan*. This is the belief that interpersonal relations are predestined. According to the traditional Buddhist belief in *karma*, fate determines what happens in a relationship. The romantic partners have little control over this process (Goodwin, 1999). If a relationship is not working, it cannot be saved; one must accept fate and the suffering that accompanies it (Rothbaum & Tsang, 1998). Although Chinese songs were sadder than American ones, there was no difference in the intensity with which love was described in the two countries. The researchers found that love in Chinese songs was as "passionate and erotic" as love expressed in American songs.

Thus, it appears that romantic love is nearly universal in the human species, but cultural rules alter how that emotional state is experienced, expressed, and remembered (Carillo, 2001; Farrer, 2002; Higgins et al., 2002; Jackson et al., 2006). As one final example, Shuangyue Zhang and Susan Kline (2009) found two major differences in American and Chinese dating couples' decisions to marry. When describing how they would decide whether or not to marry their partners, Chinese students placed a heavier emphasis on two concepts central to their collectivistic culture: *xiao* (the obedience and devotion shown by children to their parents) and *guanxi* (relationships as a network of connections). In contrast, American students placed importance on receiving support, care, and "living a better life." As Robert Moore (1998) noted in summarizing his research in the People's Republic of China, "Young Chinese do fall deeply in love and experience the same joys and sorrows of romance as young Westerners do. But they do so according to standards that require . . . the individual [to] sacrifice personal interests for the sake of the family . . . This means avoiding fleeting infatuations, casual sexual encounters, and a dating context [where] family concerns are forgotten" (p. 280).

Watch on **MyPsychLab**

For another cultural perspective on love, watch the MyPsychLab video ***Arranged Marriage: Rati and Subas, 20s.***

Attachment Styles in Intimate Relationships

Attachment Styles

The expectations people develop about relationships with others, based on the relationship they had with their primary caregiver when they were infants

Much as the culture in which we grow up shapes how we think about and experience love, so do our interactions in the early years of life with parents or caregivers. Specifically, one approach to examining intimate relationships among adults focuses on **attachment styles** and draws on the groundbreaking work of John Bowlby (1969, 1973, 1980) and Mary Ainsworth (Ainsworth et al., 1978) concerning how infants form bonds with their primary caregivers (usually their mothers or fathers).

Ainsworth and her colleagues (1978) identified three types of relationships between infants and their caregivers. Infants with a **secure attachment style** typically have caregivers who are responsive to their needs and who show positive emotions when interacting with them. These infants trust their caregivers, are not worried about abandonment, and come to view themselves as worthy and well liked. Infants with an **avoidant attachment style** typically have caregivers who are aloof and distant, rebuffing attempts to establish intimacy. These infants desire to be close to their caregiver but learn to suppress this need, as if they know that such attempts will be rejected. Infants with an **anxious/ambivalent attachment style** typically have caregivers who are inconsistent and overbearing in their affection. These infants are unusually anxious because they can never predict when and how their caregivers will respond to their needs.

Secure Attachment Style

An attachment style characterized by trust, a lack of concern with being abandoned, and the view that one is worthy and well liked

Avoidant Attachment Style

An attachment style characterized by a suppression of attachment needs because attempts to be intimate have been rebuffed; people with this style find it difficult to develop intimate relationships

Anxious/Ambivalent Attachment Style

An attachment style characterized by a concern that others will not reciprocate one's desire for intimacy, resulting in higher-than-average levels of anxiety

The key assumption of attachment theory is that the particular attachment style we learn in infancy becomes our working model or schema (as we discussed in Chapter 3) for what relationships are like. These early relationship schemas typically stay with us throughout life and generalize to adult relationships with other people (Fraley & Shaver, 2000; Hartup & Laursen, 1999; Mikulincer & Shaver, 2003, 2007; Mikulincer et al., 2009). Thus, people who as children had a secure relationship with their parents or caregivers are better able to develop mature, lasting relationships as adults; people who had avoidant relationships with their parents are less able to trust others and find it difficult to develop close, intimate relationships; and people who had anxious/ambivalent relationships with their parents want to become close to their adult partners but often worry that their partners will not return their affections (Collins & Feeney, 2000; 2004a; Rholes, Simpson & Friedman, 2006; Simpson et al., 2007). This has been borne out in numerous studies that measure adults' attachment styles with questionnaires and then correlate the styles with the quality of their romantic relationships (though, as we note below, it is *not* the case that attachment style is destiny—people who had less-happy relationships with their parents are *not* doomed to perpetually unhappy adult relationships).

In my very own self, I am part of my family.

—D. H. Lawrence

For example, researchers asked adults to choose one of the three statements shown in Table 10.3, according to how they typically feel in romantic relationships (Hazan & Shaver, 1987). Each statement was designed to capture one of the three kinds of attachment styles we described. The researchers also asked people questions about their current relationships. The results of this study were consistent with an attachment theory perspective (Feeney, Noller, & Roberts, 2000; Feeney, Cassidy, & Ramos-Marcuse, 2008; Hazan & Shaver, 1994a, 1994b; Simpson & Rholes, 1994).

Other researchers have reported similar findings: Securely attached individuals have the most enduring romantic relationships of the three attachment types. They experience the highest level of commitment to relationships as well as the highest level of satisfaction with their relationships. The anxious/ambivalently attached individuals have the most short-lived romantic relationships. They enter into relationships the most quickly, often before they know their partner well. For example, a study conducted at a marriage license bureau found that anxious men acquired marriage licenses after a shorter courtship than did either secure or avoidant men (Senchak & Leonard, 1992). They are also the most upset and angriest of the three types when their love is not reciprocated. The third category, avoidant individuals, are the least likely to enter into a relationship and the most likely to report never having been in love. They maintain their emotional distance and have the lowest level of commitment to their relationships of the three types (Campbell et al., 2005; Feeney & Noller, 1990; Keelan, Dion, & Dion, 1994).

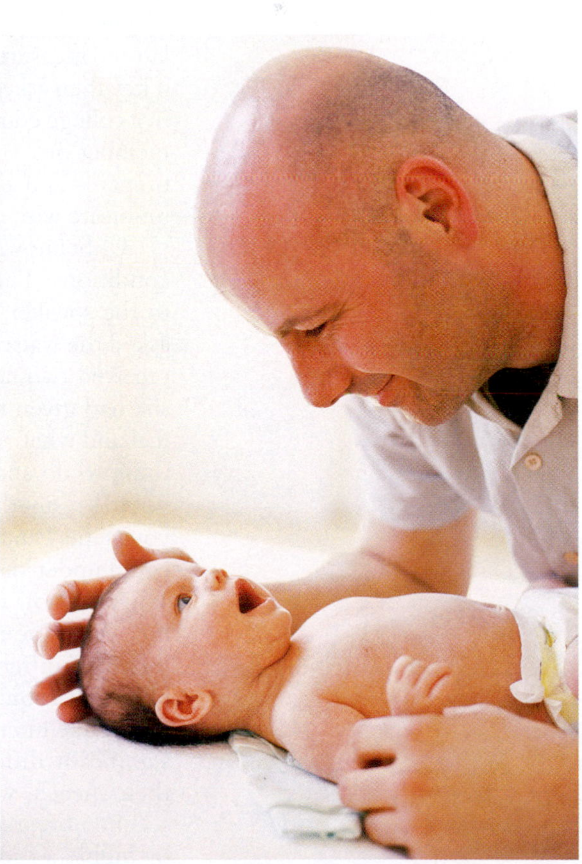

Attachment theory predicts that the attachment style we learn as infants and young children stays with us throughout life and generalizes to all of our relationships with other people.

TABLE 10.3 Measuring Attachment Styles

As part of a survey of attitudes toward love published in a newspaper, people were asked to choose the statement that best described their romantic relationships. The attachment style each statement was designed to measure and the percentage of people who chose each alternative are indicated.

Secure style	56%	"I find it relatively easy to get close to others and am comfortable depending on them and having them depend on me. I don't often worry about being abandoned or about someone getting too close."
Avoidant style	25%	"I am somewhat uncomfortable being close to others; I find it difficult to trust them completely, difficult to allow myself to depend on them. I am nervous when anyone gets close, and often love partners want me to be more intimate than I feel comfortable being."
Anxious style	19%	"I find that others are reluctant to get as close as I would like. I often worry that my partner doesn't really love me or won't stay with me. I want to merge completely with another person, and this desire sometimes scares people away."

Source: Adapted from Hazen & Shaver (1986).

Attachment in the Lab Attachment styles have also been found to affect men's and women's behavior in an experimental setting (Collins et al., 2006; Simpson, Rholes, & Nelligan, 1992). For example, researchers brought heterosexual dating couples into the lab and measured their attachment styles using a questionnaire (Collins & Feeney, 2004b). They then asked one member of each couple (the "speaker") to give a speech on the value of a college education, which would be videotaped and later judged for quality. The other member of the couple (the "waiter") was asked to sit in a waiting room while the speaker prepared and gave the speech. The couples were told that they would be allowed to communicate with each other, with the waiter sending a couple of notes to the speaker.

Unbeknownst to the participants, they had been randomly assigned to one of two conditions: The waiter would send either very supportive notes or less-supportive notes to the speaker. In fact, the experimenters had written the notes themselves, and they asked the waiters to copy the notes so they would be in their handwriting. The speakers received two notes, one while he or she prepared the speech and the other after he or she had given the speech. The supportive notes were: "Don't worry, just say how you feel and what you think and you'll do great," and "I liked your speech. That was a hard thing to do and you did a really good job." The two less supportive notes were: "Try not to say anything too embarrassing—especially since so many people will be watching your tape," and "Your speech was a little hard to follow, but I guess you did the best you could under the circumstances."

Now, how would you react to messages like these from your romantic partner? And how might your attachment style affect your perceptions? Collins and Feeney (2004b) found no differences between the participants in terms of their reactions to supportive notes; everyone felt supported by their partners, and there were no differences given their attachment styles. However, when participants received the less supportive notes, significant differences emerged. The first note, received while they were preparing their speech, was perceived the most negatively by highly avoidant participants. The second note, received after they'd given their speech, was perceived the most negatively by highly anxious participants. In both cases, these participants reported that the note was upsetting, was disappointing, and made them feel angry.

Thus, while securely attached participants reacted calmly to the less supportive messages, avoidant and anxious participants saw the same comments in a much more negative light. Avoidant individuals believe that people they are close to cannot be relied on for support or nurturance. Receiving the unsupportive note at a time when they needed support—preparing the speech—was particularly upsetting to them. Anxious individuals believe that people close to them are unpredictable and likely to reject them. Receiving the unsupportive note at a time when they needed positive feedback—after giving the speech—was particularly upsetting to them. In comparison, secure individuals took the somewhat unsupportive notes in stride, interpreting them as more neutral in tone than the avoidant or anxious participants did (Collins & Feeney, 2004b).

Attachment Style is not Destiny It is important to note, however, that attachment theory does not suggest that people who had unhappy relationships with their parents are doomed to repeat this same kind of unhappy relationship with everyone they ever meet (Simms, 2002). Some researchers have recontacted their research participants months or years after their original studies and asked them to take the attachment-style scale again. They have found that 25% to 30% of their participants have changed from one attachment style to another (Feeney & Noller, 1996; Kirkpatrick & Hazan, 1994). People can and do change; their experiences in relationships can help them learn new and healthier ways of relating to others than what they experienced as children (Baldwin & Fehr, 1995). Moreover, other research suggests that, at any given time, the attachment style that people display is the one that is called into play by their partner's behavior and the type of relationship that they've created as a couple. Thus, people may respond to situational variables in their relationships, displaying a more secure attachment style in one relationship and a more anxious one in another (Fraley, 2002; Hammond & Fletcher, 1991; Simpson et al., 2003).

Theories of Relationship Satisfaction: Social Exchange and Equity

So far, we've examined how cultural expectations and personal attachment styles predict the ways in which you define and experience love. But what aspects of your actual relationships influence relationship satisfaction? What factors determine how happy you are with your current mate or with your "love life" more generally? We turn now to theories of relationship satisfaction in the attempt to provide empirically based answers to these most intimate of questions.

Social Exchange Theory Many of the variables we discussed above as antecedents of attraction can be thought of as examples of social rewards. It is pleasing to have our attitudes validated; thus, the more similar a person's attitudes are to ours, the more rewarded we feel by spending time together. Likewise, it is rewarding to be around someone who likes us, particularly when that person is physically attractive. In other words, the more social rewards (and the fewer costs) a person provides us with, the more we like the person. The flip side of this equation is that if a relationship costs (e.g., in terms of emotional turmoil) far more than it gives (e.g., in terms of validation or praise), chances are that it will not last.

This simple notion that relationships operate on an economic model of costs and benefits, much like other marketplaces, has been expanded by researchers into complex theories of social exchange (Blau, 1964; Homans, 1961; Kelley & Thibaut, 1978; Secord & Backman, 1964; Thibaut & Kelley, 1959). **Social exchange theory** holds that how people feel about a relationship will depend on their perceptions of the rewards they receive from it, their perceptions of the costs they incur, and their beliefs regarding what kind of relationship they deserve (and the probability that they could find a better relationship with someone else). In essence, we "buy" the best relationship we can get—one that gives us the most value for our emotional dollar. The basic concepts of social exchange theory are reward, cost, outcome, and comparison level.

Love is often nothing but a favorable exchange between two people who get the most of what they can expect, considering their value on the personality market.
—Erich Fromm, *The Sane Society*, 1955

Friendship is a scheme for the mutual exchange of personal advantages and favors.
—François de La Rochefoucauld, *Maxims*, 1665

Social Exchange Theory
The idea that people's feelings about a relationship depend on their perceptions of the rewards and costs of the relationship, the kind of relationship they deserve, and their chances for having a better relationship with someone else

Rewards are the gratifying aspects of a relationship that make it worthwhile and reinforcing. They include the kinds of personal characteristics and behaviors of our relationship partner that we have already discussed, and our ability to acquire external resources by virtue of knowing this person (e.g., gaining access to money, status, activities, or other interesting people; Lott & Lott, 1974). For example, in Brazil, friendship is openly used as an exchange value. Brazilians will readily admit that they need a *pistolão* (literally, a big, powerful handgun), meaning that they need a person who will use personal connections to help them get what they want (Rector & Neiva, 1996). Costs are, obviously, the other side of the coin, and all friendships and romantic relationships have some costs attached to them, such as putting up with those annoying habits and characteristics of the other person. The outcome of the relationship is a direct comparison of its rewards and costs; you can think of it as a mathematical formula where outcome equals rewards minus costs. If you come up with a negative number, your relationship is not in good shape.

Watch on **MyPsychLab**
To learn more about how we evaluate our relationships, watch the MyPsychLab video ***What's In It For Me? Attraction.***

In addition to rewards and costs, how satisfied you are with your relationship depends on another variable: your **comparison level**, or what you *expect* the outcome of your relationship to be in terms of costs and rewards (Kelley & Thibaut, 1978; Thibaut & Kelley, 1959). Over time, you have amassed a long history of relationships with other people, and this history has led you to have certain expectations as to what your current and future relationships should be like. Some people have a high comparison level, expecting lots of rewards and few costs in their relationships. If a given relationship doesn't match this expected comparison level, they quickly will grow unhappy and unsatisfied. In contrast, people who have a low comparison level would be happy in the same relationship because they expect their relationships to be difficult and costly.

Finally, your satisfaction with a relationship also depends on your perception of the likelihood that you could replace it with a better one—or your **comparison level for alternatives**. As the saying goes, there are plenty of fish in the sea. Could a relationship with a different person give you a better outcome (i.e., greater rewards and fewer costs) than your current one? People who have a high comparison level for alternatives—either because they believe the world is full of fabulous people dying to meet them or because they know of one particular fabulous person dying to meet them—are more likely to take the plunge and hit the market for a new friend or lover. People with a low comparison level for alternatives will be more likely to stay in a costly relationship, because, in their mind, what they have may not be great, but it's better than their expectation of what they could find elsewhere (Lehmiller & Agnew, 2006; Simpson, 1987).

What, after all, is our life but a great dance in which we are all trying to fix the best going rate of exchange?
—Malcolm Bradbury, 1992

Social exchange theory has received a great deal of empirical support. Friends and romantic couples do pay attention to the costs and rewards in their relationships, and these affect how positively people feel about the status of the relationship (Bui, Peplau, & Hill, 1996; Rusbult, 1983; Rusbult, Martz, & Agnew, 1998). Such findings have been observed for intimate relationships in cultures as different as Taiwan and the Netherlands (Lin & Rusbult, 1995; Le & Agnew, 2003; Rusbult & Van Lange, 1996; Van Lange et al., 1997). Generally speaking, when relationships are perceived as offering a lot of rewards, people report feeling happy and satisfied.

However, many people do not leave their partners even when they are dissatisfied and their other alternatives look bright. Research indicates that we need to consider at least one additional factor to understand close relationships: a person's level of investment in the relationship (Impett, Beals, & Peplau, 2001–2002; Rusbult et al., 2001; Goodfriend & Agnew, 2008). In her **investment model** of close relationships, Caryl Rusbult (1983) defines *investment* as anything people have put into a relationship that will be lost if they leave it. Examples include tangible things, such as financial resources and possessions (e.g., a house), as well as intangible things, such as the emotional welfare of one's children, the time and emotional energy spent building the relationship, and the sense of personal integrity that will be lost if one gets divorced. As seen in Figure 10.3, the greater the investment individuals have in a relationship, the less likely they are to leave, even when satisfaction is low and other alternatives look promising. In short, to predict whether people will stay in an intimate relationship, we need to know (1) how satisfied they are with the relationship, (2) what they think of their alternatives, and (3) how great their investment in the relationship is.

To test this model, Rusbult (1983) asked college students involved in heterosexual dating relationships to fill out questionnaires for 7 months. Every 3 weeks, people answered questions about each of the components of the model shown in Figure 10.3.

Comparison Level
People's expectations about the level of rewards and punishments they are likely to receive in a particular relationship

Comparison Level for Alternatives
People's expectations about the level of rewards and punishments they would receive in an alternative relationship

Investment Model
The theory that people's commitment to a relationship depends not only on their satisfaction with the relationship in terms of rewards, costs, and comparison level and their comparison level for alternatives, but also on how much they have invested in the relationship that would be lost by leaving it

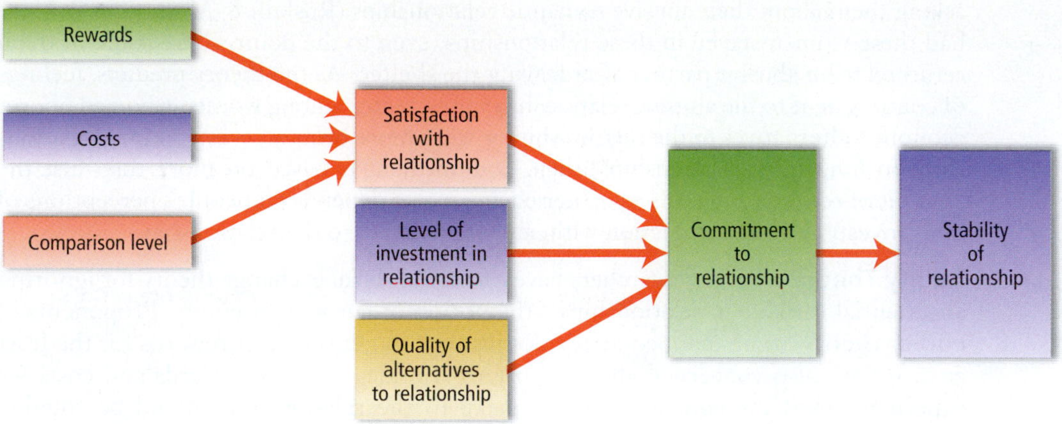

FIGURE 10.3

The Investment Model of Commitment

People's commitment to a relationship depends on several variables. First, their *satisfaction* with the relationship is based on their comparing their *rewards* to their *costs* and determining if the outcome exceeds their general expectation of what they should get in a relationship (or *comparison level*). Next, their *commitment* to the relationship depends on three variables: how *satisfied* they are, how much they feel they have *invested* in the relationship, and whether they have good *alternatives* to this relationship. These commitment variables in turn predict how *stable* the relationship will be. For example, a woman who feels her relationship has more costs and fewer rewards than she considers acceptable would have a low satisfaction. If she also felt she had little invested in the relationship and a very attractive person had just asked her for a date, she would have a low level of commitment. The end result is low stability; most likely, she will break up with her current partner.

(Adapted from Rusbult, 1983)

Rusbult also kept track of whether the students stayed in the relationships or broke up. As you can see in Figure 10.4, satisfaction, alternatives, and investments all predicted how committed people were to the relationship and whether it lasted. (The higher the number on the scale, the more each factor predicted the commitment to and length of the relationship.) Subsequent studies have found results similar to those shown in Figure 10.4 for married couples of diverse ages, lesbian and gay couples, nonsexual friendships, and residents of both the United States and Taiwan (Kurdek, 1992; Lin & Rusbult, 1995; Rusbult, 1991; Rusbult & Buunk, 1993).

Does the same model hold for destructive relationships? To find out, Rusbult and a colleague interviewed women who had sought refuge at a shelter for battered women,

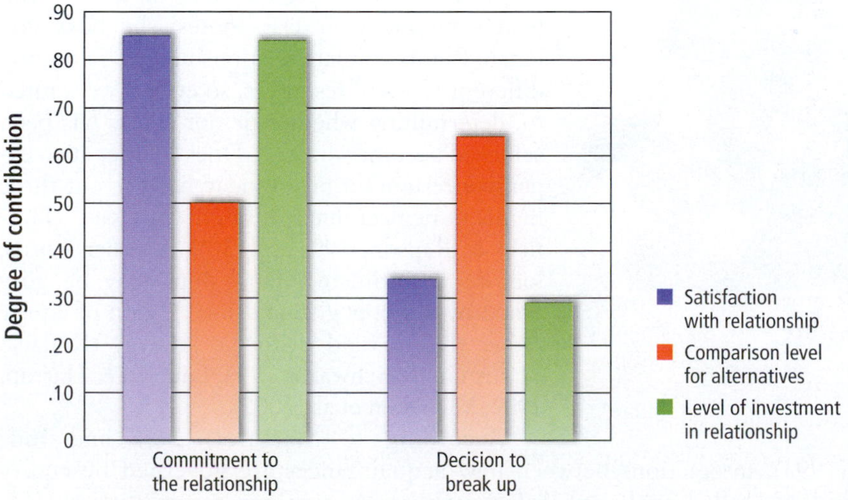

FIGURE 10.4

A Test of the Investment Model

This study examined the extent to which college students' satisfaction with a relationship, their comparison level for alternatives, and their investment in the relationship predicted their commitment to the relationship and their decision about whether to break up with their partner. The higher the number, the more each variable predicted commitment and breakup, independent of the two other variables. All three variables were good predictors of how committed people were and whether or not they broke up.

(Adapted from Rusbult, 1983)

Equity Theory

The idea that people are happiest with relationships in which the rewards and costs experienced and the contributions made by both parties are roughly equal

Exchange Relationships

Relationships governed by the need for equity (i.e., for an equal ratio of rewards and costs)

asking them about their abusive romantic relationships (Rusbult & Martz, 1995). Why had these women stayed in these relationships, even to the point where some of them returned to an abusive partner after leaving the shelter? As the theory predicts, feelings of commitment to the abusive relationship were greater among women who had poorer economic alternatives to the relationship or were more heavily invested in the relationship. In long-term relationships, then, commitment is based on more than just the amount of rewards and costs a partner elicits; it also depends on people's perceptions of their investments in, satisfaction with, and alternatives to the relationship.

Equity Theory Some researchers have criticized social exchange theory for ignoring an essential variable in relationships—the notion of fairness, or equity. Proponents of **equity theory** argue that people are not just out to get the most rewards for the least cost; we are also concerned about equity or the idea that the rewards and costs we experience (and the contributions we make to the relationship) should be roughly equal to those of the other person (Homans, 1961; Walster, Walster, & Berscheid, 1978). These theorists describe equitable relationships as the happiest and most stable (Kalmijn & Monden, 2012). In comparison, inequitable relationships result in one person feeling overbenefited (getting a lot of rewards, incurring few costs, having to devote little time or energy to the relationship) and the other feeling underbenefited (getting few rewards, incurring a lot of costs, having to devote a lot of time and energy to the relationship).

According to equity theory, both underbenefited and overbenefited partners should feel uneasy about this state of affairs, and both should be motivated to restore equity to the relationship. This makes sense for the underbenefited person—after all, who wants to feel miserable and unappreciated? But why should the overbenefited individual want to give up what social exchange theory indicates is a cushy deal: lots of rewards for little cost and little work? Theorists argue that equity is a powerful social norm and that people will eventually feel uncomfortable and guilty if they keep getting more than they deserve in a relationship. Still, being overbenefited isn't quite as bad as being underbenefited, and research has indicated that inequity is perceived as more of a problem by the underbenefited individual (Buunk & Schaufeli, 1999; Guerrero, La Valley, & Farinelli, 2008; Sprecher & Schwartz, 1994; Van Yperen & Buunk, 1990).

Of course, this whole notion of equity implies that partners in a relationship are keeping track of who is benefiting how much and who is getting shortchanged. Some might suggest that many people in happy relationships don't spend so much time and energy keeping tabs on contributions and benefits in this manner. Indeed, the more we get to know someone, the more reluctant we are to believe that we are simply exchanging favors or expecting immediate compensation for every kind gesture. Sure, in casual relationships, we trade "in kind"—you lend someone your class notes, she buys you lunch. But in intimate relationships, we're trading different types of resources, so even if we wanted to, determining whether or not equity has been achieved becomes difficult. Does "dinner at an expensive restaurant on Monday balance out three nights of neglect due to a heavy workload" (Hatfield & Rapson, 1993, p. 130)? In other words, long-term, intimate relationships may be governed by a looser give-and-take notion of equity rather than a rigid tit-for-tat strategy (Kollack, Blumstein, & Schwartz, 1994; Laursen & Hartup, 2002; Vaananen et al., 2005).

Close relationships can have either exchange or communal properties. Family relationships are typically communal.

According to Margaret Clark and Judson Mills (1993), interactions between new acquaintances are governed by equity concerns and are called **exchange relationships**. As you can see in Figure 10.5,

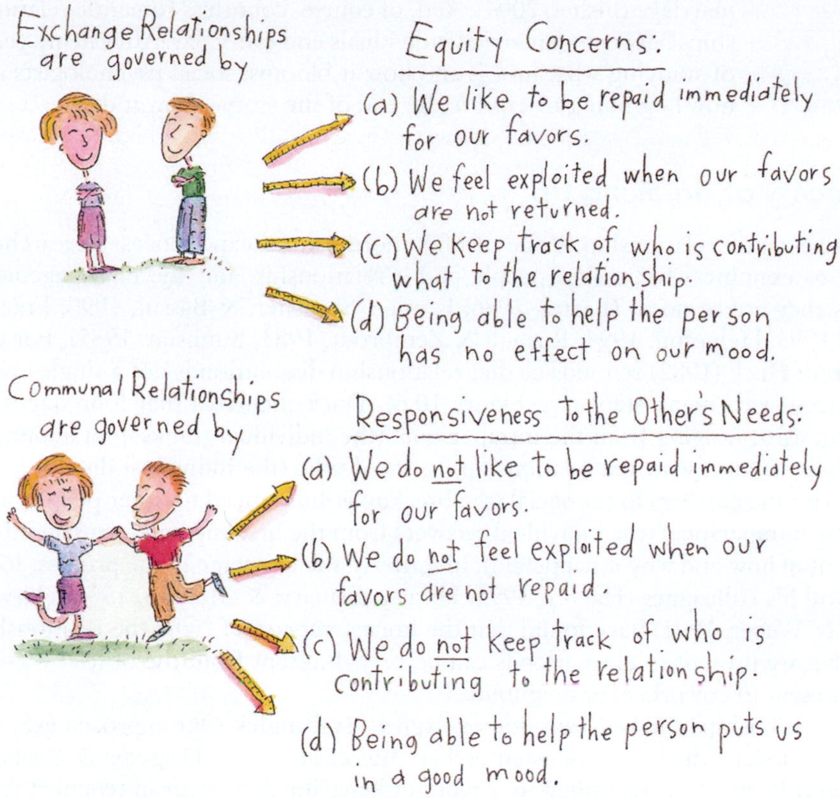

Exchange Relationships are governed by
Equity Concerns:
(a) We like to be repaid immediately for our favors.
(b) We feel exploited when our favors are not returned.
(c) We keep track of who is contributing what to the relationship.
(d) Being able to help the person has no effect on our mood.
Communal Relationships are governed by
Responsiveness to the Other's Needs:
(a) We do not like to be repaid immediately for our favors.
(b) We do not feel exploited when our favors are not repaid.
(c) We do not keep track of who is contributing to the relationship.
(d) Being able to help the person puts us in a good mood.

FIGURE 10.5
Exchange Versus Communal Relationships

in exchange relationships, people keep track of who is contributing what and feel taken advantage of when they feel they are putting more into the relationship than they are getting out of it. In comparison, longer-term interactions between close friends, family members, and romantic partners are governed less by an equity norm and more by a desire to help each other in times of need. In these **communal relationships**, people give in response to the other's needs, regardless of whether they get paid back (Clark, 1984, 1986; Clark & Mills, 1993; Mills & Clark, 1982, 1994, 2001; Vaananen et al., 2005). In this manner, communal interactions are the hallmark of long-term, intimate relationships. Research comparing heterosexual couples to same-sex couples has found that they are equally committed and communal in their relationships: if anything, gay men and lesbians report greater compatibility and less conflict than heterosexual couples do (Balsam et al., 2008; Roisman et al., 2008).

Are people in communal relationships completely unconcerned with equity? Not necessarily. As we saw earlier, people do feel distressed if they believe their intimate relationships are inequitable (Canary & Stafford, 2001; Walster et al., 1978); however, equity takes on a somewhat different form in communal relationships than it does in less-intimate ones. In communal relationships, the partners are more relaxed about what constitutes equity at any given time, believing that things will eventually balance out and a rough kind of equity will be achieved over the long run (Lemay & Clark, 2008; Lemay, Clark, & Feeney, 2007). If this doesn't happen—if they continue to feel that there is an imbalance—the relationship may ultimately end.

Ending Intimate Relationships

The American divorce rate is nearly 50% and has been for the past two decades (Thernstrom, 2003; National Center for Health Statistics, 2005). An examination of data from 58 societies, taken from the *Demographic Yearbook of the United Nations*, indicates that the majority of separations and divorces occur around the fourth year of

Communal Relationships
Relationships in which people's primary concern is being responsive to the other person's needs

Love is like war; easy to begin but very hard to stop.
—H. L. MENCKEN

marriage (Fisher, 2004). And, of course, countless romantic relationships between unmarried individuals end every day. After many years of studying what love is and how it blooms, social psychologists are now beginning to explore the end of the story—how it dies.

The Process of Breaking Up

Ending a romantic relationship is one of life's more painful experiences. Researchers continue to examine what makes people end a relationship and the disengagement strategies they use to do so (Baxter, 1986; Femlee, Sprecher, & Bassin, 1990; Frazier & Cook, 1993; Helgeson, 1994; Rusbult & Zembrodt, 1983; Simpson, 1987). For example, Steve Duck (1982) reminds us that relationship dissolution is not a single event but a process with many steps (see Figure 10.6). Duck theorizes that four stages of dissolution exist, ranging from the intrapersonal (the individual thinks a lot about his or her dissatisfaction with the relationship) to the dyadic (the individual discusses the breakup with the partner) to the social (the breakup is announced to other people) and back to the intrapersonal (the individual recovers from the breakup and forms an internal account of how and why it happened). In terms of the last stage in the process, John Harvey and his colleagues (Harvey, 1995; Harvey, Flanary, & Morgan, 1986; Harvey, Orbuch, & Weber, 1992) have found that the honest version of "why the relationship ended" that we present to close friends can be very different from the official version that we present to coworkers or neighbors.

Why relationships end has been studied from several angles. One approach uses the investment model, which we discussed earlier (Bui et al., 1996; Drigotas & Rusbult, 1992). Caryl Rusbult has identified four types of behavior that occur in troubled relationships (Rusbult, 1987; Rusbult & Zembrodt, 1983). The first two types are destructive behaviors: actively harming the relationship (e.g., abusing the partner, threatening to break up, actually leaving) and passively allowing the relationship to deteriorate (e.g., refusing to deal with problems, ignoring the partner or spending less time together,

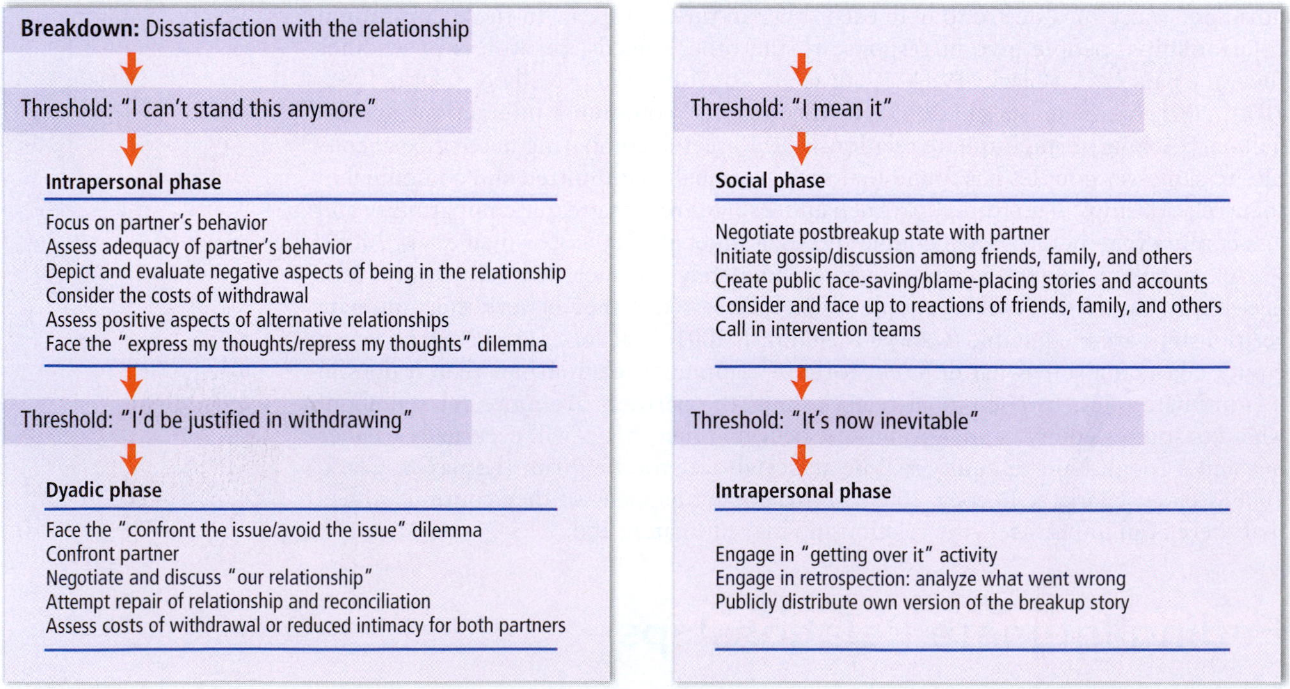

FIGURE 10.6
Steps in Dissolving Close Relationships
(Adapted from Duck, 1982)

putting no energy into the relationship). The other two responses are positive, constructive behaviors: actively trying to improve the relationship (e.g., discussing problems, trying to change, going to a therapist) and passively remaining loyal to the relationship (e.g., waiting and hoping that the situation will improve, being supportive rather than fighting, remaining optimistic). Rusbult and her colleagues have found that destructive behaviors harm a relationship a lot more than constructive behaviors help it. When one partner acts destructively and the other partner responds constructively to save the relationship (the more common pattern), the relationship is likely to continue, but when both partners act destructively, the relationship typically ends (Rusbult, Johnson, & Morrow, 1986; Rusbult, Yovetich, & Verette, 1996).

Relationships can end for many reasons. For example, in "fatal attractions," the very qualities that once attracted you ("He's so mature and wise" / "She's so young and vivacious") can become the very reason you break up ("He's too old" / "She's too immature").

Another approach to studying why relationships end considers what attracted the people to each other in the first place. For example, in one study, college men and women were asked to focus on a romantic relationship that had ended and to list the qualities that first attracted them to the person and the characteristics they ended up disliking the most about the person (Femlee, 1995, 1998a, 1988b). Thirty percent of these breakups were examples of "fatal attractions." The very qualities that were initially so attractive became the very reasons why the relationship ended. For example, "He's so unusual and different" became "He and I have nothing in common." "She's so exciting and unpredictable" became "I can never count on her." This type of breakup reminds us again of the importance of similarity between partners to successful relationships.

If a romantic relationship is in bad shape, can we predict who will end it? Much has been made about the tendency in heterosexual relationships for women to end relationships more often than men (Rubin, Peplau, & Hill, 1981). Research has found, however, that neither sex ends romantic relationships more frequently than the other (Akert, 1998; Hagestad & Smyer, 1982; Rusbult et al., 1986).

The Experience of Breaking Up

Can we predict the different ways people will feel when their relationship ends? One key is the role people play in the decision to end the relationship (Akert, 1998; Helgeson, 1994; Lloyd & Cate, 1985). For example, Robin Akert asked 344 college-age men and women to complete a questionnaire about their most important romantic relationship that had ended. One question asked to what extent they or their partner had been responsible for the decision to break up. Participants who indicated a high level of responsibility for the decision were labeled "breakers"; those who reported a low level of responsibility, "breakees"; and those who shared the decision making with their partners about equally, "mutuals."

"Somehow I remember this one differently."

Steve Duenes/The New Yorker Collection/ www.cartoonbank.com.

Akert found that the role people played in the decision to end the relationship was the single most powerful predictor of their breakup experiences. Not surprisingly, breakees were miserable; they reported high levels of loneliness, depression, and anger, and virtually all reported experiencing physical illness in the weeks after the breakup as well. Of the three groups, breakers found the end of the relationship the least upsetting, the least painful, and

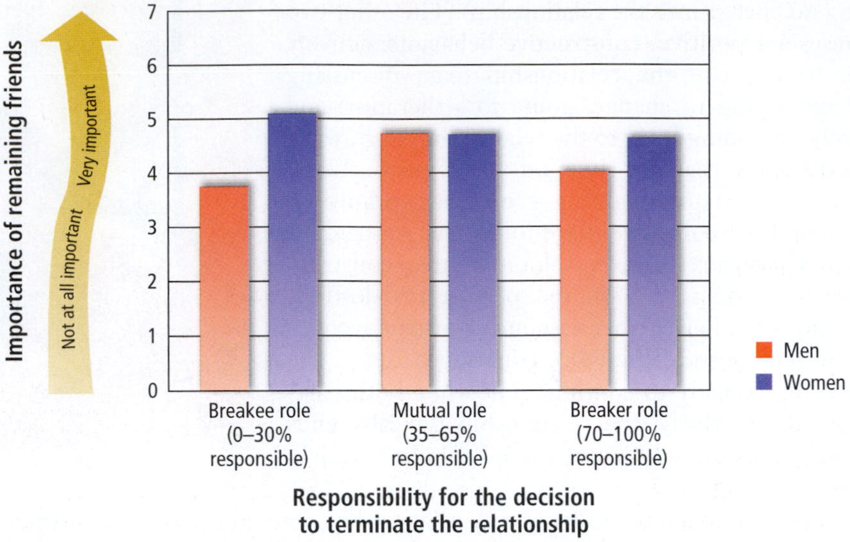

FIGURE 10.7

Importance of Remaining Friends After the Breakup

After ending a romantic relationship, do people want to remain friends with their ex-partner? It depends both on the role they played in the decision to break up and on their gender. Women are more interested than men in staying friends when they are in the breakee or breaker role; men and women are equally interested in staying friends when the relationship ends by mutual decision.

(Akert, 1998)

the least stressful. Although breakers did report feeling guilty and unhappy, they had the fewest negative physical symptoms (39%), such as headaches, stomachaches, and sleeping irregularities.

The mutual role, which carries with it a component of shared decision making, helped individuals evade some of the negative emotional and physical reactions to breaking up. Mutuals were not as upset or hurt as breakees, but they were not as unaffected as breakers. Some 60% of the mutuals reported physical symptoms, indicating that a mutual conclusion to a romantic relationship is a more stressful experience than simply deciding to end it on one's own. Finally, gender played a role in the emotional and physical responses of the respondents, with women reporting somewhat more negative reactions to breaking up than men.

Do people want to stay friends once they break up? It depends on the role played in the breakup as well as on gender. Akert (1998) found that men are not particularly interested in remaining friends with their ex-girlfriends when they are in either the breaker or the breakee role; women are more interested in remaining friends, especially when they are breakees (see Figure 10.7). Interestingly, the mutual role is the one where men's and women's interest in future friendship matches the most. These data suggest that when men experience either great control (breaker) or little control (breakee) over the end of a relationship, they tend to want to "cut their losses" and move on, severing ties with their ex-partner. In comparison, women tend to want to continue feeling connected to their ex-partner, hoping to reshape the intimate relationship into a platonic friendship. The mutual breakup is the one in which each partner effectively plays the breaker and breakee roles simultaneously, and this equality in roles appears to be important in producing an interest in future friendship among both men and women (see Figure 10.7).

Love in the Age of Technology

As this chapter details, psychologists have studied attraction and intimate relationships for decades now. And as is the case with any topic in social psychology, it is reasonable to ask whether research findings observed years and decades ago still apply to tendencies in the modern age. In particular, we now live in an era in which much of our social interaction is not of the face-to-face variety, but rather takes place via text, instant message, Internet chat room, Facebook, Twitter, interactive gaming, virtual reality, and probably even newer technologies developed since this sentence was typed. How do the principles, processes, and theories detailed in this chapter play out in this constantly evolving technological landscape? This final section provides some initial answers to this question, but clearly there is no shortage of interesting future research directions available to social psychologists interested in studying interpersonal attraction.

One question surrounding attraction is how tendencies regarding mate preference that have evolved over generations play out in the modern era of Internet dating, speed-dating events, and Facebook.

Attraction Revisited

One way to explore how our rapidly developing technological world affects the psychology of love is to revisit some of the classic findings reviewed above to see how factors like propinquity, similarity, and familiarity affect attraction in the Internet age. For example, consider how propinquity operates today, when physical distance no longer means what it once did and the Internet allows us to get to know people half a world away (Chan & Cheng, 2004; Dodds, Muhamad, & Watts, 2003). Jure Leskovec and Eric Horvitz conducted a study testing the concept that inspired the popular game "Six Degrees of Kevin Bacon." A "degree of separation" is a measure of social distance between people: You are one degree away from everyone you know, two degrees away from everyone they know, and so on. These researchers analyzed an instant-messaging network, looking at who sent messages to whom and calculating how many different people in a "chain" it would take, on average, to connect two random users to each other. After making calculations for 30 billion conversations among 240 million people, they found that the average length of a person chain was seven and that 90% of pairs could be connected in just eight "hops" (Leskovec & Horvitz, 2007). Thus, six (or seven) degrees of separation appear to explain quite well how interconnected people are in the modern era, regardless of their physical distance.

The effects of similarity have also been observed in technologically driven relationships. Earlier in this chapter, we discussed the tendency to be attracted to people of similar appearance, right down to your being attracted to others at the same level of physical attractiveness as you are. Recent research indicates that this tendency to try to date "in our own league" is little different when relationships go online. Lindsay Taylor (2011) and colleagues assessed the popularity of over 3 thousand heterosexual users of a dating Web site. They defined popularity as the number of opposite-sex individuals who sent unsolicited messages to a user. Because this measure did not include messages sent in response to contact initiated by the user or subsequent messages sent during an ongoing exchange, there was no way for the users in the study to increase their own popularity count once they posted their profile.

Taylor and colleagues (2011) found that high-popularity users of the site contacted other popular users at a rate greater than would be expected by chance—a finding that probably does not surprise you. After all, who wouldn't want to reach out to the popular potential mates? Well, the less popular users of the site, that's who. The researchers also found that users lower in popularity contacted other low-popularity users more often. A follow-up study with over 1 million users produced a comparable result: People tend to select (and be selected by) others with similar levels of popularity, and this tendency to try to "match up" with mates of comparable popularity was no different for men than for women. As the researchers concluded, "one reason that established couples tend to be similar is that matching is at play from the earliest stages of dating" (Taylor et al., 2011, p. 952).

What about familiarity? As you will recall, research has demonstrated that familiarity typically promotes attraction, to the point where even mere exposure to an object or person increases liking. But you may also recall that mere exposure works in the opposite direction when that additional exposure reveals negative characteristics of the object or person in question—a conclusion supported by another recent study of online dating. In this research, Michael Norton and colleagues (2007) gave a survey to participants both before and after going on a date. Pre-date, all that participants knew about their partner was what they had read on a Web site profile, so their ratings of how much knowledge they had about their partner increased post-date. But their ratings of how much they liked their partner *decreased* after the date, as did perceptions of how similar they were. Why? Because the more familiar participants became with their partner during the date, the more they realized that their initial impression (based on an ambiguous dating Web site profile) was not that accurate. As they obtained additional information during the date itself, they came to appreciate all the ways in which they were actually *dissimilar* to this person, which in turn decreased average liking ratings.

"On the Internet, nobody knows you're a dog."

Peter Steiner/The New Yorker Collection/ www.cartoonbank.com

The Promise and Pitfalls of Online Dating

We began this chapter with the heartwarming story of Laura and Denny Allen, Oregon retirees whose shared love of international travel, volunteer work, wild mushrooms, and pugs has translated into a happy marriage. Despite their overlapping interests and social circles, Laura and Denny wouldn't be together today if not for the help of a dating Web site. The Allens are hardly alone. A recent review of online dating reports that "by 2005, 37% of single Internet users were dating online (a percentage that is almost certainly much higher today), and, by 2007–2009, more new romantic relationships had begun online than through any means other than meeting through friends" (Finkel et al., 2012, p. 11). Attitudes toward Internet dating have never been more positive than they are today. And this is for good reason, as dating Web sites advertise three primary services for users looking for love: (1) aggregating a large number of profiles for browsing, (2) providing opportunity for computer-mediated communication with potential mates, and (3) matching users based on analyses of compatibility (Finkel et al., 2012).

Clearly, dating Web sites have a lot to offer those who are looking for love, and there is no reason to expect their popularity to stop skyrocketing anytime soon. Still, some of the promise of online dating is tempered by other psychological research findings. For example, as discussed in the opening of this chapter, the dating Web site algorithms used to match potential mates by compatibility do not lead to higher relationship success rates than older, lower-tech methods of matching such as the fix-up among friends or getting to know someone through mutual activities. Furthermore, just how honest are people when they post profiles and photos on dating Web sites anyway? Norton et al. (2007) found that learning more about a partner during a date often makes you like that person less than you did when you had only seen a profile, suggesting that perhaps the profiles aren't too accurate to begin with.

Catalina Toma and Jeffrey Hancock have conducted a series of investigations to assess these questions regarding online dating profiles. Some of their research examines potential differences in how men and women describe themselves online. In one study, they interviewed 84 online daters, presenting them with a printout of their own dating profile and asking them how accurate they believed they were in describing their height, weight, and age (Toma, Hancock, & Ellison, 2008). Of course, the researchers were able to compare these self-assessments of accuracy to objective measures of participants' actual height, weight, and age. Results indicated that a full 81% of participants provided inaccurate information in their profile for at least one characteristic, with the most lies coming about weight, followed by age, then height. Interestingly, no gender differences emerged: Men and women were equally likely to try to stretch the truth. Participants' self-reported estimates of their profile accuracy were reasonably good predictors of actual accuracy, indicating that the discrepancies observed did not result from unconscious tendencies to view the self through rose-colored glasses, but rather intentional efforts to fudge facts.

A slightly different pattern emerges from analysis of photos used in dating profiles. Here, Hancock and Toma (2009) found that distortions are often less conscious, especially among women. Following a similar procedure to their previous study, the researchers interviewed online daters about how accurate they believed their profile photo to be. They then had a separate group of college students look at a series of two images side by side: (1) each participant's dating profile photo and (2) a photo taken of each participant during the recent interview. The college students were asked to evaluate how accurate a depiction the profile photograph was of the participant's current physical appearance. In total, 32% of profile photographs were judged to be deceptive or misleading, and females' photos were found to be less accurate than males'. Common inaccuracies included daters looking thinner in the profile photo than they currently do, having more hair in the profile photo than they do now, or using profile photos that were retouched or airbrushed. Unlike with written profiles, users' self-assessed accuracy ratings were not reliable predictors of the actual accuracy of their photo (as rated by the students), particularly among female daters.

In light of these inaccuracies—both intentional and unintentional—what's a lovelorn Internet dater to do? Luckily, the same research techniques that uncovered these inaccurate profiles and photos can also be used to identify which potential online mates are the most (and least) honest. Specifically, Toma and Hancock (2012) suggest three giveaways that the profile you're checking out online may not pass a reality check. First, deceptive profiles tend to have fewer first-person pronouns like *I* and *me*. The researchers explain that this is one way for those who lie or exaggerate to distance themselves psychologically from their half-truths. Second, deceptive profiles make more use of negations, or negative turns of phrase (e.g., "not judgmental" instead of "open-minded"; "not averse to taking risks" instead of "adventurous"). Third, deceptive profiles simply include fewer total words than accurate profiles. Stretching the truth is hard work and cognitively demanding; the fewer inaccurate statements you put in your profile, the fewer fabrications you have to remember later on when you meet someone in person.

Watch on **MyPsychLab**
Consider technology's effects on romance as you watch the MyPsychLab video ***IT Video: Rules for Dating.***

In short, online dating offers users a much larger pool of potential mates than do more-traditional methods that are constrained by personal contacts and physical geography. At the same time, in some important respects, dating Web sites fall short of the promises they make to daters. Nonetheless, it's clear that online dating is here to stay. And in addition to putting an interesting new twist on the human pursuit of love and intimacy, online dating provides contemporary social psychologists with a fascinating set of questions and methods for the experimental study of attraction and relationship formation.

USE IT!

If there was ever a chapter in a textbook that had something to say about your "real" life, this is probably it. Romantic relationships and friendships are an integral part of our lives, and, wonderful as they are, they are also frequently confusing and even upsetting. While the information in this chapter could help you when you're "falling in love," you'll probably be too distracted by your new partner to even think about research studies on attraction. However, when things go bad, this information can really be of help. Apply the various terms and theories to your predicament and ask yourself "Do they help shed some light on what is going on?" For example, are you and your friend or romantic partner seeing the relationship differently, perhaps one of you as an "exchange" and the other as "communal?" Does one or the other of you have an attachment style that is causing problems? Are the two of you dissimilar in areas that are important to you? Are there cultural differences that might explain what's going on? If your loved one is thinking of ending the relationship, is it because he or she has a viable "comparison level for alternatives"? Finally, if you're one of the millions of people turning to the Internet in your search for love, specific cues can help you determine which dating profiles are likely to be most accurate.

Summary

How do humans decide whom they like and want to get to know better?

What Causes Attraction?

- **The Person Next Door: The Propinquity Effect** In the first part of this chapter, we discussed the variables that cause initial attraction between two people. One such variable is physical proximity, or the **propinquity effect**: People who you come into contact with the most are the most likely to become your friends and lovers. This occurs because of the **mere exposure effect**: Exposure to any stimulus produces liking for it.
- **Similarity** Similarity between people, whether in attitudes, values, demographic characteristics, or physical appearance is also a powerful cause of attraction and liking. Similarity is a more powerful predictor of attraction than complementarity, the idea that opposites attract.
- **Reciprocal Liking** In general, we like others who behave as if they like us.
- **Physical Attractiveness and Liking** Physical attractiveness also plays an important role in liking. People from different cultures perceive facial attractiveness quite similarly. The "what is beautiful is good" stereotype indicates that people assume that physical attractiveness is associated with other desirable traits.
- **Evolution and Mate Selection Evolutionary psychology** explains love in terms of genetic factors that have evolved over time according to the principles of natural selection. According to this perspective, which is not without its critics, men and women are attracted to different characteristics because this maximizes their reproductive success.

What is love, and how do we form close relationships?

Love and Close Relationships

- **Defining Love: Companionship and Passion** One definition of love makes a distinction between **companionate love**, feelings of intimacy that are not accompanied by intense longing and arousal, and **passionate love**, feelings of intimacy that are accompanied by intense longing and arousal.
- **Culture and Love** Although love is a universal emotion, cultural variations in the practice and definition of love do occur. Love has a somewhat different emphasis in collectivistic and individualistic cultures.
- **Attachment Styles in Intimate Relationships** People's past relationships with their parents are a significant determinant of the quality of their close relationships as adults. There are three types of attachment relationships: **secure**, **avoidant**, and **anxious/ambivalent**.
- **Theories of Relationship Satisfaction: Social Exchange and Equity Social exchange theory** states that how people feel about their relationship depends on their perception of the rewards they receive and the costs they incur. In order to determine whether people will stay in a relationship, we need to know their **comparison level** (expectations about the outcomes of their relationship), their **comparison level for alternatives** (expectations about how happy they would be in other relationships), as well as their **investment** in the relationship. **Equity theory** states that the most important determinant of satisfaction is that both parties feel comparably rewarded by the relationship. The equity of rewards and costs is different in **communal relationships** than in **exchange relationships**.

What does research tell us about romantic breakups?

Ending Intimate Relationships

- **The Process of Breaking Up** The breaking-up process is composed of stages. Strategies for responding to problems in a romantic relationship include both constructive and destructive behaviors. Fatal attractions occur when the qualities in a person that once were attractive become the very qualities that repel.
- **The Experience of Breaking Up** A powerful variable that predicts how a person will weather the breakup is the role he or she plays in the decision to terminate the relationship.

How do new technologies influence how we form close relationships?

Love in the Age of Technology

- **Attraction Revisited** Basic determinants of attraction such as propinquity, similarity, and familiarity manifest themselves differently in the modern era of text messages, the Internet, and social media.
- **The Promise and Pitfalls of Online Dating** Online dating expands your pool of potential mates, but carries its own risks; these include unproven compatibility algorithms and deceptive profile descriptions and photos.

Chapter 10 Test

Study and Review on MyPsychLab

1. Sam has his eye on Julie and wants her to like him. According to research in social psychology, which of the following is *least* likely to work? He should
   a. emphasize how similar their attitudes are.
   b. arrange to work with her on a class project so that he can spend time with her.
   c. emphasize that they have complementary personalities; after all, "opposites attract."
   d. make himself look as physically attractive as he can.

2. Rachel is considered physically attractive by her American classmates because of her large eyes and small nose—"baby face" characteristics. In another culture, she would most likely be considered
   a. unattractive because her features are not unique.
   b. unattractive because people's perceptions of beauty differ across cultures.
   c. attractive because people's perceptions of "baby face" attractiveness are similar across cultures.
   d. attractive because "baby face" characteristics appear exotic to people of other cultures.

3. Which of the following is *false?*
   a. People in communal relationships tend to keep track of who is contributing what to the relationship.
   b. People find "average" faces to be more attractive than unusual faces.
   c. People like others who like them.
   d. The more we see and interact with people, the more we will like them.

4. Kate and Jamie are dating. According to the *investment model of close relationships*, which of the following is *least* likely to influence their commitment to the relationship?
   a. Their satisfaction with the relationship
   b. Their level of investment in the relationship
   c. The availability and quality of alternative partners
   d. Their perception that what they are putting into the relationship is roughly the same as what they are getting out of it

5. __________ involves intense longing for another person, accompanied by physiological arousal, whereas __________ is the intimacy and affection we feel without arousal.
   a. passionate love, infatuation
   b. companionate love, passionate love
   c. infatuation, companionate love
   d. passionate love, companionate love

6. Which of the following statements regarding attachment style is true?
   a. Few if any individuals change their attachment style once they reach adulthood.
   b. A majority of adults have been found to exhibit an avoidant attachment style.
   c. The attachment style that adults display is shaped by their partner's behavior and the type of relationship they've created as a couple.
   d. Your attachment style as an infant typically has little to do with the attachment style you have in your adult relationships.

7. Matthew and Eric have been friends since the beginning of the school year. According to equity theory, their friendship will suffer if
   a. Eric is much more likely to help Matthew out when he needs it than Matthew is to help Eric.
   b. Eric has a "makeover" and becomes more attractive than Matthew.
   c. Eric and Matthew stop having similar interests.
   d. Eric and Matthew are romantically interested in the same person.

8. Elliot worries that his girlfriend doesn't really love him and smothers her with attention. According to attachment theory, Elliot probably has a(n) __________ attachment style, because when he was an infant, his caregivers were __________.
   a. avoidant, aloof and distant
   b. avoidant, inconsistent and overbearing
   c. anxious-ambivalent, aloof and distant
   d. anxious-ambivalent, inconsistent and overbearing
   e. secure, responsive to his needs

9. You are considering breaking up with your significant other after 1 month of being a couple. While the relationship gives you lots of rewards and has few costs, you have recently met someone new whom you anticipate will give you even more rewards for even fewer costs. Your dilemma stems from the fact that you have a __________ and a __________.
   a. low satisfaction level, high comparison level for alternatives
   b. high satisfaction level, high comparison level for alternatives
   c. low satisfaction level, low comparison level for alternatives
   d. low satisfaction level, high equity level
   e. high satisfaction level, low equity level

10. Research on the ability of dating Web sites to effectively match up mates using mathematical compatibility analyses indicates that
   a. the Web sites do a better job of matching up same-sex couples than opposite-sex couples.
   b. the Web sites produce a higher "hit rate" of happy relationships than do less-mathematical means of meeting a dating partner.
   c. the Web sites are no better at producing happy relationships than are more old-fashioned ways of meeting a dating partner, like being set up by friends.
   d. contrary to many assumptions, older individuals (e.g., senior citizens) are more likely to be successful finding love online than younger individuals (e.g., college students).

Answer Key

1-c, 2-c, 3-a, 4-d, 5-d,
6-c, 7-a, 8-d, 9-b, 10-c

11 Prosocial Behavior

Why Do People Help?

SEPTEMBER 11, 2001, WAS TRULY A DAY OF INFAMY IN AMERICAN HISTORY, WITH TERRIBLE LOSS OF LIFE AT THE WORLD TRADE CENTER, THE PENTAGON, AND THE FIELD IN PENNSYLVANIA WHERE UNITED AIRLINES FLIGHT 93 CRASHED. It was also a day of incredible courage and sacrifice by people who did not hesitate to help their fellow human beings. Many people lost their lives while helping others, including 403 New York firefighters and police officers who died trying to rescue people from the World Trade Center.

Many of the heroes of September 11 were ordinary citizens who found themselves in extraordinary circumstances. Imagine that you were working in the World Trade Center towers when they were hit by the planes and how strong the desire must have been to flee and seek personal safety. This is exactly what William Wik's wife urged him to do when he called her from the 92nd floor of the South Tower shortly after the attacks. "No, I can't do that; there are still people here," he replied (Lee, 2001, p. 28). Wik's body was found in the rubble of the South Tower after it collapsed; he was wearing work gloves and holding a flashlight.

Abe Zelmanowitz worked on the 27th floor of the North Tower and could easily have walked down the stairs to safety when the plane struck the floors above. Instead, he stayed behind with his friend Ed Beyea, a quadriplegic, waiting for help to carry him down the stairs. Both died when the tower collapsed.

Rick Rescorla was head of security for the Morgan Stanley brokerage firm. After the first plane hit the North Tower, Rescorla and the other employees in the South Tower were instructed to remain at their desks. Rescorla, who had spent years studying the security of the towers, had drilled his employees repeatedly on what to do in an emergency like this—find a partner, avoid the elevators, and evacuate the building. He invoked this plan immediately, and when the plane hit the South Tower, he was on the 44th floor supervising the evacuation, yelling instructions through a bullhorn. After most of the Morgan Stanley employees made it out of the building, Rescorla decided to do a final sweep of the offices to make sure no one was left behind, and he perished when the South Tower collapsed. Rescorla is credited with saving the lives of the 3,700 employees he guided to safety (Stewart, 2002).

And then there were the passengers on United flight 93. Based on phone calls made from the plane in the fateful minutes after it was hijacked, it appears that several passengers, including Todd Beamer, Jeremy Glick, and Thomas Burnett—all fathers of young children—stormed the cockpit and struggled with the terrorists. They could not prevent the plane from crashing, killing everyone on board, but they did prevent an even worse tragedy. The plane was headed for Washington, DC, with the White House or the U.S. Capitol the likely target.

FOCUS QUESTIONS

- What are the basic motives that determine whether people help others?
- What are some personal qualities that influence whether a given individual will help?
- In what situations are people more likely, or less likely, to help others?
- What can be done to promote prosocial behavior?

Basic Motives Underlying Prosocial Behavior: Why Do People Help?

How can we explain acts of great self-sacrifice and heroism when people are also capable of acting in uncaring, heartless ways? In this chapter, we will consider the major causes of **prosocial behavior**—any act performed with the goal of benefiting another person (Penner et al., 2005). We are particularly

Prosocial Behavior
Any act performed with the goal of benefiting another person

concerned with prosocial behavior that is motivated by **altruism**, which is the desire to help another person even if it involves a cost to the helper. Someone might act in a prosocial way out of self-interest, hoping to get something in return. Altruism is helping purely out of the desire to benefit someone else, with no benefit (and often a cost) to oneself; the heroes of September 11, who gave their lives while helping strangers, are a clear example of this.

We begin by considering the basic origins of prosocial behavior and altruism: Is the willingness to help a basic impulse with genetic roots? Must it be taught and nurtured in childhood? Is there a pure motive for helping? Or do people typically help only when there is something in it for them? Let's see how psychologists have addressed these centuries-old questions (McCullough & Tabak, 2010; Piliavin, 2009).

Evolutionary Psychology: Instincts and Genes

According to Charles Darwin's (1859) theory of evolution, natural selection favors genes that promote the survival of the individual (see Chapter 10). Any gene that furthers our survival and increases the probability that we will produce offspring is likely to be passed on from generation to generation. Genes that lower our chances of survival, such as those causing life-threatening diseases, reduce the chances that we will produce offspring and thus are less likely to be passed on. Evolutionary biologists such as E. O. Wilson (1975) and Richard Dawkins (1976) have used these principles of evolutionary theory to explain such social behaviors as aggression and altruism. Several psychologists have pursued these ideas, spawning the field of *evolutionary psychology*, which is the attempt to explain social behavior in terms of genetic factors that have evolved over time according to the principles of natural selection (Buss, 2005; Neuberg, Kenrick, & Schaller, 2010; Tooby & Cosmides, 2005). In Chapter 10, we discussed how evolutionary psychology attempts to explain love and attraction; here we discuss its explanation of prosocial behavior (Simpson & Beckes, 2010).

Altruism

The desire to help another person even if it involves a cost to the helper

Kin Selection

The idea that behaviors that help a genetic relative are favored by natural selection

Darwin realized early on that there was a problem with evolutionary theory: How can it explain altruism? If people's overriding goal is to ensure their own survival, why would they ever help others at a cost to themselves? It would seem that over the course of human evolution altruistic behavior would disappear, because people who acted that way would, by putting themselves at risk, produce fewer offspring than would people who acted selfishly. Genes promoting selfish behavior should be more likely to be passed on—or should they?

Kin Selection One way that evolutionary psychologists attempt to resolve this dilemma is with the notion of **kin selection**, the idea that behaviors that help a genetic relative are favored by natural selection (Hamilton, 1964; Vasey & VanderLaan, 2010; West & Gardner, 2010). People can increase the chances that their genes will be passed along not only by having their own children, but also by ensuring that their genetic relatives have children. Because a person's blood relatives share some of his or her genes, the more that person ensures their survival, the greater the chances that his or her genes will flourish in future generations. Thus, natural selection should favor altruistic acts directed toward genetic relatives.

According to evolutionary psychology, prosocial behavior occurs in part because of kin selection.

In one study, for example, people reported that they would be more likely to help genetic relatives than nonrelatives in life-and-death situations, such as a house fire. People did not report that they would be more likely to help genetic relatives when the situation was non-life-threatening, which supports the idea that people are most likely to help in ways that ensure the survival of their own genes. Interestingly, both males and females, and both American and Japanese participants, followed this rule of kin selection in life-threatening situations (Burnstein, Crandall, & Kitayama, 1994).

Of course, in this study people reported what they thought they would do; this doesn't prove that in a real fire they would indeed be more likely to save their sibling than their cousin. Anecdotal evidence from real emergencies, however, is consistent with these results. Survivors of a fire at a vacation complex reported that when they became aware that there was a fire, they were much more likely to search for family members before exiting the building than they were to search for friends (Sime, 1983).

Altruism based on kin selection is the enemy of civilization. If human beings are to a large extent guided to favor their own relatives and tribe, only a limited amount of global harmony is possible.

—E. O. Wilson, 1978

Evolutionary psychologists are not suggesting that people consciously weigh the biological importance of their behavior before deciding whether to help: We don't compute the likelihood that our genes will be passed on before deciding whether to help someone push his or her car out of a ditch. According to evolutionary theory, however, the genes of people who follow this "biological importance" rule are more likely to survive than the genes of people who do not. Over the millennia, kin selection may have become ingrained in human behavior (Vasey & VanderLaan, 2010; Bishop et al., 2009).

Watch on MyPsychLab

To learn more about how and why people help their own family members, watch the MyPsychLab video ***Successful Aging, Extended Family Maria, 68 Years Old.***

The Reciprocity Norm To explain altruism, evolutionary psychologists also point to the **norm of reciprocity**, which is the expectation that helping others will increase the likelihood that they will help us in the future. The idea is that as human beings were evolving, a group of completely selfish individuals, each living in his or her own cave, would have found it more difficult to survive than a group that had learned to cooperate. Of course, if people cooperated too readily, they might have been exploited by an adversary who never helped in return. Those who were most likely to survive, the argument goes, were people who developed an understanding with their neighbors about reciprocity: "I will help you now, with the agreement that when I need help, you will return the favor." Because of its survival value, such a norm of reciprocity may have become genetically based (Cosmides & Tooby, 1992; de Waal, 1996; Trivers, 1971; Zhang & Epley, 2009). Some researchers suggest that the emotion of *gratitude*—the positive feelings that are caused by the perception that one has been helped by others—evolved in order to regulate reciprocity (Bartlett & DeSteno, 2006; Grant & Gino, 2010; McCullough, Kimeldorf, & Cohen, 2008). That is, if someone helps us, we feel gratitude, which motivates us to return the favor in the future. The following Try It! describes how the reciprocity norm can work to increase helping in everyday life.

Group Selection Classic evolutionary theory argues that natural selection operates on individuals: People who have traits that make them more likely to survive are more likely to reproduce and pass those traits on to future generations. Some argue that natural selection also operates at the level of the group. Imagine two neighboring villages, for example, that are often at war with each other. Village A is made up entirely of selfish individuals who refuse to put themselves at risk to help the village. Village B, on the other hand, has selfless sentries who put their lives at risk by alerting their comrades of an invasion. Which *group* is more likely to win the war and pass on its

Norm of Reciprocity

The expectation that helping others will increase the likelihood that they will help us in the future

TRY IT! Does the Reciprocity Norm Increase Helping?

Have you ever gotten a fund-raising appeal from a charity that included a little gift, such as address labels with your name? If so, did the gift make you more inclined to donate money to the charity? If so, you were subject to the reciprocity norm; because the charity did something for you, you felt more obligated to do something for the charity. The same norm applies when stores offer free samples of a product they are selling. It can feel rude not to reciprocate by buying the product, even though these are strangers trying to sell us something, and not friends doing us a favor. What about in everyday life? Can you think of times when the reciprocity norm influenced how likely you were to help a friend? Have you found that doing a favor for a friend makes it more likely that your friend will do a favor for you? Give this a try and see if it works.

genes to later generations? The one with the selfless (altruistic) sentries, of course. Even though the *individual* sentries in Village B are at risk and likely to be captured and killed, their selfless behavior increases the likelihood that their *group* will survive—namely, the group that values altruism. Though the idea of group selection is controversial and not supported by all biologists, it is has prominent proponents (Wilson, Van Vugt, & O'Gorman, 2008; Wilson & Wilson, 2007).

In sum, evolutionary psychologists believe that people help others because of factors that have become ingrained in our genes. As we saw in Chapter 10, evolutionary psychology is a challenging and creative approach to understanding prosocial behavior, though it does have its critics (Batson, 1998; Buller, 2005; Caporael & Brewer, 2000; Confer et al., 2010; Panksepp & Panksepp, 2000; Wood & Eagly, 2002). How, for example, can evolutionary theory explain why complete strangers sometimes help each other, even when there is no reason for them to assume that they share some of the same genes or that their favor will ever be returned? It seems absurd to say that the heroes of September 11, who lost their lives while saving others, somehow calculated how genetically similar they were to the others before deciding to help. Further, just because people are more likely to save family members than strangers from a fire does not necessarily mean that they are genetically programmed to help genetic relatives. It may simply be that they cannot bear the thought of losing a loved one and therefore go to greater lengths to save the ones they love over people they have never met. We turn now to other possible motives behind prosocial behavior that do not necessarily originate in people's genes.

Let him who neglects to raise the fallen, fear lest, when he falls, no one will stretch out his hand to lift him up.
—SAADI, *THE ORCHARD*, 1257

Social Exchange: The Costs and Rewards of Helping

Although some social psychologists disagree with evolutionary approaches to prosocial behavior, they share the view that altruistic behavior can be based on self-interest. In fact, *social exchange theory* (see Chapter 10) argues that much of what we do stems from the desire to maximize our rewards and minimize our costs (Cook & Rice, 2003; Homans, 1961; Lawler & Thye, 1999; Thibaut & Kelley, 1959). The difference from evolutionary approaches is that social exchange theory doesn't trace this desire back to our evolutionary roots, nor does it assume that the desire is genetically based. Social exchange theorists assume that just as people in an economic marketplace try to maximize the ratio of their monetary profits to their monetary losses, people in their relationships with others try to maximize the ratio of social rewards to social costs.

Helping can be rewarding in a number of ways. As we saw with the norm of reciprocity, it can increase the likelihood that someone will help us in return. Helping someone is an investment in the future, the social exchange being that someday someone will help us when we need it. Helping can also relieve the personal distress of a bystander. Considerable evidence indicates that people are aroused and disturbed when they see another person suffer and that they help at least in part to relieve their own distress (Dovidio, 1984; Dovidio et al., 1991; Eisenberg & Fabes, 1991). By helping others, we can also gain such rewards as social approval from others and increased feelings of self-worth.

The other side of the coin, of course, is that helping can be costly. Helping decreases when the costs are high, such as when it would put us in physical danger, result in pain or embarrassment, or simply take too much time (Dovidio et al.,

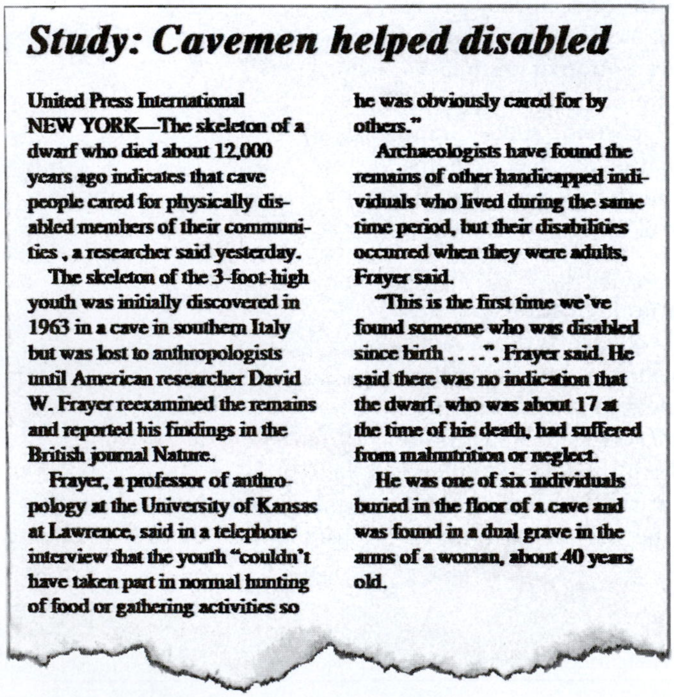

Study: Cavemen helped disabled

United Press International
NEW YORK—The skeleton of a dwarf who died about 12,000 years ago indicates that cave people cared for physically disabled members of their communities , a researcher said yesterday.

The skeleton of the 3-foot-high youth was initially discovered in 1963 in a cave in southern Italy but was lost to anthropologists until American researcher David W. Frayer reexamined the remains and reported his findings in the British journal Nature.

Frayer, a professor of anthropology at the University of Kansas at Lawrence, said in a telephone interview that the youth "couldn't have taken part in normal hunting of food or gathering activities so he was obviously cared for by others."

Archaeologists have found the remains of other handicapped individuals who lived during the same time period, but their disabilities occurred when they were adults, Frayer said.

"This is the first time we've found someone who was disabled since birth . . . .", Frayer said. He said there was no indication that the dwarf, who was about 17 at the time of his death, had suffered from malnutrition or neglect.

He was one of six individuals buried in the floor of a cave and was found in a dual grave in the arms of a woman, about 40 years old.

This touching story of early hominid prosocial behavior is intriguing to think about in terms of different theories of prosocial behavior. Evolutionary psychologists might argue that the caregivers helped the dwarf because he was a relative and that people are programmed to help those who share their genes (kin selection). Social exchange theory would maintain that the dwarf's caregivers received sufficient rewards from their actions to outweigh the costs of caring for him. The empathy-altruism hypothesis would hold that the caregivers helped out of strong feelings of empathy and compassion for him—an interpretation supported by the article's final paragraph.

1991; Piliavin et al., 1981; Piliavin, Piliavin, & Rodin, 1975). Perhaps Abe Zelmanowitz, who stayed behind with his friend Ed Beyea in the World Trade Center, found the prospect of walking away and letting his friend die too distressing. Basically, social exchange theory argues that true altruism, in which people help even when doing so is costly to them, does not exist. People help when the benefits outweigh the costs.

I once saw a man out of courtesy help a lame dog over a stile, and [the dog] for requital bit his fingers.
—William Chillingworth

What seems to be generosity is often no more than disguised ambition.
—François de La Rochefoucauld, *Maxims*, 1665

If you are like many of our students, you may think this is an overly cynical view of human nature. Is true altruism, motivated only by the desire to help someone else, really such a mythical act? Must we trace all prosocial behavior, such as large charitable gifts made by wealthy individuals, to the self-interest of the helper? Well, a social exchange theorist might reply, there are many ways in which people can obtain gratification, and we should be thankful that one way is by helping others. After all, wealthy people could decide to get their pleasure only from lavish vacations, expensive cars, and meals at fancy restaurants. We should applaud their decision to give money to the disadvantaged, even if, ultimately, it is just a way for them to feel good about themselves. Prosocial acts are doubly rewarding in that they help both the giver and the recipient of the aid. Thus, it is to everyone's advantage to promote and praise such acts.

Still, many people are dissatisfied with the argument that all helping stems from self-interest. How can it explain why people give up their lives for others, as many of the heroes of September 11 did? According to some social psychologists, some people do have hearts of gold and sometimes help only for the sake of helping.

Empathy and Altruism: The Pure Motive for Helping

C. Daniel Batson (1991) is the strongest proponent of the idea that people often help purely out of the goodness of their hearts. Batson acknowledges that people sometimes help others for selfish reasons, such as to relieve their own distress at seeing another person suffer. But he also argues that people's motives are sometimes purely altruistic, in that their only goal is to help the other person, even if doing so involves some cost to them. Pure altruism is likely to come into play, he maintains, when we feel **empathy** for the person in need of help, putting ourselves in the shoes of another person and experiencing events and emotions the way that person experiences them (Batson, 2011; Batson, Ahmad, & Stocks, 2011).

Empathy

The ability to put oneself in the shoes of another person and to experience events and emotions (e.g., joy and sadness) the way that person experiences them

Helping behavior is common in virtually all species of animals, and sometimes it even crosses species lines. In August 1996, a 3-year-old boy fell into a pit containing seven gorillas, at the Brookfield, Illinois, zoo. Binti, a 7-year-old gorilla, immediately picked up the boy. After cradling him in her arms, she placed the boy near a door where zookeepers could get to him. Why did she help? Evolutionary psychologists would argue that prosocial behavior is selected for and thus becomes part of the genetic makeup of the members of many species. Social exchange theorists would argue that Binti had been rewarded for helping in the past. In fact, because she had been rejected by her mother, she had received training in parenting skills from zookeepers, in which she was rewarded for caring for a doll (Bils & Singer, 1996).

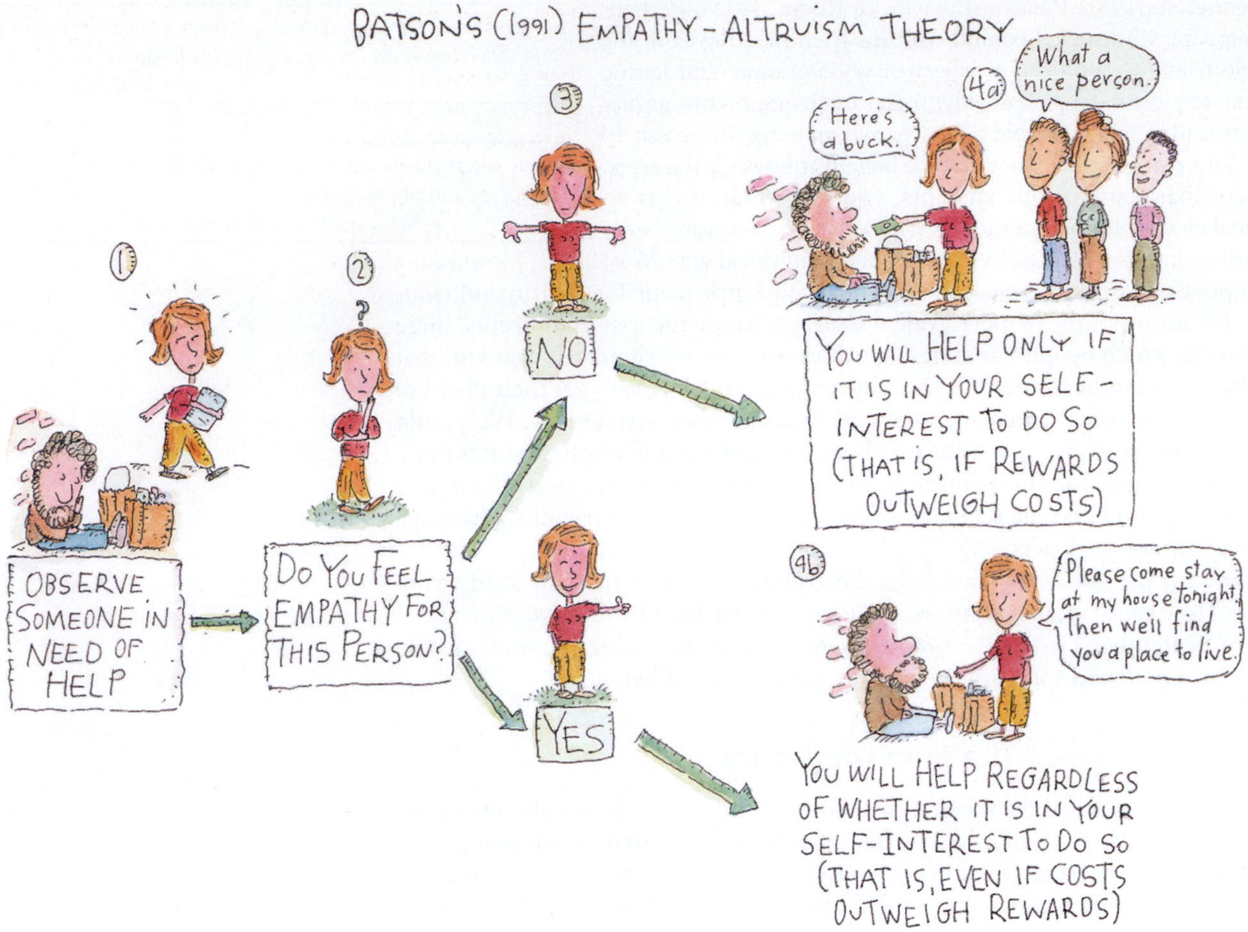

FIGURE 11.1
Empathy-Altruism Theory

Suppose that while you are food shopping, you see a man holding a baby and a bag full of diapers, toys, and rattles. As he reaches for a box of Wheat Chex, the man drops the bag, and everything spills onto the floor. Will you help him pick up his things? According to Batson, it depends first on whether you feel empathy for him. If you do, you will help, regardless of what you have to gain. Your goal will be to relieve the other person's distress, not to gain something for yourself. This is the crux of Batson's **empathy-altruism hypothesis**: When we feel empathy for another person, we will attempt to help that person for purely altruistic reasons, regardless of what we have to gain.

If you do not feel empathy, then, Batson says, social exchange concerns come into play. What's in it for you? If there is something to be gained, such as obtaining approval from the man or from onlookers, you will help the man pick up his things. If you will not profit from helping, you will go on your way without stopping. Batson's empathy-altruism hypothesis is summarized in Figure 11.1.

Batson and his colleagues would be the first to acknowledge that it can be very difficult to isolate the exact motives behind complex social behaviors. If you saw someone help the man pick up his possessions, how could you tell whether the person was acting out of empathic concern or to gain some sort of social reward? Consider a famous story about Abraham Lincoln. One day, while riding in a coach, Lincoln and a fellow passenger were debating the very question we are considering: Is helping ever truly altruistic? Lincoln argued that helping always stems from self-interest, whereas the other passenger took the view that true altruism exists. Suddenly, the men were interrupted by the screeching of a pig that was trying to save her piglets from drowning in a creek. Lincoln ordered the coach to stop, jumped out, ran down to the creek, and lifted the piglets to the safety of the bank. When he returned, his companion said, "Now, Abe, where does selfishness come in on this little episode?" "Why, bless your soul, Ed," Lincoln replied.

Empathy-Altruism Hypothesis

The idea that when we feel empathy for a person, we will attempt to help that person for purely altruistic reasons, regardless of what we have to gain

"That was the very essence of selfishness. I should have had no peace of mind all day had I gone on and left that suffering old sow worrying over those pigs. I did it to get peace of mind, don't you see?" (Sharp, 1928, p. 75).

As this example shows, an act that seems truly altruistic is sometimes motivated by self-interest. How, then, can we tell which is which? Batson and his colleagues have devised a series of clever experiments to unravel people's motives (Batson, Ahmad, & Stocks, 2004; Batson & Powell, 2003). Imagine that you were an introductory psychology student in one of these studies (Toi & Batson, 1982). You are asked to evaluate some tapes of new programs for the university radio station, one of which is called *News from the Personal Side.* There are lots of different pilot tapes for this program, and you are told that only one person will be listening to each tape. The one you hear is an interview with a student named Carol Marcy. She describes a bad automobile accident in which both of her legs were broken and talks about how hard it has been to keep up with her class work as a result of the accident, especially because she is still in a wheelchair. Carol says she is especially concerned about how far she has fallen behind in her Introductory Psychology class and mentions that she will have to drop the class unless she can find another student to tell her what she has missed.

It is one of the beautiful compensations of this life that no one can sincerely try to help another without helping himself.

—Charles Dudley Warner, 1873

After you listen to the tape, the experimenter hands you an envelope marked "To the student listening to the Carol Marcy pilot tape." The experimenter says she doesn't know what's in the envelope but was asked by the professor supervising the research to hand it out. You open the envelope and find a note from the professor, saying that he was wondering if the student who listened to Carol's tape would be willing to help her out with her psychology class. Carol was reluctant to ask for help, he says, but because she is so far behind in the class, she agreed to write a note to the person listening to her tape. The note asks if you could meet with her and share your Introductory Psychology lecture notes.

As you have probably guessed, the point of the study was to look at the conditions under which people agreed to help Carol. The researchers pitted two motives against each other: self-interest and empathy. They varied how much empathy people felt toward Carol by telling different participants to adopt different perspectives when listening to the tape. In the high-empathy condition, people were told to try to imagine how Carol felt about what had happened to her and how it had changed her life. In the low-empathy condition, people were told to try to be objective and not be concerned with how Carol felt. As expected, people in the high-empathy condition reported feeling more sympathy for Carol than people in the low-empathy condition did.

The researchers also varied how costly it would be *not* to help Carol. In one condition, participants learned that she would start coming back to class the following week and happened to be in the same psychology section as they were; thus, they would see her every time they went to class and would be reminded that she needed help. This was the high-cost condition because it would be unpleasant to refuse to help Carol and then run into her every week in class. In the low-cost condition, people learned that Carol would be studying at home and would not be coming to class; therefore, they would never have to face her in her wheelchair and feel guilty about not helping her.

When deciding whether to help Carol, did people take into account the costs involved? According to the empathy-altruism hypothesis, people should have been motivated purely by altruistic concerns and helped regardless of the costs—if empathy was high (see Figure 11.2). As you can see from the right side of Figure 11.2, this prediction was confirmed: In the high-empathy condition, about as many people agreed to help when they thought they would see Carol in class as when they thought they would not see her in class. This suggests that people had Carol's interests in mind and not their own. In the low-empathy condition, however, many more people agreed to help when they thought they would see Carol in class than when they thought they would not see her in class (see the left side of Figure 11.2). This suggests that when empathy was low, social exchange concerns came into play, in that people based their decision to help on the costs and benefits to themselves. They helped when it was in their interests to do so (i.e., when they would see Carol in her wheelchair and feel guilty for not helping), but not otherwise (i.e., when they thought they would never

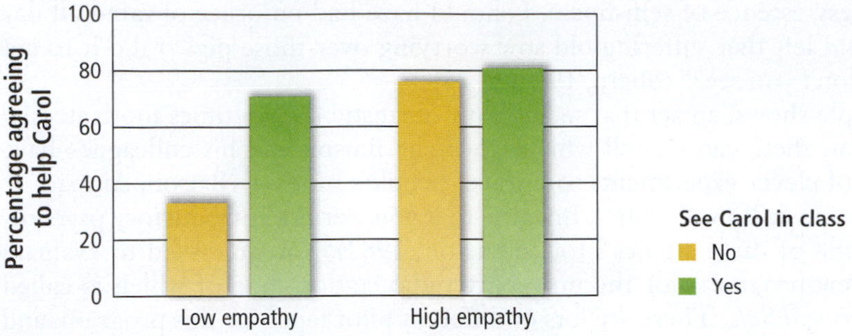

FIGURE 11.2

Altruism Versus Self-Interest

Under what conditions did people agree to help Carol with the work she missed in her introductory psychology class? When empathy was high, people helped regardless of the costs and rewards (i.e., regardless of whether they would encounter her in their psychology class). When empathy was low, people were more concerned with the rewards and costs for themselves—they helped only if they would encounter Carol in their psychology class and thus feel guilty about not helping.

(Adapted from Toi & Batson, 1982)

see her again). These results suggest that true altruism exists when people experience empathy toward the suffering of another.

To sum up, we've identified three basic motives underlying prosocial behavior:

1. Helping is an instinctive reaction to promote the welfare of those genetically similar to us (evolutionary psychology).
2. The rewards of helping often outweigh the costs, so helping is in our self-interest (social exchange theory).
3. Under some conditions, powerful feelings of empathy and compassion for the victim prompt selfless giving (the empathy-altruism hypothesis).

Each of these explanations has its supporters and critics.

Personal Qualities and Prosocial Behavior: Why Do Some People Help More Than Others?

On reflecting at dinner that he had done nothing to help anybody all day, he uttered these memorable and praiseworthy words: "Friends, I have lost a day."

—Suetonius, *Lives of the Twelve Caesars*, first century A.D.

If basic human motives are all there is to it, why are some people so much more helpful than others? Clearly, we need to consider the personal qualities that distinguish the helpful person from the selfish one.

Altruistic Personality

The qualities that cause an individual to help others in a wide variety of situations

Individual Differences: The Altruistic Personality

When you read the descriptions of the September 11 heroes at the beginning of this chapter, did you think about the personalities of the people we described? It is natural to assume that William Wik, Abe Zelmanowitz, Rick Rescorla, and the passengers of United flight 93 were cut from a different cloth—selfless, caring people who would never dream of ignoring someone's pleas for help. Psychologists have been interested in the nature of the **altruistic personality**, the qualities that cause an individual to help others in a wide variety of situations (Eisenberg, Spinrad, & Sadovsky, 2006; Mikulincer & Shaver, 2005; Penner & Orom, 2010).

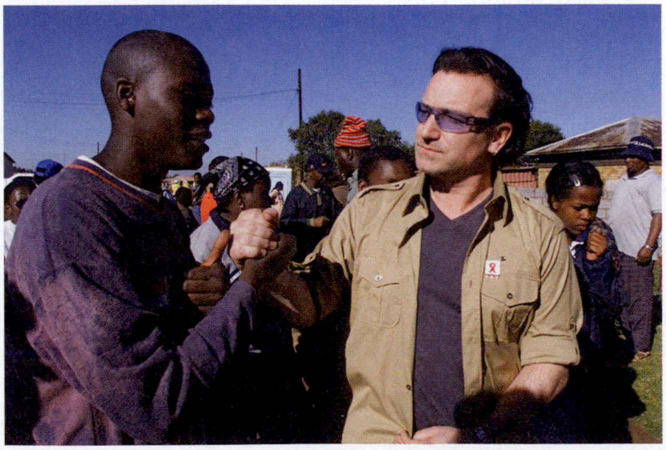

Clearly, some people have more of an altruistic personality than do others, causing them to engage in more prosocial behavior. Personality, however, is not the whole story; the nature of the social situation also determines whether people help.

Although some people are obviously more helpful than others, personality alone does not determine behavior—the pressures of the situation matter as well (as we have seen throughout this book). Predicting how helpful people will be is no exception. Studies of both children and adults, for example, find that people with high scores on personality tests of altruism are not that much more likely to help than those with lower scores (Batson, 1998; Magoo & Khanna, 1991; Piliavin & Charng, 1990). Why not? We need to consider several other critical factors as well, such as the situational pressures that are affecting people, their gender, the culture in which they grew up, how religious they are, and even their current mood (Graziano et al., 2007).

Whereas men are more likely to perform chivalrous and heroic acts, women are more likely to be helpful in long-term relationships that involve greater commitment.

Gender Differences in Prosocial Behavior

Consider two scenarios. In one, someone performs a dramatic, heroic act, like storming the cockpit of United flight 93 to fight the terrorists. In the other, someone is involved in a long-term helping relationship, such as assisting a disabled neighbor with chores around the house. Are men or women more likely to help in each situation?

The answer is males in the first situation and females in the second (Eagly, 2009; Eagly & Crowley, 1986; Eagly & Koenig, 2006). In virtually all cultures, norms prescribe different traits and behaviors for males and females, learned as boys and girls are growing up. In Western cultures, the male sex role includes being chivalrous and heroic; females are expected to be nurturing and caring and to value close, long-term relationships. Indeed, of the 7000 people who received medals from the Carnegie Hero Fund Commission for risking their lives to save a stranger, 91% have been men. In contrast, women are more likely than men to provide social support to their friends and to engage in volunteer work that involves helping others (Eagly & Koenig, 2006; McGuire, 1994; Monin, Clark, & Lemay, 2008). Cross-cultural evidence suggests the same pattern. In a survey of adolescents in seven countries, more girls than boys reported doing volunteer work in their communities (Flanagan et al., 1998).

Cultural Differences in Prosocial Behavior

Suppose you find out that a student at your university needs help because she lost all of her possession in a fire at her apartment building. She has no insurance and very little money, so a call goes out to donate to a fund to help her buy clothes and other necessities. Would you donate money? Well, let's take this example a little further: Suppose that in one case the student was very similar to you; she is of the same race and has a similar background. Alternatively, suppose that she is a member of a different cultural group. Perhaps you grew up in the United States and she is an international student, or vice versa. Would this make a difference in your willingness to help her?

On the one hand, there is ample evidence that people often favor their **in-groups**, or the groups with which they identify as a member, and discriminate against members of **out-groups**, defined as groups with which they do not identify. Indeed, as we will see in Chapter 13, there is a long history of discrimination and prejudice against out-group members, including those of other races, cultures, and genders, as well as people with different sexual orientations. But on the other hand, people often go out of their way to help out-group members. People donate to charities that help disadvantaged strangers and rise to the occasion when an individual is in need, even if he or she belongs to a different group.

Recent research resolves this conundrum. It turns out that people often do help both in-group and out-group members, but for different reasons. We are more likely to feel empathy toward members of our in-groups who are in need. Thus, if the student who lost her possessions in the apartment fire is a member of your in-group, you will probably feel empathy for her, and the more empathy you feel, the more likely you are to help. We tend to help out-group members for a different reason—we do so, to put it bluntly, when there is something in it for us, such as making us feel good about ourselves or making a good impression on others. Sound familiar? Recall that Batson's empathy-altruism theory posits two routes to helping others: When we feel empathy, we help regardless of whether there is something in it for us, but when we don't feel empathy, we help only if there is something in it for us (see Figure 11.1). Research on intergroup helping suggests that we are more likely to take the first route when the

In-Group
The group with which an individual identifies as a member

Out-Group
Any group with which an individual does not identify

person in need is an in-group member, but more likely to take the second route when the person in need is an out-group member (van Leeuwen & Täuber, 2010; Stürmer & Snyder, 2010).

More generally, are there differences in cultural values that make people in one culture more likely to help than people in another culture? One such value is *simpatía*. Prominent in Spanish-speaking countries, simpatía refers to a range of social and emotional traits, including being friendly, polite, good-natured, pleasant, and helpful toward others (interestingly, it has no direct English translation). One study tested the hypothesis that helping would be higher in cultures that value simpatía than in cultures that do not (Levine, 2003; Levine, Norenzayan, & Philbrick, 2001). The researchers staged helping incidents in large cities in 23 countries and observed what people did. In one scenario, for example, a researcher posing as a blind person stopped at a busy intersection and observed whether pedestrians offered help in crossing or informed the researcher when the light turned green.

If you look at Table 11.1, you'll see that the percentage of people who helped (averaged across the different incidents) in countries that value simpatía was higher than in countries that did not, 83% to 66%. The researchers noted that these results are only suggestive, because the five Latin American and Spanish countries differed from the others in ways other than the value they placed on simpatía. And some countries not known for their simpatía had high rates of helping. Nevertheless, if a culture strongly values friendliness and prosocial behavior, people may be more likely to help strangers on city streets (Janoff-Bulman & Leggatt, 2002).

Watch on MyPsychLab
To learn more about factors that influence helping behavior, watch the MyPsychLab video ***Private Battles***.

TABLE 11.1 Helping in Twenty-Three Cities

In 23 cities around the world, researchers observed how many people helped in three situations: helping a person with a leg brace who dropped a pile of magazines, helping someone who did not notice that he or she had dropped a pen, and helping a blind person across a busy intersection. The percentages in the table are averaged across the three situations. The cities in boldface are in countries that have the cultural value of *simpatía*, which prizes friendliness, politeness, and helping others.

City	Percent Helping
Rio de Janeiro, Brazil	**93**
San José, Costa Rica	**91**
Lilongwe, Malawi	86
Calcutta, India	83
Vienna, Austria	81
Madrid, Spain	**79**
Copenhagen, Denmark	78
Shanghai, China	77
Mexico City, Mexico	**76**
San Salvador, El Salvador	**75**
Prague, Czech Republic	75
Stockholm, Sweden	72
Budapest, Hungary	71
Bucharest, Romania	69
Tel Aviv, Israel	68
Rome, Italy	63
Bangkok, Thailand	61
Taipei, Taiwan	59
Sofia, Bulgaria	57
Amsterdam, Netherlands	54
Singapore	48
New York, United States	45
Kuala Lumpur, Malaysia	40

(Adapted from Levine, Norenzayan, & Philbrick, 2001)

Religion and Prosocial Behavior

Most religions teach some version of the Golden Rule, urging us to do unto others as we would have others do unto us. Are religious people more likely to follow this advice than nonreligious people? That is, does religion foster prosocial behavior? The answer is yes in some ways but not all (Preston, Ritter, & Hernandez, 2010). People who attend religious services report on surveys that they give more money to charity and engage in more volunteer work than do people who do not attend religious services (Brooks, 2006). When it comes to what people actually do, however—not just what they report on surveys—the story is a little more complicated. Religious people are more likely to help (e.g., raising money for a sick child) in situations in which helping makes them look good to themselves or others. They are not more likely to help, however, in private situations in which no one will know that they helped (Batson, Schoenrade, & Ventis, 1993). In terms of Batson's empathy-altruism hypothesis, which we discussed earlier, religious people do not appear to feel more empathy toward others, though they are more likely to help when it is in their best interests to do so (Norenzayan & Shariff, 2008).

The Effects of Mood on Prosocial Behavior

Imagine that you are at your local shopping mall. As you walk from one store to another, a fellow in front of you drops a manila folder and papers go fluttering in all directions. He looks around in dismay, then bends down and starts picking up the papers. Would you stop and help him? The answer might depend on what your current mood happens to be.

Effects of Positive Moods: Feel Good, Do Good In a classic study, researchers wanted to see whether people's mood influenced shoppers' likelihood of helping a stranger, much like the example we just gave (Isen & Levin, 1972). To find out, they temporarily boosted some shoppers' moods in a clever way—they left dimes in the coin-return slot of a public telephone at the mall and then waited for someone to find the coins. (Note the year this study was done; there were no cell phones, so people relied on pay phones. Also, 10 cents then would be like finding 50 cents today.) As the lucky shoppers left the phone with their newly found dime, a research assistant played the role of the man with the manila folder. He intentionally dropped the folder a few feet in front of the shopper to see whether he or she would stop and help him pick up his papers. It turned out that finding the dime had a dramatic effect on helping. Only 4% of the people who did not find a dime helped the man pick up his papers, whereas a whopping 84% of the people who found a dime stopped to help.

This "feel good, do good" effect has been replicated many times with different ways of boosting people's moods (including doing well on a test, receiving a gift, thinking happy thoughts, and listening to pleasant music; North, Tarrant, & Hargreaves, 2004) and with many different kinds of helping (including contributing money to charity, helping someone find a lost contact lens, tutoring another student, donating blood, and helping coworkers on the job; Carlson, Charlin, & Miller, 1988; Isen, 1999; Kayser et al., 2010).

Being in a good mood can increase helping for three reasons. First, good moods make us look on the bright side of life. That is, when we're in a good mood, we tend to see the good side of other people, giving them the benefit of the doubt. A victim who might normally seem clumsy or annoying will, when we are feeling cheerful, seem like a decent, needy person who is worthy of our help (Carlson et al., 1988; Forgas & Bower, 1987). Second, helping other people is an excellent way of prolonging our good mood. If we see someone who needs help, then being a Good Samaritan spawns even more good feelings, and we can walk away feeling terrific. In comparison, not helping when we know we should is a surefire "downer," deflating our good mood (Clark & Isen, 1982; Isen, 1987; Lyubomirsky, Sheldon, & Schkade, 2005). (See the following Try It! for another example of how helping others improves our moods.) Finally, good moods increase the amount of attention we pay to ourselves, and this factor in turn makes us more likely to behave according to our values and ideals (see Chapter 3). Because most of us value altruism and because good moods increase our attention to this value, good

TRY IT! Do Good, Feel Good?

Suppose you found a $20 bill on the ground and could spend it on yourself (e.g., buy yourself a nice lunch) or on someone else (e.g., treat a friend to lunch). Which would you rather do? If your goal is to improve your mood, the answer might surprise you—spend it on your friend! Research by Dunn, Aknin, and Norton (2008) found that people who spent money on others were happier than people who spent money on themselves. Try this yourself the next time you have a little extra money. Rather than buying yourself a treat, try treating a friend or donating the money to charity. You might be surprised by how good you feel!

moods increase helping behavior (Berkowitz, 1987; Carlson et al., 1988; Salovey & Rodin, 1985).

Feel Bad, Do Good What about when we are in a bad mood? Suppose that when you saw the fellow in the mall drop his folder, you were feeling down. Would this influence the likelihood that you would help the man pick up his papers? One kind of bad mood clearly leads to an increase in helping: feeling guilty (Baumeister, Stillwell, & Heatherton, 1994; Estrada-Hollenbeck & Heatherton, 1998). People often act on the idea that good deeds cancel out bad deeds. When they have done something that has made them feel guilty, helping another person balances things out, reducing their guilty feelings. For example, one study found that Catholic churchgoers were more likely to donate money to charities before attending confession than afterward, presumably because confessing to a priest reduced their guilt (Harris, Benson, & Hall, 1975). Thus, if you just realized you had forgotten your best friend's birthday and you felt guilty about it, you would be more likely to help the fellow in the mall, to repair your guilty feelings.

If you want others to be happy, practice compassion. If you want to be happy, practice compassion.
—The Dalai Lama

But suppose you were feeling sad because you just had a fight with a friend or just found out you did poorly on a test. Given that feeling happy leads to greater helping, it might seem that feeling sad would decrease helping. Surprisingly, however, sadness can also lead to an increase in helping (Carlson & Miller, 1987; Kayser et al., 2010). When people are sad, they are motivated to engage in activities that make them feel better (Cialdini & Fultz, 1990; Cialdini et al., 1987; Wegener & Petty, 1994). To the extent that helping is rewarding, it can lift us out of the doldrums.

Situational Determinants of Prosocial Behavior: When Will People Help?

Personality, gender, culture, and mood all contribute a piece to the puzzle of why people help others, but they do not complete the picture. To understand more fully why people help, we also need to consider the social situation in which people find themselves.

Environment: Rural Versus Urban

Here's another helping scenario for you. Suppose you are walking down the street one day when you see a man suddenly fall down and cry out with pain. He rolls up his pants leg, revealing a bandaged shin that is bleeding heavily. What would you do? When this event was staged in small towns, about half the people who walked by stopped and offered to help the man. In large cities, only 15% of passersby stopped to help (Amato, 1983). Other studies have found that people in small towns are more likely to help when asked to find a lost child, give directions, and return a lost letter. Helping has been found to be more prevalent in small towns in several countries, including the United States, Canada, Israel, Australia, Turkey, Great Britain, and the Sudan (Hedge & Yousif, 1992; Steblay, 1987).

Do not wait for extraordinary circumstances to do good actions; try to use ordinary situations.
—John Paul Richter, 1763

People are less helpful in big cities than in small towns, not because of a difference in values, but because the stress of urban life causes them to keep to themselves.

Why are people more likely to help in small towns? One possibility is that people who grow up in a small town are more likely to internalize altruistic values. If this were the case, people who grew up in small towns would be more likely to help, even if they were visiting a big city. Alternatively, the immediate surroundings might be the key and not people's internalized values. Stanley Milgram (1970), for example, suggested that people living in cities are constantly bombarded with stimulation and that they keep to themselves in order to avoid being overwhelmed by it. According to this **urban overload hypothesis**, if you put urban dwellers in a calmer, less stimulating environment, they would be as likely as anyone else to reach out to others. Research has supported the urban overload hypothesis more than the idea that living in cities makes people less altruistic by nature. To predict whether people will help, it is more important to know whether they are currently in a rural or urban area than it is to know where they happened to grow up (Levine et al., 1994; Steblay, 1987).

Residential Mobility

In the United States, a man will carefully construct a home in which to spend his old age and sell it before the roof is on. . . . He will settle in one place only to go off elsewhere shortly afterwards with a new set of desires.
—ALEXIS DE TOCQUEVILLE, 1835

It is not only where you live that matters, but how often you have moved from one place to another. In many areas of the world, it is common for people to move far away from where they were raised (Hochstadt, 1999). In the year 2000, for example, nearly one in five Americans (18%) were living in a different state than they were in 1995 ("Migration and Geographic Mobility," 2003), and in many urban areas, fewer than half of the residents were living in the same house as they were in 1995 (Oishi et al., 2007). As it turns out, people who have lived for a long time in one place are more likely to engage in prosocial behaviors that help the community. Residing in one place leads to a greater attachment to the community, more interdependence with one's neighbors, and a greater concern with one's reputation in the community (Baumeister, 1986; Oishi, 2010). For all these reasons, long-time residents are more likely to engage in prosocial behaviors. Shigehiro Oishi and colleagues (2007), for example, found that people who had lived for a long time in the Minneapolis-St. Paul area were more likely to purchase "critical habitat" license plates, compared to people who had recently moved to the area. (These license plates cost an extra $30 a year and provide funds for the state to purchase and manage natural habitats.)

Perhaps it is not surprising that people who have lived in one place for years feel more of a stake in their community. Oishi and his colleagues (2007) also found, though, that this increase in helping can arise quite quickly, even in a one-time laboratory setting. Imagine that you are in a study in which you are playing a trivia contest against four other students, where the winner will win a $10 gift certificate. The experimenter says that people in the group can help each other if they want, but that doing so might lower the helper's chances of winning the prize. As the game progresses, one of your

Urban Overload Hypothesis
The theory that people living in cities are constantly bombarded with stimulation and that they keep to themselves to avoid being overwhelmed by it

fellow group members keeps sighing and commenting that he doesn't know the answers to the questions. Would you offer him some help or let him continue to struggle on his own?

The answer, it turns out, depends on how long you have been in the group with the struggling student. The study by Oishi and colleagues involved a total of four tasks; the trivia contest was the last one. Half of the participants remained together and worked on all the tasks throughout the study, whereas the other half switched to a new group after each task. Thus, in the former condition people had more of an opportunity to get to know each other and form a sense of community, whereas the latter group was more analogous to moving from one community to another. As the researchers predicted, people in the "stable community" condition were more likely to help their struggling companion than were people in the "transient" group condition. Another reason that people might be less helpful in big cities, then, is that residential mobility is higher in cities than in rural areas. People are more likely to have just moved to a city and thus feel less of a stake in the community.

The Number of Bystanders: The Bystander Effect

Remember Kitty Genovese? We have just seen one reason why her neighbors turned a deaf ear to her cries for help: The murder took place in New York City, one of the most densely populated areas in the world. Perhaps her neighbors had moved to the city recently, or maybe they were so overloaded with urban stimulation that they dismissed Genovese's cries as one small addition to the surrounding din. Although it is true that people help less in urban environments, that isn't the only reason Genovese's neighbors failed to help. Her desperate cries surely must have risen above the everyday noises of garbage trucks and car horns. And there have been cases where people ignored the pleas of their neighbors even in small towns. In Fredericksburg, Virginia, a convenience store clerk was beaten in front of customers, who did nothing to help, even after the assailant had fled and the clerk lay bleeding on the floor (Hsu, 1995). Fredericksburg and its surrounding county have only about 150,000 residents. Nor are such incidents limited to the United States, as we noted in Chapter 2. In October of 2011 in Southern China, a 2-year-old girl was hit by two different vans, minutes apart, and lay in the street dying. Neither van stopped, and a dozen people walked or rode past the girl without stopping to help her (Branigan, 2011).

Bibb Latané and John Darley (1970) are two social psychologists who taught at universities in New York at the time of the Genovese murder. As we discussed in Chapter 2, they too were unconvinced that the only reason her neighbors failed to help was the stresses and stimulation of urban life. They focused on the fact that so many people heard her cries. Paradoxically, they thought, it might be that the greater the number of bystanders who observe an emergency, the less likely any one of them is to help. As Latané (1987) put it, "We came up with the insight that perhaps what made the Genovese case so fascinating was itself what made it happen—namely, that not just one or two, but thirty-eight people had watched and done nothing" (p. 78). We should note that some of the details of the Kitty Genovese story have been questioned, such as whether there really were 38 people who heard her cries and whether no one helped (Manning, Levine, & Collins, 2007). That was the story of the murder at the time, however, and the account that inspired Latané and Darley's research.

In a series of now-classic experiments, Latané and Darley (1970) found that in terms of receiving help, there is no safety in numbers. Think back to the seizure experiment we discussed in Chapter 2. In that study, people sat in individual cubicles, participating in a group discussion of college life (over an intercom system) with students in other cubicles. One of the other students suddenly had a seizure, crying out for help, choking, and finally falling silent. There was actually only one real participant in the study. The other "participants," including the one who had the seizure, were prerecorded voices. The point of the study was to see whether the real participant would attempt to help the seizure victim by trying to find him or by summoning the experimenter or whether, like Kitty Genovese's neighbors, the person would simply sit there and do nothing.

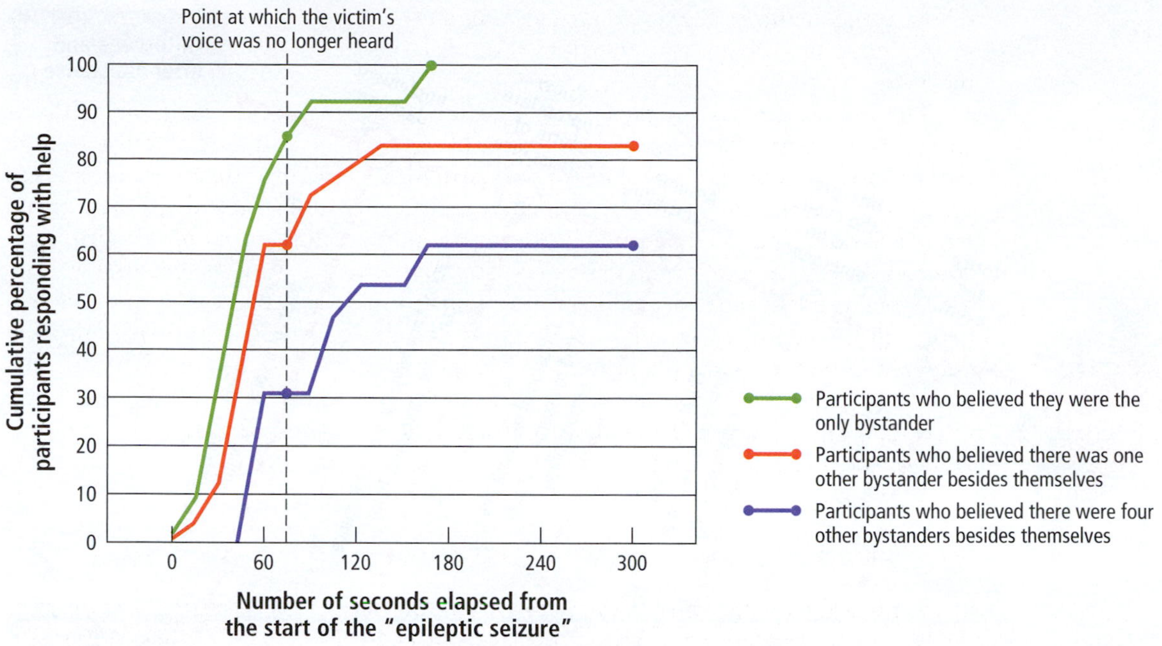

FIGURE 11.3

Bystander Intervention: The Presence of Bystanders Reduces Helping

When people believed they were the only one witnessing a student having a seizure, when they were the lone bystander, most of them helped him immediately, and all did so within a few minutes. When they believed that someone else was listening as well, that there were two bystanders, they were less likely to help and did so more slowly. And when they believed that four others were listening, that there were five bystanders, they were even less likely to help.

(Adapted from Darley & Latané, 1968)

As Latané and Darley anticipated, the answer depended on how many people the participant thought witnessed the emergency. When people believed they were the only ones listening to the student having the seizure, most of them (85%) helped within 60 seconds. By 2 1/2 minutes, 100% of the people who thought they were the only bystander had offered assistance (see Figure 11.3). In comparison, when the research participants believed there was one other student listening, fewer helped—only 62% within 60 seconds. As you can see in Figure 11.3, helping occurred more slowly when there were two bystanders and never reached 100%, even after 6 minutes, when the experiment was ended. Finally, when the participants believed there were four other students listening in addition to themselves, the percentage of people who helped dropped even more dramatically. Only 31% helped in the first 60 seconds, and after 6 minutes only 62% had offered help. Dozens of other studies, conducted in the laboratory and in the field, have found the same thing: The greater the number of bystanders who witness an emergency, the less likely any one of them is to help the victim—a phenomenon called the **bystander effect** (Fischer et al., 2011).

Why is it that people are less likely to help when others are present? Latané and Darley (1970) developed a five-step description of how people decide whether to intervene in an emergency (see Figure 11.4). Part of this description is an explanation of how the number of bystanders can make a difference. But let's begin with the first step—whether people notice that someone needs help.

Noticing an Event If you are hurrying down a crowded street, you might not notice that someone has collapsed in a doorway. Obviously, if people don't notice that an emergency situation exists, they will not intervene and offer to help. What determines whether people notice an emergency? John Darley and Daniel Batson (1973) demonstrated that something as seemingly trivial as how much of a hurry people are in can make more of a difference than what kind of people they are. These researchers conducted a study that mirrored the parable of the Good Samaritan, wherein many

Bystander Effect

The finding that the greater the number of bystanders who witness an emergency, the less likely any one of them is to help

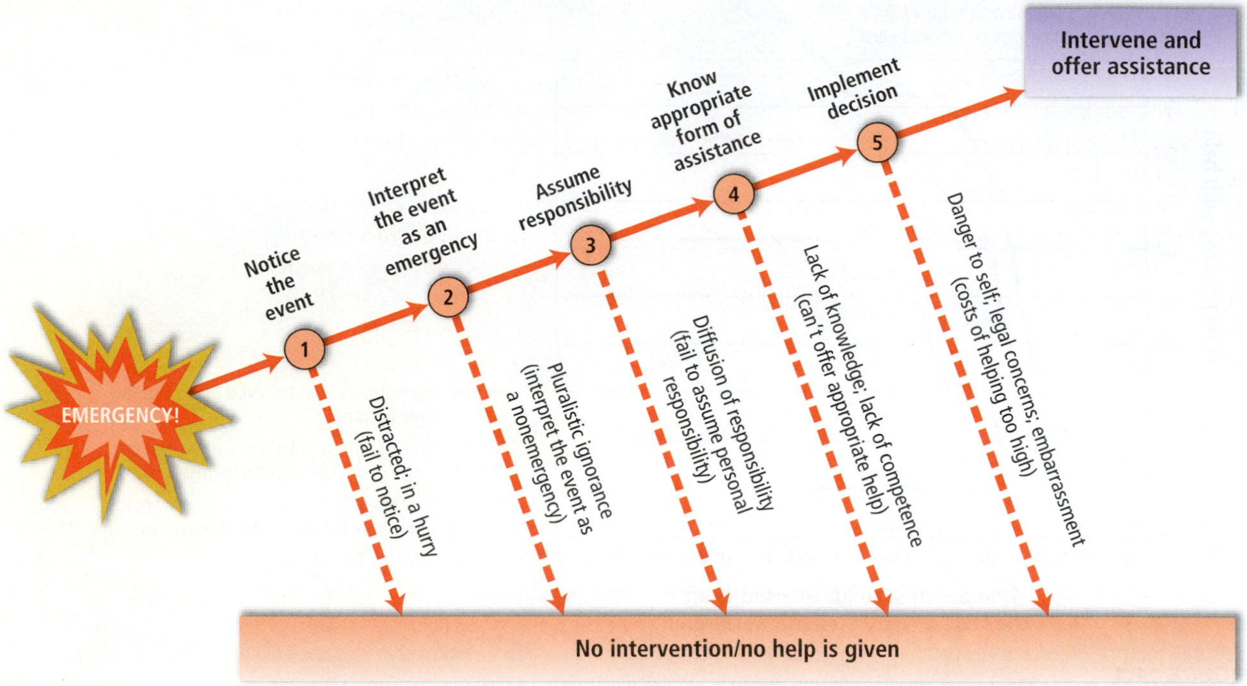

FIGURE 11.4

Bystander Intervention Decision Tree: Five Steps to Helping in an Emergency

Latané and Darley (1970) showed that people go through five decision-making steps before they help someone in an emergency. If bystanders fail to take any one of the five steps, they will not help. Each step is outlined here, along with the possible reasons why people decide not to intervene.

(Adapted from Latané & Darley, 1970)

passersby failed to stop to help a man lying unconscious at the side of the road. The research participants were people we might think would be extremely altruistic—seminary students preparing to devote their lives to the ministry. The students were asked to walk to another building, where the researchers would record them making a brief speech. Some were told that they were late and should hurry to keep their appointment. Others were told that there was no rush because the assistant in the other building was running a few minutes behind schedule. As they walked to the other building, each of the students passed a man who was slumped in a doorway. The man (an accomplice of the experimenters) coughed and groaned as each student walked by. Did the seminary students stop and offer to help him? If they were not in a hurry, most of them (63%) did. If they were hurrying to keep their appointment, however, only 10% stopped to help. Many of the students who were in a hurry did not even notice the man.

Surely if people were deeply religious, they would be less influenced by such a small matter as how hurried they were. Surprisingly, though, Darley and Batson (1973) found that the seminary students who were the most religious were no more likely to help than those who were the least religious. What about if they were thinking about helping people in need? The researchers also varied the topic of the speech they asked the students to give. Some were asked to discuss the kinds of jobs seminary students preferred; others were asked to discuss the parable of the Good Samaritan. You might think that seminary students who were thinking about the parable of the Good Samaritan would be especially likely to stop and help a man slumped in a doorway, given the similarity of this incident to the parable, but the topic of the speech made little difference in whether they helped. Students in a hurry were unlikely to help, even if they were very religious and about to give a speech about the Good Samaritan.

Interpreting the Event as an Emergency Even if people do notice someone slumped in a doorway, they might not stop and help. The next determinant of helping is whether the bystander interprets the event as an emergency—as a situation where help is needed (see Figure 11.4). Is the person in the doorway drunk or seriously ill? If we see white smoke coming out of a vent, is it something innocuous, such as mist from an air conditioner, or a sign that the building is on fire? Did that scream we just heard come from someone having a good time at a party, or is someone being attacked? If people assume that nothing is wrong when an emergency is taking place, they will not help.

When other bystanders are present, people are more likely to assume that an emergency is something innocuous. To understand why, think back to our discussion of informational social influence in Chapter 8. This type of social influence occurs when we use other people to help us define reality. When we are uncertain about what's going on, such as whether the smoke we see is a sign of a fire, one of the first things we do is look around to see how other people are responding. If other people look up, shrug, and go about their business, we are likely to assume that there is nothing to worry about. If other people look panic-stricken and yell, "Fire!" we immediately assume the building is indeed on fire. As we saw in Chapter 8, it's often a good strategy to use other people as a source of information when we are uncertain about what's going on. The danger is that sometimes no one is sure what is happening. Because an emergency is often a sudden and confusing event, bystanders tend to freeze, watching and listening with blank expressions as they try to figure out what is happening. When they glance at each other, they see an apparent lack of concern on the part of everyone else. This results in a state of **pluralistic ignorance**, wherein people think that everyone else is interpreting a situation in a certain way, when in fact they are not. When an emergency occurs, for example, bystanders often assume that nothing is wrong because no one else looks concerned—even though everyone is worried and concerned.

Consider another classic experiment by Latané and Darley (1970). You are participating in a study of people's attitudes toward the problems of urban life, and you arrive at the appointed time. A sign tells you to fill out a questionnaire while you're waiting for the study to begin, so you take a seat and get started. Then you notice something odd: White smoke is trickling into the room through a small vent in the wall. Before long, the room is so filled with smoke that you can barely see the questionnaire. What will you do?

In fact, there was no real danger—the experimenters were pumping smoke into the room to see how people would respond to this potential emergency. Not surprisingly, when people were alone, most of them took action. Within 2 minutes, 50% of the participants left the room and found the experimenter down the hall, reporting that there may have been a fire in the building; by 6 minutes, 75% of the participants had left the room to alert the experimenter.

But what would happen if people were not alone? Given that 75% of the participants who were by themselves reported the smoke, it would seem that the larger the group, the greater the likelihood that someone would report the smoke. In fact, this can be figured mathematically: If there is a 75% chance that any one person will report the smoke, then there is a 98% chance that at least one person in a three-person group will do so.

To find out if there really is safety in numbers, Latané and Darley (1970) included a condition in which three participants took part at the same time. Everything was identical except that three people sat in the room as the smoke began to seep in. Surprisingly, in only 12% of the three-person groups did someone report the smoke within 2 minutes, and in only 38% of the groups did someone report the smoke within 6 minutes. In the remaining groups, the participants sat there filling out questionnaires even when they had to wave away the smoke with their hands to see what they were writing. What went wrong?

Unsure whether the smoke signaled an emergency, participants used each other as a source of information. If the people next to you glance at the smoke and then continue filling out their questionnaires, you will feel reassured that nothing is wrong; otherwise, why would they be acting so unconcerned? The problem is that they are probably looking at you as well, and if you seem untroubled, they too are reassured that everything is OK. In short, each group member is reassured because they assume that

Pluralistic Ignorance
The case in which people think that everyone else is interpreting a situation in a certain way, when in fact they are not

Emergency situations can be confusing. Does this man need help? Have the bystanders failed to notice him, or has the behavior of the others led each of them to interpret the situation as a nonemergency—an example of pluralistic ignorance?

everyone else knows more about what's going on than they do. And when the event is ambiguous—as when smoke is coming from a vent—people in groups will convince each other that nothing is wrong (Clark & Word, 1972; Solomon, Solomon, & Stone, 1978).

Assuming Responsibility Sometimes it is obvious that an emergency is occurring, as when Kitty Genovese cried out, "Oh my God, he stabbed me! Please help me! Please help me!" (Rosenthal, 1964, p. 33). Genovese's neighbors must have believed that something terrible was happening and that she desperately needed help. That they did nothing indicates that even if we interpret an event as an emergency, we have to decide that it is *our* responsibility, not someone else's, to do something about it. Here again the number of bystanders is a crucial variable.

Think back to the Latané and Darley (1968) seizure experiment in which participants believed they were the only one listening to the student while he had a seizure. The responsibility was totally on their shoulders. If they didn't help, no one would, and the student might die. As a result, in this condition most people helped almost immediately, and all helped within a few minutes.

But what happens when there are many witnesses? A **diffusion of responsibility** occurs: Each bystander's sense of responsibility to help decreases as the number of witnesses increases. Because other people are present, no single bystander feels a strong personal responsibility to act. Recall from our earlier discussion that helping often entails costs: We might be putting ourselves in danger or end up looking foolish by overreacting or doing the wrong thing. Why should we risk these costs when many other people who can help are present? The problem is that everyone is likely to feel the same way, making all the bystanders less likely to help. This is particularly true if people cannot tell whether someone else has already intervened. When participants in the seizure experiment believed that other students were witnesses as well, they couldn't tell whether another student had already helped, because the intercom system allowed only the voice of the student having the seizure to be transmitted. Each student probably assumed that he or she did not have to help, thinking that surely someone else had already done so. Similarly, Kitty Genovese's neighbors had no way of knowing whether someone else had called the police. Most likely, they assumed that there was no need to do so, as someone else had already made the call. Tragically, everyone thought it was somebody else's responsibility to act, and Genovese was left to fight her assailant alone. The sad irony of Genovese's murder is that she probably would be alive today if fewer people had heard her cries for help.

Knowing How to Help Even if people have made it this far in the helping sequence, another condition must still be met (Step 4 in Figure 11.4): They must decide what kind of help is appropriate. Suppose that on a hot summer day you see a woman collapse in the street. No one else seems to be helping, so you decide it is up to you. But what should you do? Has the woman had a heart attack? Is she suffering from heatstroke? Should you call an ambulance, administer CPR, or try to get her out of the sun? If people don't know what form of assistance to give, obviously they will be unable to help.

Deciding to Implement the Help Finally, even if you know exactly what kind of help is appropriate, there are still reasons why you might decide not to intervene. For one thing, you might not be qualified to deliver the right kind of help. Even if the woman is complaining of chest pains, indicating a heart attack, you may not know how to give her CPR. Or you might be afraid of making a fool of yourself, of doing the wrong thing and making matters worse, or even of placing yourself in danger by trying to help. Consider the fate of three television network technicians who in 1982 saw a man beating a woman in a New York parking lot, tried to intervene, and were shot and killed by the assailant. Even when we know what kind of intervention is needed, we have to weigh the costs of trying to help.

Diffusion of Responsibility

The phenomenon wherein each bystander's sense of responsibility to help decreases as the number of witnesses increases

What about helping in situations that are not emergencies? The Latané and Darley model applies here as well. Consider an Internet chat room in which someone needs help figuring out how to use the software. Are people less likely to help each other as the number of people in the chat room increases? Researchers in one study entered chat groups on Yahoo! Chat where 2 to 19 people were discussing a wide variety of topics (Markey, 2000). The researchers posed as either a male or female participant and typed this request for help: "Can anyone tell me how to look at someone's profile?" (p. 185). The message was addressed either to the group as a whole or to one randomly selected person in the chat room. Then the researchers timed how long it took someone in the group to respond to the request for help.

When the request was addressed to the group as a whole, Latané and Darley's results were replicated closely: The more people there were in the chat room, the longer it took for anyone to respond to the request for help. But when the request was directed to a specific person, that person responded quickly, regardless of the size of the group. These results suggest that the diffusion of responsibility was operating. When a general request for help is made, a large group makes people feel that they do not have much responsibility to respond. When addressed by name, though, people are more likely to feel a responsibility to help, even when many others are present.

Even if people are by themselves, however, they can still experience a diffusion of responsibility. In a recent study, people who were asked to think about going out to dinner with 10 friends were less likely to donate money to charity or volunteer to help with another experiment than were people who were asked to think about going out to dinner with one friend (Garcia et al., 2002). Simply imagining ourselves in a group is enough to make us feel less responsible for helping others.

Simulate on **MyPsychLab**
To explore the bystander effect, try the MyPsychLab simulation ***Helping a Stranger***.

The Nature of the Relationship: Communal Versus Exchange Relationships

A great deal of research on prosocial behavior has looked at helping between strangers, such as Latané and Darley's research on bystander intervention. Although this research is very important, most helping in everyday life occurs between people who know each other well, such as family members and close friends. In Chapter 10, we distinguished between communal and exchange relationships. *Communal relationships* are those in which people's primary concern is the welfare of the other person (e.g., a child), whereas *exchange relationships* are governed by concerns about equity—that what you put into the relationship equals what you get out of it. How does helping occur in communal relationships?

Margaret Clark and Judson Mills (Clark & Mills, 2011) argue that people in communal relationships are concerned less with the benefits they will receive by helping and more with simply satisfying the needs of the other person. When parents are deciding whether to help their children, for example, they seldom think, "Well, what have they done for me lately?" Unlike in exchange relationships, where people are concerned with what they are getting in return from other people, in communal relationships people are more concerned with the welfare of the other person.

In communal relationships, such as those between parents and their children, people are concerned less with who gets what and more with how much help the other person needs.

Does this mean that people are more helpful toward friends than strangers? Yes—at least under most circumstances. We are more likely to have communal relationships with friends and are therefore more likely to help even when there is nothing in it for us. In fact, we like to help a partner in a communal relationship more than a partner in an exchange relationship (Williamson et al., 1996). There is, however, an interesting exception to this rule. Research by Abraham Tesser (1988) on self-esteem maintenance has shown that when a task is not important to us, we do indeed help friends more than strangers. But suppose that the most important thing in the world for you is to be a doctor, that you are struggling to pass a difficult premed physics course, and that two other people in the class—your best friend and a complete stranger—ask you to lend them your notes from a class they missed. According to Tesser's research, you will be more inclined to help the stranger than your friend (Tesser, 1991; Tesser & Smith, 1980). Why? Because it hurts to see a close friend do better than we do in an area of great importance to our self-esteem. Consequently, we are less likely to help a friend in these important areas than in areas we don't care as much about. To test hypotheses about helping behavior, see the Try It! on the next page.

Effects of the Media: Video Games and Music Lyrics

When we think about the effects of the media on behavior, we usually think about negative influences, such as whether violence on television or playing violent video games makes people more aggressive. There are indeed such negative effects, which we discuss in Chapter 12. But can the opposite also occur, such that seeing people act in prosocial ways or playing prosocial video games makes people more cooperative? Recent research suggests that it can.

Tobias Greitemeyer and his colleagues have conducted a number of studies that follow the same procedure: First, participants come into the lab and play a video game for about 10 minutes. Half are randomly assigned to play a game that involves prosocial acts, such as *Lemmings*, in which the goal is to care for a group of small beings and save them by helping them find the exit out of different worlds. The other half play a neutral video game such as *Tetris*, where the goal is to rotate falling geometric figures so that they cover the bottom of the screen. Participants then take part in what they think is an unrelated study, in which they are given the opportunity to help someone. The helping opportunities include relatively easy actions such as helping an experimenter pick up a cup of pencils that he or she accidentally knocked over, more time-consuming commitments such as volunteering to participate in future studies without compensation; and potentially dangerous actions such as helping a female experimenter when an ex-boyfriend enters the room and starts harassing her. As seen in Figure 11.5, people who had just played a prosocial video game were more likely to help in all of these ways than were people who had just played a neutral video game (Greitemeyer & Osswald, 2010).

It isn't just prosocial video games that can make people more helpful—listening to songs with prosocial lyrics works too. Studies have found that people who listen to such songs, such as Michael Jackson's *Heal the World* or the Beatles' *Help*, are more likely to help someone than people who listened to songs with neutral lyrics such as the Beatles' *Octopus's Garden* (Greitemeyer, 2009, 2011; North, Tarrant, & Hargreaves, 2004).

Why does playing a prosocial video game or listening to prosocial song lyrics make people more cooperative? It works in at least two ways: by increasing people's empathy toward someone in need of help and increasing the accessibility of thoughts about helping others (Greitemeyer,

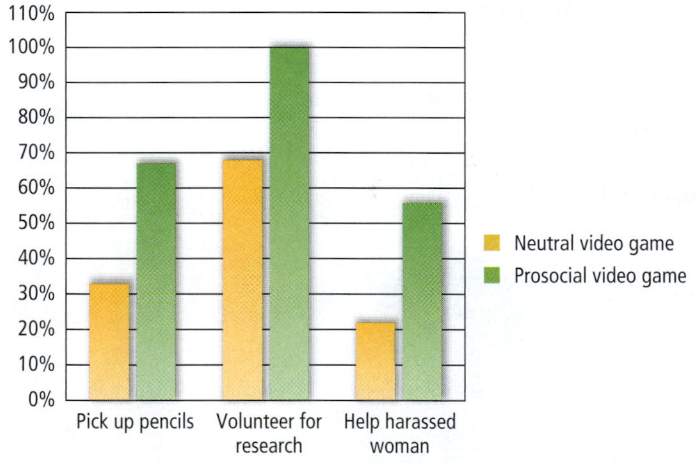

FIGURE 11.5

Effects of Playing Prosocial Video Games on the Likelihood of Helping

Participants played a prosocial video game (such as *Lemmings*) or a neutral video game (such as *Tetris*). Then, as part of what they thought was another study, they were given the opportunity to help in some way. In one study, an experimenter accidentally knocked over a jar of pencils and the researchers observed how many participants helped him or her pick them up. In another, participants were asked to volunteer to take part in future studies for no compensation. In a third, the researchers staged an event where the experimenter's ex-boyfriend charged into the room and tried to force her to leave with him. The researchers observed how many participants tried to help the experimenter in some way. As seen in the graph, playing a prosocial video game increased the likelihood that people helped in all of these situations.

(Adapted from Greitemeyer & Osswald, 2010)

TRY IT! The Lost-Letter Technique

Here's a simple technique you can use to test your own hypotheses about prosocial behavior. This procedure, called the "lost-letter technique," involves leaving stamped envelopes on the ground and seeing whether people pick them up and mail them. Stanley Milgram (1969), who first used this technique, found that people were more likely to mail letters addressed to organizations they supported. For example, 72% of letters addressed to "Medical Research Associates" were mailed, whereas only 25% of letters addressed to "Friends of the Nazi Party" were mailed (all were addressed to the same post office box so that Milgram could count how many were returned).

You can use the lost-letter technique to test some of the hypotheses about helping behavior that we have discussed in this chapter or hypotheses that you come up with on your own. Put your address on the letters so that you can count how many are returned, but vary where you put the letters or to whom they are addressed. For example, drop some letters in a small town and some in an urban area, to see whether people in small towns are more likely to mail them (be sure to mark the envelopes in some way that will let you know where they were dropped—e.g., put a little pencil mark on the back of the ones dropped in small towns). Did you replicate the finding of previous studies that people living in small towns are more likely to mail the letters (Bridges & Coady, 1996; Hansson & Slade, 1977)? Or you might vary the ethnicity of the name of the person on the address to see if people are more likely to help members of some ethnic groups more than others. Be creative!

After deciding what you want to vary (e.g., the ethnicity or gender of the addressee), be careful to place envelopes of both types (e.g., those addressed to males and females) in similar locations. It is best to use a fairly large number of letters (e.g., a minimum of 15 to 20 in each condition) to get reliable results. Obviously, you should not leave more than one letter in the same location. You might want to team up with some classmates on this project so that you can split the cost of the stamps.

Osswald, & Brauer, 2010). So, if you ever find yourself in need of help and see someone approaching who is listening to an MP3 player, hope that he or she is listening to music with prosocial lyrics!

What about prosocial lyrics and romance? If you have your eye on someone special, consider this study, which took research on song lyrics one step further (Guéguen, Jacob, & Lamy, 2010). The study was conducted in France, and the participants were female college students who were not dating anyone. When a participant arrived for the study, she was ushered into a waiting room where music happened to be playing on a sound system. For half of the participants it was a romantic song called "Je l'aime à mourir" (which loosely translates as "I love her to death"), while for the others it was a song with neutral lyrics ("L'heure du thé," or "tea time"). After a few minutes, the participant was taken to another room where she performed a consumer taste test with another participant, who happened to be a male student of average attractiveness. During a break, the man asked for the woman's phone number. "I think you are very nice and I was wondering if you would give me your phone number," he said. "I'll phone you later and we can have a drink together somewhere next week" (Guéguen, Jacob, & Lamy, 2010, p. 305). Were the women who had just listened to the romantic song more likely to say yes? Indeed they were; 52% who had

What are the effects of playing prosocial video games (such as *Lemmings*) on people's behavior? Research shows that those who have just played a prosocial video game are more likely to help others than are people who have just played a neutral video game.

listened to "Je l'aime à mourir" gave the man their number, whereas only 30% of the women who had listened to "L'heure du thé" did so.

How Can Helping Be Increased?

We would all be better off if prosocial behavior were more common than it is. How can we get people, when faced with an emergency, to act more like Abe Zelmanowitz and less like Kitty Genovese's neighbors?

Before addressing this question, we should point out that people do not always want to be helped. Imagine that you are sitting at a computer terminal at the library and are struggling to learn a new e-mail system. You can't figure out how to send and receive mail and are becoming increasingly frustrated as the computer responds with messages such as "Invalid Command." A confident-looking guy whom you know only slightly walks over to you and looks over your shoulder for a few minutes. "You have a lot to learn," he says. "Let me show you how this baby works." How would you react? You might feel some gratitude, but you will probably also feel some resentment. His offer of help comes with a message: "You are too stupid to figure this out for yourself." Because receiving help can make people feel inadequate and dependent, they do not always react positively when someone offers them aid. People do not want to appear incompetent, so they often decide to suffer in silence, even if doing so lowers their chances of successfully completing a task (Alvarez & Van Leeuwen, 2011; Brown, Nesse, & Vinokur, 2003; Halabi & Nadler, 2010).

When death, the great reconciler, has come, it is never our tenderness that we repent of, but our severity.
—George Eliot (Marian Evans), *Adam Bede*, 1859

Nevertheless, the world would be a better place if more people helped those in need. How can we increase everyday acts of kindness, such as looking out for an elderly neighbor or volunteering to read to kids at the local school? The answer to this question lies in our discussion of the causes of prosocial behavior. For example, we saw that several personal characteristics of potential helpers are important, and promoting those factors can increase the likelihood that these people will help (Clary et al., 1994; Snyder, 1993). But even kind, altruistic people will fail to help if certain situational constraints are present, such as being in an urban environment or witnessing an emergency in the presence of numerous bystanders.

Why did this person help, even when several other bystanders witnessed the same emergency and didn't help? Perhaps this person learned about the barriers to bystander intervention in a social psychology class.

Increasing the Likelihood That Bystanders Will Intervene

There is evidence that simply being aware of the barriers to helping in an emergency can increase people's chances of overcoming those barriers. A few years ago at Cornell University, several students intervened to prevent another student from committing suicide. As is often the case with emergencies, the situation was very confusing, and at first the bystanders were not sure what was happening or what they should do. The student who led the intervention said that she was reminded of a lecture she had heard on bystander intervention in her introductory psychology class a few days before and realized that if she didn't act, no one would (Savitsky, 1998). Or consider an incident at Vassar College not long ago where students saw someone being attacked by a mugger. Like Kitty Genovese's neighbors, most of them did nothing, probably because they assumed that somebody else had already called the police. One of the students, however, immediately called the campus police because she was struck by how similar the situation was to the studies on bystander intervention she had read about in her social psychology course—even though she had taken the class more than a year earlier (Coats, 1998).

These are not controlled experiments, of course, and we cannot be certain that these helpful people were spurred on by what they had learned in their psychology classes. Fortunately, this question has been addressed experimentally (Beaman et al., 1978). The researchers randomly assigned students to listen to a lecture on Latané and Darley's (1970) bystander intervention research or a lecture on an unrelated topic. Two weeks later, all the students participated in what they thought was a completely unrelated sociology study, during which they encountered a student lying on the floor. Was he in need of help? Had he fallen and injured himself, or was he simply a student who had fallen asleep after pulling an all-nighter? As we have seen, when in an ambiguous situation such as this one, people look to see how other people are reacting. Because an accomplice of the experimenter (posing as another participant) intentionally acted unconcerned, the natural thing to do was to assume that nothing was wrong. This is exactly what most participants did if they had not heard the lecture about bystander intervention research; in this condition, only 25% of them stopped to help the student. However, if the participants had heard the lecture about bystander intervention, 43% stopped to help the student. Thus, knowing how we can be unwittingly influenced by others can by itself help overcome this type of social influence. We can only hope that knowing about other barriers to prosocial behavior will make them easier to overcome as well.

Positive Psychology and Prosocial Behavior

In recent years, a new field known as *positive psychology* has emerged (Seligman, 2002; Seligman, Steen, & Park, 2005; Sheldon, Kashdan, & Steger, 2011). Martin Seligman, an influential clinical psychologist, observed that much of psychology—particularly clinical psychology—had focused on mental disorders, largely ignoring how to define and nurture psychological health. Psychology should not just be the study of "disease, weakness, and damage," he argued, but the study of "strength and virtue" (2002, p. 4). Largely through Seligman's efforts, many psychologists are now focusing on such topics as the nature of healthy human functioning, how to define and categorize human strengths, and how to improve people's lives (Lopez & Snyder, 2009).

The positive psychology movement is a useful and necessary corrective to the emphasis on mental illness in clinical psychology and has led to many fascinating research programs. As we have seen in this book, though, social psychology has not concentrated solely on negative behaviors. For many years there have been active social psychological research programs on such topics as how people develop intrinsic interest in an activity (Chapter 5), how people maintain high self-esteem (Chapter 6), and how people form impressions of and lasting relationships with others (Chapter 10). To be sure, social psychology has documented many negative behaviors that can result from powerful social influences, such as obedience to authority and other kinds of conformity (Chapter 8). By studying the basic ways in which humans process information about themselves and their social worlds, however, it has been possible to understand both the bright and the dark side of human behavior, such as when people will help others and when they will not.

An excellent example of the social psychological approach is the topic of this chapter, the study of the conditions under which people help or fail to help their fellow humans. Is this the study of positive psychology or a focus on the dark side? Both, because social psychologists study the conditions under which people are likely to help (e.g., when people feel empathy toward another) and the conditions under which they are likely to fail to help (e.g., when they experience a diffusion of responsibility).

As noted earlier, Daniel Batson and his colleagues have been the strongest proponents of the idea that many people have a pure, unselfish motive for helping others and will do so when they feel empathy (Batson, 2011). In the experiment we reviewed earlier, for example, when people felt empathy toward a classmate who had been in an automobile accident, they were willing to help her regardless of whether there was a cost to them of doing so (see Figure 11.2). Research on empathy and prosocial behavior is an excellent example of the ways in which social psychologists have been interested in positive psychology, the study of people's strengths and virtues.

Watch on **MyPsychLab**
Think about the motivations for prosocial behavior as you watch the MyPsychLab video ***Friends, Family, and Strangers***.

CONNECTIONS

Increasing Volunteerism

There are many important kinds of prosocial behavior besides intervening in emergencies, including volunteerism and community service. Social psychologists have studied this kind of helping as well, wherein people commit to helping strangers on a more long-term basis (Mannino, Snyder, & Omoto, 2011; Penner, 2004; Piliavin, 2010).

Surveys of Western European and North American countries have found that many people engage in volunteer work, with the highest rate in the United States (47%; Ting & Piliavin, 2000). Of course, that means that even in the United States more than half of the population is not volunteering, raising the question of how to increase people's willingness to spend time helping others. Some institutions have responded by requiring their members to perform community service. Some high schools, colleges, and businesses, for example, require their students or employees to engage in volunteer work.

These programs have the benefit of increasing the pool of volunteers available to help community organizations such as homeless shelters, medical clinics, and day-care centers. But the question arises as to the effect of such "mandatory volunteerism" on the motivation of the people who do the helping. Many of these organizations assume that they are increasing the likelihood that their members will volunteer in the future, even after they leave the organizations. That is, making people volunteer is assumed to foster volunteerism by enlightening people about its benefits.

An increasing number of schools and businesses are requiring people to perform community service. These programs can actually lower interest in volunteering if people feel they are helping because of an external requirement. Encouraging people to volunteer while preserving the sense that they freely choose to do so is likely to increase people's intentions to volunteer again in the future.

As we discussed in Chapter 5, however, giving people strong external reasons for performing an activity can actually undermine their intrinsic interest in that activity. This is called the *overjustification effect*: People see their behavior as caused by compelling extrinsic reasons (e.g., being required to do volunteer work), making them underestimate the extent to which their behavior was caused by intrinsic reasons (e.g., that they like to do volunteer work). Consistent with this research, the more that people feel they are volunteering because of external requirements, the less likely they are to volunteer freely in the future (Batson et al., 1978; Bringle, 2005; Kunda & Schwartz, 1983; Stukas, Snyder, & Clary, 1999). The moral is that organizations should be careful about how heavy-handedly they impose requirements to volunteer. If people feel that they are complying only because they have to, they may actually become less likely to volunteer in the future. Encouraging people to volunteer while preserving the sense that they freely choose to do so has been shown to increase people's sense of well-being and their intentions to volunteer again in the future (Piliavin, 2008; Stukas et al., 1999).

USE IT!

We hope it never happens, but suppose you are injured in an accident in a public place and need help. Based on what you have learned in this chapter, how could you make sure that someone comes to your aid as soon as possible? As we saw in the section on the bystander effect, the trick is to make sure people notice that you need help, interpret it as an emergency, and assume that they (and not someone else) is responsible for helping. One way to avoid a diffusion of responsibility is to point to one person and ask for their help. That is, instead of shouting, "Will someone please help me?" single out one person—"Hey, you in the blue shirt and sunglasses, could you please call 911?" That makes one person feel responsible and also communicates to him or her how to help. Based on what you have read in this chapter, you should also know more about what to do if you witness an emergency—don't assume that someone else will help. By the way, you might be interested to know that, contrary to what happened in the final episode of the TV show *Seinfeld*, there are no laws in the United States obligating people to help a stranger in need. Many states do have Good Samaritan laws that make it hard for a victim to sue a bystander who tries to help but causes further injury. These laws don't give bystanders complete protection, but they are meant to increase the likelihood that people will come to each other's aid.

Summary

What are the basic motives that determine whether people help others?

- **Basic Motives Underlying Prosocial Behavior: Why Do People Help?** This chapter examined the causes of **prosocial behavior**, acts performed with the goal of benefiting another person. What are the basic origins of prosocial behavior?
  - **Evolutionary Psychology: Instincts and Genes** Evolutionary theory explains prosocial behavior in four ways. The first is **kin selection**, the idea that behaviors that help a genetic relative are favored by natural selection. The second is the **norm of reciprocity**, which is the expectation that helping others will increase the likelihood that they will help us in the future. The third is *group selection*, the idea that social groups with altruistic members are more likely to survive in competition with other groups.
  - **Social Exchange: The Costs and Rewards of Helping** Social exchange theory argues that prosocial behavior is not necessarily rooted in our genes. Instead, people help others in order to maximize social rewards and minimize social costs.
  - **Empathy and Altruism: The Pure Motive for Helping** People can be motivated by **altruism**, the desire to help another person even if it involves a cost to the helper. According to the **empathy-altruism hypothesis**, when people feel **empathy** toward another person (they experience events and emotions the other person experiences), they attempt to help that person purely for altruistic reasons.

What are some personal qualities that influence whether a given individual will help?

- **Personal Qualities and Prosocial Behavior: Why Do Some People Help More Than Others?** Basic motives are not all there is to understanding prosocial behavior—personal qualities matter as well.
  - **Individual Differences: The Altruistic Personality** Although some people have personalies that make them more likely than others to help, personality factors have not been shown to be strong predictors of who will help across a variety of social situations.
  - **Gender Differences in Prosocial Behavior** In many cultures, the male sex role includes helping in chivalrous and heroic ways, whereas the female sex role includes helping in close, long-term relationships.
  - **Cultural Differences in Prosocial Behavior** People are willing to help both **in-group** and **out-group** members, but for different reasons. People are more likely to feel empathy toward members of their in-groups who are in need, and the more empathy they feel, the more likely they are to help. People help out-group members for a different reason: They do so when they have something to gain, such as feeling good about themselves or making a good impression on others.
  - **Religion and Prosocial Behavior** People who are religious report on surveys that they help more than do people who are not religious, and they actually do help more in situations in which helping makes them look good to themselves or others. They are not more likely to help, however, in private situations in which no one will know that they helped.
  - **The Effects of Mood on Prosocial Behavior** People are more likely to help if they are in especially good moods, but also if they are in especially bad moods.

In what situations are people more likely, or less likely, to help others?

- **Situational Determinants of Prosocial Behavior: When Will People Help?** To understand why people help others, we also need to consider the nature of the social situation.
  - **Environment: Rural Versus Urban** People are less likely to help in dense, urban settings because of the **urban overload hypothesis**—the idea that people living in cities are constantly bombarded with stimulation and that they keep to themselves in order to avoid being overwhelmed by it.
  - **Residential Mobility** People who have lived for a long time in one place are more likely to engage in prosocial behaviors than are people who have recently moved to an area.
  - **The Number of Bystanders: The Bystander Effect** In order to help in an emergency, people must meet five conditions: They must notice the event, interpret it as an emergency, assume responsibility, know how to help, and implement their decision to help. As the number of bystanders who witness an emergency increases, the more difficult it is to meet two of these conditions—interpreting the event as an emergency and assuming responsibility. This produces the **bystander effect**: The larger the number of bystanders, the less likely any one of them is to help.
  - **The Nature of the Relationship: Communal Versus Exchange Relationships** People in *exchange relationships*—those governed by concerns about equity—are concerned primarily with the benefits they will receive by helping others. People in *communal relationships*—those in which the primary concern is the welfare of the other person—are less concerned with the benefits they will receive and more with simply satisfying the needs of the other person.
  - **Effects of the Media: Video Games and Music Lyrics** Playing a prosocial video game or listening to a song with prosocial lyrics makes people more likely to help others in a variety of ways.

What can be done to promote prosocial behavior?

- **How Can Helping Be Increased?** Prosocial behavior can be increased in a number of ways.
  - **Increasing the Likelihood That Bystanders Will Intervene** Research shows that teaching people about the barriers to bystander intervention increases the likelihood that they will help in emergencies.
  - **Positive Psychology and Prosocial Behavior** A new field called positive psychology has emerged that focuses on people's strengths and virtues instead of mental disease. The social psychological approach is to investigate the conditions under which people act in positive (e.g., helpful) and negative (e.g., unhelpful) ways. Many of these conditions were discussed in this chapter. For example, people will help at a cost to themselves when they feel empathy toward a person in need. When they do not feel empathy, they will help only when it is in their self-interest.

Chapter 11 Test

Study and Review on MyPsychLab

1. Which of the following is *not* a way in which evolutionary theory explains prosocial behavior?
   a. social exchange
   b. kin selection
   c. the reciprocity norm
   d. group selection

2. Amy is walking across campus and sees someone on her hands and knees looking for a ring that slipped off her finger. Which of the following is *false* according to the empathy-altruism hypothesis? Amy
   a. feels empathy toward the person, so she will probably stop and help the stranger look for the ring, regardless of whether it is in her self-interest to do so.
   b. feels empathy toward the person, but she doesn't think she has much to gain by helping, so she decides not to help the person look for the ring.
   c. doesn't feel empathy toward the person but recognizes her as a TA in her English class. Amy really wants to get a good grade in that class, so she will probably stop and help her TA look for the ring.
   d. doesn't feel empathy toward the person and doesn't think she has much to gain by helping, so she decides not to help the person look for the ring.

3. Which of the following is *not* a reason why being in a good mood tends to increase prosocial behavior?
   a. Good moods make us frame situations more positively, and thus we are more likely to give people the benefit of the doubt.
   b. Helping prolongs good moods.
   c. Good moods make us pay more attention to social norms, so we will be more aware of the altruism norm.
   d. Good moods increase how much attention we pay to ourselves, which makes us more likely to act according to our values.

4. Frank has recently graduated from college and moved from New York City back to the small town in Ohio where he grew up. He now finds that he is much more inclined to engage in prosocial behavior. What is the most likely reason for this change?
   a. Growing up in a small town caused him to internalize altruistic values.
   b. The change in his immediate surroundings changed his likelihood of helping.
   c. College students are less likely to help because they are more susceptible to the bystander effect.
   d. Frank is more likely to engage in negative-state relief when he is in the small town.

5. Luke listened to a lecture in his history class that he found very confusing, but at the end of the class when the professor asked whether there was anything students didn't understand, Luke didn't raise his hand. Because no other hands were raised, Luke assumed that other students had understood the material and that he just didn't pay enough attention. In fact, many students hadn't understood the material and were in the same situation as Luke. This is an example of
   a. jigsaw classroom.
   b. self-fulfilling prophecy.
   c. ultimate attribution error.
   d. pluralistic ignorance.
   e. normative conformity.

6. Research on prosocial behavior finds that religious people
   a. help others more than nonreligious people do in virtually all ways.
   b. report on surveys that they help the same amount as do nonreligious people.
   c. actually help more than nonreligious people, but only if it makes them look good to themselves or to others.
   d. actually help others less than do nonreligious people.

7. Which of the following is most true?
   a. Listening to song lyrics with prosocial lyrics makes people more helpful.
   b. If we want someone to say yes when we ask for a date, it doesn't really work to have him or her listen to a song with romantic lyrics.
   c. Playing prosocial video games has no effect on how helpful people will be.
   d. Playing violent video games makes people more helpful.

8. Meghan lives in a single room in a college dormitory. Late one night, she hears a scream coming from just outside her dorm. She is pretty sure that the person needs help because the person yelled, "Help me! I think I broke my leg!" Meghan goes back to sleep, only to find out the next day that the person was on the ground for 45 minutes before someone helped. Which of the following best explains why Meghan didn't help?
   a. Informational influence.
   b. A diffusion of responsibility.
   c. She didn't interpret it as an emergency.
   d. Pluralistic ignorance.

9. Which of the following is true about prosocial behavior?
  a. How often people have moved from one place to another influences how helpful they are.
  b. There is no effect of personality on prosocial behavior.
  c. Being in a bad mood decreases prosocial behavior.
  d. People are much more likely to help members of their in-group than members of an out-group.

10. Which of the following is *not* true about prosocial behavior?
  a. When people are put in a good mood, they are more likely to help.
  b. People in stable communities are more likely to help than people in communities with high residential mobility.
  c. When people are put in a bad mood, they are more likely to help.
  d. Having an altruistic personality is a strong predictor of helping behavior.

Answer Key

1-a, 2-b, 3-c, 4-b, 5-d,
6-c, 7-a, 8-b, 9-a, 10-d

12 Aggression

Why Do We Hurt Other People? Can We Prevent It?

On April 20, 1999, the corridors and classrooms of Columbine High School in Littleton, Colorado, reverberated with the sound of gunshots. Two students, Eric Harris and Dylan Klebold, armed with assault weapons and explosives, had gone on a rampage, killing a teacher and several of their fellow students. They then turned their guns on themselves. After the smoke cleared, 15 people lay dead (including the shooters) and 23 others were hospitalized, some with severe wounds.

As horrendous as it was, the toll could have been much higher. The two shooters made videotapes a few weeks before the massacre, and from these we have learned that they had prepared 95 explosive devices that failed to go off. Of these, one set was placed a few miles away, intended to explode first and distract police by keeping them busy at a distance from the school. A second set was intended to explode in the cafeteria, killing a large number of students and causing hundreds to evacuate the building in terror, with Harris and Klebold waiting to gun them down. They planted a third set of explosives in their own cars in the school parking lot, timed to explode after the police and paramedics had arrived on the scene, as a way of further increasing the number of casualties and creating even more chaos. The videotape shows the perpetrators gleefully predicting that, before the day was over, they would have killed 250 people.

The Columbine massacre was the deadliest of the 15 high school shootings that had taken place in the United States over a period of a few years. In the sad aftermath of Columbine, as always happens after a violent tragedy, the country needed someone or something to blame. Almost everyone wondered whether these youngsters were crazy. How could reasonably observant parents not know that their sons kept guns in their bedrooms and were manufacturing bombs in their garage? And where were the school authorities? Didn't the teachers notice behaviors that would have predicted such violence? Some people even wondered if schools should give students personality tests to identify the teenagers most likely to commit acts of this kind.

Certain observers quickly concluded that the major cause of such violence is the easy availability of guns. Others were quick to blame the Supreme Court for outlawing prayer in the schools: Wouldn't prayer prevent this sort of outrage? Still others pointed to the prevalence of violence in films, on TV, and in video games; Harris and Klebold were devoted to violent video games. If we could ban violent entertainment, wouldn't that make our schools safe again? And some people felt that these outrageous acts grew out of a general lack of respect among teenagers in our culture. One state legislature responded to the massacre by passing a law requiring students to call their teachers "sir" or "ma'am" as a way of showing respect, as if respect can be mandated (Aronson, 2000).

In this chapter, we will focus on aggression and try to understand what causes it. Are human beings innately aggressive? Can normal people be inspired to commit violence by watching violent characters on TV or in films or by the easy availability of weapons of destruction? Can a society, a school, or a parent do anything to reduce aggression? If so, specifically what? Needless to say, we don't have all the answers, but we do have some of them. By the time you get to the end of this chapter, we hope you will have gained some insight into those issues.

FOCUS QUESTIONS

- What is aggression? Is it innate, learned, or optional?
- What are some situational influences on aggression?
- What evidence is there that aggression is learned by observing and imitating others?
- How can aggression be reduced?

Aggression
Intentional behavior aimed at causing physical harm or psychological pain to another person.

Hostile Aggression
Aggression stemming from feelings of anger and aimed at inflicting pain or injury.

Instrumental Aggression
Aggression as a means to some goal other than causing pain.

What Is Aggression?

For social psychologists, **aggression** is defined as intentional behavior aimed at causing either physical or psychological pain. It should not be confused with assertiveness, even though most people loosely refer to others as "aggressive" if they stand up for their rights, write letters to the editor complaining about real or imagined injustices, or are supremely ambitious. Some people would say that a woman who speaks her mind or disagrees with a male coworker is being "aggressive." But true aggression involves the intent to harm another. The action might be physical or verbal; it might succeed in its goal or not. If someone throws a beer bottle at your head and you duck so that the bottle misses you, it was still an aggressive act. The important thing is the intention. By the same token, if a drunk driver unintentionally runs you down while you're attempting to cross the street, that is not an act of aggression, even though the damage would be far greater than that caused by the beer bottle that missed.

It is also useful to distinguish between types of aggression (Berkowitz, 1993). **Hostile aggression** is an act of aggression stemming from feelings of anger and is aimed at inflicting pain or injury. In **instrumental aggression**, there is an intention to hurt the other person, but the hurting takes place as a means to some goal other than causing pain. In a professional football game, a defensive lineman will usually do whatever it takes to thwart his opponent (the blocker) and tackle the ball carrier. This typically includes intentionally inflicting pain on his opponent if doing so is useful in helping him get the blocker out of the way so that he can get to the ball carrier. This is instrumental aggression. By contrast, if he believes his opponent has been playing dirty, he might become angry and go out of his way to hurt his opponent, even if doing so does not increase his chances of tackling the ball carrier. This is hostile aggression.

> *Man's inhumanity to man makes countless thousands mourn.*
>
> —Robert Burns

Today, social psychologists and other social scientists have made great strides in understanding the biological, social, cultural, and situational causes of aggressive behavior.

The Evolutionary Argument

Let's begin with the obvious fact that men are more physically aggressive than women, starting in childhood. In cultures all over the world—as diverse as the United States, Switzerland, and Ethiopia—little boys are far more likely than little girls to go in for "nonplayful" pushing, shoving, and hitting (Deaux & La France, 1998; Maccoby & Jacklin, 1974). In research conducted worldwide,, men are more violent than women and also more socially dominant (Buss, 2004, 2005). In one study, teenagers from 11 different countries, mostly in Europe and Asia, read stories involving conflict among people and were asked to write their own endings (Archer & McDaniel, 1995). In every one of the 11 countries, young men showed a greater tendency toward violent solutions to conflict than young women did.

Boys are more likely than girls, the world over, to roughhouse and pummel each other. Is this evidence of hostile or instrumental aggression—or just of physical play?

Evolutionary psychologists argue that physical aggression is genetically programmed into men, because it enables them to defend their group and perpetuate their genes. (In previous chapters we have noted the evolutionary argument for prosocial behavior such as altruism and love.) Males are theorized to aggress for two reasons: first, to establish dominance over other males and secure the highest possible status. The idea here is that the female will choose the male who is most likely to provide the best genes and the greatest protection and resources for their offspring. Second, males aggress out of sexual jealousy, to ensure that their mate is not having sex with other men, thereby ensuring their paternity (Buss, 2004).

The hormone that fuels male aggression is testosterone, which both sexes have, although in higher proportion in males. Laboratory animals injected with testosterone become more aggressive (Moyer, 1983), and there is a parallel finding in humans: Naturally occurring testosterone levels are significantly higher among prisoners convicted of violent crimes than among those convicted of nonviolent crimes (Dabbs, 2000; Dabbs et al., 1995). Similarly, juvenile delinquents have higher testosterone levels than do college students (Banks & Dabbs, 1996). These studies, however, are correlational, and causality runs in both directions: That is, being in an aggressive, competitive, or sexual situation increases the production of testosterone (Thompson, Dabbs, & Frady, 1990; Mazur & Dabbs, 1992).

When people say that aggression is "natural," they often point to our primate relatives. Chimpanzees (top) are indeed pretty belligerent and aggressive, but bonobos (bottom) would rather make love than war.

Aggression in Other Animals To answer the "innate versus learned" question about aggressiveness, some scientists have turned to experiments with nonhuman species. Consider the common belief that cats will instinctively stalk and kill rats. Half a century ago, biologist Zing Yang Kuo (1961) performed a simple experiment: He raised a kitten in the same cage with a rat. Not only did the cat refrain from attacking the rat, but the two became close companions. Moreover, when given the opportunity, the cat refused either to chase or to kill other rats; thus, the benign behavior was not confined to this one buddy, but generalized to rats the cat had never met.

Although this experiment is charming, it fails to prove that aggressive behavior is not instinctive in cats; it merely demonstrates that early experience can override it. What if an organism grows up without any contact with other organisms? Will it or won't it show aggressive tendencies? It turns out that rats raised in isolation, without any experience in fighting other rats, will attack a fellow rat when one is introduced into the cage; moreover, the isolated rats use the same pattern of threat and attack that experienced rats use (Eibl-Eibesfeldt, 1963). So even though aggressive behavior can be modified by experience, as shown by Kuo's experiment, some kinds of aggressive behavior apparently do not need to be learned.

We can gain still greater insight into our own biological heritage by observing the behavior of those animals with whom we have the most genetic similarity. Our closest relatives in the animal kingdom are two primates: the chimpanzees and the bonobos. Both species have 98% of their DNA in common with human beings. The chimpanzee is known for its aggressive behavior; the females too can be pretty mean (Watts et al., 2006). It is the only nonhuman species in which groups of male members hunt and kill other members of their own kind—indeed, at about the same rate that humans in hunter-gatherer societies kill each other (Wrangham, Wilson, & Muller, 2006). Based on the research on chimps, we might conclude that humans, especially males, are genetically programmed for aggressive behavior.

However, living across the river from the chimpanzees and out of their reach are the bonobos, our equally close genetic relative. Unlike the chimp, the bonobo is known for its nonaggressive behavior. In fact, bonobos are often referred to as the "make love, not war" ape. Prior to engaging in activities that could otherwise lead to conflict, bonobos have sex, an activity that functions to diffuse potential conflict (De Waal, 1995). Thus, when the group arrives at a feeding ground, they first enjoy some sexual play and then proceed to eat peacefully. In contrast, when chimps arrive at a feeding ground, they compete aggressively for the food. Also, unlike the chimps, bonobos form female-dominated societies and are known for their sensitivity to others in their group (Parish & de Waal, 2000).

The bonobo way of life is a rare exception in the animal kingdom. The near universality of aggression strongly suggests that aggressiveness has evolved and has been maintained because it has survival value (Lore & Schultz, 1993; Buss, 2004). At the same time, nearly all organisms also seem to have evolved strong inhibitory mechanisms that enable them to suppress aggression when it is in their best interests to do so. Aggression is determined by the animal's previous social experiences as well as by the specific social context in which the animal finds itself.

The Cultural Argument

Most social psychologists, therefore, believe that aggression is an optional strategy: We humans may be born with the *capacity* for aggressive behavior, but how, whether, when, and where we express it is learned and depends on our circumstances and culture. Because of the complexity and importance of our social interactions, for human beings the social situation becomes even more important than hormones or genetic predispositions (Bandura, 1973; Berkowitz, 1993; Lysak, Rule, & Dobbs, 1989). For example, we seem to have an inborn tendency to respond to certain provocative stimuli by striking out against the perpetrator, but whether or not we actually do so depends on a complex interplay between these innate tendencies, a variety of learned inhibitory responses, and the precise nature of the social situation. You may be really, really angry if a police officer stops you for speeding, but it is likely that you will control your temper—and your behavior.

Thus, although it is true that many animals, from insects to apes, will usually attack another animal that invades their territory, we cannot conclude that human beings are likewise programmed to protect their territory and behave aggressively in response to specific stimuli. Three major lines of evidence support this view: studies of cultures across time, studies across cultures, and laboratory experiments.

Changes in Aggression Across Time Within a given culture, changing social conditions frequently lead to striking changes in aggressive behavior. Consider the Iroquois of North America. For hundreds of years, the Iroquois lived peacefully as a hunting nation, without fighting other tribes. But in the seventeenth century, barter with the newly arrived Europeans brought the Iroquois into direct competition with the neighboring Hurons over furs, which dramatically increased in value because they could now be traded for manufactured goods. A series of skirmishes with the Hurons ensued, and within a short time, the Iroquois developed into ferocious warriors. It would be hard to argue that they became ferocious warriors because of some innate aggressive instinct; rather, their aggressiveness almost certainly came about because a social change produced increases in competition (Hunt, 1940).

Differences in Aggression Across Cultures Human cultures vary widely in their degree of aggressiveness. European history, when condensed, consists of one major war after another. In contrast, cultures imbedded with cooperative, collectivist values have had lower levels of aggression than European societies (Bergeron & Schneider, 2005). Certain tribes, such as the Lepchas of Sikkim, the Pygmies of Central Africa, and the Arapesh of New Guinea, live in apparent peace and harmony, with acts of aggression being extremely rare (Baron & Richardson, 1994). In close-knit cultures that depend on cooperation for the group's survival, anger and aggression are considered dangerous and disruptive, and an offender will be ostracized or punished. But don't the men in these tribes have testosterone? Of course they do. But when men live in cultures that lack internal and external threats to their survival—and, admittedly, not many cultures are so blessed—they are not raised to be aggressive, sex differences are minimized, and cooperation is encouraged (Gilmore, 1990).

For example, the forest Teduray, a hunter-gatherer culture in the Philippine rain forest, have established institutions and norms specifically designed to prevent intragroup violence. In their societies, people are expected to pay special attention to the effect of their actions on the feelings of others. When a situation arises, such as adultery, in which there is significant risk that anger will lead to violence, specific members of a Teduray village work to placate the injured individuals. The Teduray believe that human beings are violent by nature but do all they can to reduce aggression within their group. They will, however, behave aggressively to protect themselves from aggression from outside groups (Schlegel, 1998).

Cultures of Honor and Aggression Perhaps the strongest evidence against the notion that "men are naturally aggressive because of their testosterone" comes from experiments showing how cultural norms and expectations literally "get inside" people, causing them to behave differently under similar provocation.

The early economies of the American South and West created a "culture of honor" in which a man was literally quick on the trigger if he thought another man was about to smear his reputation—or steal his cattle.

For example, in the United States there are some striking regional differences in aggressive behavior and in the kinds of events that trigger violence. Homicide rates for white southern males are substantially higher than those for white northern males, especially in rural areas. Richard Nisbett (1993) hypothesized that the higher rates of violence in the South derive from economic causes: The higher rates occur in cultures that were originally based on herding, in contrast to cultures based on agriculture. Why would this be so? People who depend economically on agriculture tend to develop cooperative strategies for survival. But people who depend on their herds are extremely vulnerable; their livelihoods can be lost in an instant by the theft of their animals. To reduce the likelihood of theft, Nisbett theorized, herders learn to be hyperalert to any threatening act (real or perceived) and respond to it immediately with force. This would explain why cattle rustling and horse thievery were capital crimes in the Old West, and why Mediterranean and Middle Eastern herding cultures even today place a high value on male aggressiveness. And indeed, when Nisbett looked at agricultural practices *within* the South, he found that homicide rates were more than twice as high in the hills and dry plains areas (where herding occurs) as in farming regions.

The emphasis on aggressiveness and vigilance in herding communities fosters, in turn, a *culture of honor* in which even small disputes put a man's reputation for toughness on the line, requiring him to respond with violence to restore his status (Cohen, 1998). Although the herding economy has become much less important in the South and West, the legacy of its culture of honor remains. These regions have rates of honor-related homicides (such as murder to avenge a perceived insult to one's family) that are five times higher than in other regions of the country. High school students in culture-of-honor states are far more likely than students from other states to bring a weapon to school and to use that weapon. These states have more than twice as many school shootings per capita than do other states (Brown, Osterman, & Barnes, 2009). Cultures of honor also have higher rates of domestic violence. Both sexes in such cultures believe it is appropriate for a man to physically assault a woman if he believes she is threatening his honor and reputation by being unfaithful or leaving him (Vandello & Cohen, 2008).

In a series of experiments with southern and northern students at the University of Michigan, Nisbett and his colleagues demonstrated how a culture of honor manifests itself in the cognitions, emotions, behaviors, and even physiological reactions of its young men. Each participant was "accidentally" bumped into by the experimenter's confederate, who then insulted him by calling him a denigrating name. Compared with northern white males, who tended to shrug off the insult, southerners were more likely to think their masculine reputation was threatened, became more upset (as shown by a rise in cortisol levels in their bloodstream), were more physiologically primed for aggression (as shown by a rise in testosterone levels in their bloodstream), became more cognitively primed for aggression, and were ultimately more likely to engage in aggressive and dominant behavior following the incident (Cohen et al., 1996).

The research on cultures of honor suggests that male aggression ("don't mess with me") fulfills a powerful part of the male role and identity. When "being a man" is defined by competitiveness and strength, men are constantly trying to "prove" their masculinity and status in displays of aggression (Bosson & Vandello, 2011).

Gender and Aggression

Nevertheless, the fact that men and boys are, on average, more *physically* aggressive does not mean that women are kinder than men or less willing to inflict harm on others. Women and girls tend to commit *relational aggression*, aggression that harms another person through the manipulation of relationships, usually in such covert acts as gossiping, backbiting, and spreading false rumors about the target person or shunning or excluding that person (Archer, 2004; Blakemore, Berenbaum, & Liben, 2009;

Males and females can be equally aggressive, when aggression is defined as intending to harm another person. But whereas men are more physically aggressive, women are more likely to indulge in "relational aggression"—backbiting, shunning, or spreading false rumors about their target.

Coie et al., 1999; Dodge & Schwartz, 1997; McFadyen-Ketchum et al., 1996; Matlin, 2012). In one sad example that went viral, Phoebe Prince, a 15-year-old Irish girl living in Massachusetts, was targeted by a group known as the "Mean Girls" after she had a brief relationship with a popular boy at her school. Seven girls and two boys began a relentless campaign against her of verbal assault (including calling her "Irish slut" and "whore" on Facebook and other social media) and threats of bodily harm. After 4 months of being slandered and harassed, Prince committed suicide.

Gender differences in physical versus relational aggression start early. In one study of 3- to 5-year-old children playing in groups of three, the kids were instructed to use a crayon to color in a picture on a white sheet of paper. Three crayons were provided, but only one was a color (orange), and the other two were white. Naturally, the children all wanted the orange crayon. The boys used physical aggression to get it, hitting or pushing the child who had the orange crayon. The girls used relational aggression, spreading rumors about the child with the orange crayon or ignoring her to make her cry (Ostrov et al., 2004).

Gender differences in physical aggression are most apparent when researchers study spontaneous, unprovoked acts, men being more likely to "pick a fight" (especially with a stranger), join in a flash mob, and commit crimes of violence (murder, aggravated assault, rape). But even in these studies, there is often great overlap between males and females. Indeed, in some studies that compared the sexes in levels of physical aggression, most of the boys and girls were similarly nonaggressive; the sex difference was primarily due to a small number of extremely aggressive boys (Archer, 2004).

Moreover, the sex difference vanishes when both sexes feel provoked (Matlin, 2012). Thus, one meta-analysis of 64 separate experiments found that although men are more aggressive than women under ordinary circumstances, the gender difference becomes much smaller when men and women are insulted and when women are given a chance to retaliate aggressively, especially when others are unaware of their gender (Bettencourt & Miller, 1996). Certainly adult women do not differ from men, on average, in their willingness to yell, be verbally abusive, humiliate or punish their children, and express aggression in similar ways (Archer, 2004).

Watch on **MyPsychLab**
To learn more, watch the MyPsychLab video ***Relational Aggression***.

Keep in mind too that just as male aggression is influenced by culture, so is female aggression. For example, in one international study women from Australia and New Zealand showed greater evidence of aggressiveness than men from Sweden and Korea (Archer & McDaniel, 1995). In a cultural community that admires physical aggression, both sexes may rely on violent tactics: Female teenage members of Mexican American gangs in Los Angeles carry any kind of weapon they can get hold of, from bats to guns, and told a researcher that they had joined not only for social support but for revenge (M. G. Harris, 1994). A study of all known female suicide bombers throughout the world since 1981 (including Afghanistan, Israel, Iraq, India, Lebanon, Pakistan, Russia, Somalia, Sri Lanka, and Turkey) found that "the main motives and circumstances that

TRY IT! Gender and Aggression

Interview several of your male friends and ask them to reflect on their childhood and adolescent experiences with physical fighting or being challenged to fight. Ask them what they think was at stake in the fight. How difficult was it to back down? Ask them to elaborate on their answers.

Now interview several of your female friends. Did any of them ever get into a physical fight with someone of the same or other sex? What experiences have they had with relational aggression, such as being shunned, gossiped about, or excluded? Did they ever treat other girls or women with those forms of aggression? If you have male and female friends of different ethnicities—or from different regions of the United States—you might ask them the same questions.

drive female suicide bombers are quite similar to those that drive men"—loyalty to their country or religion, anger at being occupied by a foreign military, and revenge for loved ones killed by the enemy (O'Rourke, 2008).

What is your own experience with gender and cultural differences in aggression? (See the Try It! on the previous page.)

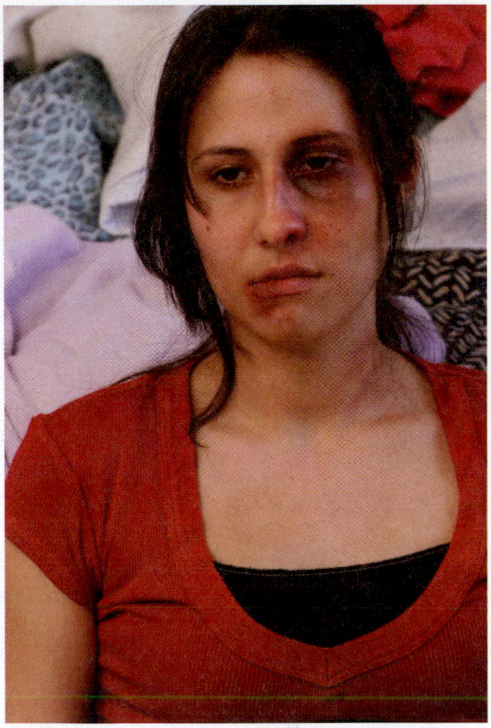

Why do some men physically abuse their partners?

Violence between Intimate Partners Finally, we must address the largest continuing gender difference in violence: that committed against intimate partners. According to the U.S. Department of Justice Statistics in 2011, of the 3.5 million violent crimes—primarily assault—committed against family members in a 5-year-period, 49% were crimes against spouses (the rest were assaults against children, parents, or other family members). Among victims of abuse by a spouse or other intimate partner, fully 84% were women. Eight in ten murderers who killed a family member were male.

Police statistics do not calculate other forms of aggression in intimate relationships. Numerous surveys in the United States and Canada report that some males begin to abuse girls as early as elementary school (with pushing, shoving, or slapping), and in high school this behavior can escalate into emotional abuse, such as publicly humiliating or degrading a girlfriend (Matlin, 2012). The rate of the physical abuse of women—beatings, stabbings, hitting, and rape—is high around the world, and highest in cultures that regard such abuse as a male prerogative (Levy, 2008). In some cultures of honor, men are legally permitted to kill their wives or daughters if they feel the women have "dishonored" them.

This gender difference in rates of domestic violence could be due, at least in part, to male physiology and men's greater average strength. Evolutionary psychologists argue that male jealousy and control of women originated as a way for men to make sure of their paternity and improve the survival chances of their progeny (Buss, 2004); other social scientists suggest that male violence against women is a means of asserting power and control (Eisenstat & Bancroft, 1999). Whatever the complex causes, however, they do not excuse violent behavior, nor do they mean that such behavior cannot be altered by a social intervention, as we shall see.

Some Physiological Influences on Aggression

It is hardly news that when people are drunk, hot, or in considerable pain, they are more likely to lash out at others, getting into fights and quarrels, than if they feel completely fine, sipping lemonade on a cool spring day. But why does the chance of aggression increase under these physical influences? Does it always?

Alcohol and Aggression As most college students know, alcohol is a social lubricant that lowers our inhibitions against acting in ways frowned on by society, including acts of aggression (Desmond, 1987; Taylor & Leonard, 1983). The link between alcohol and aggressive behavior has been well documented, and it appears even among people who have not been provoked and who do not usually behave aggressively when sober (Bailey & Taylor, 1991; Bushman & Cooper, 1990; Graham et al., 2006; Yudko et al., 1997). This might explain why fistfights frequently break out in bars and nightclubs and why family violence is often associated with alcohol abuse.

"Oh, that wasn't me talking, it was the alcohol."

Dana Fradon/The New Yorker Collection/ www.cartoonbank.com.

Why can alcohol increase aggressive behavior? Alcohol often serves as a disinhibitor: It reduces anxiety and lowers social inhibitions, making us less cautious than we usually are (MacDonald, Zanna, & Fong, 1996). But it is more than that. Alcohol also disrupts the way we usually process information, by impairing the part of the brain involved in planning and controlling behavior (Bushman, 1993, 1997; Bushman & Cooper, 1990; Hanson et al., 2011). This is why intoxicated people often respond to the earliest and most obvious aspects of a social situation and tend to miss the subtleties. If you are sober and someone steps on your toe, you would notice that the person didn't do it on purpose. But if you were drunk, you might miss the subtlety of the situation and respond as if that person had purposely stomped on your foot. If you and the offender are males, you might slug him. This response is typical of the kinds of ambiguous situations that men tend to interpret as provocative, especially under the influence of alcohol. Laboratory experiments demonstrate that when individuals drink enough alcohol to make them legally drunk, they tend to respond more violently to provocations than do people who have ingested little or no alcohol (Bushman, 1993; Lipsey et al., 1997; Taylor & Leonard, 1983).

There is another way in which alcohol facilitates aggression, however, and this is through what has been called the "think-drink" effect: When people *expect* alcohol to have certain effects on them, it often does (Marlatt & Rohsenow, 1980). Indeed, when people expect that alcohol will "release" their aggressive impulses, they often do become more aggressive—even when they are drinking something nonalcoholic. In a study of 116 men ages 18 to 45, experimenters gave one-third of the men a nonalcoholic drink, one-third a drink targeting a modest blood alcohol level, and one-third a stronger drink targeting a high blood alcohol level. Within each of these three groups, the researchers manipulated the drinkers' expectancies of how much alcohol they were getting. They then measured the men's behavior toward a person (a research confederate) who had behaved aggressively toward them. Remarkably, the actual quantity of alcohol that the men drank was less related to their aggressive behavior than their *expectations* were. The more alcohol the men believed they were drinking, the more aggressively they behaved toward the confederate (Bègue et al., 2009). Of course, as we saw, alcohol does have potent physiological effects on cognition and behavior. But those effects interact with what people have learned about alcohol, such as whether it provides an excuse to behave aggressively (or sexually) and how they expect to feel after imbibing.

Pain, Heat, and Aggression If an animal is in pain and cannot flee the scene, it will almost invariably attack; this is true of rats, mice, hamsters, foxes, monkeys, crayfish, snakes, raccoons, alligators, and a host of other creatures (Azrin, 1967; Hutchinson, 1983). In those circumstances, animals will attack members of their own species, members of different species, or anything else in sight, including stuffed dolls and tennis balls. Do you think this is true of human beings as well? A moment's reflection might help you guess that it may very well be. Most of us feel a flash of irritation when we hit our thumb with a hammer and know the feeling of wanting to lash out at the nearest available target. Indeed, in a series of experiments, students who underwent the pain of having their hand immersed in very cold water were far more likely to act aggressively against other students than were those who had not suffered the pain (Berkowitz, 1983).

Other forms of bodily discomfort—such as heat, humidity, air pollution, crowds, and offensive odors—also lower the threshold for aggressive behavior (Stoff & Cairns, 1997). During the late 1960s and early 1970s, when tensions in the United States ran high over the war in Vietnam and the rise of the civil rights movement, national leaders worried about "the long, hot summer." The phrase was a code for the fear that the summer's heat would cause simmering tensions to explode. Their fears were justified. An analysis of disturbances in 79 cities between 1967 and 1971 found that riots were far more likely to occur on hot days than on cold ones (Carlsmith & Anderson, 1979) (see Figure 12.1).

Similarly, in major American cities from Houston, Texas, to Des Moines, Iowa, the hotter it is on a given day or a given average year, the greater the likelihood that violent crimes will occur (Anderson & Anderson, 1984; Anderson, Bushman, & Groom, 1997; Rotton & Cohn, 2004). Smaller "crimes" increase, too: In the desert city of Phoenix, Arizona, drivers in non-air-conditioned cars are more likely to honk their horns in traffic jams than drivers in air-conditioned cars (Kenrick & MacFarlane, 1986). Even on the baseball field, heat and hostility go together. In major league baseball games when the temperature rises above 90 degrees, significantly more batters are hit by pitched balls and pitchers are more likely to intentionally retaliate against a batter when the pitcher's teammates have been hit by the opposing team earlier in the game (Larrick et al., 2011).

As you know by now, one must be cautious about interpreting events that take place in natural settings outside the laboratory. The scientist in you might be tempted to ask whether increases in aggression are due to the temperature itself or merely to the fact that more people are apt to be outside (getting in one another's way) on hot days than on cold or rainy days. So how might we determine that it's the heat causing the aggression

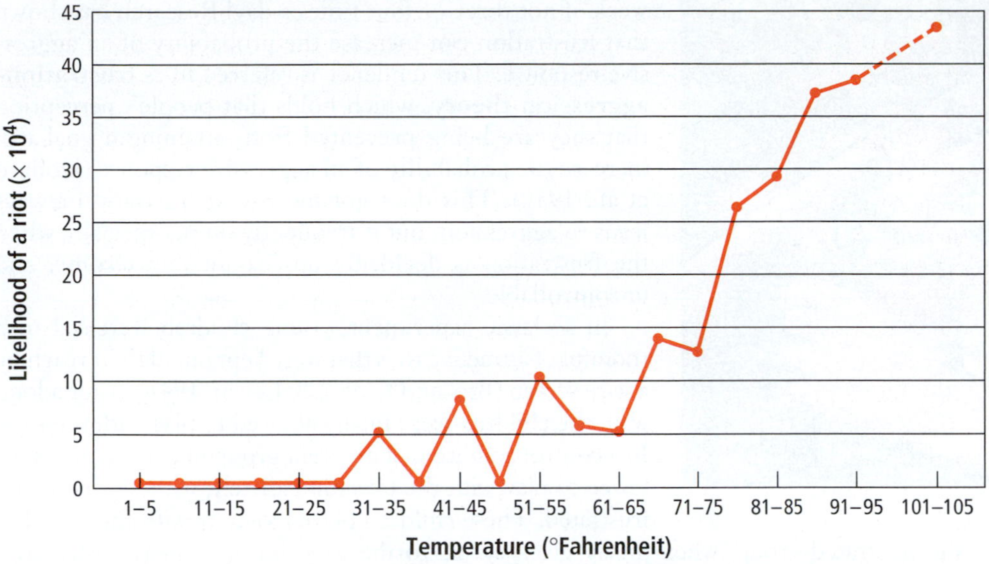

FIGURE 12.1

The Long, Hot Summer

Warm temperatures increase the likelihood that violent riots and other aggressive acts will occur.

(Adapted from Carlsmith & Anderson, 1979)

and not merely the greater opportunity for contact? We can bring the phenomenon into the laboratory; in fact, it is remarkably easy to do so. In one such experiment, students took the same test under different conditions: Some worked in a room at normal room temperature, while others worked in a room where the temperature reached 90 degrees (Griffitt & Veitch, 1971). The students in the hot room not only reported feeling more aggressive, but also expressed more hostility toward a stranger whom they were asked to describe and evaluate. Similar results have been reported by a number of investigators (Anderson, 2012; Anderson et al., 2000; Rule, Taylor, & Dobbs, 1987).

Watch on **MyPsychLab**

To learn more about physiological influences on aggression, watch the MyPsychLab video ***Heat Aggression***.

Most scientists agree that the climate will heat up due to the increase of greenhouse gasses in the atmosphere. Would you predict that global warming might have an effect on aggression as well? The answer appears to be yes. Craig Anderson (2012), the world's leading expert on the effects of climate and aggression, predicts that global warming is almost certain to produce a major increase in the rate of violent crime, for three reasons. One reason involves the effects of uncomfortable heat itself on irritability, aggression, and violence. A second involves the indirect effects global warming has on the economic and social factors known to put children and adolescents at risk for becoming violence-prone: poverty, poor prenatal and childhood nutrition, broken families, low IQ, growing up in violent neighborhoods, poor education, and living in a disorganized and unstable neighborhood. And a third involves the effects of rapid climate change on populations whose livelihoods and survival are at risk as a result of droughts, flooding, famine, and war.

Social Situations and Aggression

Imagine that your friend Sam is driving you to the airport so that you can fly home for the Christmas holidays. Sam has picked you up a bit later than you feel comfortable with; he accuses you of being overly anxious and assures you that he knows the route well and that you will arrive there with plenty of time to spare. Halfway to the airport, you are standing still in bumper-to-bumper traffic. Sam assures you that there is plenty of time, but this time he sounds less confident. After 10 more minutes, your palms are sweating. You open the car door and survey the road ahead: Not a car is moving as far ahead as you can see. You get back in the car, slam the door, and glare at Sam. He smiles lamely and says, "How was I supposed to know there would be so much traffic?" Should he be prepared to duck?

Frustration and Aggression

As this all-too-familiar story suggests, frustration is a major cause of aggression. Frustration occurs when a person is thwarted on the way to an expected goal or gratification. All of us have felt frustrated from time to time—at least three or four times a

Is road rage inevitably caused by frustration with drivers who get in the driver's way? If so, how come not every driver gets as angry as this guy?

week, if not three or four times a day! Research has shown that frustration can increase the probability of an aggressive response. This tendency is referred to as **frustration-aggression theory**, which holds that people's perception that they are being prevented from attaining a goal will increase the probability of an aggressive response (Dollard et al., 1939). This does not mean that frustration always leads to aggression, but it frequently does, especially when the frustration is decidedly unpleasant, unwelcome, and uncontrollable.

In a classic experiment, young children were led to a roomful of attractive toys that were kept out of their reach by a wire screen (Braker, Dembo, & Lewin, 1941). After a long wait, the children were finally allowed to play with the toys. In a control condition, a different group of children were allowed to play with the toys immediately, without first being frustrated. These children played joyfully with the toys, but the frustrated group, when finally given access to the toys, was extremely destructive: Many smashed the toys, threw them against the wall, stepped on them, and so forth.

Several things can increase frustration and, accordingly, will increase the probability that some form of aggression will occur. One such factor involves your closeness to the goal or the object of your desire. The closer the goal, the greater the expectation of pleasure that is thwarted; the greater the expectation, the more likely the aggression. This was demonstrated in a field experiment (Harris, 1974). A confederate cut in line in front of people who were waiting in a variety of places—for movie tickets, outside crowded restaurants, and at the checkout counter of a supermarket. On some occasions, the confederate cut in front of the second person in line; at other times, in front of the twelfth person. The results were clear: The people standing right behind the intruder were much more aggressive when the confederate cut into the second place in line.

Aggression also increases when the frustration is unexpected (Kulik & Brown, 1979). Experimenters hired students to telephone strangers and ask for donations to a charity. The students worked on a commission basis, receiving a small fraction of each dollar pledged. Some of the students were led to expect a high rate of contributions, others to expect far less success. The experiment was rigged so that none of the potential donors agreed to make a contribution. What happened? The callers with high expectations were more verbally aggressive toward the nondonors, speaking more harshly and slamming down the phone with more force, than were the callers with low expectations.

As we've said, frustration does not always produce aggression. Rather, it seems to produce anger or annoyance and a *readiness* to aggress if other things about the situation are conducive to aggressive behavior (Berkowitz, 1989, 1993; Gustafson, 1989). What are those other things? Well, an obvious one would be the size and strength of the person responsible for your frustration, as well as that person's ability to retaliate. It is undoubtedly easier to slam the phone down on a reluctant donor who is miles away and has no idea who you are than to take out your anger against your frustrator if he turned out to be the middle linebacker of the Green Bay Packers and was staring you right in the face. Similarly, if the frustration is understandable, legitimate, and unintentional, the tendency to aggress will be reduced. In one experiment, when a confederate "unwittingly" sabotaged his teammates' effort to solve a problem because his hearing aid had stopped working, the teammates' resulting frustration did not lead to a measurable degree of aggression (Burnstein & Worchel, 1962).

Frustration-Aggression Theory

The theory that frustration—the perception that you are being prevented from attaining a goal—increases the probability of an aggressive response.

We want to make it clear that frustration is not the same as deprivation: Children who don't have toys do not aggress more than children who do. In the toy experiment, frustration and aggression occurred because the children had every reason to expect to play with the toys, and their reasonable expectation was thwarted; this thwarting was what caused the children to behave destructively.

On a national scale also, thwarted expectations combined with frustration can produce riots and revolutions. Social scientists have found that it is often not *absolute* deprivation that creates anger and aggression, but *relative* deprivation, which occurs when people see a discrepancy between what they have and what they expect to have (Moore, 1978). For example, the nationwide race riots of 1967 and 1968 occurred in the middle of rising expectations and increased social spending to fight poverty. The most serious riots in that era occurred not in the geographic areas of greatest poverty, but in Los Angeles and Detroit, where things were not nearly as bad for African Americans as they were in most other large urban centers. But conditions were bad relative to the rioters' perception of how white people were doing and relative to the positive changes many African Americans had a right to expect.

A similar phenomenon occurred in Eastern Europe in 1991, when serious rebellion against the Soviet Union took place only after the government had loosened the chains controlling the population. And research on contemporary suicide bombers in the Middle East, including Mohamed Atta, who led the 9/11 attack on the World Trade Center, shows that they usually have no psychopathology and are often quite educated and affluent (Krueger, 2007; Sageman, 2008; Silke, 2003). But they were motivated by anger over the perceived discrepancy between what they had and what they felt their nation and religion were entitled to. Thus, an important cause of aggression is relative deprivation: the perception that you (or your group) have less than you deserve, less than what you have been led to expect, or less than what people similar to you have.

Evils which are patiently endured when they seem inevitable become intolerable when once the idea of escape from them is suggested.

—Alexis de Tocqueville

Provocation and Reciprocation

Suppose you are working at your part-time job behind the counter, flipping hamburgers in a crowded fast-food restaurant. Today, you are working harder than usual because the other short-order cook went home sick, and the customers are lining up at the counter, clamoring for their burgers. In your eagerness to speed up the process, you spin around too fast and knock over a large jar of pickles that smashes on the floor just as the boss enters the workplace. "Boy, are you clumsy!" he screams. "I'm gonna dock your pay $10 for that one; grab a broom and clean up, you moron! I'll take over here!" You glare at him. You'd love to tell him what he can do with this lousy job.

Nothing is more costly, nothing is more sterile, than revenge.

—Winston Churchill

Aggression frequently stems from the need to reciprocate after being provoked by aggressive behavior from another person. Although the Christian plea to "turn the other cheek" is wonderful advice, most people don't take it, as has been demonstrated in countless experiments in and out of the laboratory. Typical of this line of research is an experiment by Robert Baron (1988) in which participants prepared an advertisement for a new product; their ad was then evaluated and criticized by an accomplice of the experimenter. In one condition, the criticism, though strong, was done in a gentle and considerate manner ("I think there's a lot of room for improvement"); in the other condition, the criticism was given in an insulting manner ("I don't think you could be original if you tried"). When provided with an opportunity to retaliate, those people who were criticized harshly were far more likely to do so than those in the "gentle criticism" condition.

But even when provoked, people do not always reciprocate. We ask ourselves, was the provocation intentional or not? When we are convinced it was unintentional, or if there are mitigating circumstances, most of us will not reciprocate (Kremer & Stephens, 1983). But to curtail an aggressive response, we must be aware of those mitigating circumstances at the time of the provocation (Johnson & Rule, 1986). In one study, students were insulted by the experimenter's assistant. Half of them were first told that the assistant was upset after receiving an unfair low grade on a chemistry exam; the other students received this information only after the insult was delivered. All subjects later had an opportunity to retaliate by choosing the level of unpleasant noise

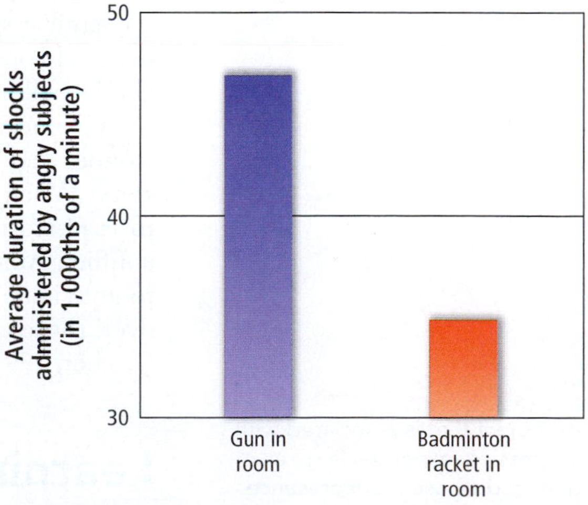

FIGURE 12.2

The Trigger Can Pull the Finger

Aggressive cues, such as weapons, tend to increase levels of aggression.

(Based on data in Berkowitz & Le Page, 1967)

TRY IT! Insults and Aggression

Think about the last time you felt insulted by another person, and note down your answers to these questions:

- Who insulted you?
- What were the circumstances?
- Did you take it personally or not?
- How did you respond?

Review your answers. How does your behavior relate to the material you have just finished reading?

with which to zap the assistant. Those students who knew about the mitigating circumstances before being insulted delivered weaker bursts of noise. Why the difference? At the time of the insult, the informed students simply did not take it personally and therefore felt no need to retaliate. This interpretation is bolstered by evidence of their physiological arousal: At the time of the insult, the heartbeat of the insulted students did not increase as rapidly if they knew about the assistant's unhappy state of mind beforehand.

Aggressive Objects as Cues

Certain stimuli seem to impel us to action. Is it conceivable that the mere presence of an **aggressive stimulus**—an object that is associated with aggressive responses—might increase the probability of aggression? (See the Try It! on this page.)

In a classic experiment, Leonard Berkowitz and Anthony Le Page (1967) purposely angered college students by insulting them. Some of the students were in a room in which a gun was left lying around (ostensibly from a previous experiment), and others in a room in which a neutral object (a badminton racket) was substituted for the gun. Participants were then given the opportunity to administer what they believed were electric shocks to a fellow college student. Those individuals who had been angered in the presence of the gun administered stronger electric shocks than those angered in the presence of the racket (see Figure 12.2 on the previous page). This provocative finding has been replicated many times in the United States and Europe (Frodi, 1975; Turner & Leyens, 1992; Turner et al., 1977). Male college students asked to interact with a gun for 15 minutes show higher testosterone levels than do students playing a children's game for the same amount of time (Klinesmith et al., 2006). Such findings point to a conclusion opposite to the familiar slogan often used by opponents of gun control, that "guns don't kill; people do." As Leonard Berkowitz (1981) put it, "The finger pulls the trigger, but the trigger may also be pulling the finger."

Violence, especially involving guns, is a major part of American society, so it is no wonder that it plays a major role in the expectations and fantasies of American youngsters. When teenagers from the United States and 10 other countries were asked to read stories involving conflict among people and to predict the outcome of the conflict, American teenagers were more likely than teenagers from other countries to anticipate a violent conclusion (Archer, 1994; Archer & McDaniel, 1995). Moreover, those conclusions were far more likely to be "lethal, gun-laden and merciless" (Archer, 1994, p. 19).

Aggressive Stimulus
An object that is associated with aggressive responses (e.g., a gun) and whose mere presence can increase the probability of aggression.

Social Learning Theory
The theory that people learn social behavior (e.g., aggression) in large part by observing others and imitating them.

Learning to Behave Aggressively

Most American children are immersed in images of violence in TV, movies, video games, pop and rap music, music videos, comics, and everywhere on the Internet. Immersed in it? They are marinated in it! They see an unending parade of murders, rapes, beatings, explosions, and bad guys committing brutal acts as well as good guys doing brutal things to catch them.

Social learning theory holds that we learn social behavior, from aggression to altruism, in large part by observing others and imitating them. Most people take their cues from others. If we want to know whether aggressive behavior is okay, we will look to see what others are doing or what others are saying about it. Thus, if a respected person or institution endorses aggression, it will have an impact on the attitudes and behavior of many people. Brad Bushman and his colleagues (2007) explored the impact of religiously sanctioned stories of violence and aggression. They found that when a violent story was attributed to the Bible and when, in that story, God sanctioned the violence, the reader was more likely to behave aggressively afterward. The effect held for nonreligious as well as religious participants.

When it comes to the imitation of aggression, the influence of others is not confined to prestigious institutions like religion. Almost anyone will do, and children are especially vulnerable to influence. Children frequently learn to solve conflicts aggressively by imitating adults and their peers, especially when they see that the aggression is rewarded. For example, in most sports the more aggressive players usually achieve the greatest fame and the highest salaries, and the more aggressive teams win more games. In sports, it usually doesn't pay to be a gentle soul. Famed baseball manager Leo Durocher once said, "Nice guys finish last," and the data bear him out. In professional hockey, those players most frequently sent to the penalty box for overly aggressive play also scored the most goals and earned the highest salaries (McCarthy & Kelly, 1978). To the extent that athletes serve as role models for children and adolescents, what is being modeled is that fame and fortune go hand in hand with excessive aggressiveness.

Similarly, if children watch their parents or other adults they admire yelling, kicking, and acting in other aggressive ways, that is the behavior they will copy. In a classic series of experiments, Albert Bandura and his associates demonstrated the power of social learning on children's aggressive behavior (Bandura, Ross, & Ross, 1961, 1963). Their basic procedure was to have an adult knock around a plastic, air-filled Bobo doll, the kind that bounces back after it's been knocked down. The adult would smack the doll around with the palm of a hand, strike it with a mallet, kick it, and yell aggressive things at it. The kids were then allowed to play with the doll. In these experiments, the children imitated the aggressive adults and treated the doll in almost exactly the same ways, as you can see in Figure 12.3. Some of them went beyond mere imitation, coming up with inventive new forms of beating up the doll. Children who did not see the aggressive adult in action almost never unleashed any aggression against the hapless doll. This research offers strong support for the social learning of aggressive behavior—the power of watching and imitating the behavior of others.

Children have never been very good at listening to their elders, but they have never failed to imitate them.

—James Baldwin, *Nobody Knows My Name*

Simulate on **MyPsychLab**

To learn more about the Bobo Doll studies, try the MyPsychLab simulation ***Aggression and Prosocial Behavior***.

Violence in the Media

If merely watching adults behave aggressively causes children to mistreat dolls, what does watching violence on television and in the movies do to them, or for that matter to all of us? What about violent video games in which children participate in the virtual destruction of cities and the lopping off of heads and limbs of characters?

For many people, it is as obvious as the Bobo doll study that children imitate the violence they see and are otherwise affected emotionally by all those exploding heads and guts. For just as many others, media violence consists of cartoon-like stories and images that everyone knows are not real. As one columnist wrote, "I grew up playing with toy guns and have never shot anybody (though I know plenty who deserve it)" (Simon, 2011). But if prosocial videos can increase helpful behavior in children who watch them (Gentile et al., 2009; Greitemeyer & Osswald, 2010; see Chapter 11), surely the far more common antisocial, violent videos can increase antisocial, violent behavior, right?

Television has brought murder back into the home—where it belongs.

—Alfred Hitchcock, 1965

In 2011, in a 7-to-2 decision, the Supreme Court overruled a California ban on the sale of violent video games to minors. The Court ruled that videos can be sold to minors no matter how violent the games are, including the popular *Mortal Kombat* and *Grand Theft Auto* series. Anthony Scalia, a conservative justice of the court, reasoned that fairy tales are also plenty violent. "Grimm's Fairy Tales are grim indeed," he wrote.

FIGURE 12.3

The Bobo Doll Experiment

Children learn aggressive behavior through imitation. In this classic study, the experimenter modeled some rather violent treatment of the doll—and the children imitated her perfectly.

"As her just deserts for trying to poison Snow White, the wicked queen is made to dance in red hot slippers until she fell dead on the floor."

Well, maybe Judge Scalia is right. But it seems reasonable to ask whether reading a fairy tale, even a violent one, is equivalent to blowing up the wicked queen yourself and watching her guts explode. How would you investigate this question, or any other effects of media violence? There are countless stories in the news that seem to provide a compelling answer. For example, several years ago, a man drove his truck through the window of a crowded cafeteria in Killeen, Texas, emerged from the cab, and began shooting people at random. He killed 22 people and then turned the gun on himself. In his pocket police found a ticket stub to *The Fisher King*, a film depicting a deranged man firing a shotgun into a crowded bar, killing several people. Dylan Klebold and Eric Harris, the Columbine killers, enjoyed the violent video game *Doom*, and the Columbine murders themselves spurred many acts of violence across the United States (Aronson, 2000). Two teenagers in Tennessee took their guns and went out sniping at passing cars on a freeway, killing one driver, because they wanted to act out their favorite video game, *Grand Theft Auto*. And then there is the case of a man who, having seen a movie showing women dancing on screen, became convinced that all women were immoral and deserved to die. He then committed four brutal rape-murders before he was caught. The film that set him off was *The Ten Commandments*.

But social scientists know that anecdotes, no matter how interesting they may be, are not sufficient to answer the question of the effects of media violence. It's too easy to cherry-pick your examples to make a case either way; you could select examples of kids who play *Grand Theft Auto* and then go off to do their homework and take piano lessons. The beauty of the laboratory experiment is that it allows us to determine whether aggressive media have any impact at all on the behavior of a random sample of people (see Chapter 2). In such an experiment, the situation is completely controlled; every factor can be held constant except for exposure to violence; and the dependent variable, the participant's behavior, can likewise be carefully measured.

Listen on **MyPsychLab**

To learn more, listen to the MyPsychLab audio ***Psychology in the News: Social Psychology—Aggression and Video Games.***

Experimental Studies of Media Violence Most of the experimental evidence demonstrates that watching violence does increase the frequency of aggressive behavior, angry emotions, and hostile thoughts (Anderson et al., 2003; Anderson et al., 2010; Cantor et al., 2001; Greitemeyer & McLatchie, 2011; Huesmann & Miller, 1994; Paik & Comstock,

1994; Wood, Wong, & Chachere, 1991). The research is not consistent, however, and two reviews of the experimental literature found minimal or no effects (Ferguson, 2007a, 2007b; Sherry, 2001). However, actively playing violent video games seems to have a stronger influence: Games that directly reward violence—for example, by awarding points or moving the player to the next level after a "kill"—are especially likely to increase feelings of hostility, aggressive thoughts, and aggressive acts (Carnagey & Anderson, 2005). Exposing children to a graphically violent video game has a direct and immediate impact on their aggressive thoughts and behavior, and this is true not only for American youngsters but also for those in other nations (Anderson et al., 2010).

Does watching violent movies make children numb to what violence really does?

In one early experiment, a group of children watched an extremely violent TV episode of a police drama. In a control condition, a similar group of children watched an exciting but nonviolent TV sporting event for the same length of time. Each child was then allowed to play in another room with a group of other children. Those who had watched the violent police drama later behaved far more aggressively with their playmates than did those who had watched the sporting event—the Bobo doll effect (Liebert & Baron, 1972).

Exposure to media violence has these effects for three reasons: It increases physiological arousal and excitement; it triggers an automatic tendency to imitate the hostile or violent characters; and it *primes* existing aggressive ideas and expectations (Anderson et al., 2003). Just as exposing young adults to rifles and other weapons left lying around the house or the laboratory has a tendency to increase the probability of an aggressive response when they are subsequently frustrated or hurt, exposing children to an endless stream of violence in films and on TV has a tendency to prime an aggressive response. Movies and games also prime our social **scripts**, approved ways of behaving socially that we learn implicitly from the culture. (Of course, scripts can prime thoughts of helping and being kind as well as being selfish and aggressive.)

The Numbing and Dehumanizing Effects of Media Violence Does watching violence have other effects? What is going on in people's heads when they are playing violent games or watching people being blown up, and with what results?

Repeated exposure to difficult or unpleasant events tends to have a numbing effect on our sensitivity to those events. In one experiment, researchers measured the physiological responses of young men while they were watching a rather brutal and bloody boxing match (Cline, Croft, & Courier, 1973). Those who had watched a lot of TV in their daily lives seemed relatively indifferent to the mayhem in the ring; that is, they showed little physiological evidence of excitement, anxiety, or other arousal. They were unmoved by the violence. But those who typically watched relatively little TV showed major physiological arousal; the violence really agitated them.

Viewing television violence can subsequently numb people's reactions when they face real-life aggression (Thomas et al., 1977). The researchers had their subjects watch either a violent police drama or an exciting but nonviolent volleyball game. After a short break, the subjects were allowed to observe a verbally and physically aggressive interaction between two preschoolers. Those who had watched the police show responded less emotionally than those who had watched the volleyball game. Viewing the initial violence seemed to have desensitized them to further acts of violence; they were not upset by an incident that by all rights should have upset them. Although such a reaction may psychologically protect us from feeling upset, it may also have the unintended effect of increasing our indifference to victims of violence and perhaps render us more accepting of violence as an aspect of life in the modern world.

This numbing effect may also make people more oblivious to the needs of others. In one field study, people who had just seen a violent movie took longer to come to the aid of a woman struggling to pick up her crutches than did people who had seen a nonviolent movie or people still waiting to see one of the two movies (Bushman & Anderson, 2009).

Scripts

Ways of behaving socially that we learn implicitly from our culture.

When you are playing a violent video game, you are likely to see yourself as the hero who is blasting those evil creatures out of existence. That's fun, as far as it goes, but some

Simulate on **MyPsychLab**
To learn more about how studies like these are conducted, try the MyPsychLab simulation ***Media Violence and Societal Aggression***.

research suggests it can go further: Once players get in the habit of dehumanizing the "enemy," that habit can be carried over into how players come to regard real people, not just robots and lifelike cartoons. In two experiments in England, researchers found that participants (male and female) who played a violent video game (*Lamers*) were later more likely to dehumanize immigrants to Britain, seeing them as somehow less human and deserving than native Britons, in contrast to the students who played a prosocial version of the game (*Lemmings*) or a neutral game (*Tetris*) (Greitemeyer & McLatchie, 2011).

Longitudinal Effects of Media Violence Taken together, these experiments show that under controlled conditions there is an impact of media violence on children and teenagers. The lab allows us to demonstrate that something of significance is happening, but it has a major limitation: Experiments cannot begin to capture the effects on a person who plays video games 20 or 30 hours a week and lives on a steady diet of action and horror films over weeks, months, and years.

To investigate that effect, we need to use longitudinal studies in which children are followed for a year or longer. The researcher has less control over the factors being studied, but it is a better way of determining the effects of what a child is *really* being exposed to. In addition, unlike most laboratory experiments that must use artificial measures of aggression (such as administering fake electric shocks or loud noises to the victim), longitudinal studies can examine seriously aggressive behavior such as assault. The disadvantage of this method is that people's lives are full of many other factors that can enhance or mitigate the effects of media violence.

Longitudinal research finds that the more violence children watch on TV, the more violence they exhibit later as teenagers and young adults (Anderson et al., 2003; Eron, 1987, 2001). For example, one study followed more than 700 families over a period of 17 years. The amount of time spent watching television during adolescence and early adulthood was strongly related to the likelihood of later committing violent acts against others, including assault. This association was significant regardless of parental education, family income, and extent of neighborhood violence (Johnson, 2002). Another, more recent study followed 430 elementary-age children in the third to fifth grades over the course of a school year. The investigators measured three types of aggression—verbal, relational, and physical—and exposure to violence in television, movies, and video games. They measured both aggressive and prosocial behaviors in the children twice during the year, interviewing the children's peers and teachers as well as observing the children directly. They found that the children's consumption of media violence early in the school year predicted higher rates of all three kinds of aggression (verbal, relational, and physical) and less prosocial behavior later in the year (Gentile, Coyne, & Walsh, 2011).

Longitudinal studies find another, unexpected consequence of watching a heavy dose of media violence: the magnification of danger. If I am watching all this murder and mayhem on the TV screen, wouldn't it be logical for me to conclude that it isn't safe to leave the house, especially after dark? That is precisely what many heavy TV viewers do conclude. Adolescents and adults who watch TV for more than 4 hours per day are more likely than light TV viewers (who watch less than 2 hours per day) to have an exaggerated view of the degree of violence taking place outside their own homes, and they have a much greater fear of being personally assaulted (Gerbner et al., 2002).

The Problem of Cause and Effect The greatest challenge involved in trying to interpret the data in most nonexperimental longitudinal studies and survey research is that of teasing apart cause and effect. The usual assumption has been that watching violence makes people more aggressive, but aggressive people are also drawn to watching violence. Moreover, another entirely independent factor may be causing both. Consider the survey research showing that people who watch a lot of TV also believe that the outside world is a dangerous place and that the crime rate is higher than it actually is. It is possible that watching TV violence made them fearful. But it is just as likely that they spend a lot of time indoors because they think there is danger in the streets; and being at home with nothing to do, they watch a lot of TV. Similarly, some children are born with a mental or emotional predisposition toward violence, or learn it as toddlers from the way they are treated by abusive parents or siblings, or in other ways develop aggressiveness as a personality trait. In turn, this trait or predisposition manifests itself in both their aggressive behavior *and* their liking for watching violence or playing aggressive games (Bushman, 1995).

Indeed, where violence in the media is concerned, causality is a two-way street. In one experiment, youngsters were exposed to either a film depicting a great deal of police violence or an exciting, nonviolent film about bike racing. The youngsters then played a game of floor hockey. Watching the violent film had the effect of increasing the number of aggressive acts committed during the hockey game, but primarily by the youngsters who had previously been rated as highly aggressive by their teachers. These kids hit others with their sticks, threw elbows, and yelled aggressive things at their opponents to a much greater extent than did either the kids rated as nonaggressive who had also watched the violent film or the kids rated as aggressive who had watched the nonviolent film (Josephson, 1987).

Does playing violent games, like paintball, make adults more prone to real violence?

Likewise, a few longitudinal studies have shown that exposure to violence in media or video games has the strongest relationship in children who are already predisposed to violence (Anderson & Dill, 2000). Thus, it may be that watching media violence merely serves to give them permission to express their aggressive inclinations (Ferguson & Kilburn, 2009). The same conclusions apply to the research on violent pornography. Meta-analyses repeatedly conclude that exposure to violent pornography has a strong effect on male viewers, increasing their hostility and aggressiveness toward women (Allen, D'Alessio, & Brezgel, 1995; Paik & Comstock, 1994). But the effects of watching violent pornography are strongest on men who already have high levels of hostility toward women and are predisposed to commit violence against them (see Chapter 2).

Does Violence Sell? Keep in mind that one reason that violence in the media is so prevalent is simply that it sells: People flock to action films with lots of killing and car chases, to horror films with lots of scary exploding body parts, and to video games that total up the kills. So it is understandable that advertisers would want to place their ads on TV shows that provide plenty of mayhem, assuming that viewers would be more inclined to see their ads and buy their products. Yet this logical assumption has an unexpected consequence. What if it turns out that certain kinds of shows produce so much mental turmoil that the sponsor's product is soon forgotten?

In one experiment, people watched TV shows that were either violent, sexually explicit, or neutral (Bushman & Bonacci, 2002). Each of the shows contained the same nine ads. Immediately after seeing the show, the viewers had to recall the brands and to pick them out from photos of supermarket shelves. Twenty-four hours later, the researchers telephoned the viewers and asked them to recall the brands they had seen during the viewing. The people who had seen the ads while watching a neutral (nonviolent, non–sexually explicit) show were able to recall the advertised brands better than did the people who saw the violent show or the sexually explicit show. This was true both immediately after viewing and 24 hours later, and was true for both men and women of all ages. It seems that watching media violence and sex impairs the memory of viewers, at least for ads that get in the way of the story! In terms of maximizing sales, advertisers might be well advised to sponsor nonviolent shows.

Conclusions: Putting Media Violence in Perspective Taking all this research together, we conclude that violent media does have an impact on average children and adolescents, but its impact is greatest on those who are already prone to violent behavior. Clearly, not all people, or even a sizable percentage of people, are motivated to commit violence as a result of watching it. People's interpretation of what they are watching, their personality dispositions, and the social context can all affect how they respond (Feshbach & Tangney, 2008). Children and teens watch many different programs and movies and have many models to observe besides those they see in the media, including parents and peers. But the fact that some people *are* influenced by violent entertainments, with tragic results, cannot be denied. As suggested throughout this discussion, there are at least five distinct reactions that explain why exposure to media violence might increase aggression in vulnerable viewers:

1. *If they can do it, so can I.* When people see characters behaving violently, it may weaken their previously learned inhibitions against violent behavior.
2. *Oh, so that's how you do it!* When people see characters behaving violently, it might trigger imitation, providing them with ideas as to how they might go about it.
3. *Those feelings I am having must be real anger rather than merely my reaction to a stressful day.* Watching violence may put people more in touch with their feelings of anger and make an aggressive response more likely through priming. Having recently viewed violence, someone might interpret his or her own feelings of mild irritation as intense anger and then be more likely to lash out.
4. *Ho-hum, another brutal beating. What's on the other channel?* Watching a lot of mayhem seems to reduce both our sense of horror about violence and our sympathy for the victims, making it easier for us to live with violence and perhaps easier for us to act aggressively.
5. *I had better get him before he gets me!* If watching a lot of TV makes people think the world is a dangerous place, they might be more apt to be hostile to a stranger who approaches them on the street.

Finally, however, let's put all of this research in larger perspective. The impact of the media pales in comparison to the biological, social, economic, and psychological factors that are far more powerful predictors of aggressive behavior: a child's genetic predispositions to violence, low feelings of self-control, being socially rejected by peers (which we will discuss further at the end of this chapter), criminal opportunity, being the victim of childhood physical abuse, and living in a violent community where aggression is a way of life (Crescioni & Baumeister, 2009; Ferguson & Kilburn, 2009).

Sexual Violence Against Women

A particularly troubling aspect of aggression is sexual violence. Why do men rape? Some men commit rape out of a desire to dominate, humiliate, or punish their victim. This motive is apparent among soldiers who rape captive women during war and then often kill them (Olujic, 1998), and among men who rape other men, usually by anal penetration (King & Woollett, 1997). The latter form of rape typically occurs in youth gangs, where the intention is to humiliate rival gang members, and in prison, where the motive, in addition to having a sexual outlet, is to conquer and degrade the victim. Far rarer are the men who commit gruesome serial rape-murders and who are mentally ill.

When most people think of a "rapist," they imagine a predatory stranger or a crazy serial killer. But the fact is that about 85% of all rapes or attempted rapes do not involve assaults by a stranger but are instances of acquaintance rape, in which the victim knows the assailant, or date rape, in which the victim may be having a relationship with the assailant (Koss, 2011). Acquaintance and date rape include direct assault: drugging the victim into a blackout with Rohypnol ("roofies"), sex with a victim who is drunk or otherwise incapacitated, and sex under physical coercion and threat.

Sexually aggressive males who commit these acts are often narcissistic, are unable to empathize with women, may feel hostility and contempt toward women, and feel entitled to have sexual relations with whatever woman they choose. (This may be why sexual violence is often committed by high-status men, including sports heroes, powerful politicians, and celebrities, who could easily find consenting sexual partners.) They misperceive women's behavior in social situations, equate feelings of power with sexuality, and accuse women of provoking them (Bushman et al., 2003; Malamuth et al., 1995; Zurbriggen, 2000). One interesting study compared men who had forcibly raped a woman with men who used manipulative techniques to have sex and with men who had had consensual sex only. The rapists were far more likely to have grown up in violent households, were more accepting of male violence, and were less likely to endorse love as a motive for sex than did the others (Lyden, White, & Kadlec, 2007).

But date rape can, unfortunately, also occur because of misunderstandings caused by the different roles that males and females play, which is why the sexes often disagree on whether or not a "rape" has occurred (Hamby & Koss, 2003). In a nationally representative survey of more than 3 thousand Americans ages 18 to 59, nearly one-fourth of the women said that a man, usually a husband or boyfriend, had forced them to do something sexually that they did not want to do, yet only about 3% of the men said they had ever forced a woman into a sexual act (Laumann et al., 1994). Conversely, however, some women are uncomfortable about or unwilling to admit that they have been raped, especially if they know their assailant (Koss, 2011). About half of all women who report a sexual assault that meets the legal definition of rape—being forced to engage in sexual acts against their will—do not label it as rape (McMullin & White, 2006; Ward & Lundberg-Love, 2006). College women tend to define rape as being forced into intercourse by an acquaintance or stranger, or as having been molested as a child. They are least likely to call their experience rape if they were sexually assaulted by a boyfriend, were drunk or otherwise drugged, or were forced to have oral sex (Kahn, 2004).

A lot of campus rapes start here.
Whenever there's drinking or drugs, things can get out of hand. So it's no surprise that many campus rapes involve alcohol.
But you should know that under any circumstances, sex without the other person's consent is considered rape. A felony, punishable by prison. And drinking is no excuse.
That's why, when you party, it's good to know what your limits are. You see, a little sobering thought now can save you from a big problem later.

A complicating factor in defining date rape stems from the different *sexual scripts* that adolescents learn as part of their gender roles in society (Gagnon & Simon, 1973; Laumann & Gagnon, 1995). Sexual scripts vary according to one's culture, sexual orientation, ethnicity, and geographic region, and they change over time. Nonetheless, one dominant script in America for young heterosexuals is that the female's role is to resist the male's sexual advances and the male's role is to be persistent. For example, an analysis of 25 primetime television shows that are most popular with teenagers found that male characters frequently act out the traditional male script by actively and aggressively pursuing sex; many female characters still play the part of "sex object" and are judged by their sexual conduct (Kim et al., 2007). (Sexual scripts for gay men and lesbians tend to be more flexible than heterosexual scripts because partners are not following traditional gender roles [Kurdek, 2005]).

The existence of scripts that dictate conventional sexual behavior may explain why there is so much confusion, anger, and joking over the meaning of the word *no*. The slogan of antirape groups—"What part of NO don't you understand?"—seems obvious. Yet, for men who are following traditional sexual scripts, "no" occasionally means "yes" or "in a little while," and many women, following their own scripts, agree with them. In one survey of high school students, although almost 100% of the males and females agreed that the man should stop his sexual advances as soon as the woman says no, nearly half of those same students also believed that when a woman says no she doesn't always mean it (Monson, Langhinrichsen-Rohling, & Binderup, 2002). The resulting confusion may also explain why some college women feel they need to be drunk in order to have sex (Cole, 2006; Howard, Griffin, & Boekeloo, 2008). After all, if they are drunk, they haven't said "yes," and if they haven't explicitly said "yes," no one can accuse them of being a slut (or one of the many other negative words often assigned to women who are sexually active). Such findings suggest that an important step toward reducing sexual aggression is for both sexes to make sure that they are following a script that is in the same play.

How to Reduce Aggression

"Stop hitting your brother!" "Turn off the TV and go to your room RIGHT NOW!" Most parents, trying to curb the aggressive behavior of their children, use some form of punishment. Some deny privileges; others shout, threaten, or use force, believing in the old saying, "Spare the rod and spoil the child." How well does punishment work? On the

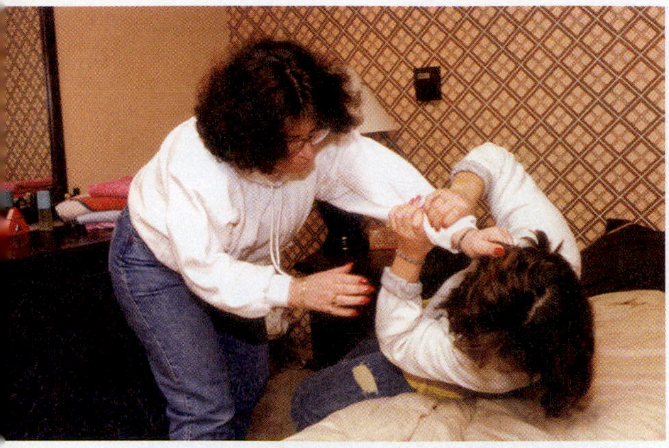

Many tired, exasperated parents punish their children's misbehavior by shouting at them or hitting or grabbing them. But this kind of punishment usually backfires, making the child angry and resentful without stopping the misbehavior. On the contrary, it teaches children what to do when they are tired and exasperated—hit someone.

one hand, you might think that punishing any behavior would reduce its frequency. On the other hand, if the punishment takes the form of an aggressive act, parents who are administering the penalty are actually modeling aggressive behavior—thereby inducing their child to imitate their action.

Does Punishing Aggression Reduce Aggression?

Let's consider the complexities of punishment. As we discussed in Chapter 6, several experiments with preschoolers demonstrated that the threat of relatively severe punishment for committing a transgression does not make the transgression less appealing to the child. But the threat of *mild* punishment, of a degree just powerful enough to get the child to stop the undesired activity temporarily, leads the child to try to justify his or her restraint and, as a result, can make the behavior less appealing (Aronson & Carlsmith, 1963; Freedman, 1965).

However, the use of *harsh* punishments to reduce aggression in children or adults usually backfires for several reasons. People may shout things they don't mean or, out of frustration, use severe methods to try to control the behavior of their children. The target of all this noise and abuse is then likely to respond with anxiety or anger, rather than with a reaction of "Thanks, I'd better correct that aggressive habit you don't like." In some cases, angry attention may be just what the offender is hoping to get. If a mother yells at her daughter who is throwing a tantrum, the very act of yelling may give her what she wants: namely, a reaction from her. Most seriously, extreme punishment—physical abuse—is a risk factor in children for the development of depression, low self-esteem, violent behavior, and many other problems (Gershoff, 2002; Widom, DuMont, & Czaja, 2007). And, finally, punishment often fails because it tells the target what not to do, but it does not communicate what the person should do. Spanking a little boy for hitting his sister will not teach him to play cooperatively with her.

Because of these drawbacks, most psychologists believe that harsh punishment is a poor way to eliminate aggressive or other unwanted behavior. In certain cases, for example when a bully is hitting a classmate, temporary physical restraint is usually called for. But is that the best strategy to keep a bully from behaving aggressively when the adult leaves the room?

All punishment is mischief; all punishment itself is evil.
—Jeremy Bentham, *Principles of Morals and Legislation*, 1789

And what if the problem is a virtual bully? Bullying, in which a stronger person intentionally humiliates or physically abuses a weaker one, has long been a fact of school life, and cyberbullying simply translates that impulse into a newer technology (Rivers, Chesney, & Coyne, 2011; Wade & Beran, 2011). Cyberbullying ranges from the less severe (prank calls and mild insults on instant messaging) to extremely severe acts (posting unpleasant or sexual photos on Web sites; sending a target photos or videos of threatening, violent scenes; and widely distributing insults, nasty text messages, rumors, and ugly accusations). It may be a one-time impulsive act or a planned campaign of harassment. According to a review prepared for the government on "Child Safety and Online Technologies," the greatest source of danger that teenagers face on the Internet does not come from pornography (which many teens themselves, usually older boys, seek out) or even from predatory adults, let alone from sexting. "Bullying and harassment, most often by peers, are the most frequent threats that minors face, both online and offline," the report found (Berkman Center for Internet & Society, 2008).

CONNECTIONS

Curbing Bullying: A Case Study in Reducing Aggression at School

Some years ago, the Norwegian government became concerned over the suicides of three young victims of bullying and the attempted suicide of several others. One sixth grader, after having been insulted, mocked, and harassed on a daily basis, was taken to the bathroom by his tormentors, who made him lie face down in the urinal. He went home and tried to kill himself. His parents found him unconscious.

Alarmed, the Norwegian government commissioned psychologist Dan Olweus (1991, 1997) to assess the problem of bullying across the entire nation and develop an intervention that might help reduce it. After surveying all of Norway's 90,000 schoolchildren, Olweus concluded that bullying was serious and widespread, that teachers and parents were only dimly aware of bullying incidents, and that even when adults were aware of these incidents, they rarely intervened. (This is also true in the United States.) The government sponsored a three-pronged campaign in every school to change the social dynamic that breeds bullies and victims.

First, community-wide meetings were held to explain the problem. Parents were given brochures detailing symptoms of victimization. Teachers received training on handling bullying. Students watched videotapes to evoke sympathy for victims of bullying. Second, students themselves, in their classes, discussed ways to prevent bullying and befriend lonely children. Teachers organized cooperative learning groups and moved quickly to stop name-calling and other aggression that escalates into bullying. Principals ensured that lunchrooms, bathrooms, and playgrounds were adequately supervised. Third, if bullying occurred despite these preventive steps, trained counselors intervened, using a combination of mild punishment and intensive therapy with the bully and counseling with the bully's parents.

Twenty months after the campaign began, acts of bullying had decreased by half, with improvements at every grade level. Olweus concluded, "It is no longer possible to avoid taking action about bullying problems at school using lack of awareness as an excuse—it all boils down to a matter of will and involvement on the part of adults" (1991, p. 415). Can you think of ways of using Olweus's techniques to reduce cyberbullying?

Using Punishment on Violent Adults The criminal justice system of most cultures administers harsh punishments both as retribution and as a means of deterring violent crimes like murder, manslaughter, and rape. Does the threat of harsh punishments make such crimes less likely? Do people who are about to commit violent crimes say to themselves, "I'd better not do this, because if I get caught I'm going to jail for a long time; I might even be executed"?

Laboratory experiments indicate that punishment can indeed act as a deterrent, but only if two conditions are met. Punishment must be both prompt and certain (Bower & Hilgard, 1981). It must follow quickly after the violence occurred, and it must be unavoidable. In the real world, these ideal conditions are almost never met, especially in a complex society with a high crime rate and a slow criminal justice system like our own. In most American cities, the probability that a person who commits a violent crime will be apprehended, charged, tried, and convicted is not high. Moreover, given the volume of cases in our courts, punishment is delayed by months or even years. Consequently, in the complex world of criminal justice, severe punishment is unlikely to have the kind of deterrent effect that it does in the controlled conditions of the laboratory.

Given these realities, severe punishment is not likely to deter violent crime. Countries that invoke the death penalty for murder do not have fewer murders per capita than those without it. American states that have abolished the death penalty have not had an increase in capital crimes, as some experts predicted (Archer & Gartner, 1984; Nathanson, 1987). A natural experiment occurred in the United States during a period that began with a national hiatus on the death penalty, resulting from a Supreme Court ruling that it constituted cruel and unusual punishment, and ended with the Court's reversal of that ruling in 1976. There was no indication that the return to capital punishment produced a decrease in homicides (Peterson & Bailey, 1988). Indeed, a study by the National Academy of Sciences demonstrated once again that consistency and certainty of punishment were far more effective deterrents of violent behavior than was severe punishment, including the death penalty (Berkowitz, 1993).

Catharsis
The notion that "blowing off steam"—by performing a verbally or physically aggressive act, watching others engage in aggressive behaviors, or engaging in a fantasy of aggression—relieves built-up aggressive energies and hence reduces the likelihood of further aggressive behavior.

Catharsis and Aggression

Conventional wisdom suggests that one way to reduce feelings of aggression is to do something aggressive. "Get it out of your system" has been common advice for decades: If you are feeling angry, yell, scream, curse, throw a dish at the wall; express the anger, and it won't build up into something uncontrollable. This belief stems from Sigmund Freud's psychoanalytic notion of **catharsis** (Dollard et al., 1939; Freud, 1933). Freud held a "hydraulic" idea of aggressive impulses: Unless people were allowed to express ("sublimate") their aggression in harmless or constructive ways, he believed, their aggressive energy would be dammed up, pressure would build, and the energy would seek an outlet, either exploding into acts of extreme violence or manifesting itself as symptoms of mental illness.

Unfortunately, Freud's theory of catharsis has been greatly oversimplified into the notion that people should vent their anger or they will suffer physically and emotionally; moreover, by venting that anger, they will become less likely to commit aggressive acts in the future. When we are feeling frustrated or angry, many of us do temporarily feel less tense after blowing off steam by yelling, cursing, or perhaps kicking the sofa. But do any of those actions reduce the chance that we will commit further aggression? Does the notion of catharsis square with the data?

The Effects of Aggressive Acts on Subsequent Aggression Following Freud, many psychoanalysts believed that playing competitive games served as a harmless outlet for aggressive energies (Menninger, 1948). But they were wrong. In fact, the reverse is true: Competitive games often make participants and observers more aggressive.

In one demonstration of this fact, the hostility levels of high school football players were measured one week before the football season began and one week after it ended. If the intense competitiveness and aggressive behavior that are part of playing football serve to reduce the tension caused by pent-up aggression, the players would be expected to show a decline in hostility over the course of the season. Instead, the results showed that feelings of hostility *increased* significantly (Patterson, 1974).

What about watching aggressive games? Will that reduce aggressive behavior? A Canadian sports psychologist tested this proposition by measuring the hostility of spectators at an especially violent hockey game (Russell, 1983). As the game progressed, the spectators became increasingly belligerent; toward the end of the final period, their level of hostility was extremely high and did not return to the pregame level until several hours after the game was over. Similar results have been found among spectators at football games and wrestling matches (Arms, Russell, & Sandilands, 1979; Branscombe & Wann, 1992; Goldstein & Arms, 1971). As with participating in an aggressive sport, watching one also increases aggressive behavior.

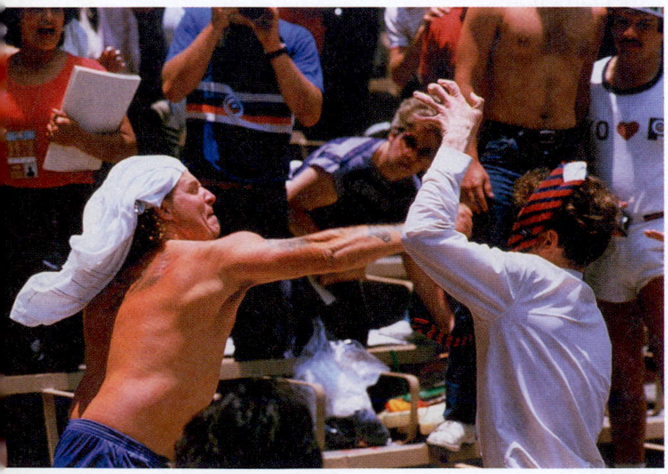

Fans watching aggressive sports do not become less aggressive; in fact, they may become more aggressive than if they hadn't watched at all.

Finally, does direct aggression against the source of your anger reduce further aggression? Again, the answer is no (Geen, 1998; Geen & Quanty, 1977). When people commit acts of aggression, such acts increase the tendency toward future aggression. In an early experiment, college students were paired with another student who was actually a confederate of the experimenters (Geen, Stonner, & Shope, 1975). First, the student was angered by the confederate; during this phase, which involved the exchanging of opinions on various issues, the student was instructed to give an electric shock to the confederate each time the confederate disagreed. (The shocks, of course, were phony.) Next, during a bogus study of "the effects of punishment on learning," the student acted as a teacher while the confederate served as learner. On the first learning task, some of the students were required to deliver electric shocks to the confederate each time he made a mistake; others merely recorded his errors. On the next task, all the students were given the opportunity to deliver shocks. If a cathartic effect were operating, we would expect the students who had previously given shocks to the confederate to administer fewer and weaker shocks the second time. This didn't happen; in fact, those students who had previously delivered shocks to the confederate expressed even greater aggression when given the subsequent opportunity to attack him.

Outside the lab, in the real world, we see the same phenomenon: Verbal acts of aggression are followed by more of the same. Many people feel worse, both physically and mentally, after an angry confrontation. When people brood and ruminate about their anger, talk to others incessantly about how angry they are, or ventilate their feelings in hostile acts, their blood pressure shoots up, they often feel angrier, and they behave even *more* aggressively later than if they had just let their feelings of anger subside (Bushman et al., 2005). Conversely, when people learn to control their tempers and express anger constructively, they usually feel better, not worse; they feel calmer, not angrier. All in all, the weight of the evidence does not support the catharsis hypothesis (Tavris, 1989).

Blaming the Victim of Our Aggression Imagine yourself in the experiments just described. After you've administered what you think are shocks to another person or have expressed hostility against someone you dislike, it becomes easier to do so a second time. Aggressing the first time can reduce your inhibitions against committing other such actions; in a sense, the aggression is legitimized, making it easier to carry out such assaults. Further, and more important, the main thrust of the research on this issue indicates that committing an overt act of aggression against a person *changes your feelings* about that person, increasing your negative feelings and making future aggression against that person more likely.

Does this material sound familiar? It should. As we saw in Chapter 6, harming someone sets in motion cognitive processes that are aimed at justifying the act of cruelty. When you hurt another person, you experience cognitive dissonance: The cognition "I hurt Charlie" is dissonant with the cognition "I am a decent, kind person." A good way for you to reduce dissonance is to convince yourself that hurting Charlie was not a bad thing to do. You can accomplish this by ignoring Charlie's virtues and emphasizing his faults, convincing yourself that Charlie is a bad person who deserved to be hurt. And you would be especially likely to reduce dissonance this way if Charlie was an innocent victim of your aggression. In the experiments described in Chapter 6, participants inflicted either psychological or physical harm on an innocent person who had not hurt them (Davis & Jones, 1960; Glass, 1964). Participants then persuaded themselves that their victims were not nice people and therefore deserved what they got. This certainly reduces dissonance, but it also sets the stage for further aggression, because once a person has succeeded in finding reasons to dislike someone, it is easier to harm that victim again.

What happens, though, if the victim isn't totally innocent? What if the victim has done something that did hurt or disturb you and therefore, in your opinion, deserves your retaliation? Here the situation becomes more complex and more interesting. Consider the results of one of the first experiments designed to test the catharsis hypothesis (Kahn, 1966). A young man, posing as a medical technician, took physiological measurements from college students. As he did, he made derogatory remarks about the students, which naturally annoyed them. In one experimental condition, the participants were allowed to vent their hostility by expressing their feelings about the technician to his employer—an action that looked as though it would get the technician into serious trouble, perhaps even cost him his job. In another condition, participants did not have the opportunity to express any aggression against the person who had aroused their anger. Those who were allowed to express their aggression subsequently felt greater dislike and hostility for the technician than did those who were blocked from expressing their aggression. In other words, expressing aggression did not "get it out of their systems"; rather, it tended to *increase* aggressive hostility—even when the target was not simply an innocent victim.

These results suggest that when people are angered they frequently respond with overkill. In this case, costing the technician his job was much more devastating than the minor offense the man committed with his insult. The overreaction, in turn, produces dissonance in much the same way that hurting an innocent person does: If there is a major discrepancy between what the person did to you and the force of your retaliation, you must justify that discrepancy by deciding that the object of your wrath really did something awful to warrant it.

"It's truly remarkable, Louis, thirty-seven years next Tuesday and never a cross word between us."

Charles Barsotti/The New Yorker Collection/ www.cartoonbank.com

What Are We Supposed to Do with Our Anger?

If violence leads to self-justification, which in turn breeds more violence, what are we to do with our angry feelings toward someone? Stifling anger, sulking around the house, and hoping the other person will read our mind doesn't seem to be a good solution, and neither are brooding and ruminating by ourselves, which just prolong and intensify the anger (Bushman et al., 2005; Rusting & Nolen-Hoeksema, 1998). But if keeping our feelings bottled up and expressing them are both harmful, what are we supposed to do?

First, it is possible to control anger by actively enabling it to dissipate. *Actively enabling* means using such simple devices as counting to 10 (or 100!) before shooting your mouth off. Taking deep breaths or getting involved in a pleasant, distracting activity (working a crossword puzzle, listening to soothing music, taking a bike ride, or even doing a good deed) are active ways of enabling the anger to fade away. If this advice sounds suspiciously like something your grandmother could have told you, well, that's because it is! Your grandmother often knows what she is talking about. But there is more to anger than merely controlling it, as you will see.

Venting Versus Self-Awareness Dissipating anger is not always best for you or for a relationship. If your close friend or partner does something that makes you angry, you may want to express that anger in a way that helps you gain insight into yourself and the dynamics of the relationship. You may also wish to express yourself in a way that solves the problem without escalating it by arousing anger in the other person. But for that to happen, you must express your feelings in a way that is neither hostile nor demeaning.

You can do this (after counting to 10) by making a clear, calm statement indicating that you are feeling angry and describing, nonjudgmentally, what you believe the other person did to bring about those feelings. Such a statement in itself will probably make you feel better to have "cleared the air," and because you haven't harmed the target of your anger with verbal or physical abuse, your response will not set in motion the cognitive processes that would lead you to justify your behavior by ridiculing your friend or escalating the argument. It is important that you speak in a way that does not cause your listener to become defensive or counterattack ("You're mad at me? Well, let me tell you where you're wrong, buster!"), but rather that invites problem solving ("Look, we seem to have different notions about housework standards. Can we figure out how to resolve this so that I don't get angry about your 'compulsive neatness' and you don't get angry with my being a 'slob'?"). Moreover, when such feelings are expressed between friends in a clear, open, nonpunitive manner, greater mutual understanding and a strengthening of the friendship can result.

> *I was angry with my friend; I told my wrath, my wrath did end.*
>
> —William Blake

Although it is probably best to reveal your anger to the friend who provoked it—at least if you are hoping to resolve the problem between you—sometimes the target of your anger is unavailable. Perhaps the person did something to you many years ago, or he or she has died or moved away. Then, research finds, it can be helpful to write down your feelings in a journal. In experiments with people undergoing a wide range of traumatic events, those who were instructed simply to write their "deepest thoughts and feelings" about the event felt healthier and even had fewer physical illnesses 6 months to a year later than did people who suffered in silence, who wrote about trivial topics, or who wrote about the details of the traumatic events without revealing their own underlying feelings. The benefits of "opening up" are due not to the venting of feeling, but primarily to the insights and self-awareness that usually accompany such self-disclosure (Pennebaker, 1990). For example, one young woman realized that she had been carrying a lot of anger since her childhood, over something another child had done to her. When she saw what she had written about the incident, she realized, "My god, we were both just kids." (See the Try It! on the next page.)

TRY IT!

Are you feeling angry about a personal matter in your life? Try to write your "deepest thoughts and feelings" about the event that has distressed you. Don't censor your feelings or thoughts. Do this for 20 minutes a day for a few days, and then reread what you have written. Can you see the situation differently? Do solutions offer themselves that you hadn't thought of?

Defusing Anger through Apology What if you are not the person who is feeling angry, but the one who caused it in someone else? Suppose you are taking a friend to a concert that starts at 8:00 P.M. She's been looking forward to it, and you've arranged to be at her house at 7:30. You leave your house with barely enough time to get there and discover that you have a flat tire. By the time you change the tire and get to her house, you are already 20 minutes late for the concert. Imagine her response if you (a) casually walk in, smile, and say, "Hey, it probably wouldn't have been such a good concert anyway. Lighten up; it's not a big deal!" or (b) run in clearly upset, show her your dirty hands, explain what happened, tell her you left your house in time to make it but got a flat, apologize sincerely, and vow to make it up to her. We predict that your friend would be prone toward aggression in the first case but not in the second, and many experiments support our prediction (Baron, 1988, 1990; Ohbuchi & Sato, 1994; Weiner et al., 1987). Typically, any apology sincerely given and in which the perpetrator took full responsibility was effective at reducing aggression.

Folklore has it that women apologize more than men do. Some observers believe the reason is that many men have trouble admitting they are wrong because of their "delicate egos" (Engel, 2001); others believe the reason is that women are more concerned than men with being courteous and maintaining smooth relations (Tannen, 2001); still others speculate that many men think it is not "manly" to apologize, a view reflected in Jim Belushi's book title *Real Men Don't Apologize* (cited in Schumann & Ross, 2010).

These explanations could conceivably play a role in the likelihood of a person apologizing, but the first question is whether the person believes an apology is even necessary. And here we see a clear gender difference. In a study in which young women and men kept daily diaries noting whether they committed an offense or experienced one, the researchers found that men simply have a higher threshold for what constitutes an offensive action warranting an apology. Moreover, when everyone was asked to evaluate actual offenses they had experienced in the past or come up with imaginary ones, again the men rated them all as being less severe than women did. You can imagine the unfortunate consequences of this discrepancy for romantic couples: A woman might feel angry or slighted that her partner doesn't even notice an offense that she thinks is serious enough to warrant an apology, and the man might feel angry that she is being oversensitive and thin-skinned (Schumann & Ross, 2010).

Given the importance of apologies in defusing anger, imagine the advantages that might be gained by equipping automobiles with apology signals! Suppose that every car came with not only a horn (an instrument of aggression worldwide), but also an apology signal; perhaps at the push of a button a little flag could pop up, saying, "Oops! Sorry!" One of our Eastern European readers wrote to tell us that in Poland and Hungary people apologize for their driving mistakes by using their emergency flashing lights; in the United States some motorists tap their chest as if to say "my fault" or make the V-sign meaning "peace." If these techniques were to become widely used, incidents of road rage might plummet.

Modeling Nonaggressive Behavior We've seen that children will be more aggressive (toward dolls as well as other children) if they have seen people behaving aggressively in similar situations. What if we reverse things and expose children to nonaggressive models—to people who, when provoked, express themselves in a restrained, rational, pleasant manner? This question has been tested in several experiments (Baron, 1972; Donnerstein & Donnerstein, 1976; Vidyasagar & Mishra, 1993). Children first watched youngsters behaving peacefully even when provoked. Later, when the children were put in a situation in which they themselves were provoked, they were much less likely to respond aggressively than were children who had not seen the nonaggressive models.

Warren Miller/The New Yorker Collection/
www.cartoonbank.com

Training in Communication and Problem-Solving Skills It is impossible to go through life without occasionally feeling frustrated, annoyed, angry, or conflicted. Feeling angry is part of being human. The problem is not anger itself, but the expression of anger in violent or cruel ways. Yet we are not born knowing how to express anger or annoyance constructively and nonviolently; we have to learn the right skills. In most societies, it is precisely the people who lack those social skills who are most prone to violent solutions to problems in relationships (Toch, 1980). One way to reduce violence, then, is to teach people such techniques as how to communicate anger or criticism in constructive ways, how to negotiate and compromise when conflicts arise, and how to be more sensitive to the needs and desires of others.

There is evidence that such formal training can be an effective means of reducing aggression (Studer, 1996). In a classic experiment, children were allowed to play in groups of four (Davitz, 1952). Some of these groups were taught constructive ways to relate to one another and were rewarded for such behavior; others were rewarded for aggressive or competitive behavior. Next, the children were deliberately frustrated: They were told that they would see some entertaining movies and would be allowed to have fun. The experimenter began to show a movie and hand out candy bars, but then he abruptly stopped the movie at the point of highest interest and took the candy bars away. Now the children were allowed to play freely as the researchers watched. The results? Children who had been taught constructive ways of behaving when they were frustrated or angry were far less aggressive than children in the other group. Many elementary and secondary schools now train students to use nonaggressive strategies for resolving conflict (Eargle, Guerra, & Tolan, 1994; Educators for Social Responsibility, 2001). Some schools have successfully reduced violence by teaching children problem-solving skills, emotional control, and conflict resolution (Reading, 2008; Wilson & Lipsey, 2007).

Man must evolve for all human conflict a method which rejects revenge, aggression, and retaliation.

—Martin Luther King, Jr., Nobel Prize acceptance speech, 1964

Countering Dehumanization by Building Empathy Picture the following scene: A long line of cars is stopped at a traffic light at a busy intersection; the light turns green and the lead car hesitates for 10 seconds. What happens? Almost inevitably, there will be an eruption of horn honking. In one experiment, when the lead car failed to move after the light turned green, almost 90% of the drivers of the second car honked their horns angrily (Baron, 1976). But if, while the light was still red, a pedestrian was hobbling across the street on crutches, only 57% of the drivers honked their horns. Seeing a person on crutches evoked feelings of empathy, which infused the consciousness of the potential horn honkers and decreased their urge to be aggressive.

Children who are taught to put themselves in others' shoes often have higher self-esteem, are more generous, and are less aggressive than children who lack skills of empathy.

As we saw, most people find it difficult to inflict pain on a stranger unless they can find a way to justify it, and the most common way of justifying it is to dehumanize the victim (Caselman, 2007; S. Feshbach, 1971). Understanding the process of dehumanization is the first step toward reversing it. By building empathy among people, aggressive acts should be more difficult to commit. The research data lend strong support to this contention. In one study, students who had been trained to empathize—that is, to take the perspective of the other person—behaved far less aggressively toward that person than did students who had not received the training (Richardson et al., 1994). In a similar study, Japanese students were told to shock another student as part of an alleged learning experiment (Ohbuchi, Ohno, & Mukai, 1993). In one condition, the "victims" first revealed something personal about themselves; in the other condition, they were not given this opportunity. Participants gave weaker shocks to the victim who had revealed personal information. It's harder to harm a stranger if you have made a personal connection with that person, and this is true whether the stranger is your neighbor, a homeless person, a sales clerk, or a civilian enemy.

CONNECTIONS

Teaching Empathy in School

"What would the world look like to you if you were as small as a cat?" "What birthday present would make each member of your family happiest?" These questions formed the basis of some of the exercises for elementary school children in Los Angeles who participated in a 30-hour program designed by Norma Feshbach (1989, 1997), who has pioneered the teaching of empathy in elementary schools. Thinking hard about the answers to such questions expands children's ability to put themselves in another's situation. The children also listened to stories and then retold them from the point of view of each of the different characters in each story. The children played the role of each of the characters and their performances were videotaped. The children then viewed the tapes and talked about how people look and sound when they express different feelings.

At the end of the program, the children not only had learned to be more empathic, but also had higher self-esteem, were more generous, and were less aggressive than were students who had not participated in the program.

At first glance, such a program may seem unrelated to academics. Yet role-playing and close analysis of stories is just what students do when putting on a play or analyzing a piece of literature. In reminiscing about his childhood, the Nobel Prize–winning physicist Richard Feynman reported that his father challenged his intellect by asking him to pretend he was a tiny creature living in their living room carpet. To do that, Feynman needed to crawl into the skin of that tiny creature and get a feel for what his life would be like in those circumstances. Such questions also encourage the kind of cognitive flexibility taught in corporate creativity programs. Accordingly, it should not surprise us to learn that students who develop greater empathic ability also tend to have higher academic achievement (Feshbach & Feshbach, 2009).

Could the Columbine Massacre Have Been Prevented?

At the beginning of this chapter we described the massacre at Columbine High School and discussed some of the speculations about what might have caused that horrifying event and the many other school shootings like it. Could these tragedies have been prevented?

One possibility is that the shooters were mentally ill. Seung-Hui Cho, the young man who murdered 32 of his fellow students at Virginia Tech in 2007, had had a lifelong history of mental problems and aberrant behavior, which had been worsening in the previous year. But it would be a mistake to dismiss the Columbine massacre and most other school shootings as being a result of individual pathology, like Cho's, and let it go at that. Such an explanation leads nowhere, because Harris and Klebold had been functioning effectively. They were getting good grades, attended class regularly, and did not present serious behavior problems to their parents or to the school authorities. True, they were loners, but so were many other students at Columbine High School; true, they dressed in Goth style, but so did other students. Their murderous spree was not readily predictable from their day-to-day interactions with parents, teachers, or friends. It was not even detected by Eric Harris's psychiatrist, who was treating the young man for depression. The adults were not negligent; Harris and Klebold's observable behavior was not far from the norm.

But more important, to dismiss this horrifying deed as "merely" the result of mental illness would lead us to miss something of vital importance, something that might help us prevent similar tragedies: the power of the social situation. Elliot Aronson (2000) argued that the school shootings were the tip of a large iceberg. Harris and Klebold were reacting in an extreme manner to a school atmosphere that creates an environment of exclusion, mockery, and taunting, making life difficult for a sizable number of students. Most high schools are cliquish places where students are shunned if they belong to the "wrong" ethnic group, come from the poor side of the tracks, wear the "wrong" clothes, or are too short, too fat, too tall, or too thin. After the shootings, Columbine students recalled that Harris and Klebold suffered greatly by being taunted and bullied by the in-group. Indeed, one in-group member justified this behavior by saying, "Most kids didn't want them there. They were into witchcraft. They were into voodoo. Sure we teased them. But what do you expect with kids who come to school with weird hairdos and horns on their hats? If you want to get rid of someone, usually you tease 'em. So the whole school would call them homos …" (Gibbs & Roche, 1999, p. 154).

How do you suppose Harris and Klebold reacted to this relentless treatment? In the video they left behind, they spoke angrily about the insults and bullying they endured at Columbine. According to psychiatrist James Gilligan (1996), the motivation behind the vast majority of rampage killings is an attempt to transform feelings of shame and humiliation into feelings of pride. "Perhaps now we will get the respect we deserve," said Klebold on the videotape, brandishing a sawed-off shotgun.

Social rejection is, in fact, the most significant risk factor for teenage suicide, despair, and violence (Crescioni & Baumeister, 2009; Leary, Twenge, & Quinlivan, 2006; Stillman et al., 2009). When a team of researchers investigated 15 school shootings that occurred between 1995 and 2001, they found that in 13 of them the killers had been angered by bullying and social rejection (Leary et al., 2003).

In the immediate aftermath of the Columbine massacre, countless young people posted messages online, describing their anguish over being rejected and taunted by their popular classmates. None of these teenagers condoned the shootings, yet their Internet postings revealed a high degree of understanding and empathy for the suffering that they assumed Harris and Klebold must have endured. A 16-year-old girl wrote: "I know how they feel. Parents need to realize that a kid is not overreacting all the time they say that no one accepts them. Also, all of the popular conformists need to learn to accept everyone else. Why do they shun everyone who is different?"

If Aronson's analysis of Columbine is correct, it should be possible to make our schools safer, as well as more pleasant and humane, by bringing about a change in the negative, exclusionary social atmosphere. Two lines of research discussed in this chapter suggest how we might achieve this goal: the success of Dan Olweus's program to reduce bullying in the schools of Norway and Norma Feshbach's successful attempt to build empathy among schoolchildren in the United States. Similarly successful programs designed to promote empathy and cooperation will be discussed in greater detail in the following chapter.

USE IT!

Imagine that you have a younger brother who is a sophomore in high school. In a phone conversation with your parents, you learn that he seems to be having a problem with anger management. He has been getting into fistfights with some of his classmates and has even beaten up on smaller boys. Your father has recommended that he try out for the high school football team as a way of "burning off" of his excess aggressive energy. Your mother is not that this is a good idea. They say to you, "You have courses in psychology. What would you recomme Based on what you have learned in this chapter, what you recommend?

Summary

What is aggression? Is it innate, learned, or optional?

- **What Is Aggression?** Aggression is intentional behavior aimed at doing harm or causing physical or psychological pain to another person. **Hostile aggression** is defined as having as one's goal the harming of another; **instrumental aggression** inflicts harm as a means to some other end. Over the centuries, philosophers and psychologists have argued about whether or not humans are aggressive by nature. Some have argued that it is in human nature to be aggressive, others that humans are malleable.
  - **The Evolutionary Argument** All over the world, males are more physically aggressive than women, starting in childhood. Evolutionary psychologists argue that aggression is genetically programmed into men because it enables them to defend their group and perpetuate their genes; males also aggress out of sexual jealousy, to protect their paternity. The hormone that fuels male aggression is testosterone. However, there is substantial variation in the degree of aggressiveness among human males and also among our two closest animal relatives, chimpanzees and bonobos. Even if aggressive behavior has survival value, nearly all animals have also evolved strong inhibitory mechanisms that enable them to suppress aggression when they need to.
  - **The Cultural Argument** Aggression is influenced by situational and cultural factors and is therefore modifiable. There is a great variation in the levels of aggression across cultures; cooperative, collectivist cultures have low levels of aggression. The degree of aggressiveness can also change within a culture over time because of changes in the situation faced by the group. In *cultures of honor*, men are raised to respond aggressively to perceptions of threat and disrespect, a response that originated in economic conditions. Multiple factors shape whether or not a culture tends to nurture aggressive behavior, including the extent to which male aggression fulfills a central part of the male role and identity.
  - **Gender and Aggression** Men and boys are much more likely than women to be physically aggressively in provocative situations, to pick a fight with strangers, and to commit crimes of violence. Men are also more likely to interpret a given situation as provocative; however, gender differences in physical aggression are reduced when women are as provoked as men or when cultural norms foster female aggression. Girls and women are more likely to commit *relational aggression*, acts that harm another person through manipulation of the relationship (backbiting, spreading rumors, shunning). Within heterosexual couples, husbands are far more likely to murder their wives than vice versa; the rate of the physical abuse of women is high around the world, especially in cultures that regard such abuse as a male prerogative.
  - **Some Physiological Influences on Aggression** Alcohol can increase aggressive behavior because it serves as a disinhibitor, reducing a person's inhibitions. Alcohol also disrupts the way people usually process information so that they may respond to the most obvious aspects of a social situation and fail to pick up its subtle elements. When people experience pain, discomfort, and heat, they are more likely to act aggressively.

What are some situational influences on aggression?

- **Social Situations and Aggression**
  - **Frustration and Aggression** The **frustration-aggression theory** states that frustration can increase the probability of an aggressive response. Frustration is more likely to produce aggression if one is thwarted on the way to a goal in a manner that is either illegitimate or unexpected. Also, *relative deprivation*—the feeling that you have less than what you deserve or less than people similar to you have—is more likely to cause frustration and aggressive behavior than absolute deprivation, as illustrated by protests and revolutions from the civil rights movement to Eastern Europe to the Middle East.
  - **Provocation and Reciprocation** Individuals frequently aggress to reciprocate the aggressive behavior of others. This response is reduced if there are mitigating circumstances or the recipient believes the other person's behavior was unintentional.
  - **Aggressive Objects as Cues** The mere presence of a gun, an aggressive stimulus, in an otherwise neutral situation increases the degree of aggressive behavior. In a classic study, participants angered in the presence of a gun administered stronger electric shocks to their "victim" than those angered in the same setting in which a tennis racket was substituted for the gun.

What evidence is there that aggression is learned by observing and imitating others?

- **Learning to Behave Aggressively** Social learning theory holds that people often learn social behavior, including aggression, by observing and imitating others.
  - **Violence in the Media** Most children are exposed to a great deal of violence in TV and movies and playing violent video games. To try to determine what effect all this violence might have on children and adults, researchers have conducted laboratory experiments and longitudinal studies. Most of the experimental evidence demonstrates that watching violence is associated with an increase in aggressive behavior, especially in children, who aren't always good at separating fantasy from reality, but not all studies find a relationship. Also, children who are already predisposed to aggression are more likely to seek out aggressive shows and games to watch and play. Exposure to violent pornography, in contrast to nonviolent erotica, increases acceptance of sexual violence toward women. As with other kinds of violent images in the media, the effects are strongest on men who are already predisposed to aggression toward women.

    In the laboratory, playing violent video games does increase hostile feelings and aggressive behavior and also has a "numbing" effect, increasing people's indifference to the needs of others. Longitudinal studies show that the more TV violence observed by children, the greater the amount of violence they exhibit as teenagers and young adults. Viewing violence also exaggerates people's perceptions of danger in the outside world and impairs their memory, making people less likely to remember a product advertised on a violent TV program.

The relationship between media violence and actual aggression is a two-way street: The former has the greatest effect on children already predisposed to violence because of a genetic predisposition, living in a violent family, or a personality trait. And many other factors have a far more powerful influence on aggression, including growing up with violent or otherwise abusive parents, living in a violent community, and being rejected socially.

- **Sexual Violence Against Women** Most crimes of rape are committed by assailants known to the victim. Acquaintance or date rape includes direct assault: drugging the victim into a blackout, sex with a victim who is drunk or otherwise incapacitated, and sex under physical coercion and threat. Sexually aggressive males who commit these acts are often narcissistic, are unable to empathize with women, may feel hostility and contempt toward women, and feel entitled to have sexual relations with whatever woman they choose. Date rape may also occur because of misunderstandings and ambiguities in the sexual **scripts** that men and women follow regarding sexual norms.

How can aggression be reduced?

■ **How to Reduce Aggression**

- **Does Punishing Aggression Reduce Aggression?** If the punishment is itself aggressive, it actually models such behavior to children and may engender greater aggressiveness. Further, severe punishment may actually enhance the attractiveness of the transgression to the child, get the attention that the child is hoping for, or backfire by making the child anxious and angry. Punishment often fails to reduce aggression because it does not communicate what the target should do, only what he or she should not do. A growing form of aggression that inflicts considerable pain on children and teenagers is cyberbullying; some interventions have been successful in reducing bullying in schools and on the Internet. For punishment to serve as a deterrent to misbehavior or criminal acts it must be both prompt and certain.
- **Catharsis and Aggression** The theory of **catharsis** predicts that venting one's anger or watching others behave aggressively would serve to make one less likely to engage in subsequent acts of aggression. Research shows the contrary: Acting aggressively or observing aggressive events or sports increases the likelihood of aggressive behavior. Ventilating anger directly toward someone who has insulted or otherwise angered you also increases blood pressure, feelings of anger, and acts of aggression. In turn, because of self-justification and the need to reduce dissonance, each act of "righteous aggression" a person commits increases the likelihood that it will be repeated.
- **What Are We Supposed to Do with Our Anger?** Venting anger usually causes more harm than good, but stifling serious feelings is often not useful either. It is more effective to become aware of the anger and then to deal with it in ways that are more constructive than yelling or hitting: cooling off; getting involved in a distracting activity; becoming more self-aware (perhaps through writing down your feelings privately); learning to communicate your feelings in a clear but nonjudgmental or insulting way; taking responsibility for acts that anger others, through understanding and apology; and strengthening empathic skills.

■ **Could the Columbine Massacre Have Been Prevented?** Social rejection is the most significant risk factor for teenage suicide, despair, and violence. Although teenagers who have committed horrifying murders in their schools had various emotional problems, what sent most of them over the edge was the anger they felt at having been bullied and rejected by their peers. Changing the atmosphere of schools is an effective way to reduce the frequency of such occurrences and improve the lives of children and teenagers.

Chapter 12 Test

Study and Review on MyPsychLab

1. ______ aggression stems from feelings of anger and is aimed at inflicting pain, whereas ______ aggression serves as a means to some goal other than pain.
   a. hostile, instrumental
   b. direct, passive
   c. instrumental, hostile
   d. passive, direct

2. Which of the following stated gender differences in aggression is *false*?
   a. Young boys tend to be more physically aggressive than young girls.
   b. Girls tend to express their aggressive feelings more covertly, such as by gossiping.
   c. Gender differences in physical aggression shrink when men and women are subjected to frustration or insults.
   d. Because violence is so rare in women, female suicide bombers are much crazier than males who carry out these attacks.

3. From a social-psychological perspective, which of the following is *not* a limitation of evolutionary theories of aggression?
   a. They fail to account for female aggression.

- **b.** They fail to account for different rates of aggression across cultures.
- **c.** They fail to account for men's sexual jealousy.
- **d.** They fail to account for differences between bonobos and chimpanzees.

4. Which of the following men is most likely to act aggressively toward someone who insults him?
- **a.** Ray, who grew up in Minnesota.
- **b.** Randy, who grew up in Louisiana.
- **c.** Richard, who grew up in Massachusetts.
- **d.** Ricky, who grew up in Maine.

5. Under which of the following conditions is John *least* likely to be aggressive?
- **a.** His boss tells him he isn't going to get a raise he was promised.
- **b.** He likes to look at nonviolent pornography.
- **c.** He is driving to work in traffic, and another driver deliberately cuts in front of him.
- **d.** He has consumed enough alcohol to make him legally drunk, and a stranger bumps into him in a crowded restaurant.

6. Which of the following statements does *not* reflect the research on media violence and young children's behavior?
- **a.** Television advertising works better when it is shown during violent shows than nonviolent shows.
- **b.** Watching violent shows increases aggressive thoughts and actions.
- **c.** Playing violent video games may have a greater impact on children than watching TV violence does.
- **d.** Viewing television violence can numb people's response to violence in real life.

7. Jim has been convicted of assault and offers many reasons for his behavior. Which of the following of Jim's arguments would a social psychologist find the *least* convincing (based upon research on aggression)?
- **a.** "There was a gun in the room when it happened."
- **b.** "I used to watch my older brother beat up neighborhood kids."
- **c.** "I had just been fired from a job I really wanted."
- **d.** "I grew up in a very cold climate, in Minnesota."
- **e.** "I was justified—the other guy started it."

8. Tiffany is angry at Whitney for forgetting her birthday. To defuse her anger, Tiffany should
- **a.** think about other times Whit annoyed her and then confront Whit with all the evidence of what a bad friend she is.
- **b.** write about her feelings privately for 20 minutes a day for a few days, to get some perspective.
- **c.** write about her feelings about Whit on her Facebook page.
- **d.** get back at Whit by complaining about her to all their mutual friends.

9. Tiffany finally decides she is ready to confront Whitney directly. How should she express her anger (assuming she wants to keep the friendship)?
- **a.** She should "let it all out" so that she will feel better and Whit will know exactly how she feels.
- **b.** She should invite Whitney to play a game of tennis and then really try to clobber her.
- **c.** She should explain why she feels upset and hurt, as calmly as she can, without blame and accusation.
- **d.** She should explain why she feels upset and hurt, but let Whit know that she blames her for her thoughtless behavior.

10. Suppose you want to reduce the chances that your children will act in aggressive ways toward other people. Which of the following is *least* likely to work?
- **a.** Be a good role model; do not yell, hit, or act in other aggressive ways.
- **b.** Limit the time you let your children play violent video games.
- **c.** Teach them how to feel empathy toward other people.
- **d.** Encourage them to play sports where they can vent their frustrations on the playing field.

Answer Key

1-a, 2-d, 3-c, 4-b, 5-b,
6-a, 7-d, 8-b, 9-c, 10-d

13 Prejudice

Causes, Consequences, and Cures

OF ALL THE SOCIAL BEHAVIORS WE DISCUSS IN THIS BOOK, PREJUDICE IS AMONG THE MOST COMMON AND THE MOST DANGEROUS. Consider these examples, which hit the news at about the same time:

- Rutgers University student Tyler Clementi committed suicide by jumping off a bridge, just a few days after his roommate had maliciously posted a video on the Internet of Clementi having sex with another man. Clementi's death was one of five suicides by gay teenagers in 3 weeks, which also included that of 13-year-old Seth Walsh, who hanged himself after having been harassed by bullies for being gay. No charges were ever filed against Seth's tormentors, but Clementi's roommate, Dharun Ravi, was subsequently convicted on 15 counts of committing a bias-motivated crime, invasion of privacy, and other charges.
- Possibly provoked by the debate over building a mosque near Ground Zero in New York City, a college student stabbed a cabdriver who said he was Muslim, and a man was arrested for entering a mosque and urinating on prayer rugs, all the while shouting anti-Muslim slurs. In Florida, a minister of a fringe Christian church urged the burning of Korans. In Tennessee, two Muslim imams were kicked off a plane when the pilot refused to fly with them. They were going to a conference on anti-Muslim prejudice.
- Clothes designer John Galliano was fired by the Christian Dior fashion house after allegedly harassing a couple—a Jewish woman and an Asian man—and using anti-Semitic and racist slurs. Eyewitnesses reported that Galliano said, "Dirty Jewish face, you should be dead" to the woman, and then shouted at her companion, "F***ing Asian bastard, I will kill you." An earlier video posted on YouTube shows Galliano yelling at a different couple, saying "I love Hitler. . . . People like you would be dead. Your mothers, your forefathers, would all be f***ing gassed." (Galliano, who is gay, apparently did not realize that he himself would have been gassed by the Nazis on that count.)
- A 2009 survey of African American college graduates looking for jobs in Chicago found that many said they had "whitened" their résumés. One young woman changed her first name (Tahani) on her application to "T. S.," and others spoke of ways in which they had disguised parts of their identities that they thought signaled their blackness, such as membership in the African American Business Students Association. The applicants were not being oversensitive. In spite of the widespread perception that affirmative action has given an advantage to black job candidates, especially those who are college graduates, statistics show that they remain at a disadvantage in tough economic times (Luo, 2009).

None of us emerges completely unscathed by prejudice; it is a problem common to all humankind. When prejudice escalates into extreme hatred, it can lead to brutality, murder, war, and even genocide. During the past half-century, social psychologists have contributed greatly to our understanding of the psychological processes underlying prejudice and have begun to identify some possible solutions. What is prejudice? How does it come about? How can it be reduced?

FOCUS QUESTIONS

- What are the three components of prejudice?
- How can we measure implicit prejudice, and what are some of the effects it can have on its victims?
- What are four aspects of social life that can cause prejudice?
- What are some conditions that can reduce prejudice?

What Is Prejudice?

THE BOSTON GLOBE THURSDAY, OCTOBER 16, 1986
In Japan, an ancient bias endures
By Tom Ashbrook Globe Staff
TOKYO – THEY WERE Japanese
INTERNATIONAL NEWS WEDNESDAY, NOVEMBER 18, 1987
Gypsies Not Welcome! Romans Say
By ROBERTO SURO
Roadblocks and banners carry a message of hate.
'That's the way it is — we're white and we're proud.'
Across the Generations, 1915 Haunts Armenians
THE NEW YORK TIMES National News TUESDAY, JANUARY 27, 1987
The Sound of Hate Reverberates in North Georgia

Prejudice exists all over the world, rising and falling with changing times and events.

Prejudice is an attitude—an emotionally powerful one. As we discussed in Chapter 7, attitudes are made up of three components: an affective or emotional component, representing both the type of emotion linked with the attitude (e.g., anger, warmth) and the intensity of the emotion (e.g., mild uneasiness, outright hostility); a cognitive component, involving the beliefs or thoughts (cognitions) that make up the attitude; and a behavioral component, relating to one's actions. People don't only hold attitudes; they usually act on them as well.

In this context, a **prejudice** is a hostile or negative attitude toward people in a distinguishable group, based *solely* on their membership in that group. Thus, when we say that someone is prejudiced against black people, we mean that he or she is primed to behave coolly or with hostility toward them and that he or she feels that they are all pretty much the same. The characteristics this individual assigns to black people are negative and applied to the group as a whole. The individual traits or behaviors of the individual target of prejudice will either go unnoticed or be dismissed. Prejudices have a cognitive element (a stereotype) and can influence behavior (in the form of discrimination).

We are all victims or potential victims of prejudice, for no other reason than our membership in an identifiable group, whether on the basis of ethnicity, skin color, religion, gender, national origin, sexual orientation, body size, or disability, just to name a few. And it is not only minority groups that are the targets of prejudice at the hands of the dominant majority. Prejudice is a two-way street; it often flows from the minority group to the majority group as well as in the other direction.

To be sure, enormous progress has been made. The numbers of people who admit to believing that blacks are inferior to whites, women inferior to men, and gays inferior to straights have been steadily dropping (Weaver, 2008). Fifty years ago, the overwhelming majority of Americans were opposed to racial integration and could not imagine ever voting for any black candidate, let alone for president of the United States, as they did for Barack Obama in 2008. Many other changes have swept the country. Fifty years ago, few could imagine that it would one day become utterly routine to see female lawyers, doctors, bartenders, Supreme Court justices, astronauts, or marine biologists. Gay men and lesbians lived in fear of anyone discovering their sexual orientation, and few could imagine that same-sex marriage would ever be a possibility, let alone actually become legal in some states and nations. Inspired by the civil rights movement, the National Association to Advance Fat Acceptance was formed in 1969, "dedicated to ending size discrimination in all of its forms," and Disability Rights Advocates likewise organized to fight discrimination against anyone with a disability.

> *We all decry prejudice, yet all are prejudiced.*
> —Herbert Spencer, 1873

And yet it's clear that prejudice continues. Surveys find that some white Americans regard racism as a zero-sum game, in which actions to improve the welfare of minority groups have been at their expense; they feel that the reduction in antiblack bias has been accompanied by a rise in antiwhite bias (Norton & Sommers, 2011). Sometimes prejudice erupts overtly, as in the stories we described above, along with hate crimes, vandalism, bigoted jokes, or the thoughtless remarks made by some celebrity, sports figure, actor, or politician. Many of its expressions are more subtle, however, having gone underground, as we will see.

Prejudice
A hostile or negative attitude toward people in a distinguishable group, based solely on their membership in that group

Stereotypes: The Cognitive Component

Close your eyes for a moment and imagine the looks and characteristics of the following people: a high school cheerleader, a compassionate nurse, a Jewish computer scientist, and a black musician. Our guess is that this task was not difficult. We all walk around with images of various types of people in our heads. Walter Lippmann (1922), a distinguished journalist who was the first to introduce the term *stereotype*, described the distinction between the world "out there" and stereotypes—"the little pictures we carry around inside our heads." Within a given culture, these pictures tend to be remarkably similar. We would be surprised if your image of the cheerleader was anything but a bouncy, pretty, nonintellectual female. We would also be surprised if the nurse was male and the Jewish computer scientist was female, or if the black musician was playing classical music.

What is this woman's occupation? Most Western non-Muslims hold the stereotype that Muslim women who wear the full-length black *niqab* must be repressed sexually as well as politically. But Wedad Lootah, a Muslim living in Dubai, United Arab Emirates, is a marriage counselor and sexual activist, author of a best-selling Arabic sex manual.

Deep down, we know that there are male cheerleaders and nurses, female Jewish computer programmers, and black classical musicians. But we tend to categorize according to what we regard as normative. And within a given culture, what people regard as normative is very similar, in part because these images are perpetuated and broadcast widely by the media. Stereotyping, however, goes a step beyond simple categorization. A **stereotype** is a generalization about a group of people, in which identical characteristics are assigned to virtually all members of the group, regardless of actual variation among the members. The stereotypic quality might be physical, mental, or occupational: blondes are ditzy bimbos, jocks are dumb, engineers are geeks. Blue-collar workers and Wall Street bankers have uncomplimentary stereotypes of each other.

Stereotype

A generalization about a group of people, in which certain traits are assigned to virtually all members of the group, regardless of actual variation among the members

Stereotyping is a cognitive process, and stereotypes can be positive as well as negative. If you like a group, your stereotype will be positive, but if you dislike the group, your stereotype *of the same behavior* will be negative. After all, you can see the same behavior as being stingy or frugal, family-loving or clannish, outgoing or pushy (Peabody, 1985). Often, stereotyping is merely a technique that all of us use to simplify how we look at the world—a useful tool in the mental toolbox. Gordon Allport (1954) described stereotyping as "the law of least effort": Because the world is too complicated for us to have a highly differentiated attitude about everything, we maximize our cognitive time and energy by developing elegant, accurate attitudes about some topics while relying on simple, sketchy beliefs for others (see Chapter 3). Given our limited capacity for processing information, it is reasonable for human beings to behave like "cognitive misers"—to take shortcuts and adopt certain rules of thumb in our attempt to understand other people (Fiske & Depret, 1996; Jones, 1990; Macrae & Bodenhausen, 2000; Taylor, 1981). Information consistent with our notions about a group will be given more attention, will be rehearsed (or recalled) more often, and will therefore be remembered better than information that contradicts those notions (Bodenhausen, 1988; Dovidio, Evans, & Tyler, 1986; Macrae & Bodenhausen, 2000). Thus, whenever a member of a group behaves as we expect, the behavior confirms and even strengthens our stereotype; but we are not inclined to seek, notice, or remember the "exceptions." Anyone who doesn't fit the stereotype can be considered an exception, so we have no need to change the stereotype.

To the extent that a stereotype is based on experience and is at all accurate, it can be an adaptive, shorthand way of dealing with complex situations. However, if the stereotype blinds us to individual differences within a class of people, it can become maladaptive, unfair, and harmful, both to the person holding the stereotype and the individuals being lumped into that category. (See the Try It! on the next page.)

Jack Ziegler/The New Yorker Collection/www.cartoonbank.com

"It's a cat calendar, so it may not be all that accurate."

TRY IT! Stereotypes and Aggression

Close your eyes. Imagine an aggressive construction worker. How is this person dressed, where is this person located, and what, specifically, is this person doing to express aggression? Write it all down, being specific about the person's actions.

Now imagine an aggressive lawyer. How is this person dressed, where is this person located, and what, specifically, is this person doing to express aggression? Write it all down, being specific about the person's actions.

If you are like the experimental subjects in one research study, your stereotypes of the construction worker and the lawyer will have influenced the way you have construed the term *aggression*: Most of the study subjects imagined the construction worker using physical aggression and the lawyer using verbal aggression (Kunda, Sinclair, & Griffin, 1997).

Illusory Correlation
The tendency to see relationships, or correlations, between events that are actually unrelated

The Illusory Correlation Human cognitive processing perpetuates stereotypical thinking through the phenomenon of **illusory correlation** (Fiedler, 2000; Garcia-Marques & Hamilton, 1996; Shavitt et al., 1999). When we expect two things to be related, we fool ourselves into believing that they are, even when they are completely unrelated. Many illusory correlations exist in our society, such as the common belief that couples who haven't been able to have children will conceive a child after they adopt one (apparently because after the adoption they feel less anxious and stressed). Guess what: This correlation is entirely illusory. Occasionally, an "infertile" couple does conceive after adopting a child, but this occurs with no greater frequency than for "infertile" couples who do not adopt. The former event, because it is so charmingly vivid, makes more of an impression on us when it happens, creating the illusory correlation (Gilovich, 1991).

What does this have to do with prejudice and stereotypes? Illusory correlations are most likely to occur when the events or people are distinctive or conspicuous, different from the run-of-the-mill, typical social scene we are accustomed to (Hamilton, 1981; Hamilton, Stroessner, & Mackie, 1993). Members of minority groups—by virtue of race, ethnicity, disability, and so on—are, by definition, distinctive compared to the majority. Other groups that are not distinctive in terms of numbers—such as women, who make up slightly more than half of the species—may nonetheless become distinctive or conspicuous because of being rare in a given occupation: for example, being a female plumber, scuba diver, or pilot. Such distinctiveness leads to the creation of and belief in an illusory correlation—a relationship between the distinctive target person and the behavior he or she displays (Hamilton & Gifford, 1976). This illusory correlation is then applied to all members of the target group.

How does this work in everyday life? Let's say you don't know many Muslims, so for you, interacting with a Muslim is a distinctive event and Muslims in general are distinctive people. You know, of course, about acts of terrorism that some Muslims in the Middle East have committed against Americans in the United States and abroad, so an illusory correlation between Muslims and violence is created. If you now hear about a young Muslim man who has tried to blow up a plane, your illusory correlation is further confirmed in your mind. The result is that in the future you will be more likely to notice situations in which Muslims are behaving violently; you will be less likely to notice situations in which they are living peacefully (all 2 billion of them!) in the United States and many other countries around the world. You will be less likely to notice all the *non-Muslims*, including Christians and Jews, who commit acts of violence in the name of their religion or political goals. You will have processed new information guided by your illusory correlation, seeing what you expect to see and confirming in your mind that your stereotype is accurate (Hamilton & Sherman, 1989; Mullen & Johnson, 1988).

I will look at any additional evidence to confirm the opinion to which I have already come.
—Lord Molson, British politician

Watch on **MyPsychLab**
To consider another example of illusory correlation, watch the MyPsychLab video ***IT Video: Stereotypes***.

What's Wrong with Positive Stereotypes? The abuse of stereotyping's mental shortcuts can be blatant and obvious, as when one ethnic group is considered lazy or another ethnic group is considered violent. But the potential abuse can be more subtle, and it might even involve a stereotype about a positive attribute.

For example, Asian Americans have often been labeled a "model minority," a culture of people who are hardworking, ambitious, and intelligent. But many Asian Americans themselves object to this blanket characterization because it sets up expectations for those who are not interested in academic achievement, who don't like science and math and don't do well in those subjects, and who in general don't appreciate being treated as a category rather than as individuals (Thompson & Kiang, 2010). Moreover, the stereotype lumps together *all* Asian Americans, ignoring differences across Asian cultures (rather like referring to Swedes, Germans, the Irish, the French, and Greeks as all one bunch of "European Americans"). A study of Cambodian, Chinese, Korean, Lao, and Vietnamese students in America found many average differences in values, motivations, and goals across these groups (Lee, 2009).

Or consider the stereotype that "white men can't jump" and its implied corollary, that black men *can* jump. Currently, more than 80% of NBA players are black, yet African Americans constitute only 13% of the U.S. population. So what here is insulting to the minority? What's wrong is that this assumption obscures the overlap in the distributions—that is, it blurs the fact that many African American kids are not adept at basketball and many white kids are. (To say that 80% of NBA players are black does not mean that 80% of all black men are capable of becoming NBA players!) Thus, a white person who meets a young African American man and is astonished at his ineptitude on the basketball court is, in a very real sense, denying him his individuality. He is also insulting him by relegating him to a category of "good athlete" rather than, say, "smart professional."

There is ample evidence that this kind of demeaning stereotyping occurs (Brinson & Robinson, 1991). In one experiment, college students listened to a 20-minute audiotape of a college basketball game. They were asked to focus on one of the players, given the name "Mark Flick," and were allowed to look at a folder containing information about him, including a photograph. Half of the participants saw a photo of an African American male; the others saw a photo of a white male. After listening to the game, the students rated Flick's performance. Their ratings reflected the prevailing stereotypes: Students who believed Flick was African American rated him as having more athletic ability and as having played a better game than did those who thought he was white. Those who thought he was white rated him as having greater hustle and greater basketball sense (Stone, Perry, & Darley, 1997).

Stereotypes of Gender Just about everyone holds stereotypes of women and men—some positive, some negative: Women are more empathic and talkative, men are more competent and aggressive (Kite, Deaux, & Haines, 2008; Matlin, 2012). But, as usual, the stereotypes exaggerate differences between the sexes, ignore differences in personality traits and abilities *within* each gender, and oversimplify (Fine, 2010). For example, are women really "more empathic" than men? Which women? Empathic toward whom? When women's and men's actual behavior is observed systematically under a variety of conditions, the sexes do not differ in having feelings of empathy or in its expression (Fine, 2010). Some supposed differences disappear on closer inspection. Consider the pop-psych stereotype that women are "more talkative" than men. To test this assumption, psychologists wired up a sample of men and women with voice recorders that tracked their conversations while they went about their daily lives. There was no significant difference in the number of words spoken: Both sexes used about 16,000 words per day on average, with large individual differences among the participants (Mehl et al., 2007).

Contrasting the stereotypes of women and men might just be a fun game if the stereotypes didn't morph into prejudices, but too often they do. For more than a decade in research involving 15,000 men and women in 19 nations, Peter Glick and Susan Fiske (2001) have

"No, this is not Mel's secretary. This is Mel."

found that around the world sexism takes two basic forms, which they call *hostile sexism* and *benevolent sexism*. Hostile sexists hold negative stereotypes of women: Women are inferior to men because they are inherently less intelligent, less competent, less brave, less capable of math and science, and so on. Benevolent sexists hold positive stereotypes of women: Women are kinder than men, more empathic, more nurturing, and so on.

According to Glick and Fiske, both sets of stereotypes are demeaning to women, because benevolent sexists, like hostile sexists, assume that women are the weaker sex. Benevolent sexists tend to idealize women romantically, may admire them as wonderful cooks and mothers, and want to protect them when they do not need protection. This type of sexism is affectionate but patronizing, conveying the attitude that women are so wonderful, good, kind, and moral that they should stay at home, away from the aggressiveness and corruption (and power and income) of public life (Glick, 2006). Because benevolent sexism lacks a tone of hostility to women, it doesn't seem like a prejudice to many people, and many women find it alluring to think that they are better than men. But both forms of sexism—whether someone thinks women are too good for equality or not good enough—legitimize discrimination against women and can be used to justify relegating them to traditional stereotyped roles (Christopher & Wojda, 2008).

Perhaps you are thinking: "Hey, what about men? There are plenty of negative stereotypes about men too—that they are sexual predators, emotionally heartless, domineering, and arrogant." In fact, when the same group of researchers completed a 16-nation study of attitudes toward men, they found that many people indeed believe that men are aggressive and predatory and overall just not as warm and kind as women (Glick et al., 2004). This attitude seems hostile to men, the researchers found, but it also reflects and supports gender inequality and prejudice against women by characterizing men as being "naturally" designed for leadership and dominance.

Emotions: The Affective Component

If you've ever argued with people who hold deep-seated prejudices, you know how hard it is to get them to change their minds. Even people who are usually reasonable about most topics become immune to rational, logical arguments when it comes to the topic of their prejudice. Why is this so? It is primarily the emotional aspect of attitudes that makes a prejudiced person so hard to argue with; logical arguments are not effective in countering emotions. If you have a stereotype of a group that you know little about, and if you are not invested emotionally in that stereotype, you are likely to be open to information that disputes it:

> *You:* Nah, I don't want to visit Norway. I hear everyone there is pretty cold and aloof. I'd be much more comfortable with those expressive Italians.
>
> *Your good friend:* Boy, are you ever wrong! I lived in Norway for 6 years and it was *fabulous*. The people are helpful, friendly, smart, and throw great parties.
>
> *You:* No kidding? I'd better rethink my view of Norwegians! When are we going?

In contrast, the difficulty of using reason to change a prejudice was beautifully illustrated by Gordon Allport (1954) in his landmark book *The Nature of Prejudice*. He reports a dialogue between Mr. X and Mr. Y:

> *Mr. X:* The trouble with the Jews is that they only take care of their own group.
>
> *Mr. Y:* But the record of the Community Chest campaign shows that they gave more generously, in proportion to their numbers, to the general charities of the community than did non-Jews.
>
> *Mr. X:* That shows they are always trying to buy favor and intrude into Christian affairs. They think of nothing but money; that is why there are so many Jewish bankers.
>
> *Mr. Y:* But a recent study shows that the percentage of Jews in the banking business is negligible, far smaller than the percentage of non-Jews.

Mr. X: That's just it; they don't go in for respectable business; they are only in the movie business or run night clubs. (pp. 13–14)

Because Mr. X is emotionally caught up in his beliefs about Jews, his responses are not logical. In effect, the prejudiced Mr. X is saying, "Don't trouble me with facts; my mind is made up." Rather than challenging the data presented by Mr. Y, he distorts the facts so that they support his hatred of Jews, or he simply ignores them and initiates a new line of attack. The prejudiced attitude remains intact, despite the fact that the specific arguments Mr. X began with are now lying in tatters at his feet.

That is the signal that emotional reasoning is at work: It is impervious to logic or evidence. Indeed, many of the stereotypes underlying anti-Semitism are mutually contradictory and constantly shift across generations and nations. Jews were attacked for being communists in Nazi Germany and Argentina, and for being greedy capitalists in the communist Soviet Union. They have been criticized for being too secular and for being too mystical, for being weak and ineffectual and for being powerful enough to dominate the world (Cohen et al., 2009).

In earlier discussions of cognitive dissonance (Chapter 6), attitudes (Chapter 7), and stereotypes (current chapter), we saw that none of us is a 100% reliable accountant when it comes to processing social information that is important to us. The human mind does not tally events objectively; our emotions, needs, and self-concepts get in the way (Fine, 2008; Gilovich, 1991; Westen et al., 2006). That is why a prejudice—a blend of a stereotype and emotional "heat" toward a particular group—is so hard to change. We only see information that confirms how right we are about "those people" and, like Mr. X, dismiss information that might require us to change our minds.

The result, as Gordon Allport observed long ago, is that "defeated intellectually, prejudice lingers emotionally." He meant that the emotional component of prejudice, its deep-seated negative feelings, may persist even when a person knows consciously that the prejudice is wrong. Thus, some social psychologists, while welcoming the evidence that *explicit*, conscious prejudices have declined, have turned to more-sophisticated measures to see whether *implicit*, unconscious negative feelings between groups have also diminished. They maintain that implicit attitudes, being automatic and unintentional, reflect lingering negative feelings that keep prejudice alive below the surface (Dovidio & Gaertner, 2008). We will soon discuss the phenomenon of implicit prejudice and the conditions under which it is activated.

Discrimination
Unjustified negative or harmful action toward a member of a group solely because of his or her membership in that group

The mind of a bigot is like the pupil of the eye; the more light you pour upon it, the more it will contract.
—Oliver Wendell Holmes, Jr., 1901

Discrimination: The Behavioral Component

Prejudice often leads to unfair treatment of a target group. We call this **discrimination**: an unjustified negative or harmful action toward the members of a group solely because of their membership in that group. Any group that is stigmatized in a society will experience discrimination, both official and subtle. In a culture that relentlessly endorses "thin is beautiful," for example, fat people are often targets of jokes, harassment, and humiliation, and they are less likely than slender people to be hired and promoted (Finkelstein, DeMuth, & Sweeney, 2007; King et al., 2006).

One unobtrusive measure of social distance and "microaggressions" is to notice how people respond, nonverbally, to people with disabilities.

Most forms of explicit discrimination in schools and the workplace are now illegal in America, but stereotypes and prejudices can "leak out" and express themselves behaviorally in potent ways. For example, blacks and whites are not treated equally in the national "war against drugs" (Fellner, 2009). Across the country, relative to their numbers in the general population and among drug offenders, African Americans are disproportionately arrested, convicted, and incarcerated on drug charges (Blow, 2011). A typical illustration comes from a study in Seattle, which is 70% white. The great majority of those who use or sell serious drugs are white, yet almost two-thirds of those who are arrested are black. Whites constitute the majority of those who use or sell methamphetamine, ecstasy, powder cocaine, and heroin; blacks are the majority of those who use or sell crack. But the police virtually ignore the white market and concentrate on crack arrests. The researchers said they could not find a "racially neutral" explanation for this difference. The focus on crack offenders did not appear to be related to the frequency of crack transactions compared to other drugs, public safety or health concerns, crime rates, or citizen complaints. The researchers concluded that the police department's drug enforcement efforts reflect racial discrimination—the unconscious impact of race on official perceptions of who is the cause of the city's drug problem (Beckett, Nyrop, & Pfingst, 2006).

Prejudice can also lead to discrimination through "microaggressions": the "slights, indignities, and put-downs" that many minorities and people with physical disabilities experience (Dovidio, Pagotto, & Hebl, 2011; Nadal et al., 2011; Sue, 2010). Derald Sue (2010) offers these examples: A white professor compliments an Asian American graduate student on his "excellent English," although the student has lived in the United States his whole life. A white woman leaving work starts to enter an elevator, sees a black man inside, covers her necklace with her hand, and "remembers" that she left something at her desk—thereby conveying to her black coworker that she thinks he is dangerous, a potential thief. Men in a discussion group completely ignore the contributions of the one female member, talking past her and paying attention only to one another.

Microaggressions take many forms (Franklin, 2000; Herek & Capitanio, 1996; Sue, 2010). In one field experiment, researchers had 16 college students (eight males and eight females), who were actually their confederates, apply for jobs at local stores (Hebl et al., 2002). In some of their interviews, the applicants were portrayed as being gay or lesbian; in others, they were not. To standardize the interactions, the applicants were all dressed similarly in jeans and pullovers. The researchers looked at two kinds of discrimination: formal and interpersonal. To gauge formal discrimination, they sought to determine if there were differences in what the employer said about the availability of jobs, in whether the employer allowed them to fill out a job application, in whether or not they received a callback, and in the employer's response to a request to use the bathroom. There was no evidence of discrimination. The employers could not be accused of treating "homosexual" applicants unjustly. However, there were strong indications of interpersonal discrimination. Compared to the way they interacted with applicants they believed to be straight, employers were less verbally positive, spent less time interviewing them, used fewer words while chatting with them, and made less eye contact with them. It was clear from their behavior that the potential employers were either uncomfortable with or felt more distant from people they believed to be gay.

The behavior of the employers reflects a kind of discrimination measured by *social distance*, a person's reluctance to get "too close" to another group. Measures of social distance can be applied in many settings: In class, is a straight man as likely to sit next to a gay student as to another heterosexual? Does a nondisabled woman move away from a woman in a wheelchair? How close will you let "those people" into your social life—work with them, live near them . . . marry them? A review of decades of representative surveys of the American population—focusing on Hispanics, whites, blacks, Jews, and Asians—found that while overt prejudice among all of these groups has declined, most people within each ethnic group are still strongly opposed to virtually all of the other ethnic groups living in their neighborhoods or marrying into their families (Weaver, 2008). But does this fact reflect a true "prejudice" or merely a comfort with and preference for people of one's own religion and ethnicity? Do you or your classmates think that you could choose a life partner of any ethnicity and that your parents would accept that person? Have your parents ever told you that you could marry anyone you loved, *except . . . ?*

Modern Racism and Other Implicit Prejudices

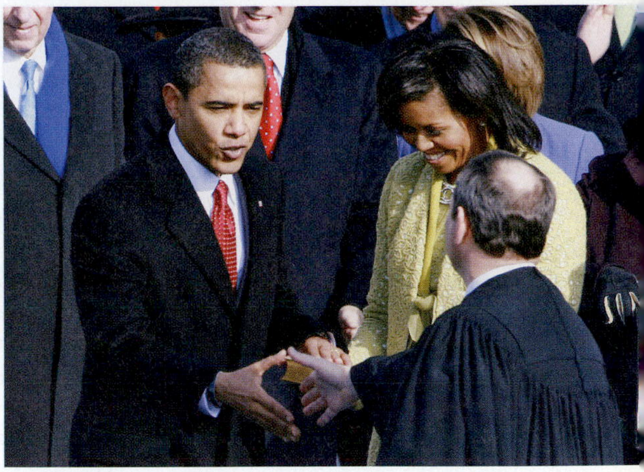

The election of America's first African American president was an exhilarating milestone for many Americans, but it awakened implicit prejudices in others.

With most forms of overt discrimination illegal, many people have become more careful, outwardly acting unprejudiced yet inwardly maintaining their prejudiced feelings. This phenomenon is known as **modern racism**, but it includes more than specifically racial prejudices. People hide their beliefs to avoid being labeled as racist, sexist, or homophobic, but when the situation becomes "safe," or their inhibitions are shed as a result of alcohol or stress, their implicit prejudice is revealed (Dovidio & Gaertner, 1996; McConahay, 1986; Pettigrew, 1989; Vala, 2009).

When Barack Obama was first elected, many people hoped the nation was entering a "post-racial" era, but before long it became apparent that we're not there yet. Highly prejudiced people realized that it would have been uncool to oppose him on transparently racial grounds, so their prejudice took the form of questioning his "Americanism": Was he born in the United States? Was he a legitimate citizen? Was he, in short, "one of us"? A study of nearly 300 students, black and white, found that for highly prejudiced whites, President Obama's perceived "non-Americanism" affected their evaluation of his performance, but not of Vice President Joe Biden's performance (Hehman, Gaertner, & Dovidio, 2011). In effect, these students could say, "I'm not prejudiced against black people—it's just that Obama isn't really an American *and* is a lousy president." In contrast, black students and unprejudiced white students could be supportive or critical of Obama, but belief in his American status was irrelevant to their evaluation of him.

Measuring Implicit Prejudices

Because most people don't want to admit their prejudices to an interviewer, modern racism is best studied with unobtrusive measures (Olson, 2009). One team of researchers created an ingenious contraption to get at people's real attitudes rather than the socially desirable ones (Jones & Sigall, 1971). They showed their study participants an impressive-looking machine, described as a kind of lie detector. In fact, this "bogus pipeline" was just a pile of electronic hardware whose dials the experimenter could secretly manipulate. Here's how researchers used the pipeline: Participants were randomly assigned to one of two conditions in which they indicated their attitudes either on a paper-and-pencil questionnaire (where it was easy to give socially correct responses) or by using the bogus pipeline (where they believed the machine would reveal their true attitudes if they lied). The students' responses showed more racial prejudice when the bogus pipeline was used (Sigall & Page, 1971; Roese & Jamieson, 1993). Similarly, college men and women expressed almost identically positive attitudes about women's rights and women's roles in society on a paper-and-pencil measure. When the bogus pipeline was used, however, most of the men displayed far less sympathy to women's issues than the women did (Tourangeau, Smith, & Rasinski, 1997).

Modern Racism

Outwardly acting unprejudiced while inwardly maintaining prejudiced attitudes

Typical stimuli used in the IAT to measure implicit racism.

The primitive bogus pipeline has since been replaced with computer-based measures, which still rely on the assumption that the study participant can't "fool" the machine. These computer tasks are designed to be difficult or impossible to consciously control (Fazio et al., 1995). The leading measure is the Implicit Association Test (IAT), which measures the speed of people's positive and negative associations to a target group (Greenwald, McGhee, & Schwartz, 1998; Greenwald et al., 2009). Its proponents maintain that if, for example, whites take longer to respond to black faces associated with positive words (e.g., *triumph*, *honest*) than to black faces associated with negative words (e.g., *devil*, *failure*), it must mean that whites have an unconscious prejudice toward blacks. Millions of people of all ages and walks of life have taken the test online, to identify their alleged prejudices toward blacks, Asians, women, old people, and people in other categories (Nosek, Greenwald, & Banaji, 2007).

Proponents of the IAT have marshaled evidence that the implicit bias it uncovers is related to how people actually behave in various situations (Greenwald et al., 2009)—for example, whether they find whites or blacks trustworthy and would be willing to invest money with them in a project (Stanley et al., 2011). But other social psychologists believe that whatever the test measures, it is not a stable prejudice (De Houwer et al., 2009). Two researchers got an IAT effect by matching target faces with nonsense words and neutral words that had no evaluative connotations at all. They concluded that the IAT does not measure emotional evaluations of the target but rather the *salience* of the word associated with it—how much it stands out. (Negative words attract more attention in general.) When the researchers corrected for these factors, the presumed unconscious prejudice faded away (Rothermund & Wentura, 2004). Other investigators think that the IAT may simply be measuring, say, white subjects' unfamiliarity with African Americans and the greater salience of white faces to them rather than a true prejudice (Kinoshita & Peek-O'Leary, 2005).

Watch on **MyPsychLab**
To learn more about this research, watch the MyPsychLab video ***Implicit Attitudes***.

Accordingly, a more compelling way of measuring implicit prejudices is by observing how people actually behave when they are stressed, angry, or otherwise not in full control of their conscious intentions.

Activating Implicit Prejudices

Late one evening in February, 1999, Amadou Diallo, an immigrant from West Africa, took in the night air on the steps of his apartment building in the South Bronx. In what was soon to become a fateful encounter, four undercover police officers on patrol, in an unmarked Ford Taurus, turned down Diallo's street. One of the officers noticed Diallo and thought that he looked like sketches of a man who had committed rapes in that area about a year earlier. The officers got out of their car and ordered Diallo to stop as he entered the vestibule of his apartment building. In fact, Diallo had no criminal record. He was working long hours as a street vendor and in his spare time was earning high school credits so that he could go to college. When the police approached him, he reached for his wallet, probably so that he could show some identification. Alarmed by the sight of a black man reaching into his pocket, the four officers did not hesitate. They fired a total of 41 shots at Diallo, killing him instantly.

Unfortunately, incidents such as this one are not rare. On the night of April 7, 2001, a Cincinnati police officer chased 19-year-old Timothy Thomas into an alley and demanded that he show him his hands. Before Thomas had a chance to comply, the officer shot and killed him. On November 25, 2006, in Queens, New York, police officers fired 50 bullets into Sean Bell in the parking lot of a strip club. Thomas and Bell were both African American, and both were unarmed.

Police officers often have to make very quick decisions under conditions of extreme stress and have little time to stop and analyze whether someone poses a threat. In the Diallo, Thomas, and Bell cases, however, many people wondered whether the officers' decisions to open fire so quickly were influenced by the victims' race. Indeed, Thomas was the 15th African American killed by the Cincinnati police in 6 years; no whites were killed by the police during that time (Singer, 2002). Would the officers have acted any differently if the men had been white?

It was this question that led researchers to try to recreate the situation in the laboratory (Correll, 2002; Payne, 2001, 2006). In one study, white participants saw photographs of young men in realistic settings, such as in a park, at a train station, and on a city sidewalk. Half of the men in the photos were African American and half were white. And half of the men in each group were holding a handgun and half were holding nonthreatening objects such as a cell phone, wallet, or camera. Participants were instructed to press a button labeled "shoot" if the man in the picture had a gun and a button labeled "don't shoot" if he did not. Like a police officer, they had very little time to make up their minds—less than a second. Participants won or lost points on each round: They won 5 points for not shooting someone who did not have a gun

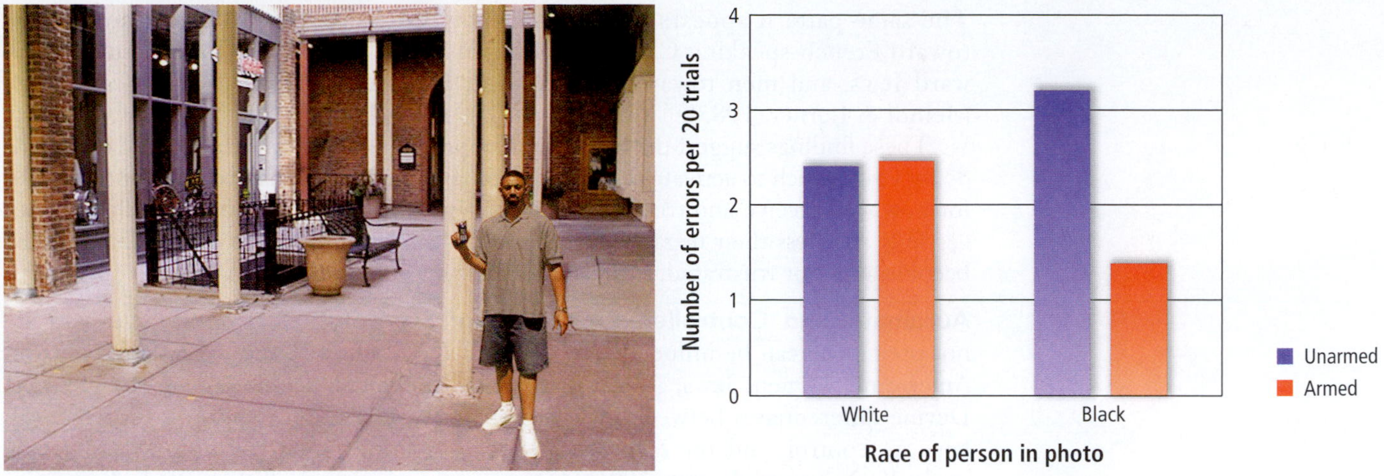

FIGURE 13.1

Errors Made in "Shooting" People in a Video Game

Participants played a video game in which they were supposed to "shoot" a man if he was holding a gun and withhold fire if he was holding a harmless object such as a cell phone. As the data graph shows, players were equally likely to "shoot" an armed white man, but much more likely to "shoot" black men who were unarmed, like the man in the photo.

(Adapted from Correll, Park, Judd, & Wittenbrink, 2002)

and 10 points for shooting someone who did have a gun; they lost 20 points if they shot someone who was not holding a gun and 40 points if they failed to shoot someone who was holding a gun (which would be the most life-threatening situation for a police officer).

The results? Participants were especially likely to pull the trigger when the people in the pictures were black, whether or not they were holding a gun. This "shooter bias" meant that people made relatively few errors when a black person was in fact holding a gun; it also meant, however, that they made the most errors (shooting an unarmed person) when a black person was not holding a gun (see Figure 13.1). When the men in the picture were white, participants made about the same number of errors whether the men were armed or unarmed. When this experiment was done with police officers, the officers showed the same association between black men and guns, taking less time to shoot an armed black man than an armed white man, even when the background situation looked safe and unthreatening (Correll et al., 2007; Correll et al., 2011; Eberhardt et al., 2004; Ma & Correll, 2011; Plant & Peruche, 2005).

Implicit prejudices can also be activated when a person is angered or insulted (Rogers & Prentice-Dunn, 1981). White students were told they would be inflicting electric shock on another student, the "learner," whom they were told was either white or African American, as part of an apparent study of biofeedback. The students initially gave a *lower* intensity of shock to black learners than to white ones—reflecting a desire, perhaps, to show that they were not prejudiced. The students then overheard the learner making derogatory comments about them, which, naturally, made them angry. Now, given another opportunity to inflict electric shock, the students who were working with a black learner administered *higher* levels of shock than did students who worked with a white learner (see Figure 13.2).

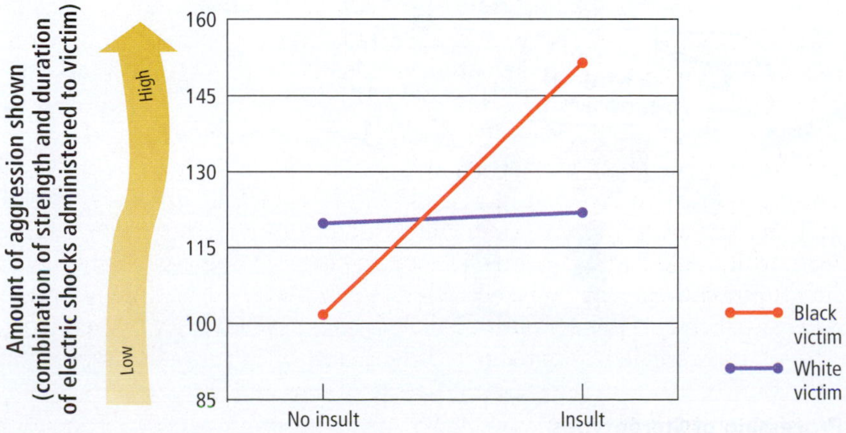

FIGURE 13.2

The Unleashing of Prejudice Against African Americans

(Adapted from Rogers & Prentice-Dunn, 1981)

The same pattern appears in studies of how English-speaking Canadians behave toward French-speaking Canadians, straights toward gays, non-Jewish students toward Jews, and men toward women (Fein & Spencer, 1997; Maass et al., 2003; Meindl & Lerner, 1985).

These findings suggest that in many of us prejudices lurk just beneath the surface. It doesn't take much to activate them, and once activated they can have dire consequences for how we perceive and treat a particular member of an out-group. Participants successfully suppress their negative feelings under normal conditions, but as soon as they become angry or frustrated, they express their implicit prejudice directly.

Automatic and Controlled Processing of Stereotypes Even people who are not prejudiced can be influenced by the archive of cultural stereotypes about African Americans, women, Jews, Asians, gay men, overweight people, and so on. Patricia Devine differentiates between the *automatic processing* of information, over which we have no control, and the *controlled processing* of information (Devine, 1989; Devine et al., 2002; Zuwerink et al., 1996). A stereotype is automatically activated when a person encounters a member of a minority group, but the stereotype can be ignored or refuted through conscious processing (see Figure 13.3). But what happens if the person is busy, overwhelmed, distracted, or not paying much attention? He or she may not be able to initiate that controlled level of processing.

To test this idea, Devine (1989) administered a test of prejudice to a large number of students and, according to their scores, divided them into high-prejudice and

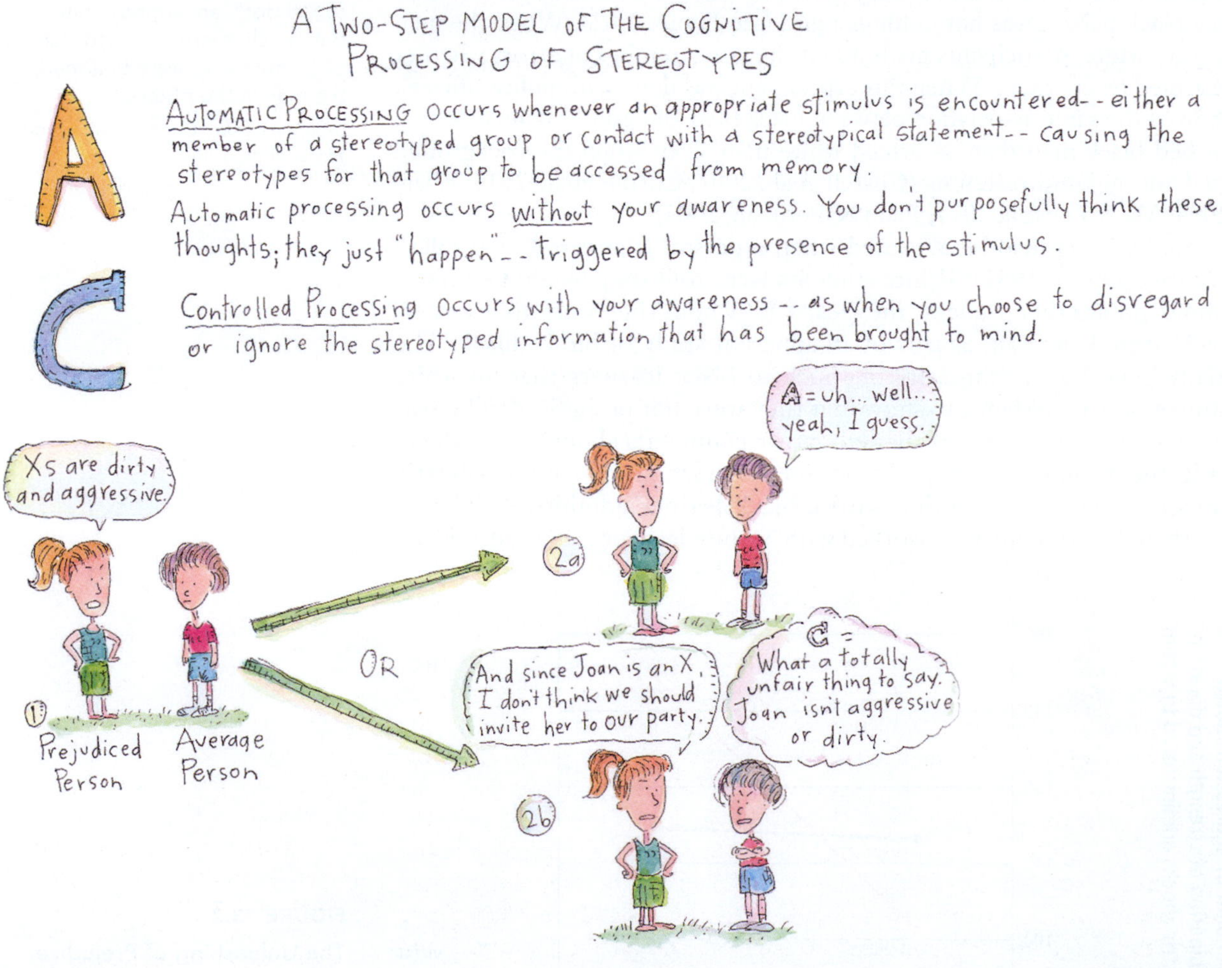

FIGURE 13.3
A Two-Step Model of the Cognitive Processing of Stereotypes

low-prejudice groups. Next, she demonstrated that both groups possessed equal knowledge of racial stereotypes. Third came the test of automatic and conscious processing: She flashed stereotyped words (e.g., *black*, *hostile*, *lazy*, *welfare*) and neutral words (e.g., *however*, *what*, *said*) on a screen so quickly that the words were just below the participants' perceptual (conscious) awareness. They saw something, but they weren't sure what. Their conscious processing couldn't identify the words; however, their automatic processing could. How could Devine be sure?

After flashing the words, she asked the participants to read a story about "Donald" (a man whose ethnicity was not mentioned) and to rate their impressions of him. Donald was described somewhat ambiguously; he did some things in the story that could be interpreted either positively or negatively. The participants who had seen the words reflecting the stereotype of black Americans interpreted Donald more negatively than those who had seen the neutral words did. Thus, for one group the negative stereotype had been primed (activated unconsciously through automatic processing); without their awareness, the participants were affected by these hostile and negative words, as revealed in their ratings of Donald. Because these stereotypes were operating outside their cognitive control, white students who were low in prejudice were just as influenced by the cultural stereotype (e.g., that blacks are hostile) as the prejudiced students were.

Simulate on **MyPsychLab**
To learn more, try the MyPsychLab simulation ***Unconscious Stereotyping***.

The Effects of Prejudice on the Victim

Thus far we have been looking at prejudice from the perspective of the perpetrator, but let's shift the focus now to the victim. One common result of being the target of prejudice is a diminution of self-esteem, internalizing society's views of one's group as being inferior, unattractive, or incompetent. Here we will discuss two kinds of self-defeating problems that can occur as a result of those internalized feelings.

Self-Fulfilling Prophecies All other things being equal, if you believe that Amy is stupid and treat her accordingly, chances are that she will not say a lot of clever things in your presence. This is the well-known **self-fulfilling prophecy**, discussed in Chapter 3. How does it work? If you believe that Amy is stupid, you probably will not ask her interesting questions, and you will not listen intently while she is talking; indeed, you might even look out the window or yawn. You behave this way because of a simple expectation: Why waste energy paying attention to Amy if she is unlikely to say anything smart or interesting? This is bound to have an important impact on Amy's behavior, for if the people she is talking to aren't paying much attention, she will feel uneasy. She will probably clam up and not come out with all the poetry and wisdom within her. This serves to confirm the belief you had about her in the first place. The circle is closed; the self-fulfilling prophecy is complete. And it is complete for Amy as well: As people continue to ignore her observations, she develops a self-concept that she is stupid and boring.

Researchers demonstrated the relevance of this phenomenon to stereotyping and discrimination in an elegant experiment (Word, Zanna, & Cooper, 1974). White college undergraduates were asked to interview several job applicants, some white, others African American. The white students displayed discomfort and lack of interest when interviewing African American applicants. They sat farther away, tended to stammer, and ended the interview far sooner than when they were interviewing white applicants. Then, in a second experiment, the researchers systematically varied the behavior of the interviewers (actually their confederates) so that it coincided with the way the original interviewers had treated the African American or white interviewees in the first experiment. But in the second experiment, all of the people being interviewed were white. The researchers videotaped the proceedings and had the applicants rated by independent judges. Applicants who were interviewed the way African Americans had been interviewed in the first experiment were judged to be far more nervous and far less effective than those who were interviewed the way white applicants had originally been interviewed. Their behavior, in short, reflected the *interviewer's* expectations (see Figure 13.4).

Self-Fulfilling Prophecy
The case wherein people have an expectation about what another person is like, which influences how they act toward that person, which causes that person to behave consistently with people's original expectations, making the expectations come true)

STUDY #1:
Interviewer sits far away and has short interview.
Applicants judged nervous, ineffective, and less competent.
Interviewer sits closer and has longer interview.
Applicants judged poised, effective, and competent.
White interviewer treats job applicants differently during interview, based on their race. Independent judges later rate black applicants as performing more poorly than white applicants.
STUDY #2:
Sits far away and has short interview.
Applicants judged nervous, ineffective, and less competent.
Sits closer and has longer interview.
Applicants judged poised, effective, and competent.
When white interviewers were trained to use one of the two interviewing "styles" from study #1, white applicants were judged as performing more poorly when they received the style previously used for blacks than when they received the style previously used for whites.

FIGURE 13.4
An Experiment Demonstrating Self-Fulfilling Prophecies

On a societal level, the insidiousness of the self-fulfilling prophecy goes even further. Suppose that there is a general belief that a particular group is irredeemably stupid, uneducable, and fit only for low-paying jobs. Why waste educational resources on them? Hence, they are given inadequate schooling. Hence, many drop out and fail to acquire the skills they need for well-paying careers. Hence, they face a limited number of jobs that are available and that they can do. Thirty years later, what do you find? For the most part, members of the targeted group will be severely limited in the jobs available to them and otherwise disadvantaged compared to the rest of the population. "See? I was right all the while," says the bigot. "How fortunate that we didn't waste our precious educational resources on such people!" The self-fulfilling prophecy strikes again.

Whether or not you feel "stereotype threat" depends on what category you are identifying with at the time. Asian women do worse on math tests when they see themselves as "women" (stereotype = poor at math) rather than as "Asians" (stereotype = good at math) (Shih, Pittinsky, & Ambady, 1999).

Stereotype Threat You might think that victims of prejudice and stereotyping would say, "Hey! I'm smarter than you think! Let me show you!" Unfortunately, the victim often internalizes these societal expectations and comes to believe them: "I guess I must be stupid if everybody thinks so."

There is a statistical difference in academic test performance among various cultural groups in the United States. Although there is considerable overlap, Asian Americans as a group perform slightly better than Anglo-Americans, who in turn perform better than African Americans. Why does this occur? There are any number of explanations—economic, cultural, historical, political. But one major contributing factor is clearly situational and stems from the anxiety produced by negative stereotypes. In a striking series of experiments, Claude Steele, Joshua Aronson, and their colleagues have demonstrated the power of what they call **stereotype threat** (Aronson et al., 1998, 1999; Steele, 1997; Steele & J. Aronson, 1995a, 1995b).

For example, when African American students find themselves in highly evaluative educational situations, most tend to experience apprehension about confirming the existing negative cultural stereotype of "intellectual inferiority." In effect, they are saying, "If I perform poorly on this test, it will reflect poorly on me and on my race." This extra burden of apprehension in turn interferes with their ability to perform well in these situations. For example, in one of their experiments, Steele and Aronson administered a difficult test (the GRE) individually to African American and white students at Stanford University. Half the students of each race were led to believe that the investigator was interested in measuring their intellectual ability. The other half were led to believe that the investigator was merely trying to develop the test itself, and because the test was not yet valid or reliable, they were assured that their performance would mean nothing in terms of their actual ability. The results confirmed the researchers' speculations. White students performed equally well (or poorly) regardless of whether or not they believed the test was being used as a diagnostic tool. The African American students who believed their abilities were not being measured performed as well as the white students. But the African American students who thought the test *was* measuring their abilities did not perform as well as the white students or as well as the African Americans in the other group. In subsequent experiments in the same series, Steele and Aronson also found that if race is made more salient, the decrease in performance among African Americans is even more pronounced.

The effects of stereotype threat generalize to other performance domains. When a game of miniature golf was framed as a measure of "sport strategic intelligence," black athletes performed worse than whites. But when the game was framed as a measure of "natural athletic ability," the pattern reversed, and the black athletes outperformed the white athletes (Stone et al., 1999).

Stereotype threat applies to gender as well (Spencer, Steele, & Quinn, 1999). The common stereotype has it that men are better at math than women are. Accordingly, when women were led to believe that a particular test was designed to show differences in math abilities between men and women, they did not perform as well as men. But in another condition, when women were told that the same test had nothing to do with male-female differences, they performed as well as men. Asian American women do worse on math tests when they are reminded of their gender (stereotype: women are poor at math) than when they are reminded of their cultural identity (stereotype: Asians are good at math; Shih, Pittinsky, & Ambady, 1999). The phenomenon applies to white males too: They performed less well on a math exam when they thought they would be compared with Asian males (J. Aronson et al., 1999). More than 3 hundred studies have shown that stereotype threat can affect the test performance not only of many African Americans and women of any ethnicity, but also of Latinos, low-income people, and the elderly—all of whom perform better when they are not feeling self-conscious about being in a negatively stereotyped group (J. Aronson, 2010; Steele, 2010). The more conscious individuals are of the stereotype about their group, the greater is the effect on their performance (Brown & Pinel, 2002).

Watch on **MyPsychLab**
To learn more, watch the MyPsychLab video ***Joshua Aronson: How does stereotype threat impact test performance?***

CONNECTIONS

Can Stereotype Threat Be Overcome?

How can the effects of stereotype threat be reversed? Joshua Aronson and his colleagues reasoned in the following way: If merely thinking about a stereotype can harm performance, then some kind of alternative mind-set ought to help performance, if it counters the stereotype. In one experimental condition, they reminded the test takers (women and men who were about to take a difficult test of spatial ability) that they were students at

Stereotype Threat
The apprehension experienced by members of a group that their behavior might confirm a cultural stereotype

a "selective northeastern liberal arts college." This reminder was enough to completely eliminate the male-female gap that occurred in the control condition, in which the test takers were merely reminded of the fact that they were "residents of the Northeast." The "I'm a good student" mind-set effectively countered the "women aren't good at math" stereotype, leading to significantly better spatial performance for the female test takers (McGlone & Aronson, 2006).

Similar results have been found for advanced calculus students at the university level (Good, Aronson, & Harder, 2007) and with middle school students on actual standardized tests (Good, Aronson, & Inzlicht, 2003). Other counter-stereotype mind-sets can enhance performance as well: being reminded that abilities are improvable rather than fixed (Aronson, Fried, & Good, 2002; Good, Aronson, & Inzlicht, 2003) and being informed that anxiety on standardized tests is normal for members of stereotyped groups (Aronson & Williams, 2009; Johns, Schmader, & Martens, 2005). An understanding of stereotype threat, then, can itself improve performance on tests and other evaluations.

Now that we have described the ubiquity and consequences of prejudice, it is time to look at some of its causes.

What Causes Prejudice?

The impulse to feel prejudice toward "outsiders"—that is, anyone not like "us"—seems to be part of a biological survival mechanism inducing us to favor our own family, tribe, or race and to protect our tribe from external threat. But that statement doesn't say much, because human beings are also biologically prepared to be friendly, open, and cooperative (Kappeler & van Schaik, 2006). That is why social psychologists strive to identify the *conditions* under which prejudice and hostility toward out-groups are fostered or reduced.

Prejudice is created and maintained by many forces in the social world. Some operate on the level of the group or institution, which demands conformity to normative standards or rules in the society (see Chapter 8). Some operate within the individual, such as in the ways we process information and assign meaning to observed events. And some forces operate on whole groups of people, such as the effects of competition, conflict, and frustration.

Pressures to Conform: Normative Rules

Children often learn prejudice from parents and grandparents.

In the 1930s, when Thurgood Marshall was a young lawyer working for the National Association for the Advancement of Colored People (NAACP), he was sent to a small town in the South to defend a black man who was accused of a serious crime. When he arrived, he was shocked and dismayed to learn that the defendant was already dead—lynched by an angry white mob. With a heavy heart, Marshall returned to the railroad station to wait for a train back to New York. While waiting, he realized he was hungry and noticed a small food stand on the platform. Walking toward the stand, he debated whether to go right up to the front and order a sandwich (as was his legal right) or to go around to the back of the stand (as was the common practice for African Americans in the South at that time). But before he reached the stand, he was approached by a large, heavyset white man who looked at him suspiciously. Marshall took him to be a lawman of some sort because he walked with an air of authority and had a bulge in his pants pocket that could only have been made by a handgun.

"Hey, boy," the man shouted at Marshall. "What are you doing here?" "I'm just waiting for a train," Marshall replied. The man scowled, took a few steps closer, glared at him menacingly, and said, "I didn't hear you. What did you say, boy?"

Marshall realized that his initial reply had not been sufficiently obsequious. "I beg your pardon, sir, but I'm waiting for a train." There was a long silence, during which the man slowly looked Marshall up and down and then said, "And you'd better catch that train, boy—and soon, because in this town, the sun has never set on a live nigger."

As Marshall later recalled, at that point his debate about how to get the sandwich proved academic. He decided not to get a sandwich at all but to catch the very next train out, no matter where it was headed. Besides, somehow he didn't feel hungry anymore (Williams, 1998).

Thurgood Marshall went on to become chief counsel for the NAACP; in 1954, he argued the case of *Brown v. Board of Education* before the U.S. Supreme Court. His victory there put an end to legalized racial segregation in public schools. Subsequently, Marshall was appointed to the Supreme Court, where he served with distinction until his retirement in 1991. We are not sure what became of the man with the bulge in his pocket.

This remarkable story illustrates the enormous power of norms: beliefs held by a society as to what is correct, acceptable, and permissible. When Thurgood Marshall was a young man, racial segregation in hotels, eating places, motion picture theaters, drinking fountains, and toilet facilities was normative in the American South. Yet in Marshall's own lifetime, that norm almost entirely evaporated, and racial segregation is not normative in the South today. Attitudes have changed as well. In fact, in 1942 fully 98% of the white population was opposed to desegregating schools (Hyman & Sheatsley, 1956), but by 1988 only 3% of white Americans said they wouldn't want their child to attend school with black children.

Most people, simply by living in a society where stereotypical information abounds and where discriminatory behavior is the norm, will develop prejudiced attitudes and behave in discriminatory ways to some extent. We call this **institutional discrimination**, including **institutionalized racism** and **institutionalized sexism**. If you grow up in a society where few minority group members and women have professional careers and where most people in these groups hold menial jobs, the likelihood of your developing certain (negative) attitudes about the inherent abilities of minorities and women will be increased. This will happen without anyone actively teaching you that minorities and women are inferior and without any law or decree banning minorities and women from college faculties, boardrooms, or medical schools. Instead, social barriers create a lack of opportunity for these groups that makes their success unlikely.

As social norms change, often as a result of changing laws and customs, so does prejudice. For decades, prejudice against gay men and lesbians has been institutionalized in law and custom, just as segregation was. "Sodomy" (anal sex and certain other forms of sexual behavior, practiced by heterosexuals as well as homosexuals) was against the law until the Supreme Court struck down state laws against sodomy in 2003. Yet as of 2012, more than half of the states permit employers to fire a worker solely because he or she is gay or lesbian. Though a handful of states recognize same-sex marriage, the federal government is currently prohibited from doing so because of the 1996 Defense of Marriage Act, which defines marriage as the union of one man and one woman. For that matter, federal laws—which forbid discrimination at work on the basis of race, national origin, sex, age, and disability—do not include sexual orientation. Government employees who are gay or lesbian are protected from job discrimination, but not workers in the private sector.

Nonetheless, institutionalized antigay prejudice is declining rapidly. The likely explanation is a generational difference in social norms, occurring when cultural changes move the younger generation in a more egalitarian direction. For example, in

Institutional Discrimination

Practices that discriminate, legally or illegally, against a minority group by virtue of its ethnicity, gender, culture, age, sexual orientation, or other target of societal or company prejudice

Institutionalized Racism

Racist attitudes that are held by the vast majority of people living in a society where stereotypes and discrimination are the norm

Institutionalized Sexism

Sexist attitudes that are held by the vast majority of people living in a society where stereotypes and discrimination are the norm

Prejudices are the props of civilization.

—André Gide, 1939

Normative Conformity
The tendency to go along with the group in order to fulfill the group's expectations and gain acceptance

2011, a national Gallup poll found that for the first time a majority of Americans (53%) supported gay marriage, up from only 27% in 1996. But gay marriage is a nonissue for most young people, whereas it remains highly contentious among many of their elders. Among those aged 18 to 34, 70% support the legalization of same-sex marriage, compared to only 39% of those over age 55 (Newport, 2011).

In Chapter 8, we discussed the tendency to go along with the group to fulfill the group's expectations and gain acceptance, a phenomenon known as **normative conformity**. An understanding of normative conformity helps explain why people who hold deep prejudices might not act on them, and why people who are not prejudiced might behave in a discriminatory way: They are conforming to the norms of their social groups or institutions. Being a nonconformist is not easy; your friends might reject you or your employer might fire you.

In the case of prejudice, many people would rather go along with the prevailing view of their friends and culture rather than rock the boat. It's as if people say, "Hey, everybody else thinks Xs are inferior; if I behave cordially toward Xs, people won't like me. They'll say bad things about me. I could lose my job. I don't need the hassle. I'll just go along with everybody else." In Little Rock, Arkansas, after the 1954 Supreme Court decision struck down school segregation, most ministers finally felt they had permission to speak out in favor of integration. They had favored equality for all American citizens, but they were afraid to support desegregation from their pulpits because they knew that their white congregations were violently opposed to it. Going against the prevailing norm would have meant losing church members and contributions, and under such normative pressure, even ministers found it difficult to do the right thing (Campbell & Pettigrew, 1959). In 1952, with racial segregation rigidly enforced throughout the South, researchers in a small mining town in West Virginia found even more dramatic evidence of the influence of social norms: African American miners and white miners worked together with total integration while they were underground but observed the norms of total segregation while they were above ground (Minard, 1952; Reitzes, 1952).

Thus, people can conform to the prejudices of others and to the pressures of institutional discrimination without being prejudiced themselves, just as they can suppress their own prejudices when the norms and situation demand. But how do prejudices get "inside" us in the first place and become so difficult to eradicate?

Because of changing norms and laws, the old stereotype of African American women, as represented by the caricature of "Aunt Jemima" many decades ago, is gone, obliterated by modern examples of glamorous, successful, powerful black women.

Social Categorization: Us Versus Them

The first step in forming a prejudice is the creation of categories—putting some people into one group based on certain characteristics and others into another group based on their different characteristics (Brewer & Brown, 1998; Dovidio & Gaertner, 2010; Wilder, 1986). We make sense out of the physical world by grouping animals and plants into taxonomies based on their physical characteristics; similarly, we make sense out of our social world by grouping people according to other characteristics, including gender, nationality, ethnicity, and so on. When we encounter people with these characteristics, we rely on our perceptions of what people with similar characteristics have been like in the past to help us determine how to react to someone else with the same characteristics (Andersen & Klatzky, 1987; Macrae & Bodenhausen, 2000). Thus, social categorization is both useful and necessary, but it has profound implications.

In-Group Bias Kurt Vonnegut captured the in-group versus out-group concept beautifully in his novel *Cat's Cradle*. A woman discovers that a person she has just met casually on a plane is from Indiana. Even though they have almost nothing else in common, a bond immediately forms between them:

> "My God," she said, "are you a Hoosier?"
>
> I admitted I was.
>
> "I'm a Hoosier too," she crowed. "Nobody has to be ashamed of being a Hoosier."
>
> "I'm not," I said. "I never knew anybody who was." (p. 90)

What is the mechanism that produces this in-group bias—positive feelings and special treatment for people we have defined as being part of our in-group and negative feelings and unfair treatment for others merely because we have defined them as being in the out-group? British social psychologist Henri Tajfel (1982a) discovered that the major underlying motive is self-esteem: Individuals seek to enhance their self-esteem by identifying with specific social groups. Yet self-esteem will be enhanced only if the individual sees his or her group as superior to other groups. Thus, for members of the Ku Klux Klan, it is not enough to believe that the races should be kept separate; they must convince themselves of the supremacy of the white race in order to feel good about themselves.

To get at the pure, unvarnished mechanisms behind this phenomenon, Tajfel and his colleagues created entities called *minimal groups* (Tajfel, 1982a; Tajfel & Billig, 1974; Tajfel & Turner, 1979). In their experiments, complete strangers are formed into groups using the most trivial criteria imaginable. For example, in one experiment participants watched a coin toss that randomly assigned them to either Group X or Group W. In another experiment, participants were first asked to express their opinions about artists they had never heard of and were then randomly assigned to a group that appreciated either the "Klee style" or the "Kandinsky style," ostensibly due to their picture preferences. The striking thing about this research is that although the participants were strangers before the experiment and didn't interact with one another during it, they behaved as if those who shared the same meaningless label were their dear friends or close kin. They liked the members of their own group better; they rated the members of their in-group as more likely to have pleasant personalities

Dressing alike is a way of demonstrating membership in an in-group.

Out-Group Homogeneity

The perception that individuals in the out-group are more similar to each other (homogeneous) than they really are, as well as more similar than members of the in-group are

and to have done better work than out-group members. Most striking, the participants allocated more money and other rewards to those who shared their label and did so in a rather hostile, cutthroat manner. For example, when given a choice, they preferred to give themselves only two dollars, if it meant giving the out-group person one dollar, over giving themselves three dollars, if that meant the out-group member received four dollars (Brewer, 1979; Hogg & Abrams, 1988; Mullen, Brown, & Smith, 1992; Wilder, 1981).

In short, even when the reasons for differentiation are minimal, being in the in-group makes you want to win against members of the out-group and leads you to treat the latter unfairly, because such tactics build your self-esteem and feeling of "belongingness." When your group does win, it strengthens your feelings of pride and identification with that group. How do you feel about being a student of your university following a winning or losing football season? Robert Cialdini and his colleagues (1976; Cialdini, 2009) counted the number of college insignia T-shirts and sweatshirts worn to classes on the Monday following a football game at seven different universities. The results? You guessed it: Students were more likely to wear their university's insignia after victory than after defeat.

Out-Group Homogeneity Besides the in-group bias, another consequence of social categorization is the perception of **out-group homogeneity**, the belief that "they" are all alike (Linville, Fischer, & Salovey, 1989; Quattrone, 1986). In-group members tend to perceive those in the out-group as more similar to each other (homogeneous) than they really are, as well as more homogeneous than in-group members are. Does your college have a traditional rival, whether in athletics or academics? If so, as an in-group member, you probably value your institution more highly than you value the rival (thereby raising and protecting your self-esteem), and you probably perceive students at this rival school to be more similar to each other than you perceive students at your own college to be.

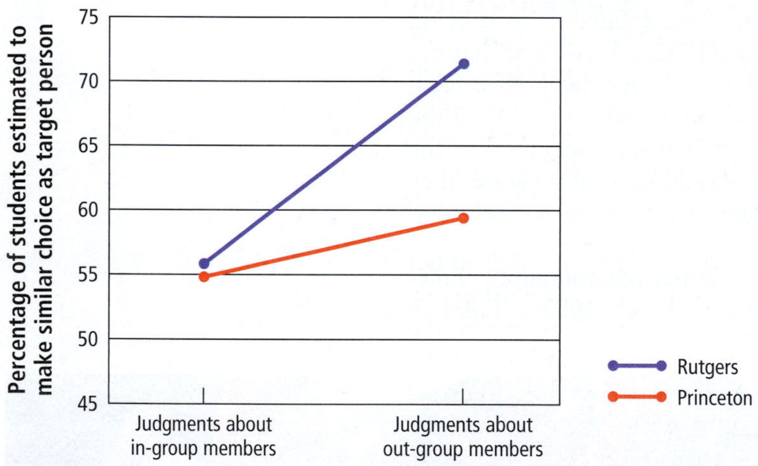

FIGURE 13.5

Judgments About In-Group and Out-Group Members

After watching the target person make a choice between two alternatives, participants were asked to estimate what percentage of students at their school (in-group) and their rival school (out-group) would make the same choice. An out-group homogeneity bias was found: Students thought that out-group members were more alike, whereas they noticed variation within their own in-group.

(Adapted from Quattrone & Jones, 1980)

Consider a study of students in two rival universities: Princeton and Rutgers (Quattrone & Jones, 1980). The rivalry between these institutions has long been based on athletics, academics, and even social-class consciousness (Princeton is private and Rutgers is public). Male students at the two schools watched videotaped scenes in which three different young men were asked to make a decision. For example, in one videotape, an experimenter asked a man whether he wanted to listen to rock music or classical music while he participated in an experiment on auditory perception. The participants were told that the man was either a Princeton or a Rutgers student, so for some of them the student in the videotape was an in-group member and for others an out-group member. Participants had to predict what the man in the videotape would choose. After they saw the man make his choice (e.g., rock or classical music), they were asked to predict what percentage of male students at that institution would make the same choice. Did the predictions vary due to the in- or out-group status of the target men?

As you can see in Figure 13.5, the results support the out-group homogeneity hypothesis: When the target person was an out-group member, the participants believed his choice was more predictive of what his peers would choose than when he was an in-group member (a student at their own school). In other words, if you know something about one out-group member, you are more likely to feel you know something about all of them. Similar results have been found in a wide variety of experiments in the United States, Europe, and Australia (Duck, Hogg, & Terry, 1995; Hartstone & Augoustinos, 1995; Judd & Park, 1988; Ostrom & Sedikides, 1992; Park & Rothbart, 1982).

How We Assign Meaning: Attributional Biases

People don't walk around with neon signs telling us everything we need to know about them. Instead, we must rely on attributional processes to try to understand why people behave as they do. Just as we form attributions to make sense out of one person's behavior, we also make attributions about whole groups of people. The attributional biases we discussed in Chapter 4 come back to haunt us now, for they underlie prejudice and discrimination.

Dispositional Versus Situational Explanations One reason stereotypes are so insidious and persistent is the human tendency to make dispositional attributions—that is, to leap to the conclusion that a person's behavior is due to some aspect of his or her personality rather than to some aspect of the situation. This is the familiar *fundamental attribution error* (see Chapter 4). Although attributing people's behavior to their dispositions is often accurate, human behavior is also shaped by situational forces. Relying too heavily on dispositional attributions, therefore, often leads us to make attributional mistakes. Given that this process operates on an individual level, you can imagine the problems and complications that arise when we overzealously act out the fundamental attribution error for a whole group of people—an out-group.

Our tendency to make dispositional attributions about an individual's negative behavior and then generalize to their entire ethnic, religious, or racial group or gender has been called the **ultimate attribution error** (Pettigrew, 1979). For example, some of the stereotypes that characterize anti-Semitism are the result of Christians committing the fundamental attribution error when interpreting the behavior of Jews. These stereotypes have a long history, extending over several centuries. When the Jews were first forced to flee their homeland some 2,500 years ago, they were not allowed to own land or become artisans in the new regions in which they settled. Needing a livelihood, some eventually took to lending money, one of the few professions to which they were allowed easy access. This choice of occupation was a by-product of restrictive laws in which Christians were not allowed to charge interest to other Christians but Jews were allowed to. The fact that Jews could lend money for interest but Christians could not led to a dispositional attribution about Jews: They were interested only in dealing with money and not in "honest" labor such as farming. As this attribution became an ultimate attribution error, Jews as a group came to be regarded as conniving, greedy moneylenders, of the kind immortalized by Shakespeare in the character of Shylock in *The Merchant of Venice* or of Fagin in Dickens's *Oliver Twist.*

Today, many white Americans make the same ultimate attribution error about African American and Hispanic men, whom they stereotype as being dispositionally prone to violence. In one study, college students playing the role of jurors in a mock trial were more likely to find a defendant guilty of a given crime if he had a Latino surname than a bland Anglo name such as Robert Johnson (Bodenhausen, 1988). They ignored any situational information or extenuating circumstances that might have explained the defendant's actions, because the dispositional attribution was stereotypically triggered by the Hispanic name.

In another study, researchers asked college students to read fictionalized files on prisoners who were being considered for parole and use that information to make a parole decision (Bodenhausen & Wyer, 1985). Sometimes the crime matched the common stereotype of the offender—for example, when a Hispanic male committed assault and battery, or when a rich Anglo-American committed embezzlement. In other instances, the crimes were inconsistent with the stereotypes. When the prisoners' crimes were consistent with participants' stereotypes, the students' recommendations for parole were harsher. Most of the students also ignored additional information that was relevant to a parole decision but was inconsistent with the stereotype, such as evidence of good behavior in prison.

When people conform to our stereotype, therefore, we tend to blind ourselves to clues about why they might have behaved as they did. Instead, we assume that something about their character or disposition, and not their situation or life circumstances, caused their behavior.

Ultimate Attribution Error

The tendency to make dispositional attributions about an entire group of people

Blaming the Victim Try as they might, people who have rarely been discriminated against have a hard time fully understanding what it's like to be a target of prejudice. Well-intentioned members of the dominant majority will sympathize with groups that are targets of discrimination, but true empathy is difficult for those who have routinely been judged on the basis of their own merit and not their racial, ethnic, religious, or other group membership. And when empathy is absent, it is hard to avoid falling into the attributional trap of **blaming the victim** for his or her plight.

Ironically, as we discuss in Chapter 4, this tendency to blame victims for their victimization—attributing their predicaments to inherent deficits in their abilities and character—is typically motivated by an understandable desire to see the world as a fair and just place, one where people get what they deserve and deserve what they get. For example, the stronger a person's belief in a just world, the more likely he or she is to blame the poor and homeless for their own plight, or to blame overweight people for being lazy, rather than consider economic conditions, genetic predispositions, mental illness, lack of opportunities, and so forth (Crandall et al., 2001; Furnham & Gunter, 1984). Similarly, most people, when confronted with evidence of an unfair outcome that is otherwise hard to explain, find a way to blame the victim (Aguiar et al., 2008; Lerner, 1980, 1991; Lerner & Grant, 1990). In one experiment, two people worked equally hard on the same task, and by the flip of a coin, one received a sizable reward and the other received nothing. After the fact, observers tended to reconstruct what happened and convince themselves that the unlucky person must not have worked as hard.

Most of us are very good at reconstructing situations after the fact to support our belief in a just world. It simply requires making a dispositional attribution (it's the victim's fault) rather than a situational one (scary, random events can happen to anyone at any time). In a fascinating experiment, college students who were provided with a description of a young woman's friendly behavior toward a man judged that behavior as completely appropriate (Janoff-Bulman, Timko, & Carli, 1985). Another group of students was given the same description, plus the information that the encounter ended with the young woman being raped by the man. This group rated the young woman's behavior as inappropriate; she was judged as having brought the rape on herself.

How can we account for such harsh attributions? When something bad happens to another person, as when someone is mugged or raped, we will feel sorry for the person but at the same time relieved that this horrible thing didn't happen to us. We will also feel scared that such a thing might happen to us in the future. We can protect ourselves from that fear by convincing ourselves that the person must have done something to cause the tragedy. We feel safer, then, because we believe that *we* would have behaved more cautiously (Jones & Aronson, 1973).

How does the belief in a just world lead to the perpetuation of prejudice? Most of us find it frightening to think that we live in a world where people, through no fault of their own, can be raped, discriminated against, deprived of equal pay for equal work, or denied the basic necessities of life. It is much more reassuring to believe that they brought their fates on themselves. One variation of blaming the victim is the "well-deserved reputation" excuse. It goes something like this: "If the Jews have been victimized throughout their history, they must have been doing something to deserve it." Such reasoning constitutes a demand that members of the out-group conform to more-stringent standards of behavior than those the majority have set for themselves.

The Justification-Suppression Model of Prejudice Prejudices support the in-group's feeling of superiority, its religious or political identity, and the legitimacy of inequality in wealth, status, and power ("our group is entitled to its greater wealth and status because 'those people' are inferior"). Wherever a majority group systematically discriminates against a minority to preserve its power—whites, blacks, Muslims, Hindus, Japanese, Hutu, Christians, Jews, you name it—they will claim that their actions are legitimate because the minority is so obviously inferior and incompetent (Jost, Nosek, & Gosling, 2008; Morton et al., 2009; Sidanius, Pratto, & Bobo, 1996). For example, in a series of experiments in Bangladesh, Muslims (who are the majority there)

Blaming the Victim

The tendency to blame individuals (make dispositional attributions) for their victimization, typically motivated by a desire to see the world as a fair place and Hindus (a minority) both revealed strong in-group favoritism, but only the majority Muslims also denigrated the minority Hindus (Islam & Hewstone, 1993). But most people who are in dominant positions in their society do not see themselves as being prejudiced; they regard *their* beliefs about the out-group as being perfectly reasonable.

Christian Crandall and Amy Eshleman (2003) argue that most people struggle between their urge to express a prejudice they hold and their need to maintain a positive self-concept as someone who is not a bigot, both in their own eyes and in the eyes of others. But suppressing prejudiced impulses requires constant energy, so people are always on the lookout for information that will enable them to convince themselves that there is a valid justification for disliking a particular out-group. Once they find that justification, they can discriminate all they want and still feel that they are not bigots (thus avoiding cognitive dissonance). Remember the experiments in which supposedly unprejudiced people administered more punishment to the out-group when they had been insulted or angered? They had a justification for their increased aggression: "I'm not a bad or prejudiced person, but he insulted me! She hurt me!" In this way, as Crandall and Eshleman (2003) put it, "Justification undoes suppression, it provides cover, and it protects a sense of egalitarianism and a non-prejudiced self-image."

Suppose you are uncomfortable about homosexuality; you dislike gay men and lesbians and do not believe they should share all of the same rights that heterosexuals enjoy. But you are suppressing those feelings and opinions because you want to preserve your self-image as a fair-minded person, and you suspect that most of your classmates won't agree with you. How might you resolve this energy-draining conflict? You might justify the expression of your antigay thoughts and feelings by citing the Bible. Through the lens of a particular reading of the Bible, an antigay stance can be defended as fighting for "family values" rather than against gays and lesbians. Certainly the Reverend Jerry Falwell, the most influential evangelist of his era, felt there was nothing wrong with expressing antigay hostility: "If you and I do not speak up now, this homosexual steamroller will literally crush all decent men, women, and children who get in its way . . . and our nation will pay a terrible price" (Falwell, quoted in *The Columbia Spectator*, April 4, 2006). The problem with using the Bible in this way is that equally religious people use the Bible to support their belief in acceptance of and equality for gay men and lesbians. In their book *What God Has Joined Together: The Christian Case for Gay Marriage*, David Myers and Letha Scanzoni (2006) argue that there are far more verses in the Bible celebrating compassion, love, and justice than the very few that refer vaguely to homosexuality.

The Bible has been used to promote tolerance and compassion—as well as to justify and inflame many prejudices.

Because the Bible is an historical as well as a spiritual document, it has been used to justify many practices that Americans no longer believe in. In the nineteenth century, American slaveholders often quoted the Bible (Exodus 21:7) as a moral justification for slavery. Prominent among these was the Reverend Thornton Stringfellow of Virginia, a distinguished theologian, who wrote a treatise (1841) designed to "rebut the palpable ignorance" of Northerners who were denouncing slavery as a sin. On the contrary, he wrote, "From Abraham's day, until the coming of Christ, a period of two thousand years, this institution found favor with God." He added that Jesus accepted slavery and never spoke out against it. Needless to say, biblical teachings about love and justice have also informed and motivated the proliferation of hospitals, the founding of universities, the fight to abolish slavery, and the modern civil rights movement. As Gordon Allport (1954, p. 444) wrote, "The role of religion is paradoxical. It makes prejudice and it unmakes prejudice."

Realistic Conflict Theory
The idea that limited resources lead to conflict between groups and result in increased prejudice and discrimination

Economic Competition: Realistic Conflict Theory

Finally, one of the most obvious sources of conflict and prejudice is competition—for scarce resources, for political power, and for social status. Indeed, whatever problems result from the simple in-group versus out-group phenomenon, they will be magnified by real economic, political, or status competition. **Realistic conflict theory** holds that limited resources lead to conflict between groups and result in prejudice and discrimination (J. W. Jackson, 1993; Sherif, 1966; White, 1977).

Economic and Political Competition In his classic study of prejudice in a small industrial town, John Dollard (1938) was among the first to document the relationship between discrimination and economic competition. At first, there was no discernible hostility toward the new German immigrants who had arrived in the town; prejudice flourished, however, as jobs grew scarce. Local whites became hostile and aggressive toward the newcomers. They began to express scornful, derogatory opinions about the Germans, to whom the native white people felt superior. "The chief element in the permission to be aggressive against the Germans," wrote Dollard, "was rivalry for jobs and status in the local woodenware plants."

Similarly, the prejudice, violence, and negative stereotyping directed against Chinese immigrants in the United States fluctuated wildly throughout the nineteenth century as a result of changes in economic competition. Chinese people who joined the California gold rush, competing directly with white miners, were described as "depraved and vicious," "gross gluttons," and "bloodthirsty and inhuman" (Jacobs & Landau, 1971, p. 71). Only a few years later, however, when they were willing to accept backbreaking work as laborers on the transcontinental railroad—work that few white Americans were willing to do—they were regarded as sober, industrious, and law-abiding. They were so highly regarded, in fact, that Charles Crocker, one of the great tycoons financing the railroad, wrote, "They are equal to the best white men . . . They are very trusty, very intelligent, and they live up to their contracts" (p. 81). At the end of the Civil War, former soldiers flooded into an already-tight job market. This influx of labor was immediately followed by an increase in negative attitudes toward the Chinese: The stereotype changed to criminal, conniving, crafty, and stupid.

Today's Chinese are Mexican, particularly the migrant workers whose labor is needed in many American states but who are perceived as costing American workers their jobs. As the American economy has worsened, violence against Latinos has risen more than 40%, and Mexicans have become the main focus of white anger about illegal immigration. These changes in the target of a majority group's anger suggest that when times are tough and resources are scarce, in-group members will feel more threatened by the out-group, and incidents of prejudice, discrimination, and violence toward out-group members will increase.

Economic competition drives a good deal of prejudice. When unemployment rises, so does resentment against minorities.

In a classic experiment, Muzafer Sherif and his colleagues (1961) tested group conflict theory using the natural environment of a Boy Scout camp. The participants in the camp were healthy, well-adjusted 12-year-old boys who were randomly assigned to one of two groups, the Eagles or the Rattlers. Each group stayed in its own cabin; the cabins were located quite a distance apart to reduce contact between the two groups. The youngsters were placed in situations designed to increase the cohesiveness of their own group. This was done by arranging enjoyable activities such as hiking and swimming and by having the campers work with their group on various building projects, preparing group meals, and so on.

After feelings of cohesiveness developed within each group, the researchers set up a series of competitive activities in which the two groups were pitted against each other—for example, in football, baseball, and tug-of-war, where prizes were awarded to the winning team. These competitive games aroused feelings of conflict and tension between the two groups. The investigators created other situations to further intensify the conflict: A camp party was arranged, but each group was told that it started at a different time, thereby ensuring that the Eagles would arrive well before the Rattlers. Also, the refreshments at the party consisted of two different kinds of food. Half the food was fresh, appealing, and appetizing, while the other half was squashed, ugly, and unappetizing. As you'd expect, the early-arriving Eagles ate well, and the late-coming Rattlers were not happy with what they found. They began to curse the Eagles for being greedy. Because the Eagles believed they deserved what they got (first come, first served), they resented the name-calling and responded in kind. Name-calling escalated into food throwing, and within a short time punches were thrown and a full-scale riot ensued.

"And see that you place the blame where it will do the most good."

Following this incident, the investigators tried to reverse the hostility they had promoted. Competitive games were eliminated, but that did not eliminate the hostility that had been engendered. Indeed, hostility continued to escalate, even when the two groups were merely watching movies together. Eventually, the investigators did manage to reduce the hostility between the two groups; exactly how will be discussed at the end of this chapter.

The Role of the Scapegoat A special consequence of the conflict that results from competition is the manufacture of *scapegoats* (Allport, 1954; Gemmill, 1989; Miller & Bugelski, 1948). People tend to lash out at members of an out-group with whom they compete directly for scarce resources, but sometimes there is no clear or logical competitor. For example, in Germany following the nation's defeat in World War I, inflation was out of control and most citizens were poor, demoralized, and hopeless. When the Nazis gained power in the 1930s, they managed to focus the frustration of the German population on the Jews—an easily identifiable, powerless out-group. The Jews were not the reason the German economy was in such bad shape, but who was? It's hard to fight back against world events or one's government, particularly when one's government is evading responsibility by blaming someone else. Thus, the Nazis created the illusion that if the Jews could be punished, deprived of their civil rights, and ultimately eliminated, all of the problems then plaguing Germany would disappear. The Jews served as a convenient scapegoat because they were easily identifiable and were not in a position to defend themselves or strike back (Berkowitz, 1962).

The research on **scapegoating** shows that individuals, when frustrated or unhappy, tend to displace aggression onto groups that are disliked, visible, and relatively powerless (Fein & Spencer, 1997). The form the aggression takes depends on what is allowed or approved by the in-group in question. In ancient Rome, Christians were the scapegoat (Allport, 1954). In America, lynchings of African Americans and pogroms against Jews were once tolerated, if not legal, but these kinds of attacks have virtually ceased because the dominant culture no longer approves of them. In many of the Eastern European countries that emerged following the fall of the former Soviet Union in 1991, new freedoms were accompanied by increased feelings of nationalism ("us versus them") that in turn intensified feelings of rancor and prejudice against out-groups. In the Baltic States and the Balkans, the rise in nationalistic feelings led to the outbreak of hostility and war among Serbs, Muslims, and Croats, Azerbaijanis and Armenians, and other groups. In these cases and many others, weak governments choose an outside scapegoat to unify their population and focus blame elsewhere (Pettigrew et al., 1998; Staub, 1999). In 2011, Serbian general Ratko Mladic was finally arrested on charges

Scapegoating
The tendency for individuals, when frustrated or unhappy, to displace aggression onto groups that are disliked, visible, and relatively powerless

After the attacks on the World Trade Center and Pentagon on 9/11, scapegoating of Muslims increased.

of committing war crimes and genocide, including the execution of more than 7 thousand Muslims at Srebrenica during the Serbian war of the 1990s. Mladic had made the Muslims the scapegoat as a way of unifying Serbians and solidifying his power.

How Can Prejudice Be Reduced?

Sometimes subtle, sometimes brutally overt, prejudice is indeed ubiquitous. The good news of declining prejudicial attitudes, greater tolerance, and an end to legal discrimination seems always to be followed by eruptions of hostility, conflict, and hatred toward the target group of the moment. Does this mean that prejudice is an essential aspect of human social interaction and will therefore always be with us? We social psychologists do not take such a pessimistic view. We tend to agree with Thoreau that "it is never too late to give up our prejudices." People can change. But how? What can we do to eliminate or at least reduce this noxious aspect of human social behavior?

One logical step might be to provide people with accurate information that refutes their stereotypes, but by now you know it is not that simple. During and after World War II, most Anglo-Americans thought that Japanese Americans were unpatriotic, potential traitors to the Allied cause. In fact, the U.S. government uprooted the Japanese Americans living on the West Coast and dispatched them to internment camps for the duration of the war. What if those prejudiced Americans learned that the most highly decorated American combat unit in World War II was composed solely of Japanese Americans? Would this information have affected their attitude toward their fellow citizens?

Not necessarily. As we saw in discussing stereotypes earlier, when people are presented with an example or two that seems to refute their existing stereotype, most of them do not change their general belief. Indeed, in one experiment, some people presented with this kind of disconfirming evidence actually *strengthened* their stereotypical belief because the disconfirming evidence challenged them to come up with additional reasons for holding on to their prejudice (Kunda & Oleson, 1997). When you offer people only two or three strong disconfirming pieces of evidence, participants can dismiss them as "the exceptions that prove the rule." That's why the most fervent racist or anti-Semite can say, "but some of my best friends are . . ."

Because stereotypes and prejudice are based on false information, for many years social activists believed that education was the answer: All we needed to do was expose people to the truth and their prejudices would disappear. But, as we saw earlier, this has proved to be a naïve expectation. Because of the underlying emotional aspects of prejudice, as well as some of the cognitive ruts we get into (including illusory correlations, attributional biases, and biased expectations), stereotypes based on misinformation are difficult to modify merely by providing people with the facts. But there is hope. As you may have experienced, repeated contact with members of an out-group can modify stereotypes and prejudice (Webber & Crocker, 1983). But mere contact is not enough; it must be a special kind of contact. What exactly does this mean?

The Contact Hypothesis

In 1954, when the U.S. Supreme Court outlawed segregated schools, social psychologists were excited and optimistic. They believed that desegregating the schools—increasing the contact between white children and black children—would increase the self-esteem of minority children and herald the beginning of the end of prejudice.

There was good reason for this optimism because not only did it make sense theoretically, but empirical evidence also supported the power of contact among races (Van Laar, Levin & Sidanius, 2008). Indeed, as early as 1951, Morton Deutsch and

Mary Ellen Collins examined the attitudes of white Americans toward African Americans in two public housing projects that differed in their degree of racial integration. In one, black and white families had been randomly assigned to separate buildings in the same project. In the other project, black and white families lived in the same building. After several months, white residents in the integrated project reported a greater positive change in their attitudes toward black neighbors than residents of the segregated project did, even though the former had not chosen to live in an integrated building initially. Similarly, when white southerners joined the U.S. Army—after army units became integrated in the early 1950s—their racism gradually decreased (Pettigrew, 1958; Watson, 1950).

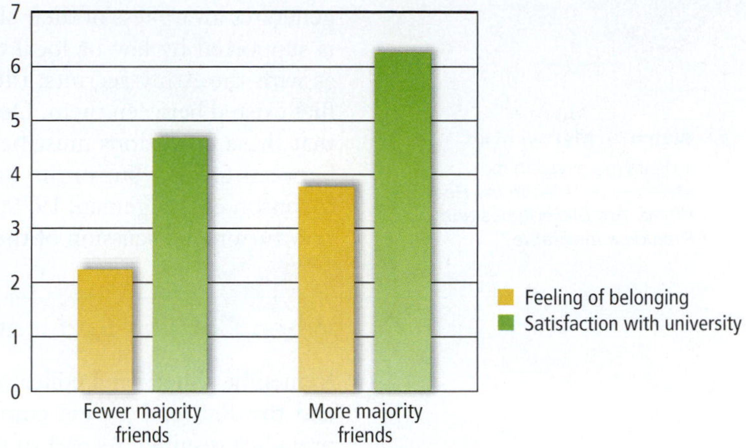

FIGURE 13.6

The Impact of Cross-Ethnic Friendships on Minority Students' Well-Being

In a longitudinal study of minority black students at a predominantly white university, many black students at first felt dissatisfied and excluded from school life. But the more white friends they made, the higher their sense of belonging (purple bar) and satisfaction with the university (green bar). This finding was particularly significant for minority students who had been the most sensitive to rejection and who had felt the most anxious and insecure about being in a largely white school. The study was later replicated with minority Latino students.

(Mendoza-Denton & Page-Gould, 2008)

The contact hypothesis has been supported by many studies in the laboratory and in the real world: young people's attitudes toward the elderly; healthy people's attitudes toward the mentally ill; nondisabled children's attitudes toward the disabled; and straight people's prejudices toward gay men and lesbians (Herek & Capitanio, 1996; Pettigrew & Tropp, 2006; Wilner, Walkley, & Cook, 1955).

Today's multiethnic college campuses are a living laboratory of the contact hypothesis. White students who have roommates, friends, and relationships across racial and ethnic lines tend to become less prejudiced and find commonalities across group borders (Van Laar et al., 2008). Cross-group friendships benefit minorities and reduce their prejudices too. Minority students who join ethnic student organizations tend to develop, over time, not only an even stronger ethnic identity, but also an increased sense of ethnic victimization. Just like white students who live in white fraternities and sororities, they come to feel that they have less in common with other ethnic groups (Sidanius et al., 2004). But a longitudinal study of black and Latino students at a predominantly white university found that friendships with white students increased their feelings of belonging and reduced their feelings of dissatisfaction with the school. This was especially true for students who had been feeling insecure and sensitive about being rejected as members of a minority (Mendoza-Denton & Page-Gould, 2008). (See Figure 13.6.)

Although contact between ethnic groups is generally a good thing, the desegregation of schools did not work as smoothly as most knowledgeable people had expected. Indeed, far from producing the hoped-for harmony, school desegregation frequently led to tension and turmoil in the classroom. In his analysis of the research examining the impact of desegregation, Walter Stephan (1978, 1985) was unable to find a single study demonstrating a significant increase in self-esteem among African American children, and 25% of the studies showed a significant decrease in their self-esteem following desegregation. In addition, prejudice was not reduced. Stephan (1978) found that in 53% of the studies prejudice actually increased; in 34% of the studies no change in prejudice occurred. And if you had taken an aerial photograph of the schoolyards of most desegregated schools, you would have found that there was very little true integration: White kids tended to cluster with white kids, black kids tended to cluster with black kids, Hispanic kids tended to cluster with Hispanic kids, and so on (Aronson, 1978; Aronson & Gonzalez, 1988; Aronson & Thibodeau, 1992; Schofield, 1986). Clearly, in this instance, mere contact did not work as anticipated.

What went wrong? Why did desegregated housing work better than desegregated schools? Let's take a closer look at the contact hypothesis. Clearly, not all kinds of contact will reduce prejudice and raise self-esteem; sometimes, contact can make intergroup relations more hostile and even increase prejudice (Saguy et al., 2011). For example, in the South, blacks and whites have had a great deal of contact, dating back to the time when Africans first arrived on American shores; however, prejudice flourished nonetheless. Obviously, the kind of contact they were having, as master and slave, was not the kind that would reduce prejudice.

Gordon Allport (1954) observed that contact can reduce prejudice only when three conditions are met: both groups are of equal status; both share a common goal that generates awareness of their shared interests and common humanity; and their contact is supported by law or local custom (social norms). Note that in the housing study, as with the Army recruits, the two groups were of equal status and no obvious conflict existed between them. Decades of research have substantiated Allport's early claim that these conditions must be met before contact will lead to a decrease in prejudice between groups, but in the intervening years, researchers have identified three more (Aronson & Bridgeman, 1979; Cook, 1985; Dovidio, Gaertner, & Validzic, 1998). Let's now turn to a discussion of these conditions.

Watch on MyPsychLab
To learn more, watch the MyPsychLab video ***In the Real World: Are Stereotypes and Prejudice Inevitable?***

When Contact Reduces Prejudice: Six Conditions

Remember Sherif and colleagues' (1961) study at the boys' camp, involving the Eagles and the Rattlers? When conflict and competition were instigated, stereotyping and prejudice resulted. As part of the study, the researchers also staged several events at the camp to reduce the prejudice they had created. Their findings tell us a great deal about what contact can and cannot do.

First, once hostility and distrust had been established, removing the conflict and the competition did not restore harmony. In fact, bringing the two groups together in neutral situations actually *increased* their hostility and distrust. The children in these groups quarreled with each other even when they were watching a movie together.

Mutual Interdependence
The situation that exists when two or more groups need to depend on one another to accomplish a goal that is important to each of them

How did Sherif succeed in reducing their hostility? He placed the two groups of boys in situations where they experienced **mutual interdependence**, the need to depend on one another to accomplish a goal that is important to both sides. One time, the investigators set up an emergency situation by damaging the water supply system; the only way the system could be repaired was if all the Rattlers and Eagles cooperated immediately. On another occasion, the camp truck broke down while the boys were on a camping trip. To get the truck going again, it was necessary to pull it up a rather steep hill. This could be accomplished only if all the youngsters pulled together, regardless of whether they were Eagles or Rattlers. Eventually, these situations brought about a diminution of hostile feelings and negative stereotyping between the two sets of campers. In fact, after these cooperative situations were introduced, the number of boys who said their closest friend was in the other group increased (see Figure 13.7). Thus, the first two of the key factors in the success of contact proved to be *mutual interdependence* and *having a common goal* (Amir, 1969, 1976).

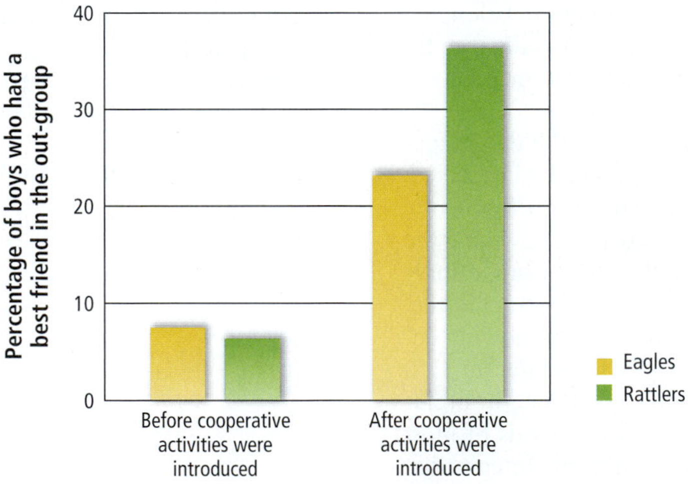

FIGURE 13.7
How Cooperation Fosters Intergroup Relations
When the Eagles and the Rattlers were in competition, very few of the boys in each group had friends from the other side. Intergroup tensions were eased only after the boys had to cooperate to get shared privileges and the boys began to make friends across "enemy lines."
(Based on data in Sherif, Harvey, White, Hood, & Sherif, 1961)

The third condition, as Allport predicted, is *equal status*. At the boys' camp (Sherif et al., 1961) and in the public housing project (Deutsch & Collins, 1951), the group members were very much the same in terms of status and power. No one was the boss, and no one was the less-powerful employee. When status is unequal, interactions can easily follow stereotypical patterns. The whole point of contact is to allow people to learn that their stereotypes are inaccurate; contact and interaction should lead to disconfirmation of negative, stereotyped beliefs. If status is unequal between the groups, their interactions will be shaped by that status difference—the bosses will act like stereotypical bosses, the employees like stereotypical subordinates—and no one will learn new, disconfirming information about the other group (Pettigrew, 1969; Wilder, 1984).

The fourth condition is that contact must occur in a *friendly, informal setting* where in-group members can interact with out-group members on a one-to-one basis (Brewer & Miller, 1984; Cook, 1984; Wilder, 1986). Simply placing two groups in contact in a room where they can remain segregated will do little to promote their understanding or knowledge of each other.

The fifth condition is that the individual learns that the out-group members he or she comes to know in that informal setting are *typical of their group*. So there must be *multiple members* of the out-group present; otherwise, the stereotype can be maintained by labeling one out-group member as the outstanding exception (Wilder, 1984). For example, when discrimination against women in the workforce became illegal, it was common for a single (brave!) woman to be hired in a field that was otherwise almost entirely male. An early study of male police officers assigned female partners in Washington, DC, found that although the men were satisfied with their female partners' performance, they still opposed hiring women police officers. Their stereotypes about women's ability to do police work hadn't changed; in fact, the stereotypes they held matched those of male officers with male partners (Milton, 1971). Why? The men assigned a female partner simply perceived her as an exception.

When women first began to work as peers with male police officers, they were often seen as the exception to the existing stereotype of women. Under what conditions will contact in the workplace reduce prejudice?

The sixth condition under which contact reduces prejudice occurs when *social norms that promote and support equality among groups* are operating in the situation (Allport, 1954; Amir, 1969; Wilder, 1984). Social norms wield great power; here they can be harnessed to motivate people to reach out to members of the out-group. For example, if the boss or the professor creates and reinforces a norm of acceptance and tolerance at work or in the classroom, group members will change their behavior to fit the norm.

To sum up, two groups are more likely to reduce their reciprocal stereotyping, prejudice, and discriminatory behavior when these six conditions of contact are met: Both sides are mutually interdependent; they share a common goal; they have equal status; they have opportunities for informal contact with one another; there are multiple members of each group; and the larger social norms promote equality.

Cooperation and Interdependence: The Jigsaw Classroom

Knowing now what conditions must exist for contact to work, we can better understand the problems that occurred when schools were first desegregated. Imagine a typical scenario. Carlos, a Mexican American sixth grader, has been attending schools in an underprivileged neighborhood his entire life. Because the schools in his neighborhood were not well equipped or well staffed, his first 5 years of education were somewhat deficient. Suddenly, without much warning or preparation, he is bused to a school in a predominantly white, middle-class neighborhood.

As you know from experience, the traditional classroom is a highly competitive environment. The typical scene involves the teacher asking a question; immediately, several hands go into the air as the children strive to show the teacher that they know the answer. When a teacher calls on one child, several others groan because they've missed an opportunity to show the teacher how smart they are. If the child who is called on hesitates or comes up with the wrong answer, there is a renewed and intensified flurry of hands in the air, perhaps even accompanied by whispered, derisive comments directed at the student who failed. Carlos finds he must compete against white, middle-class students who have had better preparation than he and who have been reared to hold white, middle-class values, which include working hard in pursuit of good grades, raising one's hand enthusiastically whenever the teacher asks a question, and so on. In effect, Carlos has been thrust into a highly competitive situation for which he is unprepared and in which payoffs are made for abilities he has not yet developed. He is virtually guaranteed to lose. After a few failures, Carlos, feeling defeated, humiliated, and dispirited, stops raising his hand and can hardly wait for the bell to ring to signal the end of the school day.

In the typical desegregated classroom, the students were not of equal status and were not pursuing common goals. Indeed, one might say that they were in a tug-of-war on an uneven playing field. When one examines the situation closely, it is easy to see why the self-esteem of minority children plummeted following desegregation (Stephan, 1978). Moreover, given the competitive atmosphere of the classroom, it is likely that the situation would have exacerbated whatever stereotypes existed before desegregation. Given that the minority kids were not prepared for the competitiveness of the classroom, it is no wonder that some of the white kids quickly concluded that the minority kids were stupid, unmotivated, and sullen, just as they had suspected (Wilder & Shapiro, 1989). For their part, the minority kids might conclude that the white kids were arrogant show-offs. This is an example of the self-fulfilling prophecy we discussed earlier.

How could we change the atmosphere of the classroom so that it comes closer to Allport's prescription for the effectiveness of contact? How could we get white students and minority students to be of equal status, mutually dependent, and in pursuit of common goals?

Setting Up the Jigsaw Classroom In 1971, Austin, Texas, desegregated its schools. Within just a few weeks, African American, white, and Mexican American children were in open conflict; fistfights broke out in the corridors and schoolyards. Austin's school superintendent called on Elliot Aronson, then a professor at the University of Texas, to find a way to create a more harmonious environment. After spending a few days observing the dynamics of several classrooms, Aronson and his graduate students were reminded of the situation that existed in the camp experiment of Sherif and colleagues (1961). With the findings of that study in mind, they developed a technique that created an interdependent classroom atmosphere designed to place the students of various racial and ethnic groups in pursuit of common goals. They called it the **jigsaw classroom** because it resembled the assembling of a jigsaw puzzle (Aronson, 1978; Aronson & Gonzalez, 1988; Aronson & Patnoe, 1997; Walker & Crogan, 1998; Wolfe & Spencer, 1996).

Here is how the jigsaw classroom works: Students are placed in diverse six-person learning groups. The day's lesson is divided into six segments, and each student is assigned one segment of the written material. Thus, if the students are to learn the life of Eleanor Roosevelt, her biography is broken into six parts and distributed to the six students, each of whom has possession of a unique and vital part of the information, which, like the pieces of a jigsaw puzzle, must be put together before anyone can view the whole picture. Each student must learn his or her own section and teach it to the other members of the group, who do not have any other access to that material. Therefore, if Debbie wants to do well on the exam about the life of Eleanor Roosevelt, she must pay close attention to Carlos (who is reciting on Roosevelt's girlhood years), to Shamika (who is reciting on Roosevelt's years in the White House), and so on.

> *Two are better than one because they have a good reward for their toil. For if they fail, one will lift up his fellow, but woe to him who is alone when he falls and has not another to lift him up. Again, if two lie together, they are warm; but how can one be warm alone?*
>
> —Ecclesiastes 4:9–12

Unlike the traditional classroom, where students are competing against each other, the jigsaw classroom has students depending on each other. In the traditional classroom, if Carlos, because of anxiety and discomfort, is having trouble reciting, the other students can easily ignore him or put him down in their zeal to show the teacher how smart they are. But in the jigsaw classroom, if Carlos is having trouble reciting, it is now in the best interests of the other students to be patient, make encouraging comments, and even ask friendly, probing questions to make it easier for Carlos to bring forth the knowledge that only he has.

Through the jigsaw process, the children begin to pay more attention to each other and to show respect for each other. A child such as Carlos would respond to this treatment by simultaneously becoming more relaxed and more engaged; this would inevitably produce an improvement in his ability to communicate. In fact, after a couple of weeks, the other students were struck by their realization that Carlos was a lot smarter than they had thought he was. They began to like him. Carlos began to enjoy school more and began to see the Anglo students in his group not as tormentors, but as helpful and responsible teammates. Moreover, as he began to feel increasingly comfortable in class and started to gain more confidence in himself, Carlos's academic performance began to improve. As his academic performance improved, so did his self-esteem. The vicious circle had been broken; the elements that had been causing a downward spiral were changed, and the spiral moved upward.

Jigsaw Classroom

A classroom setting designed to reduce prejudice and raise the self-esteem of children by placing them in small, desegregated groups and making each child dependent on the other children in the group to learn the course material and do well in the class

The formal data gathered from the jigsaw experiments confirmed the observations of the experimenters and the teachers: Compared to students in traditional classrooms, students in jigsaw groups showed a decrease in prejudice and stereotyping and an increase in their liking for their groupmates, both within and across ethnic boundaries. In addition, children in the jigsaw classrooms performed better on objective exams and showed a significantly greater increase in self-esteem than children in traditional classrooms. Children in the jigsaw classrooms also began to like school better than did the children in traditional classrooms. Moreover, children from jigsaw classrooms showed substantial evidence of true integration: In the schoolyard, there was far more intermingling among the various ethnic groups than on the grounds of schools using more-traditional classroom techniques.

When the classroom is structured so that students of various ethnic groups work together cooperatively, prejudice decreases and self-esteem increases.

Why Does Jigsaw Work? One reason for the success of this technique is that the process of participating in a cooperative group breaks down in-group versus out-group perceptions and allows the individual to develop the cognitive category of "oneness" wherein no one is excluded from group membership (Gaertner et al., 1990). In addition, the cooperative strategy places people in a "favor-doing" situation. In Chapter 6, we discussed an experiment demonstrating that people who act in a way that benefits others subsequently come to feel more favorable toward the people they helped (Leippe & Eisenstadt, 1998).

There is at least one additional reason why jigsaw learning produces such positive interpersonal outcomes: The process of working cooperatively encourages the development of empathy. In the competitive classroom, the goal is to show the teacher how smart you are. You don't have to pay much attention to the other students in your classroom. But to participate effectively in the jigsaw classroom, each student needs to pay close attention to whichever member of the group is reciting. In doing so, the participants begin to learn that great results can accrue if each of their classmates is approached in a way that is tailored to fit his or her special needs. Alicia may learn that Carlos is a bit shy and needs to be prodded gently, while Trang is so talkative that she might need to be reined in occasionally. Peter can be joked with, but Darnell responds only to serious suggestions.

If our analysis is sound, it should follow that working in jigsaw groups would lead to the sharpening of a youngster's general empathic ability, a change that will reduce the tendency to rely on stereotypes. To test this notion, Diane Bridgeman conducted a clever experiment with 10-year-old children. Just prior to her experiment, half of the children had spent 2 months participating in jigsaw classes and the other half in traditional classrooms. In her experiment, Bridgeman (1981) showed the children a series of cartoons aimed at testing children's ability to put themselves in the shoes of the cartoon characters. For example, in one cartoon, the first panel shows a little boy looking sad as he waves good-bye to his father at the airport. In the next panel, a letter carrier delivers a package to the boy. In the third panel, the boy opens the package, finds a toy airplane inside, and bursts into tears. Bridgeman asked the children why they thought the little boy burst into tears at the sight of the airplane. Nearly all of the children could answer correctly: because the toy airplane reminded him of how much he missed his father. Then Bridgeman asked the crucial question: "What did the letter carrier think when he saw the boy open the package and start to cry?"

Most children of this age make a consistent error; they assume that everyone knows what they know. Thus, the youngsters in the control group thought that the letter carrier would know the boy was sad because the gift reminded him of his father leaving. But the children who had participated in the jigsaw classroom responded differently. Because of their experience with jigsaw, they had developed the ability to take the perspective of the letter carrier—to put themselves in his shoes—and they realized that he would be confused at seeing the boy cry over receiving a nice present because he hadn't witnessed the farewell scene at the airport. (See the following Try It!)

Offhand, this might not seem very important. After all, who cares whether kids have the ability to figure out what is in the mind of a cartoon character? In point of fact, we should all care. In Chapter 12, we showed how important empathy is in curbing aggression. The extent to which children can develop the ability to see the world from the perspective of another human being has profound implications. When we develop the

TRY IT! **Jigsaw-Type Group Study**

The next time a quiz is coming up in one of your courses, try to organize a handful of your classmates into a jigsaw-type group for purposes of studying for the quiz.

Assign each person a segment of the reading. That person is responsible for becoming the world's greatest expert on that material. That person will organize the material into a report that will be given to the rest of the group. The rest of the group will feel free to ask questions to make sure they fully understand the material. At the end of the session, ask the group members the following questions:

1. Compared to studying alone, was this more or less enjoyable?
2. Compared to studying alone, was this more or less efficient?
3. How are you feeling about each of the people in the group, compared to how you felt about them prior to the session?
4. Would you like to do this again?

You should realize that this situation is probably less influential than the jigsaw groups described in this book. Why?

Listen on **MyPsychLab**
To learn more about the jigsaw technique, listen to the MyPsychLab audio ***Prejudice***.

ability to understand what another person is going through, it increases the probability that our heart will open to that person. Once our heart opens to another person, it becomes almost impossible to feel prejudice against that person, to bully that person, to taunt that person, to humiliate that person.

The Gradual Spread of Cooperative Learning The jigsaw approach was first tested in 1971; since then, educational researchers have developed a variety of similar cooperative techniques (Cook, 1985; Johnson & Johnson, 1987; Slavin & Cooper, 1999). The striking results Aronson and his colleagues obtained have now been replicated in hundreds of classrooms in all regions of the country and abroad (Jurgen-Lohmann, Borsch, & Giesen, 2001; Sharan, 1980). Cooperative learning is now generally accepted as one of the most effective ways of improving race relations, building empathy, and improving instruction in our schools (Deutsch, 1997; McConahay, 1981; Slavin, 1996). What began as a simple experiment in one school system is slowly becoming an important force in public education. Unfortunately, the operative word in the preceding sentence is *slowly*. The educational system, like all other bureaucracies, tends to resist change.

But it is a goal worth pursuing. It is impossible to overstate the power that a simple change in the classroom structure can have on the life of a child. Some three decades ago, Elliot Aronson, the designer of the jigsaw classroom, received a letter from a college student. He has saved it all these years, as an eloquent reminder that under all the scientific research and statistical analyses, there are living, breathing human beings who are affected every day by prejudice and by how the social situation treats them—individuals who can rise and flourish when the classroom structure makes it possible for them to do so. Here is the letter in its entirety:

Dear Professor Aronson:

I am a senior at ________University. Today I got a letter admitting me to the Harvard Law School. This may not seem odd to you, but let me tell you something. I am the 6th of 7 children my parents had—and I am the only one who ever went to college, let alone graduate, or go to law school.

By now, you are probably wondering why this stranger is writing to you and bragging to you about his achievements. Actually, I'm not a stranger although we never met. You see, last year I was taking a course in social psychology and we were using a book you wrote, *The Social Animal*, and when I read about prejudice and jigsaw it all sounded very familiar—and then, I realized that I was in that very first class you ever did jigsaw in—when I was in the 5th grade. And as I read on, it dawned on me that I was the boy that you called Carlos. And then I remembered you when you first came to our classroom and how I was scared and how I hated school and how I was so stupid and didn't know anything. And you came in—it all came back to me when I read your book—you were very tall—about 6 1/2 feet—and you had a big black beard and you were funny and made us all laugh.

And, most important, when we started to do work in jigsaw groups, I began to realize that I wasn't really that stupid. And the kids I thought were cruel became my friends and the teacher acted friendly and nice to me and I actually began to love school, and I began to love to learn things and now I'm about to go to Harvard Law School.

You must get a lot of letters like this but I decided to write anyway because let me tell you something. My mother tells me that when I was born I almost died. I was born at home and the cord was wrapped around my neck and the midwife gave me mouth to mouth and saved my life. If she was still alive, I would write to her too, to tell her that I grew up smart and good and I'm going to law school. But she died a few years ago. I'm writing to you because, no less than her, you saved my life too.

Sincerely,

"Carlos"

USE IT!

Is there some group of people you "can't stand"? Who evokes the strongest prejudice in you? Is it a category defined by their looks, weight, age, occupation, ethnicity, religion, sexual orientation, gender, or race? Think about the factors that cause prejudice: Which one or ones might be contributing to your negative feelings? Think about the changes in experience and attitudes that might reduce your prejudice: What would have to happen before you could let go of it?

Summary

What are the three components of prejudice?

- **What Is Prejudice?** Prejudice is a widespread phenomenon, present in all societies of the world. What varies across societies are the particular social groups that are the victims of prejudice and the degree to which societies enable or discourage discrimination. Social psychologists define **prejudice** as a hostile or negative attitude toward a distinguishable group of people based solely on their group membership. It contains cognitive, emotional, and behavioral components.
  - **Stereotypes: The Cognitive Component** A stereotype is a generalization about a group of people in which identical characteristics are assigned to virtually all members of the group, regardless of actual variation among the members. A stereotype may be positive or negative, and it can be a useful, adaptive mental tool to organize the social world. However, by obliterating individual differences within a group of people, it can be come maladaptive and unfair both to the person holding the stereotype and to the target. Human cognitive processing perpetuates stereotypes through the phenomenon of the **illusory correlation**. Even positive stereotypes of a group can be limiting and demeaning to members. Modern stereotypes of gender—which can take the form of *hostile sexism* or *benevolent sexism*—justify discrimination against women and their relegation to traditional roles.
  - **Emotions: The Affective Component** The deep emotional aspect of prejudice is what makes a prejudiced person so hard to argue with; logical arguments are not effective in countering emotions. This is the reason why prejudices can linger unconsciously long after a person wishes to be rid of them.
  - **Discrimination: The Behavioral Component** Discrimination denotes actual behavior. It is defined as an unjustified negative or harmful action towards members of a group solely because of their membership in that group. Examples include police focus on black drug users rather than on the much larger number of white drug users, and *microaggressions*, the small insults and put-downs that many members of minority groups experience. *Social distance* is another measure of how people respond to groups that are different from their own.

How can we measure implicit prejudice, and what are some of the effects it can have on its victims?

- **Modern Racism and Other Implicit Prejudices** Modern racism (or sexism) is an example of a shift in normative rules about prejudice: Nowadays, people have learned to hide their prejudices in situations where they might be labeled as racist, sexist, anti-Semitic, homophobic, and so on.
  - **Measuring Implicit Prejudices** Because many people don't want to admit their prejudices openly, researchers have developed unobtrusive measures of implicit racism and other prejudices: the "bogus pipeline" was among the first, and the Implicit Association Test (IAT) is the most widely used today. However, controversy exists about what the IAT actually measures and whether it predicts prejudiced behavior.
  - **Activating Implicit Prejudices** A more compelling way of measuring implicit prejudices is by observing how people actually behave when they are stressed, angry, have suffered a blow to their self-esteem, or otherwise are not in full control of their conscious intentions. They often behave with greater aggression or hostility toward a stereotyped target than toward members of their own group.
  - **The Effects of Prejudice on the Victim** The prevalence of stereotypes and prejudices can create **self-fulfilling prophecies** both for members of the majority and for victims of prejudice. One cause of the difference in academic performance is **stereotype threat**, the anxiety that some groups feel when a stereotype about their group is activated—e.g., that women are not as good at math as men, that Asian people are smarter than white people, that old people are less mentally competent than young people, and so on.

What are four aspects of social life that can cause prejudice?

- **What Causes Prejudice?** As a broad-based and universal attitude, prejudice may originally have served as a survival mechanism inducing people to favor their own families and tribes. But human beings are also biologically designed to be friendly and cooperative. Social psychologists strive to identify the conditions under which intergroup prejudice is fostered or reduced. This section consider four major aspects of social life that bring about prejudice: conformity to social rules, social categorization, the way we assign meaning or make attributions, and the way we allocate resources.
  - **Pressures to Conform: Normative Rules** Institutional discrimination, including institutionalized racism and sexism, are norms operating throughout the society's structure. Normative conformity, or the desire to be accepted and fit in, leads many people to go along with stereotyped beliefs and their society's dominant prejudices and not challenge them. As norms change, so, often, does prejudice.
  - **Social Categorization: Us Versus Them** Prejudice is enabled by the human tendency to organize people into in-groups and out-groups. Processes of social cognition are important in the creation and maintenance of stereotypes and prejudice. Categorization of people into groups leads to *in-group bias* (the tendency to treat members of our own group more positively than members of the out-group) and **out-group homogeneity** (the mistaken perception that "they" are all alike).
  - **How We Assign Meaning: Attributional Biases** The fundamental attribution error applies to prejudice: We tend to overestimate the role of dispositional forces when making sense out of others' behavior. The tendency to make dispositional attributions about a person's individual negative behavior and then generalize to their entire ethnic, racial, or religious group or gender is called the **ultimate attribution error**—making negative dispositional attributions about an entire out-group. When out-group members act nonstereotypically, we tend to make situational attributions about them, thereby maintaining our stereotypes. One common out-group attribution is **blaming the victim** for one's own prejudices and discriminatory behavior. Blaming the victim also promotes the in-group's feelings of superiority, its religious or political identity, and the legitimacy of its power.
  - **Economic Competition: Realistic Conflict Theory** **Realistic conflict theory** holds that prejudice is the inevitable by-product of real conflict between groups for limited resources, whether involving economics, power, or status. Competition for resources leads to derogation of and discrimination against the competing out-group, as happened with Chinese immigrants in the nineteenth century and happens with Mexican immigrants today. **Scapegoating** is a process whereby frustrated and angry people tend to displace their aggression from its real source to a convenient target—an out-group that is disliked, visible, and relatively powerless.

What are some conditions that can reduce prejudice?

- **How Can Prejudice Be Reduced?** Prejudice may be universal, but social psychologists have investigated many of the conditions under which intergroup hostility can be reduced and better relationships fostered. It is not enough simply to provide prejudiced people with information that they are stereotyping the out-group; they will often cling even more tightly to their beliefs.
  - **The Contact Hypothesis** According to the *contact hypothesis*, the most important way to reduce prejudice between racial and ethnic groups is through contact, bringing in-group and out-group members together. Such contact has been shown to be effective in many situations, from integrating housing projects and the military to fostering friendships across ethnic lines at universities. However, mere contact is not enough and can even exacerbate existing negative attitudes.
  - **When Contact Reduces Prejudice: Six Conditions** For contact between two groups to be truly successful in reducing prejudice, six conditions must be met: mutual interdependence; a common goal; equal status; informal, interpersonal contact; multiple contacts; and social norms of equality.
  - **Cooperation and Interdependence: The Jigsaw Classroom** The jigsaw classroom is a form of cooperative learning in which children from different ethnic groups must cooperate in order to learn a lesson. It has been shown to be highly effective in improving minority students' self-esteem and performance, increasing empathy, and promoting intergroup friendships.

Chapter 13 Test

Study and **Review** on **MyPsychLab**

1. According to realistic conflict theory, prejudice and discrimination are likely to increase when
   a. a country has a history of institutionalized racism.
   b. the person who holds the stereotypes is frustrated.
   c. people know that their close friends are prejudiced.
   d. there is competition over jobs in a country.
   e. prejudice is explicit rather than implicit.

2. Rebecca is covering her college's football game against its archrival for the school newspaper. At the game, she interviews several students from her college but decides she only needs to interview one or two students from the rival school to understand the general opinion of students at that school. Rebecca is demonstrating
   a. in-group bias.
   b. a perception of out-group homogeneity.
   c. the ultimate attribution error.
   d. blaming the victim.

3. Because the law has made most forms of direct prejudice and discrimination in the United States illegal, the expression of prejudice
   a. has declined markedly.
   b. is more likely to be revealed in microaggressions.
   c. has not changed.
   d. has less of an impact on minority group members.

4. Suppose you're a bartender and observe occasional fights at your establishment. Although you don't know very many people with visible tattoos, it seems to you that people with tattoos are more likely to get into fights than people without tattoos. But you are wrong; people with visible tattoos have not been more likely to get into fights. Based on the research discussed in this chapter, your faulty memory is most likely due to
   a. illusory correlation.
   b. the subliminal priming of stereotypic information.
   c. automatic activation of your stereotype.
   d. realistic conflict theory.

5. According to social psychological research, racism in America today
   a. has almost completely disappeared.
   b. results in low self-esteem for both the racists and those against whom they discriminate.
   c. has decreased more at the controlled level than at the automatic level.
   d. has remained the same at the controlled level.

6. At a party, Sam makes negative comments about gays and lesbians. According to research in social psychology, which of the following is *least* likely to explain Sam's behavior?
   a. Sam recently found out he had done poorly on an important test and was experiencing low self-esteem.
   b. Sam's friends often make similar comments and he conformed for normative reasons.
   c. When Sam was growing up, his parents often made negative comments about gays and lesbians.
   d. Sam had high self-esteem and felt very secure about his own sexuality.
   e. Sam recently applied for a job, but he learned that an openly gay man got the job instead of him.

7. According to social psychological research, which of the following is *least* likely to prevent Sam from making similar negative comments about gays and lesbians in the future?
   a. A woman Sam likes tells him that she disapproves of his negative comments.
   b. Sam finds out that a member of a rival fraternity is gay.
   c. Bob, a close friend of Sam's and a member of his fraternity, tells Sam that he (Bob) is gay.
   d. Sam is assigned a lab partner in a biology class who is openly gay. In order to get a good grade in the class, Sam must cooperate with his partner.

8. Melissa, a high school senior, doesn't get into the college she wants to attend. She blames this on affirmative action and starts to act aggressively toward the minority students at her school. Melissa's aggression can best be explained by
   a. out-group homogeneity.
   b. the ultimate attribution error.
   c. scapegoating.
   d. the illusory correlation phenomenon.

9. Which of the following is *least true* about race and stereotyping, from a social psychological perspective?
   a. Evolutionary theory holds that different human races have different genetic makeups that cause them to adopt different social behaviors.
   b. People often look for information that will allow them to convince themselves that there is a valid justification for holding a negative attitude toward a particular group.
   c. Stereotype threat has been found to lower the performance of African Americans and women.
   d. Categorizing people is a convenient way of learning about and remembering things about them.

10. Increasing contact between groups will reduce prejudice if all of the following conditions are met except one. Which one?
   a. Mutual interdependence
   b. Higher status of the minority group
   c. Multiple contacts
   d. Informal, interpersonal contact
   e. Social norms of equality

Answer Key

1-d, 2-b, 3-c, 4-a, 5-c,
6-d, 7-b, 8-c, 9-a, 10-b

SOCIAL PSYCHOLOGY IN ACTION

1 Making a Difference with Social Psychology

Attaining a Sustainable Future

THE RESIDENTS OF SHISHMAREF, AN ISLAND VILLAGE IN THE CHUKCHI SEA OFF THE WESTERN COAST OF ALASKA, RECENTLY VOTED TO ABANDON THEIR ISLAND AND MOVE TO THE MAINLAND, AT A TOTAL COST OF $200 MILLION TO $300 MILLION DOLLARS. The cause? Global warming, which in this part of the world is not a theoretical issue, but a very real problem. In the early 1990s, the villagers began to notice that the sea around the island was freezing later each fall and thawing earlier each spring, which made the island more vulnerable to sea surges during storms. In the fall of 1997, a storm washed away a 125-foot strip of land on the northern edge of the island. Four years later, 12-foot waves threatened the entire island, which rises to only 21 feet above sea level. Many feel that it is only a matter of time before the entire village is destroyed (Kolbert, 2006; "Alaskan village," 2008).

FOCUS QUESTIONS

- How can we apply what we know about social psychology to improve people's lives?
- How can social psychology help the world's people to live in a sustainable manner?
- How can we apply social psychology to make people happier?

Planet Earth has always had a supply of "greenhouse" gases that capture heat from the sun and keep the earth warm. But ever since the Industrial Revolution in the eighteenth century, humans have been adding to these gases—chiefly carbon dioxide (CO_2), which is released when we burn fossil fuels (e.g., in power plants, factories, and automobiles). The amount of CO_2 we are now releasing far exceeds the amount that the earth can absorb naturally. As a result, the global temperature has been rising at an accelerating rate. 2010, for example, tied 2005 for the warmest year on record, and was the 34th year in a row in which the average temperature was higher than the twentieth-century average ("2010 Tied For Warmest," 2011). The experience of the village of Shishmaref may signal the beginning of worldwide havoc due to global warming. Shelf ice in Antarctica and Greenland has begun to melt at an alarming rate. Although estimates of increases in sea levels over the next few decades vary widely, some argue that it could be as high as 20 feet. Twenty feet might not seem like much, but it would cause the abandonment of many of the world's greatest cities and displace as many as 2 billion people (Weart, 2003). Further, many scientists believe that the frequency and severity of hurricanes is getting worse because of a rise in ocean temperatures. In fact, the frequency of severe hurricanes has nearly doubled in the past 30 years. By some estimates, deaths attributable to global warming have already reached 300,000 people a year (Vidal, 2009).

Watch on **MyPsychLab**
To learn more watch the video *Global Warming*

Unfortunately, global warming is not the only environmental problem that human beings are causing. We are using up the world's oil, coal, fresh water, and other nonrenewable natural resources at an alarming rate. Scientists estimate that we already have or soon will reach the point of maximum oil production (Jones, 2003). Where to put all of our trash is another problem. In 1987, a barge called the *Mobro 4000* set out from New York City in search of a place to dump its cargo of trash, because landfills in that area were overflowing. It made ports of call in North Carolina, Florida, Alabama, Mississippi, Louisiana, Mexico, Belize, and the Bahamas, but no one was willing to dump New York's trash in their landfills. Finally, after a 6,000-mile voyage, the *Mobro 4000* returned home, and local authorities convinced a landfill outside of New York City to incinerate and bury the trash. Where else is our trash going? In the 1990s, researchers discovered that a huge patch of the Pacific Ocean (an area larger than the United States, by some estimates) has become an enormous garbage dump; similar "trash vortex" areas have since

Global warming has left Shishmaref, Alaska, vulnerable to sea surges. This house, for example, was upended by a storm. Villagers fear that it is only a matter of time before the entire island is submerged.

been identified in other areas of the world's oceans (Lovett, 2010). The problem is that a great deal of plastic material is produced, and it is then discarded into rivers and oceans near coastlines. Because the plastic is not biodegradable, it floats along currents into the ocean, which has become the final resting place for used toothbrushes, disposable cigarette lighters, plastic bags, and umbrella handles ("Plastic oceans," 2008).

In 1987, a barge called the *Mobro 4000* left New York City in search of a place to dump its load of trash. After traveling 6,000 miles and finding no takers, it returned to New York and dumped it in an overflowing landfill outside of the city.

The root cause of all of these environmental problems is that there are so many of us; the world-wide human population is 7 billion and counting. As seen in Figure SPA-1.1, the human population was relatively constant until the Industrial Revolution, at which point people began to reproduce like crazy. Around that time, English clergyman Thomas Malthus warned that the human population was expanding so rapidly that soon there would not be enough food to feed everyone. Malthus was wrong about when such a calamity would occur, chiefly because of technological advances in agriculture that have vastly improved grain yields. But he was right that, as the food supply has dwindled, the number of malnourished people in the world has increased. By some estimates, one out of every seven people in the world today is hungry (Lichtarowicz, 2010). Malthus's timing may have been a little off, but many scientists fear that his predictions are becoming truer every day.

What can we do? Basically, there are three solutions: First, we can try to curb population growth. The good news is that the rate of growth has slowed in the past few decades, although the population is still expanding (Rosenberg, 2006). Second, we can hope that improved technology bails us out—such as the development of more-efficient grains and renewable energy sources including wind and solar power. Although wonderful advances are being made in these areas, they are unlikely to solve environmental problems on their own. Third, people can adopt a more sustainable lifestyle by using fewer of the world's resources. This is easier said than done, of course; no one likes to be told that they have to consume less, and entrenched habits are hard to change. But if change we must, how can we encourage people to act in more–environmentally responsible ways?

By now you know that this is a classic social psychological question. In earlier chapters, we talked about how people form and change

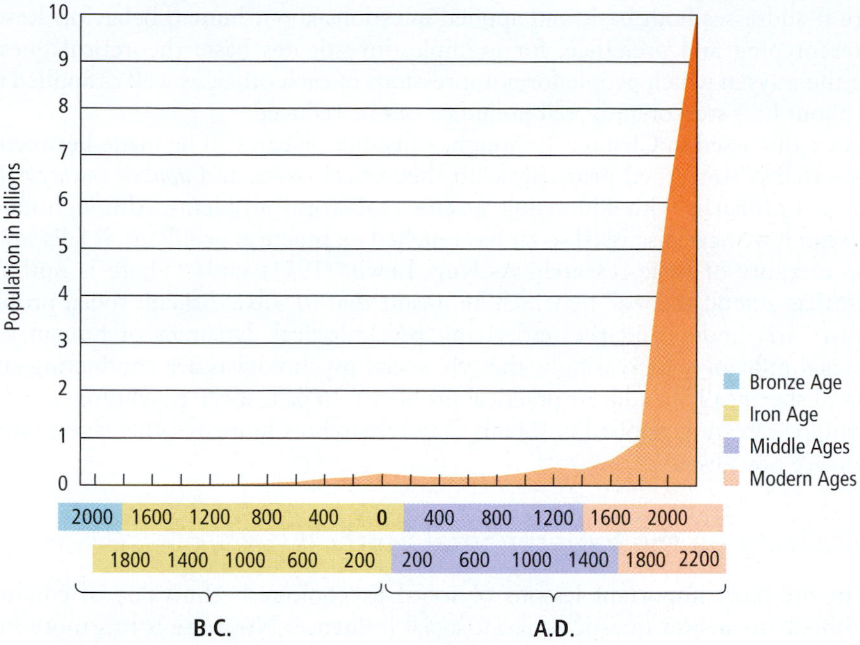

FIGURE SPA-1.1

The Growth of World Population

The size of the human race increased only very gradually until the Industrial Revolution in the eighteenth century. It has been growing exponentially ever since.

attitudes, how people are influenced by other people's behavior, the power of social norms, and so on. We turn now to a general discussion of how social psychology can be used to address social and psychological problems, followed by a specific discussion of research on how to get people to adopt more-sustainable lifestyles. Then, in the following chapters, we discuss two other major areas of applied social psychological research—namely, health and the law.

Mick Stevens/The New Yorker Collection/www.cartoonbank.com

"Gentlemen, it's time we gave some serious thought to the effects of global warming."

Applied Research in Social Psychology

Since its inception, the field of social psychology has been interested in applying what it knows to solve practical problems. Kurt Lewin (1946), generally recognized as the founder of empirical social psychology, made three key points:

- Social psychological questions are best tested with the experimental method.
- These studies can be used to understand basic psychological processes and to develop theories about social influence.
- Social psychological theories and methods can be used to address pressing social problems.

We have already touched on these issues elsewhere in the book. In Chapter 2 we saw the importance of using the experimental method to test causal hypotheses, and in subsequent chapters we saw how social psychological research has increased our understanding of important theoretical questions, such as how people think about themselves and the social world, respond to social influence, change their attitudes, and help and hurt their fellow humans. Much of this research also dealt directly with important applied issues, such as school violence, racism, bystander intervention, and decision making. To many of us in the field, the beauty of social psychology is that by its very nature it addresses both basic and applied questions about human behavior. Research on stereotyping and prejudice, for example, investigates basic theoretical questions about the ways in which people form impressions of each other, as well as applied questions about how stereotyping and prejudice can be reduced.

As we discussed in Chapter 2, though, a distinction can still be made between *basic research* that is concerned primarily with theoretical issues and *applied research* that is concerned primarily with addressing specific real-world problems. Although much of the research we have discussed so far has touched on practical problems, it falls squarely in the category of basic research. As Kurt Lewin (1951) said, "There is nothing so practical as a good theory," by which he meant that to solve difficult social problems, we must first understand the underlying psychological dynamics of human nature and social influence. Increasingly, though, social psychologists are conducting studies designed specifically to address practical problems. In fact, social psychologists are better equipped to study applied problems than researchers in many other disciplines, for reasons we now discuss.

Capitalizing on the Experimental Method

One of the most important lessons of social psychology is the value of conducting experiments to answer questions about social influence. Nowhere is this more important than in finding ways to solve applied questions, such as getting people to reduce energy consumption. Only by conducting experiments (as opposed to observational or correlational studies; see Chapter 2) can we hope to discover which solutions will work the best.

Most people seem to understand this lesson in other domains, such as research on medical treatments. Suppose that a chemist found a new compound that seems to be an effective pain killer; the initial studies with rats look very promising, but studies with people have not yet been conducted. Should we allow a drug company to go ahead and market the drug to people? Not so fast, most of us would think. Who knows how safe the drug is for humans—it might turn out to have dangerous side effects, as seems to have been the case with the pain killer Vioxx and the psoriasis drug Raptiva. There should be extensive clinical trials in humans, in which people are randomly assigned to receive the new drug or a placebo, to see whether it really does reduce pain and whether it has any serious side effects. Indeed, federal law requires extensive testing and approval by the FDA before drugs become available to the public.

We have laxer standards when it comes to testing psychological and social "treatments." If someone wants to try a new energy conservation technique, a new educational initiative, or a program to reduce prejudice, they can usually do so without a lot of rigorous testing of the intervention. A company might try a new program to reduce energy usage or institute a mandatory diversity training program, for example, before such techniques have been tested experimentally.

Well, you might think, what's the harm? Trying a new energy conservation program hardly puts people at risk, and we certainly don't want to inhibit innovation by subjecting people to cumbersome testing guidelines. And can't we find out whether these interventions work simply by interviewing people afterward or seeing whether their behavior changes (e.g., if they use less energy after the conservation program)? Unfortunately, it's not so simple. It is difficult to test the effectiveness of an intervention without a randomly assigned control group, and failing to conduct such tests can have serious consequences.

Assessing the Effectiveness of Interventions As an example, consider a psychological intervention that has been widely implemented across the world to help people who have experienced traumatic events, such as rescue workers who witness multiple deaths in a natural disaster or plane crash. The basic idea of the program, called Critical Incident Stress Debriefing (CISD), is to bring people together as soon as possible after the trauma for a 3- to 4-hour session in which participants describe their experiences in detail and discuss their emotional reactions to the events. This cathartic experience is supposed to prevent later psychiatric symptoms, including post-traumatic stress disorder (PTSD). Numerous fire and police departments have made CISD the treatment of choice for officers who witness terrible human tragedies. It is also widely used with civilians who experience traumatic events. Following the September 11, 2001, terrorist attacks, more than 9 thousand counselors rushed to New York City to help survivors deal with the trauma and stress and prevent post-traumatic stress disorder, many using psychological debriefing techniques.

Psychological debriefing makes sense, doesn't it? An ounce of prevention is worth a pound of cure, and getting people to openly discuss their reactions to traumas rather than bottling them up seems like a good thing. "Seems like" and "really is" are not the same thing, however, and an interesting thing about CISD is that it was widely implemented before social scientists conducted rigorous tests of its effectiveness.

Think for a moment about how you might go about conducting such a test. Perhaps a good place to start would be to ask people who go through CISD what they think of it. Several studies have done just that and found that participants often report that CISD was helpful. In one study, for example, 98% of police officers who had witnessed traumatic events and underwent psychological debriefing reported that they were satisfied with the procedure.

As we saw in Chapter 5, however, self-knowledge is not all that it's cracked up to be, and we should be careful about accepting these kinds of self-reports at face value. People might feel pressure to say a program that has been endorsed by their employers was helpful. More fundamentally, people might genuinely believe that the intervention was helpful, but they could be relying on theories that are incorrect. A firefighter might think, "Well, it was painful to have to rehash the fire and the deaths that I witnessed; I really would have rather gone home and played with my kids and forgotten about it. But I guess it will help me in the long run to have talked it through now." The problem is that participants can't know how they would be feeling if they had *not* undergone the CISD procedure. Maybe firefighters who go home and play with their kids *do* feel better and are at no greater risk for problems down the road.

Following the September 11, 2001, terrorists attacks, more than 9,000 counselors rushed to New York City to help survivors deal with the trauma and stress and prevent post-traumatic stress disorder. Many used a technique called Critical Incident Stress Debriefing. Was this technique adequately tested before it was widely used? Does it work or actually do harm? (See the text for the answer.)

The only way to find out is to conduct an experiment in which some people are randomly assigned to undergo CISD and others are not, and then give everyone a battery of psychological measures—ideally over a long period of time. This kind of experiment was finally conducted at various sites to test the effectiveness of CISD. The results have not been encouraging. In a comprehensive review of the literature, Harvard psychologist Richard McNally and his colleagues concluded that there is "no convincing evidence" that psychological debriefing techniques prevent post-traumatic stress disorders (McNally, Bryant, & Ehlers, 2003, p. 72).

Potential Risks of Social Interventions Even if CISD doesn't work as well as people said it did, what's the big deal? Surely getting people together to talk about their experiences can't do any harm. But here's another problem with social and psychological interventions: People use common sense to assess their effectiveness, and common sense is sometimes wrong. Not only has CISD been found to be ineffective at preventing PTSD, it may in fact do harm. In one study, participants who had been severely burned and admitted to the hospital were randomly assigned to receive CISD or to be a part of a control group that did not. All participants completed various psychological measures over the next several months and were interviewed at home by a researcher who was unaware of whether they had undergone CISD. The results were sobering: Thirteen months after the intervention, the CISD group had a significantly *higher* incidence of post-traumatic stress disorder, scored *higher* on psychological measures of anxiety and depression, and reported significantly *less* contentedness with their lives (Carlier, Voerman, & Gersons, 2000). Similar results have been found in studies testing the effectiveness of CISD with emergency workers. In their review of the literature, McNally and colleagues (2003) noted that "some evidence suggests that it [CISD] may impede natural recovery" and recommended that "for scientific and ethical reasons, professionals should cease compulsory debriefing of trauma-exposed people" (p. 72).

It turns out that right after a traumatic event, when people are experiencing considerable negative emotions, may not be the best time to focus on the event and discuss it with others. Instead, as we will see in Chapter SPA-2, people are often quite resilient when left alone (Bonanno, 2004). Forcing people to talk about and relive traumatic experiences may make them more likely to remember those experiences later. If people don't succeed in recovering on their own, they might do better to let some time pass before reliving the trauma, at a point when they have distance from it and can think about the event more objectively (Pennebaker, 2001).

Think of the consequences of implementing CISD so widely before it was adequately tested. Not only has it been a colossal waste of time, effort, and money, but also thousands of police, fire, and rescue workers have been forced to undergo a debriefing procedure that may have harmed more of them than it helped. If this were a medical intervention, there would be a huge public outcry (followed by the inevitable lawsuits).

Social Psychology to the Rescue

Social psychologists are in a unique position to find solutions to applied problems and to avoid fiascos such as the widespread use of CISD. First, the field of social psychology is a rich source of theories about human behavior that people can draw upon to devise solutions to problems. Second, and of equal importance, social psychologists know how to perform rigorous experimental tests of these solutions to see if they work (Wilson, 2011). We will see many examples of such applied research in the next two chapters. We return now to the issue with which we began this chapter: how to get people to act in ways that will help ensure a sustainable future.

Using Social Psychology to Achieve a Sustainable Future

Social psychologists have adopted a variety of approaches to get people to act in more–environmentally responsible ways. The approaches were inspired by social psychological theories and used the experimental method to see if they were successful (Oskamp, 2000; Swim, Clayton, & Howard, 2011; Steg & Vlek, 2009; Stern, 2011).

Conveying and Changing Social Norms

One approach is to remind people of social norms, the rules a group has for the acceptable behaviors, values, and beliefs of its members. As we discussed in Chapter 8, people follow two kinds of norms: *injunctive norms*, which are people's perceptions of what behaviors are approved or disapproved of by others, and *descriptive norms*, those that are people's perceptions of how people actually behave. If people believe that a certain kind of behavior is strongly frowned upon by their social group and they observe that others are obeying the norm, they are likely to follow the norm as well (Cialdini, in press; Jacobson, Mortensen, & Cialdini, 2011).

Robert Cialdini and his colleagues have illustrated the power of social norms in encouraging people to act in environmentally friendly ways. Take littering, for example. Throwing trash on the ground may not seem to be all that serious a matter. Although billboards implore us to "keep America beautiful," many people seem to think it isn't a big deal to leave their paper cup at the side of the road instead of in a trash barrel.

> *We live in an environment whose principal product is garbage.*
>
> —Russell Baker, 1968

Unfortunately, those paper cups add up. Americans discard 51 billion pieces of trash on roadsides each year, and it costs over $11 billion per year to clean up that litter ("Litter Prevention," n.d.).

In Chapter 8, we discussed a field experiment by Reno and his colleagues (1993) in which an experimental accomplice conveyed an injunctive norm against littering, by picking up a fast-food bag that had been discarded on the ground. The researchers hypothesized that seeing the accomplice pick up the bag would be a vivid reminder of the injunctive norm—that littering is bad and other people disapprove of it—and hence would lower people's inclination to litter. They were right; almost no one who saw the accomplice pick up the fast-food bag took a handbill that had been placed on the windshield of their car and tossed it on the ground. In a control condition, in which there was no bag on the ground and the accomplice simply walked by, 37% threw the handbill on the ground.

Mick Stevens/The New Yorker Collection/
www.cartoonbank.com
MStevens
"Help!"

What is the best way to communicate *descriptive* norms against littering? The most straightforward way, it would seem, would be to clean up all the litter in an environment, to illustrate that "no one litters here." In general, this is true: The less litter there is in an environment, the less likely people are to litter (Huffman et al., 1995; Krauss, Freedman, & Whitcup, 1978; Reiter & Samuel, 1980).

There is, however, an interesting exception to this finding. Cialdini, Reno, and Kallgren (1990) figured that seeing one conspicuous piece of litter on the ground spoiling an otherwise clean environment would be a better reminder of descriptive norms than seeing a completely clean environment. The single piece of trash sticks out like a sore thumb, reminding people that no one has littered here except one thoughtless person. In contrast, if there is no litter on the ground, people might be less likely to think about what the descriptive norm is. Ironically, then, littering may be more likely to occur in a totally clean environment than in one containing a single piece of litter.

To test this hypothesis, the researchers stuffed students' mailboxes with handbills and then observed from a hidden vantage point how many of the students dropped the handbills on the floor (Cialdini et al., 1990). In one condition, the researchers cleaned up the mailroom so that there were no other pieces of litter to be seen. In another condition, they placed one very noticeable piece of litter on the floor—a hollowed-out piece of watermelon. In a third condition, they not only put the watermelon rind on the floor, but also spread out dozens of discarded handbills. As predicted, the lowest rate of littering occurred in the condition where there was a single piece of trash on the floor (see Figure SPA-1.2). The single violation of a descriptive norm highlighted the fact that no one had littered but the one doofus who had dropped the watermelon rind on the floor. Now that people's attention was focused on the descriptive norm against littering, virtually none of the students littered. The highest percentage of littering occurred when the floor was littered with lots of handbills; here it was clear that there was a descriptive norm in favor of littering, and many of the students followed suit.

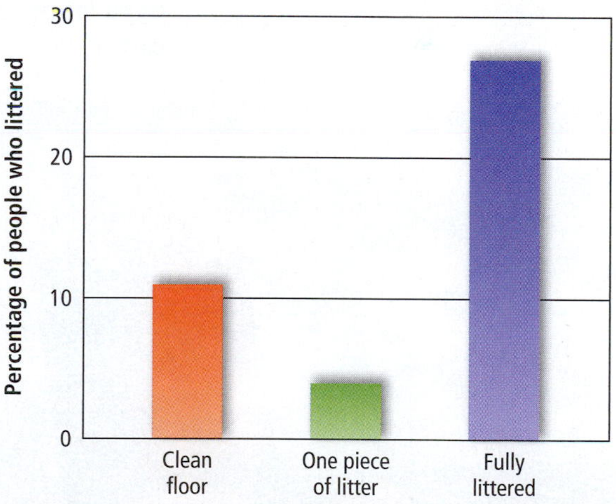

FIGURE SPA-1.2

Descriptive Norms and Littering

Who littered the least—people who saw that no one else had littered, people who saw one piece of litter on the floor, or people who saw several pieces of litter? As shown in the figure, it was people who saw one piece of litter. Seeing the single piece of litter was most likely to draw people's attention to the fact that most people had not littered, making people less likely themselves to litter.

(Adapted from Cialdini, Reno, & Kallgren, 1990)

Another way of conveying descriptive norms is simply to tell people what most others do—particularly in situations in which you can't directly observe others' behavior. If you have ever stayed in a hotel, for example, you might have seen a sign asking you to reuse your towels, because washing towels every day wastes environmental resources

TRY IT! Reducing Littering with Descriptive Norms

See if you can use the findings from the Goldstein and colleagues' (2008) hotel study to get people to act in more–environmentally friendly ways. For example, you could leave different kinds of signs in a dormitory, urging people to recycle their bottles and cans. In some locations (randomly chosen, of course), you might convey descriptive norms by saying, "Join your fellow students in helping to save the environment—75% of residents of this dorm recycle their bottles and cans." In other locations, the signs could simply say, "Help to save the environment—recycle your bottles and cans." You can then keep track of how much people recycle in each location. Be creative and try different kinds of signs!

(e.g., water and electricity). Do these appeals work? Not as much as conveying a descriptive norm about what people *actually* do. Researchers found that the standard appeal to help the environment worked less well than one that said, "Join your fellow guests in helping to save the environment" and went on to communicate that 75% of guests reuse their towels (Goldstein, Cialdini, & Griskevicius, 2008). The simple message that "other people do it" can be enough to get people to do the right thing (Nolan et al., 2008). If you would like to try to use descriptive norms in an experiment of your own, see the Try It! exercise above.

Clearly, drawing people's attention to both injunctive and descriptive norms can nudge them into acting in more–environmentally responsible ways. But what happens when there are no norms for acting in the proper way, or even norms for behaving in the opposite manner? Suppose, for example, that you are a member of a fraternity or sorority in which many people drive gas-guzzling SUVs. Perhaps that is the vehicle of choice for you and your peers; maybe it's even a sign of status and prestige. No one likes to "break the rules," and though you might have been thinking about trading in your Jeep Grand Cherokee for a smaller car with a hybrid engine, you worry about what your friends will say.

But would it really be so bad? Sometimes people overestimate the consequences of violating an injunctive norm—in other words, how much your friends would really care if you traded in your SUV. Research shows that college students overestimate other injunctive norms, such as what their friends think about drinking alcohol. Many college students believe that their peers are more in favor of drinking than they actually are (Neighbors et al., 2008; Prince & Carey, 2010). The same might be true about cars; people might not care as much as you think about what kind of car you drive.

Besides being unsightly, litter can cost millions of dollars to clean up. Social psychologists have found that emphasizing different kinds of social norms against littering is an effective way to prevent it.

Even if your friends would look disparagingly at your purchase of a hybrid car, someone has to be the first to change an injunctive norm. As we saw in Chapter 8, it is easier to buck the tide if we can get just one other person to go along with us, so you might first try to convince a friend who is looking to buy a car to consider a hybrid. If this doesn't work, just go for it. You might be surprised by how much you alone can change a norm, especially if you keep reminding people how much you are saving on gas and that SUVs are not nearly as safe as people think they are (Gladwell, 2005).

Keeping Track of Consumption

A problem with some environmental social dilemmas is that it is not easy for people to keep track of how much of a resource they are using—such as gas, electricity, or water. During a drought, for example, people may be asked to conserve water, but it is not easy for them to monitor how many gallons a month they are using. One pair of researchers reasoned that making it easy for people to keep track of their water consumption would make it easier for them to act on their concern for the greater good (Van Vugt & Samuelson, 1999). They compared two communities in the Hampshire region of England during a severe drought in the summer of 1995. The houses in one community had been equipped with water meters that allowed residents to monitor how much water they were consuming. The houses in the other community did not have meters. As expected, when people felt that the water shortage was severe, those in the metered houses consumed less water than those in the unmetered houses.

What if we got people to keep track of the energy they were saving, rather than the energy they were consuming? For example, what if we asked drivers to keep track of the miles they *avoided* driving, by walking, riding a bike, taking public transportation, or getting a ride with a friend? Making people more mindful of opportunities to avoid driving might make them more willing to leave their car at home. To find out, Graham, Koo, and Wilson (2011) asked college students to keep track of the number of miles they avoided driving and to record that figure on a Web site every other day for 2 weeks. As predicted, students who kept track of the miles they saved drove their cars less than did students in a control group who did not keep track of the miles they saved. This finding is consistent with research showing that simply keeping track of one's behavior is the first step to changing it.

Graham and colleagues (2011) also examined whether there would be an added benefit to giving the students different kinds of feedback about the miles they saved. After students entered how many miles they had avoided driving, some received feedback about how much money they had saved on gas and maintenance costs. Others received feedback about savings in air pollution (e.g., how many carbon dioxide and hydrocarbon emissions weren't emitted). Some got both kinds of feedback. It turned out that this latter group—the one that learned both how much money they had saved and how much pollution wasn't emitted—was especially likely to avoid driving their cars. Keeping track of one's behavior that avoids environmental damage and receiving concrete feedback about the savings, then, turned out to be an effective way to get college students to drive their cars less. (If you would like to try this on your own, you can download a spreadsheet with instructions how to use it at people.virginia.edu/~tdw/Driving.file.htm).

Introducing a Little Competitiveness

Other researchers have demonstrated that a little competitiveness helps people conserve energy in the workplace (Siero et al., 1996). At one unit of a factory in the Netherlands, the employees were urged to engage in energy-saving behaviors. For example, announcements were placed in the company magazine asking people to close windows during cold weather and to turn off lights when leaving a room. In addition, the employees got weekly feedback on their behavior; graphs were posted that showed how much they had improved their energy-saving behaviors, such as how often they had turned off the lights. This intervention resulted in modest improvement. By the end of the program, for example, the number of times people left the lights on decreased by 27%.

Another unit of the factory took part in an identical program, with one difference: In addition to receiving weekly feedback on their own energy-saving actions, they got to see how the other unit was doing. The researchers hypothesized that this social comparison information would motivate people to do better than their colleagues in the other unit. As seen in Figure SPA-1.3, they were right. By the end of the program, the number of times people left lights on had decreased by 61%. Engaging people's competitive spirit can have a large impact on their behavior (Staats, Harland, & Wilke, 2004).

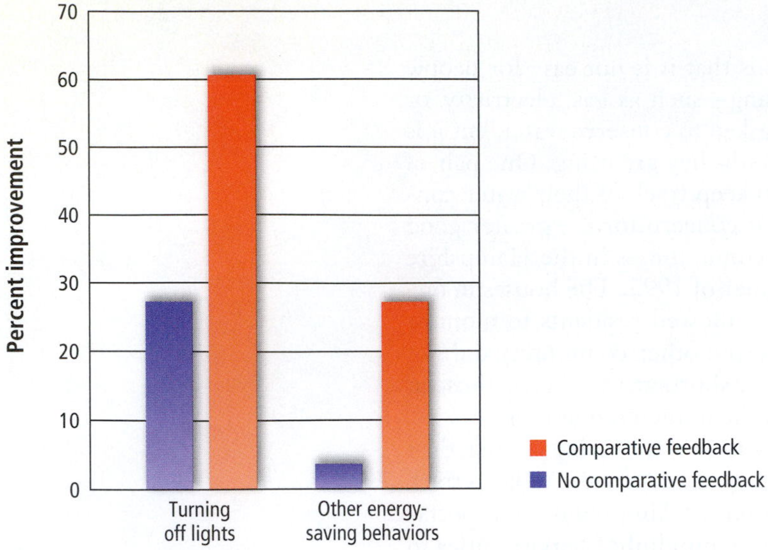

FIGURE SPA-1.3

Effects of Comparative Feedback on Energy-Saving Behaviors

Two units of a factory were urged to conserve energy and received feedback about how their unit was doing. Only one of the units, however, received comparative feedback about how it was doing relative to the other unit. As seen in the graph, this second unit improved its behavior the most, especially by turning off lights more.

(Adapted from Siero, Bakker, Dekker, & Van Den Burgh, 1996)

Inducing Hypocrisy

In many areas of the world, fresh water is becoming an increasingly scarce resource. Part of the reason is population growth in areas that have limited water supplies, such as the southwestern United States. Another cause is droughts, which are becoming increasingly frequent as the temperature of the earth rises. In 1975, 10% to 15% of the earth was drought stricken; by 2005, that figure was closer to 30% ("Drought's growing reach," 2005). It is thus important to find ways to encourage people to conserve water, especially when drought conditions exist.

Several years ago, when California was experiencing severe water shortages, administrators at one campus of the University of California realized that an enormous amount of water was being wasted by students using the university athletic facilities. The administrators posted signs in the shower rooms of the gymnasiums, exhorting students to conserve water by taking briefer, more efficient showers. The signs appealed to the students' conscience by urging them to take brief showers and to turn off the water while soaping up. The administrators were confident that the signs would be effective, because the vast majority of students at this campus were ecology minded and believed in preserving natural resources. However, systematic observation revealed that fewer than 15% of the students complied with the conservation message on the posted signs.

> *In an age where man has forgotten his origins and is blind even to his most essential needs for survival, water along with other resources has become the victim of his indifference.*
>
> —Rachel Carson, *The Silent Spring*, 1962

The administrators were puzzled; perhaps the majority of the students hadn't paid attention to the signs. After all, a sign on the wall is easy to ignore. So they made each sign more obtrusive, putting it on a tripod at the entrance to the showers so that the students needed to walk around the sign in order to get into the shower room. Although this increased compliance slightly (19% turned off the shower while soaping up), it apparently made a great many students angry; the sign was continually being knocked over and kicked around, and a large percentage of students took inordinately long showers, apparently as a reaction against being told what to do. The sign was doing more harm than good, puzzling the administrators even more. Time to call in the social psychologists.

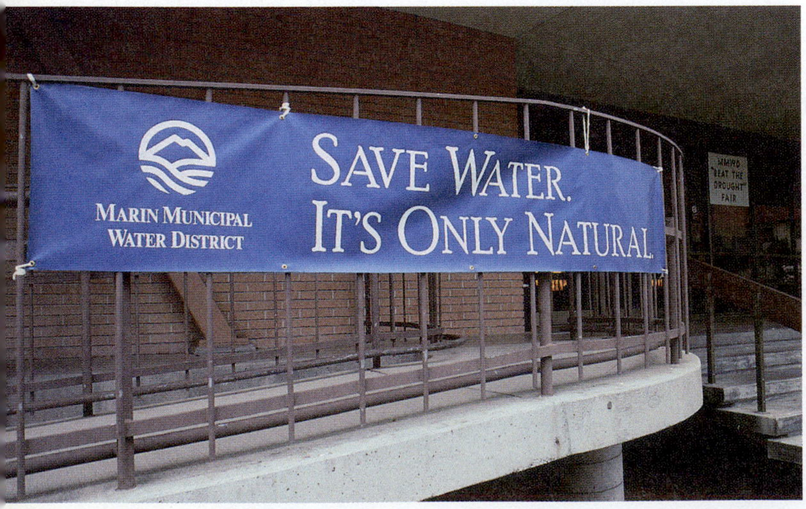

College students who were made aware that they were advocating water conservation behaviors they themselves were not practicing changed their behavior by taking shorter showers.

Elliot Aronson and his students (Dickerson et al., 1992) decided to apply a technique they had used successfully to get people to increase their use of condoms (see a description of this study in Chapter 6). The procedure involved intercepting female students who were on their way from the swimming pool to the women's shower room, introducing the experimental manipulations, and then having a research assistant casually follow them into the shower room, where she unobtrusively timed their showers. Research participants in one condition were asked to respond to a brief questionnaire about their water use, a task designed to make them mindful of how they sometimes wasted water while showering. In another condition, research participants made a public commitment, exhorting others to take steps to conserve water. Specifically, these participants were asked to sign their names to a public poster that read, "Take shorter showers. Turn shower off while soaping up. If I can do it, so can *you*!" In the crucial condition—the "hypocrisy" condition—the participants did both; that is, they were made mindful of their own wasteful behavior, and they indicated publicly (on the poster) that they were practicing water conservation. In short, they were made aware that they were preaching behavior they themselves were not practicing.

Just as in the condom study described in Chapter 6, those participants who were made to feel like hypocrites changed their behavior so that they could feel good about themselves. In this case, they took very brief showers. Indeed, the procedure was so effective that the average time students in this condition spent showering was reduced to 3.5 minutes. The hypocrisy procedure has been found to increase other environmentally sound practices as well, such as recycling (Fried & Aronson, 1995).

Removing Small Barriers to Achieve Big Changes

Sometimes the best way to change people's behavior is simply to make it easy for them to do so. Consider recycling. To reduce the amount of trash that ends up in landfills, many cities are encouraging their residents to recycle materials such as glass, paper, and aluminum. But as you know, it can be inconvenient to do so; in some areas, you have to load your car with boxes of cans and bottles and drop them off at a recycling center, which might be several miles from your house. Other cities have curbside recycling, whereby a truck picks up recycling materials that you set out at the curb on a designated day, but in most places you have to remember to separate your cans and bottles from the rest of the trash and find a place to store them until the pickup day. We thus have another social dilemma—a behavior (recycling) that, while good for us all, is effortful and unpleasant for individuals. As you might imagine, several social psychologists have turned their attention to ways of getting people to recycle more.

Watch on **MyPsychLab**
To learn more about promoting sustainable behavior, watch the MyPsychLab video ***Crack Those Recycling Codes***.

There have been two general approaches to this problem. First, some psychologists have focused on ways of changing people's attitudes and values in a proenvironment direction, with the assumption that their behavior will follow suit. This assumption is consistent with social psychological research on attitudes that has found that, under many conditions, people's attitudes are good predictors of their behavior (see Chapter 7). Several studies have found that people's attitudes toward recycling are in fact good predictors of their recycling behaviors, suggesting that a mass media campaign that targets people's attitudes is a good way to go (Knussen, Yule, & MacKenzie, 2004; Oskamp et al., 1998; Valle, Rebelo, & Reis, 2005).

Sometimes, however, we fail to act consistently with our attitudes, despite our best intentions. Perhaps the recycling center is too far away or we just can't find the time to sort our trash, even though we know we should. Kurt Lewin (1947), one of the founders of social psychology, made the observation that big social changes can sometimes occur by removing small barriers from people's environments (Ross & Nisbett, 1991). When it comes to recycling, it might be better simply to make it hassle free, such as instituting curbside recycling, than to try to change people's attitudes toward the environment. A number of studies have found this to be true. Increasing the number of recycling bins in a community, instituting curbside recycling, and allowing residents to mix materials instead of having to sort them have all been found to increase people's recycling behaviors (Domina & Koch, 2002; Ludwig, Gray, & Rowell, 1998; Schultz, Oskamp, & Mainieri, 1995).

Consider a natural experiment that was conducted in Fairfax County, Virginia (Guagnano, Stern, & Dietz, 1995). Curbside recycling had recently begun in the county, but only about a quarter of the residents had received plastic bins for collecting their recyclable materials. Others had to find their own containers in which to put their bottles and cans. Now, it might seem as if this would not be much of an impediment to recycling; if people really cared about the environment, they should be able to find their own box. As Lewin argued, however, sometimes little barriers

implementation intentions
People's specific plans about where, when, and how they will fulfill a goal

have big effects, and, indeed, the people who had the bins were much more likely to recycle.

The researchers also measured people's attitudes toward recycling, to see if those with positive attitudes were more likely to recycle than those who were not. Interestingly, people's attitudes predicted behavior only when they did *not* possess a recycling bin. When there was a barrier preventing easy compliance (e.g., people had to search through the garage to find a suitable box), only those with positive attitudes made the effort to circumvent the barrier. When there was no barrier (e.g., people had a convenient container provided by the county), attitudes did not matter as much. In this latter case, people were likely to conform even if they did not have strong proenvironmental attitudes. One study, for example, found that providing office workers with a recycling box that they could keep next to their desks dramatically increased the amount of paper they recycled (Holland, Aarts, & Langendam, 2006). The simple convenience of putting paper in a box next to their desk—as opposed to taking it to a central location—was enough to alter people's behavior.

Of course, we can't make every behavior easy to perform. How else can we nudge people into doing the right thing? The same study found that it works to get people to form **implementation intentions**, which are people's specific plans about where, when, and how they will fulfill a goal (Gollwitzer & Oettingen, 2011). The researchers also measured the extent to which people recycled plastic cups, which had to be taken to a central location (that is, the workers did not have boxes in their offices in which they could deposit used cups). Workers in the implementation intention condition were first asked to visualize and write down exactly when, where, and how they would recycle their cups, whereas workers in a control condition were not. People in the former condition recycled nearly four times as many cups as those in the latter, suggesting that the best-laid plans of mice and men often go awry (to paraphrase the poet Robert Burns), *unless* we first visualize how we are going to make those plans come true.

Now that you have read about several approaches for changing people's behavior in ways that help the environment, you are in a position to try them out yourself. See the following Try It! exercise for suggestions on how to do this.

TRY IT! Changing Environmentally Damaging Behaviors

Use the techniques discussed in this chapter to change people's behavior in ways that help the environment. Here's how to proceed.

1. *Choose the behavior you want to change.* You might try to reduce the amount of electricity used in your dorm, increase the amount that you and your roommates recycle, or increase water conservation.
2. *Choose the technique you will use to change the behavior.* For example, you might use the comparative feedback technique used by Frans Siero and colleagues (1996) to increase energy conservation. Encourage two areas of your dormitory to reduce energy usage or to recycle, and give each feedback about how it is doing relative to the other area. (To do this, you will have to have an easy, objective way of measuring people's behavior, such as the number of lights that are left on at night or the number of cans that are recycled.) Or you might try the hypocrisy technique used by Elliot Aronson and colleagues (Dickerson et al., 1992) to increase water conservation, whereby you ask people to sign a public poster that encourages recycling and have them fill out a questionnaire that makes them mindful of times they have failed to recycle. Be creative, and feel free to use more than one technique.
3. *Measure the success of your intervention.* Find an easy way to measure people's behavior, such as the amount that they recycle. Assess their behavior before and after your intervention. Best of all, include a control group of people who do not receive your intervention (randomly assigned, of course). In the absence of such a control group, it will be difficult to gauge the success of your intervention; for example, if people's behavior changes over time, you won't be able to tell if it is because of your intervention or some other factor (e.g., an article on recycling that happened to appear in the newspaper). By comparing the changes in behavior in your target group to those of the control group, you will have a better estimate of the success of your intervention.

Happiness and a Sustainable Lifestyle

The research we have been discussing thus far might seem sobering or even depressing. There are lots of environmental problems, and drastic steps are necessary to prevent them. We need to cut back on our use of energy, buy less, recycle more, and in general tighten our belts. This doesn't sound like a recipe for a happy life, does it? Actually, it might be. We end this chapter on a positive note by discussing research showing that consumption isn't nearly as important to happiness as people often assume. It is entirely possible to adopt a sustainable lifestyle and be a very happy person (Kjell, 2011).

Watch on **MyPsychLab**
To learn more about adopting a sustainable lifestyle, watch the MyPsychLab video ***Living Better Living Longer***.

What Makes People Happy?

A good place to start is with the question of what makes people happy. Philosophers and psychologists have debated this question for centuries, and there is no simple answer that applies to everyone. For one thing, some of the recipe for happiness is outside of our control. Most psychologists agree, for example, that happiness is partly genetic; some of us are born with a happier temperament than are others (Lykken & Tellegen, 1996). Further, environmental circumstances outside of our control, such as huge political upheavals in a country, can have a big impact on happiness (Inglehart & Klingemann, 2000). Nonetheless, research shows that there are things that people *can* control that influence their happiness. Three of the most important factors are having satisfying relationships with other people, pursuing something you love, and helping others.

Satisfying Relationships Perhaps the best predictor of whether someone is happy is the quality of his or her social relationships. In one study, for example, extremely happy college students were compared to their less-happy peers, and the main thing that set them apart was that happy people spent more time with other people and were more satisfied with their relationships (Diener & Biswas-Diener, 2008; Diener & Seligman, 2003). Now, being a good social psychologist, you know that this is a correlational finding and that there are three possible explanations for it: Good social relationships make people happy, happy people are more likely to have good relationships, or a third variable, such as being extraverted, makes people happier and more likely to have good relationships. These possibilities are not mutually exclusive; in fact, we suspect that all three are true. But researchers generally agree that having high-quality relationships is a major source of happiness (Baumeister & Leary, 1995; Diener & Biswas-Diener, 2008; Diener & Oishi, 2005).

Flow: Becoming Engaged in Something You Enjoy Think back to a time when you worked very hard to achieve a highly valued goal and your efforts paid off. Perhaps you were on a sports team that won a championship or in an orchestra that performed a concert to rave reviews. Now think back to when you were the happiest: Was it after you achieved the goal or while you were working toward the goal? In a sport, for example, did you feel happiest when the game ended and you were the champion, or when you were playing well and your team was ahead but you didn't know for sure whether you would win? Although it can be incredibly gratifying to have our dreams come true, there is evidence that people are happier when they are working at something they enjoy and making progress (Haidt, 2006).

There are a couple of reasons for this. First, when people are working toward a goal, they are often in a highly desired state called *flow*, which occurs when people are "lost" in a task that is challenging but attainable (Csikszentmihalyi, 1997; Csikszentmihalyi & Nakamura, 2010). Flow is what people feel when they are highly absorbed in a task and have the sense that they are making progress, such as when they are playing sports, engaged in creative activities such as writing, composing, or performing, or simply

Very happy people are more likely to spend time with other people and are more satisfied with their relationships than are less-happy people.

working on an enjoyable puzzle. Flow is such a pleasurable and absorbing state that people often lose track of how much time has passed and exactly where they are. When people achieve their goal—the game is over or they complete a work of art—the flow stops. People may be very gratified with what they have accomplished, but they are no longer "lost" in the pursuit of their goal (Keller & Bless, 2008).

Second, when people are working toward a goal but are not certain that they will obtain it, it is hard to think about anything else. The uncertainty about the outcome focuses their attention on the task, and other matters fade from view. After a goal is obtained, however, people's thoughts invariably turn to other matters—such as how much homework they have and the fact that they need to do their laundry. People usually adapt quickly to their successes, in the sense that sooner or later their accomplishment comes to seem normal, perhaps even expected, and not something that they think about all that much (Wilson & Gilbert, 2008). In short, pursuing something in an enjoyable way often makes us happier than getting it.

Things won are done; joy's soul lies in the doing.
—Shakespeare, *Troilus and Cressida*, I.ii.287

Helping Others A good way to be happy and feel better about yourself is to help other people (Aknin et al., 2011). Lyubomirsky, Sheldon, and Schkade (2005), for example, asked college students to perform five acts of kindness toward others, all in one day. Examples included donating blood, visiting an elderly relative, and helping friends with their homework. Most college students are incredibly busy, so this probably seemed like an imposition at first; imagine that you had to come up with five acts of kindness and perform them all by the end of the day. As it happened, though, the people who were randomly assigned to this condition reported that they were happier than people randomly assigned to a control group, who just went about their normal routines. In fact, the "acts of kindness" group maintained this elevated happiness for several weeks. Or consider a study by Dunn, Aknin, and Norton (2008). They gave passersby an envelope containing a small amount of cash and asked them to spend it on themselves or on someone else by 5:00 P.M. that afternoon. When the researchers telephoned people that evening, the ones that were the happiest were those who had been instructed to spend the money on someone else. Doing a good deed for others made people happier than treating themselves to a small gift.

Helping others can make people happy in a couple of ways. First, it is a way of connecting people to others and enhancing social relationships, which we've already seen is an important source of happiness. Second, people who help others are likely to come to view themselves in a more positive light—namely, as the "kind of person" who is altruistic and cares about others (see our discussion of self-perception theory in Chapter 5).

Money, Materialism, and Happiness

You may have noticed some important omissions from our recipe for happiness—especially accumulating money. Surely it is the case that people who make a lot of money are happier than those who don't? Well, the story here is not as straightforward as you might think. It is true that people who are very poor and have trouble getting food and shelter are less happy than others. After people have the basic necessities of life, however, having more money doesn't increase happiness much at all (Diener & Seligman, 2004; Howell & Howell, 2008; Kahneman & Deaton, 2010).

People who are materialistic—those who place a high value on money and possessions—tend to be less happy than people who place less value on money and possessions.

Further, there is evidence that people who are materialistic—those who place a high value on money and possessions—are *less* happy than people who place less value on money and possessions. One reason for this is that people who are materialistic have less-satisfying social relationships (Banerjee & Dittmar, 2008; Nickerson et al., 2003). Another is that a focus on money reduces people's enjoyment of everyday pleasures. That is, if people are focused on making millions and acquiring the best things that money can buy, they fail to stop and savor the little things in life that are enjoyable, such as a beautiful sunset or a bite of delicious food.

Researchers in Canada conducted a simple experiment with college students to test this. Participants first filled out a questionnaire in a binder that contained pictures from another study, which happened to be images of Canadian money or neutral pictures. Then, all participants were asked to eat some chocolate as part of a taste test. Who enjoyed the chocolate more—those who had seen the pictures of money or those who had not? As seen in Figure SPA-1.4, the people who had seen the pictures of money ate the chocolate more quickly and enjoyed it less, as rated by two objective observers. Even a reminder of wealth (the pictures of money) was enough to reduce people's interest in the small pleasures of life—in this case, a piece of chocolate (Quoidbach et al., 2010).

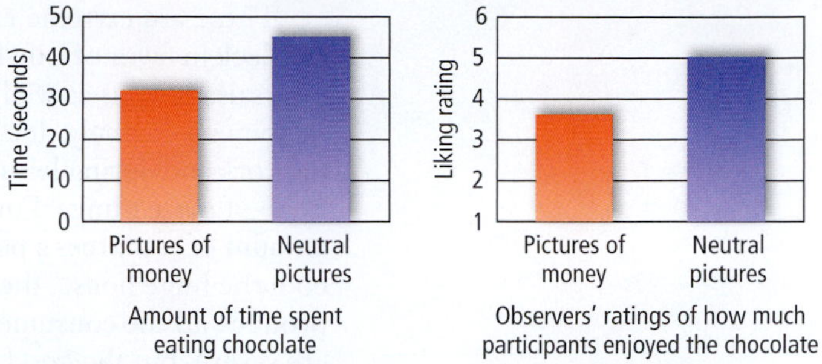

FIGURE SPA-1.4

Effects of Priming Money on the Enjoyment of Chocolate

Does being reminded of money and wealth reduce people's enjoyment of small pleasures?

After seeing pictures of money, participants ate a piece of chocolate more quickly (graph on the left) and enjoyed it less (graph on the right) than did participants who saw a neutral picture.

(Adapted from Quoidbach, Dunn, Petrides, & Mikolajczak, 2010)

Do People Know What Makes Them Happy?

Although each of us knows what makes us happy to some extent, research on **affective forecasting**—the extent to which people can predict the intensity and duration of their emotional reactions to future events—has found that we haven't figured it out completely (Gilbert, 2007; Gilbert & Wilson, 2007; Wilson & Gilbert, 2003). When it comes to understanding the recipe for happiness, sometimes we even get it backwards.

When we talk with our undergraduate advisees about their career plans, for example, many of them mention that their goal is to make a lot of money. They are not alone: Most college freshmen participating in an annual survey conducted by UCLA and the American Council of Education rated "to be able to make more money" as one of the most important reasons for going to college ("The American freshman," 2006). There is nothing wrong with wanting to achieve a comfortable lifestyle, of course. But as we have discussed, money itself does not make people happy, especially if it breeds materialism.

We also saw that one of the best predictors of happiness is having satisfying social relationships. And yet Americans are becoming increasingly isolated from each other. In the last few decades, people have become less likely to go to church, attend public meetings, get together to play cards, or entertain friends in their homes (Putnam, 2000). In 1985, about 75% of the people surveyed said they had a close friend with whom they could talk about their problems, but by 2004, only half the people said they had such a friend (Vedantam, 2006).

In short, people often strive for things that are unlikely to make them happier (e.g., earning lots of money) and overlook things that will make them happier (e.g., spending time with close friends and loved ones). And, ironically, striving for money and more consumption is a source of many environmental problems, whereas the things that really make people happy (e.g., social relationships) are not. When it comes to achieving a sustainable lifestyle, the kinds of changes we may need to make can be done without sacrificing the things that truly make people happy.

Suppose, for example, you could choose between two lives. In Life A, you live in a huge house in the suburbs and earn $500,000 a year, which you spend on lots of nice things: beautiful furniture, expensive cars, designer clothes. The downside is that you have a long commute to a job you don't really enjoy very much; you are an attorney, say, and spend most of your time researching how large corporations can pay fewer taxes. In Life B, you live in an apartment and earn $50,000 a year. You don't own a car; most days you ride your bicycle or walk the short distance to your job as a teacher. You can't wait to get to work each morning because you love what you do, especially when you see your efforts to help kids pay off. You have lots of friends at the school where you teach, as well as a tightly knit group of friends from college with whom you get together nearly every weekend. You have many interests and hobbies that keep you busy; you recently started taking salsa dance lessons, for example, and you volunteer with a literacy group that helps adults improve their reading skills.

affective forecasting
The extent to which people can predict the intensity and duration of their emotional reactions to future events

These are extreme examples, of course, and you might argue that we have stacked the deck in favor of Life B (there is no reason, for example, why our tax attorney couldn't take salsa lessons as well). But we hope the point is clear: Life B includes the recipe for happiness—namely, lots of satisfying social relationships, plenty of flow experiences (at work and during leisure time), and ample opportunities to help others. Life A satisfies none of these things. Further, Life A is much less sustainable than Life B in terms of the amount of resources a person living it would consume—the energy required to heat and cool the huge house, the gasoline needed to commute to work, the resources needed to produce all the consumer items the person buys. The environmental problems we face are severe, but the good news is that we can meet the challenges without sacrificing the things that make us truly happy.

Summary

How can we apply what we know about social psychology to improve people's lives?

- **Applied Research in Social Psychology** By its very nature, social psychology addresses both basic and applied questions about human behavior. Social psychologists have conducted a good deal of applied research on important social and psychological issues, such as how people can adopt a more sustainable lifestyle.
  - **Capitalizing on the Experimental Method** One of the most important lessons of social psychology is the value of conducting experiments to answer questions about social influence. This is important when testing the effectiveness of interventions designed to solve an applied problem. Some interventions have backfired and had negative effects because they were not adequately tested.
  - **Social Psychology to the Rescue** Social psychologists are in a unique position to find solutions to applied problems. First, the field of social psychology is a rich source of theories about human behavior that people can draw upon to devise solutions to problems. Second, social psychologists know how to perform rigorous experimental tests of these solutions to see if they work.

How can social psychology help the world's people to live in a sustainable manner?

- **Using Social Psychology to Achieve a Sustainable Future** The human population is expanding at an exponential rate, with severe environmental consequences. Famine and malnutrition are spreading, natural resources are being depleted, and global warming is an alarming, immediate problem. Social psychologists have devised several approaches to encourage people to adopt a more sustainable lifestyle.
  - **Conveying and Changing Social Norms** One approach is to remind people of both *injunctive* and *descriptive* norms against environmentally damaging acts, such as littering. For example, communicating descriptive norms—that other people act in environmentally friendly ways—has been shown to reduce the extent to which passersby litter and increase the extent to which hotel-room guests reuse their towels.
  - **Keeping Track of Consumption** One simple technique is to make it easier for people to know how much energy they are using, for example, by providing them with water meters that are easy to read. College students who kept track of the number of miles they avoided driving their cars (e.g., by walking or taking the bus) drove their cars less.
  - **Introducing a Little Competitiveness** Units in a company that were competing with each other to conserve energy were more successful than units that were encouraged to save but did not compete.
  - **Inducing Hypocrisy** It works to arouse dissonance in people by making them feel that they are not practicing what they are preaching—for example, that even though they believe in water conservation, they are taking long showers.
  - **Removing Small Barriers to Achieve Big Changes** Removing barriers that make proenvironmental behaviors difficult, such as instituting curbside recycling and providing people with recycling bins, has been shown to be effective. It also helps to get people to form **implementation intentions**, which are people's specific plans about where, when, and how they will fulfill a goal, such as the goal to recycle.

How can we apply social psychology to make people happier?

- **Happiness and a Sustainable Lifestyle** It is possible to adopt a sustainable lifestyle and be a happy person.
  - **What Makes People Happy?** Happiness is partly a matter of the temperament with which we are born and partly a matter of environmental conditions outside of our control, such as the political stability of the government. Three things we can control also influence our happiness: the quality of our social relationships, opportunities for "flow" experiences, and helping others.
  - **Money, Materialism, and Happiness** After people have the basic necessities of life, having more money doesn't increase happiness much at all. Further, people who are materialistic—those who place a high value on money and possessions—tend to be less happy than people who place less value on money and possessions.
  - **Do People Know What Makes Them Happy?** When it comes to understanding the recipe for happiness, some people get it backward: They focus too much on wealth and materialism, and too little on social relationships, flow, and helping others. The moral is that people can achieve a sustainable lifestyle without sacrificing the things that make people truly happy.

Chapter SPA-1 Test

Study and Review on MyPsychLab

1. According to what you read in this chapter, which of the following is likely to be *least* effective at solving environmental problems?
   a. Finding more-efficient ways of getting rid of the trash human beings generate.
   b. Slowing the population growth of human beings.
   c. Developing new technologies such as more-efficient grains and renewable energy sources such as wind and solar power.
   d. Getting people to adopt a more sustainable lifestyle by using fewer of the world's resources.

2. Which of the following statements is *least* true about the social psychological approach to solving applied problems?
   a. Applied questions are best tested with the experimental method.
   b. There is nothing as practical as a good theory.
   c. Social psychological theories and methods can be used to address pressing social problems.
   d. Given how pressing many problems are, it is a good idea to implement solutions before we are able to test them experimentally.

3. Meghan is a first-year college student and is trying to figure out what the norms are about dating at her school. Which of the following is the best example of an *injunctive norm*?
   a. Meghan believes that most students disapprove of people who have casual "hookups" with other people.
   b. Meghan believes that many students do hook up with other students.
   c. Meghan believes that most students do not hook up with other students.
   d. Meghan has no idea how many students hook up with other students.

4. Suppose you want people in your apartment building to stop throwing their junk mail on the floor of the mailroom. Which of the following would be *least* likely to work?
   a. Set an example by picking up the litter yourself when people are watching.
   b. Post a sign informing people that there is a recycling center on the other side of town that accepts junk mail.
   c. Clean up all the litter in the mailroom, but leave one very noticeable piece of trash on the floor.
   d. Post a sign in the mailroom that says, "Join your fellow residents in helping to keep things clean—90% of residents recycle their junk mail."

5. Suppose you live in a dorm and want to get people who live there to act in more–environmentally responsible ways, such as recycling more. Which of the following would be *least* likely to work, according to social psychological research?
   a. Measure how much the dorm recycles each month, and post graphs of these figures where everyone can see them.
   b. Set up a competition with another dorm, in which the one that recycles more each month wins free pizzas.
   c. Make a point of taking soda cans out of the trash and putting them in a recycling bin in a public area where lots of people can see you do this.
   d. Give people statistics about how much recycling saves energy and prevents landfills from overflowing.

6. Suppose you wanted to get people to use less electricity where you work by getting them to turn off lights when they leave. Which of the following is *most* likely to succeed, based on research in social psychology?
   a. Get people to sign a public pledge that they will turn off lights when they leave.
   b. Ask people to write about times when they forgot to turn off lights when they left.
   c. Ask people to do both—sign the public pledge and write about times they didn't turn off the lights.
   d. Ask people to sign the public pledge and write about times they did turn off the lights when they left.

7. Which of the following is *least* likely to make people happy?
   a. Helping other people.
   b. Having satisfying relationships with other people.
   c. Earning enough money to be able to afford a lot of luxury possessions.
   d. Having "flow" activities in which people become highly engaged.

8. Which of the following is most true about research on happiness?
   a. People have a very good idea of what will make them happy in the future.
   b. One of the best predictors of happiness is having satisfying social relationships, but Americans are becoming increasingly isolated from each other.
   c. When choosing a career, the most important thing to consider is how much money you will earn.
   d. Acting in ways that will help the environment will probably make people less happy.

Answer Key

1-a, 2-d, 3-a, 4-b, 5-d, 6-c, 7-c, 8-b

SOCIAL PSYCHOLOGY IN ACTION

2 Social Psychology and Health

JOANNE HILL SUFFERED AN UNIMAGINABLE AMOUNT OF LOSS OVER A 4-YEAR PERIOD. It began when her husband, Ken, died of heart failure at the age of 55, followed shortly by the deaths of her brother, stepfather, mother, aunt, two uncles, two cousins, her cousin's partner, her stepmother, and, finally, her son, who died suddenly of a heart attack at the age of 38. Joanne helped care for several of these loved ones before they died, including her mother, who suffered from Alzheimer's and breast cancer, her brother, who died of lung cancer, and her aunt, who died of liver cancer. "Everyone I loved seemed to need help," she said (Hill, 2002, p. 21).

How could anyone endure so much loss? Surely any one of these tragedies would stop us in our tracks, and suffering so many in such a short time would surely push most of us to the breaking point, taking a severe toll on our physical and emotional well-being. But rather than crawl under a rock, Joanne made it through what she calls her "locust years" with remarkable strength, grace, and resilience. She was the executor of several of her relatives' estates and dealt successfully with complicated legal issues. She provided help and support to numerous friends and family members. She also went back to college, traveled to Europe, and wrote a book about her experiences. Life is "filled with both bright sunny places and dark stormy times," she says. "Within each I looked for the golden nuggets of wisdom and truth that helped me grow stronger, happier and healthier" (Hill, n.d.).

Maybe Joanne is one of those rare people born with a huge reservoir of inner strength, allowing her to weather any storm. But she didn't always find it easy to deal with life's slings and arrows. She had struggled with depression in childhood and beyond, was addicted to prescription medication early in her marriage, and suffered from debilitating physical ailments—so many that she had difficulty buying life insurance. "Today," she reports in her book, "in spite of one trauma after another for several years, I am healthy in body and whole in mind. Not because of Lady Luck, but because I decided to make different choices" (p. 133). Hill attributes her survival to a series of "rainbow remedies" that she learned, through hard experience, to apply to her life.

This chapter is concerned with the application of psychology to physical and mental health, which is a flourishing area of research. We will focus primarily on topics that connect social psychology and health: how people cope with stress in their lives, the relationship between their coping styles and their physical and mental health, and how we can get people to behave in healthier ways. Along the way we will return to Joanne Hill's story, discuss her "rainbow remedies," and see that at least some of them are backed up by research in social psychology and health.

FOCUS QUESTIONS

- What effects does stress have on our health?
- What can people do to cope and recover after a stressful experience?
- How can we apply social psychology to help people live healthier lives?

People are surprisingly resilient in the face of stressful events. Studies of reactions to the 9/11 terrorist attacks, for example, have found that relatively few people showed long-term signs of depression or other mental health problems.

Stress and Human Health

There is more to our physical health than germs and disease—we also need to consider the amount of stress in our lives and how we deal with that stress (Chida & Hamer, 2008; Ganzel, Morris, & Wethington, 2010; Inglehart, 1991; Park, 2010; Segerstrom, 2010; Taylor, 2010). Early research in this area documented some extreme cases in which people's health was influenced by stress. Consider these examples, reported by psychologist W. B. Cannon (1942):

- A New Zealand woman eats a piece of fruit and then learns that it came from a forbidden supply reserved for the chief. Horrified, her health deteriorates, and the next day she dies—even though it was a perfectly fine piece of fruit.
- A man in Africa has breakfast with a friend, eats heartily, and goes on his way. A year later, he learns that his friend had made the breakfast from a wild hen, a food strictly forbidden in his culture. The man immediately begins to tremble and is dead within 24 hours.
- An Australian man's health deteriorates after a witch doctor casts a spell on him. He recovers only when the witch doctor removes the spell.

These examples probably sound bizarre, like something you would read in *Ripley's Believe It or Not.* But let's shift to the present in the United States, where many similar cases of sudden death occur following a psychological trauma. When people undergo a major upheaval in their lives, such as losing a spouse, declaring bankruptcy, or being forced to resettle in a new culture, their chance of dying increases (Morse, Martin, & Moshonov, 1991). Soon after a major earthquake in the Los Angeles area on January 17, 1994, there was an increase in the number of people who died suddenly of heart attacks (Leor, Poole, & Kloner, 1996). And many people experienced psychological and physical problems after the terrorist attacks on September 11, 2001 (Neria, DiGrande, & Adams, 2011; Silver et al., 2002). One study measured the heart rates of a sample of adults in New Haven, Connecticut, the week after the attacks. Compared to a control group of people studied before the attacks, the post–September 11 sample showed lower heart rate variability, which is a risk factor for sudden death (Gerin et al., 2005; Lampert et al., 2002). On the other hand, as we will see in a moment, studies of the long-term effects of the 9/11 attacks have found relatively little evidence of prolonged negative reactions. What exactly are the effects of stress on our psychological and physical health, and how can we learn to cope most effectively?

Resilience

The first thing to note is that humans are remarkably resilient. To be sure, we all must contend with the blows life deals us, including day-to-day hassles and major, life-altering events. And although it is true that such events can have negative effects on psychological and physical health, many people, such as Joanne Hill, cope with them extremely well. Researchers have examined people's reactions over time to major life events, including the death of loved ones and the 9/11 terrorist attacks. The most common response to such traumas is **resilience**, which can be defined as mild, transient reactions to stressful events, followed by a quick return to normal, healthy functioning (Bonanno, 2004, 2005; Bonanno, Westphal, & Mancini, 2011).

Take life's most difficult challenge—dealing with the loss of a loved one. For years, mental health professionals assumed that the "right" way to grieve was to go through an intense period of sadness and distress, in which people confronted and worked through their feelings, eventually leading to acceptance of the loss. People who did not show symptoms of extreme distress were said to be in a state of denial that would lead to greater problems down the road. When researchers looked systematically at how people respond to the death of loved ones, however, an interesting fact emerged: Many people never experienced significant distress and recovered quickly (Wortman & Silver, 1989). Studies of bereaved spouses, for example, typically find that fewer than half show signs of significant, long-term distress (Bonanno, Boerner, &

Resilience

Mild, transient reactions to stressful events, followed by a quick return to normal, healthy functioning

Wortman, 2008; Bonanno et al., 2005). The remainder, like Joanne Hill, show no signs of depression and are able to experience positive emotions.

Although one might think that such people are in a state of denial, or that they were never very attached to their spouses, there is little evidence to support these possibilities. Rather, there is increasing evidence that although life's traumas can be quite painful, many people have the resources to recover from them quickly. The same pattern has been found in people's responses to other highly stressful events, such as emergency workers' reactions to the bombing of the federal building in Oklahoma City in 1995 and New Yorkers' reactions to the 9/11 terrorist attacks. Surprisingly few people show prolonged, negative reactions to these tragedies (McNally, & Breslau, 2008; Seery et al., 2008; Updegraff, Silver, & Holman, 2008). Nonetheless, some people do have severe negative reactions to stressful events. What determines whether people bounce back quickly or buckle under stress?

Effects of Negative Life Events

Among the pioneers in research on stress is Hans Selye (1956, 1976), who defined *stress* as the body's physiological response to threatening events. Selye focused on how the human body adapts to threats from the environment, regardless of the source—be it a psychological or physiological trauma. Later researchers have examined what it is about a life event that makes it threatening. Holmes and Rahe (1967), for example, suggested that stress is the degree to which people have to change and readjust their lives in response to an external event. The more change that is required, the greater the stress we experience. For example, if a spouse or partner dies, just about every aspect of a person's life is disrupted, leading to a great deal of stress. Holmes and Rahe's definition of stress applies to happy events as well if the event causes big changes in one's daily routine. Graduating from college is a happy occasion, but it can be stressful because it is often accompanied by a separation from friends and adapting to a new situation, such as looking for a job, working full time, or going to graduate school.

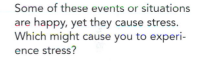

Some of these events or situations are happy, yet they cause stress. Which might cause you to experience stress?

To measure the amount of stress in your life, complete the Try It! exercise on the next page. How did you do? When the authors who developed the scale gave it to a sample of undergraduates, they found that the average score was 1,247 (Renner & Mackin, 1998). And studies have shown that the higher people score on stress inventories such as this one, the worse their mental and physical health (Almeida, 2005; Dohrenwend, 2006; Seta, Seta, & Wang, 1990).

Limits of Stress Inventories It seems pretty obvious that the more stress people are experiencing, the more likely they are to feel anxious and get sick. But the findings aren't all that straightforward. One problem, as you may have recognized, is that most studies in this area use correlational designs, not experimental designs. Just because life changes are correlated with health problems does not mean that the life changes caused the health problems (see Chapter 2 on correlation and causality). Some researchers have argued persuasively for the role of "third variables," whereby certain kinds of people are more likely to be experiencing difficult life changes and to report that they are ill (Schroeder & Costa, 1984; Watson & Pennebaker, 1989). According to these researchers, it is not life changes that cause health problems. Instead, people with certain personality traits, such as the tendency to experience negative moods, are more likely to experience life difficulties and to have health problems.

Another problem with measures such as the College Life Stress Inventory is that they focus on stressors experienced by the middle class and underrepresent stressors experienced by the poor and members of minority groups. Variables such as poverty and racism are potent causes of stress (Gibbons, Gerrard, & Cleveland, 2004; Giscombé & Lobel, 2005; Jackson et al., 1996; Myers, 2009). Moreover, the way in which these variables influence health is not always obvious. It might not surprise you to learn that the more racism minority groups experience, the worse their health. It might come as more of a surprise to learn that majority groups who express the most racist attitudes also experience diminished health (Jackson & Inglehart, 1995). Racism is often associated with hostility and aggression, and there is evidence that hostility is related to health problems such as coronary heart disease. Clearly, to understand the relationship between stress and health, we need to understand better such community and cultural variables as poverty and racism.

Perceived Stress and Health

There is another problem with measures such as the College Life Stress Inventory: They violate a basic principle of social psychology—namely, that subjective situations have more of an impact on people than objective situations (Dohrenwend, 2006; Griffin & Ross, 1991). Of course, some situational variables are hazardous to our health regardless of how we interpret them (Jackson & Inglehart, 1995; Taylor, Repetti, & Seeman, 1997). Children growing up in smog-infested areas such as Los Angeles, for example, have been found to have 10% to 15% less efficiency in their lungs than children who grow up in less-polluted areas (Peters et al., 1999). Nonetheless, some environmental events are open to interpretation and seem to have negative effects only on people who construe these events in certain ways. To some students, writing a term paper is a major hassle; for others, it's a minor inconvenience (or even an enjoyable challenge). For some people, a major life change such as getting divorced is a liberating escape from an abusive relationship; for others, it is a devastating personal failure. As recognized by Richard Lazarus (1966, 2000) in his pioneering work on stress, it is subjective, not objective, stress that causes problems. An event is stressful for people only if they interpret it as stressful; thus, we can define **stress** as the negative feelings and beliefs that occur whenever people feel unable to cope with demands from their environment (Lazarus & Folkman, 1984).

Stress
The negative feelings and beliefs that arise whenever people feel unable to cope with demands from their environment

Consider the number of losses Joanne Hill experienced in a 4-year period. According to research on life events, she should have been experiencing a great deal of stress—enough to put her at great risk for severe physical problems. The fact that she made

TRY IT! The College Life Stress Inventory

Instructions: Copy the "stress rating" number into the right column for any event that has happened to you in the past year; then add these scores.

Event	Stress Rating	Your Score
Being raped	100	______
Finding out that you are HIV-positive	100	______
Being accused of rape	98	______
Death of a close friend	97	______
Death of a close family member	96	______
Contracting a sexually transmitted disease (other than AIDS)	94	______
Concerns about being pregnant	91	______
Finals week	90	______
Concerns about your partner being pregnant	90	______
Oversleeping for an exam	89	______
Flunking a class	89	______
Having a boyfriend or girlfriend cheat on you	85	______
Ending a steady dating relationship	85	______
Serious illness in a close friend or family member	85	______
Financial difficulties	84	______
Writing a major term paper	83	______
Being caught cheating on a test	83	______
Drunk driving	82	______
Sense of overload in school or work	82	______
Two exams in one day	80	______
Cheating on your boyfriend or girlfriend	77	______
Getting married	76	______
Negative consequences of drinking or drug use	75	______
Depression or crisis in your best friend	73	______
Difficulties with parents	73	______
Talking in front of a class	72	______
Lack of sleep	69	______
Change in housing situation (hassles, moves)	69	______
Competing or performing in public	69	______
Getting in a physical fight	66	______
Difficulties with a roommate	66	______
Job changes (applying, new job, work hassles)	65	______
Declaring a major or concerns about future plans	65	______
A class you hate	62	______
Drinking or use of drugs	61	______
Confrontations with professors	60	______
Starting a new semester	58	______
Going on a first date	57	______
Registration	55	______
Maintaining a steady dating relationship	55	______
Commuting to campus or work, or both	54	______
Peer pressures	53	______
Being away from home for the first time	53	______
Getting sick	52	______
Concerns about your appearance	52	______
Getting straight A's	51	______
A difficult class that you love	48	______
Making new friends; getting along with friends	47	______
Fraternity or sorority rush	47	______
Falling asleep in class	40	______
Attending an athletic event (e.g., football game)	20	______
Sum of Your Score		______

Adopting the right attitude can convert a negative stress into a positive one.

—HANS SELYE (1978)

it through with grace and strength suggests that there are limits to trying to predict people's reactions from a count of the number of stressful events in their lives. We need to take into account how different people *interpret* disruptions and challenges in their lives.

Studies using the subjective definition of stress confirm the idea that negative life experiences are bad for our health. In fact, stress caused by negative interpretations of events can directly affect our immune systems, making us more susceptible to disease. Consider the common cold. When people are exposed to the virus that causes a cold, only 20% to 60% of them become sick. Is it possible that stress is one determinant of who will be in this category? To find out, researchers asked volunteers to spend a week at a research institute in southern England (Cohen, Tyrrell, & Smith, 1991, 1993). As a measure of stress, the participants listed recent events that had had a negative impact on their lives. (Consistent with our definition of stress, the participants listed only events they *perceived* as negative.)

The researchers then gave participants nasal drops that contained either the virus that causes the common cold or saline (salt water). The participants were subsequently quarantined for several days so that they had no contact with other people. The results? The more stress people were experiencing, the more likely they were to catch a cold from the virus (see Figure SPA-2.1).

Among people who reported the least amount of stress, about 27% came down with a cold. This rate increased steadily the more stress people reported, topping out at a rate of nearly 50% in the group that was experiencing the most stress. This effect of stress was found even when several other factors that influence catching a cold were taken into account, such as the time of year people participated and the participants' age, weight, and gender. This study, along with others like it, shows that the more stress people experience, the lower their immunity to disease (Cohen et al., 2008; O'Leary, 1990; Stone et al., 1993).

You may have noticed that the Cohen and colleagues study used a correlational design; this must make us cautious about its interpretation. The amount of stress people were experiencing was measured and correlated with the likelihood that people caught a cold. It is possible that stress itself did not lower people's immunity but rather that some variable correlated with stress did. It would have been ethically impermissible, of course, to conduct an experimental study in which people were randomly assigned to a condition in which they experienced a great deal of prolonged stress. There are studies, however, in which people's immune responses are measured before and after undergoing mildly stressful tasks in the laboratory, such as solving mental arithmetic problems continuously for 6 minutes or giving speeches on short notice. Even relatively mild stressors such as these can lead to a suppression of the immune system (Cacioppo, 1998; Cacioppo et al., 1998).

The finding that stress negatively affects health raises an important question: What exactly is it that makes people perceive a situation as stressful? One important determinant is the amount of control they believe they have over the event.

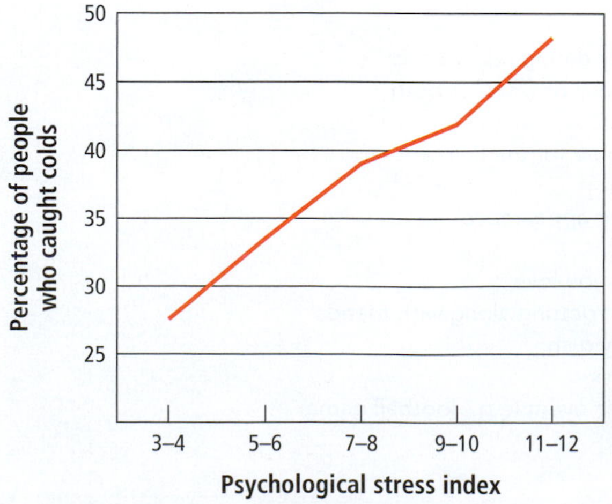

Figure SPA-2.1

Stress and the Likelihood of Catching a Cold

People were first exposed to the virus that causes the common cold and then isolated. The greater the amount of stress they were experiencing, the greater the likelihood that they caught a cold from the virus.

(Adapted from Cohen, Tyrrell, & Smith, 1991)

Feeling in Charge: The Importance of Perceived Control

"There are times in life when we feel so out of control that helplessness and hopelessness become constant companions," writes Joanne Hill. "But choice, like breath, is something that is part of us. *We always have a choice*" (Hill, 2002, p. 128). Research shows, however, that some people feel this way more than others. For example, suppose you read a series of statements and had to choose the one in each pair that you thought was more true, such as "people's misfortunes result from mistakes they make" versus "many of the unhappy things in people's lives are partly due to bad luck." Which of these two do you think is more true? These statements are part of a test of **internal-external locus of control** (Rotter, 1966), which is the tendency to believe that things happen because we control them versus believing that good and bad outcomes are out of our control. The first statement above reflects an internal locus of control, which is the belief that people can control their fates. The second statement reflects an external locus of control, which is the belief that our fates are more a matter of happenstance.

Internal-External Locus of Control

The tendency to believe that things happen because we control them versus believing that good and bad outcomes are out of our control

Perceived Control

The belief that we can influence our environment in ways that determine whether we experience positive or negative outcomes

Research by Jean Twenge and her colleagues (Twenge, Zhang, & Im, 2004) has found that between the years 1960 and 2002, college students in the United States have scored more and more on the external end of the locus-of-control scale. That is, as seen in Figure SPA-2.2, college students are becoming more convinced that good and bad things in life are outside of their control.

The reasons for this trend are not entirely clear; it may be part of an increased sense of alienation and distrust among younger generations in the United States (Fukuyama, 1999; Putnam, 2000). Whatever the reasons, research in social psychology suggests that the tendency to feel less control over one's fate is not good for our psychological and physical health. Shelley Taylor and her colleagues (Taylor, Lichtman, & Wood, 1984), for example, interviewed women with breast cancer and found that many of them believed they could control whether their cancer returned. Here is how one man described his wife: "She got books, she got pamphlets, she studied, she talked to cancer patients. She found out everything that was happening to her and she fought it. She went to war with it. She calls it 'taking in her covered wagons and surrounding it'" (quoted in Taylor, 1989, p. 178).

The researchers found that women who believed their cancer was controllable were better adjusted psychologically (Folkman & Moskowitz, 2000). Subsequent studies have found that a high sense of **perceived control**—defined as the belief that we can influence our environment in ways that determine whether we experience positive or negative outcomes—is associated with good physical and mental health (Frazier et al., 2011; Kraus, Piff, & Keltner, 2009; Leotti, Iyengar, & Ochsner, 2010; Roepke & Grant, 2011; Thompson, 1999). For example, among people who had undergone a coronary angioplasty because of diseased arteries, those who had a high sense of control over their futures were less likely to experience subsequent heart problems than people with

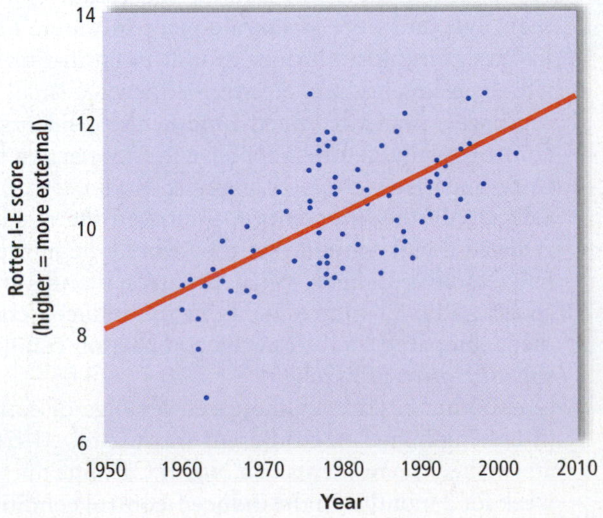

Figure SPA-2.2

Beliefs in Internal-External Locus of Control in College Students Over Time

As seen in the graph, in the past 50 years there is a trend whereby college students in the United States endorse more external beliefs about locus of control. This means that they increasingly believe that good and bad things in life are outside of their control.

(Adopted from Twenge, Zhang, & Im, 2004)

a low sense of control (Helgeson, 2003; Helgeson & Fritz, 1999). Joanne Hill recognized this lesson; one of her rainbow remedies is that the "Power of Choice is an empowering remedy that truly makes the difference whether we survive and thrive, or wither and die" (Hill, n.d.).

Increasing Perceived Control in Nursing Homes Some of the most dramatic effects of perceived control have been found in studies of older people in nursing homes. Many people who end up in nursing homes and hospitals feel they have lost control of their lives (Raps et al., 1982; Sherwin & Winsby, 2011). People are often placed in long-term care facilities against their wishes and, when there, have little say in what they do, whom they see, or what they eat. Two psychologists believed that boosting their feelings of control would help such people (Langer & Rodin, 1976). They asked the director of a nursing home in Connecticut to convey to the residents that, contrary to what they might think, they had a lot of responsibility for their own lives. Here is an excerpt of his speech:

> Take a minute to think of the decisions you can and should be making. For example, you have the responsibility of caring for yourselves, of deciding whether or not you want to make this a home you can be proud of and happy in. You should be deciding how you want your rooms to be arranged—whether you want it to be as it is or whether you want the staff to help you rearrange the furniture. You should be deciding how you want to spend your time. . . . If you are unsatisfied with anything here, you have the influence to change it. . . . These are just a few of the things you could and should be deciding and thinking about now and from time to time every day. (Langer & Rodin, 1976, pp. 194–195)

Nursing home residents who have a sense of control over their lives have been found to do better, both physically and psychologically.

The director went on to say that a movie would be shown on two nights the next week and that the residents should decide which night they wanted to attend. Finally, he offered each resident a gift of a house plant, emphasizing that it was up to the resident to decide whether to take one (they all did) and to take care of it. The director also gave a speech to residents assigned to a comparison group. This speech was different in one crucial way: All references to making decisions and being responsible for oneself were deleted. He emphasized that he wanted the residents to be happy, but he did not say anything about the control they had over their lives. He said that a movie would be shown on two nights the next week but that the residents would be assigned to see it on one night or the other. He gave plants to these residents as well but said that the nurses would take care of the plants.

The director's speech might not seem like a major change in the lives of the residents. The people in the induced-control group heard one speech about the responsibility they had for their lives and were given one plant to water. That doesn't seem like very strong stuff, does it? But to an institutionalized person who feels helpless and constrained, even a small boost in control can have a dramatic effect. Indeed, the residents in the induced-control group became happier and more active than residents in the comparison group (Langer & Rodin, 1976). Most dramatically of all, the intervention improved the residents' health and reduced the likelihood that they would die in the next year and a half (Rodin & Langer, 1977). Eighteen months after the director's speech, 15% of the residents in the induced-control group had died, compared to 30% in the comparison condition (see the left side of Figure SPA-2.3).

Another researcher increased feelings of control in residents of nursing homes in a different way (Schulz, 1976). Undergraduates visited the residents of a North Carolina nursing home once a week for 2 months. In the induced-control condition, the residents

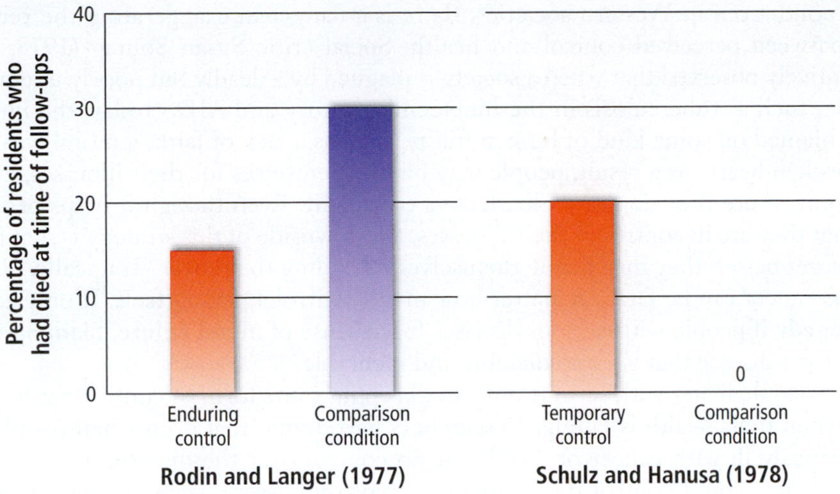

Figure SPA-2.3

Perceived Control and Mortality

In two studies, elderly residents in nursing homes were made to feel more in control of their lives. In one (Rodin & Langer, 1977), the intervention endured over time, so that people continued to feel in control. As seen on the left side of the figure, this intervention had positive effects on mortality rates. Those who received it were more likely to be alive 18 months later than those who did not. In the other study (Schulz & Hanusa, 1978), the intervention was temporary. Being given control and then having it taken away had negative effects on mortality rates, as seen on the right side of the figure.

(Adapted from Rodin & Langer, 1977; Schulz & Hanusa, 1978)

decided when the visits would occur and how long they would last. In a randomly assigned comparison condition, it was the students, not the residents, who decided when the visits would occur and how long they would last. Thus, the residents received visits in both conditions, but in only one could they control the visits' frequency and duration. This may seem like a minor difference, but again, giving the residents some semblance of control over their lives had dramatic effects. After 2 months, those in the induced-control condition were happier, healthier, more active, and taking fewer medications than those in the comparison group.

Schulz returned to the nursing home several months later to assess the long-term effects of his intervention, including its effect on mortality rates. Based on the results of the Langer and Rodin (1976) study, we might expect that the residents who could control the students' visits would be healthier and more likely still to be alive than the residents who could not. But there is a crucial difference between the two studies: The residents in the Langer and Rodin study were given an enduring sense of control, whereas the residents in the Schulz study experienced control and then lost it. Langer and Rodin's participants could continue to choose which days to participate in different activities, continue to take care of their plant, and continue to feel that they could make a difference in what happened to them, even after the study ended. By contrast, when Schulz's study was over, the student visits ended. The residents who could control the visits suddenly had that control removed.

Unfortunately, Schulz's intervention had an unintended effect: After the program ended, the people in the induced-control group did worse (Schulz & Hanusa, 1978). Compared to people in the comparison group, they were more likely to have experienced deteriorating health and zest for life, and they were more likely to have died (see the right side of Figure SPA-2.3). This study has sobering implications for the many college-based volunteer programs in which students visit residents of nursing homes, prisons, and mental hospitals. These programs might be beneficial in the short run but do more harm than good after they end.

Disease, Control, and Well-Being We end this discussion with some words of caution. First, the relationship between perceived control and distress is more important to members of Western cultures than to members of Asian cultures. One study found that Asians reported that perceived control was less important to them than Westerners did and that there was less of a relationship between perceived control and psychological distress in Asians than in Westerners (Sastry & Ross, 1998). The researchers argue that in Western cultures, where individualism and personal achievement are prized, people are more likely to be distressed if they feel that they cannot personally control their destinies. A lowered sense of control is less of an issue in Asian cultures, they argue, because Asians place greater value on collectivism and putting the social group ahead of individual goals.

Second, even in Western societies, there is a danger in exaggerating the relationship between perceived control and health. Social critic Susan Sontag (1978, 1988) perceptively observed that when a society is plagued by a deadly but poorly understood disease, such as tuberculosis in the nineteenth century and AIDS today, the illness is often blamed on some kind of human frailty, such as a lack of faith, a moral weakness, or a broken heart. As a result, people may blame themselves for their illnesses, even to the point where they do not seek effective treatment. Even though it helps people to feel that they are in control of their illnesses, the downside of this strategy is that if they do not get better, they may blame themselves for failing to recover. Tragically, diseases such as cancer can be fatal no matter how much control a person feels. It only adds to the tragedy if people with-serious diseases feel a sense of moral failure, blaming themselves for a disease that is unpredictable and incurable.

For people living with serious illnesses, keeping some form of control has benefits, even when their health is failing. Researchers have found that even when people who are seriously ill with cancer or AIDS felt no control over the disease, many of them believed they could control the consequences of the disease, such as their emotional reactions and some of the physical symptoms of the disease, such as how tired they felt. And the more people felt they could control the consequences of their disease, the better adjusted they were, even if they knew they could not control the eventual course of their illness. In short, it is important to feel in control of something, even if it is not the disease itself. Maintaining such a sense of control is likely to improve one's psychological well-being, even if one's health fails (Heckhausen & Schulz, 1995; Morling & Evered, 2006; Thompson, 2002).

Coping with Stress

No one always feels in control, of course, and sometimes it is difficult to avoid being pessimistic after something bad happens. The death of a loved one, an acrimonious divorce, and the loss of a job are extremely stressful events. Considerable research indicates that people exhibit various reactions, or **coping styles**, in the face of threatening events (Aspinwall & Taylor, 1997; Lazarus & Folkman, 1984; Lehman et al., 1993; Moos & Holahan, 2003; Salovey et al., 2000; Taylor, 2010). We examine a few coping styles here, beginning with research on gender differences in the ways people respond to stress.

Watch on **MyPsychLab**

To learn more, watch the MyPsychLab video *Coping with Stress*.

Gender Differences in Coping with Stress

If you have ever been to a dog park, you know that dogs respond in one of two ways when they are attacked: Sometimes they respond in kind, and a dogfight occurs, with owners scrambling to remove their dogs from the melee. Other times, the dog who is attacked will take off as fast as it can, tail between its legs. Walter Cannon (1932) termed this the **fight-or-flight response**, defined as responding to stress by either attacking the source of the stress or fleeing from it. For years, the fight-or-flight response has been viewed as the way in which all mammals respond to stress. When under threat, mammals are energized by the release of hormones such as norepinephrine and epinephrine, and, like the dogs in the park, they either go on the attack or retreat as quickly as they can.

That, at least, has been the accepted story for many years. Shelley Taylor and her colleagues (Taylor et al., 2000; Taylor & Master, 2011) pointed out a little-known fact about research on the fight-or-flight syndrome: Most of it has been done on males (particularly male rats). Taylor and her colleagues argue that the fight-or-flight response does not work well for females because they typically play a greater role in caring for children. Fighting is not always a good option for a pregnant female or one tending offspring. Similarly, fleeing is difficult when an adult is responsible for the care of young children or in the later months of pregnancy.

Coping Styles

The ways in which people react to threatening events

Fight-or-Flight Response

Responding to stress by either attacking the source of the stress or fleeing from it

Females are somewhat more likely than males to develop intimate friendships, cooperate with others, and focus their attention on social relationships, particularly when under stress. This is called a *tend-and-befriend* coping strategy.

Consequently, Taylor and her colleagues argue, a different way of responding to stress has evolved in females: the **tend-and-befriend response**. Instead of fighting or fleeing, women respond to stress with nurturant activities designed to protect oneself and one's offspring (tending) and creating social networks that provide protection from threats (befriending). Tending has a number of benefits for both the mother and the child (e.g., a quiet child is less likely to be noticed by predators, and nurturing behavior leads to lower stress and improved immune functioning in mammals). Befriending involves the creation of close ties with other members of the species, which also confers a number of advantages. A close-knit group can exchange resources, watch out for predators, and share child care. As we saw in Chapter 5, human females are more likely than males to develop intimate friendships, cooperate with others, and focus their attention on social relationships. This is especially so when people are under stress; under these circumstances, women are more likely to seek out others, particularly other women (Kivlighan, Granger, & Booth, 2005; Tamres, Janicki, & Helgeson, 2002; Zwolinski, 2008).

We should be careful not to oversimplify gender differences such as these. Although gender differences in coping do exist, the magnitude of these differences is not very large (Tamres et al., 2002). Further, seeking social support can benefit both women and men—as seen in the next section.

Watch on MyPsychLab
To learn more about gender differences in coping, watch the MyPsychLab interview on ***Women, Health, and Stress***.

Social Support: Getting Help from Others

Joanne Hill could not have gotten through her "locust years" without the support of a good many family members and friends. When she got the devastating news that her son had died, she was at a gathering of the National Speakers Association (NSA). Joanne turned immediately to her friend Mitchell, a man who had survived both a motorcycle accident and a plane crash. Although badly scarred and wheelchair bound, Mitchell had overcome his adversity and become a successful public speaker. On that terrible day, he held Joanne's hand, shared her grief, and rode with her to the airport. Others helped too: The president of the NSA and her husband took charge of the travel arrangements, and Barbara, a woman Joanne had met just a couple of days earlier at the convention, insisted on accompanying her home. As Joanne writes,

> In my darkest hour, I was surrounded by people . . . As word spread of the devastating news, some of the speakers came to my room to hug me and give me an encouraging word. In the days and months to come, many messages of support, hope, and love came from NSA members all over the continent . . . Strangers became friends, adding their support to those most dear to me at home, my family and long-time friends. (Hill, 2002, p. 7)

Social support, perceiving that others are responsive and receptive to one's needs, is very helpful for dealing with stress (Chaudoir & Fisher, 2010; Lakey & Orehek, 2011; Taylor, 2010; Uchino, 2009). But researchers have wondered: Does social support help people physically as well as emotionally? There is some evidence that it does. Studies have shown that interventions designed to increase social support and decrease stress in cancer patients improve the functioning of their immune systems (Antoni & Lutgendorf, 2007; Andersen et al., 2004; McGregor et al., 2004; Weihs, Enright, & Simmens, 2008). And social support seems to prolong the lives of healthy people as well. In a study of a large sample of American men and women in the years 1967

Tend-and-Befriend Response
Responding to stress with nurturant activities designed to protect oneself and one's offspring (tending) and creating social networks that provide protection from threats (befriending)

Social Support
The perception that others are responsive and receptive to one's needs

to 1969, men with a low level of social support were two to three times more likely to die over the next dozen years than men with a high level of social support (House, Robbins, & Metzner, 1982). Women with a low level of social support were one and a half to two times more likely to die than women with a high level of social support (Berkman & Syme, 1979; Schwarzer & Leppin, 1991; Stroebe & Stroebe, 1996). To get an idea of the amount of social support you feel is available in your life, complete the Try It! exercise that follows.

Friendship is a sheltering tree.
—Samuel Taylor Coleridge (1772–1834)

It may seem obvious that social support is beneficial, but it turns out that there are some interesting qualifications in when and how it helps. First, when things are tough, the kind of social support we get matters. To illustrate, imagine that you are struggling in one of your classes and attend a study session for the final exam. Sarah, a friend of yours in the group, greets you by saying, "I know you aren't doing very well in this class, so how about if we all focus on the material you don't understand and give you an extra hand?" On the one hand, you appreciate the support and extra help. But who likes being singled out as the person who "isn't doing very well"? As we saw in Chapter 11, people don't like receiving help when it comes with the message "you are too incompetent to do it yourself." Now suppose that Sarah was a little more subtle in her support. She knows that you are having trouble with the material in the last chapter of the textbook, but rather than singling you out, she says, "A lot of us are struggling with the material in Chapter 16—I know I am. How about if we focus on that?" She steers help your way without singling you out or communicating that you are incompetent.

Research has demonstrated that the latter kind of help, which they call *invisible support*, is much more effective. This kind of support provides people with assistance without sending the message that they are incapable of doing it themselves. The former

TRY IT! Social Support

This list contains statements that may or may not be true about you. For each statement that is probably true about you, circle T; for each that is probably not true about you, circle F.

You may find that many of the statements are neither clearly true nor clearly false. In these cases, try to decide quickly whether probably true (T) or probably false (F) is more descriptive of you. Although some questions will be difficult to answer, it is important that you pick one alternative or the other. Circle only one of the alternatives for each statement.

Read each item quickly but carefully before responding. This is not a test, and there are no right or wrong answers.

1.	There is at least one person I know whose advice I really trust.	T	F
2.	There is really no one I can trust to give me good financial advice.	T	F
3.	There is really no one who can give me objective feedback about how I'm handling my problems.	T	F
4.	When I need suggestions for how to deal with a personal problem, I know there is someone I can turn to.	T	F
5.	There is someone I feel comfortable going to for advice about sexual problems.	T	F
6.	There is someone I can turn to for advice about handling hassles over household responsibilities.	T	F
7.	I feel that there is no one with whom I can share my most private worries and fears.	T	F
8.	If a family crisis arose, few of my friends would be able to give me good advice about how to handle it.	T	F
9.	There are very few people I trust to help solve my problems.	T	F
10.	There is someone I could turn to for advice about changing my job or finding a new one.	T	F

Scoring instructions appear on page 431.

(Adapted from Cohen, Mermelstein, Kamarack, & Hoberman, 1985)

type of help, which they call *visible support*, is a two-edged sword, because it singles out beneficiaries as needy and as people who can't help themselves. The moral? If you have a friend who is under a great deal of stress, find a way to help him or her unobtrusively without making a big deal of it (Bolger & Amarel, 2007; Bolger, Zuckerman, & Kessler, 2000; Howland & Simpson, 2010; Maisel & Gable, 2009).

Second, social support operates differently in different cultures. Who do you think is more likely to seek support from other people when things get tough: members of Western cultures that stress individualism and independence, or members of East Asian cultures that stress collectivism and interdependence? It might seem as though cultures that stress collectivism would be more likely to seek help from each other, but research by Shelley Taylor, Heejung Kim, and David Sherman has found just the opposite: When under stress, members of East Asian cultures are *less* likely to seek social support than are members of Western cultures (Kim, Sherman, & Taylor, 2008; Taylor et al., 2004; Taylor et al., 2007). The reason? Members of collectivistic cultures are concerned that seeking support from others will disrupt the harmony of the group and open them up to criticism from others.

Does this mean that members of collectivistic cultures receive less support from others and benefit less from it when they do receive it? Not at all. The main difference is in *how* people in different cultures seek and obtain social support. Because members of collectivistic cultures are concerned with upsetting group harmony and criticism from others, they are less likely to ask directly for help in a way that shows they are having problems. For example, they are less likely to say to a friend, "Hey, I'm having a hard time here. Can you give me a hand?" They do benefit from interacting with supportive others, as long as they do not have to disclose that they are having problems (Kim et al., 2008).

Reframing: Finding Meaning in Traumatic Events

When something traumatic happens to you, is it best to try to bury it as deep as you can and never talk about it, or to spend time thinking about the event and discuss it with others? Although folk wisdom has long held that it is best to open up, only recently has this assumption been put to the test. James Pennebaker and his colleagues (Pennebaker, 1990, 1997, 2004; Sloan et al., 2008; Smyth & Pennebaker, 2008) have conducted a number of interesting experiments on the value of writing about traumatic events. Pennebaker and Beale (1986), for example, asked college students to write, for 15 minutes on each of 4 consecutive nights, about a traumatic event that had happened to them. Students in a control condition wrote for the same amount of time about a trivial event. The traumas that people chose to write about included tragedies such as rape and the death of a sibling.

Writing about these events was certainly upsetting in the short run: Students who wrote about traumas reported more-negative moods and showed greater increases in blood pressure. But there were also dramatic long-term benefits: The same students were less likely to visit the student health center during the next 6 months, and they reported having fewer illnesses. Similarly, first-year college students who wrote about the problems of entering college, survivors of the Holocaust who wrote about their World War II experiences, and patients who had had a heart attack and wrote about it improved their health over the several months after putting their experiences in writing (Pennebaker, Barger, & Tiebout, 1989; Pennebaker, Colder, & Sharp, 1990; Willmott et al., 2011).

> *If he wrote it he could get rid of it. He had gotten rid of many things by writing them.*
>
> —Ernest Hemingway, *Fathers and Sons* (1933)

What is it about opening up that leads to better health? People who write about negative events construct a more meaningful narrative or story that reframes the event. Pennebaker (1997) has analyzed the hundreds of pages of writing his participants provided and found that the people who improved the most were those who began with rather incoherent, disorganized descriptions of their problem and ended with coherent, organized stories that explained the event and gave it meaning. Subsequent research has shown that reframing is especially likely to occur when people

Research by James Pennebaker (1990) shows that there are long-term health benefits to writing or talking about one's personal traumas, particularly if enough time has passed to allow people to gain a new perspective on the traumatic events.

take a step back and write about a negative life event like an observer would, rather than immersing themselves in the event and trying to relive it (Kross & Ayduk, 2011). The result? Once people have reframed a traumatic event in this way, they think about it less and are less likely to try to suppress thoughts about it when it does come to mind. Trying to suppress negative thoughts can lead to a preoccupation with those very thoughts, because the act of trying not to think about them can actually make us think about them more, leading to intrusive memories (Wegner, 1994).

You may recall that in Chapter SPA-1 we discussed an intervention called Critical Incident Stress Debriefing (CISD), in which people who have witnessed a horrific event are asked to relive the event as soon as possible in a 3- to 4-hour session, describing their experiences in detail and discussing their emotional reactions to the event. As we saw, CISD has been shown, in well-controlled studies, *not* to be beneficial. But why does writing about an event help people recover when reliving it in a CISD session does not? One reason appears to be the timing. The writing exercise works best if enough time has passed to allow people to gain a new perspective on the incident. In contrast, right after the event occurs is not a good time to try to relive it, reframe it, or understand it in a different way. In fact, one problem with CISD is that it can solidify memories of the bad things that occurred, rather than helping people to reframe them. Thus, if you would like to try the writing exercise, allow some time to pass to make it easier to gain some perspective on what happened to you. You can find instructions about how to do the exercise on the Writing and Health section of James Pennebaker's Web site: homepage.psy.utexas.edu/homepage/Faculty/Pennebaker/Home2000/WritingandHealth.html

In sum, research shows that humans are often remarkably resilient in the face of adversity, particularly if they can maintain a sense of control. Seeking social support can help. If people continue to be troubled by the memories of stressful events, it may help to use Pennebaker's writing technique to help make sense of what happened and what it means.

Prevention: Promoting Healthier Behavior

Many serious health problems would be prevented if people adopted different habits and avoided risky behaviors. According to one estimate, the causes of half the deaths in the United States each year are preventable (Mokdad et al., 2004). More than 33 million people worldwide are currently infected with the HIV virus, and in 2008, 2 million people died of AIDS ("Global statistics," 2011). Most cases are in Sub-Saharan Africa, although no continent is free of the disease. Most of these cases could have been avoided if people had used condoms during sexual intercourse. Fortunately, the use of condoms is increasing in the United States; one survey found that among teenagers, 80% of males used a condom the first time they had sex. But that means that 20% did not (Martinez, Copen, & Abma, 2011). And although condom use is increasing in some African countries, in others it remains very low (UNAIDS Factsheet, n.d.).

Many serious health problems are preventable, including those resulting from unsafe sex, smoking, and overeating. Social psychologists have designed many successful interventions to improve health habits, such as programs that encourage people to use condoms.

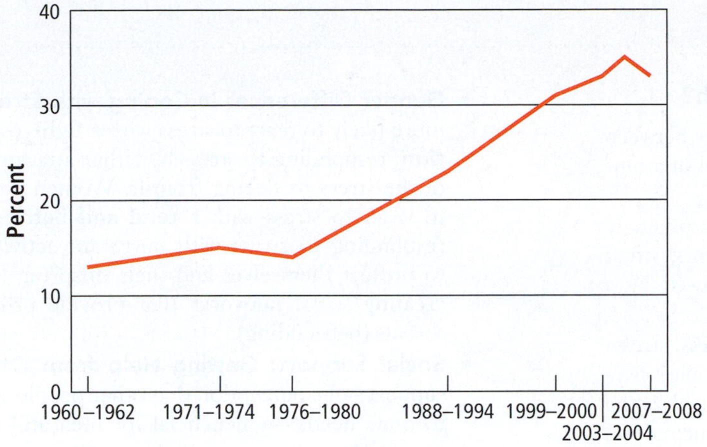

Figure SPA-2.4

Obesity Rates in the United States Over Time

The percentage of American adults who are obese (defined here as having a body mass index of 30 or above) has risen dramatically since 1960.

(Obesity and Overweight, 2011)

People could improve their health behaviors in many other areas as well, such as alcohol consumption, smoking, and overeating. Binge drinking, defined as five or more drinks in a short period of time for men and four or more for women (Wechsler & Austin, 1998), is a problem on many college campuses. Binge drinkers are at heightened risk for a number of health problems, including high blood pressure, heart disease, liver disease, meningitis, and sexually transmitted diseases. They are also more likely to be in car accidents, die by drowning, have unwanted pregnancies, experience domestic violence, and have difficulty performing sexually (Naimi et al., 2003; "Quick stats," 2008).

Americans are doing a good job of improving one unhealthy habit—namely, smoking cigarettes. Smoking rates have been declining steadily in the United States. For example, in 1995 35% of high school students reported that they smoked, but in 2009 only 20% reported that they smoked ("Trends in prevalence of tobacco use," 2009). Nonetheless, tobacco use remains the number one cause of preventable deaths in the United States. What is number two? It might surprise you to learn that it is obesity, an area in which Americans are not doing such a good job (Figure SPA-2.4). More than 1 in 3 Americans are obese, which is associated with such health problems as high blood pressure, diabetes, heart disease, and cancer of the breast, prostate, and colon ("Adult obesity," 2011). ◉

We realize that we have just maligned what many people consider to be the chief pleasures of life: sex, eating, drinking, and smoking. Health problems resulting from these behaviors are prevalent precisely because they are so pleasurable—in some cases (e.g., smoking), addictive. It is thus a challenge to find ways to change people's attitudes and behaviors in ways that lead to better health habits. How might we do so?

By now you know that this is a classic social psychological issue. It should be possible to put theories into action theories of attitude change and social influence to help people to act in healthier ways. Indeed, there is a great deal of research on this very question, and social psychologists have had considerable success in designing programs to get people to use condoms, quit smoking, drink less, and engage in a variety of preventive behaviors, such as using sunscreens (Noar, Benac, & Harris, 2007; Salovey & Rothman, 2003; Taylor, 2010). Many of these programs use social psychological principles covered elsewhere in this text—for example, the attitude-change techniques discussed in Chapter 7. Perhaps you can think of ways to adopt some of these approaches in your own life.

 Watch on **MyPsychLab**

To learn more about health behaviors, watch the MyPsychLab video *You Are What You Eat*.

"Maybe we shouldn't have kicked all our bad habits."

© Vahan Shirvanian/www.CartoonStock.com

Summary

What effects does stress have on our health?

- **Stress and Human Health** The relationship between stress and human health has received a great deal of attention from social psychologists.
  - **Resilience** People have been found to be surprisingly resilient when they experience negative events, often showing only mild, transient reactions, followed by a quick return to normal, healthy functioning.
  - **Effects of Negative Life Events** Nonetheless, stressful events can have debilitating effects on people's psychological and physical health. Some studies calculate the number of stressful events people are experiencing and use that to predict their health.
  - **Perceived Stress and Health** Stress is best defined as the negative feelings and beliefs that arise when people feel unable to cope with demands from their environment. The more stress people experience, the more likely they are to get sick (e.g., catch a cold).
  - **Feeling in Charge: The Importance of Perceived Control** People perceive negative events as stressful if they feel they cannot control them. In the last 40 years, college students have increasingly adopted an external locus of control, which is the tendency to believe that good and bad outcomes are out of their control. The less control people believe they have, the more likely it is that the event will cause them physical and psychological problems. For example, the loss of control experienced by many older people in nursing homes can have negative effects on their health.

What can people do to cope and recover after a stressful experience?

- **Coping with Stress** Coping styles refer to the ways in which people react to stressful events.
  - **Gender Differences in Coping with Stress** Men are more likely to react to stress with a **fight-or-flight reaction**, responding to stress by either attacking the source of the stress or fleeing from it. Women are more likely to react to stress with a **tend-and-befriend reaction**, responding to stress with nurturant activities designed to protect themselves and their offspring (tending) and creating social networks that provide protection from threats (befriending).
  - **Social Support: Getting Help from Others** Social support—the perception that other people are responsive to one's needs—is beneficial for men and women. The form of social support, however, is important. People react better to invisible than visible support. People from individualistic cultures react well when they directly ask for support, whereas people from collectivistic cultures react well when they get support without disclosing that they are having problems.
  - **Reframing: Finding Meaning in Traumatic Events** Other researchers focus on ways of coping with stress that everyone can adopt. Several studies show that reframing traumatic events, by writing or talking about one's problems, has long-term health benefits.

How can we apply social psychology to help people live healthier lives?

- **Prevention: Promoting Healthier Behavior** It also important to find ways to help people change their health habits more directly.

Chapter SPA-2 Test

Study and Review on MyPsychLab

1. After her husband died, Rachel did not experience significant distress. Within a few weeks she had returned to her usual activities and regained a cheerful outlook on life. Which is most true, according to research discussed in this chapter?
   a. Rachel's lack of distress indicates the likelihood of poor psychological adjustment.
   b. Because Rachel did not experience extreme grief, she was probably in a troubled marriage and did not love her husband very much.
   c. Although life's traumas can be quite painful, many people have the resources to recover from them quickly.
   d. Rachel is showing "delayed grief syndrome" and will probably experience grief later.

2. Bob's grandmother died recently, and he just found out that his girlfriend cheated on him. He is also in the middle of final exams. According to research on stress and health, which is most true?
   a. Because Bob is experiencing so many negative life events, he will almost certainly get sick.
   b. These life events will be stressful for Bob only if he interprets them as stressful—in other words, if he feels unable to cope with the events.
   c. When under stress, a person's immune system is stimulated. Therefore, Bob is less likely to get sick now than he normally would.
   d. If Bob feels more in control of these events than he really is, he is especially likely to get sick.

3. Lindsay does an internship at a nursing home. According to research discussed in this chapter, which of the following would be most likely to benefit the residents?
   a. Lindsay encourages the residents to talk to her about any stressful issues in their lives.
   b. Lindsay allows the residents to choose what time she will come to visit them, and when her internship ends, she decides to keep visiting the residents when they ask her to.
   c. Lindsay allows the residents to choose what time she will come to visit them, but when her internship ends, she doesn't visit the nursing home anymore.
   d. Lindsay gives the residents a plant and makes sure to water it for them.

4. Which of the following is *most true* about research on social support?
   a. Social support of all kinds has been found to be beneficial to people in all cultures.
   b. If you are thinking of helping someone, it is better to give them invisible rather than visible social support.
   c. If you are thinking of helping someone, it is better to given them visible rather than invisible social support.
   d. Members of East Asian cultures are more likely to seek help from others than are members of Western cultures.

5. Which of the following is *most true* of research on coping styles?
   a. Women are most likely to show the fight-or-flight response.
   b. Men are most likely to show the tend-and-befriend response.
   c. Women are mostly likely to show the tend-and-befriend response.
   d. Men and women tend to cope with stress in the same ways.

6. Michael's roommate has come down with a cold. In which of the following circumstances is Michael most likely to catch his roommate's cold?
   a. Michael's girlfriend just broke up with him, but he knew it was coming and doesn't view it as all that bad a thing.
   b. Michael's goldfish just died, which he views as a very negative event.
   c. Michael hasn't been exercising very much lately.
   d. It doesn't matter what is going on in Michael's life; all that matters is whether he is exposed to the virus that causes the cold.

7. Kate has had a hard time getting over her parents' divorce. According to social psychological research, which of the following would probably help Kate the most?
   a. She should spend 15 minutes a night on 4 consecutive nights writing about her feelings about the divorce.
   b. She should try to attribute the divorce to internal, global, stable things about herself.
   c. She should avoid talking about the divorce with her closest friends because it would probably just depress them.
   d. She should focus on the fact that she has low self-efficacy to improve her relationship with her parents.

8. Which of the following is *least true*?
   a. Although obesity is increasing in the United States, it is not a major health problem.
   b. Many serious health problems are preventable, and social psychological interventions have been developed to get people to act in healthier ways.
   c. Binge drinkers are more likely than others to have serious health problems.
   d. Although the percentage of people who smoke cigarettes is going down, tobacco use is still a major cause of preventable deaths.

Answer Key

1-c, 2-b, 3-b, 4-d, 5-c, 6-b, 7-a, 8-a

Scoring the TRY IT! exercises

Page 426

1. You get 1 point each time you answered true (T) to questions 1, 4, 5, 6, and 10 and 1 point for each time you answered false (F) to questions 2, 3, 7, 8, and 9.
2. This scale was developed to measure what the researchers call *appraisal social support*, or "the perceived availability of someone to talk to about one's problems" (Cohen et al., 1985, pp. 75–76). One of the findings was that when people were not under stress, those low in social support had no more physical symptoms than people high in social support did. When people were under stress, however, those low in social support had more physical symptoms than did people high in social support. Another finding was that women scored reliably higher on the social support scale than men did. If you scored lower than you would like, you might want to consider reaching out to others more when you are under stress.

SOCIAL PSYCHOLOGY IN ACTION

3 Social Psychology and the Law

YOU BE THE JURY AND DECIDE HOW YOU WOULD VOTE AFTER HEARING THE FOLLOWING TESTIMONY FROM AN ACTUAL CASE IN TEXAS. On a cold, dark night in November 1976, police officer Robert Wood and his partner spotted a car driving with its headlights off. Wood signaled the car to pull over, got out, and walked up to the driver's side. He intended only to tell the driver to turn on his lights, but he never got the chance. Before Wood could even speak, the driver pointed a handgun at Wood and shot him, killing him instantly. Wood's partner emptied her revolver at the car as it sped away, but the killer escaped.

A month later, the police picked up a suspect, 16-year-old David Harris. Harris admitted that he had stolen a neighbor's car and revolver the day before the murder, that this was the car Officer Wood had pulled over that night, and that he was in the car when the murder occurred. Harris denied, however, that he was the one who shot Wood. He said he had picked up a hitchhiker by the name of Randall Adams and had let Adams drive. It was Adams, he claimed, who reached under the seat, grabbed the revolver, and shot the officer.

When the police questioned Randall Adams, he admitted that he had gotten a ride from David Harris but said that Harris had dropped him off at his motel 3 hours before the murder occurred. It was Harris, he claimed, who was the murderer. Who was telling the truth? It was Harris's word against Adams's—until the police found three eyewitnesses who corroborated Harris's story. Emily and Robert Miller testified that they drove by just before Officer Wood was shot. Though it was very dark, they said they got a good look at the driver of the car, and both identified him as Randall Adams. "When he rolled down the window, that's what made his face stand out," said Robert Miller. "He had a beard, mustache, kind of dishwater blond hair" (Morris, 1988). David Harris was clean shaven, and at the time of the murder, Randall Adams did indeed fit the Millers' description (see the photos on page 434). Michael Randell, a salesman, also happened to be driving by right before the murder and claimed to have seen two people in the car. He too said the driver had long hair and a mustache.

Who do you think committed the murder? The jury believed the eyewitnesses and convicted Adams, sentencing him to death. However, as Adams languished in jail, waiting for the courts to hear his appeals, several experts began to doubt that he was guilty. New evidence came to light (largely because of a film made about the case, *The Thin Blue Line*), and it is now almost certain that David Harris was the murderer. Harris was later convicted of another murder and, while on death row, strongly implied that he, not Randall Adams, had shot Officer Wood. An appeals court finally overturned Adams's conviction. He was a free man—after spending 12 years in prison for a crime he did not commit.

If Adams was innocent, why did the eyewitnesses say that the driver of the car had long hair and a mustache? And why did the jury believe them? How common are such miscarriages of justice? In this chapter, we will discuss the answers to these questions, focusing on the role social psychological processes play in the legal system.

Let's begin with a brief review of the American justice system. When someone commits a crime and the police arrest a suspect, a judge or a grand

FOCUS QUESTIONS

- What does social psychology tell us about eyewitness testimony?
- How can social psychology help to make jury decisions more accurate?

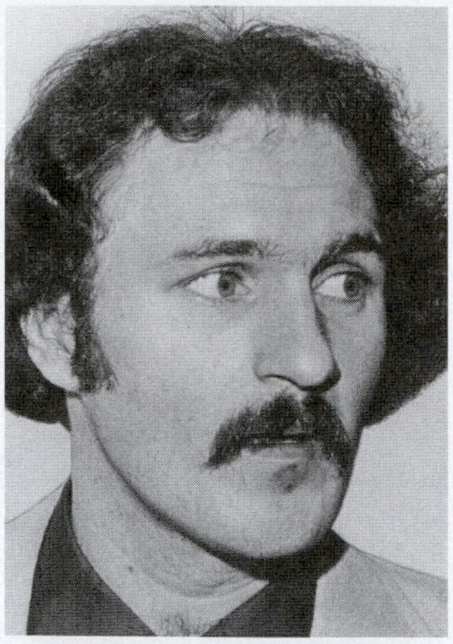

Randall Adams (top) and David Harris (bottom). The fact that eyewitnesses said the murderer had long hair and a mustache was the main reason Adams was convicted of murdering Officer Wood.

jury decides whether there is enough evidence to press formal charges. If there is, lawyers for the defense and the prosecution gather evidence and negotiate with each other. As a result of these negotiations, the defendant often pleads guilty to a lesser charge. Fewer than 10% of the cases go to trial, in which a jury decides the defendant's fate. There are also civil trials, where one party (the plaintiff) brings a complaint against another (the defendant) for violating the former's rights in some way.

Social psychologists have studied the legal system a great deal in recent years, both because it offers an excellent applied setting in which to study basic psychological processes and because of its immense importance in daily life (Kovera & Borgida, 2010). If you, through no fault of your own, become the accused in a court trial, what do you need to know to convince the system of your innocence? We will begin our discussion with eyewitness testimony, the most troubling aspect of the Randall Adams case.

Eyewitness Testimony

Randall Adams was convicted largely because of the eyewitnesses who identified him, even though in other ways the case against him was weak. Unfortunately, wrongful convictions based on faulty eyewitness identification are not uncommon. According to the Innocence Project (www.innocenceproject.org), there have been more than 250 cases in which someone has been exonerated with DNA evidence after being convicted of a crime—often, like Randall Adams, after spending years in prison. In most of these cases, the conviction was based on faulty eyewitness identification. In short, the most common cause of an innocent person being convicted of a crime is an erroneous eyewitness (Brewer & Wells, 2011; Pezdek, 2012; Sporer, Koehnken, & Malpass, 1996; Wells & Hasel, 2008).

Why Are Eyewitnesses Often Wrong?

Watch on **MyPsychLab**
To learn more about how memory functions, watch the MyPsychLab video ***Memory***.

The problem is that our minds are not like video cameras, which can record an event, store it over time, and play it back later with perfect accuracy. To be an accurate eyewitness, a person must successfully complete three stages of memory processing: acquisition, storage, and retrieval of the events witnessed. **Acquisition** refers to the process whereby people notice and pay attention to information in the environment. Because people cannot perceive everything that is happening around them, they acquire only a subset of the information. **Storage** is the process by which people store in memory information they have acquired from the environment. **Retrieval** refers to the process by which people recall information stored in their memories (see Figure SPA-3.1). Eyewitnesses can be inaccurate because of difficulties that arise at each of these three stages.

Acquisition
The process by which people notice and pay attention to information in the environment; because people cannot perceive everything that is happening around them, they acquire only a subset of the information available

Storage
The process by which people store in memory information they have acquired from the environment

Retrieval
The process by which people recall information stored in their memories

Acquisition The amount of information about a crime that people take in at the acquisition stage is limited by several factors, such as how much time they have to watch an event and the nature of the viewing conditions. As obvious as this may sound, people sometimes forget how these factors limit eyewitness reports of crimes. Crimes usually occur under the very conditions that make acquisition difficult: quickly, unexpectedly, under poor viewing conditions (e.g., at night), and under considerable stress. These conditions certainly describe the scene of the murder of Officer Wood. Eyewitnesses were driving down a dimly lit road, past a pulled-over car, when the unexpected happened—shots were fired and a police officer crumpled to the ground.

When eyewitnesses are the victims of a crime, they will be terribly afraid, and this alone can make it difficult to take in everything that is happening. The more stress people are under, the worse their memory for people involved in and the details of a crime (Deffenbacher, Bornstein, & Penrod, 2004). Another reason why victims of crimes have a poor memory for a suspect is that they focus their attention mostly on any weapon they see and less on the suspect's features (Hope & Wright, 2007; Pickel,

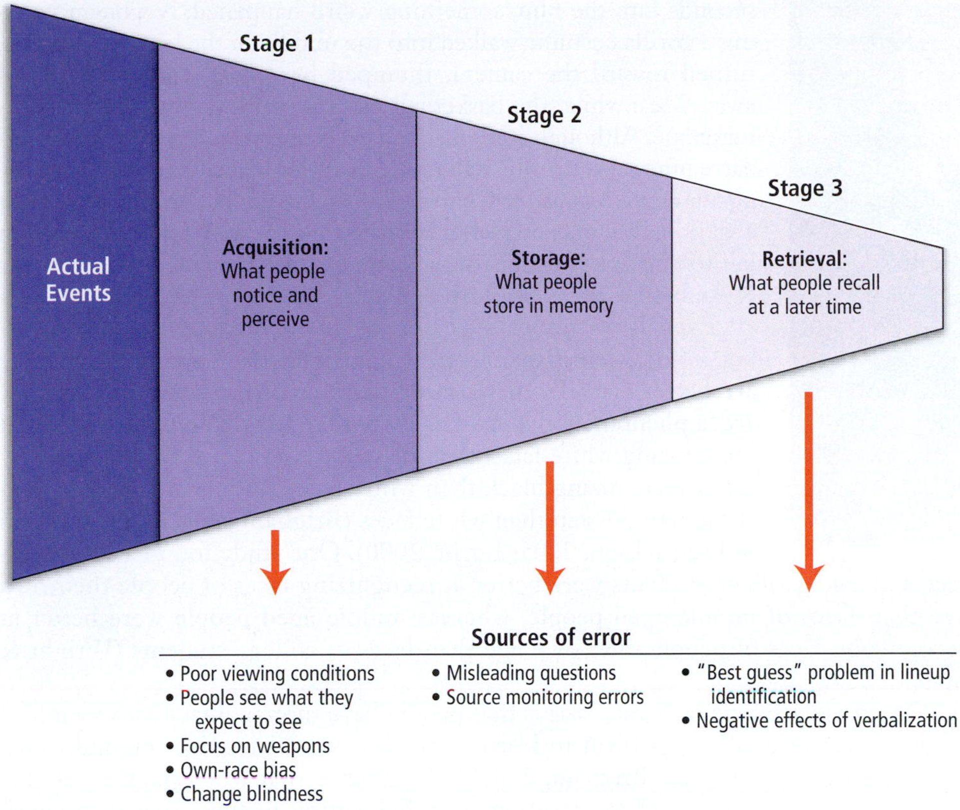

FIGURE SPA-3.1

Acquisition, Storage, and Retrieval

To be an accurate eyewitness, people must complete three stages of memory processing. Errors may creep in at each of the three stages.

2007; Saunders, 2009). If someone points a gun at you and demands your money, your attention is likely to be more on the gun than on what color the robber's eyes are.

> *When an actual perceptual fact is in conflict with expectation, expectation may prove a stronger determinant of perception and memory than the situation itself.*
>
> —Gordon Allport and Leo Postman, 1947

The information witnesses notice and pay attention to is also influenced by what they expect to see. Consider our friend Alan, a social psychologist who is an expert on social perception. One Sunday, Alan was worried because his neighbor, a frail woman in her 80s, did not appear for church. After knocking on her door repeatedly and receiving no response, Alan jimmied open a window and searched her house. Soon his worst fears were realized: The woman was lying dead on the floor of her bedroom.

Shaken, Alan went back to his house and telephoned the police. A detective spent a great deal of time in the woman's house, after which he asked Alan some pointed questions, such as whether he had noticed any suspicious activity in the past day or two. Alan was confused by this line of questioning and finally burst out, "Why are you asking me these questions? Isn't it obvious that my neighbor died of old age? Shouldn't we be notifying her family?" Now it was the detective's turn to look puzzled. "Aren't you the one who discovered the body?" he asked. Alan said he was. "Well," said the detective, "didn't you notice that her bedroom had been ransacked, that there was broken glass everywhere, and that there was a belt tied around her neck?"

It turned out that Alan's neighbor had been strangled by a man who had come to spray her house for insects. There had been a fierce struggle, and the fact that the woman was murdered could not have been more obvious. But Alan saw none of the signs. He was worried that his elderly neighbor had passed away. When he discovered that she had in fact died, he was quite upset, and the farthest thing from his mind was that she had been murdered. As a result, he saw what he expected and failed to see what he did not expect. When the police later showed him photographs of the crime scene, he felt as though he had never been there. He recognized almost nothing.

Research has confirmed that people are poor at noticing the unexpected. In one study, participants watched a videotape of two teams passing a basketball back and forth and counted the number of times one team passed the ball to the other. Thirty-five

Suppose you were watching a video of two groups of people passing a basketball back and forth and counting the number of passes one team threw to the other. Would you notice the fact that a person dressed in a gorilla suit entered the scene, faced the camera, and thumped her chest?
(From Simons & Chabris, 1999)

seconds into the film, something weird happened: A woman wearing a gorilla costume walked into the middle of the basketball game, turned toward the camera, thumped her chest, and then walked away. Meanwhile, the basketball players continued with their passing game. Although it seems as if everyone would notice such a bizarre interruption, only half did. The other half simply didn't see the gorilla at all (Simons & Chabris, 1999). Given that crimes are almost always highly unexpected events, it is no surprise that people often fail to notice key details in the crime scene (Rensink, 2002; Simons & Ambinder, 2005; Wilford & Wells, 2010).

Even if we notice a person or event, we might not remember it very well if we are unfamiliar with it. For example, people are better at recognizing faces that are of the same race as they are, a phenomenon known as **own-race bias**. Whites are better at recognizing white faces than black or Asian faces, blacks are better at recognizing black than white faces, and Asians are better at recognizing Asian than white faces (Brigham et al., 2007; Johnson & Fredrickson, 2005; Levin, 2000). One study found a similar effect with age: College students were better at recognizing faces of people their own age than faces of middle-aged people, whereas middle-aged people were better at recognizing faces of people their own age than faces of college students (Wright & Stroud, 2002).

One reason for the own-race bias is that people have more contact with members of their own race, allowing them to learn better how to distinguish one individual from another (Meissner & Brigham, 2001b). Another is that when people examine same-race faces, they pay close attention to individuating features that distinguish that face from others, such as the height of the cheekbones or the contour of the forehead. When people examine different-race faces, however, they are drawn more to features that distinguish that face from their own race, rather than individuating features (Hugenberg et al., 2010; Levin, 2000). Daniel Levin, a researcher who has investigated this hypothesis, puts it like this: "When a white person looks at another white person's nose, they're likely to think to themselves, 'That's John's nose.' When they look at a black person's nose, they're likely to think, 'That's a black nose'" (quoted in Carpenter, 2000, p. 44). Because people usually have less experience with features that characterize individuals of other races, they find it more difficult to tell members of that race apart.

Own-Race Bias

The fact that people are better at recognizing faces of their own race than those of other races

Reconstructive Memory

The process whereby memories of an event become distorted by information encountered after the event occurred

Storage In the preceding discussion of the acquisition process, we have seen that several variables limit what people perceive and thus what they are able to store in their memories. After a piece of information is in memory, it might seem as if it stays there, unaltered, until we recall it at a later time. Many people think memory is like a photograph album. We record a picture of an event, such as the face of a robber, and place it in the memory "album." In reality, few of us have photographic memories. Memories, like real photographs, fade with age. Further, it is tempting to believe that a picture, once stored, cannot be altered or retouched, and that details cannot be added to or subtracted from the image. If the robber we saw was clean shaven, surely we will not pencil in a mustache at some later time. Hence, the fact that the witnesses who testified at the Randall Adams trial remembered that the driver of the car had long hair and a mustache seems like pretty incriminating evidence against Randall Adams.

Unfortunately, however, memories are far from indelible. People can get mixed up about where they heard or saw something; memories in one "album" can get confused with memories in another. As a result, people can have quite inaccurate recall about what they saw. This is the conclusion reached after years of research on **reconstructive memory**: the distortion of memories of an event by information encountered after the event occurred (Davis & Loftus, 2007; Hirt, McDonald, & Erikson, 1995; Loftus, 1979, 2005; McDonald & Hirt, 1997). According to this research, information we obtain after witnessing an event can change our memories of the event.

Watch on **MyPsychLab**

To learn more about how memories can be inaccurate, watch the MyPsychLab video *Memory Hazards*.

> *Give us a dozen healthy memories, well-formed, and . . . we'll guarantee to take any one at random and train it to become any type of memory we might select—hammer, screwdriver, wrench, stop sign, yield sign, Indian chief—regardless of its origin or the brain that holds it.*
>
> —Elizabeth Loftus and Hunter Hoffman, 1989

In a classic study, Elizabeth Loftus showed students 30 slides depicting different stages of an automobile accident. The content of one slide varied; some students saw a car stopped at a stop sign, and others saw the same car stopped at a yield sign. After the slide show, the students were asked several questions about the car accident they had "witnessed." The key question varied how the traffic sign was described. In one version, the question asked, "Did another car pass the red Datsun while it was stopped at the stop sign?" In the other version, the question was "Did another car pass the red Datsun while it was stopped at the yield sign?" Thus, for half the participants, the question described the traffic sign as they had in fact seen it. But for the other half, the wording of the question subtly introduced new information—that they had seen a stop sign, when in fact they had seen a yield sign. Would this small change (akin to what might occur when witnesses are being questioned by police investigators or attorneys) influence people's memories of the actual event?

All the students were shown the two pictures (reproduced below) and asked which one they had originally seen. Most people (75%) who were asked about the sign they had actually seen chose the correct picture; that is, if they had seen a stop sign and were asked about a stop sign, most of them correctly identified the stop sign photograph (note that 25% made a crucial mistake on what would seem to be an easy question). However, of those who had received the misleading question, only 41% chose the correct photograph (Loftus, Miller, & Burns, 1978).

In subsequent experiments, Loftus and her colleagues found that misleading questions could change people's minds about how fast a car was going, whether broken glass was at the scene of an accident, whether a traffic light was green or red, and—of relevance to the Randall Adams trial—whether a suspect had a mustache (Loftus, 1979). Her studies show that the way in which the police and lawyers question witnesses can change the witnesses' reports about what they saw. (There is some suspicion that in the Randall Adams case the police may have led the witnesses by asking questions that implicated Adams and not Harris. At the time of the murder, Harris was a juvenile and could not receive the death penalty for killing a police officer; Adams was in his thirties and was eligible for the death penalty. According to this reasoning, Adams was a "better" suspect in the eyes of the police.)

Watch on **MyPsychLab**
To learn more about research on false memories, watch the MyPsychLab video ***Memory: Elizabeth Loftus***.

Misleading questions can cause a problem with **source monitoring**, the process people use to try to identify the source of their memories (Johnson, Hashtroudi, & Lindsay, 1993; Johnson, Verfaellie, & Dunlosky, 2008; Qin, Ogle, & Goodman, 2008). In the Loftus studies, for example, people who saw a stop sign but received the misleading question about a yield sign then had two pieces of information in memory—the stop sign and the yield sign. This is all well and good as long as they could remember where these memories came from: the stop sign from the accident they saw earlier and the yield sign from the question they were asked later. The problem is that people

Source Monitoring
The process whereby people try to identify the source of their memories

Students saw one of these pictures and then tried to remember whether they had seen a stop sign or a yield sign. Many of those who heard leading questions about the street sign made mistaken reports about which sign they had seen.

(From Loftus, Miller, & Burns, 1978)

often get mixed up about where they heard or saw something, mistakenly believing, for instance, that the yield sign looks familiar because they saw it during the slide show. This process is similar to the misattribution effects we discussed in Chapter 5, when people are unsure about what has caused their arousal. It's easy to get confused about the source of our memories as well. When information gets stored in memory, it is not always well "tagged" as to where it came from.

The implications for legal testimony are sobering. Eyewitnesses who are asked misleading questions often report seeing things that were not really there. In addition, eyewitnesses might be confused as to why a suspect looks familiar. It is likely, for example, that the eyewitnesses in the Randall Adams trial saw pictures of Adams in the newspaper before they testified about what they saw the night of the murder. When asked to remember what they saw that night, they might have become confused because of a source monitoring error. They remembered seeing a man with long hair and a mustache, but they may have gotten mixed up about where they had seen his face before.

Retrieval Suppose you are an eyewitness to a crime. The police have arrested a suspect and want to see if you identify him or her as the person you saw commit the crime. Typically, the police arrange a lineup at the police station, where you will be asked whether one of several people is the perpetrator. You might be asked to look through a one-way mirror at an actual lineup of the suspect and some foils (people known not to have committed the crime), or to examine videotapes of a lineup or photographs of the suspect and the foils. In each case, if you identify the suspect as the perpetrator, that suspect is likely to be charged and convicted of the crime. After all, if an eyewitness saw the suspect commit the crime and subsequently picked the suspect out of a lineup, that's pretty good evidence that the suspect is the guilty party, isn't it? Well, maybe not.

Just as there are problems with acquisition and storage of information, so too can there be problems with how people retrieve information from their memories (Brewer & Wells, 2011; Malpass, Tredoux, & McQuiston-Surrett, 2007; Wells & Quinlivan, 2009). Unfortunately, a number of things other than the image of a person that is stored in memory can influence whether eyewitnesses will pick someone out of a lineup. For example, witnesses often choose the person in a lineup who most resembles the criminal, even if the resemblance is not very strong.

To avoid this "best guess" problem where witnesses pick the person who looks most like the suspect, as well as other problems with lineup identifications, social psychologists have made several recommendations about how the police should conduct lineups. These are summarized in Table SPA-3.1.

Judging Whether Eyewitnesses Are Mistaken

Suppose you are a member of a jury who is listening to a witness describe a suspect. How can you tell whether the witness's memory is accurate or whether the witness is making one of the many mistakes in memory we have just documented? It might seem that the answer to this question is pretty straightforward: Pay careful attention to how confident the witness is. Consider the case of Jennifer Thompson, who was raped when she was a 22-year-old college student. During the rape, Thompson reports, she "studied every single detail on the rapist's face" to help her identify him. She was determined that if she survived, she was going to make sure he was caught and went to prison. After the ordeal, she went to the police station and looked through hundreds of police photos. When she saw Ronald Cotton's picture, she was certain that he was the rapist. "I knew this was the man. I was completely confident. I was sure."

The police brought Cotton in and put him in a lineup, and Thompson picked him out without hesitation. Certain that Cotton was the man who had raped her, she testified against him in court. "I was sure. I knew it. I had picked the right guy." On the basis of her convincing testimony, Cotton was sentenced to life in prison.

A few years later, the police asked Thompson to go to court and look at another man, Bobby Poole, who had been bragging in prison that he had committed the rape. When asked if she recognized him, Thompson replied, "I have never seen him in my life. I have no idea who he is."

TABLE SPA-3.1 Recommendations for How to Conduct Lineups

Recommendation	Why It Is Important
Make sure everyone in the lineup resembles the witness's description of the suspect.	Doing so will minimize the possibility that the witness will simply choose the person who looks most like the culprit (Wells et al., 1998).
Tell the witnesses that the person suspected of the crime may or may not be in the lineup.	If witnesses believe the culprit is present, they are much more likely to choose the person who looks most like the culprit, rather than saying that they aren't sure or that the culprit is not present. As a result, false identifications are more likely to occur when people believe the culprit is in the lineup (Clark, 2005; Malpass & Devine, 1981; Steblay, 1997; Wells et al., 1998, 2000).
Make sure that the person conducting the lineup does not know which person in the lineup is the suspect.	This avoids the possibility that the person will unintentionally communicate to the witness who the suspect is (Wells et al., 1998).
If using photographs of people, present the pictures sequentially instead of simultaneously.	Doing so makes it more difficult for witnesses to compare all the pictures and choose the one that most resembles the criminal even when the criminal is not actually in the lineup (Lindsay & Wells, 1985; Meissner, Tredoux, & Parker, 2005; Steblay, Dysart, Fulero, & Lindsay, 2001).
Avoid using composite face programs (computer programs designed to reconstruct a suspect's face according to witnesses' descriptions).	Typically, the faces that witnesses generate with these programs do not look much like the actual suspect. Also, research shows that people who give descriptions for computer-generated facial images subsequently have a worse memory for the suspect than people who do not (Wells, Charman, & Olson, 2005; Wells & Hasel, 2007). Focusing on specific features of a face, such as what the chin looked like, appears to interfere with people's original memory for the face.
Don't count on witnesses knowing whether their selections were biased.	To determine whether a witness's selection was biased, attorneys or judges sometimes ask them, for example, "Do you think your choice of suspect was influenced by how the pictures were presented or what the police told you?" Unfortunately, people are not so good at answering these questions. People don't have sufficient access to their thought processes to detect whether they were biased (Charman & Wells, 2008; Nisbett & Wilson, 1977).

As the years passed, and Cotton remained in jail for the rape, DNA testing became more widely available. The police decided to see if evidence from the case matched Cotton's or Poole's DNA. In 1995, 11 years after the crime, the police informed Thompson of the results: "I was standing in my kitchen when the detective and the district attorney visited. They were good and decent people who were trying to do their jobs—as I had done mine, as anyone would try to do the right thing. They told me: 'Ronald Cotton didn't rape you. It was Bobby Poole.'" (Thompson, 2000, p. 15). Cotton was released from prison after serving 11 years for a crime he did not commit.

> *No subjective feeling of certainty can be an objective criterion for the desired truth.*
>
> —Hugo Münsterberg, *On the Witness Stand*, 1908

This example illustrates that how confident an eyewitness is is not always a good indicator of how accurate he or she is. In fact, numerous studies have shown that witnesses' confidence is only modestly related to their accuracy (Charman, Wells, & Joy,

2011; Douglass & Pavletic, 2012; Eisenstadt & Leippe, 2010). When law enforcement officials and jurors assume that a witness who is very confident is also correct, they can make serious mistakes.

Why isn't confidence always a sign of accuracy? One reason is that the things that influence people's confidence are not necessarily the same things that influence their accuracy. After identifying a suspect, for example, a person's confidence increases if he or she finds out that other witnesses identified the same suspect and decreases if he or she finds out that other witnesses identified a different suspect (Busey et al., 2000). This change in confidence cannot influence the accuracy of the identification the person made earlier. Therefore, just because a witness is confident does not mean that he or she is accurate, as the cases of Randall Adams and Ronald Cotton illustrate so tragically. However, confidence in combination with another way of responding might indeed suggest that people are accurate—namely, if people identify a face quickly.

Responding Quickly In a study by David Dunning and Lisa Beth Stern (1994), participants watched a film in which a man stole some money from a woman's wallet; they then tried to identify the thief in a photo lineup. Some participants made their choices quickly, saying that the perpetrator's face just "popped out" at them. Others took their time, deliberately comparing one face to another. Who was more likely to correctly identify the thief? It turned out to be the fast responders, for whom the man's face "popped out." We should thus be more willing to believe a witness who says, "I knew it was the defendant as soon as I saw him in the lineup" than one who says, "I compared everyone in the lineup to each other, thought about it, and decided it was the defendant"—particularly if the first witness made his or her judgment in 10 seconds or less (Dunning & Perretta, 2002). As we saw with the example of Jennifer Thompson, even when eyewitnesses makes judgments quickly, and are very confident in their judgments, they can still be incorrect. But, witnesses who respond quickly are more likely to be correct than those who think about it for awhile.

The Problem with Verbalization It might seem that another way to improve the accuracy of eyewitness identification would be to tell people to write down a description of the suspect as soon as they can, to help them remember what they saw. Studies by Jonathan Schooler and Tonya Engstler-Schooler (1990), however, show that trying to put an image of a face into words can make people's memory worse. They showed students a film of a bank robbery and asked some of the students to write detailed descriptions of the robber's face (the verbalization condition). The others spent the same amount of time completing an unrelated task (the no-verbalization condition). All students then tried to identify the robber from a photo lineup of eight faces. The results? Only 38% of the people in the verbalization condition correctly identified the robber, compared to 64% of the people in the no-verbalization condition.

Schooler and Engstler-Schooler (1990; see also Chin & Schooler, 2008) suggest that trying to put a face into words is difficult and impairs memory for that face. Using the word *squinty* to describe a robber's eyes, for example, might be a general description of what his eyes looked like but probably does not capture the subtle contours of his eyes, eyelids, eyelashes, eyebrows, and upper cheeks. When you see the photo lineup, you look for eyes that are squinty, and doing so interferes with your attention to the finer details of the faces. If you ever witness a crime, then, you should not try to put into words what the criminal looked like. And if you hear a witness say that he or she wrote down a description of the criminal and then took a while deciding whether the person was present at a lineup, you might doubt the accuracy of the witness's identification.

To sum up, several factors make eyewitness testimony inaccurate, leading to all too many false identifications. Perhaps the legal system in the United States should rely less on eyewitness testimony than it now does. In the legal systems of some countries, a suspect cannot be convicted on the basis of a sole eyewitness; at least two independent witnesses are needed. Adopting this more stringent standard in the United States might mean that some guilty people go free, but it would avoid many false convictions. The following Try It! exercise provides an opportunity to see how accurate you and your friends are at eyewitness testimony and to illustrate some of the pitfalls.

TRY IT! The Accuracy of Eyewitness Testimony

Try this demonstration with a group of friends who you know will be gathered in one place, such as a dorm room or an apartment. The idea is to stage an incident in which someone comes into the room suddenly, acts in a strange manner, and then leaves. Your friends will then be asked to recall as much as they can about this person, to see if they are good eyewitnesses. Here are some specific instructions about how you might do this.

1. Take one friend, whom we will call the actor, into your confidence before you do this exercise. Ideally, the actor should be a stranger to the people who will be the eyewitnesses. The actor should suddenly rush into the room where you and your other friends are gathered and act in a strange (but nonthreatening) manner. For example, the actor could hand someone a flower and say, "The flower man cometh!" Or he or she could go up to each person and say something unexpected, like "Meet me in Moscow at the mosque." Ask the actor to hold something in his or her hand during this episode, such as a pencil, shoelace, or banana.
2. *Important note:* The actor should not act in a violent or threatening way or make the eyewitnesses uncomfortable. The goal is to act in unexpected and surprising ways, not to frighten people.
3. After a few minutes, the actor should leave the room. Inform your friends that you staged this event as a demonstration of eyewitness testimony and that, if they are willing, they should try to remember in as much detail as possible what occurred. Ask them to write down answers to these questions:
   a. What did the actor look like? Write down a detailed description.
   b. What did the actor say? Write down his or her words as best as you can remember.
   c. How much time did the actor spend in the room?
   d. Did the actor touch anyone? If yes, whom?
   e. What was the actor holding in his or her hand?
4. After all participants have answered these questions, ask them to read their answers aloud. How much did they agree? How accurate were people's answers? Discuss with your friends why they were correct or incorrect in their descriptions.

Note: This demonstration will work best if you have access to a video camera and can record the actor's actions. That way, you can play the tape to assess the accuracy of the eyewitnesses' descriptions. If you cannot videotape it, keep track of how much time elapsed, so that you can judge the accuracy of people's time estimates.

Judging Whether Witnesses Are Lying

There is yet another reason why eyewitness testimony can be inaccurate: Even if witnesses have very accurate memories for what they saw, they might deliberately lie when on the witness stand. After Randall Adams was tried and convicted, new evidence suggested that some of the eyewitnesses who testified against him had lied. One witness may have struck a deal with the police, agreeing to say what they wanted her to say, in return for lenient treatment of her daughter, who had been arrested for armed robbery. If this witness was lying, why couldn't the jurors tell?

> *If falsehood, like truth, had only one face, we would be in better shape. For we would take as certain the opposite of what the liar said. But the reverse of truth has a hundred thousand shapes.*
>
> —Montaigne, *Essays*, 1595

It turns out that it is harder than you might think to tell whether someone is lying. In a typical study on this topic, participants watch videos or listen to audiotapes of people who are telling the truth half the time and lying half the time, and they then try to distinguish the lies from the truths. In a review of over 250 such studies, Bond and DePaulo (2006) found that whereas people were better than chance at telling lies from truths, their level of accuracy was not impressive: On average, people were correct only 54% of the time (where 50% would be guessing at chance levels). Interestingly, people with a lot of experience in dealing with liars (e.g., law enforcement agents and employees of the CIA) are no more accurate at detecting deception than college students. It is harder than we might think to detect whether someone is lying—even if we are a seasoned police officer or judge. In fact, there is surprisingly little evidence that some people are better at detecting lies than others. Some people are better at *telling* lies, but when it comes to *detecting* lies, it simply does not appear to be the case that some people have learned to detect them better than others (Bond & DePaulo, 2008).

Polygraph
A machine that measures people's physiological responses (e.g., heart rate) while answering an operator's questions, to determine truth or deception

Because it is so difficult for humans to tell if someone is lying, researchers have developed machines to do the job. The **polygraph**, or "lie detector," is a machine that

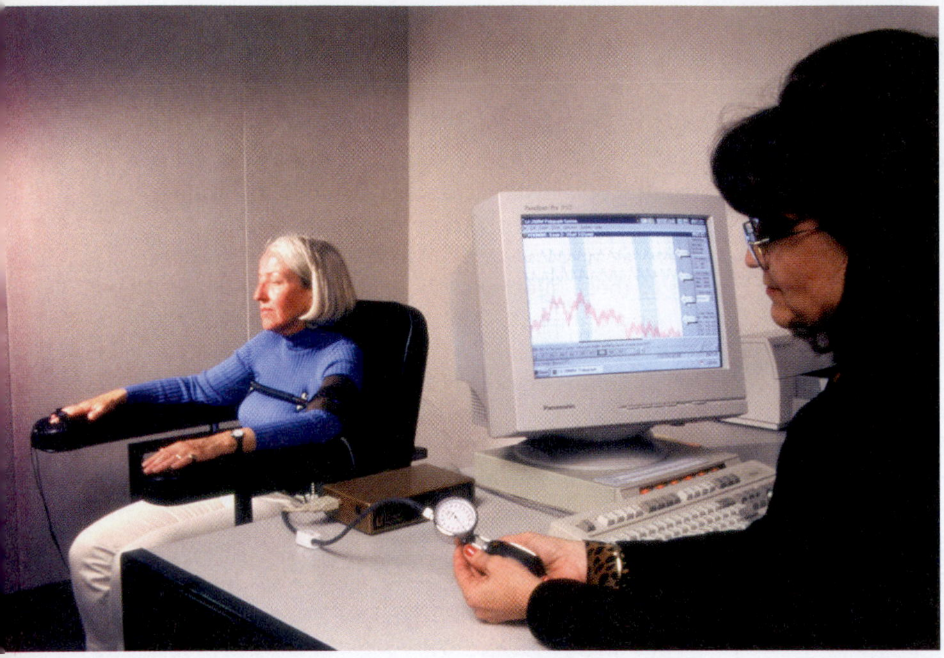

Although polygraphs can detect whether someone is lying at levels better than chance, they are far from infallible.

measures people's physiological responses, such as heart rate and breathing rate. The assumption is that when people lie, they become anxious, and this anxiety can be detected by increases in heart rate, breathing rate, and so on. How well do these tests work? The U.S. Department of Energy asked a board of distinguished scientists to address this question, and, after an extensive review, the board published a summary of its findings (National Research Council, 2003). The polygraph, they concluded, reveals whether someone is lying or telling the truth at levels better than chance. The accuracy rate, averaging over dozens of studies, was .86—that is, people were correctly labeled as lying or telling the truth 86% of the time.

Although this might seem like an impressive rate of accuracy, it still allows for a substantial number of errors, including false positives, where people who are telling the truth are incorrectly labeled as liars (Iacono, 2008; National Research Council, 2003). Think of it this way: If you were wrongly accused of a serious crime, would you be willing to take a test that had a 14% chance of landing you in prison? Because of these high error rates, polygraph evidence is inadmissible in most court trials. The National Research Council summarized it like this: "Almost a century of research in scientific psychology and physiology provides little basis for the expectation that a polygraph test could have extremely high accuracy" (p. 212).

The Recovered Memory Debate

Another form of eyewitness memory has received a great deal of attention: the case in which a person recalls having been the victim of a crime, typically sexual abuse, after many years of being consciously unaware of that fact. Not surprisingly, the accuracy of such **recovered memories** has been hotly debated (McNally, 2003; Pezdek & Banks, 1996; Schooler & Eich, 2000).

One well-known case occurred in 1988 in Olympia, Washington, when Paul Ingram's daughters accused him of sexual abuse, satanic rituals, and murder—events they claimed to have suddenly recalled years after they occurred. The police could find no evidence for the crimes, and Ingram initially denied that they had ever occurred. Eventually, though, he became convinced that he too must have repressed his past behavior and must have committed the crimes, even though he could not remember having done so. According to experts who have studied this case, Ingram's daughters genuinely believed that the abuse and killing had occurred—but they were wrong. What they thought they remembered were actually false memories (Wright, 1994).

The question of the accuracy of recovered memories is controversial. On one side are writers who claim that it is not uncommon for women who were sexually abused to repress these traumas so that they have absolutely no memory of them (Bass & Davis, 1994). The abuse and its subsequent repression, according to this view, are responsible for many psychological problems, such as depression and eating disorders. Later in life, often with the help of a psychotherapist, these events can be "recovered" and brought back into memory. On the other side of the controversy are academic psychologists and others who argue that the accuracy of recovered memories cannot be accepted on faith (e.g., Clancy & Barrett, 2005; Loftus, Garry, & Hayne, 2008; McNally & Geraerts, 2009; Ofshe & Watters, 1994; Schacter, 1996; Wegner, Quillian, & Houston, 1996). These writers acknowledge that sexual abuse and other childhood traumas are a terrible

Recovered Memories

Recollections of a past event, such as sexual abuse, that have been forgotten or repressed problem and are more common than we would like to think. They further agree that claims of sexual abuse should be investigated fully and that when sufficient evidence of guilt exists, the person responsible for the abuse should be prosecuted.

In 1988, Paul Ingram was accused by his daughters of sexual abuse, satanic rituals, and murder. His daughters claimed to have suddenly recalled these events years after they occurred, but what they thought they remembered were actually false memories.

But here's the problem: What is "sufficient evidence"? Is it enough that someone remembers, years later, that she or he has been abused, in the absence of any other evidence of abuse? According to many researchers, the answer is no, because of **false memory syndrome**: People can recall a past traumatic experience that is objectively false but that they believe is true (Kihlstrom, 1996). There is evidence that people can acquire vivid memories of events that never occurred, especially if another person—such as a psychotherapist—suggests that the events occurred (Loftus, Garry, & Hayne, 2008; Meyersburg et al., 2009, Schooler & Eich, 2000). In addition to numerous laboratory demonstrations of false memories, evidence from everyday life also indicates that memories of abuse can be false. Often, these memories are contradicted by objective evidence (e.g., no evidence of satanic murders can be found); sometimes people who suddenly acquire such memories decide later that the events never occurred; and sometimes the memories are so bizarre (e.g., that people were abducted by aliens) as to strain credibility. Unfortunately, some psychotherapists do not sufficiently consider that by suggesting past abuse they may be planting false memories rather than helping clients remember real events.

This is not to say, however, that all recovered memories are false. Although scientific evidence for repression and recovery—the idea that something can be forgotten for years and then recalled with great accuracy—is sparse, there may be instances in which people do suddenly remember abuse that really did occur (McNally & Geraerts, 2009; Schooler, 1999). Thus, any claim of abuse should be taken with the utmost seriousness. That said, we might want to be especially wary of memories of sexual abuse that are elicited by a psychotherapist.

To examine the basis of these memories, Elke Geraerts and her colleagues (2007) placed advertisements in the newspaper to recruit people who had memories of childhood sexual abuse. The researchers divided the sample into two groups: those who had continuous memories (that is, they had never forgotten their abuse) and those who had recovered a memory of abuse (that is, those who said there was a time when they believed they had not been a victim of abuse but who later recalled that they had been abused). This second group was further divided into those who recovered their memory of abuse outside of psychotherapy and those who did so in psychotherapy. All participants were asked to report any knowledge they had of corroborating evidence for the abuse, such as whether other individuals had reported being abused by the same perpetrator or if the perpetrator had confessed to the abuse. Although not perfect, the reported existence of corroborating information gives some indication of whether the memories were accurate.

As seen in Figure SPA-3.2, people whose memories of sexual abuse had been recovered in therapy were *least* likely to be able to provide corroborating evidence of the abuse; in fact, no one in this group did so. Does this prove that everyone who recovered a memory of abuse with the help of a psychotherapist was incorrect and that no such abuse occurred? Certainly not; we can't be sure how accurate people's memories are. The results suggest, however, that it can be dangerous for therapists to encourage their clients to recall memories of abuse. They may be implanting false memories in some cases, rather than eliciting memories of actual abuse. Claims of abuse cannot be taken on faith, especially if they are the result of suggestions from other people.

False Memory Syndrome

Remembering a past traumatic experience that is objectively false but is nevertheless accepted by the person as true

'Tis with our judgments as our watches, None go just alike, yet each believes his own.

—ALEXANDER POPE, *ESSAY ON CRITICISM*, 1711

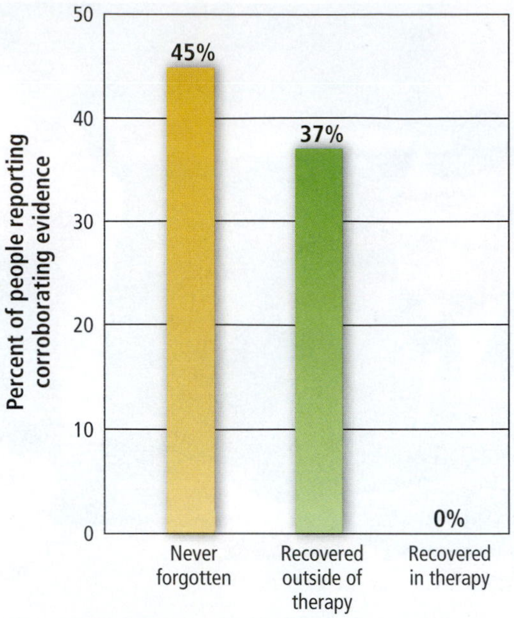

FIGURE SPA-3.2

Corroborating Evidence for Remembered Childhood Sexual Abuse

People who reported that they had been sexually abused in childhood were divided into three groups: those who had never forgotten the abuse, those who had recovered a memory of the abuse outside of psychotherapy, and those who had recovered a memory of the abuse in psychotherapy. All participants reported whether there was any corroborating evidence of the abuse, such as the perpetrator confessing. As seen here, people who recovered memories of abuse in psychotherapy were less likely to report corroborating evidence.

(Adapted from Geraerts, Schooler, Merckelbach, Jelicic, Hauer, & Ambadar, 2007)

Juries: Group Processes in Action

Ultimately, it is not a polygraph that decides whether witnesses are telling the truth, but a judge or jury. The right to be tried by a jury of one's peers has a long tradition in English and American law. Trial by jury was an established institution in England at the beginning of the seventeenth century, and the people who founded the first permanent English settlement in North America—at Jamestown, Virginia—carried this tradition with them (although, it should be noted, this right was not granted to Native Americans or other nonwhites, nor to a few rebellious English settlers who were summarily hanged).

Despite this tradition, the jury system has often come under attack. In the Randall Adams trial, it is now clear that the jury reached the wrong decision. One study found that judges who presided over criminal jury trials disagreed with the verdict rendered by the jury a full 25% of the time (Kalven & Zeisel, 1966). More-recent observers have also criticized the jury system, questioning the ability of jurors to understand complex evidence and reach a dispassionate verdict (Arkes & Mellers, 2002; Bornstein & Greene, 2011). As noted by a former dean of the Harvard Law School, "Why should anyone think that 12 persons brought in from the street, selected in various ways for their lack of general ability, should have any special capacity for deciding controversies between persons?" (Kalven & Zeisel, 1966, p. 5).

> *A court is no better than each . . . of you sitting before me on this jury. A court is only as sound as its jury, and a jury is only as sound as the [people] who make it up.*
>
> —Harper Lee, *To Kill a Mockingbird*, 1960

The jury system has its staunch supporters, of course, and few people on either side of the debate argue that it should be abolished. The point is that it is not a perfect system and that, based on research in social psychology, there are ways we might expect it to go wrong (Desmarais, & Read, 2011; Semmler, Brewer, & Douglass, 2012).

How Jurors Process Information During the Trial

How do individual jurors think about the evidence they hear during a trial? As we saw in Chapter 3, people often construct theories and schemas to interpret the world around them, and the same is true of jurors (Hart, 1995; Smith, 1991; Weinstock, 2011). Some psychologists suggest that jurors decide on one story that best explains all the evidence; they then try to fit this story to the possible verdicts they are allowed to render, and if one of those verdicts fits well with their preferred story, they are likely to vote to convict on that charge (Hastie, 2008; Hastie & Pennington, 2000). This possibility has important implications for how lawyers present their cases. Lawyers typically present the evidence in one of two ways. In the first, called *story order*, they present the evidence in the sequence in which the events occurred, corresponding as closely as possible to the story they want the jurors to believe. In the second, called *witness order*, they present witnesses in the sequence they think will have the greatest impact, even if this means that events are described out of order. For example, a lawyer might save his or her best witness for last so that the trial ends on a dramatic, memorable note, even if this witness describes events that occurred early in the alleged crime.

"Your Honor, we're going to go with the prosecution's spin."

Mike Twohy/The New Yorker Collection/www.cartoonbank.com

TABLE SPA-3.2 How Should Lawyers Present Their Cases?

Lawyers can present their cases in a variety of ways. This study found that story order, in which lawyers present the evidence in the order that corresponds most closely to the story they want the jurors to believe, works best.

Percentage of People Voting to Convict the Defendant

	Defense Evidence	
Prosecution Evidence	**Story Order (%)**	**Witness Order (%)**
Story order	59	78
Witness order	31	63

(Adapted from Pennington & Hastie, 1988)

If you were a lawyer, in which order would you present the evidence? You can probably guess which order researchers in this area hypothesized would be the most successful. If jurors are ultimately swayed by the story or schema they think best explains the sequence of events, the best strategy should be to present the evidence in story order, not witness order. To test their hypothesis, researchers asked mock jurors to listen to a simulated murder trial and varied the order in which the defense attorney and the prosecuting attorney presented their cases (Pennington & Hastie, 1988). In one condition, both used story order, whereas in another condition, both used witness order. In other conditions, one attorney used story order and the other used witness order.

The results provided clear and dramatic support for the story-order strategy. As seen in Table SPA-3.2, when the prosecutor used story order and the defense used witness order, the jurors were most likely to believe the prosecutor—78% voted to convict the defendant. When the prosecutor used witness order and the defense used story order, the tables were turned—only 31% voted to convict. One reason the conviction rate in felony trials in America is so high—approximately 80%—may be that in real trials prosecutors usually present evidence in story order, whereas defense attorneys usually use witness order. If you are a budding lawyer, remember this when you are preparing for your first trial!

Confessions: Are They Always What They Seem?

Imagine that you are a member of a jury at a murder trial. The prosecution presents what seems to be ironclad evidence—namely, a videotape of the defendant confessing to the crime. "OK, I admit it," you hear the defendant say, "I was the one who pulled the trigger." More than likely, you would vote to convict. Why would the defendant admit to the crime if he was innocent? And many cases never go to trial, because the defendant pleads guilty after confessing to the crime.

Confessions, however, are not always what they seem. Consider the case of a woman who was raped and brutally beaten while jogging in New York City's Central Park in 1989. The woman, who suffered a fractured skull and traumatic brain injuries, was in a coma for several days, and when she awoke, she had no memory of the attack. Despite the inability of the victim to point to a perpetrator, the police arrested five teenagers, African Americans and Hispanics, who had been in the park that night. The boys confessed to the crime and provided lurid details of what had happened. Four of the confessions were

"For me, a confession is much too autobiographical."

The problem with some confessions is that they are *not* autobiographical at all, but false.

Frank Cotham/The New Yorker Collection/www.cartoonbank.com

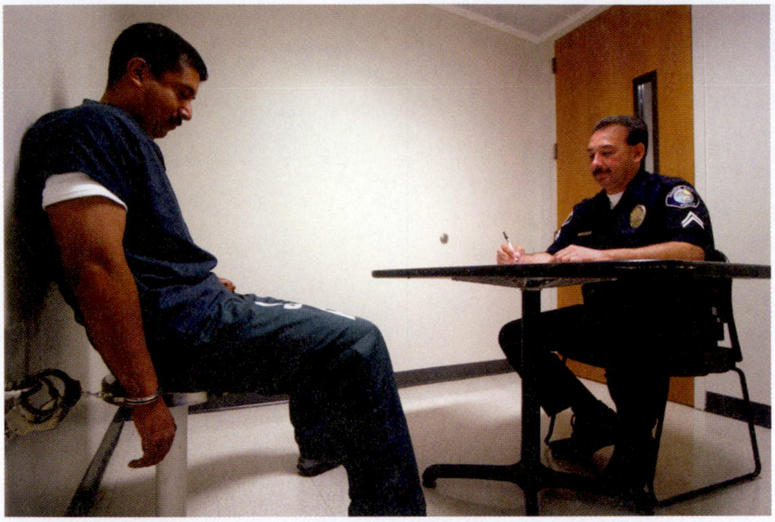

People sometimes confess to crimes they did not commit, when they are subjected to long, stressful interrogations.

videotaped and played at the trial, and largely on this basis, all of the teenagers were convicted and given long prison sentences.

The only problem is that, 13 years later, it became clear that the boys were innocent. Another man, in prison for three rapes and a murder, confessed to the crime, claiming he had acted alone. His DNA matched semen recovered from the victim (none of the teenagers' DNA matched), and he gave details of the crime scene that were known only to the police. In 2002, a judge vacated the convictions of all five boys.

If the boys were innocent, then why did they confess to the crime? Unfortunately, the police interrogation process can go wrong in ways that elicit false confessions, even to the point where innocent suspects come to believe that they actually committed the crime (Gudjonsson & Pearse, 2011; Hasel & Kassin, 2012; Kassin et al., 2010; Narchet, Meissner, & Russano, 2011). One problem is that police investigators are often convinced that the suspect is guilty, and this belief biases how they conduct the interrogation. They ask leading questions, isolate suspects and put them under considerable stress, claim that an eyewitness has identified the suspect, and sometimes make false promises. The suspects in the Central Park jogger case, for example, were questioned for up to 30 hours, and the police detectives implied that they could go home if they would sign a confession. After many hours of prolonged interrogation, innocent people can become so psychologically fatigued that they don't know what to think and may even come to believe that they are guilty. This is all well and good if the suspect really is guilty, and if the techniques succeed in making him or her confess. As we saw earlier, however, people—even trained investigators—are not very good at telling whether someone is lying, which means that innocent people are sometimes subjected to these techniques. In fact, in a large number of cases in which DNA evidence has exonerated defendants who have been falsely convicted of a crime, the defendant has confessed ("False confessions," 2006).

One solution to coerced confessions is requiring that interrogations be videotaped, so a jury can view the recording and judge for themselves whether the defendant was coerced into admitting things he or she didn't do. In 2003, the state of Illinois passed a law requiring that all police interrogations of suspects in homicide cases be electronically recorded. Although this is a step forward, it raises another potential problem. Almost all videos of interrogations focus on the suspect, rather than on the interrogator asking the questions. Well, what's wrong with that, you might wonder?

As we noted in Chapter 4, the problem is that viewers tend to think that whoever the camera is focused on is more in charge of the situation than they actually are. Some studies have showed people a video of the same confession from different camera angles and then asked them to judge how voluntary or coerced the confession was. People thought that the confession was most voluntary (i.e., the least coerced) when the camera focused on the suspect; here, people had the sense that the suspect was in charge of what was happening. When the camera showed both the suspect and the interrogator, people thought the confession was less voluntary. And when the camera focused only on the interrogator, people thought the confession was the most coerced (Lassiter, 2010). Remember, everyone heard the same confession; all that differed was their visual perspective. In part because of this research, at least one state (Wisconsin) now requires that both the suspect and the questioner be shown in videotaped interviews.

Deliberations in the Jury Room

As any trial lawyer can tell you, a crucial part of the jury process occurs out of sight, when jurors deliberate before deciding on the verdict. Even if most jurors are inclined to vote to convict, there might be a persuasive minority who change their fellow jurors' minds. Sometimes this can be a minority of one, as in the classic movie *Twelve Angry Men.* When the film begins, a jury has just finished listening to the evidence in a murder case, and all the jurors except one vote to convict the defendant. But over the course of the next 90 minutes, the lone holdout, played by Henry Fonda, persuades his peers that there is reason to doubt that the young Hispanic defendant is guilty. At first, the other jurors pressure Fonda to change his mind (using techniques of normative and informational conformity, as discussed in Chapter 8), but in the end, reason triumphs, and the other jurors come to see that Fonda is right.

In the 1954 movie *Twelve Angry Men*, Henry Fonda convinces all of his fellow jurors to change their minds about a defendant's guilt. In real life, however, cases are rare of a minority in a jury convincing the majority to change its mind.

As entertaining as this movie is, research indicates that it does not reflect the reality of most jury deliberations (Bornstein & Greene, 2011; Kalven & Zeisel, 1966; MacCoun, 1989). In the Randall Adams trial, for example, a majority of the 12-person jury (7 men and 5 women) initially voted to convict Adams. After 8 hours of deliberations, the majority prevailed: The holdouts changed their minds, and the jury voted unanimously to convict. In a study of more than 200 juries in actual criminal trials, researchers found that in 97% of the cases the jury's final decision was the same as the one favored by a majority of the jurors on the initial vote (Kalven & Zeisel, 1966). Thus, just as we saw in Chapter 8 on the subject of conformity, majority opinion usually carries the day, bringing dissenting jurors into line.

If jury deliberation is stacked toward the initial majority opinion, why not just abandon the deliberation process, letting the jury's initial vote determine a defendant's guilt or innocence? For two reasons, this would not be a good idea. First, forcing juries to reach a unanimous verdict makes them consider the evidence more carefully rather than simply assuming that their initial impressions of the case were correct (Hastie, Penrod, & Pennington, 1983). Second, even if minorities seldom succeed in persuading the majority to change their minds about guilt or innocence, minorities often do change people's minds about how guilty a person is. In criminal trials, juries usually have some discretion about the type of guilty verdict they can reach. In a murder trial, for example, they can often decide whether to convict the defendant of first-degree murder, second-degree murder, or manslaughter. One study found that people on a jury who have a minority point of view often convince the majority to change their minds about the specific verdict to render (Pennington & Hastie, 1990). Thus, while a minority of jurors is unlikely to convince a majority of jurors to change their verdict from first-degree murder to not guilty, they might well convince the majority to change the verdict to second-degree murder.

Summary

What does social psychology tell us about eyewitness testimony?

- **Eyewitness Testimony** Eyewitness testimony is often of questionable accuracy, because of the way people naturally observe and remember unexpected events.
    - **Why Are Eyewitnesses Often Wrong?** A number of factors bias the **acquisition**, **storage**, and **retrieval** of what people observe, sometimes leading to the false identification of criminals. For example, research on **own-race bias** shows that people find it more difficult to recognize members of other races than members of their own race. Research on **reconstructive memory** indicates that errors in **source monitoring** can occur when people become confused about where they saw or heard something. Recognizing the problems people have retrieving information from memory, social psychologists have issued guidelines for how police lineups should be conducted.
    - **Judging Whether Eyewitnesses Are Mistaken** There is no sure-fire way of telling whether a witness is making an accurate or inaccurate identification, although there is some evidence that people who identify a suspect from an array of pictures within 10 seconds *and* express very high confidence in their choice are especially likely to be correct.

- **Judging Whether Witnesses Are Lying** Humans are not very good at telling whether another person is lying. The **polygraph** can detect lying at above-chance levels, but is not perfect and often yields inaccurate results.
- **The Recovered Memory Debate** Although **recovered memories** may be true in some instances, they can also be the result of **false memory syndrome**, whereby people come to believe that a memory is true when it actually is not. False memories are especially likely to occur when another person, such as a psychotherapist, suggests to us that an event really occurred.

How can social psychology help to make jury decisions more accurate?

- **Juries: Group Processes in Action** Juries are of particular interest to social psychologists, because the way they reach verdicts is directly relevant to social psychological research on group processes and social interaction. Jurors are susceptible to the same kinds of biases and social pressures we have documented in earlier chapters.
  - **How Jurors Process Information During the Trial** During a trial, jurors attempt to make sense out of the testimony and often decide on one story that explains all of the evidence. Juries are thus most swayed by lawyers who present the evidence in a way that tells a consistent story.
  - **Confessions: Are They Always What They Seem?** The interrogation techniques used by the police can sometimes produce false confessions. The video recording of interrogations is a safeguard against this, although focusing the camera solely on the suspect increases the likelihood that viewers will think he or she voluntarily confessed.
  - **Deliberations in the Jury Room** During deliberations, jurors with minority views are often pressured into conforming to the view of the majority; thus, verdicts usually correspond to the initial feelings of the majority of jurors.

Chapter SPA-3 Test

Study and **Review** on **MyPsychLab**

1. Which of the following is *least* true about eyewitness testimony?
   a. Jurors and law enforcement professionals rely heavily on eyewitness testimony when they are deciding whether someone is guilty.
   b. Jurors tend to overestimate the accuracy of eyewitnesses.
   c. People are better at recognizing faces of people of their own race than faces of people of different races.
   d. Writing down a description of someone you saw will make it easier for you to recognize that person later.

2. Alicia was working the night shift at a convenience store. A man came in, pulled out a gun, and demanded that Alicia give him all the money in the cash register. When the police interview Alicia about the crime, what will she most likely be able to tell them?
   a. The kind of gun the man had.
   b. The type of clothes the man wore.
   c. The height of the man.
   d. The color of the man's eyes.

3. You are an assistant district attorney trying to decide which suspect to try for a burglary case. Each of five eyewitnesses picked a different suspect from a photo lineup. Based on social psychological research, which eyewitness would you find most credible?
   a. Beth, who carefully compared each of the faces against the others.
   b. Edward, who wrote down a description of the suspect right after the robbery.
   c. Larry, who took longer than the other witnesses to pick his suspect.
   d. Diana, who reported that the suspect's face just "popped out" at her.
   e. Fran, who said that she was "extremely confident" that she was correct.

4. Which of the following is *not* a recommendation social psychologists have made about how the police should conduct lineups?
   a. Make sure everyone in the lineup resembles the witness's description of the suspect.
   b. Tell the witness that the person suspected of the crime may or may not be in the lineup.
   c. Before seeing the lineup, have the witness reconstruct the face of the suspect, using face-composite computer programs.
   d. Do not always include the suspect in an initial lineup.
   e. Don't count on witnesses knowing whether their selections were biased.

5. Research has supported each of the following statements about recovered memories *except one*. Which one?
   a. People can recall a past traumatic experience that is objectively false but that they believe is true.
   b. People who recover memories of sexual abuse in psychotherapy are almost always correct that the abuse really occurred.
   c. There may be instances in which people do suddenly remember traumatic events that really did occur.
   d. People who, while in psychotherapy, have recovered memories of sexual abuse are less likely to report corroborating evidence for the abuse than are people who have recovered memories of sexual abuse outside of psychotherapy.

6. Which of the following recommendations have social psychologists made to the legal profession?
   a. The police should try as hard as they can to get suspects to confess to a crime, because if the suspects confess, they are surely guilty.
   b. Lawyers should present witnesses in the sequence they think will have the greatest impact, even if this means that events of the case are described out of order.

- **c.** The police should videotape all interrogations and make sure that the camera angle shows both the interrogator and the suspect.
- **d.** The results of polygraph (lie detector) tests should be allowed in trials because these tests are extremely accurate.

7. Which of the following statements is *most true* about detecting whether someone is lying?

- **a.** Juries can almost always tell whether a witness is lying.
- **b.** Polygraph machines can tell whether someone is lying with almost perfect accuracy (higher than 95% accuracy).
- **c.** College students can tell whether someone is lying with as much accuracy as law enforcement agents.
- **d.** The best indicator that someone is lying is if they look away while you are talking with them.

8. Which of the following is *most true* about research on social psychology and the law?

- **a.** In police interrogations, people sometimes confess to a crime they did not commit and even come to believe that they did commit the crime.
- **b.** When jury deliberations begin, if a couple of jurors disagree with everyone else, they often persuade the majority to change from a guilty to a not-guilty verdict.
- **c.** People have pretty good memories for events they witness, and it is hard to convince them that they saw something they did not.
- **d.** If a witness picks a suspect out of a lineup and is extremely confident that he or she has identified the right person, then he or she is almost certainly correct.

Answer Key

1-d, 2-a, 3-d, 4-c, 5-b, 6-c, 7-c, 8-a

Glossary

Accessibility The extent to which schemas and concepts are at the forefront of people's minds and are therefore likely to be used when making judgments about the social world

Affect Blend A facial expression in which one part of the face registers one emotion while another part of the face registers a different emotion

Affectively Based Attitude An attitude based more on people's feelings and values than on their beliefs about the nature of an attitude object

Aggression Intentional behavior aimed at causing physical harm or psychological pain to another person

Aggressive Stimulus An object that is associated with aggressive responses (e.g., a gun) and whose mere presence can increase the probability of aggression

Altruism The desire to help another person even if it involves a cost to the helper

Altruistic Personality The qualities that cause an individual to help others in a wide variety of situations

Analytic Thinking Style A type of thinking in which people focus on the properties of objects without considering their surrounding context; this type of thinking is common in Western cultures

Anxious/Ambivalent Attachment Style An attachment style characterized by a concern that others will not reciprocate one's desire for intimacy, resulting in higher-than-average levels of anxiety

Applied Research Studies designed to solve a particular social problem

Archival Analysis A form of the observational method in which the researcher examines the accumulated documents, or archives, of a culture (e.g., diaries, novels, magazines, and newspapers)

Attachment Styles The expectations people develop about relationships with others, based on the relationship they had with their primary caregiver when they were infants

Attitude Accessibility The strength of the association between an attitude object and a person's evaluation of that object, measured by the speed with which people can report how they feel about the object

Attitude Inoculation Making people immune to attempts to change their attitudes by initially exposing them to small doses of the arguments against their position

Attitudes Evaluations of people, objects, and ideas

Attribution Theory A description of the way in which people explain the causes of their own and other people's behavior

Automatic Thinking Thinking that is nonconscious, unintentional, involuntary, and effortless

Availability Heuristic A mental rule of thumb whereby people base a judgment on the ease with which they can bring something to mind

Avoidant Attachment Style An attachment style characterized by a suppression of attachment needs because attempts to be intimate have been rebuffed; people with this style find it difficult to develop intimate relationships

Base Rate Information Information about the frequency of members of different categories in the population

Basic Research Studies that are designed to find the best answer to the question of why people behave as they do and that are conducted purely for reasons of intellectual curiosity

Behaviorally Based Attitude An attitude based on observations of how one behaves toward an object

Behaviorism A school of psychology maintaining that to understand human behavior, one need only consider the reinforcing properties of the environment

Belief in a Just World A form of defensive attribution wherein people assume that bad things happen to bad people and that good things happen to good people

Bias Blind Spot The tendency to think that other people are more susceptible to attributional biases in their thinking than we are

Blaming the Victim The tendency to blame individuals (make dispositional attributions) for their victimization, typically motivated by a desire to see the world as a fair place

Bystander Effect The finding that the greater the number of bystanders who witness an emergency, the less likely any one of them is to help

Catharsis The notion that "blowing off steam"—by performing a verbally or physically aggressive act, watching others engage in aggressive behaviors, or engaging in a fantasy of aggression—relieves built-up aggressive energies and hence reduces the likelihood of further aggressive behavior

Causal Theories Theories about the causes of one's own feelings and behaviors; often we learn such theories from our culture (e.g., "absence makes the heart grow fonder")

Central Route to Persuasion The case in which people elaborate on a persuasive communication, listening carefully to and thinking about the arguments, which occurs when people have both the ability and the motivation to listen carefully to a communication

Classical Conditioning The phenomenon whereby a stimulus that elicits an emotional response (e.g., your grandmother) is repeatedly paired with a neutral stimulus that does not (e.g., the smell of mothballs), until the neutral stimulus takes on the emotional properties of the first stimulus

Cognitive Dissonance A drive or feeling of discomfort, originally defined as being caused by holding two or more inconsistent cognitions and subsequently defined as being caused by performing an action that is discrepant from one's customary, typically positive self-conception

Cognitively Based Attitude An attitude based primarily on people's beliefs about the properties of an attitude object

Communal Relationships Relationships in which people's primary concern is being responsive to the other person's needs

Companionate Love The feelings of intimacy and affection we have for someone that are not accompanied by passion or physiological arousal

Comparison Level for Alternatives People's expectations about the level of rewards and punishments they would receive in an alternative relationship

Comparison Level People's expectations about the level of rewards and punishments they are likely to receive in a particular relationship

Conformity A change in one's behavior due to the real or imagined influence of other people

Consensus Information Information about the extent to which other people behave the same way toward the same stimulus as the actor does

Consistency Information Information about the extent to which the behavior between one actor and one stimulus is the same across time and circumstances

Construal The way in which people perceive, comprehend, and interpret the social world

Contagion The rapid spread of emotions or behaviors through a crowd

Contingency Theory of Leadership The idea that leadership effectiveness depends both on how task-oriented or relationship-oriented the leader is and on the amount of control and influence the leader has over the group

Controlled Thinking Thinking that is conscious, intentional, voluntary, and effortful

Correlation Coefficient A statistical technique that assesses how well you can predict one variable from another—for example, how well you can predict people's weight from their height

Correlational Method The technique whereby two or more variables are systematically measured and the relationship between them (i.e., how much one can be predicted from the other) is assessed

Counterattitudinal Advocacy Stating an opinion or attitude that runs counter to one's private belief or attitude

Counterfactual Thinking Mentally changing some aspect of the past as a way of imagining what might have been

Covariation Model A theory that states that to form an attribution about what caused a person's behavior, we systematically note the pattern between the presence or absence of possible causal factors and whether or not the behavior occurs

Cover Story A description of the purpose of a study, given to participants, that is different from its true purpose and is used to maintain psychological realism

Cross-Cultural Research Research conducted with members of different cultures, to see whether the psychological processes of interest are present in both cultures or whether they are specific to the culture in which people were raised

Debriefing Explaining to participants, at the end of an experiment, the true purpose of the study and exactly what transpired

Deception Misleading participants about the true purpose of a study or the events that will actually transpire

Decode To interpret the meaning of the nonverbal behavior other people express, such as deciding that a pat on the back was an expression of condescension and not kindness

Defensive Attributions Explanations for behavior that avoid feelings of vulnerability and mortality

Deindividuation The loosening of normal constraints on behavior when people can't be identified (such as when they are in a crowd)

Dependent Variable The variable a researcher measures to see if it is influenced by the independent variable; the researcher hypothesizes that the dependent variable will depend on the level of the independent variable

Descriptive Norms People's perceptions of how people actually behave in given situations, regardless of whether the behavior is approved or disapproved of by others

Diffusion of Responsibility The phenomenon wherein each bystander's sense of responsibility to help decreases as the number of witnesses increases

Discrimination Unjustified negative or harmful action toward a member of a group solely because of his or her membership in that group

Display Rules Culturally determined rules about which nonverbal behaviors are appropriate to display

Distinctiveness Information Information about the extent to which one particular actor behaves in the same way to different stimuli

Downward Social Comparison Comparing ourselves to people who are worse than we are with regard to a particular trait or ability

Elaboration Likelihood Model A model explaining two ways in which persuasive communications can cause attitude change: *centrally*, when people are motivated and have the ability to pay attention to the arguments in the communication, and *peripherally*, when people do not pay attention to the arguments but are instead swayed by surface characteristics (e.g., who gave the speech)

Emblems Nonverbal gestures that have well-understood definitions within a given culture; they usually have direct verbal translations—such as the OK sign

Empathy-Altruism Hypothesis The idea that when we feel empathy for a person, we will attempt to help that person for purely altruistic reasons, regardless of what we have to gain

Empathy The ability to put oneself in the shoes of another person and to experience events and emotions (e.g., joy and sadness) the way that person experiences them

Encode To express or emit nonverbal behavior, such as smiling or patting someone on the back

Equity Theory The idea that people are happiest with relationships in which the rewards and costs experienced and the contributions made by both parties are roughly equal

Ethnography The method by which researchers attempt to understand a group or culture by observing it from the inside, without imposing any preconceived notions they might have

Evolutionary Approach to Mate Selection A theory derived from evolutionary biology that holds that men and women are attracted to different characteristics in each other (men are attracted by women's appearance; women are attracted by men's resources) because this maximizes their chances of reproductive success

Evolutionary Psychology The attempt to explain social behavior in terms of genetic factors that have evolved over time according to the principles of natural selection

Evolutionary Theory A concept developed by Charles Darwin to explain the ways in which animals adapt to their environments

Exchange Relationships Relationships governed by the need for equity (i.e., for an equal ratio of rewards and costs)

Experimental Method The method in which the researcher randomly assigns participants to different conditions and ensures that these conditions are identical except for the independent variable (the one thought to have a causal effect on people's responses)

Explicit Attitudes Attitudes that we consciously endorse and can easily report

External Attribution The inference that a person is behaving a certain way because of something about the situation he or she is in; the assumption is that most people would respond the same way in that situation

External Justification A reason or an explanation for dissonant personal behavior that resides outside the individual (e.g., in order to receive a large reward or avoid a severe punishment)

External Validity The extent to which the results of a study can be generalized to other situations and to other people

Extrinsic Motivation The desire to engage in an activity because of external rewards or pressures, not because we enjoy the task or find it interesting

Fear-Arousing Communication Persuasive message that attempts to change people's attitudes by arousing their fears

Field Experiments Experiments conducted in natural settings rather than in the laboratory

Fixed Mindset The idea that we have a set amount of an ability that cannot change

Frustration-Aggression Theory The theory that frustration—the perception that you are being prevented from attaining a goal—increases the probability of an aggressive response

Fundamental Attribution Error The tendency to overestimate the extent to which people's behavior is due to internal, dispositional factors and to underestimate the role of situational factors

Gestalt Psychology A school of psychology stressing the importance of studying the subjective way in which an object appears in people's minds rather than the objective, physical attributes of the object

Great Person Theory The idea that certain key personality traits make a person a good leader, regardless of the situation

Group Cohesiveness Qualities of a group that bind members together and promote liking between members

Group Polarization The tendency for groups to make decisions that are more extreme than the initial inclinations of its members

Group Three or more people who interact and are interdependent in the sense that their needs and goals cause them to influence each other

Groupthink A kind of thinking in which maintaining group cohesiveness and solidarity is more important than considering the facts in a realistic manner

Growth Mindset The idea that our abilities are malleable qualities that we can cultivate and grow

Heuristic–Systematic Model of Persuasion An explanation of the two ways in which persuasive communications can cause attitude change: either systematically processing the merits of the arguments or using mental shortcuts (heuristics), such as "Experts are always right"

Hindsight Bias The tendency for people to exaggerate how much they could have predicted an outcome after knowing that it occurred

Holistic Thinking Style A type of thinking in which people focus on the overall context, particularly the ways in which objects relate to each other; this type of thinking is common in East Asian cultures (e.g., China, Japan, and Korea)

Hostile Aggression Aggression stemming from feelings of anger and aimed at inflicting pain or injury

Hypocrisy Induction The arousal of dissonance by having individuals make statements that run counter to their behaviors and then reminding them of the inconsistency between what they advocated and their behavior. The purpose is to lead individuals to more responsible behavior

Idiosyncrasy Credits The tolerance a person earns, over time, by conforming to group norms; if enough idiosyncrasy credits are earned, the person can, on occasion, behave deviantly without retribution from the group

Illusory Correlation The tendency to see relationships, or correlations, between events that are actually unrelated

Impact Bias The tendency to overestimate the intensity and duration of one's emotional reactions to future negative events

Implicit Attitudes Attitudes that are involuntary, uncontrollable, and at times unconscious

Implicit Personality Theory A type of schema people use to group various kinds of personality traits together; for example, many people believe that someone who is kind is generous as well

Impression Management The attempt by people to get others to see them as they want to be seen

In-Group The group with which an individual identifies as a member

Independent Variable The variable a researcher changes or varies to see if it has an effect on some other variable

Independent View of the Self A way of defining oneself in terms of one's own internal thoughts, feelings, and actions and not in terms of the thoughts, feelings, and actions of other people

Individual Differences The aspects of people's personalities that make them different from other people

Informational Social Influence The influence of other people that leads us to conform because we see them as a source of information to guide our behavior; we conform because we believe that others' interpretation of an ambiguous situation is more correct than ours and will help us choose an appropriate course of action

Informed Consent Agreement to participate in an experiment, granted in full awareness of the nature of the experiment, which has been explained in advance

Ingratiation The process whereby people flatter, praise, and generally try to make themselves likable to another person, often of higher status

Injunctive Norms People's perceptions of what behaviors are approved or disapproved of by others

Institutional Discrimination Practices that discriminate, legally or illegally, against a minority group by virtue of its ethnicity, gender, culture, age, sexual orientation, or other target of societal or company prejudice

Institutional Review Board (IRB) A group made up of at least one scientist, one nonscientist, and one member not affiliated with the institution that reviews all psychological research at that institution and decides whether it meets ethical guidelines; all research must be approved by the IRB before it is conducted

Institutionalized Racism Racist attitudes that are held by the vast majority of people living in a society where stereotypes and discrimination are the norm

Institutionalized Sexism Sexist attitudes that are held by the vast majority of people living in a society where stereotypes and discrimination are the norm

Instrumental Aggression Aggression as a means to some goal other than causing pain

Insufficient Punishment The dissonance aroused when individuals lack sufficient external justification for having resisted a desired activity or object, usually resulting in individuals devaluing the forbidden activity or object

Integrative Solution A solution to a conflict whereby the parties make trade-offs on issues according to their different interests; each side concedes the most on issues that are unimportant to it but important to the other side

Interdependent View of the Self A way of defining oneself in terms of one's relationships to other people, recognizing that one's behavior is often determined by the thoughts, feelings, and actions of others

Interjudge Reliability The level of agreement between two or more people who independently observe and code a set of data; by showing that two or more judges independently come up with the same observations, researchers ensure that the observations are not the subjective, distorted impressions of one individual

Internal Attribution The inference that a person is behaving in a certain way because of something about the person, such as attitude, character, or personality

Internal Justification The reduction of dissonance by changing something about oneself (e.g., one's attitude or behavior)

Internal Validity Making sure that nothing besides the independent variable can affect the dependent variable; this is accomplished by controlling all extraneous variables and by randomly assigning people to different experimental conditions

Intrinsic Motivation The desire to engage in an activity because we enjoy it or find it interesting, not because of external rewards or pressures

Introspection The process whereby people look inward and examine their own thoughts, feelings, and motives

Investment Model The theory that people's commitment to a relationship depends not only on their satisfaction with the relationship in terms of rewards, costs, and comparison level and their comparison level for alternatives, but also on how much they have invested in the relationship that would be lost by leaving it

Jigsaw Classroom A classroom setting designed to reduce prejudice and raise the self-esteem of children by placing them in small, desegregated groups and making each child dependent on the other children in the group to learn the course material and do well in the class

Judgmental Heuristics Mental shortcuts people use to make judgments quickly and efficiently

Justification of Effort The tendency for individuals to increase their liking for something they have worked hard to attain

Kin Selection The idea that behaviors that help a genetic relative are favored by natural selection

Lowballing An unscrupulous strategy whereby a salesperson induces a customer to agree to purchase a product at a low cost, subsequently claims it was an error, and then raises the price; frequently, the customer will agree to make the purchase at the inflated price

Mass Psychogenic Illness The occurrence in a group of people of similar physical symptoms with no known physical cause

Mere Exposure Effect The finding that the more exposure we have to a stimulus, the more apt we are to like it

Meta-Analysis A statistical technique that averages the results of two or more studies to see if the effect of an independent variable is reliable

Minority Influence The case where a minority of group members influences the behavior or beliefs of the majority

Misattribution of Arousal The process whereby people make mistaken inferences about what is causing them to feel the way they do

Modern Racism Outwardly acting unprejudiced while inwardly maintaining prejudiced attitudes

Mutual Interdependence The situation that exists when two or more groups need to depend on one another to accomplish a goal that is important to each of them

Narcissism The combination of excessive self-love and a lack of empathy toward others

Natural Selection The process by which heritable traits that promote survival in a particular environment are passed along to future generations; organisms with those traits are more likely to produce offspring

Need for Cognition A personality variable reflecting the extent to which people engage in and enjoy effortful cognitive activities

Negotiation A form of communication between opposing sides in a conflict in which offers and counteroffers are made and a solution occurs only when both parties agree

Nonverbal Communication The way in which people communicate, intentionally or unintentionally, without words; nonverbal cues include facial expressions, tone of voice, gestures, body position and movement, the use of touch, and gaze

Norm of Reciprocity The expectation that helping others will increase the likelihood that they will help us in the future

Normative Conformity The tendency to go along with the group in order to fulfill the group's expectations and gain acceptance

Normative Social Influence The influence of other people that leads us to conform in order to be liked and accepted by them; this type of conformity results in public compliance with the group's beliefs and behaviors but not necessarily in private acceptance of those beliefs and behaviors

Observational Method The technique whereby a researcher observes people and systematically records measurements or impressions of their behavior

Operant Conditioning The phenomenon whereby behaviors we freely choose to perform become more or less frequent, depending on whether they are followed by a reward (positive reinforcement) or punishment

Out-Group Homogeneity The perception that individuals in the out-group are more similar to each other (homogeneous) than they really are, as well as more similar than members of the in-group are

Out-Group Any group with which an individual does not identify

Overconfidence Barrier The fact that people usually have too much confidence in the accuracy of their judgments

Overjustification Effect The tendency for people to view their behavior as caused by compelling extrinsic reasons, making them underestimate the extent to which it was caused by intrinsic reasons

Passionate Love An intense longing we feel for a person, accompanied by physiological arousal; when our love is reciprocated, we feel great fulfillment and ecstasy, but when it is not, we feel sadness and despair

Perceptual Salience The seeming importance of information that is the focus of people's attention

Performance-Contingent Rewards Rewards that are based on how well we perform a task

Peripheral Route to Persuasion The case in which people do not elaborate on the arguments in a persuasive communication but are instead swayed by peripheral cues

Persuasive Communication Communication (e.g., a speech or television ad) advocating a particular side of an issue

Pluralistic Ignorance The case in which people think that everyone else is interpreting a situation in a certain way, when in fact they are not

Postdecision Dissonance Dissonance aroused after making a decision, typically reduced by enhancing the attractiveness of the chosen alternative and devaluating the rejected alternatives

Prejudice A hostile or negative attitude toward people in a distinguishable group, based solely on their membership in that group

Priming The process by which recent experiences increase the accessibility of a schema, trait, or concept

Private Acceptance Conforming to other people's behavior out of a genuine belief that what they are doing or saying is right

Probability Level (*p*-value) A number calculated with statistical techniques that tells researchers how likely it is that the results of their experiment occurred by chance and not because of the independent variable or variables; the convention in science, including social psychology, is to consider results significant (trustworthy) if the probability level is less than 5 in 100 that the results might be due to chance factors and not the independent variables studied

Process Loss Any aspect of group interaction that inhibits good problem solving

Propinquity Effect The finding that the more we see and interact with people, the more likely they are to become our friends

Prosocial Behavior Any act performed with the goal of benefiting another person

Psychological Realism The extent to which the psychological processes triggered in an experiment are similar to psychological processes that occur in everyday life

Public Compliance Conforming to other people's behavior publicly without necessarily believing in what the other people are doing or saying

Random Assignment to Condition A process ensuring that all participants have an equal chance of taking part in any condition of an experiment; through random assignment, researchers can be relatively certain that differences in the participants' personalities or backgrounds are distributed evenly across conditions

Random Selection A way of ensuring that a sample of people is representative of a population by giving everyone in the population an equal chance of being selected for the sample

Reactance Theory The idea that when people feel their freedom to perform a certain behavior is threatened, an unpleasant state of reactance is aroused, which they can reduce by performing the threatened behavior

Realistic Conflict Theory The idea that limited resources lead to conflict between groups and result in increased prejudice and discrimination

Reasons-Generated Attitude Change Attitude change resulting from thinking about the reasons for one's attitudes; people assume that their attitudes match the reasons that are plausible and easy to verbalize

Relationship-Oriented Leader A leader who is concerned more with workers' feelings and relationships

Replications Repeating a study, often with different subject populations or in different settings

Representativeness Heuristic A mental shortcut whereby people classify something according to how similar it is to a typical case

Scapegoating The tendency for individuals, when frustrated or unhappy, to displace aggression onto groups that are disliked, visible, and relatively powerless

Schemas Mental structures people use to organize their knowledge about the social world around themes or subjects and that influence the information people notice, think about, and remember

Scripts Ways of behaving socially that we learn implicitly from our culture

Secure Attachment Style An attachment style characterized by trust, a lack of concern with being abandoned, and the view that one is worthy and well liked

Self-Affirmation In the context of dissonance theory, a way of reducing dissonance by reminding oneself of one or more of one's positive attributes

Self-Awareness Theory The idea that when people focus their attention on themselves, they evaluate and compare their behavior to their internal standards and values

Self-Esteem People's evaluations of their own self-worth—that is, the extent to which they view themselves as good, competent, and decent

Self-Fulfilling Prophecy The case wherein people have an expectation about what another person is like, which influences how they act toward that person, which causes that person to behave consistently with people's original expectations, making the expectations come true

Self-Handicapping The strategy whereby people create obstacles and excuses for themselves so that if they do poorly on a task, they can avoid blaming themselves

Self-Perception Theory The theory that when our attitudes and feelings are uncertain or ambiguous, we infer these states by observing our behavior and the situation in which it occurs

Self-Persuasion A long-lasting form of attitude change that results from attempts at self-justification

Self-Serving Attributions Explanations for one's successes that credit internal, dispositional factors and explanations for one's failures that blame external, situational factors

Social Cognition How people think about themselves and the social world; more specifically, how people select, interpret, remember, and use social information to make judgments and decisions

Social Comparison Theory The idea that we learn about our own abilities and attitudes by comparing ourselves to other people

Social Dilemma A conflict in which the most beneficial action for an individual will, if chosen by most people, have harmful effects on everyone

Social Exchange Theory The idea that people's feelings about a relationship depend on their perceptions of the rewards and costs of the relationship, the kind of relationship they deserve, and their chances for having a better relationship with someone else

Social Facilitation The tendency for people to do better on simple tasks and worse on complex tasks when they are in the presence of others and their individual performance can be evaluated

Social Impact Theory The idea that conforming to social influence depends on the group's importance, its immediacy, and the number of people in the group

Social Influence The effect that the words, actions, or mere presence of other people have on our thoughts, feelings, attitudes, or behavior

Social Learning Theory The theory that people learn social behavior (e.g., aggression) in large part by observing others and imitating them

Social Loafing The tendency for people to relax when they are in the presence of others and their individual performance cannot be evaluated, such that they do worse on simple tasks but better on complex tasks

Social Norms The implicit or explicit rules a group has for the acceptable behaviors, values, and beliefs of its members

Social Perception The study of how we form impressions of and make inferences about other people

Social Psychology The scientific study of the way in which people's thoughts, feelings, and behaviors are influenced by the real or imagined presence of other people

Social Roles Shared expectations in a group about how particular people are supposed to behave

Social Tuning The process whereby people adopt another person's attitudes

Stereotype Threat The apprehension experienced by members of a group that their behavior might confirm a cultural stereotype

Stereotype A generalization about a group of people, in which certain traits are assigned to virtually all members of the group, regardless of actual variation among the members

Subliminal Messages Words or pictures that are not consciously perceived but may nevertheless influence people's judgments, attitudes, and behaviors

Surveys Research in which a representative sample of people are asked (often anonymously) questions about their attitudes or behavior

Task-Contingent Rewards Rewards that are given for performing a task, regardless of how well the task is done

Task-Oriented Leader A leader who is concerned more with getting the job done than with workers' feelings and relationships

Terror Management Theory The theory that holds that self-esteem serves as a buffer, protecting people from terrifying thoughts about their own mortality

Theory of Planned Behavior The idea that people's intentions are the best predictors of their deliberate behaviors, which are determined by their attitudes toward specific behaviors, their subjective norms, and their perceived behavioral control

Tit-for-Tat Strategy A means of encouraging cooperation by at first acting cooperatively but then always responding the way your opponent did (cooperatively or competitively) on the previous trial

Transactional Leaders Leaders who set clear, short-term goals and reward people who meet them

Transactive Memory The combined memory of two people that is more efficient than the memory of either individual

Transformational Leaders Leaders who inspire followers to focus on common, long-term goals

Two-Factor Theory of Emotion The idea that emotional experience is the result of a two-step self-perception process in which people first experience physiological arousal and then seek an appropriate explanation for it

Two-Step Process of Attribution Analyzing another person's behavior first by making an automatic internal attribution and only then thinking about possible situational reasons for the behavior, after which one may adjust the original internal attribution

Ultimate Attribution Error The tendency to make dispositional attributions about an entire group of people

Upward Social Comparison Comparing ourselves to people who are better than we are with regard to a particular trait or ability

Urban Overload Hypothesis The theory that people living in cities are constantly bombarded with stimulation and that they keep to themselves to avoid being overwhelmed by it

Yale Attitude Change Approach The study of the conditions under which people are most likely to change their attitudes in response to persuasive messages, focusing on the source of the communication, the nature of the communication, and the nature of the audience

References

Aarts, H., Custers, R., & Holland, R. W. (2007). The nonconscious cessation of goal pursuit: When goals and negative affect are coactivated. *Journal of Personality and Social Psychology, 92*, 165–178.

Aarts, H., & Dijksterhuis, A. (2003). The silence of the library: Environment, situational norm, and social behavior. *Journal of Personality and Social Psychology, 84*, 18–28.

Abelson, R. P., Kinder, D. R., Peters, M. D., & Fiske, S. T. (1982). Affective and semantic components in political person perception. *Journal of Personality and Social Psychology, 42*, 619–630.

Abraham, M. M., & Lodish, L. M. (1990). Getting the most out of advertising and promotion. *Harvard Business Review, 68*, 50–60.

Abrams, D., Marques, J. M., Bown, N., & Henson, M. (2000). Pro-norm and anti-norm deviance within and between groups. *Journal of Personality and Social Psychology, 78*, 906–912.

Abrams, D., Viki, G. T., Masser, B., & Bohner, G. (2003). Perceptions of stranger and acquaintance rape: The role of benevolent and hostile sexism in victim blame and rape proclivity. *Journal of Personality and Social Psychology, 84*, 111–125.

Abrams, D., Wetherell, M., Cochrane, S., Hogg, M. A., & Turner, J. C. (1990). Knowing what to think by knowing who you are: Self-categorization and the nature of norm formation, conformity and group polarization. *British Journal of Social Psychology, 29*, 97–119.

Adams, G., Anderson, S. L., & Adonu, J. K. (2004). The cultural grounding of closeness and intimacy. In D. J. Mashek & A. Aron (Eds.), *Handbook of closeness and intimacy* (pp. 321–342). Mahwah, NJ: Erlbaum.

Adler, J. (1997, March 22). It's a wise father who knows . . . *Newsweek*, p. 73.

Adult obesity. (2011). Centers for Disease Control and Prevention. Retrieved November 1, 2011, from www.cdc.gov/obesity/data/adult.html

Aguiar, P., Vala, J., Correia, I., & Pereira, C. (2008). Justice in our world and in that of others: Belief in a just world and reactions to victims. *Social Justice Research, 21*, 50–68.

Aiello, J. R., & Douthitt, E. A. (2001). Social facilitation from Triplett to electronic performance monitoring. *Group Dynamics: Theory, Research, and Practice, 5*, 163–180.

Ainsworth, M. D. S., Blehar, M. C., Waters, E., & Wall, S. (1978). *Patterns of attachment: A psychological study of the strange situation.* Hillsdale, NJ: Erlbaum.

Ajzen, I. (1985). From intentions to actions: A theory of planned behavior. In J. Kuhl & J. Beckmann (Eds.), *Action control: From cognition to behavior* (pp. 11–39). Heidelberg, Germany: Springer-Verlag.

Ajzen, I., & Fishbein, M. (1980). *Understanding attitudes and predicting social behavior*. Englewood Cliffs, NJ: Prentice Hall.

Ajzen, I., & Fishbein, M. (2005). The influence of attitudes on behavior. In D. Albarracín, B. T. Johnson, & M. P. Zanna (Eds.), *The handbook of attitudes* (pp. 173–221). Mahwah, NJ: Erlbaum.

Akert, R. M. (1998). *Terminating romantic relationships: The role of personal responsibility and gender*. Unpublished manuscript, Wellesley College, Wellesley, MA.

Akert, R. M., Cheek, J. M., Rutenberg, J., Ahern-Seronde, J., & Dautoff, R. (2010). *Social intelligence and nonverbal decoding ability*. Paper presented at the meeting of the Society for Personality and Social Psychology, Las Vegas, NV.

Akert, R. M., Chen, J., & Panter, A. T. (1991). *Facial prominence and stereotypes: The incidence and meaning of face-ism in print and television media*. Unpublished manuscript, Wellesley College, Wellesley, MA.

Aknin, L. B., Sandstrom, G. M., Dunn, E. W., & Norton, M. I. (2011). Investing in others: Prosocial spending for (pro)social change. In R. Biswas-Diener (Ed.), *Positive psychology as social change* (pp. 219–234). New York: Springer. doi:10.1007/978-90-481-9938-9_13

Akrami, N., Hedlund, L., & Ekehammar, B. (2007). Personality scale response latencies as self-schema indicators: The inverted-U effect revisited. *Personality and Individual Differences, 43*, 611–618.

Alaskan village copes with real-life impacts of global climate change. (2008, July 10). *Online News Hour*. Retrieved on December 30, 2008, from www.pbs.org/newshour/bb/environment/july-dec08/alaskawarming_07-10.html

Albarracín, D., Johnson, B. T., Fishbein, M., & Muellerleile, P. A. (2001). Theories of reasoned action and planned behavior as models of condom use: A meta-analysis. *Psychological Bulletin, 127*, 142–161.

Albarracín, D., & Wyer, R. S., Jr. (2001). Elaborative and nonelaborative processing of a behavior-related communication. *Personality and Social Psychology Bulletin, 27*, 691–705.

Allen, M., D'Alessio, D., & Brezgel, K. (1995). *A meta-analysis summarizing the effects of pornography:* Vol. 2. *Aggression after exposure*. Thousand Oaks, CA: Sage.

Allen, M., Donohue, W. A., & Griffin, A. (2003). Comparing the influence of parents and peers on the choice to use drugs. *Criminal Justice and Behavior, 30*, 163–186.

Allen, V. L. (1965). Situational factors in conformity. In L. Berkowitz (Ed.), *Advances in experimental social psychology* (Vol. 2, pp. 133–175). New York: Academic Press.

Allen, V. L., & Levine, J. M. (1969). Consensus and conformity. *Journal of Personality and Social Psychology, 5*, 389–399.

Almeida, D. (2005). Resilience and vulnerability to daily stressors assessed via diary methods. *Current Directions in Psychological Science, 14*, 64–68.

Allison, P. D. (1992). The cultural evolution of beneficent norms. *Social Forces, 71*, 279–301.

Allport, G. W. (1954). *The nature of prejudice*. Reading, MA: Addison-Wesley.

Allport, G. W. (1985). The historical background of social psychology. In G. Lindzey & E. Aronson (Eds.), *The handbook of social psychology* (3rd ed., Vol. 1, pp. 1–46). New York: McGraw-Hill.

Alter, A. L., & Darley, J. M. (2009). When the association between appearance and outcome contaminates social judgment: A bidirectional model linking group homogeneity and collective treatment. *Journal of Personality and Social Psychology, 9*, 776–795. doi:10.1037/a0016957

Altman, L. K. (2000, January 18). Mysterious illnesses often turn out to be mass hysteria. *The New York Times*, pp. D7, D12.

Alvarez, K., & Van Leeuwen, E. (2011). To teach or to tell? Consequences of receiving help from experts and peers. *European Journal of Social Psychology, 41*(3), 397–402. doi:10.1002/ejsp.789

Alvarez, L. (2003, June 22). Arranged marriages get a little rearranging. *The New York Times*, p. 3.

Amato, P. R. (1983). Helping behavior in urban and rural environments: Field studies based on a taxonomic organization of helping episodes. *Journal of Personality and Social Psychology, 45*, 571–586.

Ambady, N., Bernieri, F. J., & Richeson, J. A. (2000). Toward a histology of social behavior: Judgmental accuracy from thin slices of the behavioral stream. In M. P. Zanna (Ed.), *Advances in experimental social psychology* (Vol. 32, pp. 201–271). San Diego, CA: Academic Press.

Ambady, N., & Rosenthal, R. (1992). Thin slices of expressive behavior as predictors of interpersonal consequences: A meta-analysis. *Psychological Bulletin, 111*, 256–274.

Ambady, N., & Rosenthal, R. (1993). Half a minute: Predicting teacher evaluations from thin slices of nonverbal behavior and physical attractiveness. *Journal of Personality and Social Psychology, 64*, 431–441.

The American freshman: National norms for 2005. (2006). Higher Education Research Institute, UCLA. Retrieved June 22, 2006, from www.gseis.ucla.edu/heri/PDFs/ResearchBrief05.PDF

American Psychological Association. (2010). Ethical principles of psychologists and code of conduct. Retrieved March 22, 2010, from www.apa.org/ethics/code/index.aspx

Ames, D. R., & Flynn, F. J. (2007). What breaks a leader: The curvilinear relation between assertiveness and leadership. *Journal of Personality and Social Psychology, 92*, 307–324.

Amir, I. (1969). Contact hypothesis in ethnic relations. *Psychological Bulletin, 71*, 319–342.

Amir, I. (1976). The role of intergroup contact in change of prejudice and ethnic relations. In P. A. Katz (Ed.), *Towards the elimination of racism* (pp. 245–308). New York: Pergamon Press.

Amodio, D. M., & Showers, C. J. (2005). 'Similarity breeds liking' revisited: The moderating role of commitment. *Journal of Social and Personal Relationships, 22*, 817–836.

Andersen, B., Farrar, W. B., Golden-Kreutz, D. M., Glaser, R., Emery, C. F., & Crespin, T. R. (2004). Psychological, behavioral, and immune changes after a psychological intervention: A clinical trial. *Journal of Clinical Oncology, 22*, 3570–3580.

Andersen, S. M. (1984). Self-knowledge and social inference: II. The diagnosticity of cognitive/affective and behavioral data. *Journal of Personality and Social Psychology, 46*, 294–307.

Andersen, S. M., & Bem, S. L. (1981). Sex typing and androgyny in dyadic interaction: Individual differences in responsiveness to physical attractiveness. *Journal of Personality and Social Psychology, 41*, 74–86.

Andersen, S. M., & Klatzky, R. L. (1987). Traits and social stereotypes: Levels of categorization in person perception. *Journal of Personality and Social Psychology, 53*, 235–246.

Andersen, S. M., & Ross, L. D. (1984). Self-knowledge and social inference: I. The impact of cognitive/affective and behavioral data. *Journal of Personality and Social Psychology, 46*, 280–293.

Anderson, C. A. (1995). Implicit personality theories and empirical data: Biased assimilation, belief perseverance and change, and covariation detection sensitivity. *Social Cognition, 13*, 25–48.

Anderson, C. A. (1999). Attributional style, depression, and loneliness: A cross-cultural comparison of American and Chinese students. *Personality and Social Psychology Bulletin, 25*, 482–499.

Anderson, C. A. (2012). Climate change and violence. In D. J. Christie (Ed.), *The encyclopedia of peace psychology*. New York: Wiley-Blackwell.

Anderson, C. A., & Anderson, D. C. (1984). Ambient temperature and violent crime: Tests of the linear and curvilinear hypotheses. *Journal of Personality and Social Psychology, 46*, 91–97.

Anderson, C. A., Anderson, K. B., Dorr, N., DeNeve, K. M., & Flanagan, M. (2000). Temperature and aggression. In M. P. Zanna (Ed.), *Advances in experimental social psychology* (Vol. 32, pp. 63–133). San Diego, CA: Academic Press.

Anderson, C. A., Berkowitz, L., Donnerstein, E., Huesmann, L. R., Johnson, J. D., et al. (2003). The influence of media violence on youth. *Psychological Science in the Public Interest, 4*, 81–110.

Anderson, C. A., & Bushman, B. J. (1997). External validity of "trivial" experiments: The case of laboratory aggression. *Review of General Psychology, 1*, 19–41.

Anderson, C. A., Bushman, B. J., & Groom, R. W. (1997). Hot years and serious and deadly assault: Empirical tests of the heat hypothesis. *Journal of Personality and Social Psychology, 73*, 1213–1223.

Anderson, C. A., & Dill, K. E. (2000). Video games and aggressive thoughts, feelings, and behavior in the laboratory and in life. *Journal of Personality and Social Psychology, 78*, 772–790.

Anderson, C. A., Lepper, M. R., & Ross, L. (1980). The perseverance of social theories: The role of explanation in the persistence of discredited information. *Journal of Personality and Social Psychology, 39*, 1037–1049.

Anderson, C. S., Shibuya, A., Ihori, N., Swing, E. L., Bushman, B. J., Sakamoto, A., Rothstein, H. R., & Saleem, M. (2010). Violent video game effects on aggression, empathy, and prosocial behavior in Eastern and Western countries: A meta-analytic review. *Psychological Bulletin, 136*, 151–173.

Anderson, N. B. (1989). Racial differences in stress-induced cardiovascular reactivity and hypertension: Current status and substantive issues. *Psychological Bulletin, 105*, 89–105.

Anderson, U. S., Perea, E. F., Becker, D. V., Ackerman, J. M., Shapiro, J. R., Neuberg, S. L., & Kenrick, D. T. (2010). I only have eyes for you: Ovulation redirects attention (but not memory) to attractive men. *Journal of Experimental Social Psychology, 46*, 804–808.

Andrade, E. B., & Van Boven, L. (2010). Feelings not forgone: Underestimating affective reactions to what does not happen. *Psychological Science, 21*(5), 706–711.

Angier, N. (2006, January 3). The cute factor. *The New York Times*, pp. D1–D8.

Antoni, M. H., & Lutgendorf, S. (2007). Psychosocial factors and disease progression in cancer. *Current Directions in Psychological Science, 16*, 42–46.

The AP-GfK Poll. (2011, October). Retrieved February 13, 2012, from http://ap-gfkpoll.com/main/wp-content/uploads/2011/10/AP-GfK-Poll-October-2011-Topline-FINAL_2012-FIRST-Release-10-18.pdf

Archer, D. (1991). *A world of gestures: Culture and nonverbal communication* [Videotape and manual]. Berkeley: University of California Extension Center for Media and Independent Learning.

Archer, D. (1994). American violence: How high and why? *Law Studies, 19*, 12–20.

Archer, D. (1997a). Unspoken diversity: Cultural differences in gestures. *Qualitative Sociology, 20*, 79–105.

Archer, D. (1997b). *A world of differences: Understanding cross-cultural communication* [Videotape and manual]. Berkeley: University of California Extension Center for Media and Independent Learning.

Archer, D., & Akert, R. M. (1980). The encoding of meaning: A test of three theories of social interaction. *Sociological Inquiry, 50*, 393–419.

Archer, D., & Akert, R. M. (1984). Problems of context and criterion in nonverbal communication: A new look at the accuracy issue. In M. Cook (Ed.), *Issues in person perception* (pp. 114–144). New York: Methuen.

Archer, D., Iritani, B., Kimes, D. D., & Barrios, M. (1983). Face-ism: Five studies of sex differences in facial prominence. *Journal of Personality and Social Psychology, 45*, 725–735.

Archer, D., & McDaniel, P. (1995). Violence and gender: Differences and similarities across societies. In R. B. Ruback & N. A. Weiner (Eds.), *Interpersonal violent behaviors: Social and cultural aspects* (pp. 63–88). New York: Springer-Verlag.

Archer, J. (2004). Sex differences in aggression in real-world settings: A meta-analytic review. *Review of General Psychology, 8*, 291–322.

Archer, J., & Coyne, S. M. (2005). An integrated review of indirect, relational, and social aggression. *Personality and Social Psychology Review, 9*, 212–230.

Arendt, H. (1965). *Eichmann in Jerusalem: A report on the banality of evil.* New York: Viking.

Argyle, M. (1975). *Bodily communication*. New York: International Universities Press.

Argyle, M. (1986). Rules for social relationships in four cultures. *Australian Journal of Psychology, 38*, 309–318.

Arkes, H. R., & Mellers, B. A. (2002). Do juries meet our expectations? *Law and Human Behavior, 26*, 625–639.

Arkin, R. M., & Maruyama, G. M. (1979). Attribution, affect, and college exam performance. *Journal of Educational Psychology, 71*, 85–93.

Arkin, R. M., & Oleson, K. C. (1998). Self-handicapping. In J. M. Darley & J. Cooper (Eds.), *Attribution and social interaction: The legacy of Edward E. Jones* (pp. 313–341). Washington, DC: American Psychological Association.

Arms, R. L., Russell, G. W., & Sandilands, M. L. (1979). Effects on the hostility of spectators of viewing aggressive sports. *Social Psychology Quarterly, 42*, 275–279.

Arnett, J. (1995). The young and the reckless: Adolescent reckless behavior. *Current Directions in Psychological Science, 4*, 67–71.

Aron, A., & Aron, E. N. (1996). Self and self-expansion in relationships. In G. J. O. Fletcher & J. Fitness (Eds.), *Knowledge structures in close relationships: A social psychological approach* (pp. 325–344). Mahwah, NJ: Erlbaum.

Aron, A., Aron, E. N., & Norman, C. (2004). Self-expansion model of motivation and cognition in close relationships and beyond. In M. B. Brewer & M. Hewstone (Eds.), *Self and social identity* (pp. 99–123) Malden, MA: Blackwell Publishing.

Aron, A., Dutton, D. G., Aron, E. N., & Iverson, A. (1989). Experiences of falling in love. *Journal of Social and Personal Relationships, 6*, 243–257.

Aron, A., Fisher, H., Mashek, D. J., Strong, G., Li, H., & Brown, L. L. (2005). Reward, motivation, and emotion systems associated with early-stage intense romantic love. *Journal of Neurophysiology, 94*, 327–337.

Aron, A. P., Mashek, D. J., & Aron, E. N. (2004). Closeness as including other in the self. In D. J. Mashek & A. Aron (Eds.), *Handbook of closeness and intimacy* (pp. 27–42). Mahwah, NJ: Erlbaum.

Aron, A., & Rodriguez, G. (1992). Scenarios of falling in love among Mexican, Chinese, and Anglo-Americans. In A. Aron (Chair), *Ethnic and cultural differences in love*. Symposium conducted at the Sixth International Conference on Personal Relationships, Orono, ME.

Aron, A., & Westbay, L. (1996). Dimensions of the prototype of love. *Journal of Personality and Social Psychology, 70*, 535–551.

Aronson, E. (1969). The theory of cognitive dissonance: A current perspective. In L. Berkowitz (Ed.), *Advances in experimental social psychology* (Vol. 4, pp. 1–34). New York: Academic Press.

Aronson, E. (1978). *The jigsaw classroom.* Beverly Hills, CA: Sage.

Aronson, E. (1997). The theory of cognitive dissonance: The evolution and vicissitudes of an idea. In C. McGarty & S. A. Haslam (Eds.), *The message of social psychology: Perspectives on mind in society* (pp. 20–35). Malden, MA: Blackwell.

Aronson, E. (1998). Dissonance, hypocrisy, and the self-concept. In E. Harmon-Jones & J. S. Mills (Eds.), *Cognitive dissonance theory: Revival with revisions and controversies* (pp. 21–36). Washington, DC: American Psychological Association.

Aronson, E. (1999). *The social animal* (8th ed.). New York: Worth/Freeman.

Aronson, E. (2000). *Nobody left to hate: Teaching compassion after Columbine.* New York: Worth/Freeman.

Aronson, E. (2002). Drifting my own way: Following my nose and my heart. In R. Sternberg (Ed.), *Psychologists defying the crowd: Stories of those who battled the establishment and won* (pp. 132–148). Washington, DC: American Psychological Association.

Aronson, E. (2007). The evolution of cognitive dissonance theory: A personal appraisal. In A. Pratkanis, *The science of social influence*. New York: Psychology Press.

Aronson, E. (2008) *The social animal* (11th ed.). New York: W. H. Freeman.

Aronson, E. (2010a). Fear, denial, and sensible action in the face of disasters. *Social Research.*

Aronson, E. (2010b). *Not by chance alone: My life as a social psychologist*. New York: Basic Books.

Aronson, E. (2012). *The social animal.* New York: W. H. Freeman.

Aronson, E., & Bridgeman, D. (1979). Jigsaw groups and the desegregated classroom: In pursuit of common goals. *Personality and Social Psychology Bulletin, 5*, 438–446.

Aronson, E., & Carlsmith, J. M. (1962). Performance expectancy as a determinant of actual performance. *Journal of Abnormal and Social Psychology, 65*, 178–182.

Aronson, E., & Carlsmith, J. M. (1963). Effect of severity of threat in the devaluation of forbidden behavior. *Journal of Abnormal and Social Psychology, 66*, 584–588.

Aronson, E., & Carlsmith, J. M. (1968). Experimentation in social psychology. In G. Lindzey & E. Aronson (Eds.), *The handbook of social psychology* (Vol. 2, pp. 1–79). Reading, MA: Addison-Wesley.

Aronson, E., Ellsworth, P. C., Carlsmith, J. M., & Gonzalez, M. H. (1990). *Methods of research in social psychology* (2nd ed.). New York: McGraw-Hill.

Aronson, E., Fried, C., & Stone, J. (1991). Overcoming denial and increasing the intention to use condoms through the induction of hypocrisy. *American Journal of Public Health, 81*, 1636–1638.

Aronson, E., & Gonzalez, A. (1988). Desegregation, jigsaw, and the Mexican-American experience. In P. A. Katz & D. Taylor (Eds.), *Towards the elimination of racism: Profiles in controversy* (pp. 310–330). New York: Plenum.

Aronson, E., & Linder, D. (1965) Gain and loss of esteem as determinants of interpersonal attractiveness. *Journal of Experimental Social Psychology, 1, 156–171.*

Aronson, E., & Mettee, D. (1968). Dishonest behavior as a function of differential levels of induced self-esteem. *Journal of Personality and Social Psychology, 9*, 121–127.

Aronson, E., & Mills, J. S. (1959). The effect of severity of initiation on liking for a group. *Journal of Abnormal and Social Psychology, 59*, 177–181.

Aronson, E., & Patnoe, S. (1997). *Cooperation in the classroom: The jigsaw method.* New York: Longman.

Aronson, E., Stephan, C., Sikes, J., Blaney, N., & Snapp, M. (1978). *The jigsaw classroom.* Beverly Hills, CA: Sage.

Aronson, E., & Thibodeau, R. (1992). The jigsaw classroom: A cooperative strategy for reducing prejudice. In J. Lynch, C. Modgil, & S. Modgil (Eds.), *Cultural diversity in the schools* (pp. 110–118). London: Falmer Press.

Aronson, E., Wilson, T. D., & Brewer, M. B. (1998). Experimental methods. In D. T. Gilbert, S. T. Fiske, & G. Lindzey (Eds.), *The handbook of social psychology* (4th ed., Vol. 1, pp. 99–142). New York: McGraw-Hill.

Aronson, J. (2009). Jigsaw, social psychology, and the nurture of human intelligence. In *The scientist and the humanist: A festschrift in honor of Elliot Aronson*. New York: Taylor & Francis.

Aronson, J., Fried, C. B., & Good, C. (2002). Reducing the effects of stereotype threat on African American college students by shaping theories of intelligence. *Journal of Experimental Social Psychology, 38*, 113–125.

Aronson, J., & Williams, J. (2009). *Stereotype threat: Forewarned is forearmed.* Manuscript under review.

Aronson, J. M., Cohen, G., & Nail, P. R. (1999). Self-affirmation theory: An update and appraisal. In E. Harmon-Jones & J. S. Mills (Eds.), *Cognitive dissonance: Progress on a pivotal theory in social psychology* (pp. 127–147). Washington, DC: American Psychological Association.

Aronson, J. M., Lustina, M. J., Good, C., Keough, K., Steele, C. M., & Brown, J. (1999). When white men can't do math: Necessary and sufficient factors in stereotype threat. *Journal of Experimental Social Psychology, 35*, 29–46.

Asch, S. E. (1946). Forming impressions of personality. *Journal of Abnormal and Social Psychology, 41*, 258–290.

Asch, S. E. (1951). Effects of group pressure upon the modification and distortion of judgment. In H. Guetzkow (Ed.), *Groups, leadership, and men* (pp. 76–92). Pittsburgh, PA: Carnegie Press.

Asch, S. E. (1955). Opinions and social pressure. *Scientific American, 193*, 31–35.

Asch, S. E. (1956). Studies of independence and conformity: A minority of one against a unanimous majority. *Psychological Monographs*, 7 (9, Whole No. 416).

Asch, S. E. (1957). An experimental investigation of group influence. In Walter Reed Army Institute of Research, *Symposium on preventive and social psychiatry* (pp. 15–17). Washington, DC: U.S. Government Printing Office.

Ashmore, R. D., & Longo, L. C. (1995). Accuracy of stereotypes: What research on physical attractiveness can teach us. In Y.-T. Lee, L. J. Jussim, & C. R. McCauley (Eds.), *Stereotype accuracy: Toward appreciating group difference* (pp. 63–86). Washington, DC: American Psychological Association.

Aspinwall, L. G., & Taylor, S. E. (1993). Effects of social comparison direction, threat, and self-esteem on affect, evaluation, and expected success. *Journal of Personality and Social Psychology, 64*, 708–722.

Aspinwall, L. G., & Taylor, S. E. (1997). A stitch in time: Self-regulation and proactive coping. *Psychological Bulletin, 121*, 417–436.

Associated Press. (2002, November 1). "Halloween is debated by French." *The Boston Globe*, p. A20.

Aune, K. S., & Aune, R. K. (1996). Cultural differences in the self-reported experience and expression of emotions in relationships. *Journal of Cross-Cultural Psychology, 27*, 67–81.

Avolio, B. J., Walumbwa, F. O., & Weber, T. J. (2009). Leadership: Current theories, research, and future directions. *Annual Review of Psychology*, 60, 421–449.

Axelrod, R. (1984). *The evolution of cooperation*. New York: Basic Books.

Ayman, R. (2002). Contingency model of leadership effectiveness. In L. L. Neider & C. A. Schriesheim (Eds.), *Leadership* (pp. 197–228). Greenwich, CT: Information Age.

Ayman, R., & Korabik, K. (2010). Leadership: Why gender and culture matter. *American Psychologist, 65*(3), 157–170. doi:10.1037/a0018806

Azrin, N. H. (1967, May). Pain and aggression. *Psychology Today*, pp. 27–33.

Badr, L. K., & Abdallah, B. (2001). Physical attractiveness of premature infants affects outcome at discharge from the NICU. *Infant Behavior and Development, 24*, 129–133.

Bailey, D. S., & Taylor, S. P. (1991). *Journal of research in personality, 25*(3), 334–342.

Baldwin, M. W., Keelan, J. P. R., Fehr, B., Enns, V., & Koh-Rangarajoo, E. (1996). Social-cognitive conceptualizations of attachment working models: Availability and accessibility effects. *Journal of Personality and Social Psychology, 71*, 94–109.

Banaji, M. R., & Heiphetz, L. (2010). Attitudes. In S. T. Fiske, D. T. Gilbert, & G. Lindzey (Eds.), *Handbook of social psychology* (5th ed., Vol. 1, pp. 353–393). Hoboken, NJ: Wiley.

Bandura, A. (1973). *Aggression: A social learning analysis*. Englewood Cliffs, NJ: Prentice Hall.

Bandura, A., Ross, D., & Ross, S. (1961). Transmission of aggression through imitation of aggressive models. *Journal of Abnormal and Social Psychology, 63*, 575–582.

Bandura, A., Ross, D., & Ross, S. (1963). Imitation of film-mediated aggressive models. *Journal of Abnormal and Social Psychology, 66*, 3–11.

Banerjee, R., & Dittmar, H. (2008). Individual differences in children's materialism: The role of peer relations. *Personality and Social Psychology Bulletin, 34*, 17–31.

Banks, T., & Dabbs, J. M., Jr. (1996). Salivary testosterone and cortisol in delinquent and violent urban subculture. *Journal of Social Psychology, 136*, 49–56.

Bar, M., Neta, M., & Linz, H. (2006). Very first impressions. *Emotion, 6*, 269–278.

Bar-Anan, Y., Wilson, T. D., & Hassin, R. R. (2010). Inaccurate self-knowledge formation as a result of automatic behavior. *Journal of Experimental Social Psychology, 46*(6), 884–894. doi:10.1016/j.jesp.2010.07.007

Barber, N. (1998). Secular changes in standards of bodily attractiveness in American women: Different masculine and feminine ideals. *Journal of Psychology, 132*, 87–94.

Bargh, J. A. (1996). Automaticity in social psychology. In E. T. Higgins & A. W. Kruglanski (Eds.), *Social psychology: Handbook of basic principles* (pp. 169–183). New York: Guilford Press.

Bargh, J. A., & Ferguson, M. J. (2000). Beyond behaviorism: On the automaticity of higher mental processes. *Psychological Bulletin, 126*, 925–945.

Bargh, J. A., Gollwitzer, P. M., Lee-Chai, A., Barndollar, K., & Trötschel, R. (2001). The automated will: Nonconscious activation and pursuit of behavioral goals. *Journal of Personality and Social Psychology, 81*, 1014–1027.

Bargh, J. A., & Morsella, E. (2008). The unconscious mind. *Perspectives on Psychological Science, 3*, 73–79.

Bargh, J. A., & Pietromonaco, P. (1982). Automatic information processing and social perception: The influence of trait information presented outside of conscious awareness on impression formation. *Journal of Personality and Social Psychology, 43*, 437–449.

Barker, R., Dembo, T., & Lewin, K. (1941). Frustration and aggression: An experiment with young children. *University of Iowa Studies in Child Welfare, 18*, 1–314.

Barley, S. R., & Bechky, B. A. (1994). In the backrooms of science: The work of technicians in science labs. *Work and Occupations, 21*, 85–126.

Baron, R. A. (1972). Reducing the influence of an aggressive model: The restraining effects of peer censure. *Journal of Experimental Social Psychology, 8*, 266–275.

Baron, R. A. (1976). The reduction of human aggression: A field study on the influence of incompatible responses. *Journal of Applied Social Psychology, 6*, 95–104.

Baron, R. A. (1988). Negative effects of destructive criticism: Impact on conflict, self-efficacy, and task performance. *Journal of Applied Psychology, 73*, 199–207.

Baron, R. A. (1990). Countering the effects of destructive criticism: The relative efficacy of four interventions. *Journal of Applied Psychology, 75*, 235–245.

Baron, R. A. (1997). The sweet smell of . . . helping: Effects of pleasant ambient fragrance on prosocial behavior in shopping malls. *Personality and Social Psychology Bulletin, 23*, 498–503.

Baron, R. A., & Richardson, D. R. (1994). *Human aggression* (2nd ed.). New York: Plenum.

Baron, R. M., & Misovich, S. J. (1993). Dispositional knowing from an ecological perspective. *Personality and Social Psychology Bulletin, 19*, 541–552.

Baron, R. S. (1986). Distraction/conflict theory: Progress and problems. In L. Berkowitz (Ed.), *Advances in experimental social psychology* (Vol. 19, pp. 1–40). Orlando, FL: Academic Press.

Baron, R. S. (2005). So right it's wrong: Groupthink and the ubiquitous nature of polarized group decision making. In M. P. Zanna (Ed.), *Advances in experimental social psychology* (Vol. 37, pp. 219–253). San Diego, CA: Academic Press.

Baron, R. S., Vandello, J. A., & Brunsman, B. (1996). The forgotten variable in conformity research: Impact of task importance on social influence. *Journal of Personality and Social Psychology, 71*, 915–927.

Barrouquere, B. (2006, June 15). "A call, a hoax, a nationwide search for the man on the phone." Associated Press. Retrieved August 25, 2006, from 0-web.lexis-nexis.com

Bartholomew, R. E., & Wessely, S. (2002). Protean nature of mass sociogenic illness: From possessed nuns to chemical and biological terrorism. *British Journal of Psychiatry, 180*, 300–306.

Bartlett, F. C. (1932). *Remembering*. Cambridge, UK: Cambridge University Press.

Bartlett, M. Y., & DeSteno, D. (2006). Gratitude and prosocial behavior: Helping when it costs you. *Psychological Science, 17*, 319–325.

Bass, B. M. (1990). *Bass and Stogdill's handbook of leadership: Theory, research, and managerial applications* (3rd ed.). New York: Free Press.

Bass, B. M. (1998). *Transformational leadership: Industry, military, and educational impact*. Mahwah, NJ: Erlbaum.

Bass, E., & Davis, L. (1994). *The courage to heal: A guide for women survivors of childhood sexual abuse* (3rd ed.). New York: HarperCollins.

Batson, C. D. (1991). *The altruism question: Toward a social-psychological answer*. Hillsdale, NJ: Erlbaum.

Batson, C. D. (1993). Communal and exchange relationships: What's the difference? *Personality and Social Psychology Bulletin, 19*, 677–683.

Batson, C. D. (1998). Altruism and prosocial behavior. In D. T. Gilbert, S. T. Fiske, & G. Lindzey (Eds.), *The handbook of social psychology* (4th ed., Vol. 2, pp. 282–316). New York: McGraw-Hill.

Batson, C. D. (2011). *Altruism in humans*. New York: Oxford University Press.

Batson, C. D., Ahmad, N., Lishner, D. A., & Tsang, J. (2002). Empathy and altruism. In C. R. Snyder & S. J. Lopez (Eds.), *Handbook of positive psychology* (pp. 485–498). New York: Oxford University Press.

Batson, C. D., Ahmad, N., & Stocks, E. L. (2004). Benefits and liabilities of empathy-induced altruism. In A. G. Miller (Ed.), *The social psychology of good and evil* (pp. 359–385). New York: Guilford.

Batson, C. D., Ahmad, N., & Stocks, E. L. (2011). Four forms of prosocial motivation: Egoism, altruism, collectivism, and principlism. In D. Dunning (Ed.), *Frontiers of social psychology. Social motivation* (pp. 103–126). New York: Psychology Press.

Batson, C. D., Coke, J. S., Jasnoski, M. L., & Hanson, M. (1978). Buying kindness: Effect of an extrinsic incentive for helping on perceived altruism. *Personality and Social Psychology Bulletin, 4*, 86–91.

Batson, C. D., Polycarpou, M. P., Harmon-Jones, E., Imhoff, H. J., Mitchener, E. C., Bednar, L. L., Klein, T. R., & Highberger, L. (1997). Empathy and attitudes: Can feeling for a member of a stigmatized group improve feelings toward the group? *Journal of Personality and Social Psychology, 72*, 105–118.

Batson, C. D., & Powell, A. A. (2003). Altruism and prosocial behavior. In T. Millon & M. J. Lerner (Eds.), *Handbook of psychology: Personality and social psychology* (Vol. 5, pp. 463–484). New York: Wiley.

Batson, C. D., Sager, K., Garst, E., Kang, M., Rubchinsky, K., & Dawson, K. (1997). Is empathy-induced helping due to self-other merging? *Journal of Personality and Social Psychology, 73*, 495–509.

Batson, C. D., Schoenrade, P., & Ventis, W. L. (1993). *Religion and the individual*. New York: Oxford University Press.

Battle for your brain. (1991, August). *Consumer Reports*, pp. 520–521.

Bauer, I., & Wrosch, C. (2011). Making up for lost opportunities: The protective role of downward social comparisons for coping with regrets across adulthood. *Personality and Social Psychology Bulletin, 37*, 215–228. doi:10.1177/0146167210393256

Bauer, I. M., & Baumeister, R. F. (2011). Self-regulatory strength. In K. D. Vohs & R. F. Baumeister (Eds.), *Handbook of self-regulation: Research, theory, and applications* (2nd ed., pp. 64–82). New York: Guilford.

Baumeister, R., Vohs, K., & Tice, D. (2007). The strength model of self-control. *Current Directions in Psychological Science, 16*, 351–355.

Baumeister, R. F. (1986). *Identity: Cultural change and the struggle for self*. New York: Oxford University Press.

Baumeister, R. F. (1991). *Escaping the self: Alcoholism, spirituality, masochism, and other flights from the burden of selfhood*. New York: Basic Books.

Baumeister, R. F., Campbell, J. D., Krueger, J. I., & Vohs, K. D. (2003). Does high self-esteem cause better performance, interpersonal success, happiness, or healthier lifestyles? *Psychological Science in the Public Interest, 4*, 1–44. doi:10.1111/1529-1006.01431

Baumeister, R. F., & Hetherington, T. F. (1996). Self-regulation failure: An overview. *Psychological Inquiry, 7*, 1–15.

Baumeister, R. F., & Leary, M. R. (1995). The need to belong: Desire for interpersonal attachment as a fundamental human motivation. *Psychological Bulletin, 117*, 497–529.

Baumeister, R. F., & Masicampo, E. J. (2010). Conscious thought is for facilitating social and cultural interactions: How mental simulations serve the animal–culture interface. *Psychological Review, 117*(3), 945–971. doi:10.1037/a0019393

Baumeister, R. F., Masicampo, E. J., & Vohs, K. D. (2011). Can consciousness cause behavior? *Annual Review of Psychology, 62*, 331–361.

Baumeister, R. F., Mele, A. R., & Vohs, K. D. (Eds.). (2010). *Free will and consciousness: How might they work?* New York: Oxford University Press.

Baumeister, R. F., Schmeichel, B. J., & Vohs, K. D. (2007). Self-regulation and the executive function: The self as controlling agent. In E. T. Higgins & A. W. Kruglanski (Eds.), *Social psychology: Handbook of basic principles* (2nd ed., pp. 516–534). New York: Guilford.

Baumeister, R. F., & Sommer, K. L. (1997). What do men want? Gender differences and two spheres of belongingness: Comment on Cross and Madson (1997). *Psychological Bulletin, 122*, 38–44.

Baumeister, R. F., Stillwell, A. M., & Heatherton, T. F. (1994). Guilt: An interpersonal approach. *Psychological Bulletin, 115*, 243–267.

Baumgardner, A. H., Lake, E. A., & Arkin, R. M. (1985). Claiming mood as a self-handicap. *Personality and Social Psychology Bulletin, 11*, 349–357.

Baxter, L. A. (1986). Gender differences in the heterosexual relationship rules embedded in break-up accounts. *Journal of Social and Personal Relationships, 3*, 289–306.

Bayat, M. (2011). Clarifying issues regarding the use of praise with young children. *Topics in Early Childhood Special Education, 31*, 121–128. doi:10.1177/0271121410389339

Beach, S. R. H., Tesser, A., Mendolia, M., & Anderson, P. (1996). Self-evaluation maintenance in marriage: Toward a performance ecology of the marital relationship. *Journal of Family Psychology, 10*, 379–396.

Beaman, A. L., Barnes, P. J., Klentz, B., & McQuirk, B. (1978). Increasing helping rates through informational dissemination: Teaching pays. *Personality and Social Psychology Bulletin, 4*, 406–411.

Beaman, A. L., Klentz, B., Diener, E., & Svanum, S. (1979). Objective self-awareness and transgression in children: A field study. *Journal of Personality and Social Psychology, 37*, 1835–1846.

Beauvois, J., & Joule, R. (1996). *A radical dissonance theory*. London: Taylor & Francis.

Becker, D. V., Kenrick, D. T., Neuberg, S. L., Blackwell, K. C., & Smith, D. M. (2007). The confounded nature of angry men and happy women. *Journal of Personality and Social Psychology, 92*, 179–190.

Beckett, K., Nyrop, K., & Pfingst, L. (2006). *Race, drugs, and policing: Understanding disparities in drug delivery arrests. Criminology, 44*, 105–137.

Beer, J., & Ochsner, K. (2006). Social cognition: A multi level analysis. *Brain Research, 1079*, 98–105.

Bègue, L., Subra, B., Arvers, P., Muller, D., Bricout, V., & Zorman, M. (2009). A message in a bottle: Extrapharmacological effects of alcohol on aggression. *Journal of Experimental Social Psychology, 45*, 137–142.

Bell, J. (1995). Notions of love and romance among the Taita of Kenya. In W. Jankowiak (Ed.), *Romantic passion: A universal experience?* (pp. 152–165). New York: Columbia University Press.

Bell, S. T., Kuriloff, P. J., & Lottes, I. (1994). Understanding attributions of blame in stranger-rape and date-rape situations: An examination of gender, race, identification, and students' social perceptions of rape victims. *Journal of Applied Social Psychology, 24*, 1719–1734.

Bem, D. J. (1972). Self-perception theory. In L. Berkowitz (Ed.), *Advances in experimental social psychology* (Vol. 6, pp. 1–62). New York: Academic Press.

Bem, D. J., and McConnell, H. K. (1970). Testing the self-perception explanation of dissonance phenomena: On the salience of premanipulation attitudes. *Journal of Personality and Social Psychology* 1970, Vol. 14, No. 1, 23–31.

Bender, B. (2003, June 15). Scandals rock military academies. *Boston Globe*, p. A10.

Bergeron, N., & Schneider, B. H. (2005). Explaining cross-national differences in peer-directed aggression: A quantitative synthesis. *Aggressive Behavior, 31*, 116–137.

Berke, R. L. (2000, September 12). Democrats see, and smell, "rats" in GOP ad. *New York Times on the Web*, www.nytimes.com

Berkman, L. F., & Syme, S. L. (1979). Social networks, host resistance, and mortality: A nine-year follow-up study of Alameda County residents. *American Journal of Epidemiology, 109*, 186–204.

Berkow, J. H. (1989). *Darwin, sex, and status: Biological approaches to mind and culture*. Toronto, Ontario, Canada: University of Toronto Press.

Berkowitz, L. (1962). *Aggression: A social psychological analysis*. New York: McGraw-Hill.

Berkowitz, L. (1968, September). Impulse, aggression, and the gun. *Psychology Today*, pp. 18–22.

Berkowitz, L. (1978). Whatever happened to the frustration-aggression hypothesis? *American Behavioral Scientist, 21*, 691–708.

Berkowitz, L. (1983). Aversively simulated aggression. *American Psychologist, 38*, 1135–1144.

Berkowitz, L. (1989). Frustration-aggression hypothesis: Examination and reformulation. *Psychological Bulletin, 106*, 59–73.

Berkowitz, L. (1993). *Aggression: Its causes, consequences, and control*. New York: McGraw-Hill.

Berkowitz, L., & Le Page, A. (1967). Weapons as aggression-eliciting stimuli. *Journal of Personality and Social Psychology, 7*, 202–207.

Bermeitinger, C., Goelz, R., Johr, N., Neumann, M., Ecker, U. K. H., & Doerr, R. (2009). The hidden persuaders break into the tired brain. *Journal of Experimental Social Psychology, 45*(2), 320–326. doi:10.1016/j.jesp.2008.10.001

Berns, G. S., Chappelow, J., Zink, C. F., Pagnoni, G., Martin-Skurski, M. E., & Richards, J. (2005). Neurobiological correlates of social conformity and independence during mental rotation. *Biological Psychiatry, 58*, 245–253.

Berry, D. S. (1995). Beyond beauty and after affect: An event perception approach to perceiving faces. In R. A. Eder (Ed.), *Craniofacial anomalies: Psychological perspectives* (pp. 14–29). New York: Springer-Verlag.

Berry, J. W. (1967). Independence and conformity in subsistence-level societies. *Journal of Personality and Social Psychology, 7*, 415–418.

Berscheid, E. (1985). Interpersonal attraction. In G. Lindzey & E. Aronson (Eds.), *The handbook of social psychology* (3rd ed., Vol. 3, pp. 413–484). New York: McGraw-Hill.

Berscheid, E., Boye, D., & Walster, E. (1968). Retaliation as a means of restoring equity. *Journal of Personality and Social Psychology, 10*, 370–376.

Berscheid, E., & Meyers, S. A. (1996). A social categorical approach to a question about love. *Personal Relationships, 3*, 19–43.

Berscheid, E., & Meyers, S. A. (1997). The language of love: The difference a preposition makes. *Personality and Social Psychology Bulletin, 23*, 347–362.

Berscheid, E., & Peplau, L. A. (1983). The emerging science of relationships. In H. H. Kelley, E. Berscheid, A. Christensen, J. H. Harvey, T. L. Huston, G. Levinger, E. McClintock, L. A. Peplau, & D. R. Peterson (Eds.), *Close relationships* (pp. 1–19). New York: Freeman.

Berscheid, E., & Reis, H. T. (1998). Attraction and close relationships. In D. T. Gilbert, S. T. Fiske, & G. Lindzey (Eds.), *The handbook of social psychology* (4th ed., Vol. 2, pp. 193–281). New York: McGraw-Hill.

Berscheid, E., & Walster, E. (1978). *Interpersonal attraction*. Reading, MA: Addison-Wesley.

Bettencourt, B. A., & Miller, N. (1996). Gender differences in aggression as a function of provocation: A meta-analysis. *Psychological Bulletin, 119*, 422–447.

Bettencourt, B. A., & Sheldon, K. (2001). Social roles as mechanism for psychological need satisfaction within social groups. *Journal of Personality and Social Psychology, 81*, 1131–1143.

Bickman, L. (1974). The social power of a uniform. *Journal of Applied Social Psychology, 4*, 47–61.

Biehl, M., Matsumoto, D., Ekman, P., Hearn, V., Heider, K., Kudoh, T., & Ton, V. (1997). Matsumoto and Ekman's Japanese and Caucasian facial expressions of emotion (JACFEE): Reliability and cross-national differences. *Journal of Nonverbal Behavior, 21*, 3–21.

Biek, M., Wood, W., & Chaiken, S. (1996). Working knowledge, cognitive processing, and attitudes: On the determinants of bias. *Personality and Social Psychology Bulletin, 22*, 547–556.

Biesanz, J. C., Neuberg, S. L., Smith, D. M., Asher, T., & Judice, T. N. (2001). When accuracy-motivated perceivers fail: Limited attentional resources and the reemerging self-fulfilling prophecy. *Personality and Social Psychology Bulletin, 27*, 621–629.

Bishop, D. I., Meyer, B. C., Schmidt, T. M., & Gray, B. R. (2009). Differential investment behavior between grandparents and grandchildren: The role of paternity uncertainty. *Evolutionary Psychology, 7*(1), 66–77.

Blackhart, G. C., Nelson, B. C., Knowles, M. L., & Baumeister, R. F. (2009). Rejection elicits emotional reactions but neither causes immediate distress nor lowers self-esteem: A meta-analytic review of 192 studies on social exclusion. *Personality and Social Psychology Review, 13*(4), 269–309. doi:10.1177/1088868309346065

Blakemore, J. E. O., Berenbaum, S. A., & Liben, L. S. (2009). *Gender development*. New York: Psychology Press.

Blanton, H., Buunk, B. P., Gibbons, F. X., & Kuyper, H. (1999). When better-than-others compare upward: Choice of comparison and comparative evaluation as independent predictors of academic performance. *Journal of Personality and Social Psychology, 76*, 420–430.

Blascovich, J., Ginsburg, G. P., & Veach, T. L. (1975). A pluralistic explanation of choice shifts on the risk dimension. *Journal of Personality and Social Psychology, 31*, 422–429.

Blascovich, J., Mendes, W. B., Hunter, S. B., & Salomon, K. (1999). Social "facilitation" as challenge and threat. *Journal of Personality and Social Psychology, 77*, 68–77.

Blass, T. (1991). Understanding behavior in the Milgram obedience experiment. *Journal of Personality and Social Psychology, 60*, 398–413.

Blass, T. (2000). *Obedience to authority: Current perspectives on the Milgram paradigm*. Mahwah, NJ: Erlbaum.

Blass, T. (2003). The Milgram paradigm after 35 years: Some things we now know about obedience to authority. *Journal of Applied Social Psychology, 29*, 955–978.

Blau, P. M. (1964). *Exchange and power in social life*. New York: Wiley.

Bless, H., Strack, F., & Walther, E. (2001). Memory as a target of social influence? Memory distortions as a function of social influence and metacognitive knowledge. In J. P. Forgas & W. D. Kipling (Eds.), *Social influence: Direct and indirect processes* (pp. 167–183). Philadelphia: Psychology Press.

Blow, C. (2011, June 11). Drug bust. *The New York Times*. Op-ed page.

Bochner, S. (1994). Cross-cultural differences in the self-concept: A test of Hofstede's individualism/collectivism distinction. *Journal of Cross-Cultural Psychology, 25*, 273–283.

Bodenhausen, G. V. (1988). Stereotypic biases in social decision making and memory: Testing process models of stereotype use. *Journal of Personality and Social Psychology, 55*, 726–737.

Bodenhausen, G. V., & Wyer, R. S., Jr. (1985). Effects of stereotypes on decision making and information processing strategies. *Journal of Personality and Social Psychology, 48*, 267–282.

Boduroglu, A., Shah, P., & Nisbett, R. E. (2009). Cultural differences in allocation of attention in visual information processing. *Journal of Cross-Cultural Psychology, 40*(3), 349–360. doi:10.1177/0022022108331005

Bohner, G., & Dickel, N. (2011). Attitudes and attitude change. *Annual Review of Psychology, 62*, 391–417. doi:10.1146/annurev.psych.121208.131609

Bolger, N., & Amarel, D. (2007). Effects of social support visibility on adjustment to stress: Experimental evidence. *Journal of Personality and Social Psychology, 92*, 458–475.

Bolger, N., Zuckerman, A., & Kessler, R. C. (2000). Invisible support and adjustment to stress. *Journal of Personality and Social Psychology, 79*, 953–961.

Bonanno, G. A. (2004). Loss, trauma, and human resilience: Have we underestimated the human capacity to thrive after extremely aversive events. *American Psychologist, 59*, 20–28.

Bonanno, G. A. (2005). Resilience in the face of potential trauma. *Current Directions in Psychological Science, 14*, 135–138.

Bonanno, G., A., Boerner, K., & Wortman, C. (2008). Trajectories of grieving. In M. S. Stroebe, R. O. Hansson, H. Schut, W. Stroebe, & E. Van den Blink (Eds.), *Handbook of bereavement research and practice: Advances in theory and intervention* (pp. 287–307). Washington, DC: American Psychological Association.

Bonanno, G. A., Moskowitz, J. T., Papa, A., & Folkman, S. (2005). Resilience to loss in bereaved spouses, bereaved parents, and bereaved gay men. *Journal of Personality and Social Psychology, 88*, 827–843.

Bonanno, G. A., Westphal, M., & Mancini, A. D. (2011). Resilience to loss and potential trauma. *Annual Review of Clinical Psychology, 7*, 511–535. doi:10.1146/annurev-clinpsy-032210-104526

Bond, C. F., Jr., Atoum, A. O., & Van Leeuwen, M. D. (1996). Social impairment of complex learning in the wake of public embarrassment. *Basic and Applied Social Psychology, 18*, 31–44.

Bond, C. F., Jr., & DePaulo, B. M. (2006). Accuracy of deception judgments. *Personality and Social Psychology Review, 10*, 214–234.

Bond, C. F., & DePaulo, B. (2008). Individual differences in judging deception: Accuracy and bias. *Psychological Bulletin, 134*, 477–492.

Bond, C. F., Jr., & Titus, L. J. (1983). Social facilitation: A meta-analysis of 241 studies. *Psychological Bulletin, 94*, 264–292.

Bond, M. H. (Ed.). (1988). *The cross-cultural challenge to social psychology*. Newbury Park, CA: Sage.

Bond, M. H. (1991). Chinese values and health: A culture-level examination. *Psychology and Health, 5*, 137–152.

Bond, M. H. (1996). Chinese values. In M. H. Bond (Ed.), *The handbook of Chinese psychology* (pp. 208–226). Hong Kong: Oxford University Press.

Bond, R. (2005). Group size and conformity. *Group Processes and Intergroup Relations, 8*, 331–354.

Bond, R., & Smith, P. B. (1996). Culture and conformity: A meta-analysis of studies using Asch's (1952b, 1956) line judgment task. *Psychological Bulletin, 119*, 111–137.

Bornstein, B. H., & Greene, E. (2011). Jury decision making: Implications for and from psychology. *Current Directions in Psychological Science, 20*(1), 63–67. doi:10.1177/0963721410397282

Bornstein, R. F. (1989). Exposure and affect: Overview and meta-analysis of research, 1968–1987. *Psychological Bulletin, 106*, 265–289.

Bos, M. W., & Dijksterhuis, A. (2012). Self-knowledge, unconscious thought, and decision making. In S. Vazire & T. D. Wilson (Eds.), *The handbook of self-knowledge*. New York: Guilford.

Bosson, J. K., & Vandello, J. A. (2011). Precarious manhood and its links to action and aggression. *Psychological Science, 20*, 82–86.

Botvin, G. J., & Griffin, K. W. (2004). Life Skills Training: Empirical findings and future directions. *Journal of Primary Prevention, 25*, 211–232.

Bourgeois, M. J., & Bowen, A. (2001). Self-organization of alcohol-related attitudes and beliefs in a campus housing complex: An initial investigation. *Health Psychology, 20*, 434–437.

Bower, G. H., & Hilgard, E. R. (1981). *Theories of learning* (15th ed.). Englewood Cliffs, NJ: Prentice Hall.

Bowlby, J. (1969). *Attachment and loss:* Vol. 1. *Attachment*. New York: Basic Books.

Bowlby, J. (1973). *Attachment and loss:* Vol. 2. *Separation: Anxiety and anger*. New York: Basic Books.

Bowlby, J. (1980). *Attachment and loss:* Vol. 3. *Loss*. New York: Basic Books.

Boyce, C. J., Brown, G. D. A., & Moore, S. C. (2010). Money and happiness: Rank of income, not income, affects life satisfaction. *Psychological Science, 21*, 471–475.

Boyden, T., Carroll, J. S., & Maier, R. A. (1984). Similarity and attraction in homosexual males: The effects of age and masculinity-femininity. *Sex Roles, 10*, 939–948.

Bradbury, T. N., & Fincham, F. D. (1991). A contextual model for advancing the study of marital relationships. In G. J. O. Fletcher & F. D. Fincham (Eds.), *Cognition in close relationships* (pp. 127–147). Hillsdale, NJ: Erlbaum.

Branigan, T. (2011, October 21) Chinese toddler dies after hit-and-run ordeal. *The Guardian*. Retrieved November 21, 2011, from www.guardian.co.uk/world/2011/oct/21/chinese-toddler-dies-hit-and-run

Brannon, L. A., & Brock, T. C. (1994). The subliminal persuasion controversy. In S. Shavitt & T. C. Brock (Eds.), *Persuasion: Psychological insights and perspectives* (pp. 279–293). Needham Heights, MA: Allyn & Bacon.

Branscombe, N. R., Owen, S., Garstka, T. A., & Coleman, J. (1996). Rape and accident counterfactuals: Who might have done otherwise, and would it have changed the outcome? *Journal of Applied Social Psychology, 26*, 1042–1067.

Branscombe, N. R., & Wann, D. L. (1992). Physiological arousal and reactions to outgroup members during competitions that implicate an important social identity. *Aggressive Behavior, 18*, 85–93.

Breckler, S. J., & Wiggins, E. C. (1989). On defining attitude and attitude theory: Once more with feeling. In A. R. Pratkanis, S. J. Breckler, & A. G. Greenwald (Eds.), *Attitude structure and function* (pp. 407–427). Hillsdale, NJ: Erlbaum.

Brehm, J. W. (1956). Postdecision changes in the desirability of alternatives. *Journal of Abnormal and Social Psychology, 52*, 384–389.

Brehm, J. W. (1966). *A theory of psychological reactance*. New York: Academic Press.

Brehm, J. W., & Cohen, A. R. (1962). *Explorations in cognitive dissonance*. New York: Wiley.

Brescoll, V. L., Dawson, E., & Uhlmann, E. L. (2010). Hard won and easily lost: The fragile status of leaders in gender-stereotype-incongruent occupations. *Psychological Science, 21*(11), 1640–1642. doi:10.1177/0956797610384744

Brewer, M. B. (1979). In-group bias in the minimal intergroup situation: A cognitive-motivational analysis. *Psychological Bulletin, 86*, 307–324.

Brewer, M. B. (1991). The social self: On being the same and different at the same time. *Personality and Social Psychology Bulletin, 17*(5), 475–482. doi:10.1177/0146167291175001

Brewer, M. B. (2007). The importance of being we: Human nature and intergroup relations. *American Psychologist, 62*(8), 728–738. doi:10.1037/0003-066X.62.8.728

Brewer, M. B., & Gardner, W. L. (1996). Who is this "we"? Levels of collective identity and self-representations. *Journal of Personality and Social Psychology, 71*, 83–93.

Brewer, M. B., & Miller, N. (1984). Beyond the contact hypothesis: Theoretical perspectives on desegregation. In N. Miller & M. B. Brewer (Eds.), *Groups in contact: The psychology of desegregation* (pp. 281–302). New York: Academic Press.

Brewer, N., & Wells, G. L. (2011). Eyewitness identification. *Current Directions in Psychological Science, 20*, 24–27.

Bridgeman, D. L. (1981). Enhanced role taking through cooperative interdependence: A field study. *Child Development, 52*, 1231–1238.

Bridges, F. S., & Coady, N. P. (1996). Affiliation, urban size, urgency, and cost of responses to lost letters. *Psychological Reports, 79*, 775–780.

Brigham, J., Bennett, L., Meissner, C., & Mitchell, T. (2007). The influence of race on eyewitness memory. In R. C. L. Lindsay, D. F. Ross, D. J. Read, & M. P. Toglia (Eds.). *The handbook of eyewitness psychology*, Vol. II: *Memory for people* (pp. 257–281). Mahwah, NJ: Erlbaum.

Bringle, R. G. (2005). Designing interventions to promote civic engagement. In A. M. Omoto (Ed.), *Processes of community change and social action* (pp. 167–187). Mahwah, NJ: Erlbaum.

Briñol, P., & Petty, R. E. (2009). Persuasion: Insights from the self-validation hypothesis. In M. P. Zanna (Ed.), *Advances in Experimental Social Psychology* (Vol. 41, pp. 69–118). New York: Elsevier.

Briñol, P., & Petty, R. E. (2012). Knowing our attitudes and how to change them. In S. Vazire & T. D. Wilson (Eds.), *Handbook of self-knowledge*. New York: Guilford.

Brinson, L., & Robinson, E. (1991). The African-American athlete: A psychological perspective. In L. Diamant (Ed.), *Psychology of sports, exercise, and fitness* (pp. 249–259). New York: Hemisphere.

Brislin, R. (1993). *Understanding culture's influence on behavior*. Fort Worth, TX: Harcourt Brace.

Brooke, J. (2000, January 20). Canada proposes scaring smokers with pictures on the packs. *New York Times on the Web*, www.nytimes.com

Brooks, A. (2006). *Who really cares? The surprising truth about compassionate conservatism*. New York: Basic Books.

Brophy, J. E. (1983). Research on the self-fulfilling prophecy and teacher expectations. *Journal of Educational Psychology, 75*, 631–661.

Brown, R. (1965). *Social psychology*. New York: Free Press.

Brown, R. (1986). *Social psychology* (2nd ed.). New York: Free Press.

Brown, R. P., & Pinel, E. C. (2002). Stigma on my mind: Individual differences in the experience of stereotype threat. *Journal of Experimental Social Psychology, 39*, 626–633.

Bruschke, J., & Loges, W. E. (2004). *Free press vs. fair trials: Examining publicity's role in trial outcomes*. Mahwah, NJ: Erlbaum.

Buehler, R., & Griffin, D. W. (1994). Change-of-meaning effects in conformity and dissent: Observing construal processes over time. *Journal of Personality and Social Psychology, 67*, 984–996.

Buehler, R., Griffin, D. W., & Ross, M. (2002). Inside the planning fallacy: The causes and consequences of optimistic time preferences. In T. Gilovich, D. W. Griffin, & D. Kahneman (Eds.), *Heuristics and biases: The psychology of intuitive judgment* (pp. 250–270). New York: Cambridge University Press.

Bugliosi, V. T. (1997). *Outrage: The five reasons why O. J. Simpson got away with murder*. New York: Dell.

Bui, K.-V. T., Peplau, L. A., & Hill, C. T. (1996). Testing the Rusbult model of relationship commitment and stability in a 15-year study of heterosexual couples. *Personality and Social Psychology Bulletin, 22*, 1244–1257.

Buller, D. J. (2005). *Adapting minds: Evolutionary psychology and the persistent quest for human nature*. Cambridge, MA: MIT Press.

Burger, J. M. (1981). Motivational biases in the attribution of responsibility for an accident: A meta-analysis of the defensive-attribution hypothesis. *Psychological Bulletin, 90*, 496–512.

Burns, J. M. (1978). *Leadership*. New York: Harper & Row.

Burnstein, E., Crandall, C. S., & Kitayama, S. (1994). Some neo-Darwinian decision rules for altruism: Weighing cues for inclusive fitness as a function of the biological importance of the decision. *Journal of Personality and Social Psychology, 67*, 773–789.

Burnstein, E., & Sentis, K. (1981). Attitude polarization in groups. In R. E. Petty, T. M. Ostrom, & T. C. Brock (Eds.), *Cognitive responses in persuasion* (pp. 197–216). Hillsdale, NJ: Erlbaum.

Burnstein, E., & Vinokur, A. (1977). Persuasive argumentation and social comparison as determinants of attitude polarization. *Journal of Experimental Social Psychology, 13*, 315–332.

Burnstein, E., & Worchel, P. (1962). Arbitrariness of frustration and its consequences for aggression in a social situation. *Journal of Personality, 30*, 528–540.

Busey, T. A., Tunnicliff, J., Loftus, G. R. & Loftus, E. F. (2000). Accounts of the confidence-accuracy relation in recognition memory. *Psychonomic Bulletin and Review*, 7, 26–48.

Bush, G. W. (2010). *Decision points*. New York: Crown.

Bush sought "way" to invade Iraq? (2004, January 11). Retrieved on March 8, 2006, from *www.cbsnews.com/stories/2004/01/09/60minutes/main592330.shtml*

Bushman, B. J. (1993). Human aggression while under the influence of alcohol and other drugs: An integrative research review. *Current Directions in Psychological Science, 2*, 148–152.

Bushman, B. J. (1995). Moderating role of trait aggressiveness in the effects of violent media on aggression. *Journal of Personality and Social Psychology, 69*, 950–960.

Bushman, B. J. (1997). Effects of alcohol on human aggression: Validity of proposed explanations. In M. Galanter (Ed.), *Recent developments in alcoholism:* Vol. 13. *Alcohol and violence: Epidemiology, neurobiology, psychology, family issues* (pp. 227–243). New York: Plenum.

Bushman, B. J. (2002). Does venting anger feed or extinguish the flame? Catharsis, rumination, distraction, anger, and aggressive responding. *Personality and Social Psychology Bulletin, 28*, 724–731.

Bushman, B. J., & Anderson, C. A. (2009). Comfortably numb: Desensitizing effects of violent media on helping others. *Psychological Science, 20*, 273–277.

Bushman, B. J., & Baumeister, R. F. (2002). Does self-love or self-hate lead to violence? *Journal of Research in Personality, 36*, 543–545.

Bushman, B. J., & Bonacci, A. M. (2002). Violence and sex impair memory for television ads. *Journal of Applied Psychology, 87*, 557–564.

Bushman, B. J., Bonacci, A. M., Pedersen, W. C., Vasquez, E. A., & Miller, N. (2005). Chewing on it can chew you up: Effects of rumination on triggered displaced aggression. *Journal of Personality and Social Psychology, 88*, 969–983.

Bushman, B. J., & Cooper, H. M. (1990). Alcohol and human aggression: An integrative research review. *Psychological Bulletin, 107*, 341–354.

Bushman, B. J., Ridge, R. D., Das, E., Key, C. W., & Busath, G. L. (2007). When God sanctions killing: The effect of scriptural violence on aggression. *Psychological Science, 18*(3), 204–207.

Buss D. (2005) *The handbook of evolutionary psychology*. New Jersey: John Wiley & Sons.

Buss, D. M. (1985). Human mate selection. *American Scientist, 73*, 47–51.

Buss, D. M. (1988a). The evolution of human intrasexual competition. *Journal of Personality and Social Psychology, 54*, 616–628.

Buss, D. M. (1988b). Love acts: The evolutionary biology of love. In R. J. Sternberg & M. L. Barnes (Eds.), *The psychology of love* (pp. 110–118). New Haven, CT: Yale University Press.

Buss, D. M. (1989). Sex differences in human mate preferences: Evolutionary hypotheses tested in 37 cultures. *Behavioral and Brain Sciences, 12*, 1–49.

Buss, D. M. (1996). The evolutionary psychology of human social strategies. In E. T. Higgins & A. W. Kruglanski (Eds.), *Social psychology: Handbook of basic principles* (pp. 3–38). New York: Guilford Press.

Buss, D. M. (2004). *Evolutionary psychology: The new science of the mind*, 2nd ed. Boston: Allyn & Bacon.

Buss, D. M. (Ed.). (2005). *The handbook of evolutionary psychology*. Hoboken, NJ: Wiley.

Buss, D. M., Abbott, M., Angleitner, A., Biaggio, A., Blanco-Villasenor, A., Bruchon-Schweitzer, M., et al. (1990). International preferences in selecting mates: A study of 37 cultures. *Journal of Cross-Cultural Psychology, 21*, 5–47.

Buss, D. M., & Barnes, M. L. (1986). Preferences in human mate selection. *Journal of Personality and Social Psychology, 50*, 559–570.

Buss, D. M., & Kenrick, D. T. (1998). Evolutionary social psychology. In D. T. Gilbert, S. T. Fiske, & G. Lindzey (Eds.), *The handbook of social psychology* (4th ed., Vol. 2, pp. 982–1026). New York: McGraw-Hill.

Buss, D. M., & Schmitt, D. P. (1993). Sexual strategies theory: An evolutionary perspective on human mating. *Psychological Bulletin, 100*, 204–232.

Buss, D. M., & Shackelford, T. K. (1997). From vigilance to violence: Mate retention tactics in married couples. *Journal of Personality and Social Psychology, 72*, 346–361.

Butler, D., & Geis, F. L. (1990). Nonverbal affect responses to male and female leaders: Implications for leadership evaluations. *Journal of Personality and Social Psychology, 58*, 48–59.

Buunk, A., & Gibbons, F. (2007). Social comparison: The end of a theory and the emergence of a field. *Organizational Behavior and Human Decision Processes, 102*, 3–21.

Buunk, B. P., & Schaufeli, W. B. (1999). Reciprocity in interpersonal relationships: An evolutionary perspective on its importance for health and well-being. In W. Stroebe & M. Hewstone (Eds.), *European Review of Social Psychology* (Vol. 10, pp. 259–291). New York: Wiley.

Buunk, B. P., & Van Yperen, N. W. (1991). Referential comparisons, relational comparisons, and exchange orientation: Their relation to marital satisfaction. *Personality and Social Psychology Bulletin, 17*, 709–717.

Byrne, D. (1997). An overview (and underview) of research and theory within the attraction paradigm. *Journal of Social and Personal Relationships, 14*, 417–431.

Byrne, D., & Clore, G. L. (1970). A reinforcement model of evaluative processes. *Personality, 1*, 103–128.

Byrne, D., & Nelson, D. (1965). Attraction as a linear function of positive reinforcement. *Journal of Personality and Social Psychology, 1*, 659–663.

Cacioppo, J. T. (1998). Somatic responses to psychological stress: The reactivity hypothesis. In M. Sabourin & F. Craik (Eds.), *Advances in psychological science: Biological and cognitive aspects* (Vol. 2, pp. 87–112). Hove, England: Psychology Press.

Cacioppo, J. T., Berntson, G. G., Malarkey, W. B., Kiecolt-Glaser, J. K., Sheridan, J. F., Poehlmann, K. M., Burleson, M. H., Ernst, J. M., Hawkley, L. C., & Glaser, R. (1998). Autonomic, neuroendocrine, and immune responses to psychological stress: The reactivity hypothesis. In S. M. McCann & J. M. Lipton (Eds.), *Annals of the New York Academy of Sciences* (Vol. 840, pp. 664–673). New York: New York Academy of Sciences.

Cacioppo, J. T., & Patrick, W. (2008). *Loneliness: Human nature and the need for social connection*. New York: Norton & Company.

Cacioppo, J. T., Petty, R. E., Feinstein, J., & Jarvis, B. (1996). Dispositional differences in cognitive motivation: The life and times of individuals low versus high in need for cognition. *Psychological Bulletin, 119*, 197–253.

Cafri, G., & Thompson, J. K. (2004). Measuring male body image: A review of the current methodology. *Psychology of Men and Masculinity, 5*, 18–29.

Cafri, G., Thompson, J. K., Ricciardelli, L., McCabe, M., Smolak, L., & Yesalis, C. (2005). Pursuit of the muscular ideal: Physical and psychological consequences and putative risk factors. *Clinical Psychology Review, 25*, 215–239.

Caldwell, M., & Peplau, L. A. (1982). Sex differences in same-sex friendship. *Sex Roles, 8*, 721–732.

Calvert, J. D. (1988). Physical attractiveness: A review and reevaluation of its role in social skill research. *Behavioral Assessment, 10*, 29–42.

Camille, N., Coricelli, G., Sallet, J., Pradat-Diehl, P., Duhamel, J., & Sirigu, A. (2004). The involvement of the orbitofrontal cortex in the experience of regret. *Science, 304*, 1167–1170.

Campbell, A. (2002). *A mind of her own*. New York: Oxford University Press.

Campbell, D. T. (1967). Stereotypes and the perception of group differences. *American Psychologist, 22*, 817–829.

Campbell, D. T., & Stanley, J. C. (1967). *Experimental and quasi-experimental designs for research*. Chicago: Rand McNally.

Campbell, E. Q., & Pettigrew, T. F. (1959). Racial and moral crisis: The role of Little Rock ministers. *American Journal of Sociology, 64*, 509–516.

Campbell, J., & Stasser, G. (2006). The influence of time and task demonstrability on decision-making in computer-mediated and face-to-face groups. *Small Group Research, 37*, 271–294.

Campbell, J. D., & Fairey, P. J. (1989). Informational and normative routes to conformity: The effect of faction size as a function of norm extremity and attention to the stimulus. *Journal of Personality and Social Psychology, 57*, 457–468.

Campbell, L., Simpson, J. A., Boldry, J., & Kashy, D. A. (2005). Perceptions of conflict and support in romantic relationships: The role of attachment anxiety. *Journal of Personality and Social Psychology, 88*, 510–531.

Campbell, W. K., Miller, J. D., & Buffardi, L. E. (2010). The United States and the "culture of narcissism": An examination of perceptions of national character. *Social and Personality Science, 1*, 222–229.

Canary, D. J., & Stafford, L. (2001). Equity in the preservation of personal relationships. In J. Harvey & A. Wenzel (Eds.), *Close romantic relationships: Maintenance and enhancement* (pp. 133–151). Mahwah, NJ: Erlbaum.

Cannon, W. B. (1932). *The wisdom of the body*. New York: Norton.

Cannon, W. B. (1942). "Voodoo" death. *American Anthropologist, 44*, 169–181.

Cantor, J., Bushman, B. J., Huesmann, L. R., Groebel, J., Malamuth, N. M., Impett, E. A., Donnerstein, E., & Smith, S. (2001). Some hazards of television viewing: Fears, aggression, and sexual attitudes. In D. G. Singer & J. L. Singer (Eds.), *Handbook of children and the media* (pp. 207–307). Thousand Oaks, CA: Sage.

Cantril, H. (1940). *The invasion from Mars: A study in the psychology of panic*. New York: Harper & Row.

Caporael, L. R., & Brewer, M. B. (2000). Metatheories, evolution, and psychology: Once more with feeling. *Psychological Inquiry, 11*, 23–26.

Capella, M. L., Webster, C., & Kinard, B. R. (2011). A review of the effect of cigarette advertising. *International Journal of Research in Marketing, 28*(3), 269–279. doi:10.1016/j.ijresmar.2011.05.002

Carey, B. (2006, February 14). "In music, others' tastes may help shape your own." *The New York Times*, p. D7.

Carli, L. L. (1999). Cognitive reconstruction, hindsight, and reactions to victims and perpetrators. *Personality and Social Psychology Bulletin, 25*, 966–979.

Carlier, I. V. E., Voerman, A. E., & Gersons, B. P. R. (2000). The influence of occupational debriefing on post-traumatic stress symptomatology in traumatized police officers. *British Journal of Medical Psychology, 73*, 87–98.

Carlsmith, J. M., & Anderson, C. A. (1979). Ambient temperature and the occurrence of collective violence: A new analysis. *Journal of Personality and Social Psychology, 37*, 337–344.

Carlson, M., Charlin, V., & Miller, N. (1988). Positive mood and helping behavior: A test of six hypotheses. *Journal of Personality and Social Psychology, 55*, 211–229.

Carlson, M., & Miller, N. (1987). Explanation of the relationship between negative mood and helping. *Psychological Bulletin, 102*, 91–108.

Carnagey, N. L., Anderson, C. A. (2005). The effects of reward and punishment in violent video games on aggressive affect, cognition, and behavior. *Psychological Science, 16*, 882–889.

Carnevale, P. J. (1986). Strategic choice in mediation. *Negotiation Journal, 2*, 41–56.

Carpenter, S. (2000, December). Why do "they all look alike"? *Monitor on Psychology*, pp. 44–45.

Carr, J. L., & VanDeusen, K. M. (2004). Risk factors for male sexual aggression on college campuses. *Journal of Family Violence, 19*, 279–289.

Carter, B. (2000, August 24). "CBS is surprise winner in ratings contest." *The New York Times*, p. A22.

Carter, B. (2003, May 19). Even as executives scorn the genre, TV networks still rely on reality. *The New York Times*, pp. C1, C7.

Carter, B. (2009, May 19). Upfronts: "Chuck" saved by Subway. *The New York Times*. Retrieved July 1, 2011 from: mediadecoder.blogs.nytimes.com/2009/05/19/upfronts-chuck-takes-the-subway/

Cartwright, D. (1979). Contemporary social psychology in historical perspective. *Social Psychology Quarterly, 42*, 82–93.

Caruso, E. (2008). Use of experienced retrieval ease in self and social judgments. *Journal of Experimental Social Psychology, 44*, 148–155.

Caruso, E. M. (2008). Use of experienced retrieval ease in self and social judgments. *Journal of Experimental Social Psychology, 44*(1), 148–155. doi:10.1016/j.jesp.2006.11.003

Carver, C. S. (2003). Self-awareness. In M. R. Leary & J. P. Tangney (Eds.), *Handbook of self and identity* (pp. 179–196). New York: Guilford Press.

Carver, C. S., De Gregorio, E., & Gillis, R. (1980). Ego-defensive attribution among two categories of observers. *Personality and Social Psychology Bulletin, 6*, 4–50.

Carver, C. S., & Scheier, M. F. (1981). *Attention and self-regulation: A control-theory approach to human behavior*. New York: Springer-Verlag.

Carver, C. S., & Scheier, M. F. (1998). *On the self-regulation of behavior*. New York: Cambridge University Press.

Caselman, T., (2007). *Teaching children empathy*. New York: YouthLight.

Caspi, A., & Harbener, E. S. (1990). Continuity and change: Assortive marriage and the consistency of personality in adulthood. *Journal of Personality and Social Psychology, 58*, 250–258.

Catalyst. (2011). Changing workplaces, changing lives. Retrieved July 12, 2011, from www.catalyst.org/home

Centers for Disease Control and Prevention. (n.d.). Retrieved June 6, 2011, from profiles.nlm.nih.gov/ps/access/NNBCPH.pdf

Centers for Disease Control and Prevention. (2010, January). DATA2010, The Healthy People 2010 Database. Retrieved June 6, 2011, from wonder.cdc.gov/scripts/broker.exe

Chaiken, S. (1980). Heuristic versus systematic information processing and the use of source versus message cues in persuasion. *Journal of Personality and Social Psychology, 39*, 752–766.

Chaiken, S. (1987). The heuristic model of persuasion. In M. P. Zanna, J. M. Olson, & C. P. Herman (Eds.), *Social influence: The Ontario Symposium* (Vol. 5, pp. 3–39). Hillsdale, NJ: Erlbaum.

Chaiken, S., & Baldwin, M. W. (1981). Affective-cognitive consistency and the effect of salient behavioral information on the self-perception of attitudes. *Journal of Personality and Social Psychology, 41*, 1–12.

Chaiken, S., Wood, W., & Eagly, A. H. (1996). Principles of persuasion. In E. T. Higgins & A. W. Kruglanski (Eds.), *Social psychology: Handbook of basic principles* (pp. 702–742). New York: Guilford Press.

Chambers, J. R., & Windschitl, P. D. (2009). Evaluating one performance among others: The influence of rank and degree of exposure to comparison referents. *Personality and Social Psychology Bulletin, 35*, 776–792. doi:10.1177/0146167209333044

Chan, D. K.-S., & Cheng, G. H.-L. (2004). A comparison of offline and online friendship qualities at different stages of relationship development. *Journal of Personal and Social Relationships, 21*, 305–320.

Chang, C., & Chen, J. (1995). Effects of different motivation strategies on reducing social loafing. *Chinese Journal of Psychology, 37*, 71–81.

Chapman, G. B., & Johnson, E. J. (2002). Incorporating the irrelevant: Anchors in judgments of belief and value. In T. Gilovich, D. W. Griffin, & D. Kahneman (Eds.), *Heuristics and biases: The psychology of intuitive judgment* (pp. 120–138). New York: Cambridge University Press.

Charman, S., & Wells, G. (2007). Applied lineup theory. *The handbook of eyewitness psychology*, Vol II: *Memory for people* (pp. 219–254). Mahwah, NJ: Erlbaum.

Charman, S., & Wells, G. (2008). Can eyewitnesses correct for external influences on their lineup identifications? The actual/counterfactual assessment paradigm. *Journal of Experimental Psychology: Applied, 14*, 5–20.

Charman, S. D., Wells, G. L., & Joy, S. W. (2011). The dud effect: Adding highly dissimilar fillers increases confidence in lineup identifications. *Law and Human Behavior, 35*(6), 479–500. doi:10.1007/s10979-010-9261-1

Chaudoir, S. R., & Fisher, J. D. (2010). The disclosure processes model: Understanding disclosure decision making and postdisclosure outcomes among people living with a concealable stigmatized identity. *Psychological Bulletin, 136*(2), 236–256. doi:10.1037/a0018193

Check, J. V., & Malamuth, N. M. (1983). Sex role stereotyping and reactions to depictions of stranger versus acquaintance rape. *Journal of Personality and Social Psychology, 45*, 344–356.

Chemers, M. M. (2000). Leadership research and theory: A functional integration. *Group Dynamics: Theory, Research, and Practice, 4*, 27–43.

Chemers, M. M., Watson, C. B., & May, S. T. (2000). Dispositional affect and leadership effectiveness: A comparison of self-esteem, optimism, and efficacy. *Personality and Social Psychology Bulletin, 26*, 267–277.

Chen, M., & Bargh, J. A. (1997). Nonconscious behavioral confirmation processes: The self-fulfilling consequences of automatic stereotype activation. *Journal of Experimental Social Psychology, 33*, 541–560.

Chen, N. Y., Shaffer, D. R., & Wu, C. H. (1997). On physical attractiveness stereotyping in Taiwan: A revised sociocultural perspective. *Journal of Social Psychology, 137*, 117–124.

Chen, S., & Andersen, S. M. (1999). Relationships from the past in the present: Significant-other representations and transference in interpersonal life. In M. P. Zanna (Ed.), *Advances in experimental social psychology* (Vol. 31, pp. 123–190). San Diego, CA: Academic Press.

Chen, S., & Chaiken, S. (1999). The heuristic-systematic model in its broader context. In S. Chaiken & Y. Trope (Eds.), *Dual-process theories in social psychology* (pp. 73–96). New York: Guilford Press.

Cheung, B. Y., Chudek, M., & Heine, S. J. (2011). Evidence for a sensitive period for acculturation: Younger immigrants report acculturating at a faster rate. *Psychological Science, 22*(2), 147–152. doi:10.1177/0956797610394661

Cheung, F. M., Leung, K., Fang, R. M., Song, W. Z., Zhang, J. X., & Zhang, J. P. (1996). Development of the Chinese Personality Assessment Inventory (CPAI). *Journal of Cross-Cultural Psychology, 27*, 181–199.

Chiao, J. Y., Hariri, A. R., Harada, T., Mano, Y., Sadato, N., Parrish, T. B., & Iidaka, T. (2010). Theory and methods in cultural neuroscience. *Social Cognitive and Affective Neuroscience, 5*, 356–361.

Chida, Y., & Hamer, M. (2008). Chronic psychosocial factors and acute physiological responses to laboratory-induced stress in healthy populations: A quantitative review of 30 years of investigations. *Psychological Bulletin, 134*, 829–885.

Chin, J., & Schooler, J. (2008). Why do words hurt? Content, process, and criterion shift accounts of verbal overshadowing. *European Journal of Cognitive Psychology, 20*, 396–413.

Chiu, C., Morris, M. W., Hong, Y., & Menon, T. (2000). Motivated cultural cognition: The impact of implicit cultural theories on dispositional attribution varies as a function of need for closure. *Journal of Personality and Social Psychology, 78*, 247–259.

Choi, I., Dalal, R., Kim-Prieto, C., & Park, H. (2003). Culture and judgment of causal relevance. *Journal of Personality and Social Psychology, 84*, 46–59.

Choi, I., & Nisbett, R. E. (1998). Situational salience and cultural differences in the correspondence bias and in the actor-observer bias. *Personality and Social Psychology Bulletin, 24*, 949–960.

Choi, I., Nisbett, R. E., & Norenzayan, A. (1999). Causal attribution across cultures: Variation and universality. *Psychological Bulletin, 125*, 47–63.

Choi, Y., He, M., & Harachi, T. (2008). Intergenerational cultural dissonance, parent-child conflict and bonding, and youth problem behaviors among Vietnamese and Cambodian immigrant families. *Journal of Youth and Adolescence, 37*, 85–96.

Chou, C., Montgomery, S., Pentz, M., Rohrbach, L., Johnson, C., Flay, B., & MacKinnon, D. P. (1998). Effects of a community-based prevention program in decreasing drug use in high-risk adolescents. *American Journal of Public Health, 88*, 944–948.

Christensen, L. (1988). Deception in psychological research: When is its use justified? *Personality and Social Psychology Bulletin, 14*, 664–675.

Christopher, A. N., & Wojda, M. R. (2008). Social dominance orientation, right-wing authoritarianism, sexism, and prejudice toward women in the workforce. *Psychology of Women Quarterly, 32*, 65–73.

Cialdini, R. B. (2009). *Influence: Science and practice* (5th ed.). Upper Saddle River, NJ: Prentice Hall.

Cialdini, R. B. (in press). The focus theory of normative conduct. In P. van Lange, A. Kruglanski, & T. Higgins. (Eds.), *Handbook of theories of social psychology*. London: Sage.

Cialdini, R. B., Borden, R. J., Thorne, A., Walker, M. R., Freeman, S., & Sloan, L. R. (1976). Basking in reflected glory: Three (football) field studies. *Journal of Personality and Social Psychology, 34*, 366–375.

Cialdini, R. B., Cacioppo, J. T., Basset, R., & Miller, J. (1978). Low-ball procedure for producing compliance: Commitment, then cost. *Journal of Personality and Social Psychology, 36*, 463–476.

Cialdini, R. B., & Fultz, J. (1990). Interpreting the negative mood-helping literature via "mega"-analysis: A contrary view. *Psychological Bulletin, 107*, 210–214.

Cialdini, R. B., & Goldstein, N. J. (2004). Social influence: Compliance and conformity. *Annual Review of Psychology, 55*, 591–621.

Cialdini, R. B., Kallgren, C. A., & Reno, R. R. (1991). A focus theory of normative conduct: A theoretical refinement and reevaluation of the role of norms in human behavior. In M. P. Zanna (Ed.), *Advances in experimental social psychology* (Vol. 24, pp. 201–234). San Diego, CA: Academic Press.

Cialdini, R. B., Reno, R. R., & Kallgren, C. A. (1990). A focus theory of normative conduct: Recycling the concept of norms to reduce littering in public places. *Journal of Personality and Social Psychology, 58*, 1015–1026.

Cialdini, R. B., Schaller, M., Houlihan, D., Arps, K., Fultz, J., & Beaman, A. L. (1987). Empathy-based helping: Is it selflessly or selfishly motivated? *Journal of Personality and Social Psychology, 52*, 749–758.

Cialdini, R. B., & Trost, M. R. (1998). Social influence: Social norms, conformity, and compliance. In D. T. Gilbert, S. T. Fiske, & G. Lindzey (Eds.), *The handbook of social psychology* (4th ed., Vol. 2, pp. 151–192). New York: McGraw-Hill.

Clark, M. S. (1986). Evidence of the effectiveness of manipulations of communal and exchange relationships. *Personality and Social Psychology Bulletin, 12*, 414–425.

Clark, M. S., & Isen, A. M. (1982). Toward understanding the relationship between feeling states and social behavior. In A. H. Hastorf & A. M. Isen (Eds.), *Cognitive social psychology* (pp. 73–108). New York: Elsevier.

Clark, M. S., & Mills, J. (2011). A theory of communal (and exchange) relationships. In P. A. M. Van Lange, A. W. Kruglanski, & E. T. Higgins (Eds.), *Handbook of theories in social psychology*. Thousand Oaks, CA: Sage.

Clark, R. D., III, & Hatfield, E. (1989). Gender differences in receptivity to sexual offers. *Journal of Psychology and Human Sexuality, 2*, 39–55.

Clark, R. D., III, & Maass, A. (1988). The role of social categorization and perceived source credibility in minority influence. *European Journal of Social Psychology, 18*, 347–364.

Clark, R. D., III, & Word, L. E. (1972). Why don't bystanders help? Because of ambiguity? *Journal of Personality and Social Psychology, 24*, 392–400.

Clark, S. E. (2005). A re-examination of the effects of biased lineup instructions in eyewitness identification. *Law and Human Behavior, 29*, 575–604.

Clary, E. G., Snyder, M., Ridge, R. D., Miene, P. K., & Haugen, J. A. (1994). Matching messages to motives in persuasion: A functional approach to promoting volunteerism. *Journal of Applied Social Psychology, 24*, 1129–1149.

Claypool, H. M., Hall, C. E., Mackie, D. M., & Garcia-Marques, T. (2008). Positive mood, attribution, and the illusion of familiarity. *Journal of Experimental Social Psychology, 44*, 721–728.

Cline, V. B., Croft, R. G., & Courrier, S. (1973). Desensitization of children to television violence. *Journal of Personality and Social Psychology, 27*, 360–365.

Coane, J. H., & Balota, D. A. (2009). Priming the holiday spirit: Persistent activation due to extraexperimental experiences. *Psychonomic Bulletin & Review, 16*(6), 1124–1128. doi:10.3758/PBR.16.6.1124

Coats, E. (1998, March 20). Bystander intervention [E-mail response to G. Mumford, Tobacco update]. Retrieved from www.stolaf.edu/cgibin/mailarchivesearch.pl?directory=/home/www/people/huff/SPSP&listname=archive98

Cochran, J. L., & Rutten, T. (1998). *Journey to justice*. New York: Ballantine Books.

Cohen, A. R. (1962). An experiment on small rewards for discrepant compliance and attitude change. In J. W. Brehm & A. R. Cohen (Eds.), *Explorations in cognitive dissonance* (pp. 73–78). New York: Wiley.

Cohen, D., Hoshino-Browne, E., & Leung, A. (2007). Culture and the structure of personal experience: Insider and outsider phenomenologies of the self and social world. In M. P. Zanna (Ed.), *Advances in experimental social psychology* (Vol. 39, pp. 1–67). San Diego, CA: Elsevier Academic Press.

Cohen, D., & Nisbett, R. E. (1996). *Culture of honor: The psychology of violence in the South*. Boulder, CO: Westview Press.

Cohen, D., Nisbett, R. E., Bowdle, B. F., & Schwarz, N. (1996). Insult, aggression, and the southern culture of honor: An "experimental ethnography." *Journal of Personality and Social Psychology, 70*, 945–960.

Cohen, F., Jussim, L., Harber, K. D., & Bhasin, G. (2009). Modern anti-Semitism and anti-Israeli attitudes. *Journal of Personality and Social Psychology, 97*, 290–306.

Cohen, G. L., Garcia, J., Purdie-Vaughns, V., Apfel, N., & Brzustoski, P. (2009, April 17). Recursive processes in self-affirmation: Intervening to close the minority achievement gap. *Science*, 400–403.

Cohen, J. (2001, January 18). On the Internet, love really is blind. *The New York Times*, pp. E1, E7.

Cohen, R. (1997, October 31). AH-lo-ween: An American holiday in Paris? *The New York Times*, pp. A1; A4.

Cohen, S., Alper, C., Doyle, W., Adler, N., Treanor, J., & Turner, R. (2008). Objective and subjective socioeconomic status and susceptibility to the common cold. *Health Psychology, 27*, 268–274.

Cohen, S., Evans, G. W., Krantz, D. S., Stokols, D., & Kelly, S. (1981). Aircraft noise and children: Longitudinal and cross-sectional evidence on adaptation to noise and the effectiveness of noise abatement. *Journal of Personality and Social Psychology, 40*, 331–345.

Cohen, S., Mermelstein, R., Kamarack, T., & Hoberman, H. (1985). Measuring the functional components of social support. In I. G. Sarason & B. R. Sarason (Eds.)., *Social support: Theory, research, and applications* (pp. 73–94). The Hague, Netherlands: Martines Nijhoff.

Cohen, S., Tyrrell, D. A. J., & Smith, A. P. (1991). Psychological stress in humans and susceptibility to the common cold. *New England Journal of Medicine, 325*, 606–612.

Cohen, S., Tyrrell, D. A. J., & Smith, A. P. (1993). Negative life events, perceived stress, negative affect, and susceptibility to the common cold. *Journal of Personality and Social Psychology, 64*, 131–140.

Cohen, T. R., & Insko, C. A. (2008). War and peace: Possible approaches to reducing intergroup conflict. *Perspectives on Psychological Science, 3*, 87–93.

Cohn, L. D., & Adler, N. E. (1992). Female and male perceptions of ideal body shapes. *Psychology of Women Quarterly, 16*, 69–79.

Coie, J. D., Cillessen, A. H. N., Dodge, K. A., Hubbard, J. A., Schwartz, D., Lemerise, E. D., & Bateman, H. (1999). It takes two to fight: A test of relational factors and a method for assessing aggressive dyads. *Developmental Psychology, 35*, 1179–1188.

Cole, T. B. (2006). Rape at U.S. colleges often fueled by alcohol. *Journal of the American Medical Association, 296*, 504–505.

Coleman, M. D. (2010). Sunk cost and commitment to medical treatment. *Current Psychology: A Journal for Diverse Perspectives on Diverse Psychological Issues, 29*, 121–134.

Collins, B. E., & Brief, D. E. (1995). Using person-perception vignette methodologies to uncover the symbolic meanings of teacher behaviors in the Milgram paradigm. *Journal of Social Issues, 51*, 89–106.

Collins, N. L., & Feeney, B. C. (2000). A safe haven: An attachment theory perspective on support seeking and caregiving in intimate relationships. *Journal of Personality and Social Psychology, 78*, 1053–1073.

Collins, N. L., & Feeney, B. C. (2004a). An attachment theory perspective on closeness and intimacy. In D. J. Mashek & A. Aron (Eds.), *Handbook of closeness and intimacy* (pp. 163–187). Mahwah, NJ: Lawrence Erlbaum Associates.

Collins, N. L., & Feeney, B. C. (2004b). Working models of attachment shape perceptions of social support: Evidence from experimental and observational studies. *Journal of Personality and Social Psychology, 87*, 363–383.

Collins, N. L., Ford, M. B., Guichard, A. C., & Allard, L. M. (2006). Working models of attachment and attribution processes in intimate relationships. *Personality and Social Psychology Bulletin, 32*, 201–219.

Collins, W. A., & Sroufe, L. A. (1999). Capacity for intimate relationships: A developmental construction. In W. Furman, C. Feiring, & B. B. Brown (Eds.), *Contemporary perspectives on adolescent romantic relationships*. New York: Cambridge University Press.

Confer, J. C., Easton, J. A., Fleischman, D. S., Goetz, C. D., Lewis, D. M. G., Perilloux, C., & Buss, D. M. (2010). Evolutionary psychology: Controversies, questions, prospects, and limitations. *American Psychologist, 65*(2), 110–126. doi:10.1037/a0018413

Conley, T. D., Moors, A. C., Matsick, J. L., Ziegler, A., & Valentine, B. A. (2011). Women, men, and the bedroom: Methodological and conceptual insights that narrow, reframe, and eliminate gender differences in sexuality. *Current Directions in Psychological Science, 20*, 296–300.

Conley, T. D., & Ramsey, L. R. (2011). Killing us softly? Investigating portrayals of women and men in contemporary magazine advertisements. *Psychology of Women Quarterly, 35*(3), 469–478. doi:10.1177/0361684311413383

Conway, L. G., III, & Schaller, M. (2005). When authorities' commands backfire: Attributions about consensus and effects on deviant decision making. *Journal of Personality and Social Psychology, 89*, 311–326.

Conner, M., Rhodes, R. E., Morris, B., McEachan, R., & Lawton, R. (2011). Changing exercise through targeting affective or cognitive attitudes. *Psychology & Health, 26*(2), 133–149. doi:10.1080/08870446.2011.531570

Conway, M., & Ross, M. (1984). Getting what you want by revising what you had. *Journal of Personality and Social Psychology, 47*, 738–748.

Cook, K., & Rice, E. (2003). Social exchange theory. In J. Delamater (Ed.), *Handbook of social psychology* (pp. 53–76). New York: Kluwer Academic/Plenum.

Cooley, C. H. (1902). *Human nature and social order*. New York: Scribners.

Cooper, J. (1980). Reducing fears and increasing assertiveness: The role of dissonance reduction. *Journal of Experimental Social Psychology, 47*, 738–748.

Cooper, J. (2010). Riding the D train with Elliot. In M. H. Gonzales, C. Tavris, & J. Aronson (Eds.), *The scientist and the humanist: A festschrift in honor of Elliot Aronson* (pp. 159–174). New York: Psychology Press.

Corcoran, K., & Mussweiler, T. (2009). The efficiency of social comparisons with routine standards. *Social Cognition, 27*, 939–948. doi:10.1521/soco.2009.27.6.939

Correll, J., Park, B., Judd, C., Wittenbrink, B., Sadler, M., & Keesee, T. (2007). Across the thin blue line: Police officers and racial bias in the decision to shoot. *Journal of Personality and Social Psychology, 92*, 1006–1023.

Correll, J., Park, B., Judd, C. M., & Wittenbrink, B. (2002). The police officer's dilemma: Using ethnicity to disambiguate potentially threatening individuals. *Journal of Personality and Social Psychology, 83*, 1314–1329.

Correll, J., Wittenbrink, B., Park, B., Judd, C. M., & Goyle, A. (2011). Dangerous enough: Moderating racial bias with contextual threat cues. *Journal of Experimental Social Psychology, 47*, 184–189.

Cosmides, L., & Tooby, J. (1992). Cognitive adaptations for social exchange. In J. H. Barkow, L. Cosmides, & J. Tooby (Eds.), *The adapted mind: Evolutionary psychology and the generation of culture* (pp. 163–228). New York: Oxford University Press.

Costanzo, M., & Archer, D. (1989). Interpreting the expressive behavior of others: The interpersonal perceptions task. *Journal of Nonverbal Behavior, 13*, 223–245.

Cottrell, N. B., Wack, K. L., Sekerak, G. J., & Rittle, R. (1968). Social facilitation in dominant responses by the presence of an audience and the mere presence of others. *Journal of Personality and Social Psychology, 9*, 245–250.

Courage, M. L., Edison, S. C., & Howe, M. L. (2004). Variability in the early development of visual self-recognition. *Infant Behavior and Development, 27*, 509–532.

Crandall, C. S. (1988). Social contagion of binge eating. *Journal of Personality and Social Psychology, 55*, 588–598.

Crandall, C. S., D'anello, S., Sakalli, N., Lazarus, E., Wieczorkowska, G., & Feather, N. T. (2001). An attribution-value model of prejudice: Anti-fat attitudes in six nations. *Personality and Social Psychology Bulletin, 27*, 30–37.

Crandall, C. S., & Eshleman, A. (2003). A justification-suppression model of the expression and experience of prejudice. *Psychological Bulletin, 129*(3), 414–446.

Crandall, C. S., & Greenfield, B. S. (1986). Understanding the conjunction fallacy: A conjunction of effects? *Social Cognition, 4*, 408–419.

Crandall, C. S., Silvia, P. J., N'Gbala, A. N., Tsang, J.-A., & Dawson, K. (2007). Balance theory, unit relations, and attribution: The underlying integrity of Heiderian theory. *Review of General Psychology, 11*, 12–30.

Crescioni, A. W., & Baumeister, R. F. (2009). Alone and aggressive: Social exclusion impairs self-control and empathy and increases hostile cognition and aggression. In M. J. Harris (Ed.), *Bullying, rejection, and peer victimization: A social-cognitive neuroscience perspective* (pp. 251–277). New York: Springer.

Critcher, C. R., & Gilovich, T. (2010). Inferring attitudes from mind-wandering. *Personality and Social Psychology Bulletin, 36*, 1255–1266. doi:10.1177/0146167210375434

Cross, S. E., Bacon, P. L., & Morris, M. L. (2000). The relational-interdependent self-construal and relationships. *Journal of Personality and Social Psychology, 78*, 791–808.

Cross, S. E., Hardin, E. E., & Gercek-Swing, B. (2010). The what, why, and where of self-construal. *Personality and Social Psychology Review, 15*, 142–179.

Cross, S. E., & Madson, L. (1997). Models of the self: Self-construals and gender. *Psychological Bulletin, 122*, 5–37.

Crowley, A. E., & Hoyer, W. D. (1994). An integrative framework for understanding two-sided persuasion. *Journal of Consumer Research, 20*, 561–574.

Croyle, R. T., & Jemmott, J. B., III. (1990). Psychological reactions to risk factor testing. In J. A. Skelton & R. T. Croyle (Eds.), *The mental representation of health and illness* (pp. 121–157). New York: Springer-Verlag.

Csikszentmihalyi, M. (1997). *Finding flow*. New York: Basic Books.

Csikszentmihalyi, M., & Figurski, T. J. (1982). Self-awareness and aversive experience in everyday life. *Journal of Personality, 50*, 15–28.

Csikszentmihalyi, M., & Nakamura, J. (2010). Effortless attention in everyday life: A systematic phenomenology. In B. Bruya (Ed.), *Effortless attention: A new perspective in the cognitive science of attention and action* (pp. 179–189). Cambridge, MA: MIT Press.

Cunningham, M. R. (1986). Measuring the physical in physical attractiveness: Quasi-experiments on the sociobiology of female facial beauty. *Journal of Personality and Social Psychology, 50*, 925–935.

Cunningham, M. R., Barbee, A. P., & Pike, C. L. (1990). What do women want? Facialmetric assessment of multiple motives in the perception of male facial physical attractiveness. *Journal of Personality and Social Psychology, 59*, 61–72.

Cunningham, M. R., Roberts, A. R., Barbee, A. P., Druen, P. B., & Wu, C. (1995). "Their ideas of beauty are, on the whole, the same as ours": Consistency and variability in the cross-cultural perception of female physical attractiveness. *Journal of Personality and Social Psychology, 68*, 261–279.

Curtiss, S. (1977). *Genie: A psycholinguistic study of a modern-day "wild child."* New York: Academic Press.

Cury, F., Da Fonseca, D., Zahn, I., & Elliot, A. (2008). Implicit theories and IQ test performance: A sequential mediation analysis. *Journal of Experimental Social Psychology*, 44, 783–791.

Cusumano, D. L., & Thompson, J. K. (1997). Body image and body shape ideals in magazines: Exposure, awareness, and internalization. *Sex Roles, 37*, 701–721.

Dabbs, J. M., Jr. (2000). *Heroes, rogues, and lovers*. New York: McGraw-Hill.

Dabbs, J. M., Jr., Carr, T. S., Frady, R. L., & Riad, J. K. (1995). Testosterone, crime, and misbehavior among 692 male prison inmates. *Personality and Individual Differences, 18*, 627–633.

Dabbs, J. M., Jr., Hargrove, M. F., & Heusel, C. (1996). Testosterone differences among college fraternities: Well-behaved vs. rambunctious. *Personality and Individual Differences, 20*, 157–161.

Dalbert, C., & Yamauchi, L. A. (1994). Belief in a just world and attitudes toward immigrants and foreign workers: A cultural comparison between Hawaii and Germany. *Journal of Applied Social Psychology, 24*, 1612–1626.

Dallek, R. (2002, December). The medical ordeals of JFK. *Atlantic*, pp. 49–58.

Daniels, M., & Nelson, K. (2004, 20 August). In search of rush teens risk lives surfing on cars. *Boston Globe*, pp. B1, B4.

Darley, J. M. (1992). Social organization for the production of evil. *Psychological Inquiry, 3*, 199–218.

Darley, J. M. (2004). Social comparison motives in ongoing groups. In M. B. Brewer & M. Hewstone (Eds.), *Emotion and motivation* (pp. 281–297). Malden, MA: Blackwell.

Darley, J. M., & Akert, R. M. (1993). *Biographical interpretation: The influence of later events in life on the meaning of and memory for earlier events*. Unpublished manuscript, Princeton University.

Darley, J. M., & Batson, C. D. (1973). From Jerusalem to Jericho: A study of situational and dispositional variables in helping behavior. *Journal of Personality and Social Psychology*, 27, 100–108.

Darley, J. M., & Latané, B. (1968). Bystandar intervention in emergencies: Diffusion of responsibility. *Journal of Personality and Social Psychology, 8*, 377–383.

Darwin, C. R. (1859). *The origin of species*. London: Murray.

Darwin, C. R. (1872). *The expression of the emotions in man and animals*. London: Murray.

Davidson, A. R., & Jaccard, J. J. (1979). Variables that moderate the attitude-behavior relation: Results of a longitudinal survey. *Journal of Personality and Social Psychology, 37*, 1364–1376.

Davidson, L., & Duberman, L. (1982). Friendship: Communication and interactional patterns in same-sex dyads. *Sex Roles, 8*, 809–822.

Davis, K. E., & Jones, E. E. (1960). Changes in interpersonal perception as a means of reducing cognitive dissonance. *Journal of Abnormal and Social Psychology, 61*, 402–410.

Davis, M. H., & Stephan, W. G. (1980). Attributions for exam performance. *Journal of Applied Social Psychology, 10*, 235–248.

Davitz, J. (1952). The effects of previous training on post-frustration behavior. *Journal of Abnormal and Social Psychology, 47*, 309–315.

Dawkins, R. (1976). *The selfish gene*. New York: Oxford University Press.

Dawson-Andoh, N. A., Gray, J. J., Soto, J. A., & Parker, S. (2010). Body shape and size depictions of African American women in *JET* magazine, 1953–2006. *Body Image, 8*, 86–89.

De Bono, K. G., & Snyder, M. (1995). Acting on one's attitudes: The role of a history of choosing situations. *Personality and Social Psychology Bulletin, 21*, 629–636.

Dean, K. E., & Malamuth, N. M. (1997). Characteristics of men who aggress sexually and of men who imagine aggressing: Risk and moderating variables. *Journal of Personality and Social Psychology*, 72, 449–455.

Deci, E. L., Koestner, R., & Ryan, R. M. (1999a). A meta-analytic review of experiments examining the effects of extrinsic rewards. *Psychological Bulletin, 125*, 627–668.

Deci, E. L., Koestner, R., & Ryan, R. M. (1999b). The undermining effect is a reality after all—extrinsic rewards, task interest, and self-determination: Reply to Eisenberger, Pierce, and Cameron (1999) and Lepper, Henderlong, and Gingras (1999). *Psychological Bulletin, 125*, 692–700.

De Dreu, C., Nijstad, B., & van Knippenberg, D. (2008). Motivated information processing in group judgment and decision making. *Personality and Social Psychology Review, 12*, 22–49.

De Dreu, C. K. W. (2010). Social conflict: The emergence and consequences of struggle and negotiation. In S. T. Fiske, D. T. Gilbert, & G. Lindzey (Eds.), *Handbook of social psychology* (5th ed., Vol. 2, pp. 983–1023). Hoboken, NJ: John Wiley.

De Dreu, C. K. W., & De Vries, N. K. (Eds.). (2001). *Group consensus and minority influence: Implications for innovation*. Oxford, England: Blackwell Publishers.

De Houwer, J. (in press). Evaluative conditioning: A review of procedure knowledge and mental process theories. In T. Schachtman & S. Reilly (Eds.), *Applications of learning and conditioning*. Oxford, UK: Oxford University Press.

De Houwer, J., Teige-Mocigemba, S., Spruyt, A., & Moors, A. (2009). Implicit measures: A normative analysis and review. *Psychological Bulletin, 135*, 347–368.

DeMarco, P. (1994, September 28). "Dear diary." *The New York Times*, p. C2.

DePaulo, B. M. (1992). Nonverbal behavior and self-presentation. *Psychological Bulletin, 111*, 203–243.

DePaulo, B. M., & Friedman, H. S. (1998). Nonverbal communication. In D. T. Gilbert, S. T. Fiske, & G. Lindzey (Eds.), *The handbook of social psychology* (Vol. 2, 4th ed., pp. 3–40). New York: McGraw-Hill.

DePaulo, B. M., Kenny, D. A., Hoover, C. W., Webb, W., & Oliver, P. (1987). Accuracy of person perception: Do people know what kinds of impressions they convey? *Journal of Personality and Social Psychology, 52*, 303–315.

DePaulo, B. M., Stone, J. L., & Lassiter, G. D. (1985). Deceiving and detecting deceit. In B. R. Schlenker (Ed.), *The self and social life* (pp. 323–370). New York: McGraw-Hill.

De Waal, F. B. M. (1995, March). Bonobo sex and society: The behavior of a close relative challenges assumptions about male supremacy in human evolution. *Scientific American*, 82–88.

De Waal, F. B. M. (1996). *Good natured: The origins of right and wrong in humans and other animals*. Cambridge, MA: Harvard University Press.

Dedonder, J., Corneille, O., Yzerbyt, V., & Kuppens, T. (2010). Evaluative conditioning of high-novelty stimuli does not seem to be based on an automatic form of associative learning. *Journal of Experimental Social Psychology, 46*(6), 1118–1121. doi:10.1016/j.jesp.2010.06.004

Deffenbacher, K. A., Bornstein, B. H., & Penrod, S. D. (2004). A meta-analytic review of the effects of high stress on eyewitness memory. *Law and Human Behavior, 28*, 687–706.

Dennett, D. C. (1991). *Consciousness explained*. Boston: Little, Brown.

Deppe, R. K., & Harackiewicz, J. M. (1996). Self-handicapping and intrinsic motivation: Buffering intrinsic motivation from the threat of failure. *Journal of Personality and Social Psychology, 70*, 868–876.

Dershowitz, A. M. (1997). *Reasonable doubts: The criminal justice system and the O. J. Simpson case*. New York: Touchstone.

Derzon, J. H., & Lipsey, M. W. (2002). A meta-analysis of the effectiveness of mass communication for changing substance-use knowledge, attitudes, and behavior. In W. D. Crano & M. Burgoon (Eds.), *Mass media and drug prevention: Classic and contemporary theories and research* (pp. 231–258). Mahwah, NJ: Erlbaum.

Desmarais, S. L., & Read, J. D. (2011). After 30 years, what do we know about what jurors know? A meta-analytic review of lay knowledge regarding eyewitness factors. *Law and Human Behavior, 35*(3), 200–210. doi:10.1007/s10979-010-9232-6

Desmond, E. W. (1987, November 30). Out in the open. *Time*, pp. 80–90.

Desportes, J. P., & Lemaine, J. M. (1998). The sizes of human groups: An analysis of their distributions. In D. Canter, J. C. Jesuino, L. Soczka, & G. M. Stephenson (Eds.), *Environmental social psychology* (pp. 57–65). Dordrecht, Netherlands: Kluwer.

Deutsch, M. (1973). *The resolution of conflict: Constructive and destructive processes*. New Haven, CT: Yale University Press.

Deutsch, M. (1990). Cooperation, conflict, and justice. In S. A. Wheelan, E. A. Pepitone, & V. Abt (Eds.), *Advances in field theory* (pp. 149–164). Newbury Park, CA: Sage.

Deutsch, M. (1997, April). *Comments on cooperation and prejudice reduction*. Paper presented at the symposium Reflections on 100 Years of Social Psychology, Yosemite National Park, CA.

Deutsch, M., & Collins, M. E. (1951). *Interracial housing: A psychological evaluation of a social experiment*. Minneapolis: University of Minnesota Press.

Deutsch, M., & Gerard, H. G. (1955). A study of normative and informational social influence upon individual judgment. *Journal of Abnormal and Social Psychology, 51*, 629–636.

Deutsch, M., & Krauss, R. M. (1960). The effect of threat upon interpersonal bargaining. *Journal of Abnormal and Social Psychology, 61*, 181–189.

Deutsch, M., & Krauss, R. M. (1962). Studies of interpersonal bargaining. *Journal of Conflict Resolution, 6*, 52–76.

Devine, P. G. (1989). Automatic and controlled processes in prejudice: The roles of stereotypes and personal beliefs. In A. R. Pratkanis, S. J. Breckler, & A. G. Greenwald (Eds.), *Attitude structure and function* (pp. 181–212). Hillsdale, NJ: Erlbaum.

Devine, P. G., Plant, E. A., Amodio, D. M., Harmon-Jones, E., & Vance, S. L. (2002). The regulation of explicit and implicit race bias: The role of motivations to respond without prejudice. *Journal of Personality and Social Psychology, 82*(5), 835–848.

Devos-Comby, L., & Salovey, P. (2002). Applying persuasion strategies to alter HIV-relevant thoughts and behavior. *Review of General Psychology, 6*, 287–304.

DeWall, C. N., Pond, R. S., Jr., Campbell, W. K., & Twenge, J. M. (2011, March 21). Tuning in to psychological change: Linguistic markers of psychological traits and emotions over time in popular U.S. song lyrics. *Psychology of Aesthetics, Creativity, and the Arts*. Advance online publication. doi:10.1037/a0023195

DeWall, C. N., & Richman, S. B. (2011). Social exclusion and the desire to reconnect. *Social and Personality Psychology Compass, 5*, 919–932. doi:10.1111/j.1751-9004.2011.00383.x

Dickerson, C., Thibodeau, R., Aronson, E., & Miller, D. (1992). Using cognitive dissonance to encourage water conservation. *Journal of Applied Social Psychology, 22*, 841–854.

Diedrichs, P. C., & Lee, C. (2011). Waif goodbye! Average-size female models promote positive body image and appeal to consumers. *Psychology and Health, 10*, 1273–1291.

Diener, E. (1980). Deindividuation: The absence of self-awareness and self-regulation in group members. In P. B. Paulus (Ed.), *Psychology of group influence* (pp. 209–242). Hillsdale, NJ: Erlbaum.

Diener, E., & Biswas-Diener, R. (2008). *Happiness: Unlocking the mysteries of psychological wealth*. Boston: Wiley-Blackwell. Diener, E., & Oishi, S. (2005). The nonobvious social psychology of happiness. *Psychological Inquiry, 16*, 162–167.

Diener, E., & Seligman, M. E. P. (2004). Beyond money: Toward an economy of well-being. *Psychological Science in the Public Interest, 5*, 1–31.

Diener, E., & Wallbom, M. (1976). Effects of self-awareness on antinormative behavior. *Journal of Research in Personality, 10*, 107–111.

Dietz, P. D., & Evans, B. E. (1982). Pornographic imagery and prevalence of paraphilia. *American Journal of Psychiatry, 139*, 1493–1495.

Dijksterhuis, A. (2004). Think different: The merits of unconscious thought in preference development and decision making. *Journal of Personality and Social Psychology, 87*, 586–598.

Dijksterhuis, A. (2010). Automaticity and the unconscious. In S. T. Fiske, D. T. Gilbert, & G. Lindzey (Eds.), *Handbook of social psychology* (5th ed., Vol. 1, pp. 228–267). Hoboken, NJ: Wiley.

Dijksterhuis, A., & Aarts, H. (2002). *The power of the subliminal: On subliminal persuasion and other potential applications*. Unpublished manuscript.

Dijksterhuis, A., Aarts, H., & Smith, P. K. (2005). The power of the subliminal: On subliminal persuasion and other potential applications. In R. R. Hassin, J. S. Uleman, & J. A. Bargh (Eds.), *The new unconscious* (pp. 77–106). New York: Oxford University Press.

Dijksterhuis, A., & Nordgren, L. F. (2005). *A theory of unconscious thought* (Vol. I, pp. 95–109). University of Amsterdam.

Dijksterhuis, A., & Nordgren, L. (2006). A theory of unconscious thought. *Perspectives on Psychological Science, 1*, 95–109.

Dill, J. C., & Anderson, C. A. (1995). Effects of frustration justification on hostile aggression. *Aggressive Behavior, 21*, 359–369.

Dillon, S. (2009, 23 January). Study sees an Obama effect as lifting black test-takers. *The New York Times*.

Dion, K., Berscheid, E., & Walster, E. (1972). What is beautiful is good. *Journal of Personality and Social Psychology, 24*, 285–290.

Dion, K. K., & Dion, K. L. (1993). Individualistic and collectivistic perspectives on gender and the cultural context of love and intimacy. *Journal of Social Issues, 49*, 53–69.

Dion, K. K., & Dion, K. L. (1996). Cultural perspectives on romantic love. *Personal Relationships, 3*, 5–17.

Dion, K. L. (2000). Group cohesion: From "fields of forces" to multidimensional construct. *Group Dynamics, 4*, 7–26.

Dion, K. L., & Dion, K. K. (1988). Romantic love: Individual and cultural perspectives. In R. J. Sternberg & M. L. Barnes (Eds.), *The psychology of love* (pp. 264–289). New Haven, CT: Yale University Press.

Dion, K. L., & Dion, K. K. (1993). Gender and ethnocultural comparisons in styles of love. *Psychology of Women Quarterly, 17*, 463–473.

Dionne, E. J. Jr. (2005, June 21). How Cheney fooled himself. *Washington Post*, p. A21.

Dobbs, M. (2008, June 22). Cool crisis management? It's a myth. Ask JFK. *Washington Post*, pp. B1, B4.

Dodds, D. P., Towgood, K. H., McClure, S., & Olson, J. M. (2011). The biological roots of complex thinking: Are heritable attitudes more complex? (L. G. Conway III, Illus.). *Journal of Personality, 79*(1), 101–134. doi:10.1111/j.1467-6494.2010.00690.x

Dodge, K. A., & Schwartz, D. (1997). Social information processing mechanisms in aggressive behavior. In D. M. Stoff & J. Breiling (Eds.), *Handbook of antisocial behavior* (pp. 171–180). New York: Wiley.

Dohrenwend, B. (2006). Inventorying stressful life events as risk factors for psychopathology: Toward resolution of the problem of intracategory variability. *Psychological Bulletin, 132*, 477–495.

Doi, T. (1988). *The anatomy of dependence*. New York: Kodansha International.

Dollard, J. (1938). Hostility and fear in social life. *Social Forces, 17*, 15–26.

Dollard, J., Doob, L., Miller, N., Mowrer, O. H., & Sears, R. R. (1939). *Frustration and aggression*. New Haven, CT: Yale University Press.

Domina, T., & Koch, K. (2002). Convenience and frequency of recycling: Implications for including textiles in curbside recycling programs. *Environment and Behavior, 34*, 216–238.

Donnerstein, E. (1980). Aggressive erotica and violence against women. *Journal of Personality and Social Psychology, 39*, 269–277.

Donnerstein, E., & Berkowitz, L. (1981). Victim reactions in aggressive erotic films as a factor in violence against women. *Journal of Personality and Social Psychology, 41*, 710–724.

Donnerstein, E., & Donnerstein, M. (1976). Research in the control of interracial aggression. In R. G. Green & E. C. O'Neal (Eds.), *Perspectives on aggression* (pp. 133–168). New York: Academic Press.

Donnerstein, E., & Linz, D. G. (1994). Sexual violence in the mass media. In M. Costanzo & S. Oskamp (Eds.), *Violence and the law* (pp. 9–36). Thousand Oaks, CA: Sage.

Douglass, A. B., & Pavletic, A. (2012). Eyewitness confidence malleability. In B. L. Cutler (Ed.), *Conviction of the innocent: Lessons from psychological research* (pp. 149–165). Washington, DC: American Psychological Association.

Dovidio, J. F. (1984). Helping behavior and altruism: An empirical and conceptual overview. In L. Berkowitz (Ed.), *Advances in experimental social psychology* (Vol. 17, pp. 361–427). New York: Academic Press.

Dovidio, J. F., Evans, N., & Tyler, R. B. (1986). Racial stereotypes: The contents of their cognitive representations. *Journal of Experimental Social Psychology, 22*, 22–37.

Dovidio, J. F., & Gaertner, S. L. (1996). Affirmative action, unintentional racial biases, and intergroup relations. *Journal of Social Issues, 52*, 51–75.

Dovidio, J. F., & Gaertner, S. L. (2008). New directions in aversive racism research: Persistence and pervasiveness. In C. Willis-Esqueda (Ed.), *Motivational aspects of prejudice and racism.* Nebraska Symposium on Motivation. New York: Springer Science + Business Media.

Dovidio, J. F., & Gaertner, S. L. (2010). Intergroup bias. In S. T. Fiske, D. T. Gilbert, & G. Lindzey (Eds.), *Handbook of social psychology* (5th ed., Vol. 2, pp. 1084–1121). Hoboken, NJ: John Wiley & Sons.

Dovidio, J. F., Pagotto, L., & Hebl, M. R. (2011). Implicit attitudes and discrimination against people with physical disabilities. In R. L. Wiener & S. L. Willborn (Eds.), *Disability and aging discrimination: Perspectives in law and psychology* (pp. 157–183). New York: Springer Science + Business Media.

Dovidio, J. F., Piliavin, J. A., Gaertner, S. L., Schroeder, D. A., & Clark, R. D., III. (1991). The arousal cost-reward model and the process of intervention. In M. S. Clark (Ed.), *Review of personality and social psychology* (Vol. 12, pp. 86–118). Newbury Park, CA: Sage.

Draper, R. (2008). *Dead certain*. New York: Free Press.

Drigotas, S. M., & Rusbult, C. E. (1992). Should I stay or should I go? A dependence model of breakups. *Journal of Personality and Social Psychology, 62*, 62–87.

Duck, J., Hogg, M., & Terry, D. (1995). Me, us, and them: Political identification and the third-person effect in the 1993 Australian federal election. *European Journal of Social Psychology, 25*, 195–215.

Duck, S. W. (1982). A typography of relationship disengagement and dissolution. In S. W. Duck (Ed.), *Personal relationships 4: Dissolving personal relationships* (pp. 1–32). London: Academic Press.

Duck, S. W. (1994a). *Meaningful relationships: Talking, sense, and relating*. Thousand Oaks, CA: Sage.

Duck, S. W. (1994b). Stratagems, spoils, and a serpent's tooth: On the delights and dilemmas of personal relationships. In B. H. Spitzberg & W. Cupach (Eds.), *The dark side of interpersonal communication* (pp. 3–24). Hillsdale, NJ: Erlbaum.

Dunn, E. W., Aknin, L., & Norton, M. (2008). Spending money on others promotes happiness. *Science, 319*, 1687–1688.

Dunn, E. W., Wilson, T. D., & Gilbert, D. T. (2003). Location, location, location: The misprediction of satisfaction in housing lotteries. *Personality and Social Psychology Bulletin, 29*, 1421–1432.

Dunning, D., & Perretta, S. (2002). Automaticity and eyewitness accuracy: A 10- to 12-second rule for distinguishing accurate from inaccurate positive identifications. *Journal of Applied Psychology, 87*, 951–962.

Dunning, D., & Stern, L. B. (1994). Distinguishing accurate from inaccurate eyewitness identifications via inquiries about decision processes. *Journal of Personality and Social Psychology, 67*, 818–835.

During blackout, fewer crimes than on a typical NYPD day. (2003, August 16). Retrieved from www.wnbc.com/news/2409267/detail.html

Dutton, D. G., & Aron, A. P. (1974). Some evidence for heightened sexual attraction under conditions of high anxiety. *Journal of Personality and Social Psychology, 30*, 510–517.

Duval, T. S., & Silvia, P. J. (2001). *Self-awareness and causal attributions: A dual-systems theory*. Boston: Kluwer Academic.

Duval, T. S., & Silvia, P. J. (2002). Self-awareness, probability of improvement, and the self-serving bias. *Journal of Personality and Social Psychology, 82*, 49–61.

Duval, T. S., & Wicklund, R. A. (1972). *A theory of objective self-awareness*. New York: Academic Press.

Dweck, C. S. (2006). *Mindset: The new psychology of success*. New York: Random House.

Eagly, A. H. (1987). *Sex differences in social behavior: A social-role interpretation*. Hillsdale, NJ: Erlbaum.

Eagly, A. H. (1995). The science and politics of comparing women and men. *American Psychologist, 50*, 145–158.

Eagly, A. H. (1996). Differences between women and men: Their magnitude, practical importance, and political meaning. *American Psychologist, 51*, 158–159.

Eagly, A. H. (2009). The his and hers of prosocial behavior: An examination of the social psychology of gender. *American Psychologist, 64*(8), 644–658. doi:10.1037/0003-066X.64.8.644

Eagly, A. H., Ashmore, R. D., Makhijani, M. G., & Longo, L. C. (1991). What is beautiful is good, but . . . : A meta-analytic review of research on the physical attractiveness stereotype. *Psychological Bulletin, 110*, 109–128.

Eagly, A. H., & Chaiken, S. (1975). An attribution analysis of communicator characteristics on opinion change: The case of communicator attractiveness. *Journal of Personality and Social Psychology, 32*, 136–244.

Eagly, A. H., & Chaiken, S. (1993). *The psychology of attitudes*. Fort Worth, TX: Harcourt Brace.

Eagly, A. H., & Chin, J. L. (2010). Diversity and leadership in a changing world. *American Psychologist, 65*, 216–224.

Eagly, A. H., & Crowley, M. (1986). Gender and helping behavior: A meta-analytic review of the social psychological literature. *Psychological Bulletin, 100*, 283–308.

Eagly, A. H., & Diekman, A. B. (2003). The malleability of sex differences in response to changing social roles. In L. G. Aspinwall & U. M. Staudinger (Eds.), *A psychology of human strengths: Fundamental questions and future directions for a positive psychology* (pp. 103–115). Washington, D.C.: American Psychological Association.

Eagly, A. H., Diekman, A. B., Johannesen-Schmidt, M. C., & Koenig, A. M. (2004). Gender gaps in sociopolitical attitudes: A social psychological analysis. *Journal of Personality and Social Psychology, 87*, 796–816.

Eagly, A. H., Johannesen-Schmidt, M. C., & van Engen, M. L. (2003). Transformational, transactional, and laissez-faire leadership styles: A meta-analysis comparing women and men. *Psychological Bulletin, 129*, 569–591.

Eagly, A. H., & Karau, S. J. (2002). Role congruity theory of prejudice toward female leaders. *Psychological Review, 109*, 573–598.

Eagly, A. H., & Koenig, A. M. (2006). Social role theory of sex differences and similarities: Implication for prosocial behavior. In K. Dindia & D. J. Canary (Eds.), *Sex differences and similarities in communication* (2nd ed., pp. 161–177). Mahwah, NJ: Erlbaum.

Eagly, A. H., & Steffen, V. J. (2000). Gender stereotypes stem from the distribution of women and men into social roles. In C. Stangor (Ed.), *Stereotypes and prejudice: Essential readings* (pp. 142–160). Philadelphia: Psychology Press.

Eargle, A., Guerra, N., & Tolan, P. (1994). Preventing aggression in inner-city children: Small group training to change cognitions, social skills, and behavior. *Journal of Child and Adolescent Group Therapy, 4*, 229–242.

Eberhardt, J. L., Goff, P. A., Purdie, V. J., & Davies, P. G. (2004). Seeing black: Race, crime, and visual processing. *Journal of Personality and Social Psychology, 87*, 876–893.

Educators for Social Responsibility. (2001). *About the Resolving Conflict Creatively Program.* Retrieved from www.esrnational.org/about-rccp.html

Edwards, H. (1973, July). The black athletes: 20th-century gladiators in white America. *Psychology Today*, pp. 43–52.

Edwards, K., & Smith, E. (1996). A disconfirmation bias in the evaluation of arguments. *Journal of Personality and Social Psychology, 71*, 5–24.

Egan, L. C, Santos, L. R., & Bloom, P. (2007). The origins of cognitive dissonance: Evidence from children and monkeys. *Psychological Science, 18*, 978–983.

Ehrlinger, J., Gilovich, T., & Ross, L. (2005). Peering into the bias blind spot: People's assessments of bias in themselves and others. *Personality and Social Psychology Bulletin, 31*, 680–692.

Eibl-Eibesfeldt, I. (1963). Aggressive behavior and ritualized fighting in animals. In J. H. Masserman (Ed.), *Science and psychoanalysis:* Vol. 6. *Violence and war* (pp. 8–17). New York: Grune & Stratton.

Eibl-Eibesfeldt, I. (1975). *Ethology: The biology of behavior*. New York: Holt, Rinehart & Winston.

Eisenberg, N., & Fabes, R. A. (1991). Prosocial behavior and empathy: A multimethod developmental perspective. In M. S. Clark (Ed.), *Review of personality and social psychology* (Vol. 12, pp. 34–61). Newbury Park, CA: Sage.

Eisenberg, N., Spinrad, T. L., & Sadovsky, A. (2006). Empathy-related responding in children. In M. Killen & J. G. Smetana (Eds.), *Handbook of moral development* (pp. 517–549). Mahwah, NJ: Erlbaum.

Eisend, M. (2010). A meta-analysis of gender roles in advertising. *Journal of the Academy of Marketing Science, 38*(4), 418–440. doi:10.1007/s11747-009-0181-x

Eisenstadt, D., & Leippe, M. R. (2010). Social influences on eyewitness confidence: The social psychology of memory self-certainty. In R. M. Arkin, K. C. Oleson, & P. J. Carroll (Eds.), *Handbook of the uncertain self* (pp. 36–61). New York: Psychology Press.

Eisenstat, S. A., & Bancroft, L. (1999). Domestic violence. *New England Journal of Medicine, 341*, 886–892.

Eitam, B., & Higgins, E. T. (2010). Motivation in mental accessibility: Relevance of a Representation (ROAR) as a new framework. *Social and Personality Psychology Compass, 4*(10), 951–967. doi:10.1111/j.1751-9004.2010.00309.x

Ekman, P. (1965). Communication through nonverbal behavior: A source of information about an interpersonal relationship. In S. S. Tomkins & C. E. Izard (Eds.), *Affect, cognition, and personality* (pp. 390–442). New York: Springer-Verlag.

Ekman, P. (1993). Facial expression and emotion. *American Psychologist, 48*, 384–392.

Ekman, P., & Davidson, R. J. (Eds.). (1994). *The nature of emotion: Fundamental questions*. New York: Oxford University Press.

Ekman, P., & Friesen, W. V. (1969). The repertoire of nonverbal behavior: Categories, origins, usage, and coding. *Semiotica, 1*, 49–98.

Ekman, P., & Friesen, W. V. (1971). Constants across cultures in the face and emotion. *Journal of Personality and Social Psychology*, *17*, 124–129.

Ekman, P., & Friesen, W. V. (1975). *Unmasking the face*. Englewood Cliffs, NJ: Prentice Hall.

Ekman, P., Friesen, W. V., O'Sullivan, M., Chan, A., Diacoyanni-Tarlatzis, I., Heider, K., et al. (1987). Universals and cultural differences in the judgments of facial expressions of emotions. *Journal of Personality and Social Psychology, 53*, 712–717.

Ekman, P., O'Sullivan, M., & Matsumoto, D. (1991). Confusions about content in the judgment of facial expression: A reply to "Contempt and the relativity thesis." *Motivation and Emotion, 15*, 169–176.

Elfenbein, H. A., & Ambady, N. (2002). On the universality and cultural specificity of emotion recognition: A meta-analysis. *Psychological Bulletin, 128*, 203–235.

Ellin, A. (2000, September 17). Dad, do you think I look too fat? *The New York Times*, p. 7.

Ellis, A. P. J., Porter, C. O. L. H., & Wolverton, S. A. (2008). Learning to work together: An examination of transactive memory system development in teams. In V. I. Sessa & M. London (Eds.), *Work group learning: Understanding, improving and assessing how groups learn in organizations* (pp. 91–115). New York: Erlbaum.

Ellis, J. (2002). *Founding brothers*. New York: Vintage.

Emery, N. J, & Clayton, N. S. (2005). Animal cognition. In. J. J. Bolhuis (Ed.), *Behavior of animals: Mechanisms, function, and evolution* (pp. 170–196). Malden, MA: Blackwell.

Engel, B. (2001). *The power of apology*. New York: Wiley.

Englich, B., & Mussweiler, T. (2001). Sentencing under uncertainty: Anchoring effects in the courtroom. *Journal of Applied Social Psychology, 31*, 1535–1551.

Epley, E., & Huff, C. (1998). Suspicion, affective response, and education benefit as a result of deception in psychology research. *Personality and Social Psychology Bulletin, 24*, 759–768.

Epley, N., & Gilovich, T. (2004). Are adjustments insufficient? *Personality and Social Psychology Bulletin, 30*, 447–460.

Epley, N., & Gilovich, T. (2005). When effortful thinking influences judgmental anchoring: Differential effects of forewarning and incentives on self-generated and externally provided anchors. *Journal of Behavioral Decision Making, 18*, 199–212.

Erceg, Hurn, D. M., & Steed, L. G. (2011). Does exposure to cigarette health warnings elicit psychological reactance in smokers? *Journal of Applied Social Psychology, 41*(1), 219–237. doi:10.1111/j.1559-1816.2010.00710.x

Eron, L. D. (1987). The development of aggressive behavior from the perspective of a developing behaviorism. *American Psychologist, 42*, 425–442.

Eron, L. D. (2001). Seeing is believing: How viewing violence alters attitudes and aggressive behavior. In A. C. Bohart & D. J. Stipek (Eds.), *Constructive and destructive behavior: Implications for family, school, and society* (pp. 49–60). Washington, DC: American Psychological Association.

Estrada-Hollenbeck, M., & Heatherton, T. F. (1998). Avoiding and alleviating guilt through prosocial behavior. In J. Bybee (Ed.), *Guilt and children* (pp. 215–231). San Diego, CA: Academic Press.

European Commission. (2007). *Decision-making in the Top 50 Publicly Quoted Companies*. Retrieved September 3, 2008, from europa.eu.int/comm/employment_social/women_men_stats/out/measures_out438_en.htm

Evans, J. S. B. T. (2008). Dual-processing accounts of reasoning, judgment, and social cognition. *Annual Review of Psychology, 59*, 255–278. doi:10.1146/annurev.psych.59.103006.093629

Fabrigar, L. R., & Petty, R. E. (1999). The role of affective and cognitive bases of attitudes in susceptibility to affectively and cognitively based persuasion. *Personality and Social Psychology Bulletin, 25*, 363–381.

Fabrigar, L. R., Priester, J. R., Petty, R. E., & Wegener, D. T. (1998). The impact of attitude accessibility on elaboration of persuasive messages. *Personality and Social Psychology Bulletin, 24*, 339–352.

False Confessions. (2006). Accessed on June 9, 2006, from www.innocenceproject.org/causes/falseconfessions.php

Farhi, P. (2006, Jan. 21). Deluge shuts down post blog; Ombudsman's column had sparked profane responses. *Washington Post* (p. A08).

Fazio, R. H. (1990). Multiple processes by which attitudes guide behavior: The MODE model as an integrative framework. In M. P. Zanna (Ed.), *Advances in experimental social psychology* (Vol. 23, pp. 75–109). San Diego, CA: Academic Press.

Fazio, R. H., Jackson, J. R., Dunton, B. C., & Williams, C. J. (1995). Variability in automatic activation as an unobtrusive measure of racial attitudes: A bona fide pipeline? *Journal of Personality and Social Psychology, 69*, 1013–1027.

Fazio, R. H., & Olson, M. A. (2003). Implicit measures in social cognition research: Their meaning and uses. *Annual Review of Psychology, 54*, 297–327.

Feeney, J. A., & Noller, P. (1990). Attachment style as a predictor of adult romantic relationships. *Journal of Personality and Social Psychology*, 58, 281–291.

Feeney, J. A., & Noller, P. (1996). *Adult attachment*. Thousand Oaks, CA: Sage.

Feeney, J. A., Noller, P., & Roberts, N. (2000). Attachment and close relationships. In C. Hendrick & S. S. Hendrick (Eds.), *Close relationships: A sourcebook* (pp. 185–201). Thousand Oaks, CA: Sage.

Feeney, M. (2005, October 25). Rosa Parks, civil rights icon, dead at 92. *Boston Globe*, pp. A1, B8.

Fehr, B. (1994). Prototype-based assessment of laypeople's views of love. *Personal Relationships*, 1, 309–331.

Fehr, B. (2001). The life cycle of friendship. In C. Hendrick & S. S. Hendrick (Eds.), *Close relationships: A sourcebook* (pp. 71–82). Thousand Oaks, CA: Sage.

Fehr, B., & Russell, J. A. (1991). The concept of love viewed from a prototype perspective. *Journal of Personality and Social Psychology*, 60, 425–438.

Fein, S., McCloskey, A. L., & Tomlinson, T. M. (1997). Can the jury disregard that information? The use of suspicion to reduce the prejudicial effects of pretrial publicity and inadmissible testimony. *Personality and Social Psychology Bulletin*, *23*, 1215–1226.

Fein, S., & Spencer, S. J. (1997). Prejudice as self-image maintenance: Affirming the self through derogating others. *Journal of Personality and Social Psychology*, *73*, 31–44.

Feingold, A. (1990). Gender differences in effects of physical attractiveness on romantic attraction: A comparison across five research paradigms. *Journal of Personality and Social Psychology*, 59, 981–993.

Feingold, A. (1992a). Gender differences in mate selection preferences: A test of the parental investment model. *Psychological Bulletin*, *112*, 125–139.

Feingold, A. (1992b). Good-looking people are not what we think. *Psychological Bulletin*, *111*, 304–341.

Feld, S. L. (1982). Social structural determinants of similarity among associates. *American Sociological Review*, *47*, 797–801.

Fellner, J. (2009, June 19). Race, drugs, and law enforcement in the United States. *Stanford Law and Policy Review*, *20*, 257–291.

Femlee, D. H. (1995). Fatal attractions: Affection and disaffection in intimate relationships. *Journal of Social and Personal Relationships*, *12*, 295–311.

Femlee, D. H. (1998a). "Be careful what you wish for . . .": A quantitative and qualitative investigation of "fatal attractions." *Personal Relationships*, *5*, 235–253.

Femlee, D. H. (1998b). Fatal attractions: Contradictions in intimate relationships. In J. H. Harvey (Ed.), *Perspectives on loss: A sourcebook* (pp. 113–124). Philadelphia: Brunner/Mazel.

Femlee, D. H., Sprecher, S., & Bassin, E. (1990). The dissolution of intimate relationships: A hazard model. *Social Psychology Quarterly*, *53*, 13–30.

Fenigstein, A., Scheier, M. F., & Buss, A. H. (1975). Public and private self-consciousness: Assessment and theory. *Journal of Consulting and Clinical Psychology*, *43*, 522–527.

Ferguson, C. J. (2007a). Evidence for publication bias in video game violence effects literature: A meta-analytic review. *Journal of Aggressive and Violent Behavior*, *12*, 470–482.

Ferguson, C. J. (2007b). The good, the bad and the ugly: A meta-analytic review of positive and negative effects of violent video games. *Psychiatric Quarterly*, *78*, 309–316.

Ferguson, C. J. (2009). Media violence effects: Confirmed truth or just another X-File? *Journal of Forensic Psychology Practice*, *9*, 103–126.

Ferguson, C. J. , & Kilburn, J. (2009). The public health risks of media violence: A meta-analytic review. *Journal of Pediatrics*, *154*, 759–763.

Ferris, T. (1997, April 14). The wrong stuff. *New Yorker*, p. 32.

Feshbach, N. D. (1989). Empathy training and prosocial behavior. In J. Groebel & R. A. Hinde (Eds.), *Aggression and war: Their biological and social bases* (pp. 101–111). New York: Cambridge University Press.

Feshbach, N. D. (1997). Empathy—the formative years: Implications for clinical practice. In A. C. Bohart & L. S. Greenberg (Eds.), *Empathy reconsidered: New directions in psychotherapy* (pp. 33–59). Washington, DC: American Psychological Association.

Feshbach, N. D., & Feshbach, S. (2009). Empathy and education: Social neuroscience. In J. Decety & W. Ickes (Eds.), The social neuroscience of empathy (pp. 85–97). Cambridge, MA: MIT Press.

Feshbach, S. (1971). Dynamics and morality of violence and aggression: Some psychological considerations. *American Psychologist*, *26*, 281–292.

Feshbach, S., & Tangney, J. (2008). Television viewing and aggression: Some alternative perspectives. *Perspectives on Psychological Science*, *3*, 387–389.

Festinger, L. (1954). A theory of social comparison processes. *Human Relations*, 7, 117–140.

Festinger, L. (1957). *A theory of cognitive dissonance*. Stanford, CA: Stanford University Press.

Festinger, L., & Carlsmith, J. M. (1959). Cognitive consequences of forced compliance. *Journal of Abnormal and Social Psychology*, *58*, 203–211.

Festinger, L., & Maccoby, N. (1964). On resistance to persuasive communications. *Journal of Abnormal and Social Psychology*, *68*, 359–366.

Festinger, L., Riecken, H. W., & Schachter, S. (1956). *When prophecy fails*. Minneapolis: University of Minnesota Press.

Festinger, L., Schachter, S., & Back, K. (1950). *Social pressures in informal groups: A study of human factors in housing*. New York: Harper.

Festinger, L., & Thibaut, J. (1951). Interpersonal communication in small groups. *Journal of Abnormal and Social Psychology*, *46*, 92–99.

Fiedler, F. (1967). *A theory of leadership effectiveness*. New York: McGraw-Hill.

Fiedler, F. (1978). The contingency model and the dynamics of the leadership process. In L. Berkowitz (Ed.), *Advances in experimental social psychology* (Vol. 11, pp. 59–112). Orlando, FL: Academic Press.

Fiedler, K. (2000). Illusory correlations: A simple associative algorithm provides a convergent account of seemingly divergent paradigms. *Review of General Psychology*, *4*, 25–58.

Fiedler, K., Walther, E., & Nickel, S. (1999). Covariation-based attribution: On the ability to assess multiple covariations of an effect. *Personality and Social Psychology Bulletin*, *25*, 607–622.

The financial crisis inquiry report. (2011). Washington, DC: U.S. Government Printing Office. Retrieved July 9, 2011, from www.gpoaccess.gov/fcic/fcic.pdf

Fincham, F. D., Bradbury, T. N., Arias, I., Byrne, C. A., & Karney, B. R. (1997). Marital violence, marital distress, and attributions. *Journal of Family Psychology*, *11*, 367–372.

Fine, C. (2008). *A mind of its own: How your brain distorts and deceives*. New York: W.W. Norton.

Fine, C. (2010). *Delusions of gender: The real science behind sex differences*. New York: W.W. Norton.

Fine, G. A., & Elsbach, K. D. (2000). Ethnography and experiment in social psychological theory building: Tactics for integrating qualitative field data with quantitative lab data. *Journal of Experimental Social Psychology*, *36*, 51–76.

Fink, B., & Penton-Voak, I. (2002). Evolutionary psychology of facial attractiveness. *Current Directions in Psychological Science*, *11*, 154–158.

Finkel, E. J., & Eastwick, P. W. (2009). Arbitrary social norms influence sex differences in romantic selectivity. *Psychological Science*, *20*, 1291–1295.

Finkel, E. J., Eastwick, P. W., Karney, B. R., Reis, H. T., & Sprecher, S. (2012). Online dating: A critical analysis from the perspective of psychological science. *Psychological Science in the Public Interest*. doi:10.1177/1529100612436522

Finkelstein, L. M., DeMuth, R. L. F., & Sweeney, D. L. (2007). Bias against overweight job applicants: Further explorations of when and why. *Human Resource Management*, *46*, 203–222.

Finney, P. D. (1987). When consent information refers to risk and deception: Implications for social research. *Journal of Social Behavior and Personality, 2*, 37–48.

Fischer, P., Krueger, J. I., Greitemeyer, T., Vogrincic, C., Kastenmüller, A., Frey, D., Heene, M., Wicher, M., & Kainbacher, M. (2011). The bystander-effect: A meta-analytic review on bystander intervention in dangerous and non-dangerous emergencies. *Psychological Bulletin, 137*(4), 517–537. doi:10.1037/a0023304

Fischhoff, B. (2007). An early history of hindsight research. *Social Cognition, 25*, 10–13.

Fishbein, M., Chan, D., O'Reilly, K., Schnell, D., Wood, R., Beeker, C., & Cohn, C. (1993). Factors influencing gay men's attitudes, subjective norms, and intentions with respect to performing sexual behaviors. *Journal of Applied Social Psychology, 23*, 417–438.

Fisher, J. D., & Fisher, W. A. (2000). Theoretical approaches to individual-level changes in HIV risk behavior. In J. L. Peterson & C. C. DiClemente (Eds.), *Handbook of HIV prevention* (pp. 3-55). New York: Kluwer Academic/Plenum Press.

Fisher, R. P., & Schreiber, N. (2007). Interview protocols to improve eyewitness memory. In M. P. Toglia, J. D. Read, D. F. Ross, & R. C. L. Lindsay (Eds.) *The handbook of eyewitness psychology*, Vol I: *Memory for events* (pp. 53–80). Mahwah, NJ: Erlbaum.

Fisher, W. A., & Barak, A. (2001). Internet pornography: A social psychological perspective on Internet sexuality. *Journal of Sex Research, 38*, 312–323.

Fiske, S. T., Cuddy, A. J. C., & Glick, P. (2006). Universal dimensions of social cognition: Warmth and competence. *Trends in Cognitive Sciences, 11*, 77–83.

Fiske, S. T., & Depret, E. (1996). Control, interdependence, and power: Understanding social cognition in its social context. *European Review of Social Psychology*, 7, 31–61.

Fiske, S. T., & Taylor, S. E. (1991). *Social cognition* (2nd ed.). New York: McGraw-Hill.

Flanagan, C. A., Bowes, J. M., Jonsson, B., Csapo, B., & Sheblanova, E. (1998). Ties that bind: Correlates of adolescents' civic commitments in seven countries. *Journal of Social Issues, 54*, 457–475.

Flowers, M. L. (1977). A lab test of some implications of Janis's groupthink hypothesis. *Journal of Personality and Social Psychology, 35*, 888–897.

Fointiat, V., Grosbras, J-M., Michel, S., & Somat, A. (2001). Encouraging young adults to drive carefully. The use of the hypocrisy paradigm. *Promoting Public Health*, Chambery (France), May, 10–12.

Folkman, S., & Moskowitz, J. T. (2000). The context matters. *Personality and Social Psychology Bulletin, 26*, 150–151.

Forer, B. R. (1949). The fallacy of personal validation: A classroom demonstration of gullibility. *Journal of Abnormal and Social Psychology*, 44, 118–123.

Forgas, J. P. (2011). Affective influences on self-disclosure: Mood effects on the intimacy and reciprocity of disclosing personal information. *Journal of Personality and Social Psychology, 100*(3), 449–461. doi:10.1037/a0021129

Forgas, J. P., & Bower, G. H. (1987). Mood effects on person-perception judgments. *Journal of Personality and Social Psychology, 53*, 53–60.

Förster, J., Liberman, N., & Friedman, R. (2007). Seven principles of goal activation: A systematic approach to distinguishing goal priming from priming of non-goal constructs. *Personality and Social Psychology Review, 11*(3), 211–233.

Forsterling, F. (1989). Models of covariation and attribution: How do they relate to the analogy of analysis of variance? *Journal of Personality and Social Psychology, 57*, 615–625.

Forsyth, D. R., & Burnette, J. (2010). Group processes. In R. F. Baumeister & E. J. Finkel (Eds.), *Advanced social psychology: The state of the science* (pp. 495–534). New York: Oxford.

Foster, J. D., Campbell, W. K., & Twenge, J. M. (2003). Individual differences in narcissism: Inflated self-views across the lifespan and around the world. *Journal of Research in Personality, 37*, 469–486.

Fountain, J. W. (1997, May 4). No fare. *Washington Post*, p. F1.

Fouts, G., & Burggraf, K. (1999). Television situation comedies: Female body images and verbal reinforcements. *Sex Roles, 40*, 473–479.

Fox, C. (2006). The availability heuristic in the classroom: How soliciting more criticism can boost your course ratings. *Judgment and Decision Making, 1*, 86–90.

Frager, R. (1970). Conformity and anticonformity in Japan. *Journal of Personality and Social Psychology, 15*, 203–210.

Fraidin, S. N. (2004). When is one head better than two? Interdependent information in group decision making. *Organizational Behavior and Human Decision Processes, 93*, 102–113.

Fraley, R. C. (2002). Attachment stability from infancy to adulthood: Meta-analysis and dynamic modeling of developmental mechanisms. *Personality and Social Psychology Review, 6*, 123–151.

Fraley, R. C., & Shaver, P. R. (2000). Adult romantic attachment: Theoretical developments, emerging controversies, and unanswered questions. *Review of General Psychology, 4*, 132–154.

France: An event not hallowed. (2001, November 1). *The New York Times*, p. A14.

Franich, D. (2011a, March 24). Jersey Shore recap: The missing piece. Retrieved August 3, 2011, from http://tvrecaps.ew.com/recap/jersey-shore-season

Franich, D. (2011b, February 10). Jersey Shore recap: Requiem for a sweetheart. Retrieved August 3, 2011, from http://tvrecaps.ew.com/recap/jersey-shore-season

Franklin, B. (1900). *The autobiography of Benjamin Franklin* (J. Bigelow, Ed.). Philadelphia: Lippincott. (Originally published 1868)

Franklin, K. (2000). Antigay behaviors among young adults. *Journal of Interpersonal Violence, 15*, 339–362.

Frazier, P., Keenan, N., Anders, S., Perera, S., Shallcross, S., & Hintz, S. (2011). Perceived past, present, and future control and adjustment to stressful life events. *Journal of Personality and Social Psychology, 100*, 749–765. doi:10.1037/a0022405

Frazier, P. A., & Cook, S. W. (1993). Correlates of distress following heterosexual relationship dissolution. *Journal of Social and Personal Relationships, 10*, 55–67.

Fredrickson, B. L., Roberts, T., Noll, S. M., Quinn, D. M., & Twenge, J. M. (1998). That swimsuit becomes you: Sex differences in self-objectification, restrained eating, and math performance. *Journal of Personality and Social Psychology, 75*, 269–284.

Freedman, J. L. (1965). Long-term behavioral effects of cognitive dissonance. *Journal of Experimental and Social Psychology, 1*, 145–155.

Freud, S. (1930). *Civilization and its discontents* (J. Riviere, Trans.). London: Hogarth Press.

Freud, S. (1933). *New introductory lectures on psychoanalysis*. New York: Norton.

Fried, C., & Aronson, E. (1995). Hypocrisy, misattribution, and dissonance reduction: A demonstration of dissonance in the absence of aversive consequences. *Personality and Social Psychology Bulletin, 21*, 925–933.

Friedkin, N. (2004). Social Cohesion. *Annual Review of Sociology, 30*, 409–425.

Frodi, A. (1975). The effect of exposure to weapons on aggressive behavior from a cross-cultural perspective. *International Journal of Psychology, 10*, 283–292.

Fukuyama, F. (1999). *The great disruption: Human nature and the reconstitution of social order*. New York: Free Press.

Fulero, S. M. (2002). Afterword: The past, present, and future of applied pretrial publicity research. *Law and Human Behavior, 26*, 127–133.

Fumento, M. (1997, September 12). Why we need a new war on weight. *USA Weekend*, pp. 4–6.

Funder, D. C. (1995). On the accuracy of personality judgments: A realistic approach. *Psychological Review, 102*, 652–670.

Funder, D. C., & Colvin, C. R. (1988). Friends and strangers: Acquaintanceship, agreement, and the accuracy of personality judgment. *Journal of Personality and Social Psychology, 55*, 149–158.

Furnham, A. (1993). Just world beliefs in twelve societies. *Journal of Social Psychology, 133*, 317–329.

Furnham, A., & Gunter, B. (1984). Just world beliefs and attitudes toward the poor. *British Journal of Social Psychology, 23*, 265–269.

Furnham, A., & Mak, T. (1999). Sex-role stereotyping in television commercials: A review and comparison of fourteen studies done on five continents over 25 years. *Sex Roles, 41*, 413–437.

Furnham, A., & Procter, E. (1989). Beliefs in a just world: Review and critique of the individual difference literature. *British Journal of Social Psychology, 28*, 365–384.

Fury, G., Carlson, E. A., & Sroufe, L. A. (1997). Children's representations of attachment relationships in family drawings. *Child Development, 68*, 1154–1164.

Gabbert, F., Memon, A., & Allan, K. (2003). Memory conformity: Can eyewitnesses influence each other's memories for an event? *Applied Cognitive Psychology, 17*, 533–543.

Gabriel, S., & Gardner, W. L. (1999). Are there "his" and "hers" types of interdependence? The implications of gender differences in collective versus relational interdependence for affect, behavior, and cognition. *Journal of Personality and Social Psychology, 77*, 642–655.

Gaertner, S. L., Mann, J. A., Dovidio, J. F., & Murrell, A. J. (1990). How does cooperation reduce intergroup bias? *Journal of Personality and Social Psychology, 59*, 692–704.

Gagnon, J. H., Simon, W. (1973). *Sexual conduct: The social sources of human sexuality*. Chicago: Aldine.

Gailliot, M., & Baumeister, R. (2007). The physiology of willpower: Linking blood glucose to self-control. *Personality and Social Psychology Review, 11*, 303–327.

Galati, D., Miceli, R., & Sini, B. (2001). Judging and coding facial expression of emotions in congenitally blind children. *International Journal of Behavioral Development, 25*, 268–278.

Galinsky, A. D., Mussweiler, T., & Medvec, V. H. (2002). Disconnecting outcomes and evaluations: The role of negotiator focus. *Journal of Personality and Social Psychology, 83*, 1131–1140.

Gallup, G. (1997). On the rise and fall of self-conception in primates. In J. G. Snodgrass & R. L. Thompson (Eds.), *The self across psychology: Self-recognition, self-awareness, and the self concept* (pp. 73–82). New York: New York Academy of Sciences.

Gallup, G. G., Jr., Anderson, J. R., & Shillito, D. J. (2002). The mirror test. In M. Bekoff & C. Allen (Eds.), *Cognitive animal: Empirical and theoretical perspectives on animal cognition* (pp. 325–333). Cambridge, MA: MIT Press.

Gangestad, S. W. (1993). Sexual selection and physical attractiveness: Implications for mating dynamics. *Human Nature, 4*, 205–235.

Ganzel, B. L., Morris, P. A., & Wethington, E. (2010). Allostasis and the human brain: Integrating models of stress from the social and life sciences. *Psychological Review, 117*, 134–174.

Gao, G. (1993, May). *An investigation of love and intimacy in romantic relationships in China and the United States*. Paper presented at the annual conference of the International Communication Association, Washington, DC.

Gao, G. (1996). Self and other: A Chinese perspective on interpersonal relationships. In W. B. Gudykunst, S. Ting-Toomey, & T. Nishida (Eds.), *Communication in personal relationships across cultures* (pp. 81–101). Thousand Oaks, CA: Sage.

Gao, G., & Gudykunst, W. B. (1995). Attributional confidence, perceived similarity, and network involvement in Chinese and European American romantic relationships. *Communication Quarterly, 43*, 431–445.

Garcia, L. T., & Milano, L. (1990). A content analysis of erotic videos. *Journal of Psychology and Human Sexuality, 3*, 95–103.

Garcia, S., Stinson, L., Ickes, W. J., Bissonnette, V., & Briggs, S. (1991). Shyness and physical attractiveness in mixed-sex dyads. *Journal of Personality and Social Psychology, 61*, 35–49.

Garcia, S. M., Weaver, K., Moskowitz, G. B., & Darley, J. M. (2002). Crowded minds: The implicit bystander effect. *Journal of Personality and Social Psychology, 83*, 843–853.

Garcia-Marques, L., & Hamilton, D. L. (1996). Resolving the apparent discrepancy between the incongruency effect and the expectancy-based illusory correlation effect: The TRAP model. *Journal of Personality and Social Psychology, 71*, 845–860.

Gardner, W., & Gabriel, S. (2004). Gender differences in relational and collective interdependence: Implications for self-views, social behavior, and subjective well-being. In A. H. Eagly, A. E. Beall, & R. J. Sternberg (Eds.), *The psychology of gender* (2nd ed., pp. 169–191). New York: Guilford Press.

Gardner, W., & Knowles, M. L. (2008). Love makes you real: Favorite television characters are perceived as "real" in a social facilitation paradigm. *Social Cognition, 26*, 156–168.

Gardner, W. L., & Gabriel, S. (2004). Gender differences in relational and collective interdependence: Implications for self-views, social behavior, and subjective well-being. In A. H. Eagly, A. E. Beall, & R. J. Sternberg (Eds.), *Psychology of gender* (2nd ed., pp. 169–191). New York: Guilford.

Gardner, W. L., Pickett, C. L., & Brewer, M. B. (2000). Social exclusion and selective memory: How the need to belong influences memory for social events. *Personality and Social Psychology Bulletin, 26*, 486–496.

Garfinkle, H. (1967). *Studies in ethnomethodology*. Englewood Cliffs, NJ: Prentice Hall.

Gates, H. L., Jr. (1995, October 23). Thirteen ways of looking at a black man. *New Yorker*, pp. 56–65.

Gavanski, I., & Hoffman, C. (1987). Awareness of influences on one's own judgments: The roles of covariation detection and attention. *Journal of Personality and Social Psychology, 52*, 453–463.

Gawronski, B. (2003a). Implicational schemata and the correspondence bias: On the diagnostic value of situationally constrained behavior. *Journal of Personality and Social Psychology, 84*, 1154–1171.

Gawronski, B. (2003b). On difficult questions and evident answers: Dispositional inference from role-constrained behavior. *Personality and Social Psychology Bulletin, 29*, 1459–1475.

Gawronski, B., & Bodenhausen, G. V. (2012). Self-insight from a dual-process perspective. In S. Vazire, & T. D. Wilson (Eds.), *Handbook of self-knowledge*. New York: Guilford Press.

Gawronski, B., & Payne, B. K. (Eds.). (2010). *Handbook of implicit social cognition: Measurement, theory, and applications*. New York: Guilford Press.

Geen, R. G. (1989). Alternative conceptions of social facilitation. In P. B. Paulus (Ed.), *Psychology of group influence* (2nd ed., pp. 15–51). Hillsdale, NJ: Erlbaum.

Geen, R. G. (1994). Television and aggression: Recent developments in research and theory. In D. Zillmann, J. Bryant, & A. C. Huston (Eds.), *Media, children, and the family: Social scientific, psychodynamic, and clinical perspectives* (pp. 151–162). Hillsdale, NJ: Erlbaum.

Geen, R. G., & Quanty, M. (1977). The catharsis of aggression: An evaluation of a hypothesis. In L. Berkowitz (Ed.), *Advances in experimental social psychology* (Vol. 10, pp. 1–36). New York: Academic Press.

Geen, R. G., Stonner, D., & Shope, G. (1975). The facilitation of aggression by aggression: A study in response inhibition and disinhibition. *Journal of Personality and Social Psychology, 31*, 721–726.

Gelfand, M. J., Erez, M., Aycan, Z. (2007). Cross-cultural organizational behavior. *Annual Review of Psychology, 58*, 479–514.

Gemmill, G. (1989). The dynamics of scapegoating in small groups. *Small Group Behavior, 20*, 406–418.

Gentile, D. A., Anderson, C. A., Yukawa, N., Saleem, M., Lim, K. M., Shibuya, A., et al., (2009). The effects of prosocial video games on prosocial behaviors: International evidence from correlational, longitudinal, and experimental studies. *Personality and Social Psychology Bulletin, 35*, 752–763.

Gentile, D. A., Coyne, S., & Walsh, D. A. (2011). Media violence, physical aggression, and relational aggression in school age children: A short-term longitudinal study. *Aggressive Behavior, 37*, 193–206.

George, J. M. (1990). Personality, affect, and behavior in groups. *Journal of Applied Psychology, 75*, 107–116.

Geraerts, E., Lindsay, D. S., Merckelbach, H., Jelicic, M., Raymaekers, L., Arnold, M. M., & Schooler, J. W. (2009). Cognitive mechanisms underlying recovered-memory experiences of childhood sexual abuse. *Psychological Science, 20*(1), 92–98. doi:10.1111/j.1467-9280.2008.02247.x

Geraerts, E., Schooler, J., Merckelbach, H., Jelicic, M., Hauer, B., & Ambadar, Z. (2007). The reality of recovered memories: Corroborating continuous and discontinuous memories of childhood sexual abuse. *Psychological Science, 18*, 564–568.

Gerard, H. B. (1953). The effect of different dimensions of disagreement on the communication process in small groups. *Human Relations, 6*, 249–271.

Gerard, H. B., & Mathewson, G. C. (1966). The effects of severity of initiation on liking for a group: A replication. *Journal of Experimental Social Psychology, 2*, 278–287.

Gerard, H. B., Wilhelmy, R. A., & Conolley, E. S. (1968). Conformity and group size. *Journal of Personality and Social Psychology, 8*, 79–82.

Gerbner, G., Gross, L., Morgan, M., Signorielli, N., & Shanahan, J. (2002). Growing up with television: Cultivation processes. In J. Bryant & D. Zillmann (Eds.), *Media effects: Advances in theory and research* (pp. 43–67). Mahwah, NJ: Erlbaum.

Gerdes, E. P. (1979). College students' reactions to social psychological experiments involving deception. *Journal of Social Psychology, 107*, 99–110.

Gergen, K. J., Gergen, M. M., & Barton, W. H. (1973, July). Deviance in the dark. *Psychology Today*, pp. 129–130.

Gerin, W., Chaplin, W., Schwartz, J. E., Holland, J., Alter, R., Wheeler, R., Duong, D., & Pickering, T. G. (2005). Sustained blood pressure increase after an acute stressor: The effects of the 11 September 2001 attack on the New York City World Trade Center. *Journal of Hypertension, 23*, 279–84.

Gershoff, E. T. (2002). Parental corporal punishment and associated child behaviors and experiences: A meta-analytic and theoretical review. *Psychological Bulletin, 128*, 539–579.

Gervey, B. M., Chiu, C., Hong, Y., & Dweck, C. S. (1999). Differential use of person information in decisions about guilt versus innocence: The role of implicit theories. *Personality and Social Psychology Bulletin, 25*, 17–27.

Gibbons, F. X. (1978). Sexual standards and reactions to pornography: Enhancing behavioral consistency through self-focused attention. *Journal of Personality and Social Psychology, 36*, 976–987.

Gibbons, F. X., Eggleston, T. J., & Benthin, A. C. (1997). Cognitive reactions to smoking relapse: The reciprocal relation between dissonance and self-esteem. *Journal of Personality and Social Psychology, 72*, 184–195.

Gibbons, F. X., Gerrard, M., & Cleveland, M. J. (2004). Perceived discrimination and substance use in African American parents and their children: A panel study. *Journal of Personality and Social Psychology, 86*, 517–529. www.obesity.org/subs/fastfacts/obesity_what2.shtml

Gibbs, N., & Roche, T. (1999, December 20). The Columbine tapes. *Time*, p. 154.

Gibson, B., & Poposki, E. M. (2010). How the adoption of impression management goals alters impression formation. *Personality and Social Psychology Bulletin, 36*, 1543–1554. doi:10.1177/0146167210385008

Gifford, R. (1991). Mapping nonverbal behavior on the interpersonal circle. *Journal of Personality and Social Psychology, 61*, 279–288.

Gifford, R. (1994). A lens-mapping framework for understanding the encoding and decoding of interpersonal dispositions in nonverbal behavior. *Journal of Personality and Social Psychology, 66*, 398–412.

Gigerenzer, G. (2000). *Adaptive thinking: Rationality in the real world*. Oxford: Oxford University Press.

Gigerenzer, G. (2008). Why heuristics work. *Perspectives on Psychological Science, 3*, 20–29.

Gilbert, D. T. (1989). Thinking lightly about others: Automatic components of the social inference process. In J. S. Uleman & J. A. Bargh (Eds.), *Unintended thought* (pp. 189–211). New York: Guilford Press.

Gilbert, D. T. (1991). How mental systems believe. *American Psychologist, 46*, 107–119.

Gilbert, D. T. (1993). The assent of man: Mental representation and the control of belief. In D. M. Wegner & J. W. Pennebaker (Eds.), *The handbook of mental control* (pp. 57–87). Englewood Cliffs, NJ: Prentice Hall.

Gilbert, D. T. (1998a). Ordinary personology. In D. T. Gilbert, S. T. Fiske, & G. Lindzey (Eds.), *The handbook of social psychology* (4th ed., Vol. 2, pp. 89–150). New York: McGraw-Hill.

Gilbert, D. T. (1998b). Speeding with Ned: A personal view of the correspondence bias. In J. M. Darley & J. Cooper (Eds.), *Attribution and social interaction* (pp. 5–36). Washington, DC: American Psychological Association.

Gilbert, D. T. (2006). *Stumbling on happiness*. New York: Knopf.

Gilbert, D. T. (2007). *Stumbling on happiness*. New York: Vintage.

Gilbert, D. T. (2008). *Stumbling on happiness*. New York: Vintage.

Gilbert, D. T., Ebert, E. J. (2002). Decisions and revisions: The affective forecasting of changeable outcomes. *Journal of Personality and Social Psychology, 82*(4), 503–514.

Gilbert, D. T., & Hixon, J. G. (1991). The trouble of thinking: Activation and applications of stereotypical beliefs. *Journal of Personality and Social Psychology, 60*, 509–517.

Gilbert, D. T., & Jones, E. E. (1986). Perceiver-induced constraint: Interpretations of self-generated reality. *Journal of Personality and Social Psychology, 50*, 269–280.

Gilbert, D. T., & Malone, P. S. (1995). The correspondence bias. *Psychological Bulletin, 117*, 21–38.

Gilbert, D. T., & Osborne, R. E. (1989). Thinking backward: Some curable and incurable consequences of cognitive busyness. *Journal of Personality and Social Psychology, 57*, 940–949.

Gilbert, D. T., Pelham, B. W., & Krull, D. S. (1988). On cognitive busyness: When person perceivers meet persons perceived. *Journal of Personality and Social Psychology, 54*, 733–740.

Gilbert, D. T., & Wilson, T. D. (2007). Prospection: Experiencing the future. *Science, 317*, 1351–1354.

Gilbert, S. J. (1981). Another look at the Milgram obedience studies: The role of the gradated series of shocks. *Personality and Social Psychology Bulletin, 4*, 690–695.

Gilligan, J. (1996). *Violence: Our deadly epidemic and its causes*. New York: Putnam.

Gilovich, T., & Griffin, D. W. (2002). Introduction: Heuristics and biases, now and then. In T. Gilovich, D. W. Griffin, & D. Kahneman (Eds.), *Heuristics and biases: The psychology of intuitive judgment* (pp. 1–18). New York: Cambridge University Press.

Gilovich, T., & Savitsky, K. (2002). Like goes with like: The role of representativeness in erroneous and pseudoscientific beliefs. In T. Gilovich, D. W. Griffin, & D. Kahneman (Eds.), *Heuristics and biases: The psychology of intuitive judgment* (pp. 617–624). New York: Cambridge University Press.

Girl born to Japan's princess. (2001, December 1). *The New York Times*, p. 8.

Giscombé, C., & Lobel, M. (2005). Explaining disproportionately high rates of adverse birth outcomes among African Americans: The impact of stress, racism, and related factors in pregnancy. *Psychological Bulletin, 131*, 662–683.

Gladue, B. A., Boechler, M., & McCaul, K. D. (1989). Hormonal response to competition in human males. *Aggressive Behavior, 15*, 409–422.

Gladwell, M. (2004, January 12). Big and bad: How the S.U.V. ran over automotive safety. *New Yorker*, p. 28.

Gladwell, M. (2005, January 12). Big and bad: How the S.U.V. ran over automotive safety. *New Yorker*.

Glasman, L. R., & Albarracín, D. (2006). Forming attitudes that predict future behavior: A meta-analysis of the attitude-behavior relation. *Psychological Bulletin*,*132*, 778–822.

Glass, D. C. (1964). Changes in liking as a means of reducing cognitive discrepancies between self-esteem and aggression. *Journal of Personality, 32*, 531–549.

Gleick, E. (1997, April 7). Planet Earth about to be recycled. Your only chance to survive—leave with us. *Time*, pp. 28–36.

Glick, P., & Fiske, S. (2001). An ambivalent alliance: Hostile and benevolent sexism as complementary justifications for gender inequality. *American Psychologist, 56*, 109–118.

Global statistics. (2011). Retrieved November 1, 2011, from aids.gov/hiv-aids-basics/hiv-aids-101/overview/global-statistics/

Goethals, G. R., & Darley, J. M. (1977). Social comparison theory: An attributional approach. In J. M. Suls & R. L. Miller (Eds.), *Social comparison processes: Theoretical and empirical perspectives* (pp. 259–278). Washington, DC: Hemisphere/Halsted.

Goethals, G. R., & Reckman, R. F. (1973). The perception of consistency in attitudes. *Journal of Experimental Social Psychology, 9*(6), 491–501.

Goffman, E. (1959). *Presentation of self in everyday life*. Garden City, NY: Anchor/Doubleday.

Gold, J. A., Ryckman, R. M., & Mosley, N. R. (1984). Romantic mood induction and attraction to a dissimilar other: Is love blind? *Personality and Social Psychology Bulletin, 10*, 358–368.

Goldinger, S. D., Kleider, H. M., Azuma, T., & Beike, D. R. (2003). "Blaming the victim" under memory load. *Psychological Science, 14*, 81–85.

Goldstein, J. H., & Arms, R. L. (1971). Effect of observing athletic contests on hostility. *Sociometry, 34*, 83–90.

Goldstein, N. J., Cialdini, R. B., & Griskevicius, V. (2008). A room with a viewpoint: Using social norms to motivate environmental conservation in hotels. *Journal of Consumer Research*, 35, 472–482.

Gollwitzer, P. M., & Oettingen, G. (2011). Planning promotes goal striving. In K. D. Vohs & R. F. Baumeister (Eds.), *Handbook of self-regulation: Research, theory, and applications* (2nd ed., pp. 162–185). New York: Guilford.

Good, C., Aronson, J., & Harder, J. (2007). Problems in the pipeline: Women's achievement in high-level math courses. *Journal of Applied Developmental Psychology, 29*, 17–28.

Good, C., Aronson, J., & Harder, J. (2008). Problems in the pipeline: Women's achievement in high-level math courses. *Journal of Applied Developmental Psychology, 29*, 17–28.

Good, C., Aronson, J., & Inzlicht, M. (2003). Improving adolescents' standardized test performance: An intervention to reduce the effects of stereotype threat. *Journal of Applied Developmental Psychology, 24*, 645–662.

Goode, E. (1999, February 9). Arranged marriage gives way to courtship by mail. *The New York Times*, p. D3.

Goodwin, D. K. (2006) *Team of Rivals*. New York: Simon & Schuster.

Goodwin, R. (1999). *Personal relationships across cultures*. New York: Routledge.

Gosling, S. (2008). *Snoop: What your stuff says about you*. London: Profile Books Ltd.

Gossett, J. L., & Byrne, S. (2002). "Click here": A content analysis of Internet rape cites. *Gender and Society, 16*, 689–709.

Graham, J., Koo, M., & Wilson, T. D. (2011). Conserving energy by inducing people to drive less. *Journal of Applied Social Psychology, 41*, 106–118.

Graham, K., Osgood, D. W., Wells, S., & Stockwell, T. (2006). To what extent is intoxication associated with aggression in bars? A multilevel analysis. *Journal of Studies on Alcohol, 67*, 382–390.

Granberg, D., & Bartels, B. (2005). On being a lone dissenter. *Journal of Applied Social Psychology, 35*, 1849–1858.

Granberg, D., & Brown, T. (1989). On affect and cognition in politics. *Social Psychology Quarterly, 52*, 171–182.

Grant, A. M., & Gino, F. (2010). A little thanks goes a long way: Explaining why gratitude expressions motivate prosocial behavior. *Journal of Personality and Social Psychology, 98*(6), 946–955. doi:10.1037/a0017935

Gray, K., & Wegner, D. M. (2010). Torture and judgments of guilt. *Journal of Experimental Social Psychology, 46*, 233–235.

Gray, S. (2004, March 30). Bizarre hoaxes on restaurants trigger lawsuits. *Wall Street Journal*, Retrieved on June 5, 2006, from online.wsj.com/article_print/SB108061045899868615.html

Graziano, W. G., Habashi, M. M., Sheese, B. E., & Tobin, R. M. (2007). Agreeableness, empathy, and helping: A person × situation perspective. *Journal of Personality and Social Psychology, 93*, 583–599.

Graziano, W. G., Jensen-Campbell, L. A., Shebilske, L. J., & Lundgren, S. R. (1993). Social influence, sex differences, and judgments of beauty: Putting the interpersonal back in interpersonal attraction. *Journal of Personality and Social Psychology, 65*, 522–531.

Greenberg, J., & Musham, C. (1981). Avoiding and seeking self-focused attention. *Journal of Research in Personality, 15*, 191–200.

Greenberg, J., Pyszczynski, T., & Solomon, S. (1982). The self-serving attributional bias: Beyond self-presentation. *Journal of Experimental Social Psychology, 18*, 56–67.

Greenberg, J., Solomon, S., & Pyszczynski, T. (1997). Terror management theory of self-esteem and social behavior: Empirical assessments and conceptual refinements. In M. P. Zanna (Ed.), *Advances in experimental social psychology* (Vol. 29, pp. 61–139). New York: Academic Press.

Greenwald, A. G., & Banaji, M. R. (1995). Implicit social cognition: Attitudes, self-esteem, and stereotypes. *Psychological Review, 102*, 4–27.

Greenwald, A. G., McGhee, D. E., & Schwartz, J. L. K. (1998). Measuring individual differences in implicit cognition: The Implicit Association Test. *Journal of Personality and Social Psychology, 74*, 1464–1480.

Greenwald, A. G., Poehlman, T. A., Uhlmann, E. L., & Banaji, M. R. (2009). Understanding and using the Implicit Association Test: III. Meta-analysis of predictive validity. *Journal of Personality and Social Psychology, 97*(1), 17–41. doi:10.1037/a0015575

Greenwald, A. G., Spangenberg, E. R., Pratkanis, A. R., & Eskenazi, J. (1991). Double-blind tests of subliminal self-help audiotapes. *Psychological Science, 2*, 119–122.

Greitemeyer, T. (2009). Effects of songs with prosocial lyrics on prosocial behavior: Further evidence and a mediating mechanism. *Personality and Social Psychology Bulletin, 35*(11), 1500–1511. doi:10.1177/0146167209341648

Greitemeyer, T. (2011). Exposure to music with prosocial lyrics reduces aggression: First evidence and test of the underlying mechanism. *Journal of Experimental Social Psychology, 47*(1), 28–36. doi:10.1016/j.jesp.2010.08.005

Greitemeyer, T., & McLatchie, N. (2011). Denying humanness to others: A newly discovered mechanism by which violent video games increase aggressive behavior. *Psychological Science, 22*, 659–665.

Greitemeyer, T., & Osswald, S. (2010). Effects of prosocial video games on prosocial behavior. *Journal of Personality and Social Psychology, 98*(2), 211–221. doi:10.1037/a0016997

Greitemeyer, T., Osswald, S., & Brauer, M. (2010). Playing prosocial video games increases empathy and decreases schadenfreude. *Emotion, 10*(6), 796–802. doi:10.1037/a0020194

Greitemeyer, T., & Schulz-Hardt, S. (2003). Preference-consistent evaluation of information in the hidden profile paradigm: Beyond group-level explanations for the dominance of shared information in group decisions. *Journal of Personality and Social Psychology, 84*, 322–339.

Griffin, D., & Kahneman, D. (2003). Judgmental heuristics: Human strengths or human weaknesses? In L. G. Aspinwall & U. M. Staudinger (Eds.), *A psychology of human strengths: Fundamental questions and future directions for a positive psychology* (pp. 165–178). Washington, DC: American Psychological Association.

Griffin, D. W., Gonzalez, R., & Varey, C. (2001). The heuristics and biases approach to judgment under uncertainty. In A. Tesser & N. Schwarz (Eds.), *Blackwell handbook of social psychology: Intraindividual processes* (pp. 127–133). Oxford, UK: Blackwell.

Griffin, D. W., & Ross, L. (1991). Subjective construal, social inference, and human misunderstanding. In L. Berkowitz (Ed.), *Advances in experimental social psychology* (Vol. 24, pp. 319–359). San Diego, CA: Academic Press.

Griffin, E., & Sparks, G. G. (1990). Friends forever: A longitudinal exploration of intimacy in same-sex pairs and platonic pairs. *Journal of Social and Personal Relationships, 7*, 29–46.

Griffitt, W., & Veitch, R. (1971) Hot and crowded: influences of population density and temperature on interpersonal affective behavior. *Journal of Personality and Social Psychology, 17*(1), 92–98.

Guagnano, G. A., Stern, P. C., & Dietz, T. (1995). Influences on attitude-behavior relationships: A natural experiment with curbside recycling. *Environment and Behavior, 27*, 699–718.

Gudjonsson, G. H., & Pearse, J. (2011). Suspect interviews and false confessions. *Current Directions in Psychological Science, 20*(1), 33–37. doi:10.1177/0963721410396824

Gudykunst, W. B. (1988). Culture and intergroup processes. In M. H. Bond (Ed.), *The cross-cultural challenge to social psychology* (pp. 165–181). Newbury Park, CA: Sage.

Gudykunst, W. B., Ting-Toomey, S., & Nishida, T. (1996). *Communication in personal relationships across cultures*. Thousand Oaks, CA: Sage.

Guéguen, N., Jacob, C., & Lamy, L. (2010). 'Love is in the air': Effects of songs with romantic lyrics on compliance with a courtship request. *Psychology of Music, 38*(3), 303–307. doi:10.1177/0305735609360428

Guenther, C. L., & Alicke, M. D. (2010). Deconstructing the better-than-average effect. *Journal of Personality and Social Psychology, 99*, 755–770. doi:10.1037/a0020959

Guerin, B. (1993). *Social facilitation*. Cambridge: Cambridge University Press.

Guimond, S. (1999). Attitude change during college: Normative or informational social influence? *Social Psychology of Education, 2*, 237–261.

Guisinger, S., & Blatt, S. J. (1994). Individuality and relatedness: Evolution of a fundamental dialect. *American Psychologist, 49*, 104–111.

Gully, S. M., Devine, D. J., & Whitney, D. J. (1995). A meta-analysis of cohesion and performance: Effects of level of analysis and task interdependence. *Small Groups Research, 26*, 497–520.

Gustafson, R. (1989). Frustration and successful vs. unsuccessful aggression: A test of Berkowitz's completion hypothesis. *Aggressive Behavior, 15*, 5–12.

Guyll, M., Madon, S., Prieto, L., & Scherr, K. C. (2010). The potential roles of self-fulfilling prophecies, stigma consciousness, and stereotype threat in linking Latino/a ethnicity and educational outcomes. *Journal of Social Issues, 66*(1), 113–130. doi:10.1111/j.1540-4560.2009.01636.x

Gyekye, S. A., & Salminen, S. (2004). Causal attributions of Ghanaian industrial workers in accident occurrence. *Journal of Applied Social Psychology, 34*(11), 2324–2342.

Hackman, R. J., & Katz, N. (2010). Group behavior and performance. In S. T. Fiske, D. T. Gilbert, & G. Lindzey (Eds.), *Handbook of social psychology* (5th ed., Vol. 2, pp. 1208–1251). Hoboken, NJ: Wiley.

Hafer, C. L. (2000). Investment in long-term goals and commitment to just means drive the need to believe in a just world. *Personality and Social Psychology Bulletin, 26*, 1059–1073.

Hafer, C. L., & Begue (2005). Experimental research on just-world theory: Problems, developments, and future challenges. *Psychological Bulletin, 131*(1), 128–167.

Hagestad, G. O., & Smyer, M. A. (1982). Dissolving long-term relationships: Patterns of divorcing in middle age. In S. W. Duck (Ed.), *Personal relationships:* Vol. 4. *Dissolving personal relationships* (pp. 155–188). London: Academic Press.

Hahn, R., Fuqua-Whitley, D., Wethington, H., et al. (2008). Effectiveness of universal school-based programs to prevent violent and aggressive behaviour: A systematic review. *Child: Care, Health, & Development, 34*, 139.

Haidt, J. (2006). *The happiness hypothesis: Finding modern truth in ancient wisdom*. New York: Basic Books.

Haidt, J., & Keltner, D. (1999). Culture and facial expression: Open-ended methods find more faces and a gradient of recognition. *Cognition and Emotion, 13*, 225–266.

Halabi, S., & Nadler, A. (2010). Receiving help: Consequences for the recipient. In S. Stürmer & M. Snyder (Eds.), *The psychology of prosocial behavior: Group processes, intergroup relations, and helping* (pp. 121–138). Oxford, UK: Wiley-Blackwell.

Halberstadt, J. B., & Levine, G. L. (1997). *Effects of reasons analysis on the accuracy of predicting basketball games*. Unpublished manuscript, Indiana University.

Halberstadt, J. B., & Rhodes, G. (2000). The attractiveness of nonface averages: Implications for an evolutionary explanation of the attractiveness of average faces. *Psychological Science, 11*, 285–289.

Hall, E. T. (1969). *The hidden dimension*. Garden City, NY: Doubleday.

Ham, J., & Vonk, R. (2011). Impressions of impression management: Evidence of spontaneous suspicion of ulterior motivation. *Journal of Experimental Social Psychology, 47*, 466–471. doi:10.1016/j.jesp.2010.12.008

Hamby, S. L., & Koss, M. P. (2003). Shades of gray: A qualitative study of terms used in the measurement of sexual victimization. *Psychology of Women Quarterly, 27*, 243–255.

Hamilton, D. L. (1981). Illusory correlation as a basis for stereotyping. In D. L. Hamilton (Ed.), *Cognitive processes in stereotyping and intergroup behavior* (pp. 563–571). Hillsdale, NJ: Erlbaum.

Hamilton, D. L., & Gifford, R. K. (1976). Illusory correlation in interpersonal perception: A cognitive basis of stereotypic judgments. *Journal of Experimental Social Psychology, 12*, 392–407.

Hamilton, D. L., & Sherman, S. J. (1989). Illusory correlations: Implications for stereotype theory and research. In D. Bar-Tal, C. F. Graumann, A. W. Kruglanski, & W. Stroebe (Eds.), *Stereotypes and prejudice: Changing conceptions* (pp. 59–82). New York: Springer-Verlag.

Hamilton, D. L., Stroessner, S., & Mackie, D. M. (1993). The influence of affect on stereotyping: The case of illusory correlations. In D. M. Mackie & D. L. Hamilton (Eds.), *Affect, cognition, and stereotyping: Interactive processes in group perception* (pp. 39–61). San Diego, CA: Academic Press.

Hamilton, V. L., Sanders, J., & McKearney, S. J. (1995). Orientations toward authority in an authoritarian state: Moscow in 1990. *Personality and Social Psychology Bulletin, 21*, 356–365.

Hamilton, W. D. (1964). The genetical evolution of social behavior. *Journal of Theoretical Biology, 7*, 1–52.

Hamm, M. (1999). *Go for the goal: A champion's guide to winning in soccer and life*. New York: HarperCollins.

Hammond, J. R., & Fletcher, G. J. O. (1991). Attachment styles and relationship satisfaction in the development of close relationships. *New Zealand Journal of Psychology, 20*, 56–62.

Han, S., & Shavitt, S. (1994). Persuasion and culture: Advertising appeals in individualistic and collectivistic societies. *Journal of Experimental Social Psychology, 30*, 326–350.

Hancock, J. T., & Toma, C. L. (2009). Putting your best face forward: The accuracy of online dating photographs. *Journal of Communication, 59*, 367–286.

Haney, C., Banks, C., & Zimbardo, P. (1973). Interpersonal dynamics in a simulated prison. *International Journal of Criminology and Penology, 1*, 69–97.

Hansen, C. H., & Hansen, R. D. (1988). Finding the face in the crowd: An angry superiority effect. *Journal of Personality and Social Psychology, 54*, 917-924.

Hansen, E. M., Kimble, C. E., & Biers, D. W. (2000). Actors and observers: Divergent attributions of constrained unfriendly behavior. *Social Behavior and Personality, 29*, 87–104.

Hanson, K. L., Medina, K. L., Padula, C. B., Tapert, S. F., & Brown, S. A. (2011). Impact of adolescent alcohol and drug use on neuropsychological functioning in young adulthood: 10-year outcomes. *Journal of Child & Adolescent Substance Abuse, 20*, 135–154.

Hansson, R. O., & Slade, K. M. (1977). Altruism toward a deviant in a city and small town. *Journal of Applied Social Psychology, 7*, 272–279.

Harackiewicz, J. M. (1979). The effects of reward contingency and performance feedback on intrinsic motivation. *Journal of Personality and Social Psychology, 37*, 1352–1363.

Harackiewicz, J. M., & Elliot, A. J. (1993). Achievement goals and intrinsic motivation. *Journal of Personality and Social Psychology, 65*, 904–915.

Harackiewicz, J. M., & Elliot, A. J. (1998). The joint effects of target and purpose goals on intrinsic motivation: A mediational analysis. *Personality and Social Psychology Bulletin, 24*, 675–689.

Harackiewicz, J. M., & Hulleman, C. S. (2010). The importance of interest: The role of achievement goals and task values in promoting the development of interest. *Social and Personality Psychology Compass, 4*, 42–52. doi:10.1111/j.1751-9004.2009.00207.x

Hardin, C. D., & Higgins, E. T. (Eds.). (1996). *Shared reality: How social verification makes the subjective objective*. New York: Guilford Press.

Hare, A. P. (2003). Roles, relationships, and groups in organizations: Some conclusions and recommendations. *Small Group Research, 34*, 123–154.

Harmon-Jones, E. (2010). Decisions, action, and neuroscience: A contemporary perspective on cognitive dissonance. In M. H. Gonzales, C. Tavris, & J. Aronson (Eds.), *The scientist and the humanist: A festschrift in honor of Elliot Aronson* (pp. 109–131). New York: Psychology Press.

Harmon-Jones, E., & Winkielman, P. (Eds.). (2007). *Social neuroscience: Integrating biological and psychological explanations of social behavior*. New York: Guilford.

Harrigan, J. A., & O'Connell, D. M. (1996). How do you feel when feeling anxious? Facial displays of anxiety. *Personality and Individual Differences, 21*, 205–212.

Harris M. (Ed.). (2009). *Bullying, rejection, and peer victimization: A social-cognitive neuroscience perspective* (pp. 251–277). New York: Springer.

Harris, B. (1986). Reviewing 50 years of the psychology of social issues. *Journal of Social Issues, 42*, 1–20.

Harris, C. R. (2003). A review of sex differences in jealousy, including self-report data, psychophysiological responses, interpersonal violence, and morbid jealousy. *Personality and Social Psychology Review*, 7, 102–128.

Harris, C. R., & Pashler, H. (2004). Attention and the processing of emotional words and names: Not so special after all. *Psychological Science, 15*, 171–178.

Harris, M. B. (1974). Mediators between frustration and aggression in a field experiment. *Journal of Experimental and Social Psychology, 10*, 561–571.

Harris, M. B., Benson, S. M., & Hall, C. (1975). The effects of confession on altruism. *Journal of Social Psychology, 96*, 187–192.

Harris, M. B., & Perkins, R. (1995). Effects of distraction on interpersonal expectancy effects: A social interaction test of the cognitive busyness hypothesis. *Social Cognition, 13*, 163–182.

Harris, M. G. (1994). Cholas, Mexican-American girls, and gangs. *Sex Roles, 30*, 289–301.

Harrison, J. A., & Wells, R. B. (1991). Bystander effects on male helping behavior: Social comparison and diffusion of responsibility. *Representative Research in Social Psychology, 19*, 53–63.

Hart, A. J. (1995). Naturally occurring expectation effects. *Journal of Personality and Social Psychology, 68*, 109–115.

Hart, D., & Damon, W. (1986). Developmental trends in self-understanding. *Social Cognition, 4*, 388–407.

Hart, D., & Matsuba, M. K. (in press). The development of self-knowledge. In S. Vazire & T. D. Wilson (Eds.), *The handbook of self-knowledge*. New York: Guilford.

Hart, W., Albarracín, D., Eagly, A. H., Brechan, I., Lindberg, M. J., & Merrill, L. (2009). Feeling validated versus being correct: A meta-analysis of selective exposure to information. *Psychological Bulletin, 135*, 555–588.

Harter, S. (1993). Causes and consequences of low self-esteem in children and adolescents. In R. F. Baumeister (Ed.), *Self-esteem: The puzzle of low self-regard* (pp. 87–116). New York: Plenum.

Harter, S. (2003). The development of self-representations during childhood and adolescence. In M. R. Leary & J. P. Tangney (Eds.), *Handbook of self and identity* (pp. 610–642). New York: Guilford Press.

Hartstone, M., & Augoustinos, M. (1995). The minimal group paradigm: Categorization into two versus three groups. *European Journal of Social Psychology, 25*, 179–193.

Hartup, W. W., & Laursen, B. (1999). Relationships as developmental contexts: Retrospective themes and contemporary issues. In W. A. Collins & B. Laursen (Eds.), *Relationships as developmental contexts: Minnesota Symposia on Child Psychology* (Vol. 30, pp. 13–35). Mahwah, NJ: Erlbaum.

Hartup, W. W., & Stevens, N. (1997). Friendships and adaptation in the life course. *Psychological Bulletin, 121*, 355–370.

Harvey, J. H. (1995). *Odyssey of the heart: The search for closeness, intimacy, and love*. New York: Freeman.

Harvey, J. H., Flanary, R., & Morgan, M. (1986). Vivid memories of vivid loves gone by. *Journal of Personal and Social Relationships, 3*, 359–373.

Harvey, J. H., Orbuch, T. L., & Weber, A. L. (1992). The convergence of the attribution and accounts concepts in the study of close relationships. In J. H. Harvey, T. L. Orbuch, & A. L. Weber (Eds.), *Attributions, accounts, and close relationships* (pp. 1–18). New York: Springer-Verlag.

Hasel, L. E., & Kassin, S. M. (2012). False confessions. In B. L. Cutler (Ed.), *Conviction of the innocent: Lessons from psychological research* (pp. 53–77). Washington, DC: American Psychological Association.

Hassebrauck, M., & Buhl, T. (1996). Three-dimensional love. *Journal of Social Psychology, 136*, 121–122.

Hassin, R. R., Aarts, H., Eitam, B., Custers, R., & Kleiman, T. (in press). Non-conscious goal pursuit and the effortful control of behavior. In E. Morsella, P. M. Gollwitzer & J. A. Bargh (Eds.), *The psychology of action* (Vol. 2). New York: Oxford University Press.

Hassin, R. R., Uleman, J. S., & Bargh, J. A. (Eds.) (2005). *The new unconscious*. New York: Oxford University Press.

Hastie, R. (2008). What's the story? Explanations and narratives in civil jury decisions. In B, H. Bornstein, R. L. Wiener, R. Schopp, & S. L. Willborn (Eds.), *Civil juries and civil justice: Psychological and legal perspectives* (pp. 23–34). New York: Springer.

Hastie, R., & Pennington, N. (2000). Explanation-based decision making. In T. Connolly & H. R. Arkes (Eds.), *Judgment and decision making: An interdisciplinary reader* (2nd ed., pp. 212–228). New York: Cambridge University Press.

Hastie, R., Penrod, S. D., & Pennington, N. (1983). *Inside the jury*. Cambridge, MA: Harvard University Press.

Hatfield, E. (1988). Passionate and companionate love. In R. J. Sternberg & M. L. Barnes (Eds.), *The psychology of love* (pp. 191–217). New Haven, CT: Yale University Press.

Hatfield, E., Cacioppo, J. T., & Rapson, R. L. (1993). *Emotional contagion*. New York: Cambridge University Press.

Hatfield, E., & Rapson, R. L. (1993). *Love, sex, and intimacy: Their psychology, biology, and history*. New York: HarperCollins.

Hatfield, E., & Rapson, R. L. (1996). *Love and sex: Cross-cultural perspectives*. Needham Heights, MA: Allyn & Bacon.

Hatfield, E., & Rapson, R. L. (2002). Passionate love and sexual desire: Cultural and historical perspectives. In A. L. Vangelisti, H. T. Reis, & M.

A. Fitzpatrick (Eds.), *Stability and change in relationships* (pp. 306–324). New York: Cambridge University Press.

Hatfield, E., & Sprecher, S. (1995). Men's and women's preferences in marital partners in the United States, Russia, and Japan. *Journal of Cross-Cultural Psychology, 26*, 728–750.

Hatfield, E., & Walster, G. W. (1978). *A new look at love*. Reading, MA: Addison-Wesley.

Hatoum, I. J., & Belle, D. (2004). Mags and abs: Media consumption and bodily concerns in men. *Sex Roles, 51*, 397-407.

Haugtvedt, C. P., & Wegener, D. T. (1994). Message order effects in persuasion: An attitude strength perspective. *Journal of Consumer Research, 21*, 205–218.

Hays, C. L. (2003, June 5). Martha Stewart indicted by U.S. on obstruction. *The New York Times*, pp. A1, C4.

Hazan, C., & Shaver, P. (1987). Romantic love conceptualized as an attachment process. *Journal of Personality and Social Psychology, 52*, 511–524.

Hazan, C., & Shaver, P. (1994a). Attachment as an organizational framework for research on close relationships. *Psychological Inquiry, 5*, 1–22.

Hazan, C., & Shaver, P. (1994b). Deeper into attachment theory. *Psychological Inquiry, 5*, 68–79.

Hazelwood, J. D., & Olson, J. M. (1986). Covariation information, causal questioning, and interpersonal behavior. *Journal of Experimental Social Psychology, 22*, 276–291.

Heatherton, T. F., & Sargent, J. D. (2009). Does watching smoking in movies promote teenage smoking? *Current Directions in Psychological Science, 18*, 63–67.

Hebl, M., Foster, J., Bigazzi, J., Mannix, L., & Dovidio, J. (2002). Formal and interpersonal discrimination: A field study of bias toward homosexual applicants. *Personality and Social Psychology Bulletin, 28*, 815–825.

Heckhausen, J., & Schulz, R. (1995). A life-span theory of control. *Psychological Review, 102*, 284–304.

Hedge, A., & Yousif, Y. H. (1992). Effects of urban size, urgency, and cost on helpfulness. *Journal of Cross-Cultural Psychology, 23*, 107–115.

Hehman, E., Gaertner, S. L., & Dovidio, J. F. (2011). Evaluations of presidential performance: Race, prejudice, and perceptions of Americanism. *Journal of Experimental Social Psychology, 47*, 430–435.

Heider, F. (1944). Social perception and phenomenal causality. *Psychological Review, 51*, 358–374.

Heider, F. (1958). *The psychology of interpersonal relations*. New York: Wiley.

Heine, S., Proulx, T., & Vohs, K. (2006). The meaning maintenance model: on the coherence of social motivations. *Personality and Social Psychology Review, 10*, 88–110.

Heine, S. J. (2010). Cultural psychology. In S. T. Fiske, D. T. Gilbert, & G. Lindzey (Eds.), *Handbook of social psychology* (5th ed., Vol. 2, pp. 1423–1464). Hoboken, NJ: John Wiley.

Heine, S. J., Foster, J. B., & Spina, R. (2009). Do birds of a feather universally flock together? Cultural variation in the similarity-attraction effect. *Asian Journal of Psychology, 12*, 247–258.

Heine, S. J., Kitayama, S., & Lehman, D. R. (2001). Cultural differences in self-evaluation: Japanese readily accept negative self-relevant information. *Journal of Cross-Cultural Psychology, 32*, 434–443.

Heine, S. J., Lehman, D. R., Peng, K., & Greenholtz, J. (2002). What's wrong with cross-cultural comparisons of subjective Likert scales?: The reference-group effect. *Journal of Personality and Social Psychology, 82*, 903–918.

Heine, S. J., Takemoto, T., Moskalenko, S., Lasaleta, J., & Henrich, J. (2008). Mirrors in the head: Cultural variation in objective self-awareness. *Personality and Social Psychology Bulletin. 34*, 879–887.

Heitland, K., & Bohner, G. (2010). Reducing prejudice via cognitive dissonance: Individual differences in preference for consistency moderate the effects of counter-attitudinal advocacy. *Social Influence, 5*, 164–181.

Helgeson, V. S. (1994). Long-distance romantic relationships: Sex differences in adjustment and breakup. *Personality and Social Psychology Bulletin, 20*, 254–265.

Helgeson, V. S. (2003). Cognitive adaptation, psychological adjustment, and disease progression among angioplasty patients: 4 years later. *Health Psychology, 22*, 30–38.

Helgeson, V. S., & Fritz, H. L. (1999). Cognitive adaptation as a predictor of new coronary events after percutaneous transluminal coronary angioplasty. *Psychosomatic Medicine, 61*, 488–495.

Helzer, E. G., & Pizarro, D. A. (2011). Dirty liberals! Reminders of physical cleanliness influence moral and political attitudes. *Psychological Science, 22*, 517–522.

Henderlong, J., & Lepper, M. R. (2002). The effects of praise on children's intrinsic motivation: A review and synthesis. *Psychological Bulletin, 128*, 774–795.

Hendrix, K. S., & Hirt, E. R. (2009). Stressed out over possible failure: The role of regulatory fit on claimed self-handicapping. *Journal of Experimental Social Psychology, 45*, 51–59. doi:10.1016/j.jesp.2008.08.016

Henley, N. M. (1977). *Body politics: Power, sex, and nonverbal communication*. Englewood Cliffs, NJ: Prentice Hall.

Henningsen, D., Henningsen, M., Eden, J., & Cruz, M. (2006). Examining the symptoms of groupthink and retrospective sensemaking. *Small Group Research, 37*, 36–64.

Henrich, J., Heine, S. J., & Norenzayan, A. (2010). The weirdest people in the world? *Behavioral and Brain Sciences, 33*(2–3), 61–83. doi:10.1017/S0140525X0999152X

Herek, G. M., & Capitanio, J. P. (1996). "Some of my best friends": Intergroup contact, concealable stigma, and heterosexuals' attitudes toward gay men and lesbians. *Personality and Social Psychology Bulletin, 22*, 412–424.

Hersh, S. M. (1970). *My Lai 4: A report on the massacre and its aftermath*. New York: Vintage Books.

Hersh, S. M. (2004, May 10). Torture at Abu Ghraib. *New Yorker*.

Heschl, A., & Burkart, J. (2006). A new mark test for mirror self-recognition in non-human primates. *Primates, 47*, 187–198.

Heunemann, R. L., Shapiro, L. R., Hampton, M. C., & Mitchell, B. W. (1966). A longitudinal study of gross body composition and body conformation and their association with food and activity in the teenage population. *American Journal of Clinical Nutrition, 18*, 325–338.

Hewitt, J., & Alqahtani, M. A. (2003). Differences between Saudi and U.S. students in reaction to same- and mixed-sex intimacy shown by others. *Journal of Social Psychology, 143*, 233–242.

Hewstone, M., & Jaspars, J. (1987). Covariation and causal attribution: A logical model of the intuitive analysis of variance. *Journal of Personality and Social Psychology, 53*, 663–672.

Hibbard, L. (2011, November 8). Virginia Beach high schools pay students for good grades. *Huffington Post*. Retrieved January 10, 2012, from www.huffingtonpost.com/2011/11/08/high-school-pays-students_n_1082488.html

Higgins, E. T. (1987). Self-discrepancy: A theory relating self and affect. *Psychological Review, 94*, 319–340.

Higgins, E. T. (1989). Self-discrepancy theory: What patterns of self-beliefs cause people to suffer? In L. Berkowitz (Ed.), *Advances in experimental social psychology* (Vol. 22, pp. 93–136). New York: Academic Press.

Higgins, E. T. (1996a). Knowledge application: Accessibility, applicability, and salience. In E. T. Higgins & A. R. Kruglanski (Eds.), *Social psychology: Handbook of basic principles* (pp. 133–168). New York: Guilford Press.

Higgins, E. T. (1996b). The "self-digest": Self-knowledge serving self-regulatory functions. *Journal of Personality and Social Psychology, 71*, 1062–1083.

Higgins, E. T. (1999). Self-discrepancy: A theory relating self and affect. In R. F. Baumeister (Ed.), *The self in social psychology* (pp. 150–181). Philadelphia: Psychology Press.

Higgins, E. T. (2005). Value from regulatory fit. *Current Directions in Psychological Science, 14*, 209–213.

Higgins, E. T., & Bargh, J. A. (1987). Social cognition and social perception. *Annual Review of Psychology, 38*, 369–425.

Higgins, E. T., Bond, R. N., Klein, R., & Strauman, T. (1986). Self-discrepancies and emotional vulnerability: How magnitude, accessibility, and type of discrepancy influence affect. *Journal of Personality and Social Psychology, 51*, 5–15.

Higgins, E. T., Klein, R., & Strauman, T. (1987). Self-discrepancies: Distinguishing among self-states, self-state conflicts, and emotional vulnerabilities. In K. M. Yardley & T. M. Honess (Eds.), *Self and identity: Psychosocial perspectives* (pp. 173–186). New York: Wiley.

Higgins, E. T., Rholes, W. S., & Jones, C. R. (1977). Category accessibility and impression formation. *Journal of Experimental Social Psychology, 13*, 141–154.

Hill, J. K. (n.d.). How I survived the deaths of twelve family members. Retrieved on December 21, 2008, from www.resiliencycenter.com/stories/2002stories/0201hill.shtml

Hill, J. K. (2002). *Rainbow remedies for life's stormy times*. South Bend, IN: Moorhill Communications.

Hilton, D. J., Smith, R. H., & Kim, S. H. (1995). Process of causal explanation and dispositional attribution. *Journal of Personality and Social Psychology, 68*, 377–387.

Hilton, J. L., Fein, S., & Miller, D. T. (1993). Suspicion and dispositional inference. *Journal of Personality and Social Psychology, 19*, 501–512.

Hinds, M. de C. (1993, October 19). Not like the movie: 3 take a dare and lose. *The New York Times*, pp. A1, A22.

Hirt, E. R., Kardes, F. R., & Markman, K. D. (2004). Activating a mental simulation mind-set through generation of alternatives: Implications for debiasing in related and unrelated domains. *Journal of Experimental Social Psychology, 40*, 374–383.

Hirt, E. R., & McCrea, S. M. (2009). Man smart, woman smarter? Getting to the root of gender differences in self-handicapping. *Social and Personality Psychology Compass, 3*, 260–274. doi:10.1111/j.1751-9004.2009.00176.x

Hirt, E. R., McCrea, S. M., & Boris, H. I. (2003). "I know you self-handicapped last exam": Gender differences in reactions to self-handicapping. *Journal of Personality and Social Psychology, 84*, 177–193.

Hirt, E. R., McDonald, H. E., & Erikson, G. A. (1995). How do I remember thee? The role of encoding set and delay in reconstructive memory processes. *Journal of Experimental Social Psychology, 31*, 379–409.

Hirt, E. R., Melton, J. R., McDonald, H. E., & Harackiewicz, J. M. (1996). Processing goals, task interest, and the mood-performance relationship: A mediational analysis. *Journal of Personality and Social Psychology, 71*, 245–261.

Hitler, A. (1925). *Mein kampf*. Boston: Houghton Mifflin.

Hitsch, G., Hortaçsu, A., & Ariely, D. (2010). What makes you click? Mate preferences in online dating. *Quantitative Marketing and Economics, 8*, 393–427.

Hochstadt, S. (1999). *Mobility and modernity: Migration in Germany, 1820–1989*. Ann Arbor: University of Michigan Press.

Hodges, B. H., & Geyer, A. L. (2006). A nonconformist account of the Asch experiments: Values, pragmatics, and moral dilemmas. *Personality and Social Psychology Review, 10*, 2–19.

Hodson, R. (2004). A meta-analysis of workplace ethnographies: Race, gender, and employee attitudes and behavior. *Journal of Contemporary Ethnography, 33*, 4–38.

Hoffman, C., Lau, I., & Johnson, D. R. (1986). The linguistic relativity of person cognition: An English-Chinese comparison. *Journal of Personality and Social Psychology, 51*, 1097–1105.

Hoffman, H. G., Granhag, P. A., See, S. T. K., & Loftus, E. F. (2001). Social influences on reality-monitoring decisions. *Memory and Cognition, 29*, 394–404.

Hofmann, W., De Houwer, J., Perugini, M., Baeyens, F., & Crombez, G. (2010). Evaluative conditioning in humans: A meta-analysis. *Psychological Bulletin, 136*, 390–42.

Hofstede, G. (1984). *Culture's consequences: International differences in work-related values*. Newbury Park, CA: Sage.

Hogg, M. A. (1992). *The social psychology of group cohesiveness: From attraction to social identity*. London: Harvester-Wheatsheaf.

Hogg, M. A. (1993). Group cohesiveness: A critical review and some new directions. In W. Stroebe & M. Hewstone (Eds.), *European review of social psychology* (Vol. 4, pp. 85–111). Chichester, UK: Wiley.

Hogg, M. A. (2001). A social identity theory of leadership. *Personality and Social Psychology Review, 5*, 184–200.

Hogg, M. A. (2010). Influence and leadership. In S. T. Fiske, D. T. Gilbert, & G. Lindzey (Eds.), *Handbook of social psychology* (5th ed., Vol. 2, pp. 1166–1207). Hoboken, NJ: Wiley.

Hogg, M. A., & Abrams, D. (1988). *Social identifications*. London: Routledge.

Hogg, M. A., Hohman, Z. P., & Rivera, J. E. (2008). Why do people join groups? Three motivational accounts from social psychology. *Social and Personality Psychology Compass, 2* (www.blackwellcompass.com/subject/socialpsychology/).

Hogh-Olessen, H. (2008). Human spatial behavior: The spacing of people, objects and animals in six cross-cultural samples. *Journal of Cognition and Culture, 8*, 245–280.

Holland, R. W., Aarts, H., & Langendam, D. (2006). Breaking and creating habits on the working floor: A field-experiment on the power of implementation intentions. *Journal of Experimental Social Psychology, 42*, 776–783.

Holland, R. W., Meertens, R. M., & Van Vugt, M. (2002). Dissonance on the road: Self-esteem as a moderator of internal and external self-justification strategies. *Personality and Social Psychology Bulletin, 28*, 1713–1724.

Hollander, E. P. (1960). Competence and conformity in the acceptance of influence. *Journal of Abnormal and Social Psychology, 61*, 361–365.

Hollander, E. P. (1985). Leadership and power. In G. Lindzey & E. Aronson (Eds.), *Handbook of social psychology* (3rd ed., Vol. 2, pp. 485–537). New York: McGraw-Hill.

Holmes, T. H., & Rahe, R. H. (1967). The Social Readjustment Rating Scale. *Journal of Psychosomatic Research, 11*, 213–218.

Holtz, R. (2004). Group cohesion, attitude projection, and opinion certainty: Beyond interaction. *Group Dynamics: Theory, Research, and Practice*, 8, 112–125.

Homans, G. C. (1961). *Social behavior: Its elementary forms*. New York: Harcourt Brace.

Hong, Y., Wyer, R. S., Jr., Fong, C. P. S. (2008) Chinese working in groups: Effort dispensability versus normative influence. *Asian Journal of Social Psychology, 11*, 187–195. doi:10.1111/j.1467-839X.2008.00257.x

Hong, Y.-Y., Chiu, C.-Y., & Kung, T. M. (1997). Bringing culture out in front: Effects of cultural meaning system activation on social cognition. In K. Leung, Y. Kashima, U. Kim, & S. Yamaguchi (Eds.), *Progress in Asian social psychology* (Vol. 1, pp. 135–146). Singapore: Wiley.

Hong, Y.-Y., Morris, M. W., Chiu, C.-Y., & Benet-Martinez, V. (2000). Multicultural minds: A dynamic constructivist approach to culture and cognition. *American Psychologist, 55*, 709–720.

Hoog, N., Stroebe, W., & de Wit, J. B. F. (2005). The impact of fear appeals on processing and acceptance of action recommendations. *Personality and Social Psychology Bulletin, 31*, 24–33.

Hope, L., Memon, A., & McGeorge, P. (2004). Understanding pretrial publicity: Predecisional distortion of evidence by mock jurors. *Journal of Experimental Psychology: Applied, 10*, 111–119.

Hope, L., & Wright, D. (2007). Beyond unusual? Examining the role of attention in the weapon focus effect. *Applied Cognitive Psychology, 21*, 951–961.

Hornsey, M. J., Jetten, J., McAuliffe, B. J., & Hogg, M. A. (2006). The impact of individualist and collectivist group norms on evaluations of dissenting group members. *Journal of Experimental Social Psychology, 42*, 57–68.

Hornsey, M. J., Majkut, L., Terry, D. J., & McKimmie, B. M. (2003). On being loud and proud: Non-conformity and counter-conformity to group norms. *British Journal of Social Psychology, 42*, 319–335.

House, J. S., Robbins, C., & Metzner, H. L. (1982). The association of social relationships and activities with mortality: Prospective evidence from the Tecumseh Community Health Study. *American Journal of Epidemiology, 116*, 123–140.

House, R. J., Hanges, P. J., Javidan, M., Dorfman, P. W., & Gupta, V. (2004). *Culture, leadership, and organizations: The GLOBE study of 62 societies*. Thousand Oaks, CA: Sage.

Hovland, C. I., Janis, I. L., & Kelley, H. H. (1953). *Communication and persuasion: Psychological studies of opinion change*. New Haven, CT: Yale University Press.

Hovland, C. I., & Sears, R. R. (1940). Minor studies in aggression: 6. Correlation of lynchings with economic indices. *Journal of Psychology, 9*, 301–310.

Howard, D. E., Griffin, M. A., & Boekeloo, B. O. (2008). Prevalence and psychosocial correlates of alcohol-related sexual assault among university students. *Adolescence, 43*, 733–750.

Howard, J. A., Blumstein, P., & Schwartz, P. (1987). Social or evolutionary theories? Some observations on preferences in human mate selection. *Journal of Personality and Social Psychology, 53*, 194–200.

Howell, R., & Howell, C. (2008). The relation of economic status to subjective well-being in developing countries: A meta-analysis. *Psychological Bulletin, 134*, 536–560.

Howland, M., & Simpson, J. A. (2010). Getting in under the radar: A dyadic view of invisible support. *Psychological Science, 21*(12), 1878–1885. doi:10.1177/0956797610388817

Hsu, S. S. (1995, April 8). Fredericksburg searches its soul after clerk is beaten as 6 watch. *Washington Post*, pp. A1, A13.

Huesmann, L. R., & Miller, L. S. (1994). Long-term effects of repeated exposure to media violence in childhood. In L. R. Huesmann (Ed.), *Aggressive behavior: Current perspectives* (pp. 153–186). New York: Plenum.

Huffman, K. T., Grossnickle, W. F., Cope, J. G., & Huffman, K. P. (1995). Litter reduction: A review and integration of the literature. *Environment and Behavior, 27*, 153–183.

Hugenberg, K., Young, S. G., Bernstein, M. J., & Sacco, D. F. (2010). The categorization-individuation model: An integrative account of the other-race recognition deficit. *Psychological Review, 117*(4), 1168–1187. doi:10.1037/a0020463

Hui, C. H., & Triandis, H. C. (1986). Individualism-collectivism: A study of cross-cultural researchers. *Journal of Cross-Cultural Psychology, 17*, 225–248.

Hull, J. G., Young, R. D., & Jouriles, E. (1986). Applications of the self-awareness model of alcohol consumption: Predicting patterns of use and abuse. *Journal of Personality and Social Psychology, 51*, 790–796.

Hulleman, C. S., Schrager, S. M., Bodmann, S. M., & Harackiewicz, J. M. (2010). A meta-analytic review of achievement goal measures: Different labels for the same constructs or different constructs with similar labels? *Psychological Bulletin, 136*, 422–449. doi:10.1037/a0018947

Hunt, G. T. (1940). *The wars of the Iroquois*. Madison: University of Wisconsin Press.

Huntsinger, J. & Sinclair, S. (2010). When it feels right, go with it: Affective regulation of affiliative social tuning. *Social Cognition, 28*, 290–305.

Hurley, D., & Allen, B. P. (1974). The effect of the number of people present in a nonemergency situation. *Journal of Social Psychology, 92*, 27–29.

Hurley, E., & Allen, B. (2007). Asking the how questions: Quantifying group processes behaviors. *Journal of General Psychology, 134*, 5–21.

Huston, A., & Wright, J. (1996). Television and socialization of young children. In T. M. MacBeth (Ed.), *Tuning in to young viewers: Social science perspectives on television* (pp. 37–60). Thousand Oaks, CA: Sage.

Hutchinson, R. R. (1983). The pain-aggression relationship and its expression in naturalistic settings. *Aggressive Behavior, 9*, 229–242.

Hyde, J. S. (2005). The gender similarities hypothesis. *American Psychologist, 60*, 581–592.

Hyman, J. J., & Sheatsley, P. B. (1956). Attitudes toward desegregation. *Scientific American, 195*(6), 35–39.

Iacono, W. G.. (2008). Polygraph testing. In E. Borgida and S. T. Fiske (Eds.)., *Beyond common sense: Psychological science in the courtroom* (pp. 219–235). Malden, MA: Blackwell.

Ickes, W. J., Patterson, M. L., Rajecki, D. W., & Tanford, S. (1982). Behavioral and cognitive consequences of reciprocal versus compensatory responses to preinteraction expectancies. *Social Cognition, 1*, 160–190.

IJzerman, H., & Semin, G. R. (2010). Temperature perceptions as a ground for social proximity. *Journal of Experimental Social Psychology, 46*(6), 867–873. doi:10.1016/j.jesp.2010.07.015

Imada, T., & Kitayama, S. (2010). Social eyes and choice justification: Culture and dissonance revisited. *Social Cognition, 28*, 589–608.

Imhoff, R., & Erb, H. (2009). What motivates noncomformity? Uniqueness seeking blocks majority influence. *Personality and Social Psychology Bulletin, 35*, 309–320.

Impett, E. A., Beals, K. P., & Peplau, L. A. (2001–2002). Testing the investment model of relationship commitment and stability in a longitudinal study of married couples. *Current Psychology, 20*, 312–326.

Imrich, D. J., Mullin, C., & Linz, D. G. (1995). Measuring the extent of prejudicial pretrial publicity in major American newspapers: A content analysis. *Journal of Communication, 45*, 94–117.

Inglehart, M. R. (1991). *Reactions to critical life events: A social psychological analysis*. New York: Praeger.

Inglehart, R., & Klingemann, H. (2000). Genes, culture, democracy, and happiness. In E. Diener & E. M. Suh (Eds.), *Culture and subjective well-being* (pp. 165–183). Cambridge, MA: MIT Press.

Insko, C. A., & Schopler, J. (1998). Differential trust of groups and individuals. In C. Sedikides & J. Schopler (Eds.), *Intergroup cognition and intergroup behavior* (pp. 75–107). Mahwah, NJ: Erlbaum.

Insko, C. A., Smith, R. H., Alicke, M. D., Wade, J., & Taylor, S. (1985). Conformity and group size: The concern with being right and the concern with being liked. *Personality and Social Psychology Bulletin*, 11, 41–50.

Isen, A. M. (1987). Positive affect, cognitive processes, and social behavior. In L. Berkowitz (Ed.), *Advances in experimental social psychology* (Vol. 20, pp. 203–253). San Diego, CA: Academic Press.

Isen, A. M. (1999). Positive affect. In T. Dalgleish & M. J. Power (Eds.), *Handbook of cognition and emotion* (pp. 521–539). Chichester, UK: Wiley.

Isen, A. M., & Levin, P. A. (1972). Effect of feeling good on helping: Cookies and kindness. *Journal of Personality and Social Psychology, 21*, 384–388.

Isenberg, D. J. (1986). Group polarization: A critical review and meta-analysis. *Journal of Personality and Social Psychology, 50*, 1141–1151.

Islam, M. R., & Hewstone, M. (1993). Intergroup attributions and affective consequences in majority and minority groups. *Journal of Personality and Social Psychology, 64*, 936–950.

Ivanov, B., Pfau, M., & Parker, K. A. (2009). Can inoculation withstand multiple attacks?: An examination of the effectiveness of the inoculation strategy compared to the supportive and restoration strategies. *Communication Research, 36*(5), 655–676. doi:10.1177/0093650209338909

Izard, C. E. (1994). Innate and universal facial expressions: Evidence from developmental and cross-cultural research. *Psychological Bulletin, 115*, 288–299.

Izuma, K., Matsumoto, M., Murayama, K., Samejima, K., Sadato, N., & Matsumoto, K. (2010). Neural correlates of cognitive dissonance and choice-induced preference change. *PNAS Proceedings of the National Academy of Sciences, 107*, 22014–22019.

Jackson, J. M., & Williams, K. D. (1985). Social loafing on difficult tasks: Working collectively can improve performance. *Journal of Personality and Social Psychology, 49*, 937–942.

Jackson, J. S., Brown, T. N., Williams, D. R., Torres, M., Sellers, S. L., & Brown, K. (1996). Racism and the physical and mental health status of African Americans: A thirteen-year national panel study. *Ethnicity and Disease, 6*, 132–147.

Jackson, J. S., & Inglehart, M. R. (1995). Reverberation theory: Stress and racism in hierarchically structured communities. In S. E. Hobfoll & M. W. De Vries (Eds.), *Extreme stress and communities: Impact and intervention* (pp. 353–373). Dordrecht, Netherlands: Kluwer.

Jackson, J. W. (1993). Realistic group conflict theory: A review and evaluation of the theoretical and empirical literature. *Psychological Record, 43*, 395–413.

Jackson, L. A. (1992). *Physical appearance and gender: Sociobiological and sociocultural perspectives*. Albany: State University of New York Press.

Jackson, L. A., Hunter, J. E., & Hodge, C. N. (1995). Physical attractiveness and intellectual competence: A meta-analytic review. *Social Psychology Quarterly, 58*, 108–122.

Jacobs, P., & Landau, S. (1971). *To serve the devil* (Vol. 2). New York: Vintage Books.

Jacobson, R. P., Mortensen, C. R., & Cialdini, R. B. (2011). Bodies obliged and unbound: Differentiated response tendencies for injunctive and descriptive social norms. *Journal of Personality and Social Psychology, 100*(3), 433–448. doi:10.1037/a0021470

Jacowitz, K. E., & Kahneman, D. (1995). Measures of anchoring in estimation tasks. *Personality and Social Psychology Bulletin, 21*, 1161–1166.

Jain, S. P., & Posavac, S. S. (2001). Prepurchase attribute verifiability, source credibility, and persuasion. *Journal of Consumer Psychology, 11*, 169–180.

James, L. M., & Olson, J. M. (2000). Jeer pressure: The behavioral effects of observing ridicule of others. *Personality and Social Psychology Bulletin, 26*, 474–485.

James, W. (1890). *The principles of psychology*. New York: Henry Holt.

Janis, I. L. (1972). *Victims of groupthink*. Boston: Houghton Mifflin.

Janis, I. L. (1982). *Groupthink: Psychological studies of policy decisions and fiascoes* (2nd ed.). Boston: Houghton Mifflin.

Janis, I. L., & Feshbach, S. (1953). Effects of fear-arousing communications. *Journal of Abnormal and Social Psychology, 49*, 78–92.

Janis, I. L., Mann, L (1977). Decision Making. Copyright © 1977 by The Free Press, a Division of Macmillan Publishing Co., Inc.

Jankowiak, W. R. (1995). Introduction. In W. R. Jankowiak (Ed.), *Romantic passion: A universal experience?* (pp. 1–19). New York: Columbia University Press.

Jankowiak, W. R., & Fischer, E. F. (1992). A cross-cultural perspective on romantic love. *Ethnology, 31*, 149–155.

Janoff-Bulman, R., & Leggatt, H. K. (2002). Culture and social obligation: When "shoulds" are perceived as "wants." *Journal of Research in Personality, 36*, 260–270.

Janoff-Bulman, R., Timko, C., & Carli, L. L. (1985). Cognitive biases in blaming the victim. *Journal of Experimental Social Psychology, 21*, 161–177.

Jecker, J., & Landy, D. (1969). Liking a person as a function of doing him a favor. *Human Relations, 22*, 371–378.

Jennings, K. (2011, February 16). My puny human brain. *Slate.com.* Retrieved April 18, 2011, from www.slate.com/id/2284721/

Johansson, P., Hall, L., Skiström, S., & Olsson, A. (2005). Failure to detect mismatches between intention and outcome in a simple decision task. *Science, 310*, 116–119.

Johns, M., Schmader, T., & Martens, A. (2005). Knowing is half the battle: Teaching stereotype threat as a means of improving women's math performance. *Psychological Science*, 16, 175–179.

Johnson, D. M. (1945). The phantom anesthetist of Mattoon: A field study of mass hysteria. *Journal of Abnormal and Social Psychology, 40*, 175–186.

Johnson, D. W., & Johnson, R. T. (1987). *Learning together and alone: Cooperative, competitive, and individualistic learning* (2nd ed.). Englewood Cliffs, NJ: Prentice Hall.

Johnson, F. L., & Arles, E. J. (1983). Conversational patterns among same-sex pairs of late-adolescent close friends. *Journal of Genetic Psychology, 142*, 225–238.

Johnson, J. (2011, November 4). The Lululemon murder and the pain of bystanders' inaction. *The Washington Post.* Retrieved November 21, 2011, from www.washingtonpost.com/opinions/the-bystander-effect-why-those-who-heard-the-lululemon-murder-didnt-help/2011/11/03/gIQAHIWYmM_story.html

Johnson, J. G., Cohen, P., Smailes, E. M., Kasen, S., & Brook, J. (2002). Television viewing and aggressive behavior during adolescence and adulthood. *Science, 295*, 2468–2471.

Johnson, K. J., & Fredrickson, B. L. (2005). We all look the same to me: Positive emotions eliminate the own-race bias in face recognition. *Psychological Science, 16*, 875–881.

Johnson, L. B. (1971). *The vantage point: Perspectives of the presidency, 1963–69*. New York: Holt, Rinehart and Winston.

Johnson, M., Verfaellie, M., & Dunlosky, J. (2008,). Introduction to the special section on integrative approaches to source memory. *Journal of Experimental Psychology: Learning, Memory, and Cognition, 34*, 727–729.

Johnson, M. K., Hashtroudi, S., & Lindsay, D. S. (1993). Source monitoring. *Psychological Bulletin, 114*, 3–28.

Johnson, R. D., & Downing, R. L. (1979). Deindividuation and valence of cues: Effects of prosocial and antisocial behavior. *Journal of Personality and Social Psychology, 37*, 1532–1538.

Johnson, T. E., & Rule, B. G. (1986). Mitigating circumstance information, censure, and aggression. *Journal of Personality and Social Psychology, 50*, 537–542.

Jonas, E., Martens, A., Kayser, D. N., Fritsche, I., Sullivan, D., & Greenberg, J. (2008). Focus theory of normative conduct and terror-management theory: The interactive impact of mortality salience and norm salience on social judgment. *Journal of Personality and Social Psychology Bulletin, 95*, 1239–1251.

Jones, C., & Aronson, E. (1973). Attribution of fault to a rape victim as a function of the respectability of the victim. *Journal of Personality and Social Psychology, 26*, 415–419.

Jones, D., & Hill, K. (1993). Criteria of facial attractiveness in five populations. *Human Nature, 4*, 271–296.

Jones, E. E. (1964). *Ingratiation: A social psychological analysis*. New York: Appleton-Century-Crofts.

Jones, E. E. (1979). The rocky road from acts to dispositions. *American Scientist, 34*, 107–117.

Jones, E. E. (1990). *Interpersonal perception*. New York: Freeman.

Jones, E. E., & Berglas, S. (1978). Control of attributions about the self through self-handicapping strategies: The appeal of alcohol and the role of underachievement. *Personality and Social Psychology Bulletin, 4*, 200–206.

Jones, E. E., & Harris, V. A. (1967). The attribution of attitudes. *Journal of Experimental Social Psychology, 3*, 1–24.

Jones, E. E., & Kohler, R. (1959). The effects of plausibility on the learning of controversial statements. *Journal of Abnormal and Social Psychology, 57*, 315–320.

Jones, E. E., & Nisbett, R. E. (1972). The actor and the observer: Divergent perceptions of the causes of behavior. In E. E. Jones, D. E. Kanouse, H. H. Kelley, R. E. Nisbett, S. Valins, & B. Weiner (Eds.), *Attribution: Perceiving the causes of behavior* (pp. 79–94). Morristown, NJ: General Learning Press.

Jones, E. E., & Pittman, T. S. (1982). Toward a general theory of strategic self-presentation. In J. Suls (Ed.), *Psychological perspectives on the self* (pp. 231–262). Hillsdale, NJ: Erlbaum.

Jones, E. E., & Sigall, H. (1971). The bogus pipeline: A new paradigm for measuring affect and attitude. *Psychological Bulletin, 76*, 349–364.

Jones, E. E., & Wortman, C. B. (1973). *Ingratiation: An attributional approach*. Morristown, NJ: General Learning Press.

Jones, G. (2003, Oct. 2). World oil and gas 'running out.' CNN .com/World. Retrieved on June 21, 2006, from edition.cnn.com/2003/WORLD/europe/10/02/global.warming/

Jones, M. (2006, January 15). "Shutting themselves in." *The New York Times*, Sec. 6, pp. 46–51.

Jordan, M. (1996, January 15). In Japan, bullying children to death. *Washington Post*, pp. A1, A15.

Jordan, M., & Sullivan, K. (1995, September 8). A matter of saving face: Japanese can rent mourners, relatives, friends, even enemies to buff an image. *Washington Post*, pp. A1, A28.

Josephson, W. D. (1987). Television violence and children's aggression: Testing the priming, social script, and disinhibition prediction. *Journal of Personality and Social Psychology, 53*, 882–890.

Jost, J. T., Nosek, B. A., & Gosling, S. D. (2008). Ideology: Its resurgence in social, personality, and political psychology. *Perspectives on Psychological Science, 3*, 126–136.

Jostmann, N. B., Lakens, D., & Schubert, T. W. (2009). Weight as an embodiment of importance. *Psychological Science, 20*, 1169–1174. doi:10.1111/j.1467-9280.2009.02426.x

Jowett, G. S., & O'Donnell, V. (1999). *Propaganda and persuasion*. Thousand Oaks, CA: Sage.

Judd, C. M. & Park B. (1988). Out-group homogeneity: judgments of variability at the individual and group levels. *Journal of Personality and Social Psychology, 54*(5), 778–788.

Judge rules ACLU discrimination suit against Continental Airlines can go forward. (2002). Retrieved from www.aclu.org/RacialEquality/RacialEquality.cfm?ID=10994&c=133

Judge, T. A., Bono, J. E., Ilies, R., & Gerhardt, M. W. (2002). Personality and leadership: A qualitative and quantitative review. *Journal of Applied Psychology, 87*, 765–780.

Judge, T. A., Colbert, A. E., & Ilies, R. (2004). Intelligence and leadership: A quantitative review and test of theoretical propositions. *Journal of Applied Psychology, 89*, 542–552.

Judge, T. A., Hurst, C. , & Simon, L. S. (2009). Does it pay to be smart, attractive, or confident (or all three)? Relationships among general mental ability, physical attractiveness, core self-evaluations, and income. *Journal of Applied Psychology, 94*, 742–755.

Judge, T. A., & Piccolo, R. F. (2004). Transformational and transactional leadership: A meta-analytic test of their relative validity. *Journal of Applied Psychology, 89*, 755–768.

Jürgen-Lohmann, J., Borsch, F., & Giesen, H. (2001). Kooperatives Lernen an der Hochschule: Evaluation des Gruppenpuzzles in Seminaren der Pädagogischen Psychologie. *Zeitschrift für Pädagogische Psychologie, 15*, 74–84.

Juslin, P., Winman, A., & Hansson, P. (2007). The naïve intuitive statistician: A naïve sampling model of intuitive confidence intervals. *Psychological Review, 114*, 678–703.

Jussim, L., Eccles, J., & Madon, S. (1996). Social perception, social stereotypes, and teacher expectations: Accuracy and the quest for the powerful self-fulfilling prophecy. In M. P. Zanna (Ed.), *Advances in experimental social psychology* (Vol. 28, pp. 281–388). doi:10.1016/S0065-2601(08)60240-3

Jussim, L., & Harber, K. (2005). Teacher expectations and self-fulfilling prophecies: Knowns and unknowns, resolved and unresolved controversies. *Personality and Social Psychology Review, 9*, 131–155.

Jussim, L., Robustelli, S. L., & Cain, T. R. (2009). Teacher expectations and self-fulfilling prophecies. In K. R. Wenzel & A. Wigfield (Eds.), *Educational psychology handbook series. Handbook of motivation at school* (pp. 349–380). New York: Routledge/Taylor & Francis Group.

Kahn, A. S. (2004). 2003 Carolyn Sherif Award Address: What college women do and do not experience as rape. *Psychology of Women Quarterly, 28*, 9–15.

Kahn, J. P. (2003, June 7). How the mighty have fallen. *Boston Globe*, pp. D1, D7.

Kahn, M. (1966). The physiology of catharsis. *Journal of Personality and Social Psychology, 3*, 278–298.

Kahneman, D. (2011). *Thinking, fast and slow*. New York: Farrar, Straus, & Giroux.

Kahneman, D., & Deaton, A. (2010). High income improves evaluation of life but not emotional well-being. *Proceedings of the National Academy of Sciences, 10*, 16489–16493.

Kahneman, D., & Frederick, S. (2002). Representativeness revisited: Attribute substitution in intuitive judgment. In T. Gilovich, D. W. Griffin, & D. Kahneman (Eds.), *Heuristics and biases: The psychology of intuitive judgment* (pp. 49–81). New York: Cambridge University Press.

Kahneman, D., & Miller, D. T. (1986). Norm theory: Comparing reality to its alternatives. *Psychological Review, 93*, 136–153.

Kahneman, D., & Tversky, A. (1973). On the psychology of prediction. *Psychological Review, 80*, 237–251.

Kallgren, C. A., Reno, R. R., & Cialdini, R. B. (2000). A focus theory of normative conduct: When norms do and do not affect behavior. *Personality and Social Psychology Bulletin, 26*, 1002–1012.

Kallgren, C. A., & Wood, W. (1986). Access to attitude-relevant information in memory as a determinant of attitude-behavior consistency. *Journal of Experimental Social Psychology, 22*, 328–338.

Kalmijn, M., & Monden, C. W. S. (2012). The division of labor and depressive symptoms at the couple level: Effects of equity of specialization? *Journal of Social and Personal Relationships*. doi:10.1177/0265407511431182

Kalven, H., Jr., & Zeisel, H. (1966). *The American jury*. Boston: Little, Brown.

Kameda, T., Takezawa, M., & Hastie, R. (2005). Where do social norms come from?: The example of communal sharing. *Current Directions in Psychological Science, 14*(6), 331–334. doi:10.1111/j.0963-7214.2005.00392.x

Kang, N., & Kwak, N. (2003). A multilevel approach to civic participation: Individual length of residence, neighborhood residential stability, and their interactive effects with media use. *Communication Research, 30*, 80–106.

Kappas, A. (1997). The fascination with faces: Are they windows to our soul? *Journal of Nonverbal Behavior, 21*, 157–162.

Kappeler, P., & van Schaik, C. P. (Eds.). (2006). *Cooperation in primates and humans: Mechanisms and evolution*. Berlin: Springer.

Karau, S. J., & Williams, K. D. (1993). Social loafing: A meta-analytic review and theoretical integration. *Journal of Personality and Social Psychology, 65*, 681–706.

Karau, S. J., & Williams, K. D. (2001). Understanding individual motivation in groups: The collective effort model. In M. E. Turner (Ed.), *Groups at work—theory and research: Applied social research* (pp. 113–141). Mahwah, NJ: Erlbaum.

Kassarjian, H., & Cohen, J. (1965). Cognitive dissonance and consumer behavior. *California Management Review, 8*, 55–64.

Kassin, S. M., Drizin, S. A., Grisso, T., Gudjonsson, G. H., Leo, R. A., & Redlich, A. D. (2010). Police-induced confessions, risk factors, and recommendations: Looking ahead. *Law and Human Behavior, 34*(1), 49–52. doi:10.1007/s10979-010-9217-5

Kato, M. (2009, May 19). Weight of imperial world on Princess Masako. *The Japan Times*. Retrieved March 24, 2011, from search.japantimes.co.jp/cgi-bin/nn20090519i1.html

Katz, D. (1960). The functional approach to the study of attitudes. *Public Opinion Quarterly, 24*, 163–204.

Kauffman, D. R., & Steiner, I. D. (1968). Conformity as an ingratiation technique. *Journal of Experimental Social Psychology, 4*, 404–414.

Kayser, D. N., Greitemeyer, T., Fischer, P., & Frey, D. (2010). Why mood affects help giving, but not moral courage: Comparing two types of prosocial behaviour. *European Journal of Social Psychology, 40*(7), 1136–1157. doi:10.1002/ejsp.717

Keelan, J. P. R., Dion, K. L., & Dion, K. K. (1994). Attachment style and hetereosexual relationships among young adults: A short-term panel study. *Journal of Social and Personal Relationships, 11*, 201–214.

Keller, J., & Bless, H. (2008). Flow and regulatory compatibility: An experimental approach to the flow model of intrinsic motivation. *Personality and Social Psychology Bulletin*, 34, 196–209.

Kelley, H. H. (1950). The warm-cold variable in first impressions of persons. *Journal of Personality, 18*, 431–439.

Kelley, H. H. (1955). The two functions of reference groups. In G. E. Swanson, T. M. Newcomb, & E. L. Hartley (Eds.), *Readings in social psychology* (2nd ed., pp. 410–414). New York: Henry Holt.

Kelley, H. H. (1967). Attribution theory in social psychology. In D. Levine (Ed.), *Nebraska Symposium on Motivation* (Vol. 15, pp. 192–238). Lincoln: University of Nebraska Press.

Kelley, H. H. (1972). Attribution in social interaction. In E. E. Jones, D. E. Kanouse, H. H. Kelley, R. E. Nisbett, S. Valins, & B. Weiner (Eds.), *Attribution: Perceiving the causes of behavior* (pp. 1–26). Morristown, NJ: General Learning Press.

Kelley, H. H. (1973). The process of causal attribution. *American Psychologist, 28*, 107–128.

Kelley, H. H. (1983). Love and commitment. In H. H. Kelley, E. Berscheid, A. Christensen, J. H. Harvey, T. L. Huston, G. Levinger, et al. (Eds.), *Close relationships* (pp. 265–314). New York: Freeman.

Keltner, D., & Shiota, M. N. (2003). New displays and new emotions: A commentary on Rozin and Cohen. *Emotion, 3*, 86–91.

Kenny, D. A. (1994). Using the social relations model to understand relationships. In R. Erber & R. Gilmour (Eds.), *Theoretical frameworks for personal relationships* (pp. 111–127). Hillsdale, NJ: Erlbaum.

Kenny, D. A., Albright, L., Malloy, T. E., & Kashy, D. A. (1994). Consensus in interpersonal perception: Acquaintance and the Big Five. *Psychological Bulletin, 116*, 245–258.

Kenny, D. A., & La Voie, L. (1982). Reciprocity of interpersonal attraction: A confirmed hypothesis. *Social Psychology Quarterly, 45*, 54–58.

Kenrick, D. T., & Keefe, R. C. (1992). Age preferences in mate reflect sex differences in human reproductive strategies. *Behavioral and Brain Sciences, 15*, 75–133.

Kenrick, D. T., & MacFarlane, S. W. (1986). Ambient temperature and horn honking: A field study of the heat/aggression relationship. *Environment and Behavior, 18*, 179–191.

Kernis, M. H. (2001). Following the trail from narcissism to fragile self-esteem. *Psychological Inquiry, 12*, 223–225.

Kerr, N., & Levine, J. (2008). The detection of social exclusion: Evolution and beyond. *Group Dynamics: Theory, Research, and Practice, 12*, 39–52.

Kerr, N. L., & Tindale, R. S. (2004). Groups performance and decision making. *Annual Review of Psychology, 55*, 623–655.

Key, W. B. (1973). *Subliminal seduction*. Englewood Cliffs, NJ: Signet Books.

Key, W. B. (1989). *Age of manipulation: The con in confidence and the sin in sincere*. New York: Henry Holt.

Kiesler, C. A., & Kiesler, S. B. (1969). *Conformity*. Reading, MA: Addison-Wesley.

Kihlstrom, J. F. (1996). The trauma-memory argument and recovered memory therapy. In K. Pezdek & W. P. Banks (Eds.), *The recovered memory/false memory debate* (pp. 297–311). San Diego, CA: Academic Press.

Killen, J. D., Taylor, C. B., Hayward, C., Wilson, D. M., Haydel, K. F., Hammer, L. D., et al. (1994). Pursuit of thinness and onset of eating disorder symptoms in a community sample of adolescent girls: A three-year prospective analysis. *International Journal of Eating Disorders, 16*, 227–238.

Killian, L. M. (1964). Social movements. In R. E. L. Farris (Ed.), *Handbook of modern sociology* (pp. 426–455). Chicago: Rand McNally.

Kim, H., & Markus, H. R. (1999). Deviance or uniqueness, harmony or conformity? A cultural analysis. *Journal of Personality and Social Psychology,* 77, 785–800.

Kim, H., Park, K., & Schwarz, N. (2010). Will this trip really be exciting? The role of incidental emotions in product evaluation. *Journal of Consumer Research, 36*(6), 983–991. doi:10.1086/644763

Kim, H. S., Sherman, D. K., & Taylor, S. E. (2008). Culture and social support. *American Psychologist, 63*, 518–526.

Kim, J. L., Sorsoli, C. L., Collins, K., Zylbergold, B. A., Schooler, D., & Tolman, D. L. (2007). From sex to sexuality: Exposing the heterosexual script on primetime network television. *Journal of Sex Research, 44*, 145–157.

Kim, U., & Berry, J. W. (1993). *Indigenous psychologies: Research and experience in cultural context*. Newbury Park, CA: Sage.

Kim, U., Triandis, H. C., Kagitcibasi, C., Choi, S. C., & Yoon, G. (Eds.). (1994). *Individualism and collectivism: Theory, method, and applications*. Thousand Oaks, CA: Sage.

Kimel, E. (2001, Aug. 2). Students earn cash for summer reading. *Sarasota Herald Tribune*, p. BV2.

Kinder, D. R., & Sears, D. O. (1981). Prejudice and politics: Symbolic racism versus racial threats to the good life. *Journal of Personality and Social Psychology, 40*, 414–431.

King, B., Shapiro, R., Hebl, R., Singletary, L., & Turner, S. (2006). The stigma of obesity in customer service: A mechanism for remediation and bottom-line consequences of interpersonal discrimination. *Journal of Applied Psychology, 91*, 579–593.

Kinoshita, S., Peek-O'Leary, M. (2005). Does the compatibility effect in the race Implicit Association Test reflect familiarity or affect? *Psychonomic Bulletin Review, 12*, 442–452.

Kirkpatrick, L. A., & Hazan, C. (1994). Attachment styles and close relationships: A four-year prospective study. *Personal Relationships, 1*, 123–142.

Kitayama, S., & Cohen, D. (Eds.). (2007). *Handbook of cultural psychology*. New York: Guilford.

Kitayama, S., & Markus, H. R. (1994). Culture and the self: How cultures influence the way we view ourselves. In D. Matsumoto (Ed.), *People: Psychology from a cultural perspective* (pp. 17–37). Pacific Grove, CA: Brooks/Cole.

Kitayama, S., Markus, H. R., Matsumoto, H., & Norasakkunkit, V. (1997). Individual and collective processes in the construction of the self: Self-enhancement in the United States and self-criticism in Japan. *Journal of Personality and Social Psychology,* 72, 1245–1267.

Kitayama, S., Park, H., Sevincer, A. T., Karasawa, M., & Uskul, A. K. (2009). A cultural task analysis of implicit independence: Comparing North America, Western Europe, and East Asia. *Journal of Personality and Social Psychology,* 97, 236–255.

Kitayama, S., & Uchida, Y. (2003). Explicit self-criticism and implicit self-regard: Evaluating self and friend in two cultures. *Journal of Experimental Social Psychology, 39*, 476–482.

Kitayama, S., & Uchida, Y. (2005). Interdependent agency: An alternative system for action. In R. M. Sorrentino & D. Cohen (Eds.), *Cultural and social behavior: The Ontario Symposium* (Vol. 10, pp. 137–164). Mahwah, NJ: Erlbaum.

Kite, M. E., Deaux, K., & Haines, E. L. (2008). Gender stereotypes. In F. L. Denmark & M. A. Paludi (Eds.), *Psychology of women: A handbook of issues and theories* (2nd ed., pp. 205–236). Westport, CT: Praeger.

Kivlighan, K., Granger, D., & Booth, A. (2005). Gender differences in testosterone and cortisol response to competition. *Psychoneuroendocrinology, 30*, 58–71.

Kjell, O. N. E. (2011). Sustainable well-being: A potential synergy between sustainability and well-being research. *Review of General Psychology, 15*(3), 255–266. doi:10.1037/a0024603

Klapwijk, A., & Van Lange, P. A. M. (2009). Promoting cooperation and trust in "noisy" situations: The power of generosity. *Journal of Personality and Social Psychology, 96*, 83–103.

Klein, R. (2005, November 12). President steps up attack on war critics. *The Boston Globe*. Retrieved on March 8, 2006, from www.boston.com/news/nation/washington/articles/2005/11/12/president_steps_up_attack_on_war_critics/

Kleinjan, M., van den Eijnden, R. J., & Engels, R. C. (2009). Adolescents' rationalizations to continue smoking: The role of disengagement beliefs and nicotine dependence in smoking cessation. *Addictive Behaviors, 34*, 440–445.

Klenke, K. (1996). *Women and leadership: A contextual perspective*. New York: Springer-Verlag.

Kluger, R. (1996). *Ashes to ashes: America's hundred-year cigarette war, the public health, and the unabashed triumph of Philip Morris*. New York: Knopf.

Knapp, M., & Hall, J. A. (2006). *Nonverbal communication in human interaction*. Belmont, CA: Thomson Wadsworth.

Knowles, E. D., Morris, M. W., Chiu, C., & Hong, Y. (2001). Culture and the process of person perception: Evidence for automaticity among East Asians in correcting for situational influences on behavior. *Personality and Social Psychology Bulletin, 27*, 1344–1356.

Knox, R., & Inkster, J. (1968). Postdecision dissonance at post time. *Journal of Personality and Social Psychology, 8*, 319–323.

Knussen, C., Yule, F., & MacKenzie, J. (2004). An analysis of intentions to recycle household waste: The roles of past behaviour, perceived habit, and perceived lack of facilities. *Journal of Environmental Psychology, 24*, 237–246.

Koch, I., Lawo, V., Fels, J., & Vorländer, M. (2011). Switching in the cocktail party: Exploring intentional control of auditory selective attention. *Journal of Experimental Psychology: Human Perception and Performance, 37*(4), 1140–1147. doi:10.1037/a0022189

Koehler, J. J. (1993). The base rate fallacy myth. *Psycoloquy, 4*, 49.

Koehler, J. J. (1996). The base rate fallacy reconsidered: Descriptive, normative, and methodological challenges. *Behavioral and Brain Sciences, 19*, 1–53.

Koehnken, G., Malpass, R. S., & Wogalter, M. S. (1996). Forensic applications of line-up research. In S. L. Sporer, R. S. Malpass, & G. Koehnken (Eds.), *Psychological issues in eyewitness identification* (pp. 205–231). Mahwah, NJ: Erlbaum.

Koenig, A. M., Eagly, A. H., Mitchell, A. A., & Ristikari, T. (2011). Are leader stereotypes masculine? A meta-analysis of three research paradigms. *Psychological Bulletin, 137*(4), 616–642. doi:10.1037/a0023557

Kogan, N., & Wallach, M. A. (1964). *Risk-taking: A study in cognition and personality*. New York: Henry Holt.

Kolbert, E. (2006). *Field notes from a catastrophe: Man, nature, and climate change*. New York: Bloomsbury.

Kollack, P., Blumstein, P., & Schwartz, P., (1994). The judgment of equity in intimate relationships. *Social Psychology Quarterly, 57*, 340–351.

Koranyi, N., & Rothermund, K. (2012). When the grass on the other side of the fence doesn't matter: Reciprocal romantic interest neutralizes attentional bias towards attractive alternatives. *Journal of Experimental Social Psychology, 48*, 186–191.

Koss, M. P. (2011). Hidden, unacknowledged, acquaintance, and date rape: Looking back, looking forward. *Psychology of Woman Quarterly, 35*, 348–354.

Kovera, M. B., & Borgida, E. (2010). Social psychology and law. In S. T. Fiske, D. T. Gilbert, & G. Lindzey (Eds.), *Handbook of social psychology* (5th ed., Vol. 2, pp. 1343–1385). Hoboken, NJ: John Wiley.

Kowert, P. A. (2002). *Groupthink or deadlock: When do leaders learn from their advisors?* Albany: State University of New York Press.

Krakow, A., & Blass, T. (1995). When nurses obey or defy inappropriate physician orders: Attributional differences. *Journal of Social Behavior and Personality, 10*, 585–594.

Kramer, G. P., Kerr, N. L., & Carroll, J. S. (1990). Pretrial publicity, judicial remedies, and jury bias. *Law and Human Behavior, 14*, 409–438.

Kraus, M. W., Piff, P. K., & Keltner, D. (2009). Social class, sense of control, and social explanation. *Journal of Personality and Social Psychology, 97*, 992–1004. doi:10.1037/a0016357

Krauss, R. M., & Deutsch, M. (1966). Communication in interpersonal bargaining. *Journal of Personality and Social Psychology, 4*, 572–577.

Krauss, R. M., Freedman, J. L., & Whitcup, M. (1978). Field and laboratory studies of littering. *Journal of Experimental Social Psychology, 14*, 109–122.

Kremer, J. F., & Stephens, L. (1983). Attributions and arousal as mediators of mitigation's effects on retaliation. *Journal of Personality and Social Psychology, 45*, 335–343.

Kressel, K., & Pruitt, D. G. (1989). A research perspective on the mediation of social conflict. In K. Kressel & D. G. Pruitt (Eds.), *Mediation research: The process and effectiveness of third party intervention* (pp. 394–435). San Francisco: Jossey-Bass.

Krosnick, J. A., & Alwin, D. F. (1989). Aging and susceptibility to attitude change. *Journal of Personality and Social Psychology, 57*, 416–425.

Kross, E., & Ayduk, O. (2011). Making meaning out of negative experiences by self-distancing. *Current Directions in Psychological Science, 20*(3), 187–191. doi:10.1177/0963721411408883

Krueger, A. B. (2007). *What makes a terrorist: Economics and the roots of terrorism*. Princeton, NJ: Princeton University Press.

Krueger, J., Ham, J. J., & Linford, K. (1996). Perceptions of behavioral consistency: Are people aware of the actor-observer effect? *Psychological Science, 7*, 259–264.

Krull, D. S. (1993). Does the grist change the mill? The effect of the perceiver's inferential goal on the process of social inference. *Personality and Social Psychology Bulletin, 19*, 340–348.

Krull, D. S., & Dill, J. C. (1996). On thinking first and responding fast: Flexibility in social inference processes. *Personality and Social Psychology Bulletin, 22*, 949–959.

Krull, D. S., Loy, M. H., Lin, J., Wang, C., Chen, S., & Zhao, X. (1999). The fundamental correspondence bias in individualist and collectivist cultures. *Personality and Social Psychology Bulletin, 25*, 1208–1219.

Kubitschek, W. N., & Hallinan, M. T. (1998). Tracking and students' friendships. *Social Psychology Quarterly, 61*, 1–15.

Kuhl, J. (1987). Action control: The maintenance of motivational states. In F. Halisch & J. Kuhl (Eds.), *Motivation, intention, and volition* (pp. 279–291). New York: Springer.

Kulik, J. A., & Brown, R. (1979). Frustration, attribution of blame, and aggression. *Journal of Experimental Social Psychology, 15*, 183–194.

Kunda, Z. (1999). *Social cognition: Making sense of people*. Cambridge, MA: MIT Press.

Kunda, Z., & Oleson, K. C. (1997). When exceptions prove the rule: How extremity of deviance determines the impact of deviant examples on stereotypes. *Journal of Personality and Social Psychology, 72*, 965–979.

Kunda, Z., & Schwartz, S. H. (1983). Undermining intrinsic moral motivation: External reward and self-presentation. *Journal of Personality and Social Psychology, 45*, 763–771.

Kunda, Z., Sinclair, L., & Griffin, D. W. (1997). Equal ratings but separate meanings: Stereotypes and the construal of traits. *Journal of Personality and Social Psychology, 72*, 720–734.

Kuo, Z. Y. (1961). *Instinct*. Princeton, NJ: Van Nostrand.

Kurdek, L. A. (1992). Relationship stability and relationship satisfaction in cohabitating gay and lesbian couples: A prospective longitudinal test of the contextual and interdependence models. *Journal of Social and Personal Relationships, 9*, 125–142.

Kurdek, L. A. (2005). What do we know about gay and lesbian couples? *Current Directions in Psychological Science, 14*, 251–254.

Kuykendall, D., & Keating, J. P. (1990). Altering thoughts and judgments through repeated association. *British Journal of Social Psychology, 29*, 79–86.

La France, M., Hecht, M. A., & Paluck, E. L. (2003). The contingent smile: A meta-analysis of sex differences in smiling. *Psychological Bulletin, 129*, 305–334.

La Piere, R. T. (1934). Attitudes vs. actions. *Social Forces, 13*, 230–237.

Lakoff, G., & Johnson, M. (1999). *Philosophy in the flesh: The embodied mind and its challenge to Western thought*. New York: Basic Books.

Laird, J. (2007). *Feelings: The perception of self.* New York, Oxford University Press.

Lakey, B., & Orehek, E. (2011). Relational regulation theory: A new approach to explain the link between perceived social support and mental health. *Psychological Review, 118*(3), 482–495. doi:10.1037/a0023477

Lalwani, A. K., & Shavitt, S. (2009). The "me" I claim to be: Cultural self-construal elicits self-presentational goal pursuit. *Journal of Personality and Social Psychology, 97*, 88–102. doi:10.1037/a0014100

Lambert, A. J., Burroughs, T., & Nguyen, T. (1999). Perceptions of risk and the buffering hypothesis: The role of just world beliefs and right-wing authoritarianism. *Personality and Social Psychology Bulletin, 25*, 643–656.

Lampert, R., Baron, S. J., McPherson, C. A., & Lee, F. A. (2002). Heart rate variability during the week of September 11, 2001. *Journal of the American Medical Association, 288*, 575.

Landau, M. J., Meier, B. P., & Keefer, L. A. (2010). A metaphor-enriched social cognition. *Psychological Bulletin, 136*(6), 1045–1067. doi:10.1037/a0020970

Landman, J. (1993). *Regret: The persistence of the possible*. New York: Oxford University Press.

Lane, K. A., Banaji, M. R., & Nosek, B. A. (2007). Understanding and using the implicit association test: IV: What we know (so far) about the method. In B. Wittenbrink & N. Schwarz (Eds.), *Implicit measures of attitudes* (pp. 59–102). New York: Guilford.

Langer, E. J. (1975) The illusion of control. *Journal of Personality and Social Psychology, 32*, 311–328.

Langer, E. J., & Rodin, J. (1976). The effects of choice and enhanced personal responsibility for the aged: A field experiment. *Journal of Personality and Social Psychology, 34*, 191–198.

Langlois, J. H., Kalakanis, L., Rubenstein, A. J., Larson, A., Hallam, M., & Smoot, M. (2000). Maxims or myths of beauty? A meta-analytic and theoretical review. *Psychological Bulletin, 126*, 390–423.

Langlois, J. H., Ritter, J. M., Roggman, L. A., & Vaughn, L. S. (1991). Facial diversity and infant preferences for attractive faces. *Developmental Psychology, 27*, 79–84.

Langlois, J. H., & Roggman, L. A. (1990). Attractive faces are only average. *Psychological Science, 1*, 115–121.

Langlois, J. H., Roggman, L. A., & Musselman, L. (1994). What is average and what is not average about attractive faces? *Psychological Science, 5*, 214–220.

Langlois, J. H., Roggman, L. A., & Rieser-Danner, L. A. (1990). Infants' differential social responses to attractive and unattractive faces. *Developmental Psychology, 26*, 153–159.

Larrick, R. P., Timmerman, T. A., Carton, A. M., & Abrevaya, J. (2011). Temper, temperature, and temptation: Heat-related retaliation in baseball. *Psychological Science, 22*, 423–428.

Larson, J. R., Jr., Christensen, C., Franz, T. M., & Abbott, A. S. (1998). Diagnosing groups: The pooling, management, and impact of shared and unshared case information in team-based medical decision making. *Journal of Personality and Social Psychology, 75*, 93–108.

Lassiter, G. D. (2010). Psychological science and sound public policy: Video recording of custodial interrogations. *American Psychologist, 65*(8), 768–779. doi:10.1037/0003-066X.65.8.768

Lassiter, G. D., Diamond, S. S., Schmidt, H. C., & Elek, J. K. (2007). Evaluating videotaped confessions: Expertise provides no defense against the camera perspective effect. *Psychological Science, 18*, 224–226.

Lassiter, G. D., Geers, A. L., Munhall, P. J., Ploutz-Snyder, R. J., & Breitenbecher, D. L. (2002). Illusory causation: Why it occurs. *Psychological Science, 13*, 299–305.

Lassiter, G. D., Ratcliff, J. J., Ware, L. J., & Irvin, C. R. (2006). Videotaped confessions: Panacea or Pandora's Box? *Law and Policy, 28*, 192–210.

Latané, B. (1981). The psychology of social impact. *American Psychologist, 36*, 343–356.

Latané, B. (1987). From student to colleague: Retracing a decade. In N. E. Grunberg, R. E. Nisbett, J. Rodin, & J. E. Singer (Eds.), *A distinctive approach to psychological research: The influence of Stanley Schachter* (pp. 66–86). Hillsdale, NJ: Erlbaum.

Latané, B., & Bourgeois, M. J. (2001). Successfully simulating dynamic social impact: Three levels of prediction. In J. P. Forgas & K. D. Williams (Eds.), *Social influence: Direct and indirect processes* (pp. 61–76). Philadelphia: Psychology Press.

Latané, B., & Dabbs, J. M. (1975). Sex, group size, and helping in three cities. *Sociometry, 38*, 108–194.

Latané, B., & Darley, J. M. (1968). Group inhibition of bystander intervention. *Journal of Personality and Social Psychology, 10*, 215–221.

Latané, B., & Darley, J. M. (1970). *The unresponsive bystander: Why doesn't he help?* Englewood Cliffs, NJ: Prentice Hall.

Latané, B., & L'Herrou, T. (1996). Spatial clustering in the conformity game: Dynamic social impact in electronic games. *Journal of Personality and Social Psychology, 70*, 1218–1230.

Latané, B., & Nida, S. (1981). Ten years of research on group size and helping. *Psychological Bulletin, 89*, 308–324.

Latané, B., Williams, K., & Harkins, S. (2006). Many hands make light the work: The causes and consequences of social loafing. In J. M. Levine & R. L. Moreland (Eds.), *Small groups* (pp. 297–308). New York: Psychology Press.

Lau, R. R., & Russell, D. (1980). Attributions in the sports pages: A field test of some current hypotheses about attribution research. *Journal of Personality and Social Psychology, 39*, 29–38.

Laumann, E. O., & Gagnon, J. H. (1995). A sociological perspective on sexual action. In R. G. Parker & J. H. Gagnon (Eds.), *Conceiving sexuality: Approaches to sex research in a postmodern world*. New York: Routledge.

Laumann, E. O., Gagnon, J. H., Michael, R. T., & Michaels, S. (1994). *The social organization of sexuality*. Chicago: University of Chicago Press.

Laursen, B., & Hartup, W. W. (2002). The origins of reciprocity and social exchange in friendships. In L. Brett & W. G. Graziano (Eds.), *Social exchange in development: New directions for child and adolescent development* (pp. 27–40). San Francisco: Jossey-Bass/Pfeiffer.

Lawler, E. J., & Thye, S. R. (1999). Bringing emotions into social exchange theory. *Annual Review of Sociology, 25*, 217–244.

Lazarsfeld, P. (Ed.). (1940). *Radio and the printed page*. New York: Duell, Sloan & Pearce.

Lazarus, R. S. (1966). *Psychological stress and the coping process*. New York: McGraw-Hill.

Lazarus, R. S. (2000). Toward better research on stress and coping. *American Psychologist, 55*, 665–673.

Lazarus, R. S., & Folkman, S. (1984). *Stress, appraisal, and coping*. New York: Springer-Verlag.

Le, B., & Agnew, C. R. (2003). Commitment and its theorized determinants: A meta-analysis of the investment model. *Personal Relationships, 10*, 37–57.

Le Bon, G. (1895). *The crowd*. London: Unwin.

Lea, M., & Spears, R. (1995). Love at first byte: Building personal relationships over computer networks. In J. T. Wood & S. W. Duck (Eds.), *Understudied relationships: Off the beaten track* (pp. 197–233). Thousand Oaks, CA: Sage.

Lea, M., Spears, R., & de Groot, D. (2001). Knowing me, knowing you: Anonymity effects on social identity processes within groups. *Personality and Social Psychology Bulletin, 27*, 526–537.

Leary, M. R. (2004a). *The curse of the self: Self-awareness, egotism, and the quality of human life*. New York: Oxford University Press.

Leary, M. R. (2004b). The self we know and the self we show: Self-esteem, self-presentation, and the maintenance of interpersonal relationships. In M. B. Brewer & M. Hewstone (Eds.), *Emotion and motivation* (pp. 204–224). Malden, MA: Blackwell.

Leary, M. R., & Baumeister, R. F. (2000). The nature and function of self-esteem: Sociometer theory. In M. P. Zanna (Ed.), *Advances in experimental social psychology* (Vol. 32, pp. 1–62). San Diego, CA: Academic Press.

Leary, M. R., Kowalski, R. M., Smith, L., & Phillips, S. (2003). Teasing, rejection, and violence: Case studies of the school shootings. *Aggressive Behavior, 29*, 202–214.

Leary, M. R., & Tate, E. B. (2010). The role of self-awareness and self-evaluation in dysfunctional patterns of thought, emotion, and behavior. In J. E. Maddux & J. P. Tangney (Eds.), *Social psychological foundations of clinical psychology* (pp. 19–35). New York: Guilford Press.

Leary, M. R., Twenge, J. M., & Quinlivan, E. (2006). Interpersonal rejection as a determinant of anger and aggression. *Personality and Social Psychology Review, 10*, 111–132.

Leathers, D. G. (1997). *Successful nonverbal communication: Principles and applications*. Needham Heights, MA: Allyn & Bacon.

Lee, A. Y. (2001). The mere exposure effect: An uncertainty reduction explanation revisited. *Personality and Social Psychology Bulletin, 27*, 1255–1266.

Lee, E. (2004). Effects of visual representation on social influence in computer-mediated communication: Experimental tests of the social identity model of deindividuation effects. *Human Communication Research, 30*, 234–259.

Lee, H. (1960). *To kill a mockingbird*. New York: Warner Books.

Lee, R. W. (2001). Citizen heroes. *New American, 17*, 19–32.

Lee, S. J. (2009). *Unraveling the "Model Minority" stereotype: Listening to Asian American youth* (2nd ed.). New York: Teachers College, Columbia University.

Lee, Y., & Seligman, M. E. P. (1997). Are Americans more optimistic than the Chinese? *Personality and Social Psychology Bulletin, 23*, 32–40.

Lehman, D. R., Davis, C. G., De Longis, A., & Wortman, C. B. (1993). Positive and negative life changes following bereavement and their relations to adjustment. *Journal of Social and Clinical Psychology, 12*, 90–112.

Lehman, D. R., Lempert, R. O., & Nisbett, R. E. (1988). The effects of graduate training on reasoning: Formal discipline and thinking about everyday-life events. *American Psychologist, 43*, 431–442.

Lehmiller, J. J., & Agnew, C. R. (2006). Marginalized relationships: The impact of social disapproval on romantic relationship commitment. *Personality and Social Psychology Bulletin, 32*, 40–51.

Leippe, M. R., & Eisenstadt, D. (1994). Generalization of dissonance reduction: Decreasing prejudice through induced compliance. *Journal of Personality and Social Psychology, 67*, 395–413.

Leippe, M. R., & Eisenstadt, D. (1998). A self-accountability model of dissonance reduction: Multiple modes on a continuum of elaboration. In E. Harmon-Jones & J. S. Mills (Eds.), *Cognitive dissonance theory: Revival with revisions and controversies*. Washington, DC: American Psychological Association.

Leishman, K. (1988, February). Heterosexuals and AIDS. *Atlantic*, pp. 39–57.

Leite, F. P. (2011). Larger reward values alone are not enough to entice more cooperation. *Thinking & Reasoning, 17*(1), 82–103. doi:10.1080/13546783.2010.537521

Lemay, E. P., Jr., Clark, M. S., & Greenberg, A. (2010). What is beautiful is good because what is beautiful is desired: Physical attractiveness stereotyping as projection of interpersonal goals. *Personality and Social Psychology Bulletin, 36*, 339–353.

Lemieux, R., & Hale, J. L. (1999). Intimacy, passion, and commitment in young romantic relationships: Successfully measuring the triangular theory of love. *Psychological Reports, 85*, 497–503.

Leor, J., Poole, W. K., & Kloner, R. A. (1996). Sudden cardiac death triggered by an earthquake. *New England Journal of Medicine, 334*, 413–419.

Leotti, L. A., Iyengar, S. S., & Ochsner, K. N. (2010). Born to choose: The origins and value of the need for control. *Trends in Cognitive Sciences, 14*, 457–463. doi:10.1016/j.tics.2010.08.001

Lepper, M. R. (1995). Theory by numbers? Some concerns about meta-analysis as a theoretical tool. *Applied Cognitive Psychology, 9*, 411–422.

Lepper, M. R. (1996). Intrinsic motivation and extrinsic rewards: A commentary on Cameron and Pierce's meta-analysis. *Review of Educational Research, 66*, 5–32.

Lepper, M. R., Corpus, J. H., & Iyengar, S. S. (2005). Intrinsic and extrinsic motivational orientations in the classroom: Age differences and academic correlates. *Journal of Educational Psychology, 97*, 184–196.

Lepper, M. R., Greene, D., & Nisbett, R. E. (1973). Undermining children's intrinsic interest with extrinsic reward: A test of the overjustification hypothesis. *Journal of Personality and Social Psychology, 28*, 129–137.

Lepper, M. R., Henderlong, J., & Gingras, I. (1999). Understanding the effects of extrinsic rewards on intrinsic motivation—uses and abuses of meta-analysis: Comment on Deci, Koestner, and Ryan (1999). *Psychological Bulletin, 125*, 669–676.

Lerner, J. S., & Tetlock, P. E. (1999). Accounting for the effects of accountability. *Psychological Bulletin, 125*, 255–275.

Lerner, M. J. (1980). *The belief in a just world: A fundamental decision*. New York: Plenum.

Lerner, M. J. (1991). The belief in a just world and the "heroic motive": Searching for "constants" in the psychology of religious ideology. *International Journal for the Psychology of Religion, 1*, 27–32.

Lerner, M. J. (1998). The two forms of belief in a just world. In L. Montada & M. J. Lerner (Eds.), *Responses to victimization and belief in a just world*. (pp. 247–269). New York: Plenum Press.

Lerner, M. J., & Grant, P. R. (1990). The influences of commitment to justice and ethnocentrism on children's allocations of pay. *Social Psychology Quarterly, 53*, 229–238.

Lerner, M. J., & Miller, D. T. (1978). Just world research and the attribution process: Looking back and ahead. *Psychological Bulletin, 85*, 1030–1051.

Leung, K. (1996). Beliefs in Chinese culture. In M. H. Bond (Ed.), *The handbook of Chinese psychology* (pp. 247–262). Hong Kong: Oxford University Press.

Leventhal, H., Watts, J. C., & Pagano, F. (1967). Effects of fear and instructions on how to cope with danger. *Journal of Personality and Social Psychology, 6*, 313–321.

Levin, D. T. (2000). Race as a visual feature: Using visual search and perceptual discrimination tasks to understand face categories and the cross-race recognition deficit. *Journal of Experimental Psychology: General, 129*, 559–574.

Levine, J. M. (1989). Reaction to opinion deviance in small groups. In P. B. Paulus (Ed.), *Psychology of group influence* (2nd ed., pp. 187–231). Hillsdale, NJ: Erlbaum.

Levine, J. M., Higgins, E. T., & Choi, H.-S. (2000). Development of strategic norms in groups. *Organizational Behavior and Human Decision Processes, 82*, 88–101.

Levine, J. M., & Moreland, R. L. (1998). Small groups. In D. T. Gilbert, S. T. Fiske, & G. Lindzey (Eds.), *The handbook of social psychology* (4th ed., Vol. 2, pp. 415–469). New York: McGraw-Hill.

Levine, J. M., Moreland, R. L., & Choi, S. (2001). Group socialization and newcomer innovation. In M. Hogg & S. Tindale (Eds.), *Blackwell handbook of social psychology: Group Processes* (pp. 86–106). Oxford, England: Blackwell Publishers.

Levine, J. M., & Russo, E. M. (1987). Majority and minority influence. In C. Hendrick (Ed.), *Group processes: Review of personality and social psychology* (Vol. 8, pp. 13–54). Newbury Park, CA: Sage.

Levine, R., Sato, S., Hashimoto, T., & Verma, J. (1995). Love and marriage in eleven cultures. *Journal of Cross-Cultural Psychology, 26*, 554–571.

Levine, R. A., & Campbell, D. T. (1972). *Ethnocentrism: Theories of conflict, ethnic attitudes, and group behavior*. New York: Wiley.

Levine, R. V. (2003). The kindness of strangers: People's willingness to help someone during a chance encounter on a city street varies considerably around the world. *American Scientist, 91*, 226–233.

Levine, R. V., Martinez, T. S., Brase, G., & Sorenson, K. (1994). Helping in 36 U.S. cities. *Journal of Personality and Social Psychology, 67*, 69–82.

Levine, R. V., Norenzayan, A., & Philbrick, K. (2001). Cross-cultural differences in helping strangers. *Journal of Cross-Cultural Psychology, 32*, 543–560.

Levy, B. (2008). *Women and violence*. Berkeley, CA: Seal Press.

Levy, D. A., & Nail, P. R. (1993). Contagion: A theoretical and empirical review and reconceptualization. *Genetic, Social, and General Psychology Monographs, 119*, 233–284.

Lévy-Leboyer, C. (1988). Success and failure in applying psychology. *American Psychologist*, 43, 779–785.

Lewin, K. (1943). Defining the "field at a given time." *Psychological Review, 50*, 292–310.

Lewin, K. (1946). Action research and minority problems. *Journal of Social Issues, 2*, 34–46.

Lewin, K. (1947). Frontiers in group dynamics. *Human Relations, 1*, 5–41.

Lewin, K. (1948). *Resolving social conflicts: Selected papers in group dynamics*. New York: Harper.

Lewin, K. (1951). Problems of research in social psychology. In D. Cartwright (Ed.), *Field theory in social science* (pp. 155–169). New York: Harper.

Lewis, C. C. (1995). *Educating hearts and minds: Reflections on Japanese preschool and elementary education*. Cambridge: Cambridge University Press.

Lewis, K., Belliveau, M., Herndon, B., & Keller, J. (2007). Group cognition, membership change, and performance: Investigating the benefits and detriments of collective knowledge. *Organizational Behavior and Human Decision Processes, 103*, 159–178.

Lewis, M., & Ramsay, D. (2004). Development of self-recognition, personal pronoun use, and pretend play during the 2nd year. *Child Development, 75*, 1821–1831.

Liberman, A., & Chaiken, S. (1992). Defensive processing of personally relevant health messages. *Personality and Social Psychology Bulletin, 18*, 669–679.

Liberman, V., Samuels, S. M., & Ross, L. D. (2004). The name of the game: Predictive power of reputations versus situational labels in determining Prisoner's Dilemma Game moves. *Personality and Social Psychology Bulletin, 30*, 1175–1185.

Lichtarowicz, A. (2010, October 11). Hunger index shows one billion without enough food. *BBC New Health*. Retrieved August 14, 2011, from www.bbc.co.uk/news/science-environment-11503845

Lieberman, M. D. (2010). Social cognitive neuroscience. In S. T. Fiske, D. T. Gilbert, & G. Lindzey (Eds.), *Handbook of social psychology* (5th ed., Vol. 1, pp. 143–193). Hoboken, NJ: John Wiley.

Lieberman, M. D., & Rosenthal, R. (2001). Why introverts can't always tell who likes them: Multitasking and nonverbal decoding. *Journal of Personality and Social Psychology, 80*, 294–310.

Liebert, R. M., & Baron, R. A. (1972). Some immediate effects of televised violence on children's behavior. *Developmental Psychology, 6*, 469–475.

Lim, T.-S., & Choi, H.-S. (1996). Interpersonal relationships in Korea. In W. B. Gudykunst, S. Ting-Toomey, & T. Nishida (Eds.), *Communication in personal relationships across cultures* (pp. 122–136). Thousand Oaks, CA: Sage.

Lin, Y. H. W., & Rusbult, C. E. (1995). Commitment to dating relationships and cross-sex friendships in America and China. *Journal of Social and Personal Relationships, 12*, 7–26.

Lindsay, R. C. L., & Wells, G. L. (1985). Improving eyewitness identifications from lineups: Simultaneous versus sequential lineup presentation. *Journal of Applied Psychology, 70*, 556–564.

Linville, P. W., Fischer, G. W., & Salovey, P. (1989). Perceived distributions of characteristics of in-group and out-group members: Empirical evidence and a computer simulation. *Journal of Personality and Social Psychology, 57*, 165–188.

Linz, D. G., Donnerstein, E., & Penrod, S. (1984). The effects of multiple exposures to filmed violence against women. *Journal of Communication, 34*, 130–147.

Lippmann, W. (1922). *Public opinion*. New York: Free Press.

Lipsey, M. W., Wilson, D. B., Cohen, M. A., & Derzon, J. H. (1997). Is there a causal relationship between alcohol use and violence? A synthesis of evidence. In M. Galanter (Ed.), *Recent developments in alcoholism:* Vol. 13. *Alcohol and violence: Epidemiology, neurobiology, psychology, and family issues* (pp. 245–282). New York: Plenum.

Litter prevention (n.d.). Keep America Beautiful. Retrieved September 5, 2011, from www.kab.org/site/PageServer?pagename=focus_litter_prevention#COSTS

Little, A. C., & Perrett, D. I. (2002). Putting beauty back in the eye of the beholder. *Psychologist, 15*, 28–32.

Livesley, W. J., & Bromley, D. B. (1973). *Person perception in childhood and adolescence*. New York: Wiley.

Livingston, R. W., & Pearce, N. A. (2009). The teddy-bear effect: Does having a baby face benefit black chief executive officers? *Psychological Science, 22*, 1478–1483.

Lloyd, S. A., & Cate, R. M. (1985). The developmental course of conflict in dissolution of premarital relationships. *Journal of Social and Personal Relationships, 2*, 179–194.

Locken, B., & Peck, J. (2005). The effects of instructional frame on female adolescents' evaluations of larger-sized models in print advertising. *Journal of Applied Social Psychology, 35*, 850–868.

Lodish, L. M., Abraham, M., Kalmenson, S., Lievelsberger, J., Lubetkin, B., Richardson, B., & Stevens, M. E. (1995). How TV advertising works: A meta-analysis of 389 real-world split-cable TV advertising experiments. *Journal of Marketing Research, 32*, 125–139.

Loftus, E. F. (1979). *Eyewitness testimony*. Cambridge, MA: Harvard University Press.

Loftus, E. F. (1993). The reality of repressed memories. *American Psychologist, 48*, 518–537.

Loftus, E. F. (2005). Planting misinformation in the human mind: A 30year investigation of the malleability of memory. *Learning and Memory, 12*, 361–366.

Loftus, E. F., Garry, M., & Hayne, H. (2008). Repressed and recovered memory. In E. Borgida and S. T. Fiske (Eds.)., *Beyond common sense: Psychological science in the courtroom* (pp. 177–194). Malden, MA: Blackwell.

Loftus, E. F., Miller, D. G., & Burns, H. J. (1978). Semantic integration of verbal information into a visual memory. *Journal of Experimental Psychology: Human Learning and Memory, 4*, 19–31.

Lonner, W., & Berry, J. (Eds.). (1986). *Field methods in cross-cultural research*. Beverly Hills, CA: Sage.

Lord, C. G., Lepper, M. R., & Preston, E. (1984). Considering the opposite: A corrective strategy for social judgment. *Journal of Personality and Social Psychology, 47*, 1231–1243.

Lord, C. G., Scott, K. O., Pugh, M. A., & Desforges, D. M. (1997). Leakage beliefs and the correspondence bias. *Personality and Social Psychology Bulletin, 23*, 824–836.

Lore, R. K., & Schultz, L. A. (1993). Control of human aggression. *American Psychologist, 48*, 16–25.

Lorenz, K. (1966). *On aggression* (M. Wilson, Trans.). New York: Harcourt Brace.

Lott, A. J., & Lott, B. E. (1961). Group cohesiveness, communication level, and conformity. *Journal of Abnormal and Social Psychology, 62*, 408–412.

Lott, A. J., & Lott, B. E. (1974). The role of reward in the formation of positive interpersonal attitudes. In T. L. Huston (Ed.), *Foundations of interpersonal attraction* (pp. 171–189). New York: Academic Press.

Lount, R. B., Jr., Zhong, C.-B., Sivanathan, N., & Murnighan, J. K. (2008). Getting off on the wrong foot: The timing of a breach and the restoration of trust. *Personality and Social Psychology Bulletin, 34*(12), 1601–1612. doi:10.1177/0146167208324512

Lovett, R. A. (2010, March 2). Huge garbage patch found in Atlantic too. *National Geographic News*. National Geographic Society. Retrieved March 8, 2012, from news.nationalgeographic.com/news/2010/03/100302-new-ocean-trash-garbage-patch/

Ludwig, T. D., Gray, T. W., & Rowell, A. (1998). Increasing recycling in academic buildings: A systematic replication. *Journal of Applied Behavior Analysis, 31*, 683–686.

Lumsdaine, A. A., & Janis, I. L. (1953). Resistance to "counterpropaganda" produced by one-sided and two-sided "propaganda" presentations. *Public Opinion Quarterly, 17*, 311–318.

Luo, M. (2009, December 1). In job hunt, college degree can't close racial gap. *The New York Times*, p. 1.

Lupien, S. P., Seery, M. D., & Almonte, J. L. (2010). Discrepant and congruent high self-esteem: Behavioral self-handicapping as a preemptive defensive strategy. *Journal of Experimental Social Psychology, 46*, 1105–1108. doi:10.1016/j.jesp.2010.05.022

Lykken, D., & Tellegen, A. (1996). Happiness is a stochastic phenomenon. *Psychological Science*, 7, 186–189.

Lynn, M., & Shurgot, B. A. (1984). Responses to lonely hearts advertisements: Effects of reported physical attractiveness, physique, and coloration. *Personality and Social Psychology Bulletin, 10*, 349–357.

Lysak, H., Rule, B. G., & Dobbs, A. R. (1989). Conceptions of aggression: Prototype or defining features? *Personality and Social Psychology Bulletin, 15*, 233–243.

Lyubomirsky, S., Caldwell, N. D., & Nolen-Hoeksema, S. (1993). Effects of ruminative and distracting responses to depressed mood on retrieval of autobiographical memories. *Journal of Personality and Social Psychology, 75*, 166–177.

Lyubomirsky, S., Sheldon, K. M., & Schkade, D. (2005). Pursuing happiness: The architecture of sustainable change. *Review of General Psychology, 9*, 111–131.

Ma, D. (2009). Put the brakes on car surfing among teens. *American Academy of Pediatrics News, 30*, 27.

Ma, D. S., & Correll, J. (2011). Target prototypicality moderates racial bias in the decision to shoot. *Journal of Experimental Social Psychology, 47*, 391–396.

Maass, A., Cadinu, M., Guarnieri, G., & Grasselli, A. (2003). Sexual harassment under social identity threat: The computer harassment paradigm. *Journal of Personality and Social Psychology, 85*, 853–870.

Maass, A., & Clark, R. D., III. (1984). Hidden impact of minorities: Fifteen years of research. *Psychological Bulletin, 95*, 428–450.

Maccoby, E. E., & Jacklin, C. N. (1974). *The psychology of sex differences*. Stanford, CA: Stanford University Press.

MacCoun, R. J. (1989). Experimental research on jury decision-making. *Science, 244*, 1046–1050.

MacDonald, T. K., Zanna, M. P., & Fong, G. T. (1996). Why common sense goes out the window: Effects of alcohol on intentions to use condoms. *Personality and Social Psychology Bulletin, 22*, 763–775.

Mackie, D. M. (1987). Systematic and nonsystematic processing of majority and minority persuasive communications. *Journal of Personality and Social Psychology, 53*, 41–52.

MacKinnon, C. (1993, July-August). Turning rape into pornography: Postmodern genocide. *Ms.*, pp. 24–30.

Maclean, N. (1983). *A river runs through it*. Chicago: University of Chicago Press.

MacNeil, M. K., & Sherif, M. (1976). Norm change over subject generations as a function of arbitrariness of prescribed norms. *Journal of Personality and Social Psychology, 34*, 762–773.

Macrae, C. N., & Bodenhausen, G. V. (2000). Social cognition: Thinking categorically about others. *Annual Review of Psychology, 51*, 93–120.

Madon, S., Guyll, M., Buller, A. A., Scherr, K. C., Willard, J., & Spoth, R. (2008). The mediation of mothers' self-fulfilling effects on their children's alcohol use: Self-verification, informational conformity, and modeling processes. *Journal of Personality and Social Psychology, 95*(2), 369–384. doi:10.1037/0022-3514.95.2.369

Madon, S., Guyll, M., Spoth, R. L., Cross, S. E., & Hilbert, S. J. (2003). The self-fulfilling influence of mother expectations on children's underage drinking. *Journal of Personality and Social Psychology, 84*(6), 1188–1205. doi:10.1037/0022-3514.84.6.1188

Madon, S., Smith, A., Jussim, L., Russell, D. W., Eccles, J. S., Palumbo, P., & Walkiewicz, M. (2001). Am I as you see me or do you see me as I am? Self-fulfilling prophecies and self-verification. *Personality and Social Psychology Bulletin, 27*, 1214–1224.

Madon, S., Willard, J., Guyll, M., & Scherr, K. C. (2011). Self-fulfilling prophecies: Mechanisms, power, and links to social problems. *Social and Personality Psychology Compass, 5*(8), 578–590. doi:10.1111/j.1751-9004.2011.00375.x

Madon, S., Willard, J., Guyll, M., Trudeau, L., & Spoth, R. (2006). Self-fulfilling prophecy effects of mothers' beliefs on children's alcohol use: Accumulation, dissipation, and stability over time. *Journal of Personality and Social Psychology, 90*(6), 911–926. doi:10.1037/0022-3514.90.6.911

Magaro, P. A., & Ashbrook, R. M. (1985). The personality of societal groups. *Journal of Personality and Social Psychology, 48*, 1479–1489.

Mager, J., & Helgeson, J. G. (2011). Fifty years of advertising images: Some changing perspectives on role portrayals along with enduring consistencies. *Sex Roles, 64*(3–4), 238–252. doi:10.1007/s11199-010-9782-6

Magoo, G., & Khanna, R. (1991). Altruism and willingness to donate blood. *Journal of Personality and Clinical Studies*, 7, 21–24.

Main, M., Kaplan, N., & Cassidy, J. (1985). Security in infancy, childhood, and adulthood: A move to the level of representation. In T. Bretherton & E. Waters (Eds.), *Growing points of attachment theory and research. Monographs of the Society for Research on Child Development, 50*, 66–104.

Maio, G. R., & Olson, J. M. (1995). Relations between values, attitudes, and behavioral intentions: The moderating role of attitude function. *Journal of Experimental Social Psychology, 31*, 266–285.

Maisel, N. C., & Gable, S. L. (2009). The paradox of received social support: The importance of responsiveness. *Psychological Science, 20*(8), 928–932. doi:10.1111/j.1467-9280.2009.02388.x

Major, B., & Gramzow, R. H. (1999). Abortion as stigma: Cognitive and emotional implications of concealment. *Journal of Personality and Social Psychology*, 77, 735–745.

Malamuth, N. M. (1981). Rape fantasies as a function of exposure to violent sexual stimuli. *Archives of Sexual Behavior, 10*, 33–47.

Malamuth, N. M., Addison, T., & Koss, M. (2000). Pornography and sexual aggression: Are there reliable effects and can we understand them? *Annual Review of Sex Research 11*, 26–91.

Malamuth, N. M., Linz, D. G., Heavey, C. L., Barnes, G., & Acker, M. (1995). Using the confluence model of sexual aggression to predict men's conflict with women: A 10-year follow-up study. *Journal of Personality and Social Psychology, 69*, 353–369.

Malle, B. F., & Knobe, J. (1997). Which behaviors do people explain? A basic actor-observer asymmetry. *Journal of Personality and Social Psychology*, 72, 288–304.

Malloy, T. E. (2001). Difference to inference: Teaching logical and statistical reasoning through on-line interactivity. *Behavior Research Methods, Instruments, and Computers, 33*, 270–273.

Malpass, R. S., & Devine, P. G. (1981). Eyewitness identification: Lineup instructions and the absence of the offender. *Journal of Applied Psychology, 66*, 482–489.

Malpass, R. S., Tredoux, C. G., & McQuiston-Surrett, D. (2007). Lineup construction and lineup fairness. *The handbook of eyewitness psychology*, Vol II: *Memory for people* (pp. 155–178). Mahwah, NJ: Lawrence Erlbaum.

Manning, M. (2009). The effects of subjective norms on behaviour in the theory of planned behaviour: A meta-analysis. *British Journal of Social Psychology, 48*(4), 649–705. doi:10.1348/014466608X393136

Manning, R., Levine, M., & Collins, A. (2007). The Kitty Genovese murder and the social psychology of helping: The parable of the 38 witnesses. *American Psychologist, 62*, 555–562

Mannino, C. A., Snyder, M., & Omoto, A. M. (2011). Why do people get involved? Motivations for volunteerism and other forms of social action. In D. Dunning (Ed.), *Frontiers of social psychology. Social motivation* (pp. 127–146). New York: Psychology Press.

Manstead, A. S. R. (1997). Situations, belongingness, attitudes, and culture: Four lessons learned from social psychology. In G. McGarty & H. S. Haslam (Eds.), *The message of social psychology: Perspectives on mind and society* (pp. 238–251). Oxford, UK: Blackwell.

Marion, R. (1995, August). The girl who mewed. *Discover*, pp. 38–40.

Markey, P. M. (2000). Bystander intervention in computer-mediated communication. *Computers in Human Behavior, 16*, 183–188.

Markman, K. D., Karadogan, F., Lindberg, M. J., & Zell, E. (2009). Counterfactual thinking: Function and dysfunction. In K. D. Markman, W. M. P. Klein, & J. A. Suhr (Eds.), *Handbook of imagination and mental simulation* (pp. 175–193). New York: Psychology Press.

Markoff, J. (2011, February 16). Computer wins on "Jeopardy!": Trivial, it's not. *The New York Times*. Retreived April 18, 2011, from www.nytimes.com/2011/02/17/science/17jeopardy-watson.html?pagewanted=2

Marks, J. L., Lam, C. B., & McHale, S. M. (2009). Family patterns of gender role attitudes. *Sex Roles, 61*(3–4), 221–234. doi:10.1007/s11199-009-9619-3

Markus, H. R. (1977). Self-schemata and processing information about the self. *Journal of Personality and Social Psychology, 35*, 63–78.

Markus, H. R., & Kitayama, S. (1991). Culture and the self: Implications for cognition, emotion, and motivation. *Psychological Review, 98*, 224–253.

Markus, H. R., & Kitayama, S. (2001). The cultural construction of self and emotion: Implications for social behavior. In W. G. Parrott (Ed.), *Emotions in social psychology: Essential readings* (pp. 119–137). Philadelphia: Psychology Press.

Markus, H. R., Kitayama, S., & Heiman, R. J. (1996). Culture and "basic" psychological principles. In E. T. Higgins & A. W. Kruglanski (Eds.), *Social psychology: Handbook of basic principles* (pp. 857–913). New York: Guilford Press.

Markus, H. R., & Zajonc, R. B. (1985). The cognitive perspective in social psychology. In G. Lindzey & E. Aronson (Eds.), *Handbook of social psychology* (3rd ed., Vol. 1, pp. 137–230). New York: McGraw-Hill.

Marlatt, G. A., & Rohsenow, D. J. (1980). Cognitive processes in alcohol use: Expectancy and the balanced placebo design. In N. K. Mello (Ed.), *Advances in substance abuse* (Vol. 1). Greenwich, CT: JAI Press.

Marlowe, D., & Gergen, K. J. (1970). Personality and social behavior. In K. J. Gergen & D. Marlowe (Eds.), *Personality and social behavior* (pp. 1–75). Reading, MA: Addison-Wesley.

Marques, J., Abrams, D., & Serodio, R. (2001). Being better by being right: Subjective group dynamics and derogation of in-group deviants when generic norms are undermined. *Journal of Personality and Social Psychology, 81*, 436–447.

Marqusee, M. (2005, November 9). A name that lives in infamy. *The Guardian*. Available online at www.guardian.co.uk/world/2005/nov/10/usa.iraq

Martin, A. J., Berenson, K. R., Griffing, S., Sage, R. E., Madry, L., Bingham, L. E., & Primm, B. J. (2000). The process of leaving an abusive relationship: The role of risk assessments and decision certainty. *Journal of Family Violence, 15*, 109–122.

Martin, L. L., & Tesser, A. (1996). Some ruminative thoughts. In R. S. Wyer, Jr. (Ed.), *Advances in social cognition* (Vol. 9, pp. 1–47). Hillsdale, NJ: Erlbaum.

Martin, N. G., Eaves, L. J., Heath, A. R., Jardine, R., Feingold, L. M., & Eysenck, H. J. (1986). Transmission of social attitudes. *Proceedings of the National Academy of Science, 83*, 4364–4368.

Martinez, G., Copen, C. E., & Abma J. C. (2011). Teenagers in the United States: Sexual activity, contraceptive use, and childbearing, 2006–2010 National Survey of Family Growth. National Center for Health Statistics. *Vital Health Statistics, 23*(31). Retrieved November 1, 2011, from www.cdc.gov/nchs/data/series/sr_23/sr23_031.pdf

Martinez, L. (2012, January 11). U.S. Marines allegedly urinate on Taliban corpses. ABC News. Available online at: http://abcnews.go.com/Blotter/marines-allegedly-urinate-taliban-corpes/story?id=15341700#.T1GNRcxLWpc

Martinie, M. A., & Fointiat, V. (2006). Self-esteem, trivialization, and attitude change. *Swiss Journal of Psychology, 65*, 221–225.

Masicampo, E., & Baumeister, R. (2008). Toward a physiology of dual-process reasoning and judgment: Lemonade, willpower, and expensive rule-based analysis. *Psychological Science, 19*, 255–260.

Mason, M. F., & Morris, M. W. (2010). Culture, attribution and automaticity: A social cognitive neuroscience view. *Social Cognitive and Affective Neuroscience, 5*, 292–306.

Masuda, T., Ellsworth, P. C., & Mesquita, B. (2008). Placing the face in context: Cultural differences in the perception of facial emotion. *Journal of Personality and Social Psychology, 94*(3), 365–381.

Masuda, T., & Nisbett, R. E. (2006). Culture and change blindness. *Cognitive Science: A Multidisciplinary Journal, 30*, 381–399.

Matlin, M. W. (2012). *Psychology of women* (7th ed.). Belmont, CA: Wadsworth.

Matsumoto, D., & Ekman, P. (1989). American-Japanese differences in intensity ratings of facial expressions of emotion. *Motivation and Emotion, 13*, 143–157.

Matsumoto, D., & Ekman, P. (2004). The relationship among expressions, labels, and descriptions of contempt. *Journal of Personality and Social Psychology, 87*(4), 529–540.

Matsumoto, D., & Hwang, H. S. (2010). Judging faces in context. *Social and Personality Psychology Compass, 4*, 393–402.

Matsumoto, D., & Kudoh, T. (1993). American-Japanese cultural differences in attributions of personality based on smiles. *Journal of Nonverbal Behavior, 17*, 231–243.

Matsumoto, D., Willingham, B., & Olide, A. (2009). Sequential dynamics of culturally moderated facial expressions of emotion. *Psychological Science, 20*, 1269–1274.

Mazur, A., Booth, A., & Dabbs, J. M. (1992). Testosterone and chess competition. *Social Psychology Quarterly*, 55, 70–77.

McAlister, A., Perry, C., Killen, J. D., Slinkard, L. A., & Maccoby, N. (1980). Pilot study of smoking, alcohol, and drug abuse prevention. *American Journal of Public Health, 70*, 719–721.

McAllister, H. A. (1996). Self-serving bias in the classroom: Who shows it? Who knows it? *Journal of Educational Psychology, 88*, 123–131.

McArthur, L. Z. (1972). The how and what of why: Some determinants and consequences of causal attribution. *Journal of Personality and Social Psychology, 22*, 171–193.

McArthur, L. Z., & Baron, R. M. (1983). Toward an ecological theory of social perception. *Psychological Review, 90*, 215–238.

McArthur, L. Z., & Berry, D. S. (1987). Cross cultural agreement in perceptions of babyfaced adults. *Journal of Cross-Cultural Psychology, 18*, 165–192.

McCabe, M. P., & Ricciardelli, L. A. (2003a). Sociocultural influences on body image and body changes among adolescent boys and girls. *Journal of Social Psychology, 143*, 5–26.

McCabe, M. P., & Ricciardelli, L. A. (2003b). A longitudinal study of body change strategies among adolescent males. *Journal of Youth and Adolescence, 32*, 105–113.

McCarthy, J. F., & Kelly, B. R. (1978). Aggressive behavior and its effect on performance over time in ice hockey athletes: An archival study. *International Journal of Sport Psychology, 9*, 90–96.

McCauley, C. (1989). The nature of social influence in groupthink: Compliance and internalization. *Journal of Personality and Social Psychology, 57*, 250–260.

McClellan, S. (2008). *What happened: Inside the Bush White House and Washington's culture of deception*. New York: Public Affairs.

McClellan, S. (2009). *What happened: Inside the Bush White House and Washington's culture of deception*. New York: PublicAffairs.

McConahay, J. B. (1981). Reducing racial prejudice in desegregated schools. In W. D. Hawley (Ed.), *Effective school desegregation*. Beverly Hills, CA: Sage.

McConahay, J. B. (1986). Modern racism, ambivalence, and the Modern Racism Scale. In J. F. Dovidio & S. L. Gaertner (Eds.), *Prejudice, discrimination, and racism: Theory and research* (pp. 91–125). New York: Academic Press.

McConnell, A. R., & Brown, C. M. (2010). Dissonance averted: Self-concept organization moderates the effect of hypocrisy on attitude change. *Journal of Experimental Social Psychology, 46*, 361–366.

McCrea, S., Hirt, E., & Milner, B. (2008). She works hard for the money: Valuing effort underlies gender differences in behavioral self-handicapping. *Journal of Experimental Social Psychology, 44*, 292–311.

McCrea, S. M. (2008). Self-handicapping, excuse making, and counterfactual thinking: Consequences for self-esteem and future motivation. *Journal of Personality and Social Psychology, 95*, 274–292.

McCullough, M. E., & Tabak, B. A. (2010). Prosocial behavior. In R. F. Baumeister & E. J. Finkel (Eds.), *Advanced social psychology: The state of the science* (pp. 263–302). New York: Oxford University Press.

McDonald, H. E., & Hirt, E. R. (1997). When expectancy meets desire: Motivational effects in reconstructive memory. *Journal of Personality and Social Psychology, 72*, 5–23.

McFadyen-Ketchum, S. A., Bates, J. E., Dodge, K. A., & Pettit, G. S. (1996). Patterns of change in early childhood aggressive-disruptive behavior: Gender differences in predictions from early coercive and affectionate mother-child interactions. *Child Development, 67*, 2417–2433.

McGlone, M., & Aronson, J. (2006). Social identity salience and stereotype threat. *Journal of Applied Developmental Psychology, 27*, 486–493.

McGraw, A. P., Mellers, B. A., & Tetlock, P. E. (2005). Expectations and emotions of Olympic athletes. *Journal of Experimental Social Psychology, 41*, 438–446.

McGregor, B., Antoni, M., Boyers, A., Alferi, S., Cruess, D., Kilbourn, K., et al (2004). Cognitive behavioral stress management increases benefit finding and immune function among women with early stage breast cancer. *Journal of Psychosomatic Research, 54*, 1–8.

McGuire, A. M. (1994). Helping behaviors in the natural environment: Dimensions and correlates of helping. *Personality and Social Psychology Bulletin, 20*, 45–56.

McGuire, W. J. (1964). Inducing resistance to persuasion. In L. Berkowitz (Ed.), *Advances in experimental social psychology* (Vol. 1, pp. 192–229). New York: Academic Press.

McGuire, W. J. (1968). Personality and susceptibility to social influence. In E. F. Borgatta & W. W. Lambert (Eds.), *Handbook of personality theory and research* (pp. 1130–1187). Chicago: Rand McNally.

McHugo, G. J., & Smith, C. A. (1996). The power of faces: A review of John T. Lanzetta's research on facial expression and emotion. *Motivation and Emotion, 21*, 85–120.

McMillan, W., Stice, E., & Rohde, P. (2011). High- and low-level dissonance-based eating disorder prevention programs with young women with body image concerns: An experimental trial. *Journal of Consulting and Clinical Psychology, 79*, 129–134.

McMullin, D., & White, J. W. (2006). Long-term effects of labeling a rape experience. *Psychology of Women Quarterly, 30*, 96–105.

McNally, R., & Breslau, N. (2008). Does virtual trauma cause posttraumatic stress disorder? *American Psychologist, 63*, 282–283.

McNally, R. J. (2003). *Remembering trauma*. Cambridge, MA: Harvard University Press.

McNally, R. J., Bryant, R. A., & Ehlers, A. (2003). Does early psychological intervention promote recovery from posttraumatic stress? *Psychological Science in the Public Interest, 4*, 45–79.

McNally, R. J., & Geraerts, E. (2009). A new solution to the recovered memory debate. *Perspectives on Psychological Science, 4*(2), 126–134. doi:10.1111/j.1745-6924.2009.01112.x

McNulty, J. K., O'Mara, E. M., & Karney, B. R. (2008). Benevolent cognitions as a strategy of relationship maintenance: "Don't sweat the small stuff" . . . But it is not all small stuff. *Journal of Personality and Social Psychology, 94*, 631–646.

McPherson, J. M. (1983). The size of voluntary associations. *American Sociological Review, 61*, 1044–1064.

McPherson, M., Smith-Lovin, L., & Cook, J. M. (2001). Birds of a feather: Homophily in social networks. *Annual Review of Sociology, 27*, 415–444.

Medvec, V. H., Madey, S. F., & Gilovich, T. (1995). When less is more: Counterfactual thinking and satisfaction among Olympic medalists. *Journal of Personality and Social Psychology, 69*, 603–610.

Meeus, W. H. J., & Raaijmakers, Q. A. W. (1995). Obedience in modern society: The Utrecht studies. *Journal of Social Issues, 51*, 155–175.

Mehl, M. R., Vazire, S., Ramírez-Esparza, N., & Pennebacker, J. W. (2007). Are women really more talkative than men? *Science, 317*, 82.

Mehta, M. D. (2001). Pornography in Usenet: A study of 9,800 randomly selected images. *Cyberpsychology and Behavior, 4*, 695–703.

Meier, B. P., Robinson, M. D., Carter, M. S., & Hinsz, V. B. (2010). Are sociable people more beautiful? A zero-acquaintance analysis of agreeableness, extraversion, and attractiveness. *Journal of Research in Personality, 44*, 293–296.

Meindl, J. R., & Lerner, M. J. (1985). Exacerbation of extreme responses to an out-group. *Journal of Personality and Social Psychology, 47*, 71–84.

Meissner, C. A., & Brigham, J. C. (2001). Thirty years of investigating the own-race bias in memory for faces: A meta-analytic review. *Psychology, Public Policy, and Law, 7*, 3–35.

Meissner, C. A., Tredoux, C. G., & Parker, J. F. (2005). Eyewitness decisions in simultaneous and sequential lineups: A dual-process signal detection theory analysis. *Memory and Cognition, 33*, 783–792.

Melara, R. D., De Witt-Rickards, T. S., & O'Brien, T. P. (1989). Enhancing lineup identification accuracy: Two codes are better than one. *Journal of Applied Psychology, 74*, 706–713.

Mellers, B. A. (2001). *Current Directions in Psychological Science, 10*(6), 210–214(5). Blackwell Publishing.

Mendoza-Denton, R., & Page-Gould, E. (2008). Can cross-group friendships influence minority students' well-being at historically white universities? *Psychological Science, 19*, 933–939.

Menninger, W. (1948). Recreation and mental health. *Recreation, 42*, 340–346.

Menon, T., Morris, M. W., Chiu, C., & Hong, Y. (1999). Culture and the construal of agency: Attribution to individual versus group dispositions. *Journal of Personality and Social Psychology, 76*, 701–717.

Merkle, C., & Weber, M. (2011). True overconfidence: The inability of rational information processing to account for apparent overconfidence. *Organizational Behavior and Human Decision Processes, 116*(2), 262–271. doi:10.1016/j.obhdp.2011.07.004

Merton, R. K. (1948). The self-fulfilling prophecy. *Antioch Review, 8*, 193–210.

Messick, D., & Liebrand, W. B. G. (1995). Individual heuristics and the dynamics of cooperation in large groups. *Psychological Review, 102*, 131–145.

Meston, C. M., & Frohlich, P. F. (2003). Love at first fright: Partner salience moderates roller-coaster-induced excitation transfer. *Archives of Sexual Behavior, 32*(6), 537–544.

Metcalfe, J. (1998). Cognitive optimism: Self-deception or memory-based processing heuristics? *Personality and Social Psychology Review, 2*, 100–110.

Meyersburg, C. A., Bogdan, R., Gallo, D. A., & McNally, R. J. (2009). False memory propensity in people reporting recovered memories of past lives. *Journal of Abnormal Psychology, 118*(2), 399–404. doi:10.1037/a0015371

Mezulis, A. H., Abramson, L. Y., Hyde, J. S., & Hankin, B. L. (2004). Is there a universal positivity bias in attributions? A meta-analytic review of individual, developmental, and cultural differences in the self-serving attributional bias. *Psychological Bulletin, 130*(5), 711–747.

Migration and geographic mobility in metropolitan and nonmetropolitan America, 1995–2000 (2003). United States Census Bureau. Accessed on April 16, 2006, at www.census.gov/prod/2003pubs/censr-9.pdf

Mikulincer, M., & Shaver, P. (2005). Attachment security, compassion, and altruism. *Current Directions in Psychological Science, 14*, 34–38.

Mikulincer, M., & Shaver, P. R. (2003). The attachment behavioral system in adulthood: Activation, psychodynamics, and interpersonal processes. In M. P. Zanna (Ed.), *Advances in experimental social psychology* (Vol. 35, pp. 53–152). San Diego, CA: Academic Press.

Mikulincer, M., Shaver, P. R., Sapir-Lavid, Y., & Avihou-Kanza, N. (2009). What's inside the minds of securely and insecurely attached people? The secure-base script and its associations with attachment-style dimensions. *Journal of Personality and Social Psychology, 97*, 615–633.

Milgram, S. (1961). Nationality and conformity. *Scientific American, 205*, 45–51.

Milgram, S. (1963). Behavioral study of obedience. *Journal of Abnormal and Social Psychology, 67*, 371–378.

Milgram, S. (1969, March). The lost letter technique. *Psychology Today*, pp. 30–33, 67–68.

Milgram, S. (1974). *Obedience to authority: An experimental view*. New York: Harper & Row.

Milgram, S. (1976). Obedience to criminal orders: The compulsion to do evil. In T. Blass (Ed.), *Contemporary social psychology: Representative readings* (pp. 175–184). Itasca, IL: Peacock.

Milgram, S. (1977). *The individual in a social world*. Reading, MA: Addison-Wesley.

Milgram, S., & Sabini, J. (1978). On maintaining urban norms: A field experiment in the subway. In A. Baum, J. E. Singer, & S. Valins (Eds.), *Advances in environmental psychology* (Vol. 1, pp. 9–40). Hillsdale, NJ: Erlbaum.

Mill, J. S. (1843). *A system of logic ratiocinative and inductive*. London.

Miller, A. G. (1986). *The obedience experiments: A case study of controversy in social science*. New York: Praeger.

Miller, A. G. (1995). Constructions of the obedience experiments: A focus upon domains of relevance. *Journal of Social Issues, 51*, 33–53.

Miller, A. G., Ashton, W., & Mishal, M. (1990). Beliefs concerning the features of constrained behavior: A basis for the fundamental attribution error. *Journal of Personality and Social Psychology, 59*, 635–650.

Miller, A. G., Collins, B. E., & Brief, D. E. (1995). Perspectives on obedience to authority: The legacy of the Milgram experiments. *Journal of Social Issues, 51*, 1–19.

Miller, A. G., Jones, E. E., & Hinkle, S. (1981). A robust attribution error in the personality domain. *Journal of Experimental Social Psychology, 17*, 587–600.

Miller, C. E., & Anderson, P. D. (1979). Group decision rules and the rejection of deviates. *Social Psychology Quarterly, 42*, 354–363.

Miller, C. T. (1982). The role of performance-related similarity in social comparison of abilities: A test of the related attributes hypothesis. *Journal of Experimental Social Psychology, 18*, 513–523.

Miller, D., & Taylor, B. (2002). Counterfactual thought, regret, and superstition: How to avoid kicking yourself. In T. Gilovich, D. Griffiin, & D. Kahneman (Eds.), *Heuristics and biases: The psychology of intuitive judgement* (pp. 367–378). New York: Cambridge University Press.

Miller, D. T., & Prentice, D. A. (1996). The construction of social norms and standards. In E. T. Higgins & A. W. Kruglanski (Eds.), *Social psychology: Handbook of basic principles* (pp. 799–829). New York: Guilford Press.

Miller, D. T., & Ross, M. (1975). Self-serving biases in the attribution of causality: Fact or fiction? *Psychological Bulletin, 82*, 213–225.

Miller, J. G. (1984). Culture and the development of everyday social explanation. *Journal of Personality and Social Psychology, 46*, 961–978.

Miller, N., & Bugelski, R. (1948). Minor studies in aggression: The influence of frustrations imposed by the in-group on attitudes expressed by the out-group. *Journal of Psychology, 25*, 437–442.

Miller, N., & Campbell, D. T. (1959). Recency and primacy in persuasion as a function of the timing of speeches and measurements. *Journal of Abnormal and Social Psychology, 59*, 1–9.

Miller, P. V. (2002). The authority and limitation of polls. In J. Manza, F. L. Cook, & B. I. Page (Eds.), *Navigating public opinion* (pp. 221–231). New York: Oxford University Press.

Mills, J. (1958). Changes in moral attitudes following temptation. *Journal of Personality, 26*, 517–531.

Mills, J., & Clark, M. S. (1982). Communal and exchange relationships. In L. Wheeler (Ed.), *Review of personality and social psychology* (Vol. 2, pp. 121–144). Beverly Hills, CA: Sage.

Mills, J., & Clark, M. S. (1994). Communal and exchange relationships: Controversies and research. In R. Erber & R. Gilmour (Eds.), *Theoretical frameworks for personal relationships* (pp. 29–42). Hillsdale, NJ: Erlbaum.

Milton, K. (1971). *Women in policing*. New York: Police Foundation Press.

Minard, R. D. (1952). Race relations in the Pocahontas coal field. *Journal of Social Issues, 8*, 29–44.

Mischel, W. (1968). *Personality and assessment*. New York: Wiley.

Mitchell, J., Heatherton, T., Kelley, W., Wyland, C., Wegner, D., & Macrae, C. (2007). Separating sustained from transient aspects of cognitive control during thought suppression. *Psychological Science, 18*, 292–297.

Miyamoto, Y., & Kitayama, S. (2002). Cultural variation in correspondence bias: The critical role of attitude diagnosticity of socially constrained behavior. *Journal of Personality and Social Psychology, 83*, 1239–1248.

Miyamoto, Y., Nisbett, R. E., & Masuda, T. (2006). Culture and the physical environment: Holistic versus analytic perceptual affordances. *Psychological Science, 17*, 113–119.

Modigliani, A., & Rochat, F. (1995). The role of interaction sequences and the timing of resistance in shaping obedience and defiance to authority. *Journal of Social Issues, 51*, 107–123.

Mojzisch, A., & Schulz-Hardt, S. (2010). Knowing others' preferences degrades the quality of group decisions. *Journal of Personality and Social Psychology, 98*(5), 794–808. doi:10.1037/a0017627

Mok, A., & Morris, M. W. (2010). An upside to bicultural identity conflict: Resisting groupthink in cultural ingroups. *Journal of Experimental Social Psychology, 46*(6), 1114–1117. doi:10.1016/j.jesp.2010.05.020

Mokdad, A. H., Marks, J. S., Stroup, D. F., & Gerberding, J. L. (2004). Actual causes of death in the United States. *Journal of the American Medical Association, 291*, 1238–1245.

Monin, J., Clark, M., & Lemay, E. (2008). Communal responsiveness in relationships with female versus male family members. *Sex Roles, 59*, 176–188.

Monson, C. M.; Langhinrichsen-Rohling, J. (2002). Sexual and nonsexual dating violence perpetration: Testing an integrated perpetrator typology, *Violence and Victims, 17*(4), 403–428(26). Springer Publishing Company

Montemayor, R., & Eisen, M. (1977). The development of self-conceptions from childhood to adolescence. *Developmental Psychology, 13*, 314–319.

Moore, B., Jr. (1978). *Injustice: The social bases of obedience and revolt*. White Plains, NY: Sharpe.

Moore, J. S., Graziano, W. G., & Millar, M. C. (1987). Physical attractiveness, sex role orientation, and the evaluation of adults and children. *Personality and Social Psychology Bulletin, 13*, 95–102.

Moore, R. L. (1998). Love and limerance with Chinese characteristics: Student romance in the PRC. In V. C. de Munck (Ed.), *Romantic love and sexual behavior* (pp. 251–283). Westport, CT: Praeger.

Moore, T. E. (1982). Subliminal advertising: What you see is what you get. *Journal of Marketing, 46*, 38–47.

Moors, A., & De Houwer, J. (2006). Automaticity: A theoretical and conceptual analysis. *Psychological Bulletin, 132*, 297–326.

Moos, R. H., & Holahan, C. J. (2003). Dispositional and contextual perspectives on coping: Toward an integrative framework. *Journal of Clinical Psychology, 59*, 1387–1403.

Mor, N., Doane, L. D., Adam, E. K., Mineka, S., Zinbarg, R. E., Griffith, J. W., . . . Nazarian, M. (2010). Within-person variations in self-focused attention and negative affect in depression and anxiety: A diary study. *Cognition and Emotion, 24*, 48–62. doi:10.1080/02699930802499715

Moran, S., & Ritov, I. (2007). Experience in integrative negotiations: What needs to be learned? *Journal of Experimental Social Psychology, 43*, 77–90.

Moray, N. (1959). Attention in dichotic listening: Affective cues and the influence of instructions. *Quarterly Journal of Experimental Psychology, 11*, 56–60.

Moreland, R. L. (1987). The formation of small groups. In C. Hendrick (Ed.), *Review of personality and social psychology* (Vol. 8, pp. 80–110). Newbury Park, CA: Sage.

Moreland, R. L. (1999). Transactive memory: Learning who knows what in work groups and organizations. In L. L. Thompson & J. M. Levine (Eds.), *Shared cognition in organizations: The management of knowledge* (pp. 3–31). Mahwah, NJ: Erlbaum.

Moreland, R. L. (2010). Are dyads really groups? *Small Group Research, 41*(2), 251–267. doi:10.1177/1046496409358618

Moreland, R. L., & Beach, S. R. (1992). Exposure effects in the classroom: The development of affinity among students. *Journal of Experimental Social Psychology, 28*, 255–276.

Moreland, R. L., & Topolinski, S. (2010). The mere exposure phenomenon: A lingering melody by Robert Zajonc. *Emotion Review, 2*, 329–339.

Morin, R. (2002, March 3). Bias and babies. *Washington Post*, p. B5.

Morling, B., & Evered, S. (2006). Secondary control reviewed and defined. *Psychological Bulletin, 132*, 269–296.

Morris, E. (Director). (1988). *The thin blue line* [Film]. New York: HBO Videos.

Morris, M. W., & Peng, K. (1994). Culture and cause: American and Chinese attributions for social and physical events. *Journal of Personality and Social Psychology, 67*, 949–971.

Morris, W. N., & Miller, R. S. (1975). The effects of consensus-breaking and consensus-preempting partners on reduction of conformity. *Journal of Experimental Social Psychology, 11*, 215–223.

Morry, M. M., & Staska, S. L. (2001). Magazine exposure: Internalization, self-objectification, eating attitudes, and body satisfaction in male and female university students. *Canadian Journal of Behavioural Science, 33*, 269–279.

Morse, D. R., Martin, J., & Moshonov, J. (1991). Psychosomatically induced death relative to stress, hypnosis, mind control, and voodoo: Review and possible mechanisms. *Stress Medicine, 7*, 213–232.

Morton, T. A., Postmes, T., Haslam, S. A., & Hornsey, M. J. (2009). Theorizing gender in the face of social change: Is there anything essential about essentialism? *Journal of Personality and Social Psychology, 96*, 653–664.

Moscovici, S. (1985). Social influence and conformity. In G. Lindzey & E. Aronson (Eds.), *Handbook of social psychology* (3rd ed., Vol. 2, pp. 347–412). New York: McGraw-Hill.

Moscovici, S. (1994). Three concepts: Minority, conflict, and behavioral style. In S. Moscovici, A. Mucchi-Faina, & A. Maass (Eds.), *Minority influence* (pp. 233–251). Chicago: Nelson-Hall.

Moscovici, S., Mucchi-Faina, A., & Maass, A. (Eds.). (1994). *Minority influence*. Chicago: Nelson-Hall.

Moscovici, S., & Nemeth, C. (1974). Minority influence. In C. Nemeth (Ed.), *Social psychology: Classic and contemporary integrations* (pp. 217–249). Chicago: Rand McNally.

Mostert, M. P. (2010). Facilitated communication and its legitimacy—Twenty-first century developments. *Exceptionality, 18*(1), 31–41. doi:10.1080/09362830903462524

Moyer, K. E. (1983). The physiology of motivation: Aggression as a model. In C. J. Scheier & A. M. Rogers (Eds.), *G. Stanley Hall lecture series* (Vol. 3). Washington, DC: American Psychological Association.

Mucchi-Faina, A., & Pagliaro, S. (2008). Minority influence: The role of ambivalence toward the source. *European Journal of Social Psychology, 38*, 612–623.

Mukai, T. (1996). Mothers, peers, and perceived pressure to diet among Japanese adolescent girls. *Journal of Research in Adolescence, 6*, 309–324.

Mukai, T., Kambara, A., & Sasaki, Y. (1998). Body dissatisfaction, need for social approval, and eating disturbances among Japanese and American college women. *Sex Roles, 39*, 751–771.

Mullen, B. (1986). Atrocity as a function of lynch mob composition: A self-attention perspective. *Personality and Social Psychology Bulletin, 12*, 187–197.

Mullen, B., Brown, R., & Smith, C. (1992). Ingroup bias as a function of salience, relevance, and status: An integration. *European Journal of Social Psychology, 22*, 103–122.

Mullen, B., & Cooper, C. (1994). The relation between group cohesiveness and performance: An integration. *Psychological Bulletin, 115*, 210–227.

Mullen, B., & Johnson, C. (1988). *Distinctiveness-based illusory correlation and stereotyping: A meta-analytic integration*. Unpublished manuscript, Syracuse University.

Mullen, B., Rozell, D., & Johnson, C. (2001). Ethnophaulisms for ethnic immigrant groups: The contributions of group size and familiarity. *European Journal of Social Psychology, 31*, 231–246.

Muller, D., Atzeni, T., & Fabrizio, B. (2004). Coaction and upward social comparison reduce the illusory conjunction effect: Support for distraction-conflict theory. *Journal of Experimental Social Psychology, 40*, 659–665.

Muller, D., & Butera, F. (2007). The focusing effect of self-evaluation threat in coaction and social comparison. *Journal of Personality and Social Psychology, 93*, 194–211.

Muller, D., & Fayant, M.-P. (2010). On being exposed to superior others: Consequences of self-threatening upward social comparisons. *Social and Personality Psychology Compass, 4*(8), 621–634. doi:10.1111/j.1751-9004.2010.00279.x

Muraven, M., Tice, D. M., & Baumeister, R. F. (1998). Self-control as limited resource: Regulatory depletion patterns. *Journal of Personality and Social Psychology, 74*, 774–789.

Murr, A., & Smalley, S. (2003, March 17). White power, minus the power. *Newsweek*, pp. 42–45.

Murstein, B. I. (1970). Stimulus value role: A theory of marital choice. *Journal of Marriage and the Family, 32*, 465–481.

Mushquash, A. R., Stewart, S. H., Sherry, S. B., Mackinnon, S. P., Antony, M. M., & Sherry, D. L. (2011). Heavy episodic drinking among dating partners: A longitudinal actor-partner interdependence model. *Psychology of Addictive Behaviors*. Available online. doi:10.1037/a0026653

Mussweiler, T. (2003). Comparison processes in social judgment: Mechanisms and consequences. *Psychological Review, 110*(3), 472–489.

Mussweiler, T., & Förster, J. (2000). The sex-aggression link: A perception-behavior dissociation. *Journal of Personality and Social Psychology, 79*, 507–520.

Mussweiler, T., & Strack, F. (1999). Comparing is believing: A selective accessibility model of judgmental anchoring. In W. Stroebe & M. Hewstone (Eds.), *European review of social psychology* (Vol. 10, pp. 135–167). Chichester, UK: Wiley.

Mussweiler, T., Strack, F., & Pfeiffer, T. (2000). Overcoming the inevitable anchoring effect: Considering the opposite compensates for selective accessibility. *Personality and Social Psychology Bulletin, 260*, 1142–1150.

Myers, D. G., & Scanzoni, L. D. (2006). *What God has joined together: The Christian case for gay marriage*. Harper Collins: San Francisco.

Myers, H. F. (2009). Ethnicity- and socio-economic status-related stresses in context: An integrative review and conceptual model. *Journal of Behavioral Medicine, 32*(1), 9–19. doi:10.1007/s10865-008-9181-4

Myers, T. A., & Crowther, J. H. (2009). Social comparison as a predictor of body dissatisfaction: A meta-analytic review. *Journal of Abnormal Psychology, 118*(4), 683–698. doi:10.1037/a0016763

Nadal, K., Griffin, K. E., Vargas, V. M., Issa, M., Lyons, O. B., & Tobio, M. (2011). Processes and struggles with racial microaggressions from the White American perspective: Recommendations for workplace settings. In M. A. Paludi, C. A. Paludi, Jr., & E. R. DeSouza (Eds.), *Praeger handbook on understanding and preventing workplace discrimination* (pp. 155–180). Santa Barbara, CA: Praeger/ABC-CLIO.

Nail, P. R. (1986). Toward an integration of some models and theories of social response. *Psychological Bulletin, 100*, 190–206.

Nail, P. R., McDonald, G., & Levy, D. A. (2000). Proposal of a four-dimensional model of social response. *Psychological Bulletin, 126*, 454–470.

Nail, P. R., Misak, J. E., & Davis, R. M. (2004). Self-affirmation versus self-consistency: A comparison of two competing self-theories of dissonance phenomena. *Personality and Individual Differences, 36*, 1893–1905.

Naimi, T., Brewer, B., Mokdad, A., Serdula, M., Denny, C., & Marks, J. (2003). Binge drinking among U.S. adults. *Journal of the American Medical Association, 289*, 70–75.

Narchet, F. M., Meissner, C. A., & Russano, M. B. (2011). Modeling the influence of investigator bias on the elicitation of true and false confessions. *Law and Human Behavior, 35*(6), 452–465. doi:10.1007/s10979-010-9257-x

Nasco, S. A., & Marsh, K. L. (1999). Gaining control through counterfactual thinking. *Personality and Social Psychology Bulletin, 25*, 556–568.

Natanovich, G., & Eden, D. (2008). Pygmalion effects among outreach supervisors and tutors: Extending sex generalizability. *Journal of Applied Psychology, 93*(6), 1382–1389. doi:10.1037/a0012566

Nathanson, S. (1987). *An eye for an eye? The morality of punishing by death*. Totowa, NJ: Rowman & Littlefield.

National Center for Health Statistics. (2005). Marriage and divorce. Retrieved on September 19, 2006, from www.cdc.gov/nchs/fastats/divorce.html2

National Center for Vital Statistics. (2001). *Crime facts at a glance*. Retrieved from Bureau of Justice Statistics, www.ojp.usdoj.gov/bjs/glance/hmrt.htm

National Oceanic and Atmospheric Administration. (2011, January 12). 2010 tied for warmest year on record. U.S. Department of Commerce. Retrieved August 14, 2011, from www.noaanews.noaa.gov/stories2011/20110112_globalstats.html

National Research Council (2003). *The polygraph and lie detection*. Washington, DC: National Academies Press.

Neighbors, C., O'Connor, R. M., Lewis, M. A., Chawla, N., Lee, C. M., & Fossos, N. (2008). The relative impact of injunctive norms on college student drinking: The role of reference group. *Psychology of Addictive Behaviors, 22*, 576–581.

Nel, E., Helmreich, R., & Aronson, E. (1969). Opinion change in the advocate as a function of the persuasibility of his audience: A clarification of the meaning of dissonance. *Journal of Personality and Social Psychology, 12*, 117–124.

Nelson, D. E., Bland, S., Powell-Griner, E., Klein, R., Wells, H. E., Hogelin, G., & Marks, J. S. (2002). State trends in health risk factors and receipt of clinical preventive services among US adults during the 1990s. *Journal of the American Medical Association, 287*, 2659–2667.

Nelson, M. R., (2008). The hidden persuaders: Then and now. *Journal of Advertising, 37*, 113–126. doi:10.2753/JOA0091-3367370109

Nelson, S. (Writer, Producer, Director). (2010). *Freedom riders* [motion picture]. United States: *American Experience* (Public Broadcasting Service: WGBH, Boston). Available from http://www.pbs.org/wgbh/americanexperience/freedomriders/

Nemeth, C. J., & Chiles, C. (1988). Modeling courage: The role of dissent in fostering independence. *European Journal of Social Psychology, 18*, 275–280.

Neria, Y., DiGrande, L., & Adams, B. G. (2011). Posttraumatic stress disorder following the September 11, 2001, terrorist attacks: A review of the literature among highly exposed populations. *American Psychologist, 66*(6), 429–446. doi:10.1037/a0024791

Nes, L. S., & Segerstrom, S. C. (2006). Dispositional optimism and coping: A meta-analytic review. *Personality and Social Psychology Review, 10*, 235–251.

Nestler, S., Blank, H., & Egloff, B. (2010). Hindsight ≠ hindsight: Experimentally induced dissociations between hindsight components. *Journal of Experimental Psychology: Learning, Memory, and Cognition, 36*(6), 1399–1413. doi:10.1037/a0020449

Neuberg, S. L. (1988). Behavioral implications of information presented outside of awareness: The effect of subliminal presentation of trait information on behavior in the prisoner's dilemma game. *Social Cognition, 6*, 207–230.

Neuberg, S. L., Kenrick, D. T., & Schaller, M. (2010). Evolutionary social psychology. In S. T. Fiske, D. T. Gilbert, & G. Lindzey (Eds.), *Handbook of social psychology* (5th ed., Vol. 2, pp. 761–796). Hoboken, NJ: John Wiley.

Newcomb, T. M. (1961). *The acquaintance process*. New York: Holt, Rinehart and Winston.

Newman, A. A. (2009, February 18). The body as billboard: Your ad here. *The New York Times* (p. B3). Retrieved June 6, 2011, from www.nytimes.com/2009/02/18/business/media/18adco.html

Newman, L. S. (1996). Trait impressions as heuristics for predicting future behavior. *Personality and Social Psychology Bulletin, 22*, 395–411.

Newport, F. (2011, May 20). For first time, majority of Americans favor legal gay marriage. *Gallup*. www.gallup.com/poll/147662/first-time-majority-americans-favor-legal-gay-marriage.aspx

Nichols, S. (2011). Experimental philosophy and the problem of free will. *Science, 331*(6023), 1401–1403. doi:10.1126/science.1192931

Nicholson, N., Cole, S. G., & Rocklin, T. (1985). Conformity in the Asch situation: A comparison between contemporary British and U.S. university students. *British Journal of Social Psychology, 24*, 59–63.

Nickerson, C., Schwarz, N., Diener, E., & Kahneman, D. (2003). Zeroing in on the dark side of the American Dream: A closer look at the negative consequences of the goal for financial success. *Psychological Science, 14*, 531–536.

Niedenthal, P. M., Tangney, J. P., & Gavanski, I. (1994). "If only I weren't" versus "If only I hadn't": Distinguishing shame and guilt in counterfactual thinking. *Journal of Personality and Social Psychology, 67*, 585–595.

Nielsen, K., & Cleal, B. (2011). Under which conditions do middle managers exhibit transformational leadership behaviors?—An experience sampling method study on the predictors of transformational leadership behaviors. *Leadership Quarterly, 22*(2), 344–352. doi:10.1016/j.leaqua.2011.02.009

The NIMH Multisite HIV Prevention Trial Group (1998, June 19). The NIMH Multisite HIV Prevention Trial: Reducing sexual HIV risk behavior. *Science, 280*, 1889–1894.

The NIMH Multisite HIV Prevention Trial Group (2001). Social-cognitive theory mediators of behavior change in the National Institute of Mental Health Multisite HIV Prevention Trial. *Health Psychology, 20*, 369–376.

Nisbett, R. E. (1993). Violence and U.S. regional culture. *American Psychologist, 48*, 441–449.

Nisbett, R. E. (2003). *The geography of thought: How Asians and Westerners think differently . . . and why*. New York: Free Press.

Nisbett, R. E. (2009). *Intelligence and how to get it: Why schools and cultures count*. New York: W.W. Norton.

Nisbett, R. E., Caputo, C., Legant, P., & Marecek, J. (1973). Behavior as seen by the actor and by the observer. *Journal of Personality and Social Psychology, 27*, 154–164.

Nisbett, R. E., & Cohen, D. (1996). *Culture of honor: The psychology of violence in the South*. Boulder, CO: Westview Press.

Nisbett, R. E., Fong, G. T., Lehman, D. R., & Cheng, P. W. (1987). Teaching reasoning. *Science, 238*, 625–631.

Nisbett, R. E., Peng, K., Choi, I., & Norenzayan, A. (2001). Culture and systems of thought: Holistic vs. analytic cognition. *Psychological Review, 108*, 291–310.

Nisbett, R. E., & Ross, L. (1980). *Human inference: Strategies and shortcomings of human judgment*. Englewood Cliffs, NJ: Prentice Hall.

Nisbett, R. E., & Wilson, T. D. (1977). Telling more than we can know: Verbal reports on mental processes. *Psychological Review, 84*, 231–259.

Nixon, R. M. (1990). *In the arena: A memoir of victory, defeat, and renewal*. New York: Simon & Schuster.

Noar, S. M., Benac, C. N., Harris, M. S. (2007). Does tailoring matter? Meta-analytic review of tailored print health behavior change interventions. *Psychological Bulletin, 133*, 673–693.

Nolan, J., Schultz, P., Cialdini, R., Goldstein, N., & Griskevicius, V. (2008). Normative social influence is underdetected. *Personality and Social Psychology Bulletin, 34*, 913-923.

Norenzayan, A., Choi, I., & Peng, K. (2007). Perception and cognition. In S. Kitayama & D. Cohen (Eds.), *Handbook of cultural psychology* (pp. 569–594). New York: Guilford.

Norenzayan, A., & Heine, S. J. (2005). Psychological universals: What are they and how can we know? *Psychological Bulletin, 131*, 763–784.

Norenzayan, A., & Nisbett, R. E. (2000). Culture and causal cognition. *Current Direction in Psychological Science, 9*, 132–135.

Norenzayan, A., & Shariff, A. F. (2008). The origin and evolution of religious prosociality. *Science, 322*, 58–62.

North, A. C., Tarrant, M., & Hargreaves, D. J. (2004). The effects of music on helping behavior: A field study. *Environment and Behavior, 36*, 266–275.

Norton, M. I., & Sommers, S. R. (2011). Whites see racism as a zero-sum game that they are now losing. *Perspectives on Psychological Science, 6*, 215–218.

Nosek, B. A., Greenwald, A. G., & Banaji, M. R. (2005). Understanding and using the implicit association test: II. Method variables and construct validity. *Personality and Social Psychology Bulletin, 31*, 166–180.

Nosek, B. A., Greenwald, A. G., & Banaji, M. R. (2007). The Implicit Association Test at 7: A methodological and conceptual review. In J. A. Bargh (Ed.), *Social psychology and the unconscious*. New York: Psychology Press.

Nowak, A., Szamrej, J., & Latané, B. (1990). From private attitude to public opinion: A dynamic theory of social impact. *Psychological Review, 97*, 362–376.

The number of people who say they have no one to confide in has risen. *Washington Post*, p. A3.

O'Brien, S. (2004, May 21). Researcher: It's not bad apples, it's the barrel. Retrieved on January 20, 2005, from CNN.com, www.cnn.com/2004/US/05/21/zimbarbo.access/J

O'Connor, K. M., & Carnevale, P. J. (1997). A nasty but effective negotiation strategy: Misrepresentation of a common-value issue. *Personality and Social Psychology Bulletin, 23*, 504–515.

O'Leary, A. (1990). Stress, emotion, and human immune function. *Psychological Bulletin, 108*, 363–382.

O'Rourke, L. (2008, August 2). Behind the woman behind the bomb. *The New York Times*, Op-ed page.

O'Sullivan, C. S., & Durso, F. T. (1984). Effects of schema-incongruent information on memory for stereotypical attributes. *Journal of Personality and Social Psychology, 47*, 55–70.

Obama 46%, Romney 44% in Nationwide SurveyUSA Poll. (2011, November 17). Retrieved November 21, 2011, from http://www.surveyusa.com/index.php/2011/11/16/obama-46-romney-44-in-nationwide-surveyusa-poll-cell-phone-respondents-are-difference-between-re-election-and-democrat-defeat/

Obesity and overweight (2011). National Center for Health Statistics, Center for Disease Control and Prediction. Retrieved March 13, 2011, from www.cdc.gov/nchs/fastats/overwt.htm

Ochsner, K. (2007). Social cognitive neuroscience: Historical development, core principles, and future promise. In A. W. Kruglanski & E. T. Higgins (Eds.), *Social psychology: Handbook of basic principles* (2nd ed., pp. 39–66). New York: Guilford.

Ofshe, R., & Watters, E. (1994). *Making monsters: False memories, psychotherapy, and sexual hysteria*. New York: Scribner.

Ogloff, J. R. P., & Vidmar, N. (1994). The impact of pretrial publicity on jurors: A study to compare the relative effects of television and print media in a child sex abuse case. *Law and Human Behavior, 18*, 507–525.

Ohbuchi, K., Ohno, T., & Mukai, H. (1993). Empathy and aggression: Effects of self-disclosure and fearful appeal. *Journal of Social Psychology, 133*, 243–253.

Ohbuchi, K., & Sato, K. (1994). Children's reactions to mitigating accounts: Apologies, excuses, and intentionality of harm. *Journal of Social Psychology, 134*, 5–17.

Oikawa, M., Aarts, H., & Oikawa, H. (2011). There is a fire burning in my heart: The role of causal attribution in affect transfer. *Cognition and Emotion, 25*(1), 156–163. doi:10.1080/02699931003680061

Oishi, S. (2010). The psychology of residential mobility: Implications for the self, social relationships, and well-being. *Perspectives on Psychological Science, 5*(1), 5–21. doi:10.1177/1745691609356781

Oishi, S., Rothman, A. J., Snyder, M., Su, J., Zehm, K., Hertel, A. W., et al. (2007). The socioecological model of procommunity action: The benefits of residential stability. *Journal of Personality and Social Psychology, 93*, 831–844.

Oishi, S., Schimmack, U., & Colcombe, S. J. (2003). The contextual and systematic nature of life satisfaction judgments. *Journal of Experimental Social Psychology, 39*, 232–247.

Oishi, S., Wyer, R. S., & Colcombe, S. J. (2000). Cultural variation in the use of current life satisfaction to predict the future. *Journal of Personality and Social Psychology, 78*, 434–445.

Olson, J., & Stone, J. (2005). The influence of behavior on attitudes. In D. Albarracín, B. T. Johnson, & M. P. Zanna (Eds.), *The handbook of attitudes* (pp. 223–271). Mahwah, NJ: Erlbaum.

Olson, J. M., Vernon, P. A., Harris, J. A., & Jang, K. L. (2001). The heritability of attitudes: A study of twins. *Journal of Personality and Social Psychology, 80*(6), 845–860.

Olson, M. A. (2009). Measures of prejudice. In T. Nelson (Ed.), *The handbook of prejudice, stereotyping, and discrimination*. New York: Psychology Press.

Olweus, D. (1991). Bully/victim problems among schoolchildren: Basic facts and effects of a school-based intervention program. In D. Pepler & K. Rubin (Eds.), *The development and treatment of childhood aggression* (pp. 411–448). Hillsdale, NJ: Erlbaum.

Olweus, D. (1996). Bullying at school: Knowledge base and an effective intervention program. In C. Ferris & T. Grisso (Eds.), *Understanding aggressive behavior in children* (pp. 265–276). New York: New York Academy of Sciences.

Olweus, D. (2003). Prevalence estimation of school bullying. *Aggressive Behavior 29*, 239–268.

Oppenheimer, D. M. (2004). spontaneous discounting of availability in frequency judgment tasks. *Psychological Science, 15*, 100–105.

Orvis, B. R., Cunningham, J. D., & Kelley, H. H. (1975). A closer examination of causal inference: The role of consensus, distinctiveness, and consistency information. *Journal of Personality and Social Psychology, 32*, 605–616.

Oskamp, S. (2000). A sustainable future for humanity? How can psychology help? *American Psychologist, 55*, 496–508.

Oskamp, S., Burkhardt, R. I., Schultz, P. W., Hurin, S., & Zelezny, L. (1998). Predicting three dimensions of residential curbside recycling: An observational study. *Journal of Environmental Education, 29*, 37–42.

Osofsky, M. J., Bandura, A., & Zimbardo, P. G. (2005). The role of moral disengagement in the execution process. *Law and Human Behavior, 29*, 371–393.

Ostrom, T., & Sedikides, C. (1992). Out-group homogeneity effects in natural and minimal groups. *Psychological Bulletin, 112*, 536–552.

Ostrov, J. M., Woods, K. E., Jansen, E. A., Casas, J. F., & Crick, N. R. (2004). An observational study of delivered and received aggression, gender, and social-psychological adjustment in preschool. *Early Childhood Research Quarterly, 19*, 355–371.

Oyserman, D., & Lee, S. (2008). Does culture influence what and how we think? Effects of priming individualism and collectivism. *Psychological Bulletin, 134*, 311–342.

Packer, D. J. (2009). Avoiding groupthink: Whereas weakly identified members remain silent, strongly identified members dissent about collective problems. *Psychological Science, 20*(5), 546–548. doi:10.1111/j.1467-9280.2009.02333.x

Paek, H.-J., Nelson, M. R., & Vilela, A. M. (2011). Examination of gender-role portrayals in television advertising across seven countries. *Sex Roles, 64*, 192–207.

Paik, H., & Comstock, G. (1994). The effects of television violence on antisocial behavior: A meta-analysis. *Communication Research, 21*, 516–546.

Palmer, J., & Loveland, J. (2008). The influence of group discussion on performance judgments: Rating accuracy, contrast effects, and halo. *Journal of Psychology: Interdisciplinary and Applied, 142*, 117–130.

Panksepp, J., & Panksepp, J. (2000). The seven sins of evolutionary psychology. *Evolution and Cognition, 6*, 108–131.

Parish, A. R., de Waal, F. B. M., and Haig, D. (2000). The other "closest living relative": How bonobos (*Pan paniscus*) challenge traditional assumptions about females, dominance, intra- and intersexual interactions, and hominid evolution. *Annals of the New York Academy of Sciences, 907*, 97–113.

Park, B., & Rothbart, M. (1982). Perception of out-group homogeneity and levels of social categorization: Memory for the subordinate attributes of in-group and out-group members. *Journal of Personality and Social Psychology, 42*, 1051–1068.

Park, C. L. (2010). Making sense of the meaning literature: An integrative review of meaning making and its effects on adjustment to stressful life events. *Psychological Bulletin, 136*, 257–301.

Patel, R., & Parmentier, M. J. C. (2005). The persistence of traditional gender roles in the information technology sector: A study of female engineers in India. *Information Technologies and International Development, 2*, 29–46.

Patrick, C. J., & Iacono, W. G. (1989). Psychopathy, threat, and polygraph test accuracy. *Journal of Applied Psychology, 74*, 347–355.

Patterson, A. (1974, September). *Hostility catharsis: A naturalistic quasi-experiment*. Paper presented at the annual meeting of the American Psychological Association, New Orleans.

Paulus, P. B., McCain, G., & Cox, V. (1981). Prison standards: Some pertinent data on crowding. *Federal Probation, 15*, 48–54.

Payne, B. K. (2006). Weapon bias: Split-second decisions and unintended stereotyping. *Current Directions in Psychological Science, 15*, 287–291.

Payne, B. K. (2001). Prejudice and perception: The role of automatic and controlled processes in misperceiving a weapon. *Journal of Personality and Social Psychology, 81*, 181–192.

Payne, B. K., & Gawronski, B. (2010). A history of implicit social cognition: Where is it coming from? Where is it now? Where is it going? In B. Gawronski & B. K. Payne (Eds.), *Handbook of implicit social cognition: Measurement, theory, and applications* (pp. 1–15). New York: Guilford.

Peabody, D. (1985). *National characteristics*. Cambridge, England: Cambridge University Press.

Peace in the Middle East may be impossible: Lee D. Ross on naive realism and conflict resolution. *American Psychological Society Observer, 17*, 9–11.

Pechmann, C., & Knight, S. J. (2002). An experimental investigation of the joint effects of advertising and peers on adolescents' beliefs and intentions about cigarette consumption. *Journal of Consumer Research, 29*, 5–19.

Peltokorpi, V. (2008). Transactive memory systems. *Review of General Psychology, 12*(4), 378–394. doi:10.1037/1089-2680.12.4.378

Pennebaker, J. W. (1990). *Opening up: The healing powers of confiding in others*. New York: Morrow.

Pennebaker, J. W. (1997). Writing about emotional experiences as a therapeutic process. *Psychological Science, 8*, 162–166.

Pennebaker, J. W. (2001). Dealing with a traumatic experience immediately after it occurs. *Advances in Mind-Body Medicine, 17*, 160–162.

Pennebaker, J. W. (2004). Theories, therapies, and taxpayers: On the complexities of the expressive writing paradigm. *Clinical Psychology: Science and Practice, 11*, 138–142.

Pennebaker, J. W., Barger, S. D., & Tiebout, J. (1989). Disclosure of traumas and health among Holocaust survivors. *Psychosomatic Medicine, 51*, 577–589.

Pennebaker, J. W., & Beale, S. K. (1986). Confronting a traumatic event: Toward an understanding of inhibition and disease. *Journal of Abnormal Psychology, 95*, 274–281.

Pennebaker, J. W., Colder, M., & Sharp, L. K. (1990). Accelerating t he coping process. *Journal of Personality and Social Psychology, 58*, 528–537.

Pennebaker, J. W., & Francis, M. E. (1996). Cognitive, emotional, and language processes in disclosure. *Cognition and Emotion, 10*, 601–626.

Pennebaker, J. W., & Sanders, D. Y. (1976). American graffiti: Effects of authority and reactance arousal. *Personality and Social Psychology Bulletin, 2*, 264–267.

Penner, L. A. (2000). The causes of sustained volunteerism: An interactionist perspective. *Journal of Social Issues, 58*, 447–467.

Penner, L. A. (2004). Volunteerism and social problems: Making things better or worse? *Journal of Social Issues, 60*(3), 645–666.

Penner, L. A., Dovidio, J. F., Piliavin, J. A., & Schroeder, D. A. (2005). Prosocial behavior: Multilevel perspectives. *Annual Review of Psychology, 56*, 365–392.

Penner, L. A., & Orom, H. (2010). Enduring goodness: A person-by-situation perspective on prosocial behavior. In M. Mikulincer & P. R. Shaver (Eds.), *Prosocial motives, emotions, and behavior: The better angels of our nature* (pp. 55–72). Washington, DC: American Psychological Association. doi:10.1037/12061-003

Pennington, J., & Schlenker, B. R. (1999). Accountability for consequential decisions: Justifying ethical judgments to audiences. *Personality and Social Psychology Bulletin, 25*, 1067–1081.

Pennington, N., & Hastie, R. (1988). Explanation-based decision making: Effects of memory structure on judgment. *Journal of Experimental Psychology: Learning, Memory, and Cognition, 14*, 521–533.

Pennington, N., & Hastie, R. (1990). Practical implications of psychological research on juror and jury decision making. *Personality and Social Psychology Bulletin, 16*, 90–105.

Perlstein, L. (1999, November 14). The sweet rewards of learning: Teachers motivate students with tokens for fries and candy. *Washington Post*, pp. A1, A14.

Perrett, D. I., May, K. A., & Yoshikawa, S. (1994). Facial shape and judgments of female attractiveness. *Nature, 368*, 239–242.

Persuasion: Insights from the self-validation hypothesis. In M. P. Zanna (Ed.), *Advances in Experimental Social Psychology* (Vol. 41, pp. 69–118). New York: Elsevier.

Peters, J. M., Avol, E., Gauderman, W. J., Linn, W. S., Navidi, W., London, S. J., Margolis, H., Rappaport, E., Vora, H., Gong, H. Jr., & Thomas, D. C. (1999). A study of twelve Southern California communities with differing levels and types of air pollution: II. Effects on pulmonary function. *American Journal of Respiratory and Critical Care Medicine, 159*, 768–775.

Peterson, A. A., Haynes, G. A., & Olson, J. M. (2008). Self-esteem differences in the effects of hypocrisy induction on behavioral intentions in the health domain. *Journal of Personality, 76*, 305–322.

Peterson, R. D., & Bailey, W. C. (1988). Murder and capital punishment in the evolving context of the post-Furman era. *Social Forces, 66*, 774–807.

Petrie, K. J., Booth, R. J., & Pennebaker, J. W. (1998). The immunological effects of thought suppression. *Journal of Personality and Social Psychology, 75*, 1264–1272.

Petroselli, D. M., & Knobler, P. (1998). *Triumph of justice: Closing the book on the Simpson saga*. New York: Crown.

Pettigrew, T. F. (in press). Final reflections. In U. Wagner, L. Tropp, G. Finchilescu, & C. Tredoux (Eds.), *Emerging research directions for improving intergroup relations: Building on the legacy of Thomas F. Pettigrew*. Oxford, England: Blackwell.

Pettigrew, T. F. (1958). Personality and sociocultural factors and intergroup attitudes: A cross-national comparison. *Journal of Conflict Resolution, 2*, 29–42.

Pettigrew, T. F. (1969). Racially separate or together? *Journal of Social Issues, 25*, 43–69.

Pettigrew, T. F. (1979). The ultimate attribution error: Extending Allport's cognitive analysis of prejudice. *Personality and Social Psychology Bulletin, 5*, 461–476.

Pettigrew, T. F. (1985). New black-white patterns: How best to conceptualize them? *Annual Review of Sociology, 11*, 329–346.

Pettigrew, T. F. (1989). The nature of modern racism in the United States. *Revue Internationale de Psychologie Sociale, 2*, 291–303.

Pettigrew, T. F., Jackson, J. S., Brika, J. B., Lemaine, G., Meertens, R. W., Wagner, U., & Zick, A. (1998). Outgroup prejudice in Western Europe. *European Review of Social Psychology, 8*, 241–273.

Pettigrew, T. F., & Tropp, L. R. (2006). A meta-analytic test of intergroup contact theory. *Journal of Personality and Social Psychology, 90*, 751–783.

Petty, R. E. (1995). Attitude change. In A. Tesser (Ed.), *Advanced social psychology* (pp. 195–255). New York: McGraw-Hill.

Petty, R. E., Barden, J., & Wheeler, S. C. (2009). The Elaboration Likelihood Model of persuasion: Developing health promotions for sustained behavioral change. In R. J. DiClemente, R. A. Crosby, & M. C. Kegler (Eds.), *Emerging theories in health promotion practice and research* (2nd ed., pp. 185–214). San Francisco: Jossey-Bass.

Petty, R. E., Briñol, P., Loersch, C., & McCaslin, M. J. (2009). The need for cognition. In M. R. Leary & R. H. Hoyle (Eds.), *Handbook of individual differences in social behavior* (pp. 318–329). New York: Guilford Press.

Petty, R. E., & Brock, T. C. (1981). Thought disruption and persuasion: Assessing the validity of attitude change experiments. In R. E. Petty, T. M. Ostrom, & T. C. Brock (Eds.), *Cognitive responses in persuasion* (pp. 55–79). Hillsdale, NJ: Erlbaum.

Petty, R. E., & Cacioppo, J. T. (1986). *Communication and persuasion: Central and peripheral routes to attitude change*. New York: Springer-Verlag.

Petty, R. E., Cacioppo, J. T., & Goldman, R. (1981). Personal involvement as a determinant of argument-based persuasion. *Journal of Personality and Social Psychology, 41*, 847–855.

Petty, R. E., Cacioppo, J. T., Strathman, A. J., & Priester, J. R. (2005). To think or not to think: Exploring two routes to persuasion. In T. C. Brock & M. C. Green (Eds.), *Persuasion: Psychological insights and perspectives*. Thousand Oaks, CA: Sage Publications, Inc.

Petty, R. E., Cacioppo, J. T., Strathman, A. J., & Priester, J. R. (2005). To think or not to think: Exploring two routes to persuasion. In T. C. Brock & M. C. Green (Eds.), *Persuasion: Psychological insights and perspectives* (2nd ed., pp. 81–116). Thousand Oaks, CA: Sage Publications.

Petty, R. E., Haugtvedt, C. P., & Smith, S. M. (1995). Elaboration as a determinant of attitude strength. In R. E. Petty & J. A. Krosnick (Eds.), *Attitude strength: Antecedents and consequences* (pp. 93–130). Hillsdale, NJ: Erlbaum.

Petty, R. E., & Wegener, D. T. (1999). The elaboration likelihood model: Current status and controversies. In S. Chaiken & Y. Trope (Eds.), *Dual-process theories in social psychology* (pp. 41–72). New York: Guilford Press.

Petty, R. E., & Wegener, D. T. (1999). The elaboration likelihood model: Current status and controversies. In S. Chaiken & Y. Trope (Eds.), *Dual-process theories in social psychology* (pp. 37–72). New York: Guilford Press.

Pezdek, K. (2012). Fallible eyewitness memory and identification. In B. L. Cutler (Ed.), *Conviction of the innocent: Lessons from psychological research* (pp. 105–124). Washington, DC: American Psychological Association.

Pezdek, K., & Banks, W. P. (Eds.). (1996). *The recovered memory/false memory debate*. San Diego, CA: Academic Press.

Phillips, A. G., & Silva, P. J. (2005). Self-awareness and the emotional consequences of self-discrepancies. *Personality & Social Psychology Bulletin, 31*, 703–713.

Pickel, K. (2007). Remembering and identifying menacing perpetrators: Exposure to violence and the weapon focus effect. In R. C. L. Lindsay, D. F. Ross, J. D. Read, & M. P. Toglia (Eds.), *The handbook of eyewitness psychology*, Vol. II: *Memory for people* (pp. 339–360). Mahwah, NJ: Erlbaum.

Pickett, C. L., & Gardner, W. L. (2005). The social monitoring system: Enhanced sensitivity to social cues as an adaptive response to social exclusion. In K. D. Williams, J. P. Forgas, J. P., & W. von Hippel (Eds.), *The social outcast: Ostracism, social exclusion, rejection, and bullying* (pp. 213–226). New York: Psychology Press.

Pickett, C. L., Silver, M. D., & Brewer, M. B. (2002). The impact of assimilation and differentiation needs on perceived group importance and judgments of ingroup size. *Personality and Social Psychology Bulletin, 28*, 546–558.

Pickler, N. (2011, November 29). Obama administration appeals cigarette pack ruling. *Yahoo! News*. Retrieved December 13, 2012, from news.yahoo.com/obama-administration-appeals-cigarette-pack-ruling-212530419.html

Piliavin, I. M., Piliavin, J. A., & Rodin, J. (1975). Costs, diffusion, and the stigmatized victim. *Journal of Personality and Social Psychology, 32*, 429–438.

Piliavin, J. A. (2008). Long-term benefits of habitual helping: Doing well by doing good. In B. A. Sullivan, M. Snyder, & J. L. Sullivan (Eds.), *Cooperation: The political psychology of effective human interaction* (pp. 241–258). Malden, MA: Blackwell.

Piliavin, J. A. (2009). Altruism and helping: The evolution of a field: The 2008 Cooley-Mead Presentation. *Social Psychology Quarterly, 72*(3), 209–225. doi:10.1177/019027250907200305

Piliavin, J. A. (2010). Volunteering across the life span: Doing well by doing good. In S. Stürmer & M. Snyder (Eds.), *The psychology of prosocial behavior: Group processes, intergroup relations, and helping* (pp. 157–172). Oxford, UK: Wiley-Blackwell.

Piliavin, J. A., & Charng, H. (1990). Altruism: A review of recent theory and research. *Annual Review of Sociology, 16*, 27–65.

Piliavin, J. A., Dovidio, J. F., Gaertner, S. L., & Clark, R. D., III. (1981). *Emergency intervention*. New York: Academic Press.

Piliavin, J. A., & Piliavin, I. M. (1972). The effect of blood on reactions to a victim. *Journal of Personality and Social Psychology, 23*, 253–261.

Pinel, E. C., Long, A. E., Landau, M. J., Alexander, K., & Pyszczynski, T. (2006). Seeing I to I: A pathway to interpersonal connectedness. *Journal of Personality and Social Psychology, 90*, 243–257.

Pitt, R. N. (2010). "Killing the messenger": Religious Black gay men's neutralization of anti-gay religious messages. *Journal for the Scientific Study of Religion, 49*, 56–72.

Plant, E. A., & Devine, P. G. (1998). Internal and external motivation to respond without prejudice. *Journal of Personality and Social Psychology, 75*, 811–832.

Plant, E. A., & Peruche, B. M. (2005). The consequences of race for police officers' responses to criminal suspects. *Psychological Science, 16*, 180–183.

"Plastic oceans." (2008, November 13). Spencer Michels, reporter. *The Newshour with Jim Lehrer*, Public Broadcasting System.

Pleban, R., & Tesser, A. (1981). The effects of relevance and quality of another's performance on interpersonal closeness. *Social Psychology Quarterly, 44*, 278–285.

Plotnik, J., & de Waal, F. B. M. (2006). Self-recognition in an Asian elephant. *Proceedings of the National Academy of Sciences of the United States of America, 103*(45), 17053–17057.

PollingReport.com. (2003, July 31). President Bush: Job ratings. Retrieved from www.pollingreport.com/BushJob.htm

Pomfret, J. (2005, November 20). Student turns body into billboard as the Shirtless Guy. *Washington Post*, p. A2.

Pope, H. G., Jr., Gruber, A. J., Mangweth, B., Bureau, B., de Col, C., Jouvent, R., & Hudson, J. I. (2000). Body image perception among men in three countries. *American Journal of Psychiatry, 157*, 1297–1301.

Pope, H. G., Jr., Olivardia, R., Gruber, A. J., & Borowiecki, J. (1999). Evolving ideals of male body image as seen through action toys. *International Journal of Eating Disorders, 26*, 65–72.

Pope, H. G., Jr., Phillips, K. A., & Olivardia, R. (2000). *The Adonis complex: The secret crisis of male body obsession*. New York: Freeman.

Posada, S., & Colell, M. (2007). Another gorilla (Gorilla gorilla gorilla) recognizes himself in a mirror. *American Journal of Primatology, 69*(5), 576–583.

Postmes, T., & Spears, R. (1998). Deindividuation and antinormative behavior: A meta-analysis. *Psychological Bulletin, 123*, 238–259.

Powledge, F. (1991). *Free at last? The civil rights movement and the people who made it*. Boston: Little, Brown.

Pratkanis, A. R. (1992). The cargo-cult science of subliminal persuasion. *Skeptical Inquirer, 16*, 260–272.

Predicting sporting events: Accuracy as a function of reasons analysis, expertise, and task difficulty. Unpublished manuscript, Research Institute on Addictions, Buffalo, NY.

Preston, J., & Wegner, D. (2007). The eureka error: Inadvertent plagiarism by misattributions of effort. *Journal of Personality and Social Psychology, 92*, 575–584.

Preston, J. L., Ritter, R. S., & Hernandez, J. I. (2010). Principles of religious prosociality: A review and reformulation. *Social and Personality Psychology Compass, 4*(8), 574–590. doi:10.1111/j.1751-9004.2010.00286.x

Prevalence of overweight and obesity among adults: United States, 2003–2004. National Center for Health Statistics. Retrieved on December 30, 2008, from www.cdc.gov/nchs/products/pubs/ pubd/hestats/overweight/overwght_adult_03.htm

Prince, M. A., & Carey, K. B. (2010). The malleability of injunctive norms among college students. *Addictive Behaviors, 35*, 940–947.

Prior, H., Schwarz, A., & Gunturkun, O. (2008). Mirror-induced behavior in the magpie (*Pica pica*): Evidence of self-recognition. *PLoS Biology, 6*, 1642–1650. doi:10.1371/journal.pbio.0060202

Pronin, E., Berger, J., & Moluki, S. (2007). Alone in a crowd of sheep: Asymmetric perceptions of conformity and their roots in an introspection illusion. *Journal of Personality and Social Psychology, 92*, 585–595. doi:10.1037/0022-3514.92.4.585

Pronin, E., Gilovich, T., & Ross, L. (2004). Objectivity in the eye of the beholder: Divergent perceptions of bias in self versus others. *Psychological Review, 111*, 781–799.

Pronin, E., & Kugler, M. B. (2011). People believe they have more free will than others. *Proceedings of the National Academy of Sciences.*

Pronin, E., Lin, D. Y., & Ross, L. (2002). The bias blind spot: Perceptions of bias in self versus others. *Personality and Social Psychology Bulletin, 28*, 369–381.

Proost, K., Schreurs, B., De Witte, K., & Derous, E. (2010). Ingratiation and self-promotion in the selection interview: The effects of using single tactics or a combination of tactics on interviewer judgments. *Journal of Applied Social Psychology, 40*(9), 2155–2169. doi:10.1111/j.1559-1816.2010.00654.x

Pruitt, D. G. (1998). Social conflict. In D. T. Gilbert, S. T. Fiske, & G. Lindzey (Eds.), *The handbook of social psychology* (4th ed., Vol. 2, pp. 470–503). New York: McGraw-Hill.

Puente, M. (2005, March 2). Rent this space: Bodies double as billboards. USToday.com. Retrieved on December 23, 2005, from www.usatoday.com/life/lifestyle/2005-03-02-body-ads_x.htm

Purdham, T. S. (1997, March 28). Tapes left by cult suggest comet was the sign to die. *The New York Times*, p. A2.

Putnam, R. D. (2000). *Bowling alone: The collapse and revival of American community*. New York: Simon & Schuster.

Pyszczynski, T., Greenberg, J., Solomon, S., Arndt, J., & Schimel, J. (2004). Why do people need self-esteem? A theoretical and empirical review. *Psychological Bulletin, 130*, 435–468.

Qin, J., Kimel, S., Kitayama, S., Wang, X., Yang, X., & Han, S. (2011). How choice modifies preference: Neural correlates of choice justification. *NeuroImage, 55*, 240–246.

Qin, J., Ogle, C., & Goodman, G. (2008). Adults' memories of childhood: True and false reports. *Journal of Experimental Psychology: Applied, 14*, 373–391.

Quattrone, G. A. (1982). Behavioral consequences of attributional bias. *Social Cognition, 1*, 358–378.

Quattrone, G. A. (1986). On the perception of a group's variability. In S. Worchel & W. G. Austin (Eds.), *Psychology of intergroup relations* (2nd ed.). Chicago: Nelson-Hall.

Quattrone, G. A., & Jones, E. E. (1980). The perception of variability within ingroups and outgroups: Implications for the law of small numbers. *Journal of Personality and Social Psychology, 38*, 141–152.

Quick stats binge drinking (2008). Department of Health and Human Services, Center for Disease Control and Prevention. Retrieved on December 30, 2008, from www.cdc.gov/alcohol/quickstats/ binge_drinking.htm

Quinn, A., & Schlenker, B. R. (2002). Can accountability produce independence? Goals as determinants of the impact of accountability on conformity. *Personality and Social Psychology Bulletin, 28*, 472–483.

Quoidbach, J., Dunn, E. W., Petrides, K. V., & Mikolajczak, M. (2010). Money giveth, money taketh away: The dual effect of wealth on happiness. *Psychological Science, 21*(6), 759–763.

Rajaram, S., & Pereira-Pasarin, L. P. (2010). Collaborative memory: Cognitive research and theory. *Perspectives on Psychological Science, 5*(6), 649–663. doi:10.1177/1745691610388763

Rajecki, D. W., Kidd, R. F., & Ivins, B. (1976). Social facilitation in chickens: A different level of analysis. *Journal of Experimental Social Psychology, 12*, 233–246.

Ramirez, A. (2005, December 2). New Yorkers take a tribute standing up. *The New York Times*, p. B1.

Rampell, C. (2009, February 5). As layoffs surge, women may pass men in job force. *The New York Times*. Retrieved July 6, 2011, from www.nytimes.com/2009/02/06/business/06women.html

Ramsey, S. J. (1981). The kinesics of femininity in Japanese women. *Language Sciences, 3*, 104–123.

Rapoport, A., & Chammah, A. M. (1965). *Prisoner's dilemma: A study in conflict and cooperation*. Ann Arbor: University of Michigan Press.

Raps, C. S., Peterson, C., Jonas, M., & Seligman, M. E. P. (1982). Patient behavior in hospitals: Helplessness, reactance, or both? *Journal of Personality and Social Psychology, 42*, 1036–1041.

Raskin, R., & Terry, H. (1988). A principle-components analysis of the Narcissistic Personality Inventory and further evidence of its construct validity. *Journal of Personality and Social Psychology, 54*, 890–902.

Reading, R. (2008). Effectiveness of universal school-based programs to prevent violent and aggressive behaviour: A systematic review. *Child: Care, Health and Development, 34*, 139.

Rector, M., & Neiva, E. (1996). Communication and personal relations in Brazil. In W. B. Gudykunst, S. Ting-Toomey, & T. Nishida (Eds.), *Communication in personal relationships across cultures* (pp. 156–173). Thousand Oaks, CA: Sage.

Redlawsk, D. P. (2002). Hot cognition or cool consideration? Testing the effects of motivated reasoning on political decision making. *Journal of Politics, 64*, 1021–1044.

Regan, P. C., & Berscheid, E. (1997). Gender differences in characteristics desired in a potential sexual and marriage partner. *Journal of Psychology and Human Sexuality, 9*, 25–37.

Regan, P. C., & Berscheid, E. (1999). *Lust: What we know about human sexual desire*. Thousand Oaks, CA: Sage.

Reis, H. T., & Gosling, S. D. (2010). Social psychological methods outside the laboratory. In S. T. Fiske, D. T. Gilbert, & G. Lindzey (Eds.), *Handbook of social psychology* (5th ed., Vol. 1, pp. 82–114). Hoboken, NJ: John Wiley.

Reis, H. T., & Judd, C. M. (Eds.). (2000). *Handbook of research methods in social and personality psychology*. New York: Cambridge University Press.

Reis, H. T., & Patrick, B. C. (1996). Attachment and intimacy: Component processes. In E. T. Higgins & A. W. Kruglanski (Eds.), *Social psychology: Handbook of basic principles* (pp. 523–563). New York: Guilford Press.

Reis, H. T., Wheeler, L., Speigel, N., Kernis, M. H., Nezlek, J., & Perri, M. (1982). Physical attractiveness in social interaction: 2. Why does appearance affect social experience? *Journal of Personality and Social Psychology, 43*, 979–996.

Reisman, J. M. (1990). Intimacy in same-sex friendships. *Sex Roles, 23*, 65–82.

Reiss, D., & Marino, L. (2001). Mirror self-recognition in the bottlenose dolphin: A case of cognitive convergence. *Proceedings of the National Academy of Sciences, 98*, 5937–5942.

Reiter, S. M., & Samuel, W. (1980). Littering as a function of prior litter and the presence or absence of prohibitive signs. *Journal of Applied Social Psychology, 10*, 45–55.

Reitzes, D. C. (1952). The role of organizational structures: Union versus neighborhood in a tension situation. *Journal of Social Issues, 9*, 37–44.

Renaud, J. M., & McConnell, A. R. (2002). Organization of the self-concept and the suppression of self-relevant thoughts. *Journal of Experimental Social Psychology, 38*, 79–86.

Renner, M. J., & Mackin, R. S. (1998). A life stress instrument for classroom use. *Teaching of Psychology, 25*, 46–48.

Reno, R. R., Cialdini, R. B., & Kallgren, C. A. (1993). The transsituational influence of social norms. *Journal of Personality and Social Psychology, 64*, 104–112.

Rensink, R. A. (2002). Change detection. *Annual Review of Psychology, 53*, 245–277.

Rentfrow, P. J., & Gosling, S. D. (2006). Message in a ballad: The role of music preferences in interpersonal perception. *Psychological Science, 17*, 236–242.

Rexrode, C. (2011, November 3). Twitter changes business of celebrity endorsements. *USA Today*. Retrieved December 22, 2011, from www.usatoday.com/tech/news/story/2011-11-03/celebrity-twitter-endorsements/51058228/1

Rhodes, G., Yoshikawa, S., Clark, A., Lee, K., McKay, R., & Akamatsu, S. (2001). Attractiveness of facial averageness and symmetry in non-Western cultures: In search of biologically based standards of beauty. *Perception, 30*, 611–625.

Rhodes, N., & Wood, W. (1992). Self-esteem and intelligence affect influenceability: The mediating role of message reception. *Psychological Bulletin, 111*, 156–171.

Rhodewalt, F., Sanbonmatsu, D. M., Tschanz, B., Feick, D. L., & Waller, A. (1995). Self-handicapping and interpersonal trade-offs: The effects of claimed self-handicaps on observers' performance evaluations and feedback. *Personality and Social Psychology Bulletin, 21*, 1042–1050.

Rhodewalt, F., & Vohs, K. D. (2005). Defensive strategies, motivation, and the self: A self-regulatory process view. In A. J. Elliot & C. S. Dweck (Eds.), *Handbook of competence and motivation* (pp. 548–565). New York: Guilford.

Rholes, W. S., Simpson, J. A., & Friedman, M. (2006). Avoidant attachment and the experience of parenting. *Personality and Social Psychology Bulletin, 32*, 275–285.

Ricciardelli, L. A., & McCabe, M. P. (2003). A longitudinal analysis of the role of psychosocial factors in predicting body change strategies among adolescent boys. *Sex Roles, 48*, 349–360.

Richard, F. D., Bond, C. F. Jr., & Stokes-Zoota, J. J. (2001). 'That's completely obvious . . . and important": Lay judgments of social psychological findings. *Personality and Social Psychology Bulletin, 27*, 497–505.

Richardson, D., Hammock, G., Smith, S., & Gardner, W. (1994). Empathy as a cognitive inhibitor of interpersonal aggression. *Aggressive Behavior, 20*, 275–289.

Richmond, V. P., & McCroskey, J. C. (1995). *Nonverbal behavior in interpersonal relations*. Needham Heights, MA: Allyn & Bacon.

Richter, C. P. (1957). On the phenomenon of sudden death in animals and man. *Psychosomatic Medicine, 19*, 191–198.

Riggs, J. Morgan, & Gumbrecht, L. B. (2005). Correspondence bias and American sentiment in the wake of September 11, 2001. *Journal of Applied Social Psychology, 35*(1), 15–28.

Ringelmann, M. (1913). Recherches sur les moteurs animés: Travail de l'homme [Research on driving forces: Human work]. *Annales de l'Institut National Agronomique*, series 2, *12*, 1–40.

Riordan, C. A. (1978). Equal-status interracial contact: A review and revision of a concept. *International Journal of Intercultural Relations, 2*, 161–185.

Rise, J., Sheeran, P., & Hukkelberg, S. (2010). The role of self-identity in the theory of planned behavior: A meta-analysis. *Journal of Applied Social Psychology, 40*(5), 1085–1105. doi:10.1111/j.1559-1816.2010.00611.x

Rivers, I., Chesney, T., & Coyne, I. (2011). Cyberbullying. In C. P. Monks & I. Coyne (Eds.), *Bullying in different contexts* (pp. 211–230). New York: Cambridge University Press.

Robins, R. W., & Beer, J. S. (2001). Positive illusions about the self: Short-term benefits and long-term costs. *Journal of Personality and Social Psychology, 80*, 340–352.

Robins, R. W., & Schriber, R. A. (2009). The self-conscious emotions: How are they experienced, expressed, and assessed? *Social and Personality Psychology Compass, 3*, 887–898.

Robins, R. W., Spranca, M. D., & Mendelson, G. A. (1996). The actor-observer effect revisited: Effects of individual differences and repeated social interactions on actor and observer attributions. *Journal of Personality and Social Psychology, 71*, 375–389.

Rodin, J., & Langer, E. J. (1977). Long-term effects of a control-relevant intervention with the institutional aged. *Journal of Personality and Social Psychology, 35*, 897–902.

Rodrigo, M. F., & Ato, M. (2002). Testing the group polarization hypothesis by using logit models. *European Journal of Social Psychology, 32*, 3–18.

Roepke, S. K., & Grant, I. (2011). Toward a more complete understanding of the effects of personal mastery on cardiometabolic health. *Health Psychology, 30*, 615–632. doi:10.1037/a0023480

Roesch, S. C., & Amirkhan, J. H. (1997). Boundary conditions for self-serving attributions: Another look at the sports pages. *Journal of Applied Social Psychology, 27*, 245–261.

Roese, N. J. (1997). Counterfactual thinking. *Psychological Bulletin, 121*, 133–148.

Roese, N. J., & Jamieson, D. W. (1993), Twenty years of bogus pipeline research: A critical review and meta-analysis. *Psychological Bulletin, 114*, 363–375.

Roese, N. J., & Olson, J. M. (1997). Counterfactual thinking: The intersection of affect and function. In M. P. Zanna (Ed.), *Advances in experimental social psychology* (Vol. 29, pp. 1–59). San Diego, CA: Academic Press.

Rogers, R. (1983). Cognitive and physiological processes in fear appeals and attitude change: A revised theory of protection motivation. In J. T. Cacioppo & R. E. Petty (Eds.), *Social psychophysiology: A sourcebook* (pp. 153–176). New York: Guilford Press.

Rogers, R., & Prentice-Dunn, S. (1981). Deindividuation and anger-mediated interracial aggression: Unmasking regressive racism. *Journal of Personality and Social Psychology, 41*, 63–73.

Rogers, T. B., Kuiper, N. A., & Kirker, W. S. (1977). Self-reference and the encoding of personal information. *Journal of Personality and Social Psychology, 35*, 677–688.

Rohrer, J. H., Baron, S. H., Hoffman, E. L., & Swander, D. V. (1954). The stability of autokinetic judgments. *Journal of Abnormal and Social Psychology, 49*, 595–597.

Romero-Canyas, R., Downey, G., Reddy, K. S., Rodriguez, S., Cavanaugh, T. J., & Pelayo, R. (2010). Paying to belong: When does rejection trigger ingratiation? *Journal of Personality and Social Psychology, 99*(5), 802–823. doi:10.1037/a0020013

Rooney, B. (2012, January 25). Apple tops Exxon as most valuable company. CNN Money Markets. Available at http://money.cnn.com/2012/01/25/markets/apple_stock/?hpt=hp_t2

Rosenberg, L. A. (1961). Group size, prior experience, and conformity. *Journal of Abnormal and Social Psychology, 63*, 436–437.

Rosenberg, M. (2006). Population growth rates and doubling time. Retrieved on June 21, 2006, from geography.about.com/od/populationgeography/ a/populationgrow.htm

Rosenberg, M. J., Davidson, A. J., Chen, J., Judson, F. N., & Douglas, J. M. (1992). Barrier contraceptives and sexually transmitted diseases in women: A comparison of female-dependent methods and condoms. *American Journal of Public Health, 82*, 669–674.

Rosenberg, S., Nelson, S., & Vivekananthan, P. S. (1968). A multidimensional approach to the structure of personality impressions. *Journal of Personality and Social Psychology, 9*, 283–294.

Rosenblatt, P. C. (1974). Cross-cultural perspectives on attraction. In T. L. Huston (Ed.), *Foundations of interpersonal attraction* (pp. 79–99). New York: Academic Press.

Rosenthal, A. M. (1964). *Thirty-eight witnesses*. New York: McGraw-Hill.

Rosenthal, R. (1994). Interpersonal expectancy effects: A 30-year perspective. *Current Directions in Psychological Science, 3*, 176–179.

Rosenthal, R., & Jacobson, L. (1968). *Pygmalion in the classroom: Teacher expectations and student intellectual development*. New York: Holt, Rinehart and Winston.

Ross, L. (1977). The intuitive psychologist and his shortcomings: Distortions in the attribution process. In L. Berkowitz (Ed.), *Advances in experimental social psychology* (Vol. 10, pp. 173–220). Orlando, FL: Academic Press.

Ross, L. (1998). Comment on Gilbert. In J. M. Darley & J. Cooper (Eds.), *Attribution and social interaction* (pp. 53–66). Washington, DC: American Psychological Association.

Ross, L. (2010). Dealing with conflict: Experiences and experiments. In M. H. Gonzales, C. Tavris, & J. Aronson (Eds.), *The scientist and the humanist: A festschrift in honor of Elliot Aronson* (pp. 39–66). New York: Psychology Press.

Ross, L., Amabile, T. M., & Steinmetz, J. L. (1977). Social roles, social control, and biases in social perception. *Journal of Personality and Social Psychology, 35*, 485–494.

Ross, L., & Nisbett, R. E. (1991). *The person and the situation: Perspectives of social psychology*. New York: McGraw-Hill.

Ross, L., & Ward, A. (1995). Psychological barriers to dispute resolution. In M. P. Zanna (Ed.), *Advances in experimental social psychology* (Vol. 27, pp. 255–304). San Diego, CA: Academic Press.

Ross, L., & Ward, A. (1996). Naive realism: Implications for social conflict and misunderstanding. In T. Brown, E. Reed, & E. Turiel (Eds.), *Values and knowledge* (pp. 103–135). Hillsdale, NJ: Erlbaum.

Ross, M., & Olson, J. M. (1981). An expectancy-attribution model of the effects of placebos. *Psychological Review, 88*, 408–437.

Ross, M., & Wilson, A. E. (2003). Autobiographical memory and conceptions of self: Getting better all the time. *Current Directions in Psychological Science, 12*, 66–69.

Ross, W., & La Croix, J. (1996). Multiple meanings of trust in negotiation theory and research: A literature review and integrative model. *International Journal of Conflict Management*, 7, 314–360.

Rothbaum, F., & Tsang, B. Y.-P. (1998). Lovesongs in the United States and China: On the nature of romantic love. *Journal of Cross-Cultural Psychology, 29*, 306–319.

Rothermund, K., & Wentura, D. (2004). Underlying processes in the Implicit Association Test: Dissociating salience from associations. *Journal of Experimental Psychology: General, 133*, 139–165.

Rotter, J. B. (1966). Generalized expectancies for internal versus external control of reinforcement. *Psychological Monographs, 80*, 1–28 (Whole No. 609).

Rotton, J., & Cohn, E. G. (2004). Outdoor temperature, climate control, and criminal assault: The spatial and temporal ecology of violence. *Environment & Behavior, 36*, 276–306.

Rubin, Z. (1970). Measurement of romantic love. *Journal of Personality and Social Psychology, 16*, 265–273.

Rubin, Z., Peplau, L. A., & Hill, C. T. (1981). Loving and leaving: Sex differences in romantic attachments. *Sex Roles*, 7, 821–835.

Rudman, L., Phelan, J., & Heppen, J. (2007). Developmental sources of implicit attitudes. *Personality and Social Psychology Bulletin, 33*, 1700–1713.

Rudman, L. A. (1998). Self-promotion as a risk factor for women: The costs and benefits of counterstereotypical impression management. *Journal of Personality and Social Psychology, 74*, 629–645.

Ruiter, R. A. C., Abraham, C., & Kok, G. (2001). Scary warnings and rational precautions: A review of the psychology of fear appeals. *Psychology and Health, 16*, 613–630.

Rule, B. G., Taylor, B. R., & Dobbs, A. R. (1987). Priming effects of heat on aggressive thoughts. *Social Cognition, 5*, 131–143.

Rule, N. O., & Ambady, N. (2010). First impressions of the face: Predicting success. *Social and Personality Psychology Compass, 4*, 506–516.

Rule, N. O., Ambady, N., Adams, R. B., Jr., & Macrae, C. N. (2008). Accuracy and awareness in the perception and categorization of male sexual orientation. *Journal of Personality and Social Psychology, 95*, 1019–1028.

Rule, N. O., Ambady, N., & Hallett, K. C. (2009). Female sexual orientation is perceived accurately, rapidly, and automatically from the face and its features. *Journal of Experimental Social Psychology, 45*, 1245–1251.

Rusbult, C. E. (1983). A longitudinal test of the investment model: The development (and deterioration) of satisfaction and commitment in heterosexual involvements. *Journal of Personality and Social Psychology, 45*, 101–117.

Rusbult, C. E. (1987). Responses to dissatisfaction in close relationships: The exit-voice-loyalty-neglect model. In D. Perlman & S. W. Duck (Eds.), *Intimate relationships: Development, dynamics, and deterioration* (pp. 209–237). Newbury Park, CA: Sage.

Rusbult, C. E. (1991). *Commitment processes in close relationships: The investment model.* Paper presented at the annual meeting of the American Psychological Association, San Francisco.

Rusbult, C. E., & Buunk, B. P. (1993). Commitment processes in close relationships: An interdependence analysis. *Journal of Social and Personal Relationships, 10*, 175–204.

Rusbult, C. E., Johnson, D. J., & Morrow, G. D. (1986). Impact of couple patterns of problem solving on distress and nondistress in dating relationships. *Journal of Personal and Social Psychology, 50*, 744–753.

Rusbult, C. E., & Martz, J. M. (1995). Remaining in an abusive relationship: An investment model analysis of nonvoluntary dependence. *Personality and Social Psychology Bulletin, 21*, 558–571.

Rusbult, C. E., Martz, J. M., & Agnew, C. R. (1998). The investment model scale: Measuring commitment level, satisfaction level, quality of alternatives, and investment size. *Personal Relationships, 5*, 357–391.

Rusbult, C. E., Olsen, N., Davis, N. L., & Hannon, P. (2001). Commitment and relationship maintenance mechanisms. In J. H. Harvey & A. Wenzel (Eds.), *Close romantic relationships: Maintenance and enhancement* (pp. 87–113). Mahwah, NJ: Erlbaum.

Rusbult, C. E., & Van Lange, P. A. M. (1996). Interdependence processes. In E. T. Higgins & A. W. Kruglanski (Eds.), *Social psychology: Handbook of basic principles* (pp. 564–596). New York: Guilford Press.

Rusbult, C. E., Yovetich, N. A., & Verette, J. (1996). An interdependence analysis of accommodation processes. In G. J. O. Fletcher & J. Fitness (Eds.), *Knowledge structures in close relationships: A social psychological approach* (pp. 63–90). Mahwah, NJ: Erlbaum.

Rusbult, C. E., & Zembrodt, I. M. (1983). Responses to dissatisfaction in romantic involvements: A multidimensional scaling analysis. *Journal of Experimental Social Psychology, 19*, 274–293.

Rushton, J. P. (1989). Genetic similarity, human altruism, and group selection. *Behavioral and Brain Sciences, 12*, 503–559.

Russell, G. W. (1983). Psychological issues in sports aggression. In J. H. Goldstein (Ed.), *Sports violence* (pp. 157–181). New York: Springer-Verlag.

Rusting, Cheryl L., & Nolen-Hoeksema, Susan (1998). Regulating responses of anger: Effects of rumination and distraction on angry mood. *Journal of Personality and Social Psychology*, 74, 790–803.

Ryan, B., Jr. (1991). *It works! How investment spending in advertising pays off.* New York: American Association of Advertising Agencies.

Ryan, M. K., Haslam, S. A., Hersby, M. D., & Bongiorno, R. (2011). Think crisis–think female: The glass cliff and contextual variation in the think manager–think male stereotype. *Journal of Applied Psychology, 96*(3), 470–484. doi:10.1037/a0022133

Ryan, M. K., Haslam, S. A., Hersby, M. D., Kulich, C., & Atkins, C. (2008). Opting out or pushed off the edge? The glass cliff and the precariousness of women's leadership positions. *Social and Personality Psychology Compass, 2*, www.blackwell-compass.com/subject/socialpsychology/

Ryan, R. M., & Deci, E. L. (2000). Intrinsic and extrinsic rewards: Classic definitions and new directions. *Current Educational Psychology, 25*, 54–67.

Sacks, O. (1987). *The man who mistook his wife for a hat and other clinical tales*. New York: Harper & Row.

Saffer, H. (2002). Alcohol advertising and youth. *Journal of Studies on Alcohol, 14*, 173–181.

Sagarin, B. J., & Wood, S. E. (2007). Resistance to influence. In A. R. Pratkanis (Ed.), *Frontiers of social psychology. The science of social influence: Advances and future progress* (pp. 321–340). New York: Psychology Press.

Sageman, M. (2008). *Leaderless jihad: Terror networks in the twenty-first century*. Philadelphia: University of Pennsylvania Press.

Saguy, T., Tausch, N., Dovidio, J. F., Pratto, F., & Singh, P. (2011). Tension and harmony in intergroup relations. In P. R. Shaver & M. Mikulincer (Eds.), *Human aggression and violence: Causes, manifestations, and consequences* (Herzilya series on personality and social psychology, pp. 333–348). Washington, DC: American Psychological Association.

Sakai, H. (1999). A multiplicative power-function model of cognitive dissonance: Toward an integrated theory of cognition, emotion, and behavior after Leon Festinger. In E. Harmon-Jones & J. S. Mills (Eds.), *Cognitive dissonance: Progress on a pivotal theory in social psychology* (pp. 120–138). Washington, DC: American Psychological Association.

Sakurai, M. M. (1975). Small group cohesiveness and detrimental conformity. *Sociometry, 38*, 340–357.

Salganik, M. J., Dodds, P. S., & Watts, D. J. (2006). Experimental study of inequality and unpredictability in an artificial cultural market. *Science, 311*, 854–856.

Salili, F. (1996). Learning and motivation: An Asian perspective. *Psychology and Developing Societies, 8*, 55–81.

Salovey, P., & Rodin, J. (1985). Cognitions about the self: Connecting feeling states and social behavior. In P. Shaver (Ed.), *Self, situations, and social behavior: Review of personality and social psychology* (Vol. 6, pp. 143–166). Beverly Hills, CA: Sage.

Salovey, P., & Rothman, A. J. (2003). *Social psychology of health*. New York: Psychology Press.

Salter, J. (2011, May 6). Pay-what-you-want Panera called a success. *USA Today*. Retrieved July 12, 2011, from www.usatoday.com/money/industries/food/2011-05-16-panera-pay-what-you-can_n.htm

Sampson, R. J. (1988). Local friendship ties and community attachment in mass society: A multilevel systemic model. *American Sociological Review, 53*, 766–779.

Sanger, D. E. (1993, May 30). The career and the kimono. *New York Times Magazine*, pp. 18–19.

Sanna, L. J., Meier, S., & Wegner, E. A. (2001). Counterfactuals and motivation: Mood as input to affective enjoyment and preparation. *British Journal of Social Psychology, 40*, 235–256.

Sanna, L. J., & Schwarz, N. (2004). Integrating temporal biases: The interplay of focal thoughts and accessibility experiences. *Psychological Science, 15*, 474–481.

Sanna, L. J., & Schwarz, N. (2007). Metacognitive experiences and hindsight bias: It's not just the thought (content) that counts! *Social Cognition, 25*, 185–202.

Sansone, C., & Harackiewicz, J. M. (1996). "I don't feel like it": The function of interest in self-regulation. In L. L. Martin & A. Tesser (Eds.), *Striving and feeling: Interactions among goals, affect, and self-regulation* (pp. 203–228). Mahwah, NJ: Erlbaum.

Sarche, J. (2003, June 22). For new female cadets, an Air Force Academy in turmoil. *The Boston Globe*, p. A12.

Sastry, J., & Ross, C. E. (1998). Asian ethnicity and the sense of personal control. *Social Psychology Quarterly, 61*, 101–120.

Saunders, J. (2009). Memory impairment in the weapon focus effect. *Memory & Cognition, 37*(3), 326–335. doi:10.3758/MC.37.3.326

Savitsky, K. (1998). Embarrassment study [E-mails]. Society for Personal and Social Psychology e-mail list archive. Retrieved from www.stolaf.edu/cgi-bin/mailarchivesearch.pl?directory=/home/www/people/huff/SPSP&listname=archive98

Schachter, S. (1951). Deviation, rejection, and communication. *Journal of Abnormal and Social Psychology, 46*, 190–207.

Schachter, S. (1959). *The psychology of affiliation*. Stanford, CA: Stanford University Press.

Schachter, S. (1964). The interaction of cognitive and physiological determinants of emotional state. In L. Berkowitz (Ed.), *Advances in experimental social psychology* (Vol. 1, pp. 49–80). New York: Academic Press.

Schachter, S., & Singer, J. E. (1962). Cognitive, social, and physiological determinants of emotional states. *Psychological Review, 69*, 379–399.

Schachter, S., & Singer, J. E. (1979). Comments on the Maslach and Marshall-Zimbardo experiments. *Journal of Personality and Social Psychology, 37*, 989–995.

Schafer, M., & Crichlow, S. (1996). Antecedents of groupthink: A quantitative study. *Journal of Conflict Resolution, 40*, 415–435.

Schaller, M., Asp, C. H., Rosell, M. C., & Heim, S. J. (1996). Training in statistical reasoning inhibits formation of erroneous group stereotypes. *Personality and Social Psychology Bulletin, 22*, 829–844.

Scheier, M. S., Carver, C. S., & Bridges, M. W. (2001). Optimism, pessimism, and psychological well-being. In E. C. Chang (Ed.), *Optimism and pessimism* (pp. 189–216). Washington, DC: American Psychological Association.

Schemo, D. J. (2003, July 12). Ex-superintendent of Air Force Academy is demoted in wake of rape scandal. *The New York Times*, p. A7.

Scherr, K. C., Madon, S., Guyll, M., Willard, J., & Spoth, R. (2011). Self-verification as a mediator of mothers' self-fulfilling effects on adolescents' educational attainment. *Personality and Social Psychology Bulletin, 37*(5), 587–600. doi:10.1177/0146167211399777

Schlegel, R. J., Hicks, J. A., Arndt, J., & King, L. A. (2009). Thine own self: True self-concept accessibility and meaning in life. *Journal of Personality and Social Psychology, 96*(2), 473–490. doi:10.1037/a0014060

Schlegel, S. (1998). *Wisdom from a rainforest: The spiritual journey of an anthropologist*. Athens: University of Georgia Press.

Schlenker, B. R. (2003). Self-presentation. In M. R. Leary & J. P. Tangney (Eds.), *Handbook of self and identity* (pp. 492–518). New York: Guilford.

Schlenker, B. R., & Weingold, M. F. (1989). Self-identification and accountability. In R. A. Giacalone & P. Rosenfeld (Eds.), *Impression management in the organization* (pp. 21–43). Hillsdale, NJ: Erlbaum.

Schmeichel, B. J., & Baumeister, R. F. (2004). *Self-regulatory strength*. In R. F. Baumeister & K D. Vohs (Eds.), *Handbook of self-regulation: Research, theory, and applications* (pp. 84–98). New York: Guilford.

Schmeichel, B. J., Gailliot, M. T., Filardo, E.-A., McGregor, I., Gitter, S., & Baumeister, R. F. (2009). Terror management theory and self-esteem revisited: The roles of implicit and explicit self-esteem in mortality salience effects. *Journal of Personality and Social Psychology, 96*(5), 1077–1087. doi:10.1037/a0015091

Schmitt, B. H., Gilovich, T., Goore, N., & Joseph, L. (1986). Mere presence and social facilitation: One more time. *Journal of Experimental Social Psychology, 22*, 228–241.

Schnall, S., Benton, J., & Harvey, S. (2008). With a clean conscience: Cleanliness reduces the severity of moral judgments. *Psychological Science, 19*(12), 1219–1222. doi:10.1111/j.1467-9280.2008.02227.x

Schneider, D. J. (1973). Implicit personality theory: A review. *Psychological Bulletin, 79*, 294–309.

Schneider, D. J., Hastorf, A. H., & Ellsworth, P. C. (1979). *Person perception* (2nd ed.). Reading, MA: Addison-Wesley.

Schofield, J. W. (1986). Causes and consequences of the color-blind perspective. In J. F. Dovidio & S. L. Gaertner (Eds.), *Prejudice, discrimination, and racism* (pp. 231–253). Orlando, FL: Academic Press.

Scholten, L., van Knippenberg, D., Nijstad, B. A., & De Dreu, C. K. W. (2007) Motivated information processing and group decision-making: Effects of process accountability on information processing and decision quality. *Journal of Experimental Social Psychology, 43*, 539–552.

Schooler, J. W. (1999). Seeking the core: The issues and evidence surrounding recovered accounts of sexual trauma. In L. M. Williams & V. L. Banyard (Eds.), *Trauma and memory* (pp. 203–216). Thousand Oaks, CA: Sage.

Schooler, J. W., & Eich, E. (2000). Memory for emotional events. In E. Tulving & F. I. M. Craik (Eds.), *The Oxford handbook of memory* (pp. 379–392). Oxford, UK: Oxford University Press.

Schooler, J. W., & Engstler-Schooler, T. Y. (1990). Verbal overshadowing of visual memories: Some things are better left unsaid. *Cognitive Psychology, 22*, 36–71.

Schopler, J., & Insko, C. A. (1999). The reduction of the interindividual-intergroup discontinuity effect: The role of future consequences. In M. Foddy & M. Smithson (Eds.), *Resolving social dilemmas: Dynamic, structural, and intergroup aspects* (pp. 281–293). Bristol, PA: Taylor & Francis.

Schriber, R. A., & Robins, R. W. (in press). Individual differences in self-enhancement. In Vazire, S., & Wilson, T. D. (Eds.), *Handbook of self-knowledge*. New York: Guilford.

Schriesheim, C. A., Tepper, B. J., & Tetrault, L. A. (1994). Least preferred co-worker score, situational control, and leadership effectiveness: A meta-analysis of contingency model performance predictions. *Journal of Applied Psychology, 79*, 561–573.

Schroeder, D. H., & Costa, P. T., Jr. (1984). Influence of life event stress on physical illness: Substantive effects or methodological flaws? *Journal of Personality and Social Psychology, 46*, 853–863.

Schultz, P. W., Oskamp, S., & Mainieri, T. (1995). Who recycles and when? A review of personal and situational factors. *Journal of Environmental Psychology, 15*, 105–121.

Schulz, R. (1976). Effects of control and predictability on the physical and psychological well-being of the institutionalized aged. *Journal of Personality and Social Psychology, 33*, 563–573.

Schulz, R., & Hanusa, B. H. (1978). Long-term effects of control and predictability-enhancing interventions: Findings and ethical issues. *Journal of Personality and Social Psychology, 36*, 1202–1212.

Schuman, H., & Kalton, G. (1985). Survey methods. In G. Lindzey & E. Aronson (Eds.), *Handbook of social psychology* (3rd ed., Vol. 1, pp. 635–697). New York: McGraw-Hill.

Schumann, K., & Ross, M. (2010). Why women apologize more than men: Gender differences in thresholds for perceiving offensive behavior. *Psychological Science, 21*, 1649–1655.

Schützwohl, A. (2004). Which infidelity type makes you more jealous? Decision strategies in a forced-choice between sexual and emotional infidelity. *Evolutionary Psychology, 2*, 121–2:128.

Schützwohl, A., Fuchs, A., McKibbin, W. F., & Schackelford, T. K. (2009). How willing are you to accept sexual requests from slightly unattractive to exceptionally attractive imagined requestors? *Human Nature, 20*, 282–293.

Schwartz, J. (2003, June 7). Shuttle tests seem to back foam theory in accident. *The New York Times*, p. A1.

Schwartz, J., & Wald, M. L. (2003, June 7). NASA's failings go beyond foam hitting shuttle, panel says. *The New York Times*, p. A1.

Schwartz, S. H. (1992). Universals in the content and structure of values: Theoretical advances and empirical tests in 20 countries. In M. P. Zanna (Ed.), *Advances in experimental social psychology* (Vol. 25, pp. 1–65). San Diego, CA: Academic Press.

Schwarz, N., Bless, H., Strack, F., Klumpp, G., Rittenauer-Schatka, H., & Simmons, A. (1991). Ease of retrieval as information: Another look at the availability heuristic. *Journal of Personality and Social Psychology, 61*, 195–202.

Schwarz, N., & Clore, G. L. (1988). How do I feel about it? Informative functions of affective states. In K. Fiedler & J. Forgas (Eds.), *Affect, cognition, and social behavior* (pp. 44–62). Toronto, Ontario, Canada: Hogrefe.

Schwarz, N., Groves, R. M., & Schuman, H. (1998). Survey methods. In D. T. Gilbert, S. T. Fiske, & G. Lindzey (Eds.), *The handbook of social psychology* (4th ed., Vol. 1, pp. 143–179). New York: McGraw-Hill.

Schwarz, N., & Vaughn, L. A. (2002). The availability heuristic revisited: Ease of recall and content of recall as distinct sources of information. In T. Gilovich, D. W. Griffin, & D. Kahneman (Eds). *Heuristics and biases: The psychology of intuitive judgment* (pp. 103–119). New York: Cambridge University Press.

Schwarzer, R., & Leppin, A. (1991). Social support and health: A theoretical and empirical overview. *Journal of Social and Personal Relationships, 8*, 99–127.

Scott, J. E., & Cuvelier, S. J. (1993). Violence and sexual violence in pornography: Is it increasing? *Archives of Sexual Behavior, 22*, 357–371.

Scott, J. P. (1958). *Aggression*. Chicago: University of Chicago Press.

Secord, P. F., & Backman, C. W. (1964). *Social psychology*. New York: McGraw-Hill.

Sedikides, C., & Anderson, C. A. (1994). Causal perceptions of intertrait relations: The glue that holds person types together. *Personality and Social Psychology Bulletin, 21*, 294–302.

Sedikides, C., Gaertner, L., & Yoshiyasu, T. (2003). Pancultural self-enhancement. *Journal of Personality and Social Psychology, 84*, 60–79.

Seery, M., Silver, R., Holman, E., Ence, W., & Chu, T. (2008). Expressing thoughts and feelings following a collective trauma: Immediate responses to 9/11 predict negative outcomes in a national sample. *Journal of Consulting and Clinical Psychology, 76*, 657–667.

Segerstrom, S. C. (2010). Resources, stress, and immunity: An ecological perspective on human psychoneuroimmunology. *Annals of Behavioral Medicine, 40*, 114–125.

Seligman, M. E. P. (2002). Positive psychology, positive prevention, and positive therapy. In C. R. Snyder & S. J. Lopez (Eds.), *Handbook of positive psychology* (pp. 3–9). New York: Oxford University Press.

Seligman, M. E. P., Steen, T. A., & Park, N. (2005). Positive psychology progress: Empirical validation of interventions. *American Psychologist, 60*, 410–421.

Selye, H. (1956). *The stress of life*. New York: McGraw-Hill.

Selye, H. (1976). *Stress in health and disease*. Woburn, MA: Butterworth.

Semmler, C., Brewer, N., & Douglass, A. B. (2012). Jurors believe eyewitnesses. In B. L. Cutler (Ed.), *Conviction of the innocent: Lessons from psychological research* (pp. 185–209). Washington, DC: American Psychological Association.

Senchak, M., & Leonard, K. E. (1992). Attachment styles and marital adjustment among newlywed couples. *Journal of Social and Personal Relationships, 9*, 51–64.

Sengupta, J., & Fitzsimons, G. J. (2004). The effect of analyzing reasons on the stability of brand attitudes: A reconciliation of opposing predictions. *Journal of Consumer Research, 31*, 705–711.

Senko, C., Durik, A., & Harackiewicz, J. (2008). Historical perspectives and new directions in achievement goal theory: Understanding the effects of mastery and performance–approach goals. In J. Y. Shah & W. L. Gardner (Eds.), *Handbook of motivation science* (pp. 100–113). New York: Guilford.

Seppa, N. (1997). Children's TV remains steeped in violence. *APA Monitor, 28*, 36.

Sergios, P. A., & Cody, J. (1985). Physical attractiveness and social assertiveness skills in male homosexual dating behavior and partner selection. *Journal of Social Psychology, 125*, 505–514.

Seta, C. E., & Seta, J. J. (1995). When audience presence is enjoyable: The influences of audience awareness of prior success on performance and task interest. *Basic and Applied Social Psychology, 16*, 95–108.

Seta, J. J., Seta, C. E., & Wang, M. A. (1990). Feelings of negativity and stress: An averaging-summation analysis of impressions of negative life experiences. *Personality and Social Psychology Bulletin, 17*, 376–384.

Shackleford, T. K. (2005). An evolutionary psychological perspective on cultures of honor. *Evolutionary Psychology*, 3,381–391.

Shah, A. K., & Oppenheimer, D M.. (2008). Heuristics made easy: An effort-reduction framework. *Psychological Bulletin, 134*, 207–232.

Sharan, S. (1980). Cooperative learning in small groups. *Review of Educational Research, 50*, 241–271.

Shariff, A., & Norenzayan, A. (2007). God is watching you: Priming god concepts increases prosocial behavior in an anonymous economic game. *Psychological Science, 18*, 803–809.

Sharma, D., Booth, R., Brown, R., & Huguet, P. (2010). Exploring the temporal dynamics of social facilitation in the Stroop task. *Psychonomic Bulletin & Review, 17*(1), 52–58. doi:10.3758/PBR.17.1.52

Sharp, F. C. (1928). *Ethics*. New York: Century.

Sharpe, D., Adair, J. G., & Roese, N. J. (1992). Twenty years of deception research: A decline in subjects' trust? *Personality and Social Psychology Bulletin, 18*, 585–590.

Shaver, P. R., Wu, S., & Schwartz, J. C. (1992). Cross-cultural similarities and differences in emotion and its representation. In M. S. Clark (Ed.), *Review of personality and social psychology*: Vol. 13, *Emotion* (pp. 175–212). Newbury Park, CA: Sage.

Shavitt, S. (1989). Operationalizing functional theories of attitude. In A. R. Pratkanis, S. J. Breckler, & A. G. Greenwald (Eds.), *Attitude structure and function* (pp. 311–337). Hillsdale, NJ: Erlbaum.

Shavitt, S. (1990). The role of attitude objects in attitude function. *Journal of Experimental Social Psychology, 26*, 124–148.

Shavitt, S., Sanbonmatsu, D. M., Smittipatana, S., & Posavac, S. S. (1999). Broadening the conditions for illusory correlation formation: Implications for judging minority groups. *Basic and Applied Social Psychology, 21*, 263–279.

Shaw, J. I., & Skolnick, P. (1995). Effects of prohibitive and informative judicial instructions on jury decision making. *Social Behavior and Personality, 23*, 319–325.

Sheldon, K. M., Kashdan, T. B., & Steger, M. F. (Eds.). (2011). *Designing positive psychology: Taking stock and moving forward*. New York: Oxford University Press. doi:10.1093/acprof:oso/9780195373585.003.0008

Shepperd, J., Malone, W., & Sweeny, K. (2008). Exploring causes of the self-serving bias. *Social and Personality Psychology Compass, 2*, 895–908.

Shepperd, J. A., & Taylor, K. M. (1999). Social loafing and expectancy-value theory. *Personality and Social Psychology Bulletin, 25*, 1147–1158.

Sherif, M. (1936). *The psychology of social norms*. New York: Harper.

Sherif, M. (1966). *In common predicament: Social psychology of intergroup conflict and cooperation*. Boston: Houghton Mifflin.

Sherif, M., Harvey, O. J., White, J., Hood, W., & Sherif, C. W. (1961). *Intergroup conflict and cooperation: The robber's cave experiment*. Norman: Institute of Intergroup Relations, University of Oklahoma.

Sherrod, D. R., & Cohen, S. (1979). Density, personal control, and design. In A. Baum & J. R. Aiello (Eds.), *Residential crowding and design* (pp. 217–227). New York: Plenum.

Sherry, J. L. (2001). The effects of violent video games on aggression: A meta-analysis. *Human Communication Research, 27*, 409–431.

Sherwin, S., & Winsby, M. (2011). A relational perspective on autonomy for older adults residing in nursing homes. *Health Expectations: An International Journal of Public Participation in Health Care & Health Policy, 14*, 182–190.

Shiller, R. J. (2008, November 2). Challenging the crowd in whispers, not shouts. *The New York Times*, p. BU5. Retrieved July 9, 2011, from www.nytimes.com/2008/11/02/business/02view.html?pagewanted=1&_r=1&ref=business

Shipp, E. R. (2005, October 25). Rosa Parks, 92, Intrepid pioneer of civil rights movement, is dead. *The New York Times*, pp. A1, C18.

Shotland, R. L., & Straw, M. K. (1976). Bystander response to an assault: When a man attacks a woman. *Journal of Personality and Social Psychology, 34*, 990–999.

Shteynberg, G. (2010). A silent emergence of culture: The social tuning effect. *Journal of Personality and Social Psychology, 99*, 683–689.

Shupe, L. M. (1954). Alcohol and crimes: A study of the urine alcohol concentration found in 882 persons arrested during or immediately after the commission of a felony. *Journal of Criminal Law and Criminology, 33*, 661–665.

Sidanius, J., Pratto, F., & Bobo, L. (1996). Racism, conservatism, affirmative action, and intellectual sophistication: A matter of principled conservatism or group dominance? *Journal of Personality and Social Psychology, 70*, 476–490.

Sidanius, J., Van Laar, C., Levin, S., & Sinclair, S. (2004). Ethnic enclaves and the dynamics of social identity on the college campus: The good, the bad, and the ugly. *Journal of Personality and Social Psychology, 87*, 96–110.

Siero, F. W., Bakker, A. B., Dekker, G. B., & Van Den Burg, M. T. C. (1996). Changing organizational energy consumption behavior through comparative feedback. *Journal of Environmental Psychology, 16*, 235–246.

Sigall, H., & Page, R. (1971). Current stereotypes: A little fading, a little faking. *Journal of Personality and Social Psychology, 18*, 247–255.

Sigelman, J. D., & Johnson, P. (2008). Left frontal cortical activation and spreading of alternatives: Tests of the action-based model of dissonance. *Journal of Personality and Social Psychology, 94*, 1–15.

Silke, A. (Ed.). (2003). *Terrorists, victims, and society: Psychological perspectives on terrorism and its consequences*. New York: Wiley.

Silver, R., Holman, E. A., McIntosh, D. N., Poulin, M., & Gil-Rivas, V. (2002). Nationwide longitudinal study of psychological responses to September 11. *Journal of the American Medical Association, 2882*, 1235–1244.

Silverstein, B., Perdue, L., Peterson, B., & Kelly, E. (1986). The role of the mass media in promoting a thin standard of bodily attractiveness for women. *Sex Roles, 14*, 519–532.

Silverstein, B., Peterson, B., & Perdue, L. (1986). Some correlates of the thin standard of bodily attractiveness for women. *International Journal of Eating Disorders, 5*, 895–906.

Silvia, P. J., & Abele, A. E. (2002). Can positive affect induce self-focused attention? Methodological and measurement issues. *Cognition and Emotion, 16*, 845–853.

Sime, J. D. (1983). Affiliative behavior during escape to building exits. *Journal of Environmental Psychology, 3*, 21–41.

Simmons, R. E., & Scheepers, L. (1996). Winning by a neck: Sexual selection in the evolution of giraffe. *The American Naturalist, 148*, 771–786.

Simms, L. J. (2002). The application of attachment theory to individual behavior and functioning in close relationships: Theory, research, and practical applications. In J. H. Harvey & A. Wenzel (Eds.), *A clinician's guide to maintaining and enhancing close relationships* (pp. 63–80). Mahwah, NJ: Erlbaum.

Simon, H. A. (1990). A mechanism for social selection and successful altruism. *Science, 250*, 1665–1668.

Simon, R. (2011, June 28). Supreme Court says violence OK. Sex? Maybe. Available: www.politico.com/news/stories/0611/57879.html

Simons, D., & Ambinder. M. (2005). Change Blindness: Theory and Consequences. *Current Directions in Psychological Science, 14*, 44–48.

Simons, D. J., & Chabris, C. F. (1999). Gorillas in our midst: Sustained inattentional blindness for dynamic events. *Perception, 28*, 1059–1074.

Simons, D. J., & Levin, D. T. (2005). Change blindness: Theory and consequences. *Current Directions in Psychological Science, 14*, 44–48.

Simonton, D. K. (1984). *Genius, creativity, and leadership: Historiometric inquiries*. Cambridge, MA: Harvard University Press.

Simonton, D. K. (1985). Intelligence and personal influence in groups: Four nonlinear models. *Psychological Review, 92*, 532–547.

Simonton, D. K. (1987). *Why presidents succeed: A political psychology of leadership*. New Haven, CT: Yale University Press.

Simonton, D. K. (1998). Historiometric methods in social psychology. *European Review of Social Psychology, 9*, 267–293.

Simonton, D. K. (2001). Predicting presidential performance in the United States: Equation replication on recent survey results. *Journal of Social Psychology, 141*, 293–307.

Simpson, J. (2010). A tiller in the greening of relationship science. In M. H. Gonzales, C. Tavris, & J. Aronson (Eds.), *The scientist and the humanist: A festschrift in honor of Elliot Aronson* (pp. 203–210). New York: Psychology Press.

Simpson, J. A. (1987). The dissolution of romantic relationships: Factors involved in relationship stability and emotional distress. *Journal of Personality and Social Psychology, 53*, 683–692.

Simpson, J. A., & Beckes, L. (2010). Evolutionary perspectives on prosocial behavior. In M. Mikulincer & P. R. Shaver (Eds.), *Prosocial motives, emotions, and behavior: The better angels of our nature* (pp. 35–53). Washington, DC: American Psychological Association. doi:10.1037/12061-002

Simpson, J. A., & Gangestad, S. W. (1992). Sociosexuality and romantic partner choice. *Journal of Personality, 60*, 31–51.

Simpson, J. A., & Rholes, W. S. (1994). Stress and secure base relationships in adulthood. In K. Bartholomew & D. Perlman (Eds.), *Advances in personal relationships*: Vol. 5. *Attachment processes in adulthood* (pp. 181–204). Bristol, PA: Kingsley.

Simpson, J. A., Rholes, W. S., Campbell, L., & Wilson, C. L. (2003). Changes in attachment orientations across the transition to parenthood. *Journal of Experimental Social Psychology, 39*, 317–331.

Simpson, J. A., Rholes, W. S., & Nelligan, J. S. (1992). Support seeking and support giving within couples in an anxiety-provoking situation: The role of attachment styles. *Journal of Personality and Social Psychology, 62*, 434–446.

Sinaceur, M., Thomas-Hunt, M. C., Neale, M. A., O'Neill, O. A., & Haag, C. (2010). Accuracy and perceived expert status in group decisions: When minority members make majority members more accurate privately. *Personality and Social Psychology Bulletin, 3*, 423–437.

Sinclair, R. C., Hoffman, C., Mark, M. M., Martin, L. L., & Pickering, T. L. (1994). Construct accessibility and the misattribution of arousal: Schachter and Singer revisited. *Psychological Science, 5*, 15–19.

Sinclair, S., Lowery, B. S., Hardin, C. D., & Colangelo, A. (2005). Social tuning of automatic racial attitudes: The role of affiliative motivation. *Journal of Personality and Social Psychology, 89*(4), 583–592.

Sinclair, S., & Lun, J. (2010). Social tuning of ethnic attitudes. In B. Mesquita, L. Feldman Barrett, & E. R. Smith (Eds.), *The mind in context* (pp. 214–229). New York: Guilford Press.

Singelis, T. M. (1994). The measurement of independent and interdependent self-construals. *Personality and Social Psychology Bulletin, 20*, 580–591.

Singer, M. (2002, May 20). A year of trouble. *The New Yorker*, pp. 42–46.

Sirois, F. (1982). Perspectives on epidemic hysteria. In M. J. Colligan, J. W. Pennebaker, & L. R. Murphy (Eds.), *Mass psychogenic illness: A social psychological analysis* (pp. 217–236). Hillsdale, NJ: Erlbaum.

Skinner, B. F. (1938). *The behavior of organisms: An experimental analysis*. New York: Appleton-Century-Crofts.

Skinner, E. A. (1996). A guide to constructs of control. *Journal of Personality and Social Psychology, 71*, 549–570.

Skitka, L. J. (2002). Do the means always justify the ends, or do the ends sometimes justify the means? A value protection model of justice reasoning. *Personality and Social Psychology Bulletin, 28*, 588–597.

Slavin, R. E. (1996). Cooperative learning in middle and secondary schools. (Special section: Young adolescents at risk.) *Clearing House, 69*, 200–205.

Slavin, R. E., & Cooper, R. (1999). Improving intergroup relations: Lessons learned from cooperative learning programs. *Journal of Social Issues, 55*, 647–663.

Slevec, J. H., & Tiggemann, M. (2011). Predictors of body dissatisfaction and disordered eating in middle-aged women. *Clinical Psychology Review, 31*(4), 515–524. doi:10.1016/j.cpr.2010.12.002

Sloan, D., Marx, B., Epstein, E., & Dobbs, J. (2008). Expressive writing buffers against maladaptive rumination. *Emotion, 8*, 302–306.

Slovic, P., Fischhoff, B., & Lichtenstein, S. (1976). Cognitive processes and societal risk taking. In J. S. Carroll & J. Payne (Eds.), *Cognition and social behavior* (pp. 165–184). Hillsdale, NJ: Erlbaum.

Smith, D. D. (1976). The social content of pornography. *Journal of Communication, 26*, 16–24.

Smith, M. B., Bruner, J., & White, R. W. (1956). *Opinions and personality*. New York: Wiley.

Smith, P. B., & Bond, M. H. (1999). *Social psychology across cultures* (2nd ed.). Needham Heights, MA: Allyn & Bacon.

Smith, S. S., & Richardson, D. (1983). Amelioration of deception and harm in psychological research: The important role of debriefing. *Journal of Personality and Social Psychology, 44*, 1075–1082.

Smith, V. L. (1991). Prototypes in the courtroom: Lay representation of legal concepts. *Journal of Personality and Social Psychology, 61*, 857–872.

Smyth, J., & Pennebaker, J. (2008). Exploring the boundary conditions of expressive writing: In search of the right recipe. *British Journal of Health Psychology, 13*, 1–7.

Snyder, C. R., & Higgins, R. L. (1988). Excuses: Their effective role in the negotiation of reality. *Psychological Bulletin, 104*, 23–35.

Snyder, C. R., & Lopez, S. J. (2009). *Oxford handbook of positive psychology*. New York: Oxford University Press.

Snyder, M. (1984). When belief creates reality. In L. Berkowitz (Ed.), *Advances in experimental social psychology* (Vol. 18, pp. 247–305). Orlando, FL: Academic Press.

Snyder, M. (1993). Basic research and practical problems: The promise of a "functional" personality and social psychology. *Personality and Social Psychology Bulletin, 19*, 251–264.

Snyder, M., Tanke, E. D., & Berscheid, E. (1977). Social perception and interpersonal behavior: On the self-fulfilling nature of social stereotypes. *Journal of Personality and Social Psychology, 35*, 656–666.

Sloan, D., Marx, B., Epstein, E., & Dobbs, J. (2008). Expressive writing buffers against maladaptive rumination. *Emotion, 8*, 302–306.

Solomon, L. Z., Solomon, H., & Stone, R. (1978). Helping as a function of number of bystanders and ambiguity of emergency. *Personality and Social Psychology Bulletin, 4*, 318–321.

Sommers, S. (2011). *Situations matter: Understanding how context transforms your world*. New York: Riverhead.

Sommers, S., & Kassin, S. (2001). On the many impacts of inadmissible testimony: Selective compliance, need for cognition, and the over-correction bias. *Personality and Social Psychology Bulletin, 27*, 1368–1377.

Son Hing, L. S., Li, W., & Zanna, M. P. (2002). Inducing hypocrisy to reduce prejudicial responses among aversive racists. *Journal of Experimental Social Psychology, 38*, 71–78.

Sontag, S. (1978). *Illness as metaphor*. New York: Farrar, Straus & Giroux.

Sontag, S. (1988). *AIDS and its metaphors*. New York: Farrar, Straus & Giroux.

Sorenson, T. C. (1966). *Kennedy*. New York: Bantam Books.

Sorkin, R. D., Hays, C. J., & West, R. (2001). Signal-detection analysis of group decision making. *Psychological Review, 108*, 183–203.

Spanier, G. B. (1992). Divorce: A comment about the future. In T. L. Orbuch (Ed.), *Close relationship loss: Theoretical approaches* (pp. 207–212). New York: Springer-Verlag.

Spears, T. (2008). Newspaper readers 'rational' thinkers. *Vancouver Sun*, p. A16.

Spelke, E. S. (2005). Sex differences in intrinsic aptitude for mathematics and science? *American Psychologist, 60*, 950–958.

Spencer, S. J., Steele, C. M., & Quinn, D. M. (1999). Stereotype threat and women's math performance. *Journal of Experimental Social Psychology, 35*, 4–28.

Spina, R. R., Ji, L.-J., Guo, T., Zhang, Z., Li, Y., & Fabrigar, L. (2010). Cultural differences in the representativeness heuristic: Expecting a correspondence in magnitude between cause and effect. *Personality and Social Psychology Bulletin, 36*(5), 583–597. doi:10.1177/0146167210368278

Sporer, S. L., Koehnken, G., & Malpass, R. S. (1996). Introduction: 200 years of mistaken identification. In S. L. Sporer, R. S. Malpass, & G. Koehnken (Eds.), *Psychological issues in eyewitness identification* (pp. 1–6). Mahwah, NJ: Erlbaum.

Sprecher, S., Aron, A., Hatfield, E., Cortese, A., Potapova, E., & Levitskaya, A. (1994). Love: American style, Russian style, and Japanese style. *Personal Relationships, 1*, 349–369.

Sprecher, S., & Schwartz, P. (1994). Equity and balance in the exchange of contributions in close relationships. In M. J. Lerner & G. Mikula (Eds.), *Entitlement and the affectional bond: Justice in close relationships* (pp. 11–42). New York: Plenum.

Sprecher, S., Sullivan, Q., & Hatfield, E. (1994). Mate selection preference: Gender differences examined in a national sample. *Journal of Personality and Social Psychology, 66*, 1074–1080.

Sprink, K. S., & Carron, A. V. (1994). Group cohesion effects in exercise classes. *Small Group Research, 25*, 26–42.

Staats, H., Harland, P., & Wilke, H. A. M. (2004). Effecting durable change: a team approach to improve environmental behavior in the household. *Environment and Behavior, 36*, 341–367.

Stanley, D. A., Sokol-Hessner, P., Banaji, M. R., & Phelps, E. A. (2011). Implicit race attitudes predict trustworthiness judgments and economic trust decisions. *Proceedings of the National Academy of Sciences, 108*, 7710–7715.

Stasser, G. (2000). Information distribution, participation, and group decision: Explorations with the DISCUSS and SPEAK models. In D. R. Ilgen & C. L. Hulin (Eds.), *Computational modeling of behavior in organizations: The third scientific discipline* (pp. 135–161). Washington, DC: American Psychological Association.

Stasser, G., & Birchmeier, Z. (2003). Group creativity and collective choice. In P. B. Paulus & B. A. Nijstad (Eds.), *Group creativity: Innovation through collaboration* (pp. 85–109). New York: Oxford University Press.

Stasser, G., Stewart, D. D., & Wittenbaum, G. M. (1995). Expert roles and information exchange during discussion: The importance of knowing who knows what. *Journal of Experimental and Social Psychology, 31*, 244–265.

Stasser, G., & Titus, W. (1985). Pooling of unshared information in group decision making: Biased information sampling during discussion. *Journal of Personality and Social Psychology, 48*, 1467–1478.

Staub, E. (1974). Helping a distressed person: Social, personality, and stimulus determinants. In L. Berkowitz (Ed.), *Advances in experimental social psychology* (Vol. 7, pp. 293–341). New York: Academic Press.

Staub, E. (1999). The roots of evil: Social conditions, culture, personality, and basic human needs. *Personality and Social Psychology Review, 3*, 179–192.

Steblay, N. M. (1987). Helping behavior in rural and urban environments: A meta-analysis. *Psychological Bulletin, 102*, 346–356.

Steblay, N. M. (1997). Social influence in eyewitness recall: A meta-analytic review of lineup instruction effects. *Law and Human Behavior, 21*, 283–297.

Steblay, N. M., Besirevic, J., Fulero, S. M., & Jimenez-Lorente, B. (1999). The effects of pretrial publicity on juror verdicts: A meta-analytic review. *Law and Human Behavior, 23*, 219–235.

Steblay, N. M., Dysart, J., Fulero, S. M., & Lindsay, R. C. L. (2001). Eyewitness accuracy rates in sequential and simultaneous lineup presentations: A meta-analytic comparison. *Law and Human Behavior, 25*, 459–473.

Steele, C. M., (2010). *Whistling Vivaldi: And other clues to how stereotypes affect us*. New York: W.W. Norton & Co.

Steele, C. M. (1988). The psychology of self-affirmation: Sustaining the integrity of the self. In L. Berkowitz (Ed.), *Advances in experimental social psychology* (Vol. 21, pp. 261–302). New York: Academic Press.

Steele, C. M. (1992, April). Race and the schooling of black Americans. *Atlantic*, pp. 68–78.

Steele, C. M. (1997). A threat in the air: How stereotypes shape intellectual ability and performance. *American Psychologist, 52*, 613–629.

Steele, C. M., & Aronson, J. M. (1995a). Stereotype threat and the intellectual test performance of African-Americans. *Journal of Personality and Social Psychology, 69*, 797–811.

Steele, C. M., & Aronson, J. M. (1995b). Stereotype vulnerability and intellectual performance. In E. Aronson (Ed.), *Readings about the social animal* (7th ed.). New York: Freeman.

Steele, C. M., Hoppe, H., & Gonzales, J. (1986). *Dissonance and the lab coat: Self-affirmation and the free-choice paradigm*. Unpublished manuscript, University of Washington.

Steele, C. M., Spencer, S. J., & Aronson, J. M. (2002). Contending with group image: The psychology of stereotype and social identity threat. In M. P. Zanna (Ed.), *Advances in experimental social psychology* (Vol. 34, pp. 379–440). San Diego, CA: Academic Press.

Steele, C. M., Spencer, S. J., & Josephs, R. A. (1992). *Seeking self-relevant information: The effects of self-esteem and stability of the information*. Unpublished manuscript, University of Michigan.

Steele, J. R., & Ambady, N. (2006). "Math is Hard!" The effect of gender priming on women's attitudes. *Journal of Experimental Social Psychology, 42*(4), 428–436. doi:10.1016/j.jesp.2005.06.003

Steg, L., & Vlek, C. (2009). Encouraging pro-environmental behaviour: An integrative review and research agenda. *Journal of Environmental Psychology, 29*(3), 309–317. doi:10.1016/j.jenvp.2008.10.004

Steiner, I. D. (1972). *Group process and productivity*. New York: Academic Press.

Stephan, W. G. (1978). School desegregation: An evaluation of predictions made in *Brown* v. *Board of Education*. *Psychological Bulletin, 85*, 217–238.

Stephan, W. G. (1985). Intergroup relations. In G. Lindzey & E. Aronson (Eds.), *Handbook of social psychology* (3rd ed., Vol. 2, pp. 599–658). New York: McGraw-Hill.

Stern, P. C. (2011). Contributions of psychology to limiting climate change. *American Psychologist, 66*(4), 303–314. doi:10.1037/a0023235

Sternberg, R. J. (1986). A triangular theory of love. *Psychological Review, 93*, 119–135.

Sternberg, R. J. (1988). *The triangle of love*. New York: Basic Books.

Sternberg, R. J. (1997). Construct validation of a triangular love scale. *European Journal of Social Psychology, 27*, 313–335.

Sternberg, R. J., & Vroom, V. (2002). The person versus the situation in leadership. *Leadership Quarterly, 13*, 301–323.

Stewart, D. D., & Stasser, G. (1995). Expert role assignment and information sampling during collective recall and decision making. *Journal of Personality and Social Psychology, 69*, 619–628.

Stewart, J. (2011). *Tangled webs: How false statements are undermining America*. New York: Penguin.

Stewart, J. B. (2002). *Heart of a soldier*. New York: Simon & Schuster.

Stice, E., Marti, C. N., Spoor, S., Presnell, K., & Shaw, H. (2008). Dissonance and healthy weight eating disorder prevention programs: Long-term effects from a randomized efficacy trial. *Journal of Consulting and Clinical Psychology, 76*, 329–340.

Stice, E., Rohde, P., Shaw, H., & Gau, J. (2011). An effectiveness trial of a selected dissonance-based eating disorder prevention program for female high school students: Long-term effects. *Journal of Consulting and Clinical Psychology*. Advance online publication. doi:10.1037/a0024351

Stice, E., Shaw, H., Burton, E., & Wade, E. (2006). Dissonance and healthy weight eating disorders prevention programs: A randomized efficacy trial. *Journal of Consulting and Clinical Psychology, 74*, 263–275.

Stillman, T. F., Baumeister, R. F., Lambert, N. M., Crescioni, A. W. , DeWall, C. N., & Fincham, F. D. (2009). Alone and without purpose: Life loses meaning following social exclusion. *Journal of Experimental Social Psychology, 45*, 686–694.

Stinson, D. A., Logel, C., Shepherd, S., & Zanna, M. P. (2011). Rewriting the self-fulfilling prophecy of social rejection: Self-affirmation improves relational security and social behavior up to 2 months later. *Psychological Science, 22*(9), 1145–1149. doi:10.1177/0956797611417725

Stoff, D. M., & Cairns, R. B. (Eds.). (1997). *Aggression and violence: Genetic, neurobiological, and biosocial perspectives*. Mahwah, NJ: Erlbaum.

Stone, A. A., Bovbjerg, D. H., Neale, J. M., Napoli, A., Valdimarsdottir, H., Cox, D., et al. (1993). Development of common cold symptoms following experimental rhinovirus infection is related to prior stressful life events. *Behavioral Medicine, 8*, 115–120.

Stone, J., Aronson, E., Crain, A. L., Winslow, M. P., & Fried, C. (1994). Inducing hypocrisy as a means of encouraging young adults to use condoms. *Personality and Social Psychology Bulletin, 20*, 116–128.

Stone, J., Lynch, C. I., Sjomeling, M., & Darley, J. M. (1999). Stereotype threat effects on Black and White athletic performance. *Journal of Personality and Social Psychology*, 77, 1213–1227.

Stone, J., Perry, Z., & Darley, J. (1997). "White men can't jump": Evidence for perceptual confirmation of racial stereotypes following a basketball game. *Basic and Applied Social Psychology, 19*, 291–306.

Storbeck, J., & Clore, G. L. (2008). Affective arousal as information: How affective arousal influences judgments, learning, and memory. *Social and Personality Psychology Compass, 2*(5), 1824–1843. doi:10.1111/j.1751-9004.2008.00138.x

Stormo, K. J., Lang, A. R., & Stritzke, W. G. K. (1997). Attributions about acquaintance rape: The role of alcohol and individual differences. *Journal of Applied Social Psychology, 27*, 279–305.

Storms, M. D. (1973). Videotape and the attribution process: Reversing actors' and observers' points of view. *Journal of Personality and Social Psychology*, 27, 165–175.

Story, L. (2007, January 15). Anywhere the eye can see, it's likely to see an ad. *The New York Times*. Retrieved July 12, 2011, from www.nytimes.com/2007/01/15/business/media/15everywhere.html?scp=1&sq=anywhere%20the%20eye%20can%20see&st=cse

Stouffer, S. A., Suchman, E. A., De Vinney, L. C., Star, S. A., & Williams, R. M., Jr. (1949). *The American soldier: Adjustment during army life* (Vol. 1). Princeton, NJ: Princeton University Press.

Strack, F., & Mussweiler, T. (2003). Heuristic strategies for judgment under uncertainty: The enigmatic case of anchoring. In G. V. Bodenhausen (Ed.), *Foundations of social cognition: A festschrift in honor of Robert S. Wyer Jr*. (pp. 79–95). Mahwah, NJ: Erlbaum.

Strahan, E. J., Spencer, S. J., & Zanna, M. P. (2002). Subliminal priming and persuasion: Striking while the iron is hot. *Journal of Experimental Social Psychology, 38*, 556–568.

Stringfellow, T. (1841). A brief examination of scripture testimony on the institution of slavery. *Religious Herald*. Available on Internet.

Studer, J. (1996). Understanding and preventing aggressive responses in youth. *Elementary School Guidance and Counseling, 30*, 194–203.

Stuhlmacher, A. F., & Citera, M. (2005). Hostile behavior and profit in virtual negotiation: A meta-analysis. *Journal of Business and Psychology, 20*, 69–93.

Stukas, A. A., Snyder, M., & Clary, E. G. (1999). The effects of "mandatory volunteerism" on intentions to volunteer. *Psychological Science, 10*, 59–64.

Stürmer, S., & Snyder, M. (2010). Helping "us" versus "them": Towards a group-level theory of helping and altruism within and across group boundaries. In S. Stürmer & M. Snyder (Eds.), *The psychology of prosocial behavior: Group processes, intergroup relations, and helping* (pp. 33–58). Oxford, UK: Wiley-Blackwell.

Suddendorf, T., & Collier-Baker, E. (2009). The evolution of primate visual self-recognition: Evidence of absence in lesser apes. *Proceedings of The Royal Society B: Biological Sciences, 276*, 1671–1677.

Sue, D. W. (2010). *Microaggressions in everyday life: Race, gender, and sexual orientation*. Hoboken, NJ: John Wiley & Sons.

Suls, J. M., & Fletcher, B. (1983). Social comparison in the social and physical sciences: An archival study. *Journal of Personality and Social Psychology, 44*, 575–580.

Suls, J. M., & Miller, R. L. (Eds.). (1977). *Social comparison processes: Theoretical and empirical perspectives*. Washington, DC: Hemisphere/Halstead.

Suls, J. M., & Wheeler, L. (Eds.). (2000). *Handbook of social comparison: Theory and research*. New York: Kluwer/Plenum.

Summers, G., & Feldman, N. S. (1984). Blaming the victim versus blaming the perpetrator: An attributional analysis of spouse abuse. *Journal of Social and Clinical Psychology, 2*, 339–347.

Swann, W. B., Jr. (1990). To be adored or to be known? The interplay of self-enhancement and self-verification. In E. T. Higgins & R. M. Sorrentino (Eds.), *Handbook of motivation and cognition* (Vol. 2, pp. 404–448). New York: Guilford Press.

Swann, W. B., Jr. (1996). *Self-traps: The elusive quest for higher self-esteem*. New York: Freeman.

Swann, W. B., Jr., & Pelham, B. W. (1988). *The social construction of identity: Self-verification through friend and intimate selection*. Unpublished manuscript, University of Texas, Austin.

Swim, J. K., Borgida, E., Maruyama, G., & Myers, D. G. (1989). Joan McKay vs. John McKay: Do gender stereotypes bias evaluations? *Psychological Bulletin, 105*, 409–429.

Swim, J. K., Clayton, S., & Howard, G. S. (2011). Human behavioral contributions to climate change: Psychological and contextual drivers. *American Psychologist, 66*(4), 251–264. doi:10.1037/a0023472

Symons, D. (1979). *The evolution of human sexuality*. New York: Oxford University Press.

Szalavitz, M. (2012, January 31). Mysterious tics in teen girls: What is mass psychogenic illness? *Time*. Available at http://healthland.time.com/2012/01/31/mysterious-twitching-outbreak-in-n-y-teen-girls-what-is-mass-psychogenic-illness/

Tajfel, H. (1982a). *Social identity and intergroup relations*. Cambridge: Cambridge University Press.

Tajfel, H. (1982b). Social psychology of intergroup relations. *Annual Review of Psychology, 33*, 1–39.

Tajfel, H., & Billig, M. (1974). Familiarity and categorization in intergroup behavior. *Journal of Experimental Social Psychology, 10*, 159–170.

Tajfel, H., & Turner, J. C. (1979). An integrative theory of social contact. In W. Austin & S. Worchel (Eds.), *The social psychology of intergroup relations* (pp. 162–173). Monterey, CA: Brooks/Cole.

Takaku, S. (2006). Reducing road rage: An application of the dissonance-attribution model of interpersonal forgiveness. *Journal of Applied Social Psychology, 36*, 2362–2378.

Tamres, L. K., Janicki, D., & Helgeson, V. S. (2002). Sex differences in coping behavior: A meta-analytic review. *Personality and Social Psychology Review, 6*, 2–30.

Tanford, S., & Penrod, S. D. (1984). Social influence model: A formal integration of research on majority and minority influence processes. *Psychological Bulletin, 95*, 189–225.

The tangled web of porn in the office. (2008, December 8). *Newsweek*. Retrieved March 21, 2011, from www.newsweek.com/2008/11/28/the-tangled-web-of-porn-in-the-office.html

Tannen, D. (2001). *You just don't understand: Men and women in conversation*. New York: Harper.

Ta demir, N. (2011). The relationships between motivations of intergroup differentiation as a function of different dimensions of social identity. *Review of General Psychology, 15*(2), 125–137. doi:10.1037/a0022816

Tavris, C. (1989). *Anger: The misunderstood emotion* (Rev. ed.). New York: Touchstone.

Tavris, C. & Aronson, E. (2007). *Mistakes were made (but not by me)*. New York: Harcourt.

Taylor, L. S., Fiore, A. T., Mendelsohn, G. A., & Cheshire, C. (2011). "Out of my league": A real-world test of the matching hypothesis. *Personality and Social Psychology Bulletin, 37*, 942–954.

Taylor, S. E. (2010). Health. In Fiske, S. T., Gilbert, D. T., & Lindzey, G. (Eds.). *Handbook of social psychology* (5th ed., Vol. 1, pp. 698–723). Hoboken, NJ: Wiley.

Taylor, S. E., & Brown, J. D. (1994). Positive illusions and well-being revisited: Separating fact from fiction. *Psychological Bulletin, 116*, 21–27.

Taylor, S. E., & Fiske, S. T. (1975). Point of view and perceptions of causality. *Journal of Personality and Social Psychology, 32*, 439–445.

Taylor, S. E., Klein, L. C., Lewis, B. P., Gruenewald, T. L., Gurung, R. A. R., & Updegraff, J. A. (2000). Biobehavioral responses to stress in females: Tend-and-befriend, not fight-or-flight. *Psychological Review, 107*, 411–429.

Taylor, S. E., Lichtman, R. R., & Wood, J. V. (1984). Attributions, beliefs about control, and adjustment to breast cancer. *Journal of Personality and Social Psychology, 46*, 489–502.

Taylor, S. E., & Master, S. L. (2011). Social responses to stress: The tend-and-befriend model. In R. J. Contrada & A. Baum (Eds.), *The handbook of stress science: Biology, psychology, and health* (pp. 101–109). New York: Springer.

Taylor, S. E., Repetti, R. L., & Seeman, T. (1997). Health psychology: What is an unhealthy environment and how does it get under the skin? *Annual Review of Psychology, 48*, 411–447.

Taylor, S. E., Sherman, D. K., Kim, H. S., Jarcho, J., Takagi, K., & Dunagan, M. S. (2004). Culture and social support: Who seeks it and why? *Journal of Personality and Social Psychology, 87*, 354–362.

Taylor, S. E., Welch, W., Kim, H. S., Sherman, D. K. (2007). Cultural differences in the impact of social support on psychological and biological stress responses. *Psychological Science, 18*, 831–837.

Taylor, S. P., & Leonard, K. E. (1983). Alcohol and human physical aggression. In R. G. Geen & E. Donnerstein (Eds.), *Aggression: Theoretical and empirical reviews* (pp. 77–101). New York: Academic Press.

Teger, A. L., & Pruitt, D. G. (1967). Components of group risk taking. *Journal of Experimental Social Psychology, 3*, 189–205.

Tesser, A. (1991). Emotion in social comparison and reflection processes. In J. M. Suls & T. A. Wills (Eds.), *Social comparison: Contemporary theory and research* (pp. 117–148). Hillsdale, NJ: Erlbaum.

Tesser, A. (1993). The importance of heritability in psychological research: The case of attitudes. *Psychological Review, 100*, 129–142.

Tesser, A. (2003). Self-evaluation. In M. R. Leary & J. P. Tangney (Eds.), *Handbook of self and identity* (pp. 275–290). New York: Guilford Press.

Tesser, A., Campbell, J. D., & Mickler, S. (1983). The role of social pressure, attention to the stimulus, and self-doubt in conformity. *European Journal of Social Psychology, 13*, 217–233.

Tesser, A., & Paulus, D. (1983). The definition of self: Private and public self-evaluation management strategies. *Journal of Personality and Social Psychology, 44*, 672–682.

Tesser, A., & Smith, J. (1980). Some effects of friendship and task relevance on helping: You don't always help the one you like. *Journal of Experimental Social Psychology, 16*, 582–590.

Tetlock, P. E. (1981). The influence of self-presentational goals on attributional reports. *Social Psychology Quarterly, 44*, 300–311.

Tetlock, P. E. (2002). Theory-driven reasoning about plausible pasts and probable futures in world politics. In T. Gilovich, D. W. Griffin, & D. Kahneman (Eds.), *Heuristics and biases: The psychology of intuitive judgment* (pp. 749–762). New York: Cambridge University Press.

Tetlock, P. E., Peterson, R. S., McGuire, C., Chang, S., & Field, P. (1992). Assessing political group dynamics: A test of the groupthink model. *Journal of Personality and Social Psychology, 63*, 403–425.

Teves, O. (2002, May 28). WHO warns Asia 25% of youth will die from smoking without curbed advertising. Associated Press.

The Ontario Symposium (Vol. 5, pp. 3–39). Hillsdale, NJ: Erlbaum.

Thernstrom, M. (2003, August 24). Untying the knot. *New York Times Magazine*, p. 38.

Theus, K. T. (1994). Subliminal advertising and the psychology of processing unconscious stimuli: A review. *Psychology and Marketing, 11*, 271–290.

Thibaut, J. W., & Kelley, H. H. (1959). *The social psychology of groups*. New York: Wiley.

Thomas, M. H. (1982). Physiological arousal, exposure to a relatively lengthy aggressive film, and aggressive behavior. *Journal of Research in Personality, 16*, 72–81.

Thomas, M. H., Horton, R., Lippincott, E., & Drabman, R. (1977). Desensitization to portrayals of real-life aggression as a function of exposure to television violence. *Journal of Personality and Social Psychology, 35*, 450–458.

Thomas, W. I. (1928). *The child in America*. New York: Knopf.

Thompson, J. (2000, June 18). "I was certain, but I was wrong." *The New York Times*, p. D15.

Thompson, L. (1995). They saw a negotiation: Partisanship and involvement. *Journal of Personality and Social Psychology, 68*, 839–853.

Thompson, L. (1997). *The mind and heart of the negotiator*. Upper Saddle River, NJ: Prentice Hall.

Thompson, L. L., Wang, J., & Gunia, B. C. (2010). Negotiation. *Annual Review of Psychology, 61*, 491–515. doi:10.1146/annurev.psych.093008.100458

Thompson, S. C. (1999). Illusions of control: How we overestimate our personal influence. *Current Directions in Psychological Science, 8*, 187–190.

Thompson, S. C. (2002). The role of personal control in adaptive functioning. In C. R. Snyder & S. J. Lopez (Eds.), *Handbook of positive psychology* (pp. 202–213). London: Oxford University Press.

Thompson, T. L., & Kiang, L. (2010). The model minority stereotype: Adolescent experiences and links with adjustment. *Asian American Journal of Psychology, 1*, 119–128.

Thompson, W. M., Dabbs, J. M., Jr., & Frady, R. L. (1990). Changes in saliva testosterone levels during a 90-day shock incarceration program. *Criminal Justice and Behavior*, 17, 246–252.

Thornton, D., & Arrowood, A. J. (1966). Self-evaluation, self-enhancement, and the locus of social comparison. *Journal of Experimental Social Psychology, 1*(Suppl.), 40–48.

Timaeus, E. (1968). Untersuchungen zum sogenannten konformen Verhalten [Research into so-called conforming behavior]. *Zeitschrift für Experimentelle und Angewandte Psychologie, 15*, 176–194.

Tindale, R. S. (1993). Decision errors made by individuals and groups. In N. J. Castellan Jr. (Ed.), *Individual and group decision making* (pp. 109–124). Hillsdale, NJ: Erlbaum.

Tindale, R. S., Munier, C., Wasserman, M., & Smith, C. M. (2002). Group processes and the Holocaust. In L. S. Newman & R. Erber (Eds.), *Understanding genocide: The social psychology of the Holocaust* (pp. 143–161). New York: Oxford University Press.

Ting-Toomey, S., & Chung, L. (1996). Cross-cultural interpersonal communication: Theoretical trends and research directions. In W. B. Gudykunst, S. Ting-Toomey, & T. Nishida (Eds.), *Communication in personal relationships across cultures* (pp. 237–261). Thousand Oaks, CA: Sage.

Toch, H. (1980). *Violent men* (Rev. ed.). Cambridge, MA: Schenkman.

Todd, P. M., Penke, L., Fasolo, B., & Lenton, A. P. (2007). Different cognitive processes underlie human mate choices and mate preferences. *Proceedings of the National Academy of Sciences, 104*, 15011–15016.

Todorov, A., Said, C. P., Engell, A., & Oosterhof, N. N. (2008). Understanding evaluation of faces on social dimensions. *Trends in Cognitive Sciences, 12*, 455–460.

Toi, M., & Batson, C. D. (1982). More evidence that empathy is a source of altruistic motivation. *Journal of Personality and Social Psychology, 43*, 281–292.

Toma, C., & Butera, F. (2009). Hidden profiles and concealed information: Strategic information sharing and use in group decision making. *Personality and Social Psychology Bulletin, 35*(6), 793–806. doi:10.1177/0146167209333176

Toma, C. L., & Hancock, J. T. (2012). What lies beneath: The linguistic traces of deception in online dating profiles. *Journal of Communication, 62*, 78–97.

Toma, C. L., Hancock, J. T., & Ellison, N. B. (2008). Separating fact from fiction: An examination of deceptive self-presentation in online dating profiles. *Personality and Social Psychology Bulletin, 34*, 1023–1036.

Tooby, J., & Cosmides, L. (2005). Conceptual foundations of evolutionary psychology. In D. M. Buss (Ed.), *The handbook of evolutionary psychology* (pp. 5–67). Hoboken, NJ: Wiley.

Tourangeau, R., Smith, T., & Rasinski, K. (1997). Motivation to report sensitive behaviors on surveys: Evidence from a bogus pipeline experiment. *Journal of Applied Social Psychology, 27*, 209–222.

Trappey, C. (1996). A meta-analysis of consumer choice and subliminal advertising. *Psychology and Marketing, 13*, 517–530.

Trends in cigarette smoking among high school students: United States, 1991–2002. (2002). *Centers for Disease Control, Morbidity and Mortality Weekly Report, 51*, 409–412.

Trends in the prevalence of tobacco use. (2009). National YRBS: 1991–2009. Retrieved November 1, 2011, from www.cdc.gov/healthyyouth/yrbs/pdf/us_tobacco_trend_yrbs.pdf

Triandis, H. C. (1989). The self and social behavior in differing cultural contexts. *Psychological Review, 96*, 506–520.

Triandis, H. C. (1994). *Culture and social behavior*. New York: McGraw-Hill.

Triandis, H. C. (1995). *Individualism and collectivism*. Boulder, CO: Westview Press.

Trivers, R. L. (1971). The evolution of reciprocal altruism. *Quarterly Review of Biology, 46*, 35–57.

Trivers, R. L. (1985). *Social evolution*. Menlo Park, CA: Benjamin-Cummings.

Trötschel, R., Hüffmeier, J., Loschelder, D. D., Schwartz, K., & Gollwitzer, P. M. (2011). Perspective taking as a means to overcome motivational barriers in negotiations: When putting oneself into the opponent's shoes helps to walk toward agreements. *Journal of Personality and Social Psychology, 101*, 771–790. doi:10.1037/a0023801

Tsai, J. L. (2007). Ideal affect: Cultural causes and behavioral consequences. *Perspectives on Psychological Science, 2*, 242–259.

Tsai, J. L., Knutson, B., & Fung, H. (2006). Cultural variation in affect valuation. *Journal of Personality and Social Psychology, 90*, 288–307.

Tseëlon, E. (1995). *The presentation of woman in everyday life*. Thousand Oaks, CA: Sage.

Tucker, P., Pfefferbaum, B., Doughty, D. B., Jones, D. E., Jordan, F. B., & Nixon, S. J. (2002). Body handlers after terrorism in Oklahoma City: Predictors of posttraumatic stress and other symptoms. *American Journal of Orthopsychiatry, 72*, 469–C475.

Turner, C., & Leyens, J. (1992). The weapons effect revisited: The effects of firearms on aggressive behavior. In P. Suedfeld & P. E. Tetlock (Eds.), *Psychology and social policy* (pp. 201–221). New York: Hemisphere.

Turner, C., Simons, L., Berkowitz, L., & Frodi, A. (1977). The stimulating and inhibiting effects of weapons on aggressive behavior. *Aggressive Behavior, 3*, 355–378.

Turner, F. J. (1932). *The significance of sections in American history*. New York: Henry Holt.

Turner, M., Pratkanis, A., Probasco, P., & Leve, C. (2006). Threat, cohesion, and group effectiveness: Testing a social identity maintenance perspective on groupthink. *Small Groups* (pp. 241–264). New York: Psychology Press.

Turner, M., Pratkanis, A., & Struckman, C. (2007). Groupthink as social identity maintenance. *The science of social influence: Advances and future progress* (pp. 223–246). New York: Psychology Press.

Turner, M. E., & Horvitz, T. (2001). The dilemma of threat: Group effectiveness and ineffectiveness under adversity. In M. E. Turner (Ed.), *Groups at work: Theory and research* (pp. 445–470). Mahwah, NJ: Erlbaum.

Tversky, A., & Kahneman, D. (1973). Availability: A heuristic for judging frequency and probability. *Cognitive Psychology, 5*, 207–232.

Tversky, A., & Kahneman, D. (1974). Judgment under uncertainty: Heuristics and biases. *Science, 185*, 1124–1131.

Twenge, J. M. (1997). Attitudes toward women, 1970–1995: A meta-analysis. *Psychology of Women Quarterly, 21*, 35–51.

Twenge, J. M. (2001). Changes in women's assertiveness in response to status and roles: A cross-temporal meta-analysis, 1931–1993. *Journal of Personality and Social Psychology, 81*, 133–145.

Twenge, J. M. (2006). *Generation me*. New York: Free Press.

Twenge, J. M., & Campbell, W. K. (2009). *The narcissism epidemic*. New York: Free Press.

Twenge, J. M., & Foster, J. D. (2010). Birth cohort increases in narcissistic personality traits among American college students, 1982–2009. *Social Psychological and Personality Science, 1*, 99–106.

Twenge, J. M., Konrath, S., Foster, J. D., Campbell, W. K., & Bushman, B. J. (2008). Egos inflating over time: A cross-temporal meta-analysis of the Narcissistic Personality Inventory. *Journal of Personality, 76*, 875–902. doi:10.1111/j.1467-6494.2008.00507.x

Twenge, J. M., Zhang, L., & Im, C. (2004). It's beyond my control: A cross-temporal meta-analysis of increasing externality in locus of control, 1960–2002. *Personality and Social Psychology Review, 8*, 308–319.

Tyler, J. M., & Burns, K. C. (2008). After depletion: The replenishment of the self's regulatory resources. *Self and Identity, 7*(3), 305–321. doi:10.1080/15298860701799997

U.S. Department of Justice. (2000). *Violence by intimates*. Washington, DC: Bureau of Justice Statistics.

Uchino, B. N. (2009). Understanding the links between social support and physical health: A life-span perspective with emphasis on the separability of perceived and received support. *Perspectives on Psychological Science, 4*(3), 236–255. doi:10.1111/j.1745-6924.2009.01122.x

Uleman, J. S., Saribay, S. A., & Gonzalez, C. M. (2008). Spontaneous inferences, implicit impressions, and implicit theories. *Annual Review of Psychology, 59*, 329–360. doi:10.1146/annurev.psych.59.103006.093707

UNAIDS factsheet: Sub-Saharan Africa. (n.d.). Retrieved March 13, 2012, from data.unaids.org/pub/GlobalReport/2006/200605-fs_subsaharanafrica_en.pdf

Updegraff, J., Silver, R., & Holman, E. (2008). Searching for and finding meaning in collective trauma: Results from a national longitudinal study of the 9/11 terrorist attacks. *Journal of Personality and Social Psychology, 95*, 709–722.

Uziel, L. (2010). Look at me, I'm happy and creative: The effect of impression management on behavior in social presence. *Personality and Social Psychology Bulletin, 36*(12), 1591–1602. doi:10.1177/0146167210386239

Uzzell, D. (2000). Ethnographic and action research. In G. M. Breakwell, S. Hammond, & C. Fife-Schaw (Eds.), *Research methods in psychology* (2nd ed., pp. 326–337). Thousand Oaks, CA: Sage.

Vaananen, A., Buunk, B. P., Kivimaki, M., Pentti, J., & Vahteva, J. (2005). When is it better to give than to receive: Long-term health effects of perceived reciprocity in support exchange. *Journal of Personality and Social Psychology, 89*, 176–193.

Vala Jorge, P., Cicero, C.-L., Rui C. (2009) Is the attribution of cultural differences to minorities an expression of racial prejudice? *International Journal of Psychology, 44* (1), 20–28.

Valle, P. O. D., Rebelo, E., & Reis, E. (2005). Combining behavioral theories to predict recycling involvement. *Environment and Behavior, 37*, 364–396.

Vallone, R. P., Griffin, D. W., Lin, S., & Ross, L. (1990). The overconfident prediction of future actions and outcomes by self and others. *Journal of Personality and Social Psychology, 58*, 582–592.

van de Vijver, F., & Leung, K. (1997). *Methods and data analyses for cross-cultural research*. Thousand Oaks, CA: Sage.

Van Laar, C., Levin, S., & Sidanius, J. (2008). Ingroup and outgroup contact: A longitudinal study of the effects of cross-ethnic friendships, dates, roommate relationships and participation in segregated organizations. In U. Wagner, L. R. Tropp, G. Finchilescu, & C. Tredoux (Eds.), *Improving intergroup relations: Building on the legacy of Thomas F. Pettigrew*. Malden, MA : Blackwell.

Van Laar, C., Sidanius, J., & Levin, S. (2008). Ethnic related curricula and intergroup attitudes in college: Movement towards and away from the ingroup. *Journal of Applied Social Psychology, 38* (6), 1601–1638

Van Lange, P. A. M., Rusbult, C. E., Drigotas, S. M., Arriaga, X. B., Witcher, B. S., & Cox, C. L. (1997). Willingness to sacrifice in close relationships. *Journal of Personality and Social Psychology, 72*, 1373–1395.

van Leeuwen, E., & Täuber, S. (2010). The strategic side of out-group helping. In S. Stürmer & M. Snyder (Eds.), *The psychology of prosocial behavior: Group processes, intergroup relations, and helping* (pp. 81–99). Oxford, UK: Wiley-Blackwell.

Van Reijmersdal, E., Neijens, P., & Smit, E. G. (2009). A new branch of advertising: Reviewing factors that influence reactions to product placement. *Journal of Advertising Research, 49*(4), 429–449. doi:10.2501/S0021849909091065

van Veen, V., Krug, M. K., Schooler, J. W., & Carter, C. S. (2009). Neural activity predicts attitude change in cognitive dissonance. *Nature Neuroscience, 12*, 1469–1474.

Van Vugt, M. (2006). Evolutionary Origins of Leadership and Followership. *Personality and Social Psychology Review, 10*(4), 354–371.

Van Vugt, M., & De Cremer, D. C. (1999). Leadership in social dilemmas: The effects of group identification on collective actions to provide public goods. *Journal of Personality and Social Psychology, 76*, 587–599.

Van Vugt, M., & Samuelson, C. (1999). The impact of personal metering in the management of a natural resource crisis: A social dilemma analysis. *Personality and Social Psychology Bulletin, 25*, 731–745.

Van Yperen, N. W., & Buunk, B. P. (1990). A longitudinal study of equity in intimate relationships. *European Journal of Social Psychology, 20*, 287–309.

Vansteenkiste, M., Smeets, S., Soenens, B., Lens, W., Matos, L., & Deci, E. L. (2010). Autonomous and controlled regulation of performance-approach goals: Their relations to perfectionism and educational outcomes. *Motivation and Emotion, 34*(4), 333–353. doi:10.1007/s11031-010-9188-3

Varnum, M. E. W., Grossmann, I., Kitayama, S., & Nisbett, R. E. (2010). The origin of cultural differences in cognition: The social orientation hypothesis. *Current Directions in Psychological Science, 19*(1), 9–13. doi:10.1177/0963721409359301

Vasey, P. L., & VanderLaan, D. P. (2010). An adaptive cognitive dissociation between willingness to help kin and nonkin in Samoan Fa'afafine. *Psychological Science, 21*(2), 292–297. doi:10.1177/0956797609359623

Vedantam, S. (2006, June 23). Social isolation growing in U.S.

Verwijmeren, T., Karremans, J. C., Stroebe, W., & Wigboldus, D. (2011), The workings and limits of subliminal advertising: The role of habits. *Journal of Consumer Psychology, 21*, 206–213. doi:10.1016/j.jcps.2010.11.004

Vidal, J. (2009). Global warming causes 300,000 deaths a year, says Kofi Annan thinktank. CommonDreams.org. Retrieved August 14, 2011, from www.commondreams.org/headline/2009/05/29

Vidyasagar, P., & Mishra, H. (1993). Effect of modelling on aggression. *Indian Journal of Clinical Psychology, 20*, 50–52.

Visscher, T. L. S., & Seidell, J. C. (2001). The public health impact of obesity. *Annual Review of Public Health, 22*, 355–375.

Viswesvaran, C., & Deshpande, S. P. (1996). Ethics, success, and job satisfaction: A test of dissonance theory in India. *Journal of Business Ethics, 10*, 487–501.

Vohs, K. D., & Baumeister, R. F. (2004). Sexual passion, intimacy and gender. In D. J. Mashek & A. Aron (Eds.), *Handbook of closeness and intimacy* (pp. 189–200). Mahwah, NJ: Erlbaum.

Vohs, K. D., & Baumeister, R. F. (Eds.) (2011). *Handbook of self-regulation*. New York: Guilford.

von Wittich, D., & Antonakis, J. (2011). The KAI cognitive style inventory: Was it personality all along? *Personality and Individual Differences, 50*(7), 1044–1049. doi:10.1016/j.paid.2011.01.022

Vonk, R. (1995). Effects of inconsistent behaviors on person perception: A multidimensional study. *Personality and Social Psychology Bulletin, 21*, 674–685.

Vonk, R. (1999). Effects of outcome dependency on correspondence bias. *Personality and Social Psychology Bulletin, 25*, 382–389.

Vrijheid, M., Dolk, H., Armstrong, B., Abramsky, L., Bianchi, F., Fazarinc, I., et al. (2002). Chromosomal congenital anomalies and residence near hazardous waste landfill sites. *Lancet, 359*, 320–322.

Wade, A., & Beran, T. (2011). Cyberbullying: The new era of bullying. *Canadian Journal of School Psychology, 26*, 44–61.

Wakefield, M., Flay, B., & Nichter, M. (2003). Role of the media in influencing trajectories of youth smoking. *Addiction, 98*(Suppl. 1), Special issue: Contexts and adolescent tobacco use trajectories, 79–103.

Walker, I., & Crogan, M. (1998). Academic performance, prejudice, and the jigsaw classroom: New pieces to the puzzle. *Journal of Community and Applied Social Psychology, 8*, 381–393.

Wallach, M. A., Kogan, N., & Bem, D. J. (1962). Group influences on individual risk taking. *Journal of Abnormal and Social Psychology, 65*, 75–86.

Walster, E. (1966). Assignment of responsibility for an accident. *Journal of Personality and Social Psychology, 3*, 73–79.

Walster, E., Aronson, V., Abrahams, D., & Rottman, L. (1966). Importance of physical attractiveness in dating behavior. *Journal of Personality and Social Psychology, 5*, 508–516.

Walster, E., & Festinger, L. (1962). The effectiveness of "overheard" persuasive communication. *Journal of Abnormal and Social Psychology, 65*, 395–402.

Walster, E., Walster, G. W., & Berscheid, E. (1978). *Equity: Theory and research*. Needham Heights, MA: Allyn & Bacon.

Walther, E., Bless, H., Strack, F., Rackstraw, P., Wagner, D., & Werth, L. (2002). Conformity effects in memory as a function of group size, dissenters and uncertainty. *Applied Cognitive Psychology, 16*, 793–810.

Walther, E., & Langer, T. (2010). For whom Pavlov's bell tolls: Processes underlying evaluative conditioning. In J. P. Forgas, J. Cooper, & W. D. Crano (Eds.), *The Sydney symposium of social psychology. The psychology of attitudes and attitude change* (pp. 59–74). New York: Psychology Press.

Wang, O., & Ross, M. (2007). Culture and memory. In S. Kitayama & D. Cohen (Eds.), *Handbook of cultural psychology* (pp. 645–667). New York: Guilford.

Ward, C. N., & Lundberg-Love, P. K. (2006). Sexual abuse of women. In P. K. Lundberg-Love & S. L. Marmion (Eds.), *"Intimate" violence against women: When spouses, partners, or lovers attack* (pp. 47–68). Westport, CT: Praeger.

Warneken, F., & Tomasello, M. (2008). Extrinsic rewards undermine altruistic tendencies in 20-month-olds. *Developmental Psychology, 44*(6), 1785–1788. doi:10.1037/a0013860

Warner, J. (2001, December 23). Laughter auditions: How I learned how to be a professional laugher. *LA Weekly Blogs*. Available at: blogs.laweekly.com/arts/2011/12/how_to_be_a_professional_laugh.php

Waston, J. B. (1925). *Behaviorism*. New York: Norton.

Watkins, E. R. (2008). Constructive and unconstructive repetitive thought. *Psychological Bulletin, 134*(2), 163–206. doi:10.1037/0033-2909.134.2.163

Watson, D. (1982). The actor and the observer: How are their perceptions of causality divergent? *Psychological Bulletin, 92*, 682–700.

Watson, D., & Pennebaker, J. W. (1989). Health complaints, stress, and distress: Exploring the central role of negative affectivity. *Psychological Review, 96*, 234–254.

Watson, J. (1950). Some social and psychological situations related to change in attitude. *Human Relations, 3*, 15–56.

Watson, R. I. (1973). Investigation into deindividuation using a cross-cultural survey technique. *Journal of Personality and Social Psychology, 25*, 342–345.

Watson, W. E., Johnson, L., Kumar, K., & Critelli, J. (1998). Process gain and process loss: Comparing interpersonal processes and performance of culturally diverse and non-diverse teams across time. *International Journal of Intercultural Relations, 22*, 409–430.

Wattenberg, M. P. (1987). The hollow realignment: Partisan change in a candidate-centered era. *Public Opinion Quarterly, 51*, 58–74.

Watts, D. P., Muller, M., Amsler, S. J., Mbabazi, G., and Mitani, J. C. (2006, February). Lethal intergroup aggression by chimpanzees in Kibale National Park, Uganda. *American Journal of Primatology, 68*, (2), 161–180.

Wax, E. (2008). In India, new opportunities for women draw anger and abuse from men. *Washington Post*, p. A11.

Weart, S. R. (2003). *The discovery of global warming*. Cambridge, MA: Harvard University Press.

Weary, G., & Arkin, R. C. (1981). Attributional self-presentation. In J. H. Harvey, W. J. Ickes, & R. F. Kidd (Eds.), *New directions in attribution research* (Vol. 3, pp. 223–246). Hillsdale, NJ: Erlbaum.

Weaver, C. N. (2008). Social distance as a measure of prejudice among ethnic groups in the United States. *Journal of Applied Social Psychology, 38*, 778–795.

Weaver, J. R., & Bosson, J. K. (2011). I feel like I know you: Sharing negative attitudes of others promotes feelings of familiarity. *Personality and Social Psychology Bulletin, 37*, 481–491.

Webber, R., & Crocker, J. (1983). Cognitive processes in the revision of stereotypic beliefs. *Journal of Personality and Social Psychology, 45*, 961–977.

Weber, E. U., Bockenholt, U., Hilton, D. J., & Wallace, B. (1993). Determinants of diagnostic hypothesis generation: Effects of information, base rates, and experience. *Journal of Experimental Psychology: Learning, Memory, and Cognition, 19*, 1151–1164.

Weber, E. U., & Johnson, E. J. (2009). Mindful judgment and decision making. Annual Review of Psychology, *60*, 53-85. doi:10.1146/annurev.psych.60.110707.163633

Weber, N., Brewer, N., Wells, G., Semmler, C., & Keast, A. (2004). Eyewitness Identification Accuracy and Response Latency: The Unruly 10-12-Second Rule. *Journal of Experimental Psychology: Applied, 10*, 139–147.

Webster, D. M. (1993). Motivated augmentation and reduction of the overattributional bias. *Journal of Personality and Social Psychology, 65*, 261–271.

Wechsler, H., & Austin, S. B. (1998). Binge drinking: The five/four measure. *Journal of Studies of Alcohol, 59*, 122–124.

Wechsler, H., Lee, J. E., Kuo, M., Siebring, M., Nelson, T. F., & Lee, H. (2002). Trends in college binge drinking during a period of increased prevention efforts: Findings from 4 Harvard School of Public Health college alcohol study surveys, 1993–2001. *Journal of American College Health, 50*, 203–217.

Wegener, D. T., & Petty, R. E. (1994). Mood management across affective states: The hedonic contingency hypothesis. *Journal of Personality and Social Psychology, 66*, 1034–1048.

Wegener, D. T., & Petty, R. E. (1995). Flexible correction processes in social judgment: The role of naive theories in corrections for perceived bias. *Journal of Personality and Social Psychology, 68*, 36–51.

Wegner, D. M. (1986). Transactive memory: A contemporary analysis of the group mind. In B. Mullen & G. R. Goethals (Eds.), *Theories of group behavior* (pp. 185–208). New York: Springer-Verlag.

Wegner, D. M. (1989). *White bears and other unwanted thoughts: Suppression, obsession, and the psychology of mental control*. New York: Viking.

Wegner, D. M. (1992). You can't always think what you want: Problems in the suppression of unwanted thoughts. In M. P. Zanna (Ed.), *Advances in experimental social psychology* (Vol. 25, pp. 193–225). San Diego, CA: Academic Press.

Wegner, D. M. (1994). Ironic processes of mental control. *Psychological Review, 101*, 34–52.

Wegner, D. M. (1995). A computer network model of human transactive memory. *Social Cognition, 13*, 319–339.

Wegner, D. M. (2002). *The illusion of conscious will*. Cambridge, MA: MIT Press.

Wegner, D. M. (2004). Precis of *The illusion of conscious will. Behavioral & Brain Sciences, 27*, 649–659.

Wegner, D. M., Ansfield, M., & Pilloff, D. (1998). The putt and the pendulum: Ironic effects of the mental control of action. *Psychological Science, 9*, 196–199.

Wegner, D. M., Erber, R., & Raymond, P. (1991). Transactive memory in close relationships. *Journal of Personality and Social Psychology, 61*, 923–929.

Wegner, D. M., Fuller, V. A., & Sparrow, B. (2003). Clever hands: Uncontrolled intelligence in facilitated communication. *Journal of Personality and Social Psychology, 85*, 5–19.

Wegner, D. M., Quillian, F., & Houston, C. E. (1996). Memories out of order: Thought suppression and the disturbance of sequence memory. *Journal of Personality and Social Psychology, 71*, 680–691.

Wegner, D. M., Sparrow, B., & Winerman, L. (2004). Vicarious agency: Experiencing control over the movements of others. *Journal of Personality and Social Psychology, 86*, 838–848.

Wegner, D. M., Wenzlaff, R., Kerker, M., & Beattie, A. E. (1981). Incrimination through innuendo: Can media questions become public answers? *Journal of Personality and Social Psychology, 40*, 822–832.

Wegner, D. M., Wenzlaff, R. M., & Kozak, M. (2004). Dream rebound: The return of suppressed thoughts in dreams. *Psychological Science, 15*, 232–236.

Wehrens, M. J. P. W., Kuyper, H., Dijkstra, P., Buunk, A. P., & Van Der Werf, M. P. C. (2010). The long-term effect of social comparison on academic performance. *European Journal of Social Psychology, 40*(7), 1158–1171. doi:10.1002/ejsp.706

Wehrle, T., Kaiser, S., Schmidt, S., & Scherer, K. R. (2000). Studying the dynamics of emotional expression using synthesized facial muscle movements. *Journal of Personality and Social Psychology, 78*, 105–119.

Weihs, K. L., Enright, T. M., & Simmens, S. J. (2008). Close relationships and emotional processing predict decreased mortality in women with breast cancer: Preliminary evidence. *Psychosomatic Medicine, 70*(1), 117–124. doi:10.1097/PSY.0b013e31815c25cf

Weiner, B. (1985). "Spontaneous" causal thinking. *Psychological Bulletin, 97*, 74–84.

Weiner, B. (2008). Reflections on the history of attribution theory and research. *Social Psychology, 39*, 151–156.

Weiner, B., Amirkhan, J., Folkes, V. S., & Verette, J. A. (1987). An attributional analysis of excuse giving: Studies of a naive theory of emotion. *Journal of Personality and Social Psychology, 52*, 316–324.

Weinstock, M. (2011). Knowledge-telling and knowledge-transforming arguments in mock jurors' verdict justifications. *Thinking & Reasoning, 17*(3), 282–314. doi:10.1080/13546783.2011.575191

Weir, W. (1984, October 15). Another look at subliminal "facts." *Advertising Age*, p. 46.

Wells, G. L. (1984). The psychology of lineup identifications. *Journal of Applied Social Psychology, 14*, 89–103.

Wells, G. L. (1993). What do we know about eyewitness identification? *American Psychologist, 48*, 553–571.

Wells, G. L., & Bradfield, A. L. (1998). "Good, you identified the suspect": Feedback to eyewitness reports distorts their reports of the witnessing experience. *Journal of Applied Social Psychology, 83*, 360–376.

Wells, G. L., Charman, S. D., & Olson, E. A. (2005). Building face composites can harm lineup identification performance. *Journal of Experimental Psychology: Applied, 11*, 147–156.

Wells, G. L., & Hasel, L. (2007). Facial composite production by eyewitnesses. *Current Directions in Psychological Science, 16*, 6–10.

Wells, G. L., & Hasel, L. (2008). Eyewitness identification: Issues in common knowledge and generalization. In E. Borgida & S. T. Fiske (Eds.), *Beyond common sense: Psychological science in the courtroom* (pp. 159–176). Malden : Blackwell.

Wells, G. L., & Luus, C. A. E. (1990). Police lineups as experiments: Social methodology as a framework for properly conducted lineups. *Personality and Social Psychology Bulletin, 16*, 106–117.

Wells, G. L., Malpass, R. S., Lindsay, R. C. L., Fisher, R. P., Turtle, J. W., & Fulero, S. M. (2000). From the lab to the police station. *American Psychologist, 55*, 581–598.

Wells, G. L., Olson, E. A., & Charman, S. D. (2002). The confidence of eyewitnesses in their identifications from lineups. *Current Directions in Psychological Science, 11*, 151–154.

Wells, G. L., & Quinlivan, D. S. (2009). Suggestive eyewitness identification procedures and the Supreme Court's reliability test in light of eyewitness science: 30 years later. *Law and Human Behavior, 33*, 1–24.

Wells, W. D. (Ed.). (1997). *Measuring advertising effectiveness*. Mahwah, NJ: Erlbaum.

West, S., Jett, S. E., Beckman, T., & Vonk, J. (2010). The phylogenetic roots of cognitive dissonance. *Journal of Comparative Psychology, 124*, 425–432.

Wenzlaff, R. M., & Bates, D. E. (2000). The relative efficacy of concentration and suppression strategies of mental control. *Personality and Social Psychology Bulletin, 26*, 1200–1212.

Werth, L., & Foerster, J. (2002). Implicit person theories influence memory judgments: The circumstances under which metacognitive knowledge is used. *European Journal of Social Psychology, 32*, 353–362.

West, S. A., & Gardner, A. (2010). Altruism, spite, and greenbeards. *Science, 327*(5971), 1341–1344. doi:10.1126/science.1178332

Westen, D. (2007). *The political brain: The role of emotion in deciding the fate of the nation*. New York: Public Affairs Books.

Westen, D., Kilts, C., Blagov, P., et al. (2006). The neural basis of motivated reasoning: An fMRI study of emotional constraints on political judgment during the U.S. presidential election of 2004. *Journal of Cognitive Neuroscience, 18*, 1947–1958.

Weyant, J. M. (1996). Application of compliance techniques to direct-mail requests for charitable donations. *Psychology and Marketing, 13*, 157–170.

Wheeler, D. L., Jacobson, J. W., Paglieri, R. A., & Schwartz, A. A. (1993). An experimental assessment of facilitated communication. *Mental Retardation, 31*, 49–59.

Wheeler, L., & Kim, Y. (1997). What is beautiful is culturally good: The physical attractiveness stereotype has different content in collectivistic cultures. *Personality and Social Psychology Bulletin, 23*, 795–800.

Wheeler, L., Koestner, R., & Driver, R. (1982). Related attributes in the choice of comparison others: It's there, but it isn't all there is. *Journal of Experimental Social Psychology, 18*, 489–500.

Wheeler, S. C., & DeMarree, K. G. (2009). Multiple mechanisms of prime-to-behavior effects. *Social and Personality Psychology Compass, 3*(4), 566–581. doi:10.1111/j.1751-9004.2009.00187.x

White, J. (2007). Abu Ghraib officer cleared of detainee abuse; verdict means no one in army's upper ranks will be imprisoned for the 2003 mistreatment in Iraq. *Washington Post*, p. A05.

White, J. W., Donat, P. L. N., & Humphrey, J. A. (1995). An examination of the attitudes underlying sexual coercion among acquaintances. *Journal of Psychology and Human Sexuality, 8*, 27–47.

White, K. M., Smith, J. R., Terry, D. J., Greenslade, J. H., & McKimmie, B. M. (2009). Social influence in the theory of planned behaviour: The role of descriptive, injunctive, and in-group norms. *British Journal of Social Psychology, 48*, 135–158.

White, P. A. (2002). Causal attribution from covariation information: The evidential evaluation model. *European Journal of Social Psychology, 32*, 667–684.

White, R. K. (1977). Misperception in the Arab-Israeli conflict. *Journal of Social Issues, 33*, 190–221.

Whittaker, J. O., & Meade, R. D. (1967). Social pressure in the modification and distortion of judgment: A cross-cultural study. *International Journal of Psychology, 2*, 109–113.

Wicker, A. W. (1969). Attitudes versus actions: The relationship between verbal and overt behavioral responses to attitude objects. *Journal of Social Issues, 25*, 41–78.

Wilder, D. A. (1981). Perceiving persons as a group: Categorization and intergroup relations. In D. L. Hamilton (Ed.), *Cognitive processes in stereotyping and intergroup behavior* (pp. 213–257). Hillsdale, NJ: Erlbaum.

Wilder, D. A. (1984). Intergroup contact: The typical member and the exception to the rule. *Journal of Experimental Psychology, 20*, 177–194.

Wilder, D. A. (1986). Social categorization: Implications for creation and reduction of intergroup bias. In L. Berkowitz (Ed.), *Advances in experimental social psychology* (Vol. 19, pp. 291–355). New York: Academic Press.

Wilder, D. A., & Shapiro, P. N. (1989). Role of competition-induced anxiety in limiting the beneficial impact of positive behavior by an out-group member. *Journal of Personality and Social Psychology, 56*, 60–69.

Wilford, M. M., & Wells, G. L. (2010). Does facial processing prioritize change detection? Change blindness illustrates costs and benefits of holistic processing. *Psychological Science, 21*(11), 1611–1615. doi:10.1177/0956797610385952

Willard, J., Madon, S., Guyll, M., & Spoth, R. (in press). Self-efficacy as a moderator of positive and negative self-fulfilling prophecy effects: Mothers' beliefs and children's alcohol use. *European Journal of Social Psychology*.

Williams, J. (1998). *Thurgood Marshall: American revolutionary*. New York: Times Books.

Williams, K. D., & Nida, S. A. (2011). Ostracism: Consequences and coping. *Current Directions in Psychological Science, 20*, 71–75.

Williams, L. E., & Bargh, J. A. (2008). Experiencing physical warmth promotes interpersonal warmth. *Science, 322*(5901), 606–607. doi:10.1126/science.1162548

Williams, P. (2001). *How to be like Mike: Life lessons about basketball's best*. Deerfield Beach, FL: Health Communications.

Williams, T. P., & Sogon, S. (1984). Group composition and conforming behavior in Japanese students. *Japanese Psychological Research, 26*, 231–234.

Williamson, G. M., Clark, M. S., Pegalis, L. J., & Behan, A. (1996). Affective consequences of refusing to help in communal and exchange relationships. *Personality and Social Psychology Bulletin, 22*, 34–47.

Willis, J. (2012, February 2). Companions in love and volunteering. *The Oregonian*. Available online at: http://www.oregonlive.com/living/index.ssf/2012/02/companions_in_love_and_volunte.html

Willis, J., & Todorov, A. (2006). First impressions: Making up your mind after a 100-ms exposure to a face. *Psychological Science, 17*, 592–598.

Willmott, L., Harris, P., Gellaitry, G., Cooper, V., & Horne, R. (2011). The effects of expressive writing following first myocardial infarction: A randomized controlled trial. *Health Psychology, 30*(5), 642–650. doi:10.1037/a0023519

Wilson, A. E., & Ross, M. (2000). The frequency of temporal-self and social comparisons in people's personal appraisals. *Journal of Personality and Social Psychology, 78*, 928–942.

Wilson, C. (2011, February 15). Jeopardy, Schmeopardy: Why IBM's next target should be a machine that plays poker. Slate.com. Retrieved April 18, 2011, from www.slate.com/id/2285035/

Wilson, D. K., Purdon, S. E., & Wallston, K. A. (1988). Compliance in health recommendations: A theoretical overview of message framing. *Health Education Research, 3*, 161–171.

Wilson, D. S. (1997). Altruism and organism: Disentangling the themes of multilevel selection theory. *American Naturalist, 150*, S122–S134.

Wilson, D. S., Van Vugt, M., & O'Gorman, R. (2008). Multilevel selection theory and major evolutionary transitions: Implications for psychological science. *Current Directions in Psychological Science, 17*, 6–9.

Wilson, D. S., & Wilson E. O. (2007, November 3). Survival of the selfless. *New Scientist*, 42–46.

Wilson, E. O. (1975). *Sociobiology: The new synthesis*. Cambridge, MA: Belknap Press.

Wilson, J. (2005). *The politics of truth: A diplomat's memoir.* New York: PublicAffairs.

Wilson, S. J., & Lipsey, M. W. (2007). School-based interventions for aggressive and disruptive behavior: Update of a meta-analysis. *American Journal of Preventive Medicine, 33*, S130–S143.

Wilson, T. D. (2002). *Strangers to ourselves: Discovering the adaptive unconscious*. Cambridge, MA: Harvard University Press.

Wilson, T. D. (2011). *Redirect: The surprising new science of psychological change*. New York: Little, Brown.

Wilson, T. D., Aronson, E., & Carlsmith, K. (2010). The art of laboratory experimentation. In S. Fiske, D. Gilbert, & G. Lindzey (Eds.), *Handbook of social psychology* (5th ed., pp. 49–79). New York: Wiley.

Wilson, T. D., & Bar-Anan, Y. (2008). The unseen mind. *Science, 321*, 1046–1047.

Wilson, T. D., Dunn, D. S., Kraft, D., & Lisle, D. J. (1989). Introspection, attitude change, and attitude-behavior consistency: The disruptive effects of explaining why we feel the way we do. In L. Berkowitz (Ed.), *Advances in experimental social psychology* (Vol. 19, pp. 123–205). Orlando, FL: Academic Press.

Wilson, T. D., & Dunn, E. W. (2004). Self-knowledge: Its limits, value and potential for improvement. *Annual Review of Psychology, 55*, 493–518.

Wilson, T. D., & Gilbert, D. T. (2003). Affective forecasting. In M. P. Zanna (Ed.), *Advances in experimental social psychology* (Vol. 35, pp. 345–411). San Diego, CA: Academic Press.

Wilson, T. D., Gilbert, D. T. (2005). *Current Directions in Psychological Science, 14*(3), 131–134(4). Blackwell Publishing.

Wilson, T. D., & Gilbert, D. T. (2008). Explaining away: A model of affective adaptation. *Perspectives on Psychological Science, 3*, 370–386.

Wilson, T. D., Gilbert, D. T., & Wheatley, T. (1998). Protecting our minds: The role of lay beliefs. In V. Yzerbyt, G. Lories, & B. Dardenne (Eds.), *Metacognition: Cognitive and social dimensions* (pp. 171–201). New York: Russell Sage Foundation.

Wilson, T. D., Hodges, S. D., & La Fleur, S. J. (1995). Effects of introspecting about reasons: Inferring attitudes from accessible thoughts. *Journal of Personality and Social Psychology, 69*, 16–28.

Wilson, T. D., Houston, C. E., Etling, K. M., & Brekke, N. C. (1996). A new look at anchoring effects: Basic anchoring and its antecedents. *Journal of Experimental Psychology: General, 125*, 387–402.

Wilson, T. D., Houston, C. E., & Meyers, J. M. (1998). Choose your poison: Effects of lay beliefs about mental processes on attitude change. *Social Cognition, 16*, 114–132.

Wilson, T. D., & Kraft, D. (1993). Why do I love thee? Effects of repeated introspections about a dating relationship on attitudes toward the relationship. *Personality and Social Psychology Bulletin, 19*, 409–418.

Wilson, T. D., Laser, P. S., & Stone, J. I. (1982). Judging the predictors of one's own mood: Accuracy and the use of shared theories. *Journal of Experimental Social Psychology, 18*, 537–556.

Wilson, T. D., Lindsey, S., & Schooler, T. Y. (2000). A model of dual attitudes. *Psychological Review, 107*, 101–126.

Wilson, T. D., & Linville, P. W. (1982). Improving the academic performance of college freshmen: Attribution therapy revisited. *Journal of Personality and Social Psychology, 42*, 367–376.

Wilson, T. D., & Linville, P. W. (1985). Improving the performance of college freshmen using attributional techniques. *Journal of Personality and Social Psychology, 49*, 287–293.

Wilson, T. D., Lisle, D., Schooler, J. W., Hodges, S. D., Klaaren, K. J., & La Fleur, S. J. (1993). Introspecting about reasons can reduce post-choice satisfaction. *Personality and Social Psychology Bulletin, 19*, 331–339.

Wilton, C., & Campbell, M. A. (2001). An exploration of the reasons why adolescents engage in traditional and cyber bullying. *Journal of Educational Sciences and Psychology, 1*, 101–109.

Winslow, R. W., Franzini, L. R., & Hwang, J. (1992). Perceived peer norms, casual sex, and AIDS risk prevention. *Journal of Applied Social Psychology, 22*, 1809–1827.

Wiseman, C. V., Gray, J. J., Mosimann, J. E., & Ahrens, A. H. (1992). Cultural expectations of thinness in women: An update. *International Journal of Eating Disorders, 11*, 85–89.

Wiseman, M. C., & Moradi, B. (2010). Body image and earing disorder symptoms in sexual minority men: A test and extension of objectification theory. *Journal of Counseling Psychology, 57*, 154–166.

Wittenbaum, G. M., & Moreland, R. L. (2008). Small-group research in social psychology: Topics and trends over time. *Social and Personality Psychology Compass, 2* (www.blackwell-compass.com/subject/socialpsychology/).

Wittenbaum, G. M., & Park, E. S. (2001). The collective preference for shared information. *Current Directions in Psychological Science, 10*, 72–75.

Wittenbrink, B., Judd, C. M., & Park, B. (1997). Implicit racial stereotypes and prejudice and their relationships with questionnaire measures: We know what we think. *Journal of Personality and Social Psychology, 72*, 262–274.

Wojciszke, B. (2005). Affective concomitants of information on morality and competence. *European Psychologist, 10*, 60–70.

Wolf, S. (1985). Manifest and latent influence of majorities and minorities. *Journal of Personality and Social Psychology, 48*, 899–908.

Wolfe, C., & Spencer, S. (1996). Stereotypes and prejudice: Their overt and subtle influence in the classroom. *American Behavioral Scientist, 40*, 176–185.

Wolfson, A. (2005). "A hoax most cruel." *The Courier-Journal*, October 9. Retrieved June 5, 2006, from www.courier-journal.com/ apps/pbcs.dl1/article?Date=20051009&category=NEWS01

Woll, S. (1986). So many to choose from: Decision strategies in videodating. *Journal of Social and Personal Relationships, 3*, 43–52.

Wong, E. M., Galinsky, A. D., & Kray, L. J. (2009). The counterfactual mind-set: A decade of research. In K. D. Markman, W. M. P. Klein, & J. A. Suhr (Eds.), *Handbook of imagination and mental simulation* (pp. 161–174). New York: Psychology Press.

Wong, R. Y., & Hong, Y. (2005). Dynamic influences of culture on cooperation in a Prisoner's Dilemma game. *Psychological Science, 16*, 429–434.

Wood, J. V., Taylor, S. E., & Lichtman, R. R. (1985). Social comparison in adjustment to breast cancer. *Journal of Personality and Social Psychology, 49*, 1169–1183.

Wood, W. (1982). Retrieval of attitude-relevant information from memory: Effects on susceptibility to persuasion and on intrinsic motivation. *Journal of Personality and Social Psychology, 42*, 798–810.

Wood, W. (1987). Meta-analytic review of sex differences in group performance. *Psychological Bulletin, 102*, 53–71.

Wood, W., & Eagly, A. H. (2002). A cross-cultural analysis of the behavior of women and men: Implications for the origins of sex differences. *Psychological Bulletin, 128*, 699–727.

Wood, W., Lundgren, S., Ouellette, J. A., Busceme, S., & Blackstone, T. (1994). Minority influence: A meta-analytic review of social influence processes. *Psychological Bulletin, 115*, 323–345.

Wood, W., Pool, G. J., Leck, K., & Purvis, D. (1996). Self-definition, defensive processing, and influence: The normative impact of majority and minority groups. *Journal of Personality and Social Psychology, 71*, 1181–1193.

Wood, W., & Quinn, J. M. (2003). Forewarned and forearmed? Two meta-analytic syntheses of forewarnings of influence appeals. *Psychological Bulletin, 129*, 119–138.

Wood, W., Wong, F. Y., & Chachere, J. G. (1991). Effects of media violence on viewers' aggression in unconstrained social interaction. *Psychological Bulletin*, 109, 371–383.

Woodward, B. (2004). *Plan of attack*. New York: Simon & Schuster.

Woodward, B. (2006). *State of denial*. New York: Simon & Schuster.

Wubben, M. J. J., De Cremer, D., & van Dijk, E. (2009). How emotion communication guides reciprocity: Establishing cooperation through disappointment and anger. *Journal of Experimental Social Psychology, 45*(4), 987–990. doi:10.1016/j.jesp.2009.04.010

Zajonc, R. B. (1968). Attitudinal effects of mere exposure. *Journal of Personality and Social Psychology, 9*, 1–27.

Zebrowitz, L. A., & Montepare, J. M. (2008). Social psychological face perception: Why appearance matters. *Social and Personality Psychology Compass, 2*, 1497–1517.

Zentall, S. R., & Morris, B. J. (2010). "Good job, you're so smart": The effects of inconsistency of praise type on young children's motivation. *Journal of Experimental Child Psychology, 107*(2), 155–163. doi:10.1016/j.jecp.2010.04.015

Zhang, D., Lowry, P. B., Zhou, L., & Fu, X. (2007). The impact of individualism-collectivism, social presence, and group diversity on group decision making under majority influence. *Journal of Management Information Systems, 23*, 53–80.

Zhang, Y., & Epley, N. (2009). Self-centered social exchange: Differential use of costs versus benefits in prosocial reciprocity. *Journal of Personality and Social Psychology, 97*(5), 796–810. doi:10.1037/a0016233

Zhong, C.-B., & Leonardelli, G. J. (2008). Cold and lonely: Does social exclusion literally feel cold? *Psychological Science, 19(9)*, 838–842. doi:10.1111/j.1467-9280.2008.02165.x

Zhong, C.-B., & Liljenquist, K. (2006). Washing away your sins: Threatened morality and physical cleansing. *Science, 313*, 1451–1452.

Zhu, Y., & Han, S. (2008). Cultural differences in the self: From philosophy to psychology and neuroscience. *Social and Personality Psychology Compass, 2*, 1799–1811.

Zimmer, B. (2009, October 25). On language: Ms.: The origins of the title, explained. *The New York Times*.

Credits

Text Credits

Figure 1.1, page 9 Figure from "The name of the game: Predictive power of reputations versus situational labels in determining Prisoner's Dilemma Game moves," by Verda Liberman, Steven M Samuels, and Lee Ross. *Personality and Social Psychology Bulletin*, 30.9, pp. 1175–85. Copyright © 2004 by Sage. Reprinted with permission.

Figure 3.4, page 54 Figure adapted from R. Rosenthal and L. Jacobson: *Pygmalion in the Classroom: Teacher Expectation and Pupils' Intellectual Development*. Holt, Rinehart, Winston, © 1968. Reprinted with permission of R. Rosenthal.

Figure 3.6, page 70 Figure from "Teaching Reasoning," by Nisbett, Fong, Lehman, Cheng. *Science*, 238, pp. 625–631. Copyright © 1987 by the American Association for the Advancement of Science. Reprinted with permission of AAAS.

Figure 6.6, page 153 Figure from "Inducing Hypocrisy as a Means of Encouraging Young Adults to Use Condoms," by Elliott Aronson, A. Lauren Crain, Matthew P. Winslow, and Carrie B. Fried. *Personality and Social Psychology Bulletin*, 20, 116–128. Copyright © 1994 by Sage. Reprinted with permission.

Figure 9.7, page 261 Figure from "Studies of interpersonal bargaining," by Morton Deutsch and Robert M. Krauss. *Journal of Conflict Resolution*, 6, pp. 52–76. Copyright © 1962 by Sage. Reprinted with permission.

Figure 10.2, page 279 Figure from "Arbitrary social norms influence sex difference in romantic selectivity," by Eli J. Finkel and Paul W. Eastwick. *Psychological Science*, 20, pp. 1290–1295. Copyright © 2009 by Sage. Reprinted with permission.

Photo Credits

Chapter 1 **Page xxx:** Corbis Bridge/Alamy; **Page 1:** Corbis Bridge/Alamy; **Page 2:** Norbert Schwerin/The Image Works; **Page 4:** REUTERS/Stringer; **Page 5:** Imagesource/Glow Images, Inc.; **Page 7:** Paul Chesley/National Geographic Stock; **Page 10:** Archives of the History of American Psychology-University of Akron; **Page 11 (top):** Archives of the History of American Psychology- University of Akron; **Page 11 (bottom):** Shawn Thew/EPA/Newscom; **Page 12:** Rick Friedman/Corbis; **Page 14:** JEAN-PHILIPPE KSIAZEK/AFP/Getty Images/Newscom; **Page 16:** Trudy Festinger; **Page 17:** VILLEROT/BSIP/Age Fotostock

Chapter 2 **Page 20:** Corbis Super RF/Alamy; **Page 21:** Corbis Super RF/Alamy; **Page 22:** Kyodo/Newscom; **Page 26:** Michael Newman/PhotoEdit; **Page 28:** Library of Congress; **Page 29:** Michael Newman/PhotoEdit; **Page 34:** Lewis J. Merrim/Photo Researchers, Inc.; **Page 36:** Megapress/Alamy; **Page 38:** Humayoun Shiab/EPA/Newscom; **Page 39:** Mark Harmel/Photo Researchers, Inc.; **Page 40:** ScienceCartoonsPlus.com

Chapter 3 **Page 46:** Jeopardy!/Landov; **Page 47:** Jeopardy!/Landov; **Page 48:** Sean Nel 2009. Shutterstock.com; **Page 50 (top left and right):** National Archives and Records Administration; **Page 50 (bottom):** Guido Koppes/Age Fotostock; **Page 54:** Mary Kate Denny/PhotoEdit; **Page 56:** wdstock/iStockphoto; **Page 58:** Robin Nelson/PhotoEdit; **Page 62:** Ginasander/Dreamstime; **Page 63 (top and bottom):** Takahiko Masuda; **Page 66:** Robin Nelson/PhotoEdit; **Page 68:** REUTERS/Nikola Solic

Chapter 4 **Page 74:** William D. Bird/Everett Collection; **Page 75:** William D. Bird/Everett Collection; **Page 78 (very top of page):** Courtesy of D. Vaughn Becker; **Page 78 (top middle):** UrosK/Shutterstock; **Page 78 (top right)** PhotosIndia.com RM 18/Alamy; **Page 78 (bottom left):** Guido Alberto Rossi/TIPS Images North America; **Page 78 (bottom middle):** Yuri Arcurs/Shutterstock; **Page 78 (bottom right):** Costa Manos/Magnum Photos, Inc.; **Page 79 (top):** Paul Ekman Group, LLC.; **Page 79 (bottom):** Associated Sports Photography/Alamy; **Page 80 (left and right):** Paul Ekman Group, LLC.; **Page 81 (top left):** Dmitriy Shironosov/Shutterstock; **Page 81 (bottom left):** Carol Beckwith & Angela Fisher/HAGA/The Image Works; **Page 81 (middle):** Victor Tongdee/Shutterstock; **Page 81 (top right):** Bill Bachmann/Photo Researchers, Inc.; **Page 81 (bottom right):** Sisse Brimberg/National Geographic Stock; **Page 83 (top):** Darlene Hammond/Archive Photos/Getty Images; **Page 83 (bottom):** Radius Images/Alamy; **Page 85:** AP Photo/Damian Dovarganes; **Page 88:** Bettmann/Bettmann Premium/Corbis; **Page 89:** Richard Perry/The New York Times/Redux Pictures; **Page 94 (top and bottom):** Takahiko Masuda; **Page 95:** Steve Vidler/SuperStock; **Page 96 (top left):** trubach/Shutterstock; **Page 96 (top right):** Lissandra/Shutterstock; **Page 96 (bottom left):** bigredlynx/Shutterstock; **Page 96 (bottom right):** Izmael/Shutterstock; **Page 96 (bottom of page):** violetkaipa/Shutterstock; **Page 100:** Morgan Lane Photography/Shutterstock

Chapter 5 **Page 104:** PCN Photography/Alamy; **Page 105:** PCN Photography/Alamy; **Page 106:** Eddie Lawrence/Dorling Kindersley; **Page 107:** AP Photo/Pool, Tsugufumi Matsumoto; **Page 114:** Patricia Schlein/WENN Photos/Newscom; **Page 115:** Pearson; **Page 116:** PEANUTS © (1995) Charles Schulz. Used by permission of UNIVERSAL UCLICK. All rights reserved.; **Page 119:** Deymos/Dreamstime; **Page 121:** King Features Syndicate; **Page 127 (left):** Library of Congress; **Page 127:** Lee Corkran/Sygma/Corbis; **Page 128: (right)** John F. Kennedy Presidential Library and Museum; **Page 128:** Everett Collection/SuperStock; **Page 130:** Barritt, Peter/SuperStock/Alamy

Chapter 6 **Page 136:** Aaron Horowitz/Corbis; **Page 137:** Aaron Horowitz/Corbis; **Page 139:** Powell John/Prisma/Age Fotostock; **Page 141:** Jeremy Woodhouse/Blend Images/Age Fotostock; **Page 142:** Newscast/Alamy; **Page 144:** Pixtal/Glow Images, Inc.; **Page 146:** moodboard/Fotolia; **Page 149:** Splash News/Newscom; **Page 150:** Shannon Fagan/The Image Bank/Getty Images; **Page 155:** Oasis/Photos 12/Alamy; **Page 156:** HO/AFP/GETTY IMAGES/Newscom; **Page 158:** Jose Carlos Fajardo/MCT/Newscom; **Page 159 (top left):** AP Photo/The Durango Herald; **Page 159 (top right):** AP Photo/The Denver Post; **Page 159 (bottom left):** AP Photo/Department of Motor Vehicles; **Page 159 (bottom right):** AP Photo/Tribune Newspapers

Chapter 7 **Page 164:** Pictorial Press Ltd/Alamy; **Page 165:** Pictorial Press Ltd/Alamy; **Page 166:** AP Photo/Deseret Morning News, Keith Johnson; **Page 167:** Ambient Images Inc./Alamy; **Page 169:** moodboard/Corbis; **Page 170:** AP Photo/Alex Brandon; **Page 173:** Tim Sloan/AFP/Getty Images/Newscom; **Page 177:** UPI/FDA/LANDOV; **Page 179:** Bill Aron/PhotoEdit; **Page 182:** © Screen Gems/courtesy Everett Collection; **Page 183:** REUTERS/Kenny Wu; **Page 187:** AP Photo/Calif., Dept. of Health Services; **Page 189:** Advertising Archives; **Page 190 (top):** HO/AFP/Newscom; **Page 190 (bottom):** Reprinted with permission of 4A's

Chapter 8 **Page 196:** Rich Carey/Shutterstock; **Page 197:** Rich Carey/Shutterstock; **Page 199:** HO/AFP/Getty Images/Newscom; **Page 201:** Jeremy Bembaron/Sygma/Corbis; **Page 202:** Flirt/SuperStock; **Page 204:** The Southern Standard; **Page 205:** Ricardo Azoury/Corbis; **Page 207:** Reproduced with permission. Copyright © 2012 Scientific American, Inc. All rights reserved; **Page 211:** Jeff Greenberg/Alamy; **Page 213:** INTERFOTO/Alamy; **Page 214:** Richard Heyes/Alamy; **Page 217:** Aflo Foto Agency/Alamy; **Page 220:** Pictorial Press Ltd/Alamy; **Page 221:** Craig Steven Thrasher/Alamy; **Page 224:** Prisma/Schultz Reinhard/Prisma Bildagentur AG/Alamy; **Page 226 (left and right):** From the film Obedience copyright © 1968 by Stanley Milgram. Copyright renewed 1993 by Alexandra Milgram, distributed by Penn State Media Sales.

Chapter 9 **Page 236:** REUTERS/Kevin Lamarque; **Page 237:** REUTERS/Kevin Lamarque; **Page 238:** Monkey Business/Fotolia; **Page 239:** Philip G. Zimbardo, Inc.; **Page 240:** The Washington Post/EPA/Newscom; **Page 244:** Monkey Business/Fotolia; **Page 247:** Tom Kidd/Alamy; **Page 253:** Andy Dean Photography/Shutterstock; **Page 255:** AP Photo/File; **Page 257:** Michael Reynolds/EPA/Newscom; **Page 258:** Anton Gvozdikov/Fotolia; **Page 263:** Tom McCarthy/PhotoEdit

Chapter 10 **Page 266:** Elena Elisseeva/Shutterstock; **Page 266:** Elena Elisseeva/Shutterstock; **Page 270:** Rido/Shutterstock; **Page 271 (bottom):** Willie J. Allen Jr./The New York Times/Redux Pictures; **Page 273:** Trinette Reed/Glow Images, Inc.; **Page 274 (all images):** Dr. Judith Langlois; **Page 280:** AF archive/Alamy; **Page 282:** Tomasz Trojanowski/Shutterstock; **Page 283 (top):** imagebroker/Alamy; **Page 283 (boyyom):** vario images GmbH & Co.KG/Alamy; **Page 285:** Ian Hooton/Dorling Kindersley; **Page 290:** Monkey Business Images/Shutterstock; **Page 293 (top):** Jeff Greenberg/The Image Works; **Page 295:** Exactostock/Superstock

Chapter 11 **Page 300:** AP Photo/Suzanne Plunkett; **Page 301:** AP Photo/Suzanne Plunkett; **Page 302:** wavebreakmedia ltd/Shutterstock; **Page 305:** AP Photo/WLS-TV; **Page 308:** AP Photo/Themba Hadebe; **Page 309:** Tomas Rodriguez/PicturePress/Glow Images, Inc.; **Page 313 (left):** John Lund/Drew Kelly/Sam Diephuis/Glow Images, Inc.; **Page 313 (right):** David Grossman/Alamy; **Page 218:** Steve McCurry/Magnum Photos, Inc.; **Page 319:** Floresco Productions/Corbis; **Page 321:** Kuttig-People/Alamy; **Page 322:** corepics/Shutterstock; **Page 324:** Jim West/Alamy

Chapter 12 **Page 328:** Robert Trippett/SIPA Press; **Page 329:** Robert Trippett/SIPA Press; **Page 330:** Catherine Ursillo/Photo Researchers, Inc.; **Page 331 (top and bottom):** Karl Ammann/naturepl.com; **Page 333:** Kris Hanke/iStockphoto; **Page 334:** Radius/SuperStock; **Page 335 (top):** Bonnie Kamin/PhotoEdit; **Page 338:** Vladacanon/Dreamstime; **Page 342 (all images):** From A. Bandura & R. Walters/Photo Courtesy of Albert Bandura; **Page 343:** AF archive/Alamy; **Page 345:** Sean Murphy/Stone/Getty Images; **Page 347:** Bill Aron/PhotoEdit; **Page 348:** Robert Brenner/PhotoEdit; **Page 350:** Vandystadt/Photo Researchers, Inc.; **Page 354 (bottom):** Michael Pole/Corbis

Chapter 13 **Page 360:** Lon C. Diehl/PhotoEdit; **Page 361:** Lon C. Diehl/PhotoEdit; **Page 363 (top):** Bryan Denton/The New York Times/Redux Pictures; **Page 365:** © A. Bacall. Reproduction rights obtainable from www.CartoonStock.com; **Page 367:** Sally Greenhill/Sally and Richard Greenhill/Alamy; **Page 369 (top):** 2009 Owen DB/Black Star/Newscom; **Page 369 (bottom):** William A. Cunningham, University of Toronto; **Page 371:** Copyright © [2012] by the American Psychological Association. Reproduced with permission. Correll, J., Park, B., Judd, C. M., & Wittenbrink, B. (2002). The police officer's dilemma: Using ethnicity to disambiguate potentially threatening individuals. Journal of Personality and Social Psychology, 83, 1314–1329. The use of APA information does not imply endorsement by APA. Photo by Joshua Correll.; **Page 374:** Gary Conner/PhotoEdit; **Page 376:** AP Photo/The Herald, Ross Taylor; **Page 378 (left):** Courtesy Everett Collection; **Page 378 (right):** Gene Young/Splash News/Newscom; **Page 379:** Cultura Creative/Alamy; **Page 383:** Jim West/Alamy; **Page 384:** Fort Worth Star-Telegram/MCT/Landov; **Page 386:** David Taylor Photography/Alamy; **Page 389:** Jonathan Nourok/PhotoEdit; **Page 391:** Tom Watson/Pearson

SPA 1 **Page 396:** Chico Batata/epa/Corbis; **Page 397:** Chico Batata/epa/Corbis; **Page 398 (top):** Gabriel Bouys/AFP/Getty Images/Newscom; **Page 398 (bottom):** David Bookstave/AP Images; **Page 401:** Michel Setboun/PhotoNonStop/Glow Images, Inc.; **Page 404:** Pearson; **Page 406:** Frank Pedrick/The Image Works; **Page 409:** Monkey Business Images/Shutterstock; **Page 410:** Corbis Flirt/Alamy

SPA 2 **Page 414:** Courtesy of Joanne Hill; **Page 415:** Courtesy of Joanne Hill; **Page 416:** REUTERS/Sean Adair; **Page 417 (top left):** Stephen Coburn/Shutterstock; **Page 417 (top right):** Robert Brenner/PhotoEdit; **Page 417 (bottom left):** Elena Rooraid/PhotoEdit; **Page 417 (bottom right):** Wladimir Wetzel/Fotolia; **Page 422:** Monkey Business Images/Shutterstock; **Page 425:** SuperStock/SuperStock; **Page 428 (top):** David Burch/Uppercut RF/Glow Images; **Page 428 (bottom):** Marc Hill/Alamy; **Page 429:** © Vahan Shirvanian. Reproduction rights obtainable from www.CartoonStock.com

SPA 3 **Page 432:** Blair Seitz/Stock Connection/Glow Images; **Page 433:** Blair Seitz/Stock Connection/Glow Images; **Page 434 (top and bottom):** Courtesy of The Dallas Morning News; **Page 436:** Simons, D. J., & Chabris, C. F. (1999). Gorillas in our midst: Sustained inattentional blindness for dynamic events. Perception, 28, 1059–1074. Figure provided by Daniel Simons.; **Page 437 (left and right):** Courtesy of Elizabeth Loftus; **Page 442:** Spencer Grant/PhotoEdit; **Page 443:** Steve Bloom/The Olympian; **Page 446:** Spencer Grant/PhotoEdit; **Page 447:** Photos 12/Alamy Limited

Name Index

A

B

C

D

E

F

G

H

I

J

K

L

M

N

O

P

Q

R

S

T

U

V

W

Y

Z

Subject Index

A

B

C

D

E

F

G

H

J

K

L

M

N

O

P

Q

S

T

U

V

W

Y

Z